The Vienna Rules

A Commentary on International Arbitration in Austria

KLUWER LAW INTERNATIONAL

The Vienna Rules

A Commentary on International Arbitration in Austria

Franz T. Schwarz

Christian W. Konrad

Wolters Kluwer

Law & Business

AUSTIN   BOSTON   CHICAGO   NEW YORK   THE NETHERLANDS

Published by:
Kluwer Law International
PO Box 316
2400 AH Alphen aan den Rijn
The Netherlands
Website: www.kluwerlaw.com

Sold and distributed in North, Central and South America by:
Aspen Publishers, Inc.
7201 McKinney Circle
Frederick, MD 21704
United States of America
Email: customer.care@aspenpubl.com

Sold and distributed in all other countries by:
Turpin Distribution Services Ltd.
Stratton Business Park
Pegasus Drive, Biggleswade
Bedfordshire SG18 8TQ
United Kingdom
Email: kluwerlaw@turpin-distribution.com

Printed on acid-free paper.

ISBN 978-90-411-2344-2

Printed in Great Britain.

For our parents

Preface

This book examines the new Vienna Rules and the Austrian Arbitration Act that both came into effect on 1 July 2006 as the result of a major reform. It is devoted to two principles. First, it recognizes that no two international arbitrations are the same. Arbitration thrives, and is today the predominant method of transnational dispute resolution, because it meets the demands of international business for flexibility and efficacy. Arbitration will continue to succeed if it retains those properties, allowing for the adoption of procedures that are customized to satisfy the commercial prerogatives of the individual case. This book seeks to provide its readers with a general framework, and specific instruments, to negotiate that process.

Second, this book recognizes that in today's world, a discussion of national arbitration law is incomplete without recourse to international practice and procedures. Transnational dispute resolution must be mindful of, and respect, the often different cultural and legal backgrounds and expectations of the parties, their counsel and the arbitrators. This book therefore sets out to familiarize the international user of arbitration with Austrian law, while at the same time placing the Vienna Rules and Austrian law into the context of international arbitral practice. It draws from, and seeks to reconcile, processes available in civil and common law jurisdictions in order to serve the overriding goal of ensuring that arbitration remains predicable, expeditious and fair.

We are very grateful for the critical comments and support we have received from our friends and colleagues at our respective firms Wilmer Cutler Pickering Hale and Dorr LLP and Freshfields Bruckhaus Deringer LLP. We wish to gratefully acknowledge, in particular, the mentorship of Gary Born and Georg Prantl, as well as Günther Horvath and Helmut Neudorfer. We also acknowledge the thoughtful advice of Werner Melis, Manfred Heider, Paul Oberhammer, Kurt Neuteufel, Karl Hempel, Christoph Liebscher, Kurt Heller, Jenny Power,

Anton Baier, Rudolf Fiebinger, Gerold Zeiler and Wolfgang Hahnkamper. Heidrun Halbartschlager deserves particular mention, and praise, for her meticulous research. Yvonne Schierl, Tamara Lueckoff and Marta Wrobel have assisted in the production of the manuscript with characteristic care and dedication. Gwen de Vries and Eleanor Taylor at *Kluwer Law International* provided invaluable editorial support. Finally, we are grateful for the understanding and support of our families, and in particular Eva and Johanna.

As W. Somerset Maugham wrote in the foreword of his book *Of Human Bondage*, '[a]uthors . . . are conscious how far the work on which they have spent much time and trouble comes short of their conception, and when they consider it are much more vexed with their failure . . . than pleased with the passages here and there they can regard with complacency. Their aim is perfection and they are wretchedly aware that they have not attained it'. As we entrust this work to our readers, we are sympathetic with that statement. We are grateful, therefore, for the comments that users of arbitration in Austria and elsewhere may wish to share with us.

Franz T. Schwarz   Christian W. Konrad

London, Vienna
January 2009

Table of Contents

Preface vii

List of Abbreviations xxix

Table of Cases and Awards xxxix

Bibliography lvii

Article 1
The Institution 1
I. The Jurisdiction of the VIAC 2
   A. Introduction 2
      1. Historical Background of the VIAC 3
      2. The Services Provided by the VIAC 4
         2.1. The Nature of the VIAC 5
         2.2. Administration of Dispute Settlement 5
         2.3. Cooperation with Other Arbitral Institutions 6
         2.4. Infrastructure for *Ad Hoc* Proceedings 7
         2.5. Appointing Authority 7
         2.6. Conciliation Proceedings 8
      3. The VIAC's Relationships with the Parties and
         the Arbitrators 9
         3.1. The Relationship Between the VIAC and the Parties 9
         3.2. The Relationship Between the VIAC and
         the Arbitrators 10
   B. The Arbitration Agreement 11
      1. Subjective Capacity to Conclude an Arbitration Agreement 12
         1.1. General Principles 12

		1.2.	Arbitration Agreements Concluded by Consumers	14
		1.3.	Arbitration Agreements Concluded by	
			States or State-Related Entities	17
		1.4.	Consequences of a Lack of Subjective Arbitrability	18
	2.	An Agreement Concerning a 'Specified Legal Relationship'		18
	3.	Form Requirements		20
		3.1.	Some Policy Considerations	20
		3.2.	The 'In Writing' Requirement Under the Old Regime	23
		3.3.	The 'In Writing' Requirement Under the New Regime	24
		3.4.	Conclusion of the Arbitration Agreement by an Agent	28
		3.5.	Arbitration Clauses in Statutes	31
		3.6.	Objections to Defects of Form	33
	4.	The Effect of the Arbitration Agreement		35
	5.	Interpretation of the Arbitration Agreement		37
	6.	Other Forms of Dispute Resolution		39
	7.	Third Parties		40
	8.	The VIAC's Recommended Arbitration Clause		41
C.	The Administration of 'Arbitrable' Disputes			42
	1.	Objective Arbitrability Under the Old Regime		43
	2.	Objective Arbitrability Under the New Law		46
	3.	Objective Arbitrability in Corporate Matters		49
	4.	Arbitration and Competition Law		50
	5.	When Is the New Law Applicable to Determine Objective Arbitrability?		52
	6.	Consequences of a Lack of Objective Arbitrability		52
	7.	*Ex Officio* Application by the Arbitral Tribunal		54
D.	The Administration of 'International' Disputes			55
II.	The Applicable Version of the Vienna Rules			57
A.	Previous Amendments of the Vienna Rules			57
B.	The Application of Amended Rules			58
C.	Interpretation of the Vienna Rules			59
III.	Domestic Arbitration			60

Article 2
The Place of the Arbitration   **63**
I.	Introduction			64
II.	Determining the Seat of the Arbitration			65
III.	Conducting Procedural Acts Elsewhere			67
IV.	The Impact of the Seat of the Arbitration			68
A.	Denationalization v. Territoriality			69
	1.	The Debate		69
	2.	The Emerging Compromise		73
	3.	The Approach under Austrian Law		74

B. The Seat's Impact on the Law Applicable to the
    Arbitration Agreement   75
C. The Seat's Impact on the Law Applicable to the Proceedings   78
    1. What is the *Lex Arbitri*?   78
    2. Can the Parties Choose a 'Foreign' Procedural Law?   80
    3. Mandatory Procedural Standards and Requirements   81
        3.1. Mandatory Provisions under the Old Regime   81
        3.2. Mandatory Provisions under the New Regime   82
D. The Seat's Impact on the Assistance and Intervention
    of the Courts   83
    1. Subject Matter Jurisdiction   84
    2. Assistance by the State Courts   85
    3. Challenge and Termination of the Arbitrator's Mandate   87
    4. Interim Measures   88
    5. Recourse Against the Award   89
    6. Enforcement of Foreign Awards   89
E. The Seat's Impact on the Law Applicable to the
    Substance of the Dispute   90

Article 3
The Board   **91**
I.   The Composition of the Board   91
      A. Introduction   92
      B. Number and Term of Board Members   92
II.   The President of the Board   93
III. Meetings and Decisions of the Board   94
      A. Board Meetings   94
      B. Decisions of the Board   95
IV.   Conflicts of Board Members   97
V.   Decisions by Correspondence   98
VI.   Duties of Board Members   99
      A. Standard of Performance   99
      B. Independence of Board Members   100
      C. Confidentiality Obligations   100
      D. Monitoring the Arbitration Proceedings   101

Article 4
The International Advisory Board   **103**

Article 5
The Secretary General   **105**
I.   The Appointment of the Secretary General   105
      A. Introduction   105
      B. Appointment Procedure   106
II.   Authority of the Secretary General   107
      A. Activities of the Secretariat   107

		B.	Administration of the Centre	107
		C.	Assistance to the VIAC Board	109
		D.	Further Activities of the Secretariat	109
III.			Duties of the Secretary General	111
		A.	Standard of Performance	111
		B.	Independence of the Secretary General	111
		C.	Confidentiality Obligations	112
		D.	Decisions by the Secretary General	112
IV.			Inability to Perform	113

Article 6
Languages of Correspondence   **115**
I.   Scope   115
II.   Requirements   116

Article 7
The Arbitrators   **119**
I.   Party-Autonomy in Choosing the Arbitrators   120
       A.   Introduction   120
       B.   Prerequisites for Service as Arbitrator   121
            1.   'Legal Capacity'   122
            2.   Personal and Voluntary Service   123
            3.   Active Austrian Judges   123
            4.   Expert Determination   125
            5.   Nationality of the Arbitrator   125
            6.   Non-Lawyer Arbitrators   127
            7.   Additional Requirements Imposed by Agreement   127
            8.   Practical Considerations   128
            9.   Interviewing Prospective Arbitrators   128
            10. The VIAC Roster of Arbitrators   130
II.   Institutional Requirements for Appointment   131
III.   Board Members as Arbitrators   133
IV.   The Performance of the Arbitrator's Duties   133
       A.   The Arbitrators' Duties   134
            1.   Duty to Resolve the Dispute   135
            2.   Duty to Comply with Due Process   138
            3.   Duty of Independence and Impartiality   138
            4.   Duty of Efficient Conduct   139
            5.   Duty of Secrecy   140
            6.   Duty to Meet Certain Qualification Requirements   142
            7.   Duty of Diligence   142
            8.   Ancillary and Cost-Efficiency Duties   142
            9.   Ethical Duties   143
            10. Additional Duties Imposed by the Parties in
                 the Ongoing Arbitration   144

B. The Independence and Impartiality of Arbitrators 145
1. Attempts at International Harmonization 146
2. The Standard of Impartiality and Independence in International Arbitration 148
  2.1. Impartiality and Independence 148
  2.2. Neutrality 150
3. The Standard of Independence and Impartiality Under Austrian Law 151
  3.1. The Standard of Impartiality and Independence Under the Former ZPO 152
  3.2. The Standard of Impartiality and Independence Under the New ZPO 154
4. Some Examples Regarding Impartiality and Independence 156
5. Some Particular Issues Regarding Impartiality and Independence 159
  5.1. Different Standard for Party-Appointed Arbitrators? 159
  5.2. Continuing Obligation of Impartiality 162
  5.3. The Impact of Settlement Discussions 162
  5.4. Independence in a Globally Active Legal Profession 164
  5.5. *Ex Parte* Communications 165
V. Disclosure 166
A. Disclosure Under the Former ZPO and Vienna Rules 166
B. Disclosure Under the New ZPO and Vienna Rules 166
C. The Parties' Disclosure Obligations 171
VI. The Secretary of the Tribunal 172

Article 8
The Liability of Arbitrators and the VIAC **177**
I. Arbitrator Liability 178
A. Conceptual Approaches to the Liability of Arbitrators 178
1. The Concept of Judicial Immunity 178
2. The Concept of Contractual Liability 180
B. Liability of Arbitrators Under Austrian Law 181
1. The Statute 181
2. Section 594(4) ZPO and Contractual Liability 182
3. Liability for Illegal Acts 185
C. Contractual Restriction of Liability 187
II. The Liability of the VIAC 189

Article 9
The Statement of Claims **193**
I. Filing the Statement of Claims 194

A.	Introduction	194
B.	Filing the Statement of Claims	194
	1. Designation of Addressee	195
	2. Form of Filing	196
	3. Case Administration	197
C.	Commencement of the Proceedings and Pendency of the Dispute	198
	1. Statute of Limitations	198
	2. *Lis Pendens*	202
II.	Number of Copies	211
III.	The Content of the Statement of Claims	211
A.	Mandatory Content under Austrian Law	212
B.	Required Content under the Vienna Rules	213
	1. Article 9(3)(a): The Designation of the Parties and their Addresses	216
	2. Article 9(3)(b): Specific Claim and Particulars	217
	3. Article 9(3)(c): The Amount in Dispute	218
	4. Article 9(3)(d) and (e): Specifics Regarding the Arbitrator(s)	219
C.	Additional Considerations	219
	1. Language of the Statement of Claims	219
	2. Power of Attorney	220
	3. Payment of Registration Fee	221
IV.	The Agreement Specifying the Jurisdiction of the VIAC	221
A.	Introduction	221
B.	*Prima Facie* Scrutiny of the Arbitration Agreement	222
V.	Opportunity to Remedy Defects in the Statement of Claims	226
A.	Introduction	226
B.	Failure to Provide the Arbitration Agreement	227
C.	Refusal to Proceed with the Case	227
VI.	Refusal to Administer the Case	229
A.	Introduction	229
B.	Improper Deviation from the Vienna Rules	230
C.	Procedure	232
D.	Consequences of the VIAC's Refusal	233

Article 10
Memorandum in Reply — **235**

I.	Service of the Statement of Claims	235
A.	Introduction	235
B.	Proper Statement of Claims as a Prerequisite of Service	236
C.	Service of the Statement of Claims	237
D.	The Response Period	237
E.	Extensions of the Response Period	238

II. The Memorandum in Reply   239
     A. Mandatory Content under Austrian Law   239
     B. Required Content under the Vienna Rules   240
         1. Article 10(2)(a): Reply to the Pleadings in the
             Statement of Claims   241
         2. Article 10(2)(b) and (c): Particulars Regarding
             the Number, Name and Address of the Arbitrators   242
     C. Formal Requirements   242
     D. Addressee of the Memorandum in Reply   243
     E. Failure to Submit a Proper or Timely Memorandum
         in Reply   243

Article 11
Counter-Claim, Amendments and Set-Off   **247**
I.   Jurisdiction Over Counter-Claims   247
     A. Introduction   247
     B. Jurisdiction   248
     C. Timing   249
II. Filing of the Counter-Claim   251
III. Dismissal of the Counter-Claim   251
     A. Introduction   251
     B. Same Arbitration Agreement   252
     C. Identical Parties   253
     D. Substantial Delay   253
IV. Reply to the Counter-Claim   255
V.   Amendments of Existing Claims   256
     A. Amendments under Austrian Law   257
     B. Amendments under the Vienna Rules   259
VI. Set-Off   260
     A. Jurisdiction   261
     B. Cost Implications   263

Article 12
Transmission of the File to the Arbitrators   **265**
I.   Introduction   265
II. Submission of the Files to the Arbitrators   266
     A. Statement of Claims in Due Form   267
     B. Acceptance of the Arbitrator's Mandate and
         'Confirmation of Objectivity'   268
     C. Deposit Against Costs Has Been Paid   271

Article 13
Time Limits, Service and Communications   **273**
I.   Time Limits   273
     A. Introduction   274

		B.	When Do Time Limits Commence?	274
		C.	When Are Time Limits Observed?	275
		D.	Extensions of Time Limits	276
	II.		Effective Service	278
		A.	Communications in Arbitral Proceedings	278
			1. Communications of the Parties	279
			2. Communications of and amongst the Arbitral Tribunal	280
			3. Communication with the Secretary General	281
			4. Communication with the Board	282
			5. Communication with State Courts	282
		B.	Form of Communications	282
		C.	Recipients of Delivery	284
			1. To the Address Most Recently Notified	284
			2. Actual and/or Demonstrable Transmission	286
	III.		Service to the Party Representative	287

Article 14
Nomination and Appointment of Arbitrators   **289**

I.			Number of Arbitrators	289
	A.		Introduction	290
	B.		Sole Arbitrator or Three-Member Tribunal?	290
	C.		Agreement of the Parties on the Number of Arbitrators	292
	D.		Limits of Party Autonomy	293
	E.		Recommended Arbitration Clause	294
II.			Determination by the Board	295
	A.		Procedure	295
	B.		Timing	296
	C.		Reasoned Decision	297
	D.		Criteria to Determine the Appropriate Number of Arbitrators	297
III.			Nomination or Appointment of a Sole Arbitrator	300
	A.		Terminology: Nomination and Appointment	300
	B.		Joint Nomination by the Parties	301
		1.	Joint Nomination after Board Decision on Number of Arbitrators	301
		2.	Joint Nomination if Number of Arbitrators Has Been Agreed by the Parties	302
	C.		Appointment by the Board	302
		1.	The Appointment Process	303
		2.	Culpa in Eligendo	305
	D.		Appointment by the Austrian Courts	306
IV.			Nomination and Appointment of a Co-Arbitrator	307
	A.		Nomination by the Parties	308
	B.		Appointment by the Board	309

V.   Nomination and Appointment of The Chairman   310
      A.   Nomination by the Co-Arbitrators   310
      B.   Appointment by the Board   312
      C.   Appointment by the Austrian Courts   313
VI.   Binding Effect of Nomination   313

Article 15
Multi-Party Arbitration   **315**
I.   Admissibility of Multi-Party Claims   316
      A.   Introduction   316
      B.   Admissibility of Multi-Party Arbitration under the
           Vienna Rules   318
           1.   Mandatory Requirements   318
           2.   Elective Requirements   319
                2.1. Mandatory Joinder   319
                2.2. Other Factual or Legal Connection
                      Between the Respondents   321
                2.3. Agreement   322
                2.4. Subsequent Submission by the Respondents 322
                2.5. Defaulting Respondents   322
II.   Failure to Serve the Claim on all Respondents   323
III. Determining the Number of Arbitrators in Multi-Party
      Proceedings   323
IV.   Articles 15(6)-15(7): Appointment of the Arbitrator for
      Respondents   325
      A.   *Dutco* and the Equality of the Parties in Constituting
           the Tribunal   325
      B.   Ensuring Equality Between the Parties   328
      C.   Austrian Law   330
      D.   The Vienna Rules   332
V.   Consolidation and Joinder   332
      A.   Introduction   332
      B.   Pre-Agreed Consolidation   334
      C.   Consolidation Under the Vienna Rules   335
      D.   Joinder   338
           1.   Agreement to Join a Party or an Intervener   338
           2.   Joining Non-Signatories   340
                2.1. Succession   342
                2.2. Third-Party Beneficiary   343
                2.3. Estoppel and Abuse of Law   345
                2.4. Corporate Veil Piercing   349
                2.5. Group of Companies   353
                2.6. Domestic Law or Transnational Principles? 354
VI.   Decision on Admissibility of Multi-Party Proceedings   356

Article 16
The Challenge of Arbitrators   **359**
I.   Challenging Arbitrators for Lack of Independence or
      Impartiality   359
      A. Introduction   360
      B. The Standard for Challenging an Arbitrator   360
      C. Threshold for the Challenge of a Party's Own
          Nomination   361
II.   Initiating the Challenge   363
      A. The Challenge of an Arbitrator Under Austrian Law   364
          1. Decision by the Tribunal   364
          2. Voluntary Withdrawal or Agreement   365
          3. Four Week Time Limit   365
      B. The Challenge of an Arbitrator Before the VIAC   366
          1. Reasoned Application   366
          2. Without Delay   367
          3. Waiving the Right to a Challenge and Setting
              Aside the Award   367
III. The Board's Decision on the Challenge   372
      A. Opportunity for Voluntary Withdrawal   372
      B. Decision-Making   373
      C. Remedies Before the State Courts   373
IV.   Continuation of the Proceedings During the Challenge   375

Article 17
Early Termination of the Mandate of Arbitrators   **377**
I.   Reasons for Early Termination   377
      A. Introduction   377
      B. Grounds of Termination   378
          1. Agreement on Termination   378
          2. Voluntary Withdrawal from Office   379
          3. Successful Challenge   380
          4. Removal by the Board   380
II.   Request to Remove the Arbitrator   380
      A. Grounds for Removal   381
      B. Procedure   382
      C. *Ex Officio* Removal   382
      D. Court Review   382

Article 18
Consequences of Challenge or Early Termination
of Mandate   **385**
I.   Appointing a Replacement Arbitrator   385
II.   Repeating Previous Stages of the Procedure   388

Article 19
Jurisdiction of the Arbitral Tribunal **391**
I.   Objection to Jurisdiction 391
     A.   Introduction 391
     B.   Timely Pleading 393
     C.   Admission of Delayed Objections 395
     D.   Different Treatment of Formal and Substantive
          Defects of the Arbitration Agreement 395
II. *Kompetenz-Kompetenz* 396
     A.   Introduction 396
     B.   Decision by the Arbitrator(s) 398
     C.   Court Review 398
     D.   Cost Decisions 403
III. The Doctrine of Separability 403
     A.   International Recognition 404
     B.   Presumption of Separability 405
     C.   The Separability Doctrine in Austrian Law 406
     D.   Limits of the Separability Doctrine 407

Article 20
The Conduct of the Proceedings **411**
I.   Basic Principles of Arbitral Proceedings 412
     A.   Introduction 412
     B.   Conflicting Premises 414
     C.   The Right to Fair and Equal Treatment 417
          1.   Fair Treatment in International Arbitration 417
          2.   Fair Treatment in Austrian Arbitration Law 419
          3.   Fair Treatment Under the Vienna Rules 425
     D.   The Right to Be Heard 426
          1.   Basis for the Right to Be Heard in Austrian Law 427
          2.   Scope of the Right to Be Heard 429
               2.1.   Factual Assertions 429
               2.2.   Facts in the Public Domain 431
               2.3.   Legal Issues 431
               2.4.   Issues Raised by the Arbitrators *Ex Officio* 433
          3.   The Restrictive Approach Under Austrian
               Jurisprudence 434
          4.   Recent Criticism of the Austrian *Oberster Gerichtshof* 438
          5.   The Impact of the 2006 Reform on the Previous
               Case Law 439
          6.   Causality 442
          7.   Limits to the Right to Be Heard 444
               7.1.   Evidentiary Cut-Off Date 444
               7.2.   'Reasonable Opportunity' 445
               7.3.   Irrelevant Evidence 446

		7.4.	Appropriate Time Limits		447
	E.	Controlling the Conduct of the Arbitration			447
		1.	The Arbitrators' Discretion and the Parties'		
			Agreement		448
			1.1. The Primacy of the Parties' Agreement		448
			1.2. The Arbitrator's Discretion		451
		2.	Managing the Conduct of the Arbitration		455
			2.1. The Preliminary Hearing		456
			2.2. Selected Issues of Case Management		459
			(i) Procedural Timetable		459
			(ii) Taking of Evidence		459
			(iii) Identifying the Relevant Issues		460
			(iv) Bifurcation or Other Segmentation of		
			Proceedings		460
II.	The Language of the Arbitration				461
III.	Written Submissions and the Right to an Oral Hearing				463
	A.	The Right to an Oral Hearing			464
	B.	Written Submissions in Arbitration			466
	C.	The Right to Comment			470
IV.	The Oral Hearing				471
	A.	Introduction			472
	B.	Fixing the Hearing Date and Notifying the Parties			473
	C.	Privacy of the Hearing (and Confidentiality			
		of Arbitration)			474
		1.	The Privacy of the Hearing		474
		2.	The Confidentiality of Arbitration		475
	D.	The Record of the Hearing			480
V.	The Taking of Evidence				481
	A.	Introduction			481
	B.	The Arbitrators' Right (or Duty) to Establish the			
		Relevant Facts			483
		1.	The Arbitrator's Duty to Establish the Facts		
			Under the fZPO		484
		2.	The Arbitrator's Right to Establish the Facts		
			Under the ZPO		486
	C.	Witness Testimony			490
		1.	Written Witness Testimony		492
		2.	Oral Witness Testimony		495
		3.	Witness Preparation		498
	D.	Documentary Evidence			501
		1.	Document Disclosure in Common Law and		
			Civil Law Litigation		502
		2.	Document Disclosure in International Arbitration		506
	E.	Court Intervention To Assist the Taking of Evidence			511
VI.	*Ex Parte* Proceedings				514

A.	Introduction	514
B.	No Decision by Default	514
C.	Right to Proceed with One Party Alone	518
VII.	The Obligation to Object Against Procedural Irregularities	519
A.	Objecting Against Procedural Irregularities Under the Vienna Rules	519
B.	Objecting Against Procedural Irregularities Under Austrian Law	521
VIII.	Closing the Proceedings	526

Article 21
Experts and Expert Witnesses **527**

I.	Introduction	527
II.	Experts in International Arbitration	527
III.	Experts Appointed by the Tribunal	528
IV.	Experts Appointed by the Parties	532

Article 22
Interim Measures of Protection **535**

I.	The Tribunal's Power to Grant Interim Relief	536
A.	Introduction	536
B.	The Tribunal's Authority to Grant Interim Relief	539
1.	Interim Measures in Austrian Doctrine Before the 2006 Reform	539
2.	The Basis for Interim Relief Under the ZPO	543
3.	The Basis for Interim Relief Under the Vienna Rules	545
C.	Procedural Preconditions for Interim Relief	546
1.	Power by Default	546
2.	Order Upon Application by a Party	547
3.	No *Ex Parte* Relief	548
4.	As Between the Parties	551
5.	Security	552
6.	Contractual Obligation to Comply	552
D.	Substantive Preconditions for Interim Relief	554
1.	Necessary Relief with Respect to the Subject Matter of the Arbitration	557
2.	Frustration of Final Award	559
3.	Irreparable Harm	560
4.	No Pre-Judgment of the Case	561
5.	*Prima Facie* Establishment of the Applicant's Case	562
6.	Urgency	563
7.	Balancing the parties' Interests	563
8.	Standard of Proof	564

	9.	Interim Relief Despite Jurisdictional Objection	564
	10.	Deviating from the Substantive Requirements of Section 593(1) ZPO and Article 22	565
	11.	Modifying and Terminating Interim Measures	566
E.	Categories of Interim Relief		567
	1.	Orders Ensuring Enforcement of the Final Award and Preventing Irreparable Harm	568
	2.	Orders Protecting the *Status Quo*	569
	3.	Orders Preventing the Aggravation of the Dispute	570
	4.	Orders Protecting the Taking of Evidence	570
	5.	Orders Regulating a Relationship	572
	6.	Orders Involving the Tribunal	573
	7.	Orders for Security of Costs	574

II.	Formal Considerations	576
III.	Reasoned Order	577
	A. Requirements	577
	B. Order or Award	577
IV.	Record of the Order	579
V.	Confirmation of Enforceability	580
VI.	Parallel Jurisdiction of the State Courts	580
	A. Interim Measures by State Courts	580
	B. Duty to Inform the Tribunal and the VIAC	583
VII.	Enforcing Arbitral Interim Measures in Austria	584
	1. Jurisdictional Basis	584
	2. Procedure	587
	3. Adapting Foreign Relief to the Austrian System	587
	4. Grounds to Refuse Enforcement	589
	5. Grounds to Set Aside the Enforcement	592

Article 23
Authorized Agents   **595**
I.	Introduction	595
II.	Free Choice of Party Representative	597
III.	Authorization	599

Article 24
Applicable Law and Equity   **601**
I.	The Substantive Law Applicable to the Dispute	601
	A. Introduction	601
	B. Choice of Law by the Parties	602
	1. The Choice of a National Law	604
	2. The Choice of Other Legal Rules	605
	2.1. General Principles of Law and *Lex Mercatoria*	605

2.2. Trade Usages 609
2.3. Tronc Commun and Other Special
Choice-of-Law Clauses 611
3. Restrictions on the Parties' Autonomous Choice 612
4. No *Renvoi* 616
II. Determination of the Applicable Law by the Arbitrators 616
A. Conceptual Approach 616
B. 'The Law' *v.* 'Rules of Law' 620
C. 'Incorrect' Determination by the Arbitrators 621
III. Equity-Based Decisions 621

Article 25
Termination of the Proceedings **625**
I. Introduction 626
II. Termination by Award 626
III. Termination by Settlement 627
IV. Termination by Order 628
A. Withdrawal of Claim 628
B. Agreement on Termination 629
C. Impossibility to Continue Proceedings 630
D. Failure to File the Claim 632
V. Consequences of Termination 632
A. Functus Officio 633
B. Ongoing Obligations of the Tribunal 633

Article 26
Decision Making of the Arbitral Tribunal **635**
I. Quorum 635
A. Introduction 635
B. Quorum Requirements Under Austrian Law 636
C. Quorum Requirements Under the Vienna Rules 639
D. The Tribunal's Deliberations 641
E. Dissenting Opinions 642
II. Procedural Decisions 646

Article 27
The Award **649**
I. The Reasoned Award in Writing 649
II. Statement of Date and Arbitral Seat 654
III. Signed Award 656
IV. Confirmation by the VIAC 657
V. Service and Effect of the Award 658
VI. Confirmation of Finality and Enforceability 659
VII. Partial and Interim Awards 660
VIII. Implementing the Award 662

IX.   Recourse Against an Award in the Austrian Courts   663
      A.   Jurisdiction and Proceedings   663
      B.   Grounds for Setting Aside an Arbitral Award   665
           1.   Jurisdictional Issues   666
           2.   Violation of the Right to be Heard   668
           3.   Decision *Ultra Petita*   668
           4.   Deficient Formation or Composition of the
                Arbitral Tribunal   669
           5.   *Procedural Ordre Public*   670
           6.   Reopening of Court Proceedings   671
           7.   Lack of Arbitrability   672
           8.   *Substantive Ordre Public*   672
      C.   Consequences of Setting Aside Proceedings   673
      D.   Declaration that an Award Does or Does Not Exist   673
      E.   Enforcement of Foreign Awards   674

Article 28
Settlement and Consent Award   **677**

Article 29
Correction and Interpretation of Awards   **683**
I.   Application for Correction, Interpretation or
      Supplementation of the Award   683
II.   Decision by the Tribunal   686
III. *Ex Officio* Correction   687
IV.   Application for Correction, Interpretation or
      Supplementation of the Award   688

Article 30
Publishing Awards and Decisions   **691**
I.   Publishing Awards   691
II.   Publishing Procedural Orders   693
III. Publishing Decisions of the VIAC   693

Article 31
The Award on Costs   **695**
I.   Introduction   695
II.   Determining the Costs of the Arbitration   696
III. Determining the Costs of the Parties   697
      A.   Legal Basis   698
      B.   Determining What Costs Were 'Reasonable'   702
      C.   Other Outlay Related to Arbitration Proceedings   708
IV.   Allocating the Costs Between the Parties   710
      A.   International Trends   711
      B.   The Austrian Approach   713

1.	Traditional Method of Cost Allocation in Austria	714
2.	The Modern Austrian Approach to Cost Allocation in Arbitration	716
V.	Determining the Costs Absent Jurisdiction on the Merits	716
VI.	Procedural Considerations	718
A.	Procedure	719
B.	Request for Costs	719
C.	Timing of Cost Decision	720
D.	Form of Cost Decision	721

Article 32
Categories of Costs 723

Article 33
The Registration Fee 725
I. Payment and Purpose 725
II. Increase in Multiparty Arbitrations 727
III. Deduction From Deposit 727
IV. Failure to Pay the Registration Fee 728

Article 34
The Determination of the Costs of the Arbitration and
the Deposit 731
I. Determining the Costs of the Arbitration 731
  A. Introduction 731
  B. Authority to Determine the Costs of the Arbitration 732
    1. Administrative Costs 732
    2. The Arbitrator's Fees 733
  C. Procedure for Determining the Costs of the Arbitration 735
II. The Amount of the Deposit Against Costs 736
  A. Calculation of the Amount of the Deposit 736
  B. Payment of the Deposit Against Costs 738
III. The Claimant's Failure to Pay the Deposit 739
IV. The Respondent's Failure to Pay the Deposit 740
  A. Procedural Consequences 741
  B. Remedy Against Non-Payment 741
V. Increase of the Amount in Dispute 751
VI. Additional Expenses 752

Article 35
Further Costs of Procedure 753
I. Cost Cover for all Procedural Actions 753
II. Budgeting Expenditures 754
III. Failure to pay Additional Cost Deposits 755
IV. Liability for Procedural Costs 756

Article 36
Calculating the Costs of Arbitration   **759**
I.   Determination of Arbitration Costs   759
    A.   Introduction   759
    B.   The Schedule of Arbitration Costs   760
    C.   Early Termination of the Proceedings   761
II.   Multi-Party Proceedings   762
III.   Declaration of Set-Off   763
IV.   Separate Calculations   765
V.   Partial Claim and Undervaluation   766
VI.   Raise of Fees   768
VII.   Comprehensive Cost Determination   769
VIII.   Reduction of the Amount in Dispute   769
IX.   Determination of Cash Outlays   770
X.   Value Added Tax   771

Article 37
Transitional Provisions   **773**
I.   Introduction   773
II.   The Application of Austrian Arbitration Law   774
III.   The Application of Future Versions of the Vienna Rules   775

Annexes   **779**

Annex 1a
International Arbitral Centre of the Austrian Federal
Economic Chamber Rules of Arbitration 2006
(Vienna Rules 2006)   **781**

Annex 1b
Internationales Schiedsgericht der Wirtschaftskammer
Österreich Schiedsordnung 2006 (Wiener Regeln 2006)   **803**

Annex 2a
International Arbitral Centre of the Austrian Federal
Economic Chamber Rules of Arbitration 2001
(Vienna Rules 2001)   **825**

Annex 2b
Internationales Schiedsgericht der Wirtschaftskammer
Österreich Schiedsordnung 2001 (Wiener Regeln 2001)   **843**

Annex 3a
International Arbitral Centre of the Austrian Federal
Economic Chamber Conciliation Rules 2006   **861**

Annex 3b
Internationales Schiedsgericht der Wirtschaftskammer
Österreich Schlichtungsordnung 2006   **863**

Annex 4
Arbitrator's Declaration of Acceptance, Statement of
Independence and Undertaking to Observe Rules on Costs   **865**

Annex 5
Guidelines for Arbitrators   **867**

Annex 6
Account Details   **871**

Annex 7
Schiedsgerichtsordnung für die Ständigen Schiedsgerichte
der Wirtschaftskammern 2006   **873**

Annex 8a
Code of Civil Procedure, Fourth Section: Arbitration
(Austrian Arbitration Act 2006)   **891**

Annex 8b
Zivilprozessordnung, Vierter Abschnitt: Schiedsverfahren   **913**

Annex 9a
Former Code of Civil Procedure   **935**

Annex 9b
Zivilprozessordnung (in der Fassung vor der
Schiedsrechtsänderungsreform 2006 'Alte Fassung')   **943**

Annex 10
European Convention on International Commercial
Arbitration 1961 (European Convention)   **951**

Annex 11
Convention on the Recognition and Enforcement of Foreign
Arbitral Awards 1958 (New York Convention)   **961**

Annex 12
List of Bilateral Agreements Concluded by Austria
That Refer to Arbitration   **967**

Annex 13
List of Multilateral Agreements Concluded by Austria
That Refer to Arbitration   **969**

Annex 14
List of Bilateral Investment Treaties Concluded Between
Austria and Other Countries   **973**

Annex 15
UNCITRAL Notes on Organizing Arbitral Proceedings 1996
(UNCITRAL Notes)   **975**

Annex 16
IBA Rules on the Taking of Evidence in International
Commercial Arbitration (IBA Rules of Evidence)   **1001**

Annex 17
IBA Guidelines on Conflicts of Interest in International
Arbitration (IBA Conflict Guidelines)   **1011**

Annex 18
IBA Rules of Ethics for International Arbitrators
(IBA Rules of Ethics)   **1029**

Index   **1035**

List of Abbreviations

A.C.	Appeal Cases Law Reports
AAA	American Arbitration Association
AAA Rules	AAA Commercial Arbitration Rules
AAA/ICDR	American Arbitration Association/International Centre for Dispute Resolution
AAA/ICDR Rules	AAA/ICDR International Arbitration Rules
ABA	American Bar Association
ABGB	*Allgemeines Bürgerliches Gesetzbuch* (Austrian Civil Code)
ADR	Alternative Dispute Resolution
AFCC	Austrian Federal Chamber of Commerce
AFEC	Austrian Federal Economic Chamber
AG	*Amtsgericht* (German Local Court); *also: Aktiengesellschaft* (Stock Coporation)
AHG	*Amtshaftungsgesetz* (Austrian Public Liability Act)
AHR	*Autonome Honorar-Richtlinien* (Austrian Autonomous Fee Guidelines for Attorneys)
AIAJ	Asian International Arbitration Journal
ALR	Australian Law Reports
Am Rev Int'l Arb	American Revue of International Arbitration
AnwBl	*Anwaltsblatt* (Austrian Law Journal)
App	Appendix
Arb Int'l	LCIA Arbitration International
Arb L Monthly	Arbitration Law Monthly
ArbSlg	*Sammlung arbeitsrechtlicher Entscheidungen* (Collection of Decisions on Labour Matters)

Art./Arts	Article(s)
ASA	*Association Suisse de l'Arbitrage* (Swiss Arbitration Association)
ASGG	*Arbeits- und Sozialgerichtsgesetz* (Austrian Labour and Social Courts Act)
AußStrG	*Außerstreitgesetz* (Austrian Act on Non-Contentious Matters)
BayObLG	*Bayerisches Oberstes Landesgericht* (Bavarian Highest Regional Court)
BB	*Betriebs-Berater* (German Law Journal)
Bezirksgericht	Austrian District Court
BGB	*Bürgerliches Gesetzbuch* (German Civil Code)
BGBl	*Bundesgesetzblatt* (Austrian Federal Law Gazette)
BGE	*Entscheidungen des Schweizer Bundesgerichtes* (Decisions of the Swiss Federal Supreme Court)
BGer	*Bundesgericht* (Swiss Federal Supreme Court)
BGH	*Bundesgerichtshof* (German Federal Supreme Court)
BGHZ	*Entscheidungen des Bundesgerichtshofs in Zivilsachen* (Decisions of the German Federal Supreme Court)
BLR	Building Law Reports
Brussels I Regulation	Council Regulation (EC) No 44/2001 of 22 December 2000 on Jurisdiction and the Recognition and Enforcement of Judgments in Civil and Commercial Matters
Brit YB Int'l L	British Yearbook of International Law
Brussels Convention	1968 Brussels Convention on Jurisdiction and the Enforcement of Judgments in Civil and Commercial Matters
BSG	*Bundessozialgericht* (German Federal Social Court)
Bull ASA	Bulletin de l'Association Suisse de l'Arbitrage
Bundesgericht	Swiss Federal Supreme Court
Bundesgerichtshof	German Federal Supreme Court
Bus L Int'l	Business Law International
BVerfG	*Bundesverfassungsgericht* (German Federal Constitutional Court)
BVerfGE	*Entscheidungen des Bundesverfassungsgerichts* (Decisions of the German Federal Constitutional Court)
Case W Res J Int'l L	Case Western Reserve Journal of International Arbitration
CBOE	Chicago Board Options Exchange
CCBE	Council of Bars and Law Societies of Europe
CCI	*Chambre de Commerce Internationale* (*see also*: ICC)

CEE	Central and Eastern Europe
CEPANI	*Centre belge d'arbitrage et de médiation* (Belgian Center for Mediation and Arbitration)
CEPANI Rules	CEPANI Arbitration Rules
ch.	chapter
CIDRA	Chicago International Dispute Resolution Association
CIDRA Rules	Arbitration Rules of Chicago International Dispute Resolution Association
CIETAC	China International Economic and Trade Arbitration Commission
CIETAC Rules	CIETAC Arbitration Rules
Comp L YB Int'l Bus	Comparative Law Yearbook of International Business
Columbia UP	Columbia University Press
Corte de Cassazione	Italian Supreme Court
Cour d'Appel	French Court of Appeal
Cour de Cassation 1re Ch. Civ./2e Ch. Civ.	French Supreme Court
CPR	Civil Procedure Rules
Croatian Rules	Rules of Arbitration of the Permanent Arbitration Court at the Croatian Chamber of Economy
CTR	Claims Tribunal Report
Czech Rules	Rules of the Arbitration Court attached to the Economic Chamber of the Czech Republic and Agricultural Chamber of the Czech Republic
d	deutsch(es) (German)
Dalloz	*Recueil Dalloz* (French Law Journal)
D.C. Cir.	US Court of Appeals for the D.C. Circuit
DDR	*Deutsche Demokratische Republik* (German Democratic Republic)
DHG	*Dienstnehmerhaftpflichtgesetz* (Austrian Employee Liability Act)
DIS	*Deutsche Institution für Schiedsgerichtsbarkeit* (German Institution of Arbitration)
DIS Rules	DIS Arbitration Rules
Disp Res Mag	Dispute Resolution Magazine
D. Minn	United States District Court for the District of Minessota
Doc.	Document
dRGBl.	*deutsches Reichsgesetzblatt* (German Reich Law Gazette)
e.g	exempli gratia/for example
EC	European Community
EC Treaty	Treaty establishing the European Community
ECHR	European Convention on Human Rights; *also* European Court of Human Rights

ECICA	European Convention on International Commercial Arbitration
ECJ	European Court of Justice
ecolex	*Zeitschrift für Wirtschaftsrecht* (Austrian Law Journal)
ECR	European Court Reports
ECT	Treaty establishing the European Community
E.D.Ca	United States District Court for the Eastern District of California
ed./eds	editor(s)
edn	edition
EGBGB	*Einführungsgesetz zum Bürgerlichen Gesetzbuch* (Introductory Act to the German Civil Code)
EGJN	*Einführungsgesetz zur Jurisdiktionsnorm* (Introductory Act to the Austrian Judicature Act)
EHR Court / Commission	European Court of Human Rights/European Commission of Human Rights
EHRR	European Human Rights Reports
EO	*Exekutionsordnung* (Austrian Enforcement Act)
ERCL	European Review of Contract Law
et al.	and others
et seq.	et sequentes/and the following
etc.	et cetera
EU	European Union
ECJ	European Court of Justice
European Convention	European Convention on International Commercial Arbitration (1961)
EvBl	*Evidenzblatt der Rechtsmittelentscheidungen* (Austrian Law Journal)
EWCA	Court of Appeal of England and Wales
EWHC	High Court of England and Wales
F.3d	West's Federal Reporter, Third Series
F.C.	Federal Court of Canada
F.Supp.	Federal Supplement
FCPA	Federal Corrupt Practices Act
FETAC	Foreign Economic and Trade Arbitration Commission
fn.	footnote
Fordham Urb LJ	Fordham Urban Law Journal
Forum Int'l	Forum International
fZPO	Former *Zivilprozessordnung* (former Austrian Code of Civil Procedure prior to the 2006 reform of the Austrian Arbitration Act)
GAFTA	Greater Arab Free Trade Area; *also* Grain and Free Trade Association
GebG	*Gebührengesetz* (Austrian Law on Stamp Duties)

Gericht für Arbeits- und Sozialssachen	Austrian Labour and Social Court
GesRZ	*Der Gesellschafter* (Austrian Law Journal)
GestG	*Gerichtsstandsgesetz* (Swiss Federal Statute on the Jurisdiction of Courts in Domestic Civil Matters)
GH	*Die Gerichtshalle* (Austrian Law Journal)
GIUNF	*Sammlung von zivilrechtlich Entscheidungen des k.k. Obersten Gerichtshofes* (Collection of Decisions in Civil Matters of the Austrian Imperial and Royal Supreme Court)
GmbH	*Gesellschaft mit beschränkter Haftung* (Limited Liability Company)
GmbHG	*Gesetz über die Gesellschaft mit beschränkter Haftung* (Austrian Law on Limited Liability Companies)
GPR	*Zeitschrift für Gemeinschaftsprivatrecht* (German Law Journal)
GVO-Kfz	*Verordnung (EG) Nr. 1475/95 der Kommission vom 28. Juni 1995 über die Anwendung von Artikel 85 Absatz 3 des Vertrages auf Gruppen von Vertriebs- und Kundendienstvereinbarungen über Kraftfahrzeuge* (Commission Regulation (EC) No 1475/95 of 28 June 1995 on the application of Article 85(3) of the Treaty to certain categories of motor vehicle distribution and servicing agreements)
Handelsgericht	Austrian Commercial Court
HaRÄG	*Handelsrechtsänderungsgesetz* (Revision of the Austrian Commercial Code)
HG	*Handelsgericht* (Commercial Court)
HGB	*Handelsgesetzbuch* (Austrian Commercial Code)
Hungarian Rules	Rules of Proceedings of the Arbitration Court attached to the Hungarian Chamber of Commerce and Industry
i.e.	that is
IBA	International Bar Association
IBA Guidelines	IBA Guidelines on Conflicts of Interest in International Commercial Arbitration
IBA Rules	IBA Rules on Taking of Evidence in International Commercial Arbitration
ICC	International Chamber of Commerce
ICC Ct Bull	International Chamber of Commerce Court Bulletin
ICC Pub No	International Chamber of Commerce Publication Number
ICC Rules	Rules of Arbitration of the International Chamber of Commerce
ICCA	International Council for Commercial Arbitration

ICDR	International Centre for Dispute Resolution
ICJ	International Court of Justice
ICJ Reports	International Court of Justice Reports
ICLQ	International and Comparative Law Quarterly
ICSID	International Centre for Settlement of Investment Disputes
ICSID Arbitration Rules	ICSID Rules of Procedure for Arbitration Proceedings (Arbitration Rules)
ICSID Convention	Covention on the Settlement of Investment Disputes Between States and Nationals of Other States
ICSID Rev-FILJ	ICSID Review – Foreign Investment Law Journal
IHR	*Internationales Handelsrecht – Zeitschrift für das Recht des internationalen Warenkaufs- und vertriebs* (German Law Journal)
ILA	International Law Association
ILM	International Legal Materials
Int'l Arb L Rev	International Arbitration Law Review
Int'l Bus LJ	International Business Law Journal
Int'l Fin L Rev	International Financial Law Review
IPRax	*Praxis des internationalen Privat- und Verfahrensrechts* (Austrian Law Journal)
IPRG	*Internationales Privatrechtsgesetz* (Austrian Private International Law Act)
J Chart Inst Arb	Journal of the Chartered Institute of Arbitrators
J Int'l Arb	Journal of International Arbitration
JBl	*Juristische Blätter* (Austrian Law Journal)
JCP	*La Semaine Juridique: Juris Classeur Periodique* (French Law Journal)
JDI	*Journal du Droit International* (French Law Journal)
JGS	*Justizgesetzsammlung* (Austrian Law Gazette)
JN	*Jurisdiktionsnorm* (Austrian Judicature Act)
JW	*Juristische Wochenschrift* (German Law Journal)
JZ	*Juristenzeitung* (German Law Journal)
KartG	*Kartellgesetz* (Austrian Cartel Act)
KSchG	*Konsumentenschutzgesetz* (Austrian Consumer Protection Act)
KTS	*Konkurs-, Treuhand- und Schiedsgerichtswesen* (German Law Journal)
Landesgericht	Regional Court
L & P Int'l Bus	Law and Policy in International Business
LandeskammerSG	*Landeskammer-Schiedsgericht* (Arbitral Tribunal of the Regional Economic Chamber)
LCIA	London Court of International Arbitration
LCIA Rules	LCIA Arbitration Rules
LG	*Landesgericht* (Regional Court)

Lugano Convention	Convention on Jurisdiction and the Enforcement of Judgments in Civil and Commercial Matters done at Lugano on 16 September 1988
LGZ	*Landesgericht für Zivilrechtssachen* (Regional Court for Civil Matters)
LJ	Law Yournal
Lloyd's Rep	Lloyd's Reports
LLP	Lloyd's of London Press
Ltd.	Limited
Mealy's Int'l Arb Rep	Mealy's International Arbitration Report
Mich J Int'l L	Michigan Journal of International Law
MietSlg	*Mietrechtliche Entscheidungen* (Decisions on Tenancy Matters)
MR	*Medien und Recht* (Austrian Law Journal)
MRG	*Mietrechtsgesetz* (Austrian Tenancy Act)
N.Y. App. Div.	New York Appellate Division
NAI	Netherlands Arbitration Institute
ND. Ga	United States District Court for the Northern District of Georgia
NetV	*Nova & Varia Zeitschrift des Juristenverbandes* (Austrian Law Journal)
NJW	*Neue Juristische Wochenschrift* (German Law Journal)
NJW-RR	*Neue Juristische Wochenschrift Rechtsprechungs-Report* (German Law Journal)
No(s)/no(s)	Number(s)
NY	New York
NY Convention	Convention on the Recognition and Enforcement of Foreign Arbitral Awards 1958
NY L School J Int'l Comp L	New York Law School Journal of International and Comparative Law
NY Law Journal	New York Law Journal
Oberlandesgericht	Court of Appeal
Oberster Gerichtshof	Austrian Supreme Court
OGH	*Oberster Gerichtshof* (Austrian Supreme Court)
ÖJZ	*Österreichische Juristenzeitung* (Austrian Law Journal)
OLG	*Oberlandesgericht* (Court of Appeal)
OUP	Oxford University Press
p./ pp	page/pages
para./paras.	paragraph(s)
PATV	Permanent Arbitral Tribunal of the Vienna Economic Chamber
PATV Rules	Arbitration Rules of the Permanent Arbitral Tribunal of the Vienna Economic Chamber

PCA	Permanent Court of Arbitration
PLN	Polish Zloty
Polish Rules	Rules of the Court of Arbitration at the Polish Chamber of Commerce in Warsaw
P 2d 1	Pacific Reporter, Second Series
Q.B. (Comm)	Queen's Bench
QC	Queen's Counsel
RAO	*Rechtsanwaltsordnung* (Professional Rules of the Austrian Bar)
RATG	*Rechtsanwaltstarifgesetz* (Austrian Attorney Tariff Act)
RDAI	*Revue de Droit des Affaires Internationales* (French Law Journal)
RdW	*Recht der Wirtschaft* (Austrian Law Journal)
Rev Arb	*Revue de l'arbitrage* (French Law Journal)
RG	*Reichsgericht* (Supreme Court of the German Reich)
RGBl	*Reichsgesetzblatt* (Austrian Law Gazette)
RGZ	*Entscheidungssammlung des Reichsgerichts in Zivilsachen* (Collection of Decisions of the German Reich)
RIW	*Recht der internationalen Wirtschaft* (German Law Journal)
Rsp	*Rechtsprechung* (Austrian Law Journal)
Rspr.	*Rechtsprechung* (German Law Journal)
RStDG	*Richter – und Staatsanwaltsschaftsdienstgesetz* (Austrian Law on Employment of State Court Judges and Prosecutors)
RWZ	*Österreichische Zeitschrift für Recht und Rechnungswesen* (Austrian Law Journal)
RZ	*Österreichische Richterzeitung* (Austrian Law Journal)
S.D.N.Y.	United States District Court for the Southern District of New York
SCC	Stockholm Chamber of Commerce
SCC Institute	Arbitration Institute of the Stochkholm Chamber of Commerce
SCC Rules	Arbitration Rules of the Arbitration Institute of the Stockholm Chamber of Commerce
SchiedsRÄG	*Schiedsrechtsänderungsgesetz* (Revision of the Austrian Arbitration Law)
SchiedsVZ	*Zeitschrift für Schiedsverfahren* (German Law Journal)
Sec	Section
2nd Cir./3rd Cir/ 4th Cir/10th Cir	United States Court of Appeals, Second Circuit/Third Circuit/Fourth Circuit/Tenth Circuit

SEE	South Eastern European
SIAC	Singapore International Arbitration Centre
SigG	*Signaturgesetz* (Austrian Federal Law Regarding Electronic Signatures)
Slg	*Sammlung* (Collection of judicial decisions)
Slovak Rules	Rules of Procedure of the Court of Arbitration of the Slovak Chamber of Commerce and Industry
Slovenian Rules	Rules of Arbitration of the Permanent Court of Arbitration attached to the Chamber of Commerce and Industry of Slovenia
SLR	Singapore Law Review
Swiss IPRG	*Swiss Internationales Privatrechtsgesetz* (Swiss Private International Law Act)
Swiss Rules	Swiss Rules of International Arbitration
Stockholm Arb Rep	Stockholm Arbitration Report
subs	subsection
Suppl.	Supplement
SWK	*Steuer- und Wirtschaftskartei* (Austrian Law Journal)
SZ	*Entscheidungen des österreichischen Obersten Gerichtshofes in Zivilsachen* (Decisions of the Austrian Supreme Court on Civil Matters)
TDM	Transnational Dispute Management
Tul L Rev	Tulane Law Review
U.K.	United Kingdom
U.S.	United States
U.S. S. Ct.	United States Supreme Court
UGB	*Unternehmensgesetzbuch* (Austrian Commercial Code)
UKHL	United Kingdom House of Lords
UKPC	United Kingdom Privy Council
UN	United Nations
UNCITRAL	United Nations Commission On International Trade Law
UNCITRAL Model Law	UNCITRAL Model Law On International Commercial Arbitration
UNCITRAL Notes	UNCITRAL Notes on Organizing Arbitral Proceedings 1996
UNCITRAL Rules	UNCITRAL Arbitration Rules
UNICTRAL YB	UNCITRAL Yearbook
UNTS	United Nations Treaty Series
US	United States
U.S.C.	United States Code
US FAA	United States Federal Arbitration Act
UStG	*Umsatzsteuergesetz* (Austrian Federal Law Regarding Taxation Of Turnover)

Va J Int'l Law	Virginia Journal of International Law
Vand J Transnat'l L	Vanderbilt Journal of Transnational Law
VAT	Value Added Tax
VIAC	International Arbitral Centre of the Austrian Federal Economic Chamber
VIAC Conciliation Rules	Conciliation Rules of the International Arbitral Centre of the Austrian Federal Economic Chamber
Vienna Rules	Rules of Arbitration and Conciliation of the Vienna International Arbitral Center of the Austrian Federal Economic Chamber
VO	_Verordnung_ (Regulation)
VR	_Die Versicherungsrundschau_ (Austrian Law Journal)
wbl	_Wirtschaftsrechtliche Blatter_ (Austrian Law Journal)
WIPO	World Intellectual Property Organization
WIPO Rules	WIPO Arbitration Rules
WKG	_Wirtschaftskammergesetz_ (Austrian Federal Economic Chamber Act)
WL	Westlaw
WLR	Weekly Law Reports
WM	_Wirtschafts- und Bankrecht_ (German Law Journal)
wobl	_Wohnrechtliche Blätter_ (Austrian Law Journal)
WuW	_Wirtschaft und Wettbewerb_ (German Law Journal)
YB Comm Arb	Yearbook Commercial Arbitration
YBILC	Yearbook of the International Law Commission
Zak	_Zivilrecht aktuell_ (Austrian Law Journal)
ZBl.	_Zentralblatt für die juristische Praxis_ (Austrian Law Journal)
ZfRV	_Zeitschrift für Europarecht, IPR und Rechtsvergleichung_ (Austrian Law Journal)
ZGR	_Zeitschrift für Unternehmens- und Gesellschaftsrecht_ (German Law Journal)
ZPO	_Zivilprozessordnung_ (Austrian Code of Civil Procdure)
ZPO GE	_Loi de procedure civile de Genève_ (Code of Civil Procedure of the Canton of Geneva)
ZustG	_Zustellgesetz_ (Austrian Rules of Delivery)
ZVN	_Zivil-Verfahrensnovelle_ (Revision of the Austrian Code of Civil Procedure)
ZZP	_Zeitschrift für Zivilprozessrecht_ (German Law Journal)

Table of Cases and Awards

I.   AUSTRIA*

OGH, 26 February 1901, Nr. 2164, GIUNF 1304
OGH, 5 December 1901, Nr. 14, 451, GIUNF 2543
OGH, 13 July 1904, Nr. 9722, GIUNF 2749
OGH, 28 December 1905, Nr. 19.81, GIUNF 3646
OGH, 18 May 1909, Rv I, 279/9, GIUNF 4624
OGH, 21 February 1911, Rv I, 106/11, GIUNF 5373
OGH, 1 May 1912, Rv I, 132/12, GIUNF 5896
OGH, 10 June 1913, Rv I, 580/13, GIUNF 6482
OGH, 8 July 1913, R. II, 679/13, GIUNF 6520
OGH, 13 November 1913, Ob III 709, ZBl 1923/292
OGH, 26 October 1915, JBl 238 alt
OGH, 7 May 1918, Rv I 168, ZBl 1919/222
OGH, 21 February 1922, 2 OB 17/22, SZ 4/23
OGH, 6 February 1923, Ob II 49, ZBl 1924, 206
OGH, 6 March 1923, 1 Ob 80/23, SZ 5/44
OGH, 16 January 1924, Ob I 20, ZBl 1924/92, 205
OGH, 2 September 1924, Ob III 568/24, Rsp VI, 201
OGH, 25 September 1924, Rsp 1925, 108
OGH, 3 March 1925, SZ 7/252
OGH, 17 September 1925, 3 Ob 713/25, SZ 7/279

---

* Cases cited without source are published under http://www.ris2.bka.gv.at. Translation of passages from court decisions from the German original into English were made by the authors for the purposes of this book. Users should always refer to the German original for reasons of accuracy and completeness.

OGH, 30 September 1925, 3 Ob 740/25, SZ 7/295
OGH, 18 November 1925, 25 Ob III 872, ZBl 1926, 391
OGH, 1 June 1926, Ob I 443/26, SZ 8/179
OGH, 27 October 1926, Ob II 1927/60, ZBl 1927/60
OGH, 22 December 1926, 1 Ob 1062/26, SZ 8/351
OGH, 26 April 1927, Ob III 306, ZBl 1927/222, 633
OGH, 14 December 1927, 1 Ob 1187/27, SZ 9/303
OGH, 22 August 1928, 4 Ob 243/28, Rsp 1928/349, 194
OGH, 17 October 1928, 3 Ob 573, ZBl 1929, 79
OGH, 23 October 1928, 3 Ob 648/28, SZ 10/ 303
OGH, 12 April 1929, 1 Ob 157/29, ZBl 1929/ 280, 114
OGH, 9 October 1929, 3 Ob 727/29, JBl 1930, 18
OGH, 6 November 1929, 4 Ob 490, ZBl 1930/23, 67
OGH, 19 November 1929, 1 Ob 1045/29, GH. 1930, 41
OGH, 15 October 1930, 3 Ob 784, ZBl 1931/52, 148
OGH, 28 April 1931, 2 Ob 388, ZBl 1931/222
OGH, 20 May 1931, 2 Ob 529/31, SZ 13/131
OGH, 8 July 1931, 4 Ob 362/31, Rsp 1932, 11
OGH, 4 December 1931, 3 Ob 847, ZBl 1932/306
OGH, 7 February 1933, 3 Ob 108/33, SZ XV/29
OLG Vienna, 10 February 1937, 2 R 56, EvBl 1937/270, 88
OGH, 13 June 1933, 3 Ob 419/33, Rsp 1933/234
OGH, 19 June 1934, 2 Ob 506, 507, ZBl 1934/371
OGH, 20 November 1934, 3 Ob 735/34, Rsp 1935, 11
OGH, 27 March 1935, 1 Ob 249, ZBl 1935/367, 757
OGH, 2 October 1935, 3 Ob 572/35, SZ 17/131
OGH, 29 October 1935, 1 Ob 704/35, SZ XVII/150
OGH, 16 January 1936, 1 Ob 26/36, SZ 18/12
OGH, 25 November 1936, 2 Ob 906/36, Rsp 1937/17
OGH, 9 June 1937, 3 Ob 402/37, EvBl 1937, 722, Rsp 1937/204
OGH, 5 October 1946, 1 Ob 127/46
OGH, 17 May 1950, 3 Ob 171/50
OGH, 3 June 1950, 2 Ob 276/50
OGH, 27 September 1950, 2 Ob 603/50
OGH, 12 September 1951, 1 Ob 623/51
OGH, 17 September 1952, 1 Ob 734/52
OGH, 1 October 1952, 1 Ob 803/52
OGH, 12 November 1952, 2 Ob 723/52
OGH, 21 January 1953, 1 Ob 1044/52
OGH, 10 March 1954, 1 Ob 151/54, SZ 37/31
OGH, 1 December 1954, 3 Ob 689, 690/54
OGH, 13 January 1955, 2 Ob 422/54, JBl 1955, 503
OGH, 9 February 1955, 3 Ob 37/55
OGH, 18 May 1955, 1 Ob 329/55
OGH, 11 September 1957, 2 Ob 382/57

OGH, 11 September 1957, 2 Ob 412/57, JBl 1957, 623
OGH, 5 February 1958, 1 Ob 298/58
OGH, 27 October 1960, 5 Ob 341/60
OGH, 8 March 1961, 1 Ob 98/61
OGH, 12 May 1961, 2 Ob 199/61, EvBl 1961/387
OGH, 20 September 1961, 6 Ob 305/61
OGH, 10 October 1962, 1 Ob 215/62
OGH, 20 February 1964, 6 Ob 273/63, SZ 37/31
OGH, 31 March 1966, 5 Ob 30/66
OGH, 5 April 1966, 8 Ob 92/66
OGH, 18 May 1966, 3 Ob 58/66, EvBl 1966/407
OLG Vienna, 15 December 1966, 2 R 248/66 (unpublished)
LGZ Vienna, 8 June 1967, 44 Cg 67/67, ArbSlg 8434
OGH, 12 July 1967, 6 Ob 161/67, JBl 1968, 432
OGH, 24 January 1968, 1 Ob 297/67, EvBl 1968/345
OGH, 29 January 1970, 1 Ob 252/69
OGH, 17 November 1971, 8 Ob 233/71, JBl 1974, 629
OGH, 15 December 1971, 5 Ob 208/71
OGH, 2 May 1972, 5 Ob 93/72
OGH, 23 February 1977, 8 Ob 560/76
OGH, 7 March 1977, 1 Ob 764/76, JBl 1978, 155
OGH, 7 June 1977, 4 Ob 350/77, SZ 50/83
OGH, 28 June 1977, 4 Ob 523/77, JBl 1979, 42
OGH, 10 November 1977, 6 Ob 701/77
OGH, 21 February 1978, 3 Ob 120/77
OGH, 9 May 1978, 5 Ob 580/78
OGH, 13 February 1979, 2 Ob 578/78
OGH, 7 November 1979, 3 Ob 144/79
OGH, 1 February 1980, 2 Nd 502/80
OGH, 13 March 1980, 7 Ob 13/80, ZVR 1980/304, 311
OGH, 7 July 1981, 5 Ob 633/81
OGH, 24 September 1981, 7 Ob 623/81, EvBl 1982/77
OGH, 13 October 1981, 5 Ob 673/81
OLG Vienna, 11 November 1981, 13 R 159/81, MietSlg 33.644
OGH, 18 January 1982, 8 Ob 520/82, GesRZ 1983, 102
OGH, 16 June 1982, 1 Ob 628/82
OGH, 14 October 1982, 8 Ob 556/82
OGH, 18 November 1982, 8 Ob 502/82
OGH 29 February 1984, 2 Ob 516/84
OGH, 31 August 1984, 1 Ob 20/84
OGH, 6 September 1984, 6 Ob 16/84
OGH, 6 December 1984, 8 Ob 70/84
OLG Graz, 20 February 1985, 4 R 28/85, EvBl 1985, 130
OLG Vienna, 21 February 1985, 2 R 30/85, ÖJZ 1985/120
OGH, 27 February 1985, 1 Ob 504/85

OGH, 18 April 1985, 7 Ob 551/85
OGH, 30 October 1985, 3 Ob 89/85
OGH, 26 May 1986, 8 Ob 572/86
OGH, 3 September 1986, 1 Ob 545/86
OGH, 4 November 1986, 14 Ob 136/86
OGH, 17 December 1986, 3 Ob 32/86
OGH, 9 September 1987, 3 Ob 80/87
OGH, 30 September 1987, 9 Ob A 107/87
OGH, 26 November 1987, 6 Ob 713/87
OGH, 25 January 1988, 1 Ob 297/67, JBl 1969, 669
OGH, 29 June 1988, 9 Ob A 134/88
OGH, 5 October 1988, 3 Ob 58/88
OGH, 16 November 1988, 9 Ob A 270/88
OGH, 24 May 1989, 9 Ob A 135, 136/89
OGH, 19 October 1989, 7 Ob 36/89
OGH, 19 October 1989, 7 Ob 681/89
OGH, 7 February 1990, 3 Ob 609/89
OGH, 7 June 1990, 7 Ob 584/90
OGH, 6 September 1990, 6 Ob 572/90
OGH, 14 November 1990, 1 Ob 711/89
OGH, 10 January 1991, 7 Ob 667/90, SZ 64/1
OGH, 13 February 1991, 3 Ob 507/91
OGH, 28 February 1991, 6 Ob 507, 508/90
OGH, 26 June 1991, 3 Ob 70/91
OGH, 18 September 1991, 1 Ob 582/91
OGH, 7 November 1991, 6 Ob 616/91
OGH, 27 November 1991, 3 Ob 1091/91
OGH, 9 April 1992, 3 Ob 25/92
OGH, 25 June 1992, 7 Ob 545/92
OGH, 24 September 1992, 6 Ob 533/92
HG Vienna, 16 September 1992, 24 Cg 304/92 (unpublished)
OGH, 9 March 1993, 5 Ob 503/93
OGH, 2 July 1993, 1 Ob 525/93
OGH, 14 July 1993, 7 Ob 548/93
OGH, 20 October 1993, Radenska v. Kajo, (1995) XX YB Comm Arb, 1051
OGH, 15 December 1993, 3 Ob 505/94
OGH, 16 December 1993, 8 Ob 547/92
LGZ Vienna, 26 April 1994, 43 R 2031/94, EFSlg 76.076
OGH, 12 April 1994, 4 Ob 1542/94
OGH, 22 September 1994, 2 Ob 566/94
OGH, 25 October 1994, 5 Ob 538/94
OGH, 14 December 1994, 7 Ob 604/94
OGH, 25 January 1995, 3 Ob 543/94, JBl 1995, 596
OGH, 26 January 1995, 3 Ob 221/04b
OGH, 22 March 1995, 7 Ob 647/94

OGH, 13 June 1995, 4 Ob 533/95, SZ 68/112
OGH, 29 June 1995, 2 Ob 50/95
OGH, 31 August 1995, 3 Ob 566/95
OGH, 28 November 1995, 10 Ob 1615/95
OGH, 7 December 1995, 2 Ob 89/95
OGH, 19 January 1996, 8 Ob 1211/95
OGH, 31 January 1996, 9 Ob 501/96
OGH, 21 February 1996, 3 Ob 10/96
OGH, 17 April 1996, 7 Ob 2097/96z
OGH, 5 September 1996, 2 Ob 32/95
OGH, 12 September 1996, 6 Ob 2148/96t
OGH, 7 October 1996, 3 Ob 2360/96x
OGH, 25 February 1997, 4 Ob 61/97t
OGH, 17 April 1997, 8 Ob A 2128/96s
OGH, 24 July 1997, 6 Ob 186/97i
OGH, 16 September 1997, 10 Ob 210/97y
OGH, 23 February 1998, 3 Ob 115/95
OGH, 23 February 1998, Kajo-Erzeugnisse Essenzen GmbH v. DO Zdravilisce
    Radenska (1999) XXIVa YB Comm Arb, 919
OGH, 28 April 1998, 1 Ob 253/97f
OGH, 5 May 1998, 3 Ob 2372/96m
OGH, 10 December 1998, 7 Ob 221/98w
OLG Vienna, 15 December 1998, 13 R 154/98g, ecolex 1999, 259
OGH, 13 July 1999, 5 Ob 186/99k
OGH, 5 August 1999, 1 Ob 211/99g
OGH, 5 August 1999, 1 Ob 79/99w
OGH, 1 September 1999, 9 Ob 120/99h
OGH, 26 January 2000, 7 Ob 368/98p and 7 Ob 369/98k
OGH, 8 June 2000, 2 Ob 158/00z
OGH, 16 January 2001, 4 Ob 330/00h
OGH, 27 February 2001, 1 Ob 273/00d
OGH, 3 April 2001, 4 Ob 37/01
OGH, 25 April 2001, 3 Ob 84/01a
OGH, 26 April 2001, 8 Ob 179/00g
OGH, 17 May 2001, 7 Ob 67/01f
OGH, 10 July 2001, 4 Ob 156/01x
OGH, 17 August 2001, 1 Ob 300/00z
OGH, 22 October 2001, 1 Ob 236/01i
OGH, 22 October 2001, 1 Ob 77/01g
OGH, 27 February 2002, 3 Ob 167/01g
OGH, 24 May 2002, 3 Ob 18/02x
OGH, 29 August 2002, 6 Ob 155/02s
OGH, 7 November 2002, 6 Ob 67/02z
OGH, 18 December 2002, 7 Ob 265/02z
OGH, 19 December 2002, 2 Ob 308/02m

OGH, 10 April 2003, 8 Ob 24/03t
OGH, 29 April 2003, 1 Ob 22/03x
OGH, 29 April 2003, 7 Ob 30/02t
OGH, 28 May 2003, 7 Ob 96/03y
OGH, 28 August 2003, 7 Ob 96/03y
OGH, 28 August 2003, 8 Ob A 60/03m
OGH, 2 October 2003, 6 Ob 41/03b
OGH, 2 December 2003, 6 Ob 41/03b
OGH, 16 December 2003, 1 Ob 270/03t
OGH, 13 January 2004, 5 Ob 123/03d
OGH, 19 February 2004, 6 Ob 151/03d
OGH, 18 March 2004, 2 Ob 53/04i
OGH, 21 April 2004, 9 Ob 39/04g
OGH, 24 June 2004, 6 Ob 122/04s
OGH, 29 June 2004, 3 Ob 22/04p
OGH, 15 September 2004, 9 Ob A 94/04w
OGH, 26 January 2005, 3 Ob 221/04b
OGH, 26 January 2005, 7 Ob 314/04h
OGH, 17 March 2005, 2 Ob 41/04z
OGH, 31 March 2005, 3 Ob 35/05a
OGH, 31 March 2005, 3 Ob 259/04s
OGH, 17 March 2005, 2 Ob 41/04z
OGH, 24 May 2005, 4 Ob 82/05w
OGH, 25 May 2005, 7 Ob 83/05i
OGH, 6 June 2005, 9 Ob 126/04a
OGH, 8 June 2005, 7 Ob 105/05z
OGH, 14 June 2005, 2 Ob 136/05x
OGH, 21 June 2005, 5 Ob 127/05w
OGH, 24 August 2005, 3 Ob 65/05p
OGH, 20 October 2005, 2 Ob 235/05f
OGH, 8 March 2006, 7 Ob 252/05t.
OGH, 29 March 2006, 3 Ob 290/05a
OGH, 29 March 2006, 7 Ob 64/06x
OGH, 26 April 2006, 7 Ob 236/05i
OGH, 26 April 2006, 3 Ob 211/05h
OGH, 10 May 2006, 7 Ob 42/06m
OGH, 16 May 2006, 2 Ob 226/05g
OGH, 22 May 2006, 10 Ob 3/06y
OGH, 30 May 2006, 3 Ob 87/05y
OGH, 29 June 2006, 6 Ob 145/06a
OLG Vienna, 5 July 2006, 4 R 108/06s
OGH, 21 September 2006, 8 Ob 78/06p
OGH, 24 October 2006, 10 Ob 57/06i
OGH, 30 November 2006, 6 Ob 207/06v
OGH, 18 December 2006, 8 Ob 159/06z

OGH, 20 December 2006, 9 Ob 107/06k
OGH, 22 February 2007, 3 Ob 281/06d
OGH, 20 March 2007, 10 Ob 10/07d
OGH, 20 March 2007, 10 Ob 20/07z
LGZ Vienna, 16 April 2007, 46 R 271/07d
OGH, 14 June 2007, 2 Ob 29/07i
OGH, 4 July 2007, 7 Ob 139/07b
LG Vienna, 5 July 2007, 4 R 108/06s
HG Vienna, 24 July 2007, 16 Nc 2/07w (unpublished)
OGH, 27 July 2007, 4 Ob 109/07
OGH, 7 August 2007, 4 Ob 142/07x
OGH, 30 August 2007, 7 Ob 184/06v
OGH, 29 August 2007, 7 Ob 148/07a
OGH, 13 September 2007, 6 Ob 134/07k
OGH, 18 October 2007, 2 Ob 273/06w
OGH, 23 October 2007, 3 Ob 141/07t
OGH, 12 December 2007, 7 Ob 202/07t
OGH, 17 December 2007, 2 Ob 236/07f
OGH, 22 January 2008, 4 Ob 168/07w
OGH, 24 January 2008, 6 Ob 274/07y
OGH, 5 February 2008, 10 Ob 120/07f
OGH, 28 February 2008, 8 Ob 4/08h
OGH, 1 April 2008, 5 Ob 272/07x
OGH, 9 April 2008, 7 Ob 52/08k
OGH, 10 April 2008, 2 Ob 50/08d
LG Graz, 7 May 2008, 50 Cg 235/07z (unpublished)
OGH, 11 July 2008, 3 Ob 139/08z
OGH, 28 August 2008, 4 Ob 80/08f
OGH, 3 September 2008, 3 Ob 35/08f

II.   AUSTRALIA

Resort Condominiums International Inc (USA) v. Ray Bolwell and Resort
    Condominiums (Australasia) Pty Ltd (1993) 118 ALR 655 (Supreme Court
    of Queensland)
Esso Australia Resources Ltd. and others v. The Honorable Sidney James Howard
    and others (1995) 11(3) Arb Int'l, 235, 246 *et seq.* (High Court of Australia)

III.   CANADA

Trans-Pacific Shipping Co. v. Atlantic & Orient Trust Co. Ltd, [2005] F.C. 311
    (Canadian Federal Court)

IV.   EUROPEAN COURT OF JUSTICE

ECJ, 23 March 1982, Nordsee Deutsche Hochseefischerei GmbH v. Reederei
    Mond, Case No. C-102/81, [1982] ECR I-01095
ECJ, 13 July 1995, Danvaern Production A/S v Schuhfabriken Otterbeck GmbH,
    Case No. C-341/93 [1995] ECR I-02053
ECJ, 18 November 1998, Van Uden Maritime BV, Trading as Van Uden Africa
    Line v. Kommanditgesellschaft in Firma Deco-Line, Case No. 391/95, [1998]
    ECR I 7091-7133
ECJ, 1 June 1999, Eco Swiss China Time Ltd v. Benetton International NV, Case
    No. C-126/97 [1999] ECR I-3055
ECJ, 27 January 2005, Denuit and Cordenier v. Transorient-Mosaique Voyages et
    Culture SA and Centro Mòvil Milenium, Case No. C-125/04, [2005]
    ECR I-00923

V.   EHR COMMISSION / EHR COURT

EHR Commission, 7 February 1968, X. & Co. (England) Ltd v Germany, App.
    3147/67, <http://www.echr.coe.int>
EHR Court, 25 October 1984, Bramelid and Malmström v. Sweden, App. 8588/79
    and 8589/79, (1986) 14 EHRR, 116
EHR Court, 8 July 1986, Lithgow and others v. United Kingdom, App. 9006/80,
    9262/81, 9263/81, 9265/81, 9266/81, 9319/81 and 9405/81, (1986) 8 EHRR
    329
EHR Commission, 2 October 1990, Muyldermans v Belgium, App. 12217/86,
    <http://www.echr.coe.int>
EHR Court, 27 August 1991, Demicoli v Malta, App. 13057/87, (1992) 14 EHRR,
    47
EHR Court, 29 October 1991, Jan-Ake Andersson v Sweden, App. 11274/84, ÖJZ
    1992, 304
EHR Commission, 2 December 1991, Jakob Boss Söhne KG v Germany, App.
    18479/91, <http://www.echr.coe.int>
EHR Commission, 2 December 1991, Heinz Schiebler v Germany, App. 18805/91,
    <http://www.echr.coe.int>
EHR Court, 27 October 1993, Dombo Beheer B.V. v. Netherlands, App. 14448/88,
    ÖJZ 1994, 464
EHR Commission, 12 October 1994, Fouquet v France, App. 20398/92, <http://
    www.echr.coe.int>
EHR Court, 31 January 1996, Fouquet v France, App. 20398/92, (1996) 22 EHRR,
    279
EHR Commission, 27 November 1996, L.M. Nordström-Janzon and A.M.
    Nordström-Lehtinen v the Netherlands, App. 28101/95, <http://www.echr.
    coe.int>

VI. FRANCE

Cour d'Appel de Paris, 15 June 1956, Sigma v. Bezard and Totaliment v. Comptoir Agricole du Pays-Bas Normand, [1957] Dalloz, Jur. 587, 588
Cour d'Appel de Paris, 14 June 1962, Ets. Douillet et Cie. v. Comptoirs d'Approvisionnement Pierre Four et Cie., [1962] Rev Arb, 107
Cour de Cassation, 2e Ch. Civ., 2 December 1964, S.A.R.L. Douillet et Fils v. Four et Cie., (1965) JCP, Ed. G., Pt. II, No. 14, 277 bis (1965)
Cour de Cassation, 1re Ch. Civ., 19 June 1979, SARL Primor v. Société d'Exploitation Industrielle de Bétaigne, [1979] Rev Arb, 487
Cour d'Appel de Reims, 23 July 1981, Denis Coakley Ltd. v. Sté. Michel Reverdy, (1984) IX YB Comm Arb, 400, 402
Cour de Cassation, 1re Ch. Civ., 9 October 1984, Pabalk Ticaret Sirketi v. Norsolor, [1985] Rev Arb, 431 and (1985) 2(2) J Int'l Arb, 67
Cour d'Appel de Pau, 26 November 1986, Société Sponsor A.B. v. Lestrade, [1988] Rev Arb, 153 *et seq.*
Cour d'Appel de Paris, 11 January 1990, Orri v Société des Lubrifiants Elf Aquitaine, [1992] Rev Arb, 95
Cour d'Appel de Versailles, 7 March 1990, OIAETI et Sofidif v. Cogema et al., [1991] Rev Arb, 326
Cour d'Appel de Paris, 29 March 1991, Ganz and others v. Soc. Nationale des Chemin de Fer Tunisiens, [1991] Rev Arb 478, 480
Cour de Cassation, 1re Ch. Civ., 11 June 1991, Orri v. société des Lubrifiants Elf Aquitaine, [1992] Rev Arb, 73
Cour de Cassation, 1re Ch. Civ., 7 January 1992, Siemens AG/BKMI Industrienanlagen GmbH v. Dutco Construction Company, (1993) XVII YB Comm Arb, 140
Cour d'Appel de Paris, 19 May 1993, Sté Labinal v. Stés Mors et Westland Aerospace, [1993] Rev Arb, 645
Cour de Cassation, 1re Ch. Civ., 23 March 1994, Société Hilmarton v. Société OTV, [1994] Rev Arb, 327
Cour d'Appel de Paris, 14 January 1997, République arabe d'Egypte v Société Chromalloy Aero Services, [1997] Rev Arb, 395
Cour d'Appel de Paris, 23 October 1997, IAIGG-Inter-Arab Investment Guarantee Corporation (Kuwait) v. Ball – Banque Arab et Internationale d'Investissements SA (France) (1988) XXIII YB Comm Arb, 644, 652
Cour d'Appel de Paris, 25 November 1997, Société VRV v Pharmachim, [1998] Rev Arb, 684
Cour d'Appel de Paris, 15 September 1998, Cubic Defence Systems v Chambre de Commerce International, [1999] Rev Arb, 103 with note by Lalive
Cour de Cassation, 2e Ch. Civ., 10 November 1998, Société Duarib v. Société des Etablissements Jallais, [1998] Rev Arb, 680
Cour d'Appel de Paris, 1 July 1999, Braspetro Oil Services Company – Brasoil (Cayman) v. The Management and Implementation Authority of the Great

Man-Made River Project (Libya) (1999) 14(8) Mealey's IAR, (1999) XXIVa
    YB Comm Arb, 296-302
Cour d'Appel de Paris, 29 September 2005, DAC/Dubai v. Bechtel, (2006) XXXI
    YB Comm Arb, 629
Cour de Cassation, 1re Ch. Civ., 11 July 2006, Banque populaire Loire et Iyonnais
    v Société Sangar, [2006] Rev Arb, 969

VII.   GERMANY

OLG Hamburg, 30 September 1907, Rspr. 15, 298
OLG Braunschweig, 7 June 1912, Rspr. 25, 240
OLG Stuttgart, 21 December 1927, 563/27, JW 1928, 1322
OLG Munich, 26 April 1928, 462/29 L, JW 1929, 3175
RG, 7 July 1933, VII 94/33
RG, 21 April 1936, III 161/35 in RGZ 152, 9-12
BGH, 10 October 1951, II ZR 99/51 in BGHZ 3, 215
BGH, 7 October 1953, II ZR 170/52, ZZP 71 (1958), 423, 436
BGH, 6 October 1954, II ZR 149/53 in BGHZ 15, 12, 14
BGH, 30 January 1956, II ZR 168/54 in BGHZ 20, 4
BGH, 22 May 1957, V ZR 236/56, ZZP 71 (1958) 427
BGH, 8 October 1959, VII ZR 87/58, NJW 1959, 2213
BGH, 22 November 1962, VII ZR 264/61 in BGHZ 38, 254, 257
BGH, 23 January 1963, VZR 132/55, NJW 1957, 1592
BGH, 28 May 1963, VII ZR 222/61, WM 1963, 944
BGH, 28 November 1963, VII ZR 112/62, NJW 1964, 591
LG Berlin, 4 December 1964, 81 OH 8/64, KTS 1966, 182, 184
BGH, 19 December 1968, VII ZR 83/66 in BGHZ 51, 255, 258
BGH, 27 February 1970, VII ZR 68/68 in BGHZ 53, 315; (1990) 6(1) Arb Int'l,
    79, 85
BGH, 8 July 1970, VIII ZR 28/69 in BGHZ 54, 222
BGH, 5 November 1970, VII ZR 31/69 in BGHZ 54, 392
OLG Munich, 25 February 1971, 12 W 570/71, BB 1971, 886, 887
BGH, 3 July 1975, III ZR 78/73, NJW 1976, 245, JZ 1976, 245, 247 with annota-
    tion by Schlosser
BGH, 12 February 1976, III ZR 42/74, RIW 1976, 449, 451
BGH, 5 November 1980, VIII ZR 230/79 in BGHZ 78, 318
BGH, 11 November 1982, III ZR 77/81, NJW 1983, 867.
LG Hamburg, 10 December 1985, 23 0 147/85, (1987) XII YB Comm Arb,
    487, 488
LG Dortmund, 22 April 1986, 10-0-48/68, WuW 1968, 691
BGH, 5 May 1986, III 2 R 233/84 in BGHZ 98, 32-40
BGH, 15 May 1986, III ZR 192/84, RIW 1986, 816
BGH, 3 May 1988, X ZR 99/86, ZfRV 1989, 149

BGH, 26 January, 1989, XZR 23/87, JZ 1989, 588, 589
OLG Munich, 7 April 1989, 23 U6310/88, RIW 1990, 585, 586
BGH, 11 June 1990, II ZR 159/89, NJW 1990, 3151
BGH, 12 July 1990, III ZR 174/89, NJW 1990, 3210
BGH, 14 May 1992, III ZR 169/90, NJW 1992, 2299
BGH, 4 June 1992, IX ZR 149/91, ZZP 106 (1993), 87, 88
BeVerfG, 8 June 1993, 1 BvR 878/90 in BVerfGE 89, 28, 35, NJW 1993, 2229
BGH, 15 December 1994, IZR 121/92, NJW 1995, 1677, 1679
BSG, 1 February 1996, 2 RU 7/95, NJW-RR 1997, 94
BGH, 6 June 2002, III ZB 44/01, SchiedsVZ, 2003, 39
OLG Hamburg, 30 August 2002, Case 11 Sch 02/00, Lead note available under
      <http://www.dis-arb.de>
AG Düsseldorf, 17 June 2003, 36 C 19607/02, SchiedsVZ, 2003, 240
BayObLG, 4 July 2004, 4 Z Sch 009/04, 4 Z Sch 9/04, SchiedsVZ 2004, 316
BGH, 13 January 2005, III ZR 265/03, NJW 2005, 1125
BGH, 23 February 2006, III ZB 50/05, SchiedsVZ 2006, 161, 164
BGH, 10 December 2007, II ZR 239/05, AG 2008, 256, 257

VIII.   HONG KONG

High Court of Hong Kong Special Administrative Region, 27 March 2003, Karaha
      Bodas Company LLC v. Perusahaan Minyak Pertambanga Dan Gas Bumi
      Negara, (2003) 21(3) Bull ASA, 667-684

IX.   ITALY

Italian Corte de Cassazione, 5 July 1995, Coop. Vigili Fuoco Borgotaro v. Mariani,
      No. 2304, Foro Pad. 1995, I, 206

X.   MALAYSIA

Supreme Court of Malaysia, 2 January 1990, Government of Malaysia v. Zublin-
      Muhibbah Joint Venture, consisting of Ed Zublin AG (FR Germany) and
      Muhibbah Engineering (M) Sdn Bhd. (Malaysia) (1991) XVI Y3 Comm
      Arb, 166

XI.   THE NETHERLANDS

Hoge Raad (Supreme Court of the Netherlands), 21 March 1997, Eco Swiss
      China Time Ltd. v. Benetton International NV (1998) XXIII Y3 Comm
      Arb, 180.

XII.   PCIJ / ICJ

PCIJ, 5 December 1939, The Electricity Company of Sofia and Bulgaria, [1939] 79
    Ser. A/B 194, 199
ICJ, 5 February 1970, The Barcelona Traction, Light and Power Co.(Belgium v
    Spain), (1970) ICJ, 3
ICJ, 10 May 1984, Order in Military and Paramilitary Activities in and against
    Nicaragua (Nicaragua v. United States), (1984) ICJ Reports 169, 179

XIII.   SINGAPORE

High Court of Singapore, 30 March 1988, Turner (East Asia) Pte Ltd (Singapore) v.
    Builders Federal (Hong Kong) Ltd (Hong Kong) and Josef Gartner & Co (FR
    Germany) (1988) 5(3) J Int'l Arb, 139; (1988) 3(4) Mealey's Int'l Arb Rep,
    6-9 and C1-C26; (1989) XIV YB Comm Arb, 224.
High Court of Singapore, 26 November 2003, Jurong Engineering Ltd. v. Black &
    Veatch Singapore PTE LTD, [2004] 1 SLR 333

XIV.   SWEDEN

Swedish Supreme Court, 27 October 2000, AI Trade Finance Inc. v. Bulgarian
    Foreign Trade Bank Ltd. (2001) XXVI YB Comm Arb, 291- 298

XV.   SWITZERLAND

BGer, 12 February 1958, BGE 84 I 56, 60
BGer, 11 November 1959, Vegetable Oil Products Cy c v. Sieur Elmassian, [1960]
    Rev Arb, 105, 106
BGer, 26 October 1966, BGE 92 I 271
BGer, 3 May 1967, BGE 93 I 265, 272
BGer, 12 December 1975, Provenda S.A. v Alimenta S.A. et Genève, Cour de
    justic, BGE 101 Ia 521, 526
BGer, 10 May 1982, BGE 108 Ia 197, 201
Cour de Justice de Genève, 1 June 1984, (1984) 2(3) Bull ASA, 200 (unpublished)
BGer, 14 March 1985, BGE 111 Ia 72, 74
Cour de Justice de Genève, 17 November 1989, Hilmarton v. OTV, (1994) XIX YB
    Comm Arb, 214
BGer, 17 April 1990, Hilmarton v. OTV, [1993] Rev Arb, 342 and (1994) XIX YB
    Comm Arb, 214, 220
BGer, 21 August 1990, I. v. C. SA and IHK-Schiedsgericht, BGE 116 II 373
BGer, 14 November 1990, E. AG v. K. Ltd and IHK-Schiedsgericht Zürich, (1992)
    XVII YB Comm Arb, 279, 284

BGer, 30 December 1994, F. and U. v. W Inc., (1995) 13(2) Bull ASA, 217
BGer, 16 January 1995, BGE 121 III 38
BGer, 25 April 1995, BGE 121 III 331, 334
BGer, 29 January 1996, X and XX v. Y and YY, (1996) 14(3) Bull ASA, 496, 503
BGer, 6 September 1996, X. v. Y., (1997) 15(2) Bull ASA, 291, 306
BGer, 24 March 1997, T AG v. H Company, (1997) 15(2) Bull ASA, 316
BGer, 25 July 1997, BGE 4P.221.1996, (2000) 18(1) Bull ASA, 96
BGer, 17 February 1999, G. AG (Switzerland) v. TAS (Turkey), (2000) 18(2) Bull ASA, 311
BGer, 22 February 1999, B AS (Turkey) and C AS (Turkey) v. A S.p.A. (Italy), (1999) 17(4) Bull ASA, 537
BGer, 2 March 2001, Bank Saint Petersburg PLC v. ATA Insaat Sanayi ve Ticaret Ltd., (2001) 19(3) Bull ASA, 531
BGer, 28 March 2001, Beverly Overseas SA v. Privredna Banka Zagreb d.d., (2001) 19(4) Bull ASA, 807, 814
BGer, 14 May 2001, BGE 127 III 279, (2001) 19(3) Bull ASA, 555
BGer, 11 June 2001, BGE 127 III 429, (2001) 19(3) Bull ASA, 566
BGer, 10 September 2001, BGE 127 III 576, 579
Obergericht Zürich, 11 September 2001, ZR (2002) (101) No. 21, 77
BGer, 14 March 2003, Baugenossenschaft B. v. N.K. and O.K., BGE 5 C 279/2002
BGer, 8 December 2003, BGE 4P.73.2003, (2005) 23(1) Bull ASA 119, 125
BGer, 4 August 2006, BGE 4P.105/2006, (2007) 25(1) Bull ASA, 105-122

XVI.   UNITED KINGDOM

Lord Morris in Compagnie d'Armément Maritime v. Compagnie Tunisienne de Navigation SA [1971] A.C. 572, 588 (House of Lords)
Offshore International S.A. v. Banco Central S.A. [1976] 2 Lloyd's Rep. 402, Q.B. (Comm.)
Bunge SA v. Kruse [1979] 1 Lloyd's Rep. 279, Q.B. (Comm.)
Edm. J.M. Mertens & Co. P.V.B.A. v. Veevoeder Import Export Virrex B.V. [1979] 2 Lloyd's Rep. 372 Q.B. (Comm.)
Bremer Vulkan Schiffbau und Maschinenfabrik v. South India Shipping Corp. [1981] 1 All E.R. 289, 299, 301 (House of Lords)
Channel Tunnel Group Ltd. v. Balfour Beatty Construction Ltd. [1992] 1 Q.B., 656 (Comm.)
Channel Tunnel Group Ltd. v. Balfour Beatty Construction Ltd, [1993] A.C. 334 (House of Lords)
China Agribusiness Dev. Corp. v. Balli Trading [1998] 2 Lloyd's Rep. 76 Q.B. (Comm.)
Laker Airways Inc. v. FLS Aerospace Ltd [1999] 2 Lloyd's Rep. 45, 46 Q.B. (Comm.)
Lafarge Redlands Aggregates Ltd. v. Shephard Hill Civil Engineering Ltd. [2000] 1 WLR 1621 (House of Lords)

Glencot Development and Design Co. Ltd v. Ben Barrett & Son (Contractors) Ltd [2001] BLR 207, Q.B. (TCC)

The Bay Hotel and Resort Ltd. v. Cavalier Construction Co. Ltd. [2001] UKPC 34 (Privy Council)

Mousaka Inc. v. Golden Seagull Maritime Inc. and Another [2001] 2 Lloyd's Rep. 657 Q.B. (Comm.)

Department of Economics Policy Development of the City of Moscow v. Bankers Trust Co and International industrial Bank, Unreported, Cooke J., [2003] Q.B. (Comm.) in [2003] 6(5) Int'l Arb L Rev, N-45, note by S.R. Shackleton

Associated Electric and Gas Insurance Services Ltd. v. European Reinsurance Co. of Zurich, [2003] I WLR 1041 (Privy Council)

Caterpillar Financial Services Corporation v. SNC Passion [2004] EWHC, 569 Q.B. (Comm.); case note in [2004] 4(5) Arb L Monthly, 11 *et seq.*

Peterson Farms Inc. v. C&M Farming Ltd [2004] 2 Lloyd's Rep. 603 Q.B. (Comm.)

Department of Economic Development of the City of Moscow and the Government of Moscow v. Bankers Trust Company and International Industrial Bank [2004] EWCA Civ 314 (Court of Appeal)

Econet Satellite Services Ltd v. Vee Networks Limited [2006] EWHC 1664 Q.B. (Comm.)

Fiona Trust & Holding Corp. v. Privalov [2007] UKHL 40 (House of Lords)

West Tankers Inc v. Ras Riunione Adriatica Di Sicurita Spa & ors [2007] UKHL 4 (House of Lords)

XVII.			UNITED STATES OF AMERICA

Commonwealth Coatings Corp. v. Continental Casualty Co., 393 U.S. 145 (U.S. S. Ct. 1968)

Mobil Oil Indonesia Inc. v. Asamera Oil (Indonesia) Ltd. 392 N.Y.S.2d 614, 616 (N.Y. App. Div. 1977)

Avila Group, Inc. v. Norma J. of California, 426 F. Supp. 537, 542 (S.D.N.Y. 1977)

Coastal Stares Trading Inc. v. Zenith Navigation S.A., 446 F. Supp. 330 (S.D.N.Y. 1977)

Pollux Marine Agencies, Inc. v. Louis Dreyfus Corp., 455 F. Supp. 211, 219 (S.D.N.Y.1978)

Andrew Martin Marine Corp. v. Stork-Werkspoor Diesel BV, 480 F. Supp. 1270 (E.D. La. 1979)

Schattner v. Girard, Inc., 668 F. 2d 1366 (D.C. Cir. 1981)

Williamson v. John D. Quinn Construction Corp., 537 F. Supp. 613 (S.D.N.Y 1982)

First Nat'l City Bank v. Banco Para El Comercio Exterior de Cuba, 462 U.S. 611 (U.S. S. Ct. 1983)

Mitsubishi Motors Corp. v. Soler Chrysler-Plymouth, Inc., 473 U.S. 614 (U.S. S. Ct. 1985)

United States v. Sperry Corp. et al, 493 U.S. 52, (U.S. S. Ct. 1989)

Austern v. Chicago Board Options Exchange, Inc., 898 F. 2d 882 (2nd Cir. 1990)
Westinghouse Elec. Corp. v. Republic of Philippines 951 F.2d 1414 (3rd Cir. 1991), (1992) 7(1) Mealey's Int'l Arb Rep, B-1 *et seq.*
Carte Blanche (Singapore) Pte Ltd v. Diners Club Int'l, Inc., 2 F.3d 24 (2nd Cir. 1993)
New Moon Shipping Co. v. MAN B&W Diesel AG, 121 F.3d 24 (2nd Cir. 1997)
Avedon Engineering, Inc. v. Seatex, 126 F.3d 1279 (10th Cir. 1997)
Birbrower, Montalbano, Condon & Frank, P.C. v. Superior Court of Santa Clara County, 949 P. 2d 1 (Cal. 1998)
ANR Coal Co. v. Cogentrix of North Carolina, Inc., 173 F.3d 493 (4th Cir. 1999)
Am. Bureau of Shipping v. Tencara Shipyard S.P.A., 170 F.3d 349, 353 (2nd Cir. 1999)
Comsat Corporation v. National Science Foundation, 190 F.3d 269 (4th Cir. 1999)
Int'l Paper Co. v. Schwabedissen Maschinen & Anlagen GMBH, 206 F.3d 411, 417-418 (4th Cir. 2000)
Publicis Commun. v. True North Communs. Inc., 206 F.3d 725, 729, 731 (7th Cir. 2000)
E.I. Dupont de Nemours & Co. v. Rhone Poulenc Fiber & Resin Intermediates, S.A.S., 269 F.3d 187, 200 (3rd Cir. 2001)
MAG Portfolio Consult, GmbH v. Merlin Biomed Group, LLC, 268 F.3d 58, 61 (2nd Cir. 2001)
Smoothline Ltd v. N. Am. Foreign Trading Corp., 2002 WL 31885795 (S.D.N.Y. 2002)
Intergen NV v. Grina, 344 F.3d 134, 148 (1st Cir. 2003)
China Minmetals Materials Imp. & Exp. Co. v. Chi Mei Corp., 334 F.3d 274, 288 (3rd Cir. 2003)
Prudential-Bache Securities (Hong Kong) Ltd. and Prudential-Bache International Bank Ltd. v. National Association of Securities Dealers Dispute Resolution, Inc., 289 F.Supp.2d 438 (S.D.N.Y 2003)
In re Roz Trading Ltd, 469 F. Supp. 2d 1221 (N.D. Ga. 2006)
In re Hallmark Capital Corp., 534 F.Supp.2d 951 (D.Minn. 2007)

XVIII.   AWARDS

Award in ICC Case No. 22 of 1972, (1997) 8(1) ICC Ct Bull, 52
Decision No. 22 in ICSID-Arbitration of 1972, (1994) 12(1) Bull ASA, 148, 152
Award in ICC Case No. 1434 of 1975, (1976) JDI, 978
Interim Award in ICC Case No. 2671 of 1976, Mobil Oil Indonesia v. Asamera Oil (Indonesia) Ltd., (1976) NY Law Journal, 10, col. 4
Partial Award in ICC Case No. 3896 of 1982, (1983) JDI, 914 and (1985) X YB Comm Arb, 47
Interim Award in ICC Case No. 4131 of 1982, Dow Chemical France et al. vs Isover Saint Gobain (France), (1984) IX YB Comm Arb, 131 and (1993) JDI, 899

Interim Award in Ad hoc Arbitration, 9 September 1983, German engineering
    company v. Polish buyer, (1987) XII YB Comm Arb, 63
Partial Award in ICC Case No. 4402 of 1983, (1984) IX YB Comm Arb, 138
Award in ICC Case No. 4761 of 1984, in S. Jarvin, Y. Derains and J.-J. Arnaldez,
    Collection of ICC Arbitral Awards 1986-1990 (Deventer, Kluwer Law and
    Taxation Publishers, 1994)
Interim Award in ICC Case No. 3879 of 1984, Westland Helicopters, (1984) 23
    ILM 1071
Iran-US Claims Tribunal, 7 June 1984, Bendone-Derossi Int'l v. Islamic Republic
    of Iran, Award No. ITM 40-375-1, (1984) 6 Iran-US C.T.R. 130, 131-33
Iran-US Claims Tribunal, 11 November 1985, The United States of America, on
    behalf of and for the benefit of Tadjer-Cohen Assoc. v. Islamic Republic of
    Iran, Award No. ITM 50-12118-3, (1985) 9 Iran-US C.T.R. 302-304-5
Iran-US Claims Tribunal, 27 June 1985, Sylvania Technical Systems Inc. v. The
    Government of the Islamic Republic of Iran, as reported in (1986) XI YB
    Comm Arb, 290, 301
Iran-US Claims Tribunal, 22 February 1985, Behring International, Inc. v. Iranian
    Air Force, (1985) 8 Iran-US CTR, 44
Iran-US Claims Tribunal, 10 December 1986, United Technologies International,
    Inc. v. Iran, (1986) 13 Iran-US CTR, 254
Award in ICC Case No. 5460 of 1987, Austrian franchisor v. South African fran-
    chisee, (1988) XIII YB Comm Arb, 104
Award in ICC Case No. 5505 of 1987, (1988) XIII YB Comm Arb, 110
Iran-US Claims Tribunal, 14 August 1987, Starrett Housing Corp. v. The
    Government of the Islamic Republic of Iran, Award No. 314-24-1,
    (1987)16 Iran-US CTR 112, 197
Iran-US Claims Tribunal, 1 December 1987, Arthur Young & Co. v. The Islamic
    Republic of Iran, Award No. 338-484-1, (1987) 17 Iran-US CTR 245, 253-254
Partial Award in Ad Hoc Arbitration, 5 February 1988, Wintershall AG et al v.
    Government of Qatar, (1989) 28 ILM, 798
Award in ICC Case No. 5730 of 1988, (1990) JDI 1029
Award in ICC Case No. 5103 of 1988, (1988) JDI, 1207
Award in ICC Case No. 6000 of 1988, (1991) 2(2) ICC Ct Bull, 31
Award of 15 September 1989, E. c. v. Z. ICA Z. et société M (1990) 8(3) Bull ASA,
    270, 276
Order made in 1989 by an Arbitral Tribunal composed of Rolando Forni, Pierre
    Heyer and Gabrielle Kaufmann-Kohler (1994) 12(1) Bull ASA 142, 144
Award in ICC Case No. 5894 of 1989, (1991) 2(2) ICC Ct Bull, 25
ICC Case No. 6508 of 1990, reported in (1995) JDI, 1022-1031 with comments by
    Derains
Award in ICC Case No. 5721 of 1990, (1990) JDI, 1020
ICC Case No. 5946 of 1990, (1991) XVI YB Comm Arb, 97, 112
ICC Case No. 6268 of 1990, (1991) XVI YB Comm Arb, 119, 125
Award in Ad Hoc Arbitration of 1991, Alpha S.A. v. Beta & Co and Société d'Etat
    de droit ruritane, (1992) 10(2) Bull ASA, 202

Award in ICC Case No. 5622 of 1992, (1997)8(1) ICC Ct Bull, 52
ICC Case No. 6955 of 1993, (1999) XXIVa YB Comm Arb, 107, 139
ICC Case No. 7388 of 1993, quoted by Reiner, A., 'Les mesures provisoires et
    conservatoires et L'Arbitrage international, notamment l'Arbitrage
    CCI'(1998) 4 JDI, 853, 886
Iran-US Claims Tribunal, 15 September 1993, Foremost Tehran Inc. v. The Islamic
    Republic of Iran, (1993) 3 Iran-US CTR 361, 362
Award in ICC Case No. 7047 of 1994, Westcare Investments Inc. v. Jugcimport –
    SPDR Holding Co. Ltd. & others, (1995) 13(2) Bull ASA
Award in ICC Case No. 6497 of 1994, (1999) XXIV YB Comm Arb, 71, 77-78
Final Award in ICC Case No. 7047 of 1994, (1997) 8(1) ICC Ct Bull, 62
Partial Award in ICC Case No. 8113 of 1995, (2000) XXV YB Comm Arb, 324
Award in ICC Case No. 8385 of 1995, in J.-J. Arnaldez, Y. Derains and D. Hascher,
    Collection of ICC Arbitral Awards 1996-2000 (The Hague, Kluwer Law
    International, 2003)
ICC Case No. 8113 of 1995, (2000) XXV YB Comm Arb, 324
Interim Award in ICC Case No. 7692 of 1995, (2000) 11(1) ICC Ct Bull, 623
Award in ICC Case No. 8385 of 1995, in J.J. Arnaldez, Y. Derains and D. Hascher,
    Collection of ICC Arbitral Awards 1996-2000 (The Hague, Kluwer Law
    Internationl, 2003)
Award in ICC Case Nos. 7604 and 7610 of 1995, in J.-J. Arnaldez, Y. Derains and
    D. Hascher, Collection of ICC Arbitral Awards 1996-2000 (The Hague,
    Kluwer Law International, 2003)
Interim Award in ICC Case No. 7289, 2 September 1996, [2002] Rev Arb, 1001,
    1005
Award in ICC Case No. 8486 of 1996, (1999) XXIVa YB Comm Arb, 162
Interim Award in ICC Case No. 8786 of 1996, (2000) 11(1) ICC Ct Bull, 81
Interim Award in NAI Case No. 1694, 12 December 1996, (1998) XXIII YB
    Comm Arb, 97
Award in ICC Case No. 8879 of 1998, (2000) 11(1) ICC Ct Bull, 84, 89
Award in ICC Case No. 9333 of 1998, (2001) 19(4) Bull ASA, 757, 773
Interim Award in ICC Case No. 9719 of 1999, (2005) 16(2) ICC Ct Bull, 83
Award in ICC Case No. 10169, 10 September 1999 cited and quoted in M. Secomb,
    'Awards and Orders Dealing with the Advance on Costs in ICC Arbitration:
    Theoretical Questions and Practical Problems' (2003) 14(1) ICC International
    Court of Arbitration Bulletin, 65
Award in CAS Case 96/161 of 1999, in M. Reeb, Digest of CAS Awards II 1998-
    2000, (The Hague, Kluwer Law International, 2002)
Award in NAI Case No. 2212, 28 July 1999, (2001) XXVI YB Comm Arb, 198,
    204
Award in ICC Case No. 10758 of 2000, (2005) 16(2) ICC Ct Bull, 87, 90
Partial Award in ICC Case No. 10526, 2 December 2000, [2001] JDI, 1179, 1182
Award in ICSID Case No. ARB/98/7 of 2000, Banro American Resources, Inc. and
    Société Aurifère du Kivu et du Maniema S.A.R.L. v. Democratic Republic of
    the Congo, (2002) 17 ICSID Rev – FILJ 382

Award in ICC Case No. 9762 of 2001, (2004) XXIX YB Comm Arb 40

Partial Award in ICC Case No. 10526 (Switzerland), 27 March 2001, [2002] Rev
    Arb, 1035, 1039

Award in PCA Case of 5 February 2001, Larsen v. The Hawaiian Kingdom, (2002)
    119 International Law Reports 566, 579-80

Award in ICC Case No. 11160 of 2002, (2005) 16(2) ICC Ct Bull, 99

Partial Award in ICC Case No. 11330, 17 June 2002, quoted and cited in
    M. Secomb, 'Awards and Orders Dealing with the Advance on Costs in
    ICC Arbitration: Theoretical Questions and Practical Problems' (2003)
    14(1) ICC Ct Bull, 59, 66

Partial Award in ICC Case No. 11392, 25 October 2002, cited and quoted in
    M. Secomb, 'Awards and Orders Dealing with the Advance on Costs in
    ICC Arbitration: Theoretical Questions and Practical Problems' (2003)
    14(1) ICC Ct Bull, 65 *et seq.*

Partial Award in ICC Case No. 1186, 20 December 2002, cited and quoted in
    M. Secomb, 'Awards and Orders Dealing with the Advance on Costs in
    ICC Arbitration: Theoretical Questions and Practical Problems' (2003)
    14(1) ICC Ct Bull, 65 *et seq.*

Decision on Jurisdiction in ICSID Case No. ARB/02/18 of 2004, Tokios Tokelės v.
    Ukraine, (2005) ICSID Rev 206

Order in VIAC Case No. SCH- 4750 of 2004 (unpublished)

Order in VIAC Case No. SCH-5014 of 2008 (unpublished)

Bibliography

I.   ARTICLES

Aburumieh, N., Koller, C. and Pöltner, E., 'Formvorschriften für Schiedsvereinbarungen' [2006] Österreichische Juristenzeitung.

Allison, R. and Holtzmann, H.M., 'The Tribunal's Use of Experts', in *The Iran-United States Claims Tribunal and the Process of International Claims Resolution*, Caron, D. and Crook, J. (eds) (Ardsley-on-Hudson, Transnational Publishers, 2000).

Alvarez, G.A., 'The Challenge of Arbitrators' (1990) 6(3) *LCIA Arbitration International*.

Alvarez, G.A., 'To What Extent Do Arbitrators in International Cases Disregard the Bag and Baggage of National Systems?' (1996) 8 *ICCA Congress Series* (Seoul).

Appelton, A.E. and Graf, B.U., 'Elisa María Mostaza Claro v Centro Móvil Milenium: EU Consumer Law as a Defence against Arbitral Awards, ECJ Case C-168/05' (2007) 25(1) *Bulletin ASA*.

Arfazadeh, H., 'New Perspectives in South East Asia and Delocalised Arbitration in Kuala Lumpur' (1991) 8(4) *Journal of International Arbitration*.

Aschauer, C., 'Arbitral Proceedings and the Enforcement of the Award Particularly in Relation to Austrian Law and the Rules of Arbitration of the SCC, the ICC and the Austrian Federal Economic Chamber' (2001) 2 *Stockholm Arbitration Report*.

Aschauer, C., 'Keine Klage auf Feststellung der Unzuständigkeit des Schiedsgerichts bei anhängigem Schiedsverfahren' [2003] Wirtschaftsrechtliche Blätter.

Austrian Bar Association, Statement Zl. 13/1 05/87 of 15 June 2005, <www.rakwien.at/import/documents/schiedsrechts-aenderungsgesetz2005.pdf>.

Bachner, T., 'Keine Spezialvollmacht für Vorstand und Geschäftsführer' [2005] ecolex.

Bagner, H., 'Confidentiality – A Fundamental Principle in International Commercial Arbitration?' (2001) 18(2) *Journal of International Arbitration*.

Bagner, H., 'Enforcement of International Commercial Contracts by Arbitration: Recent Developments' (1982) 14(3) *Case Western Reserve Journal of International Law*.

Bajons, E.-M., 'Zur Nationalität internationaler Schiedssachen – Der Fall "Norsolor" vor den österreichischen Gerichten' in *Festschrift für Winfried Kralik zum 65. Geburtstag*, Rechberger, W.H. and Welser, R. (eds) (Vienna, Manz, 1986).

Barceló, J.J., 'Who Decides the Arbitrator's Jurisdiction? Separability and Competence-Competence in Transnational Perspective' (2003) 36 *Vanderbilt Journal of Transnational Law*.

Beechey, J., 'Arbitrability of Anti-trust/Competition Law Issues – Common Law' (1996) 12(2) *LCIA Arbitration International*.

Benjamin, P.I., 'Notes – The European Convention on International Commercial Arbitration' (1961) 37 *British Year Book of International Law*.

Bensaude, D., 'The International Law Association's Recommendation on Res Judicata and Lis Pendens in International Commercial Arbitration' (2007) 24(4) *Journal of International Arbitration*.

Berger, B., 'Prozesskostensicherheit (cautio iudicatum solvi) im Schiedsverfahren' (2004) 22(1) *Bulletin ASA*.

Berger, K.P., 'Integration of Mediation Elements into Arbitration' (2003) 19(3) *LCIA Arbitration International*.

Berger, K.P., 'Set-Off in International Economic Arbitration' (1999) 15(1) *LCIA Arbitration International*.

Berger, K.P., 'The New German Arbitration Law in International Perspective' (2000) 26 *Forum Internationale*.

Berger, K.P., 'Schiedsrichterbestellung in Mehrparteienschiedsverfahren' [1993] Recht der Internationalen Wirtschaft.

Bishop, D. and Reed, L., 'Practical Guidelines for Interviewing, Selecting and Challenging Party-Appointed Arbitrators in International Commercial Arbitration' (1998) 14(4) *LCIA Arbitration International*.

Blackaby, N., 'Public Interest and Investment Treaty Arbitration' (2004) I(1) *Transnational Dispute Management*.

Blanke, G., 'Defining the Limits of Scrutiny of Awards Based on Alleged Violations of European Competition Law' (2006) 23(3) *Journal of International Arbitration*.

Blessing, M., 'Extension of the Arbitration Clause to Non-signatories in The Arbitration Agreement – Its Multifold Critical Aspects' (1994) *ASA Special Series No. 8*.

Blessing, M., 'Mandatory Rules of Law versus Party Autonomy in International Arbitration' (1997) 14(4) *Journal of International Arbitration*.

Blessing, M., 'The ICC Arbitral Procedure under the 1998 ICC Rules – What Has Changed?' (1997) 8(2) *ICC International Court of Arbitration Bulletin*.

Blessing, M., 'The Law Applicable to the Arbitration Clause and Arbitrability' (1999) *ICCA Congress Series No. 9.*

Böckstiegel, K.H., 'An Introduction to the New German Arbitration Act Based on the UNCITRAL Model Law' (1998) 14(1) *LCIA Arbitration International.*

Böhm, F., 'Die Rechtsschutzformen im Spannungsfeld von lex fori und lex causae', in *Festschrift für H.W. Fasching zum 65. Geburtstag*, Holzhammer, R., Jelinek, W. and Böhm, P. (eds) (Vienna, Manz, 1988).

Bond, S., 'The Nature of Conservatory and Provisional Measures', in *Conservatory and Provisional Measures in International Arbitration* (1993) ICC Publication No. 519.

Bouchez, L.J., 'The Prospects for International Arbitration: Disputes between States and Private Enterprises' (1991) 8(1) *Journal of International Arbitration.*

Branson, D.J., 'Ethics for International Arbitrators' (1987) 3(1) *LCIA Arbitration International.*

Brenn, C., 'Das österreichische Signaturgesetz – Unterschriftenersatz ir elektronischen Netzwerken' [1999] Österreichische Juristenzeitung.

Briner, R., 'Domestic Arbitration: Practice in Continental Europe and Its Lessons for Arbitration in England' (1997) 13(2) *LCIA Arbitration International.*

Brödermann, D., 'Die erweiterten UNIDROIT Prinzipien 2004' [2004] Recht der Internationalen Wirtschaft.

Brulard, Y. and Quintin, Y., 'European Community Law and Arbitration – National versus Community Public Policy' (2001) 18(5) *Journal of International Arbitration.*

Bühler, M. and Dorgan, C., 'Witness Testimony Pursuant to the 1999 IBA Rules of Evidence in International Commercial Arbitration – Novel or Tested Standards?' (2001) 17(1) *Journal of International Arbitration.*

Bühler, M., 'Awarding Costs in International Commercial Arbitration: An Overview' (2004) 22(2) *Bulletin ASA.*

Bühler, M., 'Costs in ICC Arbitration: A Practitioner's View' (1993) 3 *American Review of International Arbitration.*

Bühler, M., 'Non-payment of the Advance on Costs by the Respondent Party: Is There Really a Remedy?' (2006) 24(2) *Bulletin ASA.*

Busse, D., 'Die Bindung Dritter an Schiedsvereinbarungen' [2005] Zeitschrift für Schiedsverfahren.

Byrne, O.K., 'A New Code of Ethics for Commercial Arbitrators: The Neutrality of Party-Appointed Arbitrators on a Tripartite Panel' (2003) 30 *Fordham Urban Law Journal.*

Carter, J.H., 'The Rights and Duties of the Arbitrator: Six Aspects of the Rule of Reasonableness' (1995) ICC International Court of Arbitration Bulletin Special Supplement: The Status of the Arbitrator.

Castello, J.E., 'Ex Parte Measures – A View in Favour' (2003) 8 *LCIA Newsletter.*

Chiu, J.C., 'Consolidation of Arbitral Proceeding and International Arbitration' (1990) 7(2) *Journal of International Arbitration.*

Chiwitt-Oberhammer, T. and Oberhammer, P., '(Nicht-)Schiedssprüche in außerstreitigen Mietrechtsangelegenheiten' [2005] Wohnrechtliche Blätter.

Collins, L., 'Provisional and Protective Measures in International Litigation' (1992) 234 *Recueil des Cours*.

Crawford, J., 'Advocacy Before the International Court of Justice and Other International Tribunals in State-to-State Cases', in *The Art of Advocacy in International Arbitration*, Bishop, R. (ed.) (Huntington, Juris Publishing, 2004).

Czernich, D. and Heiss, H., 'Das Europäische Schuldvertragsübereinkommen: Neues internationales Vertragsrecht für Österreich' [1998] Österreichische Juristenzeitung.

De Groot, T.D., 'The Impact of the Benetton Decision on International Commercial Arbitration' (2003) 20(4) *Journal of International Arbitration*.

De Witt Wijnen, O.L.O., Voser, N. and Rao, N., 'Background Information on the IBA Guidelines on Conflict of Interest' (2004) 5 *Business Law International*.

Debattista, C., 'Drafting Enforceable Arbitration Clauses' (2005) 21(2) *LCIA Arbitration International*.

Delvolvé, J.-L., 'Final Report on Multi-Party Arbitration' (1995) 6(1) *ICC International Court of Arbitration Bulletin*.

Delvolvé, J.-L., 'Multipartism: The Dutco Decision of the French Cour de Cassation' (1993) 9(2) *LCIA Arbitration International*.

Departmental Advisory Committee on Arbitration Law, 1996 Report on the Arbitration Bill, Reprinted in (1997) 13(3) *LCIA Arbitration International*.

Derains, Y. and Schaf, S., 'Clauses d'arbitrage et groupes de sociétés' (1985) Revue de Droit des Affaires Internationales.

Dimolitsa, A., 'Separability and Kompetenz-Kompetenz' (1999) 9 *ICCA Congress Series* (Paris).

Ehrenhaft, P.D., 'Effective International Commercial Arbitration' (1977) 9 *Law & Policy in International Business*.

Elsing, S.H. and Townsend, J.M., 'Bridging the Common Law-Civil Law Divide in Arbitration' (2002) 18(1) *Arbitration International*.

Elsing, S.H., 'Internationale Schiedsgerichte als Mittler zwischen den prozessualen Rechtskulturen' Supplement 7 to (2002) 46 Betriebs-Berater.

Fadlallah, I., 'Payment of the Advance to Cover Costs in ICC Arbitration: the Parties' Reciprocal Obligations' (2003) 14(1) *ICC International Court of Arbitration Bulletin*.

Fasching, H.W., 'Die Form der Schiedsvereinbarung' [1989] Österreichische Juristenzeitung.

Fasching, H.W., 'Kostenvorschüsse zur Einleitung schiedsgerichtlicher Verfahren' [1993] Juristische Blätter.

Fellner, M., 'Das neue österreichische Schiedsrecht' [2007] Nova & Varia Zeitschrift des Juristenverbandes.

Folberg, J., 'Arbitration Ethics: Winds of Reform Blowing from the West' (Fall 2002) *Dispute Resolution Magazine*.

Fontaine, M., 'Drafting the Award: A Perspective from a Civil Law Jurist' (1994) 5(1) *ICC International Court of Arbitration Bulletin*.

Forbes, W., 'Rules of Ethics for Arbitrators and Their Application' (1992) 9(3) *Journal of International Arbitration*.

Franck, S., 'The Liability of International Arbitrators: A Comparative Analysis and Proposal for Qualified Immunity'(2000) 20(1) *New York Law School Journal of International and Comparative Law*.

Fremuth, A., 'Schiedsverfahren und Konkurs: Zur Bindung des Masseverwalters an Schiedsvereinbarungen des Gemeinschuldners' [1998] Österreichische Juristenzeitung.

Freyer, D.H., 'Practical Considerations in Drafting Dispute Resolution Provisions in International Commercial Arbitration Contracts: A US Perspective' (1998) 15(4) *Journal of International Arbitration*.

Fritz, C., 'Die Vorteilhaftigkeit von Schiedsgerichtsvereinbarungen im Gesellschaftsrecht' [1997] Steuer- und WirtschaftsKartei.

Gaillard, E. and Pinsolle, P., 'The ICC Pre-Arbitral Referee: First Practical Experiences' (2004) 20(1) *LCIA Arbitration International*.

Gaillard, E., 'Transnational Rules in International Arbitration' (1993) ICC Publication No. 480/4.

Geisinger, E. and Lévy, L., 'Lis Alibi Pendens in International Commercial Arbitration' (2003) *ICC International Court of Arbitration Bulletin Special Supplement: Complex Arbitration*.

Girsberger, D. and Hausmaninger, C., 'Assignment of Rights and Agreement to Arbitrate' (1992) 8(2) *LCIA Arbitration International*.

Giuliano, M. and Lagarde, P., 'Report on the Convention on the law applicable to contractual obligations' Journal Official No. C 282, 31 October 1980.

Glossner, O., 'National Report: Federal Republic of Germany' (1979) IV *Yearbook Commercial Arbitration*.

Goldman, B., 'Lex Mercatoria' (1983) 3 *Forum Internationale*.

Goldman, B., 'Provisional Measures in International Arbitration' (1993) *International Business Law Journal*.

Goldman, B., 'The Applicable Law: General Principles of Law', in *Contemporary Problems in International Arbitration*, Lew, J. (ed.) (The Hague, Kluwer Law International, 1987).

Goldman, B., 'Une bataille judiciaire autour de la lex mercatoria – L'affaire Norsolor' [1983] Revue de l'Arbitrage.

Goode, R., 'The Role of Lex Loci Arbitri in International Commercial Arbitration' (2001) 17(1) *LCIA Arbitration International*.

Gotanda, J.Y., 'Awarding Costs and Attorneys' Fees in International Commercial Arbitrations' (1999) 21(1) *Michigan Journal of International Law*.

Greenblatt, J.L. and Griffin, P., 'Towards the Harmonization of International Arbitration Rules: Comparative Analysis of the Rules of the ICC, AAA, LCIA and CIETAC' (2001) 17(1) *LCIA Arbitration International*.

Naón, G., 'Choice-of-Law Problems in International Commercial Arbitration' (2001) 289 *Recueil des Cours*.

Habscheid, W.J., 'Das Problem der Unabhängigkeit der Schiedsgerichte' [1962] Neue Juristische Wochenschrift.

Habscheid, W.J., 'Der Kostenersatzanspruch des Beklagten bei Unzuständigkeitsausspruch des Schiedsgerichtes', in *Festgabe für H. W. Fasching zum 70. Geburtstag*, Jelinek, W., Böhm, P., Konecny, A. and Buchegger, W. (eds) (Vienna, Manz, 1993).

Habscheid, W.J., 'Zur Kompetenz-Kompetenz nach dem neuen Schiedsrecht', in *Festschrift für Peter Schlosser zum 70. Geburstag*, Bachmann, B., Breidenbach, S., Coester-Waltjen, D., Hess, B., Nelle, A. and Wolf, C. (eds) (Tübingen, Mohr Siebeck, 2005).

Hamann, H. and Lenarz, T., 'Parallele Verfahren mit identischem Schiedsgericht als Lösung für Mehrparteikonflikte?' [2006] Zeitschrift für Schiedsverfahren.

Hanotiau, B., 'Complex – Multicontract-Multiparty – Arbitrations' (1998) 14(4) *LCIA Arbitration International*.

Hanusch, P., 'Challenge of Arbitrators under the New Austrian Arbitration Act', in *Austrian Arbitration Yearbook 2007*, Klausegger, C. et al. (eds) (Vienna, Manz, 2007).

Hascher, D.T., 'European Convention on International Commercial Arbitration of 1961 – Commentary' (1990) XV *Yearbook Commercial Arbitration*.

Hascher, D.T., 'The European Convention on International Commercial Arbitration (1961)' (1995) XX *Yearbook Commercial Arbitration*.

Hau, W., 'Zur Entwicklung des Internationalen Zivilverfahrensrecht in der Europäischen Union in den Jahren 2005 und 2006' [2007] Zeitschrift für Gemeinschaftsprivatrecht.

Hausmaninger, C., 'Civil Liability of Arbitrators – Comparative Analysis and Proposals for Reform' (1990) 7(4) *Journal of International Arbitration*.

Hausmaninger, C., 'Rights and Obligations of the Arbitrator with Regard to the Parties and the Arbitral Institution – A Civil Law Viewpoint' (1995) *ICC International Court of Arbitration Bulletin Special Supplement: The Status of the Arbitrator*.

Heller, K., 'Die Anfechtung von Teil- und Zwischenschiedssprüchen in Östrreich' [1994] Praxis des Internationalen Privat- und Verfahrensrechts.

Heller, K., 'Die Rechtsstellung des internationalen Schiedsgerichts der Wirtschaftskammer Österreich' [1994] Wirtschaftsrechtliche Blätter.

Hempel, K. and Welser, I., 'Das Schiedsgericht Berlin identisch mit dem Schiedsgericht bei der Kammer für Außenhandel der DDR?' [1993] Österreichische Juristenzeitung.

Hempel, K., 'Einstweiliger Rechtsschutz durch Schiedsgerichte – Cui Bono?', in *Festschrift Rudolf Welser zum 65. Geburtstag*, Fischer-Czermak, C., Kletecka, A., Schauer, M. and Zankl, W. (eds) (Vienna, Manz, 2004).

Hirsch, L., 'Remarks on the Decision of Zurich Superior Court of 11 September 2001' (2002) 20(4) *Bulletin ASA*, 702.

Hobeck, P., Mahnken, V. and Koebke, M., 'Schiedsgerichtsbarkeit im internationalen Anlagenbau – Ein Auslaufmodell?' [2007] Zeitschrift für Schiedsverfahren.

Hobér, K., 'Parallel Arbitration Proceedings – Duties of the Arbitrators', in *Parallel State and Arbitral Procedures in International Arbitration*, Cremades, B. and Lew, J. (eds) (Paris, ICC Publishing, 2005).

Holtzmann, H.M., 'Fact-Finding by the Iran-U.S. Claims Tribunal', in *Fact-Finding Before International Tribunals*, Lillich, R.B. (ed.) (Ardsley-on-Hudson, Translational Publishers, 1992).

Horvath, G.J., 'Schiedsgerichtsbarkeit und Mediation – Ein glückliches Paar?' [2005] Zeitschrift für Schiedsverfahren.

Horvath, G.J., 'The Duty of Tribunals to Render an Enforceable Award' (2001) 18(2) *Journal of International Arbitration*.

Hunter, M., 'Ethics of the International Arbitrator' (1987) 53 *Arbitration*.

Hunter, M., 'The Procedural Powers of Arbitrators Under the English 1996 Act' (1997) 13(4) *LCIA Arbitration International*.

IBA Working Party, 'Commentary on the new IBA Rules of Evidence', in *Beweiserhebung in internationalen Schiedsverfahren*, Böckstiegel, K.-H. (ed.) (Cologne, Carl Heymanns Verlag, 2001).

ICC Commission Working Party (Hunter, M., Chairman), 'Final Report on Dissenting and Separate Opinions' (1991) 2(1) *ICC International Court of Arbitration Bulletin*.

ICC Commission, '1996 ICC Final Report on the Status of the Arbitrator' (1996) 7(1) *ICC International Court of Arbitration Bulletin*.

ICC International Court of Arbitration, '2006 Statistical Report' (2007) 18(1) *ICC International Court of Arbitration Bulletin*.

Incoterms 2000 (1999) ICC Publication No. 560.

International Law Association, London Conference (2000), Interim ILA Report on Public Policy as a Bar to Enforcement of International Arbitral Awards, reprinted in (2003) 19(2) *LCIA Arbitration International*.

International Law Association, New Delhi Conference (2002), 'Final ILA Report on Public Policy as a Bar to Enforcement of International Arbitral Awards', reprinted in (2003) 19(2) *LCIA Arbitration International*.

International Law Association, Berlin Conference (2004) Interim Report: 'Res judicata and Arbitration' <www.ila-hq.org>.

International Law Association, Toronto Conference (2006), Final Report on Lis Pendens and Arbitration, <www.ila-hq.org>.

International Law Commission, Draft on Arbitral Procedure Prepared by the International Law Commission at Its Fourth Session, 1952, UN DOC. A/CN.4/59, Article 1(3), (1952) 2 *Yearbook of International Law Commission*.

International Law Commission, Memorandum on Arbitral Procedure, Prepared by the Secretariat, Doc. A/CN.4/35, (1950) II *Yearbook of International Law Commission*.

Jabornegg, P., 'Die Lehre vom Durchgriff im Recht der Kapitalgesellschaften' [1989] Wirtschaftliche Blätter.

Jarvin, S., 'The Group of Companies Doctrine' (1994) *ASA Special Series* No. 8.

Joeinig, E., 'Alternative Streitbeilegungsmöglichkeiten für Verbraucher in Österreich' [2006] Zivilrecht aktuell.

Jordans, R., 'Anmerkungen zu EuGH Rs. C-168/05 – Elisa Maria Mostaza Claro gegen Centro Movil Milenium SL' [2007] Zeitschrift für Gemeinschaftsprivatrecht.

Jud, B. and Högler-Pracher, R., 'Schiedsverfahren mit modernen Kommunikationstechniken' [1999] ecolex.

Karrer, P., 'Interim Measures Issued by Arbitral Tribunals and the Courts: Less Theory, Please' (2000) 10 *ICCA Congress Series* (New Delhi).

Kathrein, G., 'Gewährleistung im Verbrauchergeschäft' [2001] ecolex.

Kerr, M., 'Concord and Conflict in International Arbitration' (1997) 13(2) *LCIA Arbitration International*.

Klausegger, C., 'Legal Assistance by Austrian Courts in International Arbitration', in *Austrian Arbitration Yearbook 2007*, Klausegger, C. et al. (eds) (Vienna, Manz, 2007).

Klicka, T., 'Der OGH und die Schiedsklausel im Konsumentengeschäft' [1995] ecolex.

Kloiber, B., 'Vorläufige oder sichernde Massnahmen durch Schiedsgerichte' [2006] Zivilrecht aktuell.

Köhne, H.C. and Langner, S., 'Geltendmachung von Gegenforderungen im Internationalen Schiedsverfahren' [2003] Recht der Internationalen Wirtschaft.

Konecny, A., 'Zur Erweiterung der Verbesserungsvorschriften durch die Zivilverfahrens-Novelle 1983' [1984] Juristische Blätter.

Kreindler, R.H., 'Benefiting from Oral Testimony of Expert Witnesses', in *Arbitration and Oral Evidence*, Levy, L. and Veeder, V.V. (eds) (2004) ICC Dossier.

Krejci, H., 'Zum Ministerialentwurf einer HGB – Reform' [2003] Die Versicherungsrundschau.

Krejci, H., 'Zum Mitglieder- und Gläubigerschutz nach dem VerG 2002' [2003] Juristische Blätter.

Krejci, H., 'Zur Schiedsrichterhaftung' [2007] Österreichische Juristenzeitung.

Kremslehner, F., 'Lis pendens and res judicata in International Commercial Arbitration', in *Austrian Arbitration Yearbook 2007*, Klausegger, C. et al. (eds) (Vienna, Manz, 2007).

Kröll, S., 'Die Neuregelung des österreichischen Schiedsrechts – Felix Austria!?', in *Festschrift Norbert Horn, Zivil- und Wirtschaftsrecht im Europäischen und Globalen Kontext*, Berger, K.P., Borges, G., Herrmann, H., Schlüter, A. and Wackerbarth, U. (eds) (Berlin/New York, de Gruyter, 2006).

Kröll, S., 'Recourse Against Negative Decisions on Jurisdiction' (2004) 20(1) *LCIA Arbitration International*.

Kühn, W., 'Arbitrability of Antitrust Disputes in the Federal Republic of Germany' (1987) 3(3) *LCIA Arbitration International*.

Kurkela, M.S., Levin, R.C., Liebscher, C. and Sommer, P., 'Certain Procedural Issues in Arbitrating Competition Cases' (2007) 24(2) *Journal of International Arbitration*.

Kutschera, M., 'Funktion und Verwendbarkeit der elektronischen Signatur' [2000] Steuer- und WirtschaftsKartei.

Laffranque, J., 'Dissenting opinion and Judical Independence' (2003) VIII *Juridica International*.

Lalive, P., 'Inquietantes derives de l'arbitrage CCI' (1995) 13(4) *Bulletin ASA*.

Lalive, P., 'Les règles de conflit de lois appliquées au fond du litige par l'arbitre international siégeant en Suisse', in 'L'arbitrage international privé et la Suisse, Colloque des 2 et 23 avril 1976, Mémoires de la faculté de droit de Genéve', no. 53, 1977.

Lalive, P., 'Transnational (or Truly International) Public Policy and International Arbitration' (1986) 3 *ICCA Congress Series* (New York).

Lando, O., 'The Lex Mercatoria and International Commercial Arbitration' (1985) 34(4) *International & Comparative Law Quarterly*.

Landolt, P., 'Limits on Court Review of International Arbitration Awards Assessed in light of States' Interests and in particular in light of EU Law Requirements' (2007) 23(1) *Arbitration International*.

Leahy, E.R. and Bianchi, C.J., 'The Changing Face of International Arbitration' (2000) 17(4) *Journal of International Arbitration*.

Leahy, E.R. and Pierce, K.J., 'Sanctions to Control Party Misbehaviour in International Arbitration' (1986) 26 *Virginia Journal of International Law*.

Leboulanger, P., 'Multi-Contract Arbitration' (1996) 13(4) *Journal of International Arbitration*.

Legros, C., 'Garantie de passif: opposabilité de la clause d'arbitrage au bénéficiare de la stipulation pour autrui' (2006) 46 *Semaine juridique édition Générale*, II.

Level, P., 'Joinder of Proceedings, Intervention of Third Parties and Additional Claims and Counterclaims' (1996) 7(2) *ICC International Court of Arbitration Bulletin*.

Lew, J., 'Achieving the Dream: Autonomous Arbitration' (2006) 22(2) *LCIA Arbitration International*.

Lew, J., 'Commentary on Interim and Conservatory Measures in ICC Cases' (2000) 11(1) *ICC International Court of Arbitration Bulletin*.

Lew, J., 'Expert Report of Dr. Julian D.M. Lew (in Esso/BHP v. Plowman)' (1995) 11(3) *LCIA Arbitration International*.

Liebscher, C., 'European Public Policy and the Austrian Supreme Court' (2000) 16(3) *LCIA Arbitration International*.

Lindacher, W.F., 'Schiedsgerichtliche Kompetenz zur vorläufigen Entziehung der Geschäftsführungs- und Vertretungsbefugnis für Personengesellschaften' [1979] Zeitschrift für Unternehmens- und Gesellschaftsrecht.

Littman, M., 'The Arbitration Act 1996: The Parties' Right to Agree Procedure' (1997) 13(3) *LCIA Arbitration International*.

Lockerby, M.J. and Shur, K.J., 'Arbitration Fairness Act of 2007: A Trial Lawyer's Dream, a Client's Nightmare' Franchising World, November 2007, online publication <http://goliath.ecnext.com/coms2/summary_0199-7310455_ITM>.

Mänhardt, F., 'Feststellungsgerichtsbarkeit bei inländischen Schiedsverfahren –
Eine Regelungslücke?' [1989] Anwaltsblatt.

Mankowski, P., 'Die Ablehnung von Schiedsrichtern' [2004] Zeitschrift für
Schiedsverfahren.

Mann, F.A., 'Lex Facit Arbitrum', in *International Arbitration – Liber Amicorum
Martin Domke*, Sanders, P. (ed.) (The Hague, Nijhof, 1967).

Mann, F.A., 'Schiedsrichter und Recht', in *Festschrift für Werner Flume zum 70.
Geburtstag*, Ballerstedt, K., Mann, F.A., Jakobs, H.H., Knobbe-Keuk, B. and
Wilhelm, J. (Cologne, Verlag Dr. Otto Schmidt, 1978).

Mann, F.A., 'The Proper Law in the Conflict of Laws' (1987) 36(3) *International &
Comparative Law Quarterly*.

Mantilla-Serrano, F., 'Towards a Transnational Procedural Public Policy' (2004)
20(4) *LCIA Arbitration International*.

Matscher, F., 'Probleme der Schiedsgerichtsbarkeit im österreichischen Recht'
[1975] Juristische Blätter.

Matscher, F., 'Schiedsgerichsbarkeit und EMRK', in *Festschrift für Heinrich
Nagel zum 75. Geburtstag*, Haberscheid, W.J. and Schwab, K. (Münster,
Aschendorff, 1987).

Mayer, P., 'Les limites de la séparabilité de la clause compromissoire' [1997]
Revue de l'Arbitrage.

Mayer, P., 'The Limits of Severability of the Arbitration Clause' (1999) 9 *ICCA
Congress Series* (Paris).

Mayr, P., 'Schiedsklauseln in Vereinsstatuten' [2007] Recht der Wirtschaft.

Mayer, P., 'Note Cour d'Appel de Paris (1er Ch. Suppl.) 28 Novembre; Cour
d'Appel de Paris (1er Ch. Suppl.), 8 Mars 1990' [1990] Revue de l'Arbitrage.

Melis, W., 'Austria' (1979) IV *Yearbook Commercial Arbitration*.

Melis, W., 'Austria', in *International Handbook on Commercial Arbitration* (The
Hague, Kluwer Law International, Suppl. 10, 1989).

Melis, W., 'Die neue Schieds- und Schlichtungsordnung des Internationalen
Schiedsgerichts der Bundeskammer der gewerblichen Wirtschaft Wien
(Wiener Regeln)' [1991] Anwaltsblatt.

Melis, W., 'Die Schiedsgerichtsbarkeit der österreichischen Handelskammern seit
1946', in *Festschrift Seidl-Hohenveldern*, Böckstiegel, K.H., Folz, H.-E.,
Mössner, J. and Zermak, K. (eds) (Cologne, Carl Heymanns Verlag, 1988).

Melis, W., 'Function and Responsibility of Arbitral Institutions' (1991) XIII
Comparative Law Yearbook of International Business.

Melis, W., 'Überlegungen aus Anlaß des Inkrafttretens der neuen Schieds- und
Vergleichsordnung des Schiedsgerichtes der Bundeskammer der
Gewerblichen Wirtschaft' [1983] Der Gesellschafter.

Melis, W., 'Vienna Arbitration Rules Help to Resolve U.S.-European Dispute'
(1992) 47 *Arbitration Journal*.

Melis, W., 'Case Note to OGH, 18 November 1982, 8 Ob 520/82' (1984) IX
Yearbook Commercial Arbitration.

Miller, M., 'Contracting Out of Process, Contracting Out of Corporate
Accountability: An Argument against Enforcement of Pre-dispute Limits

of Process' (Tennessee Law Review Spring 2008), online publication, <http://papers.ssrn.com/sol3/papers.cfm?abstract_id=1081709>.

Mohan, R.C. and Teck, L.W., 'Some Contractual Approaches to the Problem of Inconsistent Awards in Multi-party, Multi-contract Arbitration Proceedings' (2005) 1(2) *The Asian International Arbitration Journal.*

Mustill, M.J., 'The New Lex Mercatoria: The First Twenty-five Years' in *Liber Amicorum for Lord Wilberforce*, Boss, M. and Brownlie, I. (eds) (Oxford, Clarendon Press, 1987).

Mustill, M.J., 'Transnational Arbitration and English Law' (1984) 37 *Current Legal Problems.*

Neson, T.G., '*Bridas v. Turkmenistan*: U.S. Courts Uphold an Arbitrator's Power to Hold a Foreign Sovereign Liable for the Acts of its State-Owned Enterprise' (2006) 24(3) *Bulletin ASA.*

Neuteufel, K., 'Das neue österreichische Schiedsrecht' [2006] (26) Österreichische Juristenzeitung.

Nicholas, G. and Partasides, C., 'LCIA Court Decisions on Challenges to Arbitrators: A Proposal to Publish' (2007) 23(1) *LCIA Arbitration International.*

Niklas, M., 'Schiedsverfahren via Internet nach den Wiener Regeln' [2004] Internationales Handelsrecht.

Niklisch, F., 'Schiedsgerichtsverfahren mit integrierter Schlichtung' [1998] Recht der Internationalen Wirtschaft.

Oberhammer, P., 'Fakultative Schiedsklauseln' [2000] Recht der Wirtschaft.

Oberhammer, P., 'Internationale Gerichtsstandsvereinbarungen: Konkurrierende oder ausschließliche Zuständigkeit?' [1997] Juristische Blätter.

Oberhammer, P., 'Schiedsvereinbarung und § 1016 ABGB', in *Festschrift für Rudolf Welser zum 65. Geburtstag*, Fischer-Czermak, C., Kletecka, A., Schauer, M. and Zankl, W. (eds) (Vienna, Manz, 2004).

Okekeifere, A.I., 'The Parties' Rights against a Dilatory or Unskilled Arbitrator' (1998) 15(2) *Journal of International Arbitration.*

Park, W.W., 'Non-signatories and the New York Convention' (2008) 2(1) *Dispute International.*

Park, W.W., 'An Arbitrator's Jurisdiction to Determine Jurisdiction' ICCA Congress hand-out, 2006.

Park, W.W., 'Judicial Controls in the Arbitral Process' (1989) 5(3) *LCIA Arbitration International.*

Partasides, C., 'Sections 33 and 34 of the English Arbitration Act 1996: A Potential Conflict' (1997) 13(4) *LCIA Arbitration International.*

Partasides, C., 'The Fourth Arbitrator? The Role of Secretaries to Tribunals in International Arbitration' (2002) 18(2) *LCIA Arbitration International.*

Paulsson, J. and Petrochilos, G., 'Revision of the UNCITRAL Arbitration Rules' (Paris, 2006), <www.uncitral.org/pdf/english/news/arbrules_report.pdf>.

Paulsson, J. and Rawding, N., 'The Trouble with Confidentiality' (1995) 11(3) *LCIA Arbitration International.*

Paulsson, J., 'Arbitration Unbound: Award Detached from the Law of Its Country of Origin' (1981) 30(2) *International & Comparative Law Quarterly.*

Paulsson, J., 'The Timely Arbitrator: Reflections on the Böckstiegel Method', in *Law of International Business and Dispute Settlement in the 21st Century*, Liber Amicorum K.-H. Böckstiegel, Briner, R., Fortier, L.Y., Berger, K.P. and Bredow, J. (eds) (Cologne/Berlin/Bonn/Munich, Carl Heymanns Verlag, 2001).

Peschek, R., 'Neue Möglichkeiten für Schiedsverfahren im Arbeitsrecht' [2003] Recht der Wirtschaft.

Peter, W., 'Witness Conferencing' (2002) 18(1) *LCIA Arbitration International*.

Pietrowski, R., 'Evidence in International Arbitration' (2006) 22(3) *LCIA Arbitration International*.

Pitkowitz, N. and Schmitt, M., 'Defence Tools in Arbitration Proceedings', in *Austrian Arbitration Yearbook 2007*, Klausegger, C. et al. (eds) (Vienna, Manz, 2007).

Pitkowitz, N., 'Setting Aside Arbitral Awards under the New Austrian Arbitration Act', in *Austrian Arbitration Yearbook 2007*, Klausegger, C. et al. (eds) (Vienna, Manz, 2007).

Platte, M., 'An Arbitrator's Duty to Render Enforceable Awards' (2003) 20(3) *Journal of International Arbitration*.

Platte, M., 'When Should an Arbitrator Join Cases?' (2002) 18(1) *LCIA Arbitration International*.

Polkinghorne, M. and Fitzgerald, D., 'Arbitration in Southeast Asia: Hong Kong, Singapore and Thailand Compared' (2001) 18(1) *Journal of International Arbitration*.

Polkinghorne, M., 'More Changes in Singapore: Appearance Rights of Foreign Counsel' (2005) 22(1) *Journal of International Arbitration*.

Power, J. and Konrad, C.W., 'Costs in International Arbitration: A Comparative Overview of Civil and Common Law Doctrines', in *Austrian Arbitration Yearbook 2008*, Klausegger, C. et al. (eds) (Vienna, Manz, 2008).

Power, J. and Konrad, C.W., 'Costs in International Commercial Arbitration – A Comparative Overview of Civil and Common Law Doctrines', in *Austrian Arbitration Yearbook 2007*, C. Klausegger et al. (eds) (Vienna, Manz, 2007).

Report of the Secretary-General on the Preliminary Draft Set of Arbitration Rules, Preliminary Draft Set of Arbitration Rules for an Optional Use in Ad Hoc Arbitration Relating to International Trade, UNCITRAL 8th Session, UN Doc A/CN.9/97 (1974), (1975) VI *UNCITRAL Yearbook*.

Raeschke-Kessler, H., 'Der Vergleich im Schiedsverfahren', in *Festschrift für Ottoarndt Glossner zum 70. Geburtstag*, Plantey, A., Böckstiegel, K.-H. and Bredow, J. (eds) (Heidelberg, Verlag Recht und Wirtschaft, 1994).

Rau, A.S., 'The Arbitrability Question Itself' (1999) 10 *American Review of International Arbitration*.

Rawding, N. and Seeger, K., '*Aegis v. European Re* and the Confidentiality of Arbitration Awards' (2003) 19(4) *LCIA Arbitration International*.

Rechberger, W.H. and Rami, M., 'Ablehnung von Schiedsrichtern durch die Parteien' [1999] Wirtschaftsrechtliche Blätter.

Rechberger, W.H., 'Die Widersprüchlichkeit eines Schiedsspruchs als Aufhebungsgrund nach österreichischem Recht' [2006] Zeitschrift für Schiedsverfahren.

Rechberger, W.H., 'Evergreen: Gültigkeit der Schiedsklausel', in *Festschrift für Peter Schlosser zum 70. Geburtstag*, Bachmann, B., Breidenbach, S., Coester-Waltjen, D., Heß, B., Nelle, A. and Wolf, C. (Mohr Siebek, Tübingen 2005).

Redfern, A., 'The 2003 Freshfields Lecture – Dissenting Opinions in International Commercial Arbitration: The Good, the Bad and the Ugly' (2004) 20(3) *LCIA Arbitration International*.

Reich, N., 'More clarity after "Claro"?' (2007) 3(1) *European Review of Contract Law*.

Reiner, A., 'Aufrechnung trotz (Fehlens einer) Schiedsvereinbarung nach österreichischem Recht', in *Festschrift für Dr. Karl Hempel zum 60. Geburtstag: Recht in Österreich und Europa*, Mayer, H., von Schlabrendorff, F., Spiegelfeld, B. and Welser, R. (eds) (Vienna, Manz, 1997).

Reiner, A., 'Die internationale Schiedsgerichtsbarkeit nach österreichischem und französischem Recht' [1986] Zeitschrift für Europarecht, IPR und Rechtsvergleichung.

Reiner, A., 'Les mesures provisoires et conservatoires et l'Arbitrage international, notamment l'Arbitrage CCI' (1998) *Journal du Droit International*.

Reiner, A., 'SchiedsRÄG 2006: Wissenswertes zum neuen österreichischen Schiedsrecht' [2006] ecolex.

Reiner, A., 'Schiedsverfahren und Gesellschaftsrecht' [2007] Der Gesellschafter.

Reiner, A., 'Schiedsverfahren und rechtliches Gehör' [2003] Zeitschrift für Europarecht, IPR und Rechtsvergleichung.

Reiner, A., 'The 2001 Version of the Vienna Rules' (2001) 18(6) *Journal of International Arbitration*.

Reiner, A., 'Zur Auslegung von Artikel 7 der Wiener Regeln betreffend die Frist zur Einbringung einer Widerklage' [1999] Zeitschrift für Europarecht, IPR und Rechtsvergleichung.

Reiner, A., 'Zur objektiven Schiedsfähigkeit von Streitigkeiten aus dem MRG unterliegenden Mietverträgen' [2001] Wohnrechtliche Blätter.

Rensmann, T., 'A National Arbitral Awards, Legal Phenomenon or Academic Phantom?' (1998) 15(2) *Journal of International Arbitration*.

Report from the ICC Commission on Arbitration, 'Techniques for Controlling Time and Costs in Arbitration' (2007) ICC Publication No. 843.

Report of the Secretary General, Analytical Commentary on Draft Text of a Model Law on International Commercial Arbitration, A/CN.9/264, <www.uncitral.org>.

Report of the Secretary-General on the Revised Draft Set of Arbitration Rules, UNCITRAL, 9th Session, Addendum 1 (Commentary), UN Doc. A/CN.9/112/Add. 1 (1975), (1976) VII *UNCITRAL Yearbook*.

Report of the UNCITRAL, 8th Session, Summary of Discussion of the Preliminary Draft, UN Doc. A/10017 (1975) VI *UNCITRAL Yearbook*.

Reymond, C., 'Note sur l'avance des frais de l'arbitrage et sa repartition', in *Etudes de procedure et d'arbitrage en l'honneur de Jean-Francois Poudret*, Haldy, J., Rapp, J.M. and Ferrari, P. (eds) (Lausanne, Stämpfli Verlag, 1999).

Riegler, S., 'Is Austria Any Different? The New Austrian Arbitration Law in Comparison with the UNCITRAL Model Law and the German Arbitration Law' (2006) *International Arbitration Law Review*.

Rivkin, D.W., 'Keeping Lawyers out of International Arbitration' (1990) *International Financial Law Review*.

Rivkin, D.W., 'Restriction on Foreign Counsel in International Arbitrations' (1991) XVI *Yearbook Commercial Arbitration*.

Rodriguez Iglesias, G.C., 'Der EuGH und die Gerichte der Mitgliedsstaaten – Komponenten der richterlichen Gewalt in der Europäischen Union' [2000] Neue Juristische Wochenschrift.

Rogers, C.A., 'Fit and Function in Legal Ethics: Developing a Code of Conduct for International Arbitration' (2002) *Michigan Journal of International Law*.

Rokison, K., '... Pastures New' (1998) 14(4) *LCIA Arbitration International*.

Roth, M., 'Tendenzen im internationalen Kostenrecht – erläutert am Beispiel eines neuen österreichischen Schiedsverfahrensrecht' [2004] Zeitschrift für Schiedsverfahren.

Rubino-Sammartano, M., 'The Channel Tunnel and the Tronc Commun Doctrine' (1993) 10(3) *Journal of International Arbitration*.

Rubins, N., 'In God We Trust, All Others Pay Cash: Security for Costs in International Arbitration' (2000) *American Review of International Arbitration*.

Rubins, N., Sołtysiński, S., Olechowski, M., Bagner, H. and Wiwen-Nilsson, T., 'The *CME v. Czech Republic Case* – Case summary with observations' (2003) 2 Stockholm Arbitration Report, <www.sccinstitute.com/_upload/shared_files/artiklar/tjeckiska_republiken.pdf>.

Rummel, P., 'Privates Vereinsrecht im Konflikt zwischen Autonomie und rechtlicher Kontrolle', in *Festschrift Rudolf Strasser zum 60. Geburtstag*, Schwarz, W. and Spielbüchler, K. (eds) (Vienna, Manz, 1983).

Rummel, P., 'Schiedsvertrag und ABGB' [1986] Österreichische Richterzeitung.

Sanders, P., 'L'autonomie de la clause compromissoire', in *Hommage à Frédéric Eisemann, Une initiative de la Chambre de Commerce International*, Liber Amicorum (ed.) (Paris, ICC, 1978).

Sandrock, O., ' "Intra" and "Extra-Entity" Agreements to Arbitrate and their Extension to Non-Signatories Under German Law' (2002) 19(5) *Journal of International Arbitration*.

Sandrock, O., 'The Cautio Judicatum Solvi in Arbitration Proceedings' (1997) 14(2) *Journal of International Arbitration*.

Scherer, M., 'When Should an Arbitral Tribunal Sitting in Switzerland Confronted with Parallel Litigation Abroad Stay the Arbitration?' (2001) 19(3) *Bulletin ASA*.

Schlosser, P., 'Arbitration Clauses in Maritime Contracts and Their Binding Effect on Groups of Companies' (1994) 11(4) *Journal of International Arbitration*.

Schlosser, P., 'Der Grad der Unabhängigkeit einer Schiedsvereinbarung vom Hauptvertrag', in *Law of International Business and Dispute Settlement in the 21st Century in Liber Amicorum Karl-Heinz Böckstiegel*, R. Briner et al. (eds) (Cologne, Carl Heymanns Verlag, 2001).

Schlosser, P., 'Die lange deutsche Reise in die prozessuale Moderne' [1991] Juristenzeitung.

Schlosser, P., 'Einstweiliger Rechtsschutz durch staatliche Gerichte im Dienste der Schiedsgerichtsbarkeit' [1986] Zeitschrift für Zivilprozess.

Schlosser, P., 'Schiedsgerichtsbarkeit, Schiedsgutachtenwesen und Höchstpersönlichkeit der Entscheidungsbefugnis', in *Festschrift für Norbert Horn zum 70. Geburtstag*, Berger, K.P., Borges, G., Herrmann, H., Schlüter, A. and Wackerbarth, U. (eds) (Berlin, de Gruyter Recht, 2006).

Schlosser, P., 'The 1968 Brussels Convention and Arbitration' (1991) 7(3) *LCIA Arbitration International*.

Schlosser, P., Case Note to OGH, 18 November 1982, 8 Ob 520/82 [1983] Konkurs-, Treuhand- und Schiedsgerichtswesen.

Schneider, M.E., 'Lean Arbitration: Cost Control and Efficiency Through Progressive Identification of Issues and Separate Pricing of Arbitration Services' (1994) 10(2) *LCIA Arbitration International*.

Schoible, N., 'Die Niederlassung im österreichischen Zivilprozessrecht', in *Rechtsfragen der Zweigniederlassung, 28*, Schuhmacher, W., et al. (eds) (Vienna, LexisNexis, 1993).

Schoible, N.A., 'Europäische Rechtshilfe bei der Beweisaufnahme in Zivil – und Handelssachen durch ordentliche Gerichte für Schiedsgerichte', in *Festschrift W.H. Rechberger zum 60. Geburtstag*, Bittner, L., Klicka, T., Kodek, G.E. and Oberhammer, P. (eds) (Vienna/New York, Springer, 2005).

Schöll, M., 'Set-Off Defenses in International Arbitration: Criteria for Best Practice – A Comparative Perspective', in *Best Practice in International Arbitration*, Wirth, M. (ed.) (ASA Special Series No. 26, 2006).

Schönherr, F., 'Streitigkeiten aus dem Gesellschaftsverhältnis und Schiedsgericht' [1980] Der Gesellschafter.

Schreuer, C.H., 'Commentary on the ICSID Convention, Article 47' (1998) 13 *ICSID Review* 1.

Schreuer, C.H., 'Die Durchsetzung zivilrechtlicher Ansprüche gegen ausländische Staaten' [1991] Österreichische Juristenzeitung.

Schroth, H.J., 'Einstweiliger Rechtsschutz im deutschen Schiedsverfahren' [2003] Zeitschrift für Schiedsverfahren.

Schumacher, H., 'Ein Schiedsspruch – und was nun?' [2006] Zeitschrift für Schiedsverfahren.

Schumacher, H., 'Unbestimmte Schiedsvereinbarungen und Dissens: Anknüpfungsfragen bei internationalen Sachverhalten in der Judikatur des OGH' [2005] Zeitschrift für Schiedsverfahren.

Schütze, R.A., 'Dissenting Opinions im Schiedsverfahren', in *Festschrift für Hideo Nakamura zum 70. Geburtstag*, Heldrich, A. and Uchida, T. (eds) (Tokyo, Seibundo, 1996).

Schwab, K.H., 'Einstweiliger Rechtsschutz und Schiedsgerichtsbarkeit', in *Festschrift für Fritz Baur*, Grunsky, W. (ed.) (Tübingen, Mohr Siebeck, 1981).

Schwartz, E.A., 'Multi-party Arbitration and the ICC – In the Wake of Dutco' (1993) 10(3) *Journal of International Arbitration*.

Schwartz, E.A., 'The Practices and Experience of the ICC Court', in *Conservatory and Provisional Measures in International Arbitration* (1993) ICC Publication No. 519.

Schwartz, E.A., 'The Rights and Duties of ICC Arbitrators' (1995) ICC International Court of Arbitration Bulletin Special Supplement: The Status of the Arbitrator.

Schwarz, F.T. and Beale, K., 'Disclosure in Aid of Foreign Arbitration under U.S. Law' (forthcoming).

Schwarz, F.T. and Miles, W., 'Taking of Evidence in International Commercial Arbitration', in *International Comparative Legal Guide to International Arbitration 2004* (London, Global Legal Group, 2003).

Schwarz, F.T. and Ortner, H., 'Procedural Order Public and the Internationalization of Public Policy in Arbitration', in *Austrian Arbitration Yearbook 2008*, Klausegger, C. et al. (eds) (Vienna, Manz, 2008).

Schwebel, S.M. and Lahne, S.G., 'Public Policy' (1986) 3 *ICCA Congress Series* (New York).

Seidl-Hohenveldern, I., 'Case Note to OGH, 18 November 1982, 8 Ob 520/82' [1983] Journal du Droit International (Clunet).

Smit, H., 'A-National Arbitration' (1989) 63 *Tulane Law Review*.

Smit, H., 'Confidentiality in Arbitration' (1995) 11(3) *LCIA Arbitration International*.

Smith, M.L., 'Contractual Obligations Owed by and to Arbitrators: Model Terms of Appointment' (1992) 8(1) *LCIA Arbitration International*.

Smith, M.L., 'Costs in International Commercial Arbitration', in *American Arbitration Association Handbook on International Arbitration and ADR*, Carbonneau, T.E. and Jaeggi, J.A. (eds) (Huntington, Juris Publishing, 2006).

Smith, M.L., 'Impartiality of the Party-Appointed Arbitrator' (1990) 6(4) *LCIA Arbitration International*.

Söderlund, C., 'Lis Pendens, Res Judicata and the Issues of Parallel Judicial Proceedings' (2005) 22(4) *Journal of International Arbitration*.

Stippl, C. and Öhlberger, V., 'Rendering of the Award by Multipartite Arbitral Tribunals' in *Austrian Arbitration Yearbook 2008*, Klausegger, C. et al. (Vienna, Manz, 2008).

Stockinger, S., 'Österreichisches Signaturgesetz' [1999] Medien und Recht.

Strauss, M., 'The Practice of the Iran-United States Claims Tribunal in Receiving Evidence from Parties and from Experts' (1986) 3(3) *Journal of International Arbitration*.

Tateishi, T., 'Recent Japanese Case Law in Relation to International Arbitrations' (2000) 17(4) *Journal of International Arbitration*.

Terlitza, B. and Weber, M., 'Zur Schiedsfähigkeit gesellschaftsrechtlicher Streitigkeiten nach dem SchiedsRÄG 2006' [2008] (2) Österreichische Juristenzeitung.

Thalhammer, D., 'Die Rolle der Schiedsgerichte bei der Durchsetzung von EG-Kartellrecht unter dem Regime der VO 1/2003' [2005] Wirtschaftsrechtliche Blätter.

Thöni, W., 'Zur Schiedsfähigkeit des GmbH-rechtlichen Anfechtungsstreits' [1994] Wirtschaftsrechtliche Blätter.

Triebel, V. and Coenen, T., 'Parallelität von Schiedsverfahren und staatlichem Gerichtsverfahren' Supplement 5 to (2003) Betriebs-Berater.

Triebel, V. and Zons, J., 'Discovery of Documents in international Schiedsverfahren – Theorie und Praxis' Supplement 7 to (2002) Betriebs-Berater.

Triebel, V., 'An Outline of the Swiss/German Rules of Civil Procedure and Practice Relating to Evidence' (1982) 47 *Arbitration*.

U.K. Department of Trade and Industry Consultation Document on Proposed Clauses and Schedules for an Arbitration Bill, reprinted in (1994) 10(2) *LCIA Arbitration International*.

UN Commission on International Trade Law, Working Group II (Arbitration), Note by the Secretariat, Document A/CN.9WG.II/WP.131, <www.uncitral. org/uncitral/en/commission/working_groups/2Arbitration.html>.

Uniform Customs and Practice for Documentary Credits (1983) ICC Publication No. 400.

Unteregger, S., 'Über die Wirtschaftlichkeit digitaler Signaturen' [2002] ecolex.

Van Houtte, H., 'Arbitration and Arts. 81 and 82 EC Treaty – A State of Affairs' (2005) 23(3) *Bulletin ASA*.

Van Houtte, H., 'Conduct of Arbitral Proceedings', in *Essays on International Commercial Arbitration*, Sarcevic, P. (ed.) (Leiden, Brill, 1989).

Van Houtte, H., 'Counsel-Witness Relations and Professional Misconduct in Civil Law Systems' (2003) 19(4) *LCIA Arbitration International*.

Van Houtte, H., 'Ten Reasons against a Proposal for Ex Parte Interim Measures of Protection in Arbitration' (2004) 20(1) *LCIA Arbitration International*.

Vcelouch, P., 'Interim and Protective Measures', in *Austrian Arbitration Yearbook 2007*, Klausegger, C. et al. (eds) (Vienna, Manz, 2007).

Vidal, D., 'The Extension of Arbitration Agreements within Groups of Companies: The Alter Ego Doctrine in Arbitral and Court Decisions' (2005) 16(2) *ICC International Court of Arbitration Bulletin*.

Von Hoffmann, B., 'Lex Mercatoria vor internationalen Schiedsgerichten' [1984] Praxis des Internationalen Privat- und Verfahrensrechts.

Vonkilch, A., 'Zum wirksamen Zugang von sicher signierten E-Mails' [2001] Recht der Wirtschaft.

Voser, N., 'Interessenkonflikte in der internationalen Schiedsgerichtsbarkeit – die Initiative der IBA' [2003] Zeitschrift für Schiedsverfahren.

Walter, G., 'Das Schiedsverfahren im deutsch-italienischem Rechtsverkehr' [1982] Recht der Internationalen Wirtschaft.

Walter, G. and von Hoffmann, B., 'Lex Mercatoria vor internationalen Schiedsgerichten' [1984] Praxis des Internationalen Privat- und Verfahrensrechts.

Webster, T.H., 'Evolving Principles in Enforcing Awards Subject to Annulment Proceedings' (2006) 23(3) *Journal of International Arbitration*.

Webster, T.H., 'Party Control in International Arbitration' (2003) 19(2) *LCIA Arbitration International*.

Wehrli, D., 'Zu Höhe und Umfang erstattungsfähiger Parteikosten', in *DIS-Materialien, Kosten im Schiedsverfahren – Tagungsbeiträge* (Cologne, 2005).

Weissmann, G., 'Drei Fragen zur Reform der Schiedsgerichtsbarkeit', in *Festschrift Rudolf Welser*, Fischer-Czermak, C., Kletecka, A., Schauer, M. and Zankl, W. (eds) (Vienna, Manz, 2004).

Welser, I., 'Pitfalls of Competence', in *Austrian Arbitration Yearbook 2007*, Klausegger, C. et al. (eds) (Vienna, Manz, 2007).

Welser, I., 'Vermischte Fragen aus der schiedsgerichtlichen Praxis', in *Festschrift Heinz Krejci, II*, Bernat, E., Böhler, E. and Weilinger, A. (eds) (Vienna, Verlag Österreich, 2001).

Wenger, T., 'Schiedsklausel im GmbH-Gesellschaftsvertrag' [1999] Österreichische Zeitschrift für Recht und Rechnungswesen.

Wetter, G., 'The Present Status of the International Court of Arbitration of the ICC: An Appraisal' (1990) *American Review of International Arbitration*.

Wilberforce, W., 'Written Briefs and Oral Advocacy' (1989) 5(4) *LCIA Arbitration International*.

Wilson, K., 'Saving Costs In International Arbitration' (1990) 6(2) *LCIA Arbitration International*.

Winstanley, A., 'A View from an Administering Institution' International Bar Association Conference 2002, Durban (2002) 7 LCIA News.

Wirth, M., 'Interim or Preventive Measures in Support of International Arbitration in Switzerland' (2000) 18(1) *Bulletin ASA*.

Wortmann, B., 'Choice of Law by Arbitrators: The Applicable Conflict of Laws System' (1998) 14(2) *LCIA Arbitration International*.

Yakovlev, A., 'International Commercial Arbitration Proceedings and Russian Courts' (1996) 13(1) *Journal of International Arbitration*.

Yat-Sen Li, J., 'Arbitral Immunity: A Profession Comes of Age' (1998) 64 *Arbitration*.

Zeiler, G., 'Erstmals einstweilige Massnahmen im Schiedsverfahren?' [2006] Zeitschrift für Schiedsverfahren.

Zekoll, J. and Bolt, J., 'Die Pflicht zur Vorlage von Urkunden im Zivilprozess – Amerikanische Verhältnisse in Deutschland ?' [2002] Neue Juristische Wochenschrift.

Zuberbühler, T., 'Non-signatories and the Consensus to Arbitrate' (2008) 26(1) *Bulletin ASA*.

II.   BOOKS

Aden, M., *Internationale Handelsschiedsgerichtsbarkeit* (2nd edn, Munich, C.H. Beck, 2003).

Ahrens, J.-M., *Die subjektive Reichweite internationaler Schiedsvereinbarungen und ihre Erstreckung in der Unternehmensgruppe* (Frankfurt/Main, Schriftenreihe der A.M Berges Stiftung für Arbitrales Recht, 2001).

Alvarez, H.C., Kaplan, N. and Rivkin, D., *Model Law Decisions, Cases Applying the UNCITRAL Model Law on International Commercial Arbitration (1985-2001)* (The Hague, Kluwer Law International, 2003).

Angst, P. (ed.), *Kommentar zur Exekutionsordnung* (Vienna, Manz, 2000).

Angst, P., Jakusch, W. and Mohr, F. (eds), *Exekutionsordnung* (14th edn, Vienna, Manz, 2004).

Angst, P., Jakusch, W. and Pimmer, H. (eds), *Exekutionsordnung* (14th edn, Vienna, Manz, 2006).

Arnaldez, J.-J., Derains, Y. and Hascher, D., *Collection of ICC Arbitral Awards 1996-2000* (The Hague, Kluwer Law International, 2003).

Arnold, W.-D., *Rechtsgebühren* (8th edn, Vienna, WUV, 2006).

Backhausen, G., *Schiedsgerichtsbarkeit unter besonderer Berücksichtigung des Schiedsvertragsrechts* (Vienna, Manz, 1990).

Baker, S. and Davis, M., *The UNCITRAL Arbitration Rules in Practice* (Deventer, Kluwer, 1992).

Baumbach, A. and Schwab, K.H., *Schiedsgerichtsbarkeit* (2nd edn, Munich, C.H. Beck, 1960).

Baur, F., *Neuere Probleme der privaten Schiedsgerichtsbarkeit* (Berlin/New York, de Gruyter, 1980).

Bell, A.S., *Forum Shopping and Venue in Transnational Litigation* (Oxford, OUP, 2003).

Berger, B. and Kellerhals, F., *Internationale und interne Schiedsgerichtsbarkeit in der Schweiz* (Bern/Vienna, Stämpfli Verlag/Manz, 2006).

Berger, K.P., *International Economic Arbitration* (Boston, Kluwer Law International, 1993).

Berger, K.P., *Internationale Wirtschaftsschiedsgerichtsbarkeit* (Berlin/New York, de Gruyter, 1992).

Black, H.C., *Black's Law Dictionary* (6th edn, St Paul, West Publishing Co, 1990).

Born, G.B. and Rutledge, P.B., *International Civil Litigation in United States Courts* (4th edn, New York, Aspen Publishers, 2007).

Born, G.B., *International Arbitration and Forum Selection Agreements: Drafting and Enforcing* (2nd edn, The Hague, Kluwer Law International, 2006).

Born, G.B., *International Commercial Arbitration – Commentary and Materials* (2nd edn, The Hague, Kluwer Law International, 2001).

Born, G.B., *International Commercial Arbitration – Commentary and Materials* (3rd edn, The Hague, Kluwer Law International, forthcoming).

Broches, A., *Commentary on the UNCITRAL Model Law on International Commercial Arbitration* (Deventer/Boston, Kluwer Law and Taxation Publishers, 1990).

Bühler, M. and Webster, T., *Handbook of ICC Arbitration; Commentary, Precedents, Materials* (London, Sweet & Maxwell, 2005).

Bühring-Uhle, Ch., *Arbitration and Mediation in International Business* (The Hague, Kluwer Law International, 1996).

Bydlinski, F., *Juristische Methodenlehre und Rechtsbegriff* (2nd edn, Springer, New York/Vienna, 1991).

Bydlinski, M., *Der Kostenersatz im Zivilprozess* (Vienna, Manz, 1992)

Bydlinski, S., Dehn, W., Krejci, H. and Schauer, M. (eds), *Reform-Kommentar UGB* (Vienna, Manz, 2007).

Carlston, K.S., *The Process of International Arbitration* (New York, Columbia University Press, 1946).

Caron, D., Caplan, L. and Pellonpaa, M., *The UNCITRAL Arbitration Rules: A Commentary* (Oxford, OUP, 2006).

Chiwitt-Oberhammer, T., *Der fehlerhafte Schiedsspruch* (Vienna, Verlag Österreich, 2000).

Collins, L. (Gen. eds), *Dicey, Morris and Collins on the Conflict of Laws* (14th edn, London, Sweet & Maxwell, 2006).

Craig, W.L., Park, W.W. and Paulsson, J., *International Chamber of Commerce Arbitration* (2nd edn, New York, Oceana Publications, 1990).

Craig, W.L., Park, W.W. and Paulsson, J., *International Chamber of Commerce Arbitration* (3rd edn, New York, Oceana Publications, 2000).

Czernich, D. and Heiss, H., *EVÜ: Das Europäische Schuldvertragsübereinkommen* (Vienna, LexisNexis, 1999).

Darby, W.E., *International Tribunals: A Collection of the Various Schemes Which Have Been Propounded, and of Instances since 1815 (1897)* (Whitefish, Kessinger Publishing, 2008).

De Boisseson, M., *Le Droit Francais de l'Arbitrage National et International* (Paris, GLN-éditions, 1990).

Derains, Y. and Schwartz, E.A., *A Guide to the New ICC Rules of Arbitration* (The Hague, Kluwer Law International, 1998).

Derains, Y. and Schwartz, E.A., *A Guide to the ICC Rules of Arbitration* (2nd edn, The Hague, Kluwer Law International, 2005).

Dittrich, R. and Tades, H. (eds), *Arbeitsrecht* (Vienna, Manz, 2007).

Dore, I.I., *The UNCITRAL Framework for Arbitration in Contemporary Perspective* (London, Graham & Trotman/Martinus Nijhoff, 1993).

Epping, M., *Die Schiedsvereinbarung im internationalen privaten Rechtsverkehr nach der Reform des deutschen Schiedsverfahrensrechts* (Munich, C.H. Beck, 1999).

Fasching, H.W., *Schiedsgericht und Schiedsverfahren im österreichischen und im internationalen Recht* (Vienna, Manz, 1973).

Fasching, H.W. (ed.), *Kommentar zu den Zivilprozeßgesetzen, I* (2nd edn, Vienna, Manz, 2000).

Fasching, H.W. (ed.), *Kommentar zu den Zivilprozeßgesetzen, II/1* (2nd edn, Vienna, Manz, 2002).

Fasching, H.W. (ed.), *Kommentar zu den Zivilprozeßgesetzen, II/2* (2nd edn, Vienna, Manz, 2003).

Fasching, H.W. (ed.), *Kommentar zu den Zivilprozeßgesetzen, III* (Vienna, Manz, 1966).

Fasching, H.W. (ed.), *Kommentar zu den Zivilprozeßgesetzen, III* (2nd end, Vienna, Manz, 2004).

Fasching, H.W. (ed.), *Kommentar zu den Zivilprozeßgesetzen, IV* (Vienna, Manz, 1971).

Fasching, H.W., *Lehrbuch des österreichischen Zivilprozeßrechts* (2nd edn, Vienna, Manz, 1990).

Fawcett, J.J. (ed.), *Declining Jurisdiction in Private International Law* (Oxford, OUP, 1995).

Feil, E. and Wenning, F., *Anwaltsrecht* (4th edn, Vienna, Linde Verlag, 2006).

Frank, C., *Der Durchgriff im Schiedsvertrag* (Berlin, Duncker & Humboldt, 1999).

Fremuth-Wolf, A., *Die Schiedsvereinbarung im Zessionsfall* (Vienna, Verlag Österreich, 2004).

Gaillard, E. and Savage, J. (eds), *Fouchard Gaillard Goldman On International Commercial Arbitration* (The Hague, Kluwer Law International, 1999).

Garner, B.A., *Black's Law Dictionary* (8th edn, St Pauls, Thomson West, 2004).

Gellis, M. and Feil, E., *Kommentar zum GmbH-Gesetz* (5th edn, Vienna, Verlag Linde, 2006).

Goldrein, I., *Commercial Litigation: Pre-emptive Remedies* (4th edn, London, Sweet & Maxwell, 2003).

Gotanda, J.Y., *Supplemental Damages in Private International Law* (The Hague, Kluwer Law International, 1998).

Gröben, H., Thiesing, J. and Ehlermann, C.-D. (eds), *Kommentar zum EU-/EG-Vertrag, IV* (5th edn, Baden-Baden, Nomos-Verlag, 1997).

Harris, B., Planterose, R. and Tecks, J., *The Arbitration Act 1996* (3rd edn, Oxford, Blackwell, 2003).

Hausmaninger, C., *Die einstweilige Verfügung im schiedsgerichtlichen Verfahren* (Vienna/New York, Springer, 1989).

Heller, K., *Der Verfassungsrechtliche Rahmen der Privaten Internationalen Schiedsgerichtsbarkeit* (Vienna, Manz, 1996).

Hellwig, H.-J., *Zur Systematik des zivilprozessrechtlichen Vertrages* (Bonn, Röhrscheid, 1968).

Holtzmann, H.M. and Neuhaus, J.E., *A Guide to the UNCITRAL Model Law on Commercial Arbitration: Legislative History and Commentary* (London, Kluwer Law and Taxation, 1989).

Honsell, H., Vogt, N.P., Schnyder, A.K. and Berti, S.V. (eds) *Internationales Privatrecht* (2nd edn, Basel, Helbing Lichtenhahn Verlag, 2007).

Horvath, G.J., Konrad, C.W. and Power, J., *Costs in International Arbitration – A Central and Southern Eastern European Perspective* (Vienna, Linde, 2008).

Jarvin, S. and Derains, Y., *Collection of ICC Arbitral Awards 1974-1985* (Deventer, Kluwer Law Taxation Publisher, 1990).

Jarvin, S., Derains, Y. and Arnaldez, J.-J., *Collection of ICC Arbitral Awards 1986-1990* (Deventer, Kluwer Law Taxation Publishers, 1994).

Jolidon, P., *Commentaire au Concordat Suisse sur l'Arbitrage* (Bern, Stämpfli Verlag, 1984).

Karsten, K. and Berkeley, A. (eds), *Arbitration – Money Laundering, Corruption and Fraud* (Paris, ICC Publishing, 2003).

Klauser, A. and Kodek, G., *JN-ZPO* (16th edn, Vienna, Manz, 2006).

Kloiber, B., Oberhammer, P., Rechberger, W.H. and Haller, H. (eds), *Das Neue Schiedsrecht – Schiedsrechts-Änderungsgesetz 2006* (Vienna, Manz, 2006).

Kolacny, P. and Mayr, L., *Umsatzsteuergesetz 1994* (2nd edn, Vienna, Manz, 1997).

Konrad, C.W. and Gurtner, H., *Die Umsatzsteuer im Schiedsverfahren* (Cologne/Munich, Carl Heymanns Verlag, 2008).

Koppensteiner, H.-G., GmbH-Gesetz Kommentar (2nd edn, Vienna, Orac, 1999).

Kostner, A. and Umfahrer, M., *GmbH-Handbuch für die Praxis* (5th edn, Vienna, Manz, 1998).

Koziol, H. and Welser, R., *Bürgerliches Recht I* (13th edn, Vienna, Manz, 2006).

Koziol, H. and Welser, R., *Bürgerliches Recht II* (13th edn, Vienna, Manz, 2007).

Koziol, H., Bydlinski, P. and Bollenberger, R. (eds), *Kommentar zum ABGB* (Vienna/New York, Springer, 2005).

Kreindler, R.H., Schäfer, J.K. and Wolff, R., *Schiedsgerichtsbarkeit, Kompendium für die Praxis* (Frankfurt/Main, Verlag Recht und Wirtschaft, 2006).

Kreindler, R.H., *Strafrechtsrelevante und andere anstößige Verträge als Gegenstand von Schiedsverfahren* (Frankfurt/Main, Recht und Wirtschaft, 2005).

Lachmann, J.P., *Handbuch für die Schiedsgerichtspraxis* (3rd edn, Cologne, Verlag Dr. Otto Schmidt, 2008).

Lalive, P., Poudret, J.F. and Reymond, C., *Le droit de l'arbitrage interne et international en Suisse* (Lausanne, Payot, 1989).

Lew, J. (ed.), *The Immunity of Arbitrators* (London, Lloyd's of London Press, 1990).

Lew, J., *Applicable Law in International Commercial Arbitration* (The Hague, Kluwer Law International, 1978).

Lew, J., Mistelis, L. and Kröll, S., *Comparative International Commercial Arbitration* (The Hague, Kluwer Law International, 2003).

Liebscher, C., *The Healthy Award* (The Hague, Kluwer Law International, 2003).

Liebscher, C., *The Austrian Arbitration Act 2006: Text and Notes* (The Hague, Kluwer Law International, 2006).

Lionnet, K. and Lionnet, A., *Handbuch der internationalen und nationalen Schiedsgerichtsbarkeit* (3rd edn, Stuttgart, Richard Bloorberg Verlag, 2005).

Lüke, G. and Wax, P. (eds) *Münchener Kommentar zur Zivilprozessordnung* (2nd edn, Munich, C.H. Beck 2001).

Mani, V., *International Adjudication: Procedural Aspects* (The Hague, Martinus Nijhoff Publishers, 1980).

McKinney's Consolidated Laws of New York, Book 62 1/5, Uniform Commercial Code (St. Pauls, Thomson West, 2006).

Merkin, R., *Arbitration Act 1996* (3rd edn, London, LLP, 2005).

Meyer-Hauser, F., *Anwaltsgeheimnis und Schiedsgericht* (Zürich, Schulthess, 2004).

Müller, M., *Die Zuständigkeit des Schiedsgerichts* (Bern, Haupt, 1997).

Musielak, H.J. (ed.), *Kommentar zur Zivilprozeßordnung* (6th edn, Munich, Verlag Franz Vahlen, 2008).

Mustill, M. and Boyd, S.C., *Commercial Arbitration* (2nd edn, Butterworths, London 1989).

Mustill, M. and Boyd, S.C., *Commercial Arbitration, 2001 Companion* (2nd edn, Butterworths, London, 2001).

Neuteufel, K., *Festschrift 100 Jahre Schiedsgericht der Wiener Warenbörse (1876-1975)* (Vienna, Verlag der Wiener Börsekammer, 1976).

Neuteufel, K., *Schiedsrichterliche Entscheidungen 1898-1998* (Vienna, Verlag Österreich, 2000).

Newman, L.W. and Hill, R.D. (eds), *The Leading Arbitrator's Guide to International Arbitration* (Huntington, Juris Publishing, 2004).

Oberhammer, P., *Entwurf eines neuen Schiesdvefahrensrechts* (Vienna, Manz, 2002).

Öhlinger, T., *Verfassungsrecht* (6th edn, Vienna, WUV Universitätsverlag, 2005).

Petrochilos, G., *Procedural Law in International Arbitration* (Oxford, OUP, 2004).

Poudret, J.F. and Besson, S., *Comparative Law of International Arbitration* (2nd edn, London, Sweet & Maxwell, 2007).

Power, J., *The Austrian Arbitration Act – A Practitioner's Guide to Sections 577-618 of the Austrian Code of Civil Procedure* (Vienna, Manz, 2006).

Presser, S., *Piercing the Corporate Veil* (Rev. edn., New York, West Group, 2008).

Raeschke-Kessler, H. and Berger, K.-P., *Recht und Praxis des Schiedsverfahrens* (3rd edn, Cologne, RWS Verlag, 1999).

Rechberger, W.H. (ed.), *Kommentar zur ZPO* (2nd edn, Vienna/New York, Springer, 2000).

Rechberger, W.H. (ed.) *Kommentar zur ZPO* (3rd edn, Vienna/New York, Springer, 2006).

Rechberger, W.H. and Simotta, P.A. (eds), *Grundriss des österreichischen Zivilprozeßrechts* (4th edn, Vienna, Manz, 1994).

Rechberger, W.H. and Simotta, P.A. (eds) *Grundriss des österreichischen Zivilprozeßrechts* (6th edn, Vienna, Manz, 2003).

Redfern, A., Hunter, M., Blackaby, N. and Partasides, C., *Law and Practice of International Commercial Arbitration* (3rd edn, London, Sweet & Maxwell, 1999).

Redfern, A., Hunter, M., Blackaby, N. and Partasides, C., *Law and Practice of International Commercial Arbitration* (4th edn, London, Sweet & Maxwell, 2004).

Reich-Rohrwig, J. and Zehetner, J., *Kartellrecht I* (Vienna, Linde, 2000).

Reich-Rohrwig, J., *Das österreichische GmbH-Recht, I* (2nd edn, Vienna, Manz, 1997).

Reiner, A., *Das neue österreichische Schiedsrecht/The New Austrian Arbitration Law* (Vienna, LexisNexis, 2006).

Reiner, A., _Handbuch der ICC-Schiedsgerichtsbarkeit_ (Vienna, Manz, 1989).

Riegler, S., Petsche, A., Fremuth-Wolf, A., Platte, M. and Liebscher, C. (eds), _Arbitration Law of Austria: Practice and Procedure_ (Huntington, Juris Publishing, 2007).

Rosenberg, M., Weinstein, J.B., Smit, H. and Korn, L., _Elements of Civil Procedure, Cases and Materials_ (3rd edn, Mineola, Foundation Press, 1976).

Rubino-Sammartano, M., _International Arbitration – Law and Practice_ (2nd edn, The Hague, Kluwer Law International, 2001).

Rummel, P. (ed.), _Kommentar zum ABGB, I_ (3rd edn, Vienna, Manz, 2000).

Rummel, P. (ed.), _Kommentar zum ABGB, II/1_ (3rd edn, Vienna, Manz, 2002).

Rummel, P. (ed.), _Kommentar zum ABGB, II/2_ (3rd edn, Vienna, Manz, 2002).

Säcker, F. and Rixecker, R. (eds), _Münchener Kommentar zum Bürgerlichen Gesetzbuch_ (5th edn, Munich, C.H. Beck, 2006).

Samuel, A., _Jurisdictional Problems in International Commercial Arbitration_ (Zürich, Schulthess Polypraphischer Verlag, 1989).

Sanders, P., _The Work of UNCITRAL on Arbitration and Conciliation_ (The Hague, Kluwer Law International, 2001).

Schäffler, F., _Zulässigkeit und Zweckmässigkeit der Anwendung angloamerikan- sicher Beweismethoden in deutschen und internationalen Schiedsverfahren_ (Munich, Sellier European Law Publisher, 2003).

Scheef, H.C., _Der einstweilige Rechtsschutz und die Stellung der Schiedsrichter bei dem Abschluss von Schiedsvergleichen nach dem deutschen und eng- lischen Schiedsverfahrensrecht: Eine rechtsvergleichende Untersuchung_ (Frankfurt/Main, Peter Lang Verlag, 2000).

Scheiner, M., Kolacny, P. and Caganek, E., _Kommentar zur Mehrwertsteuer – UStG 1994_ (Vienna, Verlag Orac, 2003).

Schlosser, P., _Das Recht der internationalen privaten Schiedsgerichtsbarkeit_ (2nd edn, Tübingen, Mohr Siebeck, 1989).

Schneider, B., _Die Auslegung von Parteiprozesshandlungen_ (Vienna, Verlag Österreich, 2004).

Schragel, W., _Kommentar zum Amtshaftungsgesetz_ (Vienna, Manz, 2003).

Schütze, R.A. (ed.), _Institutionelle Schiedsgerichtsbarkeit_ (Cologne, Carl Heymanns Verlag, 2006).

Schütze, R.A., _Schiedsgericht und Schiedsverfahren_ (4th edn, Munich, Beck, 2007).

Schwab, K.H. and Walter, G. (eds), _Schiedsgerichtsbarkeit_ (7th edn, Munich, C.H. Beck, 2005).

Schwebel, S., _International Arbitration: Three Salient Problems 1-3_ (Cambridge, Grotius Publications Limited, 1987).

Schwimann, M. (ed.), _Praxiskommentar zum ABGB, 6_ (3rd edn, Vienna, LexisNexis ARD ORAC, 2005).

Scoles, E.F., Hay, P., Borchers, P. and Symeonides, S.C., _Conflict of Laws_ (4th edn, London, Thomson, 2004).

Spry, I.C.F., _The Principles of Equitable Remedies_ (6th edn, LBC Information Services, 2001).

Stein, F. and Jonas. M. (eds) *Kommentar zur Zivilprozessordnung* (22nd edn, Tübingen, Mohr Siebeck, 2002).

Straube, M. (ed.), *Kommentar zum HGB, 1* (3rd edn, Vienna Manz, 2003).

Sutton, D., Gill, J. and Gearing, M., *Russell on Arbitration* (22nd edn, London, Sweet & Maxwell, 2003).

Tackaberry, J. and Marriott, A., *Bernstein's Handbook of Arbitration and Dispute Resolution Practice, I* (4th edn, London, Sweet & Maxwell, 2003).

Thomas, H. and Putzo, H., *Zivilprozessordnung – Kommentar* (26th edn, Munich, C.H. Beck, 2004).

Torggler, H. (ed.), *Schiedsgerichtsbarkeit* (Vienna, Verlag Österreich, 2007).

Van den Berg, A.J., *The New York Arbitration Convention of 1958* (The Hague, Kluwer Law International, 1981).

Van Dijk, P. and van Hoof, G.J.H., *Theory and Practice of the European Convention on Human Rights* (4th edn, Antwerpen/Oxford, Intersentia, 2006).

Van Hof, J.J., *Commentary on the UNCITRAL Arbitration Rules. The Application by the Iran-U.S. Claims Tribunal* (The Hague, Kluwer Law International, 1991).

Von Saucken, A., *Die Reform des österreichischen Schiedsverfahrensrechtes auf der Basis des UNCITRAL Modellgesetzes über die Internationale Handelsschiedsgerichtsbarkeit* (Frankfurt, Verlag Peter Lang, 2004).

Walter, R. and Mayer, H., *Grundriss des österreichischen Bundesverfassungsrechts* (10th edn, Vienna, Manz, 2007).

Weigand, F.B. (ed.), *Practitioner's Handbook on International Arbitration* (Munich, C.H. Beck, 2002).

White Book 2004, *Civil Procedure Vol 1, Lord Justice Brooke (ed.)* (London, Sweet & Maxwell, 2004).

White, G., *The Use of Experts by International Tribunals* (Syracuse, Syracuse University Press, 1965).

Zeiler, G., *Schiedsverfahren* (Vienna/Graz, Neuer Wissenschaftlicher Verlag, 2006).

Zöller, R. et al. (eds), *Zöller – Zivilprozessordnung* (26th edn, Cologne, Verlag Dr. Otto Schmidt, 2007).

Zuberbühler, T., Müller, C. and Habegger, P. (eds), *Swiss Rules of International Arbitration* (Zürich, Schulthess Verlag, 2005).

Article 1

The Institution

	Para.
I. The Jurisdiction of the VIAC	1
A. Introduction	1
1. Historical Background of the VIAC	4
2. The Services Provided by the VIAC	5
2.1. The Nature of the VIAC	6
2.2. Administration of Dispute Settlement	9
2.3. Cooperation with Other Arbitral Institutions	11
2.4. Infrastructure for *Ad Hoc* Proceedings	14
2.5. Appointing Authority	16
2.6. Conciliation Proceedings	18
3. The VIAC's Relationships with the Parties and the Arbitrators	20
3.1. The Relationship Between the VIAC and the Parties	21
3.2. The Relationship Between the VIAC and the Arbitrators	26
B. The Arbitration Agreement	30
1. Subjective Capacity to Conclude an Arbitration Agreement	32
1.1. General Principles	33
1.2. Arbitration Agreements Concluded by Consumers	37

	Para.
1.3. Arbitration Agreements Concluded by States or State-Related Entities	46
1.4. Consequences of a Lack of Subjective Arbitrability	47
2. An Agreement Concerning a 'Specified Legal Relationship'	48
3. Form Requirements	52
3.1. Some Policy Considerations	54
3.2. The 'In Writing' Requirement Under the Old Regime	61
3.3. The 'In Writing' Requirement Under the New Regime	63
3.4. Conclusion of the Arbitration Agreement by an Agent	71
3.5. Arbitration Clauses in Statutes	76
3.6. Objections to Defects of Form	79
4. The Effect of the Arbitration Agreement	85
5. Interpretation of the Arbitration Agreement	93
6. Other Forms of Dispute Resolution	97
7. Third Parties	100
8. The VIAC's Recommended Arbitration Clause	102

	Para.			Para.
C. The Administration of 'Arbitrable' Disputes 105			6. Consequences of a Lack of Objective Arbitrability 135	
1. Objective Arbitrability Under the Old Regime 109			7. *Ex Officio* Application by the Arbitral Tribunal 140	
2. Objective Arbitrability Under the New Law 119			D. The Administration of 'International' Disputes 142	
3. Objective Arbitrability in Corporate Matters 126			II. The Applicable Version of the Vienna Rules 149	
4. Arbitration and Competition Law 130			A. Previous Amendments of the Vienna Rules 151	
5. When Is the New Law Applicable to Determine Objective Arbitrability? 132			B. The Application of Amended Rules ... 154	
			C. Interpretation of the Vienna Rules 157	
			III. Domestic Arbitration 160	

I.   THE JURISDICTION OF THE VIAC

Article 1(1): The International Arbitral Centre of the Austrian Federal Economic Chamber in Vienna (the Vienna International Arbitral Centre – 'the Centre') shall make arrangements for the settlement by arbitration of disputes in which not all contracting parties that concluded the arbitration agreement had their place of business or their normal residence in Austria at the time of conclusion of that agreement. The jurisdiction of the Centre can also be agreed by parties whose place of business or normal residence is in Austria for the settlement of disputes of an international character.

A.   INTRODUCTION

1-001 Article 1 refers to the *jurisdiction* of the Vienna International Arbitral Centre (VIAC), a term that is potentially misleading. The VIAC itself has no adjudicating function and thus no jurisdiction – if jurisdiction is understood in the strict legal sense of the word as meaning the authority, over a person and subject matter, to decide a dispute.[1] Rather, jurisdiction in the sense of Article 1 describes the circumstances that must be met for a dispute to be administered under the Vienna Rules.[2]

1-002 Thus, the VIAC will administer arbitrations if the following three conditions are fulfilled: (a) there is a valid arbitration agreement; (b) there is an arbitrable

---

1. This is, in fact, arguable in the case of **Article 9** (Nomination and Appointment of Arbitrator); **Article 11** (Challenge of the Arbitrator) and **Article 12** (Termination of the Mandate of the Arbitrator). A former version of Article 1 created confusion insofar as it expressly stated that the VIAC 'has *jurisdiction* to settle disputes of a commercial nature'.

2. This is relevant under Austrian law because a reference to an institutional arbitration can only be made within the scope of the institution's jurisdiction. *See* OGH, 7 February 1990, 3 Ob 609/89.

'dispute'; and (c) the dispute is 'international' because of either the foreign status of at least one of the parties or the dispute's international character. Notwithstanding the provision of **Article 9(6)**,[3] these prerequisites are the *prima facie* elements which are scrutinized by the Secretary General;[4] if accepted, the VIAC will assume 'jurisdiction' of the case, which simply means that the VIAC agrees to administer the arbitration.[5]

In this context, it is also important to consider which law is applicable to the   **1-003** conditions established in Article 1. Which law determines what kinds of disputes can be subject to arbitration? When is an arbitration agreement valid, and what effect does it have? The issue of determining the law applicable to these questions is discussed later in the context of **Article 2**. For the purposes of discussing the three conditions of Article 1 below, it is assumed that Austrian law applies.

1.   Historical Background of the VIAC

Institutional arbitration has a remarkable tradition in Austria.[6] Initially, the   **1-004** authority to introduce arbitral institutions fell within the exclusive competence of the different Regional Economic Chambers of the Austrian Federal States (*Bundesländer*). These Chambers, following a model of the Arbitration Rules[7] issued by the Austrian Federal Chamber of Commerce[8] (AFCC) in 1949, established permanent arbitral institutions in each of the nine federal states. From 1949 to 1975, these regional arbitral institutions were responsible for handling both

---

3.   *See* **Article 9**, at paras. 088 *et seq.*
4.   *See* **Article 9**, at paras. 072 *et seq.*
5.   It must be stressed that the review of the Secretary General must not exceed such a *prima facie* evaluation – ultimately, these conditions are for the arbitrators to assess and determine. The parties' choice of the Vienna Rules implies that the parties intended to submit their disputes to arbitration only within the scope of Article 1. Therefore, a lack of the conditions set forth in Article 1 may mean that the arbitrators themselves lack jurisdiction to resolve the parties' dispute. The arbitrators' decision, in turn, would then be subject to setting aside by the state courts.
6.   Co-operative Arbitral Institutions were legitimized by the Trade Law Amendment in 1883: Subdividing tradesmen and manufacturers in co-operatives; this marks the beginning of the promotion of institutional arbitration in Austria. Nowadays, Austria has several 'compulsory arbitral tribunals', e.g. the Arbitral Tribunal of the Vienna Commodity Exchange, whose proceedings are governed by the specific legal provisions contained in the Introductory Law to the ZPO of 1 August 1985. *See in detail* W. Melis, 'Austria' (1979) IV YB Comm Arb, 21; C. Liebscher and A. Schmid in *Practitioner's Handbook on International Arbitration*, F.3. Weigand (ed.) (Munich, C.H. Beck, 2002), p. 588 and K. Neuteufel, *Festschrift 100 Jahre Schiedsgericht der Wiener Warenbörse (1876-1975)* (Vienna, Verlag der Wiener Börsekammer, 1976).
7.   *Schiedsgerichtsordnung für die Ständigen Schiedsgerichte der Kammern der gewerblichen Wirtschaft*, passed by the Board of Directors of the Austrian Federal Chamber of Commerce on 17 March 1949.
8.   Formerly called '*Handelskammer*'. The structure of the institutionalized Chamber of Commerce was reorganized in 1946 by the Federal Chamber of Commerce Act (*Handelskammergesetz* – 1946, BGBl No. 182/1946, concerning the establishment of Chambers of Commerce.)

national and international arbitration cases. However, the exclusive competence of the federal arbitration institutions could not meet the need for effective dispute resolution for various reasons. Arbitrators appointed by the Board of the AFCC were unsalaried and commonly regarded as an unreliable alternative to the well-established commercial court system in Austria. Moreover, in the early 1960's, international companies increasingly began to use Austria as a neutral venue for arbitration proceedings. The peculiar existence of nine different arbitral institutions, in addition to the AFCC's own arbitral institution, regularly caused confusion among international users, often resulting in pathological arbitration clauses with all the unintended effects. The Austrian legislature reacted to the need for a single, internationally focused arbitration forum. In 1974, the AFCC was empowered to establish a permanent arbitral tribunal for settling disputes in which at least one party had its place of business outside Austria. That same year, the Board of the AFCC agreed upon the first Rules of Arbitration and Conciliation *(Schieds- und Vergleichsordnung des Schiedsgerichts der Bundeskammer der gewerblichen Wirtschaft).*[9] The International Arbitral Centre of the AFCC opened on 1 January 1975.[10] On 3 May 2006, the General Assembly of the Austrian Federal Economic Chamber (AFEC) adopted the most recent version of the Vienna Rules of the Vienna International Arbitral Centre (VIAC), which took effect on 1 July 2006.[11]

2.   The Services Provided by the VIAC

1-005 The VIAC fulfils a statutory mission: It is a permanent arbitral institution, established to manage disputes where at least one of the contracting parties has its usual place of residence or business outside Austria. It is also competent to administer disputes between domestic parties, if their dispute has an international character.[12] The VIAC has grown in the thirty years since its inception, both in its areas of expertise and in the services it renders. The VIAC's unique legal status (as discussed below) enables it to take advantage of the services offered by the AFEC, which is the largest self-governing economic chamber in Austria, dedicated to the promotion of business interests and independent from public authorities.

---

9. Passed by the (former) Austrian Federal Economic Chamber *(Bundeskammer der Gewerblichen Wirtschaft)* on 15 November 1974 according to Section 19(3) *Handelskammergesetz,* BGBl No. 1946/182, version of BGBl No. 1974/400.
10. *See* W. Melis, 'Die Schiedsgerichtsbarkeit der österreichischen Handelskammern seit 1946' in *Festschrift Seidl-Hohenveldern,* K.H. Böckstiegel, H.-E. Folz, J. Mössner and K. Zermark (eds) (Cologne, Carl Heymanns Verlag, 1988), p. 367 with further references; W. Melis, 'Austria' (1979) IV YB Comm Arb, 21; C. Liebscher in *Institutionelle Schiedsgerichtsbarkeit,* R.A. Schütze (ed.) (Cologne, Carl Heymanns Verlag, 2006), p. 255.
11. The amendment on 3 July 1991 gave the former Rules of Arbitration and Conciliation its present name. For an overview of the amendments *see* **Article 1,** at paras. 151 *et seq.*
12. *See* Section 139(1) WKG.

As an institution dedicated to commercial arbitration, the VIAC undertakes a variety of services directly and indirectly related to arbitration.

2.1. The Nature of the VIAC

The AFEC was established under Austrian public law as a self-governing body **1-006** fulfilling a public duty. When acting within the scope of its mandate, the AFEC acts free from directives of Austrian national authorities.[13] The AFEC was specifically empowered by law to establish an arbitral institution.[14] Pursuant to this legal mandate, the Vienna International Arbitral Centre was founded in 1975.[15]

Although the VIAC is functionally and legally integrated into the AFEC, neither **1-007** the VIAC itself nor its Board members or Secretary General are in turn subject to any directives from the AFEC.[16] It is important to note that the VIAC is a structurally integrated part of AFEC, rather than a separate legal entity; therefore, when an activity of the VIAC is subject to scrutiny, the AFEC is ultimately accountable.[17] In general, however, this commentary intentionally ignores this legal distinction for the sake of simplicity, and refers only to the VIAC.

Given the public-law character of the AFEC, the question arises as to the nature **1-008** of the arbitration services offered by the VIAC. As discussed below in greater detail, these services are of a private contractual nature.[18]

2.2. Administration of Dispute Settlement

Article 1 provides that the VIAC 'shall make arrangements for the settlement by **1-009** arbitration of disputes'.[19] The administration of arbitral proceedings is indeed the core function of the VIAC as defined by the Vienna Rules. It includes all actions necessary to initiate and maintain arbitral proceedings, such as the receipt and forwarding of the statement of claims and the memorandum in reply (or

---

13. T. Öhlinger, *Verfassungsrecht* (6th edn, Vienna, WUV Universitätsverlag, 2005), p. 237; R. Walter and H. Mayer, *Grundriss des österreichischen Bundesverfassungsrechts* (10th edn, Vienna, Manz, 2007), paras. 921 *et seq.*
14. Section 19 *Handelskammergesetz* (old) with reference to Section 150(2) WKG 1998.
15. The ICC Court of International Arbitration, by contrast, is a private institution and a not-for-profit association created under the laws of France. *See* M. Bühler and S. Jarvin in *Practitioner's Handbook on International Arbitration*, F.B. Weigand (ed.) (Munich, C.H. Beck, 2002), p. 117.
16. *See also* **Article 3(6)**, at para. 028, and **Article 5(3)**, at paras. 020 *et seq.*
17. C. Liebscher in *Institutionelle Schiedsgerichtsbarkeit*, R.A. Schütze (ed.) (Cologne, Carl Heymanns Verlag, 2006), p. 17.
18. K. Heller, 'Die Rechtsstellung des internationalen Schiedsgerichts der Wirtschaftskammer Österreich' [1994] wbl, 105; C. Liebscher in *Institutionelle Schiedsgerichtsbarkeit*, R.A. Schütze (ed.) (Cologne, Carl Heymanns Verlag, 2006), p. 7.
19. In essence, this provision is comparable to Article 1 of the ICC Rules, which states that the function of the Court 'is to provide for the settlement by arbitration' of disputes.

counter-claims); the collection of the registration fees and other costs of arbitration; the substitutional appointment procedure for the arbitrator; the adjudication of challenges to arbitrators; and the replacement of arbitrators in case of incapacitation; amongst others. The VIAC also provides basic infrastructure (such as hearing facilities) and advice to the parties and arbitrators to the extent that such advice must be impartial.

1-010 However, it must be emphasized that, despite its name at least in the German language, the VIAC itself is not an arbitral tribunal (*Schiedsgericht*) within the meaning of Sections 577-618 ZPO. Thus, it is not itself involved in adjudicating the disputes submitted under the Vienna Rules; rather, it administers proceedings in international commercial arbitration in accordance with the Vienna Rules.[20] The adjudication of disputes is reserved for the arbitrators.

2.3.   *Cooperation with Other Arbitral Institutions*

1-011 The VIAC regularly cooperates with other arbitral institutions in the field of commercial arbitration.[21] At this time, the VIAC has cooperating agreements with the following institutions: the American Arbitration Association (1990); the Scottish Council (1990); the Belgian Centre for Arbitration and Mediation (1993); the Cairo Regional Centre for International Commercial Arbitration (1994); the German Institution of Arbitration (1994); the China International Economic and Trade Arbitration Commission (1994); the Croatian Chamber of Commerce (1996); the Korean Commercial Arbitration Board (1996); the Australian Centre for International Commercial Arbitration (1997); the Hungarian Chamber of Industry and Commerce (1997); the Czech Arbitration Court (1999); the Chartered Institute of Arbitrators (2002); and the Slovenian Chamber of Commerce (2003).

1-012 These cooperation agreements provide generally for reciprocal information and promotion of arbitration in each respective country. More specifically, some agreements endeavour to cooperate in the selection of arbitrators and mediators and even explicitly provide for technical assistance in commercial arbitration.[22]

---

20. This function is comparable to other arbitral institutions, such as the ICC International Court of Arbitration or the London Court of International Arbitration. The extent to which these arbitral institutions influence the decision-making of arbitrators will depend on the Rules under which they operate. *See, e.g.*, Article 27 ICC Rules, which provides that an award is subject to the scrutiny of the ICC Court.
21. As mentioned above, the VIAC is not a separate legal entity; therefore all these agreements are signed and concluded by AFEC or by the VIAC on behalf of AFEC.
22. Dependent on the status of ratification, the cooperation agreements refer to the respective arbitration conventions and/or to the Final Act of the Conference of Security and Co-operation in Europe (1975 Summit – Helsinki), which considered arbitration as an appropriate means of settling such disputes and recommended, 'where appropriate, to organizations, enterprises and firms in their countries, to include arbitration clauses in commercial contracts and industrial co-operation

The agreements with Croatia, Hungary, the Czech Republic and Slovenia contain recommendations for business entities to make use of specific arbitration agreements under the United Nations Commission on International Trade Law (UNCITRAL) Rules. Such agreements were introduced to enhance the options available to commercial parties.[23]

The applicable administrative procedure is provided by the VIAC or the counter- **1-013** part arbitral institution (e.g. by accepting either institution as the appointing authority). Most of the agreements contain a list of arbitrators, mandatory only for the institution when acting as appointing authority under such cooperation agreement, and an additional schedule of extra costs to calculate the administrative and arbitrators' fees.[24] So far, the VIAC has administered approximately 25 cases under these agreements.

2.4.   *Infrastructure for Ad Hoc Proceedings*

In addition to the services expressly mentioned in the Vienna Rules, the VIAC **1-014** offers services to any party or institution which has not submitted its dispute for resolution under the Vienna Rules as such, but seeks assistance in conducting an arbitration in Austria.

In particular, the VIAC will provide the infrastructure necessary for arbitral pro- **1-015** ceedings, such as hearing facilities, break-out rooms, translators, stenographers, and recording devices. The costs for such services are considered reasonable when compared with other venues, and the VIAC's Secretary General is well-known for offering helpful advice to both parties and arbitrators with regard to Austrian and international arbitration laws and procedures.[25]

2.5.   *Appointing Authority*

The AFEC itself also fulfils responsibilities under certain arbitration treaties, such **1-016** as the European Convention on International Commercial Arbitration (1961) (European Convention).[26] Article IV(2) to (7) of the European Convention[27]

---

contracts, or in special agreements' and that 'the provisions on arbitration should provide for arbitration under a mutually acceptable set of arbitration rules, and permit arbitration in a third country, taking into account existing intergovernmental and other agreements in this field'.

23. W. Melis, 'Überlegungen aus Anlaß des Inkrafttretens der neuen Schieds- und Vergleichsordnung des Schiedsgerichtes der Bundeskammer der Gewerblichen Wirtschaft' [1983] GesRZ, 143, 146.

24. More detailed in W. Melis, 'Vienna Arbitration Rules Help to Resolve U.S.-European Dispute' (1992) 47 Arb J, 42-45; *see also* C. Liebscher in *Institutionelle Schiedsgerichtsbarkeit*, R.A. Schütze (ed.) (Cologne, Carl Heymanns Verlag, 2006), p. 8.

25. *See also* **Article 5**, at paras. 014 *et seq.*

26. European Convention on International Commercial Arbitration (1961), Geneva, dated 21 April 1961, BGBl No. 107/1964, in force in Austria since 4 June 1964, **Annex 10**.

27. European Convention, **Annex 10**.

establishes a procedural mechanism for initiating arbitration, notwithstanding an inoperative arbitration clause or a disagreement of the parties as to the conduct of the proceedings.[28] In the case of an *ad hoc* arbitration, the European Convention provides for a specific substitutional appointment procedure administered by the President of the Chamber of Commerce of the defaulting party's country.[29]

1-017 Similarly, the AFEC acts as an appointing authority under the UNCITRAL Rules. According to unofficial statistics, the President of the AFEC administers approximately four cases per year under this provision. The AFEC currently offers these appointment services for a lump-sum fee of €2,000.00. As this service is closely connected with the administration of arbitration proceedings in general, it has so far been common practice (notwithstanding the different legal provisions involved) for parties to approach the VIAC's Secretary General for further assistance. However, an official request should be submitted directly to the President of the AFEC.

2.6. *Conciliation Proceedings*

1-018 Although its focus appears to be with arbitration proceedings, the VIAC also offers a set of Conciliation Rules.[30] Unlike arbitration which always requires a valid arbitration agreement, the conciliation procedure is more informal. The request for opening the conciliation proceedings is filed with the Secretariat, which invites the opposing party to reply to this request. In case the recourse to conciliation is accepted by all parties, the VIAC Board usually nominates one of its members to act as conciliator. After having examined the documents, the conciliator will convene with the parties and submit proposals for an amicable settlement of the dispute at bar. A settlement will typically be recorded and signed by all parties and the conciliator. Absent an agreement to the contrary, the parties are free to abort the conciliation proceedings at any time.

1-019 In case a valid arbitration agreement exists, the conciliator can, *upon joint request by the parties*, be appointed as sole arbitrator to proceed to an arbitral award (or an award by consent).[31] Absent such joint application, however, the conciliator will not be able to act as an arbitrator in subsequent arbitration proceedings. Thus, statements made by the parties in the conciliation proceedings are usually without prejudice to their position in a subsequent arbitration.[32] The costs of the conciliation (conciliator's fees and the administrative costs) are fixed by the Secretary General as a fraction of the costs calculated under the cost schedule applicable for

---

28. D.T. Hascher, 'The European Convention on International Commercial Arbitration 1961' (1995) XX YB Comm Arb, 1006, 1020.
29. K. Lionnet and A. Lionnet, *Handbuch der internationalen und nationalen Schiedsgerichtsbarkeit* (3rd edn, Stuttgart, Richard Boorberg Verlag, 2005), p. 526.
30. *See* Conciliation Rules, **Annex 3a**.
31. Article 4 Conciliation Rules, **Annex 3a**.
32. Article 5 Conciliation Rules, **Annex 3a**.

arbitration proceedings; the cost is therefore dictated by the amount in dispute. The VIAC has so far administered approximately two cases per year under these rules.

3. The VIAC's Relationships with the Parties and the Arbitrators

As an institution, the VIAC interacts with all participants in the arbitral process: the arbitrators as well as the parties. In both cases, this interaction is governed by private law contracts. **1-020**

3.1. *The Relationship Between the VIAC and the Parties*

The VIAC renders its services to the disputing parties on a contractual basis. According to Austrian scholars,[33] the VIAC and the parties to the dispute conclude an agency agreement.[34] This contract establishes duties for both the VIAC (as the agent) and the parties to the dispute (jointly as the principal) on the terms expressed in the Vienna Rules. Within the context of the institutional appointment of arbitrators (in case a party defaults on its obligation to advance a timely nomination), for example, the VIAC concludes the arbitrator's contract on behalf of the parties, with the implicit authority of each individual party as enshrined in the arbitration agreement. In such a case, the contractual relationship with the arbitrator is directly concluded as between the arbitrator and the parties represented by the VIAC.[35] **1-021**

The point at which this agency contract between the institution and the parties is concluded is subject to debate. *Heller* points out that by having the Vienna Rules available to the general public, the services of the VIAC are not initially directed at a specific party. Therefore, he considers the filing of a statement of claims as an offer by the claimant to avail itself of the services of the VIAC in compliance with the Vienna Rules. The VIAC's submission of the statement of claims to the respondent, and the concurrent notification to the claimant, is then equivalent to the VIAC's acceptance of that offer. Finally, by submitting a memorandum in reply or responding to the previous correspondence, the respondent accepts the offer *vis-à-vis* the VIAC as well. However, *Heller* also notes that, contrary to this theory, the purpose of an arbitration agreement for the parties is to avail themselves of the services of the specified institution only jointly and simultaneously. Moreover, **1-022**

---

33. H.W. Fasching, 'Kostenvorschüsse zur Einleitung schiedsgerichtlicher Verfahren' [1993] JBl, 545, 550; K. Heller, 'Die Rechtsstellung des internationalen Schiedsgerichts der Wirtschaftskammer Österreich' [1994] wbl, 105.

34. *Geschäftsbesorgungsvertrag* according to Section 1004 ABGB: 'If a reward is promised expressly or even impliedly from the perspective of the agent, for the performance of an act on behalf of another person, the contract constitutes a contract for consideration, otherwise a gratuitous contract.'

35. In OGH, 30 November 2006, 6 Ob 207/06v, this question was deliberately left open, although it had been answered in the affirmative in the preceding decision by the *Oberlandesgericht Wien* (Vienna Court of Appeal) in an unpublished case known to the authors.

once an arbitration agreement is concluded that refers a dispute to arbitration under a specified set of institutional rules, neither party can unilaterally withdraw from the agreement to arbitrate. Hence, the authority of one party to initiate arbitration proceedings lies in the conclusion of the arbitration agreement itself.[36]

1-023 *Melis*, on the other hand, takes the position that the VIAC, by publishing its rules and recommending an arbitration clause, tenders an open offer of its services to certain segments of the public, such as participants in international trade. This implies that the VIAC is bound to perform these services until a reasonable time after it has declared that it will cease to administrate its rules. *Melis* considers this relationship as a contractual relationship *sui generis*, as it embraces elements of various types of contracts, which can be differentiated by the different services performed.[37]

1-024 In practical terms, therefore, the parties are forced to accept the services of the VIAC once the Vienna Rules are agreed upon, and the VIAC is in principle under an obligation to administer the arbitration. Only if all parties were to fail to advance the deposit of institutional costs, the arbitration would not proceed.[38] However, there is an instance when the parties' relationship with the VIAC can become a contested issue. Under **Article 9(6)**, the VIAC can refuse to administer a case, even when it has been designated in the arbitration agreement, if the parties have made agreements that deviate from the Vienna Rules.[39]

1-025 Finally, and for the avoidance of doubt, the contractual relationship of the parties with the VIAC is, of course, different from the arbitration agreement between the parties themselves. The conclusion of the arbitration agreement follows mostly contractual rules, which, for Austria, are described below.

3.2.   *The Relationship Between the VIAC and the Arbitrators*

1-026 Under a previous version of the Vienna Rules, the arbitrators became 'members of the Centre for the duration of their mandate'.[40] This provision has been deleted with the penultimate amendment of the Vienna Rules.

1-027 It is accepted today that the relationship between the arbitrators and the VIAC as the arbitral institution is also contractual. Undoubtedly, mutual duties exist

---

36. For example, when the institution, through its Secretary General, collects deposits and assumes responsibility for the determination and payment of the arbitrators' fees, it also assumes the role of a trustee with regard to parties and arbitrators. *See* K. Heller, 'Die Rechtsstellung des internationalen Schiedsgerichts der Wirtschaftskammer Österreich' [1994] wbl, 105, 109.
37. W. Melis, 'Function and Responsibility of Arbitral Institutions' (1991) XIII Comp L YB Int'l Bus, 112.
38. *See* **Article 34**, at paras. 029 *et seq.*, and 033.
39. *See* discussion under **Article 9(6)**, at paras. 088 *et seq.*
40. Article 2(2) of the 1991 version of the Vienna Rules.

between the arbitrators and the VIAC which derive directly from the Vienna Rules. For example, the arbitrators have a duty to state in the award the costs fixed by the VIAC's Secretary General,[41] while the VIAC has an obligation to confirm and sign each award as being one of the Centre.[42]

By accepting their appointments on the basis of an arbitration agreement that **1-028** incorporates the Vienna Rules by reference, arbitrators

> oblige themselves to fulfil their mandate in accordance with the rules. This implies they accept the decision of the competent organs of the institution as binding upon them. The arbitral institution, on the other side, is obliged to give the arbitrators the necessary support and to determine and to pay the fees and expenses according to its rules and other directives.[43]

In practice, prospective arbitrators receive a written form,[44] by virtue of which they **1-029** expressly accept the Vienna Rules and the decisions of the VIAC as binding. Moreover, the VIAC provides a set of 'Guidelines for Arbitrators', which contain established recommendations from the VIAC in order to facilitate cooperation with it and the Secretary General.[45]

B.   THE ARBITRATION AGREEMENT

The valid arbitration agreement provides the basis for the VIAC's and the arbi- **1-030** trator's jurisdiction. As noted, the VIAC is entitled to undertake only a *prima facie* scrutiny of the arbitration agreement.[46] The detailed assessment of the arbitration agreement and, hence, the ultimate decision on jurisdiction is reserved for the arbitrators.

The following discussion considers the requirements that Austrian law imposes on **1-031** the valid formation of arbitration agreements. These include the ability of a person to enter into a legally binding agreement to arbitrate; the application of form requirements; and the requirement to specify the legal relationship that is subject to arbitration. The following section also discusses the preclusive effect of arbitration agreements in relation to state court litigation; the rules governing the interpretation of arbitration agreements; the relationship between arbitration

---

41. *See* **Article 31**, at paras. 003 *et seq.*
42. *See* **Article 27(4)**, at para. 017.
43. W. Melis, 'Function and Responsibility of Arbitral Institutions' (1991) XIII Comp L YB Int'l Bus, 114.
44. *See* Arbitrator's Declaration of Acceptance, Statement of Independence and Undertaking to Observe Rules on Costs, **Annex 4**; *see also* **Article 12**, at paras. 010 *et seq.*
45. *See* Guidelines for Arbitrators, **Annex 5**.
46. *See* **Article 9**, at paras. 072 *et seq.*

agreements and other forms of ADR; the extension of arbitration agreements to third parties;[47] and finally the arbitration clause recommended by the VIAC. The discussion examines the position both under the former Austrian arbitration law (which continues to apply to all arbitration agreements concluded prior to 1 July 2006) and the new Austrian arbitration law (which applies to all arbitration agreements concluded thereafter).[48]

1. Subjective Capacity to Conclude an Arbitration Agreement

1-032 The subjective capacity to conclude an arbitration agreement is the ability of a person to validly enter into a binding arbitration agreement and thus to refer a dispute to arbitration.[49] It is also known as 'subjective arbitrability'.

1.1. General Principles

1-033 A lack of subjective capacity is grounds for challenge under Article V (1)(a) of the New York Convention.[50] This provision contains no express definition of what constitutes such capacity, but refers instead to 'the law applicable to the person' for determining the subjective arbitrability.[51] Whether the applicable law is determined by reference to the person's nationality or their domicile or usual residence has been deliberately left open.[52] Under Austrian law, the solution follows from the Private International Law Act (*Internationales Privatrechtsgesetz* – IPRG), which, as is usual in Continental Europe, determines the law applicable to a natural person

---

47. A more detailed discussion of the extension of arbitration agreements to third parties can be found in **Article 15**, at paras. 082 *et seq.*
48. *See* Article VII ZPO, Transitional Provisions.
49. T. Chiwitt-Oberhammer, *Der fehlerhafte Schiedsspruch* (Vienna, Verlag Österreich, 2000), p. 143.
50. According to Article V(1) NY Convention, recognition and enforcement of the award may be refused at the request of the party against whom it is invoked, only if that party furnishes to the competent authority where the recognition and enforcement is sought, proof that the parties to the agreement (. . .) were, under the law applicable to them, under some incapacity, or the said agreement is not valid under the law to which the parties have subjected it or, failing any indication thereon, under the law of the country where the award was made. **Annex 11**.
51. A.J. van den Berg, *The New York Arbitration Convention of 1958* (The Hague, Kluwer Law International, 1981), p. 275.
52. It is questionable if the NY Convention, beyond the conflict of laws system of the *exequatur* state, refers also to regulations which govern the legal capacity. That is of particular concern with states which are not acquainted with the concept of *Personalstatut* but decide according to the law applicable at the place of the conclusion of the contract or the law applicable to the contract itself, as largely practiced in the US. *See* discussion in P. Schlosser, *Das Recht der internationalen privaten Schiedsgerichtsbarkeit* (2nd edn, Tübingen, Mohr Siebeck, 1989), paras. 325 *et seq.*

by reference to nationality.[53] In the case of legal entities, it is the registered main office (*Sitz der Hauptverwaltung*) that is relevant.[54]

The capacity to validly conclude an arbitration agreement has not been expressly **1-034** codified, neither under the former nor under the current arbitration law. It was derived from Section 577(1) fZPO ('as the parties are entitled to conclude a settlement')[55] and considered to be a precondition for the validity of an arbitration agreement. As the arbitration agreement is understood as a procedural contract, it presupposes legal capacity.[56] Any natural person, legal entity, or partnership fully capable of entering into a contract may conclude arbitration agreements (the exceptions under Austrian law are civil law partnerships according to general private law and so-called 'silent partnerships'). *Liebscher/Schmid* argue that entities with sovereign immunity who conclude an arbitration agreement cannot subsequently claim immunity either before the arbitral tribunal or before the courts.[57]

---

53. Section 9 IPRG freely translated: 'The personal statute (*Personalstatut*) of a natural person is the law of the state to which this person belongs. When a person holds aside from a foreign citizenship also the Austrian citizenship, the latter is relevant. For other multinationals, the citizenship of that State is relevant to which the strongest connection exists. If a person is stateless or it is not possible to determine the citizenship, then the law of the state of the usual residence is applicable.' *See* B. Verschraegen in *Kommentar zum ABGB II/2*, P. Rummel (ed.) (3rd edn, Vienna, Manz, 2002), Section 9 IPRG; *also* C. Liebscher and A. Schmid in *Practitioner's Handbook on International Arbitration*, F.B. Weigand (ed.) (Munich, C.H. Beck, 2002), p. 550.
54. *See* Section 10 IPRG.
55. Subjective arbitrability equals the ability to file a claim (*Prozessfähigkeit*). *See* W.H. Rechberger and W. Melis in *Kommentar zur ZPO*, W.H. Rechberger (ed.) (3rd edn, Vienna/New York, Springer, 2006), Section 581 ZPO, para. 7; H.W. Fasching, *Lehrbuch des österreichischen Zivilprozeßrechts* (2nd edn, Vienna, Manz, 1990) para. 2172; H.W. Fasching, *Schiedsgericht und Schiedsverfahren im österreichischen und im internationalen Recht* (Vienna, Manz, 1973), p. 13, which refers to 'personal arbitrability'.
56. H.W. Fasching, *Schiedsgericht und Schiedsverfahren im österreichischen und im internationalen Recht* (Vienna, Manz, 1973), p. 13, according to which the capacity to conclude an arbitration agreement (*persönliche Schiedsfähigkeit*) should be determined by application of Sections 1-3 ZPO whereas the capacity of foreigners should be considered under Section 3 ZPO. Different opinion by *Rechberger/Melis* according to which due to Section 611(2) no. 2 ZPO the capacity of foreigners should be determined by the conflict of laws rules (generally *Personalstatut*). *See* W.H. Rechberger and W. Melis in *Kommentar zur ZPO*, W.H. Rechberger (ed.) (3rd edn, Vienna/New York, Springer, 2006), Section 581 ZPO, para. 7; *see also* C. Liebscher and A. Schmid in *Practitioner's Handbook on International Arbitration*, F.B. Weigand (ed.) (Munich, C.H. Beck, 2002), p. 545.
57. C. Liebscher and A. Schmid in *Practitioner's Handbook on International Arbitration*, F.B. Weigand (ed.) (Munich, C.H. Beck, 2002), p. 546. For an overview of the position of the Austrian state courts to the immunity of foreign states, *see* C. Schreuer, 'Die Durchsetzung zivilrechtlicher Ansprüche gegen ausländische Staaten' [1991] ÖJZ, 41.

1-035 Subjective arbitrability can be missing where a party lacks the required legal capacity but also where a party that is not properly represented in the conclusion of the arbitration agreement.[58]

1-036 According to *Chiwitt-Oberhammer*, an award that is defective due to lack of subjective arbitrability is not automatically deemed a non-award, but is only challengeable; if neither party challenges the award, it will remain effective.[59] This is consistent with new Section 611(2) no. 1 ZPO according to which an award shall be set aside upon request if a party was not capable of concluding a valid arbitration agreement under the law which applies to that party.[60]

1.2. Arbitration Agreements Concluded by Consumers

1-037 According to former and present Austrian law, consumers can, in principle, conclude arbitration agreements. However, under the former law, an arbitration agreement with a consumer was only valid if it conformed to the restrictions of Section 14 KSchG.[61]

1-038 According to the Austrian *Oberster Gerichtshof*, this meant that:

> an arbitration agreement cannot be validly concluded when the consumer is forced to the venue of a far distant court when a competent court following legal jurisdiction regulations situated nearby is available.[62]

1-039 Many provisions appropriate for international commercial arbitration are not appropriate for the average consumer, whose expression of commercial will

---

58. *See* **Article 1**, at para. 074.
59. T. Chiwitt-Oberhammer, *Der fehlerhafte Schiedsspruch* (Vienna, Verlag Österreich, 2000), p. 145.
60. *See also* **Article 27**, at para. 045.
61. Consumer Protection Act (*Konsumentenschutzgesetz* – KSchG 1979), BGBl No. 140/1979 last amended by BGBl I No. 21/2008 introducing regulations for the protection of consumers; according to its Section 14, consumers (i) having their residence or their usual place of abode in the territory of the respective state; or (ii) who are employed in the territory of such state, may in general be sued only in the court of the district (*Sprengel*) in which they have residence, usual place of abode or place of employment. *See* translation of this section in J. Power, *The Austrian Arbitration Act – A Practitioner's Guide to Sections 577-618 of the Austrian Code of Civil Procedure* (Vienna, Manz, 2006), Section 617.
62. OGH, 25 October 1994, 5 Ob 538/94 – criticized by T. Klicka, 'Der OGH und die Schiedsklausel im Konsumentengeschäft' [1995] ecolex, 883; primarily because the consumer invoked the arbitration agreement, the court regarded Section 14 KSchG as basis for an absolute nullity of the agreement and P. Oberhammer, *Entwurf eines neuen Schiedsverfahrensrechts* (Vienna, Manz, 2002), p. 54. *See also* the restriction imposed by Section 6(2) no. 7 KSchG which basically introduces a burden of proof on the entrepreneur as to the fact that an arbitration agreement has specifically (*'im Einzelnen ausgehandelt'*) been concluded, otherwise the arbitration agreement is not binding upon the consumer. If, however, the additional requirements for the conclusion of an arbitration agreement with a consumer were observed, the consumer cannot involve the defense of an invalid arbitration agreement. *See* OGH, 20 March 2007, 10 Ob 10/07d.

may be diluted or less sophisticated and who is perceived as deserving of additional protection under the law. To protect consumers in such circumstances, Section 617 ZPO has now been introduced.[63] Under that provision, 'arbitration agreements between an entrepreneur and a consumer may validly be concluded only for disputes *that have already arisen*'. In other words, Section 617 ZPO allows for submission agreements with respect to existing disputes, but prevents the valid conclusion with consumers of an arbitration agreement for future disputes.

Further, a special form requirement, obligatory for all consumers, has been **1-040** introduced:

> Arbitration agreements with the participation of a consumer must be contained in a document which has been personally signed by the consumer. This document may not contain any agreements other than those that refer to the arbitration proceedings.[64]

Additionally, the new law requires the entrepreneur, prior to the conclusion of the **1-041** arbitration agreement, to advise the consumer in writing on the substantial differences between arbitration proceedings and proceedings before a court of law.[65] This precondition has been given particular importance as the lack of such information now constitutes a separate ground to set aside the award.[66]

In order to protect consumers from being forced to participate at great cost in an **1-042** arbitration sited in an inconvenient or distant forum, Section 617(4) ZPO requires that the seat of the arbitration must be stipulated in the arbitration agreement; the tribunal may only meet at a different place (for an oral hearing or the taking of evidence) if the consumer has consented, or if considerable difficulties prevent the parties from meeting at the location stipulated in the agreement.[67]

Indeed, under Section 617(5) ZPO, the arbitration agreement 'shall be of relevance **1-043** only if the consumer invokes it', if the consumer, at the time the arbitration agreement is concluded or when the arbitration is initiated, does not have his domicile, habitual place of residence or place of employment in the jurisdiction where the arbitration has its seat.[68] Finally, Section 617(6) ZPO broadens the grounds for

---

63. *See* Explanatory Notes to Section 617 ZPO.
64. Section 617(2) ZPO.
65. The precise extent, scope and detail of this advice is unclear. *See* J. Power, *The Austrian Arbitration Act – A Practitioner's Guide to Sections 577-618 of the Austrian Code of Civil Procedure* (Vienna, Manz, 2006), Section 617, para. 8.
66. Section 617(7) ZPO.
67. Section 617(4) ZPO.
68. Note that the ECJ – as reported in A.E. Appelton and B.U. Graf, 'Elisa María Mostaza Claro v. Centro Móvil Milenium: EU Consumer Law as a Defence against Arbitral Awards. ECJ Case C-168/05' (2007) 25(1) Bull ASA, 48 – quite recently ruled that the invalidity of an arbitration agreement can be invoked by a consumer at the stage of setting aside proceedings even if no explicit objection has been raised against the arbitral tribunal's jurisdiction in the arbitration. *See also* P. Landolt, 'Limits on Court Review of International Arbitration Awards Assessed in

challenging an award in an arbitration with a consumer, to include violations of mandatory provisions of Austrian law, which cannot be waived through the choice of law of the parties even in a case with international relevance, and the application of Section 595 fZPO, which concerns the grounds for reopening the proceedings.[69]

1-044 As a result the new arbitration law makes it practically impossible to conclude an arbitration agreement with a consumer. This is in line with the prevailing opinion, at least in Europe, that international commercial arbitration should be understood to be a dispute resolution mechanism primarily established for commercial users.[70] Note that the Austrian Consumer Protection Act (*Konsumentenschutzgesetz* – KSchG) applies to all contracts concluded between commercial enterprises and consumers.[71] According to the statutory definition, a *commercial enterprise* is a permanent organization of independent commercial activity even if it is not for profit. A *consumer* is defined as anyone who is not a commercial enterprise.[72] The application of the Consumer Protection Act is extended to transactions that

---

light of States' Interests and in particular in light of EU Law Requirements' (2007) 23(1) Arb Int'l, 63; N. Reich, 'More clarity after 'Claro'?' (2007) 3(1) ERCL, 41; R. Jordans, 'Anmerkungen zu EuGH Rs. C-168/05 – Elisa Maria Mostaza Claro gegen Centro Movil Milenium SL' [2007] GPR, 48; W. Hau, 'Zur Entwicklung des Internationalen Zivilverfahrensrecht in der Europäischen Union in den Jahren 2005 und 2006' [2007] GPR, 93.

69. According to this provision, by reference, an award can (additionally) be set aside if a party (i) has found or been put in a position to use an earlier binding decision that establishes the law between them concerning the same claim or legal relationship; or (ii) has learned of new facts or evidence or has been put in a position to use evidence that would have influenced the decision in a favourable manner to him. *See* J. Power, *The Austrian Arbitration Act – A Practitioner's Guide to Sections 577-618 of the Austrian Code of Civil Procedure* (Vienna, Manz, 2006), Section 618, para. 17.

70. For the U.S., *see* M. Miller, 'Contracting out of process, Contracting out of Corporate Accountability: An Argument against Enforcement of Pre-Dispute Limits of Process' (Tennessee Law Review Spring 2008), online publication, <http://papers.ssrn.com/sol3/papers.cfm?abstract_id=1081709>; M. J. Lockerby and K. J. Shur, 'Arbitration Fairness Act of 2007: a trial lawyer's dream, a client's nightmare', Franchising World, November 2007, online publication <http://goliath.ecnext.com/coms2/summary_0199-7310455_ITM>.

71. A different approach is taken in Germany, where the German ZPO provides for arbitration agreements entered into by consumers similar specific formal requirements. Section 1031(5) German ZPO: 'Arbitration agreements to which a consumer is a party must be contained in a document which has been personally signed by the parties. The written form pursuant to sub-section 1 may be substituted by electronic form pursuant to Section 126a German BGB.' However, the necessity to include such an agreement into a separate document can be avoided by a notarial certification. 'No agreements other than those referring to the arbitral proceedings may be contained in such a document or electronic document; this shall not apply in the case of a notarial certification.' Unlike Section 617 ZPO, the German arbitration law does not require, that the dispute has arisen prior to the conclusion of the arbitration agreement. *See also* K.H. Schwab and G. Walter (eds), *Schiedsgerichtsbarkeit* (7th edn, Munich, C. H. Beck, 2005), ch. 5 paras. 16 *et seq.*

72. Section 1 KSchG.

a natural person concludes to commence a commercial enterprise ('founding transaction' or *Gründungsgeschäfte*),[73] which may entail the conclusion of an arbitration agreement.

This could be of relevance, e.g. where a natural person acts as a shareholder or **1-045** partner (including as a silent partner or equity holder) within an incorporated or private company. In some of these cases, Austrian jurisprudence has determined the status of a person to be that of a consumer because of the lack of managing authority or effective supervisory power, even if the capital investment was clearly made for the purpose of profit.[74] Considerable caution should therefore be exercised when assessing the subjective capacity to conclude an arbitration agreement in such circumstances, as the law governing this question may expand consumer protection to persons or entities that are traditionally not perceived to be more worthy of protection than any other commercial entity.[75]

1.3.   *Arbitration Agreements Concluded by States or State-Related Entities*

The central issue regarding the subjective arbitrability of states or state entities is **1-046** the principle of *sovereignty*. Under Austrian law, entities with sovereign immunity which conclude an arbitration agreement are deemed to have waived their immunity and to submit to arbitration and to domestic courts. Such entities can no longer claim immunity before the arbitral tribunal or before the courts in arbitration-related matters.[76] Additionally, states or state-controlled entities are prevented from invoking any supposed lack of capacity under their own domestic laws,

---

73. H. Krejci in *Kommentar zum ABGB II/2*, P. Rummel (ed.) (3rd edn, Vienna, Manz, 2002), Section 1 KSchG, paras. 1 and 47 *et seq*. It is disputed whether an association (*Verein*) may be qualified as an entrepreneur. *See* H. Krejci, 'Zum Ministerialentwurf einer HGB – Reform', [2003] VR, 218; H. Krejci, 'Zum Mitglieder- und Gläubigerschutz nach dem VerG 2002' [2003] JBl, 713; P. Mayr, 'Schiedsklauseln in Vereinsstatuten' [2007] RdW, 331.
74. A. Reiner, 'Schiedsverfahren und Gesellschaftsrecht' [2007] GesRZ, 151, 165 *et seq*. with reference to OGH, 11 February 2002, 7 Ob 315/01a, OGH, 25 June 2003, 3 Ob 141/03m, OGH, 24 November 2005, 3 Ob 58/05h; *also* N. Aburumieh, C. Koller and E. Pöltner, 'Formvorschriften für Schiedsvereinbarungen' [2006] ÖJZ, 439; M. Fellner, 'Das neue österreichische Schiedsrecht' [2007] NetV, 10.
75. *See* a more recent anlysis on the qualification of shareholders as consumer in B. Terlitza and M. Weber, 'Zur Schiedsfähigkeit gesellschaftsrechtlicher Streitigkeiten nach dem SchiedsRÄG 2006' [2008] (2) ÖJZ; E. Joeinig, 'Alternative Streitbeilegungsmöglichkeiten für Verbraucher in Österreich' [2006] Zak, 366.
76. C. Liebscher and A. Schmid in *Practitioner's Handbook on International Arbitration*, F.B. Weigand (ed.) (Munich, C.H. Beck, 2002), p. 545 with reference to H.W. Fasching, *Schiedsgericht und Schiedsverfahren im österreichischen und im internationalen Recht* (Vienna, Manz, 1973), p. 14; T. Chiwitt-Oberhammer, *Der fehlerhafte Schiedsspruch* (Vienna, Verlag Österreich, 2000), p. 146; G. Zeiler, *Schiedsverfahren* (Vienna/Graz, Neuer Wissenschaftlicher Verlag, 2006), Section 577, p. 29.

given that they may not rely on their own law in order to renege on their contractual obligations.[77]

1.4.   *Consequences of a Lack of Subjective Arbitrability*

1-047 Austrian doctrine considers an award rendered in the absence of subjective arbitrability as an award, rather than a non-award, and places it in the same category as a faulty state court decision rendered in the absence of legal capacity of a party. Thus, such an award could be set aside according to Section 595(1) fZPO.[78] The new arbitration law in Section 611(2) no. 1 ZPO provides to similar effect that an award can be set aside if a 'party was not capable of concluding a valid arbitration agreement under the law which was personally relevant to that party'.[79]

2.   An Agreement Concerning a 'Specified Legal Relationship'

1-048 The arbitration agreement must contain the exact identification of the parties, the dispute or the legal relationship out of which the dispute might arise, and the submission of the parties to arbitration. It is sufficient for the identification of the dispute to be described in the underlying contract and not in the arbitration agreement itself.[80]

1-049 Facultative (or optional) arbitration agreements are agreements providing an option between state court or an arbitral tribunal and are considered to be sufficiently defined in the sense of Section 581(1) ZPO.[81] According to the Austrian *Oberster Gerichtshof*, any unspecific or unclear terms in the arbitration agreement are void, but the agreement itself is rendered inoperative only when the entire agreement is unspecific or unclear.[82] However, an agreement in general terms that all disputes that may arise between two parties for any reason shall be

---

77.   A. Reiner, *Das neue österreichische Schiedsrecht/The new Austrian Arbitration Law* (Vienna, LexisNexis, 2006), Section 577, note 195.
78.   T. Chiwitt-Oberhammer, *Der fehlerhafte Schiedsspruch* (Vienna, Verlag Österreich, 2000), p. 146; *see also* Article II (Right of Legal Persons of Public Law to Resort to Arbitration) of the European Convention: 'In the cases referred to in Article I, paragraph 1, of this Convention, legal persons considered by the law which is applicable to them as "legal persons of public law" have the right to conclude valid arbitration agreements. On signing, ratifying or acceding to this Convention any State shall be entitled to declare that it limits the above faculty to such conditions as may be stated in its declaration.' **Annex 10**.
79.   *See* **Article 27**, at para. 045.
80.   H.W. Fasching, *Schiedsgericht und Schiedsverfahren im österreichischen und im internationalen Recht* (Vienna, Manz, 1973), p. 26.
81.   In Austrian jurisprudence it is acknowledged that the agreement on two different arbitral tribunals is valid, granting the parties a right of choices. *See in detail* P. Oberhammer, 'Fakultative Schiedsklauseln' [2000] RdW, 134.
82.   *See* OGH, 9 September 1987, 3 Ob 80/87, decided under the fZPO.

submitted to arbitration would be invalid due to insufficient specificity. The legal relationship between the parties must at least be determined or determinable.[83] If an arbitration institution is not clearly specified, the dispute can be deemed as having been referred to the institution which, in line with international practice, is likely to have been agreed upon.[84]

Except for consumers, Austrian law does not conceptually distinguish between **1-050** the *submission* to arbitration of an existing dispute and an agreement stipulating arbitration for future disputes.[85] Section 577 fZPO stated that 'an arbitration agreement submitting future disputes arising from a specified legal relationship to arbitration by one or more arbitrators is also valid'. Section 581(1) ZPO now states that '[a]n arbitration agreement is an agreement by the parties to submit to arbitration all or certain disputes which have arisen or which may arise between them in respect of a defined legal relationship, whether contractual or not'. An arbitration agreement may also be concluded as to all disputes arising in connection with several legal relationships. It is advisable (but not necessary) that such multiple agreements be defined as a particular legal relationship. Additionally, the same single arbitration agreement may cover both disputes arising from contractual relationships and disputes arising from non-contractual relationships, depending on the wording of the arbitration clause.[86] Typically, an arbitration clause referring to all disputes 'arising from' or (even broader) 'in connection with' a particular agreement may cover related claims of tort. Even under the narrower phrase 'arising from', tort claims may fall within the arbitration agreement. *See* OGH, 28 August 2008, 4 Ob 80/08f.

Austrian arbitration law recognizes further ways of granting arbitrators the author- **1-051** ity to decide a dispute by arbitration. Section 581(2) ZPO grants such an authority to arbitral tribunals that are set up in a manner permitted by law, either by

---

83. *See* OLG Vienna, 10 February 1937, 2 R 56, EvBl 1937/279, 88; *also* H.W. Fasching, *Schiedsgericht und Schiedsverfahren im österreichischen und im internationalen Recht* (Vienna, Manz, 1973), p. 16.

84. OGH, 5 October 1988, 3 Ob 58/88 – in this case, the Austrian *Oberster Gerichtshof* interpreted the wording '*in eventuellen juristischen Fragen*' (in potential legal questions) as '*für alle aus dem abgeschlossenen Vertrag entstehenden Streitigkeiten*' (all disputes arising out of this contract). Additionally, the arbitration agreement contained the reference to the '*neben der Ungarischen Handelskammer wirkenden Gericht*' (besides the Hungarian Chamber acting Court). The Austrian *Oberster Gerichtshof* – referring to P. Schlosser, *Das Recht der internationalen privaten Schiedsgerichtsbarkeit* (2nd edn, Tübingen, Mohr Siebeck, 1989), para. 382, with a similar example 'Arbitrage Moskau' equals '*Außenhandels-Schiedskommission bei der Sowjetischen Industrie-Handelskammer*'; *see* OGH, 9 September 1987, 3 Ob 80/87 – considered the Permanent Arbitration Court of the Hungarian Chamber of Commerce as agreed upon.

85. W. Melis, 'Austria' in *International Handbook on Commercial Arbitration* (The Hague, Kluwer Law International, Suppl. 10, 1989), pp. 1-4 – except the specific provision of Section 9 ASGG. *See* **Article 1**, at paras. 039 and 114.

86. A. Reiner, *Das neue österreichische Schiedsrecht/The new Austrian Arbitration Law* (Vienna, LexisNexis, 2006), Section 581, note 25.

testamentary disposition[87] or by other legal transactions that are not based on the agreement of the parties. Authority is also granted to tribunals provided for by articles of incorporation.[88]

3.   Form Requirements

1-052 Arbitration agreements take disputes away from state court jurisdiction. Insofar as this is in tension with constitutional rights to have one's case heard before a court of law,[89] most legal systems impose particular formal requirements for the conclusion of an arbitration agreement,[90] notably the requirement that the arbitration agreement be concluded 'in writing'.[91]

1-053 The following discussion provides an overview of the former and new Austrian arbitration law with particular attention to the conclusion of an arbitration agreement by an agent.[92] On this occasion, reference is made again to the transitional provisions. As will be discussed below, the new arbitration law (Sections 577-618 ZPO) came into effect on 1 July 2006 and is therefore applicable to all proceedings commenced on or after that day. However, the validity (and, hence, the issue of formal requirements) of arbitration agreements concluded before 1 July 2006 will be considered under the *former* arbitration law.[93] As a result, the form requirements under the fZPO will remain relevant for a considerable period of time.

3.1.   *Some Policy Considerations*

1-054 Historically, the Austrian courts, as well as the majority of academic opinions, have placed considerable emphasis on the requirement of 'written' agreements.

---

87. It is sufficient for the testator to comply with one of the permissible forms of testamentary dispositions. *See* A. Reiner, *Das neue österreichische Schiedsrecht/The new Austrian Arbitration Law* (Vienna, LexisNexis, 2006), Section 581, note 28.
88. *See* an overview in G. Zeiler, *Schiedsverfahren* (Vienna/Graz, Neuer Wissenschaftlicher Verlag, 2006), Section 577, pp. 77 *et seq.*
89. *See also* Article 6 ECHR: 'In the determination of his civil rights and obligations or of any criminal charge against him, everyone is entitled to a fair and public hearing within a reasonable time by an independent and impartial tribunal established by law.'
90. For a short overview *see* H.W. Fasching, 'Die Form der Schiedsvereinbarung' [1989] ÖJZ, 289; *also* P. Schlosser, *Das Recht der internationalen privaten Schiedsgerichtsbarkeit* (2nd edn, Tübingen, Mohr Siebeck, 1989), para. 360.
91. *See also* Articles II(1) and (2) NY Convention: 'Each Contracting State shall recognise an agreement in writing under which the parties undertake to submit to arbitration all or any differences which have arisen or which may arise between them in respect of a defined legal relationship, whether contractual or not, concerning a subject matter capable of settlement by arbitration. The term "agreement in writing" shall include an arbitral clause in a contract or an arbitration agreement, signed by the parties or contained in an exchange of letters or telegrams.' **Annex 11**.
92. The question of which law is applicable to the conclusion of the arbitration agreement is addressed in the context of **Article 2**, at paras. 032 *et seq.*
93. *See* Article VII ZPO, Transitional Provisions.

Indeed, while the Austrian *Oberster Gerichtshof* can be qualified as 'arbitration-friendly', arbitral awards are set aside by Austrian courts much more frequently for violation of form requirements (and, hence, lack of jurisdiction) than for any other reason.

The justifications that have been advanced for this strict view on form requirements **1-055** are plenty. It has been said that the 'in writing' requirement functions as a warning, supposedly increasing the parties' awareness, when concluding an arbitration agreement, as to the consequences of their decision. The 'in writing' requirement also has an evidentiary function. Objections against a written agreement can be handled easier and more expeditiously than determining whether or not an oral arbitration agreement was formed. The clearer and less disputable the existence of an agreement, the less likely it is that one or both parties will be forced into arbitration on a questionable basis.

However, the reliance on the 'in writing' requirement is doubtful from the **1-056** perspective of modern business. It is difficult to accept that an ancillary provision such as an arbitration clause must *always* be concluded in writing – even in circumstances where the underlying main contract can be concluded orally. Indeed, many contracts are concluded without the benefit of external advice, and without much consideration given to arbitration clauses by the business people. In these circumstances, the commercial world does not fully appreciate that stringent form requirements apply beyond what is required for the main contract. Neither is the commercial world appreciative of the consequences attaching to a strict interpretation of form requirements – why should a business be 'warned' against concluding an arbitration clause when the alternative in practice oftentimes means to litigate before courts perceived as hostile in an alien jurisdiction?[94]

In that regard, the historically prominent function of the 'in writing' requirement to **1-057** warn parties of the consequences is highly anachronistic. While there can be no debate under Section 583(1) ZPO that an arbitration clause can be concluded by way of e-mail exchange,[95] no-one familiar with the practice of modern communication would characterize e-mail as a means of communication that carries a particular warning function. As *Oberhammer* eloquently puts it, a party who orally instructs his or her secretary to confirm by e-mail the content of an arbitration clause is no more 'warned' than a party who orally concludes the arbitration agreement as such.[96] Similarly, the exchange of telefaxes has been sufficient

---

94. P. Oberhammer in *Das neue Schiedsrecht – Schiedsrechts-Änderungsgesetz 2006*, B. Kloiber, W.H. Rechberger, P. Oberhammer and H. Haller (eds) (Vienna, Manz, 2006), p. 115. *See also Reiner* who notes 'a lack of legitimate admonitory purpose against arbitration agreements in case with an international connection' and postulates that this form requirement be only applied to domestic arbitration. *See* A. Reiner, *Das neue österreichische Schiedsrecht/The new Austrian Arbitration Law* (Vienna, LexisNexis, 2006), Section 583, note 43.

95. *See* **Article 1**, at paras. 064 *et seq.*

96. P. Oberhammer in *Das neue Schiedsrecht – Schiedsrechts-Änderungsgesetz 2006*, B. Kloiber, W.H. Rechberger, P. Oberhammer and H. Haller (eds) (Vienna, Manz, 2006), p. 113.

under the fZPO just as much as the new ZPO.[97] In fact, the traditional view on the function of form requirements has failed to keep pace with the continuous relaxation of form requirements in modern arbitration laws.

1-058 In short, the function of form is a myth that has, by way of doctrinal repetition, assumed a life of its own, long detached from analytical necessity. Indeed, a strict application of form requirements to arbitration clauses is not sensible when compared to the relaxed requirements applicable to forum selection clauses.[98]

1-059 A similar critique is appropriate with regard to the long-standing jurisprudence of the Austrian *Oberster Gerichtshof* holding that, apparently because an arbitration agreement is a 'procedural contract', principles of good faith cannot cure formal defects in the formation of the arbitration agreement. First, it is difficult to understand how the categorization of an arbitration agreement as a 'procedural contract' serves as a bar to general rules of contract law – it is well established that, insofar procedural rules do not assist in addressing the issues associated with an arbitration agreement, the rules of Austrian contract law apply *per analogiam*. If that is so, principles of good faith – such as *venire contra factum proprium* and others – should apply as exceptional remedies just in the same way to arbitration agreements. Certainly, the statutory form requirements should not be perceived to limit the application of good faith arguments; rather, form requirements constitute but a part of contract law; they still allow for the individual circumstances to be taken into account in order to determine who really is deserving of protection in a particular case.

1-060 Indeed, it has been a less than glorious feature of (previous) Austrian arbitration law to allow a respondent to fully litigate the merits of a case without ever raising an objection to the tribunal's jurisdiction, or indeed for the claimant to rely on an arbitration agreement – just to turn around, when the case is lost, to apply to the courts to have the award set aside because the arbitration agreement suffered from formal defects resulting in a lack of jurisdiction. While this is no longer possible under the new ZPO (or the Vienna Rules),[99] the hostility towards a more relaxed and contract-based assessment of form requirements with regard to arbitration agreements ought to be re-considered in general. Indeed, new provisions in the ZPO seem to support the argument that good faith principles should be applied to the formation of arbitration agreements as well.[100] It is also comforting that recent case law indicates that the Austrian *Oberster Gerichtshof* appears increasingly prepared to do so.[101]

---

97. Under the regime of the former arbitration law this has, however, only been addressed by an *obiter dictum* in OGH, 2 July 1993, 1 Ob 525/93, whereas Section 583(1) ZPO has now explicitly clarified the sufficiency of telefax transmissions.
98. *See* Article 23(1) Brussels I Regulation and Article 17(1) Brussels Convention/Lugano Convention. *See* also **Article 15**, at paras. 083 *et seq.*
99. *See* **Article 19**, at paras. 006 *et seq.*
100. *See* Sections 583(3), 584(5) and 592(2) ZPO.
101. OGH, 26 April 2006, 7 Ob 236/05i, curing a formal defect in the arbitration agreement on the basis of the principles of *non venire contra factum proprium* and abuse of rights (*Rechtsmissbrauch*).

3.2.   The 'In Writing' Requirement Under the Old Regime

Prior to the 2006 reform, the form requirements attaching to arbitration agreements **1-061** were amended twice,[102] in order to bring Austrian arbitration law in line with the formal requirements of Article II New York Convention.[103] According to Section 577(3) fZPO, the arbitration agreement was required to be 'in writing or be contained in telegrams,[104] telexes or in electronic representations exchanged by the parties'. Commentators extended these provisions to apply to telefaxes as well.[105] The party's handwritten signature was *not* required, however, because the main purpose of Section 577(3) fZPO was to clarify the content of the agreement. In case of electronic data transmission, there was also no need for a signature; the function of the personal signature to identify the party is replaced by the indication in the e-mail of the name of the party to the contract.[106]

Interestingly, the Austrian *Oberster Gerichtshof* also ruled that the formal require- **1-062** ments of an arbitration agreement should be determined *exclusively* by Article II New York Convention (which therefore overrides national Austrian law) if the recognition and enforcement procedure of an Austrian arbitral award is possible in another country that has ratified the New York Convention, and if the matter has an international character. Austrian jurisprudence thereafter attempted to apply Article II New York Convention to modern business life on a case-by-case basis.[107] While an arbitration clause contained in general terms and conditions

---

102. ZVN 1983 in BGBl No. 135/1983 and in BGBl I No. 152/2001.
103. A. von Saucken, *Die Reform des österreichischen Schiedsverfahrensrechtes auf der Basis des UNCITRAL-Modellgesetzes über die Internationale Handelsschiedsgerichtsbarkeit* (Frankfurt, Verlag Peter Lang, 2004), p. 65; B. Jud and R. Högler-Pracher, 'Schiedsverfahren mit modernen Kommunikationstechniken' [1999] ecolex, 601; NY Convention, **Annex 11**.
104. *See also* OGH, 12 November 1952, 2 Ob 723/52.
105. W.H. Rechberger and W. Melis in *Kommentar zur* ZPO, W.H. Rechberger (ed.) (2nd edn, Vienna, Manz, 2000), Section 577, para. 9; *see* H.W. Fasching, 'Die Form der Schiedsvereinbarung' [1989] ÖJZ, 289; *see also* **Article 1**, at para. 057.
106. *See* C. Liebscher and A. Schmid in *Practitioner's Handbook on International Arbitration*, F.B. Weigand (ed.) (Munich, C.H. Beck, 2002), p. 542 with further annotations; *see also* OGH, 2 July 1993, 1 Ob 525/93.
107. OGH, 17 November 1971, 8 Ob 233/71, JBl 1974, 629; *see* for instance in OGH, 16 January 1924, Ob I 20, ZBl 1924/92, 205 and OGH, 11 September 1957, 2 Ob 412/57; OGH, 28 December 1905, Nr. 19.981, GIUNF 3646 (no valid conclusion of an arbitration clause by oral agreement); OGH, 26 April 1927, Ob III 306, ZBl 1927/222, 633 (required content of an arbitration agreement); OGH, 1 May 1912, Rv I, 132/12, GIUNF 5896; OGH, 9 October 1929, 3 Ob 727/29, JBl 1930, 18; OGH, 21 February 1978, 3 Ob 120/77 (arbitration agreement contained in letter and counter-letter can be sufficient when both contain the same arbitration agreement); OGH, 18 May 1909, Rv I, 279/9, GIUNF 4624 (different when arbitration agreement solely contained in confirmation letter); OGH, 15 October 1930, 3 Ob 784, ZBl 1931/52, 148 (arbitration agreement in an unsigned protocol); OGH, 21 February 1996, 3 Ob 10/96 (arbitration agreement concluded by third party); OGH, 17 September 1952, 1 Ob 734/52 (arbitration agreement contained in two different documents); OGH, 21 February 1911,

was considered to be invalid if the main contract made only vague references to those terms,[108] the Austrian *Oberster Gerichtshof* has taken the position in more recent decisions that a general reference is sufficient when the terms and conditions are directly attached to the signed contract.[109] As discussed above, however, the Austrian *Oberster Gerichtshof* appears in general reluctant to relax the form requirements imposed by the statute.[110]

3.3.   The 'In Writing' Requirement Under the New Regime

1-063 The formal requirements under Austrian law have more recently been criticized as being too rigid.[111] As discussed in the introduction to this section, a strict

---

Rv II, 106/11, GIUNF 5373 (the exchange of the one party's signed application and the other party's insurance policy, both containing the arbitration agreement, is a valid conclusion of an arbitration agreement); OGH, 9 April 1992, 3 Ob 25/92 (when to apply the form requirement in accordance with NY Convention); OGH, 7 November 1979, 3 Ob 144/79 (the *tacet* acceptance of an order confirmation containing an arbitration agreement is not a written agreement according to Article II NY Convention); OGH, 17 May 1950, 3 Ob 171/50; OGH, 8 March 1961, 1 Ob 98/61; OGH, 18 May 1966, 3 Ob 58/66, EvBl 1966/407 and *also* OGH, 2 May 1972, 5 Ob 93/72; OLG Vienna, 15 December 1998, 13 R 154/98g, ecolex 1999, 259 (the conclusion of an arbitration agreement by reference); OGH, 13 July 1904, Nr. 9722, GIUNF 2749; OGH, 8 July 1913, R. II, 679/13, GIUNF 6520; OGH, 10 March 1954, 1 Ob 151/54, SZ 37/31 (the conclusion of statutory arbitration agreements); OGH, 29 October 1935, 1 Ob 704/35, SZ XVII/150 (signature by stamp is not sufficient to substitute a signature under an arbitration agreement); OGH, 10 June 1913, Rv I, 580/13, GIUNF 6482; OGH, 12 April 1929, 1 Ob 157/29, ZBl 1929/280, 114; OGH, 20 February 1964, 6 Ob 273/63, SZ 37/31; OGH, 10 November 1977, 6 Ob 701/77 (arbitration agreements related to associations); OGH, 9 June 1937, 3 Ob 402/37, Rsp 1937/204, 162 (for a company arbitration agreement, it is sufficient that the accessor signs a written declaration of accession and is informed about its acceptance in writing) – *see* more detailed list in K. Neuteufel, *Schiedsrechtliche Entscheidungen 1898-1998* (Vienna, Verlag Österreich, 2000).

108. OGH, 18 May 1966, 3 Ob 58/66, EvBl 1966/407.
109. Recently confirmed in OGH, 24 May 2005, 4 Ob 82/05w; *see also* OGH, 18 March 2004, 2 Ob 53/04i; *see* further C. Liebscher and A. Schmid in *Practitioner's Handbook on International Arbitration*, F.B. Weigand (ed.) (Munich, C.H. Beck, 2002), p. 542 with reference to OGH, 31 August 1984, 1 Ob 20/84, and OGH, 2 May 1972, 5 Ob 93/72 with further annotations and cases; detailed analysis in G. Backhausen, *Schiedsgerichtsbarkeit unter besonderer Berücksichtigung des Schiedsvertragsrechts* (Vienna, Manz, 1990), p. 11.
110. In OGH, 26 January 2000, 7 Ob 368/98p, 7 Ob 369/98k it was reiterated that the relief for the conclusion of an arbitration agreement relaxes the prevailing formalities only for those methods where a signature is technically not possible (telegrams, etc.). Where an approximation to a signature is possible (telecopy, electronic data transmission, etc.), the formal requirements need to be fully observed. *See* OGH, 24 May 2005, 4 Ob 82/0w, emphasizing the importance of the warning function with reference to more recent doctrine.
111. P. Oberhammer, 'Schiedsvereinbarung und § 1016 ABGB' in *Festschrift Rudolf Welser zum 65. Geburtstag*, C. Fischer-Czermak, A. Kletecka, M. Schauer and W. Zankl (eds) (Vienna, Manz, 2004), p. 758; S. Riegler, 'Is Austria any different? The new Austrian arbitration law in

application of formal requirements made arbitration awards challengeable even where the main contract was validly concluded and the parties, at the time of conclusion, had no doubts that they had agreed to arbitration.

In line with the international trend, the formal requirements for the conclusion of an **1-064** arbitration agreement have been relaxed and further developed.[112] The Working Group's draft had suggested a more liberal approach, beyond Article 7 UNCITRAL Model Law, which provides that the arbitration agreement should be given effect if it was valid under the law chosen by the parties, or under the law applicable to the merits, or under Austrian law.[113] Regrettably, this approach was eventually rejected by the legislature, which deliberately deviated from the Working Group draft.[114] Section 583(1) ZPO now provides:

> The arbitration agreement must be contained in either a document signed by the parties or in letters, faxes, e-mails, or other forms of communication exchanged between them that provide proof of the existence of the agreement.

The form requirements can therefore be fulfilled in two ways ('either (...) or'). **1-065** First, the form requirement can be met by the signature of the parties on the document containing the arbitration agreement. This arguably includes every adequate form of electronic signature.[115]

The second – and *notabene* separate – means to conclude an arbitration agreement **1-066** is by exchange of letters, faxes, e-mails or other forms of communication exchanged by the parties that provide 'proof of the existence of the agreement'.[116]

---

comparison with the UNCITRAL Model Law and the German arbitration law' (2006) Int'l Arb L Rev, 69.

112. *See also* the latest developments of the UNCITRAL Working Group with regard to Article II NY Convention.

113. Draft Section 583 ZPO had provided: (1) 'The arbitration agreement shall be in writing. This requirement is satisfied by any form of record, in particular through electronic, optical, or another form of data processing. A signature is not required. (2) A written arbitration agreement pursuant to subs. 1 also exists, in particular, when the recorded wording of an arbitration agreement in terms of Section 581 which corresponds to the form requirements of subs. 1 became part of a contract or otherwise binding, even if the contract itself does not correspond to this form requirement. (3) Subs. 1 does not apply to the authorization to conclude an arbitration agreement. (4) In all other aspects the arbitration agreement is valid provided it complies with the law chosen by the parties, with the law applicable to the merits, in particular that applicable to the principal contract, or with Austrian Law.'

114. Explanatory Notes to Section 583 ZPO.

115. E-mails have again expressly been inserted in this provision as they were already contained in a former version of Section 577 (' (...) *elektronisch Erklärung*', BGBl I No 152/2001); hence, they will not fall under the fall-back provision of 'other forms of communication'. *See* discussion to the old law in B. Jud and R. Högler-Pracher, 'Schiedsverfahren mit modernen Kommunikationstechniken' [1999] ecolex, 601 *et seq.*

116. This corresponds with Article II NY Convention in which scope it has been argued that the declarations contained in the exchanged documents refer to each other. The arbitration

In other words, the parties must choose a mode of transmitting the information that documents the text of the agreement. It is not sufficient for a letter, facsimile, e-mail, or other form of written communication to be accepted orally – rather, the acceptance must be in writing as well.[117] Electronic storage, such as on a CD-ROM or computer hard disc, should however be sufficient.[118] In fact, any form of communication that provides a record of the agreement or is otherwise accessible so as to be usable for subsequent reference would suffice.[119]

1-067 It bears emphasis that the form requirements of Section 583 ZPO do not impose a particular evidentiary rule; they only apply to the conclusion of the arbitration agreement. It is therefore possible to prove the formation of a valid arbitration agreement (originally concluded 'in writing' within the meaning of Section 583(1) ZPO) by way of oral testimony, for example, in cases where the original can no longer be found or has been destroyed.[120]

1-068 Section 583(2) ZPO goes on to address separate arbitration agreements, as opposed to arbitration clauses contained in a contract:

> When an agreement which fulfils the form requirements of paragraph 1 refers to a document which contains an arbitration agreement, it shall constitute an arbitration agreement if the reference is such that it makes the arbitration agreement part of the contract.

---

agreement would have to be covered by the pertaining declarations of the parties. Whether or not these declarations are congruent has to be judged by the law governing the arbitration agreement. *See* U. Haas in *Practitioner's Handbook on International Arbitration*, F.B. Weigand (ed.) (Munich, C.H. Beck, 2002), p. 442.

117. A. Reiner, *Das neue österreichische Schiedsrecht/The new Austrian Arbitration Law* (Vienna, LexisNexis, 2006), Section 583, note 42.

118. J. Power, *The Austrian Arbitration Act – A Practitioner's Guide to Sections 577-618 of the Austrian Code of Civil Procedure* (Vienna, Manz, 2006), Section 583, para. 3.

119. The exchange of the means of communication does not require that both parties mention the arbitration agreement. *See* M. Roth in *Practitioner's Handbook on International Arbitration*, F.B. Weigand (ed.) (Munich, C.H. Beck, 2002), p. 1191; *see also* P. Oberhammer, *Entwurf eines neuen Schiedsverfahrensrechts* (Vienna, Manz, 2002), pp. 43 *et seq.* Von Saucken considers it essential that, despite which (future) method of communication is used, the issues of secured transmission, locked storage and proof of origin are complied with. *See* A. von Saucken, *Die Reform des österreichischen Schiedsverfahrensrechtes auf der Basis des UNCITRAL-Modellgesetzes über die Internationale Handelsschiedsgerichtsbarkeit* (Frankfurt, Verlag Peter Lang, 2004), p. 68. Although it was inserted in the *Ministerialentwurf*, the so-called '*halbe Schriftform*', as seen in Section 1031(2) German ZPO, had not been adopted. *See* R. Geimer in *Zöller – Zivilprozessordnung*, R. Zöller *et al.* (eds) (26th edn, Cologne, Verlag Dr. Otto Schmidt, 2007), Section 1031, para. 29.

120. A. Reiner, *Das neue österreichische Schiedsrecht/The new Austrian Arbitration Law* (Vienna, LexisNexis, 2006), Section 583, note 39. Under the former arbitration law, the Austrian *Oberster Gerichtshof* ruled similarly that the written arbitration agreement need not necessarily to be produced, as the 'in writing' requirement can be proven by all legal means possible. *See* OGH, 17 September 1952, 1 Ob 734/52 (this by explicit renunciation of an opposing decision rendered on 29 August 1916).

This provision seems to be modelled as a circular definition.[121] However, the **1-069** provision clarifies that the requirement of physically attaching the arbitration agreement to the signed document is obsolete.[122] What is decisive is the nature of the reference to the separate document – it must be such as to make the separate document 'part of the contract'. Whether that is so, appears to be a question of the substantive law applicable to the arbitration agreement.[123]

It is noteworthy that Section 583 ZPO is not only applicable when the seat of the **1-070** tribunal is within Austria.[124] According to Section 577(2) ZPO, it also applies when the place of arbitration is not in Austria, or even not yet determined. However, Section 583 ZPO does not establish a conflict of laws rule regarding form and issues of conclusion of arbitration agreements. Instead, it was intended to clarify that an arbitration agreement referring to an arbitral tribunal situated outside of Austria has the same effect on substantive claims before courts as an arbitration agreement referring to a tribunal situated in Austria.[125]

---

121. *See also* A. Reiner, *Das neue österreichische Schiedsrecht/The new Austrian Arbitration Law* (Vienna, LexisNexis, 2006), Section 583, note 44.

122. According to *Liebscher*, it was not intended that an independent arbitration term ('reference') be created. The effective incorporation of an arbitration agreement depends upon the general rules (*e.g*, provisions on general terms and conditions). *See* C. Liebscher, *The Austrian Arbitration Act 2006: Text and Notes* (The Hague, Kluwer Law International, 2006), Annotated Text to Section 583(2) ZPO. The *Ministerialentwurf* initially provided a stricter approach. It reads: 'An arbitration agreement which is contained in standard terms and conditions or in standard form contracts must be individually negotiated; this has to be recorded in accordance with the formal requirement under subs. 1.' This additional requirement was abolished after massive criticisms has been voiced, *inter alia* by the Vienna Bar Association. *See* Statement Zl 13/1 05/87 of 15 June 2005 <http://www.rakwien.at/import/documents/schiedsrechts-aenderungsgesetz2005.pdf>.

123. Under Austrian law, with the arbitral seat in Austria, Section 583(2) ZPO therefore overrides Section 864a ABGB, whereas Section 879(3) ABGB still persists in applying a limit to content. *See in detail* A. von Saucken, *Die Reform des österreichischen Schiedsverfahrensrechtes auf der Basis des UNCITRAL-Modellgesetzes über die Internationale Handelsschiedsgerichtsbarkeit* (Frankfurt, Verlag Peter Lang, 2004), p. 82.

124. *See* Section 577(1) ZPO.

125. That follows, according to *Oberhammer*, Article 178(2) Swiss IPRG, in the sense of a *favor validatis*, determines alternative nexus to different legal systems. Hence, the validity of arbitration agreements, referring to a foreign seat of an arbitration, need not be determined according to Section 583 ZPO. *See* P. Oberhammer, *Entwurf eines neuen Schiedsverfahrensrechts* (Vienna, Manz, 2002), p. 31. *Kröll* considers this to be 'a clear and specific conflict of law rule' which leads to a welcome synchronisation of form requirements in the defence proceedings of an existing arbitration agreement (*Einredesituation*) and the *exequatur* proceedings. *See* S. Kröll, 'Die Neuregelung des österreichischen Schiedsrechts – Felix Austria!?' in *Festschrift Norbert Horn, Zivil- und Wirtschaftsrecht im Europäischen und Globalen Kontext*, K.P. Berger, G. Borges, H. Herrmann, A. Schlüter and U. Wackerbarth (eds) (Berlin/New York, de Gruyter, 2006), p. 991.

3.4.   *Conclusion of the Arbitration Agreement by an Agent*

1-071 The question of agency in relation to the formation of arbitration agreements is a particularly controversial issue under Austrian law. Thankfully, the recent amendments have addressed the issue, and liberalized the regime significantly for commercial parties.[126]

1-072 As always in international arbitration the starting point is the search for the applicable law. It is acknowledged that law governing the question of agency is separate from, and does not overlap with, the law governing the subject matter of the contract.[127] Under Austrian law, officers (such as managing directors) authorized to act for commercial entities are also entitled to conclude arbitration agreements unless the corporate charter or statute provides otherwise.[128] However, it was a peculiar, yet extremely important, characteristic of the former Austrian law to impose special requirements on agents who concluded arbitration agreements on behalf of a principal.[129] In such cases, the principal was only bound by the arbitration agreement, if the agent had a *written* power of attorney (mirroring the form requirements for arbitration agreements).[130] *In addition*, this power of attorney was required to *specifically* include, and to refer to, the power to conclude an arbitration agreement (*schriftliche Spezialvollmacht*) according to Section 1008 ABGB.[131] This provision did not cover what Austrian law calls *Prokura*, which is a specific legally defined power of attorney granted to a *Prokurist*, as the person holding such special statutory authority.[132] Those *Prokuristen* did therefore not require an additional written power of attorney according to Section 1008

---

126. At least for those falling under the new Austrian Commercial Code (*Unternehmensgesetzbuch –* UGB).
127. *See* P. Schlosser, *Das Recht der internationalen privaten Schiedsgerichtsbarkeit* (2nd edn, Tübingen, Mohr Siebeck, 1989), para. 352. In Austria (partly) regulated in Section 49 IPRG. *See* B. Verschraegen in *Kommentar zum ABGB II/2*, P. Rummel (ed.) (3rd edn, Vienna, Manz, 2002), Section 49 IPRG.
128. OGH, 29 March 2006, 7 Ob 64/06x; OGH, 7 November 2002, 6 Ob 67/02z; OGH, 26 April 2006, 7 Ob 236/05i; *see also* G. Zeiler, *Schiedsverfahren* (Vienna/Graz, Neuer Wissenschaftlicher Verlag, 2006), Section 583, p. 103; T. Bachner, 'Keine Spezialvollmacht für Vorstand und Geschäftsführer' [2005] ecolex, 282.
129. Mostly by a contractually authorized agent.
130. *See* OGH, 26 January 2000, 7 Ob 368/98p and 7 Ob 369/98k; *see* H.W. Fasching, 'Die Form der Schiedsvereinbarung' [1989] ÖJZ, 289; C. Liebscher and A. Schmid in *Practitioner's Handbook on International Arbitration*, F.B. Weigand (ed.) (Munich, C.H. Beck, 2002), p. 543; P. Oberhammer, 'Schiedsvereinbarung und § 1016 ABGB' in *Festschrift für Rudolf Welser zum 65. Geburtstag*, C. Fischer-Czermak, A. Kletecka, M. Schauer and W. Zankl (eds) (Vienna, Manz, 2004), pp. 759 *et seq.*
131. Section 1008 ABGB refers *inter alia* to the authority 'to chose an arbitrator'. This was gradually extended by jurisprudence to the authority to conclude an arbitration agreement.
132. OGH, 23 October 1928, 3 Ob 648/28, Rsp 1928/379. This is a power of attorney granted to a '*Prokurist*' under the Austrian Commercial Code (*Unternehmensgesetzbuch –* UBG), conferring authority to act on behalf of the principal.

ABGB. The same was argued for the commercial power of attorney (*Handlungsvollmacht*); however, whether this also comprised the conclusion of an arbitration agreement needed to be assessed on a case-to-case basis.[133]

Using a general or oral power of attorney could have serious consequences; **1-073** the Austrian *Oberster Gerichtshof* has set aside awards on this basis, for lack of a valid arbitration agreement.[134] It would be wrong to assume in this regard that this provision by its very nature is not applicable to non-Austrian parties. This may depend on the conflict of laws rules applied in a particular case.[135] However, credit should be given to the ruling of the Austrian *Oberster Gerichtshof* of 17 November 1971.[136] In this case, as discussed above, the Austrian *Oberster Gerichtshof* held applying the former arbitration law, that the application of formal requirements to the arbitration agreement should be assessed exclusively under Article II New York Convention[137] in all cases where an Austrian arbitral award will possibly (because of an international connection of the matter) be recognized or enforced in a third country that, in turn, has ratified the New York Convention. In these cases it has been argued that the form requirement under Article II (1) New York Convention should not be applied to the form requirement otherwise applicable to powers of attorney under Austrian law.[138]

---

133. The *Prokura* and the commercial power of attorney were both expressly named in the *4. Ein-führungsverordnung zum Handelsgesetzbuch*, dRGBl. I S 1999/1938, cancelled with BGBl. I No. 120/2005 to Sections 49 and 54 HGB (*Prokura und Handlungsvollmacht*): For those transactions and legal acts, which are authorized by a prokura or a general power of attorney (*Handlungsvollmacht*), a specific power of attorney under Section 1008 ABGB is not required. However, some decisions suggested that the authorized agent requires a written power of attorney. *See* OGH, 6 February 1923, Ob II 49, ZBl 1924, 206 and a confirmation by the *Oberlandesgericht Graz* (*Graz* Court of Appeal) that the power of attorney used by a commercial agent despite the explicit legal provision unalteredly requires *to be in writing*. *See* OLG Graz, 20 February 1985, EvBl 1985, 130. The same applies in cases where statutory organs of the company are only entitled to collective representation (*Kollektivvertretung*). In such cases an oral power of attorney of one organ to the other would not suffice to conclude the arbitration agreement. *See*, with regard to shareholders, OGH, 2 September 1924, Ob III 568/24, Rsp VI, 201 and with regard to general managers, OGH, 13 November 1913, Ob III 709, ZBl 1923/292. If the commercial power of attorney also granted the right to conclude an arbitration agreement, this has to be specified in each individual case. *See* Explanatory Notes to Section 583 ZPO; *also* G. Zeiler, *Schiedsverfahren* (Vienna/Graz, Neuer Wissenschaftlicher Verlag, 2006), Section 583, p. 104. *See also* OGH, 20 October 2005, 2 Ob 235/05f, a decision dealing with the question of valid representation by high officials of an Austrian Ministry, also addressing the issue that the party introducing the arbitration agreement into the contract is in essence not entitled to rely on an invalid representation according to Section 1008 ABGB.
134. *See* **Article 1**, at para. 072.
135. J. Power, *The Austrian Arbitration Act – A Practitioner's Guide to Sections 577-618 of the Austrian Code of Civil Procedure* (Vienna, Manz, 2006), Section 584, para. 9.
136. OGH, 17 November 1971, 8 Ob 233/71, JBl 1974, 629.
137. NY Convention, **Annex 11**.
138. P. Oberhammer, 'Schiedsvereinbarung und § 1016 ABGB' in *Festschrift für Rudolf Welser zum 65. Geburtstag*, C. Fischer-Czermak, A. Kletecka, M.Schauer and W. Zankl (eds)

1-074 It is evident that the peculiar requirement of a specific power of attorney deviated from international standards and did not reflect the otherwise arbitration-friendly position of Austrian law and the Austrian courts. Naturally, this requirement often came as a surprise to international parties. Therefore, the Working Group draft proposed to dispense entirely with this requirement.[139] However, the solution proposed by the Working Group was regrettably not adopted by the Austrian legislature.[140] Instead, the new law still requires, as a matter of principle, that a power of attorney specifically confer the authority on the agent to conclude an arbitration agreement on behalf of the principal. Importantly, however, the new law now expressly exempts persons acting under a commercial power of attorney (*Handlungsvollmacht*) or with *Prokura*.[141] This exception is important and should render the application of Section 1008 ABGB moot in the context of commercial transactions, even in purely domestic cases.[142] In such cases, a general power of attorney will be sufficient, as will be an oral power of attorney. Even where the principal has not actually extended a power of attorney, but is at fault for creating the impression that such a power of attorney exists (*Duldungs- oder Anscheinsvollmacht*, apparent agency), the principal will arguably be bound by the arbitration agreement so concluded.[143] However, whether other entities

---

(Vienna, Manz, 2004), p. 770. In OGH, 26 April 2006, 7 Ob 236/05i, the Austrian *Oberster Gerichtshof* noted that *Oberhammer's* criticism is 'significant'. If, however, the requirement of Section 1008 ABGB should not be applied in these circumstances has not yet been finally decided.

139. Section 583(3) draft ZPO referred to the idiosyncratic provisions regarding the powers of attorney and states clearly that these formal requirements do not apply 'to the authorization to conclude an arbitration agreement'.

140. *See* Statement Z1.13/1 05/87 of Vienna Bar Association of 15 June 2005 <http://www.rakwien.at/import/documents/schiedsrechts-aenderungsgesetz2005.pdf>. *Neuteufel* speaks of an '*Austriacum ganz besonderer Art*'. *See* K. Neuteufel, 'Das neue österreichische Schiedsrecht' [2006] (26) ÖJZ.

141. This was done by inserting an explicit clarification in Section 54 UGB: 'No special power of attorney is required for such transactions and legal acts under Section 1008 ABGB.' Note that the UGB (*Handelsrechts-Änderungsgesetz* – HaRÄG, BGBl I No. 120/2005) came into force on 1 January 2007, leaving a time gap between the coming into effect of the new Arbitration Act on 1 July 2006.

142. A. Reiner, *Das neue österreichische Schiedsrecht/The new Austrian Arbitration Law* (Vienna, LexisNexis, 2006), Section 583, note 43; P. Oberhammer in *Das neue Schiedsrecht – Schiedsrechts-Änderungsgesetz 2006*, B. Kloiber, W.H. Rechberger, P. Oberhammer and H. Haller (eds) (Vienna, Manz, 2006), pp. 108 *et seq.*

143. *See* Explanatory Notes to Section 583 ZPO: 'As in the scope of Section 362a HGB, the provision of Section 1008 ABGB has been declared non-applicable, there do remain two areas for the form requirements of a power of attorney: in case a written power of attorney in specific detail is still necessary for the conclusion of an arbitration agreement, the form requirement of the new Section 583(1) 1 ZPO will be applicable to the power of attorney likewise; in the scope of Section 362a HGB, however, there will be no specific form requirement as there is no pertaining indication in the wording. The power of attorney can be granted orally or can even be a power of attorney by estoppel or an apparent power of attorney.'

perhaps outside the scope of Austrian commercial law (e.g. state entities) are also exempt *per analogiam* from the requirements of Section 1008 ABGB still remains uncertain.[144]

In any event, a defect in, or lack of, the required power of attorney can be cured **1-075** pursuant to Section 1016 ABGB. Thus, even where no power of attorney existed, or where the power of attorney failed to meet the form requirements of Section 1008 ABGB, the arbitration agreement is not invalid, but merely suspended (*schwebend unwirksam*). As such, it can be subsequently approved by the principal, which, according to general rules of agency, cures any such defect. However, it has been argued that, in order not to undermine the warning purpose associated with the form requirements under Austrian arbitration law, the principal's approval must follow the same form requirements as are imposed by Section 1008 ABGB: thus, the approval must be in writing and must 'specifically' refer to the arbitration agreement at issue.[145] However, courts have also considered as sufficient the approval by an (Austrian) attorney on behalf of the principal (his client) on the record of the arbitration.[146]

3.5. Arbitration Clauses in Statutes

Section 581(2) ZPO contains an express provision, similar to Section 599(1) fZPO, **1-076** addressing in particular arbitration clauses in corporate statutes (such as deeds of formations or articles of association). It provides:

> The provisions of this section shall also apply accordingly to arbitral tribunals that are, in a manner permitted by law, imposed by testamentary disposition or by other legal transactions that are not based on agreements of the parties, or that are provided for by articles of incorporation.

While under its express terms, this provision appears to extend generally the **1-077** provisions of the arbitration law to such clauses as well, it bears emphasis that

---

144. *See* Statement Z1.13/l 05/87 of Vienna Bar Association of 15 June 2005 to Section 362a HGB <http://www.rakwien.at/import/documents/schiedsrechts-aenderungsgesetz2005.pdf>.
145. OGH, 26 January 2000, 7 Ob 368/98p (7 Ob 369/98k). In this decision, the Austrian *Oberster Gerichtshof* also suggested (under the previous arbitration law) that the approval by the principal could only occur until the engagement of the merits in the arbitration (*Streiteinlassung*), although it did not provide reasons for why this should be so. The better view is to allow the principal (if it wants to rely on the arbitration agreement) to cure any defect, under general rules of agency but in the appropriate form, at the latest immediately upon the defect being raised. *See also* P. Oberhammer, 'Schiedsvereinbarung und § 1016 ABGB' in *Festschrift für Rudolf Welser zum 65. Geburtstag*, C. Fischer-Czermak, A. Kletecka, M. Schauer, and W. Zankl (eds) (Vienna, Manz, 2004). Under the new law, formal defects that are not raised at the first appearance are deemed cured anyway under Section 583(3) ZPO.
146. OGH, 28 February 1991, 6 Ob 507/90 (6 Ob 508/90).

this provision refers to arbitration clauses that are 'imposed' (*angeordnet*) and thus 'not based on the agreement of the parties'.[147]

1-078 This raises the question whether a distinction must be made regarding form requirements between arbitration agreements and statutory arbitration clauses; in practice, this question is particularly acute with respect to corporate articles of incorporation.[148] There is a strong argument that where a company's statute contains an arbitration clause, this arbitration clause binds (or rather is, within the meaning of Section 581(2) ZPO, 'imposed' on) any party operating within the scope of the statute – without the need for a separate accession in writing to the statutory arbitration clause. This would include the company itself, members of the company (such as shareholders), their legal successors and assignees, but also, arguably (and in particular where the substantive law governing the company's corporate affairs so suggests[149]) putative shareholders. While there appears to be growing consensus that this should be so,[150] the Austrian *Oberster Gerichtshof* has so far left the question open.[151]

147. It is sufficient for the testator to comply with one of the permissible forms of testamentary dispositions. *See* A. Reiner, *Das neue österreichische Schiedsrecht/The new Austrian Arbitration Law* (Vienna, LexisNexis, 2006), Section 581, note 28.

148. For an overview, *see* G. Zeiler, *Schiedsverfahren* (Vienna/Graz, Neuer Wissenschaftlicher Verlag, 2006), Section 581, pp. 77 *et seq.*

149. While historically and also in Austria, the place of the arbitration determined the law applicable to the formation, validity and effect of the arbitration agreement, a more nuanced view seems to be developing. As regards arbitration clauses of corporate statutes, the effect of clauses may well be informed by the legal effect of the statute itself – which would usually be determined by the law of incorporation. *See* B. Kloiber and H. Haller in *Das neue Schiedsrecht – Schiedsrechts-Änderungsgesetz 2006*, B. Kloiber, W.H. Rechberger, P. Oberhammer and H. Haller (eds) (Vienna, Manz, 2006), p. 39.

150. P. Rummel, 'Privates Vereinsrecht im Konflikt zwischen Autonomie und rechtlicher Kontrolle' in *Festschrift Rudolf Strasser zum 60. Geburtstag*, W. Schwarz and K. Spielbüchler (eds) (Vienna, Manz, 1983), p. 832; A. Reiner, *Das neue österreichische Schiedsrecht/The new Austrian Arbitration Law* (Vienna, LexisNexis, 2006), Section 581, note 30, and (uniformly) German doctrine to Section 1066 German ZPO. An opposing view is presented by G. Zeiler, *Schiedsverfahren* (Vienna/Graz, Neuer Wissenschaftlicher Verlag, 2006), Section 581, p. 78. This view is not fully convincing, because it does not take into account that the effects of a statutory clause under Section 581(2) ZPO may well be informed by applicable corporate law.

151. OGH, 25 January 1995, 3 Ob 543/94, JBl 1995, 596 with annotation by *Rummel*. In this case, the Austrian *Oberster Gerichtshof* considered the possibility of the direct effect of a statutory arbitration clause but held that in the case at bar, the written declaration of an entity to join a *Genossenschaft* as a member (a legal form under Austrian law with elements of both a partnership and a corporation) in and of itself satisfied any 'in writing' requirement as regards the arbitration clause contained in the corporate charter.

3.6. Objections to Defects of Form

The consequences attaching to a formally invalid arbitration agreement are severe. **1-079** Such arbitration agreements are considered to have no legal effect[152] and result in a lack of jurisdiction on the part of the tribunal.

Indeed, as noted, it was possible under the old regime to participate in arbitration **1-080** proceedings without questioning the formal validity or invalidity of the arbitration agreement, and to raise the issue only afterwards in proceedings to set aside the award.[153] As also noted, the Austrian *Oberster Gerichtshof* has traditionally been reluctant to loosen the strict form requirements and ruled that the reliance of one party on a showing of good faith does not cure the violation of the form requirements under Austrian law.[154] Only a joint procedural declaration of the parties to submit the dispute to arbitration could cure a defect in the form of the arbitration agreement.[155] However, following extensive and very persuasive criticism by *Oberhammer*,[156] the Austrian *Oberster Gerichtshof* recently accepted that a party cannot invoke an arbitration agreement only to later successfully challenge the resulting award by relying on a formal defect in the arbitration agreement.[157]

In any event, this uncertainty is now expressly resolved by the new arbitration law. **1-081** Section 583(3) ZPO provides that

> [a] defect of form of the arbitration agreement shall be cured in the arbitration proceedings by entering an appearance in the case, if a notification of the defect is not made earlier or at the latest together with entering an appearance.[158]

---

152. C. Liebscher and A. Schmid in *Practitioner's Handbook on International Arbitration*, F.B. Weigand (ed.) (Munich C.H. Beck, 2002), p. 543 with reference to OGH, 19 January 1996, 8 Ob 1211/95; OGH, 28 February 1991, 6 Ob 507, 508/90; OGH, 23 October 1928, 3 Ob 648/28, SZ X/303; OGH, 7 February 1933, 3 Ob 108/33, SZ XV/29; OGH, 27 March 1935, 1 Ob 249, ZBl 1935/367, 757; OGH, 14 October 1982, 8 Ob 556/82; OGH, 26 January 2000, 7 Ob 368/98p; OGH, 27 February 2001, 1 Ob 273/00d; OGH, 17 May 2001, 7 Ob 67/01f; OGH, 31 August 1984, 1 Ob 20/84 – recently confirmed in OGH, 21 June 2005, 5 Ob 127/05w ; OGH, 20 October 2005, 2 Ob 235/05f; in this case, however, more limited as the public hand attempted to rely on this *per analogiam. See* detailed list in K. Neuteufel, *Schiedsrechtliche Entscheidungen 1898-1998* (Vienna, Verlag Österreich, 2000).
153. *See* G. Weissmann, 'Drei Fragen zur Reform der Schiedsgerichtsbarkeit' in *Festschrift Rudolf Welser zum 65. Geburtstag*, C. Fischer-Czermak, A. Kletecka, M. Schauer and W. Zankl (eds) (Vienna, Manz, 2004), p. 1153; *see also* G. Zeiler, *Schiedsverfahren* (Vienna/Graz, Neuer Wissenschaftlicher Verlag, 2006), Section 583, p. 103.
154. OGH, 14 October 1982, 8 Ob 556/82; OGH, 21 June 2005, 5 Ob 127/05w.
155. OGH, 28 February 1991, 6 Ob 507, 508/90.
156. P. Oberhammer, 'Schiedsvereinbarung und § 1016 ABGB' in *Festschrift Rudolf Welser zum 65. Geburtstag*, C. Fischer-Czermak, A. Kletecka, M. Schauer and W. Zankl (eds) (Vienna, Manz, 2004), pp. 759 *et seq.*
157. OGH, 26 April 2006, 7 Ob 236/05i, introducing the principle of *non venire contra factum proprium*, mainly arguing that such conduct amounts to an abuse of rights (*Rechtsmissbrauch*).
158. *See also* **Article 19**, at para. 014.

1-082 According to Section 592(2) ZPO, purely procedural acts (such as the appointment of an arbitrator) do not represent the entering of an appearance in the case within the meaning of this provision.[159] The 'appearance' thus refers to a party's submission on the merits (which in the case of the Vienna Rules is typically the memorandum in reply).

1-083 If a party fails to raise a timely objection, it is generally barred from raising this defence at a later stage. This clearly facilitates legal certainty and should help to restrict the use of dilatory tactics, which could be too easily pursued under the old regime.

1-084 This is also reinforced by Section 584(5) ZPO which introduces for the first time the principle of '*non venire contra factum proprium*'[160] or 'good faith'[161] in Austrian arbitration law (which ought to establish a general principle to this effect beyond the strict scope of these provisions). Specifically, Section 584(5) ZPO provides that once a party has invoked the existence of an arbitration agreement at one stage in the proceedings, it cannot subsequently claim that such an agreement does not exist (unless the relevant circumstances have changed).[162] From the wording of this provision, a party is only precluded from challenging the existence of an arbitration agreement if it previously relied on it in the '*proceedings*'; hence, the invoking of formal defects of the arbitration agreement seems arguably *not* precluded merely by reliance on the arbitration agreement in pre-trial correspondence or conduct.[163] It bears emphasis, however, that Section 583(3) ZPO only governs *formal* defects in the arbitration agreement. *Substantive* deficiencies of the arbitration agreement – such as alleged invalidity due to error, fraud, or duress – are subject to Section 592(2) ZPO.[164]

---

159. The first entering of an appearance in the case will generally occur in the answer to the complaint pursuant to Section 597(1) ZPO. *See* C. Liebscher, *The Austrian Arbitration Act 2006: Text and Notes* (The Hague, Kluwer Law International, 2006), Annotated Text to Section 583(3) ZPO.

160. *See* OGH, 26 April 2006, 7 Ob 236/05i; *also* C. Liebscher *The Austrian Arbitration Act 2006: Text and Notes* (The Hague, Kluwer Law International, 2006), Annotated Text to Section 583(3) ZPO.

161. A. Reiner, *Das neue österreichische Schiedsrecht/The new Austrian Arbitration Law* (Vienna, LexisNexis, 2006), Section 584, note 64.

162. As the exception to an important principle, this *clausula rebus sic stantibus* must be read narrowly. Conceivable changed circumstances might be the subsequent annulment of the arbitration agreement or a party's insolvency. *See* G. Zeiler, *Schiedsverfahren* (Vienna/Graz, Neuer Wissenschaftlicher Verlag, 2006), Section 584, p. 114 with reference to P. Oberhammer, *Entwurf eines neuen Schiedsverfahrensrechts* (Vienna, Manz, 2006), p. 52.

163. *See* J. Power*, The Austrian Arbitration Act – A Practitioner's Guide to Sections 577-618 of the Austrian Code of Civil Procedure* (Vienna, Manz, 2006), Section 584, para. 16.

164. A. Reiner, *Das neue österreichische Schiedsrecht/The new Austrian Arbitration Law* (Vienna, LexisNexis, 2006), Section 583, note 45. Section 592(2) ZPO reads: 'An objection to the jurisdiction of the arbitral tribunal shall be raised no later than the first pleading in the matter. A party is not precluded from raising such objection by the fact that it has appointed, or

4.   The Effect of the Arbitration Agreement

The arbitration agreement has two different procedural effects: First, it has the **1-085** positive effect of constituting the foundation of the arbitral tribunal's jurisdiction. Second, the arbitration agreement has a negative effect in that it serves as a procedural bar to proceedings before the state courts whose jurisdiction is excluded as a result of the parties' agreement to arbitrate.

Under the former arbitration law, when a claim was filed with a national court **1-086** despite an arbitration agreement governing the dispute, this constituted according to prevailing opinion merely a waivable lack of jurisdiction (*prorogable Unzuständigkeit*); the jurisdiction of the arbitral tribunal is based on the parties' consent, and can again be amended by them.[165] This means that a respondent party (which is being sued in state courts despite the existence of an arbitration agreement) could choose not to invoke the arbitration agreement but to litigate the matter in the state courts instead. If a respondent party wanted to raise the existence of the arbitration agreement as a jurisdictional defence, it was required to do so no later than at the first hearing.[166] Relying on Section 41 JN, Austrian scholars argued that state courts could take the issue even with a waivable absence of jurisdiction *ex officio* at the time the suit is filed until (and including) the first hearing.[167] However, the Austrian *Oberster Gerichtshof* denied an *ex officio* application by the state courts.[168]

Now, Section 584 ZPO explicitly deals with the 'Arbitration Agreement **1-087** and Substantive Claim before Court' abandoning uncertainty of an *ex officio*

---

participated in the appointment of, an arbitrator. An objection that the arbitral tribunal is exceeding the scope of its authority shall be raised as soon as the matter alleged to be beyond the scope of its authority is raised during the arbitral proceedings. In either case, a later objection shall not be permitted; however, if the arbitral tribunal considers the delay justified, the objection can still be raised by the party.'

165. For many others, *see* OGH, 29 March 2006, 7 Ob 64/06x. An arbitration agreement causes not the inadmissibility of the recourse to the courts, but a waivable lack of jurisdiction; an erroneous titulation of this objection is considered irrelevant according to OGH, 2 October 2003, 6 Ob 41/03b.

166. OGH, 27 September 1950, 2 Ob 603/50; OGH, 5 February 1958, 5 Ob 2/58, EvBl 1958/103; OGH, 12 July 1967, 6 Ob 161/67, JBl 1968, 432. According to *Dolinar and Holzhammer*, the conclusion of an arbitration agreement amounts in a waiver of state administration of justice (*staatliche Rechtspflege*), hence a claim in court lacks legal interest. *See* W.H. Rechberger and W. Melis in *Kommentar zur ZPO*, W.H. Rechberger (ed.) (2nd edn, Vienna/New York, Springer 2000), Section 577, para. 12.

167. H.W. Fasching, *Schiedsgericht und Schiedsverfahren im österreichischen und im internationalen Recht* (Vienna, Manz, 1973), p. 35. The authority of an arbitral tribunal will also be constituted if the arbitration agreement is concluded during a claim pending with a state court. In such a case, the state court would have to reject the claim.

168. *See* OGH, 5 February 1958, 1 Ob 298/58.

consideration of the arbitration agreement by the courts.[169] With regard to a timely objection, the arbitration agreement is now treated as an unwaivable lack of jurisdiction (*unprorogable Unzuständigkeit*).[170] Thus, if an action in a matter that is the subject of an arbitration agreement is brought before the court, the court can reject the claim *in limine*, i.e. until an oral hearing is scheduled or a party is ordered to answer – provided the respondent does not submit a pleading in the subject matter, or orally pleads before the court, without objecting to the court's jurisdiction. If the court does not reject the claim upon its own motion and if the respondent enters an appearance without objecting, then an objection to the jurisdiction of the court can no longer be made.[171]

1-088 In such a case, the arbitration agreement is deemed to be inoperative, but only for the purposes of the pending court proceedings. Thus, the respondent to such proceedings may neither challenge the jurisdiction of the court on that basis at any later stage in the proceedings, nor file a request for arbitration relating to the dispute before the court.[172] This does not apply if the court establishes that the arbitration agreement does not exist or is incapable of being performed, which is aimed at particular situations where it is apparent that the arbitration agreement has been invoked for the sole purpose of aggravating or frustrating the enforcement of the other party's claim.[173]

1-089 Section 584 ZPO also seeks to avoid parallel proceedings as much as possible and gives preference to arbitration over court proceedings if there is a valid arbitration agreement. Any action brought on the grounds of the same claim is to be rejected by the courts if an arbitration is pending; no other legal dispute may be carried out before a court – or indeed before another arbitral tribunal (Section 584(3) ZPO) – with respect to the asserted claim.[174] However, this does not apply if a timely objection to the jurisdiction of the arbitral tribunal

---

169. A. von Saucken, *Die Reform des österreichischen Schiedsverfahrensrechts auf der Basis des UNCITRAL-Modellgesetzes über die Internationale Handelsschiedsgerichtsbarkeit* (Frankfurt, Verlag Peter Lang, 2004), p. 99.

170. According to Section 104(3) JN. *See* P. Oberhammer in *Das neue Schiedsrecht – Schiedsrechts-Änderungsgesetz 2006*, B. Kloiber, P. Oberhammer, W.H. Rechberger and H. Haller (eds) (Vienna, Manz, 2006), p. 195.

171. C. Liebscher, *The Austrian Arbitration Act 2006: Text and Notes* (The Hague, Kluwer Law International, 2006), Annotated Text to Section 584(1) ZPO.

172. J. Power, *The Austrian Arbitration Act – A Practitioner's Guide to Sections 577-618 of the Austrian Code of Civil Procedure* (Vienna, Manz, 2006), Section 584, para. 3.

173. A. von Saucken, *Die Reform des österreichischen Schiedsverfahrensrechts auf der Basis des UNCITRAL-Modellgesetzes über die Internationale Handelsschiedsgerichtsbarkeit* (Frankfurt, Verlag Peter Lang, 2004), p. 100.

174. Section 584(3) ZPO. According to C. Liebscher, *The Austrian Arbitration Act 2006: Text and Notes* (The Hague, Kluwer Law International, 2006), Annotated Text to Section 584(3) ZPO: This provision, in connection with para. (1) results in a de facto precedence of arbitration over court proceedings. According to *Reiner*, this may result in a 'race to court or arbitration' who considers the application of this provision as too far in that it tells arbitral tribunals sitting outside Austria how they must proceed if another arbitration is pending (where the same claims

was raised with the arbitral tribunal but a decision of the arbitral tribunal on the matter could not be obtained within a reasonable period of time.[175] In this regard, it bears emphasis that the courts have the last word on the existence or non-existence of an arbitration agreement.[176] Thus, jurisdictional decisions of the arbitral tribunal can be reviewed by the state courts under Section 611 ZPO.

Also, the initiation of state court proceedings does not establish *lis pendens* with **1-090** respect to arbitration. Arbitral proceedings may therefore be commenced, continued, or even concluded.[177] In cases where a partial or final award has been rendered, the state court proceedings should be stayed until a final decision has been reached (be it by challenging the award or by a lapse of the time limit for bringing a challenge). If the award is set aside due to lack of the arbitral tribunal's jurisdiction, the state court proceedings will have to be resumed. By analogy, arbitration proceedings in Austria should be permitted to proceed even if court proceedings before a non-Austrian court are pending with respect to the same subject matter.[178]

To ensure that parties do not end up without a forum, state courts are bound by a **1-091** decision of the arbitral tribunal denying jurisdiction. In such cases, the court may not reject an action on the grounds that an arbitral tribunal is in fact competent to hear the matter.[179]

Finally, it bears emphasis that Section 584 ZPO is also applicable if the place of **1-092** arbitration is outside Austria or has not yet been determined.[180]

5.   Interpretation of the Arbitration Agreement

Under traditional Austrian doctrine, the interpretation of an arbitration agreement **1-093** is in principle a question of procedural law.[181] However, *Fasching* admits that arbitration agreements are typically embedded in contracts of substantive law and, with regard to their validity, 'it would lead to an unbearable result if a procedural interpretation with regard to the scope of the arbitration agreement would lead to a different result than the interpretation according to the true will of the parties in

---

       are being assessed). *See* A. Reiner, *Das neue österreichische Schiedsrecht/The new Austrian Arbitration Law* (Vienna, LexisNexis, 2006), Section 584, note 56 *et seq.*

175.   Section 584(2) ZPO: Section 584 additionally contains provisions concerning the Statute of Limitations, which are dealt with under **Article 9**, at paras. 016 *et seq.*

176.   C. Liebscher, *The Austrian Arbitration Act 2006: Text and Notes* (The Hague, Kluwer Law International, 2006), Annotated Text to Section 584 ZPO.

177.   *See* Section 584(1) ZPO and the discussion on *lis pendens* under **Article 9**, at paras. 023 *et seq.*

178.   A. Reiner, *Das neue österreichische Schiedsrecht/The new Austrian Arbitration Law* (Vienna, LexisNexis, 2006), Section 584, note 53.

179.   The right of the claimant to make an application under Section 611 ZPO of this law to set aside the decision with which the arbitral tribunal denied its competence shall expire with the bringing of an action in court; Section 584(2) ZPO.

180.   Section 577(2) ZPO.

181.   *See* G. Zeiler, *Schiedsverfahren* (Vienna/Graz, Neuer Wissenschaftlicher Verlag, 2006), Section 581, p. 58.

accordance with Section 914 ABGB'.[182] According to this statutory rule regarding the interpretation of contracts, not only the formal wording but also the true intention of the parties as well as the principles of fair business conduct have to be taken into consideration.[183] Case law has extended this to the business practice which the parties have introduced between themselves,[184] as well as the subsequent conduct of the parties;[185] a merely literal interpretation is not sufficient.[186]

1-094 Therefore, an arbitration agreement has to be interpreted in accordance with the will of the parties and with regard to fair business conduct and trade usages.[187] Consideration should be given to a reasonable interpretation that favours the validity of the arbitration agreement.[188] *Fasching's* opinion can be considered to be the current prevailing doctrine in Austria.[189]

1-095 The courts have adopted this approach over time, but were in the past not completely coherent. It was ruled that arbitration agreements are considered to be procedural acts; therefore interpretation should be made in accordance with procedural law.[190] However, the interpretation rules of the general private law were held to apply *per analogiam*.[191] Hence, the Austrian courts agree that the intention of the parties and the principle of fair business conduct have to be taken into consideration.[192] In 7 Ob 310/02t, 29 April 2003, the Austrian *Oberster Gerichtshof* clearly put it as follows:

> [a]rbitration agreements are to be interpreted according to the will of the parties; decisive for the jurisdiction of the arbitral tribunal is the wording

---

182. H.W. Fasching, *Schiedsgericht und Schiedsverfahren im österreichischen und im internationalen Recht* (Vienna, Manz, 1973), p. 31.

183. P. Rummel in *Kommentar zum ABGB I*, P. Rummel (ed.) (3rd edn, Vienna, Manz, 2000), Section 914.

184. OGH, 13 October 1981, 5 Ob 673/81, JBl 1983, 97.

185. OGH, 6 March 1923, 1 Ob 80/23, SZ 5/44; OGH, 24 July 1997, 6 Ob 186/97i.

186. OGH, 23 February 1977, 8 Ob 560/76; OGH, 13 February 1979, 2 Ob 578/78.

187. H.W. Fasching, *Schiedsgericht und Schiedsverfahren im österreichischen und im internationalen Recht* (Vienna, Manz, 1973), p. 31.

188. H.W. Fasching, *Schiedsgericht und Schiedsverfahren im österreichischen und im internationalen Recht* (Vienna, Manz, 1973), p. 152.

189. N.A. Schoible, 'Die Niederlassung im österreichischen Zivilprozessrecht' in *Rechtsfragen der Zweigniederlassung, 28*, W. Schuhmacher, M. Gruber *et al.* (eds) (Vienna, LexisNexis, 1993), pp. 159 *et seq.*; D.-A. Simotta in *Kommentar zu den Zivilprozeßgesetzen I*, H.W. Fasching (ed.) (2nd edn, Vienna, Manz, 2000), Section 104 JN, paras. 9 *et seq.*; H.-J. Hellwig, *Zur Systematik des zivilprozessrechtlichen Vertrages* (Bonn, Röhrscheid, 1968), pp. 95 *et seq.*; P. Oberhammer, 'Internationale Gerichtsstandsvereinbarungen: Konkurrierende oder ausschließliche Zuständigkeit?' [1997] JBl, 434; G. Zeiler, *Schiedsverfahren* (Vienna/Graz, Neuer Wissenschaftlicher Verlag, 2006), Section 581, pp. 58 *et seq.* For a different opinion, see F. Matscher, 'Probleme der Schiedsgerichtsbarkeit im österreichischen Recht' [1975] JBl, 412; an overview also in B. Schneider, *Die Auslegung von Parteiprozesshandlungen* (Vienna, Verlag Österreich, 2004), pp. 227 *et seq.*

190. OGH, 9 March 1993, 5 Ob 503/93.

191. OGH, 17 May 2001, 7 Ob 67/01f.

192. OGH, 3 September 1986, 1 Ob 545/86, with further references.

of the arbitration agreement with consideration given to reasonable interpretation that favours the validity of the arbitration agreement.[193]

The wording of the agreement limits the possible interpretation; but within those **1-096** boundaries, it is again the will of the parties that is decisive.[194] The interpretation of an arbitration agreement should be in favour of the jurisdiction of the arbitral tribunal.[195] In case of two equal possibilities of interpretation, the interpretation that favours the validity and application of the arbitration agreement should be given preference.[196] Even a gap-filling interpretation should be permissible,[197] including where the scope of the arbitration agreement has to be determined.[198]

6. Other Forms of Dispute Resolution

Increasingly, arbitration agreements provide for escalation mechanisms, postpon- **1-097** ing recourse to arbitration until after preliminary steps have been taken by the parties to resolve their disputes.[199] These typically involve mediation, or other forms of conciliation procedures (which are sometimes considered, depending on the wording of the clause, to constitute an additional condition for the tribunal's jurisdiction).[200] The admissibility of such procedures is undisputed and has been recognized by Austrian jurisprudence.[201] In terms of drafting, parties should take care in ensuring that the arbitration agreement remains operable.[202]

Under Austrian law, there is an important distinction between a proper arbitration **1-098** agreement (*Schiedsvereinbarung*) on the one hand and an agreement for expert

---

193. OGH, 29 April 2003, 7 Ob 30/02t; recently confirmed by OGH, 26 August 2008, 4 Ob 80/08f.
194. OGH, 24 June 2004, 6 Ob 122/04s; OGH, 21 April 2004, 9 Ob 39/04g; OGH, 29 August 2002, 6 Ob 155/02s.
195. OGH, 3 April 2001, 4 Ob 37/01; OGH, 5 May 1998, 3 Ob 2372/96m.
196. OGH, 17 May 2001, 7 Ob 67/01f; OGH, 5 May 1998, 3 Ob 2372/96m.
197. OGH, 29 August 2002, 6 Ob 155/02s; OGH, 15 December 1971, 5 Ob 208/71.
198. OGH, 22 December 1926, 1 Ob 1062/26, SZ 8/351.
199. C. Debattista, 'Drafting Enforceable Arbitration Clauses' (2005) 21(2) Arb Int'l, 233; *also* A. Redfern, M. Hunter, N. Blackaby and C. Partasides, *Law and Practice of International Commercial Arbitration* (4th edn, London, Sweet & Maxwell, 2004), para. 1-95.
200. For example, if a clause suggests that a dispute can be referred to arbitration only after mediation has been attempted, the tribunal may take the view that it has no jurisdiction to hear the case before such an attempt is made. The difficulty, of course, is in establishing precise enough parameters for determining whether the 'attempt' was sufficient within the meaning of the clause. *See* D.H. Freyer, 'Practical Considerations in Drafting Dispute Resolution Provisions in International Commercial Arbitration Contracts: A US Perspective' (1998) 15(4) J Int'l Arb, 7.
201. In OGH, 17 April 1997, 8 Ob A 2128/96s, where it was held that mediation clauses (*Schlichtungsklauseln*) do not result in the lack of jurisdiction of a state court, but in lack of due date, therefore in a dismissal of the claim.
202. When parties deviate from the model clause suggested by the VIAC, they should bear **Article 9(6)** in mind. It is generally advisable for parties to seek professional assistance in drafting such clauses.

determination (*Schiedsgutachten*) on the other. The latter is generally an agreement whereby a third person is called to give an opinion concerning questions of fact; contrary to a proper arbitration agreement, it is not aimed at finally deciding a dispute with binding effect. Special cases of such expert opinions are expert determinations that assert legal conclusions. Thereby, a third party is entrusted to adapt an existing contractual obligation to a change in circumstances. In such cases, the expert is not only asked to ascertain existing facts, but also to draw legal conclusions – a task usually reserved for arbitrators or judges. However, the authority to draw legal conclusions alone does not result in an arbitration agreement.[203] According to jurisprudence, the decisive criterion is whether the decision can be challenged only on the grounds for setting aside an arbitration award or if, additionally, the state court should have the authority to review the case on the merits.[204]

1-099 The distinction is essential, as expert agreements do not fall under the scope of Sections 577-618 ZPO; hence, they are not, *inter alia*, covered by any specific legal form requirements.[205] Contrary to arbitration agreements (which result in a waivable bar to the court's jurisdiction),[206] a claim that is subject to expert determination is simply not due for as long as the expert procedure is not completed.[207]

7.   Third Parties

1-100 In light of the increasing complexity of disputes referred to arbitration, the question if and to what extent third parties, in particular non-signatories, are bound by an arbitration agreement is an important issue of modern arbitration law and currently subject of intense debate.[208] This includes the question of whether or not an

---

203. OGH, 27 February 1985, 1 Ob 504/85.
204. OGH, 17 August 2001, 1 Ob 300/00z. In case it is in doubt whether one deals with an expert opinion or an arbitration award, Section 612 ZPO now explicitly allows for an application to the state court for the determination of the existence or non-existence of an award if the applicant has a legal interest therein.
205. W. Melis, 'Austria' in *International Handbook on Commercial Arbitration* (The Hague, Kluwer Law International, Suppl. 10, 1989), p. 2; H.W. Fasching, *Schiedsgericht und Schiedsverfahren im österreichischen und im internationalen Recht* (Vienna, Manz, 1973), p. 25; C. Liebscher and A. Schmid in *Practitioner's Handbook on International Arbitration*, F.B. Weigand (ed.) (Munich, C.H. Beck, 2002), p. 542 and F. Matscher, 'Probleme der Schiedsgerichtsbarkeit im österreichischen Recht' [1975] JBl, 412, 416; for a detailed list of case law *see* G. Zeiler, *Schiedsverfahren* (Vienna/Graz, Neuer Wissenschaftlicher Verlag, 2006), Section 581, p. 78.
206. *See* **Article 1**, at paras. 085 *et seq.*
207. OGH, 17 August 2001, 1 Ob 300/00z with reference to EvBl 1985, 119; SZ 62/167; 3 Ob 507/91, 8 Ob A 2128/96s and 1 Ob 211/99g.
208. For a discussion on various such theories, *see, e.g.*, J. Lew, L. Mistelis and S. Kröll, *Comparative International Commercial Arbitration* (The Hague, Kluwer Law International, 2003), paras. 7-36 *et seq.*; E. Gaillard and J. Savage (eds), *Fouchard Gaillard Goldmann On*

arbitration agreement concluded by a company can be considered binding on one of its affiliates, usually the group's ultimate controlling shareholder.[209] The party seeking to 'pierce the corporate veil' attempts to emphasize the legitimacy of addressing the 'true' party in interest, often the financially better-situated member of a group of companies. This typically meets the objection that corporate identity is created precisely for the purpose of confining personal liability within a corporate entity.[210]

The issue of extending the arbitration agreement to third parties – so-called 'non-signatories', such as assignees, members of the same group of companies, and third party beneficiaries – is discussed in detail *below*, in the context of multi-party arbitrations under **Article 15**. **1-101**

8. The VIAC's Recommended Arbitration Clause

For institutional arbitration, it is necessary for the parties to refer the dispute to a specific institution. By virtue of such reference, the parties incorporate the rules of that institution into their arbitration agreement. The VIAC recommends that parties use the following clause: **1-102**

> Alle Streitigkeiten, die sich aus diesem Vertrag ergeben oder auf dessen Verletzung, Auflösung oder Nichtigkeit beziehen, werden nach der Schieds- und Schlichtungsordnung des Internationalen Schiedsgerichts der Wirtschaftskammer Österreich in Wien (Wiener Regeln) von einem oder mehreren gemäß diesen Regeln ernannten Schiedsrichtern endgültig entschieden.

and provides the following translation from the authentic[211] German text: **1-103**

> All disputes arising out of this contract or related to its violation, termination or nullity shall be finally settled under the Rules of Arbitration and Conciliation of the International Arbitral Centre of the Austrian Federal Economic Chamber in Vienna (Vienna Rules) by one or more arbitrators appointed in accordance with these Rules.

As appropriate supplementary provisions, the VIAC further recommends that the agreement also indicates the number of arbitrators (absent such agreement, **1-104**

International Commercial Arbitration (The Hague, Kluwer Law International, 1999), para. 500; W.L. Craig, W.W. Park and J. Paulsson, *International Chamber of Commerce Arbitration* (3rd edn, New York, Oceana Publications, 2000), pp. 74-75, pp. 171-179; O. Sandrock, ' "Intra" and "Extra-Entity" Agreements to Arbitrate and their Extension to Non-Signatories Under German Law' (2002) 19(5) J Int'l Arb, 423.

209. For details *see* B. Hanotiau, 'Complex – multicontract-multiparty – arbitrations' (1998) 14(4) Arb Int'l, 369.

210. A. Redfern, M. Hunter, N. Blackaby and C. Partasides, *Law and Practice of International Commercial Arbitration* (4th edn, London, Sweet & Maxwell, 2004), para. 3-31.

211. The authenticity of the German version of the Vienna Rules is discussed under **Article 1**, at para. 157.

the VIAC will determine the number under **Article 14(2)**). Amongst other things, the parties are free to agree upon the place of the arbitration; the language to be used in the arbitral proceedings;[212] and the laws applicable to the substance of the dispute.[213] In case parties deviate from the recommended arbitration clause, consideration should be given to the Board's authority under **Article 9(6)** to refuse to administer the proceedings.[214]

C.   THE ADMINISTRATION OF 'ARBITRABLE' DISPUTES

1-105 The existence of an arbitration agreement is not enough; Article 1 also requires the existence of a dispute. Although this term is quite commonly used in international arbitration rules,[215] there is no express definition of what constitutes a dispute. The Vienna Rules do not even specify that the dispute must be of a commercial nature.[216] The term 'dispute' should be interpreted broadly to include any disagreement or controversy between the parties.[217]

1-106 Of course, Article 1 only applies to disputes that can be resolved by arbitration. Therefore, the reference to 'disputes' under Article 1 is in fact related to the general issue of *arbitrability* under the applicable law.

1-107 Here, the contractual freedom of the parties and the impositions of mandatory law meet head on. Arbitrability involves the ostensibly simple question of which issues can and cannot be submitted to arbitration. On the one hand, party autonomy espouses the right of parties to submit any dispute to arbitration. It is the parties' right to opt out of the customary national court jurisdiction.[218] On the other hand, whether or not a particular type of dispute is 'arbitrable' under a given law is, in essence, a matter of public policy that the law must determine.[219] For that reason,

---

212. In this context, the VIAC rightly proposes that consideration should be given to the possible application of the United Nations Convention on Contracts for the International Sale of Goods, 1980.
213. *See* **Article 24**, at paras. 004 *et seq.*
214. *See* **Article 9(6)**, at paras. 088 *et seq.*
215. *See* Article 1 ICC Rules; Article 1(1)(c) LCIA Rules and Article 1(1) AAA/ICDR Rules.
216. *See, e.g.*, Article 1(1) ICC Rules and Y. Derains and E.A. Schwartz, *A Guide to the ICC Rules of Arbitration* (2nd edn, The Hague, Kluwer Law International, 2005), p. 11 with further references.
217. Black's Law Dictionary defines dispute as 'conflict or controversy, especially one that has given rise to a particular lawsuit'. *See* B.A. Garner, *Black's Law Dictionary* (8th edn, St. Pauls, Thomson West, 2004).
218. J. Lew, L. Mistelis and S. Kröll, *Comparative International Commercial Arbitration* (The Hague, Kluwer Law International, 2003), para. 9-1; J.P. Lachmann, *Handbuch für die Schiedsgerichtspraxis* (3rd edn, Cologne, Verlag Dr. Otto Schmidt, 2008), p. 77.
219. *Redfern/Hunter* indicate categories which typically fall outside the scope of arbitration such as patents, trademarks and copyrights, antitrust and competition laws, securities transactions, bribery and corruption and fraud. *See* A. Redfern, M. Hunter, N. Blackaby and C. Partasides, *Law and Practice of International Commercial Arbitration* (4th edn, London, Sweet & Maxwell, 2004), para. 3-15.

Article 1(5) of the UNCITRAL Model Law did not, as one might expect, provide a list of non-arbitrable matters. Instead, it relies on the domestic provisions on arbitrability of the enacting state.[220]

An award on a non-arbitrable matter is subject to being set aside by the Austrian **1-108** courts.[221] The following section provides a general overview (rather than a conclusive description) of the former and current legal position under Austrian law. Given their practical importance, a few topics, such as arbitrability in corporate matters and cartel law, are addressed separately.

1.   Objective Arbitrability Under the Old Regime

Under the former Austrian arbitration law, *objective arbitrability* required that the **1-109** dispute in question be capable of settlement, which in turn presupposes that the subject matter of the dispute is at the disposition of the parties.[222]

Section 577(1) fZPO provided: **1-110**

> An agreement that a legal dispute shall be settled by one or more arbitrators (an arbitration agreement) is valid insofar as the parties are entitled to conclude a settlement concerning the subject matter of the dispute.

Objective arbitrability is the characteristic *sine qua non* for a legal matter in order **1-111** to be the subject of an arbitration agreement. Should this characteristic be missing with regard to the matter of the dispute, the arbitration agreement is considered null and void.

According to *Fasching*, the objective limits of arbitrability were defined in **1-112** Sections 577(1) and (2) fZPO itself. It was therefore necessary that the subject matter of a dispute is referred to a *decision on the merits*, in respect of which the parties are entitled to conclude a *settlement*. Requests by parties for mere procedural declarations therefore did not even raise the question of arbitrability. Arbitration agreements referring only parts of a dispute to arbitration, on the other hand, are permissible insofar as this constitutes a request for a decision *in rem* (similar to partial judgments according to Section 391 ZPO). Agreements that limit the authority of the arbitral tribunal to a decision either on liability or on quantum are therefore admissible.[223]

---

220. Although the drafters regarded it as desirable to limit the number of non-arbitrable subject matters. *See* M. Roth in *Practitioner's Handbook on International Arbitration*, F.B. Weigand (ed.) (Munich, C.H. Beck, 2002), p. 1172. For an overview of the different approaches taken in England, France and Switzerland, *see* C. Liebscher, *The Healthy Award* (The Hague, Kluwer Law International, 2003), pp. 169 *et seq.*
221. *See* **Article 1**, at para. 138 and **Article 27**, at paras. 058 *et seq.*
222. K. Heller, *Der verfassungsrechtliche Rahmen der Privaten Internationalen Schiedsgerichtsbarkeit* (Vienna, Manz, 1996), p. 32.
223. H.W. Fasching, *Schiedsgericht und Schiedsverfahren im österreichischen und im internationalen Recht* (Vienna, Manz, 1973), p. 15.

1-113 Additionally, the dispute must, as a threshold requirement, concern a subject matter that can be the subject of a court decision within the meaning of Section 1 JN (*bürgerliche Rechtssache*).[224] Arbitration agreements which attempt to refer a claim to an arbitral tribunal for which there is no legal recourse to a national court are void; any awards based on such agreements are, according to *Fasching*, subject to challenge.[225] If a subject matter is inadmissible in proceedings before the state courts (e.g. issues of administrative law), it is therefore always inadmissible in arbitration proceedings. In such cases, where a court's decision is neither permissible nor possible, a 'legal dispute' within the meaning of Section 577 fZPO does not exist.[226]

1-114 The term 'legal dispute' shall be understood as a synonym for legal proceedings, but does not necessarily mean that the claim in question is actually disputed. The arbitration agreement is also effective when the matter in dispute has been accepted before proceedings were initiated or the claim has been amicably settled.[227] Future disputes can be referred to arbitration as long as the subject matter is sufficiently specified.[228]

1-115 Austrian commentators have been reluctant to identify specific guidelines for the requirement that arbitrable disputes are those that are 'capable of settlement'. An overview of case law and commentary addressing the former ZPO may still be informative.

1-116 Arbitration agreements that concern matters of procedure seem problematic insofar as such matters are reserved for the state courts. In similar vein, arbitration agreements which intend to override state court procedural measures, such as those concerning claims under the Enforcement Code (*Exekutionsordnung* – EO), are not permissible. *Fasching* also indicates that the legal effect (*Rechtskraft*) of a decision is beyond the parties' disposition. Arbitrations deciding on the alleged nullity of a court decision are therefore not possible. The same is true for the decision on re-opening the proceedings after a final award has been rendered.[229] On the other hand, the parties are not prevented from concluding an arbitration agreement on the

---

224. H.W. Fasching, *Schiedsgericht und Schiedsverfahren im österreichischen und im internationalen Recht* (Vienna, Manz, 1973), p. 16.

225. H.W. Fasching, *Schiedsgericht und Schiedsverfahren im österreichischen und im internationalen Recht* (Vienna, Manz, 1973), p. 16. For a discussion on the consequences of a decision in a non-arbitrable subject *see* **Article 1**, at paras. 135 *et seq.* and **Article 27**, at paras. 058 *et seq.*

226. This means, for example, that a mere dispute as to a claim of facts (with certain exceptions, e.g. the authenticity of a document) lacks objective arbitrability, just as if it were a dispute about an abstract legal question. Courts will not hear requests to ascertain legal facts, or evaluate legal principles; in the abstract; arbitral tribunals cannot be used to undertake what courts will not do.

227. For a discussion on the requirement of defined legal relationship, *see* **Article 1**, at paras. 048 *et seq.*

228. H.W. Fasching, *Schiedsgericht und Schiedsverfahren im österreichischen und im internationalen Recht* (Vienna, Manz, 1973), p. 16.

229. *See* OGH, 5 December 1901, Nr. 14, 451, GlUNF 2543.

legal consequences of changes in the facts of the dispute after an award has become final.[230]

According to Austrian jurisprudence, matters of so-called 'non-contentious pro- **1-117** ceedings' (*Außerstreitsachen*) are arbitrable if the parties are capable to settle such disputes.[231] *Fasching* offers a more differentiated view and considers arbitration agreements on matters of 'non-contentious proceedings' not permissible: (1) when the public interest is effected, such that proceedings are, or can be, commenced *ex officio* by the state courts (e.g. matters of inheritance or civil guardianship); (2) when *ex officio* participation of a state representative is necessary to protect the public interest, so that arbitrators cannot decide matters only a state court vested with public authority can decide (e.g. matters regarding the public land register; the commercial register; the validity of public documents; or the determination of a person's civil status); or (3) cases of special protection of juveniles or curatorship.[232]

In Austrian case law, several categories of disputes have so far *not* been considered **1-118** *arbitrable* under the old regime, such as claims to nullify or set aside a judgment; compensation claims against managing directors of a limited liability company,[233] claims to extract a share of the capital of a limited liability company and claims by a shareholder of a limited liability company concerning the recognition of a loan as a contribution-in-kind.[234] Furthermore, issuance of interim measures or other security measures,[235] enforcement claims,[236] certain disputes in land leasehold and tenant relations,[237] and specific labour disputes were not deemed arbitrable under

---

230. H.W. Fasching, *Schiedsgericht und Schiedsverfahren im österreichischen und im internationalen Recht* (Vienna, Manz, 1973), p. 13.
231. OGH, 6 September 1984, 6 Ob 16/84.
232. H.W. Fasching, *Schiedsgericht und Schiedsverfahren im österreichischen und im internationalen Recht* (Vienna, Manz, 1973), p. 15.
233. *See* OGH, 14 July 1993, 7 Ob 548/93. But claims arising out of the termination of an employment contract by shareholders' agreement have been considered arbitrable. *See* OGH, 10 December 1998, 7 Ob 221/98w. Differentiating positions when the obligation to contribute to the application to the Commercial Register is concerned. *See* OGH, 29 April 2003, 1 Ob 22/03x.
234. OGH, 14 July 1993, 7 Ob 548/93.
235. *See* OGH, 7 June 1977, 4 Ob 350/77, SZ 50/83; OLG Vienna, 22 January 1947, I R 37, EvBl 1947, 100.
236. *See* Sections 35, 36, 37, 233 and 258 EO and claims in connection with Section 308 EO.
237. For leasehold relations *see* OGH, 26 May 1986, 8 Ob 572/86 and OGH, 26 May 1986, 8 Ob 572/86; for tenancy matters *see* OGH, 8 June 2000, 2 Ob 158/00z; OGH, 5 October 1946, 1 Ob 127/46 and OGH, 28 November 1995, 10 Ob 1615/95; OGH, 13 July 1999, 5 Ob 186/99k; W.H. Rechberger and W. Melis in *Kommentar zur ZPO*, W.H. Rechberger (ed.) (2nd edn, Vienna/New York, Springer, 2000), Section 577, para. 5. Even certain disputes under so-called 'non-contentious proceedings' (*Außerstreitverfahren*) in respect to Section 37 MRG are considered not to be arbitrable; C. Liebscher and A. Schmid in *Practitioner's Handbook on International Arbitration*, F.B. Weigand (ed.) (Munich, C.F. Beck, 2002), p. 546, with

the old law.[238] As arbitral disputes have to be capable of settlement, certain disputes in connection with marriage and family law are also not arbitrable,[239] and the same holds for criminal matters, matters of public law, and certain disputes relating to insolvency[240] and equalization.[241] Disputes regarding intellectual property rights are, in principle, capable of being referred to arbitration.[242]

2. Objective Arbitrability Under the New Law

1-119 The approach adopted under the former arbitration law was somewhat casuistic. The intention of the Austrian legislature was therefore 'to create a clear and, also for international users, unambiguous solution to avoid problems of interpretation'.[243] Section 582(1) ZPO now provides:

> Any claim involving an economic interest that lies within the jurisdiction of the courts of law can be the subject of an arbitration agreement. An arbitration agreement on claims which do not involve an economic interest shall be legally effective insofar as the parties are capable of concluding a settlement on the issue in dispute.

1-120 This provision follows the solution adopted in Germany, which addresses the issue of arbitrability by expressly declaring that 'any claim involving an economic interest (*vermögensrechtlicher Anspruch*) can be the subject of an arbitration

---

reference to OGH, 8 June 2000, 2 Ob 158/00z; A. Reiner, 'Zur objektiven Schiedsfähigkeit von Streitigkeiten aus dem MRG unterliegenden Mietverträgen' [2001] wobl, 161; G. Backhausen, *Schiedsgerichtsbarkeit unter besonderer Berücksichtigung des Schiedsvertragsrechts* (Vienna, Manz, 1990), pp. 107 *et seq.* with further annotations; K. Lionnet and A. Lionnet, *Handbuch der internationalen und nationalen Schiedsgerichtsbarkeit* (3rd edn, Stuttgart, Richard Boorberg Verlag, 2005), pp. 39 *et seq.*, providing an overview over German, French, Swiss and US tendencies.

238. Although the amendment of Section 9(2) ASGG extended the scope of arbitrability to future labour disputes of managing directors and board members. *See* R. Peschek, 'Neue Möglichkeiten für Schiedsverfahren im Arbeitsrecht' [2003] RdW, 153; R. Dittrich and H. Tades (eds), *Arbeitsrecht* (Vienna, Manz, 2007), p. 2064; W.H. Rechberger and W. Melis in *Kommentar zur ZPO*, W.H. Rechberger (ed.) (2nd edn, Vienna/New York, Springer, 2000), Section 577, para. 7; also OGH, 29 June 1988, 9 Ob A 134/88 and OGH, 16 November 1988, 9 Ob A 270/88.

239. Such as disputes about the cancellation of a marriage, divorce claims or claims about acknowledgement of paternity.

240. A. Fremuth, 'Schiedsverfahren und Konkurs: Zur Bindung des Masseverwalters an Schiedsvereinbarungen des Gemeinschuldners' [1998] ÖJZ, 848.

241. H.W. Fasching, *Lehrbuch des österreichischen Zivilprozeßrechts* (2nd edn, Vienna, Manz, 1990), para. 2174 with further annotations.

242. However, disputes about the valid grant or revocation of intellectual property rights, e.g. trademarks and patents, are not considered to be arbitrable. *See* C. Liebscher and A. Schmid in *Practitioner's Handbook on International Arbitration*, F.B. Weigand (ed.) (Munich, C.H. Beck, 2002), p. 546 with further references.

243. Explanatory Notes to Section 582.

agreement'.[244] According to *Liebscher*, the phrase 'claim involving an economic interest' should be interpreted broadly. It also encompasses claims that are not aimed at a payment – such as claims for the challenge of a shareholder resolution.[245]

The second sentence of Section 582(1) ZPO also follows Section 1030 German **1-121** ZPO and mirrors the wording of Section 577 fZPO.[246] Hence, claims that do not involve an economic interest are legally subject to an arbitration agreement 'insofar as the parties are capable of concluding a settlement on the issue in dispute'.

According to *Oberhammer*, such (non-economic) disputes will rarely be subject to **1-122** arbitration. The direct reference to 'non-economic interest' was added to explicitly make claims arbitrable that do not involve an economic interest, or where it is at least difficult to ascertain such an economic interest. Thus, if the claim can be settled by an agreement, it is arbitrable, even though this claim might not involve an economic interest.[247]

Indeed, *Liebscher* considers this additional wording as 'meant to keep the circle of **1-123** claims that are not objectively arbitrable as small as possible'. In his opinion, claims that are to be decided by Austrian administrative authorities (e.g. disputes between Austrian local authorities involving an economic interest) are non-arbitrable.[248] *Reiner* also applies this to administrative claims that must be decided by regulatory or supervisory authorities (anti-trust, public procurement, or telecommunications) as well as claims under the Patent Office (abandonment, revocation or denial of patents, cancellation of a trademark).[249] Thus, only claims that

---

244. Section 1030 German ZPO: (1) Any claim involving an economic interest (*vermögensrechtlicher Anspruch*) can be the subject of an arbitration agreement. An arbitration agreement concerning claims not involving an economic interest shall have legal effect to the extent that the parties are entitled to conclude a settlement on the issue in dispute. (2) An arbitration agreement relating to disputes on the existence of a lease of residential accommodation within Germany shall be null and void. This does not apply to residential accommodation as specified in Section 549(2) nos 1-3 of the Civil Code. (3) Statutory provisions outside this Book by virtue of which certain disputes may not be submitted to arbitration, or may be submitted to arbitration only under certain conditions, remain unaffected.
245. C. Liebscher, *The Austrian Arbitration Act 2006: Text and Notes* (The Hague, Kluwer Law International, 2006), Annotated Text to Section 582(1) ZPO.
246. *See* **Article 1**, at paras. 109 *et seq.*
247. P. Oberhammer additionally admits that sentence 2 is in fact superfluous, as practically all disputes – due to the broad understanding of the term – which are considered arbitrable should be covered. In order to avoid a too narrow interpretation of the term 'claim that involves an economic interest', it was deliberately chosen to leave this as extra clarification. *See* P. Oberhammer, *Entwurf eines neuen Schiedsverfahrensrechts* (Vienna, Manz, 2002), pp. 40 *et seq.*
248. C. Liebscher, *The Austrian Arbitration Act 2006: Text and Notes* (The Hague, Kluwer Law International, 2006), Annotated Text to Section 582(1) ZPO.
249. A. Reiner, *Das neue österreichische Schiedsrecht/The new Austrian Arbitration Law* (Vienna, LexisNexis, 2006), Section 582, note 33.

involve an economic interest that are based on civil law and fall under the jurisdiction of the national civil courts are arbitrable; claims which must be submitted to administrative authorities are excluded, so as to prevent parties from using arbitration to evade provisions of mandatory public policy.[250]

1-124 In addition, the ZPO now includes a catalogue of subject matters that are excluded from arbitration.[251] These are, according to Section 582(2) ZPO:

> Claims involving family law, as well as all claims arising out of contracts that are even only partially subject to the Landlord and Tenant Act or the Limited-Profit Housing Act, including disputes about the conclusion, existence, termination, and legal classification of such contracts, and all claims involving condominium law, cannot be the subject of an arbitration agreement. Statutory provisions outside this section by virtue of which certain disputes may not be submitted to arbitration, or may be submitted to arbitration only under certain conditions, shall remain unaffected.

1-125 The last sentence of Section 582(2) ZPO, by referring to other provisions that 'remain unaffected', makes clear that the enumeration of non-arbitrable matters in this provision is not exclusive. This refers in particular to employment law matters, which have been included in Chapter 10 (special provisions), Section 618 ZPO. This provision, by reference to Sections 617(2)-(7) ZPO (a special provision for consumers) introduces specific form requirements and procedural rules for arbitration with employees.[252] Limited in scope, it only applies to arbitration proceedings in labour law matters within the meaning of Section 50(1) ASGG.[253] As Section 9(2) ASGG remained largely unchanged, the main issue for non-executive employees is that arbitration agreements in employment matters will continue to be valid only for disputes that exist at the time the arbitration agreement was concluded; future disputes in employment matters cannot be referred to arbitration. However, after the amendment of the Labour and Social Courts Act (*Arbeits- und Sozialgerichtsgesetz* – ASGG) in 2002, this position changed for managing directors of limited liability companies and members of the Board of a joint stock company, who may now validly conclude an arbitration agreement before a dispute arises.[254]

---

250. *See* draft of the commentary to Section 582 ZPO.
251. Some Model Law States expressly stipulate that the fact that an enactment confers jurisdiction with respect to any matter on a court or other tribunal does not refer to determination by arbitration does not, by itself, indicate that a dispute about that matter is non-arbitrable. *See* M. Roth in *Practitioner's Handbook on International Arbitration*, F.B. Weigand (ed.) (Munich, C.H. Beck, 2002), p. 1173.
252. *See* in more detail **Article 1**, at paras. 037 *et seq.*
253. Section 618 ZPO. Labour law matters within the meaning of Section 50(1) ASGG are, in particular, disputes between employers and employees in connection with an employment relationship or its initiation.
254. In these cases, particular caution is advisable with regard to the place of arbitration as one might not know in what country the manager or Board member has his or her place of

3. Objective Arbitrability in Corporate Matters

In the last few years, more and more questions have arisen concerning arbitration **1-126** agreements in corporate matters. In international transactions, this has become the standard rather than the exception, and business entities have started including arbitration agreements in their charters, statutes and company agreements.

The issue of objective arbitrability has been discussed mostly in connection with **1-127** the arbitrability of defective shareholder resolutions according to Section 41 GmbHG.[255] In 2 Ob 276/50, 3 June 1950, the Austrian *Oberster Gerichtshof* confirmed the objective arbitrablity of such disputes and held that parties could validly agree to refer a dispute about an action for annulment of a shareholders' resolution to arbitration. It reasoned that the parties could enter into a valid arbitration agreement as long as the subject matter is capable of settlement, such as the action for annulment of a resolution. In 1 Ob 22/03x, 29 April 2003, the Austrian *Oberster Gerichtshof* confirmed the objective arbitrability of such disputes and held that the company agreement gives rise to an implied duty of the shareholder to support the registration into the commercial register and confirmed that disputes of this matter are capable of settlement, and hence, arbitrable. However, in this decision, the Austrian *Oberster Gerichtshof* also held that disputes are not arbitrable when they involve mainly public interests or the protection of specific groups of persons. As previously discussed, arbitration agreements are invalid when the public interest is affected in such a way that requires the *ex officio* commencement of proceedings or participation of a public interest representative, or if the decision at bar could only be rendered by a national court.

Thoeni's in-depth analysis in 1994 introduced a differentiated conclusion: An **1-128** action for annulment of a shareholders' resolution is, in principle, arbitrable insofar as the shareholders are capable of settling the dispute amongst themselves by simply repeating the internal procedure for adopting shareholder resolutions in order to cure previous defects. This is the case with resolutions that have legal effect only as amongst the shareholders themselves.[256] In 7 Ob 221/98w,

---

residence, domicile or centre of business activities at the time of commencing the arbitration. *See* A. Reiner, *Das neue österreichische Schiedsrecht/The new Austrian Arbitration Law* (Vienna, LexisNexis, 2006), Section 618, note 236. Additionally, the competency to set aside arbitral awards has been fully assigned to the Regional Courts functionally acting as Labour and Social Courts. *See in detail* J. Power, *The Austrian Arbitration Act – A Practitioner's Guide to Sections 577-618 of the Austrian Code of Civil Procedure* (Vienna, Manz, 2006), Section 618, paras. 1 *et seq.*

255. *See in detail* H.-G. Koppensteiner, *GmbH-Gesetz Kommentar* (2nd edn, Vienna, Orac, 1999), Section 41, pp. 430 *et seq.*; M. Gellis and E. Feil, *Kommentar zum GmbH-Gesetz* (5th edn, Vienna, Verlag Linde, 2006), Section 41, pp. 508 *et seq.*

256. W. Thöni, 'Zur Schiedsfähigkeit des GmbH-rechtlichen Anfechtungsstreits' [1994] wbl, 298; *T. Wenger* draws further practical conclusions from this decision and considers a dispute as arbitrable if those affected (in particular all shareholders) have agreed to refer the dispute to arbitration. If the arbitration agreement was included in the articles of association or company

10 December 1998, the Austrian *Oberster Gerichtshof* addressed this point and additionally discussed the *res judicata* effect of an arbitration award on a party who was not provided the right to be heard:

> The right to participate in the proceedings is properly granted, when the other shareholders *could* – like in an action for annulment – join the proceedings in a third-party intervention, whereas the arbitrator has no discretionary power not to allow such a participation.

1-129 This decision requires that, where participation of all shareholders is mandated by statutory law (such as Section 42 GmbHG), all shareholders have the opportunity to participate in the arbitration. This presumes necessarily that all shareholders are parties to the same arbitration agreement – which is typically the case if the relevant arbitration clause is contained in the statute (articles) of the company concerned. Based on this decision, therefore, arbitral tribunals have in practice regularly requested the claimant party to provide separate proof that all shareholders of the company's resolution involved have been given the right to participate in the proceedings. It should be noted, therefore, that answering the question of arbitrability does not necessarily answer the question of which person should actually participate in the arbitration proceeding. Hence, although the objective arbitrability of disputes has now been expanded to 'claims involving an economic interest',[257] arbitrators in such circumstances need to carefully ensure the participation of all shareholders concerned, for example, by way of interventions in order to make certain that the award has a *res judicata* effect on third persons.[258] Indeed, where the applicable substantive law requires the participation of all shareholders, claims against only some of them may have to be dismissed on the merits.[259]

4.   Arbitration and Competition Law

1-130 The role of arbitrators in disputes that involve or are subject to competition law, either directly or indirectly, has provoked considerable debate.[260] The *former*

---

agreement (*Gesellschaftsvertrag*), this condition is satisfied. Therefore, every shareholder must consent if an arbitration agreement is included in the articles of association at a later date. *See* T. Wenger, 'Schiedsklausel im GmbH-Gesellschaftsvertrag' [1999] RWZ, 108. Reference is made to the difficulty to conclude an arbitration agreement when consumers are participating in the arbitration agreement. *See* **Article 1**, at paras. 037 *et seq.*

257. *See* objective arbitrability under the new regime at **Article 1**, at paras. 119 *et seq.* and a more recent analysis on the objective arbitrability in corporate matters in B. Terlitza and M. Weber, 'Zur Schiedsfähigkeit gesellschaftsrechtlicher Streitigkeiten' [2008] (2) ÖJZ.

258. Explanatory Notes to Section 582 ZPO.

259. *See* also **Article 15**, at paras. 013 *et seq.*

260. *See* discussion in H. van Houtte, 'Conduct of Arbitral Proceedings' in *Essays on International Commercial Arbitration*, P. Sarcevic (ed.) (Leiden, Brill, 1989); H. van Houtte, 'Arbitration and Arts. 81 and 82 EC Treaty – A State of Affairs' (2005) 23(3) Bull ASA, 431; T.D. de Groot, 'The impact of the Benetton Decision on International Commercial Arbitration' (2003) 20(4) J Int'l Arb, 365; G. Blanke, 'Defining the limits of scrutiny of awards based on alleged violations of

Austrian Cartel Act (*Kartellgesetz* – KartG),[261] and specifically Section 124 KartG restricted the arbitrability of such matters. Under this old regime, a party faced with a dispute arising from a cartel agreement,[262] which contained an arbitration clause was not prevented from requesting a court decision, as long as it had not yet nominated an arbitrator or applied for the nomination or decision of an arbitrator or a tribunal.

Furthermore, arbitrators had the duty to verifiably inform the opposing party of its **1-131** right to apply to a state court before granting the requesting party its right to be heard.[263] This attracted considerable criticism,[264] and with good reason. The last major amendment of the Cartel Act,[265] which came into effect on 1 January 2006, thus abolished this restriction, bringing Austrian law in line with the laws of

European Competition Law' (2006) 23(3) J Int'l Arb, 249; Y. Brulard and Y. Quintin, 'European Community Law and Arbitration – National versus Community Public Policy' (2001) 18(5) J Int'l Arb, 533; J. Beechey, 'Arbitrability of Anti-trust/Competition Law Issues – Common Law' (1996) 12(2) Arb Int'l, 179 and M.S. Kurkela, R.C. Levin, C. Liebscher and P. Sommer, 'Certain Procedural Issues in Arbitrating Competition Cases' (2007) 24(2) J Int'l Arb, 189; for Austria, *see* C. Liebscher, 'European Public Policy and the Austrian Supreme Court' (2000) 16(3) Arb Int'l, 357; D. Thalhammer, 'Die Rolle der Schiedsgerichte bei der Durchsetzung von EG-Kartellrecht unter dem Regime der VO 1/2003' [2005] wbl, 62.

261. BGBl. No. 600/1988 in its version of BGBl No. 693/1993.
262. Particularly referring to a contractual penalty or stoppage.
263. If the party was not represented by a lawyer and the tribunal failed to instruct the party on its special right verifiably, this party might have requested a court decision until the rendering of the award (Section 124(2) KartG; furthermore, enforcing an award in this matter required certain notification procedure in advance, Section 125 KartG); an award contradicting Article 81 ECT would violate the *ordre public* and be subject to vacatur. *See* J. Reich-Rohrwig and J. Zehetner, *Kartellrecht I* (Vienna, Linde, 2000), pp. 397 *et seq.* Rather recently, the Austrian *Oberster Gerichtshof* ruled in 1 Ob 270/03t, 16 December 2003, that this provision was not applicable to vertical distribution agreements (*vertikale Vertriebsvereinbarungen*). The Austrian *Oberster Gerichtshof* argued that such agreements – contrary to cartels, which need to be notified and authorized – do only have to be notified and, as long as not prohibited, can be freely agreed upon. Furthermore, there exist block exemptions for the automobile industry. In the explanatory of the transitional provisions it had been clarified that notified agreements will seize to be considered as cartels anymore. As already expressed in 1 Ob 300/00z, 17 August 2001, the Austrian *Oberster Gerichtshof* ruled that - according to the explanatory notes - the precedence of the national courts is justified by the public interest and the continuity in the decision-making. *In concreto* this public interest was not affected to such an extent that an exclusion of arbitration would have been necessary. In 1 Ob 300/00z, 17 August 2001, the Austrian *Oberster Gerichtshof* further ruled that an agreement to jointly appoint an expert in compliance with Section 5(3) GVO-Kfz 1995 shall be construed as an arbitrator's expert opinion (*Schiedsgutachterabrede*).
264. A. von Saucken, *Die Reform des österreichischen Schiedsverfahrensrechts auf der Basis des UNCITRAL-Modellgesetzes über die Internationale Handelsschiedsgerichtsbarkeit* (Frankfurt, Verlag Peter Lang, 2004), p. 58.
265. BGBl. I No. 61/2005.

Germany and Switzerland, where no restriction on the arbitrability of competition law issues exists.[266]

5. When Is the New Law Applicable to Determine Objective Arbitrability?

1-132 The new ZPO came into force as of 1 July 2006. According to Article VII(2) of the Transitional Provisions, the provisions previously in force apply to arbitration proceedings that were commenced prior to 1 July 2006. Also, according to Article VII(3), the effectiveness of arbitration agreements concluded prior to 1 July 2006 are governed by the provisions of the former ZPO as well.

1-133 This raises interesting questions regarding the law applicable to objective arbitrability. Insofar as objective arbitrability is perceived as a requirement that determines the validity of an arbitration agreement – as the wording of both Section 577(1) fZPO and Section 582(1) ZPO suggests[267] – then objective arbitrability must be assessed according to the former law with respect to all arbitration agreements concluded before 1 July 2006, irrespective of when the arbitration proceedings are eventually initiated. This appears to have been the intention of the legislature.[268]

1-134 However, there are credible arguments to detach, at least in part, the question of objective arbitrability from the validity of the arbitration agreement. Under this view, objective arbitrability is a prerequisite for conducting an arbitration beyond the existence of an arbitration agreement. Indeed, insofar the concept of objective arbitrability protects public policy interests, it may well be perceived as an inherent condition of the proceeding in general and not merely an element in the analysis of whether a valid arbitration agreement was formed. This argument appears to be supported by Section 611(2) no. 7 ZPO which provides that 'an award shall be set aside if the subject matter of the dispute is not arbitrable under Austrian law'[269] – in addition to the provision of Section 611(2) no. 1 ZPO which more generally provides for *vacatur* 'if a valid arbitration agreement does not exist'. If that is so, the new ZPO applies to the question of objective arbitrability with regard to all proceedings commenced after 1 July 2006, irrespective of when the arbitration agreement is concluded. The ultimate answer, of course, will be for the courts to give.

6. Consequences of a Lack of Objective Arbitrability

1-135 The requirement of objective arbitrability becomes particularly important when an award has been rendered on the subject of a non-arbitral matter. How should such

---

266. W. Kühn, 'Arbitrability of Antitrust Disputes in the Federal Republic of Germany' (1987) 3(3) Arb Int'l, 226; M. Blessing, 'Mandatory Rules of Law versus Party Autonomy in International Arbitration' (1997) 14(4) J Int'l Arb, 23.
267. *See also* Article II(1) of the NY Convention, **Annex 11**.
268. Explanatory Notes to Article VII ZPO, Transitional Provisions.
269. *See* **Article 27**, at paras. 058 *et seq.*

an award be treated? Neither Austrian doctrine nor case law on the former arbitration law had in the past presented a unified view on this matter. According to *Backhausen*, such an award was to be considered a 'non-award', ineffective *ipso facto*, which did not even require a challenge according to Section 595 fZPO.[270]

Fasching argued that, because an arbitral award has the same judicial effect of a **1-136** decision *in rem* that attaches to a state court judgment, the basic conditions of existence must be met both for a state court judgment and an arbitral award. If a matter cannot be the subject of court or arbitral proceedings, he also assumed a non-award.[271] *Chiwitt-Oberhammer* was of the opinion that a lack of objective arbitrability generally leads to a successful challenge or *non-exequatur* of the award, but absent any challenge, the arbitral award exists.[272] The same view was expressed by *Rechberger/Melis*;[273] this seemed to reflect modern international doctrine as well.[274]

As regards case law under the former ZPO, the Austrian *Oberster Gerichtshof* **1-137** initially followed *Rechberger/Melis* in 2 Ob 158/00z, 8 June 2000, and considered such an award challengeable under Section 595(1) no. 1 fZPO. However in 5 Ob 123/03d, 13 January 2004, the Austrian *Oberster Gerichtshof* expressly renounced this view and concluded:

> [T]he lack of any basic condition for a formal valid decision leads to a non-award, being ipso facto ineffective, without separate challenge under Section 595 ZPO. In all these cases mandatory law is concerned in the public interest. Therefore,

270. G. Backhausen, *Schiedsgerichtsbarkeit unter besonderer Berücksichtigung des Schiedsvertragsrechts* (Vienna, Manz, 1990), p. 114.

271. H.W. Fasching, *Schiedsgericht und Schiedsverfahren im österreichischen und im internationalen Recht* (Vienna, Manz, 1973), p. 135.

272. T. Chiwitt-Oberhammer, *Der fehlerhafte Schiedsspruch* (Vienna, Verlag Österreich, 2000), p. 136 with further references.

273. W.H. Rechberger and W. Melis, *Kommentar zur ZPO*, W.H. Rechberger (2nd edn, Vienna/New York, Springer, 2000), Section 595, para. 5.

274. *Born* notes that in case a party does not challenge the arbitrability of a particular dispute, it may later be deemed to have waived jurisdictional objections thereto *See* G.B. Born, *International Commercial Arbitration – Commentary and Materials* (2nd edn, The Hague, Kluwer Law International, 2001), p. 880. This seems to suggest that the award would be voidable rather than void. It can therefore not be treated as *non-est*, since the conduct of parties may clearly serve to give it the status of an enforceable award. Most notable is the landmark decision of the US Supreme Court in *Mitsubishi Motors Corp. v Soler Chrysler-Plymouth, Inc.*, 473 U.S. 614 (U.S. S. Ct. 1985). In this regard, *see also Schattner v Girard, Inc.*, 668 F. 2d 1366 (D.C. Cir. 1981). For a civil law approach, *see* decision of the Cour d'Appel de Paris, 15 June 1956, *Sigma v. Bezard* and *Totaliment v. Comptoir Agricole du Pays-Bas Normard* [1957] Dalloz, Jur 587, 588, and J. Robert's note. *Compare*, concerning another French award, regarding exports, with Cour de Cassation, 2e Ch. Civ., 2 December 1964, *S.A.R.L. Douillet et Fils v. Four et Cie.*, (1965) JCP, Ed. G., Pt. II, No. 14, 277 bis, affirming Cour d'Appel de Paris, 14 June 1962, *Ets. Douillet et Cie. v. Comptoirs d'Approvisionnement Pierre Four et Cie.* [1962] Rev Arb, 107; both cited from E. Gaillard and J. Savage (eds), *Fouchard Gaillard Goldman On International Commercial Arbitration* (The Hague, Kluwer Law International, 1999), para. 565.

it cannot be in the parties' discretion to divert such non-awards into valid arbitral awards by simply neglecting to file a challenge. The possibility of the challenge presupposes the validity of the arbitral award.[275]

1-138 The new Austrian arbitration law, however, has put an end to the ongoing discussion and change in jurisprudence. As discussed, Section 611(2) no. 7 ZPO now explicitly provides that 'an award shall be set aside if the subject matter of the dispute is not arbitrable under Austrian law'.[276] The concern voiced by the Austrian *Oberster Gerichtshof* was that parties should not be given the possibility to circumvent the limits of objective arbitrability by simply not setting aside the award and 'curing' such a defect. Section 613 ZPO, therefore, allows for an *ex officio* application of this challenge by any court or authority, providing that

> [i]f a court or another authority determines in another proceeding, for instance in an enforcement proceeding, that there is a reason for setting aside under Section 611(2) nos 7-8, then the award shall be disregarded in this proceeding.

1-139 A similar provision already existed for foreign awards in *exequatur* proceedings.[277]

7.   *Ex Officio* Application by the Arbitral Tribunal

1-140 In principle, arbitrators act within the scope of the parties' request for relief. This follows from the contractual nature of arbitration proceedings. However, there are issues which are regularly addressed by arbitral tribunals *sua sponte*, without any application by the parties. Amongst such issues is often the question of objective arbitrability.[278] Arbitrators may feel they are exceeding their jurisdiction by adjudicating an issue that the parties have not included, or could not include, in the arbitrator's mandate. The issue is particularly difficult where a subject matter is not arbitrable under the *lex loci arbitri*, at the seat of the arbitration (which is relevant for a possible challenge to the award), but *is* arbitrable at the likely place of enforcement.

1-141 However, the question of objective arbitrability of a given dispute is necessarily outside the reach of party autonomy; thus, it should be ascertained by the arbitrators irrespective of the parties' applications. According to *Lew/Mistelis/Kröll*, 'irrespective of the wishes of the parties, the tribunal should always verify the

---

275. With critical remarks T. Chiwitt-Oberhammer and P. Oberhammer, '(Nicht-)Schiedssprüche in außerstreitigen Mietrechtsangelegenheiten' [2005] wobl, 181.

276. *See* **Article 27**, at paras. 058 *et seq.*

277. *Reiner* criticizes that this was done within the framework of the ZPO, as this section conflicts with Sections 606 and 607 ZPO, both dealing with the binding effect of an arbitration award upon the parties. Additionally, this section will be applicable to arbitral settlements according to Section 605 ZPO. *See* A. Reiner, *Das neue österreichische Schiedsrecht/The new Austrian Arbitration Law* (Vienna, LexisNexis, 2006), Section 613, notes 212 and 214.

278. J. Lew, L. Mistelis and S. Kröll, *Comperative International Commercial Arbitration* (The Hague, Kluwer Law International, 2003), paras. 9-39 *et seq.* and 14-8.

arbitrability of a dispute *ex officio*, and should decline jurisdiction if the dispute is not arbitrable.'[279]

D.   THE ADMINISTRATION OF 'INTERNATIONAL' DISPUTES

A further prerequisite for the application of the Vienna Rules and the 'jurisdiction' **1-142** of the VIAC under Article 1 is that the dispute referred to arbitration is 'international'.

This is so if 'not all contracting parties that concluded the arbitration agreement **1-143** have their place of business or their normal residence in Austria'. As the authentic German version of the Vienna Rules demonstrates, the 'place of business' of a contracting party refers to the '*Sitz*',[280] that is, the 'seat' of the contracting parties as determined by applicable corporate law. At least one party's seat needs to be outside Austria, but only *at the time of the conclusion* of the arbitration agreement.[281]

Potentially problematic cases were conceivable where an Austrian company – i.e., **1-144** a company with its legal seat in Austria – has a branch office (rather than a subsidiary) outside the federal territory of Austria, or *vice versa*, where a foreign company maintains a branch office in Austria. It is debatable whether these cases fall within the scope of Article 1; it is even more uncertain whether these types of cases would allow a challenge to the jurisdiction of the tribunal, or support the setting aside or resistance to the enforcement of the award. Some guidance can be found in Article 1(4) of the UNCITRAL Model Law, which states that if a party has more than one place of business, the relevant place of business is the location which has the closest connection to the arbitration agreement.

Indeed, Article 1(1), in its previous form, proved more and more difficult to **1-145** apply, as it made jurisdiction of the VIAC solely dependent on the question of a foreign place of business or normal residence outside Austria. Otherwise

---

279. J. Lew, L. Mistelis and S. Kröll, *Comparative International Commercial Arbitration* (The Hague, Kluwer Law International, 2003), para. 14-8; C. Liebscher and A. Schmid in *Practitioner's Handbook on International Arbitration*, F.B. Weigand (ed.) (Munich, C.H. Beck, 2002), p. 546. According to *Fasching*, the question of subjective arbitrability, and thereby the question of proper authorization, also has to be addressed without any party application. *See* H.W. Fasching, *Schiedsgericht und Schiedsverfahren im österreichischen und im internationalen Recht* (Vienna, Manz, 1973), p. 101. Similar *Lew/Mistelis/Kröll* for issues of EC competition law. *See* J. Lew, L. Mistelis and S. Kröll, *Comparative International Commercial Arbitration* (The Hague, Kluwer Law International, 2003), paras. 19-38 *et seq.* with further references.
280. Section 5(4) GmbHG states clearly that only a place in Austria can be determined as seat of the company. *See* A. Kostner and M. Umfahrer, *GmbH-Handbuch für die Praxis* (5th edn, Vienna, Manz, 1998), paras. 93 *et seq.*; J. Reich-Rohrwig, *Das österreichische GmbH-Recht, I* (2nd edn, Vienna, Manz, 1997), paras. 1/155 *et seq.*
281. Article 1(1), stipulates generally 'that agreement'.

clearly international disputes simply fell outside the jurisdiction of the VIAC because both parties had their place of business or their normal residence in Austria. These problems were addressed with an amendment of Section 139 *Handelskammergesetz*, which in turn led to an amendment of the Vienna Rules in 2000, which clarified the VIAC's mandate under its founding legislation to administer disputes of an international character. Thus, Article 1(1) was amended to allow 'disputes of an international character' to be referred to the VIAC even if both parties have their place of business or normal residence in Austria.

1-146 Again, Article 1(3) of the UNCITRAL Model Law can provide some guidance on what makes a dispute international in character.[282] Irrespective of the parties' place of business, a dispute has an international nature, *inter alia*, if a substantial part of the obligations of the commercial relationship is to be performed outside Austria; if the subject matter of the dispute is outside Austria; or, perhaps, if the parties have expressly stipulated that the subject matter of the arbitration agreement relates to a place outside Austria or if they have agreed on the application of a foreign law.

1-147 In its *prima facie* review, the VIAC interprets this provision broadly, accepting jurisdiction as long as there is at least some international element in the case in question.[283] Thus, the VIAC has in the past accepted jurisdiction where the arbitration clause provided for a procedural language other than German. Similarly, if a company was Austrian at the time of the conclusion of the arbitration agreement but, because of subsequent changes, had its seat outside Austria at the commencement of the proceedings, the dispute should fall within the scope of Article 1(1) because a change of seat accords an international character to the dispute.

1-148 If there are doubts as to whether a dispute is of international character, it is advisable to provide further explanations in the statement of claims. Additionally, if, following a *prima facie* assessment of the statement of claims, the VIAC Secretary General considers the dispute of *national* character, he will draw the claimant's attention to the fact that a regional chamber is competent to decide the dispute. However, as noted previously, the Secretary General undertakes only a *prima facie* assessment; the VIAC is not entitled to make a final decision on this point. Rather, the claimant has the right to demand that an arbitral tribunal be established under the provisions of the Vienna Rules to decide upon jurisdiction, including the international character of the dispute at bar. If the tribunal denies jurisdiction solely

---

282. According to this provision an arbitration is international if (a) the parties to an arbitration agreement have, at the time of the conclusion of that agreement, their places of business in different states; or (b) one of the following places is situated outside the state in which the parties have their places of business: (i) the place of arbitration if determined in, or pursuant to, the arbitration agreement; (ii) any place where a substantial part of the obligations of the commercial relationship is to be performed or the place with which the subject-matter of the dispute is most closely connected; or (c) the parties have expressly agreed that the subject-matter of the arbitration agreement relates to more than one country.

283. *See also* C. Liebscher in *Institutionelle Schiedsgerichtsbarkeit*, R.A. Schütze (ed.) (Cologne, Carl Heymanns Verlag, 2006), p. 13.

on the grounds that the dispute is national, it is debatable whether the dispute should be transferred to the competent regional chamber of commerce, or whether the arbitration tribunal should stay in place to decide the dispute under the (then applicable) set of domestic rules.

II. THE APPLICABLE VERSION OF THE VIENNA RULES

Article 1(2): If the parties have agreed to the jurisdiction of the Centre, these arbitration rules ('Vienna Rules') shall thereby apply in the version valid at the time of commencement of the proceedings.

All arbitral institutions face the same difficulty: In adopting institutional rules, they **1-149** need to strike a balance between reflecting accepted practice and suggesting improvements. Only after several years of experiencing rules in practice can possible deficiencies be removed. Also, arbitration institutions are not entities operating in isolation; they are called upon to take into consideration amendments of the national arbitration law, most immediately of the country where they are established, as well as developments in international arbitral practice.

Amendments to the rules may cause problems for parties who concluded arbitra- **1-150** tion agreements under a certain version of the Vienna Rules without anticipating subsequent changes. This issue is discussed below and in the context of **Article 37**.

A. PREVIOUS AMENDMENTS OF THE VIENNA RULES

From the beginning of the VIAC's activities in 1975 until today, the Vienna Rules **1-151** have been amended five times. The original version was passed by the Board of the AFCC on 15 November 1974 and became effective of 1 January 1975. This date also marked the beginning of the operative activity of the VIAC.

The first amendment, which was actually a complete revision of the Vienna Rules, **1-152** was passed on 17 June 1983; it did not contain any provisions regarding the application of different versions of the Vienna Rules. The second amendment, passed on 3 July 1991, became effective on 1 September 1991. The third amendment was passed on 5 December 1996, taking effect on 1 January 1997. This amendment only revised the costs schedule; the substantive rules remained unchanged.

The fourth amendment was passed on 30 November 2000, taking effect on **1-153** 1 January 2001. The fifth (and, so far, most recent) amendment of the Vienna Rules was in fact a complete revision of the Rules, passed on 3 May 2006 and taking effect on 1 July 2006. The changes in the last amendment were made to bring the Vienna Rules in line with the new Austrian arbitration law.[284]

---

284. *See* **Article 1**, at para. 004.

B.   THE APPLICATION OF AMENDED RULES

1-154 Between the time the arbitration agreement is concluded and the actual dispute arises, a considerable time span, often of many years, may elapse. As a rule, the parties who originally concluded the arbitration agreement had a particular set of rules in mind: those applicable at the specific time of their agreement. A dispute arising subsequently, after the rules have changed, can cause unpleasant surprises; the parties generally assume that the set of rules originally agreed upon will continue to be valid.

1-155 Yet, arbitral institutions have a choice to make. They can either allow for the application of the rules valid at the conclusion of the arbitration agreement, or they can apply the rules valid at the commencement of the proceedings. The Vienna Rules, in Article 1(2), have opted for this latter alternative and provide that the Rules apply in the version valid at the time of 'commencement of the proceedings';[285] this could be understood to be either the date of the filing of the statement of claims with the Secretary General (according to **Article 9**) or the date when the file is transmitted to the arbitral tribunal (according to **Article 12**). **Article 37** clarifies that the new version of the Vienna Rules applies to all proceedings in which the claim was filed after 30 June 2006, hence, the decisive point in time is the filing of the statement of claims with the Secretary General. This also underscores the proposition that the contractual relationship between the institution and the parties commences at the time of first contact of the parties with the institution.[286]

1-156 However, Article 1(2) does not fully resolve the issue. According to **Article 37**, the current version of the Vienna Rules applies to all proceedings in which the claim was filed after 30 June 2006. A similar provision was already included in the 2001 version of the Vienna Rules. Former Article 25 permitted the parties to agree that the proceedings will be conducted according to the rules valid at the date the arbitration agreement was concluded. This approach seems more comprehensive as it gave the parties a choice to opt for that set of rules they had in mind when

---

285.   In essence, this solution follows Article 6(1) ICC Rules which states: 'Where the parties have agreed to submit to arbitration under the Rules they shall be deemed to have submitted ipso facto to the Rules in effect on this date of commencement of the arbitration proceedings unless they have agreed to submit to the Rules in effect on the date of their arbitration agreement.' When the ICC Rules were amended in 1988, the Court followed the policy of applying the amended rules to all arbitration proceedings commenced after the effective date of the new rules. *See* M. Bühler and S. Jarvin in *Practitioner's Handbook on International Arbitration*, F.B. Weigand (ed.) (Munich, C.H. Beck, 2002), p. 156; Y. Derains and E.A. Schwartz, *A Guide to the ICC Rules of Arbitration* (2nd edn, The Hague, Kluwer Law International, 2005), p. 75; a similar approach can be found in Article 1(2) DIS Rules; Article 1(1) AAA/ICDR Rules and in the introduction to the LCIA Rules.

286.   *See* **Article 1**, at paras. 022 *et seq*; K. Hempel and I. Welser, 'Das Schiedsgericht Berlin identisch mit dem Schiedsgericht bei der Kammer für Außenhandel der DDR?' [1993] ÖJZ, 413.

concluding the arbitration agreement.[287] This was and is still particularly necessary for those arbitration agreements concluded prior to 1 January 2001 as the parties at that time cannot conceivably have incorporated Article 1(2) of the *new* Rules. In these cases, the parties should still be entitled to jointly agree to opt for the set of arbitration rules valid at the date of the conclusion of the arbitration agreement. As no procedure for a potential dispute about the question of applicability is or was provided, it can be assumed that the arbitrators must ultimately decide which version of the rules applies.[288]

C.   INTERPRETATION OF THE VIENNA RULES

The Vienna Rules are a set of procedural rules the parties have agreed upon. The **1-157** only authentic version of these rules is the one published in the German language by the VIAC. However, as the Vienna Rules by their very nature are addressing the international business community, they are available in different languages. Currently the VIAC provides its Rules in English, Russian and Czech language translations. An Italian translation is being considered. In case the translation deviates from the German original, the authentic German version will prevail.

There are no formal requirements as to how the arbitration rules or their transla- **1-158** tions have to be published. In the past, the VIAC has, as soon as an amendment has been adopted, distributed written copies and, more recently, also published the latest version on its website.

There may be situations where a strict and verbatim application of the Vienna **1-159** Rules is not possible because the Rules or not clearly worded, or otherwise ambiguous, or else because a literal application would lead to a systematically unsatisfactory result. The question which method of interpretation should then apply mainly depends on whether one takes a contractual or statutory approach. On the one hand, the Vienna Rules can be considered to form part of the parties' arbitration agreement, incorporated by explicit reference. On the other hand, the Vienna Rules can also be considered to form a separate statute by which a third party, an institution, is called upon to administer a case. In that sense, the parties agree to the Vienna Rules as a regulatory framework similar to a choice of law. The better view is to treat the Vienna Rules as a statute for the purposes of interpretation. Once agreed, the parties can control the process only insofar as the Vienna Rules so permit. Indeed, insofar as administrative tasks are concerned, any deviation from the Vienna Rules would require the consent of the VIAC, or else run the risk of the VIAC refusing to administer the arbitration under **Article 9(6)**. Under

---

287. It also declared the former provisions of Articles 21-24 (costs of the proceedings) automatically applicable. **Annex 2a**.
288. This, however, will only be feasible where the existing arbitration law does not contradict such assumption.

Austrian law, the Vienna Rules therefore have to be interpreted according to their literal and systemic meaning and the clear intent of the drafters.[289]

III.   DOMESTIC ARBITRATION

Article 1(3): If parties which had their place of business or normal residence in Austria at the time of conclusion of the arbitration agreement have agreed that their disputes should be finally settled by a sole arbitrator or an arbitral tribunal to be appointed according to the Vienna Rules, and if the dispute is not international in character, the Permanent Arbitral Tribunal of the Vienna Economic Chamber, or, if another venue in Austria has been agreed, of the regional economic chamber in whose territorial jurisdiction the agreed venue is situated, shall be competent to make arrangements for settlement by arbitration. The latter tribunal shall conduct the proceedings in accordance with the rules of arbitration for the Permanent Arbitral Tribunals of the regional economic chambers.

1-160 This provision is the corollary of Article 1(1). Intended as a catch-all for disputes that lack the international character required for administration by the VIAC,[290] Article 1(3) ensures that the domestic nature of an Austrian dispute, despite the parties' agreement on the (international) Vienna Rules, will not result in a pathological or invalid arbitration agreement.[291]

1-161 Article 139(1) WKG enables each regional chamber, with authorization from the economic parliament (*Wirtschaftsparlament*), to establish a regional arbitral institution for disputes in which all parties have their place of business or habitual residence in Austria at the time of the conclusion of the arbitration agreement. These regional institutions will administer domestic Austrian arbitrations. Because parties, when considering the Vienna Rules, regularly choose Vienna as the venue for the arbitration proceedings, the Permanent Arbitral Tribunal of the Vienna Economic Chamber (PATV) will often be the competent body to conduct the proceedings in accordance with its own set of arbitration rules.[292] Any other Regional Economic Chamber, in whose territorial jurisdiction the arbitration is sited, equally may have jurisdiction.

---

289. *See* Section 6 ABGB.
290. *See* **Article 1**, at paras. 005 and 142 *et seq.* Although the wording of Article 1(3) only refers to arbitration agreements that provide for final settlement 'by a sole arbitrator or an arbitral tribunal', the section will apply when the agreement refers to the Vienna Rules without choosing the exact numbers of arbitrators.
291. *See, e.g.*, OGH, 7 February 1990, 3 Ob 609/89, holding that an arbitration agreement between two Austrian undertakings was invalid because it had failed to specify the jurisdiction of an Austrian arbitral institution (*LandeskammerSG*).
292. PATV Rules in force since 1 July 2006, **Annex 7**.

It is conceivable that the jurisdictions of the VIAC and PATV overlap as Article **1-162** 2(3) PATV Rules bases the jurisdiction of the Regional Chamber only on the residence or usual business place of the parties at the time of the conclusion of the arbitration agreement. In case domestic parties have a dispute of an international character, both institutions are in essence competent to administer such a case. Hence, it will depend on which institution was chosen in the arbitration agreement.

Sometimes parties simply overlook that the statement of claims that was filed with **1-163** the VIAC in fact relates to a domestic dispute in the sense of Article 1(3). In such cases, both institutions take a pragmatic approach. The Secretary General of the VIAC will notify the claimant that according to a *prima facie* assessment the case falls within the jurisdiction of the PATV. If the claimant agrees, the file, together with the registration fee, will then be submitted to the PATV where it receives a new file number and where it will subsequently be administered. If the claimant insists on the administration by the VIAC, it will ultimately be for the arbitrators to decide if they are competent to hear the dispute under the jurisdiction of the VIAC or not. If the arbitral tribunal raises this issue in the course of the proceedings or the respondent objects to the tribunal's jurisdiction on this ground, the claimant will be entitled to apply for a transferral of the case to the PATV.[293] In case such application is found to be justified, any deposit on costs, registration fees and other payments will then be transferred to the PATV, which will take over the administration of the case at the exact same stage of the proceedings.

---

293. This approach seems to be inspired by Section 260(6) ZPO which permits a similar procedure in state court proceedings.

Article 2

The Place of the Arbitration

		Para.
I.	Introduction	1
II.	Determining the Seat of the Arbitration	4
III.	Conducting Procedural Acts Elsewhere	10
IV.	The Impact of the Seat of the Arbitration	13
	A. Denationalization v. Territoriality	17
	1. The Debate	18
	2. The Emerging Compromise	25
	3. The Approach under Austrian Law	29
	B. The Seat's Impact on the Law Applicable to the Arbitration Agreement	32
	C. The Seat's Impact on the Law Applicable to the Proceedings	37
	1. What is the *Lex Arbitri*?	38
	2. Can the Parties Choose a 'Foreign' Procedural Law?	41

		Para.
	3. Mandatory Procedural Standards and Requirements	45
	3.1. Mandatory Provisions under the Old Regime	46
	3.2. Mandatory Provisions under the New Regime	47
D.	The Seat's Impact on the Assistance and Intervention of the Courts	51
	1. Subject Matter Jurisdiction	53
	2. Assistance by the State Courts	55
	3. Challenge and Termination of the Arbitrator's Mandate	63
	4. Interim Measures	64
	5. Recourse Against the Award	68
	6. Enforcement of Foreign Awards	69
E.	The Seat's Impact On The Law Applicable to the Substance of the Dispute	72

Article 2: Unless the parties have agreed otherwise:

(a) the place of arbitration shall be Vienna

(b) the sole arbitrator (arbitral tribunal) may conduct procedural acts at any place where he deems appropriate.

The arbitral tribunal may in any case meet at any place to consult in any way.

I.   INTRODUCTION

2-001 In arbitration agreements, parties regularly specify the 'place', 'seat' or '*situs*' of the arbitration; and are well advised to do so. The seat of the arbitration ought not to be a question of convenience, determined by weather forecasts, preferences of cuisine or cultural offerings. It may be, in fact, one of the most important choices for the parties to make in international arbitration.

2-002 This is because of the potential impact of the law of the arbitral seat, the importance of which becomes visible at various levels. The law of the host state may provide the law applicable to the arbitration agreement and determine its validity. The *lex loci arbitri* may, through mandatory procedural provisions, also impact on the arbitration process itself, by providing standards for arbitrators and parties to comply with and by regulating the intervention of local courts in the arbitral process. The law of the *situs* may also, through conflicts of law rules or through certain mandatory provisions and *ordre public*, impact on the substantive law governing the parties' dispute. Finally, the place of arbitration provides the law and venue for setting aside the award; and it plays an important role in enforcement proceedings under the New York Convention.[1]

2-003 Some commentators, therefore, regard the seat of the arbitration as the 'vital territorial link' between the arbitration proceedings and the law of the place where these proceedings are legally situated; the '*formal legal domicile*' of the arbitration.[2] This 'territorial' approach of arbitration has been for a long time the accepted standard by international doctrine. However, in more recent times, there is an effort to detach – and thus delocalize – international arbitration as much as possible from the seat of the arbitration. This trend is also reflected in modern arbitral legislation, including the new ZPO. Although Section 577 ZPO provides that its provisions shall apply 'if the seat of the arbitration is within Austria', it goes on to limit the interference by the local Austrian courts, and Austrian law, to an arbitration-friendly minimum. The courts may only become active in matters governed by the ZPO and only if the law expressly provides so.[3] Finally, the trend of delocalization may also indicate how arbitrators interpret and apply legal rules to the arbitration. The following section examines first how the seat of the arbitration is determined and considers then the competing concepts of

---

1. A. Redfern, M. Hunter, N. Blackaby and C. Partasides, *Law and Practice of International Commercial Arbitration* (4th edn, London, Sweet & Maxwell, 2004), para. 2-11 with further notes. 'The vital role of the arbitral *situs* in the viability of international arbitration derives in large measure from the enforcement scheme of the New York Arbitration Convention.' *See* W.W. Park, 'Judicial Controls in the Arbitral Process' (1989) 5(3) Arb Int'l, 230, 255; NY Convention, **Annex 11**.
2. K. Lionnet and A. Lionnet, *Handbuch der internationalen und nationalen Schiedsgerichtsbarkeit* (3rd edn, Stuttgart, Richard Boorberg Verlag, 2005), p. 117.
3. Section 578 ZPO reads: 'The court may only become active in matters governed by this section if this section provides therefore.'

territoriality and delocalization. Finally, it addresses the impact of the seat of arbitration on arbitrations placed in Austria and conducted under the Vienna Rules.

II. DETERMINING THE SEAT OF THE ARBITRATION

Under the new Austrian arbitration law, Section 595(1) ZPO provides the basic **2-004** rule:

> The parties are free to agree on the seat of the arbitral tribunal. They may also allow the seat of the arbitral tribunal to be determined by an arbitral institution. Failing such agreement, the seat of the arbitral tribunal shall be determined by the arbitral tribunal having regard to the circumstances of the case, including the convenience of the seat for the parties.[4]

Thus, the parties are free to choose the seat of the arbitration;[5] absent their agree- **2-005** ment, the seat is determined by the tribunal. It is argued that this determination is not a procedural question within the meaning of Section 604(1) ZPO and can therefore not be delegated to the chairperson of an arbitral tribunal.[6]

Section 595(1) ZPO also permits the parties to delegate the determination of the **2-006** seat of the arbitration to an arbitral institution (which only states the obvious, namely the parties' freedom to agree on this issue). Article 2 in turn, provides that the place of arbitration shall be Vienna (unless the parties have agreed otherwise). This reflects the reality that the vast majority of all arbitrations under the Vienna Rules are sited in Vienna.

Of course, the default seat of Vienna gives way to the parties' agreement. This is **2-007** in line with all major rules that provide the parties the freedom to choose the seat of the arbitration.[7] Various rules provide different solutions, however, as to the situation where the choice of seat is not made by the parties. Under Article 14 ICC Rules, for instance, the place of the arbitration is fixed by the

---

4. This provision follows Article 20 UNCITRAL Model Law.
5. Note that the provision refers to the 'seat' rather than the 'place' of the arbitration, confirming that the seat is a legal concept detached from where the arbitration actually 'takes place'.
6. C. Liebscher, *The Austrian Arbitration Act 2006: Text and Notes* (The Hague, Kluwer Law International, 2006), Annotated Text to Section 595 ZPO.
7. This approach is well established in various arbitration rules, *e.g.* Article 16 LCIA Rules – Rules of London Court of International Arbitration; Article 5(1) Polish Rules – Rules of the Court of Arbitration at the Polish Chamber of Commerce in Warsaw; Article 4 Croatian Rules – The Rules of Arbitration of the Permanent Arbitration Court at the Croatian Chamber of Economy; Article 5 Czech Rules – The Rules of the Arbitration Court attached to the Economic Chamber of the Czech Republic and Agricultural Chamber of the Czech Republic; Article 11 Slovenian Rules – Rules of Arbitration of the Permanent Court of Arbitration attached to the Chamber of Commerce and Industry of Slovenia; Article 1 Slovak Rules – Rules of Procedure of the Court of Arbitration of the Slovak Chamber of Commerce and Industry.

Court (unless it is agreed upon by the parties). In doing so, the Court will consider the specific circumstances of a case; the law applicable to the dispute; accessibility and convenience; neutrality; and other relevant aspects.[8] Under Article 20 UNCITRAL Model Law, the arbitral tribunal will determine the place of arbitration, in the absence of an agreement by the parties.[9] In this case, the arbitral tribunal will determine the seat most appropriate under the circumstances of the case, following similar considerations as the ICC Court. Similarly, under the regime of the European Convention the President or the Special Committee is entitled 'to determine the place of arbitration, provided that the arbitrator(s) may fix another place of arbitration'.[10]

2-008 As noted, Article 2 adopts a different approach, as it makes Vienna the default place of the arbitration, from which the parties can deviate. This provision is, perhaps, not entirely appropriate for an international institution such as the VIAC, particularly in Central and Eastern Europe. There may well be cases where the parties fail to choose the seat of the arbitration, but Vienna is in fact not the most appropriate *situs* for the proceedings. In such cases, by providing for Vienna by default, arbitrators have no authority to determine a more appropriate seat for the arbitration. For an international institution that by its very nature does not want to be too closely linked to any given place, this approach appears somewhat outdated.[11]

2-009 Of course, should the parties fail to determine a seat at the outset, they may do so *after* the commencement of the proceedings, arguably also after the arbitral tribunal has been constituted.

---

8. *See in detail* Y. Derains and E.A. Schwartz, *A Guide to the ICC Rules of Arbitration* (2nd edn, The Hague, Kluwer Law International, 2005), pp. 213 *et seq.* A similar approach is taken by Article 13 AAA/ICDR Rules and Article 21 DIS Rules, providing that in the absence of a party agreement, the place of the arbitration, shall be determined by the arbitral tribunal.

9. *Roth* considers the place of arbitration of particular importance in three respects. Firstly, it is important for the UNCITRAL Model Law's territorial scope of application. Secondly, it establishes the international character of the arbitration proceedings. Thirdly, pursuant to Article 31(3) UNCITRAL Model Law, the award is deemed to have been made at the place of arbitration as determined in accordance with Article 20 UNCITRAL Model Law. Therefore, the place of origin of the award is relevant in recognition and enforcement proceedings. *See* M. Roth in *Practitioner's Handbook on International Arbitration*, F.B. Weigand (ed.) (Munich, C.H. Beck, 2002), p. 1233.

10. *See* Article IV(4)(c) European Convention, **Annex 10**.

11. The recent amendment of the Vienna Rules has at least abolished an unpleasant ambiguity. Article 2 of the Vienna Rules 2001 stipulated that arbitration proceedings are to take place 'at the seat of the Centre'. **Annex 2a**. It could be argued that this might not be a clear indication as to the seat of the arbitration itself. However, this provision was clearly inserted to provide a fallback default route in case the parties failed to agree on the place of arbitration. Indeed, the former version of Article 2 provided that 'the parties can agree that the proceedings be conducted at a different place'. Given the development of Article 2 over time however, there was no doubt that the provision gives the parties the freedom to choose a seat other than Vienna.

III.   CONDUCTING PROCEDURAL ACTS ELSEWHERE

The legal seat of the arbitration must not be confused with the physical loca- **2-010**
tion of where the proceedings are, entirely or in part, actually conducted. It
is well-established that individual procedural acts can be conducted in places
other than the seat of arbitration. Article 2 thus provides that the parties can
agree – and (unless the parties have restricted the arbitrator's authority in this
regard) the arbitrators can determine – that meetings, hearings or the taking
of evidence can be conducted elsewhere, even if the seat of the arbitration,
by agreement or default, is in Vienna. In similar vein, Section 595(2) ZPO
provides:

> Notwithstanding the provisions of paragraph 1 of this section, the arbitral
> tribunal may, unless otherwise agreed by the parties, meet at any place it
> considers appropriate for conducting proceedings, especially for deliberation,
> making decisions, conducting oral hearings and the taking of evidence.

In that sense, the seat of the arbitration is a legal fiction, and conceptually detached **2-011**
from the place where the arbitration is actually conducted.[12] Under the Vienna
Rules, the arbitrators need to be aware that in cases which require the proceedings
to be relocated, they must make arrangements to cover the expected costs in
accordance with **Article 35(1)**. In any event, arbitrators should consult with the
parties on such relocation in advance.[13]

If, however, both parties oppose the relocation, arbitrators cannot hold meet- **2-012**
ings at another place as their right to do so exists only unless both parties have
agreed otherwise. For the sake of clarification, Article 2 hastens to add that
the arbitral tribunal may in any event consult at any place it deems appropriate
- a right of the arbitral tribunal that no one would seriously call into question.
In that regard, it does not matter where the tribunal's consultation takes place,
or where the award is physically written and produced; the award is deemed
to be made at the seat of the arbitration (and it must state so according to
Article 27(2)).

---

12. It is therefore better to speak of the 'seat' of the arbitration, rather than the 'place' of the
     arbitration.
13. Article 14(2) ICC Rules, for example, allows the arbitral tribunal to conduct hearings and
     meetings at any location it considers appropriate. This is again under the reservation that nothing
     else has been agreed by the parties. Unlike for instance Article 13(2) AAA/ICDR Rules or
     Article 16(2) UNCITRAL Rules, the ICC Rules give the tribunal an obligation to consult with
     the parties. This is considered to be generally sufficient to discourage the most blatant abuses.
     See Y. Derains and E.A. Schwartz, *A Guide to the ICC Rules of Arbitration* (2nd edn, The
     Hague, Kluwer Law International, 2005), pp. 219 *et seq.*

IV.   THE IMPACT OF THE SEAT OF THE ARBITRATION

2-013 Each state will make its own determination of what laws it will adopt to govern arbitration proceedings seated within its own territory, thus defining the scope of the *lex arbitri*. Even where modern legislatures reduce the impact of their local arbitration laws to an arbitration-friendly minimum, such laws apply and cannot be ignored. Thus, 'it may well be that the *lex arbitri* will govern with a very free reign, but it will govern nonetheless'.[14] Recognizing this, the New York Convention provides in Article V(1)(d)[15] that the

> recognition and enforcement of the award may be refused (. . .) if (. . .) the composition of the arbitral authority or the arbitral procedure was not in accordance with the agreement of the parties, or failing such agreement, was not in accordance with the law of the country where the arbitration took place.[16]

2-014 Typically, the *lex loci arbitri* will extend to three important categories. First, it will usually provide rules governing the arbitration agreement. This may include conflict of laws rules as to what law applies to the arbitration agreement; or may be of a substantial nature, governing directly questions of capacity; arbitrability of disputes; form; validity; and effect of the arbitration agreement. It will often also regulate if arbitrators have the competence to decide on the validity and scope of the arbitration agreement, thus determining their own jurisdiction.

2-015 Second, the *lex loci arbitri* regularly also addresses procedural issues. It may include safeguards for due process, such as the parties' right to be heard; determine the scope of what parties can agree in deviation of the default rules of local arbitration law; define the powers that arbitrators have (such as the power to grant interim relief); regulate the intervention of state courts in, or in support of, the arbitration; and may provide rules for the form, challenge and enforcement of awards. In that regard, the *lex loci arbitri* is not purely 'procedural'. For example, the possibility of setting aside an award because it violates (Austrian) public policy is incorporating by reference fundamental principles of Austrian substantive law that form the pertinent *ordre public*.[17]

---

14. A. Redfern, M. Hunter, N. Blackaby and C. Partasides, *Law and Practice of International Commercial Arbitration* (4th edn, London, Sweet & Maxwell, 2004), paras. 2-13, 2-14, and note 27 with reference to further reading on the impact of the seat of the arbitration.
15. NY Convention, **Annex 11**.
16. A similar provision is contained in Article IX(1) European Convention, **Annex 10** and applied under the Geneva Convention of 1927; *See* A.J. van den Berg, *The New York Arbitration Convention of 1958* (The Hague, Kluwer Law International, 1981), p. 323 with further reference.
17. *See* A. Redfern, M. Hunter, N. Blackaby and C. Partasides, *Law and Practice of International Commercial Arbitration* (4th edn, London, Sweet & Maxwell, 2004), para. 2-19.

Third, and finally, the host state may also, through its conflict of laws rules, provide **2-016** the law applicable to the substance of the dispute. The position under Austrian law with respect to these three categories is discussed below. As a preliminary matter, this section first examines some conceptual trends ranging from a territorial approach, linked intrinsically to the seat of the arbitration, to a delocalized view of arbitration; these concepts are useful to understand the choices made by the Austrian legislature in the new ZPO.

A.   DENATIONALIZATION V. TERRITORIALITY

There has been substantial debate in international legal literature as to whether **2-017** international arbitration is necessarily embedded in national procedural law (*territorialism*) or whether it can exist, given its international character, independently of national laws as 'delocalized', 'stateless' or 'a-national arbitration' (*delocaliza- tion*).[18] This question is closely linked to the impact of the seat of the arbitration, which gives the proceedings their 'formal legal domicile'.[19] On the one hand, the state hosting an arbitration will want to assert control over the proceedings on its territory, ensuring minimum procedural standards of fairness and safeguarding its *ordre public*. On the other hand, it is not easy to argue why, for example, Austria should be much concerned with an arbitration between an English and a Peruvian party, under German substantive law, that results in an award to be enforced in the United States only because parties met in a Viennese hotel. International arbitration will often have a very attenuated connection to the seat of the arbitration. The following discusses the arguments advanced by the two sides of the debate, and seeks to stake the claim for an emerging compromise, as reflected in modern legislation.

1.   The Debate

A famous proponent of territorialism, emphasizing the impact of the seat of the **2-018** arbitration, is *F.A. Mann*. His opposition to the concept of delocalized arbitration is set out in two famous articles of 1967 and 1978.[20] According to *Mann*, the

---

18. H. Smit, 'A-National Arbitration' (1989) 63 Tul L Rev, 629, note 1 with further reference. The theory of a-national arbitration procedures corresponds with the theory of a-national arbitration decisions. This concept is relevant to the question of enforcement of arbitration decisions and will be dealt with later under **Article 2**, at paras. 023-024. *See also* W.W. Park, 'Judicial Controls in the Arbitral Process' (1989) 5(3) Arb Int'l, 230 and more recently H. Arfazadeh, 'New Perspectives in South East Asia and Delocalised Arbitration in Kuala Lumpur' (1991) 8(4) J Int'l Arb, 103; G.A. Alvarez, 'To What Extent Do Arbitrators in International Cases Disregard the Bag and Baggage of National Systems?' (1996) 8 ICCA Congress Series (Seoul), 139; J. Lew, 'Achieving the Dream: Autonomous Arbitration' (2006) 22(2) Arb Int'l, 179.

19. K. Lionnet and A. Lionnet, *Handbuch der internationalen und nationalen Schiedsgerichtsbar- keit* (3rd edn, Stuttgart, Richard Boorberg Verlag, 2005), p. 117.

20. F.A. Mann, 'Schiedsrichter und Recht' in *Festschrift für Werner Flume zum 70. Geburtstag*, K. Ballerstedt, F.A. Mann, H.H. Jakobs, B. Knobbe-Keuk and J. Wilhelm (Cologne, Verlag

so-called 'international arbitration does not exist at all; every arbitration is always national'.[21] The nationality of arbitration is determined by the law of the country where the arbitration takes place and, which is in control of the arbitration in relation to procedural and substantive law, the composition of the tribunal, the proceedings, the choice of curial law and arbitral decisions, and which defines the circumstances under which parties can exercise autonomy, making their own arrangements.[22] And further:

> The control that can be exercised over local[23] arbitral decisions which cannot be extended over foreign arbitral decisions shows clearly two things: every arbitral decision has essentially a national character that belongs always and only to that state whose courts are competent and obliged to revoke the same under certain conditions which differ from country to country. If somebody declares that arbitral decisions can live in a vacuum, because they are 'international' or 'a-national,' and the national sovereignty is of no concern to the international arbitration, he is simply denying inevitable legal facts.[24]

2-019 Thus, since each country can set the rules governing all activities occurring on its territory, each country can subject arbitrators, parties and arbitral proceedings, if they take place on the territory, to local procedural law.[25] According to *Mann*, the liberty to embellish the proceedings[26] presumably guaranteed by Article V(1)(d) of the New York Convention[27] is given under the 'obvious provisions

Dr. Otto Schmidt, 1978); F.A. Mann, 'Lex Facit Arbitrum' in *International Arbitration – Liber Amicorum for Martin Domke*, P. Sanders (ed.) (The Hague, Martinus Nijhoff, 1967).

21. F.A. Mann, 'Schiedsrichter und Recht' in *Festschrift für Werner Flume zum 70. Geburtstag*, K. Ballerstedt, F.A. Mann, H.H. Jakobs, B. Knobbe-Keuk and J. Wilhelm (Cologne, Verlag Dr. Otto Schmidt, 1978), p. 595 and note 10 with further reference.

22. F.A. Mann, 'Schiedsrichter und Recht' in *Festschrift für Werner Flume zum 70. Geburtstag*, K. Ballerstedt, F.A. Mann, H.H. Jakobs, B. Knobbe-Keuk and J. Wilhelm (Cologne, Verlag Dr. Otto Schmidt, 1978), p. 598.

23. Domestic from the perspective of the state in which the arbitral tribunal is located.

24. F.A. Mann, 'Schiedsrichter und Recht' in *Festschrift für Werner Flume zum 70. Geburtstag*, K. Ballerstedt, F.A. Mann, H.H. Jakobs, B. Knobbe-Keuk and J. Wilhelm (Cologne, Verlag Dr. Otto Schmidt, 1978), p. 598. Elsewhere: '[E]ven the idea of the autonomy of the parties exists only by virtue of a given system of municipal law and in different systems may have different characteristics and effects (. . .). Every right or power a private person enjoys is inexorably conferred by or derived from a system of municipal law which may be conveniently and in accordance with tradition be called *lex fori*, though it would be more exact (but also less familiar) to speak of the lex arbitri (. . .)'. *See* F.A. Mann, 'Lex Facit Arbitrum' in *International Arbitration – Liber Amicorum for Martin Domke*, P. Sanders (ed.) (The Hague, Martinus Nijhoff, 1967), p. 159.

25. F.A. Mann, 'Lex Facit Arbitrum' in *International Arbitration – Liber Amicorum for Martin Domke*, P. Sanders (ed.) (The Hague, Martinus Nijhoff, 1967), p. 159.

26. *See* **Article 2**, at para. 023.

27. NY Convention, **Annex 11**.

of the nationality of the award and they are valid and effective under law of the arbitral *situs*'.[28]

Smit argues that the question of a-national arbitral decisions does not arise when the respective collision provisions are properly applied.[29] **2-020**

> A-national arbitration was developed to permit escape from unduly limiting provisions of the law of the nationality of the award, which was considered to be the law of the arbitral *situs*. But such provisions can more properly be avoided by applying under appropriate choice of law rules, the law of a state other than the *lex loci arbitri*. In any event even the most elaborate institutional rules cannot avoid drawing on some body of law for their effectiveness. Arbitration does not proceed in a legal vacuum. Ultimately, it must rely for its existence in the legal order on some law rendering it valid and effective. As will be demonstrated, this law is national law. (...) A-national arbitration neither exists nor is it needed.[30]

It is also demonstrated by *Smit* that arbitration procedures cannot exist outside of their local legal context. In the case of institutional arbitration, the arbitration agreement and the arbitral award draw their efficacy and validity not from these institutions, but by being embedded in established national law, which grants them such validity and effect. This is applicable both to procedural and substantive provisions of arbitration rules in so far as their enforcement depends on national law. *Smit* admits, on the other hand, that an unreflected application of the law of the seat of the arbitration (*lex loci arbitri*) may lead to dissatisfactory results.[31] **2-021**

Indeed, difficulties arise from differences in the procedural law of the *situs* state and the law of the state of enforcement. Article V(1)(d) of the New York Convention[32] provides: **2-022**

> Recognition and enforcement of the award may be refused (...) if (...) the composition of the arbitral authority or the arbitral procedure was not in accordance with the agreement of the parties, or failing such agreement, was not in accordance with the law of the country where the arbitration took place.[33]

Mann is of the opinion that the international recognition and enforcement of arbitral awards 'is a completely different question which the arbitrators could and actually must disregard, because they cannot nor do they need to know in **2-023**

---

28. F.A. Mann, 'Schiedsrichter und Recht' in *Festschrift für Werner Flume zum 70. Geburtstag*, K. Ballerstedt, F.A. Mann, H.H. Jakobs, B. Knobbe-Keuk and J. Wilhelm (Cologne, Verlag Dr. Otto Schmidt, 1978), p. 604.
29. H. Smit, 'A-National Arbitration' (1989) 63 Tul L Rev, 629.
30. H. Smit, 'A-National Arbitration' (1989) 63 Tul L Rev, 629, 631.
31. H. Smit, 'A-National Arbitration' (1989) 63 Tul L Rev, 629, 630 and notes 38-41.
32. NY Convention, **Annex 11**.
33. Similar provision is contained in Article IX(1) of the European Convention, **Annex 10**.

which countries the arbitration award should be recognized'.[34] However, the crucial point here is that the New York Convention provides that enforcement *may* be refused if the arbitration violated *lex loci arbitri*.[35] In other words, countries are free under the New York Convention to enforce awards even though they go against the law of the state that provided the arbitral seat. This is illustrated in particular by arbitral awards that are set aside in accordance with the law of the arbitral seat, but are nevertheless enforced in third countries.[36] If the courts of the host state set aside the award under *lex loci arbitri*, territorialists would argue that such a 'non-existent' arbitral award ought not to be enforceable in third states. Such cases therefore obviously contradict the traditional theory of territoriality, holding that every arbitral award is embedded in the law of the state of the arbitral proceedings, so that its legal existence emanates from that law.

2-024 Drawing from such precedent, *Paulsson*, a prominent advocate of the theory of delocalized arbitral procedure, in particular disputes the application of a single exclusive *lex arbitri*.[37] Even when an arbitral award does not have binding effect under the *lex loci arbitri*, it is left to the liberty of any third state to recognize the award as binding and enforceable in accordance with its *own* law.[38] This clearly shows that the existence and effectiveness of the award does not depend on a single national law: *Lex arbitri* cannot be equated with *lex loci arbitri* in all instances. Territorialism in its purest form is therefore wrong because it incorrectly presupposes that a single national law exclusively governs the arbitral procedure.[39]

---

34. F.A. Mann, 'Schiedsrichter und Recht' in *Festschrift für Werner Flume zum 70. Geburtstag*, K. Ballerstedt, F.A. Mann, H.H. Jakobs, B. Knobbe-Keuk and J. Wilhelm (Cologne, Verlag Dr. Otto Schmidt, 1978), p. 596.

35. Note that this is based on the English text of the NY Convention. There are indications that the Austrian *Oberster Gerichtshof* takes a different view. *See* OGH, 29 June 2004, 3 Ob 22/04p, although the Austrian *Oberster Gerichtshof* has failed to date to use consistent terminology: 'may' (OGH, 26 April 2006, 3 Ob 211/05h; OGH, 22 October 2001, 1 Ob 236/01i; OGH, 17 December 1986, 3 Ob 32/86), 'can' (OGH, 25 June 1992, 7 Ob 545/92) and 'must' (OGH, 29 June 2004, 3 Ob 22/04p; OGH, 21 February 1978, 3 Ob 120/77).

36. *See*, famously, Cour de Cassation, 1re Ch. Civ., 9 October 1984, *Pabalk Ticaret Sirketi v. Norsolor* [1985] Rev Arb, 431; (1985) 2(2) J Int'l Arb, 67; and Cour de Cassation, 1er Ch. Civ., 23 March 1994, *Société Hilmarton v. Société OTV* [1994] Rev Arb, 327; Cour d'Appel de Paris, 14 January 1997, *République arabe d'Egypte v. Société Chromalloy Aero Services* [1997] Rev Arb, 395. More recently, *see* T.H. Webster, 'Evolving Principles in Enforcing Awards Subject to Annulment Proceedings' (2006) 23(3) J Int'l Arb, 213 referring to Cour d'Appel de Paris, 29 September 2005, *DAC/Dubai v. Bechtel*. (2006) XXXI YB Comm Arb, 629. For an Austrian award enforced in Austria (under the European Convention that was set aside in Slovenia), *see* OGH, 20 October 1993, *Radenska v. Kajo* (1995) XX YB Comm Arb, 1051.

37. J. Paulsson, 'Arbitration Unbound: Award Detached From The Law of its Country of Origin' (1981) 30(2) ICLQ, 363.

38. J. Paulsson, 'Arbitration Unbound: Award Detached From The Law of its Country of Origin' (1981) 30(2) ICLQ, 363.

39. J. Paulsson, 'Arbitration Unbound: Award Detached From The Law of its Country of Origin' (1981) 30(2) ICLQ, 361.

2. The Emerging Compromise

In practical terms, parties and arbitrators are well advised to consider the effect of **2-025** the arbitral seat by way of applicable local law, despite the merits of a delocalized approach. The choice of the seat remains, therefore, an important one.

In any event, the debate about delocalizing arbitration has had an impact on the law **2-026** and practice of international arbitration. First, it appears that modern arbitration laws seek to limit their impact as the *lex loci arbitri* to a minimum. Modern legislatures seem more confident to permit parties to isolate substantial aspects of the arbitration from the local law of the seat, and will intervene, through mandatory law and their court system, only in support of arbitration or when *procedural* or *substantive ordre public* so require. For example, the Working Group intended to provide in Section 583(4) draft ZPO that an arbitration agreement would be valid if it complies with the law chosen by the parties, the law applicable to the substance of the dispute, or Austrian law.[40] Provisions such as these underscore a trend away from a strict application of territoriality, by providing parties with the freedom to opt out of the application of the national law of the arbitral seat.

Second, international arbitrators tend to think less and less in terms of national **2-027** procedural law, and more in terms of delocalized standards. Thus, the embrace of arbitral procedure by the host state was likened to the myth of Prokrustes who waylaid unassuming wanderers, forced them to lie in his bed and then cut or stretched their bodies to size[41] – an approach inappropriate for international proceedings that, by virtue of the parties' and the arbitrators' nationality, have only an attenuated nexus to the place of arbitration.[42] *Lalive* argues in this respect that the legal basis of the arbitrator's activity is distinct from the activity of the national judge. Whereas the national judge is bound to implement the rules of the law that determines his jurisdiction, the jurisdiction of the arbitrator derives exclusively from an agreement concluded by the parties under private law. Therefore, the international arbitrator's authority does not exist by virtue of national law alone.[43] In the words of *Paulsson*:

> Whilst, if [the parties'] contract had stipulated the jurisdiction of that country's courts, they may have expected the local judge to fit the Procrustean bed

---

40. Regrettably, the Austrian legislature did not accept this approach, *see* **Article 1**, at para. 064.
41. P. Lalive, 'Les règles de conflit de lois appliquées au fond du litige par l'arbitre international siégeant en Suisse' in 'L'arbitrage international privé et la Suisse, Colloque des 2 et 23 avril 1976, Mémoires de la faculté de droit de Genéve', (1977) no. 53, 50-105.
42. R. Goode, 'The Role of Lex Loci Arbitri in International Commercial Arbitration' (2001) 17(1) Arb Int'l, 19, 32-33.
43. '[I]t would be a rather artificial interpretation to deem [the arbitrator's] power to be derived (...) from a tolerance of the State of the place of arbitration.' *See* P. Lalive, 'Les règles de conflit de lois appliqués au fond du litige par l'arbitre international siégeant en Suisse' in 'L'arbitrage international privé et la Suisse, Colloque des 2 et 23 avril 1976, Mémoires de la faculté de droit de Genéve', (1997) no. 53, 1977, 50-105.

of the municipal legal system, which would be his exclusive source of authority, the same need not be true with respect to arbitrators whom the parties, as it were, brought along.[44]

2-028 Thus, unlike state court judges, arbitrators do not see themselves wedded to a national system. Indeed, some commentators argue that international arbitrators, by definition, do not have a *lex fori*.[45]

3.   The Approach under Austrian Law

2-029 Austrian law has, in principle, adopted the concept of territoriality by linking the applicability of its arbitration law to the seat of the arbitration ('The provisions of this section shall apply if the seat of the arbitral tribunal is within Austria'). The term 'seat' is not defined. It can be inferred from Section 595(2) ZPO that 'seat' has a purely legal meaning ('fictional seat'). As noted above, it is not necessary that any actions take place at the location designated as the seat.[46]

2-030 Interestingly, Austrian arbitration law also provides, in Section 577(2) ZPO, for an extra-territorial application of some provisions even where the seat of the arbitral tribunal is not within Austria (or has not yet been determined). The provisions listed in Section 577(2) ZPO concern the permissibility of court intervention,[47] the receipt of written communications,[48] the form of the arbitration agreement,[49] the effect of arbitration agreements in court proceedings,[50] unimpeded access to the courts for provisional measures,[51] the enforcement of provisional measures rendered by the arbitral tribunal,[52] court assistance,[53] the determination of the existence or non-existence of an award[54] and the recognition and enforcement of foreign awards.[55] This is intended to 'integrate the phenomenon of arbitration' and to assist the arbitral tribunal:[56] Section 577(2) ZPO allows the Austrian courts

---

44. J. Paulsson, 'Arbitration Unbound: Award Detached From The Law of its Country of Origin' (1981) 30(2) ICLQ, 363.
45. A. Redfern, M. Hunter, N. Blackaby and C. Partasides, *Law and Practice of International Commercial Arbitration* (4th edn, London, Sweet & Maxwell, 2004), para. 2-80.
46. C. Liebscher, *The Austrian Arbitration Act 2006: Text and Notes* (The Hague, Kluwer Law International, 2006), Annotated Text to Section 577(1) ZPO; B. Kloiber and H. Haller in *Das Neue Schiedsrecht – Schiedsrechts-Änderungsgesetz 2006*, B. Kloiber, P. Oberhammer, W.H. Rechberger and H. Haller (eds) (Vienna, Manz, 2006), p. 14.
47. *See* Section 578 ZPO.
48. *See* Section 580 ZPO.
49. *See* Section 583 ZPO.
50. *See* Section 584 ZPO.
51. *See* Section 585 ZPO.
52. *See* Sections 593(3) to (6) ZPO.
53. *See* Section 602 ZPO.
54. *See* Section 612 ZPO.
55. *See* Section 614 ZPO.
56. B. Kloiber and H. Haller in *Das Neue Schiedsrecht – Schiedsrechts-Änderungsgesetz 2006*, B. Kloiber, P. Oberhammer, W.H. Rechberger and H. Haller (eds) (Vienna, Manz, 2006), p. 14.

to assist arbitral tribunals that have their seat elsewhere, or to grant interim relief to parties to foreign arbitration.

Yet in line with the modern trend outlined above, Austria's territorial approach is **2-031** self-restrained. It is an overriding feature of the new Austrian arbitration law that it affords the parties significant freedom to customize the proceedings according to their own designs and agree between them on a wide spectrum of issues. At the same time, the new Austrian arbitration law limits the intervention by the state courts to only a few pre-specified instances; the courts may only become active if the arbitration law expressly so provides.[57] Conceptually, the Austrian legislature's self-imposed restriction recognizes arbitration as a separate and independent form of dispute resolution that is in principle protected from national interference except for some instances of supervision and support.

B.   THE SEAT'S IMPACT ON THE LAW APPLICABLE TO THE ARBITRATION
            AGREEMENT

The position of Austrian law as to the capacity to enter into an arbitration agree- **2-032** ment; the arbitrability of disputes; formal requirements; the effect of the arbitration agreement; and how the arbitrators and the courts might interpret the arbitration agreement has been discussed in the context of **Article 1**. Now, in the context of Article 2 and the seat of the arbitration, it is assessed whether or not Austrian law in fact governs these questions.

Arbitration agreements are regarded under most national laws as separate from the **2-033** underlying contract in which they appear. This *doctrine of separability* of the arbitration agreement is well established in Austrian jurisprudence[58] and scholarship.[59] One consequence of this is that the arbitration agreement *may* be governed by a different national law than that which applies to the contract. The arbitration agreement is a separate contract which may be governed by one of four possible laws: by the law chosen by the parties specifically to govern the arbitration agreement itself; the law of the arbitral seat; the law governing the parties' underlying contract; or the law of the forum in which judicial enforcement of the agreement is sought.[60]

---

57. *See* Section 578 ZPO.
58. OGH, 18 April 1985, 7 Ob 551/85; OLG Vienna, 15 December 1966, 2 R 248/66; OGH, 9 October 1929, 3 Ob 727/29, JBl 1930, 18.
59. *See* **Article 19**, at para. 042. *See also* W.H. Rechberger and W. Melis in *Kommentar zur ZPO*, W.H. Rechberger (ed.) (2nd edn, Vienna/New York, Springer, 2000), Section 577 para. 16; H.W. Fasching, *Schiedsgericht und Schiedsverfahren im österreichischen und im internationalen Recht* (Vienna, Manz, 1973), p. 30; G. Backhausen, *Schiedsgerichtsbarkeit unter besonderer Berücksichtigung des Schiedsvertragsrechts* (Vienna, Manz, 1990), p. 98; C. Liebscher and A. Schmid in *Practitioner's Handbook on International Arbitration*, F.B. Weigand (ed.) (Munich, C.H. Beck, 2002), p. 546.
60. G.B. Born, *International Commercial Arbitration – Commentary and Materials* (2nd edn, The Hague, Kluwer Law International, 2001), p. 43. According to *van den Berg*, the most important

2-034 The basic principle under Austrian law in this context is, as elsewhere,[61] party autonomy. Arbitration itself is indeed predicated on the autonomy of the parties, therefore, the arbitrator will in the first instance have to apply the law chosen by the parties.[62] This approach is reflected in Article VI(2) of the European Convention[63] and Article V(1)(a) of the New York Convention, which provide that recognition

---

issue for the enforcement of the arbitration agreement is the law applicable to the arbitration agreement, which, according to the NY Convention, is 'the law to which the parties have subjected it or, failing any indication thereon, (. . .) the law of the country where the award was made'. *See* A.J. van den Berg, *The New York Arbitration Convention of 1958* (The Hague, Kluwer Law International, 1981), p. 123. Swiss law indicates that the validity of an arbitration clause may be determined either by (1) the law chosen by the parties, or (2) the law governing the main contract or (3) the law of the seat of the arbitration. *See* W. Wenger and C. Müller in *Internationales Privatrecht*, H. Honsell, N.P. Vogt, A.K. Schnyder and S.V. Berti (eds) (2nd edn, Basel, Helbing Lichtenhahn Verlag, 2007), p. 1523; *Lew/Mistelis/Kröll* distinguish between law governing the arbitration agreement, law applicable to formal validity, law applicable to capacity of the parties or law applicable to substantive validity of the arbitration agreement. *See* J. Lew, L. Mistelis and S. Kröll, *Comparative International Commercial Arbitration* (The Hague, Kluwer Law International, 2003), paras. 6-1 *et seq.* Furthermore, in the opinion of the authors, international arbitration practice shows that the primary factor in determining the applicable law to substantive validity of the arbitration agreement is the autonomy of the party. Where the parties have not chosen the applicable law, there are other relevant factors for such a determination as, for example, the place of arbitration, the place where the arbitration agreement has been concluded, the law governing the main contract, the law of the place of enforcement as well as the combination of some of those factors. *See* J. Lew, L. Mistelis and S. Kröll, *Comparative International Commercial Arbitration* (The Hague, Kluwer Law International, 2003), para. 6-68; M. Mustill and S.C. Boyd, *Commercial Arbitration* (2nd edn, Butterworths, London 1989), p. 62; E. Gaillard and J. Savage (eds), *Fouchard Gaillard Goldman On International Commercial Arbitration* (The Hague, Kluwer Law International, 1999), para. 425; G.B. Born, *International Commercial Arbitration – Commentary and Materials* (2nd edn, The Hague, Kluwer Law International, 2001), p. 95.

61.   *See, e.g.,* J. Lew, L. Mistelis and S. Kröll, *Comparative International Commercial Arbitration* (The Hague, Kluwer Law International, 2003), para. 6-68.

62.   This follows the concept of Section 35 IPRG. OGH, 8 March 1961, 1 Ob 98/61, with an exposition of the prevalent legal doctrine at the time, but ultimately concurring. *See* **Article 24**, at paras. 004 *et seq.*

63.   The European Convention is an example of a legal instrument containing a special provision for decisions concerning the existence or the validity of an arbitration agreement. Article VI(2) of the European Convention provides that '[i]n taking a decision concerning the existence or the validity of an arbitration agreement, courts of Contracting States shall examine the validity of such agreement with reference to the capacity of the parties, under the law applicable to them, and with reference to other questions: (a) under the law to which the parties have subjected their arbitration agreement; (b) failing any indication thereon, under the law of the country in which the award is to be made; (c) failing any indication as to the law to which the parties have subjected the agreement, and where at the time when the question is raised in court the country in which the award is to be made cannot be determined, under the competent law by virtue of the rules of conflict of the court seized of the dispute. The courts may also refuse recognition of the

and enforcement of the award may be refused *inter alia* 'if the said agreement is not valid under the law to which the parties have subjected it'[64]. Where there is no choice of law in a contract, Article V(1)(a) New York Convention provides that the enforcement of the award may be refused if the parties have not agreed on a choice of law; the arbitration agreement 'is not valid under the law of the country where the award was made'.[65] Similarly, the Austrian *Oberster Gerichtshof* has held that:

> the validity or non-validity, as far as it is not concerning the personal capability to conclude the arbitration agreement, has to be judged by the law of the country where the award is made.[66]

Therefore, the substantive validity of an arbitration agreement will in principle be **2-035** assessed by the arbitrators or the courts under Austrian law, if the arbitration has its seat in Austria[67] and if the parties have not themselves chosen a different law to be applicable to their agreement to arbitrate.[68]

---

arbitration agreement if under the law of their country the dispute is not capable of settlement by arbitration.' **Annex 10**.

64. NY Convention, **Annex 11**.
65. A.J. van den Berg, *The New York Arbitration Convention of 1958* (The Hague, Kluwer Law International, 1981), p. 291; U. Haas, in *Practitioner's Handbook on International Arbitration*, F.B. Weigand (ed.) (Munich, C.H. Beck, 2002), p. 450. The provision of Article V(1)(a) NY Convention is exclusively covering the *exequatur* perspective. It follows, however, the spirit of the NY Convention to consider parties' choice of law via Article 2 NY Convention also for the arbitration agreement. *See, e.g.*, K.H. Schwab and G. Walter (eds), *Schiedsgerichtsbarkeit* (7th edn, Munich, C.H. Beck, 2005), ch. 43 para. 2; M. Epping, *Die Schiedsvereinbarung im internationalen privaten Rechtsverkehr nach der Reform des deutschen Schiedsverfahrensrechts* (Munich, C.H. Beck, 1999), pp. 40 *et seq.* with further reference. Therefore, note in particular Article VI(2)(a) European Convention which applies to all different stages of the proceedings. German jurisprudence (to the old arbitration law) unanimously considered the arbitration agreement to be under the same law as the main contract. *See, e.g.*, BGH, 28 November 1963, VII ZR 112/62, NJW 1964, 591; BGH, 12 February 1976, III ZR 42/74, RIW 1976, 449, 451; OLG Munich, 7 April 1989, 23 U6310/88, RIW 1990, 585, 586; R. Geimer in *Zöller – Zivilprozessordnung*, R. Zöller *et al.* (eds) (26th edn, Cologne, Verlag Dr. Otto Schmidt, 2007), Section 1025, para. 10 with further reference; M. Epping, *Die Schiedsvereinbarung im internationalen privaten Rechtsverkehr nach der Reform des deutschen Schiedsverfahrensrechts* (Munich, C.H. Beck, 1999), p. 53 with further reference.
66. Already in OGH, 8 March 1961, 1 Ob 98/61; but mostly noted in OGH, 17 November 1971, 8 Ob 233/71, JBl 1974, 629 where this was confirmed with clear reference as to the question of the certainty of the arbitration agreement; OGH, 22 September 1994, 2 Ob 566/94; OGH, 19 February 2004, 6 Ob 151/03d and recently in OGH, 24 August 2005, 3 Ob 65/05p and OGH, 26 January 2005, 7 Ob 314/04h.
67. Or even when the arbitration proceeding is taking place outside Austria, as far as formal requirement of the arbitration agreement is concerned. *See* Section 577(2) ZPO.
68. In such cases, however, the question of arbitrability will still be assessed under Austrian law, as an agreement referring a non-arbitrable dispute to arbitration is invalid. *See* **Article 1**, at paras. 135 *et seq.*

2-036 The current position in Austrian jurisprudence seems to be that a (general) choice of law clause in the main contract also governs the arbitration agreement.[69] However, this is currently the subject of debate.[70] The ZPO Working Group discussed including separate conflict of law rules for the law applicable to the arbitration agreement. However, it was noted that this issue is 'currently developing in the international debate' and it would be more appropriate to leave further solutions to jurisprudence and doctrine.[71] As far as the formal validity of arbitration agreements is concerned, there is also some support that the provisions of Article II of the New York Convention override Austrian law in cases of an international nature.[72]

C.   THE SEAT'S IMPACT ON THE LAW APPLICABLE TO THE PROCEEDINGS

2-037 Arbitrations conducted in Austria are embedded within the Austrian legal framework. Thus, Austrian law is applicable to arbitrations conducted on its territory. The question as to what exactly constitutes the *lex loci arbitri* and how, if at all, the parties can deviate from it, is discussed below.

1.   What is the *Lex Arbitri*?

2-038 Former (Sections 577-599 ZPO) and current (Sections 577-618 ZPO) Austrian arbitration law governs 'arbitral proceedings'. These provisions are, therefore, part of the Austrian Code of Civil Procedure (*Zivilprozeßordnung* – ZPO).

---

69. That was ruled in OGH, 26 January 2000, 7 Ob 368/98p / 7 Ob 369/98k without any further explanation.

70. *See* W.H. Rechberger, 'Evergreen: Gültigkeit der Schiedsklausel' in *Festschrift für Peter Schlosser zum 70. Geburtstag*, B. Bachmann, S. Breidenbach, D. Coester-Waltjen, B. Heß, A. Nelle and C. Wolf (Mohr Siebeck, Tübingen, 2005), pp. 733, 736; F. Böhm, 'Die Rechtsschutzformen im Spannungsfeld von lex fori und lex causae' in *Festschrift für H.W.Fasching zum 65. Geburtstag*, R. Holzhammer, W. Jelinek, P. Böhm (eds) (Vienna, Manz,1988), pp. 107, 134; H. Schumacher, 'Unbestimmte Schiedsvereinbarungen und Dissens: Anknüpfungsfragen bei internationalen Sachverhalten in der Judikatur des OGH' [2005] SchiedsVZ, 54, 54; in Germany: K. Lionnet and A. Lionnet, *Handbuch der internationalen und nationalen Schiedsgerichtsbarkeit* (3rd edn, Stuttgart, Richard Boorberg Verlag, 2005), p. 170 with further reference; *also* P. Schlosser, *Das Recht der internationalen privaten Schiedsgerichtsbarkeit* (2nd edn, Tübingen, Mohr Siebeck, 1989), para. 254 with further reference; *also* A. Redfern, M. Hunter, N. Blackaby and C. Partasides, *Law and Practice of International Commercial Arbitration* (4th edn, London, Sweet & Maxwell, 2004), para. 2-86 with further reference.

71. The draft Section 583(4) ZPO intended to loosen the link between the law applicable to the arbitration agreement and Austrian law as the *lex loci arbitri* significantly. It provided: '[In all other aspects] the Arbitration agreement is valid provided it complies with the law chosen by the parties, with the law applicable on the merits, in particular that applicable to the principal contract, or with the Austrian law.' *See* P. Oberhammer, *Entwurf eines neuen Schiedsverfahrensrechts* (Vienna, Manz, 2002), p. 48.

72. *See* **Article 1**, at paras. 062 and 073; NY Convention, **Annex 11**.

Yet this does not mean that the rules governing arbitration proceedings as such are systemically linked to the provisions regarding civil procedure before Austrian state courts. Rather, it is accepted in Austria, as elsewhere, that these provisions form a distinct, separate and self-contained normative framework for arbitration proceedings, independent of state court rules.[73] This is an important distinction. Traditional territorialism supported the analogous application of rules of civil procedure to arbitration proceedings, to fill gaps in the typically vague normative framework provided by the arbitration law.[74]

In this regard, the modern approach of delocalization appears more appropriate. As **2-039** *Oberhammer* noted:

> Time is not yet ripe for procedural conflict law in Austria. Theoretically there is still the perception that procedural questions should on an abstract level always follow the *lex arbitri*. This sometimes leads to the dramatically false approach of filling gaps in the applicable law with recourse to the procedural rules of the curial law as applicable before the state courts. Also, the *lex-fori* rule for the law applicable to the proceedings is more of a necessary rule of thumb rather than a dogmatic dictum. In the context of international arbitration, it is even less clear why procedural questions should be determined according to the law of the seat of the arbitration.[75]

If parties had wished to apply the rules of civil procedure of a particular country, **2-040** they should and could have agreed to litigation before the courts of the host state. By agreeing to arbitration, however, parties opted merely for the application of those provisions of the law of the arbitral seat that directly pertain to arbitration. Indeed, there is no reason to assume that international parties had any wish or intention to incorporate Austrian court rules into their dispute resolution by choosing Austria as the seat for their arbitration. As far as procedural issues such as the taking of evidence; security for cost; and others are concerned, arbitrators are therefore well advised to apply rules of local civil procedure not at all, or only with the greatest of caution if the circumstances of the individual case provide a basis for an analogous application. The preferable approach is for arbitrators to seek agreement amongst the parties on such issues; and if such agreement cannot be achieved, to resort to a solution that takes account of the parties' legitimate

---

73. *See*, for Germany, J.P. Lachmann, *Handbuch für die Schiedsgerichtspraxis* (3rd edn., Cologne, Verlag Dr. Otto Schmidt, 2008), pp. 55, 318.
74. H.W. Fasching, *Schiedsgericht und Schiedsverfahren im österreichischen und im internationalen Recht* (Vienna, Manz, 1973), p. 99; *see also* B. Kloiber and H. Haller in *Das Neue Schiedsrecht – Schiedsrechts-Änderungsgesetz 2006*, B. Kloiber, P. Oberhammer, W.H. Rechberger and H. Haller (eds) (Vienna, Manz, 2006), p. 38; W.H. Rechberger in *Das Neue Schiedsrecht – Schiedsrechts-Änderungsgesetz 2006*, B. Kloiber, P. Oberhammer, W.H. Rechberger and H. Haller (eds) (Vienna, Manz, 2006), p. 84.
75. P. Oberhammer in *Das Neue Schiedsrecht – Schiedsrechts-Änderungsgesetz 2006*, B. Kloiber, P. Oberhammer, W.H. Rechberger and H. Haller (eds) (Vienna, Manz, 2006), p. 134.

expectations, based on their own legal background. *See* **Article 20**, at paras. 101 *et seq*. In short, therefore, as far as the *lex arbitri* is concerned, Austria's impact on the arbitration is reduced to those provisions directly pertinent to arbitration.

2.   Can the Parties Choose a 'Foreign' Procedural Law?

2-041 Some national procedural laws leave it to the parties – also in liberal interpretation of Article V(1)(d) of the New York Convention[76] – to agree amongst themselves the law of which country, and even which kind of foreign curial law, shall apply.[77] Even in these states the selection of a foreign procedural law will not render the law of the arbitral seat entirely irrelevant.[78]

2-042 In practice, the majority of international arbitration clauses do not contain a procedural choice of law clause.[79] Where they do, the choice of the law applicable to the arbitration can raise difficult issues. First, it is not always possible to determine clearly whether the parties, in choosing a particular curial law, intended to apply the civil procedure law of a certain state or intended to only apply its arbitration law.[80] Second, the attempt to isolate arbitration entirely from national procedural law may not always be advisable, particularly when the parties rely on the assistance of local courts or established law to ascertain their rights.[81] As *Lord Mustill* noted in *Channel Tunnel Group Ltd v. Balfour Beatty Construction Ltd*:[82]

> The parties chose an indeterminate law to govern their substantive rights, an elaborate process for ascertaining those rights and a location for that process outside the territories of the participants. The conspicuously neutral, a-national and extra-judicial structure may well have been the right choice for the special needs of the Channel Tunnel venture. But whether it was right or wrong, it is the choice which the parties made. The appellants now regret that choice (. . .). [T]hey now wish to obtain far-reaching relief through judicial means which they have been so scrupulous to exclude.[83]

---

76. NY Convention, **Annex 11**.
77. *See* Article 182 Swiss IPRG.
78. G.B. Born, *International Commercial Arbitration – Commentary and Materials* (2nd edn, The Hague, Kluwer Law International, 2001), p. 415; Articles 1693, 1694 Belgian Code of Civil Procedure.
79. *See Preliminary Award in ICC Case No. 5505 of 1987*, (1988) XIII YB Comm Arb 110.
80. G.B. Born, *International Commercial Arbitration – Commentary and Materials* (2nd edn, The Hague, Kluwer Law International, 2001), pp. 415 *et seq*.
81. T. Rensmann, 'Anational Arbitral Awards, Legal Phenomenon or Academic Phantom?' (1998) 15(2) J Int'l Arb, 37.
82. *Channel Tunnel Group Ltd. v. Balfour Beatty Construction Ltd*, [1993] A.C. 334 (House of Lords).
83. Quoted in T. Rensmann, 'Anational Arbitral Awards, Legal Phenomenon or Academic Phantom?' (1998) 15(2) J Int'l Arb, 65.

In fact, this case reveals the difficulties parties might occur when a different **2-043** procedural law has been chosen and the assistance of a state court becomes necessary during the arbitral process.[84] If parties find a particular *lex arbitri* attractive, it is therefore far more recommendable to locate the arbitration in that particular jurisdiction than opting for that set of rules in a differing forum.

In any event, the new Austrian arbitration law has put an end to the debate of **2-044** potentially incorporating foreign procedural rules. Under Section 577 ZPO, the choice of foreign law applying to the arbitral procedure, to the exclusion of mandatory provisions of Austrian arbitration law, is not possible, when the seat of the arbitration is in fact in Austria. The Working Group considered not much need for this in practice and stressed the intricacies that could arise with regard to mandatory provisions of national law.[85] Note, however, that the mandatory provisions under Austrian arbitration law impose only a general minimum standard of fairness leaving it to the parties to agree on deviating rules with respect to a wide spectrum of issues.[86]

3.   Mandatory Procedural Standards and Requirements

An important function of the *lex loci arbitri* is to provide safeguards for due **2-045** process; and to determine the scope of party autonomy and the powers of the arbitrators in regulating the procedure. It follows from Section 577(1) ZPO that, for proceedings where the seat is in Austria, the mandatory provisions of Austrian arbitration law must always be applied.[87] Hence, it is necessary to establish which rules of the *lex loci arbitri* are in fact to be considered mandatory and which are not.

3.1.   Mandatory Provisions under the Old Regime

The former arbitration law did not contain an explicit list specifying which provi- **2-046** sions were mandatory. Following *Fasching*, the mandatory provisions of Austrian arbitration law concerned the decision-making of the tribunal, the capacity to be a party to or conduct legal proceedings, the right to be heard, the arbitrators' duty to establish the facts of the case, and the prohibition on default decisions.[88] Provisions

---

84. See A. Redfern, M. Hunter, N. Blackaby and C. Partasides, *Law and Practice of International Commercial Arbitration* (4th edn, London, Sweet & Maxwell, 2004), para. 2-20.
85. P. Oberhammer in *Das Neue Schiedsrecht – Schiedsrechts-Änderungsgesetz 2006*, B. Kloiber, P. Oberhammer, W.H. Rechberger and H. Haller (eds) (Vienna, Manz, 2006), p. 160.
86. Explanatory Notes to Section 577 ZPO.
87. C. Liebscher, *The Austrian Arbitration Act 2006: Text and Notes* (The Hague, Kluwer Law International, 2006), Annotated Text to Section 577 ZPO.
88. H.W. Fasching, *Schiedsgericht und Schiedsverfahren im österreichischen und im internationalen Recht* (Vienna, Manz, 1973), pp. 101 *et seq.*

concerning the formal requirements and the challenge of the award were also considered mandatory.[89]

3.2.   Mandatory Provisions under the New Regime

2-047   The Working Group discussed the inclusion of a list of mandatory provisions in the new Arbitration Act.[90] In the end, this idea was not pursued as it was considered to be impossible to set up an exhaustive list of such provisions. It was argued that such a 'lithified approach' would hamper jurisprudence and doctrine to develop a catalogue, free of statutory restrictions and open to new developments. A logistical categorization of each scenario that might amount to an infringement of mandatory law was therefore considered to be a tedious task leading to 'doubtful results'.[91]

2-048   The Austrian legislator considers the mandatory provisions to be rather limited and refers to the parties' freedom to amend non-mandatory provisions.[92] Non-mandatory are certainly those provisions that, by statute, are open to the disposition of the parties. The statute uses wording such as 'unless otherwise agreed' or 'if nothing else has been agreed upon' and thereby clarifies that these provisions are within the disposition of the parties, hence non-mandatory.[93]

2-049   The new arbitration law contains only a few sections where mandatory provisions can be inferred by the language used. Section 594(2) ZPO, for example, reintroduces

89.   W. Jakusch in *Kommentar zur EO*, P. Angst (Vienna, Manz, 2000), Section 1, para. 89.
90.   That was in fact done in Section 4 (Schedule 1) English Arbitration Act 1996.
91.   P. Oberhammer in *Das Neue Schiedsrecht – Schiedsrechts-Änderungsgesetz 2006*, B. Kloiber, P. Oberhammer, W.H. Rechberger and H. Haller (eds) (Vienna, Manz, 2006), p. 149.
92.   Explanatory Notes to Section 577 ZPO.
93.   That could (non-exclusively) be argued for the following provisions of the ZPO under the new Austrian Arbitration Act: Section 580(1) (Receipt of written communication), Section 586 (Number of arbitrators), Section 587 (Procedure of appointing the arbitrator), Section 589(1) (Procedure of challenging an arbitrator – however, note the reservation made with respect to para. 3), Section 591(2) (Procedure after the appointment of a substitute arbitrator), Section 593(1) (ordering of provisional or protective measures), Section 595 (Seat of the arbitral tribunal and place of conduct of proceedings), Section 596 (Language to be used in the proceedings), Section 597(2) (Period of time for statements of claim and defence and for amendments or supplement of the claim), Section 598 (whether to hold oral hearings or conduct the proceedings in writing), Section 600(2) (consequences of the respondents' failure to respond within the determined period of time, or the failure of a party to perform any other procedural act), Section 601(Appointment and oral hearings of experts by the arbitral tribunal and each party's right to produce reports from its own experts), Section 603 (Law applicable to substance of dispute), Section 604 (Procedure of decision making by the panel of arbitrators), Section 606 (requirements regarding the signature of the award in arbitral proceedings with more than one arbitrator and the statement of reasons upon which the award is based), Section 609(1) (Decision of the arbitral tribunal on the obligation to reimburse the costs of the proceeding), Section 610 (Period of time in which a party can request the tribunal to correct, to give an interpretation or to make an additional award).

the principle of equal treatment and the right to be heard, two mandatory provisions.[94] However, this provision goes further and extends the parties' right to be represented or advised by persons of their own choosing. Here, the law clearly indicates its mandatory character as 'this right cannot be excluded or restricted'. Other provisions merely use indicative language, such as Section 599(1) or Section 601(3) ZPO. But does this mean that all non-mandatory provisions are expressly labelled as such and, by reverse, the remainder is mandatory?[95] This is not necessarily the case. It will, as noted by the drafters of the new Arbitration Act, to a greater extent be left to jurisprudence to determine the distinction.[96]

The arbitral procedure under Austrian law is discussed in detail in the content of **Article 20**. It bears emphasis that – subject to the mandatory provisions of the arbitration law – the parties are free to determine the rules of procedure, for example by incorporating the Vienna Rules.[97] Any changes the parties make to the Vienna Rules, however, will be tested under the threshold established in **Article 9(6)**.[98] **2-050**

D.   THE SEAT'S IMPACT ON THE ASSISTANCE AND INTERVENTION OF THE COURTS

The *lex loci arbitri* also typically regulates the intervention of state courts in, or in aid of, the arbitration; and it provides the rules for the challenge and enforcement of awards before the courts of the forum state. In Austria, the ZPO now addresses the question of court interference expressly, limiting the instances of court assistance and intervention to those expressly stipulated by the statute.[99] Thus, as noted, Section 578 ZPO states: **2-051**

> The court may only become active in matters governed by this section if this section so provides.

This provision prevents courts from interfering with the arbitral process outside the scope of the fourth section of the ZPO ('Arbitration Procedure') in any way unless there is a specific statutory basis in Austrian law that would expressly allow the courts to intervene.[100] As this provision is also applicable if the seat of the arbitral **2-052**

---

94. *See* **Article 20**, at para. 019.
95. *See* C. Liebscher, *The Austrian Arbitration Act 2006: Text and Notes* (The Hague, Kluwer Law International, 2006), Annotated Text to Section 594 ZPO.
96. *See* G. Zeiler, *Schiedsverfahren* (Vienna/Graz, Neuer Wissenschaftlicher Verlag, 2006), Section 594, p. 198, who considers additionally 'at least' Sections 597, 599, 602 and 617 ZPO as mandatory.
97. Section 594(1) ZPO.
98. *See* **Article 9(6)**, at paras. 091 *et seq.*
99. Under the former arbitration law that approach was only reflected in jurisprudence. *See* OGH, 12 April 1994, 4 Ob 1542/94.
100. *See* C. Liebscher, *The Austrian Arbitration Act 2006: Text and Notes* (The Hague, Kluwer Law International, 2006), Annotated Text to Section 578 ZPO.

tribunal is not within Austria or has not yet been determined, Austrian courts will also assist arbitral tribunals seated outside the territory of Austria, but only in those cases where they are expressly authorized to do so by the statute.[101] Below, those statutory provisions that still provide for the intervention of the Austrian courts are discussed together with those situations that typically arise in arbitration proceedings and require state court assistance.

1.   Subject Matter Jurisdiction

2-053   Under the previous regime of the fZPO, Austrian courts were, after some debate, willing to accept international jurisdiction in matters relating to international arbitration proceedings. For example, as to the challenge of an award, the Austrian courts have long accepted jurisdiction for international cases that have no nexus to Austria other than the seat of the arbitration. This has been clarified by the Austrian *Oberster Gerichtshof* in the famous case of *Norsolor I*[102] and others.[103]

2-054   While Section 577 ZPO thus expressly submits certain arbitration matters within the ambit of Austrian law, Section 578 ZPO provides, as noted previously, that the courts may only act in matters relating to arbitration where this is expressly permitted by the law. This provision, while deriving essentially from basic legal principles,[104] puts an affirmative limit on the jurisdiction of Austrian courts to hear arbitration-related matters. This is in line with the modern approach of voluntary denationalization of municipal systems to limit the interference of their courts with the arbitral process to a minimum.[105] As a result of this provision, claims to the state courts requesting a declaration that an arbitration agreement exists, or that it does not exist, are not permissible because there is no basis for such a procedure in the law.[106] For similar reasons, procedural orders by arbitral tribunals cannot be appealed before the state courts.[107]

---

101.   *See* Section 577(2) ZPO. In principle that was already possible before the enactment of the new ZPO. *See* P. Oberhammer, *Entwurf eines neuen Schiedsverfahrensrechts* (Vienna, Manz, 2002), p. 106.

102.   OGH, 1 February 1980, 2 Nd 502/80. The parties were French and Turkish and had no further connection with Austria, besides the ICC proceedings (with the award rendered herein) having taken place in Vienna. The losing French party commenced setting aside proceedings in accordance with Sections 596(1), 582 ZPO. *See* with detailed discussion and further annots E.-M. Bajons, 'Zur Nationalität internationaler Schiedssachen – Der Fall "Norsolor" vor den österreichischen Gerichten' in *Festschrift für Winfried Kralik zum 65. Geburtstag*, W.H. Rechberger und R. Welser (eds) (Vienna, Manz, 1986), p. 3.

103.   OGH, 25 June 1992, 7 Ob 545/92 and the detailed discussion of K. Heller, 'Die Anfechtung von Teil- und Zwischenschiedssprüchen in Östrreich' [1994] IPRax 142; *see also* OGH, 26 November 1987, 6 Ob 713/87; *also* OLG Vienna, 21 February 1985, 2 R 30/85, ÖJZ 1985/120.

104.   P. Oberhammer in *Das Neue Schiedsrecht – Schiedsrechts-Änderungsgesetz 2006*, B. Kloiber, P. Oberhammer, W.H. Rechberger and H. Haller (eds) (Vienna, Manz, 2006), p. 165.

105.   P. Oberhammer, *Entwurf eines neuen Schiedsverfahrensrechts* (Vienna, Manz, 2002), p. 32.

106.   *See* **Article 19**, at para. 026.

107.   That was ruled under the fZPO. *See* OGH, 12 April 1994, 4 Ob 1542/94.

2.   Assistance by the State Courts

There are circumstances in which an arbitral tribunal is asked to perform judicial **2-055**
acts that are by virtue of their nature reserved for the state courts (such as the
summoning of unwilling witnesses), typically because these acts involve some
measure of force that the arbitral tribunal is naturally not authorized to apply, or
because the judicial act would concern third parties that are not privy to the arbitration agreement and therefore outside the tribunal's jurisdictional reach. In such
cases, the state courts are available to assist the tribunal in the administration of
justice.[108] This was already provided for by Section 589 fZPO[109] and is now
confirmed in Section 602 ZPO:

> The arbitral tribunal, arbitrators who have been accordingly authorized by
> the arbitral tribunal, or a party with the approval of the arbitral tribunal,
> may request from a court the performance of judicial acts for which the arbitral
> tribunal has no authorization. The judicial assistance may also consist of the
> court requesting a foreign court or a public agency to conduct such acts.
> Section 37, paragraphs 2 to 5 and Sections 38, 39 and 40 JN shall apply
> accordingly, provided that the arbitral tribunal and the parties to the arbitral
> proceedings shall have the right to appeal in accordance with Section 40 JN.
> The arbitral tribunal or an arbitrator mandated by the arbitral tribunal and the
> parties may participate in the taking of evidence by the court and may pose
> questions. Section 289[110] of this law shall apply accordingly.

The reference to provisions in the Judicature Act (*Jurisdiktionsnorm* – JN) **2-056**
elevates such requests to the level of a legal obligation for state courts to assist.

---

108. Bi- and multilateral treaties govern the relationship between the state courts. With the intro-
      duction of Council Regulation No 1206/2001 of 28 May 2001 on cooperation between the
      courts of the Member States in the taking of evidence in civil or commercial matters, trans-
      national legal assistance between state courts has increasingly become more effective. For an
      overview on the impact, *see* N.A. Schoibl, 'Europäische Rechtshilfe bei der Beweisaufnahme
      in Zivil – und Handelssachen durch ordentliche Gerichte für Schiedsgerichte' in *Festschrift für
      W.H. Rechberger zum 60. Geburtstag*, L. Bittner, T. Klicka, G.E. Kodek and P. Oberhammer
      (eds) (Vienna/New York, Springer, 2005), pp. 513 *et seq.*
109. Section 589 fZPO: 'Those judicial acts considered necessary by the arbitrators but which they
      have no jurisdiction to undertake will be carried out by the State Court which has jurisdiction
      on the application of the arbitrators. In case of doubt the application is to be made to the District
      Court in whose district the act is to be carried out or the evidence to be taken. The Court to
      which the application is made shall accede to it insofar as it is not legally inadmissible. In
      particular the Court shall also take those decisions regarding taking of evidence which are
      reserved by the present statute in the case of taking of evidence on commission to the Court
      hearing the case.' In connection with Article XIII EGJN, *see* W.H. Rechberger and W. Melis in
      Kommentar zur ZPO, W.H. Rechberger (ed.) (2nd edn, Vienna/New York, Springer, 2000),
      Section 589, para 1.
110. Section 602 ZPO. This provision governs the taking of evidence.

In fact, the court is obliged to take all necessary steps to fulfil the requests of the arbitral tribunal *ex officio*. It may thereby also deviate from the rules of civil procedure, in case the request asked for requires procedural acts unknown to Austrian and is still in accordance with the law.

2-057 The right to request judicial assistance is vested with the arbitral tribunal which shall, on its own account, decide whether it wants to authorize just one member of the tribunal to participate in such proceedings alone. The parties themselves are entitled to request the court's assistance only with the approval of the arbitral tribunal; the process is therefore controlled by the tribunal.[111]

2-058 Jurisdiction for the requested judicial act lies with the district court located at the place where the act will be performed.[112] As most of the arbitral proceedings under the Vienna Rules are seated in Vienna, it is likely that one of the thirteen District Courts in Vienna[113] is competent for such a request.[114]

2-059 The request must comply with the form requirements of the ZPO. Therefore, irrespective of the language used in the arbitration proceedings, such request needs to be drafted in the German language.[115] In order to facilitate an effective consideration by the state court, it is recommendable to accompany such request with the arbitration agreement, an overview of the arbitral proceedings, a brief description of the subject-matter of the dispute, documentation of the constitution of the arbitral tribunal, documents evidencing the state court's jurisdiction, a statement of the arbitral tribunal as to why it considers itself not authorized to take the requested action and those parts of the arbitration file which are required or helpful for the court to execute the request.[116] The requested court is also competent to decide on the costs which might arise as a result of its assistance. In the end the

---

111. That can only apply to instances where the arbitral tribunal has no judicial authority for certain acts, such as summoning witnesses. This does in particular not apply to the parties' right to apply for interim measures in accordance with **Article 22**.

112. Section 37(2) JN; W.H. Rechberger and W. Melis *in Kommentar zur ZPO*, W.H. Rechberger (ed.) (3rd edn, Vienna/New York, Springer, 2006), Section 37 JN, para. 2.

113. There exist 142 District Courts in Austria and 13 District Courts in Vienna: District Court for the Innere Stadt, Josefstadt, Favoriten, Meidling, Hietzing, Fünfhaus, Hernals, Döbling, Leopoldstadt, Floridsdorf, Donaustadt, Liesing and one district court in commercial matters (*Bezirksgericht für Handelssachen in Wien*).

114. In matters relating to the Austrian Companies Register the *Handelsgericht Wien* (Commercial Court of Vienna) will be competent. *See* C. Klausegger, 'Legal Assistance by Austrian Courts in International Arbitration Proceedings' in *Austrian Arbitration Yearbook 2007*, C. Klausegger *et al.* (eds) (Vienna, Manz, 2007), p. 287.

115. B. Kloiber and H. Haller in *Das Neue Schiedsrecht – Schiedsrechts-Änderungsgesetz 2006*, B. Kloiber, P. Oberhammer, W.H. Rechberger and H. Haller (eds) (Vienna, Manz, 2006), p. 46.

116. C. Klausegger, 'Legal Assistance by Austrian Courts in International Arbitration Proceedings' in *Austrian Arbitration Yearbook 2007*, C. Klausegger *et al.* (eds) (Vienna, Manz, 2007), p. 287.

arbitral tribunal will decide which party has to refund those costs to the other party.[117]

The courts will only deny their assistance if this would violate a legal prohibition **2-060** under Austrian law.[118] Any disputes that might arise between the parties or the arbitral tribunal, on the one hand, and the court to which the request is made, on the other hand, will be decided by the Court of Appeal, in most cases the *Handelsgericht Wien* (Commercial Court of Vienna).[119]

The parties can be present when the court takes the evidence[120] and have a right to **2-061** ask the judge to put certain questions to witnesses and experts.[121] Direct examination by the parties (or their counsels) is only allowed with permission from the judge.[122]

In practice, there are cases where foreign state courts refuse their assistance to **2-062** arbitral tribunals. Hence, judicial assistance may also consist of the Austrian court formally requesting the assistance of a foreign court or a public agency under international agreements and diplomatic protocol. With this in mind, the Working Group discussed the possibility to enable an arbitral tribunal to request a preliminary ruling of the ECJ with regard to a specific question of EU law.[123] In the end, this idea was not pursued; however, it was deliberately left open if and how an arbitral tribunal might convince an Austrian court to follow such a request to this effect under Section 602 ZPO.[124]

3.   Challenge and Termination of the Arbitrator's Mandate

The Austrian courts are also authorized to review the challenge of a party against an **2-063** arbitrator (because the arbitrator lacks the required independence and impartiality

---

117. H. W. Fasching, *Kommentar zu den Zivilprozeßgesetzen IV* (Vienna, Manz, 1971), Section 589, p. 798.
118. Section 38(2) no. 2 JN.
119. Section 40 JN.
120. C. Liebscher, *The Austrian Arbitration Act 2006: Text and Notes* (The Hague, Kluwer Law International, 2006), Annotated Text to Section 614 ZPO.
121. Section 289(2) ZPO.
122. C. Klausegger, 'Legal Assistance by Austrian Courts in International Arbitration Proceedings' in *Austrian Arbitration Yearbook 2007*, C. Klausegger *et al.* (eds) (Vienna, Manz, 2007), p. 294.
123. *See* the opposing ruling of the ECJ, 23 March 1982, *Nordsee Deutsche Hochseefischerei GmbH v. Reederei Mond*, Case No. 102/81, [1982] ECR-01095 and ECJ, 1 June 1999, *Eco Swiss China Time Ltd v. Benetton International NV*, Case No. C-126/97, [1999] ECR I-3055 and rather recently in ECJ, 27 January 2005, *Denuit and Cordenier v. Transorient-Mosaique Voyages et Culture SA and Centro Móvil Milenium, Case No. 125/04*, [2005] ECR I-00923; *see also* T.D. De Groot, 'The Impact of the Benetton Decision on International Commercial Arbitration' (2003) 20(4) J Int'l Arb, 365, 370.
124. P. Oberhammer in *Das Neue Schiedsrecht – Schiedsrechts-Änderungsgesetz 2006*, B. Kloiber, P. Oberhammer, W.H. Rechberger and H. Haller (eds) (Vienna, Manz, 2006), p. 282.

or fails to meet other requirements agreed by the parties),[125] as well as requests to terminate an arbitrator's mandate.[126] Further, to the extent the parties have delegated these functions to arbitral institutions, the courts can be asked to review the institution's decision on such matters.[127]

4.   Interim Measures

2-064   Section 585 ZPO establishes parallel jurisdiction of state courts and arbitral tribunals with regard to interim measures in cases where the subject matter of the dispute falls within the scope of an arbitration agreement. It states:

> It is not incompatible with an arbitration agreement for a party to request from a court, before or during arbitral proceedings, an interim measure of protection and for a court to grant such measure.

2-065   Section 585 ZPO is addressed both to parties (who are free to apply to the state courts despite the existence of a pertinent arbitration agreement) and the state courts (who are permitted to grant interim relief in such circumstances). As such, Section 585 ZPO is an application of Section 578 ZPO. The considerations attaching to this parallel jurisdiction are discussed in greater detail below in the context of **Article 22**.

2-066   A more difficult question is raised by the notion of anti-suit injunctions. It has been argued that such injunctions are not permissible because there is no statutory basis for such injunctions in the law.[128] However, anti-suit injunctions can be considered a form of interim relief – and as such, there is in principle a statutory basis for them in Section 585 ZPO.[129] This provision expressly allows parties to apply to the state courts for interim measures of protection even where the subject matter of their dispute (and hence the protective measure sought) falls within the scope of an existing arbitration agreement. In principle, therefore, parties could arguably base their request for an anti-suit injunction on Section 585 ZPO.

2-067   Thus, the argument that anti-suit injunctions that seek to prevent parties from arbitrating ought not to be permissible requires qualification. It is true that, where an arbitration agreement exists, parties cannot, and should not, be prevented by virtue of an anti-suit injunction from arbitrating their claims. This, indeed, would be an undue interference with the arbitral process – not because of Section 578 ZPO, but because Section 584(1) ZPO affirmatively provides that even when the arbitration agreement is disputed in state court proceedings, an arbitration can be commenced, continued and concluded. It is therefore because

---

125. *See* **Article 16**, at para. 019.
126. *See* **Article 17**, at para. 021.
127. *See* **Article 16**, at paras. 047 *et seq.* and **Article 17**, at paras. 021 *et seq.*
128. *See* G. Zeiler, *Schiedsverfahren* (Vienna/Graz, Neuer Wissenschaftlicher Verlag, 2006), Section 578, pp. 34 *et seq.*
129. *See* **Article 22**, at paras. 122 *et seq.*

of Section 584(1) ZPO that an anti-suit injunction seeking to prevent the commencement, continuation or conclusion of an arbitration is not permissible under Austrian law. However, the situation is different if the anti-suit injunction seeks to prevent litigation or arbitration of a matter that is already subject to an arbitration. Section 584(3) ZPO – which applies even if the seat of the arbitration is outside Austria or not yet determined[130] – provides that, where an arbitration is pending, the claim cannot be made the subject of state court litigation, or indeed another arbitration. Where the arbitration is already pending, it might therefore be conceivable that a party can apply to the state courts (or an arbitral tribunal) based on Section 584(3) in conjunction with Section 585 ZPO for an anti-suit injunction seeking to enjoin the other party from arbitrating or litigating the same claim elsewhere. However, this may raise issues of European law (which are currently pending before the ECJ).[131]

5. Recourse Against the Award

One of the most important functions of state courts is the limited control over **2-068** awards, as exercised in setting aside proceedings. Here, the intervention of state courts is considered justified to protect basic norms of due process and public policy. Setting aside proceedings according to Section 611 ZPO with respect to awards rendered in Austria are discussed in detail in the context of **Article 27**, at paras. 033 *et seq.*

6. Enforcement of Foreign Awards

National arbitration awards do not require any *exequatur* to be enforceable in **2-069** Austria.[132] An arbitral award is considered to be 'national' if the place of arbitration is seated in Austria.[133] The place stated in the award is deemed to have been the seat of the arbitration.[134]

As foreign awards do not fall under the challenge regime of Section 611 ZPO, they **2-070** need to be declared enforceable in an *exequatur* proceeding in accordance with the provisions of the Austrian Enforcement Act (*Exekutionsordnung* – EO).[135] The

---

130. Section 577(2) ZPO.
131. *See West Tankers Inc v Ras Riunione Adriatica Di Sicurita Spa & ors* [2007] UKHL 4.
132. P. Angst, W. Jakusch and H. Pimmer, *Exekutionsordnung* (14th edn, Vienna, Manz, 2006), Section 1 no. 16, pp. 33 *et seq. See also* OGH, 24 May 2002, 3 Ob 18/02x.
133. *See* Section 577 ZPO.
134. *See* Section 606(3) ZPO.
135. Unless otherwise provided in international law or in legal acts of the European Union. *See* Section 614 ZPO. According to W.H. Rechberger and W. Melis in *Kommentar zur ZPO*, W.H. Rechberger (ed.) (3rd edn, Vienna/New York, Springer, 2006), Section 614, para. 2, the last part of this sentence is meant to cover future regulations of this issue by the EC. The recognition of the foreign arbitral awards takes effect *ipso jure*, however, not its enforcement. *See* G. Zeiler, *Schiedsverfahren* (Vienna/Graz, Neuer Wissenschaftlicher Verlag, 2006),

Austrian Enforcement Act is largely superseded by the substantial provisions of international conventions dealing with recognition and enforcement of arbitral awards, most notably the New York Convention.[136] The formal requirements can be fulfilled either by compliance with the provisions of the New York Convention or, cumulatively, by fulfilling both standards established under Austrian law and under the law applicable to the arbitration agreement.[137] The latter applies only if these provisions are more favourable than the New York Convention.

2-071 The new ZPO (Section 614 ZPO), recognizing the international trend of liberalization, states that presentation of the original arbitration agreement or a certified copy thereof,[138] is only necessary if requested by the court. This should facilitate the enforcement where no written arbitration agreement exists, for example when one party has impliedly accepted the arbitral tribunal's jurisdiction by not expressing any objections.[139] This abolishment of the strict form requirement however, does not mean that the existence of the arbitration agreement does not have to be proven when the opposing party raises pertinent objections in the *exequatur* proceeding.[140]

E.   THE SEAT'S IMPACT ON THE LAW APPLICABLE TO THE SUBSTANCE
                OF THE DISPUTE

2-072 Above, the impact of Austrian law as the *lex loci arbitri* on the arbitration agreement and on the arbitral procedure has been discussed. However, the seat of the arbitration may also impact on the applicable substantive law, for example by importing local conflict of law rules. Austrian law has now limited the impact of the choice of Austria as the seat of the arbitration by refraining from imposing its own conflict of law rules with respect to the substantive law governing the parties' relationship. This is discussed in the context of **Article 24**.

Section 614, p. 288. The *exequatur* proceedings are vital to afford such foreign awards legal effect. *See* OGH, 28 April 1931, 2 Ob 388, ZBl 1931/222.

136. *See* NY Covention, **Annex 11**. Note also pertaining provisions under the European Convention, **Annex 10**.

137. This ZPO draft initially sought to unify the form requirements and to expressly exclude the application of the NY Convention. *See* P. Oberhammer, *Entwurf eines neuen Schiedsverfahrensrechts* (Vienna, Manz, 2002). The final version actually introduced a more restrictive approach for foreign awards. *See* J. Power, *The Austrian Arbitration Act – A Practitioner's Guide to Sections 577-618 of the Austrian Code of Civil Procedure* (Vienna, Manz, 2006), Section 614, para. 4. A foreign arbitral award may also be declared partially enforceable. *See* A. Reiner, *Das neue österreichische Schiedsrecht/The new Austrian Arbitration Law* (Vienna, LexisNexis, 2006), Section 614, note 219 with reference to OGH, 26 January 1995, 3 Ob 221/04b.

138. As required by Article IV 1(b) of the NY Convention, **Annex 11**.

139. *See* **Article 19**, at paras. 006 *et seq.*

140. P. Oberhammer in *Das Neue Schiedsrecht – Schiedsrechts-Änderungsgesetz 2006*, B. Kloiber, P. Oberhammer, W.H. Rechberger and H. Haller (eds) (Vienna, Manz, 2006), p. 343.

Article 3
The Board

		Para.				Para.
I.	The Composition of the Board	1	V.	Decisions by Correspondence		21
	A. Introduction	1	VI.	Duties of Board Members		25
	B. Number and Term of Board			A. Standard of Performance		26
	Members	3		B. Independence of Board		
II.	The President of the Board	8		Members		28
III.	Meetings and Decisions of the			C. Confidentiality		
	Board	10		Obligations		31
	A. Board Meetings	10		D. Monitoring the Arbitration		
	B. Decisions of the Board	12		Proceedings		33
IV.	Conflicts of Board Members	16				

I. THE COMPOSITION OF THE BOARD

Article 3(1): The Board of the Centre shall have at least five members. They shall be appointed for a period of office of five years by the Extended Board of the Austrian Federal Economic Chamber by recommendation of the President of the Centre and can be reappointed. If there is no new appointment by the time of the expiration of a period of office, the members of the Board shall remain in office until a new Board is appointed. If a member of the Board is permanently incapacitated during his period of office (for instance, by resignation or death), a substitute member can be appointed for the remainder of the period of office of the serving Board.

A.   INTRODUCTION

3-001 The VIAC operates through two executive entities, the Secretary General and the Board, a collective organ. Most arbitral institutions employ organizational structures similar to those of the VIAC to allocate jurisdiction for various matters within their organization. Thus, the Board of the VIAC shares a number of common features with other equivalent organs, such as the International Court of Arbitration of the ICC or the Court of the London Court of International Arbitration.

3-002 There are, however, some noteworthy differences, which are partly due to the different organizational structure, and partly due to the specific powers entrusted, or not entrusted, to the Board under the Vienna Rules. Thus, the VIAC Board has no jurisdiction to approve terms of reference,[1] to formally scrutinize the award,[2] to decide upon the cost of the arbitration[3] or to interfere with the time limits in the expedited constitution of a tribunal.[4] In sum, therefore, the functions of the VIAC Board arise from, and cannot exceed, the powers conferred upon the Board by virtue of the Vienna Rules. These powers are perhaps limited in comparison with similar bodies of other prominent arbitral institutions, which leaves the VIAC Board entrusted only with certain key functions within the arbitral process. These are discussed in greater detail in the appropriate context of the Vienna Rules; the following section considers the general obligations applying to the Board and its members.

B.   NUMBER AND TERM OF BOARD MEMBERS

3-003 The VIAC Board members are appointed by the Board of the AFEC. This is consistent with Section 139 WKG, according to which the Extended Board of the Federal Chamber of Commerce must establish the Board of the VIAC. As discussed, the VIAC is thus structurally – but, given the independence of the VIAC's Board members, not functionally – integrated into AFEC.[5]

3-004 Also, the members of the VIAC Board are not simultaneously employees of AFEC; they are simply appointed 'on a private contractual basis'.[6] The terms of their service arise directly from the Vienna Rules and by accepting their appointment, the members of the Board undertake to provide certain services as set out in the

---

1. *See* Articles 18 and 19 ICC Rules.
2. *See* Article 27 ICC Rules.
3. *See* Articles 30 and 31 ICC Rules.
4. *See* Article 9 LCIA Rules.
5. For a more detailed discussion, *see* **Article 1**, at para. 007.
6. K. Heller, 'Die Rechtsstellung des Internationalen Schiedsgerichts der Wirtschaftskammer Österreich' [1994] wbl, 105, 108.

Vienna Rules. Board membership is an unpaid honorary office.[7] A discharge procedure is not provided for; the office simply expires with the end of the term or voluntary withdrawal from office. In case of a dispute amongst the Board members, the President of the Board will assume the role of an amiable adjudicator.

Article 3(1) provides that the Board 'shall have *at least* five members'. In practice, **3-005** the number of Board members has steadily increased over the years. At the time of the completion of this book, the Board of the VIAC consisted of eight members, prominent in the field of arbitration and elected from various professions, including academic and private practice.[8]

This also provides a pragmatic solution for the case of a Board member becoming **3-006** permanently unable to perform his office. Article 3(1) provides that in such a case, 'a substitute member can be appointed', but this will hardly become relevant in practice because the overall number of Board members is likely to remain at or above the minimum number of five Board members for the remainder of the office period.

An office term of five years serves to maintain continuity within the VIAC. This is **3-007** conducive to better administration and thus beneficial to the parties, and some of the Board's current members have already been acting for several office periods since the formation of the VIAC in the year 1975. The next re-appointment is scheduled for 2009.

II.   THE PRESIDENT OF THE BOARD

Article 3(2): The members of the Board shall elect one of their number to act as President for the duration of their term of office. Where the President is prevented, the member who is oldest by age shall take over his tasks.

While earlier versions of the Vienna Rules provided that the Board of AFEC **3-008** appoint the Chairman of the VIAC Board (as he was formerly called), the election of the President now exclusively falls to the VIAC Board members. This approach seems more appropriate because it underscores the VIAC's independence; the Board itself is most likely best suited to know who of its members will be most appropriate to serve as its President.

---

7. K. Heller, 'Die Rechtsstellung des Internationalen Schiedsgerichts der Wirtschaftskammer Österreich' [1994] wbl, 105, 108.
8. The Board currently consists of the following members: DDr. Werner Melis (President), Univ. Prof. Dr. Josef Aicher, Dr. Anton Baier, Hon. Prof. Dr. Gerhard Hopf, Dr. Günther Horvath, Gen. Sekr. Dr. Kurt Neuteufel, Univ. Prof. Dr. Walter H. Rechberger and Hofrat d. OGH Dr. Erich Schwarzenbacher.

3-009 Although the function of the President is expressly mentioned in the Vienna Rules, he cannot be considered to be a separate organ of the VIAC.[9] The function of the President is of a merely administrative nature, although it entails significant responsibilities.[10] Apart from the administrative tasks explicitly conferred by Article 3(3), the President serves as a link between the Secretary General and the other Board members, ensuring the seamless operation of the VIAC. Under the current practice, meetings of the Board are thus usually planned and prepared jointly by the President and the Secretary General. The President also plays a vital role in representing the VIAC externally. He presides over conferences sponsored by the VIAC and attends conferences and gatherings in the international arbitration community abroad on behalf of the VIAC. Also on behalf of the VIAC, the President usually signs bilateral agreements and initiates cooperation with other arbitral institutions.[11]

III.   MEETINGS AND DECISIONS OF THE BOARD

Article 3(3): The meetings of the Board are convened by the President, and presided over by the President or in his absence, by the most senior member by age present who is eligible to vote. The Board can validly take decisions if more than half of its members are present. It shall take decisions by a simple majority of the members present who are eligible to vote (see paragraph 4). In the event of a tie in voting, the Chairman shall have a casting vote.

A.   BOARD MEETINGS

3-010 Following the example of most arbitral institutions, the VIAC acts through its Board which in turn decides by majority vote during its meetings. These meetings are not open to the public, and all matters discussed are treated as confidential by the VIAC. Minutes of the meetings are prepared by the Secretary General, also on a confidential basis. The VIAC Board meetings are usually held every four to six weeks or on an *ad hoc* basis, if special occasions so demand.[12] The authority to

---

9. This can be derived from the Vienna Rules themselves, which do not specifically include the President in the liability exemption of **Article 8**. A different view is expressed by K. Heller, 'Die Rechtsstellung des Internationalen Schiedsgerichts der Wirtschaftskammer Österreich' [1994] wbl, 105, 108.

10. In similar vein, Article 1(3) ICC Rules provides that: 'The Chairman of the Court or, in the Chairman's absence or otherwise at his request, one of its Vice-Chairman shall have the power to take urgent decisions on behalf of the court, provided that any such decision is reported to the Court at its next session.'

11. *See* **Article 1**, at paras. 011 *et seq.*

12. This is in line with international practice. For example, the ICC Court holds monthly meetings as well as, on a more frequent basis, committee meetings. The plenary sessions are presided by the Chairman, or, in his absence, a Vice-Chairman.

convene such meetings is vested with the President. This was clarified with the last amendment of the Vienna Rules. However, each Board member has the right to request that such a meeting is held. In practice, the quorum requirements under Article 3(3) regarding the presence of a certain number of Board members have little relevance, as, according to Article 3(4), it is possible to adopt decisions by written circular. Article 3(3) also clarifies that in case of the President's absence, the most senior member attending shall preside over the meeting. This member shall also have the right to vote and, in the event that votes are tied, shall have the decisive vote.[13]

It is standing practice that the Board meetings are also attended by the Secretary **3-011** General who, at the beginning of the meetings, reports on pending cases. Thus, the Board has an up-to-date overview of pending cases, their status and their progress.

B.   DECISIONS OF THE BOARD

Under the current version of the Vienna Rules, no time limits apply to the Board's **3-012** decision-making process. This means that the parties, in principle, have no express ground in the Vienna Rules to complain about the Board's failure to decide a matter in a timely fashion.[14] However, it can be derived from the overall structure and purpose of the Vienna Rules that the parties and the arbitrators are entitled to Board decisions being made in due course. Provided there is no delay caused by a party or an arbitrator, the Board can in practice be expected to make a decision within four weeks.

According to Article 3(6), decisions of the Board are treated as confidential by the **3-013** VIAC, and the Board's reasoning is usually not made public. Nevertheless, it is common practice for the Board to substantiate and explain its decisions to the extent possible, so that the VIAC's rational becomes accessible to the parties and the arbitrators.[15] In past practice, the Board has in particular provided reasons for its decisions under **Article 16** (Challenge of Arbitrators) and **Article 17** (Early Termination of the Mandate of Arbitrators).[16] Where the Board is entitled to exercise discretion, it usually puts the parties on advance notice and offers them

---

13. As of the completion of this book, the current translation of this paragraph erroneously refers to the Chairman and not the President.

14. This could be debatable under Section 587(3) no. 3 ZPO pursuant to which any party may request a state court where a third party fails to perform a function (e.g. the substitutional appointment) within three months. *See* **Article 14**, at paras. 019 *et seq.*

15. *Bühler/Jarvin* have argued with regard to decisions by the ICC Court that '[t]his does not mean that the ICC Court can, in the exercise of the discretion which is afforded by the Parties under the Rules, render arbitrary decisions. It also does not mean that certain standards of due process (fairness) do not have to be satisfied.' *See* M. Bühler and S. Jarvin in *Practitioner's Handbook on International Arbitration*, F.B. Weigand (ed.) (Munich, C.H. Beck, 2002), p. 124.

16. *See* **Article 16**, at para. 045.

an opportunity to comment on the matter. Moreover, in the case of a challenge to the arbitrators, the parties will both have commented on the alleged challenge and will have seen the concerned arbitrator's comments as well. The factual account so developed can later be used by the parties before the state courts.

3-014 Beyond that, however, for example, in the case of the appointment of substitute arbitrators, specific reasons for Board decisions are not provided. This corresponds with the practice of other arbitral institutions and is intended to protect the Board from frivolous challenges of its decisions by frustrated parties. Since Board members confirm that meetings are often characterized by intense debate, the VIAC's reluctance to give reasoned decisions or provide board minutes also results from the desire to prevent parties from relying on differences of opinion between Board members.[17] Such differences are ultimately irrelevant; the decision is one of the Board, as a collective organ, and not of individual members. It also follows from the non-judicial nature of Board decisions that the decisions do not necessarily need to set forth certain reasoning and are typically (unless expressly provided for by mandatory law[18]) not open to challenge by the courts.[19]

3-015 Beyond the perspective of the individual case, however, it would facilitate arbitration under the Vienna Rules if Board decision(s) were published at least in anonymous format. This would lead, particularly in the case of **Article 9(6)** (refusal of administration) or the Board's assessment of independence and or impartiality of arbitrators, to increased transparency of the arbitral process, and hence to greater confidence by parties and arbitrators in the application of the Vienna Rules.

---

17. *Aden* has argued that provisions about the internal organization 'unnecessarily expose [the VIAC] insofar as the losing arbitration party will clutch at any straw to expose an irregularity'. *See* M. Aden, *Internationale Handelsschiedsgerichtsbarkeit* (2nd edn, Munich, C.H. Beck, 2003), p. 515. *Aden* alludes in particular to the possibility that, if the organizational rules of Article 3 were violated, parties could challenge an award on the basis that the constitution of the Tribunal was tainted and conceivably, a party could argue that an appointment by the VIAC in violation of, for example, the quorum requirement, leads to the constitution of a tribunal in violation of the parties' agreement in accordance with Section 611(2) no. 4 ZPO. This is doubtful at best. Not only is it debatable how an error of a clerical nature that does not violate equal opportunity or other core values in the appointment process can constitute a basis to challenge an award, moreover, the VIAC does not disclose its quorum that was actually present with respect to individual decisions. This would make it virtually impossible for an aggrieved party to rely on a decision by the Board when seeking to set aside the award. *See also* C. Liebscher in *Institutionelle Schiedsgerichtsbarkeit*, R.A. Schütze (ed.) (Cologne, Carl Heymanns Verlag, 2006), p. 266.

18. *See, e.g.,* **Article 16**, at paras. 047 *et seq.* for court review of a failed challenge; or **Article 17**, at paras. 021 *et seq.* for the court review of decisions denying the early termination of an arbitrator's mandate.

19. *See also* Article 7(4) ICC Rules: 'The decisions of the court as to the appointment, confirmation, challenge or replacement of an arbitrator shall be final and the reasons for such decisions shall not be communicated.' Also Article 29(1) LCIA Rules which provides for the decisions of the LCIA Court, which have an administrative nature, are conclusive and binding and the court shall not be required to give any reasons for such decisions.

IV.   CONFLICTS OF BOARD MEMBERS

Article 3(4): Members of the Board who are parties to particular arbitration proceedings in any capacity whatsoever shall be excluded from decisions pertaining to those proceedings, however they are to be counted for the presence quorum.

It is axiomatic that members of an arbitral institution ought not to participate in decisions in which they have a personal interest. However, given the lack of constitutional or statutory guarantees regarding the impartiality of the members of the arbitral institution, this principle needed to be set forth in express terms. This paragraph, together with **Article 7(3)**, thus demonstrates that the VIAC endeavours to ensure impartiality both at the level of the arbitrators and at Board level; this corresponds with the practice of other international arbitral institutions.[20] **3-016**

The official English translation of this paragraph is somewhat misleading, in that it suggests a more limited obligation of impartiality than is in fact imposed by the authentic German version. The English translation excludes members from the Board's decision-making in particular arbitration proceedings, 'who are parties' to such proceedings (albeit 'in any capacity whatsoever'). By contrast, the authentic German version excludes any Board member who is *involved* in the relevant arbitration in any capacity whatsoever.[21] Thus, a Board member will be conflicted if he or she is involved in the relevant arbitration in a capacity other than party or arbitrator, for example, as an expert witness or if he or she has any other personal interest in the arbitration or its outcome. Moreover Article 3(4) must be read together with Article 3(6), first sentence, which requires, *inter alia*, that Board members must act 'independently'. These provisions encourage a broad reading. **3-017**

---

20. *See, e.g.*, the approach of Article 2 App. II of ICC Rules: 'The chairman and the members of the Secretariat of the Court may not act as arbitrators or as counsel in cases submitted to ICC arbitration. The Court shall not appoint Vice-Chairman or members of the court as arbitrators. They may, however, be proposed for such duties by one or more of the parties, or pursuant to any other procedure agreed upon by the parties, subject to confirmation. When the Chairman, a Vice-Chairman or a member of the Court or of the Secretariat is involved in any capacity whatsoever in proceedings pending before the Court, such person must inform the Secretary General of the Court upon becoming aware of such involvement. Such person must refrain from participating in the discussions or in the decisions of the Court concerning the proceedings and must be absent from the courtroom whenever the matter is considered. Such person will not receive any material documentation or information pertaining to such proceedings.' *See* also Section 14(6) of the Statutes of the German Institution of Arbitration: 'The members of the "Appointing Committee" who participate in any function in arbitral proceedings before the DIS cannot participate in decisions regarding such arbitral proceedings. A member of the "Appointing Committee" may not be nominated as arbitrator pursuant to subsection 2 of this section.'
21. Article 3(4): 'Mitglieder des Präsidiums, die in irgendeiner Eigenschaft an einem Schiedsverfahren *beteiligt sind*, sind bei Entscheidungen, die dieses Verfahren betreffen, nicht stimmberechtigt, sind aber auf das Anwesenheitserfordernis anzurechnen.'

In particular, it can be inferred from the meaning typically attached to the notion of independence in international arbitration that a conflict of a Board member should be determined according to the same criteria used to asses the independence and impartiality of the arbitrators under **Articles 7** and **16**.

3-018 Article 3(4) and (6) also imply a duty for Board members to carefully scrutinize and disclose a potentially relevant involvement in the arbitration in question, and, in case of conflict, decline at their own volition to participate in the decision-making process of the Board with respect to this matter. Article 3 is drafted as a self-executing provision, and no particular act needs to be performed by the Board to exclude a Board member from the decision-making.

3-019 The last half sentence of Article 3(4) regarding the calculation of the presence quorum has been inserted with the last amendment, reflecting the VIAC's former decision-making practice. Following a literal interpretation of this provision, a Board member, although being excluded from the decision-making, may physically still be present at the decision-making and, arguably, during the foregoing debate on that issue. In order not to allow the pertaining Board member to gain any additional information, it is, however, standing practice that this person simply leaves the room as soon as the case is about to be discussed. For purposes of quorum, he is still counted as present.

3-020 There is no provision in the Vienna Rules for a dispute within the Board as to whether a member should be excluded or not. Given the Board members' reputation and experience in arbitration, such disputes are unlikely. Following a systematic approach to the Vienna Rules, it can be assumed that the President of the Board is arguably entitled to resolve such issues.

V.   DECISIONS BY CORRESPONDENCE

Article 3(5): Decisions may be made by correspondence. In this case the President shall submit a written proposal to the members and shall set a time limit for voting by correspondence. Paragraph 3, sub-sections 3. and 4. shall apply accordingly. Each member has the right to request a meeting regarding the written proposal.

3-021 As already mentioned, the VIAC Board is comprised of prominent practitioners and academics in the field of national and international commercial arbitration. This paragraph is therefore a pragmatic solution to the logistic issues arising from the international composition of the Board and facilitates swift decision-making.

3-022 The former version contained an indication that the relevant rules for such a decision by correspondence shall be determined by the Board. This was in fact done with the last amendment of this paragraph. It now describes the authority and the mode of decision-making.

In practice, the President, in co-ordination with the Secretary General, prepares a **3-023** draft decision that is circulated by fax to the individual Board members. The draft decision allows the recipient Board member to choose between the following three options: to agree with the draft decision, to object or to request a Board meeting. A personal meeting is compulsory, if it is requested by at least one Board member. There is no requirement to give specific reasons for the request.

Relatively routine decisions, such as decisions on the number of arbitrators under **3-024** **Article 14**, are usually made by correspondence. However, where an arbitrator is challenged under **Article 16** or the termination of the mandate is requested under **Article 17**, the Board typically meets in person.

VI.   DUTIES OF BOARD MEMBERS

Article 3(6): The members of the Board must perform their duties to the best of their ability; they are independent and are not subject to any directives in that respect. They are bound to secrecy on all matters coming to their notice in the course of their duties.

The Board's most important function is 'to allow for the arbitrators to commence **3-025** and continue their work'.[22] Its general duties arise directly from the Vienna Rules and will be discussed in detail where appropriate. Article 3(6) applies to the Board's discharge of all its functions, requiring that Board members: (i) perform their duties to the best of their ability; (ii) are and remain independent and (iii) are bound to secrecy on all matters coming to their notice in the course of carrying out their duties. All three requirements are discussed below. In addition, however, the following section also considers the Board's implied duty to ensure that arbitration proceedings administered by the VIAC comply with the Vienna Rules.

A.   STANDARD OF PERFORMANCE

Besides the duties that are imposed directly by the Vienna Rules, such as the **3-026** substitutional appointment[23] or the challenge procedure of arbitrators,[24] there is an implied obligation of the Board members to regularly attend the Board meetings and to support the decision finding process to the best way possible.

The addendum that the Board members must perform all of their duties 'to the best **3-027** of their ability' mainly serves the purpose to emphasize the particularly diligent

---

22. *See* K. Heller, 'Die Rechtsstellung des Internationalen Schiedsgerichts der Wirtschaftskammer Österreich' [1994] wbl, 105, 116.
23. *See* **Article 14**, at paras. 037 *et seq.*, 056 *et seq.* and 064 *et seq.*
24. *See* **Article 16**, at paras. 040 *et seq.*

modus operandi of its members. It raises the standard of duties of the members to an obligation in the true sense of the word.

B.   INDEPENDENCE OF BOARD MEMBERS

3-028 The independence of each Board member is grounded in the legal relationship between the Board members and the AFEC. Article 3(6), to a certain extent, implements Section 139(4) WKG according to which the organs of the VIAC are, with regard to their office, independent and not bound to follow any directives. This provision cannot be considered to merely afford a privilege; it also imposes the additional obligation for each Board member to remain independent during his or her term of office.

3-029 As soon as a Board member notices that he or she may have an interest in an arbitration proceeding to which the decision relates, he or she must disclose this fact to the Secretary General and to the President of the Board immediately.

3-030 The provision of **Article 7(3)** reinforces the principle of independence, as it permits Board members only to act as Chairman or sole arbitrator in arbitration proceedings under the Vienna Rules.[25] In practice, the Board endeavours to avoid the impression that 'friendly appointment' procedures are applied whereby Board members would be favoured in substitutional appointment procedures. Hence, it is established practice that in principle Board members will not be appointed in substitutional appointment procedures, unless this is particularly appropriate in the specific circumstances of the individual case.

C.   CONFIDENTIALITY OBLIGATIONS

3-031 Confidentiality obligations imposed on the arbitral institution and its officers accord the parties' and the arbitrators' additional comfort.[26] *Liebscher* rightly notes that confidentiality obligations are already enshrined in Section 69 WKG as an administrative provision of public law.[27] Therefore, Article 3(6) introduces an *additional* obligation under private law which affords the parties a right to

---

25. *See* **Article 7(3)**, at paras. 043 *et seq.*
26. In similar vein, *see, e.g.,* Article 31(2) LCIA Rules: 'After the award has been made (. . .), neither the LCIA, the LCIA Court (including its President, Vice-Presidents and individual members), the Registrar, any deputy Registrar, any arbitrator and any expert to the Arbitral Tribunal shall be under any legal obligation to make any statement to any person about any matter concerning the arbitration, nor shall any party seek to make any of these persons a witness in any legal or other proceedings arising out of the arbitration.'
27. M. Aden, *Internationale Handelsschiedsgerichtsbarkeit* (2nd edn, Munich, C.H. Beck, 2003), p. 515. According to *Aden,* however, these confidentiality obligations arise from public administrative law and confer no individual rights on the parties.

confidentiality as against the Board members. Consequently, a release from confidentiality requires the consent of all parties.[28]

The duty of confidentiality is not absolute, however. **Article 30** entitles the Board **3-032**
to publish awards in an anonymous form, unless the parties object to such a
publication.[29]

D.   Monitoring the Arbitration Proceedings

Most arbitral institutions consider themselves not only to serve as the administrator **3-033**
of the dispute, but also to ensure that the arbitration complies with 'their' set of
rules.[30] Indeed, some other arbitration rules specifically require the institution to
execute its functions in the spirit of the rules.[31] For the VIAC, such a duty could
follow from the wording of **Article 1** which provides that it 'shall make arrangements for settlement by arbitration'. It is indeed a decisive question how far the
institution is willing to actively insert itself into the arbitration, for example, when
the institution realizes that the arbitrators persistently ignore the arbitration rules or
that they apply them incorrectly. This presents a particularly difficult situation to
the institution where the arbitrator has been appointed by the VIAC itself. The
current President of the VIAC's Board takes the following position:

> The question still arises as to how an arbitral institution shall react if it dis-
> covers that an arbitrator has, nevertheless, made a mistake in the application of
> its rules. I think that, in this event, if it discovers the mistake in time for
> possible correction, it will have to consider the following: whether or not
> the deviation from its rules can adversely affect the validity of the award, if
> it is attacked by a party on these grounds. In this case, it will have to react in
> order to save the situation. The same will apply when the deviation might

---

28. C. Liebscher in *Institutionelle Schiedsgerichtsbarkeit*, R.A. Schütze (ed.) (Cologne, Carl Hey-
    manns Verlag, 2006), p. 266.
29. *See* **Article 30**, at para. 003.
30. *See* Article 1(1) App. I ICC Rules: 'The function of the International Court of Arbitration of the
    International Chamber of Commerce (the 'Court') is to ensure the application of the Rules of
    Arbitration of the International Chamber of Commerce, and it has all the necessary powers of
    that purpose.' The intention of this provision was to affirm the role of the Court as an admin-
    istrator of the Rules and to confirm the court's authority to require that the parties and arbitrators
    comply with provisions of these Rules. *See* in detail Y. Derains and E.A. Schwartz, *A Guide to
    the ICC Rules of Arbitration* (2nd edn, The Hague, Kluwer Law International, 2005), p. 19.
31. *See* Article 35 ICC Rules: 'In all matters not expressly provided for in these Rules, the Court and
    the Arbitral Tribunal shall act in the spirit of these Rules (. . .).' Also, Article 32(2) LCIA: 'In all
    matters not expressly provided for in these Rules, the LCIA Court, the Arbitral Tribunal and the
    parties shall act in the spirit of these Rules and shall make every reasonable effort to ensure that
    an award is legally enforceable.' Similarly, in Article 36 AAA/ICDR Rules: 'The Tribunal shall
    interpret and apply these rules insofar as they relate to its powers and duties. The administrator
    shall interpret and apply all other rules.'

create some other damages to a party. In other cases of minor deviations, it might sometimes be prudent not to interfere, in order not to endanger the climate of an arbitration. In any case, it will not always be easy for an arbitration institution to take the appropriate decision.[32]

3-034 The authority to directly interfere with the arbitration is in any event not entirely alien to the Vienna Rules. **Article 9(6)**, for example, allows the Board to refuse the administration of a case when the parties made agreements that deviate from the Vienna Rules. Where the Board is unable to amicably convince the arbitrator to comply with the Rules, it can in very grave cases also consider relieving the arbitrator of his office under **Article 17(1)(d)** and **(2)**. However, cases of deliberate misconduct are rare; most problems arise in connection with the speed the arbitration proceedings are conducted.

3-035 In this context it must be asked if the VIAC has in fact a duty to monitor the arbitration proceedings administered under its Rules. This is arguably the case. Indeed, **Article 17** confirms the VIAC's commitment to a swift conduct of the arbitration proceedings as an arbitrator mandate may be terminated, *inter alia*, if he or she 'unduly delays the proceedings'. On this ground, the Board can even terminate an arbitrator's mandate *ex officio* if it considers the reasons for the undue delay to be permanent.[33] In practice, an institution will only cautiously exercise this power, as the appointment of a replacement arbitrator may cause considerable delay in and of itself.

---

32. W. Melis, 'Function and Responsibility of Arbitral Institutions' (1991) XIII Comp L YB Int'l Bus 115.
33. *See* **Article 17**, at paras. 019 *et seq.*

Article 4

The International Advisory Board

Article 4: The International Advisory Board consists of international arbitration experts who may be invited by the respective Board of the Centre for the duration of its period of office. Its purpose is to discuss factual issues of immediate interest.

With the new provision of Article 4, the VIAC has now established an International Advisory Board, designed to enable the VIAC to facilitate the exchange of expertise on a regular and formalized basis. With Article 4, the VIAC follows the example of other institutions that want to impress upon their international users that their institutional horizon reaches beyond the borders of the institution's host country. However, the Advisory Board is not part of the institution's decision-making process as such; it is clear that its role is merely advisory and no further powers have been vested with the Advisory Board through other provisions of the Vienna Rules. **4-001**

At the time of publication, the first Advisory Board under the new rules was in the process of being established. Evidently, clear specifications about member qualifications were deliberately avoided in order to maintain the highest amount of flexibility in the selection process. It is also not clear at first sight who should be responsible for appointing the Advisory Board members and how this would occur. Systematically, it is safe to assume that this authority is vested with the VIAC Board. **4-002**

Article 4 provides that advisory experts will be 'invited by the respective Board of the Centre for the duration of its period of office'. This can be understood as meaning that each new Board of the VIAC can and will appoint its own advisory panel. Consequently, the mandate of the previous Advisory Board members will expire automatically, and simultaneously, with the end of the VIAC Board's term. A separate act of termination will not be required. **4-003**

4-004 The function of the Advisory Board member is an honorary, unsalaried position. It can be expected that VIAC will not adopt a too narrow reading of this provision and will, besides 'factual issues of immediate interest', also discuss those topical issues of arbitration that have a long-term impact on the process beyond the day-to-day operations and thus deserve in-depth examination and discussion.

Article 5

The Secretary General

		Para.				Para.
I.	The Appointment of the Secretary General	1		D.	Further Activities of the Secretariat	14
	A. Introduction	1	III.	Duties of the Secretary General		18
	B. Appointment Procedure	2		A. Standard of Performance		18
II.	Authority of the Secretary General	5		B. Independence of the Secretary General		20
	A. Activities of the Secretariat	5		C. Confidentiality Obligations		24
	B. Administration of the Centre	7		D. Decisions by the Secretary General		25
	C. Assistance to the VIAC Board	11	IV.	Inability to Perform		27

I. THE APPOINTMENT OF THE SECRETARY GENERAL

Article 5(1): The Secretary General of the Centre shall be appointed by the Extended Board of the Austrian Federal Economic Chamber for a period of office of five years by recommendation of the Board of the Arbitral Centre; he can be reappointed. The third sentence of Article 3 paragraph 1, shall apply by analogy.

A. INTRODUCTION

The Secretary General is, in addition to the Board, the second executive entity **5-001** through which the VIAC operates.[1] The Secretary General's position is at the heart

---

1. It was with the last amendment of the Vienna Rules that the Secretary was renamed into Secretary General. This position is currently occupied by Dr. Manfred Heider.

of the arbitral process. Overseeing the Secretariat, he or she will be the first point of contact for the parties when approaching the institution, whether on an informal basis with general inquiries about arbitrating under the Vienna Rules, or whether by filing a statement of claims. The Secretary General is exclusively responsible for the administrative functions of the VIAC, such as processing the statement of claims (*see* **Article 9**), collecting the registration fee, requesting the memorandum in reply (*see* **Article 10**), obtaining the arbitrators' acceptance of mandate and declaration of independence (*see* **Article 7**), and submitting the file to the Arbitral Tribunal (*see* **Article 11**). He is in direct contact with the arbitrator(s) when determining the cost of the arbitration (*see* **Article 34**) and is entitled to fix the amount in dispute when it was obviously undervalued by the parties (*see* **Article 36**). The Secretary General also assists the parties, alone or even sometimes together with the Arbitral Tribunal, in complying with whatever further formalities or requests might arise in the process. Hence, the Secretary General can be considered the *anima* of the arbitral administration. His role and functions under the Vienna Rules are discussed below.

B.   APPOINTMENT PROCEDURE

5-002   Given the important functions of the Secretary General, the Board needs to be in a position to assure that only the best and most suitable candidates are elected. Despite this, other versions of the Vienna Rules afforded no rights to the VIAC Board. With the 2001 amendment the Board obtained the right to propose the Secretary General to the AFEC. This proposal is not binding upon the AFEC. In practice, however, the AFEC has always followed the proposals of the VIAC Board in the past and is likely to continue that practice in the future.[2]

5-003   The Secretary General, unlike the members of the VIAC Board, is a paid position, in a direct employment contract with the Economic Chamber. Albeit being an employee of the AFEC, the Secretary General enjoys special rights with regard to confidentiality and independence, discussed further below. The Secretary General's term of office is for the same period of five years as for the Board members. (Unlimited) re-appointment is permissible.

5-004   The reference to the analogous application of the third sentence of **Article 3(1)** is in fact a false translation of the authentic German version of this Article. In reality, the analogous application of the second sentence of **Article 3(1)** is intended, which provides for the Board that in case there is no new appointment by the time the term of the office expires, the members of the Board shall remain in office until a new Board is appointed. The same, therefore, applies to the Secretary General by analogy. Interestingly, this is the only place where the Vienna Rules make explicit

---

2.   Note, however, that it is not the extended Board of the AFEC that is competent for this appointment, as it is for the Board members under **Article 3**.

reference to an *analogous* application of another provision, at least in the context of determining the appointment procedure of its executive organs.[3]

II.   AUTHORITY OF THE SECRETARY GENERAL

Article 5(2): The Secretary General shall direct the activities of the Secretariat and shall perform the administrative tasks of the Centre insofar as they are not reserved to the Board of the Centre.

A.   ACTIVITIES OF THE SECRETARIAT

Although the Vienna Rules make a distinction between the Secretary General and **5-005** the Secretariat, the latter is not a separate organ of the VIAC. Rather, it serves as the executive arm of the Secretary General, assisting him in the execution of his duties under the Vienna Rules. Hence, any act of the Secretariat can be considered to be executed on behalf of the Secretary General. The staff of the Secretariat is, again, in a direct employment relationship with the AFEC. The duties of confidentiality, explicitly imposed upon the Secretary General by Article 5(3), also apply to the staff without any restriction. The privilege of independency remains limited by the statutory provisions of Austrian labour law.

The VIAC is under no obligation to provide for a specific number of personnel for **5-006** its Secretariat. However, due to the contractual relation between it and the parties, and the statutory mission it fulfils, there exists a duty to provide and secure infrastructure that permits the proper administration of the arbitral process. This includes the ability to provide assistance to the parties and the arbitrators. Given the increasing caseload the VIAC has to administer, it is perhaps surprising that the Secretariat of the VIAC consists of a relatively small team of personnel, individually referred to as file managers.

B.   ADMINISTRATION OF THE CENTRE

The Secretary General shall perform the administrative task 'insofar as they are not **5-007** reserved for the Board'. This clarifies that the Secretary General has, in principle, a subsidiary power for all administrative matters of the VIAC.[4] As a default rule, this

---

3.   *See* **Article 1**, at para. 159.
4.   This is in line with other prominent arbitral institutions. Under the ICC Rules, there is no explicit provision dealing with the competence of the Secretary General. However, several administrative tasks can be found in the pertaining Articles, such as the confirmation of the arbitrators (Article 9(2) ICC Rules), certification of additional copies of the award (Article 28(2) ICC Rules) or requesting the claimant for paying a provisional advance for costs of arbitration (Article 30(1) ICC Rules). Furthermore, 'the Secretariat may, with the approval of the Court, issue notes and other documents

includes all matters even if they are of an administrative nature not explicitly attributed to the Secretary General.

5-008 The administration of the Centre can be seen to comprise everything that requires an administrative act which is based on, or results from, the application of the Vienna Rules. This agenda can be divided into 'introductory' and 'concluding' tasks. The former set the arbitration proceeding in motion. This part of the proceedings requires the Secretary General to play an active role in order to facilitate the swift commencement of the process. It includes the *prima facie* scrutiny and collection of the statements of claims; its delivery upon the respondent; the arbitrator's contract; and the determination and the collection of the deposit of costs.

5-009 Once the file has been transmitted to the arbitrator(s), the Secretary General will usually not be required to engage directly in the proceedings, save where the parties or the arbitrators require him to do so (e.g. when the amount in dispute has been increased, cash outlays need to be reimbursed, etc.). At the end of the proceedings, shortly before the award will be rendered, the Secretary General will then determine the costs of the arbitration,[5] confirm the award and deliver it upon the parties.[6]

5-010 The tasks conferred upon the Secretary General are, however, of a purely administrative nature, in the sense that he is not included in the decision-making process of the Arbitral Tribunal or the VIAC Board. Arguably, the line between administrative and non-administrative tasks might not always be easy to draw, for example, when the Secretary General undertakes a *prima facie* scrutiny of the statement of claims and thereby exercises in fact a 'semi-jurisdictional authority' to decline acceptance of the statement of claims.[7] Similarly, a decision whether a declaration to offset is in fact and in law with or without connection to the main claim, exceeds the notion of 'administration'.[8] The same applies when the Secretary General, on

---

for the information of the parties and the arbitrators, or as necessary for the proper conduct of the arbitral proceedings' (Article 5(2) App. II to the ICC Rules). Under the LCIA Rules, the administrative functions, such as communication, sending and receipt of communication are in the responsibility of the Registrar. Under the DIS Rules the administrative functions are administered by the Secretariat. Under the AAA/ICDR Rules it is also an Administrator that is responsible for the administrative tasks of the Secretariat, such as the receipt of the notice of arbitration, statement of defence or counter-claims as well as the publishing of the award (Article 27(8) AAA/ICDR Rules), arrangement and substitute establishment of compensation of arbitrators (Article 32 AAA/ICDR Rules), requesting the filing party for the advance for the costs of arbitration (Article 33 AAA/ ICDR Rules). Note, however, the Administrator is also responsible for substitutional procedures, such as the determination and appointment of the arbitrator(s) and the decision on the challenge of the arbitrators as well as the interpretation and application of all other rules.

5. *See* **Article 34**, at paras. 001 *et seq.*
6. *See* **Article 27**, at paras. 017 and 019.
7. *See* discussion under **Article 9**, at paras. 008 and 072 *et seq.*
8. *See* **Article 36(3)**, at paras. 012 *et seq.*

his own motion, deviates from the statement of the parties and fixes the amount in dispute based on his own calculation.[9] All these acts have potentially significant impact on the proceedings and are by their appearance and effect rather of jurisdictional than administrative nature. Still, they lie in the sole and express authority of the Secretary General. The better way to describe his function is therefore not only the administration of the Centre, but more generally the exercise of his rights and obligations as explicitly foreseen under the Vienna Rules.

C.   ASSISTANCE TO THE VIAC BOARD

In those matters that are reserved to the Board of the Centre, it is standing practice **5-011** that the Secretary General also facilitates the correspondence of the Board and administers the preparation of the decision-making process.[10] By doing so, he will not interfere with the merits of the Board's decision-making and will restrict his activities to the practical implementation and execution of the Board's instructions.

Although the Board always maintains the authority to exercise its rights under the **5-012** Vienna Rules in complete independence, it is in fact dependant on the Secretary General, not so much for reasons of convenience, but, in particular, for process-related considerations. It is the Secretary General who will first encounter the arbitration agreement in order to assess if it deviates from the Vienna Rules to such an extent that the Board might refuse administering the case under **Article 9(6)**. It will also be the Secretary General who will notice disagreement between the parties regarding their choice on the number, or the identity of the arbitrators and inform the Board about the necessity to make a default decision in accordance with **Article 14**.

This ultimately leads again to the question if the VIAC, through its Secretary **5-013** General, has a duty to monitor the arbitration proceedings administered under its rules. As already discussed such a duty arguably exists. The Secretary General can be seen in the most practical position to facilitate this obligation. In order to increase the necessary exchange of information the Secretary General regularly attends the Board meetings, in an advisory capacity.[11]

D.   FURTHER ACTIVITIES OF THE SECRETARIAT

In addition to those activities explicitly mentioned in the Vienna Rules, the **5-014** Secretary General is available to the parties and the arbitrators for information and advice with regard to the administrative practice of the VIAC. This is an

---

9. *See* **Article 36(5)**, at paras. 023 *et seq.*
10. *See* **Article 3**, at para. 023.
11. This was explicitly foreseen in the 1991 version of the Vienna Rules, which stipulated in its Article 4 that 'the Secretary shall attend the meetings of the Board in an advisory capacity'.

important auxiliary function which serves to increase the parties' confidence in choosing the Vienna Rules for the resolution of their dispute. However, any advice given by the Secretary General has to strike a delicate balance between being practical and helpful and at the same time maintaining the required neutrality of the arbitral institution. For example, it is perceived to be acceptable for the Secretary General to assist a party more directly with the formal requirements of commencing the arbitration rather than during the course of the proceedings.

> For an institution, there will often be a temptation to provide advice to a party that will help to ensure that the arbitration will result in an award that is enforceable. Indeed, many parties consider that this is one of the functions of an institution and that, as guardians of the arbitration process, institutions should actively preserve and protect its efficacy and credibility through not only advice but action, as required.[12]

5-015 To that extent the Secretary General will strive to provide assistance to the parties in the arbitration, provided that he or she does not jeopardize the required neutrality he owes to the parties and the arbitrators.

5-016 As an arbitral institution dedicated to international commercial arbitration, the VIAC not only administers arbitration proceedings under the Vienna Rules, but also offers its assistance to any party seeking advice in arbitration matters, in particular where Austrian parties or Vienna as a seat of the arbitration are involved. The VIAC also regularly provides infrastructure for *ad hoc* arbitration proceedings or for arbitrations under other rules according to international cooperation agreements with other arbitral institutions.[13] Assistance is also offered when the AFEC is approached to act as the appointing authority under the UNCITRAL Rules, or the President of the Chamber of Commerce is requested to facilitate the substitutional appointment procedure in accordance with the European Convention.[14] Technically speaking, these requests are based on different legal provisions and are not directly addressed to the VIAC and thus not within the scope of its powers. However, as this service is closely connected with the administration of arbitration proceedings in general, it has so far been common practice (notwithstanding the different legal provisions involved) for parties to approach the VIAC's Secretary General for further assistance.

5-017 It bears emphasis that the VIAC is also actively involved in the organization and promotion of international conferences[15] and seminars[16] dedicated to commercial arbitration.[17]

---

12. *See* Y. Derains and E.A. Schwartz, *A Guide to the ICC Rules of Arbitration* (2nd edn, The Hague, Kluwer Law International, 2005), p. 27. *See also* under **Article 3**, at paras. 025 and 033 *et seq.*, where the Board's duty to safeguard the proceedings is discussed.
13. *See* **Article 1**, at paras. 014 *et seq.*
14. *See* **Article 1**, at paras. 016 *et seq.*; European Convention, **Annex 10**.
15. *See* **Article 3**, at para. 009.
16. The VIAC regularly invites young practitioners to seminars in Herrnstein.
17. In the past these events were always a remarkable success and marked by the attendance of distinguished practitioners and experts in the field of international arbitration.

III.   DUTIES OF THE SECRETARY GENERAL

Article 5(3): The Secretary General must perform his duties to the best of his ability and is not subject to any directives in that respect. He is bound to secrecy on all matters coming to his notice in the course of his duties.

A.   STANDARD OF PERFORMANCE

As discussed, the Secretary General can be seen as the *anima* of the arbitral **5-018** process. His most important function is to facilitate the administration of the proceedings and organize the correct application of the Vienna Rules. His general duties arise directly from the Vienna Rules and will be discussed in detail where appropriate. Article 5(3) applies to the Secretary General's discharge of all his functions, requiring that he (i) performs his duties to the best of his abilities; (ii) is not subject to any directives and (iii) is bound to secrecy on all matters coming to his notice in the course of carrying out his duties. All three requirements are discussed below. In addition, however, the Secretary General has an implied duty to assist the Board to ensure that arbitration proceedings administered by the VIAC comply with the Vienna Rules.

The addendum that the Secretary General must perform all of his duties 'to the best **5-019** of his ability' mainly serves the purpose to emphasize the particularly diligent *modus operandi* of this particular organ of the VIAC. As with the VIAC Board members, this raises the standard of performance to an obligation in the true sense of the word.

B.   INDEPENDENCE OF THE SECRETARY GENERAL

The independence of the Secretary General is grounded in the legal relationship **5-020** between the Board members and the AFEC. Article 5(3), to an extent, implements Section 139(4) WKG according to which the organs of the VIAC are, with regard to their office, independent and not bound to follow any directives.

Interestingly, Article 5 does not – or at least not in terms quite as express as **5-021** **Article 3** for the members of the VIAC Board – directly convey the privilege of independence to the Secretary General. This is only granted by indirect reference that this organ 'is not subject to any directives in that respect'. This is because the Secretary General stands in a direct working relation with the AFEC and, thus, his independence can only be granted within the limits imposed by the mandatory provisions of Austrian labour law.

In any case, AFEC is not entitled to give directions to the Secretary General as far **5-022** as the performance of his duties under the Vienna Rules is concerned. This independence, however, is limited to those tasks that are entrusted to him, either by way of direct submission by the Vienna Rules or by way of the default rule discussed under paragraph 2. In case the Secretary General acts for or on behalf of the VIAC

Board, he is confined to the directives issued by this organ. Outside the scope of these tasks, the Board also has no authority either in a supervisory or any other instructing function over the Secretary General.[18]

5-023 Article 5(3) cannot be considered to merely afford a privilege; it also imposes the obligation on the Secretary General to remain independent during his or her term of office. Hence, any sort of involvement in arbitration proceedings under the Vienna Rules, other than in his professional capacity as Secretary General, would undermine his ability to perform his duties and arguably trigger the consequences of Article 5(4). Thus, as soon as a the Secretary General notices that he may have an interest in an arbitration proceeding to which the decision relates, he must disclose this fact to the VIAC Board immediately. As a result, although there is in fact no provision which explicitly bars the Secretary General to act either as arbitrator or party counsel (or in any other capacity) in arbitration proceedings under the Vienna Rules, Artcile 5(3) can be seen as an implied restriction, applicable for all arbitration cases which became pending during the office of the Secretary General.

C.   CONFIDENTIALITY OBLIGATIONS

5-024 As discussed, confidentiality obligations imposed on the arbitral institution and its officers afford the parties and the arbitrators additional comfort.[19] Article 5(3) introduces an independent obligation under private law which affords the parties a right to confidentiality as against the Secretary General. Consequently, a release from confidentiality requires the consent of all parties; the same standards that apply to the VIAC Board members are also applicable to the Secretary General.[20] This obligation of confidentiality is important, in particular when third parties, which were not involved in the arbitration process, approach the VIAC and request the release of confidential information.

D.   DECISIONS BY THE SECRETARY GENERAL

5-025 The Secretary General decides alone and in his own right, and is not required to consult with the Board on issues entrusted to him (although he will do so in

---

18. Different approach can be found under Article 3(2) LCIA Rules, where 'the functions of the Registrar under these Rules shall be performed by the Registrar or any deputy Registrar of the LCIA Court under the supervision of the LCIA Court.'
19. *See, e.g.*, Article 31(2) LCIA Rules: 'After the award has been made (. . .), neither the LCIA, the LCIA Court (including its President, Vice-Presidents and individual members), the Registrar, any deputy Registrar, any arbitrator and any expert to the Arbitral Tribunal shall be under any legal obligation to make any statement to any person about any matter concerning the arbitration, nor shall any party seek to make any of these persons a witness in any legal or other proceedings arising out of the arbitration.'
20. *See also* **Article 3**, at paras. 031 *et seq.*

sensitive cases, as a matter of good practice). Under the current version of the Vienna Rules, no time limits apply to the Secretary General's decision-making. As with the decisions of the VIAC Board, a party will have no express basis in the Vienna Rules to complain about a delay in reaching a decision in a timely manner. However, the Secretary General operates under the assumption that a party is entitled to a decision in due course. Depending on the nature of the decision and the circumstances of the case, the time for a decision by the Secretary General will usually not exceed four weeks.

Although the Vienna Rules do not expressly address this issue, it is common **5-026** practice of the current Secretary General to substantiate and explain his decision, so that the rationale behind it becomes accessible and transparent to the parties and the arbitrators. This is of particular importance where the Secretary General is entitled to exercise discretion in his decision-making.[21] In that case, the parties usually will have an opportunity to comment on the specific matter. Beyond that, the reasons provided for a decision will be limited to a statement of the factual circumstances.[22] The decisions of the Secretary General are not subject to appeal and are therefore binding on the parties.

IV.   INABILITY TO PERFORM

> **Article 5(4): If the Secretary General is unable to perform his duties or if he is permanently incapacitated, a member of the Board of the Centre, appointed by that Board, shall perform the relevant functions until a Secretary General is appointed.**

The office of the Secretary General does not allow for any permanent vacancy. **5-027** Arbitration proceedings, regardless if pending or commencing, usually require a swift decision-making of the institution entrusted with its administration.[23] Thus, the rule of vacancy under Article 5(4) is a practical compromise to facilitate an efficient and transparent transition in the administration of the VIAC member of the VIAC Board and will be best suited to continue the administrative agenda of the Secretariat. This interim solution was applied once in the past.

From the wording of Article 5 it is unclear if the Board member called to stand in as **5-028** Secretary General will actually remain a member of the VIAC Board for the tenure of his substitutional appointment. Considering the nature of work involved, the two

---

21. For example with regard to the *prima facie* scrutiny under **Article 9** or the deviation from the amount in dispute under **Article 36(5)**.
22. *See* **Article 10**, at para. 014, for the practice with regard to the memorandum in reply and **Article 13**, at para. 010, with regard to the extension of time limits.
23. *See* Article 5(1) App. II to the ICC Rules: 'In case of absence, the Secretary General may delegate to the General Counsel and Deputy Secretary General the authority to confirm arbitrators, to certify true copies of Awards and to request the payment of a provisional advance, respectively provided for in Article 9(2), 28(2) and 30(1) of these Rules.'

functions are most likely incompatible, although nothing would restrict the member to resume his role with the Board after a new Secretary General has been appointed. Hence, during office, the member of the Board will most likely be exempted from its rights under **Article 3**, but will stay governed by the confidentiality and independency obligations of Article 5.

5-029 The incapacitation of the acting Secretary General must be of a permanent nature, hence holiday breaks or temporary illnesses would naturally not fall under this category. The 'inability to perform the duties' could arguably be seen to allow a restriction to administer a case on an individual basis. This is in theory conceivable where the Secretary General might have a personal interest in a particular case and could therefore not be involved in its administration. In such a case he or she would be excluded to administer this individual case and would have it transferred to the interim administration by a Board member appointed under Article 5(4). The decision on whether the prerequisites for an interim Secretary General have been met, will ultimately fall to the VIAC Board.

Article 6

Languages of Correspondence

	Para.		Para.
I. Scope	1	II. Requirements	4

Article 6: Correspondence by the Parties with the Board and the Secretary General shall be conducted in German or English.

I.   SCOPE

As an institution dedicated to international commercial arbitration, the VIAC **6-001** administers proceedings with parties of diverse nationality and background. Article 6 was inserted with the 2001 amendment of the Vienna Rules[1] in order to facilitate correspondence between the parties and the Board or the Secretary General by establishing two official institutional working languages.

Importantly, Article 6 *only* applies to correspondence between the parties and the **6-002** organs of the VIAC, that is, the Board and the Secretary General, and *vice versa*. Thus, Article 6 does not apply to what is commonly referred as the 'language of the arbitration', that is, procedural correspondence between the parties, and between the parties and the tribunal. On its terms, Article 6 does also not mandatorily apply to correspondence between the arbitrators and the VIAC, or to correspondence amongst the arbitrators themselves.

This distinction is important. The parties are, as a matter of course, free under the **6-003** Vienna Rules to agree on any language they deem appropriate for their arbitration.

---

1. Article 4a Vienna Rules 2001, **Annex 2a**.

Absent such agreement, the arbitrators will determine the language of the arbitration pursuant to **Article 20(2)**.[2] In doing so, the arbitrators will choose a language that both parties and their counsel of choice are familiar with and that is convenient in terms of the relevant documentation of the case. The language of the arbitration will then extend to the parties' submission on procedural and substantive matters, as well as the taking of evidence through documents or witness testimony. In practice, the vast majority of international arbitrations are conducted in English.

II.   REQUIREMENTS

6-004 While the distinction between the language of the arbitration and the language of the parties' correspondence with the VIAC is important, there is some conceivable overlap.[3] Specifically, the Board and the Secretary General of the VIAC must be able to fulfil their functions properly under the Vienna Rules. Thus, it is the standing practice of the Secretary General to insist that, at the time of filing of the statement of claims under **Article 9**, the essential passages of the arbitration agreement shall be provided in English or German in order to enable the VIAC to undertake a *prima facie* assessment of its jurisdiction.[4] This may be cumbersome where none of the parties has any knowledge of the German or English language and the arbitration agreement provides, for example, for proceedings in the Russian language. However, the VIAC must be enabled to assess on a preliminary basis its authority to administer the arbitration proceeding[5] or to find out if the parties made agreements that deviate from the Vienna Rules.[6] The same applies to circumstances where the Board is by virtue of the Vienna Rules entrusted with certain decisions, such as the institutional appointment of arbitrators[7] or the challenge procedure of the arbitrators[8] (but not of experts[9]). Insofar as the parties have submitted documents pertaining to such issues, these documents or relevant parts thereof will have to be submitted in English or German.

---

2. *See* **Article 20**, at paras. 120 *et seq.*
3. Indeed, it is not unheard of to link the language of the arbitration and the language to be used in correspondence with the institution. *See, e.g.,* Article 8 Hungarian Rules: 'All documents pertaining to the institution at the initiation or in the course of proceedings (. . .) shall be submitted in the language which the parties determined for the proceedings. If no such determination was made, the documents shall, until the arbitral tribunal determines the language of the proceedings (. . .), be submitted either in the Hungarian, the German or the English language depending on the decision of the Arbitration Court.'
4. *See* **Article 9**, at para. 066.
5. *See* **Article 9**, at paras. 066 and 072 *et seq.*
6. *See* **Article 9**, at paras. 088 *et seq.*
7. *See* **Articles 14**, at paras. 037 *et seq.*, 056 and 064 *et seq.* and **Article 15**, at paras. 032 *et seq.*
8. *See* **Article 16**, at paras. 040 *et seq.*
9. *See* **Article 21**, at para. 014.

It can therefore be taken as a rule that whenever correspondence is addressed to the **6-005** specific attention of the Secretary General or the Board, it will need to be in English or German. As far as the arbitration itself is concerned, however, the arbitrators or parties are not obliged to provide English or German translations of their submissions by way of courtesy copy to the Secretary General to keep in his mirror file.[10] Only insofar direct correspondence with the organs of the VIAC is concerned and the document is submitted in a 'third' language, the Board or the Secretary General, respectively, may in reliance on Article 6 return the document and request a translation. If a party refuses to comply, the document may be deemed as not having been properly submitted, and may effectively be excluded from the proceedings. Naturally, the parties agree to Article 6 by incorporating the Vienna Rules in their arbitration agreement.

While this provision may seem rather rigid, one should bear in mind that, because **6-006** of the diversity of the parties in international commercial arbitration, the VIAC would, without Article 6, be required to employ, or have available, staff or translators for an unspecified variety of different languages, incurring considerable additional costs. Not surprisingly, this burden is considered unacceptable by other institutions as well. Irrespective of the language chosen as the language of the arbitration, the ICC Court and Secretariat, for example, are under no obligation to use any other language than the ICC's working languages, English and French.[11] Article 6 thus shifts the burden of costs associated with third languages from the VIAC to the parties. However, while each party will therefore typically have to bear its own cost for any translation required by the VIAC, it may be possible to claim these costs as disbursements related to the arbitration proceedings from the other party in the final award.[12]

In practice, the VIAC tries to apply Article 6 rather flexibly and seeks to accom- **6-007** modate parties speaking languages other than English or German.[13]

---

10. *See* **Article 12**, at para. 021 and **Article 13**, at para. 019.
11. Y. Derains and E.A. Schwartz, *A Guide to the ICC Rules of Arbitration* (2nd edn, The Hague, Kluwer Law International, 2005), p. 233.
12. *See* **Article 32(b)**, at para. 003.
13. *See* **Article 1**, at para. 157.

Article 7

The Arbitrators

		Para.
I.	Party-Autonomy in Choosing the Arbitrators	1
	A. Introduction	1
	B. Prerequisites for Service as Arbitrator	5
	1. 'Legal Capacity'	6
	2. Personal and Voluntary Service	10
	3. Active Austrian Judges	13
	4. Expert Determination	17
	5. Nationality of the Arbitrator	18
	6. Non-Lawyer Arbitrators	23
	7. Additional Requirements Imposed by Agreement	26
	8. Practical Considerations	28
	9. Interviewing Prospective Arbitrators	31
	10. The VIAC Roster of Arbitrators	38
II.	Institutional Requirements for Appointment	40
III.	Board Members as Arbitrators	43
IV.	The Performance of the Arbitrator's Duties	46
	A. The Arbitrators' Duties	49
	1. Duty to Resolve the Dispute	52
	2. Duty to Comply with Due Process	57
	3. Duty of Independence and Impartiality	58
	4. Duty of Efficient Conduct	59
	5. Duty of Secrecy	63
	6. Duty to Meet Certain Qualification Requirements	68
	7. Duty of Diligence	69

		Para.
	8. Ancillary and Cost-Efficiency Duties	71
	9. Ethical Duties	73
	10. Additional Duties Imposed by the Parties in the Ongoing Arbitration	78
	B. The Independence and Impartiality of Arbitrators	80
	1. Attempts at International Harmonization	83
	2. The Standard of Impartiality and Independence in International Arbitration	90
	2.1. Impartiality and Independence	92
	2.2. Neutrality	97
	3. The Standard of Independence and Impartiality Under Austrian Law	99
	3.1. The Standard of Impartiality and Independence Under the Former ZPO	100
	3.2. The Standard of Impartiality and Independence Under the New ZPO	105
	4. Some Examples Regarding Impartiality and Independence	110
	5. Some Particular Issues Regarding Impartiality and Independence	115

	Para.		Para.
5.1. Different Standard for Party-Appointed Arbitrators?	116	V. Disclosure	133
		A. Disclosure Under the Former ZPO and Vienna Rules	133
5.2. Continuing Obligation of Impartiality	121	B. Disclosure Under the New ZPO and Vienna Rules	134
5.3. The Impact of Settlement Discussions	123	C. The Parties' Disclosure Obligations	149
5.4. Independence in a Globally Active Legal Profession	129	VI. The Secretary of the Tribunal	152
5.5. *Ex Parte* Communications	131		

I.   PARTY-AUTONOMY IN CHOOSING THE
                 ARBITRATORS

Article 7(1): The parties shall be free to appoint the arbitrators. Any person having legal capacity – irrespective of nationality – may be an arbitrator, provided the parties have not agreed upon any special additional qualification requirements.

A.   INTRODUCTION

7-001 The parties' choice to appoint a particular arbitrator is considered one of the most critical steps in any arbitration. The identity of the arbitrators will invariably affect the character and quality of the arbitral proceedings and may directly impact their outcome.[1] It reflects the importance of the arbitrator's appointment as well as the inherently consensual nature of arbitration to leave it, in the first instance, to the parties to select the arbitrators they deem to be the most appropriate choice in the circumstances of their case. The appointment of arbitrators is therefore a core application of party autonomy in arbitration.

7-002 National legislatures and arbitral institutions have therefore been rightly hesitant to impose preconditions that would unduly restrict the parties' right to elect an arbitrator of their choosing to decide their dispute. In fact, arbitral institutions rarely impose any special preconditions for prospective arbitrators.[2] Where they do, those requirements appear to be more of a general nature to ensure the overall integrity of the process. Article 8 Schedule C of the ICSID Arbitration Additional Facility

---

1. G.B. Born, *International Commercial Arbitration – Commentary and Materials* (2nd edn, The Hague, Kluwer Law International, 2001), pp. 620-629; A. Redfern, M. Hunter, N. Blackaby and C. Partasides, *Law and Practice of International Commercial Arbitration* (4th edn, London, Sweet & Maxwell, 2004), para. 4-39.
2. *See* Article 9(5) ICC Rules; Article 6 LCIA Rules and Article 11 UNCITRAL Model Law basically refer to the nationality of the arbitrator. Article 6(4) AAA/ICDR Rules empowers the administrator to select suitable arbitrators.

Rules[3] for instance states that '[a]rbitrators shall be persons of high moral character and recognized competence in the fields of law, commerce, industry or finance, who may be relied upon to exercise independent judgment'. Article 4 Hungarian Rules requires, *inter alia*, that the arbitrator 'commands the necessary level of legal, economic and other knowledge to enable him to resolve legal disputes' and that 'he possesses the required language skills'. Similarly, a former version of Article 7 of the Vienna Rules stated that 'arbitrators should have specific knowledge and experience in legal, commercial or other pertinent matters'.

These 'requirements' are hardly offensive, but they appear more programmatic than normative. The resolution of disputes may be an art, but it is not a natural science; and reasonable people may disagree as to who is suitable to hear a given dispute. In that sense, requirements such as that the arbitrator must have the *necessary level of legal, economic and other knowledge to enable him to resolve legal disputes* are not helpful in practice. Such requirements lead inevitably to the intricate question of subjective evaluation as to whether adequate knowledge of an arbitrator exists and whether it is backed up by the required professional experience. In case of appointment of the arbitrator by the institution, it is conceivable that a party aggrieved by the award could seek to blame the institution for making an inappropriate choice that violates the selection criteria set out in the applicable rules (*culpa in eligendo*). **7-003**

Thus, Article 7(1) intentionally requires of the arbitrator no more than legal capacity. In reality, of course, the VIAC, like any arbitral institution, strives to appoint arbitrators of quality, as a poor selection and offended parties will reflect badly on the institution's reputation. In addition, as discussed in greater detail below, prospective arbitrators are under a duty, *qua culpa in contrahendo*, not to accept an appointment if they know that they lack the skills or abilities to hear a particular case.[4] This, of course, is different from setting out selection criteria at the outset that may restrict the parties' choice. The solution adopted in Article 7(1) is therefore preferable, because it subjects the appointment of the arbitrators to the free discretion of the parties, hence making it their responsibility as well. **7-004**

B.   PREREQUISITES FOR SERVICE AS ARBITRATOR

The principal requirement for service as an arbitrator is 'legal capacity'. The following section examines this requirement under Austrian law and analyzes **7-005**

---

3. The Administrative Council of the Centre has adopted Additional Facility Rules authorizing the Secretariat of ICSID to administer certain categories of proceedings between states and nationals of other states that fall outside the scope of the ICSID Convention. The Additional Facility Rules comprise a principal set of Rules Governing the Additional Facility and their three schedules: Fact-Finding Rules (Schedule A), Conciliation Rules (Schedule B) and Arbitration Rules (Schedule C). On 29 September 2002, the Administrative Council approved amendments of the Additional Facility Rules. These amendments came into effect on 1 January 2003.
4. *See also* IBA Rules of Ethics item 2, **Annex 18**.

ancillary requirements and considerations implied by Austrian law or international practice.

1.   'Legal Capacity'

7-006 The Vienna Rules require that the arbitrator has 'legal capacity'. The ZPO does not specify any such requirement, but the condition of legal capacity is implied as a matter of course. In line with most national laws, institutional rules and modern doctrine, this is the only requirement an arbitrator needs to meet.

7-007 Legal capacity in Austria is understood to mean, at a minimum, *Geschäftsfähigkeit*, which refers to the status allowing a person to make, by his or her own will, legally binding commitments. Under Austrian law, this status is conferred on all mentally capable persons aged 18 and older. For non-Austrian arbitrators, legal capacity (*Geschäftsfähigkeit*) is determined by their own national law (*Personalstatut*).[5] Commentators have argued, quite sensibly, that the arbitrator's legal capacity also implies the capacity to engage in proceedings (*Prozessfähigkeit*)[6] and to be capable of pleading (*Verhandlungsfähigkeit*).[7]

7-008 Since neither the ZPO nor the Vienna Rules contain more extensive provisions regarding the mandatory qualification of an arbitrator, it has been argued that a legal entity, such as a company or association, also could be appointed as an arbitrator.[8] In such cases, it is assumed that the person assigned by statute, agreement or charter to legally represent such entity would be responsible for rendering the arbitral award.[9] Whether that assumption is justified, and whether the appointment of a legal entity reflects the nature of the arbitral process and decision-making, remains doubtful yet poses a largely academic question; such appointments are exceedingly rare in practice.[10] An arbitration agreement appointing an

---

5. This derives from Section 12 IPRG which refers to the general capacity to act in such a way as to produce legal consequences (*Handlungsfähigkeit*). This is understood to comprise also the question of the personal legal capacity to be determined by the personal statute of the individual person. Section 9 IPRG links this personal statute to the nationality of the individual. *See in detail* B. Verschraegen in *Kommentar zum ABGB II/2*, P. Rummel (ed.) (3rd edn, Vienna, Manz, 2002), Sections 9 IPRG *et seq.*

6. *See* Section 1 ZPO which considers a person capable to act as party in proceedings as far as this person can independently enter into a valid commitment.

7. *See* Section 185 ZPO which refers to the ability to express oneself comprehensibly. *See* W. Schragel in *Kommentar zu den Zivilprozeßgesetzen II/2*, H.W. Fasching (ed.) (2nd edn, Vienna, Manz, 2003), Section 185; H.W. Fasching, *Schiedsgericht und Schiedsverfahren im österreichischen und im internationalen Recht* (Vienna, Manz, 1973), p. 57.

8. H.W. Fasching, *Schiedsgericht und Schiedsverfahren im österreichischen und im internationalen Recht* (Vienna, Manz, 1973), pp. 56 *et seq.*

9. H.W. Fasching, *Schiedsgericht und Schiedsverfahren im österreichischen und im internationalen Recht* (Vienna, Manz, 1973), p. 57.

10. P. Schlosser, 'Schiedsgerichtsbarkeit, Schiedsgutachtenwesen und Höchstpersönlichkeit der Entscheidungsbefugnis' in *Festschrift für Norbert Horn zum 70. Geburtstag*, K.P. Berger, G. Borges, H. Herrmann, A. Schlüter and U. Wackerbarth (eds) (Berlin, de Gruyter Recht, 2006), p. 1025.

administrative agency or a state court as 'arbitrator' was considered invalid under the former Austrian arbitration law.[11]

Lack of legal capacity is in fact the only instance where the VIAC itself can *ex officio* **7-009** reject a nominee that is put forward by the parties or, in the case of the chairperson, by the co-arbitrators. All other prerequisites, in particular the required independence and impartiality, are examined by the Board only upon application by the parties.[12]

2.   Personal and Voluntary Service

The function of an arbitrator is a highly personal service *intuitu personae*, to be **7-010** exclusively performed by the nominated person.[13] As such, the arbitrator cannot delegate his function to anyone else.[14]

Possibly for this reason, Section 579 fZPO provided that 'no-one is obliged to accept **7-011** the appointment as an arbitrator'. An arbitration agreement violating this principle of voluntary service was, under Austrian law, considered to be ineffective. This includes agreements in a corporate charter or in the articles that a certain officer of the company, e.g. the chairman of the supervisory board, is obliged to assume the function of arbitrator in certain cases. A person refusing to accept a nomination was thus neither liable for damages nor could he or she be compelled to accept the appointment.[15]

The new ZPO does not contain a similar provision. However, given the nature of **7-012** arbitral appointments, there is no doubt that the rule of voluntary service applies under the new ZPO as well.

3.   Active Austrian Judges

According to Section 578 fZPO, active state judges were excluded from an arbi- **7-013** tration appointment:

> Judicial officers may not accept appointment as arbitrators during their tenure of judicial office.

This provision was interpreted narrowly. First, it applied only to *Austrian* state judges. **7-014** Thus, the participation of a foreign state judge in an arbitration sited in Austria did not

---

11. H.W. Fasching, *Schiedsgericht und Schiedsverfahren im österreichischen und im internationalen Recht* (Vienna, Manz, 1973), p. 57.
12. *See* **Article 16**, at paras. 014 *et seq.*
13. P. Schlosser, 'Schiedsgerichtsbarkeit, Schiedsgutachtenwesen und Höchstpersönlichkeit der Entscheidungsbefugnis' in *Festschrift für Norbert Horn zum 70. Geburtstag*, K.P. Berger, G. Borges, H. Herrmann, A. Schlüter and U. Wackerbarth (eds) (Berlin, de Gruyter Recht, 2006), pp. 1023 *et seq.*
14. *See* **Article 7**, at paras. 052 and 152.
15. H.W. Fasching, *Schiedsgericht und Schiedsverfahren im österreichischen und im internationalen Recht* (Vienna, Manz, 1973), p. 58.

affect the validity of the award so rendered. Similarly, if a non-Austrian active judge, in compliance with the law applicable to the proceedings, had participated as arbitrator in an arbitration sited outside Austria, the recognition or enforcement of this award in Austria was not precluded.[16] Second, the restriction of Section 578 fZPO applied only to state judges in the technical sense. Aspirants or trainees for judicial appointments, laypersons serving on juries or as part of a judicial panel together with judges did not fall within the scope of this provision.[17] Third, the prohibition immediately ceased to be effective upon (permanent or temporary) retirement, and presumably also for the period of suspension or removal from judicial office.

7-015 Participation by an active Austrian judge in making an arbitral award could, according to *Fasching*, have led to a successful challenge of the award under Section 595(1) no. 3 fZPO,[18] even when the parties have waived this ground for challenge. Most other Austrian scholars were of the opinion that this regulation was to be interpreted as disciplinary provision, for which violation of the Austrian judge could face disciplinary sanctions, but would not constitute a reason for setting aside the award.[19] Similarly, an arbitration agreement requiring that a judge be appointed as arbitrator was not *per se* invalid. In this context, the Austrian *Oberster Gerichtshof* held that

> the provision that an independent judge of [the court of X] must be a member of the Arbitral Tribunal, does not invalidate the arbitration clause, as it could be interpreted that it has to be a person that was holding office in the past and therefore affords enhanced guarantee for impartiality. Such terminology is of insignificant importance.[20]

7-016 The new ZPO does not contain a restriction comparable to Section 578 fZPO. Instead, a prohibition has now been inserted in Section 63(5) RStDG[21] which

---

16. H.W. Fasching, *Schiedsgericht und Schiedsverfahren im österreichischen und im internationalen Recht* (Vienna, Manz, 1973), p. 58.

17. H.W. Fasching, *Schiedsgericht und Schiedsverfahren im österreichischen und im internationalen Recht* (Vienna, Manz, 1973), p. 57.

18. Section 595(1) no. 3 fZPO reads: 'The award shall be set aside if statutory or contractual provisions regarding the composition of the arbitral tribunal or the method of reaching a decision have been infringed or if the original of the award has not been signed in accordance with the provisions of Section 592(2).'

19. W.H. Rechberger and W. Melis in *Kommentar zur ZPO*, W.H. Rechberger (ed.) (2nd edn, Vienna/New York, Springer, 2000), Section 578, para. 1; affirmative F. Matscher, 'Probleme der Schiedsgerichtsbarkeit im österreichischen Recht' [1975] JBl, 412, 452, 456; T. Chiwitt-Oberhammer, *Der fehlerhafte Schiedsspruch* (Vienna, Verlag Österreich, 2000), pp. 102 *et seq.*, with express reference to the legal situation in Germany.

20. OGH, 18 May 1955, 1 Ob 329/55.

21. Section 63(5) RStDG reads: 'State court judges are not permitted to accept an appointment as an arbitrator within the meaning of the Fourth Section of the Sixth Part of the ZPO, (RGBl. No. 113/1895).'

can be seen as an endorsement of the argument that participation of an active state court judge as arbitrator merely results in disciplinary proceedings against the judge and not in a challengeable award.

4. Expert Determination

Under Austrian Law, a distinction is made between an arbitrator *strictu sensu* and an 'arbitral expert' *(Schiedsgutachter)*.[22] The latter is informally appointed to determine certain disputed facts without adjudicating the dispute as such. *Fasching* proposes to examine if the task entrusted to the expert constitutes a distinct claim that could successfully be filed with the courts for adjudicating. If the courts were likely to decline subject-matter jurisdiction, the task assigned to the expert is likely to be of a non-judicial nature; hence, it is a case of expert determination and not arbitration. As a practical consequence, an agreement referring issues to expert determination does not have to meet the mandatory formal requirements applicable to arbitration agreements, nor is the expert determination subject to the provisions of Sections 577 *et seq.* ZPO.[23]

7-017

5. Nationality of the Arbitrator

The nationality of arbitrators is sometimes viewed as an issue of neutrality.[24] The argument is made that an arbitrator having a different nationality than the parties will be more neutral or impartial than an arbitrator who shares the same passport with one of the parties. This is mostly a matter of perception:

7-018

> In an ideal world, the nationality of a sole arbitrator, or of the presiding arbitrator, should be irrelevant. The qualifications, experience and integrity of the arbitrator are the factors which should count. The country in which he was born, or the passport that he carries should be irrelevant.[25]

---

22. *See also* **Article 1**, at paras. 098 *et seq.*
23. H.W. Fasching, *Schiedsgericht und Schiedsverfahren im österreichischen und im internationalen Recht* (Vienna, Manz, 1973), p. 10; *see* OGH, 9 May 1978, 5 Ob 580/78; OGH 13 March 1980, 7 Ob 13/80, ZVR 1980/304, 311; OGH, 27 February 1985, 1 Ob 504/85; OGH, 4 November 1986, 14 Ob 136/86; OGH, 14 December 1994, 7 Ob 604/94; more detailed list in K. Neuteufel, *Schiedsrechtliche Entscheidungen 1898-1998* (Vienna, Verlag Österreich, 2000); W.H. Rechberger and W. Melis in *Kommentar zur ZPO*, W.H. Rechberger (ed.) (2nd edn, Vienna/New York, Springer, 2000), Section 577, para. 20; C. Liebscher and A. Schmid in *Practitioner's Handbook on International Arbitration*, F.B. Weigand (ed.) (Munich, C.H. Beck, 2002), p. 542. The mere fact that professionals are sometimes referred to as arbitrators does not automatically convey on them the benefits of arbitral immunity *See* C. Hausmaninger, 'Civil Liability of Arbitrators – Comparative Analysis and Proposals for Reform' (1990) 7(4) J Int'l Arb, 7, 23.
24. *See also* the discussion of impartiality under **Article 7**, at paras. 080 *et seq.*
25. A. Redfern, M. Hunter, N. Blackaby and C. Partasides, *Law and Practice of International Commercial Arbitration* (4th edn, London, Sweet & Maxwell, 2004), para. 4-58.

7-019 This approach is clearly reflected in Article 11(1) UNCITRAL Model Law which provides that 'no person shall be precluded by reason of his nationality from acting as an arbitrator, unless otherwise agreed by the parties'. Yet some major institutional rules require that the sole or presiding arbitrator must, under certain circumstances, be someone of a different nationality than those of the parties.²⁶

7-020 Article 7(1) provides that anyone having legal capacity can serve as an arbitrator 'irrespective of nationality'. Thus, the VIAC takes the position that nationality as such is not a determinative factor in appointing arbitrators, as long as the Vienna Rules' provisions on impartiality and independence of arbitrators are complied with.

7-021 Notwithstanding this, the VIAC Board will take the nationality of a prospective arbitrator into account when making appointments. In many cases, therefore, it will endeavour to appoint chairpersons of arbitral tribunals who have a different nationality than the parties, simply to increase the perception of neutrality. In other cases, it may be more appropriate to appoint an arbitrator who comes from the same country as one of the parties, if, for example, the evidence to be taken or the applicable substantive law have a strong connection to a certain country, or if the appointment of an arbitrator from that country enhances the efficiency of the arbitration and saves costs. Since there is no obligation imposed on the Board to regard nationality, the Board is free to do so.²⁷

7-022 The fZPO did not contain any requirement as to nationality. Article 11(5) of the UNCITRAL Model Law, which formed the basis for Section 587(8) of the new ZPO, requires that 'in the case of a sole or a third arbitrator, the court shall take into account as well the advisability of appointing an arbitrator of a nationality other than those of the parties'. This particular element of Article 11(5) of the UNCITRAL Model Law was eventually not adopted in Austria. Section 587(8) ZPO only requires the court to ensure that the arbitrators meet any particular qualification requirements on which the parties have agreed, and that generally the importance of having an independent and impartial arbitrator is considered. Nationality as such is therefore no consideration implied by Austrian law.

---

26. *See, e.g.*, Article 9(5) ICC Rules: 'The sole arbitrator or the chairman of the tribunal shall be of a nationality other than those of the parties. However, in suitable circumstances and provided that neither of the parties objects within the time limit fixed by the Court, the sole arbitrator or the chairman may be chosen from a country of which any of the parties is a national'. Or the similar provision of Article 6 LCIA Rules, which includes the clarification that 'the nationality of the parties shall be understood to include that of controlling shareholders or interests. For the purpose of this Article, a person who is a citizen of two or more states shall be treated as a national of each state; and citizens of the European Union shall be treated as nationals of its different Member States and shall not be treated as having the same nationality'.
27. *See also* **Article 14**, at para. 038.

6.   Non-Lawyer Arbitrators

Unless the parties have imposed specific requirements or arbitrators in their arbitra- **7-023**
tion agreement, any person having legal capacity can be appointed as an arbitrator.
Specifically, there is no requirement under the Vienna Rules or Austrian law that an
arbitrator needs a law degree or is admitted to a bar. In particular, in construction or
industrial engineering cases turning on points of technical expertise rather than law,
the parties may arguably feel better served by having individuals with specific technical expertise decide their dispute. In that regard, the Vienna Rules fully respect party
autonomy.

Other rules seem to have a built-in bias in favour of lawyers. Article 2(2) DIS **7-024**
Rules, e.g. provides that '[u]nless otherwise agreed by the parties, the chairman of
the arbitral tribunal or the sole arbitrator, as the case may be, shall be a jurist'.
While this provision also appears to honour the parties' freedom to agree
otherwise, the solution adopted under the Vienna Rules seems preferable because
it gives the VIAC the authority, absent agreement by the parties, to appoint who-
ever they deem is best suited to resolve the parties' dispute, whether lawyer or not.

In practice, of course, the vast majority of arbitrators, under the Vienna Rules and **7-025**
elsewhere, are jurists, practicing attorneys or legal scholars.[28] This may be for good
reason because arbitrators with a legal background will usually deal more comfortably with the kind of procedural and conflict of laws issues that invariably tend
to arise in international arbitration. For the same reason, a party may not want to
appoint an engineer or commercial person to a tribunal of which the remaining
members are lawyers. Such a mixed tribunal can lead to difficult dynamics, often
leaving the non-lawyer arbitrator disadvantaged on points of law or procedure.

7.   Additional Requirements Imposed by Agreement

The parties are of course free to impose additional requirements on arbitrators, in **7-026**
terms of professional training, qualification or experience, language skills or industry expertise.[29] When including such additional requirements in their arbitration
agreement, parties should be careful, however, not to unduly limit the pool of
potentially available arbitrators at the outset.

Where such additional requirements are specified, the (prospective) arbitrator has **7-027**
the duty to make necessary disclosures as to whether he or she meets these requirements, and indeed has a duty not to accept an appointment if he or she fails to do
so.[30] For this reason, arbitrators should not accept an appointment without first

---

28. Specifically, members of the legal academic community play an important role in international
     arbitration as counsel, advisers and arbitrators.
29. *See also* Section 587(8) ZPO.
30. A. Philip, 'The Duties of an Arbitrator' in *The Leading Arbitrators' Guide to International
     Arbitration*, L.W. Newmann and R.D. Hill (eds) (Huntington, Juris Publishing, 2004), p. 72; *see
     also* IBA Rules of Ethics item 2, **Annex 18**.

consulting the arbitration agreement, failing which the arbitrator can be challenged and removed. This is discussed further below.[31]

8.   Practical Considerations

7-028 Apart from the requirements imposed by law, the Vienna Rules or the parties' agreement, there are a number of other considerations that determine whether a person be a suitable arbitrator, in general as well as in a particular case.

7-029 In general terms, parties are well advised to choose arbitrators that have the experience, outlook and training required for the case at bar. Knowledge of the language of the arbitration or the languages of correspondence with the VIAC is not mandatorily required,[32] but it is of course preferable if the arbitrators are able to speak the language of the arbitration to avoid costly and inefficient translations and interpreters. In many cases, it may be advisable to choose arbitrators who have knowledge of a potentially relevant 'background language' – that is a language other than the language of the arbitration that features in the documentary evidence of the case.

7-030 The sole or presiding arbitrator should have practical experience in international arbitral procedure. This is an important point, sometimes neglected by the parties, as 'presiding over the conduct of an international commercial arbitration is no less skilled than driving a car or flying an aircraft'.[33] Thus, knowledge of the substantive law or the relevant industry may well not be enough; in fact, practical exposure to international arbitration may be preferable to specific knowledge of a national law because international arbitration practitioners are used to applying a variety of laws, in a multitude of commercial sectors.

9.   Interviewing Prospective Arbitrators

7-031 It has become a practice in recent years for counsel to interview prospective arbitrators prior to appointment. U.S. lawyers in particular have regarded this as a normal exercise of 'due diligence'. Given that the parties' right to appoint an arbitrator of their choosing and given the substantial sums of money often entrusted to the arbitrator's authority, the practice of getting to know the arbitrator before making the appointment through an interview is now widespread.[34]

---

31. *See* **Article 16**, at paras. 001 and 004.
32. C. Liebscher and A. Schmid in *Practitioner's Handbook on International Arbitration*, F.B. Weigand (ed.) (Munich, C.H. Beck, 2002), p. 550.
33. A. Redfern, M. Hunter, N. Blackaby and C. Partasides, *Law and Practice of International Commercial Arbitration* (4th edn, London, Sweet & Maxwell, 2004), para. 4-47.
34. *See* Chartered Institute of Arbitrators, Practice Guidelines 16: The Interviewing of Prospective Arbitrators, para. 2(c).

The obvious difficulty with interviews is, however, that they are usually conducted **7-032** *ex parte* so that the other side does not know what is being said. This makes the process susceptible to being manipulated or abused.

The most critical factor to determine if an interview is appropriate is, therefore, **7-033** the scope of the discussion.[35] For example, the Chartered Institute of Arbitrators has recently adopted Practice Guidelines on The Interviewing of Prospective Arbitrators, which set forth a fairly strict regime governing such interviews, prohibit a discussion of the specific circumstances or facts giving rise to the dispute; the positions or arguments of the parties; and the merits of the case. In order to determine the prospective arbitrator's suitability in terms of expertise, experience, language proficiency and conflict status, it is permissible to discuss the names of the parties in dispute and any third parties involved or likely to be involved; the general nature of the dispute; the expected timetable of the proceedings; the language, governing law, seat of and rules applicable to the proceedings if agreed, or the fact that some or all of these are not agreed; the interviewee's experience, expertise and availability; and 'sufficient detail, but no more than necessary, of the project to enable both interviewer and interviewee to assess the latter's suitability for the appointment'. In addition, parties are permitted to ask questions to test the prospective arbitrator's knowledge and understanding of the nature and type of project in question; of the particular area of law applicable to the dispute; of the interviewee's publishing history (if any); and of arbitration law, practice and procedure in general.[36]

In more general terms, but similar spirit, the IBA Guidelines on Conflicts of **7-034** Interest in International Arbitration (IBA Conflict Guidelines)[37] permit interviews as part of the Green List,[38] provided the interview

> is limited to the arbitrator's availability and qualifications to serve or to the names of possible candidates for a chairperson and [does] not address the merits or procedural aspects of the dispute.

Similarly, the ABA's 'Code of Ethics for Arbitrators in Commercial Disputes' **7-035** states:

> When the appointment of a prospective arbitrator is being considered, the prospective arbitrator: (a) may ask about the identities of the parties, and the general nature of the case; and (b) may respond to inquiries from a

---

35. *See, e.g.,* A. Redfern, M. Hunter, N. Blackaby and C. Partasides, *Law and Practice of International Commercial Arbitration* (4th edn, London, Sweet & Maxwell, 2004), para. 4-50 ('However, it is hard to perceive the practice [*i.e.,* of interviews] as being objectionable in principle, provided that it is not done in a secretive way and that the scope of the discussion is appropriately restricted.').
36. *See* Chartered Institute of Arbitrators, Practice Guidelines 16: The Interviewing of Prospective Arbitrators, paras. 9-11.
37. IBA Conflict Guidelines, **Annex 17**.
38. For a discussion of the scope and terminology of the Guidelines, *see* **Article 17**, at paras. 086 *et seq.*

party or its counsel designed to determine his or her suitability and availability for the appointment. In any such dialogue, the prospective arbitrator may receive information from the party or its counsel disclosing the general nature of the dispute but should not permit them to discuss the merits of the case.[39]

7-036 Applied in this proper manner, the arbitrator interview can be a useful tool.[40] Finding out in advance in a personal meeting or telephone call about the qualification, experience and availability of a prospective arbitrator will enable a party to make an informed choice.

7-037 Discussions going beyond the scope set forth in the IBA Conflict Guidelines may well be problematic. As with every *ex parte* communication, anything that cannot be done in the open should not be done at all.[41] Arbitrators should therefore not discuss anything in the course of the interview that they do not feel entirely comfortable to disclose to the other party to the proceedings. In fact, arbitrators may want to make clear to interviewing counsel at the outset that they will fully disclose the content of the interview if called upon to do so.[42] For more elaborate interviews of the sole arbitrator or chairperson, there is a trend for counsel for both sides to conduct the interview jointly.

10.   The VIAC Roster of Arbitrators

7-038 Article 5(2) of the previous version of the Vienna Rules had provided for the VIAC Board to 'draw up a list of arbitrators every three years, to be valid for three calendar years in each case. Inclusion in the list of arbitrators shall not be a prerequisite for appointment as an arbitrator'.[43]

7-039 This provision has now been deleted. As a matter of practice, however, the VIAC will continue to maintain a list of potential arbitrators deemed suitable for arbitral

---

39. Canon III, Paragraph B(1) ABA Code of Ethics for Arbitrators in Commercial Disputes.
40. *See also* Article 7(2) AAA/ICDR Rules: 'No party or anyone acting on its behalf shall have any *ex parte* communication relating to the case with any arbitrator, or with any candidate for appointment as party-appointed arbitrator except to advise the candidate of the general nature of the controversy and of the anticipated proceedings and to discuss the candidate's qualifications, availability or independence in relation to the parties, or to discuss the suitability of candidates for selection as a third arbitrator where the parties or party-designated arbitrators are to participate in that selection.'
41. A.F. Lowenfeld, 'The Party-Appointed Arbitrator: Further Reflections' in *The Leading Arbitrators' Guide to International Arbitration*, L.W. Newman and R.D. Hill (eds) (Huntington, Juris Publishing, 2004), p. 44.
42. *See also* Chartered Institute of Arbitrators, Practice Guidelines 16: The Interviewing of Prospective Arbitrators, para. 7.
43. Vienna Rules 2001, **Annex 2a.**

practice.[44] This is done to assist users of arbitration in selecting an arbitrator. Now more than ever, this list will have to be viewed as a non-committal recommendation.[45] At present, the list (which was last amended in 2007) contains over 200 internationally and nationally renowned professionals in the field of commercial arbitration.[46]

II. INSTITUTIONAL REQUIREMENTS FOR APPOINTMENT

Article 7(2): The requirements for the appointment as arbitrator are:

a) **A written statement as to his impartiality and independence in accordance with paragraph 5. The Secretary General shall transmit to the parties a copy of the form in which the sole arbitrator (all members of the arbitral tribunal) has (have) confirmed his (its) impartiality and independence.**

b) **A written statement to submit to these Rules of Arbitration including to the provisions on the costs of the proceedings.**

The Austrian *Oberster Gerichtshof* has held unambiguously that 'the agreement **7-040** with the arbitrators, which determined the legal relationship between the arbitrators and the parties is, in any case, of private law nature'.[47] Thus, the relationship between the arbitrator and the parties is defined through a contract under which the arbitrator's rights, obligations and duties arise. Again, the contract can contain

---

44. Typically, the VIAC Board examines the candidacy of a potential arbitrator on the basis of a *curriculum vitae* and proof of arbitral practice. Subsequently, informal information will be issued stating that admission was granted (or not). A second invitation for inclusion in the list is, in general, not forthcoming, however, listed arbitrators are regularly invited to update their contact details and professional credentials.

45. Such compulsory lists are used in *e.g.*, Articles 17 and 20(2) Polish Rules; Article 15(3) Slovenian Rules and Article 18(1) Hungarian Rules, but are also employed by the AAA/ICDR which maintain that an exclusive, mandatory list gives the institution greater control over the quality of the arbitration. However, in some jurisdictions, compulsory appointment from the institutional list is (or can be seen as) limiting appointments to local 'cliques'.

46. The sanction of 'deletion from the list' as referred to in a former version of Article 5(2) is no longer applied. Should the Board consider that a listed arbitrator should no longer appear on the list, the person concerned will simply not be listed again when the new list is drawn up.

47. OGH, 28 April 1998, 1 Ob 253/97f with reference to W.H. Rechberger and P.A. Simotta (eds), *Grundriss des österreichischen Zivilprozessrechts* (4th edn, Vienna, Manz, 1994), para. 961; H.W. Fasching, *Schiedsgericht und Schiedsverfahren im österreichischen und im internationalen Recht* (Vienna, Manz, 1973), p. 69; P. Schlosser, *Das Recht der internationalen privaten Schiedsgerichtsbarkeit* (2nd edn, Tübingen, Mohr Siebeck, 1989), para. 491; H.W. Fasching, *Lehrbuch des österreichischen Zivilprozeßrechts* (2nd edn, Vienna, Manz, 1990), para. 2198, referring to A. Baumbach and K.H. Schwab, *Schiedsgerichtsbarkeit* (2nd edn, Munich, C.H. Beck, 1960), p. 90 – that, according to private international law, the law applicable to the arbitration agreement applies to the agreement with the arbitrators.

express terms or can incorporate the terms of the Vienna Rules by reference. The precise contents of the arbitrator contract, in terms of express or implied obligations and rights, will be discussed in detail immediately below. The issue of the arbitrator's liability is discussed further at **Article 8**.

7-041 In *ad hoc* arbitration, the arbitrator's contract can be concluded explicitly as well as in an implied manner.[48] Under the Vienna Rules, there is usually no contractual relationship between the parties and the arbitrators until the time of appointment of the arbitrators. The statement of claims must contain, *inter alia*, particulars regarding the number of arbitrators; if a decision by three arbitrators is requested, the claimant – and later the respondent – must each nominate one arbitrator.[49] The Secretary General then requests the sole arbitrator,[50] or, as the case may be, the arbitral tribunal, to confirm that they accept their mandate (and that they are therefore able and willing to fulfil it),[51] and that they are independent and impartial. This acceptance is declared by the arbitrators on a form issued by the Centre which constitutes the arbitrator's contract.[52] Thus, the appointment affects and defines the arbitrator's legal status and relationship to the parties in two distinct ways. First, the arbitrator's appointment transfers on him or her the authority to settle disputes in place of a state court. It legitimates the arbitrator *externally* as holder of quasi-judicial power. Second, the arbitrator's appointment, when accepted by the arbitrator, typically concludes the arbitrator's contract with the parties. This concept is in line with a decision of the Austrian *Oberster Gerichtshof* which held that

> the contractual relationship between the arbitrators and the parties has become effective, (. . .) by the selection of the arbitrators and their acceptance of their mandate; it is irrelevant whether the arbitrator was appointed by one or another of the parties or a third party.[53]

7-042 Article 7(2) formalizes this process. The appointment of an arbitrator is therefore perfected only if the arbitrator submits in writing to the Vienna Rules (which therefore form part of his or her contract with the parties) and if the arbitrator confirms his or her independence and impartiality.[54]

---

48. H.W. Fasching, *Kommentar zu den Zivilprozeßgesetzen, IV* (Vienna, Manz, 1971), Section 579, p. 749; *also* OGH, 7 July 1981, 5 Ob 633/81.
49. **Article 9(3)(d)**, at paras. 062 *et seq.* and **Article 9(3)(e)**, at paras. 062 *et seq.*
50. This applies if the Secretary General has received a claim in due form pursuant to **Article 9** and the cost deposits pursuant to **Article 34** are fully paid.
51. *See also* IBA Rules of Ethics item 2, **Annex 18**.
52. *See* Arbitrator's Declaration of Acceptance, Statement of Independence and Undertaking to Observe Rules on Costs, **Annex 4**. The practical procedure of the acceptance of the arbitrator's mandate is discussed under **Article 12**, at paras. 010 *et seq.*
53. OGH, 28 April 1998, 1 Ob 253/97f.
54. *See* **Article 7(4)**, at paras. 046 *et seq.* and 080 *et seq.*

III.   BOARD MEMBERS AS ARBITRATORS

Article 7(3): A member of the Board may act only as Chairman of an arbitral tribunal or sole arbitrator.

This provision was already contained in the former version of the Vienna Rules and 7-043 is meant to facilitate, in principle, the independence and impartiality of the members of the VIAC Board. As discussed, **Article 3(4)** expressly provides that members of the Board who are involved in particular arbitration proceedings in any capacity whatsoever shall be excluded from decisions pertaining to those proceedings. Article 7(3) takes this further by preventing a VIAC Board member, even if he has no personal interest in the arbitration, to act as co-arbitrator.

Following a literal interpretation of that provision, this restriction would only be 7-044 applicable during active participation as Board member. Should a person be newly appointed to the VIAC Board during pending arbitration proceedings under the Vienna Rules, that person would eventually have to resign as co-arbitrator in this matter; or rather, given his or her duties to the parties, would conceivably not be able to accept the appointment to the Board. Contrarily, the termination of Board membership would immediately allow participation as co-arbitrator.

In practice, the VIAC Board applies Article 7(3) broadly and beyond its literal 7-045 scope; it has therefore only in exceptional cases appointed one of its own members as arbitrator when called upon to make an institutional appointment.

IV.   THE PERFORMANCE OF THE ARBITRATOR'S DUTIES

Article 7(4): The arbitrators must perform their duties in complete independence and impartiality, to the best of their ability, and are not subject to any directives in that respect. They are bound to secrecy in respect of all matters coming to their notice in the course of their duties.

Article 7(4) sets out certain requirements which the arbitrators must meet when 7-046 performing 'their duties', but it does not list what these duties are. Different layers of express or implied duties can be considered 'primary duties' that concern the arbitrators' obligation to render a final award; duties that are otherwise imposed by institutional rules or applicable law; (further) duties imposed by the arbitration agreement; and, conceivably, duties that arise from international practice. Each layer poses the additional question of what consequences attach to the breach of the arbitrators' duties: the arbitrator could be removed; the award could be challenged; or, conceivably, the arbitrators could be liable for damages.[55]

---

55. J. Lew, L. Mistelis and S. Kröll, *Comparative International Commercial Arbitration* (The Hague, Kluwer Law International, 2003), paras. 12-31 *et seq.*; *see also* **Article 8**, at paras. 003 *et seq.*, for a detailed discussion of arbitrator immunity.

7-047 This section examines the duties that an arbitrator owes to the parties which flow from the contractual relationship between the arbitrators and the parties and may also arise from applicable mandatory law and institutional rules. Particular emphasis is given to the discussion of the arbitrators' duty to discharge their obligations impartially and independently. Some of the duties set out below are, on the other hand, the by-product of the arbitrators' procedural obligations; these are mentioned here in brief, but discussed in more detail elsewhere.[56]

7-048 In addition, this section is informed by some notable international instruments; in particular by the 1977 IBA Rules of Ethics for International Arbitrators,[57] the 1996 ICC Final Report on the Status of the Arbitrator, the 1996 UNCITRAL Notes on Organizing Arbitral Proceedings,[58] the AAA Code of Ethics (effective as of March 2004), and the IBA Guidelines on Conflicts of Interest in International Arbitration (adopted on 22 May 2004).[59] Where appropriate, these are addressed below as well.

A.   THE ARBITRATORS' DUTIES

7-049 As discussed above, the arbitrators' duties flow, first and foremost, from their contract with the parties, complemented by mandatory provisions of the applicable *lex arbitri*.[60] Further, by virtue of accepting their appointment under the auspices of the VIAC, obligations arising from the Vienna Rules are also incorporated into the arbitrators' mandate.[61]

7-050 The most important duty of the arbitrator is to 'act judicially', that is, to resolve the parties' dispute. Other requirements may be imposed or implied by applicable law, such as the requirement under the fZPO that arbitrators establish the facts of the case;[62] or that arbitrators treat the parties fairly and equally.[63]

7-051 Other duties may be imposed by the arbitration agreement, or, by reference, the applicable institutional rules. These are discussed below, the point being here that the arbitrators must make themselves familiar with the arbitration agreement and the applicable rules to determine if they can or should accept the appointment.

---

56. *See*, in particular, **Article 20**, regarding the conduct of the proceedings.
57. *See* IBA Rules of Ethics **Annex 18**.
58. *See* UNCITRAL Notes **Annex 15**.
59. *See* IBA Conflict Guidelines, **Annex 17**.
60. *See also* M.L. Smith, 'Contractual Obligations Owed by and to Arbitrators: Model Terms of Appointment' (1992) 8 Arb Int'l, 17-40.
61. *See* at **Article 12**, at para. 011; *see also* G.J. Horvath, 'The Duty of the Tribunal to Render an Enforceable Award' (2001) 18(2) J Int'l Arb, 135.
62. *See* the discussion in **Article 20**, at paras. 181 *et seq.*
63. *See* the discussion in **Article 20**, at paras. 015 *et seq.*

Similarly, parties should give the arbitrators sufficient information prior to appointment so that arbitrators can make an informed decision.[64]

1.   Duty to Resolve the Dispute

The foremost duty of an arbitrator is to complete his or her mandate by finally resolving the parties' dispute; that is, to make an award.[65] Under Austrian law, the legal nature of an arbitrator's contract can therefore be considered to constitute a contract for work and services (*Werkvertrag*) with elements of an agency contract (*Geschäftsbesorgungsvertrag*) to which the provisions of Sections 1165 to 1171, and 1002 *et seq.* ABGB will apply,[66] provided that Sections 577 ZPO *et seq.* do not stipulate otherwise.[67] Arbitrators are personally appointed; they are not entitled to delegate their primary judiciary function to third parties (such as arbitral secretaries).[68] **7-052**

Each arbitrator – whether party-appointed or not – owes the performance of this duty to both parties.[69] An arbitrator who fails to perform – that is generally, who fails to render an award – may incur liability under Austrian law.[70] A necessary **7-053**

---

64. A. Redfern, M. Hunter, N. Blackaby and C. Partasides, *Law and Practice of International Commercial Arbitration* (4th edn, London, Sweet & Maxwell, 2004), para. 5-11.

65. H.W. Fasching, *Schiedsgericht und Schiedsverfahren im österreichischen und im internationalen Recht* (Vienna, Manz, 1973), pp. 68, 70; J. Lew, L. Mistelis and S. Kröll, *Comparative International Commercial Arbitration* (The Hague, Kluwer Law International, 2003), para. 12-12; A. Philip, 'The Duties of an Arbitrator' in *The Leading Arbitrators' Guide to International Arbitration*, L.W. Newman and R.D. Hill (eds) (Huntington, Juris Publishing, 2004), p. 79. However, under Austrian law, the arbitrator cannot be compelled by the courts to perform this duty. *See* H.W. Fasching, *Schiedsgericht und Schiedsgerichtsbarkeit im österreichischen und im internationalen Recht* (Vienna, Manz, 1973), p. 70, with reference to Sections 579 and 584(2) fZPO.

66. *See* H.W. Fasching, *Schiedsgericht und Schiedsverfahren im österreichischen und im internationalen Recht* (Vienna, Manz, 1973), p. 69; H.W. Fasching, *Lehrbuch des österreichischen Zivilprozeßrechts* (2nd edn, Vienna, Manz, 1990), para. 2198; H.W. Fasching, 'Kostenvorschüsse zur Einleitung schiedsgerichtlicher Verfahren' [1993] JBl, 545, 548-549; W.H. Rechberger and W. Melis in *Kommentar zur ZPO*, W.H. Rechberger (ed.) (2nd edn, Vienna/ New York, Springer, 2000), Section 579 ZPO, para. 4; OGH, 2 October 2003, 6 Ob 41/03b; OGH, 7 March 1977, 1 Ob 764/76, JBl 1978, 155.

67. OGH, 7 March 1977, 1 Ob 764/76, JBl 1978, 155 with reference to H.W. Fasching, *Schiedsgericht und Schiedsverfahren im österreichischen und im internationalen Recht* (Vienna, Manz, 1973), p. 69 and OGH, 26 October 1915, JBl 238 alt.

68. *See* **Article 7**, at paras. 010 and 152. On behalf of many, *see* E.A. Schwartz, 'The Rights and Duties of ICC Arbitrators' (1995) ICC Ct Bull Special Supplement: The Status of the Arbitrator, 67.

69. H.W. Fasching, *Schiedsgericht und Schiedsverfahren im österreichischen und im internationalen Recht* (Vienna, Manz, 1973), p. 67; J. Lew, L. Mistelis and S. Kröll, *Comparative International Commercial Arbitration* (The Hague, Kluwer Law International, 2003), para. 12-6. As soon as the appointment of the arbitrator has been notified to the other party, the appointing party cannot unilaterally cause an arbitrator not to reach a decision on the dispute. *See* OGH, 6 November 1929, 4 Ob 490, ZBl 1930/23, 67.

70. *See* **Article 8**, at paras. 008 *et seq.*

corollary of the arbitrator's duty to render an award is the arbitrator's duty not to retire from the arbitration without good cause.[71] Although the Vienna Rules are silent on this matter, the arbitrators' contract with the parties, as a multilateral contractual relationship, cannot be unilaterally terminated by the arbitrator without compelling reason.[72] Conversely, an arbitrator must resign if he or she is no longer able to properly perform his or her duties, be it that he or she is incapacitated either permanently or in a way that would unduly delay the proceedings, or be it that he or she is no longer impartial or independent.

7-054 It is sometimes suggested that arbitrators have the duty to render an *enforceable* award.[73] However, a distinction must be made between the *validity* (and resulting enforceability) of the award in its country of origin (that is, the country in which the arbitration is seated) and the *international enforceability* of the award outside the country of origin. As to the validity of the award in its country of origin, the arbitrator must take care to ensure that the final award is not subject to *vacatur*.[74] Thus, the (foreign) arbitrator must inform himself about the mandatory provisions of the applicable *lex arbitri*, must conduct the arbitration in compliance with these provisions and must render the award in the form prescribed. The arbitrator may also have to take (mandatory) public policy into account that applies at the arbitral *situs*.[75] On the other hand, the arbitrator does not have a duty to render an award that is enforceable in any number of countries outside the award's country of origin. Indeed, the arbitrator will often be unable to anticipate the countries in which the parties will seek to enforce the award; and, despite international harmonization, the requirements for, and restrictions on, enforcement may still differ widely.[76] As far as international enforceability is concerned, therefore, the arbitrator can be expected to safeguard due process and the parties' right to

---

71. C. Hausmaninger, 'Rights and Obligations of the Arbitrator with Regard to the Parties and the Arbitral Institution – A Civil Law Viewpoint' (1995) ICC Ct Bull Special Supplement: The Status of the Arbitrator, 36, 39 *et seq.*

72. J. Lew, L. Mistelis and S. Kröll, *Comparative International Commercial Arbitration* (The Hague, Kluwer Law International, 2003), para. 12-15.

73. For a broad and instructive discussion of the subject, *see* G.J. Horvath, 'The Duty of Tribunals to Render an Enforceable Award' (2001) 18(2) J Int'l Arb 135; *see also* A. Philip, 'The Duties of an Arbitrator' in *The Leading Arbitrators' Guide to International Arbitration*, L.W. Newman and R.D. Hill (eds) (Huntington, Juris Publishing, 2004), p. 75.

74. J. Lew, L. Mistelis and S. Kröll, *Comparative International Commercial Arbitration* (The Hague, Kluwer Law International, 2003), para. 12-12.

75. For example, arbitrators may, as a matter of public policy, have to address EC competition law issues even when they have not been raised by the parties: *See* ECJ, 1 June 1999, Case No. C-126/97, *Eco Swiss China Time Ltd v. Benetton International NV*, [1999] ECR I-3055 (for a more detailed discussion of this case and its implications for the parties' right to be heard, *see* **Article 20**, at para. 047; *see also* G.J. Horvath, 'The Duty of Tribunals to Render an Enforceable Award' (2001) 18(2) J Int'l Arb, 135, 146-147).

76. J. Lew, L. Mistelis and S. Kröll, *Comparative International Commercial Arbitration* (The Hague, Kluwer Law International, 2003), para. 12-14, with a brief discussion of instructive examples, such as the potentially limited enforceability of punitive damages or interest.

be heard to ensure enforcement under the New York Convention.[77] Beyond this, however, the arbitrator is only obligated to use his best efforts to ensure that the award is internationally enforceable (as opposed to being liable for the result).[78]

Under **Article 24**, the arbitrators also have the duty to base their award on the applicable law, rather than reaching their decision *ex aequo et bono.*[79] For the arbitrators to properly complete their mandate, the award should dispose of all the relief requested by the parties. By the same token, the arbitrators must not exceed their authority under the arbitration agreement (*ultra petita*)[80] or applicable law (by disregarding applicable rules of arbitrability)[81] failing which the award may be subject to setting aside.[82] Under Austrian law and **Article 27(1)**, the award must also be reasoned (which should, at least as a matter of good practice, include a description of the history and status of the proceedings, the parties' claims and the reasons for the arbitrators' decision, including a weighing of the evidence), and must comply with a number of formal requirements.[83] Further, **Article 29** requires the arbitrators to make corrections to the award, if a party so requests. **7-055**

With regards to the consequences of a breach of the arbitrator's primary duty to resolve the parties' dispute, Section 583(2) no. 2 fZPO provided that the courts, upon application by a party, can terminate the arbitration agreement if an arbitrator refuses to perform, or unreasonably delays the performance of, his duties.[84] Under the previous Vienna Rules, the parties could apply to the VIAC to have the non-performing arbitrator removed and replaced by a suitable candidate under former Articles 12 and 13.[85] However, there were no Austrian cases on point.[86] Following the 2006 reforms of Austrian arbitration law and the Vienna Rules, **Article 17** and **7-056**

---

77. M. Platte, 'An Arbitrator's Duty to Render Enforceable Awards' (2003) 20(3) J Int'l Arb, 307.
78. G.J. Horvath, 'The Duty of Tribunals to Render an Enforceable Award' (2001) 18(2) J Int'l Arb, 135.
79. *See* **Article 24**, at paras. 048 *et seq.*
80. Although arbitrators may have to go beyond the relief requested by the parties. *See* ECJ, 1 June 1999, Case No. C-126/97, *Eco Swiss China Time Ltd v. Benetton International NV*, [1999] ECR I-3055; for a more detailed discussion of this case and its implications for the parties' right to be heard, *see* **Article 20**, at para. 047.
81. *See* **Article 1**, at paras. 105 *et seq.*
82. Article V(1)(c) New York Convention, **Annex 11**; *see also* J. Lew, L. Mistelis and S. Kröll, *Comparative International Commercial Arbitration* (The Hague, Kluwer Law International, 2003), para. 12-13.
83. H.W. Fasching, *Schiedsgericht und Schiedsverfahren im österreichischen und im internationalen Recht* (Vienna, Manz, 1973), p. 70. Under the old law should an arbitrator refuse to sign, the parties could apply to the courts. *See* OGH, 29 January 1970, 1 Ob 252/69.
84. OGH, 25 February 1997, 4 Ob 61/97t.
85. Vienna Rules 2001, **Annex 2a**.
86. C. Liebscher and A. Schmid in *Practitioner's Handbook on International Arbitration*, F.B. Weigand (ed.) (Munich, C.H. Beck, 2002), p. 555.

Section 590 ZPO provide for the removal of an arbitrator who fails to perform his or her primary duties.[87]

2.   Duty to Comply with Due Process

7-057 As a matter of principle, and to ensure the validity of their award, arbitrators must comply with due process, and thus must treat the parties fairly and equally and afford each party an opportunity to present its case.[88] For a detailed discussion of mandatory requirements of due process under Austrian law, *see* **Article 20** below.[89]

3.   Duty of Independence and Impartiality

7-058 Article 7(4) expressly requires arbitrators to be impartial and independent in the performance of their duties. It is indeed an undisputed premise of international arbitration that arbitrators[90] – whether party-appointed or presiding – have the duty to act impartially and independently from the parties.[91] This duty applies at the time of the appointment and continues throughout the proceedings until a final award is rendered.[92] A necessary corollary of the duty of impartiality and independence is the arbitrator's duty to make the appropriate disclosures to allow the parties (and, as the case may be, the arbitral institution) to adequately assess his or her impartiality.[93] Similarly, the arbitrator should seek to avoid any *appearance* of

---

87.   *See* **Article 17**, at paras. 015 *et seq.* For liability of arbitrators in case of non-performance, *see* **Article 8**, at paras. 008 *et seq.*

88.   A. Philip, 'The Duties of an Arbitrator' in *The Leading Arbitrators' Guide to International Arbitration*, L.W. Newman and R.D. Hill (eds) (Huntington, Juris Publishing, 2004), p. 75.

89.   *See* **Article 20**, at paras. 015 *et seq.* and 029 *et seq.*

90.   For a practical 'code of conduct' as to how to maintain independence as an arbitrator. *See* G. Aksen, 'The Tribunal's Appointment' in *The Leading Arbitrators' Guide to International Arbitration*, L.W. Newman and R.D. Hill (eds) (Huntington, Juris Publishing, 2004), p. 31; A.F. Lowenfeld, 'The Party-Appointed Arbitrator: Further Reflections' in *The Leading Arbitrators' Guide to International Arbitration*, L.W. Newman and R.D. Hill (eds) (Huntington, Juris Publishing, 2004), p. 41.

91.   C. Hausmaninger, 'Rights and Obligations of the Arbitrator with Regard to the Parties and the Arbitral Institution – A Civil Law Viewpoint' (1995) ICC Ct Bull Special Supplement: The Status of the Arbitrator, 36, 43; A. Philip, 'The Duties of an Arbitrator' in *The Leading Arbitrators' Guide to International Arbitration*, L.W. Newman and R.D. Hill (eds) (Huntington, Juris Publishing, 2004), p. 68.

92.   J. Lew, L. Mistelis and S. Kröll, *Comparative International Commercial Arbitration* (The Hague, Kluwer Law International, 2003), para. 12-17; *see also* IBA Conflict Guidelines, General Standard 1, **Annex 17**. The Second Draft of the IBA Conflict Guidelines recommended that arbitrators remain impartial and independent until the period for filing an application for *vacatur* has elapsed. This was abandoned; but, of course, the duty of impartiality is reborn if the award is set aside and the case referred back to the arbitrators.

93.   *See, e.g.*, IBA Conflict Guidelines, General Standard 7(c): 'An arbitrator is under a duty to make reasonable enquiries to investigate any potential conflict of interest, as well as any facts or circumstances that may cause his or her impartiality or independence to be questioned. Failure

impartiality, and should refrain from *ex parte* communications with any one party.[94] The arbitrator's impartiality is expressly prescribed, as a matter of mandatory Austrian law, by Section 588 ZPO. For a detailed discussion of the concept of impartiality and independence, *see* **Article 7**, at paras. 080 *et seq.*; as to the challenge of a biased arbitrator, and consequences attaching to the arbitrator's bias under Austrian law, *see* **Article 16** below.

4.   Duty of Efficient Conduct

Justice delayed is justice denied, and the speed of arbitral proceedings has been **7-059** termed one of arbitration's *raisons d'être* when compared to state court litigation.[95] While more complex disputes and more litigious parties result in longer proceedings, it is still commonly accepted that an arbitrator has the duty to proceed speedily and efficiently, and to ensure that the parties' dispute is finally resolved within a reasonable period of time. Thus, it is the arbitrators' – and oftentimes in particular the chairman's – duty to organize the proceedings efficiently; establish and follow a timetable; counter any one party's attempt to delay and obstruct the proceedings; and write and issue an award within a reasonable period of time. The arbitrators' duty to effect a speedy arbitration must, of course, be balanced against the parties' right to be heard and to have a reasonable opportunity to present their case.[96]

By way of sanction, a party may request the removal of an arbitrator under **Article** **7-060** **17** if the arbitrator is responsible for unduly delaying the proceedings. Under Section 590 ZPO, parties also have the possibility to apply to the Austrian courts for removal of an arbitrator who does not perform his duties 'within reasonable time'.[97]

As a consequence, an arbitrator also has the duty *not to accept* an appointment **7-061** if, due to other commitments, he or she cannot devote an adequate portion of their time to the parties' dispute; as well as the duty to reserve the adequate time once he or she has accepted the appointment.[98] This also includes a duty not to

---

to disclose a potential conflict is not excused by lack of knowledge if the arbitrator makes no reasonable attempt to investigate.' **Annex 17**.

94. J. Lew, L. Mistelis and S. Kröll, *Comparative International Commercial Arbitration* (The Hague, Kluwer Law International, 2003), para. 12-17.

95. C. Hausmaninger, 'Rights and Obligations of the Arbitrator with Regard to the Parties and the Arbitral Institution – A Civil Law Viewpoint' (1995) ICC Ct Bull Special Supplement: The Status of the Arbitrator, 36, 41.

96. *See* **Article 20**, at paras. 076 *et seq.*

97. For a more detailed discussion of this provision, *see* **Article 17**, at paras. 014 *et seq.*

98. *See* IBA Rules of Ethics item 2, **Annex 18**; *see also* A. Philip, 'The Duties of an Arbitrator' in *The Leading Arbitrators' Guide to International Arbitration*, L.W. Newman and R.D. Hill (eds) (Huntington, Juris Publishing, 2004), p. 71; A.I. Okekeifere, 'The Parties' Rights Against A Dilatory or Unskilled Arbitrator' (1998) 15(2) J Int'l Arb, 130.

cause delay to the arbitral process by resigning as an arbitrator without good cause.[99]

7-062 The duty of efficiency is also expressed in international instruments, such as the 1996 UNCITRAL Notes on Organizing Arbitral Proceedings,[100] and Article 7 of the IBA Rules of Ethics for International Arbitrators.[101] For a more detailed discussion of how to organize arbitration proceedings efficiently, *see* **Article 20** below.[102]

5.   Duty of Secrecy

7-063 Article 7(4) expressly provides that the arbitrators 'are bound to secrecy in respect of all matters coming to their notice in the course of their duties'. Thus, the Vienna Rules impose a far-reaching obligation of confidentiality on the arbitrators regarding *all* information they receive in the course of the arbitral proceedings, be it in the form of documents, witness testimony, submissions or otherwise.[103]

7-064 The duty of secrecy under Article 7(4) goes further than the widely supported principle that not only the award,[104] but also the deliberations of the arbitrators are confidential.[105] By way of example, Article 9 of the IBA Rules of Ethics[106] provides:

> The deliberations of the arbitral tribunal, and the contents of the award itself, remain confidential in perpetuity unless the parties release the arbitrators from

---

99. A. Philip, 'The Duties of an Arbitrator' in *The Leading Arbitrators' Guide to International Arbitration*, L.W. Newman and R.D. Hill (eds) (Huntington, Juris Publishing, 2004), p. 74. Indeed, the arbitrator should not excuse himself hastily. *See Laker Airways Inc. v. FLS Aerospace Ltd* [1999] 2 Lloyd's Rep. 45, 46 Q.B. (Comm.); J. Lew, L. Mistelis and S. Kröll, *Comparative International Commercial Arbitration* (The Hague, Kluwer Law International, 2003), para. 12-15 with further references. This is a natural consequence of the arbitrator's duty to complete his or her mandate.
100. UNCITRAL Notes **Annex 15**.
101. IBA Rules of Ethics **Annex 18**.
102. *See* **Article 20**, at paras. 101 *et seq.*
103. J. Lew, L. Mistelis and S. Kröll, *Comparative International Commercial Arbitration* (The Hague, Kluwer Law International, 2003), para. 12-20.
104. *See*, however, **Article 30**, at paras. 001 *et seq.*
105. *See* E. Gaillard and J. Savage (eds), *Fouchard Gaillard Goldman On International Commercial Arbitration* (The Hague, Kluwer Law International, 1999), para. 1374 ('Although again most laws do not explicitly require deliberations in international arbitrations to be secret, such secrecy is generally considered to be the rule. This means that views exchanged during the deliberations cannot be communicated to the parties.'); A. Redfern, 'The 2003 Freshfields Lecture – Dissenting Opinions in International Commercial Arbitration: The Good, the Bad and the Ugly' (2004) 20(3) Arb Int'l, 223 (referring to M. Boisséson, *Le Droit Francais de l'arbitrage interne et international* (Paris, GLN-éditions, 1990), p. 296 ('[T]he rule that such a "deliberation" should be, and should remain secret, is a "fundamental principle", which constitutes one of the mainsprings of arbitration, as it does of all judicial decisions')).
106. IBA Rules of Ethics **Annex 18**.

this obligation. An arbitrator should not participate in, or give any information for the purpose of assistance in, any proceedings to consider the award unless, exceptionally, he considers it his duty to disclose any material misconduct or fraud on the part of his fellow arbitrators.[107]

The scope of this principle of secrecy, in order for it to be effective, necessarily **7-065** extends to less formal aspects of the deliberation process such as informal discussions held amongst the arbitrators.[108]

The arbitrators' duty to keep the proceedings and in particular the deliberation **7-066** of the tribunal confidential does not end with the arbitration. Therefore, arbitrators should not divulge the content of their deliberations in setting aside proceedings before national courts (unless arguably in a case of allegations of criminal behaviour). However, this principle has recently been subject to some debate. Tension over the extent of this confidentiality arises in particular when the due process of the arbitrators' deliberations is called into question, usually by one of the arbitrators in a dissenting opinion, resulting in the initiation of setting aside proceedings before a national court.[109]

This situation occurred recently in a famous case in the Swedish Court of **7-067** Appeal.[110] The Swedish courts took the position that the obligation to testify before a court as contained in the Swedish Procedural Code overrides any principle of confidentiality and may be enforced by fines and ultimately detention. The court held that this provision of the Code was applicable to the deliberations of an arbitral tribunal sitting in Stockholm. The arbitrators provided oral testimony and their correspondence was submitted into evidence. The court also stated, however, that it would not impose sanctions on the arbitrators if they failed to co-operate, although it did say that negative inferences might be drawn from any refusal by an arbitrator to answer a question.[111] The questions raised by this case have not yet been addressed by the Austrian courts. However, they go to the core of the judicial nature of arbitration. If one accepts that arbitrators perform a quasi-judicial function, there are good arguments to extend to the arbitrators the privilege of

---

107. *See also* Rule 15(1) ICSID Arbitration Rules: 'The deliberations of the Tribunal shall take place in private and remain secret'.
108. *See, e.g.,* A. Redfern, 'The 2003 Freshfields Lecture – Dissenting Opinions in International Commercial Arbitration: The Good, the Bad and the Ugly' (2004) 20(3) Arb Int'l, 223 (quoting Sir Robert Jennings QC's decision concerning the U.S. government's challenge of Judge Bengt Broms as an arbitrator of the US-Iran Claims Tribunal).
109. *See* the discussion about dissenting opinions under **Article 26** at paras. 024 *et seq.*
110. *See* N. Rubins, S. Sołtysinski, M. Olechowski, H. Bagner and T. Wiwen-Nilsson, 'The CME v. Czech Republic Case – Case summary with observations' (2003) 2 Stockholm Arb Rep <www.sccinstitute.com/_upload/shared_files/artiklar/tjeckiska_republiken.pdf>.
111. *See* N. Rubins, S. Sołtysinski, M. Olechowski, H. Bagner and T. Wiwen-Nilsson 'The CME v. Czech Republic Case – Case summary with observations' (2003) 2 Stockholm Arb Rep <www.sccinstitute.com/_upload/shared_files/artiklar/tjeckiska_republiken.pdf>, p 244.

keeping their deliberations secret.[112] After all, the confidentiality of deliberations is well recognized with respect to state court judges. Absent a statutory provision guaranteeing that privilege for arbitrators, however, Austrian courts may be prepared to hear arbitrators as witnesses, including with respect of testimony regarding the tribunal's deliberations.

6.   Duty to Meet Certain Qualification Requirements

7-068   As discussed in some detail above, parties may impose certain particular requirements on arbitrators. Thus, the (prospective) arbitrator has the duty to make himself familiar with the arbitration agreement, make necessary disclosures as to whether he meets these requirements, and indeed not to accept an appointment if he fails to do so.[113] An arbitrator who fails to meet the qualifications agreed by the parties may be challenged under **Article 16** and Section 589 ZPO.[114]

7.   Duty of Diligence

7-069   In addition, Article 7(4) requires the arbitrators to conduct the arbitration 'to the best of their ability'. This amounts to a duty of diligence and care which requires the arbitrators, amongst other things, to prepare the case adequately and to familiarize themselves with the files when hearing the parties and taking evidence.[115]

7-070   The duty of diligence may well include the duty for arbitrators to consciously familiarize themselves with the duties they may have in a particular case. Some commentators therefore suggest that arbitrators draw up a list of duties as applicable under the relevant law, the parties' arbitration agreement and applicable institutional rules.[116]

8.   Ancillary and Cost-Efficiency Duties

7-071   The Vienna Rules also imply a series of ancillary duties, including the arbitrator's duty to go to the seat of the arbitration (**Article 2**), or, as the case may be, to co-operate in the constitution of the tribunal.[117]

---

112.   Note also that similar privileges were recently afforded to Austrian mediators.
113.   A. Philip, 'The Duties of an Arbitrator' in *The Leading Arbitrators' Guide to International Arbitration*, L.W. Newman and R.D. Hill (eds) (Huntington, Juris Publishing, 2004), p. 71.
114.   *See* **Article 16**, at paras. 001 and 004.
115.   *See also* IBA Rules of Ethics item 7, **Annex 18**.
116.   A. Redfern, M. Hunter, N. Blackaby and C. Partasides, *Law and Practice of International Commercial Arbitration* (4th edn, London, Sweet & Maxwell, 2004), para. 5-11.
117.   C. Hausmaninger, 'Rights and Obligations of the Arbitrator with Regard to the Parties and the Arbitral Institution – A Civil Law Viewpoint' (1995) ICC Ct Bull Special Supplement: The Status of the Arbitrator, 36, 40.

Arbitrators are also considered to be under a duty to conduct the arbitration in a **7-072** cost-efficient manner, and specifically to 'do their best to conduct the arbitration in such a manner that costs do not rise to an unreasonable proportion of the interests at stake'.[118] Arbitrators are also under a duty to keep proper record of the costs and expenses incurred in the course of the arbitration, and to make their records available for inspection by the VIAC (or, in the case of *ad hoc* arbitration, by the parties).[119] Arguably, arbitrators are also under a duty to provide a proper invoice for their services in case they requested the parties to pay VAT on their fees.[120] Indeed, **Article 35** requires the arbitrator to inform the Secretary General of all procedural steps that would incur further costs.[121] Such steps may be taken only if the costs are covered in the cost deposit advanced by the parties under **Article 34**.[122]

9.   Ethical Duties

In recent years, the discussion of an arbitrator's duties has focused on ethical **7-073** obligations as the 'foundation of the arbitral process'.[123] Most of these are concerned with the arbitrator's impartiality and related problems, such as *ex parte* communications.[124] Some question whether ethical norms in arbitration proceedings are of great importance. However, ethical norms produce faith in the arbitration system and offer a reliable basis upon which to structure specific mechanisms for dispute resolution.[125]

For an arbitrator who is a member of a national bar, ethical obligations can arise **7-074** from local bar rules and professional codes of conduct. In international arbitration, however, the application of local rules suffers from the lack of international harmonization.[126] In view of this, international organizations have adopted general ethical principles to guide international arbitrators. Notable examples are the ABA/AAA's Code of Ethics for Arbitrators in Commercial Arbitration (which was adopted in 1977 and substantially revised in 2004), the IBA Rules of Ethics for International Arbitrators (adopted in 1987),[127] and the IBA Guidelines

---

118. IBA Rules of Ethics item 7, **Annex 18**.
119. H.W. Fasching, *Schiedsgericht und Schiedsverfahren im österreichischen und im internationalen Recht* (Vienna, Manz, 1973), p. 72.
120. *See* **Article 36(10)**, at para. 043; C.W. Konrad and H. Gurtner, *Die Umsatzsteuer im Schiedsverfahren* (Cologne/Munich, Carl Heymanns Verlag, 2008).
121. *See* **Article 35**, at para. 003.
122. *See* **Article 34**, at paras. 019 *et seq.*, and 059 *et seq.*
123. W. Forbes, 'Rules of Ethics for Arbitrators and their Application' (1992) 9(3) J Int'l Arb, 5-26.
124. *See, e.g.*, IBA Rules of Ethics item 5, **Annex 18**.
125. O.K. Byrne, 'A New Code of Ethics for Commercial Arbitrators: The Neutrality of Party-Appointed Arbitrators on a Tripartite Panel' (2003) 30 Fordham Urb LJ, 1815, 1817.
126. *See*, however, the Code of Conduct for lawyers in the European Union, as adopted by the Council of the Bass and Law Societies of he European Union.
127. IBA Rules of Ehtics, **Annex 18**.

on Conflicts of Interest in International Commercial Arbitration (adopted 22 May 2004).[128]

7-075 Ethical obligations may also arise if the arbitration 'is high-jacked for a criminal purpose'.[129] Increasingly, arbitrators are faced with parties who assert fraud or corruption as the basis for their claim, which raises difficult questions for arbitrators who lack the resources and powers of state prosecutors to adequately deal with such allegations. Even more difficult questions arise in the – in practice highly relevant – context of money laundering. Parties could, for example, abuse the arbitration by obtaining an award by consent which *prima facie* provides a legitimate title for monetary payments. Such a 'settlement' in the form of an internationally enforceable award is obviously an attractive instrument to whitewash criminal proceeds.

7-076 How are arbitrators supposed to react if they harbour a suspicion that the arbitration is abused for such a purpose? EU Directive No. 2001/97/EC requires that 'members of the legal profession' have an obligation to report 'any fact which might indicate money laundering and provide the authorities with any information requested'. Arbitrators are well advised to check, at least when sitting within the European Union, how this directive has been implemented locally and if it is understood to apply to arbitrators as well.

7-077 Such reporting requirements do not sit comfortably with arbitrators whose mandate is premised upon the parties' trust. Arbitrators are often hesitant to abuse that trust by reporting to the authorities behind the parties' backs. Yet the issue is serious, and, if it persists, may undermine the credibility of the arbitral process in the eyes of national legislatures. Obviously, an award based on criminal conduct will be subject to setting aside and may be denied enforcement.[130] Recently, therefore, the ICC has published a dossier on *Arbitration – Money Laundering, Corruption and Fraud*;[131] and in 2004, the ICC has established a Working Group on Criminal Law and Arbitration, whose mission is to provide guidance to arbitrators on this issue.

10.   Additional Duties Imposed by the Parties in the Ongoing Arbitration

7-078 Apart from requirements and duties laid out by the parties in their arbitration agreement, the parties may agree on some additional duties for the arbitrators in the course of an already pending arbitration. Such additional duties require the

---

128. IBA Conflict Guidelines, **Annex 17**; *see* the detailed discussion at **Article 7**, at paras. 086 *et seq.*
129. A. Redfern, M. Hunter, N. Blackaby and C. Partasides, *Law and Practice of International Commercial Arbitration* (4th edn, London, Sweet & Maxwell, 2004), para. 5-28.
130. *See* **Article 27**, at para. 060 *et seq.*
131. K. Karsten and A. Berkeley (eds), *Arbitration – Money Laundering, Corruption and Fraud* (Paris, ICC Publishing, 2003).

consent of the arbitrators who have agreed to accept their appointment on the terms valid as of the time of that appointment.

Some Austrian commentators argue that the arbitrators have the duty to follow the parties' joint instructions.[132] In principle, rather than allowing the parties to 'instruct' the arbitrators (which may well be problematic in view of the judicial nature of the arbitrators' function and which is in any event restricted to subject matters that are at the parties' disposal under applicable law), the better dogmatic view (although arriving at the similar result) is that parties are free to jointly amend the arbitration agreement, which in turn may restrict the arbitrators' powers and jurisdiction.[133] If both parties insist on a particular modification, this approach leaves the arbitrator who finds himself unable to perform under such changed circumstances the freedom to resign.[134] **7-079**

B. THE INDEPENDENCE AND IMPARTIALITY OF ARBITRATORS

In order to ensure that the arbitration tribunal has the full trust and confidence of the parties, arbitrators must be in a position to carry out their functions impartially and without bias. As a matter of principle, the impartiality of arbitrators is an integral prerequisite of due process, ensuring that arbitration is indeed a reliable alternative to state court litigation.[135] On the level of the individual arbitration, it ensures the enforceability of the arbitral award. On the other hand, applying too stringent a standard for disqualification (and for disclosure of circumstances possibly leading to disqualification) may unduly diminish the parties' right to select arbitrators of their choosing. Thus, ensuring a non-partisan decision-making process has been called the 'crux of arbitration'.[136] **7-080**

All of this may be trite to state. Of course, parties, when entrusting the resolution of their dispute to 'private' persons, will expect that these persons reach their decision without bias towards either party.[137] And yet, the trivial can turn complex and subtle in practice. On a general level, there are many, and oftentimes different, perceptions in the international arena as to what makes an arbitrator partial or dependent. Also, in the world of international law firms with offices around the **7-081**

---

132. H.W. Fasching, *Schiedsgericht und Schiedsverfahren im österreichischen und im internationalen Recht* (Vienna, Manz, 1973), p. 74; H.W. Fasching, *Lehrbuch des österreichischen Ziviprozessrechts* (2nd edn, Vienna, Manz, 1990), para. 2202.
133. C. Liebscher and A. Schmid in *Practitioner's Handbook on International Arbitration*, F.B. Weigand (ed.) (Munich, C.H. Beck, 2002), p. 555.
134. For a detailed discussion, *see* **Article 20**, at paras. 098 *et seq.*
135. *See, e.g.*, Article 6 ECHR which requires a hearing by 'an independent and impartial tribunal'.
136. F. Matscher, 'Schiedsgerichtsbarkeit und EMRK' in *Festschrift für Heinrich Nagel zum 75. Geburtstag*, W.J. Haberscheid and K. Schwab (Münster, Aschendorff, 1987), p. 236.
137. Y. Derains and E.A. Schwartz, *A Guide to the ICC Rules of Arbitration* (2nd edn, The Hague, Kluwer Law International, 2005), p. 116.

globe, conflict of interest issues are not academic, but very real and increasingly difficult to manage for arbitrators working in such settings.

7-082 As a preliminary matter, this section examines recent efforts of harmonization attempting to define a common standard for impartiality and independence of arbitrators; it then discusses the nature and different possible standards of bias in international arbitration; and finally, on the basis of that discussion, approaches these issues from the perspective of Austrian law. The discussion in this chapter needs to be read in context with **Article 16**, which sets forth the mechanics for challenging a biased arbitrator.

1.   Attempts at International Harmonization

7-083 When parties opt for arbitral proceedings in preference over litigation in national courts, they do not waive their right to independent and impartial adjudicators.[138] As the use of arbitration as a means to settle international disputes continues to grow, however, the concern with arbitrators meeting standards of impartiality and independence has also increased:

> Problems of conflicts of interest increasingly challenge international arbitration. Arbitrators are often unsure about what facts need to be disclosed, and they may make different choices about disclosure than other arbitrators may make about the same situation. The growth of international business and the manner in which it is conducted, including interlocking corporate relationships and larger international law firms, has caused more disclosures and has created more difficult issues to determine. Reluctant parties have more opportunities to use challenges of arbitrators to delay arbitrations or to deny the opposing party the arbitrator of its choice.[139]

7-084 At the heart of the problem, therefore, lies a lack of standardization. Different arbitrators will apply different standards as to the circumstances that should lead to disclosure or indeed to disqualification. It is also true that obstructive parties have learned to exploit that lack of clarity to bring challenges against arbitrators as a dilatory tactic.

7-085 Different arbitral organizations and legislatures have, therefore, recently increased efforts to define a standard of impartiality and independence.[140] Notable examples of this tendency are recent Californian legislation (providing for strict ethical standards for private arbitrators, which, if violated, would be grounds for

---

138. G.A. Alvarez, 'The Challenge of Arbitrators' (1990) 6(3) Arb Int'l, 203.
139. IBA Conflict Guidelines, Introduction, **Annex 17**.
140. Arguably, at least for the time being, these standards provide competing systems; until any one standard prevails, they are thus unlikely to end the uncertainty surrounding the definition of bias and of the standard for disclosure.

disqualification and *vacatur*)[141] and the revised Code of Ethics which was adopted by the American Arbitration Association in conjunction with the American Bar Association effective as of 1 March 2004.[142]

The internationally most important initiative came from the International Bar Association, which, on 22 May 2004, adopted Guidelines on Conflicts of Interest in International Arbitration (IBA Conflict Guidelines), dealing specifically with the issue of arbitrators' impartiality, independence, and disclosure.[143] **7-086**

The IBA Conflict Guidelines in their present form are the result of the dedicated effort of a Working Group established under IBA Committee D and comprised of experts from both civil law and common law jurisdictions. The Working Group invited debate and comments from international arbitration practitioners and arbitral institutions and produced three drafts reflecting the comments it received.[144] **7-087**

The IBA Conflict Guidelines now provide for seven General Standards, which set out the principles applying to the issue of impartiality. Following each General Standard, the Guidelines also contain Explanatory Notes. In lists annexed to the General Standards, the Guidelines also provide a non-exhaustive enumeration of circumstances in which the arbitrator must decline to act (non-waivable Red List); the arbitrator can act only if he or she obtains, after full disclosure of the relevant facts, the express consent of both parties (waivable Red List); the arbitrator can act if, after the arbitrator makes a disclosure, no party objects within 30 days (Orange List); and circumstances in which the arbitrator can act without having to make a disclosure (Green List). **7-088**

The approach adopted by the IBA Conflict Guidelines has attracted some controversy. It has been argued that the examples in the lists provide obstructive parties with a checklist to launch a challenge. Yet the IBA Conflict Guidelines further an important goal in setting out for the first time in considerable detail what could be a harmonized and transparent standard for impartiality and disclosure in international arbitration. Through the discussion surrounding their adoption, the guidelines certainly have increased awareness in the arbitration community. Whatever one makes of them, it can be expected that the IBA Conflict Guidelines will feature prominently in the considerations and arguments of parties, arbitrators, institutions, and **7-089**

---

141. J. Folberg, 'Arbitration Ethics: Winds of reform blowing from the West' (Fall 2002) Disp Res Mag, 5.
142. For a download of the 2004 Code of Ethics (and related explanatory notes and materials), *see* the AAA's website <http:www.adr.org>.
143. *See* IBA Conflict Guidelines, **Annex 17**.
144. For a summary of the drafting process and useful assistance for interpreting the Guidelines, *see* O.L.O. De Witt Wijnen, N. Voser and N. Rao, 'Background Information on the IBA Guidelines on Conflicts of Interest' (2004) 5 Bus L Int'l, 444; *see also* N. Voser, 'Interessenkonflikte in der internationalen Schiedsgerichtsbarkeit – die Initiative der IBA' [2003] SchiedsVZ, 59.

perhaps even national courts.[145] For that reason, these Guidelines are incorporated into the discussion of impartiality, independence and disclosure below.

2.   The Standard of Impartiality and Independence in International Arbitration

7-090 All major institutional arbitration rules impose some standard of neutrality on the arbitrator, but there is no unified terminology. Arbitrators acting under ICC Rules must be, and remain throughout the case, 'independent of the parties involved in the arbitration';[146] arbitrators may be challenged before the ICC Court for lack of 'independence and otherwise'. Arbitrators acting under LCIA Rules 'shall be and remain at all times impartial and independent of the parties; and none shall act in the arbitration as advocates for any party'.[147] Arbitrators acting under UNCITRAL Rules may be challenged for lack of 'impartiality and independence'.[148] The Vienna Rules appear to apply a particularly strict standard, requiring the arbitrators to 'perform their duties in *complete* independence and impartiality'.[149]

7-091 None of these rules, however, give any guidance as to what 'impartiality' or 'independence' mean. These terms were developed in academic writing and by the courts, and are – together with the related concepts of 'neutrality' and 'bias' – discussed below.

2.1.   Impartiality and Independence

7-092 The differences between being 'independent' or 'impartial' may seem mere semantics.[150] Some argue that the concepts of impartiality and independence are interrelated,[151] some that it is of little consequence what particular terms are used, as these terms refer 'not so much to a rule of law as an internalized ethos that is an amalgam of impartiality and independence'.[152] However, whether real or perceived, the lack of uniformity of institutional rules and legal standards has caused a significant measure of controversy and debate in the international community.[153]

---

145. For the application of the IBA Conflict Guidelines in Austria, *see* **Article 7**, at para. 109.
146. Article 7(1) ICC Rules.
147. Article 5(2) LCIA Rules.
148. Article 10 UNCITRAL Rules.
149. **Article 7**, at para. 122.
150. G.B. Born, *International Arbitration and Forum Selection Agreements: Drafting and Enforcing* (2nd edn, The Hague, Kluwer Law International, 2006), p. 72.
151. D. Bishop and L. Reed, 'Practical Guidelines for Interviewing, Selecting and Challenging Party-Appointed Arbitrators in International Commercial Arbitration' (1998) 14(4) Arb Int'l, 395, 396.
152. G. Aksen, 'The Tribunal's Appointment' in *The Leading Arbitrators' Guide to International Arbitration*, L.W. Newman and R.D. Hill (eds) (Huntington, Juris Publishing, 2004), p. 32.
153. G. Aksen, 'The Tribunal's Appointment' in *The Leading Arbitrators' Guide to International Arbitration*, L.W. Newman and R.D. Hill (eds) (Huntington, Juris Publishing, 2004), p. 32.

In trying to give meaning to the differences in terminology, impartiality is **7-093** described as the arbitrator's ability to assume a neutral position with respect to the subject matter of the dispute. It is thus a state of mind,[154] in which the arbitrator does not adopt a position favourable to either of the parties until the case has been heard and argued in full.[155] Impartiality is therefore considered the 'essential duty of the arbitrator'.[156] It enables the arbitrator to conduct a truly fair proceeding, to approach the case unbiased and to give the parties 'equal opportunities to present their case and persuade the decision-makers'.[157] In the case of the party-appointed arbitrator, impartiality implies the freedom of thought to decide against the nominating party if the opposing party has a better case.[158]

Independence, on the other hand, refers to the relationship between the arbitrator **7-094** and the parties. Independence thus means the absence of a close, substantial, recent and proven relationship between a party and a prospective arbitrator. It has also been described as 'the obligation to remain free of any undisclosed relationship likely to give rise to a personal interest in the result of the arbitration'.[159] Accordingly, the arbitrator's relationships with the parties in personal, social, and financial contexts are an indicator for his or her independence. The closer the relationship becomes, the more dependent the arbitrator is considered to be.[160] It appears to be in the nature of these descriptors, however, that they do not resolve the struggle of determining how close is too close a relationship. At a minimum, arbitrators are prohibited from having any direct relationship with the parties that would give rise to a financial, business or professional interest by the arbitrator.[161] Obviously, a close private relationship to one of the parties may also affect the arbitrator's freedom of judgment.[162] In practice, every case needs to be carefully evaluated on its own merits.

---

154. G. Aksen, 'The Tribunal's Appointment' in *The Leading Arbitrators' Guide to International Arbitration*, L.W. Newman and R.D. Hill (eds) (Huntington, Juris Publishing, 2004), p. 32.
155. D. Bishop and L. Reed, 'Practical Guidelines for Interviewing, Selecting and Challenging Party-Appointed Arbitrators in International Commercial Arbitration' (1998) 14(4) Arb Int'l, 395, 396.
156. G.A. Alvarez, 'The Challenge of Arbitrators' (1990) 6(3) Arb Int'l, 203, 214; D. Bishop and L. Reed, 'Practical Guidelines for Interviewing, Selecting and Challenging Party-Appointed Arbitrators in International Commercial Arbitration' (1998) 14(4) Arb Int'l, 395, 398; D.J. Branson, 'Ethics for International Arbitrators' (1987) 3(1) Arb Int'l, 72, 73.
157. C.A. Rogers, 'Fit and Function in Legal Ethics: Developing a Code of Conduct for International Arbitration' [2002] Mich J Int'l L, 341, 362.
158. M.L. Smith, 'Impartiality of the Party-Appointed Arbitrator' (1990) 6(4) Arb Int'l, 320, 323.
159. M.L. Smith, 'Impartiality of the Party-Appointed Arbitrator' (1990) 6(4) Arb Int'l, 320, 323.
160. O.K. Byrne, 'A New Code of Ethics for Commercial Arbitrators: The Neutrality of Party-Appointed Arbitrators on a Tripartite Panel' (2003) 30 Fordham Urb LJ, 1815, 1829.
161. G.B. Born, *International Arbitration and Forum Selection Agreements: Drafting and Enforcing* (2nd edn, The Hague, Kluwer Law International, 2006), p. 72.
162. Y. Derains and E.A. Schwartz, *A Guide to the ICC Rules of Arbitration* (2nd edn, The Hague, Kluwer Law International, 2005), p. 127. In this regard, it is irrelevant if the arbitrator is biased against or in favour of either party.

7-095 U.S. courts have developed a four factor test to determine bias which also strongly focuses on the concept of independence: the extent and character of the arbitrator's personal interest; the directness of the arbitrator's relationship to the allegedly favoured party; the relationship's link to the arbitration; and the proximity in time between the relationship and the arbitration.[163] The ICC Rules also focus on the test of independence which, it is considered, can be determined by objective standards, whereas the arbitrator's impartiality, as a state of mind, is considered an inherently subjective notion more difficult to assess.[164] The ICC thus requires arbitrators to disclose 'any past or present relationship, direct or indirect, with any of the parties, their counsel, whether financial, professional or of another kind'.[165]

7-096 The ICC's approach has force in that it is practical. However, impartiality should not be omitted from the applicable test because, in truth, it is the decisive standard. The arbitrator's independence from the parties – that is, the lack of financial, social or other ties – is only an *indicator* of the arbitrator's impartiality. In other words, the closer the relationship is, the higher is the suspicion of dependency and, in turn, the appearance of partiality. Thus, parties may usually waive the requirement of independence upon proper disclosure of connections between a party and an arbitrator. However, that does not mean that the party intends to waive the requirement of impartiality as well.[166] In sum, while there is no harm in including, as the Vienna Rules do, the requirement of independence, it is ultimately the arbitrator's impartiality that is decisive.

2.2.   *Neutrality*

7-097 Occasionally, in particular in the United States, impartiality and neutrality are used synonymously to describe the obligation not to favour one of the parties or prejudge an issue. In addition, neutrality is often used to refer to *national* neutrality. The perception is that the sole or presiding arbitrator, to be neutral, ought to come

---

163. *See ANR Coal Co. v. Cogentrix of North Carolina, Inc.*, 173 F.3d 493 (4th Cir. 1999).
164. D. Bishop and L. Reed, 'Practical Guidelines for Interviewing, Selecting and Challenging Party-Appointed Arbitrators in International Commercial Arbitration' (1998) 14(4) Arb Int'l, 395, 397.
165. ICC Form 'Arbitrator's Declaration of Acceptance and Statement of Independence' reprinted in (1995) 6(2) ICC Ct Bull, 79.
166. M.L. Smith, 'Impartiality of the Party-Appointed Arbitrator' (1990) 6(4) Arb Int'l, 320, 323. For these reasons, the English Arbitration Act 1996 requires in Section 24(1), 'impartiality'. The Drafting Committee explained this as follows: '101. (. . .) It seems to us that lack of independence, unless it gives rise to justifiable doubts about the impartiality of the arbitrator, is of no significance. The latter is, of course, the first of our grounds for removal. If lack of independence were to be included, then this could only be justifiable if it covered cases where the lack of independence did not give rise to justifiable doubts about impartiality, for otherwise there would be no point including lack of independence as a separate ground.' *See* Departmental Advisory Committee on Arbitration Law, 1996 Report on the Arbitration Bill', reprinted in (1997) 13(3) Arb Int'l, 275, 292.

from a different country than either party.[167] Some institutional rules specifically require the presiding arbitrator to be of a different country than the parties. Under the ICC Rules, for example, the sole or presiding arbitrator, when appointed by the ICC Court, 'shall be of a nationality other than those of the parties' although he or she may be a national of one of the parties in case the parties do not object.[168]

The term 'neutral' or 'non-neutral' arbitrator is also commonly used in domestic **7-098** U.S. arbitration. Under that concept, a party-appointed arbitrator may be non-neutral, and, as such, predisposed towards a party. At least conceptually, the idea of a non-neutral arbitrator is difficult to understand, or endorse, from a European perspective. Indeed, the recently adopted ABA/AAA Code of Ethics for Arbitrators have abandoned the previously applicable principle that party-nominated arbitrators are non-neutral in favour of an assumption of neutrality; thus, parties have to expressly agree to non-neutral arbitrators.

3. The Standard of Independence and Impartiality Under Austrian Law

As a matter of course, it is accepted in Austria that all members of the tribunal must **7-099** be impartial.[169] Insofar as an arbitrator performs a judicial function that is given effect by national law as if it were a state court judgment, it is argued that the impartiality and independence of arbitrators are a constitutional requirement.[170] Although different standards may be applicable to state court litigation as opposed to arbitration,[171] the legislator is under an obligation, both as a matter of constitutional law and the ECHR, to ensure through appropriate legislation the impartiality and independence of arbitrators[172] and to provide mechanisms for control and supervision.[173]

---

167. For nationality requirements, *see* **Article 7**, at paras. 018 *et seq.*
168. D. Bishop and L. Reed, 'Practical Guidelines for Interviewing, Selecting and Challenging Party-Appointed Arbitrators in International Commercial Arbitration' (1998) 14(4) Arb Int'l, 395, 399. For the Vienna Rules and Austrian law, *see* **Article 7**, at paras. 018 *et seq.*
169. W.H. Rechberger and M. Rami, 'Ablehnung von Schiedsrichtern durch die Parteien' [1999] wbl, 103, 105, with reference to a phrase coined by *Habscheid*.
170. For Germany: K.H. Schwab and G. Walter (eds), *Schiedsgerichtbarkeit* (7th edn, Munich, C.H. Beck, 2005), ch. 9, para. 4 with reference to Article 97 German GG.
171. K. Heller,'Die Rechtsstellung des internationalen Schiedsgerichts der Wirtschaftskammer Österreich' [1994] wbl, 105, 116 *et seq.*
172. K.H. Schwab and G. Walter (eds), *Schiedsgerichtbarkeit* (7th edn, Munich, C.H. Beck, 2005), ch. 9, para. 4; R. Geimer in *Zöller – Zivilprozessordnung*, R. Zöller *et al.* (eds) (26th edn, Cologne, Verlag Dr. Otto Schmidt, 2007), Section 1036, para. 8; BVerfG, 8 June 1993, 1 BvR 878/90 in BVerfGE 89, 28, 35, NJW 1993, 2229; BGH, 15 December 1994, IZR 121/92, NJW 1995, 1677, 1679.
173. K. Heller, *Der Verfassungsrechtliche Rahmen der Privaten Internationalen Schiedsgerichtsbarkeit* (Vienna, Manz, 1996), p. 50.

3.1.   *The Standard of Impartiality and Independence Under the*
            Former ZPO

7-100 The standard for the independence and impartiality of arbitrators, imposed by the mandatory provision of Section 586 fZPO, provided that arbitrators could be challenged on the same grounds as state court judges according to Sections 19 and 20 JN. These provisions differentiated between compulsory grounds that automatically exclude the judge from acting on a case (*Ausschließungsgründe*) and grounds on which a judge can be challenged by the parties (*Befangenheitsgründe*). *Fasching* considered this equality with state court judges justified because of the arbitrators' judicial function.[174]

7-101 The first category (*Ausschließungsgründe*), contained in Section 20 JN and Section 537 ZPO, essentially prohibit the judge to act in his or her own matters, if the judge him or herself was a party to the dispute at bar; if the judge was related to one of the parties; if the judge was or had been the representative of one of the parties;[175] if the judge shared rights or obligations with one of the parties;[176] or if the judge participated in a lower court decision and is now asked to hear the appeal. These grounds are absolute, in that they do not require a further showing that they actually lead to impartiality in the circumstances of the case.[177] These grounds also apply *ex officio* at all stages of the proceeding, that is, even without a party's application, and indeed, if not applied, result in the absolute nullity of the state court proceedings.[178] In that regard, these grounds appear comparable to the Non-Waivable Red List contained in the IBA Conflict Guidelines.[179]

7-102 Second, Section 19 no. 2 JN contains the catch-all provision allowing for the challenge of a judge if 'there is a sufficient ground to doubt the impartiality'. According to established doctrine and case law, this provision rests on an objective standard, requiring disqualification of the judge if it must be feared, as the result of

---

174. H.W. Fasching, *Schiedsgericht und Schiedsverfahren im österreichischen und im internationalen Recht* (Vienna, Manz, 1973), p. 63. It has been debated, however, if the trust placed by the parties in the arbitrators, in conjunction with a lack of judicial control, would require that stricter standards are applied to arbitrators than to judges on the other hand, the parties' direct participation in the appointment process may justify a larger measure of generosity than would be displayed towards state court judges. *See* W.H. Rechberger and M. Rami, 'Ablehnung von Schiedsrichtern durch die Parteien' [1999] wbl, 103, 106.

175. H.W. Fasching, *Schiedsgericht und Schiedsverfahren im österreichischen und im internationalen Recht* (Vienna, Manz, 1973), p. 63, with further references.

176. *See* H.W. Fasching, *Schiedsgericht und Schiedsverfahren im österreichischen und im internationalen Recht* (Vienna, Manz, 1973), p. 63.

177. C. Liebscher, *The Healthy Award* (The Hague, Kluwer Law International, 2003), p. 274, with further references.

178. Section 477(1) no. 1 ZPO.

179. IBA Conflict Guidelines, **Annex 17**.

an objective analysis, that the judge's impartiality is tainted.[180] Although the standard is objective, the appearance of impartiality is sufficient in the interest of the integrity of the judiciary.[181] These *Befangenheitsgründe* do not result in absolute nullity; in state court proceedings, they must be raised at the earliest opportunity,[182] failing which they are considered to be cured.

By virtue of Section 586 fZPO, both categories applied to determine the impartiality **7-103** of arbitrators.[183] However, with respect to arbitrators, neither category automatically *excluded* the arbitrator from acting (the only arguable exception was the prohibition that the arbitrator must not be a party to the dispute).[184] In all other cases, the aggrieved party was *required* – without delay[185] – to *challenge* the arbitrator.[186] This was also confirmed by Section 595(1) no. 4 fZPO which provided for the setting aside of the award only if an arbitrator was challenged, but the challenge was wrongfully rejected. This did not mean that an arbitrator could ignore grounds for challenge if they were not advanced by a party. Rather, the arbitrator owed to the parties a duty of good faith to refrain from adjudicating a dispute if he or she is biased, failing which the arbitrator may be liable to the parties.

The requirement that the aggrieved party must make an affirmative challenge to **7-104** preserve its right to vacate the award recognized the prominent role of party autonomy in arbitration.[187] This was reinforced by Section 586(2) fZPO which provided specifically for arbitration that the party that appointed an arbitrator (whether alone or in agreement with the other side) could only challenge that arbitrator 'if the basis for the challenge has come into existence, or has become known to the party, after that arbitrator's appointment'.[188] Again, Section 586(2)

---

180. P.G. Mayr, in *Kommentar zur ZPO*, W.H. Rechberger (ed.) (3rd edn, Vienna/New York, Springer, 2006), Section 19 JN, para. 4, with further references.

181. P.G. Mayr, in *Kommentar zur ZPO*, W.H. Rechberger (ed.) (3rd edn, Vienna/New York, Springer, 2006), Section 19 JN, para. 4.

182. Section 21(2) JN.

183. *See* W.H. Rechberger and M. Rami, 'Ablehnung von Schiedsrichtern durch die Parteien' [1999] wbl, 103.

184. H.W. Fasching, *Schiedsgericht und Schiedsverfahren im österreichischen und im internationalen Recht* (Vienna, Manz, 1973), p. 62. Under the new ZPO, the participation of an arbitrator who is also a party to the dispute would probably lead to *vacatur* as a violation of *procedural ordre public*.

185. *See* **Article 16**, at paras. 023 *et seq.*

186. H.W. Fasching, *Schiedsgericht und Schiedsverfahren im österreichischen und im internationalen Recht* (Vienna, Manz, 1973), p. 62; W.H. Rechberger and W. Melis in *Kommentar zur ZPO*, W.H. Rechberger (ed.) (2nd edn, Vienna/New York, Springer, 2000), Section 586, para. 2. Apparently of contrary opinion, C. Liebscher, *The Healthy Award* (The Hague, Kluwer Law International, 2003), pp. 274-275.

187. H.W. Fasching, *Schiedsgericht und Schiedsverfahren im österreichischen und im internationalen Recht* (Vienna, Manz, 1973), p. 62.

188. Similarly, Article 11(3) Vienna Rules 2001 provided that '[a] challenge is inadmissible if the party making the challenge has taken part in the proceedings notwithstanding the knowledge which it already had or ought to have had of the grounds of challenge relied upon, or if the party making the challenge notified the grounds of challenge with undue delay'. **Annex 2a.**

fZPO did *not* differentiate between the (extreme) cases of *Ausschließungsgründe*, on the one hand, and sufficient grounds to doubt the arbitrator's impartiality, on the other hand. Therefore, the aggrieved party needed to complain irrespective of whether there was a ground for exclusion or merely a ground to doubt the arbitrator's impartiality – failing which the defect was healed. This is different from grounds for exclusion of state court judges (Section 20 JN) which cannot be waived and always provide a basis for nullity. Again, however, Austrian doctrine and the courts did not apply the requirement of Section 586(2) fZPO to situations where arbitrators served in a dispute to which they themselves were parties.[189]

3.2.   *The Standard of Impartiality and Independence*
                 Under the New ZPO

7-105 Section 588(2) ZPO now provides, in terms identical to **Article 16**:

An arbitrator may be challenged only if circumstances exist that give rise to justifiable doubts as to its impartiality or independence, or if it does not possess qualifications agreed to by the parties.

7-106 Section 588(2) ZPO sets out an objective standard. A challenge will be successful only if the circumstances of the case *objectively* lead to justifiable doubts. Thus, a challenge ought not to turn on whether a party has doubts regarding the arbitrator's impartiality, but on whether such doubts are justified in the eyes of a reasonable person.[190]

7-107 This approach is warranted by the wording of Section 588(2) ZPO (and **Article 16**), which require that circumstances *exist* – rather than circumstances are *perceived to*

---

189. H.W. Fasching, *Schiedsgericht und Schiedsverfahren im österreichischen und im internationalen Recht* (Vienna, Manz, 1973), pp. 62 *et seq.* with further references; *see also* W.H. Rechberger and M. Rami, 'Ablehnung von Schiedsrichtern durch die Parteien' [1999] wbl, 103, with further references. *See*, however, the German BGH decision: BGH, 3 July 1975, III ZR 78/73, NJW 1976, 245, JZ 1976, 245, 247 (with annotation by *Schlosser*), in which the challenge of an arbitrator was rejected, even though the arbitrator was the legal representative of a party, only because that arbitrator reached a decision against the party that appointed him and whose representative he was. As W.H. Rechberger and M. Rami, 'Ablehnung von Schiedsrichtern durch die Parteien' [1999] wbl, 103, 105 point out, it may be irrelevant which decision the arbitrator reached in the end. The arbitrator deciding against 'his party' to demonstrate his 'independence' is just as biased as the arbitrator who is favourably inclined. In extreme cases, it may therefore be indeed justified to abstract from the circumstances of the individual case to safeguard the integrity of the arbitral process.

190. M. Platte in *Arbitration Law of Austria: Practice and Procedure*, S. Riegler, A. Petsche, A. Fremuth-Wolf, M. Platte and C. Liebscher (eds) (Huntington, Juris Publishing, 2007), Section 588, p. 258; G. Zeiler, *Schiedsverfahren* (Vienna/Graz, Neuer Wissenschaftlicher Verlag, 2006), Section 588, p. 151; J. Power, *The Austrian Arbitration Act – A Practicioner's Guide to Sections 577-618 of the Austrian Code of Civil Procedure* (Vienna, Manz, 2006), Section 588, para. 8.

exist in the eyes of the parties – that give rise to *justifiable* doubts. Within the system of Austrian procedural law, such an objective standard has always been applied with respect to state court judges. As noted above, doctrine and case law require disqualification of the judge if it must be feared, as the result of an objective analysis, that the judge's impartiality is tainted.[191] In other words, for a challenge to be successful, it is not enough that such doubts are 'sufficient' in the eyes of an aggrieved party – rather, they must be objectively sufficient from the perspective of a neutral and informed third-party observer.[192] This objective standard puts Austrian law in line with the objective test suggested by IBA Conflict Guidelines, which provide in General Standard 2(c) that '[d]oubts are justifiable if a reasonable and informed third party would reach the conclusion that there was a likelihood that the arbitrator may be influenced by factors other than the merits of the case as presented by the parties in reaching his or her decision'.[193] Given the identical wording, the same standard of impartiality and independence applies to Section 588(2) ZPO and **Article 16** of the Vienna Rules.

It can be expected that for the application of Section 588(2) ZPO, case law **7-108** rendered under the fZPO will still have some impact.[194] Indeed, all reasons that automatically would exclude an Austrian state court judge from hearing a case (*Ausschließungsgründe* in Section 20 JN and Section 537 ZPO) by their nature adversely affect an arbitrator's independence and impartiality. In one of the first decisions under Section 589(3) ZPO, reviewing a challenge rejected by the VIAC, the *Handelsgericht Wien* (Commercial Court of Vienna) indeed equated the concept of 'impartiality and independence' under Section 588 ZPO with the grounds of challenge under Sections 19, 20 JN.[195] In that decision, the court also expressly (and correctly) recognized that Section 588 ZPO set an objective standard, which is however satisfied by an appearance of partiality in the eyes of an objective observer.

The *Handelsgericht Wien* also considered the application of the IBA Conflict **7-109** Guidelines in the context of Section 588 ZPO. It recognized that the legislature intended, with the 2006 reform, an internationalization of Austrian arbitration law, but rejected the application of the IBA Conflict Guidelines on the basis that the legislative materials did not specifically refer to them in the context of Section 588 ZPO. This analysis is not convincing. The Austrian legislature specifically changed the existing terminology for arbitrators. The law no longer refers to '*Unbefangenheit*' (the term used in Section 19 JN), but to '*Unparteilichkeit und Unabhängigkeit*' – that is, impartiality and independence. These terms should be interpreted in an international light, because they were borrowed from Article 12

---

191. P.G. Mayr, in *Kommentar zur ZPO*, W.H. Rechberger (ed.) (3rd edn, Vienna/New York, Springer, 2006), Section 19 JN, para. 4, with further references.
192. *See* OGH, 15 September 2004, 9 Ob A 94/04w.
193. *See* IBA Conflict Guidelines, **Annex 17**.
194. P. Oberhammer, *Entwurf eines neuen Schiedsverfahrensrechts* (Vienna, Manz, 2002), p. 69.
195. HG Vienna, 24 July 2007, 16 Nc 2/07w.

of the UNCITRAL Model Law.[196] The terminology of Article 12 of the UNCITRAL Model Law influenced in turn the applicable international standard under other instruments, including the IBA Conflict Guidelines.[197] As a result – while recognizing that the Austrian legislature did not intend to change the essence of the applicable substantive standards[198] – it is arguably permissible to use international precedent as persuasive authority to shed further light on Section 588 ZPO, reducing possible municipal peculiarities for the international user.

4.   Some Examples Regarding Impartiality and Independence

7-110 As discussed, case law rendered under the fZPO will arguably continue to impact the application of Section 588(2) ZPO. All reasons that would automatically exclude an Austrian state court judge from hearing a case (*Ausschließungsgründe* in Section 20 JN and Section 537 ZPO) by their nature adversely affect an arbitrator's impartiality. As also discussed, these grounds essentially include cases in which the arbitrator were him or herself a party to, or had a direct interest in, the dispute at bar;[199] these grounds appear comparable to the non-waivable Red List contained in the IBA Conflict Guidelines.[200] Any of these factors are perceived to indicate, in and of themselves, a measure of dependence that 'objectively indicates partiality'.[201] Under the framework of the IBA Conflict Guidelines, these grounds of impartiality are so severe that they cannot be waived by the parties (for the discussion of waiver under Austrian law, *see* **Article 16** below[202]). It is even conceivable that the prohibition on being a judge in one's own case forms part of the *procedural ordre public* in Austria, which could be relevant for the purposes of Section 611(2) no. 5 ZPO.[203] Other rare cases will be examples of actual bias demonstrated by an arbitrator in the conduct of an ongoing proceeding. These are hard to prove, but if established, will have to result in the arbitrator's disqualification.

7-111 Other cases must be decided on an individual basis, inferring from the particular circumstances whether an arbitrator is impartial and independent or not.[204] In this regard, the IBA Conflict Guidelines contain an Orange List,[205] providing examples

---

196. P. Oberhammer, *Entwurf eines neuen Schiedsverfahrensrechts* (Vienna, Manz, 2002), p. 69.
197. *See* IBA Conflict Guidelines, Explanation to General Standard 1, **Annex 17**.
198. P. Oberhammer, *Entwurf eines neuen Schiedsverfahrensrechts* (Vienna, Manz, 2002), p. 69.
199. *See* **Article 7**, at para. 101.
200. IBA Conflict Guidelines, **Annex 17**.
201. D. Bishop and L. Reed, 'Practical Guidelines for Interviewing, Selecting and Challenging Party-Appointed Arbitrators in International Commercial Arbitration' (1998) 14(4) Arb Int'l, 395, 406.
202. *See* **Article 16**, at paras. 026 *et seq.*
203. *See* at **Article 27**, at paras. 054 *et seq.*; F.T. Schwarz and H. Ortner, 'Procedural Ordre Public and the Internationalization of Public Policy in Arbitration' in *Austrian Arbitration Yearbook 2008*, C. Klausegger *et al.* (Vienna, Manz, 2008).
204. For a discussion of terminology, *see* **Article 7**, at paras. 090 *et seq.*
205. IBA Conflict Guidelines, **Annex 17**.

that in and of themselves would not give rise to objective justifiable doubts relating to the arbitrator's impartiality (and that, as such, would not justify a challenge), but that require disclosure because *in the eyes of the parties* justifiable doubts may arise. Although not necessarily weighing conclusively against the appointment of an arbitrator, these facts will typically merit close scrutiny in light of particular circumstances. If a matter can be considered a 'grey area', careful assessment by the appointing party and full disclosure on the side of the nominated arbitrator are particularly important.[206] Indeed, in international practice, an arbitrator's failure to make an appropriate disclosure is often seen to constitute in itself a ground for challenge.[207] The argument goes that the arbitrator who fails to make a disclosure probably has a reason to hide particular circumstances or facts which indicate his or her partiality. The IBA Conflict Guidelines' Green List,[208] finally, includes examples of instances that should not normally taint an arbitrator's impartiality.

It can also be assumed that, because of strong similarities in statute and system, **7-112** German and Swiss precedent may well carry persuasive authority with the Austrian courts. Under Section 1036 German ZPO, arbitrators were disqualified because of a personal friendship between the arbitrator and one of the parties;[209] the arbitrator was a tenant or debtor of a party;[210] the arbitrator was employed by one of the parties;[211] the wife of an arbitrator was employed by the law firm representing one of the parties;[212] an arbitrator had a conversation about the merits of the arbitration with one of the parties (or their counsel);[213] an arbitrator had *ex parte* communications with one of the parties alone and undertook certain procedural measures with only one party present;[214] an arbitrator risked financial losses if a party lost the arbitration because the arbitrator held shares in this party;[215] an arbitrator had personally witnessed facts relevant to the dispute;[216] the arbitrator was a member of a law firm which advised the holding company of one of the parties;[217] the arbitrator regularly appeared as a lawyer (in unrelated matters) for the appointing party;[218] and where the

---

206. D. Bishop and L. Reed, 'Practical Guidelines for Interviewing, Selecting and Challenging Party-Appointed Arbitrators in International Commercial Arbitration' (1998) 14(4) Arb Int'l, 395, 414.
207. *See, e.g., Commonwealth Coatings Corp. v. Continental Casualty Co.*, 393 U.S. 145 (U.S. S. Ct. 1968).
208. IBA Conflict Guidelines, **Annex 17**.
209. K.H. Schwab and G. Walter (eds), *Schiedsgerichtbarkeit* (7th edn, Munich, C.H. Beck, 2005), ch. 14, para. 8; OLG Stuttgart, 21 December 1927, 563/27, JW 1928-1322.
210. OLG Stuttgart, 21 December 1927, 563/27, JW 1928, 1322.
211. LG Dortmund, 22 April 1986, 10-0-48/68, WuW 1968, 691.
212. BGer, 26 October 1966, BGE 92 I 271.
213. OLG Munich, 25 February 1971, 12 W 570/71, BB 1971, 886, 887.
214. OLG Hamburg, 30 September 1907, Rspr. 15, 298.
215. BGer, 14 March 1985, BGE 111 Ia 72, 74.
216. RG, 7 July 1933, VII 94/33 (unpublished).
217. OLG Braunschweig, 7 June 1912, Rspr. 25, 240.
218. RG, 21 April 1936, III 161/35 in RGZ 152, 9-12.

non-party-appointed arbitrator described himself as the personal representative of the party who appointed him.[219] By contrast, arbitrators were considered not to be biased where counsel for one of the parties and a prospective arbitrator met for an initial discussion in which the merits of the case were not discussed; personal friendship between the arbitrator and counsel for one of the parties existed;[220] and where a previous business relationship between an arbitrator and the appointing party was found to have existed for a considerable time prior to the dispute at bar.[221]

7-113 Austrian case law on the impartiality and independence of arbitrators is scarce.[222] In determining whether 'circumstances exist which, on objective examination, give rise as to justifiable doubts' regarding the arbitrator's impartiality and independence, the Austrian *Oberster Gerichtshof* has held that the principles developed for judges should hold true for arbitrators as well.[223] The Austrian *Oberster Gerichtshof* has held that harsh statements of the arbitrator *vis-à-vis* a party are not sufficient to assume partiality, nor are informal discussions between only two of the arbitrators. In this decision, the Austrian *Oberster Gerichtshof* was apparently guided by the concern that parties could tactically provoke arbitrators into inappropriate responses solely to challenge them.[224] It is also established that it is no ground for challenge if arbitrators and parties are acquainted socially or through business contacts. As the *Handelsgericht Wien* has held, 'in arbitrations, in which each side nominates an arbitrator, these arbitrators will oftentimes be attached to the same circles; as long as there are not particular reasons to assume the personal impartiality or prejudice of that arbitrator, this does not as such constitute a ground for challenge'.[225] In a recent decision, the Austrian *Oberster Gerichtshof* has also held that an arbitrator is not deemed impartial by virtue of the fact that he had once represented the party nominating him in an entirely unrelated matter, and not against the other party in the arbitration.[226] However, as another recent decision

---

219. OLG Munich, 26 April 1928, 462/29 L, JW 1929, 3175.
220. K.H. Schwab and G. Walter (eds), *Schiedsgerichtbarkeit* (7th edn, Munich, C.H. Beck, 2005), ch. 14, para. 8.
221. W.L. Craig, W.W. Park and J. Paulsson, *International Chamber of Commerce Arbitration* (3rd edn, New York, Oceana Publications, 2000), p. 229; *Health Service Management Corp. v. Hughes*, 975 F.2d 1253 (7th Cir. 1992).
222. *See also* the discussion in P. Hanusch, 'Challenge of Arbitrators under the New Austrian Arbitration Act' in *Austrian Arbitration Yearbook 2007*, C. Klausegger *et al.* (eds) (Vienna, Manz, 2007), pp. 71-74.
223. OGH, 15 September 2004, 9 Ob A 94/04w.
224. OGH, 7 June 1990, 7 Ob 584/90.
225. HG Vienna, 16 September 1992, 24 Cg 304/92, as cited in K. Heller, 'Die Rechtsstellung des internationalen Schiedsgerichts der Wirtschaftskammer Österreich' [1994] wbl, 105, 117. For judges, membership in the same association as one of the parties (OGH, 7 November 1991, 6 Ob 616/91) or a particular affiliation with a political party (OGH, 30 September 1987, 9 Ob A 107/87) does as such not justify a challenge, but a close personal relationship to the party or a witness may be relevant (OGH, 24 May 1989, 9 Ob A 135, 136/89).
226. OGH, 28 May 2003, 7 Ob 96/03y.

has held, an arbitrator who for eight years has acted as counsel in all matters for the party nominating him, is not impartial and independent.[227]

While the VIAC as a matter of practice gives reasoned decisions to the parties **7-114** under **Article 16** regarding the challenge of arbitrators, it does not publish these decisions, in redacted form or otherwise. In addition to other arguments for increased institutional transparency, this is unfortunate because a body of publicly available precedent would advance the uniform application of the relevant standards of impartiality and independence.[228] In a case known to the authors, the VIAC has disqualified an arbitrator who was a partner in the same firm as the main expert on whose opinion the appointing party had based its entire case.[229] In this case, the Austrian *Oberster Gerichtshof* effectively confirmed the VIAC's decision when the arbitrator, once removed, unsuccessfully sought to recover his fees from the institution.[230] By contrast, the VIAC has rejected challenges where a party-appointed arbitrator had previously participated as an arbitrator in related arbitration proceedings;[231] in one of the first cases under Section 589 ZPO, the VIAC's decision was confirmed.[232]

5. Some Particular Issues Regarding Impartiality and Independence

The following discussion examines some specific issues of impartiality and **7-115** independence that frequently arise in international arbitration proceedings.

5.1. *Different Standard for Party-Appointed Arbitrators?*

There is some debate, fuelled by different perceptions in different cultures and **7-116** jurisdictions as to whether the presiding arbitrator ought to adhere to a higher standard of impartiality than the party-appointed arbitrators. As *Fasching* has noted, a certain proximity of party-appointed arbitrators to 'their' parties does not necessarily result in disqualification because such disadvantages are compensated

---

227. OGH, 15 September 2004, 9 Ob A 94/04w.
228. For a persuasive argument in favour of transparency, *see* G. Nicholas and C. Partasides, 'LCIA Court Decisions on Challenges to Arbitrators: A Proposal to Publish' (2007) 23 Arb Int'l, 1.
229. Decision not published.
230. OGH, 30 November 2006, 6 Ob 207/06v.
231. In these cases (which are also known to the authors), the challenge was brought when the arbitrator was appointed for the third time by the same party. In the first arbitration, there was a unanimous award against the appointing party; in the second arbitration, there was a unanimous award partly in favour of the appointing party. Also, the third arbitration, while based on the parties' previous litigious history, raised new issues of law and fact which were not as such prejudged in the previous proceedings.
232. HG Vienna, 24 July 2007, 16 Nc 2/07w.

by the other side's arbitrator.[233] That suggestion must be viewed with a measure of suspicion. In principle, an arbitrator is either impartial or not; and as a matter of fundamental procedural fairness, the requirement of impartiality must extend equally to all decision-makers administering a quasi-judicial function.[234]

7-117 This being said, the impartiality of the presiding arbitrator may be simply more important as a practical matter, because the presiding arbitrator must be expected to counter attempts by partisan party-appointed arbitrators to unduly influence the adjudication of the dispute. Following the principle that justice not only needs to be done, but that it must be seen to be done, there is certainly a practical 'importance of the appearance as well as the actuality of absolute impartiality and independence for presiding arbitrators'.[235]

7-118 On the other hand, party-appointed arbitrators, while fully agreeing that the party with the better case must win,[236] may understandably feel obliged to ensure that the arguments of the party that appointed him or her are adequately considered.[237] Indeed, arbitrators will often have an inherent commercial interest to be appointed again.[238] By the same token, parties (and their counsel) will want to appoint arbitrators, whose cultural or professional background and past conduct indicates that they will view the own case favourably. In this respect, there is a fine line between making sure that the appointing party's arguments receive sufficient attention from the tribunal as opposed to influencing the tribunal's decision in an inappropriate manner. As *Martin Hunter* has famously put it:

> [I]t seems clear that a party may nominate an arbitrator who is predisposed toward him personally in a very general sense, or as regards his position in the

233. H.W. Fasching, *Schiedsgericht und Schiedsverfahren im österreichischen und im internationalen Recht* (Vienna, Manz, 1973), p. 62.
234. O.L.O. De Witt Wijnen, N.Voser and N. Rao, 'Background Information on the IBA Guidelines on Conflict of Interest' (2004) 5 Bus L Int'l 444-445; *see also* M. L.Smith 'Impartiality of the Party-Appointed Arbitrator' (1990) 6(4) Arb Int'l, 320; G. Aksen, 'The Tribunal's Appointment' in *The Leading Arbitrators' Guide to International Arbitration*, L.W. Newman and R.D. Hill (eds) (Huntington, Juris Publishing, 2004), p. 31; A.F. Lowenfeld, 'The Party-Appointed Arbitrator: Further Reflections' in *The Leading Arbitrators' Guide to International Arbitration*, L.W. Newman and R.D. Hill (eds) (Huntington, Juris Publishing, 2004), p. 41. However, *see* BGH, 5 November 1970, VII ZR 31/69 in BGHZ 54, 392 in Germany, which required a stricter standard for presiding arbitrators.
235. D. Bishop and L. Reed, 'Practical Guidelines for Interviewing, Selecting and Challenging Party-Appointed Arbitrators in International Commercial Arbitration' (1998) 14(4) Arb Int'l, 395, 399.
236. D. Bishop and L. Reed, 'Practical Guidelines for Interviewing, Selecting and Challenging Party-Appointed Arbitrators in International Commercial Arbitration' (1998) 14(4) Arb Int'l, 395, 399. *See also* the discussion of non-neutral arbitrators at **Article 7**, at para. 098.
237. G.A. Alvarez, 'The Challenge of Arbitrators' (1990) 6(3) Arb Int'l, 203, 217.
238. P. Mankowski, 'Die Ablehnung von Schiedsrichtern' [2004] SchiedsVZ, 304, 309 with further references.

dispute, provided that the nominee is at the same time capable of applying his mind judicially and impartially to the evidence and arguments submitted by both parties. Indeed, when I am representing a client in an arbitration, what I am really looking for in a party-nominated arbitrator is someone with the maximum predisposition towards my client, but with the minimum appearance of bias. At first sight, this may sound a little shocking – and indeed it would not be an appropriate approach in considering the appointment of a presiding arbitrator. However, although the terms 'neutral' and 'non-neutral' suggest a difference as marked as night and day, in reality this is not so. Most non-neutral arbitrators will not allow the fact of their appointment by one party to dictate the outcome of the proceedings. They may be favourably disposed to the party who appointed them, but they will not allow this to override their conscience and professional judgment if they believe that the other party has made the better case.[239]

Hunter's pragmatic characterization distinguishes between impartiality and a **7-119** measure of predisposition. This is not inconsistent with a strict understanding of impartiality, as it should be possible for an arbitrator to contribute without bias to the tribunal's decision-making process while ensuring that the legal position of the party that appointed him is considered adequately.[240] In that sense, as *Hunter* also points out, no predisposition can or should be expected from the presiding arbitrator. Thus, commentators have argued that a

> tribunal comprised of the usual three, in which the party-appointed arbitrators see the truth – the law under the circumstances – from the parties' perspective, while the chairman looks 'in its face' may be particularly well-suited to make a just and correct award.[241]

In practice, the degree of bias attributable to a party-appointed arbitrator might **7-120** take different forms and range from a 'covert sympathy' with the party's case to an 'overt taking of instructions from, and offering of advice to, the nominating party'.[242] Where the latter is the case, the line to improper conduct has long been crossed.

---

239. M. Hunter, 'Ethics of the International Arbitrator' (1987) 53 *Arbitration*, 219, 222-223.
240. A.F. Lowenfeld, 'The Party-Appointed Arbitrator: Further Reflections' in *The Leading Arbitrators' Guide to International Arbitration*, L.W. Newman and R.D. Hill (eds) (Huntington, Juris Publishing, 2004), p. 46. Indeed, some consider this to be an 'extra duty' of the party-appointed arbitrator. A. Philip, 'The Duties of an Arbitrator', in *The Leading Arbitrators' Guide to International Arbitration*, L.W. Newman and R.D. Hill (eds) (Huntington, Juris Publishing, 2004), p. 80.
241. W.J. Habscheid, 'Das Problem der Unabhängigkeit der Schiedsgerichte' [1962] NJW, 5, 9.
242. M.L. Smith, 'Impartiality of the Party-Appointed Arbitrator' (1990) 6(4) Arb Int'l, 320.

5.2.   *Continuing Obligation of Impartiality*

7-121 General Standard 1 of the IBA Conflict Guidelines[243] provides that

> an arbitrator shall be impartial and independent of the parties at the time of accepting an appointment to serve and shall remain so during the entire arbitration proceeding until the final award has been rendered or the proceeding has otherwise finally terminated.[244]

7-122 The Vienna Rules do not contain a similar express provision, but provide in Article 7(4) that arbitrators 'must perform their duties in complete independence and impartiality'. The Vienna Rules make equally clear, therefore, that impartiality and independence are not merely a requirement for appointment, but need to persist throughout the arbitration.

5.3.   *The Impact of Settlement Discussions*

7-123 Quite often, parties enter into settlement negotiations during the course of the arbitration. Indeed, it is often said to be a major advantage of arbitration that it encourages the amicable settlement of disputes, enabling the parties to continue their business relationship and thus benefiting both the litigants and their macro-economic environment.[245] In such cases, parties may understandably feel that the arbitrators, being familiar with the circumstances of the dispute, may be well suited to mediate between them. This is indeed quite common in some jurisdictions, but it raises quite serious issues of bias that require careful attention.

7-124 By way of illustration, an English court held with respect to an arbitrator who attempted to mediate a settlement between the parties and, having failed with the mediation, proceeded to issue an award that, because of the attempted mediation, there were 'real prospects of success in establishing that [the arbitrator] was no longer impartial [and that] any fair minded and informed observer would conclude that [because of the arbitrator's] participation in [the mediation] there was a real possibility of him being biased'. The court explained that mediation is 'concerned with the commercial interests of the parties which may not be synonymous with their legal rights and obligations. Thus such a person will or may have to listen to arguments and hear things which may be completely irrelevant to the dispute in the adjudication but which might be prejudicial to its determination.'[246] The question

---

243. IBA Conflict Guidelines, **Annex 17**.
244. The Second Draft of the Guidelines imposed a duty of independence 'even after the arbitration proceedings have ended' for the period of setting aside proceedings. This was abandoned in the final version, but it is clear that, if the award is vacated and the proceeding referred back to the arbitrators, a fresh duty of independence arises.
245. G.J. Horvath, 'Schiedsgerichtsbarkeit und Mediation – Ein glückliches Paar?' [2005] SchiedsVZ, 292, 293.
246. Lloyd J JH QC in *Glencot Development and Design Co. Ltd v. Ben Barrett & Son (Contractors) Ltd* [2001] BLR 207, Q.B. (TCC).

posed, therefore, is whether or not an arbitrator is still impartial after having heard arguments and concessions in the course of a mediation or settlement negotiation that the parties would not have made in strictly contentious proceedings.

If this is right, some settlement discussions may be more appropriate for arbitrators **7-125** to conduct or facilitate than others. If the arbitrator merely suggests settlement discussions between the parties, perhaps providing them with some discussion items, without being present when these discussions take place, this may cause little concern. If, on the other hand, the arbitrator were to utilize mediation techniques such as caucusing involving separate *ex parte* meetings with each side, this can raise significant problems.[247]

In terms of solutions, it has been suggested that the arbitrator and the parties agree **7-126** prior to the mediation what will happen to the information exchanged between them should the mediation fail. Some authors suggest that it should be agreed at the outset that, if the mediation fails, neither the arbitrators nor the parties should be permitted to rely on any information that has been obtained in the course of the settlement discussions and that would otherwise not have been accessible.[248] More often than not, however, this will miss the point how can the arbitrators actually 'forget' information about a case once they have read a document or heard a statement?

Where settlement discussions can be properly conducted by the arbitrators, the **7-127** rules governing these discussions as well as the parties' consent should be recorded in advance. General Standard 4(d) of the IBA Conflict Guidelines proposes that:

> An arbitrator may assist the parties in reaching a settlement of the dispute at any stage of the proceedings. However, before doing so, the arbitrator should receive an express agreement by the parties that acting in such a manner shall not disqualify the arbitrator from continuing to serve as arbitrator. Such express agreement shall be considered to be an effective waiver of any potential conflict of interest that may arise from the arbitrator's participation in such process or from information that the arbitrator may learn in the process. If the assistance by the arbitrator does not lead to final settlement of the case, the parties remain bound by their waiver. However, consistent with General Standard 2(a) and notwithstanding such agreement, the arbitrator shall resign if, as a consequence of his or her involvement in the settlement process, the arbitrator develops doubts as to his or her ability to remain impartial or independent in the future course of the arbitration proceedings.[249]

---

247. *See also* G.J. Horvath, 'Schiedsgerichtsbarkeit und Mediation – Ein glückliches Paar?' [2005] SchiedsVZ, 292, 298 and note 68 with further references.
248. G.J. Horvath, 'Schiedsgerichtsbarkeit und Mediation – Ein glückliches Paar?' [2005] SchiedsVZ, 292, 301.
249. IBA Conflict Guidelines, **Annex 17**.

7-128 This solution is premised on the parties' informed consent. The consent needs to be given prior to the mediation taking place, and it needs to be express, that is, in writing or recorded in the minutes or the transcript of the hearing.[250] This raises the question, however, if or to what extent parties can effectively waive issues of impartiality, depriving themselves of their right to challenge the award on the grounds of bias (*see* **Article 16** below).[251]

5.4.   Independence in a Globally Active Legal Profession

7-129 Large law firms pose increasing risks of conflicts, particularly in the context of international arbitration. In recent years, senior practitioners who serve mostly as arbitrators rather than party representatives have established niche practices to avoid the conflicts that attached to their previous mega-firms. General Standard 6 of the IBA Conflict Guidelines seeks to address that dilemma:

(a) When considering the relevance of facts or circumstances to determine whether a potential conflict of interest exists or whether disclosure should be made, the activities of an arbitrator's law firm, if any, should be reasonably considered in each individual case. Therefore, the fact that the activities of the arbitrator's firm involve one of the parties shall not automatically constitute a source of such conflict or a reason for disclosure.

(b) Similarly, if one of the parties is a legal entity which is a member of a group with which the arbitrator's firm has an involvement, such facts or circumstances should be reasonably considered in each individual case. Therefore, this fact alone shall not automatically constitute a source of a conflict of interest or a reason for disclosure.

(c) If one of the parties is a legal entity, the managers, directors and members of a supervisory board of such legal entity and any person having a similar controlling influence on the legal entity shall be considered to be the equivalent of the legal entity.

7-130 This provision has caused some controversy; it has been argued that it favours large firms over smaller ones. Indeed, as the IBA Working Group recognized, an arbitrator should 'in principle be considered as identical to his or her law firm'.[252]

---

250. *See* IBA Conflict Guidelines, Explanation to General Standard 4(d), **Annex 17** and O.L.O. De Witt Wijnen, N.Voser and N. Rao, 'Background Information on the IBA Guidelines on Conflict of Interest' (2004) 5 Bus L Int'l, 451.

251. For a recent analysis of arbitrators' bias in the arbitration context, *see* G.J. Horvath, 'Schiedsgerichtsbarkeit und Mediation – Ein glückliches Paar?' [2005] SchiedsVZ, 292 *et seq.*, with further references; *in part.*: F. Niklisch, 'Schiedsgerichtsverfahren mit integrierter Schlichtung' [1998] RIW, 169; K.P. Berger, 'Integration of Mediation Elements into Arbitration' (2003) 19(3) Arb Int'l, 387; H. Raeschke-Kessler, 'Der Vergleich im Schiedsverfahren' in *Festschrift für Ottoarndt Glossner zum 70. Geburtstag*, A. Plantey and K.-H. Böckstiegel and J. Bredow (eds) (Heidelberg, Verlag Recht und Wirtschaft, 1994), p. 259.

252. *See* IBA Conflict Guidelines, Explanation to General Standard 6, **Annex 17**.

If that is so, it is not easy to see why relevant involvement of the arbitrator's law firm should 'not automatically lead to the disqualification of the arbitrator'. The IBA Conflict Guidelines suggest that the 'nature, timing and scope of the work by the law firm, should be reasonably considered in each individual case'.[253] However, requiring a case-by-case examination of the circumstances does not provide much in terms of general guidance. A perhaps preferable solution would have been to reverse the burden of proof, stating that the involvement of an arbitrator's law firm in the case leads to the presumption of a conflict which can be overcome if the circumstances of the case so justify. This would have set an ethically strict standard, but would have allowed to accommodate commercial reality where no improprieties exist.[254]

5.5.   Ex Parte Communications

What cannot be done in the open, before the eyes of all parties, should not be done at all. Thus, there should not be any *ex parte* communication between an arbitrator and one party.[255] The only generally accepted exception regards contacts of a party with a prospective arbitrator to assess his or her qualifications and availability, and to discuss the appointment of the presiding arbitrator (*see* **Article 7**, at paras. 031 *et seq*).[256] **7-131**

According to one opinion, the conversation should be limited to thirty minutes;[257] others might argue that it is more reasonable to determine the appropriate time for such a conversation with reference to the complexity of the case. Under no circumstances should an arbitrator discuss the merits of the case with one party alone.[258] If a party approaches an arbitrator in any fashion during the arbitration, the arbitrator is well advised to communicate that approach to the other arbitrators and the other parties, in order to avoid any appearance of inappropriate conduct on his or her part. Discussion with prospective arbitrators may have to be disclosed as well.[259] Some cases, in particular jurisprudence in France, suggest that *ex parte* communications between the arbitrators or the chairman of the tribunal and one party to the exclusion of the other side may also violate a party's right to be heard.[260] **7-132**

---

253. *See* IBA Conflict Guidelines, Explanation to General Standard 6, **Annex 17**.
254. For a more liberal approach, *see* P. Mankowski, 'Die Ablehnung von Schiedsrichtern' [2004] SchiedsVZ, 304, 310 with further references.
255. *See* IBA Rules of Ethics item 5.3, **Annex 18**.
256. *See* ABA Code of Ethics for Arbitrators in Commercial Disputes.
257. J.P. Lachmann, *Handbuch für die Schiedsgerichtspraxis* (3rd edn, Cologne, Verlag Dr. Otto Schmidt, 2008), p. 128.
258. J.P. Lachmann, *Handbuch für die Schiedsgerichtspraxis* (3rd edn, Cologne, Verlag Dr. Otto Schmidt, 2008), p. 218.
259. *See* IBA Rules of Ethics item 5.1, **Annex 18**.
260. Cour de Cassation, 2e Ch. Civ., 10 November 1998, *Société Duarib v. Société des Etablissements Jallais* [1998] Rev Arb, 680.

V.   DISCLOSURE

Article 7(5): When a person is approached in connection with his possible appointment as arbitrator, he shall disclose any circumstances likely to give rise to doubts as to his impartiality or independence or that are in conflict with the agreement of the parties. An arbitrator, from the time of his appointment and throughout the arbitral proceedings, shall without delay disclose any such circumstances to the parties unless they have already been informed of them by him.

A.   Disclosure Under the Former ZPO and Vienna Rules

7-133 The fZPO did not contain specific requirements for disclosure, and neither did the Vienna Rules in their previous version. Yet there was consensus that arbitrators had the implied obligation to disclose to the parties circumstances relevant to assess their impartiality. Indeed, such requirements apply to Austrian state court judges in the context of Sections 19 and 20 JN who must disclose circumstances that lead to their exclusion or that result in justifiable doubts as to their impartiality.[261] Thus, the duty to disclose has always been considered a necessary corollary of the duty to be impartial and independent; one cannot exist without the other.[262] Only proper disclosure enables the VIAC and the parties to make an informed decision if the appointment, or the challenge, of an arbitrator is appropriate under the circumstances. As a matter of practice, therefore, the VIAC has traditionally required arbitrators to sign a statement of impartiality prior to appointment by the institution; this is now affirmatively prescribed by Article 7(2)(a).

B.   Disclosure Under the New ZPO and Vienna Rules

7-134 Section 588(1) ZPO and the identical provision of Article 7(5) now provide, based on Article 12 of the UNCITRAL Model Law:

When a person is approached in connection with his possible appointment as arbitrator, he shall disclose any circumstances likely to give rise to doubts as to his impartiality or independence, or that are in conflict with the agreement of the parties. An arbitrator, from the time of his appointment and throughout the

---

261. P.G. Mayr, in *Kommentar zur ZPO*, W.H. Rechberger (ed.) (3rd edn, Vienna/New York, Springer, 2006), Section 19 JN, para. 1.
262. In Switzerland, the *Bundesgericht* has found that the duty to disclose is an implied contractual duty of the arbitrator. *See* O.L.O. De Witt Wijnen, N.Voser and N. Rao, 'Background Information on the IBA Guidelines on Conflict of Interest' (2004) 5 Bus L Int'l, fn. 13.

arbitral proceedings, shall without delay disclose any such circumstances to the parties unless they have already been informed of them by him.

As discussed above, a prospective arbitrator needs to carefully examine his or her **7-135** relationship to the parties and the circumstances of the case to ensure that there are no conflicts that would prevent his accepting the appointment.[263] Thus, 'an arbitrator shall decline to accept an appointment or, if the arbitration has already been commenced, to refuse to continue to act as an arbitrator if he or she has any doubts as to his or her ability to be impartial or independent'.[264]

However, the arbitrator cannot be the only instance to judge whether his or her **7-136** service is appropriate under the circumstances. Rather, the parties and, where applicable, the administering institution need to be given the opportunity to assess the arbitrator's impartiality and independence prior to appointment, but also during the course of the arbitration if new circumstances arise. The parties (and the institution) can only do so in an informed and meaningful fashion if the arbitrator discloses relevant facts and circumstances.

Most major institutional rules therefore contain express provisions setting forth **7-137** terms under which a prospective arbitrator is required to make a disclosure. Article 7 ICC Rules, for example, provides:

> Before appointment or confirmation, a prospective arbitrator shall sign a statement of independence and disclose in writing to the Secretariat any facts or circumstances which might be of such a nature as to call into question that arbitrator's independence in the eyes of the parties. The Secretariat shall provide such information to the parties in writing and fix a time limit for any comments from them. (. . .) An arbitrator shall immediately disclose in writing to the Secretariat and to the parties any facts or circumstances of a similar nature which may arise during the arbitration.

Other major rules contain similar requirements.[265]   **7-138**

---

263. G.A. Alvarez, 'The Challenge of Arbitrators' (1990) 6(3) Art Int'l, 203, 217.
264. IBA Conflict Guidelines, General Standard 2, **Annex 17**.
265. Article 5(3) LCIA Rules provides in quite similar terms that prior to appointment, 'each arbitrator shall sign a declaration to the effect that there are no circumstances known to him likely to give rise to any justified doubts as to his impartiality or independence, other than any circumstances disclosed by him in the declaration. Each arbitrator shall also assume a continuing duty to disclose any such circumstances to the LCIA Court, to any other members of the Arbitral Tribunal and to all the parties if such circumstances should arise after the date of such declaration and before the arbitration is concluded'. Article 7(1) AAA/ICDR Rules requires that '[p]rior to accepting appointment, a prospective arbitrator shall disclose to the administrator any circumstance likely to give rise to justifiable doubts as to the arbitrator's impartiality or independence. If at any stage during the arbitration, new circumstances arise that may give rise to such doubts, an arbitrator shall disclose such circumstances to the parties and to the administrator. Upon receipt of such information the administrator shall communicate it to the other parties and to the tribunal.'

7-139 The standard of disclosure is subject to debate, however. That standard could be an *objective* one; an arbitrator needs to disclose circumstances that, from the objective perspective of an informed and neutral observer, give rise to justifiable doubts as to the arbitrator's impartiality and independence. On the other hand, a subjective standard would require arbitrators to disclose those circumstances that give rise to doubts from the parties' perspective. Such a subjective standard is expressly embraced by Article 7(2) ICC Rules which requires the disclosure of facts 'which might be of such a nature as to call into question that arbitrator's independence *in the eyes of the parties*'.

7-140 After some discussion, the IBA Working Group on Conflicts of Interest in International Arbitration has adopted a subjective standard as well. General Standard 3(a) of the IBA Conflict Guidelines provides:

> If facts or circumstances exist that may, in the eyes of the parties, give rise to doubts as to the arbitrator's impartiality or independence, the arbitrator shall disclose such facts or circumstances to the parties, the arbitration institution or other appointing authority (if any, and if so required by the applicable institutional rules) and to the co-arbitrators, if any, prior to accepting his or her appointment or, if thereafter, as soon as he or she learns about them.[266]

7-141 With the introduction of Section 588 ZPO, this debate has now reached Austria. Some authors argue that the standard of disclosure should be an *objective* one: an arbitrator needs to disclose circumstances that, from the objective perspective of an informed and neutral observer – the perspective of that impressive reasonable person – give rise to justifiable doubts as to the arbitrator's impartiality and independence.[267] As a result, it is argued that the same criteria should be applied to determine both whether an arbitrator has to disclose a particular fact and whether he must be disqualified.[268]

7-142 This view raises serious questions. For the reasons detailed below, the arguably better view is that Article 7(5) and Section 588(1) ZPO contain a subjective element as well.

7-143 If there are, from an objective perspective, justifiable doubts of bias, the arbitrator should simply not serve. However, if one were to require disclosure under the same criteria that apply to disqualification, *every* disclosure by an arbitrator would necessarily lead to disqualification. This is a highly unattractive proposition.

---

266. IBA Conflict Guidelines, **Annex 17**.
267. A similar view appears to be taken by M. Platte in *Arbitration Law of Austria: Practice and Procedure*, S. Riegler, A. Petsche, A. Fremuth-Wolf, M. Platte and C. Liebscher (eds) (Huntington, Juris Publishing, 2007), Section 588, p. 256 and P. Hanusch, 'Challenge of Arbitrators under the New Austrian Arbitration Act' in *Austrian Arbitration Yearbook 2007*, C. Klausegger *et al.* (eds) (Vienna, Manz, 2007), p. 59, 64.
268. G. Zeiler, *Schiedsverfahren* (Vienna/Graz, Neuer Wissenschaftlicher Verlag, 2006), Section 588, p. 153.

There ought to be many instances where arbitrators, as a matter of caution, choose to, and should, disclose a fact even though that fact should not and does not lead to disqualification.[269] This, then, calls for some distinction in the applicable standard.

While it is true that Article 7(5) and Section 588(1) ZPO do not expressly refer to **7-144** facts relevant 'in the eyes of the parties', there are some important distinctions in the text. Based on Article 12 of the UNCITRAL Model Law, Article 7(5) and Section 588(1) ZPO requires *disclosure* of any circumstances that *likely* give rise to *doubts*, whereas an arbitrator will be *disqualified* if the circumstances actually *exist* that give rise to *justifiable doubts*.[270] If one assumes that this difference in wording is intentional, one ought to give meaning to the difference. Thus, the assessment as to whether certain facts *may* give rise to doubts is broader and more subjective than the assessment as to whether certain facts *actually* give rise to justifiable (i.e. reasonable) doubts. In that sense, the threshold for a successful challenge is more difficult to meet than the test for requiring disclosure. By setting different standards for disclosure as opposed to disqualification, not every disclosure automatically leads to disqualification. This approach is certainly endorsed by the VIAC which distinguishes between grounds for challenge and circumstances that should be disclosed. Thus, when accepting the mandate, each prospective arbitrator can either confirm that no grounds for challenge exist, or else that:

> There are no circumstances known to me which would justify a challenge to my acting as arbitrator in these proceedings pursuant to Article 16 of the Vienna Rules. However, I would like to disclose the following circumstances which, *from the perspective of the parties*, could possibly call my independence into question.[271]

Indeed, an arbitrator who makes a disclosure typically assumes that he or she can **7-145** act; otherwise the arbitrator should simply not accept the appointment in the first place. In that sense, General Standard 3(b) of the IBA Conflict Guidelines emphasizes the distinction between the different standards:

> [A]n arbitrator who has made a disclosure considers himself or herself to be impartial and independent of the parties despite the disclosed facts and therefore capable of performing his or her duties as arbitrator. Otherwise, he or she

---

269. *See* IBA Conflict Guidelines, General Standard 3(a) which clarifies: 'If facts or circumstances exist that may, in the eyes of the parties, give rise to doubts as to the arbitrator's impartiality or independence, the arbitrator shall disclose such facts or circumstances to the parties, the arbitration institution or other appointing authority (if any, and if so required by the applicable institutional rules) and to the co-arbitrators, if any, prior to accepting his or her appointment or, if thereafter, as soon as he or she learns about them.' **Annex 17**.

270. For a detailed discussion of various standards in different jurisdictions, *see* O.L.O. De Witt Wijnen, N.Voser and N. Rao, 'Background Information on the IBA Guidelines on Conflict of Interest' (2004) 5 Bus L Int'l, 448.

271. *See* Arbitrator's Declaration of Acceptance, Statement of Independence and Undertaking to Observe Rules on Costs, **Annex 4**.

would have declined the nomination or appointment at the outset or resigned.[272]

7-146 Applying a less stringent standard for disclosure and a stricter standard for disqualification also facilitates the policy aim of encouraging disclosures in case of doubt[273] and at all stages of the arbitration.[274]

7-147 The subjective standard also makes the most of the consensual nature of arbitration. The prospective arbitrator, if intending to accept the appointment,[275] should therefore disclose all circumstances that 'are likely to' (rather than those that *actually will*) justify doubts as to the arbitrator's impartiality. Only if the parties know of those circumstances which, from their perspective, give rise to doubts as to the arbitrator's impartiality and independence, can they determine if, in their eyes, such circumstances warrant a challenge to the arbitrator – regardless of whether or not that challenge will ultimately be successful.[276] This will of course require the arbitrator to make all reasonable enquiries as to whether such circumstances exist.[277]

7-148 In short, arbitrators are well advised to err on the side of caution and to make a disclosure in cases of doubt.[278] A failure to make an appropriate disclosure may be interpreted as a strong indicator that the arbitrator sought to 'hide' disqualifying circumstances. This in itself may constitute evidence of bias. According to a recent Austrian *Oberster Gerichtshof* decision, an arbitrator who fails to disclose upon appointment relevant facts to the institution forfeits his claim for remuneration if successfully challenged.[279] Conversely, if an arbitrator has disclosed all relevant facts and circumstances and the parties participated in the arbitration without

---

272. IBA Conflict Guidelines, **Annex 17**.
273. IBA Conflict Guidelines, General Standard 3(c) provides: 'Any doubt as to whether an arbitrator should disclose certain facts or circumstances should be resolved in favour of disclosure.' **Annex 17**.
274. IBA Conflict Guidelines, General Standard 3(d) provides: 'When considering whether or not facts or circumstances exist that should be disclosed, the arbitrator shall not take into account whether the arbitration proceeding is at the beginning or at a later stage.' **Annex 17**.
275. The arbitrator obviously can decline the appointment without giving any reasons, and thus, without disclosing potentially disqualifying circumstances. *See* P. Oberhammer, *Entwurf eines neuen Schiedsverfahrensrechts* (Vienna, Manz, 2002), p. 69.
276. G.A. Alvarez, 'The Challenge of Arbitrators' (1990) 6(3) Arb Int'l, 203, 217; *see also* IBA Conflict Guidelines, General Standard 2, **Annex 17**.
277. *See, e.g.*, IBA Conflict Guidelines, General Standard 7(c) ('An arbitrator is under a duty to make reasonable enquiries to investigate any potential conflict of interest, as well as any facts or circumstances that may cause his or her impartiality or independence to be questioned. Failure to disclose a potential conflict is not excused by lack of knowledge if the arbitrator makes no reasonable attempt to investigate.') **Annex 17**.
278. *See* IBA Conflict Guidelines, General Standard 3(c), **Annex 17**; *see also* IBA Rules of Ethics item 4. **Annex 18**.
279. OGH, 30 November 2006, 6 Ob 207/06v.

objection, subsequent challenges on the same set of facts during or after the proceedings should be unsuccessful.[280]

C. THE PARTIES' DISCLOSURE OBLIGATIONS

Interestingly, the IBA Conflict Guidelines appear to impose disclosure obligations **7-149** not only on the arbitrator, but also on the parties. General Standard (7) provides:

(a) A party shall inform an arbitrator, the Arbitral Tribunal, the other parties and the arbitration institution or other appointing authority (if any) about any direct or indirect relationship between it (or another company of the same group of companies) and the arbitrator. The party shall do so on its own initiative before the beginning of the proceeding or as soon as it becomes aware of such relationship.

(b) In order to comply with General Standard 7(a), a party shall provide any information already available to it and shall perform a reasonable search of publicly available information.[281]

As the Explanation to General Standard (7) details, this provision was included to **7-150** reduce the risk of abuse through unmeritorious challenges of an arbitrator's impartiality or independence. There have been cases where parties were aware of facts that could be grounds for challenge but chose to rely on these facts only at a tactically convenient time. As discussed under **Article 16**, a party appointing an arbitrator has to bring a challenge at the earliest opportunity.

In addition, General Standard (7)(d) requires any party or potential party to an **7-151** arbitration at the outset to make a reasonable effort to ascertain and to disclose publicly available information that, applying the general standard, might affect the arbitrator's impartiality and independence. It is the (prospective) arbitrator's obligation to make similar enquiries and to disclose any information that may cause his or her impartiality or independence to be called into question.[282] This approach is innovative[283] and sensible. There is indeed an argument that, just as disclosure is an implied obligation of the arbitrator under his or her contract with the parties, the parties themselves have an implied duty of good faith under the arbitration agreement obliging them to make transparent all circumstances that present a potential conflict of interest for the arbitrators and that, as a result, could endanger the enforceability of the final award. That parties search available public information prior to an appointment is simply a matter of due diligence. Of course, no such duty

---

280. A. Redfern, M. Hunter, N. Blackaby and C. Partasides, *Law and Practice of International Commercial Arbitration* (4th edn, London, Sweet & Maxwell, 2004), para. 4-61.
281. IBA Conflict Guidelines, **Annex 17**.
282. IBA Conflict Guidelines, Explanation to General Standard 7, **Annex 17**.
283. A. Winstanley, 'A view from an administering institution' (IBA Conference 2002, Durban) (2002) 7 LCIA News, 24.

could go beyond what is without difficulty publicly available; parties cannot be expected to investigate, or intrude into, prospective arbitrators' personal background.[284]

VI.   THE SECRETARY OF THE TRIBUNAL

7-152 Especially in complex, fact-intensive and document-heavy international arbitrations, tribunals increasingly tend to appoint a (usually legally trained) 'administrative secretary' to support their work. The appointment of a secretary can raise a number of issues. On the one hand, the parties appoint an arbitrator because of his or her individual qualifications. The arbitrator is (therefore) not allowed to delegate his mandate to decide the parties' legal dispute,[285] the arbitrator's mission is considered *intuitu personae*.[286] With the increasing use of secretaries concerns grow, therefore, that their involvement contradicts the principle that the arbitrator has to perform his task in person.[287] This has led to motions to dismiss the arbitrator;[288] or to the ICC Court requesting a tribunal to replace its secretary (who was himself known as an arbitrator).[289] On the other hand, administrative secretaries can make the arbitration more effective and perhaps more cost-efficient as arbitrators are released from administrative tasks. It is also important to note that appointments as administrative secretaries provide a fertile training ground for prospective arbitrators.[290]

7-153 There are no rules in the ZPO (or in the Vienna Rules) with respect to the arbitral secretary. The ICC Court, however, has issued a Note (dated 1 October 1995) setting forth some ground rules for the involvement of administrative secretaries, which is usually provided to arbitrators with their appointment papers. The Note emphasizes:

---

284. *See* A. Reiner, *Das neue österreichische Schiedsrecht/The new Austrian Arbitration Law* (Vienna, LexisNexis, 2006), Section 588, note 81.

285. *See* **Article 7**, at paras. 010 and 052. On behalf of many, *see* E.A. Schwartz, 'The Rights and Duties of ICC Arbitrators' (1995) ICC Ct Bull Special Supplement: The Status of the Arbitrator, 67.

286. C. Partasides, 'The Fourth Arbitrator? The Role of Secretaries to Tribunals in International Arbitration' (2002) 18(2) Arb Int'l, 147 with further references; P. Schlosser, 'Schiedsgerichtsbarkeit, Schiedsgutachtenwesen und Höchstpersönlichkeit der Entscheidungsbefugnis' in *Festschrift für Norbert Horn zum 70. Geburtstag*, K.P. Berger, G. Borges, H. Herrmann, A. Schlüter and U. Wackerbarth (eds) (Berlin, de Gruyter Recht, 2006), pp. 1027 *et seq.*

287. C. Partasides, 'The Fourth Arbitrator? The Role of Secretaries to Tribunals in International Arbitration' (2002) 18(2) Arb Int'l, 147.

288. C. Partasides, 'The Fourth Arbitrator? The Role of Secretaries to Tribunals in International Arbitration' (2002) 18(2) Arb Int'l, 147.

289. E.A. Schwartz, 'The Rights and Duties of ICC Arbitrators' (1995) ICC Ct Bull Special Supplement: The Status of the Arbitrator, 67, 86.

290. P. Lalive, 'Inquietantes derives de l'arbitrage CCI' (1995) 13(4) Bull ASA, 634.

The duties of the administrative secretary must be strictly limited to administrative tasks. The choice of the person is important. Such person must not in any way influence in any manner whatsoever the decisions of the arbitral tribunal. In particular, the administrative secretary must not assume the functions of an arbitrator, notably by becoming involved in the decision-making process of the tribunal or expressing opinions with respect to the issues in question.

The ICC's position reflects good practice. Given the particular nature of the arbitrator's engagement, it allows arbitrators only to delegate administrative tasks to the secretary. The UNCITRAL Notes however, appear to be less strict. Article 4(26) states: **7-154**

> Administrative services might be secured by engaging a secretary of the arbitral tribunal (also referred to as registrar, clerk, administrator or rapporteur), who carries out the tasks under the direction of the arbitral tribunal. Some arbitral institutions routinely assign such persons to the cases administered by them. In arbitrations not administered by an institution or where the arbitral institution does not appoint a secretary, some arbitrators frequently engage such persons, at least in certain types of cases, whereas many others normally conduct the proceedings without them.[291]

Unlike the ICC Note, Article 4(27) of the UNCITRAL Notes then goes on to address the controversial question as to what constitutes 'administrative' tasks: **7-155**

> To the extent the tasks of the secretary are purely organizational (e.g. obtaining meeting rooms and providing or coordination secretarial services), this is usually not controversial. Differences in views, however, may arise if the tasks include legal research and other professional assistance to the arbitral tribunal (e.g. collecting case law or published commentaries on legal issues defined by the arbitral tribunal, preparing summaries from case law and publications, and sometimes also preparing drafts of procedural decisions or drafts of certain parts of the award, in particular those concerning the facts of the case). Views or expectations may differ especially where a task of the secretary is similar to professional functions of the arbitrators. Such role of the secretary is in the view of some commentators inappropriate or is appropriate only under certain conditions, such as that the parties agree thereto. However, it is typically recognized that it is important to ensure that the secretary does not perform any decision-making function of the arbitral tribunal.[292]

---

291. UNCITRAL Notes **Annex 15**.
292. UNCITRAL Notes **Annex 15**.

7-156 Thus, in the view of some arbitrators, the scope of administrative support extends from legal research to the drafting of legal opinions. Others consider this inappropriate because these tasks already involve an assessment of the law and – in some cases – of the facts.[293] Yet it is those tasks that are particularly helpful to the arbitrator; mere logistics can, to some extent, be handled through the arbitral institution as well. It is not surprising, therefore, that in many jurisdictions, including Austria, even judges regularly use law clerks. Their functions usually include the drafting of legal decisions (*Entscheidungsentwürfe*) without violating the right to be heard by a statutory designated judge.[294]

7-157 In light of the uncertainty attached to this issue, it is highly advisable for arbitrators to obtain the parties' consent prior to the secretary's involvement. The parties' advance approval may also be necessary for cost reasons, depending on whether the involvement of the secretary should be treated as an additional expense or whether the costs should be borne out of the arbitrator's fee.[295] The ICC Note states:

> It shall normally be the arbitral tribunal's responsibility, however, to pay the administrative secretary out of the fees awarded to the arbitrators by the Court, the amount of which shall be solely for the Court to decide in accordance with Article 20.2 of the ICC Rules. The fees of the administrative secretary shall therefore not normally be treated as expenses of the arbitral tribunal.

7-158 Indeed, when determining the arbitrators' fees, the ICC Court will normally be concerned to ensure that the engagement of such person does not increase the cost of the arbitration to the parties. Arbitrators wishing to appoint an administrative secretary should therefore assume that any amounts payable to the administrative secretary will be deducted from the fee awarded to them.[296] It seems to be the

---

293. P. Lalive, 'Inquietantes derives de l'arbitrage CCI' (1995) 13(4) Bull ASA, 634.

294. This function is performed as part of the legal training by *Rechtsreferendaren* in Germany and by *Rechtspraktikanten* in Austria. In the U.S. even at the Supreme Court *law clerks* draft legal decisions. Critical: C. Partasides, 'The Fourth Arbitrator? The Role of Secretaries to Tribunals in International Arbitration' (2002) 18(2) Arb Int'l, 147, 148 *et seq.*

295. C. Partasides, 'The Fourth Arbitrator? The Role of Secretaries to Tribunals in International Arbitration' (2002) 18(2) Arb Int'l, 147, 160.

296. However, treating the cost of a secretary as an additional expense will only increase the cost of the arbitration in case the arbitrators' fees are calculated on an *ad valorem* basis (as in ICC arbitration). In case of the arbitrators' fees being calculated on an hourly basis (as in LCIA arbitration) the result depends on the hourly rate of the arbitrators as well as their secretaries and can be less expensive for the parties. *See* C. Partasides, 'The Fourth Arbitrator? The Role of Secretaries to Tribunals in International Arbitration' (2002) 18(2) Arb Int'l, 147, 161.

ICC's policy that the parties should not be put in the awkward position of having to negotiate the payment of the secretary with the arbitral tribunal.[297] The VIAC's present Secretary General has in practice taken a similar view as the ICC and has considered any additional costs caused by any such person as not recoverable under **Article 32(a)**.[298]

---

297. C. Partasides, 'The Fourth Arbitrator? The Role of Secretaries to Tribunals in International Arbitration' (2002) 18(2) Arb Int'l, 147, 160 with further references.
298. However, where the assistance by arbitrators' internal personnel simply substitutes the involvement of otherwise necessary assistants to the arbitral proceedings, e.g. court reporters, it has been the Secretary General's practice to reimburse the hours spent by such internal personnel on the basis of average fees usually charged by external professionals. *See also* **Article 34**, at paras. 004 *et seq.*

Article 8

The Liability of Arbitrators and the VIAC

		Para.				Para.
I.	Arbitrator Liability	1		1. The Statute	9
	A. Conceptual Approaches to the			2. Section 594(4) ZPO	
	Liability of Arbitrators	3		and Contractual	
	1. The Concept of Judicial			Liability	11
	Immunity	4		3. Liability for Illegal	
	2. The Concept of Contractual			Acts	20
	Liability	6		C. Contractual Restriction of	
	B. Liability of Arbitrators Under			Liability	25
	Austrian Law	8	II.	The Liability of the VIAC	28

Article 8: Liability of the arbitrators, the Secretary General, the Board and its members and the Austrian Federal Economic Chamber and its employees for any act or omission in relation to arbitration proceedings, insofar as such liability may be admissible by law, shall be excluded.[1]

---

1. The English version of the Vienna Rules currently posted in the VIAC's website reads: 'Liability of the arbitrators, the Secretary General, the Board and its members and the Austrian Federal Economic Chamber and its employees for any act or omission in relation to arbitration proceedings, *insofar as such liability may be admissible by law*, shall be excluded'. A comparison with the authentic German version of the 2006 Vienna Rules makes clear that this translation fell victim to a clerical error; the highlighted part of Article 8 is about the admissibility of the *exclusion* of liability.

I.   ARBITRATOR LIABILITY

8-001 Ours is a litigious world, and parties – scorned by an unfavourable result – may blame the arbitrators or the institution rather than the weakness of their case. In line with similar provisions adopted by other arbitral institutions, the VIAC adopted Article 8 with the 2001 amendment of the Vienna Rules,[2] in order to protect arbitrators conducting proceedings under their rules as well as the institution itself, including its employees and officers, from lawsuits initiated by disgruntled litigants or third parties.

8-002 The following discussion addresses the basic principles in common and civil law jurisdictions governing the liability of arbitrators and arbitral institutions. The analysis below will also set out Austrian doctrine. It will show that while Austrian law, in line with most civil law jurisdictions, adopts primarily a contractual viewpoint, it nevertheless applies the doctrine of judicial immunity to significantly restrict the exposure of arbitrators.

A.   Conceptual Approaches to the Liability of Arbitrators

8-003 As regards the liability of arbitrators, there are in principle two concepts, one contractual and one functional. The contractual approach focuses on the contractual relationship between the arbitrator and the parties, and assesses liability according to the applicable rules of contract law. The functional approach postulates, based on the quasi-judicial function of the arbitrator, that arbitrators, save for exceptional circumstances, must be immune from liability similar to state court judges. This approach is frequently referred to as the concept of judicial immunity of arbitrators.

1.   **The Concept of Judicial Immunity**

8-004 The doctrine of judicial immunity in arbitration views arbitrators as functionally comparable to judges. The fact that arbitrators are contractually chosen by parties as substitutes for state judges does not alter their essential function of finally resolving disputes between parties with a binding effect that is recognized by the law.[3] Arbitrators 'act as judges, but as private judges. They assume a judicial function, but are generally paid, under contract, to perform that function. As a

---

2. Article 5 Vienna Rules 2001, **Annex 2a**.
3. As *Hausmaninger* puts it, 'arbitrators are granted broad discretion in the fashioning of legal remedies as long as they represent a fair solution. Arbitral solutions are judged to be a welcome and adequate substitute to judicial proceedings, and arbitrators are viewed as judges to be chosen by the parties'. *See* C. Hausmaninger, 'Civil Liability of Arbitrators – Comparative Analysis and Proposals for Reform' (1990) 7(4) J Int'l Arb, 7, 15. According to *Fouchard/Gaillard/Goldman*, the principle of the immunity of arbitrators is primarily found in common law countries. *See* E. Gaillard and J. Savage (eds), *Fouchard Gaillard Goldman On International Commercial Arbitration* (The Hague, Kluwer Law International, 1999), para. 1086.

result, they provide services to the parties and to the arbitral instituticn'[4] and 'should benefit from protection similar to that enjoyed by judges, both during and after the proceedings'.[5] In other words, arbitrators should, just like judges, in principle not be exposed to civil liability arising from erroneous decisions, nor for the manner in which they perform their judicial functions.[6] 'Arbitral immunity' is thus seen to support and uphold the integrity of the arbitral process.[7] The functional approach of judicial immunity appears to have been first developed primarily by courts and commentators in common law jurisdictions. However, similar solutions have been adopted in civil law jurisdictions as well.[8]

The concept of judicial immunity for state judges is enshrined in Austrian law **8-005** in the Public Liability Act (*Amtshaftungsgesetz* – AHG) which regulates the liability of organs of the state, including members of the judiciary.[9] According to the majority view, arbitrators are considered to discharge their judicial authority not by

---

4. E. Gaillard and J. Savage (eds), *Fouchard Gaillard Goldman On International Ccmmercial Arbitration* (The Hague, Kluwer Law International, 1999), para. 1017.

5. E. Gaillard and J. Savage (eds), *Fouchard Gaillard Goldman On International Ccmmercial Arbitration* (The Hague, Kluwer Law International, 1999), para. 1074.

6. This is also sometimes referred to as the 'status school' which is based on the performance by arbitrators of a judicial or quasi-judicial function. *See* A. Redfern, M. Hunter, N. Blackaby and C. Partasides, *Law and Practice of International Commercial Arbitration* (4th edn, London, Sweet & Maxwell, 2004), paras. 5-17. On this issue, the position seems to have changed in common law systems, which were initially in favour of the principle of arbitrator immunity. A number of more recent decisions, notably in England, have held that the situation of the arbitrators is governed by contract, and that by accepting their appointment and remuneration, the arbitrators undertake to perform their obligation diligently. *See* E. Gaillard and J. Savage (eds), *Fouchard Gaillard Goldman On International Commercial Arbitration* (The Hague, Kluwer Law International, 1999), para. 1148.

7. *See also* J. Yat-Sen Li, 'Arbitral Immunity: A Profession Comes cf Age' (1998) 64 Arbitration, 51. In *Arenson v. Casson Beckmann Rutley & Co*, Lord Kilbadron ruled that arbitrators should be liable like any other professional person selected for his expertise. *See* J. Lew, L. Mistelis, S. Kröll, *Comparative International Commercial Arbitration* (The Hague, Kluwer Law International, 2003), para. 12-40. In the recent case of *Prudential-Bache Securities (Hong Kong) Ltd. and Prudential-Bache International Bank Ltd. v. National Association of Securities Dealers Dispute Resolution, Inc.*, 289 F. Supp. 2d 438 (S.D.N.Y 2003), the plaintiffs sought to enjoin the defendant, an arbitral institution, from proceeding with an arbitration commenced against them. The US District Court for the Southern District of New York held that arbitrators are immune from suit for jurisdictional determinations made in their capacity as arbitrators.

8. For Germany, *see* R.H. Kreindler, J.K. Schäfer and R. Wolff, *Schiedsgerichtsbarkeit, Kompendium für die Praxis* (Frankfurt/Main, Verlag Recht und Wirtschaft, 2006), para. 582 with further annotations. For a comparative overview, *see* S. Franck, 'The Liability of Internaticnal Arbitrators: A Comparative Analysis and Proposal for Qualified Immunity' (2000) 20(1) NY L School J Int'l Comp L.

9. According to Section 1(1) AHG, the Federal Republic of Austria is liable for any financial damages to persons which one of its authorities has wrongfully caused in the execution of the laws pursuant to the general provision of tort under Austrian civil law. *See* W. Melis in *The Immunity of Arbitrators*, J. Lew (ed.) (London, Lloyd's of London Press, 1990), para. 3.3; in further detail W. Schragel, *Kommentar zum Amtshaftungsgesetz* (Vienna, Manz, 2003).

virtue of an act of state but by virtue of private act of contractual appointment (even if, in the context of *ad hoc* arbitration, the arbitrator is appointed by a national court in the absence of appointment by the parties).[10] While arbitrators are therefore not considered '*executive organs*' within the Public Liability Act and their liability is assessed predominantly under contractual theories, Austrian scholars have relied on the Public Liability Act *per analogiam*, to restrict the civil law liability of arbitrators.[11] This is discussed further below in the context of Austrian statute and case law.[12] *Hausmaninger*, going further still than *Fasching*, proposes a direct application of the Public Liability Act. He argues that arbitrators could well be regarded as an executive organ falling within this law.[13] This approach raises practical difficulties. Under Section 1(1) AHG, a state entity will be liable for errors of its organs. Specifically, the Federal Republic of Austria is liable for errors of the members of its judiciary.[14] Yet, in the case of arbitrators, no such state entity is available to satisfy an aggrieved party's claims. In that sense, the analogous application of the Public Liability Act (or its principles) appears preferable as it allows the parties to direct their claims directly against the arbitrators.

2.   **The Concept of Contractual Liability**

8-006 In discussing the issue of arbitrator liability, commentators in civil law countries typically focus on the contractual nature of arbitration and the parties' relationship to the arbitrators. According to *Hausmaninger*,

> [i]n civil law countries the powers of the arbitrator are more limited and they are primarily viewed as experts whose liability for wrongful acts should, similar to other professionals providing services for compensation, be determined by the terms of their appointment contract (*receptum arbitri*) concluded with the parties. This contractual approach, [in Austria] reflected in Section 584(2) ZPO, is based on the idea that in determining a liability standard for arbitrators, one should not be looking at the quasi judicial function the arbitrator has to perform, but rather at the contractual character and origin of his appointment.[15]

---

10. H.W. Fasching, *Schiedsgericht und Schiedsverfahren im österreichischen und im internationalen Recht* (Vienna, Manz, 1973), p. 72.
11. W. Schragel, *Kommentar zum Amtshaftungsgesetz* (Vienna, Manz, 2003); H.W. Fasching, *Schiedsgericht und Schiedsverfahren im österreichischen und im internationalen Recht* (Vienna, Manz, 1973), p. 72.
12. OGH, 17 October 1928, 3 Ob 573, ZBl 1929, 79; *see* **Article 8**, at paras. 011 *et seq.*
13. C. Hausmaninger, 'Civil Liability of Arbitrators – Comparative Analysis and Proposals for Reform' (1990) 7(4) J Int'l Arb, 7, 38.
14. W. Melis in *The Immunity of Arbitrators*, J. Lew (ed.) (London, Lloyd's of London Press, 1990), para. 3.4.
15. C. Hausmaninger, 'Civil Liability of Arbitrators – Comparative Analysis and Proposals for Reform' (1990) 7(4) J Int'l Arb, 7, 19.

Under the contractual approach, therefore, arbitrators can incur civil liability **8-007** because 'a fault committed in conducting the arbitral proceedings constitutes a breach of contract, and as remunerated providers of services the arbitrators are accountable for such breaches under the ordinary law of contract'.[16] Thus, Austrian law has traditionally looked at the parties' contract with the arbitrators as the basis for the arbitrator's liability. A purely contractual approach is obviously based on the premise that all parties to the arbitration (including the party who has not nominated the arbitrator concerned) are parties to the contract with the arbitrator; thus, the arbitrator owes his or her duties to all parties of the arbitration.[17] As will be discussed below, however, Austrian statute and case law severely limit the arbitrator's contractual liability to approximate judicial immunity.

B. LIABILITY OF ARBITRATORS UNDER AUSTRIAN LAW

With Section 594(4) ZPO, Austrian arbitration law contains a statutory provision **8-008** specifically addressing the issue of arbitrator liability. However, the literal meaning of this provision *prima facie* appears to limit its application to the arbitrator's unjustified refusal to perform his or her obligation to issue an award, or to do so without unreasonable delay. The relationship between Section 594(4) ZPO, an arbitrator's general contractual liability and the entitlement to judicial immunity is, therefore, not spelled out clearly in the statute. This relationship is discussed below in the context of Austrian case law and academic writing.

1. The Statute

While the academic discussion of arbitrator liability emphasizes the contractual **8-009** nature of the contract between the arbitrators and the parties, less attention is devoted to the ZPO which contains an express provision on point. Section 594(4) ZPO, a mandatory provision which incorporates (without changes) Section 584(2) fZPO,[18] states:

> An arbitrator who does not at all or who does not timely fulfil the obligations resulting from the acceptance of his appointment shall be liable to the parties for all damage caused by his culpable refusal or delay.

---

16. E. Gaillard and J. Savage (eds), *Fouchard Gaillard Goldman On International Commercial Arbitration* (The Hague, Kluwer Law International, 1999), para. 1144.
17. H.W. Fasching, *Kommentar zu den Zivilprozeßgesetzen, IV* (Vienna, Manz, 1971), Section 579, pp. 748 *et seq; see also* **Article 7**, at para. 053.
18. J. Power, *The Austrian Arbitration Act – A Practitioner's Guide to Sections 577-618 of the Austrian Code of Civil Procedure* (Vienna, Manz, 2006), Section 594, para. 7; A. von Saucken, *Die Reform des österreichischen Schiedsverfahrensrechts auf der Basis des UNCITRAL-Modellgesetzes über die Internationale Handelsschiedsgerichtsbarkeit* (Frankfurt, Verlag Peter Lang, 2004), pp. 147 *et seq.*

8-010 The scope of this provision is subject to some debate, and decisions addressing liability under this provision sporadic. The provision seems to apply only to an unjustified refusal by the arbitrator to perform his or her obligations 'at all' or with delay; but the statute does not say what these obligations are (other than stating that they arise from the arbitrator's appointment). In line with general rules of contractual liability, the arbitrator must be at fault for such failures, but the statute does not say expressly which degree of fault is sufficient to result in liability. Thus, the relationship of Section 594(4) ZPO to the concepts of contractual liability and arbitrator immunity is unclear. It is fair to assume that the Austrian courts have not yet spoken the last word on the matter, but the following considerations might provide guidance to the application of Section 594(4) ZPO.

2.   Section 594(4) ZPO and Contractual Liability

8-011 It is easy to see how Section 594(4) ZPO would apply to cases where the arbitrator simply refuses to act, or acts with delay, or withdraws from office without good cause.[19] Such cases would meet the provision's basis – non-fulfilment or delay – in the most literal sense, and would give rise to liability insofar as the arbitrator is at fault for the non-fulfilment or delay within the meaning of Section 1295 ABGB. In this regard, *Fasching* argues that the fault must reach or exceed the level of gross negligence.[20]

8-012 It is more difficult, however, to establish the relationship between Section 594(4) ZPO and the arbitrator's general contractual liability. Insofar as non-performance and delay could easily be addressed under general rules of contractual liability, Section 594(4) ZPO appears somewhat redundant.[21] Yet, the traditional view has been to apply Section 594(4) ZPO (or rather, its predecessor) exclusively to cases of non-fulfilment or delay, as specified in Section 594(4) ZPO and to accept that in addition, the arbitrator's liability arising from a failure to make a correct award,[22] or to observe applicable procedural rules, would follow general rules of the law of damages.[23]

---

19. OGH, 7 May 1918, Rv I 168, ZBl 1919/222.
20. H.W. Fasching, *Schiedsgericht und Schiedsverfahren im österreichischen und im internationalen Recht* (Vienna, Manz, 1973), p. 73.
21. G. Weissmann, 'Drei Fragen zur Reform der Schiedsgerichtsbarkeit' in *Festschrift für Rudolf Welser zum 65. Geburtstag*, C. Fischer-Czermak, A. Kletecka, M. Schauer and W. Zankl (eds) (Vienna, Manz, 2004), para. 1160.
22. H.W. Fasching, *Schiedsgericht und Schiedsverfahren im österreichischen und im internationalen Recht* (Vienna, Manz, 1973), p. 73; C. Liebscher and A. Schmid in *Practitioner's Handbook on International Arbitration*, F.B. Weigand (ed.) (Munich, C.H. Beck, 2002), p. 555; G. Weissmann, 'Drei Fragen zur Reform der Schiedsgerichtsbarkeit' in *Festschrift für Rudolf Welser zum 65. Geburtstag*, C. Fischer-Czermak, A. Kletecka, M. Schauer and W. Zankl (eds) (Vienna, Manz, 2004), para. 1149.
23. A. von Saucken, *Die Reform des österreichischen Schiedsverfahrensrechts auf der Basis des UNCITRAL-Modellgesetzes über die Internationale Handelsschiedsgerichtsbarkeit* (Frankfurt, Verlag Peter Lang, 2004), p. 147.

In that regard, it has been noted that under Section 1299 ABGB, the arbitrator may **8-013** be exposed to a higher standard of diligence in light of his or her expert status.[24] On the other hand, commentators have sought to restrict the application of contractual liability by reference to the concept of arbitrator immunity. *Fasching* thus argues that the personal liability of an arbitrator should not exceed the liability of a professional state judge.[25] Indeed, German authorities consider this an implied term of the arbitrator's contract with the parties.[26] Good policy reasons support that argument: an extended civil liability would unduly impede the arbitrator's decision-making; would deter suitable persons from accepting appointments; and would without cause discriminate against arbitrators when they fulfil the same judicial function as state court judges.

As a result, a decision that is objectively incorrect, even if it contradicts established **8-014** case law, will not be sufficient to result in liability – unless it is an outright inconceivable legal position (*unvertretbar*) in the circumstances.[27] Procedural or evidentiary errors will generally also not give rise to liability of the arbitrator unless they are the result of gross negligence (*grobes Verschulden*).[28] For both procedural errors and incorrect decisions on the merits, *Fasching* postulates the additional (cumulative) condition that the arbitrator's error in law or procedure

---

24. Section 1299 ABGB reads: 'A person who claims in public to have knowledge of a function (*Amt*), an art, a trade or a handicraft, or who accepts without necessity voluntarily an undertaking which requires special skills or exceptional diligence demonstrates that he believes to possess the necessary diligence and the required unusual skills. He is, therefore, liable for their absence.' This provision imposes an objectively more severe standard for the assessment of the diligence to be exercised by experts and the assessment of their abilities and their knowledge for whose lack they will have to account for. Translation of Section 1299 ABGB from W. Melis in *The Immunity of Arbitrators*, J. Lew (ed.) (London, Lloyd's of London Press, 1990), para. 3.7.
25. H.W. Fasching, *Schiedsgericht und Schiedsverfahren im österreichischen und im internationalen Recht* (Vienna, Manz, 1973), p. 73.
26. BGH, 6 October 1954, II ZR 149/53 in BGHZ 15, 12, 14 *et seq* ; R.H. Kreindler, J.K. Schäfer and R. Wolff, *Schiedsgerichtsbarkeit, Kompendium für die Praxis* (Frankfurt/Main, Verlag Recht und Wirtschaft, 2006), para. 582.
27. For state judges, Section 3 AHG provides: '(1) Provided that the legal entity has indemnified the injured person under the provisions of the subject Federal Act, it is entitled to claim reimbursement from the persons who acted as its organs and committed or caused the respective violation of the law **with intent or gross negligence**. (2) In case the organ committed or caused the violation of the law **grossly negligent**, the court may mitigate such reimbursement on grounds of equity. For such purpose the court is bound to consider accordingly the circumstances as listed in Section 2 para. 2 DHG, BGBl No. 80/1965 last amended by BGBl. No. 159/1983.'
28. Austrian commentators have defined gross negligence as 'negligence so severe that a diligent person would never act like this in the circumstances'. *See* E. Karner in, *Kommentar zum ABGB*, H. Koziol, P. Bydlinski and R. Bollenberger (eds) (New York/Vienna, Springer, 2005), Section 1294 ABGB, para. 11. Note, however, that in OGH, 17 October 1928, 3 Ob 573, ZBl 1929, 79, it was held that ordinary negligence (*leichte Fahrlässigkeit*) should be sufficient. *See* also C. Liebscher and A. Schmid in *Practitioner's Handbook on International Arbitration*, F.B. Weigand (ed.) (Munich, C.H. Beck, 2002), p. 555.

leads to the award being successfully set aside. In principle, therefore, as long as the award survives, the arbitrator has discharged his or her primary duties – and a party that fails to challenge the award within the time limits provided under the law has foregone its right to hold the arbitrator liable.[29]

8-015 As discussed in great detail in German doctrine, the privilege of a rather restricted liability accorded to arbitrators extends only to those activities of the arbitrator that relate directly to the decision-making process, that is, the arbitrators' taking of the evidence and their establishing the facts; the application of the law to the facts and their conduct of the proceedings. By the same token, it is argued that obligations that are ancillary to the decision-making itself – such as the duty to disclose conflicts – do not enjoy the privilege of an analogous application of judicial immunity.[30]

8-016 In any event, however, Austrian case law clearly indicates that a successful challenge of the award is a necessary prerequisite for arbitrator liability. In one of the rare decisions on the issue of arbitrator liability, dating from 1928, the Austrian *Oberster Gerichtshof* stated:

> Even on the supposition that the arbitrator renders his award not only in compliance with a private contract but also in execution of a public function derived from acceptance of the appointment, one cannot conclude that he should not be liable for damage caused by unlawful conduct of his arbitral duties. Even when Section 584 [f]ZPO solely refers to unlawful refusal or delay only, this does not imply that he cannot be charged with liability for other breaches of duties. However, the arbitral award, similar to a judicial ruling, can be set aside only for reasons specifically mentioned in Section 595 [f]ZPO and cannot be contested because of any mistake in law, wrongful evaluation or essential defects in the proceedings. It can therefore be concluded that the arbitrator is generally accountable for intentional infringement of the principles and rules pertaining to arbitral proceedings but that the arbitrator will be liable for damage only when his action leads to the inoperability of the award.[31]

8-017 A more recent decision by the Austrian *Oberster Gerichtshof* confirms this. In 9 Ob 126/04a, 6 June 2005, the Austrian *Oberster Gerichtshof* was presented with a liability dispute that arose between a bank institute (as the claimant) against two members (one of them the chairman) of an arbitral tribunal. The tribunal had decided against the claimant in a preceding arbitration, denying the request for payment of a contractual penalty. Discontent with this outcome, the claimant requested from the arbitrators damages in the amount of the penalty that it was

---

29. H.W. Fasching, *Schiedsgericht und Schiedsverfahren im österreichischen und im internationalen Recht* (Vienna, Manz, 1973), p. 74.
30. H.J. Musielak and W. Voit, *Kommentar zur Zivilprozessordnung* (5th edn, Munich, Verlag Franz Vahlen, 2006), Section 1035 ZPO, para. 25 with further references.
31. OGH, 17 October 1928, 3 Ob 573, ZBl 1929, 79.

not awarded, along with the costs of the arbitration. The claimant argued that the two arbitrators had committed fundamental procedural errors, especially by disregarding various evidentiary applications, and that they had interpreted the applicable law in an unjustifiable manner. By doing so, the claimant argued, the arbitrators had violated their contractual obligations to the parties and had to be held liable for any resulting damages. It bears emphasis, however, that the claimant had not even attempted to set aside the arbitral award, due to alleged 'hopelessness'.

The Austrian *Oberster Gerichtshof* dismissed the claim. In its reasoning, the **8-018** Austrian *Oberster Gerichtshof* stated that, whether under Section 584(2) fZPO (now Section 594(4) ZPO) or under contractual theories, an arbitrator can as a matter of principle only be held liable if the award has been set aside for reasons for which the arbitrator is at fault.[32] As regards this requirement, it would constitute an unjustifiable paradox if liability under Section 584(2) fZPO (now Section 594(4) ZPO) depended on a successful challenge to the award (as is the majority view in Austria), but alleged contractual violations did not. This decision makes sense of the purpose of Section 594(4) ZPO in that – even if the violation is of a contractual nature – the annulment of the award could be understood as non-performance within the meaning of that provisioning. Insofar as the subjective element of personal fault is also present to the required degree, this may then give rise to liability.[33]

Notably, the Austrian legislature did include the provision of Section 584(2) fZPO **8-019** in the new Arbitration Act (now Section 594(4) ZPO) precisely and expressly to ensure that courts would not interpret its absence as an incentive to expand arbitrators' liability.[34]

3.   Liability for Illegal Acts

Finally, it is fairly obvious that the arbitrator does not fulfil his or her duties – **8-020** under Section 594(4) ZPO or indeed any contractual theory – if the arbitrator perverts the judicial mandate received from the parties, e.g., by accepting a bribe. This is the dominating position in Germany where only illegal conduct by the arbitrator pierces the protective veil of quasi-judicial immunity and gives rise to liability.[35]

---

32. OGH, 6 June 2005, 9 Ob 126/04a; *see also* H. Krejci, 'Zur Schiedsrichterhaftung' [2007] ÖJZ, 87 and OGH, 28 February 2008, 8 Ob 4/08h.
33. A. Reiner, *Das neue österreichische Schiedsrecht/The new Austrian Arbitration Law* (Vienna, LexisNexis, 2006), Section 594, note 114.
34. Explanatory Notes to Section 594(4) ZPO.
35. BGH, 6 October 1954, II ZR 149/53 in BGHZ 15, 12, 14; R.H. Kreindler, J.K. Schäfer and R. Wolff, *Schiedsgerichtsbarkeit, Kompendium für die Praxis* (Frankfurt/Main, Verlag Recht und Wirtschaft, 2006), para. 582 and note 47 with further annotations.

8-021 In a recent and internationally observed decision, a German company sought before the Austrian courts to recover damages allegedly caused by an arbitrator in his capacity as chairman of an arbitral tribunal.[36] The Austrian *Oberster Gerichtshof*, applying German law to the arbitrator's contract, explained that

> according to the general principles of [German] contract law, an arbitrator is liable for damages caused by fault (*Verschulden*). Only in case of fault in connection with the making of the award does he enjoy in principle, in view of the nature of the arbitral proceedings, the same exclusion of liability accorded to judges by Section 839(2) BGB. The 'judicial privilege' – that is, the limitation of the liability of the judge when deciding on a dispute to the case of intentional misapplication of the law – is not, according to German doctrine and jurisprudence, extended to arbitrators on the basis of an application by analogy of Section 839(2) BGB; rather, it is derived from the contractual position accorded to arbitrators. (...) A neglect of duty in the making of the award can consist of mistakes regarding the merits of the decision as well as defects in the measures establishing the basis for that decision. Hence, in connection with the decision-making process there is only a liability for (intentionally) perverting the course of justice. (...) The arbitrator's activities which do not pertain to the decision-making process consequently, that is, all arbitral behaviour which does not concern the making of the award, or establishing the basis for the award – are not subject to the exclusion of liability. Among these activities and omissions not subject to exclusion are in particular those where the arbitrator is to fault for giving rise to a ground for challenge, for instance by having secret contacts with one party only.

8-022 In limiting the arbitrator's liability with regards to the decision-making process to cases of illegal conduct, German law restricts arbitrator liability further than Austrian law. However, Austrian law, too, will deny the privilege of quasi-judicial immunity in cases of illegal conduct, and expose the arbitrator to liability for intentional or fraudulent actions that are not merely errors in law or fact. From a civil law perspective, *Fouchard/Gaillard/Goldman* emphasize convincingly that

> authors and practitioners seeking to determine when arbitrators will not enjoy immunity are broadly in agreement: any intentional fault, and any misrepresentative or fraudulent conduct will render them liable. In such cases, the arbitrators violate their judicial obligations to act fairly and treat the parties equally, and they therefore no longer deserve to be protected in the same way as a judge. Personal faults of that kind are separable from the arbitrator's

---

36. OGH, 28 April 1998, 1 Ob 253/97f.

professional role, and do not even require proof of a contractual basis in order for the arbitrators to be liable.[37]

It is clear, therefore, that even where applied, liability restrictions – whether based **8-023** on the concept of judicial immunity or on contractual theories – do not confer unlimited freedom on the arbitrator. Rather, the immunity of arbitrators is

> an exception to the general principle of liability for breach of an implied contractual duty of care which will not be given any wider application than is necessary to meet the demands of public policy.[38]

Thus, arbitral immunity facilitates the public interest in the finality and legal **8-024** certainty of arbitral proceedings; it also allows arbitrators to remain independent in exercising their judicial function.[39] By the same token, the restrictions on arbitrator liability extend only insofar as is necessary to reach these public policy goals,[40] and they do not hand arbitrators a *card blanche* to break the law.

C.   CONTRACTUAL RESTRICTION OF LIABILITY

Article 8 provides that the 'liability of the arbitrators (. . .) for any act or omission **8-025** related to the arbitration proceedings, insofar as such exclusion is admissible by law, *will be excluded*'.[41] This Article thus amounts to a contractual restriction of the arbitrator's liability, insofar as the Vienna Rules are incorporated by reference into the arbitration agreement and, in turn, into the arbitrator's contract with the parties.

Naturally, exclusions of liability are permitted only within the framework of the **8-026** applicable law.[42] Which law, then, governs the determination of the arbitrator's

---

37. E. Gaillard and J. Savage (eds), *Fouchard Gaillard Goldman On International Commercial Arbitration* (The Hague, Kluwer Law International, 1999), para. 1099.
38. M.L. Smith, 'Contractual Obligations Owed by and to Arbitrators: Model Terms of Appointment' (1992) 8(1) Arb Int'l, 17.
39. M.L. Smith, 'Contractual Obligations Owed by and to Arbitrators: Model Terms of Appointment' (1992) 8(1) Arb Int'l, 17.
40. J. Lew, L. Mistelis and S. Kröll, *Comparative International Commercial Arbitration* (The Hague, Kluwer Law International, 2003), para. 12-39.
41. As discussed in **Article 8**, at fn 1, the English version of the Vienna Rules currently posted in the VIAC's website reads: 'Liability of the arbitrators, the Secretary General, the Board and its members and the Austrian Federal Economic Chamber and its employees for any act or omission in relation to arbitration proceedings, **insofar as such liability may be admissible by law,** shall be excluded'. A comparison with the authentic German version of the 2006 Vienna Rules makes clear that this translation fell victim to a clerical error; the highlighted part of Article 8 is about the admissibility of the exclusion of liability.
42. C. Hausmaninger, 'Civil Liability of Arbitrators – Comparative Analysis and Proposals for Reform' (1990) 7(4) J Int'l Arb, 7, 21.

liability[43] is subject to debate.[44] In this regard, the Austrian *Oberster Gerichtshof* has held that 'the agreement with the arbitrators, which determines the legal relationship between the arbitrators and the parties is, in any case, one of private law; hence, it is subject to the rules of private international law rather than to the *lex fori* principle of procedural law. As the agreement with the arbitrators is of contractual nature, the international rules regarding the law of obligations apply'.[45] The Austrian *Oberster Gerichtshof* has also suggested that the arbitrator's contract is subject to the provisions of the law applicable to the arbitration agreement.[46]

8-027 Under Austrian law, parties in a commercial setting are at liberty to limit liability, save that liability for intentional wrongdoing cannot be excluded in advance; the exclusion of liability for grossly negligent conduct is disputed.[47] The situation is, as in many jurisdictions, more problematic with respect to consumer contracts.[48] From a purely contractual standpoint, therefore, it is doubtful if the absolute exclusion of arbitrator liability is valid as a matter of law.[49] Yet, this exclusion must be

---

43. *Fouchard/Gaillard/Goldman* point out that neither the Brussels Convention nor the Lugano Convention on Jurisdiction and Enforcement in Civil and Commercial Matters appear to apply to such disputes and suggest that 'one should therefore apply either other treaties on international jurisdiction that do cover arbitration, or the rules adopted on this issue in the country where the action is heard'. *See* E. Gaillard and J. Savage (eds), *Fouchard Gaillard Goldman On International Commercial Arbitration* (The Hague, Kluwer Law International, 1999), para. 1012.

44. C. Hausmaninger, 'Civil Liability of Arbitrators – Comparative Analysis and Proposals for Reform' (1990) 7(4) J Int'l Arb, 39.

45. OGH, 28 April 1998, 1 Ob 253/97f, with reference to W.H. Rechberger and P.A. Simotta (eds), *Grundriss des österreichischen Zivilprozessrechts* (4th edn, Vienna, Manz, 1994) para. 961; H.W. Fasching, *Schiedsgericht und Schiedsverfahren im österreichischen und im internationalen Recht* (Vienna, Manz, 1973), p. 69; P. Schlosser, *Das Recht der internationalen privaten Schiedsgerichtsbarkeit* (2nd edn, Tübingen, Mohr Siebeck, 1989), para. 491; H.W. Fasching, *Lehrbuch des österreichischen Zivilprozeßrechts* (2nd edn, Vienna, Manz, 1990), para. 2198, referring to A. Baumbach and K.H. Schwab, *Schiedsgerichtbarkeit* (2nd edn, Munich, C.H. Beck, 1960), p. 90 – that, according to private international law, the law applicable to the arbitration agreement also applies to the agreement with the arbitrators.

46. H.W. Fasching, *Schiedsgericht und Schiedsverfahren im österreichischen und im internationalen Recht* (Vienna, Manz, 1973), p. 69; T. Chiwitt-Oberhammer, *Der fehlerhafte Schiedsspruch* (Vienna, Verlag Österreich, 2000), p. 62, with reference to the position under German law.

47. H.W. Fasching, *Schiedsgericht und Schiedsverfahren im österreichischen und im internationalen Recht* (Vienna, Manz, 1973), p. 72. In some cases, even this can be possible. *See also* C. Liebscher and A. Schmid in *Practitioner's Handbook on International Arbitration*, F.B. Weigand (ed.) (Munich, C.H. Beck, 2002), pp. 541 *et seq.*; C. Liebscher in *Institutionelle Schiedsgerichtsbarkeit*, R.A. Schütze (ed.) (Cologne, Carl Heymanns Verlag, 2006), p. 271.

48. In Austria, *see, e.g.*, G. Kathrein, 'Gewährleistung im Verbrauchergeschäft' [2001] ecolex, 426.

49. E. Gaillard and J. Savage (eds), *Fouchard Gaillard Goldman On International Commercial Arbitration* (The Hague, Kluwer Law International, 1999), para. 1154, with specific reference to common law countries and the 1996 English Arbitration Act.

seen in the context of judicial immunity, as discussed above, which may limit the arbitrator's liability to 'intentionally perverting the course of justice'.[50] Although institutional arbitration rules, insofar as they are private instruments of a contractual nature, do in and of themselves not have the power to confer judicial immunity on the arbitrators, such judicial immunity could either be inferred by operation of law, or it could become, as a matter of public policy, a term of the arbitrator's contract with the parties. As discussed, this approach appears to have been adopted in Germany where arbitrators are considered to agree to arbitrate on the understanding that they be held liable only to the extent judges are liable. Thus, the terms of the appointment should be interpreted as affording them with '*quasi-judicial*' immunity.[51] In light of *Fasching's* and *Hausmaninger's* (analogous or direct) application of the Public Liability Act to arbitrator liability, Article 8 can probably be interpreted in that light as well.

II.   THE LIABILITY OF THE VIAC

Parties dissatisfied with the outcome or the conduct of the arbitration have also **8-028** tried to recover damages from the institution under whose rules the proceedings were conducted, particularly for the institution's appointment of the 'wrong' arbitrators.[52]

Arbitral institutions perform services which operate as quasi-judicial organiza- **8-029** tions that uphold and protect the integrity of the arbitral process. This might lead to the conclusion that the institution enjoys similar immunity to the courts, at least in exercise of such activities. Some courts have already accepted this view.[53]

---

50. *See* OGH, 28 April 1998, 1 Ob 253/97f.
51. C. Hausmaninger, 'Civil Liability of Arbitrators – Comparative Analysis and Proposals for Reform' (1990) 7(4) J Int'l Arb, 7, 20; similar J.P. Lachmann, *Handbuch für die Schiedsgerichtspraxis* (3rd edn, Cologne, Verlag Dr. Otto Schmidt, 2008), p. 932. The well-established case law limiting arbitrator liability dates back to the times of the former German Supreme Court, the '*Reichsgericht*'. Given that broad and far-reaching privilege granted as a matter of law, contractual reductions and exclusions of arbitrator's liability are, according to German scholars, unusual and unnecessary. *See* W. Wagner in *Practitioner's Handbook on International Arbitration*, F.B. Weigand (ed.) (Munich, C.H. Beck, 2002), p. 730, with further references.
52. J. Lew, L. Mistelis and S. Kröll, *Comparative International Commercial Arbitration* (The Hague, Kluwer Law International, 2003), para. 12-62.
53. The basis for the immunity of arbitral institutions in common law jurisdictions is different from that relating to arbitrators: it is based on the fact that they operate as quasi-judicial organizations in order to protect those functions that are closely related to the arbitral process and sufficiently related to the adjudicative phase of the arbitration. *See* A. Redfern, M. Hunter, N. Blackaby and C. Partasides, *Law and Practice of International Commercial Arbitration* (4th edn, London, Sweet & Maxwell, 2004), para. 5-21. According to *Hausmaninger*, in particular US courts 'in

8-030 In any event, arbitral institutions have reacted to these increasing pressures and have, in more or less detail, inserted clauses in their rules that seek to limit, or exclude altogether, the liability of the institution. Some clauses provide for a complete, unconditional exemption,[54] others limit liability for damage caused by intentional or grossly negligent breaches of institutional duties,[55] or accept liability only for deliberate wrongdoing.[56]

8-031 As with claims against arbitrators, parties often base their claim on an alleged violation of the contract concluded between them and the institution.[57] As already discussed, there is indeed a contractual relationship between the VIAC and the parties.[58] The VIAC owes the parties the fulfilment of this contract on the terms defined by the Vienna Rules. For example, while the VIAC cannot be held responsible for acts that are committed by the arbitrators, the VIAC could conceivably be held liable for *culpa*

---

their eagerness to ensure effectiveness of arbitration, have held that arbitral immunity should extend beyond the arbitrators themselves and not merely shield arbitrators from actions involving alleged torts. Thus arbitral immunity has been extended to various parts of the arbitral proceedings'. *See* C. Hausmaninger, 'Civil Liability of Arbitrators – Comparative Analysis and Proposals for Reform' (1990) 7(4) J Int'l Arb, 39. In *Austern v. Chicago Board Options Exchange, Inc.*, 898 F. 2d (2nd Cir. 1990), an award rendered by a tribunal acting under the rules of the CBOE had been vacated on the grounds that the composition of the tribunal was contrary the arbitration rules. Claimant brought an action for damages against the CBOE which was rejected by the Court of Appeal granting the CBOE immunity for all functions that are integrally related to the arbitration. *See* J. Lew, L. Mistelis and S. Kröll, *Comparative International Commercial Arbitration* (The Hague, Kluwer Law International, 2003), para. 12-66.

54. Article 34 ICC Rules: 'Neither the arbitrators, nor the Court and its members, nor the ICC and its employees, nor the ICC National Committees shall be liable to any person for any act or omission in connection with the arbitration.'

55. Article 44(1) DIS Rules: 'All liability of an arbitrator for any act in connection with deciding a legal matter in excluded, provided such act does not constitute an intentional breach of duty. All liability of the arbitrators, the DIS, its officers and its employees for any other act or omission in connection with arbitral proceedings is excluded, provided such acts do not constitute an intentional or grossly negligent breach of duty.'

56. Article 35 AAA/ICDR Rules: 'The members of the tribunal and the administrator shall not be liable to any party for any act or omission in connection with any arbitration conducted under these rules, except that they may be liable for the consequences of conscious and deliberate wrongdoing'. *See also* Article 31 LCIA Rules: 'None of the LCIA, the LCIA Court (including its President, Vice-Presidents and individual members), the Registrar, any deputy Registrar, any arbitrator and any expert to the Arbitral Tribunal shall be liable to any party howsoever for any act or omission in connection with any arbitration conducted by reference to these Rules, save where the act or omission is shown by that party to constitute conscious and deliberate wrongdoing committed by the body or person alleged to be liable to that part'.

57. *See* J. Lew, L. Mistelis and S. Kröll, *Comparative International Commercial Arbitration* (The Hague, Kluwer Law International, 2003), para. 12-62.

58. Please note that the reference to the VIAC is made for reasons of simplicity. As discussed, the contractual relation exists between the parties and AFEC; therefore, a reference to the VIAC has rightly not been included within Article 8.

in eligendo or for neglecting the qualifications required of the arbitrator by the agreement of the parties when making an institutional appointment.[59]

According to *Heller*, the liability of the institution is only conceivable if there is a **8-032** valid arbitration agreement which requires the organs of the VIAC to fulfil their duties under the Vienna Rules.[60] This is debatable. If a claim is raised under the Vienna Rules, with the claimant having paid the deposit on costs and the registration fee, and the VIAC accepts the administration of the case, there are strong arguments to assume an obligation of the VIAC to act in accordance of the Vienna Rules irrespective of whether there is a valid arbitration agreement or not. Arguably, the contract concluded between the parties and the institution is separate from the arbitration agreement.

Potential liability could also arise if the VIAC delays its decisions without proper **8-033** justification. The Vienna Rules do not provide any time limits in this respect, but it would be fair to assume that any institutional decision-making is required within reasonable time, as indicated by the circumstances of each case.[61]

It has also been argued that the VIAC does not incur liability for any decisions that **8-034** involve the exercise of discretion, proposing to apply Section 594(4) ZPO (Section 584(2) fZPO) *per analogiam*. Under that view, the VIAC would be liable for an unjustified failure to meet its obligations under the Vienna Rules timely or at all, but would not incur liability for decisions that are simply incorrect.[62] Applying the principles developed above with respect to arbitrator liability, and the recent case law on Section 584(2) fZPO, however, it is conceivable to assume institutional liability where an award is set aside as a result of a profoundly erroneous decision of the VIAC, provided the VIAC acted intentionally or with gross negligence.

Article 8 not only exempts the institution but also its employees from liability; this **8-035** benefits in particular the case managers and the Secretary General. Both also enjoy the statutory privileges accorded to employees under Austrian law, pursuant to the Employee Liability Act (*Dienstnehmerhaftpflichtgesetz* – DHG).

---

59. *See* **Article 14**, at paras. 043 *et seq.* In some countries, the appointment of the arbitrator is expressly excluded from the institutional liability, such as Section 74 English Arbitration Act.
60. K. Heller, 'Die Rechtsstellung des Internationalen Schiedsgerichts der Wirtschaftskammer Österreich' [1994] wbl, 105, 111, 115. *Melis* considers the arbitral institution under a duty to verify the existence of the arbitration agreement. In his opinion it shall only accept cases where the claimant can give *prima facie* evidence of a valid arbitration agreement. It will 'refuse to accept a case, if the claimant is unable to produce a document which is, at least, of such a nature as to indicate the jurisdiction of the institution is not impossible'. *See* W. Melis, 'Function and Responsibility of Arbitral Institutions' (1991) XIII Comp L Y3 of Int'l Bus, 113.
61. *See* **Article 14**, at paras. 019 *et seq.*, 037, 056 and 064
62. K. Heller, 'Die Rechtsstellung des Internationalen Schiedsgerichts der Wirtschaftskammer Österreich' [1994] wbl, 105, 115.

8-036 The liability exemption applies further to the VIAC Board as a whole, as it is a collective organ.[63] Nevertheless, each member of the Board has specific duties to fulfil which conceivably could result in liability. It is most likely that in such a case the Board would be held liable *in toto*, with possible recourse against individual members. The privilege of the Employee Liability Act is not applicable because the function of the Board member is honorary unpaid office.[64]

---

63. *See* **Article 3**, at paras. 001 and 014.
64. *See* **Article 3**, at para. 004. However, it could be argued that the Board members due to their unpaid honorary office are not exposed to the same level of liability such as arbitrators. *See* Section 1300 ABGB in F. Harrer in *Praxiskommentar zum ABGB*, 6, M. Schwimann (ed.) (3rd edn, Vienna, LexisNexis ARD ORAC, 2005).

Article 9

The Statement of Claims

			Para.
I.	Filing the Statement of Claims		1
	A.	Introduction	1
	B.	Filing the Statement of Claims	3
		1. Designation of Addressee	5
		2. Form of Filing	10
		3. Case Administration	13
	C.	Commencement of the Proceedings and Pendency of the Dispute	15
		1. Statute of Limitations	16
		2. *Lis Pendens*	23
II.	Number of Copies		41
III.	The Content of the Statement of Claims		44
	A.	Mandatory Content under Austrian Law	44
	B.	Required Content under the Vienna Rules	46
		1. Article 9(3)(a): The Designation of the Parties and their Addresses	53
		2. Article 9(3)(b): Specific Claim and Particulars	57
		3. Article 9(3)(c): The Amount in Dispute	59

			Para.
		4. Article 9(3)(d) and (e): Specifics Regarding the Arbitrator(s)	62
	C.	Additional Considerations	64
		1. Language of the Statement of Claims	65
		2. Power of Attorney	68
		3. Payment of Registration Fee	69
IV.	The Agreement Specifying the Jurisdiction of the VIAC		70
	A.	Introduction	70
	B.	*Prima Facie* Scrutiny of the Arbitration Agreement	72
V.	Opportunity to Remedy Defects in the Statement of Claims		80
	A.	Introduction	80
	B.	Failure to Provide the Arbitration Agreement	82
	C.	Refusal to Proceed with the Case	84
VI.	Refusal to Administer the Case		88
	A.	Introduction	88
	B.	Improper Deviation from the Vienna Rules	91
	C.	Procedure	97
	D.	Consequences of the VIAC's Refusal	100

I.   FILING THE STATEMENT OF CLAIMS

Article 9(1): Arbitral proceedings are commenced when a statement of claims is filed with the Secretariat. The proceedings become pending on receipt of the statement of claims by the Secretariat.

A.   INTRODUCTION

9-001 The first procedural step in most institutionalized arbitrations is the submission of a document variably referred to as the 'request for arbitration' or the 'notice of arbitration',[1] or, in the case of the Vienna Rules, the 'statement of claims'. All of these documents serve the same basic functions as a civil complaint or writ in national litigation. They notify the respondent that the action has been brought and formally mark the commencement of the arbitration, including its pendency for Statute of Limitations purposes. In addition, these documents typically identify the claimant's claims (with more or less particularity) and the relief requested, make reference to the arbitration agreement as the basis for the tribunal's jurisdiction, and often are required to include the claimant's nomination of an arbitrator or the claimant's position concerning the number, and appointment mechanism, of the arbitrators.[2]

9-002 This chapter sets out the content requirements for the statement of claims under the Vienna Rules and Austrian law. It concentrates, in particular, on describing the role of the Secretary General of the VIAC as the parties' first point of contact with the institution. The responsibilities of the Secretary General to conduct the *prima facie* scrutiny of the statement of claims are significant. Finally, this chapter discusses the legal consequences of commencing arbitration and creating a 'pending case', including the effect on the Statute of Limitations and the question of *lis pendens*.

B.   FILING THE STATEMENT OF CLAIMS

9-003 The Vienna Rules expressly state that a statement of claims must be addressed to the *Secretariat* of the VIAC. Accordingly, a statement of claims is not served on the respondent(s) when it is initially filed. This requirement – that a statement of claims first be filed only with the VIAC – was chosen for several reasons. First, it allows the Secretary General to determine, at the time that the statement of claims

---

1.   *See* Article 3 ICC Rules; Article 3 UNCITRAL Rules; Article 2 AAA/ICDR Rules and Article 1 LCIA Rules.
2.   This seems to be common ground. *See* Article 3 UNCITRAL Rules; Article 3 ICC Rules and Article 2 AAA/ICDR Rules.

is received, whether this submission complies with the minimum standards set out in Article 9(3).[3] Second, it enables the VIAC Board to determine, when appropriate, whether the parties' arbitration agreement complies with the requirements of Article 9(6) or whether the parties have made agreements deviating irreconcilably with the Vienna Rules.[4] All of this is done before the respondent is notified that the arbitration has been commenced.

After receipt of a statement of claims, the VIAC's initial focus clearly lies on **9-004** ensuring compliance with the formal requirements – in particular with the mandatory requirements set out in Article 9(3) and (4) – under the Vienna Rules. Hence, the Secretary General will (merely) confirm to the claimant that its statement of claims has been received, but will not immediately inform the respondent that a statement of claims has been filed. Instead, the respondent will normally learn of the claim against it only after the Secretary General has determined that the statement of claims formally complies with the Vienna Rules; only following this determination will the Secretary General serve it on the respondent in accordance with **Article 10(1)**. If the Secretary General determines that the statement of claims does not comply with the Vienna Rules, its further treatment will depend on the reason for such non-compliance. The most important cases for arbitral practice are discussed below.

1.   Designation of Addressee

A statement of claims should be addressed to: **9-005**

The Secretariat of the International Arbitral Centre
of the Austrian Federal Economic Chamber
Postfach 319
Wiedner Hauptstrasse 63
1045 Vienna
Austria

The requirement that within the VIAC a statement of claims must be addressed to **9-006** 'the Secretariat' should not be interpreted too narrowly and a failure to address a statement of claims to the Secretariat does not necessarily mean that the arbitration will not go forward. For instance, the VIAC will allow an arbitration to proceed even if the statement of claims is addressed to the Board, to the VIAC itself, or, as

---

3. Such minimum standards are a common feature in the rules of most leading arbitral institutions. *See, e.g.,* Article 4 ICC Rules; Article 1 LCIA Rules; Article 6 DIS Rules and Article 2 AAA/ ICDR Rules. For similarities in Central European arbitral rules *see* Article 21 Polish Rules; Article 13 Croatian Rules; Article 17 Czech Rules; Article 22 Hungarian Rules; Article 28 Slovenian Rules and Article 13 Slovak Rules.
4. *See* **Article 9(6)**, at paras. 088 *et seq.*

the case may, be to the AFEC. Usually, statements of claims that are not filed directly with the Secretariat are passed on to the Secretary General, which is generally sufficient for the commencement of an arbitration. This reflects standard practice of the VIAC. However, the Secretariat is expressly nominated as recipient under the Vienna Rules, and any other service of the claim might open debate on the issue of pendency.

9-007   Difficulties also can arise when a statement of claims is addressed to an incorrect recipient that does not or cannot automatically forward it to the Secretary General, for instance, when a statement of claims is directed to the national committee of the ICC (that happened to be located at the same address as the VIAC), or to another arbitral institution. Occasionally, statements of claims are sent to the VIAC's address to the 'arbitration court' or to 'the arbitration tribunal'. If a statement of claims and the underlying arbitration agreement clearly indicate that the VIAC should administer the arbitration, this should suffice to commence arbitration proceedings. Additionally, the Secretary General can, when in doubt, request the claimant to clarify its statement of claims within a set period of time.

9-008   As discussed, the Vienna Rules do not provide for the direct submission of a statement of claims to the respondent or to the respondent's counsel. This follows from the necessity that, pursuant to the Vienna Rules, the Secretary General should perform his *prima facie* scrutiny of the statement of claims before it is transmitted to the respondent. In practice, it is sometimes the case that a statement of claims is erroneously delivered directly to the respondent (or to respondent's counsel), who might then bring it to the attention of the VIAC. In such cases, the standard practice of the present Secretary General has been not to consider this as proper notice for commencing the arbitration. Hence, the respondent will only be notified in accordance with the Vienna Rules once the Secretary General is satisfied that the statement of claims complies with the Vienna Rules.

9-009   In any event, the Vienna Rules do not obligate the respondent to reply to a statement of claims that was delivered to it directly by the claimant. Only the proper notification by the Secretary General triggers the time period for the respondent to submit the memorandum in reply, pursuant to **Article 10**.

2.   Form of Filing

9-010   The Vienna Rules do not specify the form of submission for a statement of claims. It is established practice that the Secretary General applies the form requirements set out in **Article 13(2)**. Accordingly and by analogous application, a statement of claims can be submitted in writing by registered letter, fax or courier service. In the past, alternative means of submitting a statement of claims have been rejected. If a statement of claims were submitted in electronic form, the Secretary General usually would request that the claimant provide a hard-copy version of the submission. However, in view of the recent amendment of the Vienna Rules, **Article 13** now allows for 'means of communication that guarantee evidence of transmission'.[5] Perhaps, this should open the door for a more flexible approach in administering electronic submissions. Notwithstanding the paramount importance of electronic submissions, in practice, statements of claims are almost always submitted in hard-copy format (even if they are additionally submitted electronically).

The Vienna Rules do not specifically state that a statement of claims must be **9-011** signed by the claimant or its representative.[6] Therefore, a signature on a statement of claims usually will not be requested. Indeed, as a signature is not a mandatory requirement under Article 9(3) and (4), and its absence cannot prevent the statement of claims from being processed.

Additionally, it is not mandatory that a statement of claims be expressly labelled as **9-012** such. Accordingly, parties frequently refer to their initial submissions as a 'notice' or 'request' of arbitration, or use similar titles. Under the principle of *falsa demonstratia non nocet*, false terminology should be irrelevant, so long as the statement of claims meets the mandatory requirements of Article 9 in terms of informational content.

3.   Case Administration

Upon receipt of a statement of claims, the Secretary General will assign a file **9-013** number to the case and will insert the case into the internal list of pending cases.

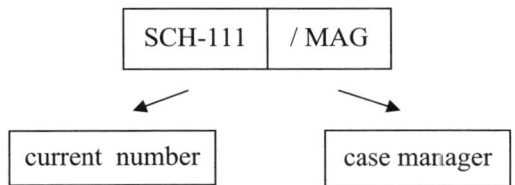

Each case's file number carries the abbreviation 'SCH' for the German word for **9-014** 'arbitration' (*'Schiedsverfahren'*), along with a consecutive number. After the number there are several letters, which indicate the case manager appointed to the case. This unique file number remains with the case until the end of the arbitral proceedings. If a counter-claim is filed, or if multiparty proceedings are involved, there will usually be a joint file (meaning that all proceedings are registered under the same file number), or else each claim can receive a separate file number. As the file number identifies the proceedings, it should be included in all written submissions related to a particular VIAC arbitration.

---

5. *See* **Article 13**, at paras. 031 *et seq.*
6. *See likewise* Article 17(1) Czech Rules; Article 22(1) Hungarian Rules and Article 13(1) Slovak Rules.

C.   COMMENCEMENT OF THE PROCEEDINGS AND PENDENCY
                          OF THE DISPUTE

9-015 Under the arbitration rules of most leading arbitral institutions, arbitration proceedings are commenced when a statement of claims is filed with the relevant institution.[7] The same is true under the Vienna Rules. However, under the Vienna Rules a distinction has been drawn between the date of the commencement of the proceedings and the date that the proceedings become pending. The former occurs when a statement of claims is *filed*, while the latter occurs when the statement of claims is effectively *received* by the Secretariat. The time difference between dispatch and receipt might often be marginal. However, the distinction can be of particular relevance when statutes of limitations or the pendency of the dispute are concerned.

1.   Statute of Limitations

9-016 When a claim is filed with an arbitral institution, a regular question of great practical importance arises: Does this filing interrupt the Statute of Limitations? When arbitral proceedings are commenced, there are several moments in time that could conceivably serve as the point where the Statute of Limitations is interrupted (e.g. when the claim is initially filed, when it is received by the arbitral institution, when it is delivered to the respondent, when the arbitral tribunal is constituted, etc.).

9-017 Article 9(1) states that proceedings are *pending* as soon as the statement of claims is *received* by the Secretariat. This concept clearly derives from Austrian notions regarding pending disputes, whereby as soon as a state court receives a claim, a concrete procedural relationship (between the court and plaintiff) is established and the Statute of Limitations is interrupted according to Section 1497 ABGB.[8] This interruption of the Statute of Limitations occurs as soon as the claimant has, from its point of view, done 'everything necessary' (*'alles aus seiner Sicht Notwendige'*) to commence the arbitration proceedings.[9] Accordingly the

---

7. *See* Article 4(2) ICC Rules; Article 6(1) DIS Rules; Article 3(2) CIDRA Rules and Article 1(2) LCIA Rules.
8. *See* M. Bydlinski in *Kommentar zum ABGB, II/1*, P. Rummel (ed.) (3rd edn, Vienna, Manz, 2002), Section 1497, para. 6; W. Dehn in *Kommentar zum ABGB*, H. Koziol, P. Bydlinski and R. Bollenberger (eds) (Vienna/New York, Springer, 2005), Section 1497, para. 5.
9. P. Oberhammer in *Das neue Schiedsrecht – Schiedsrechts-Änderungsgesetz 2006*, B. Kloiber, W.H. Rechberger, P. Oberhammer and H. Haller (eds) (Vienna, Manz, 2006), p. 202; I. Welser, 'Vermischte Fragen aus der schiedsgerichtlichen Praxis' in *Festschrift Heinz Krejci, II*, E. Bernat, E. Böhler and A. Weilinger (eds) (Vienna, Verlag Österreich, 2001), p. 1892. Note that under Austrian law settlement talks could lead to a toll of the Statute of Limitations period. *See, e.g.*, OGH, 5 September 1996, 2 Ob 32/95. For a general overview on Statute of Limitations under Austrian law, *see* H. Koziol and R. Welser, *Bürgerliches Recht I* (13th edn, Vienna, Manz, 2006), pp. 224 *et seq.*; M. Bydlinski in *Kommentar zum ABGB, II/1*, P. Rummel (ed.) (3rd edn, Vienna, Manz, 2002), Sections 1451 *et seq.*, pp. 556 *et seq.*

Statute of Limitations is interrupted when the Secretariat of the VIAC *receives* the statement of claims.[10]

According to Austrian jurisprudence, proceedings before an arbitral tribunal can **9-018** also interrupt the limitations period.[11] However, it is debatable if this also applies to cases where the statement of claims is filed with an arbitral tribunal that ultimately lacks jurisdiction in the subject matter. Under Austrian law, the interruption of the Statute of Limitations will only take effect if the claim is filed with a competent court that has jurisdiction in the matter.[12] The Explanatory Notes to the new Austrian Arbitration Act note that where the arbitral tribunal was found to lack jurisdiction, the Statute of Limitations will remain interrupted, provided that the claim is subsequently filed with the national court without *unjustified* delay.[13] This is inferred by reference to 5 Ob 30/66, 31 March 1966.[14] However, in 8 Ob A 60/03m, 28 August 2003, the Austrian *Oberster Gerichtshof* clearly ruled to the contrary. The court held that in case the claim is filed with an arbitral tribunal that lacks jurisdiction 'the Statute of Limitations is not interrupted from the very beginning'.[15] The Austrian *Oberster Gerichtshof* reached its decision mainly with reference to

---

10. In OGH, 18 March 2004, 2 Ob 53/04i, the Austrian *Oberster Gerichtshof* argued that *unless the parties have agreed otherwise* the dispute becomes pending only when the statement of claims has been received by the respondent. As parties under the Vienna Rules have incorporated all the provisions, including Article 9(1), this provision can be seen as such an agreement between the parties with regard to the pendency of the dispute. This is also in line with initially proposed amendment of Section 1497 ABGB: 'If the right is to be asserted in an arbitration, then the interruption shall occur at the point in time at which the defendant or a third party, *including an institution*, who is appointed for this according to the arbitration agreement, receives the written request for the institution of the arbitral proceedings (Section 580 ZPO). (. . .).'
11. OGH, 31 March 1966, 5 Ob 30/66.
12. W. Dehn in *Kommentar zum ABGB*, H. Koziol, P. Bydlinski and R. Bollenberger (eds) (Vienna/ New York, Springer, 2005), Section 1497, para. 5.
13. *See* Explanatory Notes to Section 584(4).
14. *See* OGH, 31 March 1966, 5 Ob 30/66. The dispute arose out of a sales contract for seeds; the claim was filed with the Permanent Court of Arbitration of the Chamber of Commerce of Lower Austria. The arbitral tribunal rendered its arbitral award dividing damages between claimant and respondent. As the arbitral award was successfully set aside, claimant sued respondent for damages with the state courts. The Austrian *Oberster Gerichtshof* held that where the arbitral award is set aside due to the tribunal's violation of mandatory provisions of the substantive law, the Statute of Limitations remains interrupted, provided that the claim is subsequently filed with the state court without *unjustified* delay. Although the published facts of this decision do not make clear why the arbitral tribunal effectively lacked jurisdiction, some Austrian scholars have adopted the view expressed in the Explanatory Notes. *See* B. Kloiber and H. Haller in *Das neue Schiedsrecht – Schiedsrechts-Änderungsgesetz 2006*, B. Kloiber, P. Oberhammer, W.H. Rechberger and H. Haller (eds) (Vienna, Manz, 2006) p 24.
15. Free translation of the authentic German text: 'Die Schiedsklage beim unzuständigen Schiedsgericht unterbrach daher von allem Anfang an die Verjährung nicht.'

Section 261(6) ZPO, indicating that a transferral from the forum lacking jurisdiction to the correct forum (e.g. state court to arbitral tribunal or *vice versa*) was not foreseen under Austrian procedural law.[16]

9-019 The new arbitration law addresses this issue with respect to the interplay of the arbitration agreement and the state courts. Section 584(4) ZPO, which also applies when the place of arbitration is not within Austria or has not yet been determined,[17] provides the following:

> When an action is rejected by a court of law due to jurisdiction of an arbitral tribunal or by an arbitral tribunal due to jurisdiction of a court of law or of another arbitral tribunal or when in proceedings for the setting aside of an award an arbitral award is set aside due to lack of jurisdiction of the arbitral tribunal, the proceedings shall be deemed to be orderly continued if the action is immediately brought to the competent court of law or arbitral tribunal.

9-020 This passage clarifies on a statutory basis that the Statute of Limitations is interrupted even when an incompetent forum is first invoked.[18] To avoid preclusion however, the requirement of an immediate subsequent filing with the competent court or tribunal remains. The exact timing of this second filing has been deliberately left unspecified.[19]

9-021 It is and remains subject to debate if proceedings are considered to properly have become pending and the Statute of Limitations therefore interrupted if the statement of claims fails to satisfy the requirements of Article 9(3) and (4) in part or in full. The 1996 version of Article 9 provided in this regard that 'the provisions of the second sentence of paragraph 1 [identical to actual Article 9(1)] shall not be affected if the statement of claims is defective or incomplete or if copies of documents or enclosures are missing'. The current version no longer contains such clarification. This, however, does not render a defective statement of claims

---

16. *See also* A. Fremuth-Wolf in *Arbitration Law of Austria: Practice and Procedure*, S. Riegler, A. Petsche, A. Fremuth-Wolf, M. Platte and C. Liebscher (eds) (Huntington, Juris Publishing, 2007), Section 584, p. 197.
17. *See* Section 577(2) ZPO.
18. *See* A. Reiner, 'SchiedsRÄG: Wissenswertes zum neuen österreichischen Schiedsrecht' [2006] ecolex, 468.
19. *Reiner* is of the opinion that a period of two months 'will always suffice'. *See* A. Reiner, *Das neue österreichische Schiedsrecht/The new Austrian Arbitration Law* (Vienna, LexisNexis, 2006), Section 584, note 59; B. Kloiber and H. Haller in *Das neue Schiedsrecht – Schiedsrechts-Änderungsgesetz 2006*, B. Kloiber, P. Oberhammer, W.H. Rechberger and H. Haller (eds) (Vienna, Manz, 2006) p. 24. The Working Group initially suggested a three months period – proposed amendment of Section 1497(2) ABGB: 'The interruption shall continue if, within three months after a decision with which the arbitral tribunal denies its jurisdiction becomes unappealable, or with final and binding force of a court decision on the lack of jurisdiction of an arbitral tribunal, an action is brought before a court. This applies *mutatis mutandis* if a court dismisses an action because the subject-matter is the subject-matter of an arbitration agreement.'

without legal effect. In Austrian state court proceedings, in case a defective but curable complaint is filed, the judge will set a time limit in which the party can remedy the defects. If the party complies and remedies these defects in time, then the statement of claims is deemed to have been submitted in due form at the initial time of its filing. The corollary is that – in case the remedy is fully complied within a timely manner – the Statute of Limitations continues to be interrupted.[20] Similarly, insofar as the claimant complies in time with the Secretary General's instructions to cure the defects, the claimant should be able to benefit from the date of the original filing for the purpose of the limitation period.[21] Thus, as even a faulty statement of claims results in administered activity, the proceedings have arguably become pending.

However, even where parties comply with the time-limits for the submission of a **9-022** statement of claims under Article 9, the submission may still be declared inadmissible under the law governing the substance of the contract.[22] This relates to the question whether time-limits are classified as matters of procedure, arguably to be governed by the law of the place of arbitration, or as matters of substance, governed by the law applicable to the merits. Civil law countries, like Austria, tend to classify provisions relating to time-limits as substantive, while the approach of common law countries was to treat questions relating to time-limits as procedural.[23] However, the modern tendency in common law countries is also to classify foreign laws governing time-limits as matters of substance.[24] A typical example of the potential relevance of this distinction will be where the law governing a contract provides that actions in respect of damages must be brought within a certain time-limit. Apart from complying with the relevant procedural rules, arbitrators, when ruling on the merits of a dispute arising out of such contract, will have to decide on a failure to meet those deadlines by applying the consequences of that failure as prescribed by the law governing the contract.[25]

---

20. *See* OGH, 6 December 1984, 8 Ob 70/84. There is no ground for the extension of such time limit. *See* A. Konecny, 'Zur Erweiterung der Verbesserungsvorschriften durch die Zivilverfahrens-Novelle 1983' [1984] JBl, 13, 19; *see* OGH, 6 December 1984, 8 Ob 70/84 more grounds in E. Gitschthaler in *Kommentar zur ZPO*, W.H. Rechberger (ed.) (3rd edn, Vienna/New York, Springer, 2006), Sections 84-85, para. 11.
21. *See* **Article 9(5)**, at para. 087.
22. E. Gaillard and J. Savage (eds), *Fouchard Gaillard Goldman On International Commercial Arbitration* (The Hague, Kluwer Law International, 1999), para. 1216.
23. J. Lew, L. Mistelis and S. Kröll, *Comparative International Commercial Arbitration* (The Hague, Kluwer Law International, 2003), paras. 20-10 *et seq.*; *See* also P. Schlosser, *Das Recht der internationalen privaten Schiedsgerichtsbarkeit* (2nd edn, Tübingen, Mohr Siebeck, 1989), para. 436.
24. A. Redfern, M. Hunter, N. Blackaby and C. Partasides, *Law and Practice of International Commercial Arbitration* (4th edn, London, Sweet & Maxwell, 2004), paras. 4-04 *et seq.*
25. E. Gaillard and J. Savage (eds), *Fouchard Gaillard Goldman On International Commercial Arbitration* (The Hague, Kluwer Law International, 1999), para. 1216.

2.   *Lis Pendens*

9-023 The doctrine of *lis pendens* in general provides a basis for suspending or staying legal proceedings in light of other pending proceedings that involve the same or very similar parties, issues, or relief.[26] The main concern is to avoid situations in which two (equally final and enforceable but perhaps contradicting) decisions exist within the same legal system.[27] *Lis pendens* traditionally forms part of the domestic procedural arsenal of countries with well-developed legal traditions.[28] However, no universally accepted concept of *lis pendens* exists on the international level,[29] providing a clearly defined rule in what cases the doctrine applies and what the precise consequences are. Diverging decisions in different legal cultures, creating legal uncertainty, are the result. What is more, there is no generally accepted terminology. It seems, however, that in legal doctrine the terms *lis pendens*[30] and *lis alibi pendens*[31] are used interchangeably; with the term *lis alibi pendens* more often being used in common law jurisdictions and *lis pendens* in civil law countries.[32]

9-024 For the principle of *lis pendens* to be applicable, the following three criteria have been identified:[33] (i) the disputes deal with the same (relevant) subject matter,

---

26. A. S. Bell, *Forum Shopping and Venue in Transnational Litigation* (Oxford, OUP, 2003); J.J. Fawcett (ed.), *Declining Jurisdiction in Private International Law* (Oxford, OUP, 1995); B.A. Garner, *Black's Law Dictionary* (8th edn, St. Paul, Thomson West, 2004) explains the concept as referring to a 'lawsuit [that] is pending elsewhere'.
27. While the principle of *lis pendens* deals with parallel proceedings, *res judicata* deals with the effects that prior decisions have to subsequent proceedings. The term *res judicata* refers to the general doctrine that an earlier and final adjudication by a court or arbitration tribunal is conclusive in subsequent proceedings involving the same subject matter or relief, the same legal ground and the same parties. It is described as a consequence of the principle of finality. Without the notion of *res judicata*, no dispute could ever be solved and the parties would be tempted to resubmit their claims to the same or a different forum in case of defeat. *See* Interim Law Association, Berlin Conference (2004) '*Res judicata* and Arbitration', p. 2; E. Geisinger and L. Lévy, '*Lis Alibi Pendens* in International Commercial Arbitration' (2003) ICC Ct Bull Special Supplement: Complex Arbitration, p.53, 55.
28. C. Söderlund, 'Lis Pendens, Res Judicata and the Issues of Parallel Judicial Proceedings' (2005) 22(4) J Int'l Arb, 301.
29. F. Kremslehner, '*Lis Pendens* and *Res Judicata* in International Commercial Arbitration' in *Austrian Arbitration Yearbook 2007*, C. Klausegger *et al.* (eds) (Vienna, Manz, 2007), p. 128.
30. *Lis pendens*, *e.g.*, in P. Schlosser, 'The 1968 Brussels Convention and Arbitration' (1991) 7(3) Arb Int'l, 238.
31. *Lis alibi pendens*, *e.g.*, in E. Geisinger and L. Lévy, '*Lis Alibi Pendens* in International Commercial Arbitration' (2003) ICC Ct Bull Special Supplement: Complex Arbitration, 53.
32. The term *litis pendens* is mentioned mostly to describe 'the time during which a lawsuit is pending'. According to the rule of *litis pendens*, it is possible that an arbitral tribunal posterior to another arbitral tribunal concerned with the same relevant subject matter has to reject the request for arbitration.
33. F. Kremslehner, '*Lis Pendens* and *Res Judicata* in International Commercial Arbitration' in *Austrian Arbitration Yearbook 2007*, C. Klausegger *et al.* (eds) (Vienna, Manz, 2007), pp. 134-136.

(ii) they are between the same parties and (iii) they involve the same cause of action. Concerning the first prerequisite, the term 'subject matter' may not only include the factual and legal basis of a claim, but also the specific relief sought. The connotation of the term 'relevant' differs among the legal cultures. In civil law systems, it is theoretically possible to force a court to rehear a case if a new action is based on additional factual allegations, or on new grounds of action, or on another relief. The common law approach looks at the 'cause of action', which in England is understood to comprise all claims that are based on substantially the same facts and evidence. In summary, the scope of the 'same relevant subject matter' is conceivably narrower in civil law than in common law jurisdictions.

On the second premise, the term 'same parties' includes the claimant and the **9-025** respondent of the proceedings *in personam*. In common law jurisdictions, the binding effects even include parties that are closely related to the dispute, for example, partners of a partnership as well as beneficiaries and trustees under the law of England and Wales. In civil law jurisdictions, such parties are typically not bound by the principle of *lis pendens*. On the third premise, in civil law jurisdictions, the 'cause of action' is usually understood broadly as the legal grounds that justify a claim and the relief requested in an action. However, there is no prevalent consensus whether the term also includes the factual grounds on which the claim is based.

The doctrine of *lis pendens* can operate in various contexts in which two or more **9-026** parallel or subsequent proceedings take place: trials before state courts, proceedings before a national state court and an arbitral tribunal as well as proceedings before arbitral tribunals.[34] The doctrine of *lis pendens* was initially developed to deal with concurrent proceedings in front of different national state courts on a national level. In this context, in civil law jurisdictions[35] usually a 'first-in-time

---

34. F. Kremslehner, '*Lis Pendens* and *Res Judicata* in International Commercial Arbitration' in *Austrian Arbitration Yearbook 2007*, C. Klausegger *et al.* (eds) (Vienna, Manz, 2007), pp. 127 *et seq.*

35. *See, e.g.*, in Switzerland the rule of *lis pendens* forms part of the public policy and is embodied in Article 9 IPRG. It was disputed, whether the concept of *lis pendens* applies in relation between foreign state courts and arbitral tribunals. Legal authorities were undecided on this issue. *See* M. Scherer, 'When Should an Arbitral Tribunal Sitting in Switzerland Confronted with Parallel Litigation Abroad Stay the Arbitration?' (2001) 19(3) Bull ASA, 451. The Swiss *Bundesgericht* has now ruled that Article 9 IPRG does apply to arbitration proceedings. *See* BGer, 14 May 2001, BGE 127 III 279, (2001) 19(3) Bull ASA, 555. 'An arbitral tribunal sitting in Switzerland must stay the arbitration proceedings if the same matter is pending between the same parties abroad and if the foreign decision could be recognized in Switzerland.' If there are two arbitration proceedings pending within Switzerland legal authorities apply Section 35 GestG *per analogiam*. According to this provision, the state court to which the claim was filed subsequently, has to reject the claim, if the prior court or arbitral tribunal has confirmed its jurisdiction. *See*, B. Berger and F. Kellerhals, *Internationale und interne Schiedsgerichtsbarkeit in der Schweiz* (Bern/Vienna, Stämpfli Verlag/Manz, 2006), para. 638.

rule' applies,[36] meaning the court where the proceedings start first, has jurisdiction over the subject matter. Courts in common law jurisdictions are prepared to focus more on substantive justice,[37] attempting to settle the dispute in the most suitable forum.[38] On the international level, *lis pendens* related issues have been addressed in international treaties and conventions; within Europe there has been a notable success in harmonizing the pertinent rules, culminating in Article 27 of Council Regulation (EC) No. 44/2001, also providing for a 'first-in-time rule'.[39]

9-027 When applied in settings involving state courts and arbitral tribunals, there is a broad consensus on the international level to employ a strong *favor arbitri* in conflicts between arbitral tribunals and state courts. Some authors have even argued that the dogmatic basis for this preferential treatment of arbitration is such as to render the doctrine of *lis pendens* unnecessary.[40] That doctrine is

---

Germany applies a narrow concept of *lis pendens* not permitting the analogous application of Section 263(3) no. 1 German ZPO, but addressing the issue under Section 1032(3) German ZPO. *See* A. Baumbach, W. Lauterbach, J. Albers and P. Hartmann, *Zivilprozessordnung* (66th edn, Munich, C.H. Beck, 2008), Section 1032, para. 10. In case the dispute is pending before the arbitral tribunal prior to the state court there is no express provision in the German ZPO. The corollary is parallel proceeding, a situation deliberately accepted by the German legislature. *See* V. Triebel and T. Coenen, 'Parallelität von Schiedsverfahren und staatlichem Gerichtsverfahren' Supplement 5 to (2003) BB, 1; *also* P. Schlosser, *Das Recht der internationalen privaten Schiedsgerichtsbarkeit* (2nd edn, Tübingen, Mohr Siebeck, 1989), para. 616.

36. F. Kremslehner, '*Lis Pendens* and *Res Judicata* in International Commercial Arbitration' in *Austrian Arbitration Yearbook 2007*, C. Klausegger *et al.* (eds) (Vienna, Manz, 2007), p. 133.

37. *See also* International Law Association, Toronto Conference (2006), 'Final Report on *Lis Pendens* and Arbitration', p. 5.

38. In common law jurisdictions this is sometimes referred to as the doctrine of *forum non conveniens*. This theory is premised on the doctrine that for every dispute there is a natural claimant, a natural defendant and a natural forum. There have to be strong arguments to allow a claimant to litigate the case in a different forum. *See also* F. Kremslehner, '*Lis Pendens* and *Res Judicata* in International Commercial Arbitration' in *Austrian Arbitration Yearbook 2007*, C. Klausegger *et al.* (eds) (Vienna, Manz, 2007), p. 132.

39. Article 27 Council Regulation (EC) No. 44/2001 provides: (1) 'Where proceedings involving the same cause of action and between the same parties are brought in the Courts of different member states, any court other than the court first seized shall of its own motion stay its proceedings until such time as the jurisdiction of the court first seized is established. (2) Where the jurisdiction of the court first seized is established, any court other than the court first seized shall decline jurisdiction in favour of that court.'

40. *See Award in ICC Case No. 5103 of 1988* (1988) JDI, 1207 (*lis pendens* is only applicable to concurrent judicial proceedings, not arbitration); International Law Association, Toronto Conference (2006), 'Final Report on *Lis Pendens* and Arbitration', Sections 1.7-9. ('There is (...) limited need to have a rule which determines which of two legitimate *fora* should proceed to determine the dispute, because the jurisdiction of the Arbitrator will trump the jurisdiction of any court.'); E. Geisinger and L. Lévy, '*Lis Alibi Pendens* in International Commercial Arbitration' (2003) ICC Ct Bull Special Supplements: Complex Arbitration, 53 ('*lis alibi pendens* (...) presupposes that the two courts have equal jurisdiction. In arbitration, on the other hand, there can be no question of two equally competent bodies: (...) one of the main legal

premised on the existence of two presumptively competent *fora* (e.g. two competing state courts),[41] whereas in the constellations under consideration here, by definition, only the arbitral tribunal is competent[42] if a valid arbitration agreement exists.

This *favor arbitri*, whenever there is a (valid) arbitration agreement, is enshrined **9-028** prominently in the New York Convention which prescribes in Article 2(3)[43] that court proceedings should be dismissed on the basis of an arbitration agreement.[44] The European Convention even expressly addresses the subject of *lis pendens* for cases in which the arbitration proceedings have been commenced prior to state court proceedings. Article VI(3) of the European Convention provides:[45]

> Where either party to an arbitration agreement has initiated arbitration proceedings before any resort is had to a court, courts of Contracting States subsequently asked to deal with the same subject-matter between the same parties or with the question whether the arbitration agreement was non-existent or null and void or had lapsed, shall stay their ruling on the arbitrator's jurisdiction until the arbitral award is made, unless they have good and substantial reasons to the contrary.[46]

---

consequences of such an [arbitration] agreement is precisely that it evicts the jurisdiction of national courts.').

41. G.B. Born and P.B. Rutledge, *International Civil Litigation in United States Courts* (4th edn, New York, Aspen Publishers, 2007), p. 522.

42. In the words of C. Söderlund, '*Lis Pendens, Res Judicata* and the Issue of Parallel Judicial Proceedings' (2005) 22(4) J Int'l Arb, 321, 'state court proceedings and arbitral proceedings are conducted, as it were, in different realms as a necessary outflow of their separate underpinnings'.

43. NY Convention, **Annex 11**.

44. A. J. van den Berg, *The New York Arbitration Convention of 1958* (The Hague, Kluwer Law International, 1981), pp. 129 *et seq.*, explains that this provision entails a stay of the state court proceedings on the merits and has the effect of a partial incompetence of the court. *See* A. Redfern, M. Hunter, N. Blackaby and C. Partasides, *Law and Practice of International Commercial Arbitration* (4th edn, London, Sweet & Maxwell, 2004), para. 1-147. The same is true for most national laws (*see* Article 8 UNCITRAL Model Law). If the litigation is not dismissed, any resulting judgment is in violation of the agreement to arbitrate (and the NY Convention), and should not be entitled to any preclusive effect in the arbitral proceeding. *See* G.B. Born, *International Commercial Arbitration – Commentary and Materials* (3rd edn, The Hague, Kluwer Law International, forthcoming), ch. 16.

45. European Convention, **Annex 10**.

46. *See* P.I. Benjamin, 'Notes – The European Convention on International Commercial Arbitration' (1961) 37 Brit YB Int'l L, 478, 489 *et seq.*; D.T. Hascher, 'European Convention on International Commercial Arbitration of 1961 – Commentary' (1990) XVYB Comm Arb, 624, 646 *et seq.*

9-029 The same mindset is further reflected in arbitral practice, including under the ICC Rules,[47] in line with the predominant view among arbitration practitioners that international arbitrators have a 'duty to proceed with the arbitration irrespective of the pendency of a judicial proceedings or injunctions contesting [their] (...) jurisdiction'.[48] This approach is also mirrored in Article 8(2) of the UNCITRAL Model Law which states that when an action before a national court is brought while arbitral proceedings are ongoing, the latter may nevertheless be continued and an award may be made, while the issue is pending before the court.[49]

9-030 In line with this strong *favor arbitri* on the international level, the general principle in Austrian arbitration law is also that in case of pending arbitral proceedings (*Schiedshängigkeit*), the state courts' or another arbitral tribunal's jurisdiction is excluded.[50] Section 584(3) ZPO provides:

> When an arbitration procedure is pending, no other legal dispute may be carried out before a court or an arbitral tribunal on the asserted claim. Any action brought on the grounds of the same claim[51] is to be rejected. This shall not apply if an objection to the jurisdiction of the arbitral tribunal was raised to the arbitral tribunal at the latest together with entering an appearance in the case and a decision of the arbitral tribunal on this matter cannot be obtained within a reasonable period of time.

9-031 According to the third sentence of this provision, notwithstanding such arbitration proceedings, an Austrian state court might not reject the same claim in case the (timely raised) objection against the arbitral tribunal's jurisdiction cannot be obtained within a reasonable period of time. How long an arbitral tribunal can

---

47. W.L. Craig, W.W. Park and J. Paulsson, *International Chamber of Commerce Arbitration* (3rd edn, New York, Oceana Publications, 2000), p. 170.
48. Except possibly in the case of a direct order emanating from a competent court at the seat of the arbitration. *See* Y. Derains and E.A. Schwartz, *A Guide to the ICC Rules of Arbitration* (2nd edn, The Hague, Kluwer Law International, 2005), p. 108; W.L. Craig, W.W. Park and J. Paulsson, *International Chamber of Commerce Arbitration* (3rd edn, New York, Oceana Publications, 2000), p. 171.
49. Paragraph 1 provides that the national court before which an action is brought in a matter which is the subject of an arbitration agreement shall (if a party so requests) refer the parties to arbitration (unless it finds that the agreement is null and void, inoperative or incapable of being performed). *See* J. Lew, L. Mistelis and S. Kröll, *Comparative International Commercial Arbitration* (The Hague, Kluwer Law International, 2003), para. 14-20.
50. B. Kloiber and H. Haller in *Das neue Schiedsrecht – Schiedsrechts-Änderungsgesetz 2006*, B. Kloiber, P. Oberhammer, W.H. Rechberger and H. Haller (eds) (Vienna, Manz, 2006), p. 23; I. Welser, 'Pitfalls of Competence' in *Austrian Arbitration Yearbook 2007*, C. Klausegger *et al.* (eds) (Vienna, Manz, 2007), p. 15.
51. Even though not explicitly mentioned in the wording of Section 584(3) ZPO, the identity of the parties must be considered an implicit element of the 'same claim' in line with the generally acknowledged criteria for the application of the *lis pendens* doctrine.

in fact 'reasonably' wait with its decision on jurisdiction, has been left open,[52] the Explanatory Notes only refer to Article 6 ECHR in this regard.[53] The basic idea of this provision is to prevent parties from initiating arbitral proceedings just to obstruct the pursuit of the claim with the state court. Hence, under these circumstances, two parallel proceedings based on the grounds of the same claim are conceivable.[54]

The strong *favor arbitri* of the Austrian legislature is also clearly mirrored in Section 584(1) ZPO. The last sentence of this paragraph provides that, notwithstanding pending state court proceedings (*Streitanhängigkeit*), arbitration proceedings may be commenced or continued and an award may be made.[55] Thus, the Austrian legislature's 'arbitration friendly' approach even permits parallel state court and arbitration proceedings in this case.[56] This provision is supported by two fundamental ideas regarding the jurisdiction of the arbitral tribunal. First, an arbitration proceeding cannot be impeded by a court proceeding. On the other hand, the state court has the last word on the existence or non-existence of an arbitration agreement.[57] Hence, once the court's decision on the arbitral tribunal's jurisdiction has become final, the arbitral tribunal is bound by it. Also, in case a state court (or a foreign court whose decision is to be recognized in Austria) renders a final and binding judgment in the subject matter, an arbitral tribunal is bound by the *res judicata* effect and may not decide in the same subject matter, constituting grounds for challenge according to Section 611(2) no. 8 ZPO.[58] **9-032**

As seen from the wording of Section 584(3) ZPO, this provision also applies to the third area of the doctrine's scope of application, parallel proceedings before two arbitral tribunals. Compared to the area of application just discussed, there is much less reference to this constellation in international instruments. However, the ILA Final Report on *Lis Pendens* and Arbitration (Toronto Conference 2006) **9-033**

---

52. *See* discussion under **Article 19**, at para. 019. Once pendency of the dispute has been established, the mere inactivity of the arbitrators will not adverse this effect. *See* OGH, 2 October 2003, 6 Ob 41/03b.
53. *See* Explanatory Notes to Section 584 ZPO.
54. Critical A. Reiner, *Das neue österreichische Schiedsrecht/The new Austrian Arbitration Law* (Vienna, LexisNexis, 2006), Section 584, note 58.
55. The assessment of pendency is independent with whether proceedings between the same parties are pending before the two domestic courts or a domestic court and an arbitral tribunal. *See* OGH, 24 September 1992, 6 Ob 533/92.
56. B. Kloiber and H. Haller in *Das neue Schiedsrecht – Schiedsrechts-Änderungsgesetz 2006*, B. Kloiber, P. Oberhammer, W.H. Rechberger and B. Haller (eds) (Vienna, Manz, 2006) p. 23; I. Welser, 'Pitfalls of Competence' in *Austrian Arbitration Yearbook 2007*, C. Klausegger *et al.* (eds) (Vienna, Manz, 2007), p. 15.
57. *See* C. Liebscher, *The Austrian Arbitration Act 2006: Text and Notes* (The Hague, Kluwer Law International, 2006), Annotated Text to Section 584 ZPO.
58. *See* A. Fremuth-Wolf in *Arbitration Law of Austria: Practice and Procedure*, S. Riegler, A. Petsche, A. Fremuth-Wolf, M. Platte and C. Liebscher (eds) (Huntington, Juris Publishing, 2007), Section 584, p. 190.

recently addressed this issue. Together with the clear provision in Section 584(3), its recommendations in Resolution No. 1/2006 provide useful guidance for arbitral tribunals seated in Austria.

9-034 As discussed, the first sentence of Section 584(3) ZPO clearly provides that '[w]hen an arbitration procedure is pending, no other legal dispute may be carried out before (. . .) an arbitral tribunal on the asserted claim. Any action brought on the grounds of the same claim is to be rejected.' Thus, the general rule under Austrian law is that pending arbitral proceedings bar the commencement of parallel arbitral proceedings on the 'same claim'.[59]

9-035 The meaning of this term in Section 584(3) ZPO is not explicitly defined by the legislature or Austrian commentary discussing this provision. It is best understood, however, in line with the concept of 'matter in dispute' (*Streitgegenstand*) used in connection with other provisions of the ZPO, such as Section 411 (which deals with *res judicata*).[60] As applied by the Austrian *Oberster Gerichtshof, Streitgegenstand* is a three-tier concept consisting of the (i) factual predicate, (ii) prayer for relief, and (iii) legal categorization of the type of matter (if specified by the claimant).[61] This approach results in a narrow understanding of the 'matter in dispute',[62] such that two proceedings will only rarely really concern the 'same claim'. Only if this strict standard is met in a particular case, the rigid 'first-in-time rule', provided for in Section 584(3) ZPO applies.

9-036 However, whenever these narrow criteria are not met, there is still room for arbitral tribunals seated in Austria to be guided by the ILA's recommendations in their decision how to deal with such 'parallel proceedings in a broader sense'. The latter are defined in the ILA recommendations as 'any other proceedings pending before (. . .) another arbitral tribunal in which the parties and one or more of the issues are

---

59. J. Power, *The Austrian Arbitration Act – A Practitioner's Guide to Sections 577-618 of the Austrian Code of Civil Procedure* (Vienna, Manz, 2006), Section 584, para. 8.
60. The use of the term in connection with Section 411 ZPO is especially instructive, because of the close connection to the notion of *lis pendens*; just *see* International Law Association, Toronto Conference (2006), 'Final Report on *Lis Pendens* and Arbitration', *sub* I, 1.4.
61. W. H. Rechberger and T. Klicka in *Kommentar zur ZPO*, W. H. Rechberger (ed.) (3rd edn, Vienna/New York, Springer, 2006) Introduction to Section 226, paras. 14 *et seq.* F. Kremslehner, '*Lis Pendens* and *Res Judicata* in International Commercial Arbitration' in *Austrian Arbitration Yearbook 2007*, C. Klausegger *et al.* (eds) (Vienna, Manz, 2007), pp. 127, 142, considers only circumstances in which 'each of the arbitrators deals with the same factual and legal issues and the same claims and the same request for relief between the same parties' as 'obvious' cases of the *lis pendens* doctrine's application.
62. To the contrary the International Law Association, Toronto Conference (2006), 'Final Report on *Lis Pendens* and Arbitration', *sub* V.B, 5.6. explicitly states that Recommendation 1 defines 'parallel proceedings in terms of parties and issues that are the same or substantially the same, rather than in terms of the triple identity test (of identical parties, causes of action and relief)'.

the same or substantially the same as the ones before the arbitral tribunal in the Current Arbitration'.[63] In the case of such parallel proceedings in a broader sense, the ILA recommendations on *lis pendens* should be looked to by the arbitrators 'as reference for sound case management'.[64]

For these situations, the ILA does not advocate a rigid 'first-in-time rule' but **9-037** emphasizes that the arbitral tribunal should have 'considerable discretion to order a stay of the arbitration on such terms as it sees fit'.[65] This flexible approach is mirrored in Recommendation No. 5 of Resolution No. 1/2006, which provides for cases in which parallel proceedings have been commenced prior to the arbitration in question[66] and are pending before a separate arbitral tribunal,

> the arbitral tribunal should decline jurisdiction or stay the Current Arbitration, in whole or in part, and on such conditions as it sees fit, for such duration as it sees fit (such as until a relevant determination in the Parallel Proceedings), provided that it is not precluded from doing so under the applicable law and provided that:
> 5.1 the arbitral tribunal in the Parallel Proceedings has jurisdiction to resolve the issues in the Current Arbitration; and
> 5.2 there will be no material prejudice to the party opposing the request because of (i) an inadequacy of relief available in the Parallel Proceedings; (ii) a lack of due process in the Parallel Proceedings; (iii) a risk of annulment or non-recognition or non-enforcement of an award that has been or may be rendered in the Parallel Proceedings; or (iv) some other compelling reason.[67]

However, this is not the end of the analysis an arbitral tribunal seated in Austria **9-038** should apply in case of multiple arbitration proceedings. There is a third step to the cascade of legal standards a tribunal should refer to in dealing with *lis pendens*-related constellations. There can be situations which do not even correspond to this wider notion of 'parallel proceedings'.[68]

---

63. International Law Association Resolution No. 1/2006, Annex 1 at para. 1, <http://www.ila-hq.org>
64. F. Kremslehner, '*Lis pendens* and *Res Judicata* in International Commercial Arbitration' in *Austrian Arbitration Yearbook 2007*, C. Klausegger *et al.* (eds) (Vienna, Manz, 2007), pp. 127, 145.
65. International Law Association, Toronto Conference (2006), 'Final Report on *Lis Pendens* and Arbitration', *sub* V.B., 5.10.
66. This first in time argument does not seem to appear in the Recommendation regarding a stay for procedural efficiency reasons.
67. International Law Association Resolution No. 1/2006, Annex 1 at para. 5, <http://www.ila-hq.org>.
68. International Law Association, Toronto Conference (2006), 'Final Report on *Lis Pendens* and Arbitration', *sub* IV.B, 4.47 mentions as examples 'arbitrations between the same parties raising different claims, albeit closely related', or 'arbitrations between the same parties in which each relies on different formulations of the agreement to arbitrate', or a 'situation (. . .) where closely related disputes are running in parallel between parties that are not identical'.

9-039 Also for this third scenario, the ILA has proposed criteria designed to strike a reasonable balance in view of procedural efficiency considerations. Recommendation No. 6 of its Resolution No. 1/2006 contemplates the stay of an arbitration proceeding where a similar but not parallel proceeding is taking place[69] 'as a matter of sound case management, or to avoid conflicting decisions, to prevent costly duplication of proceedings or to protect a party from oppressive tactics'.[70] In this 'case management' or 'procedural efficiency' scenario, the arbitral tribunal may stay its proceedings so long as it is:

> 6.1 not precluded from doing so under applicable law;
> 6.2 satisfied that the outcome of the other pending proceedings or settlement process is material to the outcome of the Current Arbitration; and
> 6.3 satisfied that there will be no material prejudice to the party opposing the stay.[71]

9-040 The Committee emphasized that a stringent standard should be applied when scrutinizing whether these prerequisites are given in a specific case: '(...) the Committee envisages such power [to stay the proceedings] being exercised very sparingly'.[72]

---

69. In the words of International Law Association, Toronto Conference (2006), 'Final Report on *Lis Pendens* and Arbitration', *sub* V.B., 5.11: 'The Committee concluded that arbitral tribunals should have confidence to exercise case management powers and be empowered to stay their own proceedings, even when the situation did not fulfill the traditional criteria of *lis pendens*.'

70. International Law Association Resolution No. 1/2006, Annex 1 at para. 6, <http://www. ila-hq.org>. International Law Association, Toronto Conference (2006), 'Final Report on *Lis Pendens* and Arbitration', *sub* IV.B, 4.49 states that 'in some circumstances [of similar but not parallel proceedings], arbitral efficiency and doing justice between the parties should persuade tribunals to stay their own proceedings'. And it reads *sub* V.B, 5.7 that the Committee 'recognized the important policy objectives of arbitral efficiency, the avoidance of conflicting decisions, and the avoidance of costly duplication and oppressive tactics (...)'. *See also* K. Hobér, 'Parallel Arbitration Proceedings – Duties of the Arbitrators' in *Parallel State and Arbitral Procedures in International Arbitration*, B. Cremades and J. Lew (eds) (Paris, ICC Publishing, 2005), p. 254. ('In situations where all the different tribunals are equally appropriate, or where the claimants have legitimate interests to pursue all the different proceedings (...) joinder of additional parties to an existing dispute or consolidation of separate proceedings would generally appear as the most efficient way of coordinating parallel or multiple proceedings.').

71. International Law Association Resolution No. 1/2006, Annex 1 at para. 6, <http://www. ila-hq.org>. *See also* D. Bensaude, 'The International Law Association's Recommendation on *Res judicata* and *Lis Pendens* in International Commercial Arbitration' (2007) 24(4) J Int'l Arb, 415, 422, who considers this Recommendation to be 'of substantial assistance to arbitrators (...) [which] help to guide their thinking'.

72. International Law Association, Toronto Conference (2006), 'Final Report on *Lis Pendens* and Arbitration', *sub* V.B.5.11.

II. NUMBER OF COPIES

Article 9(2): One copy of the statement of claims together with enclosures must be submitted for each Respondent, arbitrator and the Secretariat.

This provision was already contained in the former version of the Vienna Rules,[73] **9-041** and it reflects a practical concern about the dissemination of the statement of claims and enclosures. Although a statement of claims does not need to contain other content than required by Article 9(3) and (4), statements of claims and related enclosures can be quite extensive and voluminous. In such cases, it would be impractical to burden the institution with doing large scale copying work that is the responsibility of the claimant.

As Article 9(5) contains a direct reference to 'copies of documents or missing **9-042** enclosures'; the claimant can therefore expect that if it fails to provide sufficient copies after it is given an opportunity to remedy the situation, its case may not proceed.

It is possible that at the commencement of the proceedings, the exact number of **9-043** arbitrators is uncertain, as it may not have been specified in the arbitration agreement. If the claimant wants a three-person tribunal, it will be requested to provide an appropriate number of copies. If the VIAC Board subsequently decides the number of arbitrators under **Article 14**, and if the claimant did not originally provide enough copies for the fully constituted tribunal, the Secretary General will also request the claimant to provide sufficient copies.[74]

III. THE CONTENT OF THE STATEMENT OF CLAIMS

Article 9(3): The statement of claims must include:

(a) The designation of the parties and their addresses;
(b) A specific statement of claims and the particulars and supporting documents on which the claims are based;
(c) The amount in dispute at the time of submission of the statement of claims, unless the claims are not related exclusively to a specific sum of money;

---

73. Article 6(2) Vienna Rules 2001, **Annex 2a**.
74. As a request of this sort will only be made after the statement of claims has been delivered to the respondent, it is debatable if, in the event of non-compliance by the claimant, the VIAC can refuse to proceed with the arbitration. In any event, however, the claimant is well advised not to risk a bad first impression with the tribunal when asked to provide sufficient copies of his statement of claims.

(d) **Particulars regarding the number of arbitrators in accordance with Article 14;**

(e) **If a decision by three arbitrators is requested, the nomination of an arbitrator and the address of that person.**

A.   MANDATORY CONTENT UNDER AUSTRIAN LAW

9-044 What is required – and equally important, what is permitted – content of the document initiating the arbitration may vary depending on the parties' arbitration agreement,[75] applicable institutional rules[76] and applicable national law.[77] Any or all of these sources may require that a request for or notice of arbitration includes specified information.

9-045 National arbitration legislation sometimes addresses the contents of a request for arbitration (at least in *ad hoc* arbitrations, where the parties have not agreed otherwise). In general, national laws impose relatively few requirements with regard to the request for arbitration. For example, under French law, a request for arbitration must (unless otherwise agreed) state an unequivocal intention to refer a dispute to arbitration (but is not required to include much else).[78] Under German law, which amended the UNCITRAL Model Law in this regard, a request for arbitration must set forth the parties, the nature of the dispute and a reference to the arbitration agreement.[79] Under Austrian law, Section 597(1) ZPO provides that the claimant shall state its claim and the facts supporting its claim. Further, the parties may submit with their statements all documents they consider to be relevant or may add a reference to the documents or other evidence they will submit. However, as opposed to proceedings before courts, arbitration proceedings do not necessarily commence with an action. In *ad hoc* proceedings, arbitration proceedings might already begin with the receipt of a demand to appoint an arbitrator

---

75. Arbitration agreements generally do not impose requirements for the contents of a request for arbitration. Occasionally, an arbitration agreement will require that the request for arbitration nominate a co-arbitrator or (less frequently) identify the alleged dispute and the exhaustion of contractual ADR procedures.

76. *E.g.*, Article 3(3) UNCITRAL Rules and Article 4(3) ICC Rules.

77. Civil law systems and practice will often favor more detailed initial notices (or submissions), supported by documentary evidence, while common law systems may incline towards relatively skeletal 'notice' pleading. *See* S. Elsing and J.M. Townsend, 'Bridging the Common Law-Civil Law Divide in Arbitration' (2002) 18(1) Arb Int'l, 59.

78. E. Gaillard and J. Savage (eds), *Fouchard Gaillard Goldman On International Commercial Arbitration* (The Hague, Kluwer Law International, 1999), para. 1213.

79. Section 1044 German ZPO.

pursuant to Section 587(2) ZPO,[80] which on its own might not be sufficient to interrupt the Statute of Limitations.[81]

B.   REQUIRED CONTENT UNDER THE VIENNA RULES

Most arbitral institutions provide mandatory content requirements for statements **9-046** of claim, sometimes suggesting additional information that would be useful to include, such as the place of arbitration,[82] the applicable law or languages of the arbitral proceedings,[83] and information about the parties' legal representatives.[84]

The Vienna Rules' content requirements are in fact more detailed than those under **9-047** both the former and current Austrian arbitration law.[85] Article 9 is mandatory and provides *minimum standards* for a statement of claims. It does not, however, provide guidance as to what is appropriate to include in addition to those mandatory requirements, or indeed what detail is required to satisfy them in the first place. Certainly, the Vienna Rules do not prohibit a party from producing a statement of claims that is more detailed than Article 9(3) requires. On the other hand, it is quite conceivable that the information required – the parties and their addresses; a description of the claim; the amount in dispute; a view on the

---

80. C. Liebscher, *The Austrian Arbitration Act 2006: Text and Notes* (The Hague, Kluwer Law International, 2006), Annotated Text to Section 597 ZPO.
81. *See* G. Zeiler, *Schiedsverfahren* (Vienna/Graz, Neuer Wissenschaftlicher Verlag, 2006), Section 584, p. 112.
82. Article 4(3) ICC Rules; Article 1(1) LCIA Rules; Article 6(2) and (3) DIS Rules; Article 2(3) AAA/ICDR Rules; Article 21(2) Polish Rules; Article 13(2) Croatian Rules; Article 17 Czech Rules; Article 22 Hungarian Rules; Article 28 Slovenian Rules and Article 13 Slovak Rules. By contrast, **Article 2** of the Vienna Rules makes this, in principal, dispensable.
83. Article 4(3) ICC Rules; Article 1(1) LCIA Rules; Article 6(3) DIS Rules; Article 2(3) AAA/ICDR Rules and Article 21(2) Polish Rules.
84. Article 1(1) LCIA Rules; Article 28(1) Slovenian Rules and Article 13(1) Slovak Rules. It is common practice for the Secretary to request proof of power of attorney, *see* **Article 9**, at para. 068.
85. With regard to the former Arbitration law, *Fasching* considered that the required content (in *ad hoc* proceedings) is a written request to the other party to appoint its arbitrator and the indication of one's own arbitrator. *See* H.W. Fasching, *Schiedsgericht und Schiedsverfahren im österreichischen und im internationalen Recht* (Vienna, Manz, 1973), p. 85. A description of the dispute is only required when several disputes exist and doubts could arise about which of them is the subject of the arbitration proceeding. *See* C. Liebscher in *Institutionelle Schiedsgerichtsbarkeit*, R.A. Schütze (ed.) (Cologne, Carl Heymanns Verlag, 2006), p. 274. Likewise, pursuant to Section 587(2) ZPO of the new arbitration law, *ad hoc* proceedings will commence on receipt of a demand to appoint an arbitrator. Pursuant to Section 597 ZPO, the parties may agree, or failing agreement, the arbitrators may determine the period of time within which the claimant shall state its claim and the facts supporting its claim. The parties may submit with their statements all documents which they consider to be relevant, or may add a reference to the documents or other evidence that they will submit.

appropriate number of arbitrators; and, if a decision by three arbitrators is requested, the nomination of an arbitrator – can be submitted only on a few pages. Indeed, a claimant may have good reasons, including tactical ones, to delay the presentation of the full details of its case until a later point in the proceedings – and there is a very credible argument that nothing in the Vienna Rules requires the claimant to prematurely let down its guard in full. However, the claimant will have to consider that holding back *essentialia* to determine the scope and nature of the dispute might result in lack of pendency as, depending on the law applicable to this question, the claim might not have been sufficiently particularized.[86]

9-048 It is instructive in this context to consider the different approach adopted by the UNCITRAL Rules, which contemplate that the claimant will submit, at some point after the notice of arbitration, a 'statement of claim' that more fully describes the legal and factual basis of its claims.[87] In that regard, the Vienna Rules appear to follow more the example of the ICC (or the AAA/ICDR) Rules which contemplate a single document – the request for arbitration – addressing the claim and the requested relief in a more detailed fashion at the outset.[88] Thus, no further pleading is prescribed by the Vienna Rules prior to specific directions from the tribunal on written submissions.

9-049 In practice, however, all of these documents tend to look more or less the same; they all serve the basic purpose of according the respondent a reasonable understanding of the claims brought against it. It is this purpose that should guide the claimant under the Vienna Rules as well. Whatever the tactical considerations may be, providing too little information about the particulars of the facts and thus leaving the respondent in the dark, may provoke discussions of pendency and be perceived as unfair by the tribunal once constituted.[89] Also, the more details provided with the statement of claims, the easier it will be for the parties (or, in the

---

86. *See* **Article 9**, at paras. 057 *et seq.*
87. Article 18 UNCITRAL Rules. The LCIA Rules are to the same effect, *see* Article 15(2) LCIA Rules.
88. Article 4 ICC Rules. *See* W.L. Craig, W.W. Park and J. Paulsson, *International Chamber of Commerce Arbitration* (3rd edn, New York, Oceana Publications, 2000), p. 148; Y. Derains and E.A. Schwartz, *A Guide to the ICC Rules of Arbitration* (2nd edn, The Hague, Kluwer Law International, 2005), p. 41. The AAA/ICDR Rules are similar to the ICC Rules in their contemplation of a single, comparatively-detailed statement of claim (Article 2 AAA/ICDR Rules). The ICC and AAA's approach to the request for arbitration has been criticized on the grounds that the claimant has essentially unlimited time to prepare its request setting forth its claims in detail, while the respondent (under current ICC Rules, *see* Article 9) has only 30 days to prepare what should be an equally detailed reply. *See* G. Wetter, 'The Present Status of the International Court of Arbitration of the ICC: An Appraisal' (1990) Am Rev Int'l Arb, 98 *et seq.*
89. As discussed below, the mandatory contents of the statement of claims are limited, and if a party chooses, it can submit a very 'short-form' document, particularly if it wants to withhold aspects of its case for tactical or other reasons. Experienced arbitral tribunals exercise care to ensure that these sorts of 'ambush' tactics are not permitted to cause unfair surprise and disadvantage. *See*

case of a substitutional appointment, for the VIAC Board) to select a suitable presiding arbitrator.

The claimant may also be well advised to anticipate the influence of different legal **9-050** cultures on the case, in the form of arbitrators, experts and counsel from different legal systems. Thus, the ideal statement of claims will describe the 'relevant facts, agreements and claims in language accessible to lawyers from diverse jurisdictions'.[90] It will often be appropriate to also append the principal documents in the case in addition to the arbitration agreement (together with translations, where necessary).[91] In addition, a thorough statement of claims will often set forth the claimant's legal theory, often in skeleton form, but perhaps with citations to relevant statutes and other authorities, and request particular relief.[92] In general, the statement of claims

> should avoid the types of boiler-plate formalisms that sometimes prevail in domestic litigation. Counsel should strive to produce a document that will be understandable and persuasive to readers from other legal and linguistic backgrounds. (Of course, the request – and other written submissions – must satisfy the formal requirements of the applicable institutional rules, but as discussed above, these requirements are minimal.)[93]

Detailed argumentation, however, is usually left to briefs or memorials at **9-051** subsequent points in the arbitration. It is for the arbitrators to ensure that such further submissions are presented in due course and in the appropriate manner.[94]

Under the current practice of the Secretariat, the VIAC tends towards a liberal **9-052** interpretation of whether statement of claims comply with the relevant provisions of Article 9. Indeed, if a respondent feels that a statement of claims fails to meet the requirements of Article 9, there is little he can do as, in accordance with **Article 10(1)**, the respondent will be served with the statement of claims only *after* the Secretary General has already considered the statement of claims to be in due form. After transmission of the file to it, it will be for the tribunal to address the respondent's procedural complaints.

G.B. Born, *International Commercial Arbitration – Commentary and Materials* (2nd edn, The Hague, Kluwer Law International, 2001), p. 452.

90. *See* G.B. Born, *International Commercial Arbitration – Commentary and Materials* (2nd edn, The Hague, Kluwer Law International, 2001), p. 452.
91. Generally, a party need only attach the principal contract from which the parties' dispute arises and in which the arbitration agreement appears (together with any amendments). *See also* S. Elsing and J.M. Townsend, 'Bridging the Common Law-Civil Law Divide in Arbitration' (2002) 18(1) Arb Int'l, 102.
92. *See* G.B. Born, *International Commercial Arbitration – Commentary and Materials* (2nd edn, The Hague, Kluwer Law International, 2001), p. 452.
93. *See* G.B. Born, *International Commercial Arbitration – Commentary and Materials* (2nd edn, The Hague, Kluwer Law International, 2001), p. 452.
94. *See* **Article 20**, at paras. 133 *et seq.*

1.   **Article 9(3)(a): The Designation of the Parties and their Addresses**

9-053 Besides being an explicit mandatory requirement of the statement of claims, the names and addresses of the parties are essential. Parties to the proceedings against whom an award will be rendered need to be properly identified in order to ensure recognition and enforcement of the final award.[95] In the past the Secretary General has taken a strict approach to the question of who is effectively identified as a party in the statement of claims. Where a party is not a natural person, it is in the claimant's interests to describe the legal nature of the entity and provide a company registration number if available. It might also be helpful, in particular for a substitutional appointment process and attending conflict checks, to include details about the parties' corporate affiliations. Where the party is a natural person, full name and date of birth should be provided.

9-054 The address provided must be sufficiently specified to make service possible. Although providing the respondent's correct address of service is essentially the claimant's responsibility, the VIAC is often able to offer assistance through Austria's Foreign Trade Offices and Embassies or other connections available to the AFEC.[96] Where difficulties in serving documents are anticipated, claimants should keep in contact with the Secretary General.[97]

9-055 In practice, parties sometimes foresee that deliveries (of any kind and in accordance with the contract) may validly be effected if they are submitted to an address expressly stipulated in the contract. It is debatable if, in this case, the claimant can or should be burdened with a respondent party that (intentionally or unintentionally) 'disappears' or whether the mere submission to this address should suffice to validly serve the statement of claims on the respondent. The default rule under **Article 13(2)** does not seem to cover this situation.[98] Section 580(2) ZPO even requires a party to have *actual knowledge* of the arbitration before any default

---

95. The correct identification of the party is of paramount importance, not only at the enforcement stage. As *Aschauer* rightly says, the state court, on application for enforcement of the award, will apply the *lex fori* with regard to procedural matters pursuant to Article III NY Convention. From an Austrian perspective, Section 7 EO, provides that the person against whom the enforcement is sought must be identical to the persons indicated in the enforceable instrument, *e.g.* an arbitral award. *See* C. Aschauer, 'Arbitral Proceedings and the Enforcement of the Award Particularly in Relation to Austrian Law and the Rules of Arbitration of the SCC, the ICC and the Austrian Federal Economic Chamber' (2001) 2 Stockholm Arb Rep, 38; *see also, e.g.*, Article 4(3) ICC Rules ('the name in full, description and address of each of the parties'); Article 1(1) LCIA Rules ('the names, addresses, telephone, facsimile, telex and e-mail numbers (if known) of the parties to the arbitration and of their legal representatives') and Article 2(3) AAA/ICDR Rules ('the names, addresses and telephone numbers of the parties.').

96. *See* **Article 1**, at para. 006.

97. *See* **Article 10**, at para. 008.

98. *See* **Article 13**, at paras. 037 *et seq.*

delivery process can take effect.[99] Given that provision,[100] and assuming that Austrian law is applicable in the specific case, the claimant has a vested interest that respondent has effectively been served the statement of claims and thereby received proper notice of the arbitration proceedings.[101]

In the absence of any other provision, the Vienna Rules give the Secretary General **9-056** discretion as to how many times delivery must be attempted. However, if the claimant continually provides incorrect addresses and thereby delays the delivery process, the Secretary General may increase the deposit of costs under **Article 34(6)**.[102]

2. Article 9(3)(b): Specific Claim and Particulars

The statement of claims should provide at least a brief factual account of the **9-057** dispute. Whether tactical considerations warrant a brief or a more extended statement of claims, the respondent should be put in a position to understand what claims are being raised against him; the dispute needs to be sufficiently particularized. Also, the factual account given in the statement of claims, will help the institution to understand the nature of the dispute and thus appoint the appropriate arbitrator, should this become necessary. There are, however, under the Vienna Rules, no sanctions for the failure to provide a fairly detailed factual account, and the Secretary General is neither required nor entitled to engage in the merits of the case. Parties ought to give special attention to drafting their prayers for relief with precision, as inaccuracies may cause difficulties at a later stage, particularly during the enforcement of any future award.[103]

---

99. Section 580(2) ZPO reads: 'If the addressee has knowledge of the arbitral proceedings, and if, despite reasonable investigation, his residence or the residence of an authorized recipient remains unknown, then any written communication is deemed to have been received, on the day on which a proper delivery was verifiably attempted at a location that was specified at the conclusion of the arbitration agreement or that the addressee subsequently gave to the other party or to the arbitral tribunal as the address and that has not yet been revoked by giving a new address.' In order to ensure due process of law, an attempt of service at the places specified in this provision shall only suffice if the addressee has knowledge of the arbitration. It does not matter how this knowledge was acquired. If a party is not at all reachable, a *curator absentis* can be appointed pursuant to Section 276 ABGB. In this context, one must take into consideration that, according to Section 110 JN, in general Austrian jurisdiction exists only if the party for which a *curator absentis* is supposed to be appointed is an Austrian citizen or has its seat or ordinary residence in Austria. *See* C. Liebscher, *The Austrian Arbitration Act 2006: Text and Notes* (The Hague, Kluwer Law International, 2006), Annotated Text to Section 580(2) ZPO.
100. *See in detail* **Article 13**, at paras. 042 *et seq.*
101. *See* Article V(1)(b) NY Convention, **Annex 11** and Article IX(1)(b) European Convention, **Annex 10**.
102. *See* **Article 10**, at para. 008.
103. *Aschauer* considers this requirement to be inspired by Section 226 ZPO, which requires a specific statement of claims to be indicated for claims at state court. He proposes, *inter alia*, to

9-058 The relevant 'particulars' refer to all necessary factual elements on which the claim is based. However, the English translation 'supporting documents' for the German 'evidence requested' (*'beantragten Beweise'*) is not entirely accurate. The idea that a party would have to 'request evidence' at this stage is an anachronistic remnant of Austrian civil procedure, inappropriate for international arbitration rules. If the claimant does not request in its statement of claims that particular evidence is taken, this does not preclude it from proffering evidence at a later stage.[104] It is advisable to produce at least the disputed contract (if different from the arbitration agreement) with the statement of claims, and indicate that the production of further evidence is reserved for a later stage.

3.   Article 9(3)(c): The Amount in Dispute

9-059 The Vienna Rules, like the rules of most leading arbitral institutions, state that the 'amount in dispute' shall be specified at 'the time of submission of the statement of claims, unless the claims are not related exclusively to a specific sum of money'. Despite the difficulties in assessing the amount in dispute at the beginning of the proceedings (and the sometimes deliberate omission of the amount in dispute, referring to placeholders such as 'damages to be quantified'), the present Secretary General insists on the amount in dispute being specified.

9-060 The claimant should take particular care to provide an accurate assessment. Pursuant to **Article 36(8)**, a reduction of the amount in dispute will only be taken into consideration in calculating the arbitrator's fees and administration costs if the reduction was made prior to the transmission of the files to the arbitral tribunal.

9-061 While specifying the amount in dispute is simple when the prayer for relief demands payment, difficulties may arise where the prayer for relief does not seek payment of a certain sum, e.g. in cases of declaratory claims. In such cases, it is advisable to disclose in the statement of claims the evaluation method used to calculate the amount in dispute. Otherwise the Secretary General may seek further details pursuant to paragraph 5, or, in the case of non-compliance, fix the amount in dispute at his discretion.[105]

---

indicate any amount payable in numbers and not by a proportion or percentage of another amount. Where an order for specific performance is requested, it is advisable to describe the obligation in general and specific terms. Reference is made to OGH, 16 September 1997, 10 Ob 210/97y, where the duty to perform had been phrased inaccurately and later adjustment was not permitted during the enforcement stage. *See* C. Aschauer, 'Arbitral Proceedings and the Enforcement of the Award Particularly in Relation to Austrian Law and the Rules of Arbitration of the SCC, the ICC and the Austrian Federal Economic Chamber' (2001) 2 Stockholm Arb Rep, 38. *See also* C. Liebscher in *Institutionelle Schiedsgerichtsbarkeit*, R.A. Schütze (ed.) (Cologne, Carl Heymanns Verlag, 2006), p. 273.

104. *See* however **Article 20**, at paras. 071 *et seq.* This may also help the Secretary General has to fix the amount of the deposit against the expected cost of the arbitration pursuant to **Article 34(2)**.

105. *See* **Article 36(5)**, at paras. 023 *et seq.*

4. **Article 9(3)(d) and (e): Specifics Regarding the Arbitrator(s)**

Article 9(3)(d) and (e) require the claimant to specify in the statement of claims the **9-062** 'particulars regarding the number of arbitrators in accordance with **Article 14** and, if a decision by three arbitrators is requested, the nomination of an arbitrator and the address of that person'. Arguably, this provision is not a mandatory requirement of the statement of claims. If the claimant fails to address the mechanism for the arbitrator appointment, or to specify the number of arbitrators, **Article 14** will apply by default. In that sense, Article 9(3)(d) affords the claimant an opportunity to participate in the constitution of the tribunal rather than requiring the claimant, strictly speaking, to provide this information. It is therefore debatable whether the Secretary General should refuse to proceed with the case, if the claimant maintains its silence on the points; the better view is that the constitution of the tribunal should follow **Article 14**.

It is rare that a claimant will not make use of its right to nominate an arbitrator. **9-063** Sometimes a claimant merely specifies qualifications for potential arbitrators, such as language requirements and specific additional professional qualifications. Although the claimant cannot unilaterally alter the arbitration agreement and impose conditions for arbitrators on which both parties have not agreed, the VIAC Board will endeavour to take this information into account when administering a substitutional appointment procedure pursuant to **Article 14**. The claimant may also simply reserve the right to nominate an arbitrator at a later stage, and request that it be afforded a certain time to do so, a course of action that is common practice with the present Secretariat. After all, it is in the interest of the claimant to provide a proper statement of claims in order to accelerate the proceedings. Where the number of arbitrators has already been agreed upon in the arbitration agreement, a simple reference to the clause will be sufficient. If the case is that one arbitrator will decide the dispute, the claimant is also entitled to nominate an arbitrator at this stage. Often the other party will not accept this proposal and the substitutional appointment procedure under **Article 14** will be followed.

C. ADDITIONAL CONSIDERATIONS

Besides the content requirements explicitly mentioned in Article 9(3), there are **9-064** other issues that should as a matter of practice be considered when drafting a statement of claims.

1. **Language of the Statement of Claims**

In an earlier version of the Vienna Rules 'the statement of claims had to be drawn **9-065** up in German or in one of the languages of the arbitration agreement'.[106] This

---

106. Article 6(1) Vienna Rules 1996.

mandatory requirement has (deliberately) been omitted in the current version. The reference to the language of the arbitration agreement found in the 1996 version of the Vienna Rules could not match the practical reality of arbitration proceedings. There have been cases where the arbitration agreement was, for example, drafted in French, but the agreed language of the proceedings was English. Under the old Vienna Rules, in a case of that sort, the statement of claims had to be drawn up in German or French, even though the parties for the arbitration had chosen neither of these languages.

9-066 In the current version of the Vienna Rules, there is no indication as to what language the statement of claims should be written in. Where the language of the arbitration is not specified in the arbitration agreement, this can pose difficulties. **Article 6**, which limits correspondence by the parties to German or English, does not appear to apply, as the statement of claims cannot, at first glance, be considered to be 'correspondence' in that sense. However, the Secretary General, who is the first person to receive a statement of claims on behalf of the VIAC, must be in a position to effectively conduct the *prima facie* scrutiny that is described in greater detail below. Thus, although the language of the statement of claims is not prescribed by Article 9(3), it has nevertheless been the Secretary General's practice to return a statement of claims not drafted in English or German and to request that the claimant resubmit the statement of claims in either language, so that the Secretary General may determine whether the contents requirements of Article 9 are met.[107]

9-067 There have also been cases where the claimant filed a statement of claims in a language that the respondent allegedly did not understand. When the language of the arbitration proceedings was not then determined in the arbitration agreement, but the contract itself in the English language, the Secretary General has requested that the claimant provide an English translation of the statement of claims.[108] In light of a party's right to be heard, it is understandable that, at the outset of arbitral proceedings, the VIAC should attempt to ensure that all parties have a reasonable opportunity to learn of the commencement of arbitral proceedings.

2.   Power of Attorney

9-068 Although this is not expressly addressed in Article 9, it is obvious that a party representative, whether a lawyer or not, is entitled to submit a statement of claims on behalf of the claimant.[109] While it is sufficient for Austrian lawyers in litigation before a national court, to simply refer to the power of attorney granted to them

---

107. *See* **Article 6**, at para. 004.
108. In principle, the parties are free to agree upon the language of the proceedings, *see also, e.g.*, Article 16 ICC Rules; Article 17 LCIA Rules; Article 22 DIS Rules; Article 14 AAA/ICDR Rules; Section 20 Polish Rules; Article 9 Hungarian Rules and Article 12 Slovenian Rules.
109. *See* **Article 23**, at paras. 004 *et seq.*

pursuant to Section 8 RAO,[110] representatives in international arbitration are typically required to present an actual copy (or sometimes even an original) of the power of attorney. Indeed, the Secretary General's current practice is to request a copy of the power of attorney when a statement of claims is filed. The failure to provide a power of attorney will not prevent the arbitral proceedings from commencing, however, it is questionable whether the Secretary General is entitled to investigate the status of party representatives. It is arguable that the Secretary General lacks such authority, as Article 9(3) does not require proof of the power of attorney to be submitted along with the statement of claims. It is, nevertheless, advisable for party representatives to comply with this request to avoid delays. The arbitral tribunal will usually ensure that counsels are duly authorized to represent the parties in the proceedings.

3.   Payment of Registration Fee

The registration fee is payable on submission of the statement of claims pursuant to **9-069** **Article 33**. It is recommended, although not required, to provide evidence of payment with the statement of claims in order to expedite the proceedings.[111] Note should be taken that the registration fee is subject to a 10% increase for each additional party, and that cases will not be dealt with until payment is made.[112]

IV.   THE AGREEMENT SPECIFYING THE JURISDICTION
        OF THE VIAC

Article 9(4): A copy of the agreement specifying the jurisdiction of the Arbitral Centre must be attached to the statement of claims.

A.   INTRODUCTION

The mandatory requirement to produce evidence of the VIAC's jurisdiction was **9-070** already contained in the 1996 version of the Vienna Rules.[113] Surprisingly, it did not foresee any sanction in case such document was ultimately not submitted. Even the most recent version is not entirely clear on that point, as the requirement under

---

110. Professional Rules of the Austrian Bar (*Rechtsanwaltsordnung* – RAO 1868), RGBl, No. 96/ 1868 last amended by BGBl No. 68/2008; E. Feil and F. Wennig, *Anwaltsrecht* (4th edn, Vienna, Linde, 2006), pp. 43 *et seq.*
111. *See* Article 1(1) LCIA Rules; Article 17 Czech Rules and Article 13(2) Slovak Rules for an alternative approach.
112. *See* **Article 33(2)**, at para. 006 and **Article 33(4)**, at paras. 009 *et seq.*
113. Article 6(3) Vienna Rules 1996 reads: 'The statement of claims must include the document or documents giving evidence of the jurisdiction of the Centre'.

paragraph 4 has not been explicitly included into those provisions which would entitle the Secretary General to request claimant to remedy such defect.[114]

9-071 Under the new ZPO, the requirements as to the form of an arbitration agreement have been noticeably relaxed.[115] Unlike the rules of most leading arbitral institutions, the Vienna Rules contain no express requirement for the arbitration agreement to be in writing.[116] They do, however, require the parties to produce a *copy* of such an agreement. Thus, the implication is that, in practice, the agreement has to be made in writing or at least be capable of being produced in a written format. Consequently, it seems likely that problems will arise in the future when determining what constitutes an acceptable *copy* of an agreement. Ultimately, this leads to the question on how to proceed in case the arbitration agreement has been concluded in a different manner than in written format or is (intentionally or unintentionally) 'lost' before the proceedings have even commenced. On its face, the Vienna Rules seem to exclude the possibility of witnesses to evidence the existence of the arbitration agreement. Given the relaxation of the form requirement for the valid conclusion of arbitration agreements under Austrian law, any form that provides proof of the existence of the VIAC's jurisdiction should arguably be sufficient.

B.   *Prima Facie* Scrutiny of the Arbitration Agreement

9-072 Before it proceeds with administrating an arbitration referred to it, the VIAC must ensure that it has the proper jurisdiction within the meaning of **Article 1** to administer with the dispute.[117] Therefore, the institution needs to establish at the earliest possible stage in the proceedings that the arbitration agreement in question properly refers to the Vienna Rules. It follows that in order for the VIAC to conduct this *prima facie* assessment, the claimant must attach a copy of the agreement to its statement of claims or at least provide sufficient evidence in favour of this assessment.[118] The Vienna Rules do not sufficiently allocate the task of this

---

114. *See* discussion under **Article 9(5)**, at paras. 080 *et seq.*
115. *See* discussion under **Article 1**, at paras. 063 *et seq.*
116. *See, e.g.*, Article 7(2) UNCITRAL Model Arbitration Law; Introduction to LCIA Rules; Article 1(1) AAA/ICDR Rules and the 'Form of agreement' attached to the DIS Rules.
117. *See* W. Melis, 'Function and Responsibility of Arbitral Institutions' (1991) XIII Comp L YB Int'l Bus 113. The VIAC itself has no adjudicating function and no jurisdiction in the strict legal sense of the word as meaning the authority, in terms of the scope and subject matter, to decide a dispute. *See* discussion under **Article 1**, at paras. 001 *et seq.*
118. A similar, more direct approach can be found in Article 1(6) Hungarian Rules: 'The Arbitration Court considers the existence of its jurisdiction on its own motion. The jurisdiction of the Arbitration Court includes the ability to determine the existence or lack of its own jurisdiction and furthermore, to judge an objection concerning the existence or the validity of an agreement to submit a legal dispute to arbitration. (...) A decision of the Arbitration Court according to

prima facie assessment. As this task is not expressly conferred upon the VIAC Board, it is therefore, pursuant to **Article 5(2)**, for the Secretary General to undertake.

The Vienna Rules in general, and Article 9(4) in particular, are also silent with respect **9-073** to the manner and scope of the required *prima facie* scrutiny of the arbitration agreement with regard to the VIAC's jurisdiction. No procedure is prescribed, no guidelines are available, and no sanctions can be determined. This is in marked contrast to other institutional rules.[119] Article 6 of the ICC Rules, for example, provides a clear procedure, allocating the authority to make a *prima facie* decision on jurisdiction to the ICC Court. Specifically, according to Article 6(2) of the ICC Rules, in case the respondent does not file an answer to the request or if one party raises one or more pleas concerning the existence, validity or scope of the agreement, the court may decide, if it is *prima facie* satisfied that a valid agreement exists, that the proceedings shall continue. All this is without prejudice to the admissibility or the merits of the plea(s). It is then for the arbitral tribunal to rule on its own jurisdiction. As *Derains/ Schwartz* point out, the ICC Court almost always sets arbitrations in motion, even if, for example, the arbitration agreement was not included in a signed but only in a draft contract.[120] In reality, 'it is extremely unusual for a party to file a request for arbitration with the ICC in the absence of any evidence at all of an arbitration agreement'.[121] The same is true for proceeding under the Vienna Rules.

In addition, while such *prima facie*-powers are not expressly specified in the **9-074** Vienna Rules, they appear to be implied.[122] As the relationship between the parties and the arbitral institution is of a contractual nature, the VIAC can only be required to perform its administrative tasks under such terms as are initially set out in its offer to contract under the Vienna Rules.[123] As already discussed, this contract establishes duties for both the VIAC (as the agent) and the parties to the dispute (jointly as the principal) on the terms expressed in the Vienna Rules. By virtue of this contract the VIAC, for example, in the course of the substitutional appointment procedure, concludes the arbitrator's contract on behalf of the parties, with the implicit authority of each individual party as enshrined in the arbitration

---

which a contract is considered as invalid does not imply *ipso iure* the invalidity of an agreement to submit a legal dispute to arbitration.'

119. *See, e.g.*, Article 16(1) Rules of Arbitration of the Court of International Commercial Arbitration attached to the Chamber of Commerce and Industry of Romania.

120. *See* Y. Derains and E.A. Schwartz, *A Guide to the ICC Rules of Arbitration* (2nd edn, The Hague, Kluwer Law International, 2005), pp. 83 *et seq.*

121. Y. Derains and E.A. Schwartz, *A Guide to the ICC Rules of Arbitration* (2nd edn, The Hague, Kluwer Law International, 2005), p. 83.

122. *See* C. Liebscher in *Arbitration Law of Austria: Practice and Procedure*, S. Riegler, A. Petsche, A. Fremuth-Wolf, M. Platte and C. Liebscher (eds) (Huntington, Juris Publishing, 2007), p. 622.

123. *See* K. Heller, 'Die Rechtsstellung des Internationalen Schiedsgerichts der Wirtschaftskammer Österreich' [1994] wbl, 105, 111.

agreement. In practical terms, therefore, the parties are forced to accept the services of the VIAC once the Vienna Rules are agreed upon, and the VIAC is in principle under an obligation to administer the arbitration.[124] Most fundamentally, this includes an assessment on the part of the VIAC, as one of the contracting parties, whether the dispute falls within the terms of its jurisdiction under **Article 1** of the Vienna Rules. *Melis* has taken the following view:

> The power of an arbitral institution is based on the existence of a valid arbitration agreement. It is, for this reason, its duty to verify the existence of such an agreement. It shall, therefore, only accept a case when the claimant gives *prima facie* evidence of the existence of a valid arbitration agreement (. . .) [VIAC should] refuse to accept a case if the claimant is unable to produce a document which is, at least, of such a nature as to indicate that the jurisdiction of the institution is not impossible.[125]

9-075 The difficulty for any institution is to determine what constitutes sufficient *prima facie* evidence of the existence of an arbitration agreement. In any case, the overriding principle must be that it is ultimately only for the tribunal to determine its jurisdiction. Indeed, both **Article 19** of the Vienna Rules and Section 592(1) ZPO reserve such jurisdictional decisions to the arbitrators. Also, at the point in time the VIAC considers its *prima facie* jurisdiction – which is before the statement of claims is served on the respondent – it cannot even know whether or not the respondent will raise a jurisdictional objection in the first place. When determining whether to accept the administration of a dispute, an arbitral institution should therefore exercise great caution not to interfere with the authority of the tribunal to determine its jurisdiction. It is the parties' right to have such decision rendered by the tribunal rather than the institution. In case of doubt, therefore, the arbitral institution should accept to administer an arbitration and leave it to the arbitrators to resolve any uncertainty or dispute as to jurisdiction.

9-076 *Melis* describes this institutional caution well when he argues that any document is sufficient 'which is, at least, of such a nature as to indicate that the jurisdiction of the institution is not impossible'.[126] There is much to be said in favour of a negative test. Rather than requiring the institution to take an affirmative view on whether there is jurisdiction, it should merely satisfy itself that jurisdiction is not outright impossible. That is also in line with the practice of other arbitral institutions. The ICC, for example, has in the past set arbitrations in motion 'unless it is evident that there is no ICC arbitration agreement between the parties'.[127] For example, clauses

---

124. *See* discussion under **Article 1**, at paras. 021 *et seq.*
125. W. Melis, 'Function and Responsibility of Arbitral Institutions' (1991) XIII Comp L YB Int'l Bus, 113.
126. *See* W. Melis, 'Function and Responsibility of Arbitral Institutions' (1991) XIII Comp L YB Int'l Bus, 113.
127. Y. Derains and E.A. Schwartz, *A Guide to the ICC Rules of Arbitration* (2nd edn, The Hague, Kluwer Law International, 2005), p. 79.

referring to 'arbitration in Paris in the chamber of arbitration,' 'a Commission of Arbitration of French Chamber of Commerce, Paris' or 'the Geneva Court of International Arbitration' were held to be 'sufficiently valid' to be administered under the ICC Rules.[128] On this issue, the Austrian *Oberster Gerichtshof* ruled in 1989[129] that in case of doubt it is 'always the arbitration institution that is typically chosen in international commerce that has been meant'.[130]

That way, the institution is not drawn into the merits of the dispute, on a question such as: is the arbitration agreement valid; was it signed by authorized persons; or is the particular dispute referred in this instance arbitrable? All of these questions, and many others going to the core of any jurisdictional issue, are for the arbitrators to decide. Thus, only if the claimant fails to specify any jurisdictional basis so that the jurisdiction is 'impossible', should the institution deny administration of the case. **9-077**

In such cases, it is the practice of the VIAC to inform the claimant. If the claimant insists on proceeding, the VIAC may still defer this question to the tribunal, at the claimant's obvious risk to be liable for costs. *Melis* has suggested that **9-078**

> the refusal to accept a case can create hardship for a party. In practice, an arbitral institution should attempt first to obtain agreement of the parties which confirms their jurisdiction. If this is not possible, the institution might accept the case and constitute a tribunal, provided that the claimant, in full knowledge of the risks which this involves, makes such an application.[131]

Questions arise as to the claimant's remedies if the VIAC wrongfully refuses to administer the case, incorrectly assuming that it lacks jurisdiction. There is no precedent on this point in Austria. If one accepts the contractual nature of the relationship between the parties and the institution, it is conceivable that a party able to show that jurisdiction in fact exists could apply to the Austrian courts requesting the VIAC to perform its obligations and administer the arbitration.[132] The consequence of the claimant's failure to provide documents evidencing the arbitration agreement is discussed in the following section. **9-079**

---

128. *See* Y. Derains and E.A. Schwartz, *A Guide to the ICC Rules of Arbitration* (2nd edn, The Hague, Kluwer Law International, 2005), p. 86.
129. OGH, 5 October 1988, 3 Ob 58/88.
130. Free translation of the authentic German text: 'Die Vereinbarung eines Schiedsgerichtes der vorliegenden Art entspricht nämlich im Ost-West-Handel einer ständigen Übung (..), sodaß im Zweifel immer die im internationalen Verkehr typische institutionelle Schiedsgerichtsbarkeit gemeint ist'.
131. W. Melis, 'Function and Responsibility of Arbitral Institutions' (1991) XIII Comp L YB Int'l Bus, 114.
132. *See* discussion under **Article 9(6)**, at paras. 100 *et seq.*

V.   OPPORTUNITY TO REMEDY DEFECTS IN THE
                                STATEMENT OF CLAIMS

**Article 9(5): If the statement of claims does not comply with the provisions
of paragraph 3 of the present Article or if copies of documents or enclosures are missing, the Secretary General shall request the claimant to
remedy the defect or to submit the necessary documents or enclosures.
The claimant is to be informed that until the defects have been remedied,
the claim shall not be processed.**

A.   INTRODUCTION

9-080   The rules of most leading arbitral institutions allow the claimant to remedy
        defective statement of claims.[133] Similarly, the Vienna Rules require the
        Secretary General to accord the claimant the opportunity to remedy any defect
        of the statement of claims by providing the information required by Article 9(3)
        lit (a) to (e) that was missing when the statement of claims was originally filed.
        Further, as discussed, other defects that may lead to the request for remedy include
        the absence of a translation of the arbitration agreement,[134] and the failure to pay the
        registration fee.

9-081   The Secretary General has no discretion in the matter, except as to set out appro-
        priate time limit, and must invite the claimant to do so. The time limit usually
        granted is fifteen days, depending on the kind of defect or missing information,
        with a discretion to grant an extension under **Article 13**.[135] Unsurprisingly, an
        extension is more likely to be granted where information regarding the address of
        the parties or arbitrators is missing than, for example, if the claimant consistently
        refuses to reveal the standards of evaluation of its claim.[136]

---

133. Article 6(4) DIS Rules; Article 29(5) Polish Rules; Article 19(1) Czech Rules; Article 24(1)
     Hungarian Rules; Article 28(3) Slovenian Rules and Article 15(1) Slovak Rules.
134. As already mentioned, the claimant, in line with **Article 6**, has to ensure that the arbitration
     agreement is translated into English or German. It can be argued that the language requirement
     is not part of the requirement catalogue of paragraph 3. Hence, if arbitration proceedings are
     agreed to be conducted in another language, it would not be mandatory to provide the arbi-
     tration agreement even for partial translation. As already discussed, in so far as jurisdiction of
     the VIAC is concerned, this will be deemed to be part of the correspondence with the VIAC,
     consequently **Article 6** has to apply to the arbitration agreement accordingly. *See* **Article 6**,
     at para. 004.
135. The international arbitration practice varies, for instance, Article 19(1) Czech Rules and
     Article 15(1) Slovak Rules limit the additional time limit up to 2 months; Article 28(3) Slo-
     venian Rules provides 15 days, whereas Article 24(1) Hungarian Rules limits up to 60 days;
     Article 4(4) ICC Rules solely refers to the submission of copies and payment of advance
     administrative costs.
136. The second sentence of this paragraph has been amended in 2006. The wording of former
     Article 6(5) Vienna Rules 2001, **Annex 2a**, referred to remedy 'within the time limit(s)' which

B.   FAILURE TO PROVIDE THE ARBITRATION AGREEMENT

Provision of a copy of the arbitration agreement is currently not a mandatory **9-082**
requirement under Article 9(3). Instead, it is mentioned separately in Article
9(4) which could give rise to the argument that, if no proof of the arbitration
agreement is provided, the Secretary General cannot request the claimant to
remedy this defect.

On the other hand however, a copy of the arbitration agreement is vital for the **9-083**
VIAC to determine its *prima facie* jurisdiction. Such a copy can therefore be
considered a 'supporting document' for the purposes of Article 9(3)(b) and
thus, as a mandatory attachment to the statement of claims. Although admittedly,
such an interpretation would run contrary to the plain words of Article 9, it has the
better argument for it.[137] Difficulties would arise in the application of Article 9
(and in particular Article 9(6)) if the Secretary General did not have the power to
request proof of the arbitration agreement (and, failing the provision of sufficient
proof, the right to refuse to administer the case under Article 9(5)). Indeed, prior to
the transfer of the files to the arbitration tribunal, only the Secretary General can
advise the Board that the parties' arbitration agreement deviates from the Vienna
Rules.

C.   REFUSAL TO PROCEED WITH THE CASE

Under the former Article 6(5), the Secretary General had the authority to 'delete **9-084**
the case from the list of pending cases' if the claimant did not remedy the defects
of the statement of claims upon request. This raised a number of questions regarding the then Secretary's authority as an administrative organ to effectively refuse
access to legal protection. *Fasching* considered whether the 'deletion of the list'
was comparable to the instrument of the withdrawal of a claim without prejudice
(*Klagsrücknahme ohne Anspruchsverzicht*) or the dismissal of a claim with
prejudice (*Klagszurückweisung*). Although *Fasching*, on the basis of a historical
interpretation of the statute, construed the deletion from the list as a dismissal of the
claim with prejudice,[138] the better view was to allow a re-filing of the claim.
Indeed, according to Article 17a of the Vienna Rules 2001,[139] the deletion from
the list of pending cases was not an inherent obstacle to properly re-filing the claim

---

lead to the conclusion that more prolongations of the time limits were permissible and that
different time limits for various defects could in fact be granted.

137. This provisions should therefore be included in the catalogue of mandatory requirements of
Article 9(5).
138. *See* H.W. Fasching, 'Kostenvorschüsse zur Einleitung schiedsgerichtlicher Verfahren' [1993]
JBl, 545, 558 *et seq.*
139. Vienna Rules 2001, **Annex 2a**.

at a later stage; and construing the deletion as a sanction with prejudice would not have done justice to the administrative character of the decision which simply seeks to sanction a claimant's failure to properly pursue its claim.

9-085 In any event, the sanction of deleting a case from the list of pending cases was abolished in light of new Section 608 ZPO, which exhaustively lists the ways arbitral proceedings may be terminated.[140] Instead, in line with the rules of most leading arbitral institutions,[141] if a claimant fails to remedy the defects, the claim will simply not proceed.[142]

9-086 Thus, for as long as the defects of the statement of claims remain unresolved, the claim will not go forward, hence, it will not be served on the respondent, nor will there be any substitutional appointment procedure of the arbitral tribunal. *Arguendo e contrario*, the claimant can (at any later stage) reactivate the claim by remedying the defects identified by the Secretary General. Given that the Secretary General lacks the power to terminate the proceedings,[143] the claimant has virtually unlimited time to keep the proceedings at such a stage alive. In many ways, it would make more sense in such a case to require the claimant to file an entirely new statement of claims, rather than re-activating the defective old one.

---

140. *See* G. Zeiler, *Schiedsverfahren* (Vienna/Graz, Neuer Wissenschaftlicher Verlag, 2006), Section 608, p. 251. According to Section 608 the arbitral proceedings may be terminated by the award on the merits, by an award by consent, or by an order of the arbitral tribunal in case the claimant fails to file its claim, the claimant withdraws its claim (unless the respondent objects thereto and the arbitral tribunal recognizes a legitimate interest on its part in obtaining a final settlement of the dispute), the parties agree on the termination of the proceedings and communicate this to the arbitral tribunal or the arbitral tribunal finds that the continuation of the proceedings has become impossible, in particular when the parties so far active in the proceedings, do not continue the arbitral proceedings despite a written request from the arbitral tribunal, in which it refers to the possibility of termination of the proceedings.

141. For instance, in case of non-compliance, Article 6(4) DIS Rules declares the proceedings *terminated*; or Article 4(4) ICC Rules: 'In the event that the Claimant fails to comply with either of these requirements, the Secretariat may fix a time limit within which the Claimant must comply, failing which the file shall be closed without prejudice to the right of the Claimant to submit the same claims at a later date in another Request.'
    Different approaches can be found, *e.g.*, in Article 19(2) Czech Rules where notwithstanding the correction of his claim 'the Plaintiff can insist on continuation of the proceedings' or according to Article 15(2) Slovak Rules where claimant can insist 'that the dispute be heard'.

142. *See* **Article 33(4)**, at paras. 009 *et seq.*, regarding the claimant's failure to meet his financial obligation to pay the registration fee, or, **Article 34(3)**, at paras. 029 *et seq.*, the amount of deposit.

143. This is not the case in *ad hoc* proceedings. Here, Section 600 ZPO permits the arbitral tribunal to terminate the proceedings in case the claimant fails to file his statement of claim in accordance with Section 597(1).

If the Secretary General sets time limits, the claimant must observe them, or else **9-087** run the risk of raising the question whether the dispute has become pending or whether he has duly pursued the proceedings, which is under Austrian law, a requirement to benefit from the interruption of the Statute of Limitations.[144]

VI.   REFUSAL TO ADMINISTER THE CASE

Article 9(6): The Board can refuse to carry out proceedings if the parties have designated the International Arbitral Centre of the Austrian Federal Economic Chamber in the arbitration agreement but have made agreements that deviate from the Vienna Rules.

A.   INTRODUCTION

Arbitral institutions are often confronted with arbitration agreements which differ **9-088** markedly from the model agreements proposed by the institution, or indeed from what is customary in Austrian or international arbitration practice. Parties' motivations to amend the recommended model agreements differ and do not always seem to be the result of diligent consideration. Parties are well advised to use the institution's model clause as a starting point, and deviate from the template suggested by the institution only with caution and with the advice of experienced arbitration counsel.

Deviations from the model clause create a tension between the procedural flexi- **9-089** bility rightly expected by parties to be one of the hallmarks of arbitration and the expectation of legal certainty and predictability of the institution. On the one hand, parties should be given the opportunity to tailor the arbitral process to their specific needs without being trapped in a corset of predetermined procedural rules; and most rules specifically allow the parties to 'provide otherwise' and thus modify the default regime set forth in the institutional rules. On the other hand, an institution wants to retain a measure of freedom to refuse the administration of a particular case in particular procedural circumstances, in order not to be forced to administer an arbitration governed by rules which irreconcilably conflict with its own tried and tested procedures.

Of course, for an institution to refuse the administration of a case is a serious **9-090** sanction. It may deprive the parties of the possibility to arbitrate and eventually force them into state courts against their will. In practice, therefore, while some major institutions contain provisions similar to Article 9(6), the VIAC and other

---

144. *See* OGH, 29 June 1995, 2 Ob 50/95, *see also* the discussion about Statute of Limitations, **Article 9**, at paras. 016 *et seq.*

institutions rarely ever invoke their right to refuse administration on that ground.[145] Much will depend therefore on the degree of the amendment or variation, and whether the arbitration resulting from such an agreement cannot be administered, or is otherwise truly incompatible with the spirit of the institutional rules.

B.   IMPROPER DEVIATION FROM THE VIENNA RULES

9-091 Article 9(6) is clearly intended to vest the Board with the power to refuse the administration of arbitrations which cannot be administered due to agreements that 'deviate from' the Vienna Rules. The former version of Article 9(6) vested the Board with the authority to 'return the statement of claims to the claimant as unsuitable for further action if the parties have designated the International Arbitral Centre of the Austrian Federal Economic Chamber in the arbitration agreement but have made agreements that conflict with the Vienna Rules'.[146] On its face, the new Article 9(6) appears to extend the scope of this provision in that agreements must no longer 'conflict' with the Vienna Rules but can simply 'deviate' from the Vienna Rules for Article 9(6) to apply. This wording suggests a broad scope of this provision, and the Vienna Rules offer no indication with respect to evaluating which kind of 'deviation' is permissible, and which will result in an application of Article 9(6).

9-092 As discussed, this is problematic as parties should not easily be denied the possibility to arbitrate and to refer their dispute to the chosen institution. Indeed, it is the nature of arbitration that proceedings are by far more flexible and adaptable to individual circumstances than state court proceedings. As also discussed, the institution, having offered its services to the public under pre-determined circumstances described in its rules, is under a duty (discussed in the context of **Article 1**)[147] to conclude a contract (*Kontrahierungszwang*) which is in tension with the VIAC's power under Article 9(6) to refuse administration of a case. For that reason, the VIAC should only refuse to administer the case in exceptional circumstances.

---

145. When adding language to, or varying a model arbitration clause proposed by an institution, *Derains/Schwartz* consider it 'essential to ensure that the language being added does not conflict with the arbitration rules being selected'. The ICC Court, e.g., may refuse to accept an arbitration when the amendments to the ICC Rules are found to be 'incompatible' with the ICC Rules. *See* Y. Derains and E.A. Schwartz, *A Guide to the ICC Rules of Arbitration* (2nd edn, The Hague, Kluwer Law International, 2005), p. 388.

146. The expression 'return the statement of claims' was intentionally chosen in contrast to the 'dismissal' of a claim, as the latter would not have lied within the Board's jurisdiction. The question of the legal consequence of the 'return' or the deletion of the claim was not clearly answered. Article 17(a) Vienna Rules 2001, **Annex 2a**, clarified that such a deletion was inherently not an obstacle to refile a claim.

147. *See* **Article 1**, at paras. 021 *et seq.*

As a result, Article 9(6) requires a narrow reading. Every deviation from the model **9-093** clause requires an interpretation of the Vienna Rules, both literal and systematic, to assert a conflict that justifies the application of Article 9(6). *Melis* appears to restrict Article 9(6) to cases where the deviation from the rules is such that the case cannot be administered in the spirit of the rules.[148] While *Melis* seems to favour a narrow reading of this provision, this criterion alone is not entirely instructive. As a starting point, one needs to look at the freedom both Austrian law and the Vienna Rules afford the parties. Most provisions of the Vienna Rules allow the parties to provide otherwise, and agreements which simply aim at facilitating the proceedings, the taking of evidence or the general conduct of the arbitration can hardly be offensive – parties can not only be expected, but are to be encouraged to agree on bespoke procedures that fit their case. To postulate a general principle therefore, agreements of the parties relating the procedural conduct of the arbitration that affect only their relationship as adversaries should not give rise to the application of Article 9(6).

Such agreements need to be distinguished from agreements that affect the role of **9-094** the institution. If parties accept arbitration under the Vienna Rules, they have to accept in principle the institutional framework as it stands. Agreements therefore, that seek to restrict the powers of the VIAC Board, or of the Secretary General, may well raise concerns under Article 9(6) unless such deviating agreements are expressly permissible under the Vienna Rules. Such agreements do not primarily concern the freedom of the parties to customize the procedural conduct of the arbitration to their needs, but concern the legitimate interest of the institution to be able to administer an arbitration according to their standards. It will thus be difficult to require the VIAC to conduct proceedings according to the ICC Rules or even the UNCITRAL Rules, or to take away the Board's power to determine the challenge of an arbitrator.

In addition, agreements that are in the words of *Heller*, 'legally unclear', may also **9-095** raise concerns although a perceived lack of clarity may be overcome by resorting to the default rules of the institution, or leaving it to the arbitrators to exercise their discretion and find an appropriate solution.[149]

Cases on this issue are exceedingly rare. *Heller* reports a case where the parties **9-096** referred the arbitration to the VIAC but nominated the President of the Vienna Bar as the appointing authority. The parties did not clarify whether the President of the Vienna Bar was supposed to decide all other questions concerning the appointment of arbitrators (such as challenge or removal) in lieu of the VIAC Board. In addition, the parties had agreed that the award ought to be rendered within six months but

---

148. With reference to the former version of Article 9(6). *See* W. Melis, 'Function and Responsibility of Arbitral Institutions' (1991) XIII Comp L YB Int'l Bus, 113.
149. K. Heller, 'Die Rechtsstellung des Internationalen Schiedsgerichts der Wirtschaftskammer Österreich' [1994] wbl, 105, 110.

gave the VIAC Board power to extend the time limit on application. Applying a former version of Article 9(6) however, the VIAC Board returned the statement of claims, holding that it was not clear whether the parties would leave the power to extend the deadline for the award to the Board's discretion or whether the parties had intended to bind themselves to some objective standard.[150] Without knowing the factual background of that case in detail, it is difficult to make an instructive observation. The nomination of a different appointing authority does not necessarily cause insurmountable difficulties (although one would advise parties against drafting an institutional arbitration agreement in that way). Similarly, imposing a certain time limit for the rendering of the award is not uncommon; and the underlying intention to facilitate an expeditious arbitration is not *prima facie* objectionable as creating 'legal uncertainties,'[151] but other factors may ultimately have influenced the Board's decision in that case.

C.   PROCEDURE

9-097 In considering whether additional agreements fall under this paragraph, the Secretary General, in the course of his *prima facie* scrutiny,[152] and in accordance with Article 9(5), identifies agreements that deviate from the Vienna Rules and forwards them to the Board. It appears from the placement of this authority in Article 9 (dealing with the 'Commencement of the Proceedings') and from the system of **Article 10** that Board decisions on Article 9(6) can only be made *prior* to the submission of the statement of claims to the respondent.

9-098 Given that the Vienna Rules do not expressly provide that only the Secretary General is entitled to inform the Board about deviating agreements, the respondent could arguably invoke Article 9(6) and also request a decision of the Board. However, Article 9(6) is designed to protect the institution from having to administer arbitrations that conflict with its rules – it is not primarily designed to protect the parties. A direct application of the respondent to the Board under Article 9(6) is therefore questionable. The Vienna Rules do not provide a time limit for a Board decision. It can only be inferred from **Article 3** that the admissibility of a statement

---

150. K. Heller, 'Die Rechtsstellung des Internationalen Schiedsgerichts der Wirtschaftskammer Österreich' [1994] wbl, 105, 110.
151. This time restriction to render an award is not unfamiliar in international arbitration practice, *see*, *e.g.*, Article 24 ICC Rules and Article 10 Hungarian Rules – six months or Article 33 DIS Rules 'within a reasonable period of time'; 30 days within Section 31 Slovak Rules ('after termination of proceedings') and also under Article 35 Polish Rules ('after closure of hearings' but 'in the event that the arbitral tribunal does not issue an award within the period of time (. . .), the Presidium of the Court may issue a decision on divesting the presiding arbitrator and the other arbitrators of the right to the honorarium, to which they are entitled in respect of participation in the proceedings before the Court, in part or in full.').
152. *See* **Article 9**, at paras. 072 *et seq.*

of claims will be decided in due course.[153] As the Board's decision is generally not subject to any appeal, and thus an erroneous refusal might deprive a party from any form of reasonable legal relief, the Board will not lightly make use of this authority, and will inform the claimant and the potential respondent about its intention to refuse to conduct the proceedings.[154] In order to give the parties an opportunity to reach an understanding that the conflicting agreement(s) shall no longer apply, the Board must specify which of the agreements are of such nature that administration will be refused (and give reasons) in its notification.

In summary, if parties choose to make arrangements deviating from the Vienna **9-099** Rules, it is advisable to do so with awareness of the applicable mandatory arbitration law.[155] While parties enjoy a significant degree of freedom to deviate from the Vienna Rules as far as the procedural conduct of the arbitration is concerned, they should be cautious to interfere with the powers of the institution and its organs. In cases of doubt, advice should be sought from the VIAC beforehand.[156]

D.   CONSEQUENCES OF THE VIAC'S REFUSAL

As discussed, the VIAC renders its services to the disputing parties on a contractual **9-100** basis, which is considered to be either an *agency agreement* or a contractual relationship *sui generis*, as it embraces elements of various types of contracts, which can be differentiated by the different services performed.[157] In practical terms, therefore, the parties are forced to accept the services of the VIAC once the Vienna Rules are agreed upon, and the VIAC is in principle under an obligation to administer the arbitration. In case the parties deviate from the Vienna Rules, they thereby create from a contractual point of view, an offer to the VIAC to conclude a new contractual relationship which is based on those amended terms that the parties have previously concluded. By executing its right of refusal of carrying out the proceedings under Article 9(6), the VIAC effectively refuses to accept this offer. As a corollary, no contract is concluded between the VIAC and the parties and therefore no access is granted to arbitration under the Vienna Rules.

---

153. *See* **Article 3**, at para. 012.
154. *See*, however, **Article 17**, at paras. 021 (and all the other instances where the Board's decision can be reviewed).
155. *See* **Article 2**, at paras. 045 *et seq.*
156. As there is often a considerable delay between the time when entering into the arbitration agreement and the time when proceedings are effectively commenced, such advice would be limited in its efficiency, it is unlikely that either the Secretary General or the Board would consider giving binding advice as to the conformity of the deviation in question with the Vienna Rules. The Members of these organs might, in case the dispute arises, be different from those originally agreed to in the contemplated agreements.
157. *See* **Article 1**, at paras. 021 *et seq.*

9-101 As already discussed, the VIAC does not lightly make use of this power and cases of such refusal are exceedingly rare. However, in the past there are reported cases where parties to ICC arbitration who considered their access to administered arbitration unrightly denied, approached the state court in an attempt to hold the ICC to its contractual promise. The Paris *Tribunal de Grande Instance* refused to force the ICC to administer arbitration proceedings.[158] There are no cases reported where the VIAC was ever involved in such state court proceedings.

9-102 Finally, given the clear distinction of the contractual relationship of the parties with the VIAC and the relationship between the parties themselves, it is worth to consider the impact of the VIAC's decision on the arbitration agreement itself. The agreement to submit a dispute to arbitration which is administered under the auspices of the VIAC can be seen as an arbitration agreement which is concluded under a condition subsequent.[159] In case the VIAC refuses to carry out the administration of the particular case, the condition has been met and the arbitration agreement is dissolved. However, another approach would be to let the parties' intention to submit their dispute to arbitration proceedings prevail. In such case, the factual impossibility of arbitration proceedings administered by the VIAC would eventually lead to arbitration on an *ad hoc* basis. In any case, the effect of the institutional refusal on the validity of the arbitration agreement will ultimately have to be considered under the law applicable to the arbitration agreement, and the weight given to the parties' intentions.[160]

---

158. This happened in the 'Cekobanka' case, where a Lebanese bank, the respondent, had through the course of exchanged telexes offered the claimant, Cekobanka, to have their dispute settled by arbitration under the ICC Rules. It was only after the claimant had accepted the respondent's offer to ICC arbitration that the respondent argued the invalidity of its offer. *See* Y. Derains and E.A. Schwartz, *A Guide to the ICC Rules of Arbitration* (2nd edn, The Hague, Kluwer Law International, 2005), p. 85.

159. Conditional arbitration agreements have been considered permissible under Austrian law. *See* H.W. Fasching, *Schiedsgericht und Schiedsverfahren im österreichischen und im internationalen Recht* (Vienna, Manz, 1973), pp. 25 *et seq.*

160. *See* **Article 2**, at paras. 032 *et seq.*

Article 10

Memorandum in Reply

		Para.			Para.
I.	Service of the Statement of Claims......	1	1.	Article 10(2)(a): Reply to the Pleadings in the Statement of Claims	19
	A. Introduction.....................................	1			
	B. Proper Statement of Claims as a Prerequisite of Service	3	2.	Article 10(2)(b) and (c): Particulars Regarding the Number, Name and Address of the Arbitrators...................	23
	C. Service of the Statement of Claims	7			
	D. The Response Period.......................	9			
	E. Extensions of the Response Period....	12	C.	Formal Requirements	26
II.	The Memorandum in Reply..................	16	D.	Addressee of the Memorandum in Reply....-...............................	29
	A. Mandatory Content under Austrian Law	16	E.	Failure to Submit a Proper or Timely Memorandum in Reply	31
	B. Required Content under the Vienna Rules	17			

I.   SERVICE OF THE STATEMENT OF CLAIMS

Article 10(1): If the claim is not to be dealt with under Article 9 paragraphs 5 and 6, the Secretary General shall make service to the Respondent of the statement of claims and one copy each of the rules of arbitration and shall invite the Respondent to submit a memorandum in reply within a period of thirty days, in the number of copies required under Article 9 paragraph 2.

A.   INTRODUCTION

Article 10 has been largely unaffected by the last amendment of the Vienna Rules. **10-001** The 'defendant' of the previous version of the Vienna Rules is now termed 'respondent', as is customary in international arbitration. Further, the rules regarding the transmission of the file to the arbitrators have been placed into a separate provision (**Article 12**), where they remain essentially unaltered in substance.

10-002 This chapter gives an overview of the practical implications relevant to a respondent receiving a statement of claims under the Vienna Rules. However, the important changes in the Vienna Rules regarding objections against the arbitral tribunal's jurisdiction are discussed in the context of **Article 19**.

B.　　　　　PROPER STATEMENT OF CLAIMS AS A PREREQUISITE OF SERVICE

10-003 Article 10(1) makes clear that the Secretary General may only process the statement of claims, and thus serve it on the respondent, if it does not fall within **Article 9(5)** and **(6)**. As discussed above, **Article 9(5)** allows the Secretary General to return the statement of claims to the claimant if it does not meet the mandatory requirements of the Vienna Rules as to form and content. As also discussed above, **Article 9(6)** allows the VIAC to refuse the administration of a case altogether if the arbitration agreement deviates from the Vienna Rules. Article 10(1) should be read to refer to '**Article 9** paragraphs **5** *or* **6**'. It will be very rare that the claimant does not comply with a request to rectify a defect in the statement of claims *and* the Board additionally refuses the administration of the claim.

10-004 Under the structure of Article 10, the statement of claims will therefore only be served on the respondent if the Secretary General is satisfied that the statement of claims complies with **Article 9**. Notably, the Vienna Rules do not provide that the Secretary General separately confirms that the statement of claims has been filed in 'due form'. The fact that the statement of claims is served on the respondent in accordance with Article 10 is, however, implicit confirmation that it complies with the formal requirements of **Article 9**.

10-005 Thus, as soon as a statement of claims is delivered to the respondent(s), the parties can draw the following conclusions. Firstly, the claim fulfils the mandatory requirements under **Article 9(3)**. Secondly, the Board is *prima facie* satisfied with the arbitration agreement submitted by the claimant and is willing to administer the case. Thirdly, the deposit of costs has been paid by the claimant(s), which as required by **Article 33(1)**.

10-006 If the respondent considers the VIAC to have overlooked defects in the statement of claims that should have prevented the claimant's submission from being processed under Article 10, there is in principle no procedure available to address this with the VIAC. However, in practice, the respondent can of course always attempt to address the VIAC (or, after transmission of the file to the arbitrators, perhaps more properly, the arbitral tribunal) on such issues.

C. SERVICE OF THE STATEMENT OF CLAIMS

As previously mentioned, it is the claimant's obligation (and in its genuine interest) **10-007**
that the respondent is properly identified and designated and their address included
in the statement of claims. On the basis of this information, service of the statement
of claims is effected through the Secretariat.

The Secretary General will assist the claimant with the delivery.[1] Several delivery **10-008**
attempts may become expensive and the claimant might therefore be asked to pay
an additional advance on costs even at this stage of the proceedings. There is no
indication in the Vienna Rules as to the number of times the Secretary General
must attempt to effect service on the respondent. It is the current practice of the
Secretariat that, should there be delay or difficulty in serving the statement of
claims, the claimant is as a matter of course given the opportunity to improve
on the contact details of the respondent.[2] In practice, therefore, multiple requests
for service will usually been granted, but it falls on the claimant to inquire, and
provide, improved particulars of the respondent's address to the Secretariat. The
claimant's failure to provide an address fit for service would entitle the Secretary
General not to proceed with the statement of claims in accordance with **Article 9(5)**.[3]

D. THE RESPONSE PERIOD

Being served with a statement of claims may not come as a surprise to a belligerent **10-009**
party. Oftentimes, conflicts emerge over a long period of time, ultimately culminating in the filing of a statement of claims. In practice, commercial parties will
have instructed in-house lawyers or external counsel to assess, and prepare for, the
dispute long before the arbitration actually commences.

However, parties, less litigant or perhaps less accustomed to arbitration proceedings, **10-010**
may just as well be taken by surprise by being confronted with a statement of claims
and an 'invitation' to submit a memorandum in reply. In this case, fairness demands
that the respondent must be put on notice that important time-limits (e.g. for the
nomination of the number or the appointment of the arbitrators[4]) commence from the
date of receipt of the statement of claims delivered by the Secretary General.

The Secretary General therefore delivers the statement of claims together with a **10-011**
copy of the Vienna Rules and the VIAC's list of arbitrators. The Secretary General

---

1. In contrast, Article 2(1) AAA/ICDR Rules requires the claimant to simultaneously serve the
   statement of defence to the administrator as well as to the respondent, a similar procedure can be
   found in Article 5(1) DIS Rules. Article 3(6) Swiss Rules provides that the arbitral tribunal shall
   deliver the statement of defence without delay.
2. *See* **Article 9**, at paras. 053 *et seq.*
3. For a more detailed discussion of effective service of the statement of claims under the Vienna
   Rules, *see* **Article 9**, at paras. 003 *et seq.*
4. *See* **Article 14**, at paras. 006, 032 and 052.

also expressly advises the respondent to file the memorandum in reply within thirty days, and, where applicable, to nominate an arbitrator within that time. As discussed further below, the respondent must then decide, on the basis of legal and tactical considerations, which course of action is most advantageous to its position, and must carefully consider the appointment of a suitable arbitrator.[5]

E.   EXTENSIONS OF THE RESPONSE PERIOD

10-012 Although the 30-day period to produce a memorandum in reply corresponds with international standards and other arbitration rules,[6] the respondent will often find this time-limit too brief for comfort. In such cases, the respondent will be well advised to contact the Secretary General at an early stage (and not on the expiry date of thirty-day time-limit) and apply for an extension for the preparation of the memorandum in reply.[7]

10-013 Such requests for extension follow the provision of **Article 13**. Unlike Article 5(2) ICC Rules, the respondent need not comment on 'the particulars regarding the numbers of the arbitrators' before applying for an extension of the time-limit.[8] This opens the door to dilatory tactics. **Article 13** therefore provides that a request for extension of time must provide 'sufficient grounds' for the requested extension. Although, according to **Article 13**, documentary evidence is in principle not required, it is still advisable to explain in detail the difficulties encountered in preparing the memorandum in reply.

10-014 It is the practice of the present Secretary General to grant extensions for 30 days, unless special circumstances require otherwise. An almost automatic first extension is usually granted upon the respondent's application, which is usually not forwarded to the claimant for further comment. This practice is problematic; the

---

5. *See* **Article 7**, at para. 028.
6. Same time-limits in Article 5(1) ICC Rules; Article 2(1) LCIA Rules; Article 3(1) AAA/ICDR Rules; Article 20(2) Czech Rules; Article 25(2) Hungarian Rules; Article 29(2) Slovenian Rules – within 15 days for domestic disputes Article 29(1) Slovenian Rules; an exceptionally short time-limit of 10 days can be found in Article 16(2) Slovak Rules; *in contrast*, there are institutions with a discretionary element, such as, *e.g.*, Article 9 DIS Rules; Article 32(1) Polish Rules and Article 14 Croatian Rules.
7. The ability to apply for a time-extension is also found in Article 5(2) ICC Rules (with the Secretariat); Article 3(4) AAA/ICDR Rules (with the arbitral tribunal or the administrator); Article 29(3) Slovenian Rules (with the Secretary of the Court); Article 20(2) Czech Rules; Article 25(2) Hungarian Rules (with a maximum extension of 30 days) and Article 16(2) Slovak Rules (with a very strict maximum extension of 10 days).
8. Article 5(2) ICC Rules reads: 'The Secretariat may grant the Respondent an extension of the time-limit for filing the Answer, provided the application for such an extension contains the Respondent's comments concerning the number of arbitrators and their choice, and, where required (. . .) the nomination of an arbitrator. If the Respondent fails to do so, the Court shall proceed in accordance with these rules'.

better view may be for the Secretariat to always seek the claimant's comment. The claimant – having access to information not available to the Secretariat – may be able to demonstrate convincingly that, in the circumstances of the case, particular urgency is required or that the respondent is engaging in dilatory tactics. With respect to the appointment of the respondent's co-arbitrator in the memorandum in reply, the automatic grant of an extension is also problematic in light of **Article 14(4)** which provides that, if the 30 day time limit is missed, 'the arbitrator *shall* be appointed by the Board'. As the wording of this provisions suggests, the thirty day time period is, in principle, mandatory, and, as the agreed rule, arguably affords the claimant a contractual entitlement *vis-à-vis* both the respondent and the VIAC to that effect. Automatic extensions therefore may run foul of the strong principle embodied in **Article 14**, and undermine the requirement of **Article 13** to show 'sufficient grounds' for an extension.

In any event, while the VIAC is lenient with initial requests for extensions, it is **10-015** more conservative as far as further requests are concerned. In such cases, it will usually hear the claimant before making a decision, and it is likely to grant only shorter extensions of fifteen days.

II.   THE MEMORANDUM IN REPLY

Article 10(2): The memorandum in reply must include:

(a) A reply to the pleadings in the statement of claims;
(b) Particulars regarding the number of arbitrators in accordance with Article 14;
(c) Indication of the name and address of an arbitrator, if a decision by an arbitral tribunal is requested or if a decision by three arbitrators has been agreed upon in the arbitration agreement.

A.   MANDATORY CONTENT UNDER AUSTRIAN LAW

As with the statement of claims, the required – and equally important, permitted – **10-016** content for the respondent's first submission may vary depending on the parties' arbitration agreement,[9] applicable institutional rules[10] and applicable national law.[11] This submission is sometimes, because of the practice under other institutional

---

9. Arbitration agreements generally do not impose requirements for the contents of a request for arbitration, even less frequently, for the memorandum in reply.
10. Article 2 LCIA Rules; Article 5 ICC Rules; Article 3 AAA/ICDR Rules and Article 19 UNCITRAL Rules.
11. Civil law systems and practice will often favour more detailed initial notices (or submissions), supported by documentary evidence, while common law systems may incline towards relatively

rules, referred to as the respondent's 'Answer'.[12] National arbitration legislation also sometimes addresses the contents of a memorandum in reply (at least in *ad hoc* arbitrations, where the parties have not otherwise agreed). In general, national laws impose relatively few requirements for such submissions. Under Austrian law, Section 597(1) ZPO provides for a 'statement of defence' without actually setting out much guidance as to its contents:

> Within the period of time agreed by the parties or determined by the arbitral tribunal, the claimant shall state its claim and the facts supporting its claim, and the respondent shall respond thereto. The parties may submit with their statements all documents they consider to be relevant or may add a reference to the documents or other evidence they will submit.[13]

B.   REQUIRED CONTENT UNDER THE VIENNA RULES

10-017 The content requirements for the memorandum in reply, as stipulated in Article 10, are rather restrained.[14] Article 10 does not even mention that any evidence has to be provided in the memorandum in reply, so that the respondent does not, at this stage, run the risk of prejudicing its position. Again, it is left to the respondent's discretion and tactical assessment to decide upon the level of detail of its submission.

10-018 Having said this, a former version of Article 10 contained even less guidance in terms of content requirements and therefore left it entirely to the respondent to decide how to comment on the claimant's pleading.[15] The current version of the Vienna Rules has, for the sake of clarification and possibly in light of Section 597

---

skeletal 'notice' pleading. *See* S. Elsing and J.M. Townsend, 'Bridging the Common Law-Civil Law Divide in Arbitration' (2002) 18(1) Arb Int'l, 59.

12. Article 5 ICC Rules.
13. This provision is almost literally identical to Article 23(1) UNCITRAL Model Law.
14. By contrast, Article 5 ICC Rules asks additionally for 'any comments as to the place of arbitration, the applicable rules of law and the language of the arbitration'. Similarly Article 3(3) AAA/ICDR Rules provides that '[a] respondent shall respond (. . .) to any proposals the claimant may have made as to the number of arbitrators, the place of the arbitration or the language(s) of the arbitration, except to the extent that the parties have previously agreed as to these matters'.
15. Article 7 of a former version of the Vienna Rules provided: 'The Secretary shall make services to the Defendant of the statement of the claims and one copy each of the Rules of arbitration and the list of arbitrators and shall invite the defendant to submit a memorandum in reply within a period of 30 days; including where appropriate a counter-claim accompanied by the number of copies required in accordance with Article 6 paragraph 2, and to state its wishes with regard to the number of arbitrators in accordance with Article 9. If a decision by three arbitrators is requested, an arbitrator shall be nominated in the memorandum in reply and the address of that person shall be stated.'

ZPO, added at least minimum requirements. Under the Vienna Rules, the respondent is also entitled to raise a counter-claim in the memorandum in reply.[16]

1. Article 10(2)(a): Reply to the Pleadings in the Statement of Claims

Article 10(2)(a) provides, rather vaguely, that the memorandum in reply should **10-019** contain a 'reply to the pleadings in the statement of claims'. As discussed, this leaves a substantial measure of discretion to the respondent to structure the memorandum in reply depending on tactical considerations. For example, a very brief reply essentially only 'rejecting' the claimant's pleadings would be sufficient.[17] Perhaps surprisingly, and in contrast to the requirements pertaining to the statement of claims under **Article 9**, evidence need not be referred to, much less attached.[18]

However, the respondent should consider carefully the impression it wishes to **10-020** make on the arbitral tribunal. A comprehensive reply also facilitates the drawing up of an accurate timetable for the proceedings. The Secretary General will typically also appreciate more detailed pleadings, making it easier for the VIAC to estimate the possible costs of proceedings and consider the amount of the advance, for example, with respect to more complex applications for the taking of evidence that will likely involve significant costs.[19]

Further, the respondent is entitled under **Article 11** to advance a set-off defence or **10-021** to file an affirmative counter-claim.[20] This could influence the calculation of the costs of the deposit and the administrative charges but will typically not delay the proceedings.[21]

It may also happen occasionally that, after receipt of the statement of claims, the **10-022** respondent is prepared to concede the claimant's claim in full or to agree to satisfy at least part of the claim. If such (full or partial) admission occurs, the Secretary General will notify the claimant and inquire whether the claimant wishes to continue the proceedings or, where applicable, whether it wishes to pursue the unsatisfied portion of the claim. In principle, also after the respondent's admissions, the claimant may be entitled to an enforceable award and might, therefore, have a legitimate interest in continuing the proceedings.

---

16. See **Article 11**, at paras. 002 *et seq.*
17. This is similar under Article 5(1) ICC Rules outlines only minimal requirements for the content of the reply to the pleadings, referred to as answer to the request, and how much a respondent chooses to state in an answer depends on the circumstances of the case, including the content of the request. See Y. Derains and E.A. Schwartz, *A Guide to the ICC Rules of Arbitration* (2nd edn, The Hague, Kluwer Law International, 2005), pp. 63-72.
18. C. Liebscher in *Arbitration Law of Austria: Practice and Procedure*, S. Riegler, A. Petsche, A. Fremuth-Wolf, M. Platte and C. Liebscher (eds) (Huntington, Juris Publishing, 2007), p. 626.
19. See **Article 34**, at paras. 019 *et seq.*
20. See **Article 11**, at paras. 001 *et seq.*, and 043 *et seq.*
21. See in detail **Article 34**, at paras. 019 *et seq.*

2.   **Article 10(2)(b) and (c): Particulars Regarding the
              Number, Name and Address of the Arbitrators**

10-023 With the memorandum in reply, the respondent is also required to comment on the
particulars regarding the number of arbitrators and the claimant's proposal in this
respect. Where a tribunal of three has been agreed in the arbitration agreement, or
where the decision of such a tribunal is requested, the respondent must also name
its co-arbitrator. In essence, the commentary on **Article 9(3)(d)** and **(e)** applies
mutatis mutandis.[22]

10-024 Where the indication of the number of arbitrators in the statement of claims contradicts the indication in the memorandum in reply, or where such an indication is
lacking, the matter is referred to the VIAC Board to make a binding decision on the
number of arbitrators pursuant to **Article 14.**[23]

10-025 Also, if an arbitrator has been nominated by the claimant, and the respondent
objects to this nomination, the respondent is advised to notify his objection
immediately. Failure to do so runs the risk that the Board may assume pursuant
to **Article 16(1)** that the respondent participated in the appointment procedure and
thus waived its right to challenge the claimant's co-arbitrator.[24]

C.   FORMAL REQUIREMENTS

10-026 As regards requirements of form, the same considerations apply to the memorandum in reply that have been discussed in the context of the statement of claims.
Thus, a memorandum in reply will be accepted if it is submitted in compliance
with **Article 13**, that is, by registered letter, courier service, fax or by any other
means of communication that guarantees evidence of transmission.[25] Attaching
a different, and strictly speaking incorrect, terminology such as 'Answer' or
'Statement of Defence' will not affect the admissibility of the submission.
However, the reference to **Article 9(2)** obliges the respondent to include a sufficient
number of copies of the submission with enclosures for each party, each arbitrator
and the Secretariat.

10-027 As with the statement of claims, the Vienna Rules do not specifically require that
the memorandum in reply be signed by the respondent or its representative.[26]

---

22. *See* **Article 9**, at paras. 062 *et seq.*
23. *See* **Article 14**, at paras. 015 *et seq.*
24. For a detailed discussion of the challenge procedure and the issue of waiver, *see* **Article 16**, at
    paras. 026 *et seq.* For the substantive standards of arbitrator impartiality and independence, *see*
    Article 7, at paras. 080 *et seq.*
25. *See* **Article 9**, at para. 010.
26. *See likewise* Article 17(1) Czech Rules; Article 22(1) Hungarian Rules and Article 13(1) Slovak
    Rules.

Therefore, a signature will not be requested. Indeed, because a signature is not a mandatory requirement under Article 10, the lack of a signature cannot prevent the memorandum in reply from being processed.

Although not explicitly mentioned, it is recommended that a respondent's counsel **10-028** also submit proof of its power of attorney. This will facilitate the proceedings for the arbitral tribunal, although no sanction applies to a failure to do so.

D.   ADDRESSEE OF THE MEMORANDUM IN REPLY

The Vienna Rules contain no indication as to the destination to which the **10-029** respondent must submit the memorandum in reply. The standard cover letter sent by the Secretary General to effect service of the statement of claim on the respondent requests that the memorandum in reply be addressed to the Secretariat. Although there is no express provision on point, it then falls as a matter of course to the Secretary General to deliver the memorandum in reply to the claimant(s).

It is standing practice, however, that the respondent delivers a copy of his submis- **10-030** sion directly to the claimant's counsel named in the statement of claims. It is recommended that this kind of direct delivery is noted in the respondent's cover letter to the VIAC. With the delivery of the memorandum in reply to the claimant, the Secretary General usually calls for payment of the advance of costs. Also, insofar as the parties have not nominated their co-arbitrators (or agreed on a sole arbitrator), the Secretary General sets in motion the nomination procedure for constituting the tribunal in accordance with **Article 14**.

E.   FAILURE TO SUBMIT A PROPER OR TIMELY MEMORANDUM IN REPLY

Whereas the Secretary General's power to address defects in the statement of claims **10-031** has explicitly been provided for in **Article 9**, Article 10 remains silent on this point. As discussed above there is – under the present concept – literally no sanction in the Vienna rules for a defective memorandum in reply.[27] Nevertheless, it is the current practice of the Secretary General to request an additional copy of the memorandum in reply from the respondent, if such copy is missing under the calculus of **Article 9(2)**, even though no sanction will be imposed.

The Vienna Rules also do not provide express sanctions in case of delay or **10-032** outright failure to submit a memorandum in reply; the proceeding will simply

---

27.   *See*, however, the discussion about the jurisdiction of the arbitral tribunal in **Article 19**, at paras. 011 *et seq.*

continue even if no memorandum in reply is filed.[28] To an extent, this reflects the somewhat distorted translation of the authentic German version of Article 10 into English. The authentic German version provides, arguable in stronger terms, that the Secretary General '*auffordert*' (that is, requests) the submission of a memorandum in reply, whereas the current English translation has the Secretary General merely 'invite' submission of the memorandum in reply, which arguably does not carry the same sense of obligation as the German original.

10-033 Absent express sanctions, the respondent can (theoretically) file the memorandum in reply even beyond the expiry of the 30-day time-limit (or a possible extension). The Secretary General would not be in a position to reject this submission but would have to notify the claimant to include it in the case file for transmission to the arbitral tribunal. Such a late submission is conceivable until the arbitral tribunal makes appropriate procedural orders prohibiting late filings ('cutting-off orders').[29] In the absence of an agreement between the parties, the Vienna Rules leave it to a great extent to the arbitral tribunal to decide and rule on appropriate and adequate procedure,[30] and to address late filings by the parties. Arbitrators will normally be concerned that the parties have had a reasonable opportunity to present their case, and are unlikely to penalize the respondent's failure to comply with the prescribed time-limit by refusing to accept a late submission.

10-034 However, submitting no memorandum in reply, or doing so only late, creates serious risks for the respondent. First, the respondent will, unless very good reasons prevented it from a timely submission, make a negative impression on the tribunal. Second, the VIAC will not consider the respondent's position concerning the number of arbitrators, and, as discussed below in **Article 14**, can determine the number of arbitrators without further notice to the defaulting party.[31] Also, the VIAC will be entitled under **Article 14** to proceed with the constitution of the tribunal, or the appointment of the sole arbitrator, even if no memorandum in reply is filed. Third, once the tribunal is constituted, the

---

28. C. Liebscher in *Arbitration Law of Austria: Practice and Procedure*, S. Riegler, A. Petsche, A. Fremuth-Wolf, M. Platte and C. Liebscher (eds) (Huntington, Juris Publishing, 2007), p. 626. Unlike other arbitration rules, the ICC Rules include explicit measures to continue with the proceedings in the case that the respondent refuses to participate or attempts to delay the tribunal. Article 6(3) ICC Rules provides that if a party refuses to take part in the arbitration, the proceedings will proceed *ex parte*. Where a sole arbitrator is provided in an arbitration agreement or it is deemed appropriate by the court, an arbitrator will be appointed by the court on behalf of the respondent. The awards rendered under these conditions are no less enforceable than those in an active adversarial proceeding. *See* W.L. Craig, W.W. Park and J. Paulsson, *International Chamber of Commerce Arbitration* (3rd edn, New York, Oceana Publications, 2000), pp. 151-153.
29. *See* **Article 20**, at paras. 071 *et seq.*
30. *See* **Article 20**, at paras. 093 *et seq.*
31. *See* **Article 14**, at para. 017.

arbitration will continue even without the respondent's participation.[32] This is addressed in **Article 20(6)**[33] and in line with Section 600(2) ZPO which provides:

> If the respondent fails to respond in accordance with Section 597, paragraph 1 of this law during the agreed or determined period of time, the arbitral tribunal shall, unless the parties have agreed otherwise, continue the proceedings without treating such failure in itself as an admission of the claimant's allegations. The same shall apply where a party has failed to perform any other procedural act. The arbitral tribunal may continue the proceedings and may make an award on the basis of the evidence taken. If a failure to perform a procedural act has been excused to the arbitral tribunal's satisfaction, it may then be performed by the party.

The respondent's failure to submit a memorandum in reply does not cause the proceedings to be terminated. Rather, the arbitral tribunal must continue the proceedings. If the respondent does not respond to claims made by the claimant, the tribunal will not take these claims on face value or automatically accept them to be true. If the proceeding is conducted in its entirety without the submission of a memorandum in reply, the arbitral tribunal is still required to obtain as much information as possible and to evaluate the case in a fair and balanced manner.[34] The tribunal may thus allow the respondent to submit a memorandum in reply at a later time if its default is excused.[35] **10-035**

---

32. The impact of an untimely objection to the jurisdiction of the arbitral tribunal is discussed under **Article 19**, at para. 010.

33. *See* **Article 20**, at paras. 257 *et seq*. *See* also Article 6(3) of the ICC Rules which provides that if a party refuses to take part in the arbitration, the proceedings will proceed *ex parte*. *See* W.L. Craig, W.W. Park and J. Paulsson, *International Chamber of Commerce Arbitration* (3rd edn, New York, Oceana Publications, 2000), pp. 151 *et seq*.

34. *See* **Article 20**, at paras. 257 *et seq*. Under the former arbitration law, it was argued that in arbitration proceedings the claimant could in case of respondent's default, not apply for a default judgment in accordance with Section 396 fZPO. The same is true under the new Arbitration Act, *see* Section 600(2) ZPO, however permitting parties to 'agree otherwise'.
   See H.W. Fasching, *Schiedsgericht und Schiedsverfahren im österreichischen und im internationalen Recht* (Vienna, Manz, 1973), p. 127.

35. M.Platte in *Arbitration Law of Austria: Practice and Procedure*, S. Riegler, A. Petsche, A. Fremuth-Wolf, M. Platte and C. Liebscher (eds) (Huntington, Juris Publishing, 2007), Section 600, p. 387.

Article 11

Counter-Claim, Amendments and Set-Off

		Para.				Para.
I.	Jurisdiction Over Counter-Claims	1	IV.	Reply to the Counter-Claim		27
	A. Introduction	1	V.	Amendments of Existing Claims		29
	B. Jurisdiction	4		A. Amendments under Austrian		
	C. Timing	7		Law		32
II.	Filing of the Counter-Claim	13		B. Amendments under the Vienna		
III.	Dismissal of the Counter-Claim	15		Rules		39
	A. Introduction	15	VI.	Set-Off		43
	B. Same Arbitration Agreement	17		A. Jurisdiction		45
	C. Identical Parties	20		B. Cost Implications		51
	D. Substantial Delay	23				

I.   JURISDICTION OVER COUNTER-CLAIMS

Article 11(1): Claims by the Respondent against the Claimant that are based on an arbitration agreement which constitutes the jurisdiction of the International Arbitral Centre of the Austrian Federal Economic Chamber can be raised as counter-claims up to the time of closure of the evidentiary proceedings.

A.   INTRODUCTION

Procedural provisions governing counter-claims (and amendments of existing **11-001** claims) need to strike a difficult, but highly-relevant balance. They should allow for the full and final disposition of the parties' pending disputes in one proceeding, yet also facilitate a speedy and efficient dispute resolution that discourages dilatory tactics.

11-002 Article 11 regulates the admissibility of counter-claims under the Vienna Rules. In essence, this provision allows arbitrators to determine the admissibility of such claims at their discretion, provided that they have jurisdiction over the counter-claim and that the counter-claim does not unacceptably protract the proceedings.

11-003 Article 11 does not expressly address the requirements for the amendment of the parties' existing claims in the course of the proceedings. While this silence is unfortunate (and atypical for modern arbitration rules), the criteria set out in Article 11 provide useful guidance for this issue as well. Article 11 also appears to be the appropriate place for a discussion of the admissibility of set-off (although, again, the Vienna Rules are silent on the issue).[1]

B.   JURISDICTION

11-004 The ZPO (whether under its former or present version) is silent on the admissibility of counter-claims in arbitration proceedings. Under the present regime, the general provision of Section 594 ZPO applies, so that 'the parties are free to determine the rules of procedure', including by 'refer[ing] to other rules of procedure' such as the Vienna Rules. Although the ZPO does not specifically address counter-claims, it allows parties in Section 597 ZPO to 'amend or supplement its claim or pleadings during the course of the arbitral proceedings unless the arbitral tribunal considers this inappropriate due to delay.'

11-005 Under the ZPO, Austrian commentators have traditionally taken a somewhat restrictive approach to counter-claims. *Fasching* appeared to allow counter-claims only if they seek a declaration that is *prejudicial* to the main claim, or if they are connected to the claim *and* covered by the same arbitration agreement.[2]

11-006 However, the Vienna Rules in their present version do not require that the counter-claim be prejudicial to, or connected with, the main claim in the arbitration. Indeed, with the adoption of Article 11, the regime has been significantly liberalized. Specifically, this Article replaces Article 7a of the Vienna Rules 2001[3] (which in turn was introduced to amend the somewhat unsatisfactory regime contained in Article 7 of the Vienna Rules 1991).[4] Article 7a(1) required that the counter-claim fall within the scope of the *same* arbitration agreement governing the main claim,

---

1.   The cost implication of set-off defences are dealt with under **Article 36(3)**, at paras. 012 *et seq.*
2.   H.W. Fasching, *Schiedsgericht und Schiedsverfahren im österreichischen und im internationalen Recht* (Vienna, Manz, 1973), p. 27.
3.   Vienna Rules 2001, **Annex 2a**.
4.   A. Reiner, 'Zur Auslegung von Artikel 7 der Wiener Regeln betreffend die Frist zur Einbringung einer Widerklage' [1999] ZfRV, 169.

thereby requiring *de facto* a connection with the main claim at bar. This position has now been abandoned, with Article 11(1) simply requiring that the counter-claim fall within *any* arbitration agreement that confers jurisdiction upon the VIAC – and not just the arbitration agreement under which the claimant's claim was brought. The arbitration agreement is thus perceived as the central, and perhaps the only relevant, connecting link between the parties, and hence, between the parties' respective claims against each other. By not relying on a substantive connection between claim and counter-claim, but rather the jurisdictional ambit of the parties' arbitration agreements, the Vienna Rules facilitated the full and final disposition of *all* the parties' current disputes in one proceeding, which seems to better serve the needs of commercial reality. This approach appears to be in line with international practice and major arbitration rules.[5]

C.   TIMING

Under the Vienna Rules, counter-claims can, in principle, be raised until 'the **11-007** closure of the evidentiary proceeding'. This most likely refers to the tribunal's declaration to close the proceedings pursuant to **Article 20(8)**,[6] although that provision refers to the 'closure of the proceedings', which is arguably a wider notion.[7] Absent post-hearing submissions, this may coincide with the end of the proceedings as such, and will in any event be at a very advanced stage in the proceedings.

In this point, Article 11 appears to have been modelled after Section 233(2) ZPO **11-008** which sets a similar deadline for counter-claims in litigation before the Austrian courts,[8] as do various institutional rules in the region.[9] It is debatable, however, whether allowing counter-claims until the closure of the evidentiary proceeding facilitates the efficiency of the arbitral process.

This approach appears at odds with most modern institutional arbitration rules. **11-009** Article 19 of the ICC Rules, for example, provides that no counter-claim may be

---

5. *See, e.g.*, Article 19 ICC Rules, which permits the tribunal to admit counter-claims not listed in the terms of reference against the objection of one party. According to *Bühler/Jarvin*, such liberty also enhances the predictability and transparency of the arbitral process. *See* M. Bühler and S. Jarvin in *Practitioner's Handbook on International Arbitration*, F.B. Weigand (ed) (Munich, C.H. Beck, 2002), p. 112; *see also* Article 19 UNCITRAL Rules.
6. *See* **Article 11**, at paras. 288 *et seq.*
7. C. Liebscher in *Arbitration Law of Austria: Practice and Procedure*, S. Riegler, A. Petsche, A. Fremuth-Wolf, M. Platte and C. Liebscher (eds) (Huntington, Juris Publishing, 2007), p. 627.
8. Section 233(2) ZPO provides: 'After the proceedings have been commenced, the defendant may submit a counter claim with the court, before which the main claim is pending, if the statutory jurisdictional requirements are met, as long as the oral hearing before the court of first instance has not been closed.'
9. *See, e.g.*, Article 34(1) of the Hungarian Rules.

introduced after the Terms of Reference have been signed, unless, based on a particular justification in the given circumstances, the tribunal permits otherwise. The ICC Rules obviously aim at deterring a party from concealing its counter-claim in order to present them at a later stage in the proceedings, which inevitably causes disruption to the arbitral process.[10]

11-010 Article 2(1)(b) of the LCIA Rules goes even further: it requires the respondent to submit 'a brief statement describing the nature and circumstances of any counter-claims' as part of the response to the claimant's request for arbitration – which is thirty days after the request has been served. Failure to do so does not preclude the advancement of a counter-claim in the arbitration,[11] but leaves it to the arbitrators' discretion whether to admit the counter-claim.[12] Similarly, Article 3 of the AAA/ ICDR Rules requires counter-claims to be filed 'at the time a respondent submits its statement of defence', again within thirty days of the commencement of the arbitration.[13] Finally, the UNCITRAL Rules provide that a counter-claim may be made 'in [the] statement of defence, or at a later stage in the arbitral proceedings if the arbitral tribunal decides that the delay was justified under the circumstances'.[14]

11-011 The major arbitration rules, therefore, while maintaining some flexibility, require as a principle that counter-claims be filed at an early stage in the proceedings, usually with the respondent's first submission, whereas no such principle is established by Article 11.[15]

11-012 However, in order to avoid the potentially disruptive effect caused by the late filing of counter-claims, Article 11(1) must be read in close connection with the restrictions imposed by Article 11(3), including, in particular, the requirements that counter-claims that cause substantial delay must be referred to separate proceedings (which is discussed in detail below). *De lege ferenda*, Article 11 should be amended by either establishing an early deadline (which can be deviated from should the given circumstances so require) or, at minimum, by consolidating Article 11(1) with the criteria set out in Article 11(3). It is difficult (although not impossible) to conceive as a matter of principle a counter-claim filed just before 'the time of closure of the evidentiary proceedings' that would not cause significant delay, and additional cost and prejudice to the claimant.

---

10. M. Bühler and S. Jarvin in *Practitioner's Handbook on International Arbitration*, F.B. Weigand (ed.) (Munich, C.H. Beck, 2002), p. 237.
11. Article 2(3) LCIA Rules.
12. The tribunal can 'adopt procedures suitable to the circumstances of the arbitration, avoiding unnecessary delay or expense, so as to provide a fair and efficient means for the final resolution of the parties' dispute'. *See* Article 14(1) LCIA Rules.
13. Article 3 AAA/ICDR Rules.
14. Article 19(3) UNCITRAL Rules.
15. *See* Y. Derains and E.A. Schwartz, *A Guide to the ICC Rules of Arbitration* (2nd edn, The Hague, Kluwer Law International, 2005), p. 267.

II.   FILING OF THE COUNTER-CLAIM

Article 11(2): Counter-claims must be submitted to the Secretariat of the Centre and must be forwarded by the latter to the sole arbitrator (arbitral tribunal) for further action after the deposit against costs has been paid.

The counter-claim must be submitted to the Secretariat before it can be introduced **11-013** in the proceedings. As with a statement of claims, the counter-claim is subject to the same formal and content requirements articulated under **Article 9**. The Secretary General will therefore conduct a *prima facie* assessment of the VIAC's jurisdiction.[16] If the counter-claim is defective, the Secretary General will request that the counter-claimant remedy such defect within a certain time limit.[17] Ultimately, however, the Secretary General has no power, beyond a 'conservative *prima facie* assessment', to evaluate the admissibility under any of the restrictions imposed by Article 11(1) and (3) – this power is vested exclusively with the tribunal.[18]

The Secretary General must forward the counter-claim to the tribunal as soon as the **11-014** deposit of costs has been paid.[19] For the computation of costs under the Vienna Rules, *see* **Article 36(3)**.

III.   DISMISSAL OF THE COUNTER-CLAIM

Article 11(3): If the claim designated as a counter-claim is not based on an arbitration agreement which constitutes the jurisdiction of the International Arbitral Centre of the Austrian Federal Economic Chamber, if the parties are not identical, or if the submission of a counter-claim after transmission of the files to the sole arbitrator (arbitral tribunal) would lead to a substantial delay in the main proceedings, the sole arbitrator (arbitral tribunal) must return the claim to the Secretariat to be dealt with in separate proceedings.

A.   INTRODUCTION

Article 11(3), which is directed at the tribunal, imposes further restrictions as to the **11-015** admissibility of the counter-claim. The tribunal may exercise free discretion in

---

16. *See* **Article 9**, at paras. *046 et seq.*
17. *See* **Article 9**, at paras. *080 et seq.*
18. *See* **Article 1**, at paras. *002, 030* and *148* and **Article 9**, at paras. *072 et seq.*
19. This provision is valid under Austrian law only insofar as it does not infringe the respondent's/ counter-claimant's right to be heard in the ongoing arbitral proceeding. *See* C. Liebscher and A. Schmid in *Practitioner's Handbook on International Arbitration*, F.B. Weigand (ed.) (Munich, C.H. Beck, 2002), p. 575. For the counter-claimant's and the counter-respondent's failure to pay the deposit, *see,* **Article 34**, at paras. *029 et seq.,* and *032 et seq.*

assessing these restrictions. However, once it has found that one of the restrictions applies, the tribunal has no discretion as to the legal consequence. Article 11(3) provides that the tribunal '*must*' return the claim to the Secretariat to be dealt with in separate proceedings. Arguably, therefore, the tribunal has to apply the requirements of Article 11(3) *ex officio*, even if no objections are raised by the counter-respondent.[20] This is certainly so where the tribunal lacks jurisdiction or where the parties are not identical; the notion of delay is inherently subjective and will leave a greater extent of discretion to the tribunal.

11-016 By contrast, it is argued that, if the conditions for dismissal of the counter-claim under **Article 10** are not met, the arbitrators are under an obligation to hear and decide upon the counter-claim as well (if the separate deposit on costs is being paid by the respondent/counter-claimant).[21] In any event, the dismissal of the counter-claim under Article 11(3) is *without prejudice*. The counter-claimant expressly retains the possibility to assert the counter-claim in a separate proceedings.

B.   SAME ARBITRATION AGREEMENT

11-017 As noted above, a substantive connection between counter-claim and main claim is not required. The counter-claim must be dismissed, however, 'if the claim designated as a counter-claim is not based on an arbitration agreement which constitutes the jurisdiction of the International Arbitral Centre of the Austrian Federal Economic Chamber'. This repeats the jurisdictional requirement set out in Article 11(1).[22] As noted, the previous regime under Article 7a(1)[23] required that the counter-claim fall within the scope of the *same* arbitration agreement governing the main claim. Article 11 now only requires that the counter-claim falls within *any* arbitration agreement that confers jurisdiction upon the VIAC.

11-018 With this liberalization, the Vienna Rules seek to facilitate the full and final disposition of *all* the parties' current disputes in one proceeding, which seems to better serve the needs of commercial reality. While the tribunal is not a standing

---

20. If, however, the tribunal admits a counter-claim that does not meet the requirements of Article 11 and the counter-defendant fails to raise a jurisdictional objection, the counter-defendant may be precluded from later relying on this procedural error under Section 579 ZPO. *See* **Article 19**, at paras. 006 *et seq.* for a detailed discussion.
21. N. Pitkowitz and M. Schmitt, 'Defence Tools in Arbitration Proceedings' in *Austrian Arbitration Yearbook 2007*, C. Klausegger *et al.* (eds) (Vienna, Manz, 2007), p. 203, with reference to OGH, 2 December 2003, 6 Ob 41/03b.
22. This is another reason for why Article 11(1) and (3) should be consolidated in the next revision of the Vienna Rules. As such, however, the requirement that counter-claims be based on the same arbitration agreement is quite standard. *See, e.g.,* Article 19(3) UNCITRAL Rules ('may make a counter-claim arising out of the same contract') and R. Trittmann and C. Duve in *Practitioner's Handbook on International Arbitration*, F.B. Weigand (ed.) (Munich, C.H. Beck, 2002), p. 346.
23. Vienna Rules 2001, **Annex 2a**.

institution to decide any and all disputes between the parties, it should be able to resolve disputes that arise out of the parties' contractual relationship efficiently – i.e. in one proceeding.

If the claimant (counter-respondent) expressly agrees (arguably in writing or on **11-019** the record) that a counter-claim be admitted and thus agrees on the jurisdiction of the VIAC, even though the counter-claim is not based on the same arbitration agreement, the counter-claim should also be allowed.[24]

C.   IDENTICAL PARTIES

The counter-claim must be dismissed if the parties are not identical. Thus, a **11-020** counter-claimant is not allowed, even if the tribunal otherwise has jurisdiction over the counter-claim and the parties involved, to disrupt the ongoing arbitral process by introducing new parties, not identified as a claimant or respondent in the statement of claims, to the arbitration. This is in line with other institutional arbitration rules. For example, the ICC Rules have long been understood as preventing a respondent from asserting counter-claims against a 'new' party.[25]

This limitation makes sense. The addition of a new party to arbitral proceedings by **11-021** way of counter-claim will often raise serious issues of equal treatment, because the newly-added party may not have an appropriate opportunity to participate in the constitution of the arbitral tribunal.[26]

A more difficult situation can arise in a multi-party situation, for example, where the **11-022** respondent directs the counter-claim only against one of two or more claimants. Are the parties 'identical' within the meaning of Article 11? As no new parties are introduced, such counter-claims should in principle be allowed, subject to Article 15 (Multi-Party Proceedings)[27] and the effects such a counter-claim may have on the allocation of costs, and, more generally, the delay caused to the pending proceedings.

D.   SUBSTANTIAL DELAY

A counter-claim must be dismissed if it is submitted 'after the transmission of the **11-023** files to the sole arbitrator (arbitral tribunal)' *and* if it 'would lead to a substantial

---

24. M. Aden, *Internationale Handelsschiedsgerichtsbarkeit* (2nd edn, Munich, C.H. Beck, 2003), p. 523.
25. Y. Derains and E.A. Schwartz, *A Guide to the ICC Rules of Arbitration* (2nd edn, The Hague, Kluwer Law International, 2005), pp. 70-71; W.L. Craig, W.W. Park and J. Paulsson, *International Chamber of Commerce Arbitration* (3rd edn, New York, Oceana Publications, 2000), p. 151.
26. For issues of joinder, *see* also **Article 15**, at paras. 074 *et seq.*
27. M. Aden, *Internationale Handelsschiedsgerichtsbarkeit* (2nd edn, Munich, C.H. Beck, 2003), p. 524.

delay in the main proceedings.' This provision is particularly important as a matter of practice. Specifically, it serves as a counter-balance to the (perhaps unusually) generous principle established by Article 11(1) that counter-claims may be raised until the evidentiary hearing is closed.

11-024 It is for the tribunal to decide,[28] on a case-by-case basis and in its own discretion,[29] what constitutes 'substantial delay'; the tribunal must take into account that the delay has to be 'substantial.' The tribunal's judgment could be guided, for example, by considering:

    (i) whether the counter-claim is specifically aimed at delaying the arbitral proceeding;

    (ii) whether there is reasonable justification for why the counter-claim has not been raised earlier;[30]

    (iii) if there is an overlap between the main claim and the counter-claim regarding the issues and evidence at hand;[31]

    (iv) to what procedural stage the proceedings have progressed (including the extent to which evidence has been taken); as well as

    (v) the extent to which further submissions need to be made and further evidence needs to be taken as a result of the counter-claim.[32]

11-025 In assessing whether the delay is 'substantial' within the meaning of Article 11(3), it also appears fair for the arbitrators to contrast the cost and delay caused by the counter-claim against the costs and delays that would be caused by a new and separate arbitral proceeding possibly before a different tribunal, which might be less informed about the parties and the history of their dispute. If these costs and delays would frustrate otherwise achievable synergies and would outweigh the additional costs and delays resulting from the amended claim, separate

---

28. This discretion to allow counter-claims at a later stage in the proceedings, if justified under the circumstances of the case, is a customary power of tribunals in international arbitration and is reflected in other rules. *See, e.g.*, Article 19(3) UNCITRAL Rules ('may make a counter-claim (. . .) at a later stage in the arbitral proceedings *if the tribunal decides that the delay was justified under the circumstances*'). *See also* Section 1046(2) German ZPO.

29. *See* R. Trittmann and C. Duve in *Practitioner's Handbook on International Arbitration*, F.B. Weigand (ed.) (Munich, C.H. Beck, 2002), p. 347.

30. For (i) and (ii), *see* R. Trittmann and C. Duve in *Practitioner's Handbook on International Arbitration*, F.B. Weigand (ed.) (Munich, C.H. Beck, 2002), p. 346.

31. M. Aden, *Internationale Handelsschiedsgerichtsbarkeit* (2nd edn, Munich, C.H. Beck, 2003), p. 525.

32. As to what constitutes significant obstruction or delay, the Austrian courts have held that 'an obstruction or delay in the proceedings within the meaning of Section 235(3) ZPO is to be assumed if the proceeding has matured so far that a decision can be issued, and the proceeding would have to be conducted entirely differently in view of the amended claim which has been introduced at the very end of the proceeding, and the evidence that has already been collected cannot be used for the new claim'. *See* LGZ Vienna, 26 April 1994, 43 R 2031/94, EFSlg 76.076.

proceedings may frustrate the overall aim of Article 11 to allow the resolution of the parties' disputes in a single forum.[33] As a general rule, the further the proceedings have progressed, the higher the standards which the tribunal should apply to the admissibility of the counter-claim have to be.[34]

Other rules in the region employ different mechanisms to safeguard the arbitral **11-026** proceeding against unjustified delay.[35] Article 34(1) of the Hungarian Rules, for example, allow the defendant to bring a counter-claim 'before the close of the hearing on the principal claim' (if, of course, the tribunal has jurisdiction), but permits the tribunal to order the counter-claimant to pay the costs resulting from any unjustified delay in bringing the counter-claim. This appears to include the costs incurred by the other party as well,[36] but may ultimately not deter cash-rich defendants from delaying the arbitral process.

IV.   REPLY TO THE COUNTER-CLAIM

Article 11(4): The sole arbitrator (arbitral tribunal) must give the Counter-Respondent to an admissible counter-claim the opportunity to submit a memorandum in reply in writing and must set a time-limit for that purpose.

A counter-claim is a separate and independent affirmative claim, establishing *lis* **11-027** *pendens* and capable of *res judicata* effect.[37] As a matter of course, therefore, the claimant (counter-respondent) has the right to be heard separately on the counter-claim. Article 11(4) adds the additional qualification that the counter-respondent can exercise this right by submitting a written memorandum in reply. **Article 10** applies *mutatis mutandis*.[38] The time limit will usually follow the thirty-day rule under **Article 10**, but the tribunal is entitled to set a different time limit if the circumstances of the case so demand.

---

33. OLG Vienna, 11 November 1981, 13 R 159/81, MietSlg 33.644.
34. K.P. Berger, *International Economic Arbitration* (Boston, Kluwer Law International, 1993), p. 464.
35. Article 25 Slovak Rules allows for a counter-claim to be asserted without any qualifications other than that the counter-claim is within the tribunal's jurisdiction. Article 30 Slovenian Rules does so as well, although this appears to be inconsistent with the *telos* expressed in Article 32 Slovenian Rules, according to which the tribunal is not to admit an amendment to an existing claim, if the amendment 'would cause undue delay of the proceedings, or if there are other justified reasons for such denial'.
36. *See, e.g.*, Article 28 Czech Rules.
37. *See, e.g.*, ECJ, 13 July 1995, Case No. C-341/93, *Danvaern Production A/S v Schuhfabriken Otterbeck GmbH*, [1995] ECR I-02053. *See* also **Article 9**, at paras. 023 *et seq.*
38. *See* **Article 10**, at paras. 001 *et seq.*

11-028 Article 11(4) appears to limit the counter-respondent's right to be heard to an *'admissible'* counter-claim. However, the counter-respondent should also be heard precisely on whether or not the counter-claim is admissible in the first place.

V.   AMENDMENTS OF EXISTING CLAIMS

11-029 The admissibility of an amendment to an existing claim raises issues similar to the introduction of a counter-claim. On the one hand, arbitration is being lauded for its informality and flexibility, allowing parties to escape the procedural rigidity associated with state court litigation.[39] Particular formality in pleading is therefore not required by most international arbitration rules and is seldom rigorously observed in practice.[40] In arbitration, parties therefore enjoy, as a matter of principle, substantial freedom to amend their pleadings and change or supplement their legal arguments and factual allegations.[41]

11-030 On the other hand, the flexibility of arbitration can come at the price of delay and obstruction, in particular where irresponsible or incompetent parties are involved.[42] Deliberate disregard for deadlines, substantial eleventh-hour changes to pleadings, and the late introduction of evidence can all compromise the arbitral process.[43] Again, therefore, any provision regulating the amendment of the parties' pleadings must aim at avoiding disruption and delay, while allowing legitimate amendments where they are preferable for reasons of procedural efficacy.

11-031 The Vienna Rules do not expressly address a party's right to amend its claim. This is atypical. Many major rules contain specific provisions regarding the amendment of pending claims,[44] as do most rules in the region.[45] Article 20 UNCITRAL Rules provides, for example that 'during the course of the arbitral proceedings either party may amend or supplement his claim or defence unless the arbitral tribunal considers it inappropriate to allow such amendment having regard to the delay in making it or prejudice to the other party or any other circumstances.'[46] However, following the 2006 reform, Section 597 ZPO and the criteria set out in Article 11(3)

---

39. *See* **Article 9**, at para. 092.
40. G.B. Born, *International Commercial Arbitration – Commentary and Materials* (3rd edn, The Hague, Kluwer Law International, forthcoming). ch. 14.
41. G.B. Born, *International Commercial Arbitration – Commentary and Materials* (3rd edn, The Hague, Kluwer Law International, forthcoming), ch. 14.
42. *See* E.R. Leahy and K.J. Pierce, 'Sanctions to Control Party Misbehaviour in International Arbitration' (1986) 26 Va J Int'l Law, 292.
43. G.B. Born, *International Commercial Arbitration – Commentary and Materials* (3rd edn, The Hague, Kluwer Law International, forthcoming), ch. 14.
44. *See, e.g.,* Rule 6 AAA Commercial Arbitration Rules and Mediation Procedures; Article 4 AAA/ICDR Rules and Article 22(1)(a) LCIA Rules.
45. *See, e.g.,* Article 26 Hungarian Rules and Article 32 Slovenian Rules.
46. Article 20 UNCITRAL Rules.

provide a suitable guideline for when parties should be permitted to amend their existing claims.

A.   AMENDMENTS UNDER AUSTRIAN LAW

It may depend on applicable procedural law, or, as the case may be, the tribunal's **11-032** inclination,[47] whether a change of an existing claim constitutes an 'amendment' or rather a new claim, and whether that distinction makes a difference.[48] For state court litigation, the ZPO contains a broad definition of 'amendment'. Under Austrian law, an amendment is either: (a) an amendment of the relief requested; (b) an amendment of the factual basis for the claim or (c) an amendment of both the requested relief and the underlying facts.[49] It as been argued that the ZPO requires the Austrian courts to permit parties to make amendments to their original claims whenever possible, because

> [t]he economy of legal proceedings and the public interest in an efficient jurisprudence favour the admissibility of amendments of complaints. While under the wording of Section 235(3) ZPO[50] the admissibility seems to be subject to the discretion of the court, it appears from the overall context of the procedural rules that this 'discretion' is narrow and that 'can' really means here 'shall'. The Court therefore ought to admit the amendment to the complaint always, if it does not create a change in its jurisdiction and if it does not cause a significant obstruction or delay of the proceeding.(. . .) It is therefore only decisive whether the amendment to the complaint is an successful instrument to finally resolve the parties legal dispute.[51]

Regarding arbitration, Austrian commentators have therefore traditionally advo- **11-033** cated taking a liberal approach in permitting parties to amend their claims, save

---

47.   Y. Derains and E.A. Schwartz, *A Guide to the ICC Rules of Arbitration* (2nd edn, The Hague, Kluwer Law International, 2005), p. 268.
48.   *See, e.g.*, Article 19 ICC Rules, which does not speak of an amendment, but of a 'new claim'. For a detailed discussion, *see* Y. Derains and E.A. Schwartz, *A Guide to the ICC Rules of Arbitration* (2nd edn, The Hague, Kluwer Law International, 2005), pp. 268 *et seq.*
49.   For state court litigation, all of these amendments are in principle admissible under Section 235(3) ZPO.
50.   Section 235(3) provides: 'The Court can admit an amendment even after the proceeding has started and against the objections of the adversary party, if through the amendment the jurisdictional scope of the court is not exceeded and a significant obstruction or delay of the proceeding is not to be feared.'
51.   H.W. Fasching, *Lehrbuch des österreichischen Zivilprozeßrechts* (2nd edn, Vienna, Manz, 1990), para. 1240; *see also* A. Klauser and G. Kodek, *JN-ZPO* (16th edn, Vienna, Manz, 2006), Section 235(3), E 171 *et seq.*

where the amendments exceed the scope of the arbitration agreement or violate procedural rules agreed to by the parties:

> The amendment of a complaint is admissible within the scope and limits of the arbitration agreement even without the consent of the adversary party, if the amendment were to exceed the scope of the arbitration agreement, the arbitration agreement would have to be amended accordingly. The Tribunal can reject the amendment to the complaint only if the amended complaint exceeded the scope of the arbitration agreement or if the possibility of an amendment were limited under the procedural rules of the arbitration agreement.[52]

11-034 A liberal approach to the admissibility of amended claims is also consistent with general international arbitration practice.[53] While the ICC Rules, for example, have historically limited the power of a party to introduce new claims following signing the Terms of Reference (which rule has attracted considerable criticism), this regime has been significantly modified in the most recent version of the ICC Rules in order to allow reasonable amendments more liberally.[54] This approach seems to reflect the acknowledgement that it can be more efficient, and ultimately less costly for the parties, to avoid the commencement of a new arbitration proceeding with respect to the amended claim.

11-035 The 2006 reform introduced a specific provision governing the amendment of claims in arbitral proceedings. Pursuant to Section 597(2) ZPO, a party can

> amend or supplement its claim or pleadings during the course of the arbitral proceedings unless the arbitral tribunal considers this inappropriate due to delay.

11-036 In effect, Section 597(2) ZPO follows Article 23(2) UNCITRAL Model Law, on which it is based. It covers both *amendments* (that is, modifications of the claim or the relief requested) and *supplemental* (that is, additional) pleadings, such as new factual or legal arguments with regard to existing claims.[55]

---

52. H.W. Fasching, *Schiedsgericht und Schiedsverfahren im österreichischen und im internationalen Recht* (Vienna, Manz, 1973), p. 101.
53. *See, e.g.*, the practice of tribunals in the Iran-United States Claims Conference, applying Article 20 of the UNCITRAL Rules. Although Article 20 gives the tribunal broader discretion than it has under Austrian law (*see* **Article 20**, at paras. 093 *et seq.*), 'the tribunal's authority [to admit amendments] is not meant to discourage legitimate amendments to claims or defences', as 'in principle, the parties were entitled to amend.' *See* S. Baker and M. Davis, *The UNCITRAL Arbitration Rules in Practice* (Deventer, Kluwer, 1992), pp. 91-92.
54. *See* Y. Derains and E.A. Schwartz, *A Guide to the ICC Rules of Arbitration* (2nd edn, The Hague, Kluwer Law International, 2005), p. 267; Article 19 ICC Rules.
55. B. Kloiber and H. Haller in *Das Neue Schiedsrecht – Schiedsrechts-Änderungsgesetz 2006*, B. Kloiber, P. Oberhammer, W.H. Rechberger and H. Haller (eds) (Vienna, Manz, 2006), p. 41.

The Drafting Commission of the new Austrian arbitration law had originally **11-037** intended to permit the tribunal to reject amendments *without* regard to the delay that the amendment would cause. The Drafting Commission considered that the claimant does not have an obligation to amend its claim and that it could therefore be irrelevant whether the claimant should have amended its claim at an earlier stage in the proceeding.[56] This is not entirely persuasive. As the Drafting Committee recognized, the factor 'delay' also has an objective element when measured against the status of the proceeding at the time the claim is amended.[57] Also, the claimant may well have an obligation to conduct the arbitration in good faith and, therefore, to avoid unnecessary delay. For good reason, therefore, the factor of delay was included in the final version of Section 597(2) ZPO.

By not referring to delay, but simply stating that the arbitrators could permit or **11-038** reject an amendment, the Drafting Commission also wanted to give the tribunal an entirely free hand to decide the admissibility of amended claims in order to protect the arbitrators from having to resolve new and additional claims which the arbitrators did not agree, and would perhaps not have agreed, to adjudicate at the time of their appointment.[58] This consideration does not now appear to be reflected in the text of Section 597(2) ZPO which seems to allow the arbitrators to reject an amendment only 'due to delay'. It is still argued that arbitrators cannot be forced to hear an entirely new claim that was not originally referred to them and which they did not agree to hear.[59] As a matter of the contract formed between the arbitrators and the parties, this argument has force, although the arbitrators' duty to resolve the dispute referred to them may require them, as a contractual matter, to more liberally accept the introduction of new or amended claims.[60] As a judicial matter, the delay caused by the amendment is therefore the most relevant factor for the admissibility of amendments.

B.   AMENDMENTS UNDER THE VIENNA RULES

Based on the considerations discussed above, Article 11 provides guidance on the **11-039** admissibility of an amended claim. If anything, an amendment should be admitted even more liberally than a counter-claim.[61]

---

56. P. Oberhammer, *Entwurf eines neuen Schiedsverfarhensrechts* (Vienna, Manz, 2002), p. 98.
57. Section 235 ZPO. *See* **Article 11**, at paras. 023 *et seq.*
58. P. Oberhammer, *Entwurf eines neuen Schiedsverfahrensrechts* (Vienna, Manz, 2002), p. 98.
59. M. Platte in *Arbitration Law of Austria: Practice and Procedure*, S. Riegler, A. Petsche, A. Fremuth-Wolf, M. Platte and C. Liebscher (eds) (Huntington, Juris Publishing, 2007), Section 597, p. 359.
60. N. Pitkowitz and M. Schmitt, 'Defence Tools in Arbitration Proceedings' in *Austrian Arbitration Yearbook 2007*, C. Klausegger *et al.* (eds) (Vienna, Manz, 2007), p. 203, with reference to OGH, 2 December 2003, 6 Ob 41/03b.
61. OLG Vienna, 11 November 1981, 13 R 159/81, MietSlg 33.644.

11-040 Applied *mutatis mutandis* to amendments of claims, Article 11 requires that, following the amendment, the claim must still fall within an arbitration agreement conferring jurisdiction to the VIAC (in other words, the standing tribunal must have jurisdiction over the amended claim) and that the amended claim be between the same parties. Further, Article 11 requires that an amendment to a claim after the transmission of a file to the arbitrators be dismissed if it would cause 'substantial delay' in the main proceedings. As with counter-claims, the tribunal has discretion in assessing what constitutes a substantial delay, but if this restriction (or either of the other two restrictions) applies, it *'must'* dismiss the amendment without prejudice to be dealt with in separate proceedings. For assessing the threat of 'substantial delay', the tribunal should exercise its discretion according to the same guiding principles discussed above with respect to Article 11.

11-041 It is debatable to what extent Article 11(2) is applicable to the amendment of existing claims. Where the amendment affects the calculation of the administrative costs of the arbitration and the arbitrators' fees, the Secretariat must at least be notified so that it can request an additional deposit, if appropriate, under the procedure set out in **Article 34(5)**.[62]

11-042 If the amendment is admitted, the respondent must be given the right to be heard on the amended claim 'in writing' pursuant to Article 11(4) of the Vienna Rules and to general principles of due process under applicable law.[63]

VI.   SET-OFF

11-043 Article 11 does not address claims which the respondent may raise as a *defence* (as opposed to a separate, affirmative counter-claim) by deducting the set-off claim from the *quantum* requested by the claimant. Austrian law is perhaps peculiar in this regard because it distinguishes between two kinds of set-off. First, the so-called declaration of set-off (*Aufrechnungserklärung*) raised outside litigation proceedings. Such a set-off declaration serves as substitute form of payment[64] and, importantly, is premised on an acknowledgment that the principal claim exists.[65] Second, Austrian law recognizes the set-off raised as procedural plea by the defendant in litigation. This procedural set-off defence (*Aufrechnungseinrede*) does not require the respondent to acknowledge the principal claim: rather, this set-off will only apply if the court finds in favour of the claimant with regard to the

---

62. *See* **Article 34**, at paras. 056 *et seq.*
63. *See* **Article 20**, at paras. 037 *et seq.*
64. *See* S. Dullinger in *Kommentar zum ABGB, II/1*, P. Rummel (ed.) (3rd edn, Vienna, Manz, 2002), Section 1438, p. 487.
65. *See* I. Griss in *Kommentar zum ABGB*, H. Koziol, P. Bydlinski and R. Bollenberger (eds) (Vienna/New York, Springer, 2005), Section 1438, pp. 1581 *et seq.*; other opinion: S. Dullinger in *Kommentar zum ABGB, II/1*, P. Rummel (ed.) (3rd edn, Vienna, Manz, 2002), Section 1438, p. 487.

principal claim, in which case the set-off claim (if found to exist) will be deducted.[66]

The discussion below is only concerned with this procedural set-off defence. In this **11-044** regard, it has been suggested that the Vienna Rules' silence on the admissibility of set-off defence constitutes an inadvertent *lacuna*. This has been doubtful under the previous version of the Vienna Rules; it certainly is not the case under the Vienna Rules 2006. Despite the extensive discussion of this point,[67] the VIAC plainly chose not to address the admissibility of set-off in the new rules.[68] Indeed, arbitral rules are not necessarily the appropriate place to regulate the admissibility of a set-off, as it is for applicable *substantive* law to determine whether or not a set-off is permissible in the first place.[69] In Austria, for example, the substantive requirements for set-off are regulated in Section 1438 ABGB, which requires a claim that is due and of 'similar kind'.[70] Procedural law, by contrast, only determines whether or not a set-off defence can, *as a matter of jurisdiction*, be asserted before the arbitral tribunal that was constituted to adjudicate the claimant's claim.[71] This is discussed below.

A.   JURISDICTION

Like the Vienna Rules, the ZPO is silent on the admissibility of set-off defences. **11-045** Some authors take silence to mean that only extraneous *declarations of set-off* (*Aufrechnungserklärungen*) shall be admissible in arbitration proceedings (which would force the respondent to acknowledge the principal claim).[72] This is not convincing: absent a particular provision in the ZPO, a set-off defence is simply subject to the same jurisdictional considerations as any other claim.

---

66. W.H. Rechberger in *Kommentar zur ZPO*, W.H. Rechberger (ed.) (3rd edn, Vienna, Manz, 2006), Sections 391-392, para. 10.
67. C. Liebscher in *Arbitration Law of Austria: Practice and Procedure*, S. Riegler, A. Petsche, A. Fremuth-Wolf, M. Platte and C. Liebscher (eds) (Huntington, Juris Publishing, 2007), p. 628 with further references.
68. The cost implication of set-off defence are dealt with under **Article 36(3)**, at paras. 012 *et seq.*
69. OGH, 14 November 1990, 1 Ob 711/89; OGH, 22 October 2001, 1 Ob 77/01g; in Germany, *see* BGH, 22 November 1962, VII ZR 264/61 in BGHZ 38, 254, 257 with a discussion of Section 389 BGB and its procedural ramifications; *see also* H.C. Köhne and S. Langner, 'Geltendmachung von Gegenforderungen im Internationalen Schiedsverfahren' [2003] RIW, 361, 362-363 and K.P. Berger, 'Set-Off in International Economic Arbitration' (1999) 15(1) Arb Int'l, 53-84.
70. H. Koziol and R. Welser, *Bürgerliches Recht II* (13th edn, Vienna, Manz, 2007), pp. 103 *et seq.*
71. M. Aden, *Internationale Handelsschiedsgerichtsbarkeit* (2nd edn, Munich, C.H. Beck, 2003), pp. 523 *et seq.*
72. *See* G. Zeiler, *Schiedsverfahren* (Vienna/Graz, Neuer Wissenschaftlicher Verlag, 2006), Section 597, p. 209.

11-046 Under Austrian procedural law, set-offs in arbitration[73] are therefore in principle admissible if the set-off claim is covered by the parties' arbitration agreement,[74] lest as a matter of principle the tribunal lacks the necessary jurisdiction to adjudicate the set-off claim.[75] This appears to be consistent with the position under German law.[76] Under the systemic principle now expressed in Article 11, however, the set-off claim need not fall under the *same* arbitration agreement that covers the claimant's principal claim; it only needs to fall under *any* arbitration agreement between the parties that confers jurisdiction on the VIAC.

11-047 If the set-off claim is outside an appropriate arbitration agreement, the failure to object against the set-off claim may extend the arbitration agreement to such claim.[77]

11-048 In Germany, commentators have argued to permit a set-off which is based on claim outside the arbitration agreement if the set-off claim has been confirmed through a final judgment, or if it is undisputed, or if the claimant has not objected against the defendant's set-off; or if the parties have extended their arbitration agreement to the set-off claim through express or implied agreement.[78] Some commentators want to admit set-off claims based in contracts that do not contain an arbitration or forum selection clause and that are 'closely related' to the dispute at hand.[79] The argument is one of procedural efficiency (although procedural efficiency may not be able to overcome jurisdictional concerns).[80]

---

73. It is possible for a defendant in litigation before the Austrian national courts to rely on a set-off, if the set-off claim is covered by an arbitration agreement. *See* OGH, 14 November 1990, 1 Ob 711/89.

74. H.W. Fasching, *Schiedsgericht und Schiedsverfahren im österreichischen und im internationalen Recht* (Vienna, Manz, 1973), p. 27; H.W. Fasching, *Kommentar zu den Zivilprozeßgesetzen III* (Vienna, Manz, 1966), post Section 391, p. 577.

75. H.W. Fasching, *Kommentar zu den Zivilprozeßgesetzen III* (Vienna, Manz, 1966), post Section 391, p. 577; H.W. Fasching, *Schiedsgericht und Schiedsverfahren im österreichischen und im internationalen Recht* (Vienna, Manz, 1973), p. 27; *see also* G. Backhausen, *Schiedsgerichtsbarkeit unter besonderer Berücksichtigung des Schiedsvertragsrechts* (Vienna, Manz, 1998), pp. 140 *et seq.* Only *Matscher*, referring to the function of a set-off claim as a defence, wants to allow set-off under all circumstances. *See* F. Matscher, 'Probleme der Schiedsgerichtsbarkeit im österreichischen Recht' [1975] JBl, 412, 416 *et seq.*

76. H.C. Köhne and S. Langner, 'Geltendmachung von Gegenforderungen im Internationalen Schiedsverfahren' [2003] RIW, 361, 362.

77. M. Aden, *Internationale Handelsschiedsgerichtsbarkeit* (2nd edn, Munich, C.H. Beck, 2003), p. 523.

78. H.C. Köhne and S. Langner, 'Geltendmachung von Gegenforderungen im Internationalen Schiedsverfahren' [2003] RIW, 361.

79. M. Schöll, 'Set-Off Defenses in International Arbitration: Criteria for Best Practice – A Comparative Perspective' in *Best Practice in International Arbitration*, M. Wirth (ed.) (ASA Special Series No. 26, 2006), p. 98.

80. For a detailed discussion of these issues, *see* N. Pitkowitz and M. Schmitt, 'Defence Tools in Arbitration Proceedings' in *Austrian Arbitration Yearbook 2007*, C. Klausegger *et al.* (eds) (Vienna, Manz, 2007), pp. 195 *et seq.*

Reiner has argued that set-off claims should be admissible even if arising from **11-049** contracts that contain a different arbitration or even a forum selection clause.[81] In doing so, *Reiner* applies *per analogiam* Austrian case law which allows a defendant to rely on a set-off defence in state court litigation even where the set-off arises from a contract subject to an arbitration agreement.[82] This argument has force in light of the nature of the set-off as a defence which, if so mandated as a matter of *substantive* law, should in principle be available to the respondent. For this reason, it is not convincing to state that 'the cross-claim [being] subject to a different dispute settlement clause clearly expresses that the parties did not want the set-off defence to be decided by an arbitral tribunal'.[83] The parties will have expressed a view that affirmative claims be subject to a certain dispute resolution mechanism, but it is less clear that they would not have permitted to advance defences (that are available under substantive law) in a single forum.

In sum, the issue is still disputed. As with all jurisdictional issues, proceeding to an **11-050** award without sound jurisdictional basis runs the risk of *vacatur*. A respondent may therefore want to consider asserting the set-off in the course of a parallel proceeding before competent state courts. Alternatively, at least if the respondent is not permitted to advance the set-off in the arbitration, the respondent may be able under Austrian law, by way of so-called *Oppositionsklage*, to raise a set-off available under substantive law against the enforcement of an arbitral award.[84]

B.   COST IMPLICATIONS

A set-off claim may have cost implications under **Article 36(3)**, at least if the set- **11-051** off claim is not closely connected to the main claim. The argument seems to be that if the set-off involves similar factual arguments and evidence or legal considerations, a separate and additional cost deposit is not justified.[85]

---

81. A. Reiner, 'Aufrechnung trotz (Fehlens einer) Schiedsvereinbarung nach österreichischem Recht' in *Festschrift für Dr. Karl Hempel zum 60. Geburtstag: Recht in Österreich und Europa*, H. Mayer, F. von Schlabrendorff, B. Spiegelfeld and R. Welser (eds) (Vienna, Manz, 1997), pp. 110 *et seq.*
82. *See, e.g.*, OGH, 27 February 2002, 3 Ob 167/01g.
83. M. Platte in *Arbitration Law of Austria: Practice and Procedure*, S. Riegler, A. Petsche, A. Fremuth-Wolf, M. Platte and C. Liebscher (eds) (Huntington, Juris Publishing, 2007), Section 597, p. 364.
84. H.C. Köhne and S. Langner, 'Geltendmachung von Gegenforderungen im Internationalen Schiedsverfahren' [2003] RIW, 361, 366; *see also* N. Pitkowitz and M. Schmitt, 'Defence Tools in Arbitration Proceedings' in *Austrian Arbitration Yearbook 2007*, C. Klausegger *et al.* (eds) (Vienna, Manz, 2007), p. 206; OGH, 29 March 2006, 3 Ob 290/05a; *see also* OGH, 12 September 1951, 1 Ob 623/51.
85. N. Pitkowitz and M. Schmitt, 'Defence Tools in Arbitration Proceedings' in *Austrian Arbitration Yearbook 2007*, C. Klausegger *et al.* (eds) (Vienna, Manz, 2007), p. 202.

11-052 It appears that, as a matter of practice, the Secretary General adds the amount claimed as set-off to the main claim, and invoices half of the resulting deposit fee to each of the parties. However, before doing so, the Secretary General usually inquires with the arbitrators whether the set-off claim will be admitted to the proceedings. In 3 Ob 84/01a, 25 April 2001, the Austrian *Oberster Gerichtshof* also held, in the context of enforcement proceedings relating to a foreign award, that it does not violate the *ordre public* if a tribunal makes the admission of a set-off contingent on the payment of a separate cost advance.[86]

---

86. *See also* **Article 36**, at para. 018.

Article 12

Transmission of the File to the Arbitrators

		Para.			Para.
I.	Introduction..	1	B.	Acceptance of the Arbitrator's Mandate and 'Confirmation of Objectivity'..	10
II.	Submission of the Files to the Arbitrators...	4			
	A. Statement of Claims in Due Form..	7	C.	Deposit Against Costs Has Been Paid	22

Article 12: The Secretary General shall transmit the files to the sole arbitrator (arbitral tribunal) as soon as a statement of claims (counterclaim) has been received in due form, the sole arbitrator (all members of the arbitral tribunal) has (have) confirmed acceptance of the mandate and his (its) objectivity, using a form issued by the Centre (Article 7 paragraph 2), and the deposit for costs has been paid (Article 34). The proceedings before the sole arbitrator (arbitral tribunal) shall thereby commence.

I.   INTRODUCTION

Article 12, which used to form part of Article 7(3) of the Vienna Rules 2001,[1] has **12-001** now been extracted into a separate provision. Article 12 marks the important procedural point when the file is transmitted to the arbitrators. From this date onwards, it is the arbitral tribunal (and no longer the Secretary General) who determines the conduct of the proceedings, within the framework of **Article 20**. Also from this date, any subsequent reduction of the amount in dispute will,

---

1. Vienna Rules 2001, **Annex 2a**.

according to **Article 36(8)**, no longer be considered for the purposes of calculating the costs of the arbitration. The same is true with respect to the calculation of costs pursuant to additional parties under **Article 36(2)**.[2] However, despite the wording of Article 12, transmission of the file to the arbitrators does not 'commence' the arbitration as such, with consequences for the statute of limitations and *lis pendens*. As discussed in the context of **Article 9**, the arbitration is already properly commenced when the statement of claims is duly received by the Secretariat.[3]

12-002   The exact time at which the file is considered to be transmitted is the moment at which the file is (demonstrably) handed over to the arbitrator. In case of a tribunal, the file needs to have been transmitted to all arbitrators, so the date on which the last member of the tribunal receives the file is the date of transmission.[4] The Secretary General keeps the relevant records in his files, should the exact date of transmission become relevant.

12-003   The following section gives an overview on how the Secretary General practically approaches potential arbitrators at the beginning of the proceedings, collects the deposit against costs and, finally, transfers the files of the case to the arbitrator(s).

II.   SUBMISSION OF THE FILES TO THE ARBITRATORS

12-004   Under the Vienna Rules, the statement of claims is not served on the respondent but is submitted to the Secretary General.[5] The Secretary General then manages the file until four conditions are met and the file is transferred to the arbitrators. First, a statement of claims must have been received in proper form complying with **Article 9**.[6] Second, the arbitrator(s) must have confirmed their acceptance of the mandate as well as their 'objectivity'.[7] Third, the cost deposit must have been paid. Fourth, and finally, the time limit for submitting a memorandum in reply must have expired.[8]

12-005   This last condition is not explicitly mentioned in Article 12 but derives directly from **Article 10**. On the one hand, the arbitrators should receive a full file that includes the memorandum in reply. Also, in a typical arbitration, the respondent's co-arbitrator will be nominated with the memorandum in reply. On the other hand, the respondent's failure to submit a memorandum in reply (or to nominate a co-arbitrator) will not stop the file from being transmitted to the tribunal (once constituted).

---

2. *See* **Article 36(2)**, at para. 011.
3. *See* **Article 9**, at para. 015.
4. To ensure parity on the tribunal, the file is transmitted on the same day to all arbitrators.
5. *See* **Article 9**, at para. 003.
6. *See* **Article 9**, at paras. 046 *et seq.*
7. For the arbitrators' duty to be, and remain, independent and impartial, *see* **Article 7**, at paras. 058 and 080 *et seq.* For a discussion of the term 'objectivity' as used in Article 12, *see* **Article 12**, at para. 012.
8. Or there is sufficient indication that respondent will not participate in the arbitration proceeding.

The English language version of the Vienna Rules refers to the *files* (plural) to be **12-006** submitted. Of course, each case is allocated a single case number constituting a single file.[9] However, it is clear from the authentic German version that the Secretary General transmits 'the documents pertaining to the case' *('Unterlagen zum Fall')* to the arbitrators, thus including any further correspondence that has occurred in addition to the statement of claims and the memorandum in reply. Naturally, the Secretary General has the obligation to submit the complete file, including these additional documents, to the arbitrator(s). Indeed, the Vienna Rules do not distinguish between correspondence between the parties and correspondence between the parties and the VIAC. For this reason, the arbitrator can assume that the file transmitted by the Secretary General contains all relevant correspondence which has occurred by that point in time.

A.   STATEMENT OF CLAIMS IN DUE FORM

The *prima facie* scrutiny of the statement of claims performed by the Secretary **12-007** General has been addressed in the context of **Article 9**. However, there is no clear indication in the text that the statement of claims must have been served on the respondent for the file to be transmitted to the arbitrator. Indeed, the authentic German version of this provision merely provides that the statement of claims has 'to be available' *('vorliegen')*, without addressing the question of service at all.[10]

A systemic interpretation of the Vienna Rules leaves no doubt, however, that the **12-008** respondent must have been served with the statement of claims before the file can be transmitted to the tribunal. First, Section 580(2) ZPO requires that the respondent has 'knowledge of the proceedings'.[11] Second, if the statement of claims were not delivered, the respondent would obviously not have been able to nominate its own co-arbitrator, leading to a substitutional appointment under **Article 14**. This provision applies only, however, if the respondent is *in default* with respect to nominating its co-arbitrator. As a rule, the Secretary General requests the respondent to nominate an arbitrator together with serving the statement of claims. If, for whatever reason, neither the statement of claims nor the request to nominate an arbitrator have effectively been served on the respondent, a substitute appointment under **Article 14** is not permissible.[12]

In short, the Secretary General can transmit the file to the arbitrators not merely **12-009** after having received the statement of claims in due form, but only after the

---

9. *See* **Article 9**, at paras. 013 *et seq.*
10. *See* **Article 10**, at paras. 007 *et seq.*, on the question of delivery of the statement of claims to the respondent.
11. *See* **Article 9**, at para. 055 and **Article 13**, at para. 042.
12. It is conceivable that the parties have, although this happens rarely, appointed a specific arbitrator in their arbitration agreement. In this case, it is possible that the file is handed to the arbitrator without prior submission of the statement of claims to the respondent. However, in such rare circumstances the arbitrator(s) would be well advised to ensure that the respondent's right to be heard is not infringed through *ex parte* proceedings.

statement of claims has been served on the respondent, the time limit for submitting a memorandum in reply has expired, and the tribunal has been constituted, either through party nominations or through substitute appointments pursuant to **Article 14** or, for multi-party cases, under **Article 15**.

B.   ACCEPTANCE OF THE ARBITRATOR'S MANDATE AND
                                'CONFIRMATION OF OBJECTIVITY'

12-010 For the file to be transmitted to the arbitrators, Article 12 also requires that the arbitrators have accepted their mandate and confirmed their 'objectivity'. The task to approach the arbitrators for this purpose lies with the Secretary General.[13] Usually, the Secretary General will direct a request in writing to the candidate, with notice that he or she has been elected by one or all parties, or else been proposed by the Board for substitute appointment. This request is accompanied by the form asking the candidate to accept the mandate in compliance with the Vienna Rules, if he or she wishes to do so, by signing and returning the form to the Secretariat. A template of this form is produced as **Annex 4**.

12-011 Article 12 requires the arbitrator to produce a two-pronged confirmation. First, by signing the form, the arbitrator accepts the mandate, and thus accepts to conduct the arbitration pursuant to the Vienna Rules. Hence, the form provides a separate space for the arbitrator to expressly accept the appointment, to submit to the Vienna Rules and to confirm that he or she has taken notice of the Guidelines for Arbitrators dated July 2007.[14] A necessary corollary of the arbitrator's general submission to the Vienna Rules is the separate undertaking to specifically observe the rules on costs. The form thus additionally requires the arbitrator to acknowledge that determinations as to cost advances, arbitrators' fees and administrative costs in the arbitration shall be made exclusively by the Secretary General (pursuant to **Articles 34** and **36**) and that such determinations are recognized as binding on the arbitrator. Further, the arbitrator has to acknowledge that he or she may not take any action that will incur costs (such as, for example, the appointment of experts) before appropriate arrangements to cover the expected costs have been made.[15] The arbitrator's right and duties, and the contractual relationship between the arbitrator and the parties and the VIAC, respectively, are further discussed in detail in the context of **Article 7**.

12-012 Second, by signing the form and returning it to the Secretariat, the arbitrator also confirms that he or she is independent. The form provides that there are no circumstances known to him or her that would justify a challenge to his or her acting as an arbitrator pursuant to **Article 16**. It is noteworthy that Article 12 itself requires the arbitrator to confirm his or her 'objectivity' thus introducing a different term compared to the arbitrators 'impartiality and independence' under

---

13. *See* **Article 5**, at para. 001.
14. Guidelines for Arbitrators, **Annex 5**.
15. *See* **Article 35(1)**, at paras. 001 *et seq.*

Article 7(2)(b) and **Article 16**. The term 'objectivity' is also alien to Section 588 ZPO which refers to impartiality and independence as well. However, the confirmation form used by the VIAC leaves no doubt that 'objectivity' within the meaning of Article 12 is supposed to refer to impartiality and independence. Thus, the use of 'objectivity' appears to be an editorial mistake and is not meant to introduce an additional standard of neutrality.[16]

The importance of impartiality under Austrian law and international practice is **12-013** discussed in detail in the context of **Article 7**. In the context of the confirmation required under Article 12, it bears emphasis that the arbitrator is entitled to request all information necessary to assess his or her independence and impartiality, and to make the necessary disclosures. Prudent arbitrators will therefore typically inquire into the full identity of the parties and will want to review the arbitration agreement.[17]

In practice, the Secretary General has upon the request of prospective arbitrators **12-014** also provided them with copies of the submissions from the parties. Such an informal exchange of information does not constitute 'transmission' within the meaning of Article 12, nor does it have the effect of 'commencing the proceedings'.[18] Assuming that the arbitrator then, for whatever reason, decides not to accept the mandate, there is an implied undertaking to keep any information so received strictly confidential.[19]

Usually, the potential arbitrator either rejects his or her appointment due to **12-015** potential conflicts or else accepts unconditionally.[20] Sometimes, however,

---

16. *See also* C. Liebscher in *Arbitration Law of Austria: Practice and Procedure*, S. Riegler, A. Petsche, A. Fremuth-Wolf, M. Platte and C. Liebscher (eds) (Huntington, Juris Publishing, 2007), p. 629, who argues that 'objectivity' is an umbrella term comprising both independence and impartiality.

17. As noted at **Article 7**, at paras. 027 *et seq.*, the arbitration agreements may contain additional requirements imposed on prospective arbitrators. Prior to accepting their mandate, arbitrators are therefore well advised to review the arbitration agreement. If the parties have agreed on particular qualifications or additional skills the arbitrator would have to meet, the arbitrator is under an obligation to ensure his or her suitability for the particular case, irrespective of whether the arbitrator was proposed and agreed upon by the parties or whether the candidate is approached in the course of a substitute appointment by the Board (although in the latter case, the Secretary General will, qua *culpa in eligendo*, have a corresponding duty to investigate on a preliminary basis whether the candidate matches the criteria the parties have agreed upon.)

18. C. Liebscher in *Arbitration Law of Austria: Practice and Procedure*, S. Riegler, A. Petsche, A. Fremuth-Wolf, M. Platte and C. Liebscher (eds) (Huntington, Juris Publishing, 2007), p. 629.

19. The same has been argued under German law. *See* W. Voit in *Kommentar zur Zivilprozessordnung*, H.-J. Musielak (ed.) (6th edn, Munich, Verlag Franz Vahlen, 2008), Section 1035 ZPO, para. 24.

20. This approach reflects international practice, as for example Article 7(2) ICC Rules reads: 'Before his appointment, an arbitrator shall sign a statement of independence and disclose in writing to the Secretariat any facts and circumstances which might call into question the

arbitrators declare their acceptance of the mandate, but feel compelled to simultaneously disclose a certain relationship with one of the parties, therefore accepting the mandate 'with reservation'. The new 'declaration of independence'[21] under the Vienna Rules therefore contains a separate column for the candidate to declare that there are no circumstances known to him or her that would require disqualification while at the same time enabling the disclosure of facts that 'from the perspective of the parties, could possibly call the independence into question'.

12-016 In this case, and as discussed in greater detail in the context of **Article 16**, the Secretary General has to forward the arbitrator's notification to the parties and request their comments as to whether the parties agree to the appointment despite the potential conflict. In this event, the parties will have to declare, within the time limit set by the Secretary General, whether they accept the reservation to the arbitrator's independence, impartiality or lack of specific qualification. The party concerned is well advised to comply with this time limit, as belated pleadings could be considered inadmissible under **Article 16(1)**.

12-017 The arbitrator is not entitled to compensation for inquiring into the circumstances of the case, assessing his or her impartibility and impendence and, where necessary, making the appropriate disclosure. This is an arbitrator's duty *in contrahendo*; a prospective arbitrator is of course free to refuse the mandate from the outset, thus avoiding any inquiries of this sort.

12-018 The Vienna Rules contain no time limit within which prospective arbitrators have to confirm to the Secretary General that they accept the mandate. It is the Secretary General's practice, in order to expedite the proceedings, to set a time limit that is brief.[22] In case the candidate nominated by the parties is unable or unwilling to accept the mandate, the Secretary General has to inform the parties immediately. In modern practice, however, parties will oftentimes approach potential arbitrators to clear conflicts, and establish those arbitrators' willingness to accept the mandate, before making a nomination.[23]

---

independence of the arbitrator.' Similar in Article 5(3) LCIA Rules where before appointment, each arbitrator shall provide the Registrar with 'a written resume of his past and present professional positions' and he shall sign a 'declaration to the effect that there are no circumstances known to him likely to give rise to any justified doubts as to his impartiality or independence, other than any circumstances disclosed by him in the declaration'. Similar also Article 7 AAA/ICDR Rules 'Prior to accepting appointment, a prospective arbitrator shall disclose to the administrator any circumstances likely to give rise to justifiable doubts as to the arbitrator's impartiality or independence.'

21. *See* Arbitrator's Declaration of Acceptance, Statement of Independence and Undertaking to Observe Rules on Costs, **Annex 4**.

22. *See, e.g.*, Article 16(1) DIS Rules which provides that 'each person who is nominated as arbitrator shall *without undue delay* notify the DIS Secretariat of his acceptance of the office as arbitrator and declare whether he fulfils the qualifications agreed upon by the parties. Such person shall disclose all circumstances which are likely to give rise to doubts as to his impartiality or independence.'

23. For the limits of such *ex parte* approaches, *see* **Article 7**, at paras. 032 *et seq.*

If the prospective arbitrator refuses to accept the mandate, or if the acceptance is **12-019** not forthcoming within the time limit set by the Secretary General (or, where no time limit is set, a reasonable period of time), parties should be permitted to nominate a different arbitrator without the substitute appointment procedure under **Article 14** to take effect.[24] However, it is arguable, on the basis of **Article 18(1)** last sentence,[25] that each party is given no more than two chances to nominate an arbitrator in order to avoid any unnecessary delay in the proceedings.

When the file has been transmitted to the arbitrators, the Secretary General will **12-020** provide the parties with a copy of the arbitrators' declaration of independence. At this occasion, the Secretary General officially puts the parties on notice that the file has been handed over to the arbitrators and invites the parties to direct all future correspondence regarding the conduct of the proceedings to the tribunal.[26]

The Secretary General regularly requests the arbitrators to submit copies of all their **12-021** procedural orders, in particular copies of all summons, to the Secretariat, in order to keep a shadow file for all cases. Although the Vienna Rules do not expressly provide for this, the Secretary General also requests the parties to send courtesy copies of all submissions together with all enclosures, to the Secretariat which can in any event be considered good practice in institutional arbitration proceedings.[27]

C. DEPOSIT AGAINST COSTS HAS BEEN PAID

Article 12 provides that the file may only be handed to the arbitrators once the **12-022** deposit against costs has been paid; the deposit has to be paid in full. This provision must be read together with **Article 34(2)** vesting the Secretary General with the authority to determine, and then collect, the deposit against the expected costs of arbitration.[28]

The last amendment of the Vienna Rules included the (potential) VAT on the **12-023** arbitrator's fees as part of the costs of the proceedings. Thus, the Secretary

---

24. A different approach can be found in Article 11(3) Schedule B – Conciliation (Additional Facility) Rules of ICSID which reads: 'If a conciliator fails to accept his appointment within 15 days, the Secretary General shall promptly notify the parties, and if appropriate the Chairman, and invite them to proceed to the appointment of another conciliator in accordance with the method followed for the previous appointment.'
25. 'If a new arbitrator nominated has also been successfully challenged, the right to nominate a new arbitrator shall lapse and the new arbitrator shall be appointed by the Board.'
26. Of course, there are submissions that by their very nature, as typically recognized by the Vienna Rules, continue to be directed to the VIAC, such as the challenge of an arbitrator under **Article 14**.
27. *See, e.g.,* the express obligation in this respect under Article 3 ICC Rules. *See* Y. Derains and E.A. Schwartz, *A Guide to the ICC Rules of Arbitration* (2nd edn, The Hague, Kluwer Law International, 2005), p. 211.
28. *See* **Article 34**, at paras. 019 *et seq.*

General, before requesting the parties to pay the shares of the deposit, will informally approach the arbitrators to inquire the tax rate which the arbitrators consider
applicable to their fee. This amount will now be included in the calculation of the
deposit of costs.[29]

12-024 It is of no relevance for the purposes of Article 12 whether all parties have honoured the request to pay the deposit or whether the claimant has provisionally paid
the outstanding share for respondent.

12-025 As **Article 34** (in connection with Article 12) allows the Secretary General only to
proceed with the administration of the case once the full amount of the deposit has
been paid, this entails the risk of delaying the constitution of the tribunal.[30] To
mitigate that risk, the Secretary General presently follows the practice to approach
the arbitrators *before* the deposit of costs has been paid in full. In such a case, the
candidates are informed about the financial status of the case and that their appointment is conditional upon the receipt of the full deposit. Once the deposit is then
paid in full, the file can be transmitted to the arbitrators without further delay.

---

29. *See* **Article 36(10)**, at para. 041 *et seq.*
30. Note the two different thirty day time limits under **Article 34**, at paras. 029 *et seq.*, and 033.

Article 13

Time Limits, Service and Communications

		Para.
I.	Time Limits	1
	A. Introduction	1
	B. When Do Time Limits Commence?	4
	C. When Are Time Limits Observed?	6
	D. Extensions of Time Limits	9
II.	Effective Service	15
	A. Communications in Arbitral Proceedings	15
	1. Communications of the Parties	18
	2. Communications of and amongst the Arbitral Tribunal	21

		Para.
	3. Communication with the Secretary General	25
	4. Communication with the Board	28
	5. Communication with State Courts	29
	B. Form of Communications	30
	C. Recipients of Delivery	35
	1. To the Address Most Recently Notified	37
	2. Actual and/or Demonstrable Transmission	44
III.	Service to the Party Representative	48

I.   TIME LIMITS

Article 13(1): A time-limit shall be deemed to have been observed if the document is dispatched as provided under paragraph 2 of the present Article on the last day of the period set. Time-limits can be prolonged by the Secretary General on sufficient grounds; after the transmission of the files to the sole arbitrator (arbitral tribunal), the sole arbitrator (arbitral tribunal) shall be competent to prolong time-limits (except in the cases covered by Article 34 paragraphs 5 and 6).

A.   INTRODUCTION

13-001 The rules governing time limits are naturally important in any arbitration, and they have to strike a delicate balance. On the one hand, time management is plainly essential in arbitration proceedings. The parties involved have to be provided with a workable tool to expedite proceedings and to exclude dilatory tactics to the largest possible extent. On the other hand, the rules have to guarantee that the right to be heard will not be compromised in favour of these considerations of procedural efficiency.

13-002 The following section will discuss how time limits are determined, how submissions are served, and how information is exchanged and communicated between the players of an international arbitration under the Vienna Rules. Article 13(1) refers expressly only to time limits set by the Secretary General and the arbitral tribunal, but there is no doubt that the scope of this provision also covers any time limits set by the Board of the VIAC.

13-003 It bears emphasis in this context that the parties, as a result of party autonomy, and the arbitrators, within the scope of **Article 20**, are free to enter into their own (deviating) procedural arrangements. Their discretion is limited, of course, in so far as the VIAC itself is concerned, as neither the parties nor the arbitrators can impose on the conduct of the institution.[1]

B.   WHEN DO TIME LIMITS COMMENCE?

13-004 The Vienna Rules, unlike other arbitration rules, do not contain any indication as to when a time limit is deemed to have commenced. Article 18(2) AAA/ICDR Rules, for example, provides that time limits 'shall begin to run on the day following the day when a notice, statement or written communication is received'. Article 3(4) ICC Rules states in similar vein that time periods 'shall start to run on the day following the date a notification or communication is deemed to have been made (. . .)' which is[2] 'on the day, when it was received by the party itself or by its representatives, or would have been received (. . .).'[3]

13-005 Given the uniform approach of major institutions, it appears sensible to assume for arbitrations under the Vienna Rules as well that time limits commence on the day following the date when the document is deemed to have been received.[4] As

---

1. Furthermore, any arrangement deviating, supplementing or complementing the Vienna Rules has ultimately to be measured against the threshold of **Article 9(6)**.
2. According to Article 3(3) ICC Rules.
3. Similar provisions can be found, *inter alia*, in Article 3(1) UNCITRAL Model Law; Article 4(3) LCIA Rules and Article 5(3) DIS Rules.
4. This is in line with the Austrian Rules of Delivery (*Österreichisches Zustellgesetz* – ZustG). According to Section 13 ZustG, a submission is considered to be effectively served when it was

discussed further below, Section 580 ZPO now clarifies for arbitrations sited in Austria that any written communication is deemed to have been received on the day on which it is delivered to the addressee or to an authorized recipient or, if this was not possible, to the registered office, place of residence or habitual residence of the recipient.[5] Article 13(2) and (3), discussed further below, extend the possibilities of validly effecting delivery.[6]

C.   WHEN ARE TIME LIMITS OBSERVED?

There is also some ambiguity between the authentic German version and the **13-006** official English translation of Article 13. The authentic German version of Article 13(1) reads: '*Eine Frist ist gewahrt, wenn das Schriftstück am letzten Tag der Frist in einer in Abs 2 vorgesehenen Weise versendet wird.*' Translated into English, this reads: 'A time limit *is observed*, if the document is dispatched on the last day.' However, the official English translation published by the VIAC provides that a 'time limit shall be *deemed to have been observed* if (. . .)'. This appears to suggest that the observance of a time limit is merely a legal fiction that can be disproved.[7] This is not the case – a time limit under the Vienna Rules is plainly observed when the document is '*dispatched*' (as opposed to being '*received*') either by registered letter, courier service, telefax or by any other means of communication that guarantee evidence of transmission. As a result, observance of a time limit hinges on two conditions: first, on the dispatch (rather than the receipt) of the communication; and second, on the dispatch being made in a way and form recognized under the Vienna Rules.

Naturally, even though Article 13(1) only refers to the *dispatch* (and not the **13-007** receipt) of communications, there is no doubt that a time limit can also be observed if the document has been demonstrably and in actual fact delivered on the last day of the time period.

---

handed over at the place of delivery. Substitutional deliveries are, under certain circumstances, possible. The time limit commences with the valid delivery, the day of delivery is usually not accounted for. Therefore, it commences with the day following the day of delivery at 00:00 hour. Holidays do not effect the commencement of time limit. In case of day and week time limits the day of delivery has to be added on to the duration of time limit (in number of days). When it extends beyond the end of the month the number of days of the month preceding has to be deducted. Month and annual time limits end with the expiration of the day of the last week or the month which was declared by name or by number as the day of commencement. In case this day falls in the last month of the time limit, the time limit will end with the expiration of the last day of this month. *See* E. Gitschthaler in *Kommentar zur ZPO*, W.H. Rechberger (ed.) (3rd edn, Vienna/New York, Springer, 2006), Sections 125 *et seq.*

5. This is under the assumption that the parties have made no deviating agreement.
6. *See* **Article 13**, at paras. 030 *et seq.*, and 048 *et seq.*
7. Assuming that the provision does not contain a *praesumptio iuris et de iure.*

13-008 The Vienna Rules do not contain a rule providing for the situation that the last day of the time limit is an official holiday or non-business day. All major arbitration rules provide for such a case that the time limit should expire at the end of the first business day thereafter.[8] Given the strong precedent in other rules, one can assume that this principle constitutes established international practice. For this purpose, it is the sender's schedule of public holidays that is relevant, not the receiving party's.[9]

D.   EXTENSIONS OF TIME LIMITS

13-009 Article 13(1) makes clear that time limits set under the Vienna Rules are not of an absolute nature that would preclude any possibility of extension.[10] Rather, time limits can be extended 'on sufficient grounds'. Naturally, the party requesting that a deadline be extended will have to substantiate those 'sufficient grounds' and offer adequate proof to justify the extension. In principle, the longer the requested extension, the higher the need to substantiate the grounds for it. The Secretary General usually grants extensions in increments of 15 or 30 days, unless the requesting party can (convincingly) show that further extension is necessary. The Secretary General will also take into account the impact of the extension on the proceedings. Thus, extensions will be more liberally granted to remedy defects in the statement of claims,[11] and less liberally where the parties are late in appointing an arbitrator[12] or in effecting the payment of the advance on costs.[13]

13-010 It is the Secretary General's current practice to allow the first extension without need for much explanation.[14] However, as discussed in the context of

---

8. *See, e.g.*, Article 3(4) ICC Rules; Article 4(6) LCIA Rules or Article 18(2) AAA/ICDR Rules.
9. In international arbitration, sender and recipient will often reside in different countries with different public holidays. As Article 13 refers to the dispatch of the communication, the rule only makes sense if the sender is given an additional day to effect such dispatch if the last day is a public holiday in the sender's country.
10. *See also* W. Melis, 'Die neue Schieds- und Schlichtungsordnung des Internationalen Schieds-gerichts der Bundeskammer der gewerblichen Wirtschaft Wien (Wiener Regeln)' [1991] AnwBl, 776, 778.
11. *See* **Article 9**, at para. 081.
12. *See* **Article 14**, at paras. 037 and 056.
13. *See* **Article 34**, at paras. 030 and 033.
14. This could of course vary in case the urgency of the matter demands it. Other arbitration rules include as a further requirement that an extension of time must not delay the proceedings, as, for example, Article 18(1) Croatian Rules states explicitly: 'The parties may agree to prolong the time limit for the performance of certain procedural actions by the parties (. . .)' furthermore, 'the Secretary of the Arbitration Court and the arbitral tribunal are authorised in justified cases, within the limits of their jurisdiction, to extend the time limits for the performance of certain procedural actions determined in the Rules or by a conclusion of the arbitral tribunal, taking care to prevent undue delays of the proceedings'. A more general approach is adopted in Article 32(2) ICC

Article 10, this can be problematic.[15] While certain extensions may have a lesser disruptive effect than others, the other parties should in principle be given the opportunity to be heard, and thus to point out particular circumstances (of which the VIAC or the arbitrators may not otherwise be aware) that advocate for denying the extension. In any event, it is standing practice for the Secretary General to submit a second request for an extension to the other party for comment before reaching a decision. Such additional time extensions will have to overcome a higher threshold, both in terms of substance and evidence.

Arbitral tribunals will typically provide the other party with an opportunity to **13-011** comment on an application for a time extension. While the Vienna Rules do not impose a duty on the tribunal to justify a decision granting (or denying) an extension, it is advisable to provide such reasons in particular where the granted extension causes substantial delay, or, conversely, where the denial of the extension could be seen to affect a party's right to be heard. In the end, decisions on the extension of time limits are discretionary, and will depend on the circumstances of the case, and in particular on the stage of, and the disruptive effect on, the proceedings.

The Vienna Rules do not regulate whether the extension of a time limit has to be **13-012** requested before its expiry or whether it is permissible to apply for an extension after the original time limit has expired. Notably, the previous reference to the possibility to extend time limits 'possibly after their expiry' has been abandoned in the 2006 rules.[16] Although this could be interpreted to indicate that such exclusions are not longer permissible, the better view is to admit late applications for an extension, but only if they are particularly well founded.[17]

After transmission of the file to the arbitrators pursuant to **Article 12**, the VIAC's **13-013** jurisdiction to extend time limits is necessarily restricted to instances where such authority is conferred upon the VIAC (and its organs) by virtue of express provisions of the Vienna Rules. Article 13(1) mentions one such instance – namely

---

Rules: 'The Court, on its own initiative, may extend any time limit which have been modified (. . .) if it decides that it is necessary to do so in order that the Arbitral Tribunal and the Court may fulfil their responsibilities in accordance with these Rules.' Or even Article 17(2) AAA/ICDR Rules, limited to written Statements, '(. . .) the tribunal may extend such time limits if it considers such extension justified.' Or similar in Article 3(4) AAA/ICDR Rules solely for the Statement of Defence and the Counter-claim: 'The arbitral tribunal, or the administrator if the arbitral tribunal has not yet been formed, may extend any of the time limits (. . .) if it considers such an extension justified.'

15. See **Article 10**, at para. 014.
16. The 1991 version of this provision reads: 'Time-limits provided for in the rules of arbitration or set by the Secretary can be prolonged by the latter on request or on his own initiative – possibly also after their – expiry if he considers that the reasons that are presented or that come to his notice in other ways are worthy of consideration.'
17. C. Liebscher in *Institutionelle Schiedsgerichtsbarkeit*, R.A. Schütze (ed.) (Cologne, Carl Heymanns Verlag, 2006), p. 279.

Article 34(5) and **(6)** – but others exist.[18] More accurately, **Article 3(1)** should therefore provide generally that after transmission of the file it is for the arbitrators to extend time limits 'unless the Vienna Rules provide otherwise'.

13-014   Under the Vienna Rules, there is also no provision on whether the parties are in fact entitled to shorten time limits after they have been established. Typically, the cutting-short of already established deadlines would have to be grounded in the mutual consent of the parties. Indeed, international practice and professional courtesy suggest that deviations from established schedules would have to meet the approval of the arbitrators (whose personal timetable might be affected) or of the VIAC insofar as time limits set by the institution are concerned.[19]

II.   EFFECTIVE SERVICE

> **Article 13(2): Communications shall be considered as having been validly served if they are forwarded by registered letter, courier service, telefax or by other means of communication that guarantee evidence of transmission to the address most recently notified in writing to the sole arbitrator (arbitral tribunal) by the addressee as the address for service, or if the document to be served has been demonstrably transmitted.**

A.   COMMUNICATIONS IN ARBITRAL PROCEEDINGS

13-015   The wording chosen for Article 13 clearly indicates that it is not confined to particular types of submissions, but intended to apply to any sort of communication occurring in the arbitral process. This covers party submissions, decisions of the VIAC's organs, orders of the tribunal and the delivery of the award. Article 13(2) addresses, first and foremost, the form in which submissions under the Vienna Rules must be made and thereby intends to ensure that there is a sufficient record evidencing the transmission.

---

18.   *See, e.g.*, the Secretary General's authority to fix the amount in dispute also after transmission of the file under **Article 36(5)** or time limits set by the Board in the context of the challenge of an arbitrator under **Article 16**.

19.   According to Article 32 ICC Rules, for example, the parties may also shorten the various time limits, but 'any such agreement entered into subsequent to the constitution of an Arbitral Tribunal shall become effective only upon the approval of the Arbitral Tribunal'. However, 'the Court, on its own initiative, may extend any time limit which has been modified pursuant to Article 32(1) if decides that it is necessary to do so'. Article 4(7) LCIA Rules explicitly empowers the arbitral tribunal to 'extend (even where the period of time has expired) or abridge any period of time prescribed under these Rules or under the Arbitration Agreement for the conduct of the arbitration, (...)'. Article 17(2) AAA/ICDR Rules concerning the conduct of the arbitration – written statements in addition to statements of claims and counter-claims and statements of defence limits the period fixed by the tribunal to 45 days but leaves the possibility to extend if the tribunal 'considers such an extension justified'.

The following graphic illustrates the typical communication channels in arbitration **13-016** proceedings.

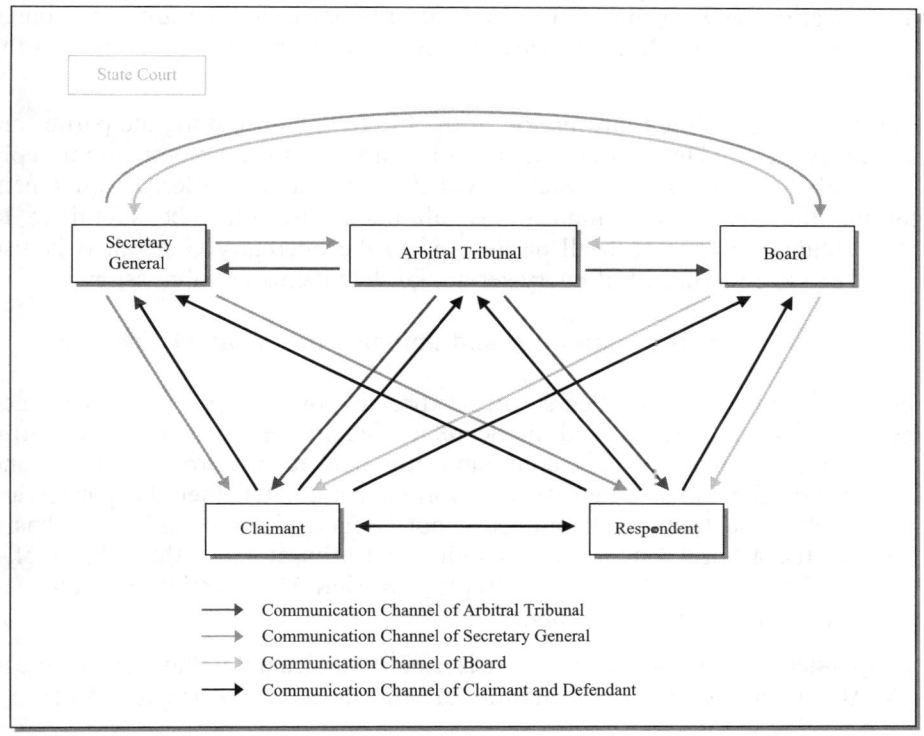

These channels of communication, and the practice established in this regard under **13-017** the Vienna Rules, are addressed below.

1.   Communications of the Parties

Article 13 concerns the parties' correspondence with the VIAC (Board and **13-018** Secretary General) and with the arbitral tribunal as well as, absent a different agreement, the correspondence between the parties insofar as it relates to the arbitration.

Although not explicitly provided for in the Vienna Rules, it is established practice **13-019** that copies of all submissions made in the course of the proceedings are sent to each party, to each arbitrator and, by way of courtesy copy, also to the Secretary General.[20] The Secretary General regularly invites the parties and the arbitrators

---

20.   *See*, *e.g.*, Article 3(1) ICC Rules where 'all pleadings and other written communications sub-
       mitted by any party, as well as all documents annexed thereto, shall be supplied in a number of

to submit copies of the documents in order to keep a mirror file for the institution. It is also common practice that arbitral tribunals allow a party to directly serve a submission on the other party, with copy to the tribunal.[21] The proper form of communication between the parties and the tribunal is for the arbitral tribunal to establish under **Article 20(1)** *after* the Secretary General has transmitted the file to it.[22]

13-020 By contrast, *prior* to the transmission of the file to the arbitrators, the parties are mandatorily required to file the statement of claims and the memorandum in reply solely with the Secretary General.[23] Absent a procedural order or agreement regarding the parties' communications, all documents must be submitted to each individual arbitrator, to all parties and to the Secretary General. It is also advisable to keep a receipt of every service of documents or submissions.

2.   Communications of and amongst the Arbitral Tribunal

13-021 There is no provision in the Vienna Rules expressly governing the correspondence between the arbitral tribunal and the Secretary General or the Board, or the arbitrators amongst themselves. The communication between the arbitral tribunal and the Secretary General is often of an informal nature; whether the parties are informed about such communications or not is decided on an individual basis. Insofar as the arbitral tribunal or an individual arbitrator are the subject of a provision of the Vienna Rules, for example in **Article 16** or **Article 17**, however, the regime of Article 13 will apply.[24]

13-022 Correspondence amongst the arbitrators is usually carried out without disclosure to the VIAC, much less the parties. Drafts of procedural orders are dispatched per

---

copies sufficient to provide one copy for each party, plus one for each arbitrator, and one for the Secretariat. A copy of any communication from the Arbitral Tribunal shall be sent to the Secretariat.' Article 1(2) LCIA Rules: 'The Request (including all accompanying documents) should be submitted to the Registrar in two copies where a sole arbitrator (. . .)' is appointed and in four copies, where there are three arbitrators. The same is valid for the Response; if the communication concerns the tribunal and parties simultaneous copies have, according to Article 13(2) LCIA Rules, to be submitted to the Registrar. In Article 13(3) LCIA Rules this obligation goes further, as when the Registrar sends any written communication to one party on behalf of the Arbitral Tribunal, he shall then send a copy to each of the other parties. Where any party sends to the Registrar any communication (including Written Statements and Documents), it shall include a copy for each arbitrator; and it shall also send copies directly to all other parties and confirm to the Registrar in writing that it has done or is doing so. Article 4 DIS Rules provides: 'All written pleadings and attachments shall be submitted in a number of copies at least sufficient to provide one copy for each arbitrator, for each party and, in case the pleadings are filed with the DIS, one copy for the latter.'

21. This is sometimes subject to furnishing proof of the delivery to the tribunal, in particular when there is a time limit attached to this particular submission.
22. *See* **Article 12**, at para. 001.
23. *See* discussion under **Article 9**, at para. 003.
24. *See* **Articles 16**, at paras. 001 *et seq.*, and **17**, at paras. 001 *et seq.*

telefax or e-mail. Telephone conferences or personal meetings are held to discuss individual issues, results of which are often recorded in internal memoranda. The deliberations of the tribunal are usually considered secret.[25]

The relationship between Article 13 and **Article 20** is not entirely clear. While **13-023** Article 13 sets forth certain rules of communication, **Article 20(1)** refers to the arbitral tribunal's *'absolute discretion'* in conducting the proceedings.[26] However, the tribunal can exercise its discretion only within the confines of the Vienna Rules, and is thus bound by the procedural rules of communication as set forth in Article 13. This does not prevent the arbitral tribunal to adopt additional practical arrangements, such as, for example, particular arrangements with regard to the time when the request for the extension must be made.[27] The communication channels between the parties and the VIAC, however, are not at the discretion of the arbitral tribunal.

Where communication from the tribunal to the parties contains time limits, the **13-024** arbitral tribunal will use those means of communication described in Article 13(2) in order to prove their transmission and receipt.

3.   Communication with the Secretary General

In principle, the correspondence between the Secretary General and the parties also **13-025** follows Article 13. However, the Secretary General will sometimes have to discuss issues other than those explicitly provided for in the Vienna Rules. In the course of the proceedings, situations may arise calling for informal exchange of views with the VIAC. *Derains/Schwartz's* analysis of the function of the ICC's Secretary equally applies to the Secretary General of the VIAC:

> There may nevertheless be circumstances in which parties should be permitted to communicate with the Secretariat on a confidential basis. In this connection, it has to be recognized that the Secretariat plays a fundamentally different role from the arbitrators in the arbitration process. Arguably, by dealing with parties on an *ex parte* basis in certain circumstances, the Secretariat can facilitate the process. Thus, for example, parties may be concerned about the conduct of an arbitrator, but may feel reluctant to disclose this. By allowing the parties to air their concern in confidence, the ecretariat may not only receive information that might otherwise not have come to its attention, but it may be in a position to defuse possible difficulties that could otherwise eventually disrupt the arbitration (. . .).[28]

---

25. *See* **Article 7**, at para. 064.
26. *See* C. Liebscher in *Institutionelle Schiedsgerichtsbarkeit*, R.A. Schütze (ed.) (Cologne, Carl Heymanns Verlag, 2006), p. 279.
27. So, for example, if the extension can also be made after the expiry of the initial time limit.
28. Y. Derains and E.A. Schwartz, *A Guide to the ICC Rules of Arbitration* (2nd edn, The Hague, Kluwer Law International 2005), p. 35.

13-026 Since the Secretary General is not involved with the decision *in merito*, he may be able to offer the opportunity for informal and neutral discussions of procedural issues. Nevertheless, it will be the Secretary General's endeavour to keep his communications with the parties as transparent as possible in order to avoid the appearance of partiality or of preferential treatment of a certain party.

13-027 The correspondence between the Secretary General and the arbitral tribunal is often of an informal nature. Such correspondence will be brought to the parties' knowledge on an individual and discretionary basis. Formal communications between the Secretary General and the Board are unlikely and rarely happen in practice.

4.   Communication with the Board

13-028 When the Board is called upon to act – for example, when the statement of claims is returned under **Article 9(6)**,[29] in case of substitutional nomination or appointment of the arbitrator(s),[30] in case of an arbitrator's challenge[31] or termination of its mandate[32] – the Secretary General, in accordance with **Article 5(2)** will administer the correspondence of the Board and in doing so, will follow the regime of Article 13. The communications between the Board and the Secretary General is informal and will be conducted by internal postal service or oral discussions.

5.   Communication with State Courts

13-029 In some situations national courts play a vital role in assisting the arbitration; and national courts will of course be relevant for the annulment and the enforcement of the award.[33] The provisions concerning delivery and time limits will be based on the procedural rules as applicable to the proceedings before that national court.[34] The national court might, however, have to take Article 13 into consideration, for example, in order to assess if and when the award was properly delivered to a party and if for this reason a claim for setting aside the award has been made within the prescribed time limit.[35]

B.   FORM OF COMMUNICATIONS

13-030 Article 13(2) sets out the formal requirements for communications in proceedings under the Vienna Rules. It provides for three *specific* means of communication that

---

29. *See* **Article 9(6)**, at paras. 088 *et seq.*
30. *See* **Article 14**, at paras. 037 *et seq.*, 056 *et seq.*, and 064 *et seq.*
31. *See* **Article 16**, at paras. 040 *et seq.*
32. *See* **Article 17**, at paras. 012 *et seq.*
33. *See* **Article 2**, at paras. 055 *et seq.*, 068 and 069 *et seq.*
34. Note that according to Section 580(3) ZPO (Receipt of written communications), paragraphs 1 and 2 are not applicable to communications in court proceedings.
35. *See* **Article 2**, at para. 068 and **Article 27**, at paras. 033 *et seq.*

constitute valid and effective service: (i) service by registered letter, (ii) by courier, and (iii) by telefax. Finally, the Vienna Rules also provide a general *catch-all* clause, permitting in addition any other means of communication that ensures evidence of transmission.

Service under the Vienna Rules is valid if the submission is 'forwarded' in a particular form and to a particular address (discussed above at **Article 9**).[36] 'Forwarded' is equal to 'being sent'; actual receipt by the addressee is in principle not required. **13-031**

On first sight, the reference to registered letters and courier service seems rather restricted. Based on the wording of Article 13, it could be questioned if an unregistered letter or a personal delivery, for example, by employees of the sender, constituted a valid delivery. However, the better view is that the forms of communications explicitly mentioned in Article 13 are simply those that attach the immediate assumption of formal validity. Thus, if a party for whatever reason decides to use different forms of communication, it bears the risk that the validity of its submission is contested in which case it will have to proffer evidence of the transmission if necessary. In other words, the opposing party cannot really complain that an unregistered letter would have any adverse affect on it; but use of such means of communications can lead to a tiresome dispute about whether the submission was actually sent, or whether it was sent in time. Arbitrators frequently combine the forms of communications by ordering, for example, that the parties' submissions be sent by courier and advance facsimile. **13-032**

The *catch-all* provisions of 'other means of communication that guarantee evidence of transmission' was inserted with the last amendment of the Vienna Rules, intended to cover in particular e-mail communications.[37] Although, contrary to the new Austrian arbitration law,[38] e-mail is not expressly mentioned, it is certain that e-mail communications can serve as a valid tool of communication since this form of communication create a sufficient record of transmission, in particular when secured e-mail signatures are being used. **13-033**

Article 13 only requires evidence of transmission, not of receipt. Indeed, in particular with respect to unsecured e-mail, is easier to ensure and demonstrate that a message has been sent than that it has actually been received. Although the 'dispatch' rather than the receipt is relevant for the compliance with time limits under Article 13(1), the exact date a submission is received can still be relevant in arbitration proceedings. Thus, regular unsecured e-mail may not always provide sufficient security to the parties and the arbitrators. In practice, certain informal communication between the parties and the arbitral tribunal are certainly permissible via e-mail without separate explicit agreements. However, should arbitrators **13-034**

---

36. *See* **Article 9**, at paras. 003 *et seq.*, and 053 *et seq.*
37. The Vienna Rules thus reacted to technical changes; the former version of this provision included the telex as a means of communications.
38. *See* Section 583(1) ZPO.

intend to conduct the entire or significant parts of the arbitration electronically, they should clarify the exact technical specifications the exchange of electronic information has to follow, possibly including provisions regarding confirmations of receipt.[39]

C.   RECIPIENTS OF DELIVERY

13-035 Article 13(2) and (3) address the question on whom submissions under the Vienna Rules should be properly served. Article 13(2) provides that parties can rely on the address most recently notified by that party to the arbitrators, and that, irrespective of the address, a submission is validly served if it is actually received by the recipient. Article 13(3) adds that parties can also deliver submissions to the other party's representative on record.

13-036 The Vienna Rules do not appear to accord a particular priority to any of these recipients so that service to either recipient constitutes a valid way to deliver a submission under the Vienna Rules. However, there will often be procedural arrangements between the parties, or determined by the tribunal, that will establish some priority as to one of the possible recipients; usually, service only to the party representatives will be agreed as sufficient.

1.   To the Address Most Recently Notified

13-037 As in any other legal proceedings one always runs the risk that a party may (intentionally or unintentionally) 'disappear' in the course of the proceedings, so that no submissions can be served on it, sometimes to argue later that its right to be heard was violated. In such a case it would be intolerable to burden the other party with the risk of effecting valid service.

13-038 Article 13(2) provides the assumption that the 'address most recently notified' is considered to be a valid address of delivery. Hence, a submission delivered to such an address, in the forms discussed above, can be considered as having been validly

---

39.   *See* the Federal Law regarding electronic signatures (*Signaturgesetz* – SigG), BGBl I No 190/ 1999, implementing Directive 1999/93/EC of the European Parliament and of the Council of 13 December 1999 on a Community framework for electronic signatures, which grants legal recognition to electronic signatures under certain circumstances. *See* in detail C. Brenn, 'Das österreichische Signaturgesetz – Unterschriftenersatz in elektronischen Netzwerken' [1999] ÖJZ, 587; M. Kutschera, 'Funktion und Verwendbarkeit der elektronischen Signatur' [2000] SWK, W 7; S. Stockinger, 'Österreichisches Signaturgesetz' [1999] MR, 203; S. Unteregger, 'Über die Wirtschaftlichkeit digitaler Signaturen' [2002] ecolex, 571; A. Vonkilch, 'Zum wirksamen Zugang von sicher signierten E-Mails' [2001] RdW, 578. More and more arbitrations are conducted in an 'unsecured' electronic form. *See also* M. Niklas, 'Schiedsverfahren via Internet nach den Wiener Regeln' [2004] IHR, 103; C. Liebscher in *Institutionelle Schiedsgerichtsbarkeit*, R.A. Schütze (ed.) (Cologne, Carl Heymanns Verlag, 2006), p. 279.

served upon the other party, even if this party is no longer resident at this address. By submitting to the Vienna Rules, the parties accept the obligation to notify the arbitrators of their current address, failing which they agree to the last notified address as the proper address of service. Given the parties' express consent to the Vienna Rules, the failure to notify a new service precludes a party from challenging the award on the basis that it has not received certain submissions in the course of the proceedings.

The address must be notified 'to the arbitrator'. The authentic German version **13-039** provides in addition for the VIAC to be notified, which was erroneously left out of the English translation.[40] Additionally, the notification must be made in writing in the form provided by Article 13(2).

It has been debated whether a parties' notification of no more than a fax number is **13-040** sufficient notice of a serviceable address within the meaning of Article 13(2). However, as Article 13(2) expressly mentions service via telefax as a proper form of service, it could well be argued that the sole provision of a fax number should suffice – even though Article 13(2) goes on to refer to the 'address for service'.

Similarly, an address repeatedly used by a party itself in the course of the proceed- **13-041** ings should constitute a valid delivery address for that party, even when it was not expressly labelled as the address for service. Given that Article 13(2) seems to require a written notification, information concerning a new address that is provided merely orally may not suffice, except when stated into the record during an arbitration hearing. Notifications provided by a third party are also generally not sufficient.[41]

As discussed, the notification during the course of the proceedings must be made **13-042** either to the VIAC or to the arbitrators.[42] An explicit revocation of an address is only relevant if the party simultaneously indicated a new and valid delivery address.[43] This is in line with Section 580(2) ZPO which provides: 'If the addressee has knowledge of the arbitral proceedings, and if, despite reasonable investigation,

---

40. The VIAC should therefore always be notified; indeed, it is the only conceivable recipient of such a notification where the tribunal has not yet been constituted.
41. Other approach in Article 3(2) ICC Rules which also explicitly permits delivery to an address notified by another party. All notifications or communications from the Secretariat and the Arbitral Tribunal shall be made to the last address of the party or its representative for whom the same are intended, as notified either by the party in question or by the other party. Such notification or communication may be made by delivery, against receipt, registered post, courier, facsimile transmission – find also in Article 4(2) LCIA Rules; Article 5(2) DIS Rules; Article 18(1) AAA/ICDR Rules; Article 3(1) UNCITRAL Model Law; Article 6(2) Polish Rules and Article 9(1) Czech Rules.
42. The question of how to commence arbitration proceedings against a 'vanished' party has been addressed under **Article 9**, at paras. 053 *et seq.*
43. *See* A. Reiner, *Das neue österreichische Schiedsrecht/The new Austrian Arbitration Law* (Vienna, LexisNexis, 2006), Section 580, note 20.

his residence or the residence of an authorized recipient remains unknown, then any written communication is deemed to have been received, on the day on which a proper delivery was verifiably attempted at a location that was specified at the conclusion of the arbitration agreement or that the addressee subsequently gave to the other party or to the arbitral tribunal as the address and that has not yet been revoked by giving a new address.'[44]

13-043 It bears emphasis that, unlike Section 580(2) ZPO, Article 13(2) does not require a party to undertake a *reasonable investigation* of the other party's address of service or actual residence before being able to rely on the fallback position of the last notified address (although it is in any case advisable to do so).[45] The rationale behind the assumption of Article 13(2) is to oblige a party to an arbitration to stay available in the course of the proceedings, but only to the extent that the party has initially been informed that such proceedings are effectively taking place. Hence, the reliance on an address that was notified *before* the commencement of the proceedings (but is not the actual residence) is not sufficient to effect valid delivery.

2.   Actual and/or Demonstrable Transmission

13-044 Arbitration proceedings markedly differ from court proceedings as they allow for a greater degree of flexibility. When the parties and the arbitrators are in direct contact, for example during the arbitration hearing, it is therefore permissible and a valid service under Article 13(2) to directly transmit a document directly to its recipient, rather than sending it through the VIAC.

13-045 Article 13(2) goes even further. It deems any delivery valid if the submission has been 'demonstrably transmitted'. The meaning of this phrase flows from the authentic German version of Article 13(2), following which it is sufficient that the document is 'handed over to the recipient' (*ausgehändigt*). This phrase therefore entails first and foremost situations in which the submission may have been sent to the wrong address, but it was actually received by the addressee regardless. Clearly, if the recipient has *actually* received it, it does not matter that the submission was not sent to the proper address on record. Article 13(2) also provides a

---

44. The knowledge of the arbitration proceedings serves to ensure due process of law. *See* C. Liebscher, *The Austrian Arbitration Act 2006: Text and Notes* (The Hague, Kluwer Law International, 2006), Annotated Text to Section 580(2) ZPO. Note the different approach under Section 1028 German ZPO that does not explicitly require the party to have knowledge of the proceedings. *See* R. Geimer in *Zöller – Zivilprozessordnung*, R. Zöller *et al.* (eds) (26th edn, Cologne, Verlag Dr. Otto Schmidt, 2007), Section 1028, para. 1.

45. Section 580 ZPO is insofar considered to be not mandatory. *See* P. Oberhammer, *Entwurf eines neuen Schiedsverfahrensrechts* (Vienna, Manz, 2002), p. 33; A. Reiner, *Das neue österreichische Schiedsrecht/The new Austrian Arbitration Law* (Vienna, LexisNexis, 2006), Section 580, note 20.

second option for cases in which no address of service has been notified to the arbitrators and the VIAC.

The authentic German version ('handed over'/'*ausgehändigt*') does not appear to **13-046** require proof of delivery. Hence, following a literal interpretation, the mere allegation that a document has been handed over to the recipient would at first glance satisfy the delivery requirements (and allow for timely observation of a time limit). The English version suggests what is advisable in practice in any event: for the sender to be able to *demonstrate* that the recipient has actually received the submission. In that regard, the registered letter, courier service, telefax or any 'other means of communication that guarantee evidence of transmission' should provide the required demonstration that the submission was actually received.

In sum, if the submission is sent to the address properly notified, it is sufficient for **13-047** the sender to show that it has been *sent* in a form permitted by the Vienna Rules (in order for the submission to be validly served and for time limits to be observed). However, if the submission is sent to another address (or if no address of service has been notified at all), the sender must show that the submission was actually received by the addressee. In the latter case, the use of electronic messages raises particular questions. It could as well be argued that using e-mail as communication tool enables the recipient to get hold of the document as soon as it lands on the recipient's server (having entered the recipient's sphere), thereby satisfying the requirement of being 'handed over' ('*ausgehändigt*') within the meaning of Article 13(2). Yet this may be difficult to prove in a reliable or verifiable fashion. As discussed above, if arbitrators intend to conduct the entire or significant parts of the arbitration by exchange of electronic submissions only, they are well advised to clarify the technical parameters, specifications and requirements with the parties in advance.

III.   SERVICE TO THE PARTY REPRESENTATIVE

Article 13(3): As soon as a party has appointed a representative, service to the most recently indicated address of that representative shall be considered as having been made to the party represented.

This provision has been newly inserted with the 2001 amendment of the Vienna **13-048** Rules[46] and seeks to extend, beyond the scope of Article 13(2), the possibilities of valid service. In addition to service by actual transmission and service to the address most recently notified, service can also be effected if made to the address of the recipient's representative most recently indicated.

In practice, this is the most important way to serve submissions in the course of an **13-049** arbitration, often without copying the parties themselves at all. Counsel notifies at

---

46. Article 8(3) Vienna Rules 2001, **Annex 2a.**

the very outset of the proceedings that they are entitled to act for and on behalf of a party, which authority includes the valid acceptance of service in the parties' name.

13-050 It can be assumed that, when a party terminates the mandate of its counsel during the arbitration, counsel's address remains a valid address for delivery for as long as the termination of the mandate has not been notified to the arbitrators and the VIAC. In such a case, the address of the former representative would remain the address 'most recently indicated' by the party. Following this interpretation, Article 13(2) secures the effective delivery of submissions and goes even beyond the duties lawyers usually owe to their client, at least under Austrian law.[47] This might serve as an additional disincentive for parties 'to disappear' at a certain stage in the proceedings.

---

47. Under Austrian law, a lawyer whose mandate is terminated in the course of the proceedings is nevertheless obliged to continue representation for a fortnight as far as is necessary to protect the (former) client from legal disadvantages. *See* Section 36(2) ZPO and Section 11(2) RAO. Externally, the termination of the mandate will only come into effect upon delivery of a written notification or, in case the lawyer's representation is mandatory in this proceeding, a new lawyer has been formally appointed and such appointment has been notified.

Article 14

Nomination and Appointment of Arbitrators

		Para.
I.	Number of Arbitrators	1
A.	Introduction	1
B.	Sole Arbitrator or Three-Member Tribunal?	3
C.	Agreement of the Parties on the Number of Arbitrators.	6
D.	Limits of Party Autonomy	10
E.	Recommended Arbitration Clause	13
II.	Determination by the Board	15
A.	Procedure	15
B.	Timing	19
C.	Reasoned Decision	24
D.	Criteria to Determine the Appropriate Number of Arbitrators	26
III.	Nomination or Appointment of a Sole Arbitrator	29
A.	Terminology: Nomination and Appointment	29
B.	Joint Nomination by the Parties	31
1.	Joint Nomination after Board Decision on Number of Arbitrators	32

		Para.
2.	Joint Nomination if Number of Arbitrators Has Been Agreed by The Parties	35
C.	Appointment by the Board	37
1.	The Appointment Process	38
2.	Culpa in Eligendo	43
D.	Appointment by the Austrian Courts	45
IV.	Nomination and Appointment of a Co-Arbitrator	50
A.	Nomination by the Parties	51
B.	Appointment by the Board	56
V.	Nomination and Appointment of the Chairman	57
A.	Nomination by the Co-Arbitrators	57
B.	Appointment by the Board	64
C.	Appointment by the Austrian Courts	66
VI.	Binding Effect of Nomination	67

I.   NUMBER OF ARBITRATORS

Article 14(1): The parties can agree that their dispute is to be decided either by a sole arbitrator or by an arbitral tribunal that shall consist of three arbitrators.

A.   INTRODUCTION

14-001 The parties' right to nominate their own arbitrator is fundamental. Equally important is the parties right to freely agree on a particular procedure to constitute the
tribunal. Only where the parties do not agree, in their arbitration agreement or at the
outset of the arbitration, on the specifics of the tribunal, default rules either of
applicable law or agreed institutional rules take effect. These default provisions
need to ensure that the constitution of the tribunal can proceed promptly, without
disruption by an unwilling party, while safeguarding the equality of the parties.[1]
Thus, whilst the effects of an obstructive attitude by one or several of the parties
regarding the number of arbitrators or their nomination must be minimized,
fundamental procedural rights of the parties to participate in the constitution of
the tribunal must be observed at the same time.

14-002 The following section looks at the institutional constitution of the tribunal under
the Vienna Rules and Austrian law, from the determination of the number of
arbitrators, to the nomination of co-arbitrators and presiding arbitrators.

B.   SOLE ARBITRATOR OR THREE-MEMBER TRIBUNAL?

14-003 The Vienna Rules make it clear that it is primarily the parties' choice if the dispute
is to be decided by a sole arbitrator or by an arbitral tribunal consisting of three
arbitrators.[2] It is often perceived to be a major advantage of appointing a sole
arbitrator that he or she will cost only a third of the expense incurred by a
three-member tribunal. Indeed, cost might be a legitimate consideration in smaller
cases, although, at least under the Vienna Rules, smaller amounts in dispute lead to
smaller fees for the arbitrators in any event.[3]

14-004 A sole arbitrator may also be able to resolve the dispute more speedily. There is no
need to coordinate the schedules of three busy arbitrators to find time for the

---

1. *See* **Article 15** on Multiparty Proceedings where equal opportunities to participate in the constitution of the tribunal raise particular issues.
2. That is international arbitration practice, *see, e.g.*, Article 7(6) ICC Rules: 'Insofar as the parties
   have not provided otherwise, the Arbitral Tribunal shall be constituted in accordance with the
   provisions (. . .)'. Similar Article 11(2) UNCITRAL Model Law: 'The parties are free to agree
   on a procedure of appointing the arbitrator or arbitrators, subject to the provisions (. . .)'. Or
   Article 6(1) AAA/ICDR Rules: 'The parties may mutually agree upon any procedure for appointing arbitrators and shall inform the administrator as to such procedure.' And Article 17 Slovak
   Rules 'Parties to the proceedings may agree in the arbitration agreement (clause) on the person
   of arbitrator (arbitrators) or on the manner of their subsequent appointment'. On the contrary
   Article 4 Hungarian Rules reads: 'The formation of the arbitral tribunal or the appointment of the
   sole arbitrator shall occur according to the present Rules of Proceedings'. This is also in line with
   Section 587 ZPO.
3. Even where there is a substantial amount at stake financially, but the issues are not complex, the
   parties may prefer the efficiency of appointing a sole arbitrator. *See* W.L. Craig, W.W. Park and

hearing, or for deliberations both on procedural matters as they occur during the arbitration and on the merits of the case. Also, there is no chance that a party appointed arbitrator will employ delaying tactics. It is also argued, sometimes, that appointing a sole arbitrator removes the likelihood of an award that is a compromise between the interests of both parties – a tendency argued to be inherent in tribunals with two 'adverse' party appointed members, with a chairperson seeking to negotiate two opposing positions.[4]

Despite this, there is a strong preference in modern arbitration for a three-member **14-005** tribunal, certainly in bigger and more complex cases. Specifically, it is argued that such a choice facilitates a higher degree of quality in the award, in particular where the case concerns different legal areas and the arbitrators, due to their possibly different areas of experience and expertise, are able to complement each other in the decision-making process. With three arbitrators deliberating, and discussing each other's approaches,[5] a three-member tribunal is vested with a powerful dynamic of internal quality control.[6] These deliberations can reduce the risk of misunderstandings, facilitate the use of more sophisticated expertise, and, as is generally the case with diverse panels, take account of the different national and legal backgrounds of the parties which in turn may make the award of the tribunal more acceptable to the parties.[7] On balance, these quality considerations off-set some disadvantages associated with three-member tribunals, in particular the risk of higher costs and the potential for delay.[8]

J. Paulsson, *International Chamber of Commerce Arbitration* (3rd edn, New York, Oceana Publications, 2000), p. 190.

4. *See* Y. Derains and E.A. Schwartz, *A Guide to the ICC Rules of Arbitration* (2nd edn, The Hague, Kluwer Law International, 2005), p.147; J. Lew, L. Mistelis and S. Kröll, *Comparative International Commercial Arbitration* (The Hague, Kluwer Law International, 2003), paras. 10-11 *et seq.*; W.L. Craig, W.W. Park and J. Paulsson, *International Chamber of Commerce Arbitration* (3rd edn, New York, Oceana Publications, 2000), p. 190.

5. *See* W.L. Craig, W.W. Park and J. Paulsson, *International Chamber of Commerce Arbitration* (3rd edn, New York, Oceana Publications, 2000), p. 191.

6. J. P. Lachmann, *Handbuch für die Schiedsgerichtspraxis*, (3rd edn, Cologne, Verlag Dr. Otto Schmidt, 2008), p. 208. There is a preference visible in common law countries to choose a sole arbitrator, whereas, in civil law countries preference is made to an arbitral tribunal. *See* J. Lew, L. Mistelis and S. Kröll, *Comparative International Commercial Arbitration* (The Hague, Kluwer Law International, 2003), para. 10-10 commenting that a three-member tribunal also allows the appointment of arbitrators with particular scientific or technical knowledge when required. *See* para. 10-18.

7. *See* W.L. Craig, W.W. Park and J. Paulsson, *International Chamber of Commerce Arbitration* (3rd edn, New York, Oceana Publications, 2000), p. 191; J. Lew, L. Mistelis and S. Kröll, *Comparative International Commercial Arbitration* (The Hague, Kluwer Law International, 2003), para. 10-18.

8. J. Lew, L. Mistelis and S. Kröll, *Comparative International Commercial Arbitration* (The Hague, Kluwer Law International, 2003), para. 10-19.

C.   AGREEMENT OF THE PARTIES ON THE NUMBER OF ARBITRATORS

14-006 The current concept of the Vienna Rules does not give an indication with respect to the form and timing of the parties' agreement. It is common practice that the parties agree on the number of the arbitrators in the arbitration agreement. However, it is also possible – and the provisions dealing with the commencement of the proceedings (**Articles 9** and **10**) provide nothing to the contrary – for the parties to reach a subsequent agreement on the number of arbitrators *after* submission of the statement of claims and the memorandum in reply. However, the 'particulars regarding the numbers of arbitrators' are mandatory content of the statement of claims and the memorandum in reply under **Article 9** and **10**, respectively, so that the parties are in principle required to set forth their respective positions in their initial submissions. The Secretary General also usually requests the respondent, when serving the statement of claims, to comment on the claimant's position in the memorandum in reply. Yet, the principle of party autonomy prevails; therefore the parties are not prevented to conclude, even after exchange of the statement of claims and memorandum in reply, an agreement on the number of arbitrators. This is permissible until the Board has reached a decision in accordance with Article 14(2).[9] At this stage, unilateral requests to extend time limits to reach a decision on the number of arbitrators are rarely granted, in order not to delay the constitution of the proceedings.

14-007 If there is no apparent consent on the number of the arbitrators in the arbitration agreement and one party alleges that there has been such agreement in pre-arbitral correspondence, and the other party contests this allegation, there is dissent between the parties. In such a case, the Secretary General will, without further request but giving notice to the parties, draw this fact to the Board's attention in order for the institutional determination of the number of arbitrators to commence pursuant to Article 14(2). Note that under the current practice of the VIAC an implied expression of will by a party is usually not considered to be sufficient. Thus, if an arbitration agreement does not indicate for the size of the tribunal, the claimant in its statement of claims suggests a three-member tribunal and the respondent simply remains silent after receipt of the statement of claims, the Secretary General will nevertheless submit the case to the Board for substitutional determination.[10]

14-008 An explicit agreement to a certain number of arbitrators in the arbitration clause is a valid commitment by the parties and will need to be respected by the VIAC in the nomination and appointment procedure. It is thus questionable if a party can deviate from an agreement which has already been concluded in the arbitration agreement. This might be conceivable in cases where the opposing party contests the

---

9. *See* **Article 14**, at paras. 015 *et seq.*
10. In such a case, the Board intends to follow the claimant's request as it will most likely not be disputed by the respondent.

validity or conclusion of the arbitration agreement as such. In such case it is arguable that no binding effect to the agreement on the number of arbitrators can be assumed in such circumstances, as the agreement on a number of arbitrators arguably forms an integral part of the agreement to arbitrate – the existence of which is contested. In case the objection is raised that the arbitration agreement has never been validly concluded, this might therefore affect the validity of the choice on the size of the tribunal.

A jurisdictional objection does not automatically entail the contestation regarding **14-009** the number of arbitrators. This would need to be raised separately by the opposing party. In this case the Board, through its Secretary General, has the obligation to scrutinize the arbitration agreement and other parties' agreements, consider the objection raised and examine the parties' possible consensus or dissent to the extent as is necessary for a *prima facie* preparation of the proceedings. It is neither in the interest of an efficient proceeding to permit detailed inquiries into the parties will, nor is this provided for in Article 14. Hence, the assessment is on a *prima facie* basis only. As discussed, if there is no clear consent on the number of arbitrators, the VIAC will proceed with a substitutional determination.

D.   LIMITS OF PARTY AUTONOMY

While the parties are in principle free to agree on the procedure for constituting the **14-010** tribunal as an important element of party autonomy, there may be certain limits imposed by applicable law or the Vienna Rules. Specifically, any agreement that deviates from the Vienna Rules will ultimately be tested against the threshold of **Article 9(6)**. After passing this test, it will be for the arbitrator-nominate to decide whether he or she is willing to accept the mandate under the conditions agreed by the parties. Hence, parties are well advised to act cautiously when deviating from the Vienna Rules or imposing additional conditions in their arbitration agreement.

Sometimes parties agree that the arbitral tribunal should consist of two arbitrators. **14-011** However, this would contradict the mandatory provision of Section 586 ZPO.[11] The former legislation did not contain any such restriction, and the parties could agree on an even number of arbitrators. Where such an even number could not reach a majority decision on the merits of the dispute, a party could request the court to declare the arbitration agreement void with regard to the particular dispute.[12] In order to overcome such a deadlock situation, Section 586 ZPO now

---

11. This provision mandatorily provides for an uneven number. *See* C. Liebscher, *The Austrian Arbitration Act 2006: Text and Notes* (The Hague, Kluwer Law International, 2006), Annotated Text to Section 586 ZPO.

12. J. Power, *The Austrian Arbitration Act - A Practitioner's Guide to Sections 577-618 of the Austrian Code of Civil Procedure* (Vienna, Manz, 2006), Section 586, para. 2.

provides that 'if the parties have, however, agreed on an even number of arbitrators, then these shall appoint a further person as chairman'.[13]

14-012 Sometimes parties also agree that the arbitration should be decided by a panel consisting of more than three members. While an agreement on any odd number of arbitrators is in principle permissible under Austrian law, such an agreement on more than three arbitrators would most likely not be administered by the VIAC. That would lead to intricate difficulties in the course of nomination or costs determination. To this extent the Vienna Rules clearly limit the parties' autonomy to freely choose the size of their arbitral panel. Finally, any agreement by the parties regarding the constitution of the tribunal (including an agreement regarding the number of arbitrators) needs to ensure a fair and balanced trial within the meaning of Article 6 ECHR.[14]

E.   Recommended Arbitration Clause

14-013 As an addendum to the recommended arbitration clause,[15] the VIAC suggests to specify the number of arbitrators in the following way: 'The number of arbitrators shall be (one or three).'

14-014 However, arbitration agreements do not always follow the institutional recommendation. Contracts often contain more or less sophisticated appointment procedures that deviate from the default procedure of Article 14 (and perhaps also from other provisions of the Vienna Rules).[16] For example, parties sometimes agree on a certain threshold regarding the amount in dispute; disputes below this threshold are then to be decided by a sole arbitrator, and disputes exceeding that threshold by an arbitral tribunal. Typically, however, parties would in such situations not specifically address how additional claims, reductions of the claim, counter-claims or set-off impacts on the constitution of the tribunal.[17] In practice, particular care should be given to any deviation from tried and tested 'standard' procedures, in

---

13. There is some debate on the question of how much time should be granted to the even number of arbitrators to appoint a presiding chairman. As the statutory provisions do not address this specific question, it has been argued *per analogiam* to Section 587 ZPO that the even numbered arbitrators will have to reach a conclusion within four weeks. After expiry of this time period, the default appointment of the courts will take effect.

14. Austrian jurisprudence has addressed this issue on a case to case basis. *See, e.g.,* OGH, 16 January 1936, 1 Ob 26/36, SZ 18/12; OGH, 31 January 1996, 9 Ob 501/96; OGH, 17 March 2005, 2 Ob 41/04z and more recently in OGH, 22 May 2006, 10 Ob 3/06y. For a detailed discussion of this point, *see* **Article 15**, at paras. 032 *et seq.*

15. *See* **Article 1**, at para. 104.

16. *See* for possible consequences **Article 9(6)**, at paras. 088 *et seq.*

17. C. Liebscher in *Institutionelle Schiedsgerichtsbarkeit*, R.A. Schütze (ed) (Cologne, Carl Heymanns Verlag, 2006), p. 280.

order to avoid the risk that further disputes occur regarding the constitution of the tribunal or that the arbitration clause becomes in part inoperable.[18]

II.   DETERMINATION BY THE BOARD

Article 14(2): When no such agreement has been made and the parties do not agree on the number of arbitrators, the Board shall determine whether the dispute is to be decided by a sole arbitrator or by an arbitral tribunal. In that context, the Board shall take into consideration in particular the difficulty of the case, the magnitude of the amount in dispute and the interest of the parties in a rapid and cost-effective decision.

A.   PROCEDURE

Absent agreement by the parties, the number of arbitrators is determined by the Board, with the Secretary General, according to **Article 5(2)**, preparing the Board's decision. To make that determination, the Board must first decide whether or not to initiate the substitutional appointment procedure under Article 14 at all; thus, the Board is vested with the authority to decide if an agreement between the parties about the number of arbitrators exists or not.   **14-015**

As discussed, it is standing practice that the Board will not conduct a lengthy, investigative procedure to clarify this issue. If the submission of the statement of claims and the memorandum in reply and the *prima facie* scrutiny of the arbitration agreement indicate a potential *dissens* between the parties, the Secretary General, without further request, but with separate notice to the parties, will draw this fact to the Board's attention. The procedure under Article 14 is thereby initiated.   **14-016**

However, the wording of Article 14(1) ('and the parties do not agree on the number of arbitrators') could also be interpreted to mean that, *after* the exchange of the initial submissions, the Board should give the parties another opportunity to reach an understanding on the number of arbitrators. In practice, contradicting declarations in the initial submissions of the parties suffice, and usually no further request to consult on this issue will be directed at the parties. This clearly reflects the Board's intention to expedite the constitution of the tribunal as much as possible.   **14-017**

Article 14(1) not only vests the Board with an authority, but also imposes a duty. At the outset of arbitration proceedings, where either inadvertent or deliberate delays by the parties are increasingly common, the swift determination of the number of arbitrators is important. As discussed, the Board is entitled, according   **14-018**

---

18. A guide to drafting arbitration clauses is provided by G.B. Born, *International Arbitration and Forum Selection Agreements: Drafting and Enforcing* (2nd edn, The Hague, Kluwer Law International, 2006).

to **Article 3(5)**, to adopt decisions by correspondence, so it is not necessary for the Board to wait for the next formal meeting.

B.   TIMING

14-019 The Vienna Rules do not contain, as one might expect, a time period for the Board to determine the number of arbitrators. However, Section 587(3) ZPO has introduced an important three-month time limit in this regard:

> If, under an appointment procedure agreed upon by the parties, a third party, fails to perform any function entrusted to it under such procedure within three months of receipt of a written notification to that respect; then any party may request the court to order the necessary measures, unless the agreement on the appointment procedure provides other means for securing the appointment.

14-020 Originally, the Drafting Committee had proposed to specify that 'a third party' should expressly include a reference to an arbitral institution. Although this wording was not adopted, the Explanatory Notes clarify that an arbitral institution is considered a third party within the meaning of this provision;[19] and given that parties most often grant such functions to arbitral institutions, this is in any event the most natural reading of Section 587(3) ZPO. There is also no doubt that the determination of the number of arbitrators is a preliminary, but necessary 'function' relating to the appointment of arbitrators. As a result, Section 587(3) ZPO applies if the VIAC fails to determine the number of arbitrators within three months.

14-021 The prescription of the three-month period in Section 587(3) ZPO appears to be mandatory in that it is not linked to a caveat of 'unless the parties provide otherwise'.[20] However, it has been argued that the parties are free to agree on a different specified period of time;[21] and it is indeed difficult to understand why this period should be outside the parties' disposition. Certainly, the parties are free to agree on 'other means for securing the appointment'.

14-022 According to Section 587(3) ZPO, the time limit commences upon 'the receipt of a written notification to that respect'. The procedure under the Vienna Rules does not provide for a written notification specifically on the topic of determining the number of arbitrators. The VIAC usually becomes active after the parties' disagreement on this point has become evident. This is typically after the parties have expressed their divergent positions in the statement of claims (pursuant to **Article 9**) and memorandum in reply (pursuant to **Article 10**), respectively. Typically, therefore, the time period for the purposes of Section 587(3) ZPO will run from the date the memorandum in reply is submitted. In case the respondent fails to submit a

---

19. Explanatory Notes to Section 587 ZPO.
20. *See* the discussion about mandatory provision under **Article 2**, at paras. 045 *et seq.*
21. *See also* A. Reiner, *Das neue österreichische Schiedsrecht/The new Austrian Arbitration Law* (Vienna, LexisNexis, 2006), Section 587, note 71.

memorandum in reply, the three-month time period should run from the date the memorandum in reply should have been submitted, either under the thirty day period of **Article 10**, or any extension granted by the Secretary General. If the Board fails to determine the number of arbitrators within this three-month time limit either party is entitled to apply to the Austrian courts for such determination.

In practice, the Board of the VIAC regularly attempts to carry out its responsibilities under Article 14 without delay, and usually reaches a decision within three weeks. Therefore, the fall back provision of Section 587(3) ZPO will hardly become relevant. Indeed, the possibility of a three-month time limit ought not be any incentive for arbitral institutions not to make decision on a quicker pace than statutorily allowed. **14-023**

C. Reasoned Decision

The Vienna Rules specify no obligation for the Board to state reasons for its determination of the number of arbitrators, and no reasons are given in practice.[22] It is argued that substantiating the reasoning of its decision would expose the VIAC to critique from a disgruntled party. **14-024**

It is difficult to see how the VIAC Board could effectively be criticized for what is in essence a discretionary decision. As with all procedural decisions by an institution, providing reasons – if the reasons are well articulated – may actually increase the parties' acceptance of an institutional determination that, absent reasons, might otherwise seem arbitrary. Reasoned procedural decisions by institutions also increase procedural transparency and would provide a body of precedence on which parties could rely in planning for their disputes. As such, providing reasons would increase procedural predictability and legal certainty. Indeed, although most arbitral institutions have historically been reluctant to justify their decisions, there is arguably a (positive) trend towards greater transparency, by not only providing the parties with reasons but also by making the decision available in anonymous form to the interested public.[23] **14-025**

D. Criteria to Determine the Appropriate Number of Arbitrators

Other major rules contain an express preference for sole arbitrators,[24] at least on paper. By contrast, Section 586(2) ZPO contains a clear preference for a **14-026**

---

22. See also C. Liebscher in *Institutionelle Schiedsgerichtsbarkeit*, R.A. Schütze (ed.) (Cologne, Carl Heymanns Verlag, 2006), p. 280.
23. See **Article 16**, at para. 046 and **Article 30**, at paras. 006 *et seq.*
24. Article 8 ICC Rules provides that in the absence of a party agreement on the number of arbitrators, the Court 'shall appoint a sole arbitrator, save where it appears to the Court that

three-member tribunal.[25] This is not so under the Vienna Rules which leave this issue completely open and afford the parties the benefit of an independent determination with reference to objective criteria. Thus, unlike under some other rules, a party need not necessarily be forced to accept a number of arbitrators that may be inappropriate for a case simply because it has been unable to agree on the number with the other party.[26]

14-027 When determining the number of arbitrators, Article 14 merely requires 'the Board [to] take into consideration in particular the difficulty of the case, the magnitude of the amount in dispute and the interest of the parties in a rapid and cost-effective decision'. The enumeration of specific factors (introduced with the amendment of the Vienna Rules in 2001[27]) that the Board has to take into account is not exclusive; the Board may, and should, generally consider all circumstances of the case and decide on its own merits. The specification of certain factors was simply meant to make the process more transparent.[28] In reality, the relative importance of these factors is uncertain. The 'magnitude of the amount in dispute' seems to be the most relevant factor for most institutions, in that a small monetary claim is often said not to justify the expense of a three-member tribunal. This is obviously because the size of the tribunal appointed will have a substantial impact on the cost of the arbitration. When a three-member tribunal, rather than a sole arbitrator, is appointed, the fees and costs of the tribunal are multiplied by a factor of three.[29] In addition, the time required to conduct the case is ordinarily prolonged, due to the need to coordinate the schedules of three busy arbitrators and the need, in such case, for deliberations. In a small and simple case, therefore, there will rarely be any justification for the appointment of more than one arbitrator. But when substantial sums are in dispute, the case for the appointment of three arbitrators is

---

the dispute is such as to warrant the appointment of three arbitrators'. Article 5(4) LCIA Rules: 'A sole arbitrator shall be appointed unless the parties have agreed in writing otherwise, or unless the LCIA Court determines that in view of all the circumstances of the case a three-member tribunal is appropriate'. Article 5 AAA/ICDR Rules: 'If the parties have not agreed on the number of arbitrators, one arbitrator shall be appointed unless the administrator determines in its discretion that three arbitrators are appropriate because of the large size, complexity or other circumstances of the case.'
25. Section 586(2) ZPO reads: 'Unless the parties have determined otherwise, three arbitrators are to be appointed.'
26. *See* Y. Derains and E.A. Schwartz, *A Guide to the ICC Rules of Arbitration* (2nd edn, The Hague, Kluwer Law International, 2005), p. 147.
27. Article 9(2) Vienna Rules 2001, **Annex 2a**.
28. Standards of value in determining the number of arbitrators are not uncommon in other arbitration rules, *e.g.*, in Article 5 AAA/ICDR Rules: '(. . .) the administrator determines in its discretion that three arbitrators are appropriate because of the large size, complexity or other circumstances of the case'. More unclear in Article 8(2) ICC Rules where 'the Court shall appoint a sole arbitrator, save where it appears to the Court that the dispute is such as to warrant the appointment of three arbitrators'.
29. *See* **Article 36(6)**, paras. 028 *et seq.*

ordinarily much more compelling.[30] As an unofficial rule of thumb, the Board appears to allocate disputes amounting up to € 1 Million in principle to a sole arbitrator and any dispute exceeding that threshold to an arbitral tribunal.[31] However, it is not clear that the amount in dispute should automatically trump the 'difficulty of the case'; small cases can raise very difficult issues of procedure, evidence or law, and would clearly benefit from a panel. As to costs, the smaller the amount in dispute, the smaller the fees for the arbitrators,[32] although a sole arbitrator will always attract less fees. The special reference to the 'interest of a party in a rapid and cost effective decision' is somewhat self-serving; one would not assume the contrary.

In sum, the Board enjoys relative discretion in its decision-making. One can **14-028** assume that the Board will take into account the considerations that normally drive the parties to agree on one or three arbitrators in the arbitration agreement.[33] As discussed above, a sole arbitrator may be able to resolve the dispute more speedily, as there is no need to coordinate the schedules of three arbitrators. A sole arbitrator also removes the potential risk of delaying tactics by a party appointed arbitrator, and it reduces the risk of a compromise decision (a tendency argued to be inherent in three-member tribunals).[34] By contrast, as also discussed above,[35] it is argued that three-member tribunals ensure a higher degree of quality in the award and are better able to accommodate the different national and legal backgrounds of the parties.[36] On balance, these quality considerations off-set some

---

30. *See* Y. Derains and E.A. Schwartz, *A Guide to the ICC Rules of Arbitration* (2nd edn, The Hague, Kluwer Law International, 2005), p. 147.
31. Comparable approach with a lower threshold in Article 6 Croatian Rules: 'If the parties have not come to a prior agreement on the number of arbitrators and if (. .) in disputes where the foreign currency value of the subject of the dispute does not exceed 50,000 EUR, the arbitration shall be conducted by a sole arbitrator, whilst in other disputes, the arbitration shall be conducted by an arbitration panel of three arbitrators'. The ICC Court has for many years applied a similar rule of thumb with a threshold of USD 1 Million. According to Y. Derains and E.A. Schwartz, *A Guide to the ICC Rules of Arbitration* (The Hague, Kluwer Law International, 2005), p 148, '[i]n recent years, however, the Court's approach has become more flexible (and arguably less predictable)'.
32. *See* **Article 36**, at para. 002.
33. *See* **Article 14**, at paras. 003 *et seq.*
34. *See* Y. Derains and E.A. Schwartz, *A Guide to the ICC Rules of Arbitration* (2nd end, The Hague, Kluwer Law International, 2005), p. 147; J. Lew, L. Mistelis and S. Kröll, *Comparative International Commercial Arbitration* (The Hague, Kluwer Law International, 2003), paras. 10-11 *et seq.*; W.L. Craig, W.W. Park and J. Paulsson, *International Chamber of Commerce Arbitration* (3rd edn, New York, Oceana Publications, 2000), p. 190.
35. *See* **Article 14**, at para. 005.
36. *See* W.L. Craig, W.W. Park and J. Paulsson, *International Chamber of Commerce Arbitration* (3rd edn, New York, Oceana Publications, 2000), p. 191; J. Lew, L. Mistelis and S. Kröll, *Comparative International Commercial Arbitration* (The Hague, Kluwer Law International, 2003), para. 10-18.

disadvantages associated with three-member tribunals, in particular the risk of higher costs and the potential for delay.[37]

III.   NOMINATION OR APPOINTMENT OF A SOLE
                          ARBITRATOR

Article 14(3): The parties shall be notified of the decision of the Board pursuant to paragraph 2 of the present Article; in the event that proceedings before a sole arbitrator are decided upon, the parties shall be requested to agree on a sole arbitrator and to indicate that person's name and address within thirty days after service of the request. If no such indication is made within that period, the sole arbitrator shall be appointed by the Board.

A.   Terminology: Nomination and Appointment

14-029 Different arbitration rules use different terminology when referring to the nomination or appointment of arbitrators. Under the ICC Rules, parties nominate arbitrators, which are then appointed by the ICC Court by way of confirmation, having checked the arbitrator's impartiality against ICC standards.[38]

14-030 Under the Vienna Rules, the parties will *nominate* arbitrators, i.e. put forward certain candidates, but this nomination will, unlike in other arbitration rules, not be subject to any acceptance or confirmation by the VIAC. Where the parties fail to nominate a co-arbitrator, or jointly nominate a sole arbitrator, the VIAC will make an *appointment*. This difference in terminology simply denotes whether an arbitrator is put forward by a party (nomination) or, by way of imposing a substitute arbitrator where the parties fail to put forward a candidate within the applicable time period, by the Board (appointment).[39]

---

37. J. Lew, L. Mistelis and S. Kröll, *Comparative International Commercial Arbitration* (The Hague, Kluwer Law International, 2003), paras. 10-19 *et seq.*
38. Different approaches also under the LCIA Rules, where the party and other nominations need to be appointed by the LCIA Court – Articles 5 and 7 LCIA, or the DIS Rules, where the nomination of arbitrator has to be confirmed by the DIS Secretary General or DIS Appointing Committee – Article 17 DIS Rules.
39. The English version of Article 14(4) states for a parties' failure to nominate a co-arbitrator, '[i]f the party has not **appointed** an arbitrator within that time-limit, the arbitrator shall be appointed by the Board'. This is the only time where Article 14 speaks of an appointment by a party (as opposed to a nomination). This appears to be a clerical error. Indeed, the authentic German version consistently, including in Article 14 (4), refers to '*benennen*' (for party nominations) and '*bestellen*' (for appointments by the Board).

B.   JOINT NOMINATION BY THE PARTIES

There are two situations conceivable in which the parties can be asked to jointly **14-031**
nominate an arbitrator. First, if there was no agreement already on the number of
arbitrators, and the Board determined according to Article 14(1) that the dispute
will be decided by a single arbitrator. Second, the parties have already agreed to
refer their dispute to a sole arbitrator. For structural reasons discussed in more
detail below, these two situations are examined separately.

**1.   Joint Nomination after Board Decision on Number
of Arbitrators**

The Board will provide the parties with its determination that the dispute will be **14-032**
decided by a sole arbitrator together with a request to agree on, and jointly nominate, a candidate within thirty days. In multi-party proceedings, this time limit
should run with the receipt of the request by the last party pursuant to **Article 15**.
The time period for the joint nomination of the sole arbitrator can be extended upon
application, which in line with the VIAC's present practice will be decided by the
Secretary General.[40]

The parties are absolutely free in choosing the arbitrator.[41] The VIAC has no **14-033**
authority to review qualifications of the arbitrator nominated by the parties.[42]
Neither the nationality[43] nor the VIAC's (informal) roster[44] have to be considered.
In a case where the parties already put forward certain candidates in the statement
of claims or in the memorandum in reply, even though the number of arbitrators
was unresolved, this 'nomination' is considered preliminary and non-binding on
the parties, despite Article 14(6). Only once the VIAC has decided whether the
dispute will be decided by a sole arbitrator or a panel of three, the parties are
required to consult and agree on a joint nomination.

Paragraph 3 only requires the parties to agree upon a person and to indicate its name. **14-034**
It does not require the arbitrator to accept the mandate within this time limit. In case
the parties have reached an understanding on a sole arbitrator and this person either
declines the appointment or accepts the mandate under unacceptable reservations
the question will occur if and how often the parties should be given an opportunity to
attempt another nomination. The Vienna Rules do not specifically address this
situation. One can conclude by analogy from **Article 18** that the parties will have
at least one other opportunity to nominate a candidate. However, if either one party
objects to this procedure, the Board will have to decide without further delay.

---

40. This practice is debatable as the substitutional appointment procedure is entrusted to the Board.
41. *See* **Article 7**, at paras. 001 *et seq.*
42. C. Liebscher in *Arbitration Law of Austria: Practice and Procedure*, S. Riegler, A. Petsche,
     A. Fremuth-Wolf, M. Platte and C. Liebscher (eds) (Huntington, Juris Publishing, 2007), p. 633.
43. *See* **Article 7**, at paras. 018 *et seq.*
44. *See* **Article 7**, at paras. 039.

2.   Joint Nomination if Number of Arbitrators Has Been Agreed by the Parties

14-035 The Vienna Rules do not appear to provide an express authorization to the Board to appoint an arbitrator if the parties have agreed that a sole arbitrator should decide the dispute, but fail to agree on a candidate. Article 14(1) provides that '[t]he parties can agree that their dispute is to be decided (. . .) by a sole arbitrator'. Next, Article 14(2) provides that where 'no such agreement has been made and the parties do not agree on the number of arbitrators, the Board shall determine whether the dispute is to be decided by a sole arbitrator or by an arbitral tribunal'. Article 14(3) then states simply that

> [t]he parties shall be notified of the decision of the Board pursuant to paragraph 2 of the present Article; in the event that proceedings before a sole arbitrator are decided upon, the parties shall be requested to agree on a sole arbitrator.

14-036 From that structure, it appears that Article 14(3) only requires the parties to agree on a joint nomination if the VIAC has previously 'decided' that the dispute will be heard before a sole arbitrator. This Article does not appear to apply if the parties had agreed on a sole arbitrator in the first place, either in their original arbitration agreement or subsequently.[45] By contrast, for the appointment of a three-member panel, Article 14(4) simply applies 'if the dispute is to be decided by an arbitral tribunal', leaving it open if that is because of the parties' agreement or a determination of the Board pursuant to Article 14(2). The apparent *lacuna* in Article 14(3) is an editorial error. It is clear that, when the parties have agreed that the dispute is to be decided by a sole arbitrator, the Board will in analogous application of Article 14(4) request the parties to jointly nominate a sole arbitrator within thirty days, failing which the Board will proceed to a substitute appointment pursuant to Article 14(3).

C.   APPOINTMENT BY THE BOARD

14-037 After expiration of the thirty days time limit (or any extension granted by the Secretary General, or else after such an extension has expired), the Board will

---

45. Similarly, the authentic German version requests the parties to jointly nominate the sole arbitrator once the number of arbitrators has been decided (*entschieden*), rather than agreed. The English version of this provision, however, uses a semicolon to separate the Board's determination of the number of arbitrators, on the one hand, from the nomination of the sole arbitrator, on the other hand: 'The parties shall be notified of the decision of the Board pursuant to paragraph 2 of the present Article; in the event that proceedings before a sole arbitrator are decided upon (. . .)'. The authentic German version of this provision contains no semicolon and connects the decision on the number of arbitrators with the request to agree upon the joint nomination of the arbitrator.

appoint the sole arbitrator on behalf of the defaulting parties according to Article 14(3).[46] As discussed, there is no fixed time limit in the Vienna Rules for the Board to determine the number of arbitrators. The same is true for the substitutional appointment of a sole arbitrator. In practice, the Board attempts to carry out its duties under this provision without undue delay, and usually reaches a decision within three to four weeks. The introduction of Section 587(3) ZPO and the new three-month time limit should be equally applicable to the Board's decision to appoint a sole arbitrator.[47] In case the parties fail to jointly nominate the sole arbitrator, this three-month time period will commence after the time limit set under Article 14(3) has expired. However, the parties' time limit to jointly nominate an arbitrator is not absolute. Therefore, even after its expiry, the parties are not considered to have forfeited their right for a joint nomination. A late nomination would still be accepted if made prior to the Board's appointment of an arbitrator.[48]

1.   The Appointment Process

While Article 14 does not provide specific factors that the VIAC has to take into account when appointing the sole arbitrator, Section 587(3) no. 8 ZPO imposes a clear obligation for state courts to 'have due regard to any qualifications required of the arbitrator by the agreement of the parties and to such considerations as are likely to secure the appointment of an independent and impartial arbitrator'. This in fact reflects the Board's previously applied practice. Additionally, although not being required to do so under **Article 7**,[49] the Board will attempt to carefully assess the impact of the nationality of the parties involved.[50] For example, in disputes between an Austrian and a non-Austrian party, the VIAC would usually appoint a sole arbitrator from a third country.[51] It is also a common practice that arbitrators

14-038

---

46. In ICC practice the parties jointly agree on a sole arbitrator in fewer than 30% of the cases. Hence, the substitutional appointments seems to be the rule than the exception. *See* Y. Derains and E.A. Schwartz, *A Guide to the ICC Rules of Arbitration* (2nd edn, The Hague, Kluwer Law International, 2005), p. 150. *See also* E. Schäfer, H. Verbist and C. Imhoos, *ICC Arbitration in Practice* (The Hague, Kluwer Law International, Stämpfli, Bern, 2005), p. 50.

47. *See discussion* at **Article 14**, at paras. 019 *et seq.* Section 587 (3) ZPO now provides: 'If, under an appointment procedure agreed upon by the parties, 3. a third party fails to perform any function entrusted to it under such procedure within three months of receipt of a written notification to that respect, then any party may request the court to take the necessary measure, unless the agreement on the appointment procedure provides other means for securing the appointment.'

48. C. Liebscher in *Institutionelle Schiedsgerichtsbarkeit*, R.A. Schütze (ed.) (Cologne, Carl Heymanns Verlag, 2006), p. 280.

49. *See* **Article 7**, at paras. 020 *et seq.*

50. W. Melis, 'Die Schiedsgerichtsbarkeit der österreichischen Handelskammern seit 1946' in *Festschrift Seidl-Hohenveldern*, K.H. Böckstiegel, H.-E. Folz, J. Mössner and K. Zermak (eds) (Cologne, Carl Heymanns Verlag, 1988), 373; *see also* C. Liebscher in *Institutionelle Schiedsgerichtsbarkeit*, R.A. Schütze (ed.) (Cologne, Carl Heymanns Verlag, 2006), p. 280.

51. This will, subject to the rule of thumb (€ 1 Million) mentioned under paragraph 2, in case of a lower amount in dispute presumably not justify the increased travel costs of the foreign

will be familiar with the field (e.g., financing, energy, construction) that is the subject of the arbitration. In appointing arbitrators, the Board therefore generally endeavours to identify a person knowledgeable in the relevant area and also experienced in the field of international arbitration. According to *Derains/Schwartz*, 'this is a widespread view, particularly in regard to a sole arbitrator or chairman of an Arbitral Tribunal. It is, moreover, generally considered that any such arbitration experience should include experience of international arbitration accompanied by both managerial ability and "international mindedness" for untold damage can be done to the international arbitration process when an arbitrator's attitude and approach to a case are unduly parochial or chauvinistic'.[52]

14-039 From a practical point of view the Board will strive to ensure that only such a person is chosen that will be able to perform his or her function as an arbitrator efficiently and effectively. Thereby language capabilities will need to be equally considered as the availability to conduct the proceedings without delay due to conflicting other commitments. In short, the Board will endeavour to take all circumstances of the dispute into account in order to appoint a person that is suited to the specific particulars of the case. In this context, it is helpful if the parties provide details of the nature of the dispute in the statement of claims and the memorandum in reply, respectively. Should the Board conclude that the available background information is insufficient for making an appropriate appointment, the Board could conceivably request the parties to provide further information.

14-040 The VIAC will take into consideration the arbitrators listed on its roster, but does not considers itself limited to the candidates on that list.[53] The VIAC will generally follow accepted international practice, as reflected in the provisions of most major rules.[54] Expressing these standards more clearly in Article 14 would perhaps further increase transparency and the confidence of the parties in the process.

---

arbitrator. *See* C. Liebscher in *Institutionelle Schiedsgerichtsbarkeit*, R.A. Schütze (ed.) (Cologne, Carl Heymanns Verlag, 2006), p. 280.

52. *See* Y. Derains and E.A. Schwartz, *A Guide to the ICC Rules of Arbitration* (2nd edn, The Hague, Kluwer Law International, 2005), p. 163 with reference to the appointment practice of the ICC Court which is comparable in that respect.

53. *See* **Article 7**, at paras. 038 *et seq.*

54. Different institutions have inserted various standards of value, *e.g.*, Article 9(1) ICC Rules: 'In confirming or appointing arbitrators, the Court shall consider the prospective arbitrator's nationality, residence and other relationship with the countries of which the parties or the other arbitrators are nationals and the prospective arbitrator's availability and ability to conduct the arbitration in accordance with these Rules.' In Article 5(5) LCIA Rules: 'The LCIA Court will appoint arbitrators with due regard for any particular method or criteria of selection agreed in writing by the parties. In selecting arbitrators consideration will be given to the nature of the transaction, the nature and circumstances of the dispute, the nationality, location and language of the parties (. . .). Article 6(4) AAA/ICDR Rules provides: 'In making such appointments, the administrator, after inviting consultation with the parties, shall endeavour to select suitable arbitrators. At the request of any party or on its own initiative, the administrator may appoint nationals of a country other than that of any of the parties.' *See also* Article 11(5) UNCITRAL Model Law.

Should it be impossible, or unreasonably difficult, to find an arbitrator who meets **14-041** the particular requirements the parties have specified beforehand, the arbitration agreement could be pathological. To avoid this outcome, the Board will in such cases usually invite the parties to alter their agreement accordingly, or to accept a deviating appointment (and thereby waiving the requirements they had originally provided).[55]

Once the Board has identified a candidate, the Secretary General will approach that **14-042** person to see whether that candidate would be willing and able to accept the appointment if put forward by the Board.[56] If that is so, the Secretary General will submit the candidate to the Board for a resolution that appointment conforming, which can be adopted either at the next meeting of the Board or by circular. After the formal declaration of independence has been signed by the arbitrator,[57] the Secretary General will inform the parties of the appointment and provide them with a copy of the arbitrator's acceptance of the mandate.[58]

2.   Culpa in Eligendo

The question can be raised whether the Board has to satisfy a special duty of **14-043** diligence when appointing an arbitrator. Given that the parties have virtually no influence on the appointment procedure,[59] they have to rely entirely on the good judgment of the Board. It is clear that under **Article 3(6)**, Board members must perform their duties to the best of their ability.[60] Under Austrian law, Section 1315 ABGB[61] establishes liability when someone makes use of an incompetent, or knowing use of a dangerous person, in conducting his affairs.[62] One could see how under these provisions, the Board would conceivably be liable for appointing a blatantly unsuitable person as arbitrator.[63]

The standard of what constitutes a suitable arbitrator is expressed in **Article 7** **14-044** which sets forth the requirements an arbitrator has to meet in order to serve under the Vienna Rules. Notably, an arbitrator has to be, and remain, impartial

---

55. *See* **Article 16**, at para. 026.
56. *See* **Article 7**, at para. 041.
57. *See* **Article 12**, at paras. 010 *et seq.*
58. *See* **Article 7**, at paras. 040 *et seq.*
59. The parties are free to challenge an arbitrator appointed by the Board pursuant to **Article 16**. However, such a challenge can occur only after the arbitrator has been appointed.
60. *See* **Article 3(6)**, at paras. 025 *et seq.*
61. Section 1315 ABGB (freely translated): 'In general, someone who avails himself of an incompetent or, knowingly, of a dangerous person to take care of his own affairs, is liable for the damage caused by such person to a third party in doing so.'
62. R. Reischauer in *Kommentar zum ABGB, II/1*, P. Rummel (ed.) (3rd edn, Vienna, Manz, 2002), Section 1315. It is, however, besides the limits of liability imposed by **Article 8**, doubtful at best how far the Board is, in the course of substitutional appointments, conducting its own affairs.
63. Regarding general provisions on the liability of the VIAC, *see* **Article 8**, at paras. 028 *et seq.*

and independent. In the context of appointment by the Board under Article 14, the Board will therefore exercise some caution. If an arbitrator is in principle prepared to accept the appointment but, as it happens in practice, may express some reservations concerning his or her impartiality, the Board will typically not proceed with the appointment, simply to limit its exposure to claims that is had made an inappropriate choice. The Board could also bring this reservation to the parties' attention, seeking their consent, but the usual, route for the Board is simply to appoint an arbitrator who is able to offer an unconditional declaration of independence and impartiality.

D.   APPOINTMENT BY THE AUSTRIAN COURTS

14-045   As discussed, the 2006 reform has introduced a new time limit in which an appointment procedure agreed upon by the parties must be able to perform its function successfully. As such, Section 587(3) ZPO establishes a definite three-month time limit for the appointment of arbitrators and the determination on the number of arbitrators. The former legislation provided for a similar procedure in Section 581(1) fZPO, with a relatively short period of 14 days. A more serious drawback of the former legislation was Section 583(1) fZPO, according to which the court could terminate an arbitration agreement at the request of a party if the parties could not reach an agreement on an arbitrator jointly to be appointed.[64]

14-046   Section 587(3) ZPO limits the 'third party's' failure to perform the function entrusted to it to the receipt of a written notification in that respect. Such separate notification would not fit into the procedure under Article 14. Hence, depending on the action to be taken by the Board (determination of the number of arbitrators – according to Article 14(2); the choice of a sole arbitrator or three-member panel – according to Article 14(3); and, ultimately, the appointment of co-arbitrators according to Article 14(4) and/or a chairman according to Article 14(5)), the commencement of those time limits vary and have been addressed at the appropriate section. It has been emphasized that the Board regularly attempts to carry out its responsibilities under Article 14 without delay, and usually reaches a decision within a maximum of three weeks. Therefore, the fall back provision will most likely not be of practical relevance in arbitrations administered by the VIAC.

14-047   In brief, the request must be directed in general civil law matters to the civil court with jurisdiction for such matters as specified in the arbitration agreement or whose jurisdiction was agreed upon in accordance with Section 104 JN, or, failing such specification or agreement, the court in whose district the arbitral tribunal has its seat, regardless of the value in dispute. If the seat of the arbitral tribunal has not yet been determined, or if, in the case of Section 612 ZPO, it is not within Austria,

---

64.   *See* J. Power, *The Austrian Arbitration Act – A Practitioner's Guide to Sections 577-618 of the Austrian Code of Civil Procedure* (Vienna, Manz, 2006), Section 587, para. 3.

then the *Handelsgericht Wien* (Commercial Court of Vienna) shall have jurisdiction. If the legal matter in dispute underlying the award is a matter of commercial law within the meaning of Section 51 JN,[65] then, acting as commercial courts, the regional court shall have jurisdiction, in Vienna this is, again, the *Handelsgericht Wien*; for labour law matters within the meaning of Section 50(1) ASGG, the regional courts acting as labour and social courts shall have jurisdiction. In Vienna this is the *Gericht für Arbeits - und Sozialsachen Wien* (Labour and Social Court of Vienna).[66]

The request to the court must also state which claim is being asserted and which **14-048** arbitration agreement the party is invoking. If the belated appointment of the Board takes place prior to the first instance decision and a party proves this, then the application will be dismissed.

By virtue of Section 587(9) ZPO no appeal is permitted against court decisions by **14-049** which arbitrators are appointed. Such decisions cannot be considered binding as to the question of jurisdiction (or lack thereof) of an arbitral tribunal so appointed. Consequently, when courts undertake an examination of the validity of the arbitration agreement within the context of a proceeding to appoint an arbitrator, this will necessarily be limited to a summary review.[67]

IV.   NOMINATION AND APPOINTMENT OF A
           CO-ARBITRATOR

Article 14(4): If the dispute is to be decided by an arbitral tribunal, the party that has not yet nominated an arbitrator shall be requested to indicate the name and address of an arbitrator within thirty days after service of the request. If the party has not appointed an arbitrator within that time-limit, the arbitrator shall be appointed by the Board.

Article 14(4) applies whenever the dispute is decided by an arbitral tribunal, **14-050** whether as a result of the parties' arbitration agreement or subsequent consent, or whether in the absence of any such agreement this has been determined by the VIAC pursuant to Article 14(2).

---

65. Section 615(2) ZPO. The *Handelsgericht Wien* or the regional courts, in exercise of their jurisdiction in commercial law matters, generally have jurisdiction over the proceeding to set aside an award when the underlying dispute is a transaction related to a business and the statement of claim was directed against a business entity registered in the commercial register. Pursuant to Section 1(2) UGB, a business is any organization of commercial activity created on a permanent basis, even if it is non-profit.
66. Section 615 ZPO.
67. A. Reiner, *Das neue österreichische Schiedsrecht/The new Austrian Arbitration Law* (Vienna, LexisNexis, 2006), Section 587, note 79.

A.   NOMINATION BY THE PARTIES

14-051 As the agreement on the number of arbitrators can be reached at different stages of the process, the parties' right to nominate their co-arbitrator needs to be considered at various levels. **Article 9(3)(d)** and **(e)** require the claimant to specify in the statement of claims the 'particulars regarding the number of arbitrators in accordance with Article 14 and, if a decision by three arbitrators is requested, the nomination of an arbitrator and the address of that person'. As discussed, this provision is not a mandatory requirement of the statement of claims. Hence, if the claimant fails to address the mechanism for the arbitrator appointment, or to specify the number of arbitrators, Article 14 will apply by default.

14-052 In that sense, **Article 9(3)(d)** affords the claimant an opportunity to participate in the constitution of the tribunal rather than requiring the claimant, strictly speaking, to do so.[68] In case a three-member tribunal has been pre-determined in the arbitration agreement and the claimant does not nominate its arbitrator in the statement of claims, the Secretary General will set a short time limit, usually not exceeding 15 days, and request such nomination separately from the claimant. In case of non-compliance, the decision will be made by the Board without further delay, hence requests for time extensions are rarely granted at this stage. The same procedure applies to the respondent who has not made use of its right to nominate its arbitrator in the memorandum in reply.

14-053 In case either or both parties have reserved their right to nominate an arbitrator at a later stage, the Secretary General will approach the parties with the nomination request as soon as the number of arbitrators has been determined either by the parties or by the Board pursuant to Article 14(2).

14-054 In case the parties both nominate their respective co-arbitrators with their initial submissions under **Articles 9** and **10**, the parties are bound by that nomination pursuant to Article 14(6), and the VIAC will approach the co-arbitrators under Article 14(5) to nominate a presiding arbitrator. Indeed, even where the parties, absent agreement on that point, argue for a panel and at the same time nominate a co-arbitrator, they are bound by that nomination pursuant to Article 14(6) if the VIAC determines that the dispute shall be decided by three arbitrators. In this case, too, no further request will be directed at the parties, and the VIAC will approach the co-arbitrators to nominate a presiding arbitrator pursuant to Article 14(5).

14-055 Article 14(4) only requires the parties to nominate an arbitrator and to indicate his or her name to the VIAC and the other party.[69] It does not require the arbitrator to

---

68. *See* **Article 9**, at para. 062.
69. Note that the English translation of this paragraph is not correct as it (correctly) refers in its first sentence to the 'nomination' of the arbitrator but continues in the second sentence: 'If the party has not appointed an arbitrator'. This distinction finds no basis in the authentic German version of this Article which refers to '*benennen*', *i.e.* nomination.

accept the mandate within this time limit. In case the party has nominated an arbitrator and this person either declines the appointment or accepts the mandate under unacceptable reservations the question will arise if and how often the parties should be given an opportunity to attempt another nomination. The Vienna Rules do not specifically address this situation. One can conclude by analogy from **Article 18** that the party will have at least one other opportunity to nominate a candidate, failing which the Board will have to decide in accordance with Article 14(4).[70]

B.   APPOINTMENT BY THE BOARD

In case either party fails to submit its nomination within the time limit set by the   **14-056**
Secretary General, the Board will proceed with the substitutional appointment procedure. As discussed, there is no fixed time limit in the Vienna Rules for the Board to pursue the default proceedings. In practice, the Board attempts to carry out its duties under this provision without undue delay. Once more, the introduction of Section 587(3) ZPO and the new three-month time limit should be equally applicable to the Board's decision to appoint a co-arbitrator on behalf of a defaulting party.[71] In this case, the time limit will commence as soon as a party failed to nominate the co-arbitrator within the time limit set by the Secretary General.

---

70. For the sake of completeness, it should be noted that the recent amendment of the Vienna Rules abandoned the curious provision of the former version of Article 9(4). This provision stipulated that, where the claimant had not appointed an arbitrator within thirty days after service of the pertaining request and did not expressly leave his appointment to the Board, the case was deleted from the list of pending cases. This provision was a systemic anomaly under the Vienna Rules, and unusual when compared to other major arbitration rules. It also gave rise to absurd results. If the claimant requested a decision by a sole arbitrator and failed to indicate a name of the arbitrator, the Board would have appointed an arbitrator on behalf of the claimant but not imposed any other sanction. Only in case of an arbitral tribunal, the claimant was compelled to nominate an arbitrator or else face deletion from the list of pending cases (rather than a substitute appointment of the co-arbitrator by the VIAC). This made no sense, and this procedure was removed from Article 14, as was the instrument of deletion from the list of pending cases. Former Article 9(4) Vienna Rules 2001 read: 'If the dispute is to be decided by an arbitral tribunal, the party that has not yet nominated an arbitrator shall be requested to indicate the name and address of an arbitrator within thirty days after service of the request. If the Claimant has not appointed an arbitrator within that time-limit and does not expressly leave the appointment to the Board, the case must be deleted from the list of pending cases. However, if the Defendant fails to appoint an arbitrator within that time-limit, the arbitrator shall be appointed by the Board.' **Annex 2a**.

71. *See* **Article 14**, at paras. 019 *et seq*. Section 587(3) ZPO now provides: 'If, under an appointment procedure agreed upon by the parties, 3. a third party fails to perform any function entrusted to it under such procedure within three months of receipt of a written notification to that respect, then any party may request the court to take the necessary measure, unless the agreement on the appointment procedure provides other means for securing the appointment.'

However, the parties' time limit to nominate a co-arbitrator is not absolute. Therefore, even after its expiry, the parties are not considered to have forfeited their right for a nomination. A late nomination would still be accepted if made prior to the Board's appointment.

V.   NOMINATION AND APPOINTMENT OF THE
            CHAIRMAN

Article 14(5): If the dispute is to be decided by an arbitral tribunal, the arbitrators nominated by the parties or appointed by the Board shall be requested to agree on a Chairman and to indicate his name and address within thirty days after service of the request. If no such indication is made within that period, the Chairman shall be appointed by the Board.

A.   NOMINATION BY THE CO-ARBITRATORS

14-057 As in other arbitration rules, the appointment of the presiding arbitrator is initially entrusted to the two party-nominated arbitrators.[72] This approach is most respectful of party-autonomy, and limits the influence of the arbitral institution to cases where no agreement on a joint nomination can be reached.

14-058 The procedure to nominate a presiding arbitrator is started by the VIAC sending a request to the co-arbitrators to agree on a suitable candidate. From the receipt of this request, the co-arbitrators have thirty days to reach an agreement. The request could conceivably arrive at different times with the two co-arbitrators, in which case the thirty day period begins to run only once both co-arbitrators have received it.

14-059 This thirty day period does not count toward the three-month period under Section 587(3) ZPO as far as the VIAC is concerned. In principle, the time limit can be extended by the VIAC under **Article 13** if sufficient reasons are given. However, the time limit available to the co-arbitrators to agree on a chairman cannot be extended to exceed three months, as this would arguably trigger Section 587(3) ZPO. If both arbitrators agree prior to the end of the deadline

---

72. *See, e.g.,* Article 11(3) UNCITRAL Model Law; Article 12(2) DIS Rules; Article 22 Polish Rules or Article 18(4) Hungarian Rules; a different approach can be found in Article 8(4) ICC Rules where 'the third arbitrator, who will act as a chairman of the Arbitral Tribunal, shall be appointed by the Court, unless the parties have agreed upon another procedure for such appointment (. . .)'. And similar in Article 5(6) LCIA Rules: 'In the case of a three-member Arbitral tribunal, the chairman (who will be not a party-nominated arbitrator) shall be appointed by the LCIA Court' or even in Article 6(3) AAA/ICDR Rules 'the administrator shall (. . .) appoint the arbitrator(s) and designate the presiding arbitrator'.

that they are unable to reach an agreement, the Board can immediately proceed to make an appointment.

It bears emphasis that Article 14(5) only obliges the co-arbitrators to agree on a **14-060** chairman and indicate his or her name and address to the VIAC. It does not demand that the appointment is actually accepted by the proposed chairman within this time limit. In case the (potential) chairman refuses to accept or accepts under unacceptable conditions, there is no express solution offered under the present wording of Article 14. Indeed, the Board's authority to substitutionally appoint the chairman only appears to arise 'if no (...) indication [of agreement on a suitable chairperson, his name and address] is made' by the arbitrators. This provision encourages a broad reading, however. In case the joint nomination by the co-arbitrators of a chairman has not led to an acceptance of the mandate within reasonable time after the nomination, the Board shall be entitled to proceed to make an institutional appointment. At a minimum, the two co-arbitrators will have to nominate a presiding arbitrator who meets the requirements of **Article 7** and is not subject to challenge for lack of impartiality and independence under **Article 16**,[73] including by meeting any additional requirements for the chairman that the parties have specified in their agreement.[74] In this context, they will consider the candidate's nationality,[75] but will generally not have to investigate any potential conflict that a chairman could face. This is ultimately the chairman's responsibility when accepting the nomination. Beyond this, the two co-arbitrators are free to nominate any person they think is suitable for the task. In practice, both co-arbitrators will have to feel comfortable with the choice on a personal and professional level.

In practice, most co-arbitrators, insofar as they are able to reach agreement, also **14-061** approach the candidate and ask him or her whether there are conflicts preventing the appointment, whether his or her professional background meets the requirements of the case, and whether he or she is willing to accept the appointment. In these circumstances it is common for the co-arbitrators to reveal the identity of the parties in order to enable the candidate to facilitate a conflict check. On this issue, all people involved must maintain strict standards of confidentiality.[76] Although the VIAC is also prepared to approach any candidates, it can accelerate the

---

73. *See* the standard imposed on the state court in Section 587(8) ZPO.
74. Explicitly mentioned, *e.g.*, in Article 12(2) DIS Rules, where the arbitrators when appointing the chairman 'should take into account concurring proposals by the parties'. *See also* C. Hausmaninger, 'Rights and Obligations of the Arbitrator with Regard to the Parties and the Arbitral Institution – A Civil Law Viewpoint' (1995) ICC Ct Bull Special Supplement: The Status of the Arbitrator, 36, 40.
75. That follows the concept of Article 11(5) UNCITRAL Model Law, which was initially inserted in Section 587(7) draft ZPO, where the nationality other than those of the parties shall be taken into consideration. The same approach can be found in Article 9(5) ICC Rules; Article 6(1) LCIA Rules or in Article 6(4) AAA/ICDR Rules.
76. *See* **Article 7**, at paras. 063 *et seq.*

constitution of the tribunal if the co-arbitrators not merely reach agreement, but also, within the thirty-day time limit, eliminate candidates that are conflicted, are otherwise unavailable and ultimately arrive at a candidate who is able and willing to accept the nomination.

14-062 The process of joint nomination under Article 14 rests in principle entirely with the co-arbitrators, and does not foresee the involvement of the parties, or the VIAC.[77] It is accepted, however, that the co-arbitrators are free to discuss potential candidates with the parties that nominated them.[78] Indeed, it is legitimate for parties to have a say with respect to the constitution of the tribunal to suit their needs. Parties will often be guided by the applicable substantive law, procedural preferences and other factors; and will be concerned with the overall dynamics on the panel. For example, if the applicable law is Austrian law; and one party-nominated co-arbitrator is Austrian while the other is English, would the nomination of an Austrian chairman tactically disadvantage the party that nominated the English co-arbitrator, who might find it more difficult to impact the chairman's analysis of Austrian law *vis-à-vis* the Austrian counterpart? These, and many other, considerations will in practice affect the consultation process. Ultimately, however, it is clear under Article 14(5) that the nomination is the co-arbitrators' responsibility; and the arbitrators do not have to substantiate the reason for their nomination to the parties or the VIAC.[79]

14-063 As soon as both arbitrators have agreed upon a chairman and indicated the nomination to the VIAC, the Secretary General will arrange for the declaration of independence to be signed by the presiding arbitrator, pursuant to **Articles 7** and **12**. Only then will the parties be informed about the co-arbitrators' joint nomination of, and the acceptance by, the chairman.

B.   APPOINTMENT BY THE BOARD

14-064 When the Board is called upon to appoint the chairman, the same procedure as for the appointment of the co-arbitrators is applicable. Hence, reference can be made to the comments above at **Article 14**, at paras. 056 *et seq.* In addition, the Board

---

77. Even the presiding arbitrator's election by draw may be permissible: *see* jurisprudence under the former ZPO *e.g.*, OGH, 29 February 1984, 2 Ob 516/84.

78. C. Hausmaninger, 'Rights and Obligations of the Arbitrator with Regard to the Parties and the Arbitral Institution – A Civil Law Viewpoint' (1995) ICC Ct Bull Special Supplement: The Status of the Arbitrator, 36, 40 with reference to Rule 5(2) of the 1987 IBA Rules of Ethics for International Arbitrators.

79. That corresponds with the concept of most of the prominent arbitration rules; an interesting exception can be found in Article 18(4) Hungarian Rules where in case 'the arbitrators appointed by the parties elect a presiding arbitrator not included in the roll of arbitrators, they shall notify the Presidium of the Arbitration Court thereof, designating the reasons for such election'.

will place particular emphasis on questions such as arbitral expertise, neutrality and managerial skills as the appointment of a suitable chairman is certainly one of the most decisive decision to make in the arbitral process. At this stage, it is not common that the co-arbitrators or the parties are involved in the decision-making process. Hence, they will officially be informed about the Board's decision when the chairman's declaration of independence becomes available.

As this paragraph does not provide any time limit for the Board to make the appointment, the three-month time limit of Section 587(3) ZPO applies; it will commence as soon as the time limit for the co-arbitrators has expired without resulting in a joint nomination, or as soon as the co-arbitrators notify the VIAC prior to the expiry of the time limit that they are unable to reach an agreement.[80] **14-065**

C.   APPOINTMENT BY THE AUSTRIAN COURTS

Article 14(5) is in line with Section 587(2) no. 2 ZPO which in turn stipulates that 'in an arbitration with three arbitrators, each party shall appoint one arbitrator. The two arbitrators thus appointed shall appoint the third arbitrator who shall preside over the arbitral tribunal'. In case the arbitrators are unable to reach an agreement, any party may request the court to take the necessary measure and make the appointment on behalf of the defaulting party or institution. This court decision, again, is not subject to any appeal. **14-066**

VI.   BINDING EFFECT OF NOMINATION

Article 14(6): The parties are bound by their nomination of arbitrators as soon as the identity of the arbitrator nominated has been made known to the other party.

This paragraph had been newly inserted with the amendment of the Vienna Rules in 2001.[81] It is clearly intended to accelerate the proceedings. Neither party should have the possibility of recalling nominations and thereby unnecessarily delaying the constitution of the tribunal, or subsequently disrupting the arbitration. **14-067**

Systemically, this provision has to be read in conjunction with **Article 16** regarding the challenge of arbitrators. **Article 16** is conceptually only needed if the parties are bound by their respective nominations; where the parties are not already bound by their appointment (e.g. the opposing party was not yet notified of the appointment), a challenge of the appointed arbitrator is not required. In such cases, the party is free to nominate a different arbitrator. **14-068**

---

80. *See* **Article 14**, at para. 059.
81. Article 9(6) Vienna Rules 2001, **Annex 2a.**

14-069 The wording of Article 14(6) is broad and refers to the identity of the arbitrator having 'been made known to the other party'. Arguably even a nomination prior to the commencement of the arbitration proceedings as, for example, in a demand letter may already have a binding effect on a party. This has not been intended by drafters of the Vienna Rules. Article 14(6) will apply only at or after the arbitration proceedings are commenced, that is, when the statement of claims is received by the VIAC (*see* **Article 9**, at para. 015). After commencement of the arbitration, however, the binding effect of any notification applies automatically as soon as the identity of the arbitrator is disclosed; it makes no difference if the notification was served on the other party directly, or via the VIAC.

14-070 A party's nomination is in principle binding irrespectively of whether this nomination is challenged by the other party or not. However, this principle has limits in party autonomy. Hence, should a party object to the other party's nomination of an arbitrator on the basis of **Article 12**, the nominating party should be allowed to withdraw its nomination and propose a new candidate. It makes no sense to force the parties through challenge proceedings if the nominating party agrees to revoke and renew its nomination.

14-071 The binding effect of the nomination of an arbitrator is, as a matter of course, also limited by operation of other provisions in the Vienna Rules (or applicable law). A party is not bound to its original nomination if, for example, the arbitrator had been successfully challenged or removed from his office, or resigned. The binding effect does also not extend to other arbitrations under the Vienna Rules between the same parties.

Article 15

Multi-Party Arbitration

		Para.				Para.
I.	Admissibility of Multi-Party Claims	1	B.	Ensuring Equality Between the Parties	41
	A. Introduction	1	C.	Austrian Law	46
	B. Admissibility of Multi-Party Arbitration under the Vienna Rules	6	D.	The Vienna Rules	53
			V.	Consolidation and Joinder	55
	1. Mandatory Requirements	8		A. Introduction	55
	2. Elective Requirements	11		B. Pre-Agreed Consolidation	59
	2.1. Mandatory Joinder	13		C. Consolidation Under the Vienna Rules	66
	2.2. Other Factual or Legal Connection Between the Respondents	19		D. Joinder	74
	2.3. Agreement	21		1. Agreement to Join a Party or an Intervener	75
	2.4. Subsequent Submission by the Respondents	23		2. Joining Non-Signatories	82
	2.5. Defaulting Respondents	24		2.1. Succession	84
II.	Failure to Serve the Claim on all Respondents	26		2.2. Third-Party Beneficiary	86
III.	Determining the Number of Arbitrators in Multi-Party Proceedings	28		2.3. Estoppel and Abuse of Law	94
				2.4. Corporate Veil Piercing	104
IV.	Articles 15(6)-15(7): Appointment of the Arbitrator for Respondents	32		2.5. Group of Companies	109
	A. *Dutco* and the Equality of the Parties in Constituting the Tribunal	33		2.6. Domestic Law or Transnational Principles?	112
			VI.	Decision on Admissibility of Multi-party Proceedings	118

I.   ADMISSIBILITY OF MULTI-PARTY CLAIMS

Article 15(1): A claim against two or more Respondents shall be admissible only if the Centre has jurisdiction for all of the Respondents, and, in the case of proceedings before an arbitral tribunal, if all Claimants have nominated the same arbitrator, and:

(a) **If the applicable law positively provides that the claim is to be directed against several persons; or**

(b) **If all Respondents are by the applicable law in legal accord or are bound by the same facts or are joint and severally bound; or**

(c) **If the admissibility of multiparty proceedings has been agreed upon; or**

(d) **If all Respondents submit to multiparty proceedings and, in the case of proceedings before an arbitral tribunal, all Respondents nominate the same arbitrator; or**

(e) **If one or more of the Respondents on whom the claim was served fails or fail to provide the particulars mentioned in Article 10 paragraph 2, b) and c) within the thirty-day time-limit (Article 10 paragraph 1).**

A.   INTRODUCTION

15-001   Disputes reflect the realities of commercial life. As commerce becomes increasingly complex, so do disputes. Thus, an arbitration may not arise simply between two parties to a contract, but between multiple parties. This is typical for joint venture agreements; arbitration clauses contained in articles of association;[1] distribution agreements; construction projects (which typically include the principal, one or more contractors and possibly subcontractors);[2] and many other forms of commercial contracts. As a particular form of multiparty-arbitrations,[3] commercial arrangements also give rise to multi-contract arbitration between two or more parties, who have entered into a number of different contracts all providing for arbitration.[4]

15-002   There is a lot to be said in favor of establishing one tribunal instead of several different ones to settle disputes that are commercially related. First, a single

---

1. J. Lew, L. Mistelis and S. Kröll, *Comparative International Commercial Arbitration* (The Hague, Kluwer Law International, 2003), para. 16-7.

2. Ch. Bühring-Uhle, *Arbitration and Mediation in International Business* (The Hague, Kluwer Law International, 1996), p. 65.

3. J. Lew, L. Mistelis and S. Kröll, *Comparative International Commercial Arbitration* (The Hague, Kluwer Law International, 2003), para. 16-1.

4. J. Lew, L. Mistelis and S. Kröll, *Comparative International Commercial Arbitration* (The Hague, Kluwer Law International, 2003), para. 16-5.

tribunal would gain full knowledge of relevant facts and circumstances and would likely be able to see the 'larger picture' of the parties' dispute. Second, to consolidate multiple disputes in one arbitration will often save the parties a significant amount of time and other resources. Third, resolving multi-party disputes in a single forum resolves the risk that different tribunals reach inconsistent or contradictory conclusions with regard to the same matter.[5]

In the context of arbitration, however, multi-party (and multi-contract) proceedings raise some difficult issues. First, the arbitration agreement must be valid and applicable in scope to all the parties to the dispute.[6] Second, all the parties must have been given proper notice of the arbitration and have had an equal opportunity to present their cases.[7] Finally, and this has caused some debate in international arbitration, all parties must have an equal opportunity to participate in the constitution of the tribunal.[8] **15-003**

These questions are not always easy to answer. How to provide, for example, two claimants and three respondents with an equal right to nominate the arbitrator of their choice? Similar issues, albeit on a more managerial scale, arise during the process: should all parties to the arbitration be granted an equal time to present their cases although there is an uneven number of claimants and respondents? **15-004**

For the Vienna Rules, Article 15 sets out the conditions under which multi-party arbitration is admissible. Article 15 also takes into account the difficulties that can result from the participation of multiple parties to the same proceedings and contains default rules for such situations. Article 15(1) lists the circumstances in which multi-party arbitration is admissible. Article 15(2) contains provisions regarding a failure to serve the claim on all respondents; followed by provisions on the number of arbitrators (Article 15(3)-(5)) and the substitute appointment of arbitrators in proceedings with multiple parties (Article 15(6)-(7)). Article 15(8) contains rules on consolidation, which also serves as the appropriate place to discuss the concepts of joinder, intervention and the extension of the arbitration agreement to non-signatory parties. Article 15(9), finally, addresses the tribunal's power to decide on the admissibility of multi-party arbitration. **15-005**

---

5. P. Level, 'Joinder of Proceedings, Intervention of Third Parties and additional Claims and Counterclaims' (1996) 7(2) ICC Ct Bull, 27 *et seq.*; ICC Commission on International Arbitration (Chairman: J.-L. Delvolvé), 'Final Report on Multi-Party Arbitration' (1995) 6(1) ICC Ct Bull, 26, 35.
6. *See* Article V(1)(a) NY Convention, **Annex 11**.
7. *See* Article V(1)(b) NY Convention, **Annex 11**.
8. *See* Article V(1)(d) NY Convention, **Annex 11**.

B.   ADMISSIBILITY OF MULTI-PARTY ARBITRATION UNDER
             THE VIENNA RULES

15-006 The provisions related to multi-party arbitration in most arbitration rules only deal with the constitution of the tribunal and provide default rules for situations where the parties cannot agree on the appointment of arbitrators. Rules containing other provisions related to multi-party arbitration, such as rules on the admissibility of such proceedings are rare.[9]

15-007 Article 15(1) addresses the admissibility of multi-party proceedings under the Vienna Rules in what is one of the more complex solutions available anywhere. Structurally, Article 15 provides for certain mandatory conditions, each of which must always be met for a multi-party arbitration to be admissible under the Vienna Rules. In addition, Article 15(1)(a)-(e) provides for several elective conditions, only one of which needs to be met in addition to the mandatory conditions.

1.   **Mandatory Requirements**

15-008 Article 15(1) lays out the basis for the admissibility of multi-party arbitration. First, in order for multiple respondents to be parties to the same proceedings, the Centre must have jurisdiction over all of them.[10] In line with other provisions of the Vienna Rules,[11] it is not required that all the respondents are subject to the same arbitration agreement. It is merely required that they are all subject to an arbitration agreement that provides for arbitration under the Vienna Rules. Although not expressly mentioned, multiple claimants must also all be within the subjective scope of an arbitration agreement conferring jurisdiction on the VIAC, or else they will lack the standing to bring a claim under the Vienna Rules. Whatever jurisdictional objections exist, they must be raised, in accordance with **Article 19**, and hence with the first submission on the merits (usually the memorandum in reply).[12]

15-009 Second, if there are multiple claimants, they must all jointly agree on the same arbitrator. The nomination of an arbitrator by the claimant is straightforward when there are multiple respondents to the dispute but only one claimant. In cases where there are several claimants, agreement on a single arbitrator can be more difficult to achieve. In order for the claimants to be able to have the dispute settled by one arbitral tribunal, the claimants must consent on a joint arbitrator, or at least appoint the same arbitrator in different but related proceedings in order to make use of the

---

9. *See, e.g.,* Article 13(3) DIS Rules: 'The arbitral tribunal decides on the admissibility of the multi-party proceedings.'
10. *See* **Article 1**, at paras. 001 *et seq.*
11. *See, e.g.,* **Article 11**, at para. 006.
12. A. Fremuth-Wolf in *Arbitration Law of Austria: Practice and Procedure*, S. Riegler, A. Petsche, A. Fremuth-Wolf, M. Platte and C. Liebscher (eds) (Huntington, Juris Publishing, 2007), Section 592, p. 301; Section 1040(2) German ZPO explicitly refers to the statement of defense.

possibility of consolidation under Article 15(8) at a later stage.[13] The consent of multiple claimants to jointly appoint an arbitrator is not only a prerequisite for the claims to be admissible,[14] but also saves time in the constitution of the tribunal.

The mandatory charcter of these requirements derives form a textual interpretation **15-010** that connects the requirement of jurisdiction and joint nomination by the claimant in cumulative fashion ('and').

2.   Elective Requirements

In addition to the mandatory conditions discussed above, Article 15(1)(a)-(e) list **15-011** several elective requirements. Only one of these requirements must be met, in addition to the mandatory requirements, for the arbitration to be admissible under Article 15.

The structure of Article 15 is problematic, however. It is difficult to understand **15-012** why the additional requirements of Article 15(1)(a)-(e) are needed, or what purpose they serve, in particular where some of these requirements can raise problems of their own. A simplified solution would rest on the jurisdictional scope of the arbitration clause that is being invoked. Where that clause (or those clauses) vests the tribunal with jurisdiction as against multiple parties (whether on the claimants' or the respondents' side), additional conditions seem an artificial imposition rather than helpful clarification. For good reasons, other arbitral rules have stayed away from this sort of regime.

2.1.   *Mandatory Joinder*

Article 15(1)(a) stipulates that multi-party proceedings are admissible '[i]f the **15-013** applicable law positively provides that the claim is to be directed against several persons.'

Article 15(1)(a) follows the concept of uniform party (*einheitliche Streitpartei*) **15-014** and mandatory joinder (*notwendige Streitgenossenschaft*), as laid out in Section 14 ZPO.[15] The wording of litera a) of the English translation of the rules could be clearer in its reference to the applicable law 'positively' providing for the admissibility of multi-party arbitration. From the German wording of the same provision,

---

13. *See* **Article 15**, at paras. 055 *et seq.*
14. *See* discussion on **Article 15(1)**, at para. 007.
15. Section 14 JN provides: 'If, due to the nature of the legal relationship in dispute or by virtue of a statutory provision, the effect of the judgment to be delivered extends to all co-participants (*Streitgenossen*), [such co-participants] shall constitute a single party to the dispute. Even if certain individual co-participants are belated, the effect of the procedural acts undertaken by the active co-participants also extend to them.' *See* R. Fucik in *Kommentar zur ZPO*, W.H. Rechberger (3rd edn, Vienna/NewYork, Springer, 2006), Section 14; G. Schubert in *Kommentar zu den Zivilprozeßgesetzen, II/1*, H.W. Fasching (2nd edn, Vienna, Manz, 2002), Section 14.

it is clear that the drafters made reference to cases where the applicable law affirmatively *requires* a certain group to be named as respondents.[16]

15-015 It is therefore up to the arbitral tribunal to establish the applicable legal system and determine whether the term 'applicable law' refers to procedural or substantive law.[17] Usually, the 'applicable law' that requires such a joinder is a rule of substantive law. This is most likely but not necessarily the law applicable to the contract, but may also be a corporate regime applicable to the respondents and their relationship towards each other. Austrian law 'positively' requires, for instance, that certain corporate disputes between shareholders must include all shareholders of the company, such as disputes concerning the validity of shareholders' resolutions.[18]

15-016 Problems arise if a claim must, as a matter of applicable substantive law, be directed against several persons, but only some of them are parties to the arbitration agreement. It has been suggested that in such a case, the dispute is no longer arbitrable,[19] but that is inaccurate terminology. Section 582 ZPO contains the exclusive definition of arbitrability, providing that

> [a]ny claim involving an economic interest that lies within the jurisdiction of the courts of law can be subject of an arbitration agreement. An arbitration agreement concerning claims not involving an economic interest shall have legal effect to the extent that the parties are entitled to conclude a settlement on the subject-matter in dispute.[20]

15-017 As a conceptual matter, the dispute therefore remains objectively arbitrable, even where not all necessary parties are parties to the arbitration agreement. Arbitrability under Section 582 ZPO is determined solely with regard to whether or not the dispute involved 'an economic interest' or whether 'the parties are entitled to conclude a settlement on the subject-matter in dispute.' As *Reiner* argues convincingly, '[o]ne of the most fundamental changes introduced by the new arbitration law is the more liberal approach to arbitrability (. . .). There can no longer be any doubt that all corporate law disputes, which always involve an economic interest, are objectively arbitrable. The question of arbitrability must be distinguished from the question of how the arbitration agreement and the

---

16. Article 15(1)(a): 'Eine Schiedsklage gegen zwei oder mehrere Beklagte ist nur zulässig, sofern das Schiedsgericht für alle Beklagten zuständig ist, bei einem Verfahren vor einem Schiedsrichtersenat alle Kläger denselben Schiedsrichter benennen und a) die Klage nach dem anzuwendenden Recht zwingend gegen mehrere Personen zu richten ist; (. . .).'

17. C. Liebscher in *Arbitration Law of Austria: Practice and Procedure*, S. Riegler, A. Petsche, A. Fremuth-Wolf, M. Platte and C. Liebscher (eds) (Huntington, Juris Publishing, 2007), p. 635 *et seq.*

18. OGH, 27 July 2007, 4 Ob 109/07; OGH, 16 December 1993, 8 Ob 547/92; OGH, 19 October 1989, 7 Ob 681/89. *See* also **Article 1**, at para. 129.

19. OGH, 10 December 1998, 7 Ob 221/98w.

20. Section 582 ABGB.

proceedings must be structured in order to justify the extension of *res judicata* required by corporate law.'[21]

Thus, where the applicable substantive law mandates the participation of certain **15-018** 'necessary' parties, because a decision can otherwise not be made, the absence of such parties does not lead to the objective non-arbitrability of the matter, but may lead to the dismissal of the claim for lack of standing, or for lack of substantive basis. Obviously, the award would have no effect against those parties that were unable to participate in proceedings;[22] there is therefore no need for such parties to have the right to challenge such an award.[23]

2.2.   Other Factual or Legal Connection Between the Respondents

Article 15(1)(b) further stipulates that multi-party proceedings are admissible '[i]f **15-019** all Respondents are by the applicable law in legal accord or are bound by the same facts or are joint and severally bound.'[24]

The English translation of this provision is not entirely clear.[25] The aim of the **15-020** drafters was to grant jurisdiction over a group of respondents that form, on the basis of the applicable (substantive) law, one legal entity. Joint proprietors would, for example, constitute such a *Rechtsgemeinschaft*. It has been argued that this provision reflects the concept of 'material joinder' contained in Section 11(1) ZPO (*Rechtsgemeinschaft*),[26] but the wording of Article 15(1)(b) goes further, allowing for multi-party arbitration where the respondents 'are bound by the same facts.' Given the problematic nature of limiting the admissibility of multi-party arbitration in the first place,[27] a broad reading appears preferable. Thus, as long as there is some sort of factual connection between the respondents and the claim advanced against them, the arbitration should be permissible under Article 15. Indeed, both respondents must be subject to an arbitration agreement conferring jurisdiction on the VIAC. It is unlikely in such circumstances that a claimant would choose to pursue an arbitration against two respondents even though their relationship to each other, or to the claimant, or to the claim, does not arise from the same factual matrix.

---

21. A. Reiner, 'Schiedsverfahren und Gesellschaftsrecht' [2007] GesRZ, 151, 151 *et seq.*
22. *See* Section 607 ZPO and **Article 27**, at para. 020.
23. *See also* **Article 1**, at para. 129.
24. This is a new provision, not previously contained in the predecessor of Article 15, namely Article 10(1)(b) of the 2001 Vienna Rules. **Annex 2a.**
25. The German version of Article 15(1)(b) reads: 'Eine Schiedsklage gegen zwei oder mehrere Beklagte ist nur zulässig, sofern das Schiedsgericht für alle Beklagten zuständig ist, bei einem Verfahren vor einem Schiedsrichtersenat alle Kläger denselben Schiedsrichter benennen und b) die beklagten Parteien nach dem anzuwendenden Recht in Rechtsgemeinschaft stehen oder aus demselben tatsächlichen Grund oder solidarisch verpflichtet sind; (. . .).'
26. C. Liebscher in *Arbitration Law of Austria: Practice and Procedure*, S. Riegler, A. Petsche, A. Fremuth-Wolf, M. Platte and C. Liebscher (eds) (Huntington, Juris Publishing, 2007), p. 636.
27. *See* **Article 15**, at para. 012.

2.3.   *Agreement*

15-021 Article 15(1)(c) stipulates that multi-party proceedings are admissible '[i]f the admissibility of multiparty proceedings has been agreed upon.' Of the specifications contained in Article 15, this one is the most straightforward: under this requirement, the admissibility of multiparty arbitration is simply based on the agreement of the parties.

15-022 Article 15(1)(c) does not require an explicit agreement. If more than two parties jointly concluded an arbitration agreement, this would typically imply that they agree to arbitrate claims as against each other, including in the same arbitration.[28] Thus, arbitration clauses contained in a company's articles of associations typically must be interpreted to allow for multi-party arbitration as between all shareholders.

2.4.   *Subsequent Submission by the Respondents*

15-023 Article 15(1)(d) stipulates that multi-party proceedings are admissible '[i]f all Respondents submit to multiparty proceedings and, in the case of proceedings before an arbitral tribunal, all Respondents nominate the same arbitrator.' Article 15(1)(d) addresses the situation that no specific agreement on multi-party arbitration exists, but after the disputes have arisen, the respondents either agree to it or fail to raise a timely objection against the tribunal's jurisdiction.[29] In addition, the respondents must be prepared to jointly nominate the same arbitrator.

2.5.   *Defaulting Respondents*

15-024 Finally, Article 15(1)(e) stipulates that multi-party proceedings are admissible '[i]f one or more of the Respondents on whom the claim was served fails or fail to provide the particulars mentioned in Article 10 paragraph 2 b) and c) within the thirty-day time-limit (Article 10 paragraph 1).' Article 10(2) requires a respondent to nominate the arbitrator in its memorandum in reply. Pursuant to Article 15(1)(e), if a respondent fails to take a position in the memorandum in reply with respect to the number of arbitrators, and, where applicable, the identity of the arbitrator it wants to nominate, it is deemed to have consented to the admissibility of multi-party arbitration.

15-025 In practice, this provision allows the arbitration to proceed if one of two respondents does not submit a memorandum in reply at all. In such a case, the solution is sensible; a defaulting respondent should not be allowed to block a proceeding. However, this provision raises serious questions in case of larger numbers of respondents. Assuming, for example, that of four respondents, one respondent

---

28. C. Liebscher in *Arbitration Law of Austria: Practice and Procedure*, S. Riegler, A. Petsche, A. Fremuth-Wolf, M. Platte and C. Liebscher (eds) (Huntington, Juris Publishing, 2007), p. 636.
29. *See* **Article 19**, at paras. 006 *et seq.*

fails to submit a memorandum in reply, the effect under Article 15 on the other respondents is unclear. According to the wording of Article 15(1)(e), as long as they are subject to an arbitration agreement conferring jurisdiction on the VIAC, the other three respondents seem to have lost their right to protest against the admissibility of multi-party proceedings – simply because 'one or more of the Respondents on whom the claim was served fails' to provide a statement of defense – even if none of the other requirements of Article 15(1)(a)-(d) is met. Systemically, that frustrates the purpose of Article 15(1); it is additional support for the proposition that, as long as the arbitrators have jurisdiction over all the respondents, additional requirements are not needed and may indeed prove an undue restriction on the arbitral process.

II.   FAILURE TO SERVE THE CLAIM ON ALL RESPONDENTS

Article 15(2): Where a claim against a number of Respondents cannot be served on all Respondents, the arbitral proceedings shall, upon application of the Claimant (the Claimants), be continued against those Respondents on whom the claim was served. The claim against those Respondents to which the claim could not be served shall be subject to separate proceedings.

Of course, no arbitration can be conducted without proper service of the statement **15-026** of claims, which puts the respondent on notice that proceedings are initiated against it, so that it can participate in the constitution of the tribunal and prepare, and then advance, its defense. A failure to observe these basic principles may result in the setting-aside of the award *vis-à-vis* the respondent party that was not even notified of the existence of the arbitration.[30]

Article 15(2) allows the proceedings to continue, at least against the other respon- **15-027** dents, even if it is impossible to serve the statement of claims on all of the respondents. Those respondents, against whom service could not be effected, must be pursued in a separate forum.

III.   DETERMINING THE NUMBER OF ARBITRATORS IN MULTI-PARTY PROCEEDINGS

Article 15(3): If multiparty proceedings are admissible, the Respondents must agree among themselves whether they wish to have the dispute decided by one arbitrator or by three arbitrators, and, if a decision by three arbitrators is desired, must jointly nominate an arbitrator.

Article 15(4): In the case covered by paragraph 3 of the present Article, if there is no agreement among the Respondents concerning the number of arbitrators, the Respondents shall be requested by the Secretary General

---

30. *See* **Article 9**, at para. 055.

to provide evidence of such agreement within thirty days after service of the request.

Article 15(5): If no evidence of agreement on the number of arbitrators is presented within the period mentioned in paragraph 4 of the present article, the Board shall determine whether the dispute is to be decided by one arbitrator or by an arbitral tribunal.

15-028 According to **Article 14**, the parties can agree on the number of arbitrators.[31] Where no such agreement exists, the claimant (or multiple claimants jointly) need to propose a number in the statement of claims. Indeed, in case the claimants propose a three-arbitrator panel, Article 15(1) requires them to make a joint nomination. Thus, the Vienna Rules do not provide for the case where multiple claimants are unable to reach agreement on the number of arbitrators. In this case, the claimants could only initiate separate proceedings, each against the same respondents. The only way in which these proceedings could later be consolidated, would be by appointing the same arbitrators in the different cases, which the respondents can easily sabotage by nominating different arbitrators for each case.[32]

15-029 Article 15(3) Vienna Rules provides essentially the same for the respondents, who, in the absence of an agreement between the parties, need to take a joint position on whether they want the dispute decided by one arbitrator or a panel of three arbitrators. Where the respondents prefer a tribunal of three, they need to make a joint nomination (failing which the VIAC will make the appointment for them). This is in line with the discernible trend. Other arbitration rules also tend to require the parties' common decision on the number of arbitrators, treating multiple claimants and respondents as the collective claimant and the collective respondent.[33]

15-030 Article 15(4) requires the Secretary General to set an additional thirty day deadline to the respondents by which they must reach agreement on the number of arbitrators. It is not entirely clear, and does not aid the expeditious constitution of the tribunal, why the respondents need an extra thirty days to reach that agreement; they already have thirty days to prepare their statement of defense which they could use to discuss amongst themselves the number of arbitrators as well. In any event, if no evidence for such agreement is forthcoming within that deadline, the Board will determine whether the case will be heard by one arbitrator or a tribunal of three arbitrators.[34] In essence, therefore, Article 15(3) requires the agreement of all claimants and all respondents on the number of arbitrators. Where one respondent takes a different position, the number of arbitrators will be determined by the Board, similar to the procedure under Article 14(2). As discussed there, the

---

31. *See* **Article 14**, at paras. 006 *et seq.*
32. *See* **Article 15(8)**, at paras. 055 *et seq.*
33. *See* Article 10(1) ICC Rules; Article 8(1) LCIA Rules; Article 24(1) CIETAC Rules; Article 8(1) SIAC Rules; Article 13(4) SCC Rules; Article 8(3) Swiss Rules and Article 18 WIPO Rules.
34. *See* also **Article 14**, at paras. 015 *et seq.*

trend in modern rules is not for such determination to take place, but to provide, absent agreement by the parties, for a default number in the rules, which can save considerable time.[35]

Article 14(2) provides that in determining the number of arbitrators, the Board **15-031** 'shall take into consideration in particular the difficulty of the case, the magnitude of the amount in dispute and the interest of the parties in a rapid and cost-effective decision'.[36] The same considerations will guide the Board's determination under Article 15(3).

IV.   ARTICLES 15(6)-15(7): APPOINTMENT OF THE
       ARBITRATOR FOR RESPONDENTS

> **Article 15(6): If the Respondents have agreed that the dispute is to be decided by an arbitral tribunal, but without nominating an arbitrator, they shall be requested by the Secretary General to indicate the name and address of an arbitrator within thirty days after service of the request.**

> **Article 15(7): If no arbitrator is jointly nominated within the period mentioned in paragraph 6 of the present Article and if the dispute is to be decided by an arbitral tribunal, the Board shall appoint the arbitrator for the defaulting Respondents.**

The composition of the arbitral tribunal – and in particular the appointment of an **15-032** arbitrator where multiple parties on one side fail to agree on a joint nomination – is a prime area of concern in multi-party arbitrations.[37] The essential pattern of 'one party – one arbitrator' appointment will not work where there are more than two parties, for example in an 'asymmetric' arbitration with one claimant and multiple respondents, in particular if those multiple respondents do not share the same interests. This raises concerns because the principle of equal treatment of the parties also applies to the constitution of the tribunal.[38]

A.   *DUTCO AND THE EQUALITY OF THE PARTIES IN CONSTITUTING THE TRIBUNAL*

One of the fundamental principles of commercial arbitration is the equal treatment **15-033** of the parties, as well as the parties' freedom to agree upon the arbitral procedure.[39]

---

35. *See, e.g.*, Article 8 ICC Rules; Articles 5 and Article 8(1) LCIA Rules and Article 12 SCC Rules. The Vienna Rules do not set a time limit for decisions taken by the Board.
36. *See* **Article 14(2)**, at paras. 026 *et seq.*
37. J. Lew, L. Mistelis and S. Kröll, *Comparative International Commercial Arbitration* (The Hague, Kluwer Law International, 2003), para. 16-11.
38. *See* discussion on *Dutco* decision at **Article 15**, at paras. 033 *et seq.*
39. G.B. Born, *International Commercial Arbitration – Commentary and Materials* (3rd edn, The Hague, Kluwer Law International, forthcoming), ch. 14.

It is generally accepted that these principles also apply to the appointment of arbitrators, requiring for multi-party cases that the parties should be treated equally when appointing arbitrators. At the same time, applicable rules should ensure that unwilling parties do not abuse the added complexity of constituting a tribunal in multi-party cases to obstruct or delay the process.[40]

15-034 The issue is illustrated by the famous case of *Siemens AG/BKMI Industrienanlagen GmbH v. Dutco Construction Company* decided by the French *Cour de Cassation* in 1992.[41] In this case, the Court was asked to consider the issue of equal treatment of the parties with regard to the constitution of an arbitral tribunal.

15-035 The problem arose as a result of a three party consortium contract containing an ICC arbitration clause making reference to a three-person tribunal. The consortium, formed in 1981, consisted of *Siemens AG, BMKI* and *Dutco. Dutco* commenced an ICC arbitration against *Siemens AG* and *BKMI* in 1986. Pursuant to the ICC Rules in force at the time, the respondents had to jointly nominate one arbitrator for 'their side'. *Siemens AG* and *BKMI* did so, with the caveat that in their view the procedure imposed by the ICC Rules constituted a procedural irregularity and grounds for challenging the award. In essence, the two respondents argued that although they were both opposing *Dutco's* claim, their interests were not entirely aligned, as each of the respondents alleged to have different obligations under the relevant contract. They should therefore not be forced to jointly appoint a single arbitrator.[42]

15-036 The arbitral tribunal decided in a partial award that it had been validly and properly constituted and that the proceedings could continue as a multiparty arbitration. The respondents challenged this decision in the French courts. Ultimately, the French *Cour de Cassation* found that the constitution of the tribunal had been unfair to the respondents. The court set aside the award reasoning that 'the principle of the equality of the parties in the appointment of arbitrators is a matter of public policy (*ordre public*) [and] can be waived only after a dispute has arisen'.[43] According to the court, the appointment of the arbitral tribunal was unfair because it afforded

---

40. J. L. Greenblatt and P. Griffin, 'Towards the Harmonization of International Arbitration Rules: Comparative Analysis of the Rules of the ICC, AAA, LCIA and CIETAC' (2001) 17(1) Arb Int'l, 101, 102.

41. *See* Cour de Cassation, 1re Ch. Civ., 7 January 1992, *Siemens AG/BKMI Industrienanlagen GmbH v. Dutco Construction Company* (1993) XVII YB Comm Arb, 140-142.

42. The then applicable, long-standing ICC practice had been – in the absence of a clause such as Article 10 ICC Rules of the currently applicable rules – to require joint nominations of arbitrators in cases with multiple respondents, allowing 'each party' to nominate one arbitrator. This created uncertainty in multi-party context because the wording 'each party' was ambiguous: it was unclear whether it made reference to 'each side' or 'every party'. *See also* J. Lew, L. Mistelis and S. Kröll, *Comparative International Commercial Arbitration* (The Hague, Kluwer Law International, 2003), para. 16-27.

43. *See* Cour de Cassation, 1re Ch. Civ., 7 January 1992, *Siemens AG/BKMI Industrienanlagen GmbH v. Dutco Construction Company* (1993) XVII YB Comm Arb, 140-142.

Dutco a better position to influence the final outcome of the arbitration. The court considered that the parties could not waive the right to equal treatment through their arbitration agreement and their submission to the ICC Rules prior to the dispute arising because all parties to an arbitration agreement should have the same right to contribute to the constitution of the arbitral tribunal.

This decision established two principles, at least for French law. First, should the **15-037** parties not have had an equal opportunity to influence the constitution of the tribunal, the award can be annulled on public policy grounds.[44] Second, as this is a principle of public policy, the parties cannot waive that protection before the dispute has arisen.[45]

Commentators have correctly noted, however, that the *Dutco* decision of the **15-038** French *Cour de Cassation* does not establish an irrevocable right for each party involved in an arbitration to appoint its 'own' arbitrator – if that were true, the tribunal could easily consist of an unmanageably large number of arbitrators.[46] Indeed, such a solution would violate the principle of equality giving one 'side' to the dispute (the claimants or respondents) more influence on the composition of the tribunal.[47]

The Italian *Corte de Cassazione* confirmed in its *Borgotaro* judgment[48] the require- **15-039** ment that the parties are to be placed on an equal footing with regard to the appoint-ment of arbitrators.[49] In a decision from 2001, the *Obergericht Zürich* (Zurich Superior Court)[50] followed the same principle of equality of the parties as the French *Cour de Cassation* did in the *Dutco*-case, albeit applied to a different factual situation, and suggesting a more nuanced approach focusing on the interests of the parties. Holding that the principle of equality of the parties could not be waived by an agreement between the parties, the *Obergericht Zürich* found that the necessary balance between the parties would be jeopardized by an agreement allowing the two respondents to appoint two arbitrators and the single claimant only one arbitrator, thus giving the respondents more influence on the appointment of the chairman, who is appointed by the selected arbitrators. The court also found, however, that the two respondents in that case had the same interests and positions, and therefore

---

44. J.-L. Delvolvé, 'Multipartism: The *Dutco* Decision of the French Cour de Cassation' (1993) 9(2) Arb Int'l, 197.
45. E. Gaillard and J. Savage (eds), *Fouchard Gaillard Goldman On International Commercial Arbitration* (The Hague, Kluwer Law International, 1999), para. 1436.
46. F.B. Weigand in *Practitioner's Handbook on International Arbitration*, F.B. Weigand (ed.) (Munich, C.H. Beck, 2002), p. 184.
47. J. Lew, L. Mistelis and S. Kröll, *Comparative International Commercial Arbitration* (The Hague, Kluwer Law International, 2003), para. 16-12.
48. Italian *Corte de Cassazione*, 5 July 1995, *Coop. Vigili Fuoco Borgotaro v. Mariani*, No. 2304, Foro Pad. 1995, I, 206.
49. Y. Derains and E.A. Schwartz, *A Guide to the ICC Rules of Arbitration* (2nd edn, The Hague, Kluwer Law International, 2005), p. 115 *et seq.*
50. Obergericht Zürich, 11 September 2001, ZR 2002(101) No. 21, 77.

concluded that it was reasonable to expect the parties to agree on a joint appointment. In the case of a conflict of interests between the respondents, however, it would have been more in line with the principle of equality of the parties to permit the appointment of an arbitrator by each of the three parties.[51] This decision suggests that the right of equality of the parties in the designation of the arbitrators would not be considered to be violated where a joint nomination or appointment of an arbitrator is required to be made by entities that are under common control, or that otherwise have identical interests in the outcome of the arbitration.[52] In these cases close ties usually exist between the members of the group, which may justify an obligation for those parties to agree on a single arbitrator.[53]

15-040 Although the *Dutco*-case can be considered a precedent in the field of multiparty arbitration, there are a number of court decisions that do not adopt the same understanding of the principle of equality of the parties.[54]

B.   ENSURING EQUALITY BETWEEN THE PARTIES

15-041 Whatever its merits, the decision in *Dutco* had an enormous impact on institutional arbitration rules. Almost all major institutions introduced specific provisions for multiparty arbitration, especially for the appointment of a tribunal by a multitude of parties.[55]

15-042 Conceptually, there are two models to ensure a fair appointment process for multiple parties. Both models proceed on the basis that multiple claimants and multiple respondents must jointly agree on the nomination of an arbitrator for each side. This premise is sensible.[56] Obviously, it treats both parties the same,

---

51. L. Hirsch, 'Remarks on the Decision of Zurich Superior Court of 11 September 2001' (2002) 20(4) Bull ASA, 702 *et seq.*

52. E. A. Schwartz, 'Multi-Party Arbitration and the ICC – In the Wake of *Dutco*' (1993) 10(3) J Int'l Arb, 5.

53. J. Lew, L. Mistelis and S. Kröll, *Comparative International Commercial Arbitration* (The Hague, Kluwer Law International, 2003), para. 16-28; *see also* J.L. Greenblatt and P. Griffin, 'Towards the Harmonization of International Arbitration Rules: Comparative Analysis of the Rules of the ICC, AAA, LCIA and CIETAC' (2001) 17(1) Arb Int'l, 101, 103; Y. Derains and E.A. Schwartz, *A Guide to the ICC Rules of Arbitration* (2nd edn, The Hague, Kluwer Law International, 2005), p. 115 *et seq.*

54. *See* High Court of the Hong Kong Special Administrative Region, 27 March 2003, *Karaha Bodas Company LLC v. Perusahaan Minyak Pertambanga Dan Gas Bumi Negara*, (2003) 21(3) Bull ASA, 667-684; *see also* BGer, 4 August 2006, BGE 4P.105/2006, (2007) 25(1) Bull ASA, 105-122; *see* J. Lew, L. Mistelis and S. Kröll, *Comparative International Commercial Arbitration* (The Hague, Kluwer Law International, 2003), para. 16-27.

55. *See*, e.g., Article 8 LCIA Rules; Article 18 WIPO Rules; Article 10 ICC Rules; Article 13 DIS Rules; Article 8 Swiss Rules; Article 9 SIAC Rules; Article 24 CIETAC Rules; Article 12 CEPANI Rules; Article 23 Polish Rules.

56. J. Lew, L. Mistelis and S. Kröll, *Comparative International Commercial Arbitration* (The Hague, Kluwer Law International, 2003), para. 16-22.

although, as the *Dutco* case illustrates, the claimants' interests will naturally be aligned (or else they would not have chosen to jointly bring a claim) whereas the respondents' interest might not be. It also does not violate the *Dutco* rationale, as each claimant can make an informed decision to join the proceedings with other claimants *after* a particular dispute has arisen; it therefore does not waive its right to an individual appointment in advance.

Thus, the decisive question is how to address the respondents' failure to make a joint appointment. Here, the two models differ. Under the first, and predominant, approach, the institution will proceed to appoint an arbitrator for the respondents *and* the claimants (even where the claimants have made a joint nomination), or indeed proceed to immediately appoint all three arbitrators. That way, both sides are treated equally, because both sides are faced with an institutional appointment,[57] in what is a prompt and unequivocal solution that uniformly applies to all cases.[58] Of course, this solution imposes most directly on the claimants who were able to make a joint appointment, but who loose that right if the respondents cannot make a joint appointment as well. Some have also raised concerns that this solution is unfair because by deliberately not agreeing on an arbitrator, the respondents could effectively cancel the appointment of the claimants' arbitrator.[59]   **15-043**

This model has been adopted by the ICC, with its 1998 revision of the rules, as a direct reaction to *Dutco*. Under Article 10 of the ICC Rules, the ICC has the right to nominate the entire panel of three arbitrators if one side with multiple parties fails to put forward a joint nomination. Equality thus translates into both claimant(s) and respondents loosing their right to nominate an arbitrator; the entire panel will be appointed by the ICC Court.[60] This standard has also been adopted by the LCIA, CEPANI, SIAC, as well as other arbitration centers; and in somewhat modified form by the DIS Rules[61] and the WIPO Rules. Some national laws follows a similar approach. The English Arbitration Act from 1996, for example, vests the English courts with the power to revoke an appointment of an arbitrator that has already been made in order to guarantee equal treatment of the parties.[62]   **15-044**

---

57. *See* P. Oberhammer in *Das neue Schiedsrecht – Schiedsrechts-Änderungsgesetz 2006*, B. Kloiber, P. Oberhammer, W.H. Rechberger and H. Haller (eds) (Vienna, Manz, 2006), p. 132.

58. K.-P. Berger, 'Schiedsrichterbestellung in Mehrparteienschiedsverfahren' [1993] RIW, 702.

59. P. Oberhammer in *Das neue Schiedsrecht – Schiedsrechts-Änderungsgesetz 2006* B. Kloiber, P. Oberhammer, W.H. Rechberger and H. Haller (eds) (Vienna, Manz, 2006), p. 132.

60. J.L. Greenblatt and P. Griffin, 'Towards the Harmonization of International Arbitration Rules: Comparative Analysis of the Rules of the ICC, AAA, LCIA and CIETAC' (2001) 17(1) Arb Int'l, 101, 103.

61. Under Article 13 DIS Rules, if multiple respondents fail to jointly appoint an arbitrator, the institution will set aside the claimant's appointment and nominate two arbitrators; but the institution will not appoint the presiding arbitrator.

62. The Departmental Advisory Committee on Arbitration Law, '1996 Report on the Arbitration Bill' reprinted in (1997) 13(3) Arb Int'l, 275, 290: 'It will be noted that we have given the Court the power to revoke any appointments already made. This is to cover the case where unless the Court took this step it might be suggested thereafter that the parties had not been fairly treated, since one had its own choice arbitrator while the other had an arbitrator imposed on him by the

15-045 The other model, which is less favored today, takes the more traditional approach of leaving the claimants' joint appointment in place, and making an institutional appointment only on behalf of the respondents. Here, the claimants' right to appoint an arbitrator of their choosing is left intact. On the other hand, it could be argued, as was the case in *Dutco*, that respondents (whose interests may not be aligned) are treated worse than claimants (whose interest are aligned). The second model has been adopted as the default rule in some national laws[63] including in Austria, and under the Vienna Rules.[64]

C.   AUSTRIAN LAW

15-046 Austrian law also recognizes the equality of the parties as an overriding principle of fairness with respect to the constitution of the tribunal. For this reason, the Austrian *Oberster Gerichtshof* has rendered invalid an appointment mechanism that gave one party the right to appoint the chairman.[65] Similar considerations would apply if, for example, the claimant had the right to appoint the sole arbitrator, or the entire tribunal. Such a mechanism is argued to violate the right to a fair trial under Article 6 ECHR, and would constitute a violation of Section 879 ABGB. Indeed, the equality of the parties in the constitution of the tribunal is sometimes considered part of the *procedural ordre public*,[66] and thus protected by the right to challenge an award rendered in violation of this principle.[67]

15-047 Section 587(5) ZPO now addresses the appointment of arbitrators in a multi-party context:

> If several parties who together must appoint one or more arbitrators cannot agree on the appointment(s) within four weeks of receipt of a written request to do so, then the arbitrator(s) shall be appointed by a court in response to a request by a party, unless the agreement on the appointment procedure provides other means for securing the appointment.

15-048 By adopting Section 587(5) ZPO, the Austrian legislator did not aim at regulating or resolving all aspects of multiparty arbitration, but merely addressed the central

---

Court in circumstances that were no fault of his own. This situation in fact arose in France in the *Dutco* case, where an award was invalidated for this reason.'

63. *See, e.g.,* Article 360 Draft 2006 of Swiss ZPO.
64. *See also* Article 8(5) Swiss Rules which provides: 'Where a party or group of parties fail(s) to designate an arbitrator in multiparty proceedings, the Chambers *may* appoint all three arbitrators.'
65. OGH 17 March 2005, 2 Ob 41/04z.
66. *See* G. Zeiler, *Schiedsverfahren* (Vienna/Graz, Neuer Wissenschaftlicher Verlag, 2006), Section 587, p. 130 with further reference; F.T. Schwarz and H. Ortner, 'Procedural Ordre Public and the Internationalization of Public Policy' in *Austrian Arbitration Yearbook 2008*, C. Klausegger *et al.* (eds) (Vienna, Manz, 2008).
67. M. Platte in *Arbitration Law of Austria: Practice and Procedure*, S. Riegler, A. Petsche, A. Fremuth-Wolf, M. Platte and C. Liebscher (eds) (Huntington, Juris Publishing, 2007), Section 587, p. 233.

question of appointment of arbitrators that ensure the constitution of the tribunal.[68] This fall-back provision applies only absent a specific agreement by the parties on the appointment of arbitrators in a multi-party scenario:[69] and as such, does not prevent parties from agreeing (within the confines of equality principles) a different procedure on the appointment of tribunals for multi-party cases, including by reference to institutional rules.

Section 587(5) ZPO becomes applicable where several parties that 'together must **15-049** appoint one or more arbitrators' cannot reach agreement on the appointment. The law does not specify the cases in which parties 'together must appoint one or more arbitrators,' but it is assumed in the literature that this applies to both claimants and respondents, following the classic model of one arbitrator for each 'side'.[70] Where no joint nomination is made, any party, whether from the claimants' or the respondents' side, can apply to the courts.[71]

Although parties joined on the side of either claimants or respondents are well **15-050** advised to do so, they may not always be in communication with each other. If one of those parties nominates an arbitrator, the other parties will have to object in order for the appointment to be considered ineffective.[72] Otherwise, their silence could be considered as implicit acceptance to the arbitrator's appointment.[73]

Where one 'side' – either all the claimants or all the respondents together – fails to **15-051** appoint an arbitrator, the appointment will be made by the court. Austrian law has therefore rejected the solution that the entire panel is appointed by the court (or an institution, where so agreed) if several parties fail to make a joint appointment. The same approach is adopted in Article 15(6), as discussed below.[74]

The ZPO does not regulate any other aspects of multi-party arbitration It was a **15-052** conscious decision of the legislator not to deal with such other issues, including third party intervention (*Nebenintervention*) in the law.[75]

---

68. P. Oberhammer in *Das neue Schiedsrecht – Schiedsrechts-Änderungsgesetz 2006*, B. Kloiber, P. Oberhammer, W.H. Rechberger and H. Haller (eds) (Vienna, Manz, 2006), pp. 131 *et seq.*
69. A. Reiner, *Das neue österreichische Schiedsrecht/The new Austrian Arbitration Law* (Vienna, LexisNexis, 2006), Section 587, note 73.
70. Specifically, it is argued that when Section 587(2) requires each party to appoint an arbitrator, it is really referring to each 'side' of the dispute. *See* G. Zeiler, *Schiedsverfahren* (Vienna/Graz, Neuer Wissenschaftlicher Verlag, 2006), Section 587, p. 137.
71. A. Reiner, *Das neue österreichische Schiedsrecht/The new Austrian Arbitration Law* (Vienna, LexisNexis, 2006), Section 587, note 73, correctly pointing to an error in the Explanatory Notes.
72. M. Platte in *Arbitration Law of Austria: Practice and Procedure*, S. Riegler, A. Petsche, A. Fremuth-Wolf, M. Platte and C. Liebscher (eds) (Huntington, Juris Publishing, 2007), Section 587, p. 239.
73. *See* OGH 25 November 1936, 2 Ob 906/36, Rsp 1937/17.
74. *See* at **Article 15**, at para. 054.
75. P. Oberhammer in *Das neue Schiedsrecht – Schiedsrechts-Änderungsgesetz 2006*, B. Kloiber, P. Oberhammer, W.H. Rechberger and H. Haller (eds) (Vienna, Manz, 2006), p. 132. For the old law, *see* OGH, 10 December 1998, 7 Ob 221/98w.

D.   THE VIENNA RULES

15-053 Article 15(6) provides for an additional extension of times afforded to the respondents if they have agreed on the number of arbitrators but failed to jointly nominate an arbitrator. This rule causes unnecessary delay to the constitution of the tribunal. In extreme cases, it will take over three months for the Board to make an institutional appointment in a multi-party scenario. It would be equally possible to require the respondents to agree on the number of arbitrators, and make a joint nomination, together with their statement of defense (and hence thirty days after receipt of the statement of claim), failing which the Board could immediately proceed to make an appointment on the respondents' behalf. In all likelihood, the VIAC felt that additional time provided to multiple respondents may shield the institutional appointment process from claims of unfairness.

15-054 Article 15(7) provides that, where the respondents fail to make a joint nomination, the Board will appoint an arbitrator for them.[76] As discussed, this provision goes against the trend of other modern rules; it is, however, consistent with Section 587(5) ZPO.

V.   CONSOLIDATION AND JOINDER

Article 15(8): In cases other than those mentioned in paragraph 1 of the present Article, the consolidation of two or more disputes shall be admissible only if the same arbitrators have been appointed in all the disputes that are to be consolidated and if all parties and the sole arbitrator (arbitral tribunal) agree.

A.   INTRODUCTION

15-055 As discussed at the outset, the classic scenario of one claimant against one respondent will not always reflect commercial reality. In addition to the scenarios discussed above, disputes may not only arise between multiple parties, but also on the basis of multiple contracts. The most frequent examples of multi-contractual relationships are found in engineering, construction, raw materials, mining and the oil and gas sectors,[77] as well as in joint ventures and complex corporate transactions.[78] Often, there is a strong incentive on both sides to arbitrate between all the parties, under a variety of different (but related) contracts, in a single arbitration,

---

76. For institutional appointments in general *see also* **Article 14**, at paras. 037 *et seq.*, 056 *et seq.* and 064 *et seq.*
77. P. Leboulanger, 'Multi-Contract Arbitration' (1996) 13(4) J Int'l Arb, 43.
78. H. Hamann and T. Lenarz, 'Parallele Verfahren mit identischem Schiedsgericht als Lösung für Mehrparteikonflikte?' [2006] SchiedsVZ 289, 291.

for example to avoid the risk of contradicting decisions in case of separate proceedings,[79] or to avoid duplication of cases and costs.[80]

Different instruments are conceivable to bring several disputes and parties together **15-056** in one forum. Consolidation denotes the act or process of uniting several arbitrations which are pending or initiated into a single set of proceedings before the same panel of arbitrators.[81] Its purpose is to prevent related issues from being determined separately, and with the potential of contradicting awards.[82] Consolidation is conceivable both to concentrate several proceedings that are pending between two parties; or to bring together disputes that involve a number of different parties.[83]

The instrument of joinder serves to add one or more parties to an existing pro- **15-057** ceeding. The figure of necessary joinder – whereby usually substantive legal rules determine that a party is 'necessary' to resolve a particular dispute – has been discussed above.[84] Beyond those considerations, there may be other reasons, perhaps of a pragmatic or strategic nature, to add other parties to the arbitration whose presence is desirable because it will facilitate the complete resolution of the dispute, secure justice between the parties by avoiding conflicting decisions for related issues, and serve procedural efficiency as well as time and costs by co-ordinating the taking of evidence.[85] Parties should be aware, however, that in some circumstances, the expected benefits can turn in to disadvantages.[86]

The discussion below examines contractual mechanisms to ensure the consolidated **15-058** resolution of disputes under related contracts through pre-agreed arbitration clauses; the solution for consolidation under the Vienna Rules; the concept of joinder; and the extension of arbitration clauses to non-signatory parties.

---

79. P. Level, 'Joinder of Proceedings, Intervention of Third Parties and Additional Claims and Counterclaims' (1996) 7(2) ICC Ct Bull, 27, 36 *et seq.*; ICC Commission on International Arbitration (Chairman: J.-L. Delvolvé); 'Final Report on Multi-Party Arbitration' (1995) 6(1) ICC Ct Bull, 26, 35.
80. J. Tackaberry and A. Marriott, *Bernstein's Handbook of Arbitration and Dispute Resolution Practice, I* (4th edn, London, Sweet & Maxwell, 2003), para. 2-645.
81. M. Platte, 'When Should an Arbitrator Join Cases?' (2002) 18(1) Arb Int'l, 67, 68.
82. J.C. Chiu, 'Consolidation of Arbitral Proceeding and International Arbitration' (1990) 7(2) J Int'l Arb, 53, 56; P. Leboulanger, 'Multi-Contract Arbitration' (1996) 13(4) J Int'l Arb, 43.
83. M. Platte, 'When Should an Arbitrator Join Cases?' (2002) 18(1) Arb Int'l, 67, 68.
84. *See* **Article 1**, at paras. 128 *et seq.*, and **Article 15**, at paras. 013 *et seq.*
85. J.C. Chiu, 'Consolidation of Arbitral Proceeding and International Arbitration' (1990) 7(2) J Int'l Arb, 53, 55-56; A. Redfern, M. Hunter, N. Blackaby and C. Partasides, *Law and Practice of International Commercial Arbitration* (4th edn, London, Sweet & Maxwell, 2004) paras. 3-73 *et seq.*
86. R.C. Mohan and L.W. Teck, 'Some Contractual Approaches to the Problem of Inconsistent Awards in Multi-party, Multi-contract Arbitration Proceedings' (2005) 1(2) AIAJ, 161, 165. For example, the costs of a longer multi-party proceeding can be in some situations exceed the cost of an unconsolidated arbitration; or the parties may not be able to achieve consent on the person of the joint arbitrator and may be faced with an unwelcome institutional appointment.

B.   PRE-AGREED CONSOLIDATION

15-059 Many commercial relationships are contained in several contractual instruments, often between multiple parties. While such contracts exist each for itself, they all are integrated parts of a single commercial transaction.[87] In such circumstances, it may well be preferable to consolidate disputes that arise under several of these related contracts in one forum.[88]

15-060 A specific provision for consolidation in an arbitration agreement that covers not one, but all of the related contracts between the parties, might be the most effective way to ensure the proper consolidation of future disputes. It is based on the advance consent of all of the parties to concentrate disputes arising under any of their agreements before one tribunal.[89] Compared to any procedural consolidation that is attempted after the dispute has arisen, a solution agreed in advance allows the parties to create a regime adapted to the special circumstances of their contractual relationship.

15-061 It may not be easy, however, to draft appropriate consolidation clauses in arbitration agreements,[90] and several decisions tell of the non-trivial difficulties that drafters will face.[91] This does not mean that consolidation clauses are impossible to draft, or not worth the effort. Parties should consider provisions on the scope of consolidated proceedings; the circle of parties to be included; the nomination/appointment process for the tribunal; and the joinder of certain parties to, the proceedings.[92]

15-062 For example, a pre-agreed consolidation clause could read:[93]

> If more than one arbitration is begun under this Agreement, the [second Agreement], and/or the [third Agreement] and any Party contends that two or more arbitrations are substantially related and that the issues should be heard in one proceeding, the Arbitral Tribunal appointed in the first-filed of such proceedings shall have the power to determine whether, in the interests of

---

87. P. Leboulanger, 'Multi-Contract Arbitration' (1996) 13(4) J Int'l Arb, 43.
88. J. Lew, L. Mistelis and S. Kröll, *Comparative International Commercial Arbitration* (The Hague, Kluwer Law International, 2003), para. 16-38.
89. P. Leboulanger, 'Multi-Contract Arbitration' (1996) 13(4) J Int'l Arb, 43, 70 *et seq.*
90. J.C. Chiu, 'Consolidation of Arbitral Proceeding and International Arbitration' (1990) 7(2) J Int'l Arb 53, 71; A. Redfern, M. Hunter, N. Blackaby and C. Partasides, *Law and Practice of International Commercial Arbitration* (4th edn, London, Sweet & Maxwell, 2004), para. 3-84.
91. *See, e.g., Lafarge Redlands Aggregates Ltd. v. Shephard Hill Civil Engineering Ltd.* [2000] 1 WLR 1621 (House of Lords); *The Bay Hotel and Resort Ltd. v. Cavalier Construction Co. Ltd.* [2001] UKPC 34 (Privy Council).
92. H. Hamann and T. Lenarz, 'Parallele Verfahren mit identischem Schiedsgericht als Lösung für Mehrparteikonflikte?' [2006] SchiedsVZ, 289, 295 *et seq.*
93. Naturally, any template for an arbitration clause such as this should not be applied indiscriminately. Users should make sure that such a clause is adopted to comply with the circumstances of the case and applicable law.

justice and efficiency, the proceedings should be consolidated before that Arbitral Tribunal.

Another example, consolidating arbitrations between different parties, but under the same agreement, reads as follows: **15-063**

> Each Party agrees that it may be joined as an additional party to an arbitration involving other Parties under this Agreement. If more than one arbitration is begun under this Agreement and any Party contends that two or more arbitrations are substantially related and that the issues should be heard in one proceeding, the Arbitral Tribunal appointed in the first-filed of such proceedings shall have the power to determine whether, in the interests of justice and efficiency, the proceedings should be consolidated before that Arbitral Tribunal.

Even where no express agreement has been concluded, it is conceivable that an implied agreement may exist. Such an implied agreement has been assumed if all contracts concluded between the different parties in connection with a single economic venture contain identically worded arbitration clauses, or when the 'heads of agreement' of a specific project contained an arbitration clause to which the subsequently executed contracts referred.[94] On the other hand, if multiple contracts contain arbitration clauses that differ in such matters as the chosen seat or the applicable law, usually no consolidation agreement can be implied.[95] **15-064**

An agreement to consolidate allows the parties to initiate the arbitration from the outset as a concentrated procedure addressing several claims under several contracts. Pre-agreed arbitration under such contractual regimes resolves some of the issues arising from Article 15(8) which applies to the consolidation of separate proceedings after they have been initiated. **15-065**

C.   Consolidation Under the Vienna Rules

Article 15(8) provides, for 'cases other than those mentioned in paragraph 1', that 'the consolidation of two or more disputes shall be admissible only if the same arbitrators have been appointed in all the disputes that are to be consolidated and if all parties and the sole arbitrator (arbitral tribunal) agree.' **15-066**

Article 15(8) therefore applies to the scenario that several arbitrations have been initiated and are now pending in parallel. It does not suggest substantive standards for consolidation (such as recommending consolidation for reasons of **15-067**

---

94. J. Lew, L. Mistelis and S. Kröll, *Comparative International Commercial Arbitration* (The Hague, Kluwer Law International, 2003), para. 16-56.
95. J. Lew, L. Mistelis and S. Kröll, *Comparative International Commercial Arbitration* (The Hague, Kluwer Law International, 2003), para. 16-59; *see also* Cour d'Appel de Versailles, 7 March 1990, *OIAETI et Sofidif v. Cogema et al.*, [1991] Rev Arb, 326.

procedural efficiency and the like), but is merely concerned with the consent of all those involved. Thus, consolidation requires the consent of all the parties (of all the proceedings that are to be consolidated),[96] so the arbitrators do not have the power to consolidate proceedings without the parties' agreement. Likewise, it is not sufficient for the parties to agree on consolidation; the arbitrators (who must be the same arbitrators for all proceedings to be consolidated) must agree as well.

15-068 In practice, consolidation under the Vienna Rules will rarely occur under these restrictive standards. It almost defeats the purpose of consolidation to require an identity of arbitrators; the agreement of the parties should, at most, be the decisive standard, even if that results in one tribunal becoming defunct.

15-069 Indeed, some modern legislations and rules do not even require the parties' consent for consolidation. For example, Article 1046 of the Netherlands Arbitration Law, and the Arbitration Ordinance in Hong Kong, instead vest the local courts with the power to consolidate two or more arbitrations.[97] Article 14 CEPANI Rules A[98] and Article 12 CEPANI Rules B[99] vest the institution (but not the tribunal) with the power to consolidate several arbitration proceedings in case of closely related contracts containing a CEPANI arbitration clause.[100] They also contain the possibility to extend the size of the tribunal to a maximum of five arbitrators as a result of the consolidation. As another example, the recently-adopted Swiss Rules provide in Article 4(1):

> Where a Notice of Arbitration is submitted between parties already involved in other arbitral proceedings pending under these Rules, the Chambers may decide, after consulting with the parties to all proceedings and the Special Committee, that the new case shall be referred to the arbitral tribunal already

---

96. H. Hamann and T. Lenarz, 'Parallele Verfahren mit identischem Schiedsgericht als Lösung für Mehrparteikonflikte?' [2006] SchiedsVZ, 289, 295; J. Lew, L. Mistelis and S. Kröll, *Comparative International Commercial Arbitration* (The Hague, Kluwer Law International, 2003), para. 16-50.
97. A. Redfern, M. Hunter, N. Blackaby and C. Partasides, *Law and Practice of International Commercial Arbitration* (4th edn, London, Sweet & Maxwell, 2004), para. 3-82.
98. For disputes not exceeding €12,500.
99. For disputes exceeding €12,500. The Belgian Centre for Mediation and Arbitration multiparty proceedings provisions set: 'When several contracts containing a CEPANI arbitration clause give rise to disputes that are closely related or indivisible, the Appointments Committee or the Chairman is empowered to order the joinder of the arbitration proceedings. This decision shall be taken either at the request of the Arbitral Tribunal, or, prior to any other issue, at the request of the parties or of the most diligent party, or upon CEPANI's own motion. (. . .) They may not order the joinder of disputes in which an interim award or an award on admissibility or on the merits of the claim has already been rendered.'
100. B. Hanotiau, 'Complex – Multicontract-Multiparty – Arbitrations' (1998) 14(4) Arb Int'l, 369, 380.

constituted for the existing proceedings. The Chambers may proceed likewise where a Notice of Arbitration is submitted between parties that are not identical to the parties in the existing arbitral proceedings. When rendering their decision, the Chambers shall take into account all circumstances, including the links between the two cases and the progress already made in the existing proceedings. Where the Chambers decide to refer the new case to the existing arbitral tribunal, the parties to the new case shall be deemed to have waived their right to designate an arbitrator.

Thus, the Swiss Chambers are empowered to decide on the consolidation of **15-070** different proceedings,[101] after consultation with all parties involved and the arbitral tribunal. Consolidation can be ordered against the will of one of the parties. Also, the provision allows for consolidation of a proceedings between non-identical parties, even though the party in the new proceedings may have to abstain from appointing its own arbitrator.[102]

These perhaps more innovative rules better reflect the realities of modern **15-071** commercial life. Disputes will often benefit from consolidation even if the arbitrators in those disputes are not identical. Equally, to not allow consolidation only because one party objects facilitates obstruction and fails to do justice to the overriding considerations of fairness and efficiency often associated with consolidation.

At least, Article 15(8) does not require that the parties to the parallel arbitrations **15-072** must be identical for consolidation to be possible.[103] Also, Article 15(8) – which appears to distance itself from Article 15(1) as a textual matter – does not require that the proceedings must all be governed by arbitration clauses that confer jurisdiction to the VIAC. Because Article 15(8) requires that all parties and all arbitrators must agree to the consolidation, such agreements amongst all involved could be treated as a submission under the Vienna Rules, even where one of the proceedings was originally conducted as an *ad hoc* arbitration or perhaps under different institutional rules.

In practice, where formal consolidation is not possible, the parties may still request **15-073** (and the tribunal may still order where appropriate) a *de facto* consolidation of the

---

101. P. Karrer in *Institutionelle Schiedsgerichtsbarkeit*, R.A. Schütze (ed.) (Cologne, Carl Heymanns Verlag, 2006), p. 321.

102. H. Hamann and T. Lenarz, 'Parallele Verfahren mit identischem Schiedsgericht als Lösung für Mehrparteikonflikte?' [2006] SchiedsVZ, 289, 295. This will exclude the *Dutco*-principle;' when the very close relation between the parties will make the entering party to accept the done nomination.

103. *See*, for contrast, Article 4(6) ICC Rules which reads: 'When a party submits a Request in connection with a legal relationship in respect of which arbitration proceedings between the same parties are already pending under these Rules, the Court may, at the request of a party, decide to include the claims contained in the Request in the pending proceedings provided that the Terms of Reference have not been signed or approved by the Court.'

proceedings, resulting at least in the co-ordination between the different arbitral tribunals that deal with the related disputes.[104] For such cases, some commentators have raised the issue of possible bias in parallel arbitrations with identical or different parties, but at least partially overlapping factual or legal issues, where one party appoints the same arbitrator in all proceedings, but other arbitrators are different. Will the one arbitrator sitting in all arbitrations be biased, because he has formed an opinion in one arbitration that may (unduly?) influence him, or through him his co-arbitrators, in the other proceedings? It has been argued convincingly that such a multiple appointment absent other, aggravating circumstances does not result in bias, as long as all parties have an opportunity to be heard on the information that forms the basis for the award.[105] Naturally, the arbitrator cannot consider information from other arbitrations if such information has not also been put before the tribunal in the case before him; it is for the parties to make sure all relevant information and evidence is produced in all arbitrations.

D.   Joinder

15-074 The instrument of joinder is not concerned with bringing together several disputes, but seeks to add, sometimes even during the arbitration, another party to the proceedings.[106] This raises issues of consent; as a principle, no party can be forced to arbitrate without its agreement.

1.   **Agreement to Join a Party or an Intervener**

15-075 As a consequence of the consensual nature of arbitration, at least under the traditional view, a joinder requires a corresponding consent of the parties. This consent can be given expressly, implied in certain contracts or provisions or by reference to arbitration rules, which provide for joinder.[107] This consent can be given either at the time the request for joinder is made or at an earlier stage in the contract itself.[108] Depending once more on the circumstances of the case and the applicable law, a pre-agreed joinder provision could read:[109]

---

104. *See also* P. Leboulanger, 'Multi-Contract Arbitration' (1996) 13(4) J Int'l Arb, 43, 70 *et seq.*; M. Platte, 'When Should an Arbitrator Join Cases?' (2002) 18(1) Arb Int'l, 67, 80.

105. *See* W.H. Rechberger and M. Rami, 'Ablehnung von Schiedsrichtern durch die Parteien' [1999] wbl, 103, 106 and note 45 with further reference. This approach has also been confirmed in recent decisions of the Austrian courts.

106. M. Platte, 'When Should an Arbitrator Join Cases?' (2002) 18(1) Arb Int'l, 67, 68.

107. M. Platte, 'When Should an Arbitrator Join Cases?' (2002) 18(1) Arb Int'l, 67, 69.

108. J. Lew, L. Mistelis and S. Kröll, *Comparative International Commercial Arbitration* (The Hague, Kluwer Law International, 2003), paras. 16-40, 16-42.

109. Templates for arbitration agreements should be applied with caution and only after considering whether or ot they are appropriate in the individual case and under the applicable law.

Each Party agrees that it may be joined as an additional party to an arbitration involving other Parties under this Agreement, [or Agreement X and Agreement Y].

Under Austrian law, the issue is discussed in the context of the intervention of a third **15-076** party that has an interest in the arbitration. It is argued that such a third party intervener must be a party to the arbitration agreement or otherwise submit to the jurisdiction of the tribunal;[110] that all parties, including the intervener, must agree to the intervention;[111] that, if the tribunal has already been constituted, the intervener must waive its right to participate in the tribunal's constitution;[112] but that the intervener, once joined to the proceedings, is essentially treated like a party and enjoys all basic procedural rights, such as the right to be heard.[113] If the intervener has participated in the proceedings and is affected by the award, the intervener has therefore also the right, in principle, to challenge the award in the Austrian courts.[114] If the intervener is refused access to the arbitration, the award will not have any effects against it, so that a right to challenge the award is in principle not necessary.[115] For a discussion of mandatory joinder, *see* **Article 15(1)**, at paras. 013 *et seq.*[116]

Although Article 15(8) addresses consolidation of proceedings, and not the joinder **15-077** of additional parties, there is a systemic argument under the Vienna Rules that the joinder of additional parties requires consent. If the standard of Article 15(8) is applied to the joinder of a third party during already pending proceedings, all parties – that is, the existing claimant and respondent along with the party to be joined – must consent. Under that standard, the arbitrators must consent as well,

---

110. M. Platte in *Arbitration Law of Austria: Practice and Procedure*, S. Riegler, A. Petsche, A. Fremuth-Wolf, M. Platte and C. Liebscher (eds) (Huntington, Juris Publishing, 2007), Section 587, p. 242 with reference to OGH, 10 December 1998, 7 Ob 221/98w (holding that an arbitration clause in the statute of a company applies to all shareholders who therefore can be joined together in one arbitration).

111. M. Platte in *Arbitration Law of Austria: Practice and Procedure*, S. Riegler, A. Petsche, A. Fremuth-Wolf, M. Platte and C. Liebscher (eds) (Huntington, Juris Publishing, 2007), Section 587, p. 242. For a more differentiated view, *see* H.W Fasching, *Schiedsgericht und Schiedsverfahren im österreichischem und im internationalen Recht* (Vienna, Manz, 1973), p. 100, who argues that if both parties oppose the joinder, it is included; if only one party opposes the joinder, the tribunal may order it.

112. M. Platte in *Arbitration Law of Austria: Practice and Procedure*, S. Riegler, A. Petsche, A. Fremuth-Wolf, M. Platte and C. Liebscher (eds) (Huntington, Juris Publishing, 2007), Section 587, p. 243; *see also* G. Zeiler, *Schiedsverfahren* (Vienna/Graz, Neuer Wissenschaftlicher Verlag, 2006), Section 607, p. 248 and Section 594, p. 201.

113. G. Zeiler, *Schiedsverfahren* (Vienna/Graz, Neuer Wissenschaftlicher Verlag, 2006), Section 594, p. 201.

114. M. Platte in *Arbitration Law of Austria: Practice and Procedure*, S. Riegler, A. Petsche, A. Fremuth-Wolf and C. Liebscher (eds) (Huntington, Juris Publishing, 2006), Section 587, pp. 243 *et seq.*; G. Zeiler, *Schiedsverfahren* (Vienna/Graz, Neuer Wissenschaftlicher Verlag, 2006), Section 611, p. 274.

115. G. Zeiler, *Schiedsverfahren* (Vienna/Graz, Neuer Wissenschaftlicher Verlag, 2006), Section 611, p. 248; *see also* Section 607 ZPO and **Article 15**, at para. 018.

116. *See* **Article 15**, at paras. 013 *et seq.*

although that is an unnecessary restriction that is disputed for arbitration in Austria outside the context of the Vienna Rules.[117] Indeed, as discussed, Article 15(8) contains a restrictive standard that would make the joinder of third party to pending proceedings highly unlikely under the Vienna Rules. Again, such a standard may be too restrictive to satisfy the commercial needs of businesses to bring multiple parties together in one forum, even where one party disagrees.

15-078 Modern arbitration rules therefore take a different approach, Article 22(1)(h) of the LCIA Rules provides, for example:

> the Arbitral Tribunal shall have the power, on the application of any party or of its own motion, but in either case only after giving the parties a reasonable opportunity to state their views: to allow, only upon the application of a party, one or more third persons to be joined in the arbitration as a party provided any such third person and the applicant party have consented thereto in writing, and thereafter to make a single final award, or separate awards, in respect of all parties so implicated in the arbitration.

15-079 Article 22(1)(h) LCIA Rules thus requires the consent of the third party to be joined as well as of the party applying for a joinder – but not of the other party to the arbitration (which has already consented to the tribunal's power under Article 22(1)(h) by agreeing to the LCIA Rules).

15-080 Another very modern approach to joinder is contained in Article 4(2) Swiss Rules which reads:

> Where a third party requests to participate in arbitral proceedings already pending under these Rules or where a party to arbitral proceedings under these Rules intends to cause a third party to participate in the arbitration, the arbitral tribunal shall decide on such request, after consulting with all parties, taking into account all circumstances it deems relevant and applicable.

15-081 Here, the tribunal is given broad discretion to join a third party, after consultation with all parties, but even without their consent.[118] Provisions such as these are preferable to the static model of requiring express consent of all parties to joinder or consolidation after the dispute has arisen.

2.   Joining Non-Signatories

15-082 The instrument of 'joinder' is also used to refer to the addition of parties that have not signed the arbitration agreement, so-called 'non-signatories'.[119] To be clear, forcing a party that has never consented to arbitration to join the proceedings will

---

117. OGH, 10 December 1998, 7 Ob 221/98w.

118. H. Hamann and T. Lenarz, 'Parallele Verfahren mit identischem Schiedsgericht als Lösung für Mehrparteikonflikte?' [2006] SchiedsVZ, 289, 293.

119. For an overview of the debate in Austria, *see* A. Fremuth-Wolf in *Arbitration Law of Austria: Practice and Procedure*, S. Riegler, A. Petsche, A. Fremuth-Wolf, M. Platte and C. Liebscher (eds) (Huntington, Juris Publishing, 2007), p. 672 *et seq.*

raise jurisdictional issues, and risk a challenge to the award. As the Commission on International Arbitration considered in its Final Report on Multi-party Arbitrations:

> The difficulties of multi-party arbitrations all result from a single cause. Arbitration has a contractual basis; only the common will of the contracting parties can entitle a person to bring a proceeding before an arbitral tribunal against another person and oblige the other person to appear before it. The greater the number of such persons, the greater the degree of care which should be taken to ensure that none of them is joined in the proceeding against its will.[120]

However, there are several theories, some of them well-established under Austrian **15-083** law, to extend arbitration clauses to parties that have not signed the original arbitration agreement, on the basis of implied consent. Indeed, in light of the growing complexity of disputes referred to arbitration, the question if and to what extent third parties, in particular non-signatories, are bound by an arbitration agreement, is an important issue of modern arbitration law.[121] This includes questions of whether or not an arbitration agreement concluded by a company can be considered binding on one of its affiliates, usually the group's ultimate controlling shareholder.[122] The party seeking to 'pierce the corporate veil' attempts to emphasize the legitimacy of addressing the 'true' party in interest, often the financially better-situated member of a group of companies. This typically meets the objection that corporate identity is created precisely for the purpose of confining personal liability within a corporate entity.[123] In practice, much depends on the drafting of the arbitration agreement, and the circumstances at the conclusion and performance of the underlying contract.[124] However, the number of cases in which the arbitration agreement has been extended to third parties is remarkably large.[125]

---

120. ICC Commission on International Arbitration (Chairman: J.-L. Delvolvé), 'Final Report on Multi-party Arbitrations' (1994) 6(1) ICC Ct Bull, 26.
121. For a discussion on various such theories, *see, e.g.*, J. Lew, L. Mistelis and S. Kröll, *Comparative International Commercial Arbitration* (The Hague, Kluwer Law International, 2003), paras. 7-34 *et seq.*; E. Gaillard and J. Savage (eds), *Fouchard Gaillard Goldman On International Commercial Arbitration* (The Hague, Kluwer Law International, 1999), para. 500; W.L. Craig, W.W. Park and J. Paulsson, *International Chamber of Commerce Arbitration* (3rd edn, New York, Oceana Publication, 2000), pp. 74 *et seq.* and pp. 171 *et seq.*; O. Sandrock, "Intra' and 'Extra-Entity' Agreements to Arbitrate and their Extension to Non-Signatories Under German Law' (2002) 19(5) J Int'l Arb, 423.
122. For details, *see* B. Hanotiau, 'Complex – Multicontract-Multiparty – Arbitrations' (1998) 14(4) Arb Int'l, 49-99.
123. A. Redfern, M. Hunter, N. Blackaby and C. Partasides, *Law and Practice of International Commercial Arbitration* (4th edn, London, Sweet & Maxwell, 2004), para. 3-31.
124. E. Gaillard and J. Savage (eds), *Fouchard Gaillard Goldman On International Commercial Arbitration* (The Hague, Kluwer Law International, 1999), paras. 501 *et seq.*
125. *See* D. Busse, 'Die Bindung Dritter an Schiedsvereinbarungen' [2005] SchiedsVZ, 118, 121. The leading case on the 'group of companies doctrine' is *Dow Chemical v. Isover St. Gobain*. *See Interim Award in ICC Case No. 4131 of 1982, Dow Chemical France et al. v. Isover Saint Gobain (France)*, (1984) IX YB Comm Arb, 131 and (1993) JDI, 899 *et seq.*

2.1.   Succession

15-084 The most non-controversial form of joining a non-signatory relates to a legal successor – undoubtedly a non-signatory to the arbitration clause – who must be held to arbitrate when it assumes the legal position of one of the original signatories of the arbitration agreement. The rationale for this is obvious: the legal successor has to accept the legal position, and all attending rights and obligations, as they were originally created and as it finds them. Where those rights and obligations contain the obligation to arbitrate, the legal successor is therefore bound by an existing arbitration clause without ever having signed it.[126] As the Austrian *Oberster Gerichtshof* has held, 'the parties' arbitration clause also binds anyone who assumes the rights and obligations of the original party;'[127] 'the single successor of a contracting party also becomes a party to the arbitration agreement; there is no need for a separate acceptance by the single successor of the arbitration agreement in the sense of [then] Section 577(3) ZPO.'[128]

15-085 This rationale has been applied to all forms of legal succession, such as universal and specific successors-in-law as well as assignees that are uniformly considered to be bound by an arbitration agreement concluded by their legal predecessors without having signed it. Austrian jurisprudence[129] and scholarly writing[130] therefore accept that an assignee of a claim (*Zessionar* in the sense of Sections 1393 *et seq.* ABGB) is bound by an arbitration agreement contained in the contract between the debtor and the assignor. This is also true for statutory assigments (*Legalzessionar*)[131] and the redemption of a debt (*Einlösung einer Forderung*) according to Section 1422 ABGB.[132] The assignee of a debt (*privater Schuldübernehmer*) according to Sections 1405 *et seq.* ABGB is equally bound by an arbitration agreement contained in the contract between the creditor and the debtor.[133] The same applies in case of a judicial conferment of a debt (*richterliche Schuldübertragung*), such as the conferment of a right or obligation for collection according to Section 308 EO, where the

---

126. OGH, 13 June 1995, 4 Ob 533/95.
127. OGH, 18 March 2004, 2 Ob 53/04i.
128. OGH, 26 April 2001, 8 Ob 179/00g.
129. *See, e.g.*, OGH, 18 March 2004, 2 Ob 53/04i; OGH, 17 May 2001, 7 Ob 67/01f; OGH, 26 April 2001, 8 Ob 179/00g.
130. W.H. Rechberger and W. Melis in *Kommentar zur ZPO*, W.H. Rechberger (ed.) (3rd edn, New York/Vienna, Springer, 2006), Section 581, para. 12; G. Zeiler, *Schiedsverfahren* (Vienna/ Granz, Neuer Wissenschaftlicher Verlag, 2006), Section 581, p. 72; H.W. Fasching, *Schiedsgericht und Schiedsverfahren im österreichischen und im internationalen Recht* (Vienna, Manz, 1973), p. 27;
131. G. Zeiler, *Schiedsverfahren* (Vienna/Graz, Neuer Wissenschaftlicher Verlag, 2006); H.W. Fasching, *Schiedsgericht und Schiedsverfahren im österreichischen und im internationalen Recht* (Vienna, Manz, 2006), p. 27.
132. A. Fremuth-Wolf, *Die Schiedsvereinbarung im Zessionsfall* (Vienna, Verlag Österreich, 2004), p. 207.
133. P. Rummel, 'Schiedsvertrag und ABGB' [1986] RZ, 146, 151.

enforcing creditor (*Überweisungsgläubiger*) is bound by the arbitration agreement of 'his' debtor *vis-à-vis* the third party debtor.[134] Those legal successors assume all rights and duties, including the obligation to arbitrate, as it was originally concluded.[135]

2.2. Third-Party Beneficiary

More recent Austrian case law takes the rationale that binds a legal successor even **15-086** further. In case 4 Ob 533/95, 13 June 1995, the Austrian *Oberster Gerichtshof* held, for the first time, that an arbitration agreement has a binding effect on a non-signatory ***third party*** if that party exercises rights under the contract that contains the arbitration clause.[136] In this case, a claim was brought before an Austrian court by a third-party beneficiary against the buyer of the shares of an Austrian limited liability company. In the share purchase agreement, the buyer had agreed to indemnify the sellers and the third-party beneficiary (not a signatory of the share purchase agreement) with respect to any liabilities of the sold company arising out of a loan agreement. The share purchase agreement contained an arbitration agreement providing that all disputes arising out of or in connection with the agreement were subject to a resolution by an arbitral tribunal.

The Austrian *Oberster Gerichtshof* in principle confirmed the requirement of a **15-087** written arbitration agreement but held as follows in relevant part:

> The reasons for extending the arbitration agreement to a third party beneficiary are essentially the same as for the legal successor. Both take a legal position, which was created without their own active conduct; hence, such parties have to accept this position as it was contractually concluded. (...) Arbitration agreements and the granting of a right [to a third party] are not divisible; the third party cannot reject one [the arbitration agreement], but accept the other [the granted right].[137]

---

134. OGH, 18 March 2004, 2 Ob 53/04i; A. Fremuth-Wolf, *Schiedsvereinbarung im Zessionsfall* (Vienna, Verlag Österreich, 2004), p. 208.
135. OGH, 17 September 1925, 3 Ob 713/25, SZ 7/279; OGH, 16 January 1936, 1 Ob 25/36, SZ 18/12; OGH, 13 June 1995, 4 Ob 533/95, SZ 68/112 recently confirmed by OGH, 18 March 2004, 2 Ob 53/04i with reference to jurisprudence dating back to G.UNF 5796 (21 February 1912). *See also* H.W. Fasching, *Schiedsgericht und Schiedsverfahren im österreichischen und im internationalen Recht* (Vienna, Manz, 1973), p. 27; C. Liebscher and A. Schmid in *Practitioner's Handbook on International Arbitration*, F.B. Weigand (ed.) (Munich, C.H. Beck, 2002), p. 544 and G. Zeiler, *Schiedsverfahren* (Vienna/Graz, Neuer Wissenschaftlicher Verlag, 2006), Section 581, p. 71. A detailed analysis is given in A. Fremuth-Wolf, *Die Schiedsvereinbarung im Zessionsfall* (Vienna, Verlag Österreich, 2004) with further annotations.
136. OGH, 13 June 1995, 4 Ob 533/95.
137. OGH, 13 June 1995, 4 Ob 533/95.

15-088 Thus, the Austrian *Oberster Gerichtshof* – by express reference to the prevailing opinion in Germany[138] and in clear rejection of more traditional Austrian commentaries[139] – confirmed that third-party beneficiaries are bound by an arbitration agreement. This position has already been confirmed by subsequent decisions,[140] and has been extended to apply to lease agreements.[141] *Fremuth-Wolf* provides a good overview of the current status of the debate.[142]

15-089 The rationale applied in these cases is compelling. Where a party assumes the legal rights and obligations of another, by whatever substantive legal mechanism, it must accept those rights and obligations as it finds them. It would be inequitable in the extreme for a party to pick and choose certain advantages of the legal position that it enters, but to reject the obligations and disadvantages that attend that legal position.

15-090 On that basis, the Austrian *Oberster Gerichtshof* held that a third party, which chooses to benefit from rights contained in a contract with an arbitration clause, must accept 'the rights afforded to it jointly with all their contractual properties.'[143] As a result, the third party is bound by an arbitration clause contained in the contract: the third party 'assumes a legal position which was created without [its] contribution; [it] must accept that legal position as it exists, including the contractual dispute resolution mechanism.'[144]

15-091 This decision expressly rejected the traditional Austrian rule[145] that, because of the strict formal requirements of a written arbitration agreement, the arbitration clause can have no effect as against a non-signatory third party. As the Austrian *Oberster Gerichtshof* has recognized, the protective purposes that attend the requirement of written arbitration agreements are fully satisfied in the case of third party beneficiaries. To the extent a non-signatory party benefits from a contract, it is still fully

---

138. *See* K.H. Schwab and G. Walter (eds), *Schiedsgerichtsbarkeit* (7th edn, Munich, C. H. Beck, 2005), pp. 60-61, 65. In most jurisdictions, it is generally accepted that non-signatory third party beneficiaries from a contract including an arbitration agreement are bound to the arbitration agreement. *See* D. Busse, 'Die Bindung Dritter an Schiedsvereinbarungen' [2005] SchiedsVZ, 118, 123, also with reference to international case law.

139. See H.W. Fasching, *Schiedsgericht und Schiedsverfahren im österreichischen und im internationalen Recht* (Vienna, Manz, 1973), p. 28.

140. OGH, 05 August 1999, 1 Ob 79/99w.

141. OGH, 28 August 2003, 7 Ob 96/03y. Note that in cases where the parties to the arbitration agreement require certain prerequisites, it is debatable if the arbitration agreement is effectively applicable in case of assignment. *See* P. Rummel, 'Schiedsvertrag und ABGB' [1986] RZ, 146.

142. *See* A. Fremuth-Wolf in *Arbitration Law of Austria: Practice and Procedure*, S. Riegler, A. Petsche, A. Fremuth-Wolf, M. Platte and C. Liebscher (eds) (Huntington, Juris Publishing, 2007), p. 672 *et seq.*

143. OGH, 13 June 1995, 4 Ob 533/95.

144. OGH, 13 June 1995, 4 Ob 533/95.

145. D. Girsberger and C. Hausmaninger, 'Assignment of Rights and Agreement to Arbitrate' (1992) 8(2) Arb Int'l, 121; G. Backhausen, *Schiedsgerichtsbarkeit unter besonderer Berücksichtigung des Schiedsvertragsrechts* (Vienna, Manz, 1990), p. 62 *et seq.*; P. Rummel, 'Schiedsvertrag und ABGB' [1986] RZ, 146.

protected. Because the contract and the arbitration clause it contains exist in writing, the evidentiary function is also fully satisfied. By contrast, it is not necessary to protect the third party beneficiary from a hurried decision to agree to arbitration. The third party is entirely free as to whether or not it wishes to exercise rights under the contract.

A third party beneficiary has a choice, therefore. It can either reject the right that is **15-092** afforded to it by the original parties of the contract – or it can accept those rights. If it does accept them, it can accept them only together with all their contractual properties, including an attending arbitration clause. As the Austrian *Oberster Gerichtshof* held in conclusion,

> an arbitration clause and a contractual right are not divisible in the sense that the third party reject the one but accept the other. Rather, the arbitration clause determines how the right afforded can be claimed – so that the third party only has the option to exercise the rights under the contract with that property or to reject them altogether.[146]

With this line of jurisprudence, the Austrian *Oberster Gerichtshof* follows a substantial **15-093** body of international precedent.[147] Conceptually, the findings of the Austrian *Oberster Gerichtshof* are important because they underscore that the consent to arbitrate need not be express consent (much less consent expressed in writing). Although the third party beneficiary never expressly (let alone in written form) consents to arbitration, that consent is implied – it is deemed to have consented because it voluntarily decided to exercise rights under the contract in question. That voluntary choice is sufficient to bind the third party to the effects of the arbitration clause.

2.3. *Estoppel and Abuse of Law*

International precedent also compels non-signatories to arbitrate if their resistance **15-094** to arbitration would amount to an abuse of law, under theories of estoppel or (in civil law jurisdictions) of *venire contra factum proprium*.

For example, courts in the United States have held that '[e]quitable estoppel pre- **15-095** cludes a party from asserting rights he otherwise would have had against another when his own conduct renders assertion of those rights contrary to equity. In the arbitration context, the doctrine recognizes that a party may be estopped from asserting that the lack of his signature on a written contract precludes enforcement of the contract's arbitration clause when he has consistently maintained that other

---

146. OGH, 13 June 1995, 4 Ob 533/95.
147. P. Schlosser, *Das Recht der internationalen privaten Schiedsgerichtsbarkeit* (2nd edn, Tübingen, Mohr Siebeck, 1989), para. 425; W. Voit in *Kommentar zur Zivilprozessordnung*, H.-J. Musielak (6th edn, Munich, Verlag Franz Vahlen, 2008) Section 1031, para. 3; Cour de Cassation, 1re Ch. Civ., 11 July 2006, *Banque populaire Loire et Iyonnais v. Société Sangar* [2006] Rev Arb, 969; C. Legros, Garantie de passif: opposabilité de la clause d'arbitrage au bénéficiaire de la stipulation pour autrui' (2006) 46 JCP G, II 10183.

provisions of the same contract should be enforced to benefit him;'[148] or that a 'non-signatory is estopped from refusing to comply with an arbitration clause when it receives a direct benefit from a contract containing an arbitration clause.'[149]

15-096 These notions directly relate to the principle of good faith. In the words of one renowned commentator,

> the 'heart' of all the above notions or doctrines [of non-signatory status] clearly is the *bona fides* principle, respectively the requirement to act in good faith and the notion that positions or defenses which stand in contradiction to the exigencies to act in good faith will not deserve legal (or arbitral) protection.[150]

15-097 Unlike the courts in Germany,[151] Austrian courts have exercised resistance against the notion of good faith as applied to arbitration agreements, in particular with respect to formal defects.[152] However, there are several good reasons not to apply those cases to assess the binding effect of an arbitration agreement on non-signatory parties.

15-098 First, the basis for the resistance is unfounded. The Austrian *Oberster Gerichtshof* has argued,[153] and prevailing doctrine seems to accept,[154] that an arbitration

---

148. *Int'l Paper Co. v. Schwabedissen Maschinen & Anlagen GMBH*, 206 F.3d 411, 417-418 (4th Cir. 2000);

149. *Am. Bureau of Shipping v. Tencara Shipyard S.P.A.*, 170 F.3d 349, 353 (2nd Cir. 1999); *see also Avila Group, Inc. v. Norma J. of California*, 426 F. Supp. 537, 542 (S.D.N.Y. 1977); *MAG Portfolio Consult, GmbH v. Merlin Biomed Group, LLC*, 268 F.3d 58, 61 (2nd Cir. 2001); *see also E.I. Dupont de Nemours & Co. v. Rhone Poulenc Fiber & Resin Intermediates, S.A.S.*, 269 F.3d 187, 200 (3rd Cir. 2001) ('Under the [direct benefits] theory, courts prevent a non-signatory from embracing a contract, and then turning its back on the portions of the contract, such as an arbitration clause, that it finds distasteful.').

150. M. Blessing, 'Extension of the Arbitration Clause to Non-Signatories in The Arbitration Agreement – Its Multifold Critical Aspects' (1994) ASA Special Series No. 8, 151, 162.

151. *See* W. Voit in *Kommentar zur Zivilprozeßordnung*, H.J. Musielak (ed.) (6th edn, Munich, Verlag Franz Vahlen, 2008), Section 1031, para. 16.

152. OGH, 21 June 2005, 5 Ob 127/05w ('Reliance by the contractual partner on an external fact or an argument based on good faith cannot [be used to justify] the violation of such a written form requirement.'). *See also* OGH, 14 October 1982, 8 Ob 556/82; OGH, 26 January 2000, 7 Ob 368/98p ('According to unanimous Austrian case law and legal doctrine so far [on this point], the authority to enter into an arbitration agreement is subject to the same form requirement as the main contract itself. The power of attorney must also comprise special authority to conclude an arbitration agreement pursuant to Section 1008 ABGB. This is typically justified by reference to the fact that with respect to contracts that are subject to form requirements – on the basis of the protection against hurried decisions (*Übereilungsschutz*) –, the authority to enter into a contract is subject to the same form requirement as the conclusion of the contract itself.').

153. OGH, 17 May 2001, 7 Ob 67/01f; OGH, 24 July 1997, 6 Ob 186/97i; OGH, 3 September 1986, 1 Ob 545/86.

154. G. Zeiler, *Schiedsverfahren* (Vienna/Graz, Neuer Wissenschaftlicher Vertrag, 2006), Section 581, p. 50; W.H. Rechberger and W. Melis in *Kommentar zur ZPO*, W.H. Rechberger (ed.) (3rd edn,

agreement, given its effect of excluding the courts and its regulative roots in the ZPO,[155] is a procedural contract and thus governed by the rules of the ZPO alone (which apparently do not accept the notion of good faith). This analysis falls short. Save for the issues of the formal 'in-writing' requirement and arbitrability,[156] the ZPO is entirely insufficient to assess the validity of any contract or agreement, whether termed (somewhat artificially) procedural or substantive. Indeed, it is fully accepted that, to the extent that procedural rules are silent, rules of substantive contract law apply to the arbitration agreement *per analogiam*.[157] Thus, questions of offer and acceptance, interpretation, rescission, and the like, are examined under substantive contractual rules, precisely because the ZPO fails to provide any meaningful guidance on any of these issues.

Indeed, the Austrian *Oberster Gerichtshof* has recently confirmed specifically in **15-099** the context of extending the arbitration agreement to a third party beneficiary that, although an arbitration agreement is a procedural contract which must be interpreted according to the procedural rules of Austrian arbitration law, rules of private contract apply *per analogiam* to the extent that those rules are insufficient.[158] As a result, there is no systemic difficulty that would prevent the application of substantive rules to the question of whether it would be an abuse of right, or a case of *venire contra factum proprium*, for a non-signatory party to refuse to be bound by an arbitration agreement.

Second, as a related matter, it is wrong to look at these issues as purely procedural. **15-100** The traditional view in Austria would have denied that a legal successor is bound by the arbitration clause concluded by its predecessor, supposedly because he did not sign it and thus failed to satisfy the formal requirements imposed by procedural law.[159] This view has now been rejected both by the courts[160] and in academic

---

Vienna, Manz, 2006), Section 581, para. 5; P. Rummel, 'Schiedsvertrag und ABGB' [1986] RZ, 146.

155. A. Fremuth-Wolf, in *Arbitration Law of Austria: Practice and Procedure*, S. Riegler, A. Petsche, A. Fremuth-Wolf, M. Platte and C. Liebscher (eds) (Huntington, Juris Publishing, 2007), p. 675.

156. A. Fremuth-Wolf, in *Arbitration Law of Austria: Practice and Procedure*, S. Riegler, A. Petsche, A. Fremuth-Wolf, M. Platte and C. Liebscher (eds) (Huntington, Juris Publishing, 2007), p. 675.

157. W.H. Rechberger and W. Melis in *Kommentar zur ZPO*, W.H. Rechberger (ed.) (3rd edn, NewYork/Vienna, Springer, 2006), Section 581, para. 5; S. Riegler in *Arbitration Law of Austria: Practice and Procedure*, S. Riegler, A. Petsche, A. Fremuth-Wolf, M. Platte and C. Liebscher (eds) (Huntington, Juris Publishing, 2007), Section 609, p. 483; P. Rummel, 'Schiedsvertrag und ABGB' [1986] RZ, 146.

158. OGH, 13 June 1995, 4 Ob 533/95. *See* also **Article 1**, at para. 059.

159. G. Backhausen, *Schiedsgerichtsbarkeit unter besonderer Berücksichtigung des Schiedsvertragsrechts* (Vienna, Manz, 1990), p. 62 *et seq*; P. Rummel, 'Schiedsvertrag und ABGB' [1986] RZ, 146; Girsberger and C. Hausmaninger, 'Assignment of Rights and Agreement to Arbitrate' (1992) 8(2) Arb Int'l, 121, 144.

160. *See, e.g.*, OGH, 26 April 2001, 8 Ob 179/00g with further references.

discussion.[161] There is no dispute that the legal successor of a party to an arbitration agreement assumes the obligation to arbitrate if the succession was valid as a matter of *substantive* law. A *substantively* valid assignment is sufficient; formal requirements of a signature to the arbitration agreement are no longer required. Thus, it is conceptually flawed to apply procedural law to issues of good faith, because principles of good faith go to the substantive validity of the arbitration agreement and its effect towards third party non-signatories. As a procedural contract, the arbitration agreement has been validly concluded – that is no longer the question. Rather, the question is whether or not a third party, by some mechanism of substantive law, assumes the obligation to arbitrate.

15-101 Third, the Austrian case law discussed above that extends the binding effect of arbitration agreements to non-signatory successors and third party beneficiaries effectively rests on doctrines of abuse of right and estoppel. As discussed above, the Austrian *Oberster Gerichtshof* applied the arbitration clause to non-signatories precisely because a party claiming an existing legal position is bound on exactly the same terms that defined that position in the first place. Such a third party cannot pick and choose the properties of that position; it cannot assume the advantageous rights and reject at the same time some unwelcome obligations that attend those rights. Thus, every party that enters into, or claims, a legal position that is governed by an arbitration clause must accept that arbitration clause against it without having been a signatory of the original agreement. These considerations, as they were applied by the Austrian *Oberster Gerichtshof*, are a classic expression of fundamental fairness and the prohibition on abuse of law. Once that basic rationale is accepted, as it should be, there is no reason to restrict it to cases of legal succession or third party beneficiary in the strict sense.[162]

15-102 Fourth, even if this issue were considered as one of procedural law and form, recent Austrian case law suggests that the Austrian *Oberster Gerichtshof* is willing to accept a notion of abuse of right with respect to the effect of arbitration agreements. In a landmark decision of 26 April 2006,[163] the Austrian *Oberster Gerichtshof* specifically held that principles of good faith, and a party's conduct, can overcome formal defects in the conclusion of an arbitration agreement. This decision arose when a party argued that it was not bound by an arbitration agreement because, when that agreement was concluded, its agent acted on the basis of a formally-defective power of attorney. Under previous Austrian authority,[164] the party's 'factual behavior' would have been insufficient to cure any formal defects.[165] Despite this, the Austrian *Oberster Gerichtshof* expressly declined to adopt

---

161. A. Fremuth-Wolf, *Die Schiedsvereinbarung im Zessionsfall* (Vienna, Verlag Österreich, 2004), pp. 140 *et seq.* with further references.
162. It would therefore be an abuse of right, for example, if a third party were to claim the status as a shareholder, yet refused to be bound by an arbitration clause in the deed of formation.
163. OGH, 26 April 2006, 7 Ob 236/05i.
164. OGH, 21 June 2005, 5 Ob 127/05w; OGH 14 October 1982, 8 Ob 556/82.
165. OGH, 21 June 2005, 5 Ob 127/05w ('Reliance by the contractual partner on an external fact or an argument based on good faith cannot [be used to justify] the violation of such a written form

restrictive view of form requirements. Rather, the Austrian *Oberster Gerichtshof* held that the party in question and its agents

> acted through the years in a way that there was no doubt that they considered themselves bound by the agreement and the arbitration clause contained therein. In the circumstances it constitutes contradictory conduct and violates in the extreme the prohibition on *venire contra factum proprium* for the party to later rely on formal defects in the conclusion of the agreement and the arbitration clause contained therein (...) this must be deemed abuse of law.[166]

The Austrian *Oberster Gerichtshof* thus recognized that formal defects in an arbitration agreement may be cured on the basis of principles of good faith and estoppel. Its decision leaves no question but that an entity may be held party to an arbitration agreement, based on principles of estoppel and good faith, even where the arbitration agreement is subject to formal requirements. That conclusion is correct, and in line with international precedent.[167] **15-103**

2.4. Corporate Veil Piercing

Modern arbitral doctrine also applies the notion of corporate veil piercing to international arbitration agreements. This notion results in disregarding a subsidiary's separate corporate identity and attaching liability for the subsidiary's obligations to a parent company. In the context of agreements to arbitrate, a corporation may, in appropriate circumstances, be bound by the arbitration agreements of its affiliates. **15-104**

As a matter of substantive law, most developed legal systems recognize the principle of corporate veil piercing. As the Austrian *Oberster Gerichtshof* has held, '[t]he underlying principle of piercing the corporate veil is that no one may use a legal entity in order to damage a third party, or in order to evade the law.'[168] Or, as a leading Austrian authority has reasoned '[t]he aspect of an abuse of law must be taken into account because, in any context, the legal system will oppose to an abusive behavior, particularly through liabilities. One would virtually have to invent reasons why, in the context of corporate veil piercing, this should not **15-105**

---

requirement.'). *See also* OGH, 14 October 1982, 8 Ob 556/82; OGH, 26 January 2000, 7 Ob 368/98p ('According to unanimous Austrian case law and legal doctrine so far [on this point], the authority to enter into an arbitration agreement is subject to the same form requirement as the main contract itself. The power of attorney must also comprise special authority to conclude an arbitration agreement pursuant to Section 1008 ABGB. This is typically justified by reference to the fact that with respect to contracts that are subject to form requirements – on the basis of the protection against hurried decisions (*Übereilungsschutz*) – the authority to enter into a contract is subject to the same form requirement as the conclusion of the contract itself.').

166. OGH, 26 April 2006, 7 Ob 236/05i.
167. W. Voit in *Kommentar zur Zivilprozeßordnung*, H.J. Musielak (ed.) (6th edn, Munich, Verlag Franz Vahlen, 2008), Section 1031, para. 16; BGer, 16 January 1995, BGE 121 III 38.
168. OGH, 19 December 2002, 2 Ob 308/02m.

be the case.'[169] Similar positions are taken in related jurisdictions, such as Germany[170] and Switzerland.[171] The underlying principle is the prevention of an abuse of law;[172] because of its uniform application in common and civil law systems, corporate veil piercing has been accepted in arbitral awards as a principle of transnational application.[173]

15-106 There is a growing body of precedent in international arbitration that applies such principles of corporate veil piercing not only to a parent company's substantive liability, but to matters of jurisdiction, particularly in the context of agreements to arbitrate. Thus, international arbitral awards have frequently applied veil piercing principles in considering the tribunal's jurisdiction over

---

169. P. Jabornegg, 'Die Lehre vom Durchgriff im Recht der Kapitalgesellschaften' [1989] wbl, 1, 6.
170. BGH, 10 December 2007, II ZR 239/05, AG 2008, 256, 257 ('According to established jurisprudence, only the corporation itself, not its members are liable for the corporation's debts. An exemption from this principle can only exceptionally be admitted, if the use of legal separateness between the legal entity and the person behind constitutes an abuse of law.'). *See also* BGH, 30 January 1956, II ZR 168/54 in BGHZ 20, 4 ('The corporate entity may only be acknowledged insofar, as it is being used in accordance with the law. It is not sufficient that a corporate entity is being used in accordance with its own purposes'). *See also* BGH, 8 July 1970, VIII ZR 28/69 in BGHZ 54, 222, 224 ('The senate adheres to principle repeatedly pronounced by the Reichsgerichtshof and the Bundesgerichtshof (RGZ 156, 271, 277; 169, 240, 248; BGHZ 20, 4, 11; 26, 31,37) that one may not easily set aside the legal form of a corporate entity. Therefore, only the association (*eingetragener Verein*) itself is liable for debts, not its members. However, there must be an exception, if an application of this rule would generate results that are not consistent with the principle of good faith, and when relying on the separateness between a legal entity and the persons behind would constitute an abuse of law'.). *See also* BGH, 5 November 1980, VIII ZR 230/79 in BGHZ 78, 318 ('[O]ne may not easily set aside the legal form of a corporate entity (. . .). However, there must be an exception, if an application of this rule would generate results that are not consistent with the principle of good faith, and when relying on the separateness between a legal entity and the persons behind would constitute an abuse of law'). *See also* D. Reuter in *Münchener Kommentar zum Bürgerlichen Gesetzbuch*, F. Säcker and R. Rixecker (eds) (5th edn, Munich, C.H. Beck, 2006) introductory remarks to Section 21, at para. 47 ('Of course, amongst others, the individual abuse of law also confines reliance on legal separateness of a legal entity').
171. BGer, 29 January 1996, *X and XX v. Y and YY*, (1996) 14(3) Bull ASA, 496, 503.
172. BGer, 14 March 2003, *Baugenossenschaft B. v. N.K. and O.K.*, BGE 5C.279/2002.
173. S. Presser, Piercing the Corporate Veil (Rev. edn., New York, West Group, 2008), Section 5.1; *see also Interim Award in ICC Case No. 3879 of 1984, Westland Helicopters*, (1984) 23 ILM 1071, 1084; *Interim Award in ICC Case No. 9719 of 1999*, (2005)16(2) ICC Ct Bull, 83; *Award in ICC Case No. 8385 of 1995*, in J.-J. Arnaldez, Y. Derains and D. Hascher, *Collection of ICC Arbitral Awards 1996-2000* (The Hague, Kluwer Law International, 2003), pp. 474 *et seq.*; *Award in Ad Hoc Arbitration of 1991, Alpha S.A. v. Beta & Co and Société d'Etat de droit ruritane*, (1992) 10(2) Bull ASA 202; *see also Decision on Jurisdiction in ICSID Case No. ARB/02/18 of 2004, Tokios Tokeles v. Ukraine*, (2005) ICSID Rev 206, para. 23; *Award in ICSID Case No. ARB/98/7 of 2000, Banro American Resources, Inc. and Société Aurifère du Kivu et du Maniema S.A.R.L. v. Democratic Republic of the Congo*, (2002) 17 ICSID Rev – FILJ 382.

non-signatory parties.[174] As one award has held, '[t]he final question is to what extent the juridical fiction which is the basis of legal entities must give way to the reality of human behavior and cease to protect those who hide behind the corporate veil in order to promote their own interests at the cost of those who dealt with the company.'[175] In the same vein, a German author explains that

> it remains true for the arbitration agreement that its extension represents the only sensible sanction. (...) Specifically in international commerce, the legal result can only consist in an extension of the arbitration clause; otherwise the abuse would be warranted with the 'home field advantage' of public proceedings, which can in itself be decisive. (...) Reliance on the assumption not to be bound to the arbitration agreement, only including the controlled entity as party, is therefore considered as an abuse of law.[176]

Thus, a substantive veil piercing, in cases of abuse, may also extend the arbitration **15-107** clause from the subsidiary to the parent company.[177] Under basic concepts of abuse of law, the corporate veil of a subsidiary will be pierced for jurisdictional purposes, and a non-signatory parent will be required to arbitrate, where the non-signatory parent so dominates and controls the signatory subsidiary and its operations that the latter can be regarded as a mere instrumentality or agency of the former.[178] The corporate veil of a subsidiary could also be pierced for jurisdictional purposes

---

174. *Award in ICC Case No. 8385 of 1995*, in J.J. Arnaldez, Y. Derains and D. Hascher, *Collection of ICC Arbitral Awards 1996-2000* (The Hague, Kluwer Law Internationl, 2003), pp. 474 *et seq.* (applying *lex mercatoria* to pierce the corporate veil, and thereby finding the Tribunal had jurisdiction over the non-signatory).

175. *Award in ICC Case No. 8385 of 1995*, in J.-J. Arnaldez, Y. Derains and D. Hascher, *Collection of ICC Arbitral Awards 1996-2000* (The Hague, Kluwer Law International, 2003), pp. 474 *et seq.*

176. C. Frank, *Der Durchgriff im Schiedsvertrag* (Berlin, Duncker & Humboldt, 1999), p. 300.

177. *Raeschke-Kessler/Berger* agree and state that '[t]he extension of the arbitration clause to a third party is substantively unobjectionable, if the respective applicable law provides for apparent agency or corporate veil piercing.') *See* H. Raeschke-Kessler and K. Berger, *Recht und Praxis des Schiedsverfahrens* (3rd edn, Cologne, RWS Verlag, 1999), para. 302; M. Blessing, 'The Law Applicable to the Arbitration Clause and Arbitrability', (1999) ICCA Congress Series No. 9, 169 *et seq.*; B. Berger and F. Kellerhals, *Internationale und interne Schiedsgerichtsbarkeit in der Schweiz* (Bern/Vienna, Stämpfli Verlag/Manz, 2006), para. 528; T. Zuberbühler, 'Non-Signatories and the Consensus to Arbitrate' (2008) 26(1) ASA Bull, 33; J.-M. Ahrens, *Die subjektive Reichweite internationaler Schiedsvereinbarungen und ihre Erstreckung in der Unternehmensgruppe* (Frankfurt/Main, Schriftenreihe der A.M Berges Stiftung für Arbitrales Recht, 2001), p. 187 *et seq.*

178. *Intergen NV v. Grina*, 344 F.3d 134, 148 (1st Cir. 2003); *Interim Award in ICC Case No. 4131 of 1982, Dow Chemical France et al. v. Isover Saint Gobain (France)*, (1984) IX YB Comm Arb, 131 and (1983) JDI, 899; *Trans-Pacific Shipping Co. v. Atlantic & Orient Trust Co. Ltd*, [2005] F.C. 311 (Canadian Federal Court) (permitting veil-piercing claims to proceed); P. Schlosser, 'Arbitration Clauses in Maritime Contracts and Their Binding Effect on Groups of Companies' (1994) 11(4) J Int'l Arb. 127, 129 *et seq.*; *Award in Ad Hoc Arbitration of 1991, Alpha S.A. v. Beta & Co and Société d'Etat de droit ruritane*, (1992) 10(2) Bull ASA, 202;

where its corporate parent or affiliate abuses the subsidiary's corporate form for illegitimate, inequitable, tortuous or fraudulent purposes.[179] Moreover, the corporate veil of a subsidiary could be pierced for jurisdictional purposes if the non-signatory parent is substantively liable for its subsidiary's contractual obligations – in such cases, the procedural obligation to arbitrate is indivisibly associated, and therefore travel together, with the substantive liability.[180]

15-108 In Austria, there is little discussion of this issue, although there has been some support in recent writing.[181] Its opponents will argue that corporate veil piercing is built on notions of abuse of right which, under traditional Austrian precedent, have no application to arbitration agreements.[182] However, this view is anachronistic, isolated in the international context, and fails to persuade even within the existing system of Austrian law.[183]

T.G. Neson, 'Bridas v. Turkmenistan: U.S. Courts Uphold an Arbitrator's Power to Hold a Foreign Sovereign Liable for the Acts of its State-Owned Enterprise' (2006) 24(3) Bull ASA 584, 595; *Carte Blanche (Singapore) Pte Ltd v. Diners Club Int'l, Inc.*, 2 F.3d 24 (2nd Cir. 1993); *Smoothline Ltd v. N. Am. Foreign Trading Corp.*, 2002 WL 31885795 (S.D.N.Y. 2002); *Andrew Martin Marine Corp. v. Stork-Werkspoor Diesel BV*, 480 F.Supp. 1270 (E.D. La. 1979); *Coastal Stares Trading Inc. v. Zenith Navigation S.A.*, 446 F. Supp. 330 (S.D.N.Y. 1977).

179. ICJ, 5 February 1970, *The Barcelona Traction, Light and Power Co.(Belgium v Spain)*, (1970) ICJ., 3; *Interim Award in ICC Case No. 9719 of 1999*, (2005) 16(2) ICC Ct Bull, 83; *Interim Award in ICC Case No. 3879 of 1984, Westland Helicopters*, (1984) 23 ILM 1071, 1087; *Award in ICC Case No. 8385 of 1995*, in J.-J. Arnaldez, Y. Derains and D. Hascher, *Collection of ICC Arbitral Awards 1996-2000*, (The Hague, Kluwer Law International, 2003), pp. 474 *et seq.*; *Award in Ad Hoc Arbitration of 1991, Alpha S.A. v. Beta & Co and Société d'Etat de droit ruritane*, (1992) 10(2) Bull ASA, 202; *Award in CAS Case 96/161 of 1999* in M. Reeb (ed.), *Recueil des sentences du TAS/Digest of CAS Awards II 1998-*2000, (The Hague, Kluwer Law International, 2002), pp. 3 *et seq.*; *Award in ICC Case No. 10758 of 2000*, (2005) 16(2) ICC Ct Bull, 87, 90; *Award of 15 September 1989, E.c. v. Z.. ICA Z. et société M* (1990) 8(3) Bull ASA, 270, 276; OGH, 19 December 2002, 2 Ob 308/02m; Cour d'Appel de Paris, 29 March 1991, *Ganz and others v. Soc. Nationale des Chemin de Fer Tunisiens*, [1991] Rev Arb 478, 480; Cour de Cassation, 1re Ch. Civ., 11 June 1991, *Orri v. société des Lubrifiants Elf Aquitaine*, [1992] Rev Arb, 73; BGH, 8 July 1970, VIII ZR 28/69 in BGHZ 54, 222; BSG, 1 February 1996, 2 RU 7/95, NJW-RR 1997, 94; BGer, 14 March 2003, *Baugenossenschaft B. v N.K. and O.K.*, BGE 5 C 279/2002.

180. *Award in Ad Hoc Arbitration of 1991, Alpha S.A. v. Beta & Co. and Société d'Etat de droit ruritane*, (1992) 10(2) Bull ASA 202, 229. In *ALPHA S.A.*, an undisclosed country, 'Ruritania', established the company *ETA* to commercialize the product X after a fixed price. Looking for an intermediary to sell *X* at market rate after a significant price hike, *ETA* created a foreign subsidiary, *ZETA* to sell *X* to *ALPHA*, which could offer it on the free market. Subsequent problems led *ALPHA* to initiate arbitration against *BETA*, the legal successor in rights to *ETA*, based on the arbitration clause signed by *ALPHA* and *ZETA*. *See also Award in ICC Case No. 9762 of 2001*, (2004) XXIX YB Comm Arb 40; BGer, 29 January 1996, *X and XX v. Y and YY*, (1996) 14(3) Bull ASA 496, 503,

181. A. Reiner, 'Schiedsverfahren und Gesellschaftsrecht' [2007] GesRZ, 151, 159.

182. OGH, 21 June 2005, 5 Ob 127/05w; OGH 14 October 1982, 8 Ob 556/82.

183. *See* **Article 15**, at paras. *097 et seq.*

2.5.   *Group of Companies*

The doctrine of jurisdictional veil piercing is related in modern arbitral practice to **15-109** the 'Group of Companies' doctrine. The Group of Companies doctrine is particularly well-accepted in the law and jurisprudence of France, but also accepted in other developed jurisdictions. It has been forcefully rejected elsewhere [184]

In many instances, the Group of Companies doctrine involves analysis that is **15-110** distinguishable from that under veil piercing principles – focusing on the relations and dealings between separate corporate entities, rather than on setting aside or piercing the separate corporate forms.[185] Nonetheless, as leading commentators have observed, there are circumstances in which the Group of Companies doctrine is invoked in conjunction with principles of veil piercing, with tribunals or courts relying on the doctrine to set aside a company's separate legal identity.[186]

Thus, some awards consider, similar to veil piercing doctrines, the principles **15-111** against abuse of right to form the basis for a 'group of companies' analysis;[187] other tribunals have held that the juridical independence of a person could exceptionally be disregarded if it appeared as 'the linchpin of the contractual setup' and

---

184. *Peterson Farms Inc. v. C&M Farming Ltd* [2004] 2 Lloyd's Rep. 603 Q.B. (Comm.).
185. *See, e.g., Award in ICC Case No. 6000 of 1988*, discussed in Grigera Naón, 'Choice-of-Law Problems in International Commercial Arbitration' (2001) 289 Recueil des Cours, 127 ([I]t is largely admitted that by virtue of an usage of the international trade, where a contract, including an arbitration clause, is signed by a company which is a party to a group of companies, the other company or companies of the group which are involved in the execution, the performance and/or the termination of the contract are bound by the arbitration clause, provided the common will of the parties does not exclude such an extension, and even more so where the common will of the parties does not exclude such an extension, and even more so where the common will of the parties was to include a company of the group in the contractual relationship, even if such company did not formally sign the contract'). *See also Award in ICC Case Nos. 7604 and 7610 of 1995*, in J.-J. Arnaldez, Y. Derains and D. Hascher, *Collection of ICC Arbitral Awards 1996-2000* (The Hague, Kluwer Law International, 2003), pp. 510 ('[A]lthough the existence of a group is the first condition for joining a third party to the arbitration proceedings, it is also necessary to determine the parties' actual intention at the time of the facts or, at the very least the intention of the non-signatory third party.'). *See also Award in ICC Case No. 5894 of 1989*, (1991) 2(2) ICC Ct Bull, 25; *Award in ICC Case No. 1434 of 1975*, (1976) JDI, 978; *Award in ICC Case No. 6000 of 1988*, (1991) 2(2) ICC Ct Bull, 31, 34; *Award in ICC Case No. 11160 of 2002*, (2005) 16(2) ICC Ct Bull, 99; Cour d'Appel de Pau, 26 November 1986, *Société Sponsor A.B. v. Lestrade*, [1988] Rev Arb, 153 *et seq.*
186. D. Vidal, 'The Extension of Arbitration Agreements within Groups of Companies: The Alter Ego Doctrine in Arbitral and Court Decisions' (2005) 16(2) ICC Ct Bull, 63.
187. *See, e.g., Interim Award in Ad hoc Arbitration 1983, German engineering company v. Polish buyer*, (1987) XII YB Comm Arb 63; *Award in ICC Case No. 5730 of 1988*, (1990) JDI 1029 *et seq.* (Tribunal held that the signatory to the arbitration agreement could be seen as authorized by Respondent either in fact or at least following the principle of apparent authority. The Tribunal added that, if by not signing the contract itself, Respondent had wanted to

notably if there was 'confusion entertained' as between the members of the group or its majority shareholder.[188] These cases complement the basic principle that the corporate form of the subsidiary may be disregarded in certain cases to bind the parent to the subsidiary's obligation to arbitrate.

2.6.   *Domestic Law or Transnational Principles?*

15-112 There is a growing body of authority suggesting that the appropriate law governing the application of valid international arbitration clauses to non-signatories is prescribed by transnational or international standards, rather than domestic law.[189] These transnational standards are said to be particularly appropriate to, and tailored for, application in international disputes, where multiple national jurisdictions have different connecting factors to the issues in dispute.[190]

15-113 By agreeing to arbitrate an international dispute in a neutral arbitral seat, parties deliberately select an international means of dispute resolution, in significant part to avoid the jurisdictional and choice-of-law uncertainties and complexities that arise in national courts. In these circumstances, it is arguably appropriate to apply international or transnational principles to determine the subjective scope of a valid international arbitration agreement: doing so provides a uniform body of law tailored to the parties' needs and expectations in international business transactions and avoids the idiosyncrasies and uncertainties of domestic law. Several arbitral awards have therefore applied international or transnational principles to the

---

evade its personal responsibility, such behavior would have to be regarded as fraudulent and not meriting legal protection). *See also* Cour d'Appel de Paris, 11 January 1990, *Orri v Société des Lubrifiants Elf Aquitaine*, [1992] Rev Arb, 95 *et seq*. The Court held that arbitration clause could be extended to the 'parties directly involved in the execution of the contract and the disputes that could result from it, once it is established that the contractual situation, the activities and usual commercial relationships between the parties justify the assumption that they have accepted the arbitration clause of which they knew the existence and scope'. It also confirmed that if the signature by the Respondent's employee was meant to dissimulate the real party to the contract such behavior constituted a fraud which could not have any legal effect, making the Respondent a party to the contract. It added that this was further justified by the 'group of companies' doctrine.

188.   *Award in ICC Case No. 5721 of 1990*, (1990) JDI, 1020.
189.   Y. Derains and S. Schaf, 'Clauses d'arbitrage et groupes de sociétés' (1985) RDAI, 231, 236-237.
190.   S. Jarvin, 'The Group of Companies Doctrine' (1994) ASA Special Series No. 8, 181; G. Naón, 'Choice of Law Problems in International Commercial Arbitration' (2001) 289 Recueil, 181; Y. Derains and S. Schaf, 'Clauses d'arbitrage et groupes de societes,' (1985) RDAI 1985, 231, 236-37; A. Redfern, M. Hunter, N. Blackaby and C. Partasides, *Law and Practice of International Commercial Arbitration* (4th edn, London, Sweet & Maxwell, 2004), para. 2-83.

question of whether an arbitration clause binds non-signatories on the basis of jurisdictional veil-piercing, group of companies, estoppel or other theories.[191]

By contrast, the law of the place of incorporation of the non-signatory (*lex societis*) **15-114** has been rejected in determining the subjective scope of an arbitration agreement, even with regard to questions of corporate veil-piercing, because the question of whether to bind a non-signatory to an arbitration agreement is derived from the parent's dominant position, abusive behavior or fraud – and not the capacity or authority of the non-signatory.[192] For example, the U.S. Supreme Court has refused to apply the law of the parent company's state of incorporation, holding:

> As a general matter, the law of the state of incorporation normally determines issues relating to the internal affairs of a corporation. Application of that body of law achieves the need for certainty and predictability of result while generally protecting the justified expectations of parties with interests in the corporation. (...). Different conflicts principles apply, however, where the rights of third parties external to the corporation are at issue.[193]

Likewise, arbitral tribunals frequently reject application of the law of the place of **15-115** incorporation of the signatory subsidiary to the question of whether to bind a non-signatory parent corporation. One arbitral award held:

> Whereas it can be regarded as fair and reasonable to subject a company and its shareholders, directors and managers to the law of the place of incorporation for their internal relations, third parties who deal with the corporations cannot properly be regarded to have united themselves with the corporation in a venture to be controlled by the law of the corporation's creation. This is especially true of third parties from other countries that are necessarily less acquainted with the law of the state of incorporation.
>
> Indeed, in an international relations context, the Tribunal prefers to apply rules that are well-adapted to the international market environment and which achieve a reasonable balance between the corporation's trust in its separate legal personality and the protection of persons, which can be victims of manipulations by a corporation or its subsidiary in order to deprive a creditor of his benefits.[194]

---

191. M. Blessing, 'Extension of the Arbitration Clause to Non-Signatories in The Arbitration Agreement – Its Multifold Critical Aspects' (1994) ASA Special Series No. 8. 175-178; *Interim Award in ICC Case No. 4131 of 1982, Dow Chemical France et al. v. Isover Saint Gobain (France)*, (1985) IX YB Comm Arb, 131 and (1983) JDI, 899; *see also Award in ICC Case No. 10758 of 2000*, (2005) 16(2) ICC Ct Bull, 87-88.

192. *Award in Ad Hoc Arbitration of 1991, Alpha S.A. v. Beta & Co. and Société d'Etat de droit ruritane*, (1992) 10(2) Bull ASA, 202.

193. *First Nat'l City Bank v. Banco Para El Comercio Exterior de Cuba*, 462 U.S. 611, 621 (U.S. S. Ct. 1983).

194. *Award in ICC Case No. 8385 of 1995*, in J.J. Arnaldez, Y. Derains and D. Hascher, *Collection of ICC Arbitral Awards 1996-2000* (The Hague, Kluwer Law International, 2003), pp. 474.

15-116 There are therefore credible reasons for applying international standards to issues of jurisdictional veil piercing, and other non-signatory doctrines, in the context of international arbitration agreements. As *Park* argues:

> [Transnational] norms can justify themselves as the best calculus for determining reasonable expectations of litigants from diverse legal cultures. In appropriate circumstances, they apply not because any authority says they must, but *faute de mieux*, for want of any better way to promote dispute resolution in a global community where not all commercial actors accept the parochial standards of a single national law. Intensely fact-based, transnational norms applied in joinder cases draw their content and value from consensus in the decisions of a wide range of national courts and arbitral proceedings. These decisions tend to work themselves into an emerging framework to guide principled decision-making in international arbitration.'[195]

15-117 There is little debate of this issue in Austria so far. On the one hand, the Austrian *Oberster Gerichtshof* holds that, absent choice of law by the parties, the validity of an arbitration agreement is in principle governed by Austrian law if Austria is the seat of the arbitration;[196] but it has also held under the former arbitration law that international principles under the New York Convention override national Austrian law as far as the formal validity of arbitration agreements is concerned, where the dispute is of an international character.[197] In any event, those decisions address the formal validity of arbitration agreements, which may miss the point in many cases of succession, estoppel, and veil piercing – which present questions of substantive law.

VI.   DECISION ON ADMISSIBILITY OF MULTI-PARTY
                   PROCEEDINGS

Article 15(9): The decision whether multiparty proceedings, as per paragraph 1 of this Article, are admissible, shall be taken by the sole arbitrator (the arbitral tribunal) upon application of one of the Respondents. If the

---

195. W.W. Park, 'Non-Signatories And The New York Convention' (2008) 2(1) Dispute International, 95; *see also* J. Lew, L. Mistelis and S. Kröll, *Comparative International Commercial Arbitration* (The Hague, Kluwer Law International, 2003), para. 17-53; B. Wortmann, 'Choice of Law by Arbitrators: The Applicable Conflict of Laws System' (1998) 14 Arb Int'l, 106-107.
196. *See, e.g.,* OGH, 19 February 2004, 6 Ob 151/03d; OGH, 22 September 1994, 2 Ob 566/94. For a detailed discussion, *see* **Article 2**, at paras. 032 *et seq.*
197. OGH, 17 November 1971, 8 Ob 233/71, JBl 1974, 628; *see also* OGH, 26 April 2006, 7 Ob 236/05i; P. Oberhammer, 'Schiedsvereinbarungen und § 1016 ABGB' in *Festschrift für Rudolf Welser zum 65. Geburtstag*, C. Fischer-Czermak, A. Kletecka, M. Schauer, W. Zankl (eds) (Vienna, Manz, 2004), pp. 761 *et seq.*

admissibility of multiparty proceedings is denied, the arbitral proceedings return to the stage they were in for the Respondents before the sole arbitrator (the arbitral tribunal) was appointed.

Article 15(9) expressly provides that it is for the tribunal, not the institution, to **15-118** decide on whether or not multi-party proceedings are applicable. This is not a discretionary decision; the tribunal has to follow the standard set by Article 15(1), with respect to both the mandatory[198] and the elective[199] requirements set out in that provision.

As a textual matter, Article 15 uses the term 'admissibility', which could lead to the **15-119** conclusion that the tribunal is deciding a purely procedural issue. More precisely, however, Article 15 addresses a jurisdictional matter. For some elements of Article 15(1) – such as the requirement that all parties must be subject to an arbitration agreement referring the dispute to the VIAC[200] – this is an obvious conclusion. But even more generally, the requirements set out in Article 15(1) describe the circumstances in which the tribunal is authorized to hear a dispute between multiple parties. Where those requirements are not met, the Tribunal lacks the authority to hear the dispute. The nature of Article 15 is therefore jurisdictional. As a result, the approach of Article 15(9), in vesting the tribunal with the authority to determine the matter, is correct because it should always be the tribunal who decides, in the first instance, on its own jurisdiction.[201]

The qualification of Article 15 as raising issues of jurisdiction has several impor- **15-120** tant consequences. First, it means that the time limits for jurisdictional objections apply.[202] Thus, a respondent who considers that the requirements of Article 15(1) are not met, and that the tribunal therefore has no authority to conduct a multi-party arbitration, must object before making submissions on the merits, or else be deemed to have accepted the Tribunal's jurisdiction.[203] Secondly, the Tribunal should decide on the admissibility of multi-party arbitration in the form of an award that, like any jurisdictional award, can be reviewed by the courts under Section 611(2) no. 1 ZPO.[204]

Article 15(9) appears to operate on the premise that the arbitrators' decision on the **15-121** 'admissibility' of multi-party proceedings is final. It provides, in terms of consequences, that '[i]f the admissibility of multiparty proceedings is denied, the arbitral proceedings return to the stage they were in for the Respondents before the sole arbitrator (the arbitral tribunal) was appointed.' Although the wording of that provision is not entirely clear, it appears to mean, in effect, that the tribunal

---

198. *See* **Article 15**, at paras. 008 *et seq.*
199. *See* **Article 15**, at paras. 011 *et seq.*
200. *See* **Article 15**, at paras. 008 *et seq.*
201. *See* **Article 19**, at paras. 015 *et seq.*
202. *See* **Article 19**, at paras. 006 *et seq.*
203. *See* **Article 19**, at para. 010.
204. *See* **Article 19**, at paras. 021 *et seq.*

becomes defunct. If the claimant accepts the tribunal's decision that a single arbitration against multiple respondents is not possible under the Vienna Rules, it will consider whether to withdraw its statement of claim as against some of the respondents (for which the requirements of Article 15 or not met); or to file a new statement of claim against some or all of the respondents, but, depending on the grounds for denial of multi-party jurisdiction, in separate proceedings. If the claimant does not accept the tribunal's decision, it should challenge the award. If the award is set aside because the courts find that the tribunal had no reason to deny its jurisdiction, the claimant should be able to refile its claims against the multiple respondents. In that case, a new tribunal will have to be constituted in accordance with Article 15(2) *et seq.*

Article 16

The Challenge of Arbitrators

	Para.			Para.
I. Challenging Arbitrators for Lack of Independence or Impartiality	1	B. The Challenge of an Arbitrator Before the VIAC	20
A. Introduction	1	1. Reasoned Application	21
B. The Standard for Challenging an Arbitrator	3	2. Without Delay	23
C. Threshold for the Challenge of a Party's Own Nomination	5	3. Waiving the Right to a Challenge and Setting Aside the Award	26
II. Initiating the Challenge	13	III. The Board's Decision on the Challenge	40
A. The Challenge of an Arbitrator Under Austrian Law	13	A. Opportunity for Voluntary Withdrawal	41
1. Decision by the Tribunal	14	B. Decision-Making	43
2. Voluntary Withdrawal or Agreement	16	C. Remedies Before the State Courts	47
3. Four Week Time Limit	19	IV. Continuation of the Proceedings During the Challenge	55

I. CHALLENGING ARBITRATORS FOR LACK OF INDEPENDENCE OR IMPARTIALITY

Article 16(1): An arbitrator may be challenged only if circumstances exist that give rise to justifiable doubts as to his impartiality or independence, or that are in conflict with the agreement of the parties. A party may challenge an arbitrator appointed by him, or in whose appointment he participated, only for reasons of which he becomes aware after the participation in the appointment or after the appointment has been made.

A.   Introduction

16-001 Previously, Article 11 of the Vienna Rules 2001[1] simply provided that '[a]n arbitrator may be challenged if there are sufficient grounds for doubting his independence or impartiality'. Closely mirroring the 2006 reform, Article 16 now allows challenges for lack of impartiality and independence, as well as for cases where arbitrators fail to meet the requirements for this office as agreed by the parties. The new legal environment in Austria also provides for significant procedural changes. Under Section 595(1) no. 4 fZPO, the participation of an arbitrator who proceeded to an award in the face of an unsuccessful, but justified, challenge gave rise to *vacatur*. Under that system, the setting aside proceedings *de facto* served as an appeal mechanism for the challenge procedure. The obvious disadvantage of that system was the uncertainty attaching to any decision denying a challenge and proceeding with the arbitration to a final award – which could then be challenged in setting aside proceedings. Section 589 ZPO now provides both for a detailed challenge procedure and for the immediate one-stop appeal to the state courts regarding the challenge of an arbitrator, with no possibility of further revision. Thus, the participation of a biased arbitrator will only in exceptional circumstances justify the setting aside of the award under the provision of Section 611(2) nos 4 and 5 ZPO.[2]

16-002 As discussed in detail in the context of **Article 7**, the independence and impartiality of arbitrators is a fundamental premise of the arbitral process. It preserves the integrity of arbitration and thus, its credibility in the eyes of its users as a trustworthy alternative to litigation before national courts.[3] This chapter examines the procedure for challenging arbitrators for lack of impartiality and independence, or for their failure to meet agreed requirements, under Austrian law and the Vienna Rules. The discussion set out below should be read together with the commentary on the arbitrator's duty to be, and to remain, impartial and independent in the context of **Article 7**. The consequences of a successful challenge are considered in the context of **Article 18**.

B.   The Standard for Challenging an Arbitrator

16-003 As discussed above,[4] it is accepted in Austria that all members of the tribunal must be impartial and independent – that is, able and willing to reach an unbiased decision.[5] Austrian law has traditionally defined the standard for the independence

---

1. Vienna Rules 2001, **Annex 2a**.
2. *See* **Article 16**, at paras. 026 *et seq.*
3. *See* the discussion of the arbitrators' duties under **Article 7**, at paras. 049 *et seq.*
4. *See* **Article 7**, at paras. 058 and 099 *et seq.*
5. W.H. Rechberger and M. Rami, 'Ablehnung von Schiedsrichtern durch die Parteien' [1999] wbl, 103, 105 with reference to a phrase coined by *Habscheid*.

and impartiality of arbitrators similar to the standard applicable to state court judges, applying a two-pronged test of grounds for *exclusion*, on the one hand, and for *bias*, on the other hand.[6] Section 588(2) ZPO now provides, in line with international standards, that '[a]n arbitrator may be challenged only if circumstances exist that give rise to justifiable doubts as to its impartiality or independence, or if it does not possess qualifications agreed to by the parties.' As also discussed in detail in the context of **Article 7**, Section 588(2) ZPO therefore provides an objective standard for the disqualification of an arbitrator. A challenge ought not to turn on whether *a party* has doubts regarding the arbitrator's impartiality, but on whether such doubts are justified in the eyes of a reasonable person. According to established doctrine and case law, such an objective standard also fits best into the systemic approach that Austrian law has traditionally adopted with respect to the bias of state court judges;[7] it is also the approach taken by the IBA Guidelines on Conflict of Interest in International Arbitration (IBA Conflict Guidelines).[8]

Where Article 11(1) of the Vienna Rules 2001[9] premised a challenge on *sufficient* doubts as to the arbitrator's impartiality and independence, Article 16(1) now mirrors the standard provided by Section 588(2) ZPO. As discussed, Article 16 has, compared to Article 11(1) of the Vienna Rules 2001, also been expanded to allow for a challenge not only for lack of impartiality, but also if the arbitrator lacks agreed qualifications, thereby reflecting the standard of Section 588(2) ZPO. This clarification is welcome, as the lack of agreed qualifications was previously not regulated by the Vienna Rules at all. As the wording of Article 11(1) of the Vienna Rules 2001 was unambiguous, it was arguably not possible for the VIAC to assume jurisdiction for challenges against arbitrators who lack the qualifications agreed by the parties. From both a systemic and an institutional perspective, it is of course preferable to have all challenges to arbitrators, on whatever grounds they may be raised, uniformly decided by one forum. Article 16(1) now expressly allows this. **16-004**

C.   THRESHOLD FOR THE CHALLENGE OF A PARTY'S OWN NOMINATION

Article 16(1) also provides that '[a] party may challenge an arbitrator appointed by him, or in whose appointment he participated, only for reasons of which he becomes aware after the participation in the appointment or after the appointment has been made'. This mirrors the statutory provision contained in the last sentence **16-005**

---

6. Section 586 fZPO in conjunction with Sections 19 and 20 JN.
7. P.G. Mayr in *Kommentar zur ZPO*, W.H. Rechberger (ed.) (3rd edn, Vienna/New York, Springer, 2006), Section 19 JN, para. 4 with further reference.
8. *See* **Article 7**, at paras. 100 *et seq.*, 108 and 110. The IBA Conflict Guidelines provide in General Standard 2(c) that '[d]oubts are justifiable if a reasonable and informed third party would reach the conclusion that there was a likelihood that the arbitrator may be influenced by factors other than the merits of the case as presented by the parties in reaching his or her decision.' **Annex 17**.
9. Vienna Rules 2001, **Annex 2a**.

of Section 588(2) ZPO. The Vienna Rules 2001 contained a similar (but not identical) provision in Article 11(3).[10]

16-006 Article 16(1) and Section 588(2) ZPO concern the admissibility of a challenge, rather than its merits; as such, they address a threshold issue. If a challenge is not admissible for violation of Article 16(1) (or Section 588(2) ZPO), the merits of the challenge cannot be considered by the VIAC. Whether the conditions of Article 16(1) and Section 588(2) ZPO are met, is for the VIAC to decide in the first instance, but, if the challenge is not successful, this result is subject to review by the Austrian state courts pursuant to Section 589(3) ZPO.[11]

16-007 It is not entirely clear whether this provision of Section 588(2) ZPO is mandatory or not. If it is, then, for arbitrations sited in Austria, Section 588(2) ZPO must be applied cumulatively with Article 16. On the other hand, it is conceivable to argue that Section 588(2) ZPO is *replaced*, for arbitrations under the Vienna Rules, by Article 16(1), since Section 589(1) ZPO expressly allows the parties to agree on a procedure different from the one provided by the law. On balance, although the principle of party autonomy holds strong force in the context of arbitration, it is doubtful that the Austrian legislature perceived the issue of admissibility under Section 588(2) ZPO to form part of the dispositive procedure referred to in Section 589(1) ZPO. A cumulative application of both provisions is most sensible for arbitrations sited in Austria and conducted under the Vienna Rules.

16-008 In substance, a party who knowingly procures the appointment of an arbitrator cannot later challenge the arbitrator on grounds known to it that would otherwise justify a challenge. This applies not only for the immediate nomination by a party of an arbitrator (such as in the case of a co-arbitrator on a three arbitrator panel), but also to any participation by a party in the nominating process (such as a party's agreement to a sole arbitrator despite the knowledge of disqualifying grounds). For good reasons, this provision is therefore designed to keep obstructive and dilatory tactics at bay.

16-009 It is suggested, based on the wording of Article 16 and Section 588(2) ZPO, that only *actual* knowledge of a disqualifying ground prevents a party from a subsequent challenge, and that even gross negligence does not suffice.[12] In that sense, Article 16 presents a change from the Vienna Rules 2001, which provided in Article 11(3)[13] that a party participating in the arbitration although it '*should have known*' about disqualifying grounds is prevented from bringing a subsequent challenge. This

---

10. Article 11(3) Vienna Rules 2001 provided: 'A challenge is inadmissible if the party making the challenge has taken part in the proceedings notwithstanding the knowledge which it already had or ought to have had of the grounds of challenge relied upon, or if the party making the challenge notified the grounds of challenge with undue delay.' **Annex 2a**.
11. *See* **Article 16**, at paras. 047 *et seq.*
12. M. Platte in *Arbitration Law of Austria: Practice and Procedure*, S. Riegler, A. Petsche, A. Fremuth-Wolf, M. Platte and C. Liebscher (eds) (Huntington, Juris Publishing, 2007), Section 588, p. 262.
13. Vienna Rules 2001, **Annex 2a**.

appeared to impose an obligation on the parties to make, at their own initiative, reasonable inquiries into the arbitrator's background and circumstances, or else run the risk not to be able to subsequently challenge the arbitrator. The Vienna Rules 2001 were quite groundbreaking in this respect. More recently, General Standard No. 7 of the IBA Conflict Guidelines has followed suit, imposing a duty on the parties to disclose circumstances known to them – and to make a reasonable inquiry into the public domain.[14] Of course, this duty imposed on the parties does not release the arbitrators from the obligation to make appropriate disclosures.

Although, in light of considerations of procedural efficiency, it is debatable why a **16-010** party should deserve protection if it nominates an arbitrator that it *should have known*, had it observed only a minimum of due diligence, was not impartial or independent, the view to restrict Article 16 (and Section 588(2) ZPO) to cases of actual knowledge ultimately has the better arguments for it.[15] Most importantly, the responsibility not to accept a mandate when there are justifiable doubts rests firmly with the arbitrator, and should in principle not be shifted to the nominating party.

Article 16 uses the term 'appointment' rather than 'nomination': A party may **16-011** challenge an arbitrator *appointed* by him, or in whose *appointment* he participated, only for reasons of which he becomes aware after the participation in the *appointment* or after the *appointment* has been made'. This is inconsistent with the terminology used in **Article 14** regarding the constitution of the tribunal. Arbitrators are, under the concept of the Vienna Rules, *nominated* by the parties (or the co-arbitrators with respect to the presiding arbitrator), and, where the parties (or the co-arbitrators) fail to do so, *appointed* by the VIAC. To make sense, Article 16 must be interpreted to apply to any nomination by a party, or any participation of a party in a joint nomination.

In sum, a party that knows of a disqualifying ground but nevertheless acquiesces in **16-012** the nomination of an arbitrator is barred, by operation of Section 588(2) ZPO, to rely on that ground when it later becomes convenient for tactical reasons. It is debatable, however, if there are limits to that principle under *ordre public* considerations. These limits are discussed at **Article 16**, at 026 *et seq.*

II.   INITIATING THE CHALLENGE

Article 16(2): If a party challenges an arbitrator, it must without delay inform the Secretary General thereof, stating the grounds for the challenge.

---

14. *See* IBA Conflict Guidelines, **Annex 17**. *See also* the recent decision by the Swiss *Bundesgericht* on the parties duty to make resonable investigations with regard to the appointment of their own arbitrator. BGer, 20 March 2008, 4A 506/2007, BGer, 4 April 2008, 4A 528/2007.
15. J. Power, *The Austrian Arbitration Act – A Practitioner's Guide to Sections 577-618 of the Austrian Code of Civil Procedure* (Vienna, Manz, 2006), Section 588, para. 11.

A.   THE CHALLENGE OF AN ARBITRATOR UNDER AUSTRIAN LAW

16-013 Section 589 ZPO, based on Article 13 of the UNCITRAL Model Law, addresses the procedure for challenging arbitrators under Austrian law. It provides, first, that '[t]he parties are free to agree on a procedure for challenging an arbitrator, subject to the provisions of subs. 3 of this section'. In other words, Section 589 ZPO is not mandatory, and the parties can agree on their own mechanism or procedure for challenging arbitrators that lack the required impartiality and independence, or that fail to meet any additional requirements on which the parties have agreed. Typically, parties will agree to such a procedure by incorporating a set of institutional arbitration rules. Section 589(3) ZPO, however, provides for an appeal mechanism before the Austrian state courts that is mandatory.[16] This is discussed at **Article 16** at paras. 047 *et seq.*

1.   Decision by the Tribunal

16-014 If the parties have not agreed on a procedure (such as Article 16) then Section 589(2) ZPO provides that

> a party who intends to challenge an arbitrator shall, within four weeks after becoming aware of the composition of the arbitral tribunal or after becoming aware of any circumstances referred to in Section 588(2), send a written statement of the reasons for the challenge to the arbitral tribunal. Unless the challenged arbitrator withdraws from its office or the other party agrees to the challenge, the arbitral tribunal shall decide on the challenge.

16-015 Absent an agreement or a reference to institutional rules, Section 589(2) ZPO, by way of default, authorizes the arbitral tribunal, including the challenged arbitrator,[17] to hear and to decide upon the challenge. Notably, the decision on the merits of the challenge is made by the tribunal, including the arbitrator that is challenged. This is, in principle, similar to the situation in *ad hoc* arbitrations under the fZPO,[18] where the challenged arbitrator would have also participated in this decision and, indeed, the challenged sole arbitrator would alone have decided if the challenge directed against him or her was justified.[19]

---

16. M. Platte in *Arbitration Law of Austria: Practice and Procedure*, S. Riegler, A. Petsche, A. Fremuth-Wolf, M. Platte and C. Liebscher (eds) (Huntington, Juris Publishing, 2007), Section 589, p. 272.

17. *See* Explanatory Notes to Section 589 ZPO.

18. Although there is no such express provision in the ZPO, this follows clearly from Section 595(1) no. 4 fZPO. *See also* W.H. Rechberger and M. Rami, 'Ablehnung von Schiedsrichtern durch die Parteien' [1999] wbl, 103, 104. This has been confirmed by the courts, most recently: *See* OGH, 17 March 2005, 2 Ob 41/04z.

19. It is disputed, from a policy perspective, whether that rule is just, and Austrian scholars have taken issue with it. *See, e.g.* A. Reiner, 'Die internationale Schiedsgerichtsbarkeit nach

2.   Voluntary Withdrawal or Agreement

Section 589(2) ZPO contains some additional elements First, it expressly allows **16-016** an arbitrator to withdraw from office which obviously makes the challenge moot. This provision serves clarification purposes only: if an arbitrator is aware of disqualifying circumstances, he or she is in any event under an obligation to withdraw.[20] However, if the challenge is brought at the start of the proceeding, following the nomination of the arbitrator, then an arbitrator's withdrawal cannot considerably disrupt the proceedings, and an arbitrator exposed to such a challenge may wish to consider whether a withdrawal would help the dynamics on the tribunal and protect the integrity of the process (even where the challenge is in his or her view not justified). To protect an arbitrator in these circumstances, Section 590(3) ZPO provides that the withdrawal 'does not imply acceptance of the validity of any ground' suggestive of the lack of impartiality or independence.

On the other hand, if there are no objectively disqualifying circumstances, an **16-017** arbitrator arguably has a duty to remain in office to discharge his or her judicial function to both parties, maintaining the appointing party's right to have an arbitrator of its choosing hear the case, and avoiding the delay and obstruction of having to appoint a replacement.[21] For unjustified challenges launched at later stages of the proceeding, these considerations may well compel the arbitrator not to withdraw if he thinks the challenge is unjustified, lest he might be considered in violation of his contractual duty to render an award.[22]

Second, under Section 589(2) ZPO, the arbitrator can also be removed, without a **16-018** formal challenge procedure, if the other party agrees to it. This confirms that, in particular as far as the constitution of the tribunal is concerned, the parties are the masters of the procedure. If all parties are in agreement regarding the unsuitability of an arbitrator, the arbitrator is required to resign.

3.   Four Week Time Limit

Section 589(2) ZPO requires the aggrieved party to bring the challenge 'within **16-019** **four weeks** after becoming aware of the composition of the arbitral tribunal or after

---

österreichischem und französischem Recht' [1986] ZfRV, 162, 194; *also* W.H. Rechberger and M. Rami, 'Ablehnung von Schiedsrichtern durch die Parteien' [1999] wbl, 103, fn. 24. However, in the case of a three-arbitrator tribunal it will take at least two concurring votes to decide on the challenge, which should severely limit the risk of abuse. This is obviously not so in the case of a sole arbitrator. *De lege ferenda*, for reasons also discussed below, it will be preferable to grant the parties effective relief before the state courts, so that a challenge can be resolved fast, effectively, finally and with a minimum of disruption to the arbitration. *See* **Article 16**, at para. 047.

20. *See* **Article 7**, at paras. 027, 053 and 135; *see also* IBA Conflict Guidelines, Explanation to General Standard No. 2(a) and No. 3(d), **Annex 17**.
21. *See* **Article 7**, at para. 053.
22. *See* **Article 7**, at paras. 052 *et seq.*

becoming aware of [the arbitrator's lack of impartiality or independence as defined in] Section 588(2)'. The Working Group had originally proposed to provide for an even shorter time period of only 14 days for any challenge.[23] Now, a challenge must be brought no later than four weeks after the party becomes aware of the grounds for the challenge, which is either as early (but arguably not earlier)[24] as the notification to the party of the tribunal's constitution, or at a later stage in the proceedings when the disqualifying circumstances first become known to the party.[25] As discussed,[26] actual knowledge of the disqualifying circumstances is required. A party who fails to bring a challenge within the prescribed time period cannot later apply to the court under Section 589(3) ZPO,[27] or challenge the award on the basis that a biased arbitrator participated in the decision-making, save perhaps for exceptional circumstances discussed in greater detail at **Article 16**, at 026 *et seq.*

B.   THE CHALLENGE OF AN ARBITRATOR BEFORE THE VIAC

16-020 By agreeing to the application of the Vienna Rules, in their arbitration agreement or otherwise, the parties incorporate by reference the challenge procedure of Article 16. Under Section 589(1) ZPO, they are free to do so; however, a decision of the VIAC rejecting a challenge is subject to appeal to the state courts under the mandatory provision of Section 589(3) ZPO, discussed further below.[28]

1.   Reasoned Application

16-021 Article 16(2) requires that the challenging party provides the VIAC with the grounds on which it bases the allegation of bias. An unsubstantiated submission can be dismissed by the Board; in practice, the Secretary General (before forwarding the challenge to the Board for a decision) or the Board will return it to the challenging party with the request to substantiate the challenge within a certain period of time. The ultimate decision to accept or dismiss the challenge is, in any case, for the Board to make, and not the Secretary General, pursuant to Article 16(3).

---

23. P. Oberhammer, *Entwurf eines neuen Schiedsverfahrensrechts* (Vienna, Manz, 2002), p. 70.
24. The constitution of the tribunal is arguably the earliest point in time for launching a challenge. Before the tribunal is constituted, there is no body to receive, much less hear, a challenge. *See* M. Platte in *Arbitration Law of Austria: Practice and Procedure*, S. Riegler, A. Petsche, A. Fremuth-Wolf, M. Platte and C. Liebscher (eds) (Huntington, Juris Publishing, 2007), Section 589, p. 274. For a different view, *see* A. Reiner, *Das neue österreichische Schiedsrecht/The new Austrian Arbitration Law* (Vienna, LexisNexis, 2006), Section 589, note 84.
25. *See* Section 1036 German ZPO with a similar provision. *See* J.P. Lachmann, *Handbuch für die Schiedsgerichtspraxis* (3rd edn, Cologne, Verlag Dr. Otto Schmidt, 2008), p. 276.
26. *See* **Article 16**, at paras. 009 *et seq.*
27. J. Power, *The Austrian Arbitration Act – A Practitioner's Guide to Sections 577-618 of the Austrian Code of Civil Procedure* (Vienna, Manz, 2006), Section 589, para. 5.
28. Section 589(3) ZPO provides: 'The parties are free to agree on a procedure for challenging an arbitrator, subject to the provisions of subs. 3 of this section.'

As is also clear from Article 16(3), a challenging party can, and should in practice **16-022** be encouraged, to substantiate its challenge to the greatest extent possible, including by submitting evidence. Indeed, it has been suggested that, because the Board must consider the evidence attached to the challenge, a challenge without evidence is not admissible. This is too far-fetched. A challenge can be substantiated, setting out specific grounds for disqualification, even without proffering evidence; such a challenge will have to be considered by the Board. Whether a challenge is persuasive without attaching any evidence will depend on the circumstances; where possible, the parties are of course well advised to offer any evidence they might have at the outset.

2. Without Delay

According to Section 589(1) ZPO, the parties are free to agree on a procedure for **16-023** the challenge of an arbitrator that deviates from the mechanism established by Section 589 ZPO. Therefore, the parties can provide for a stricter procedure, *inter alia* by requiring that any challenge be brought within a shorter time frame than the four week period under Section 589(2) ZPO.

Arguably, Article 16(2) imposes such stricter conditions, requiring that any **16-024** challenge be brought 'without delay'. It is unfortunate that the Vienna Rules do not provide for a fixed period, such as two weeks, or the four weeks suggested by the statute. Arguably, the phrase 'without delay' means that parties have to bring a challenge immediately upon becoming aware of any disqualifying circumstances; a fairly strict standard would also best serve the underlying purpose of Article 16 to resolve any challenges expeditiously and with minimum disruption to the arbitration. On the other hand, a party ought to be given reasonable time to formulate its challenge in a substantiated manner. A challenge brought after four weeks from actual knowledge of disqualifying circumstances will, in view of Section 589(2) ZPO, be most likely 'delayed' within the meaning of Article 16.

A party who fails to bring a challenge within the prescribed time period cannot later **16-025** challenge the award on the basis that a biased arbitrator participated in the decision-making. In principle, save perhaps for exceptional circumstances discussed in greater detail below, an application for *vacatur* under Section 611 ZPO should not be permissible for a party who failed to comply with the time limits provided by Section 589(2) ZPO or Article 16(2) respectively.

3. Waiving the Right to a Challenge and Setting Aside the Award

A party becoming aware of disqualifying circumstances has a choice *not* to make a **16-026** challenge. This choice could be tactically motivated: if an arbitrator's bias is obvious enough, the other arbitrators on the tribunal may not give credibility to that arbitrator's position in the course of the tribunal's deliberations. However, under Austrian law, this choice has significant consequences. As discussed, a party that participates in the nomination of an arbitrator although it knows of disqualifying circumstances can no longer rely on these circumstances to raise a subsequent challenge.[29] Similarly, a party who waits beyond the four week period under Section 589(2) ZPO, or is otherwise delayed within the meaning of Article 16(2), cannot later raise a challenge. By missing the relevant time periods, parties forego their right to a challenge; and if their choice is deliberate, they affirmatively waive their right to a challenge.

16-027 Yet from a public policy perspective, the impartiality of arbitrators is not only designed to protect the parties, for example, in light of requirements of fair trial under Article 6 ECHR; it is also aimed at safeguarding the overall integrity of the process. It is conceivable, therefore, that certain severe instances of bias – such as a violation of the prohibition not to be a judge in one's own case – raise concerns of the *procedural ordre public*, which is now recognized as a ground for setting aside an award under Section 611(2) no. 5 ZPO.[30] Based on this rationale, the IBA Conflict Guidelines contain a Non-Waivable Red List[31] which exemplifies circumstances which must lead to the disqualification of an arbitrator; they are perceived as violations of impartiality so egregious as to prevent a waiver of the parties' right to a challenge with regard to these circumstances. In these cases, party autonomy is most likely superseded by public interest.

16-028 Of course, the IBA Conflict Guidelines do not have the force of law, in Austria or elsewhere,[32] and there is ongoing debate how this principle of non-waivable instances of bias, if it exists at all, fits into the Austrian legal system.[33] Under the fZPO, parties were always required to affirmatively challenge arbitrators; even in the presence of disqualifying circumstances, arbitrators were therefore not excluded from hearing a case unless a challenge was made.[34] Section 595(1) no. 4 fZPO provided for *vacatur* only if an arbitrator was challenged during the arbitration and the challenge was wrongfully rejected. The Austrian courts did also not allow for the challenge of an award on the basis that the arbitrator lacked contractually-agreed attributes, if the party was aware of these deficiencies at

---

29. *See* **Article 16**, at paras. 008 *et seq.*
30. F.T. Schwarz and H. Ortner, 'Procedural Ordre Public and the Internationalization of Public Policy in Arbitration' in *Austrian Arbitration Yearbook 2008*, C. Klausegger *et al.* (eds) (Vienna, Manz, 2008).
31. *See* IBA Conflict Guidelines, **Annex 17**.
32. *See* in detail **Article 7**, at paras. 083 *et seq.*, and 109.
33. F. T. Schwarz and H. Ortner, 'Procedural Ordre Public and the Internationalization of Public Policy in Arbitration' in *Austrian Arbitration Yearbook 2008*, C. Klausegger *et al.* (eds) (Vienna, Manz, 2008).
34. H.W. Fasching, *Schiedsgericht und Schiedsverfahren im österreichischen und im internationalen Recht* (Vienna, Manz, 1973), p. 62; W.H. Rechberger and W. Melis in *Kommentar zur ZPO*, W.H. Rechberger (ed.) (2nd edn, Vienna/New York, Springer, 2000), Section 586, para. 2. Apparently of contrary opinion, C. Liebscher, *The Healthy Award* (The Hague, Kluwer Law International, 2003), p. 274-5.

the time of the appointment.[35] Austrian doctrine, in requiring the aggrieved party to make an affirmative challenge to preserve its right to vacate the award, thus recognized the prominent role of party autonomy in arbitration.[36] If a party failed to make a (timely) complaint, the defect of bias was considered healed.

However, some commentators argued that there ought to be an exception to this **16-029** principle: the prohibition that the arbitrator must not be a party to the dispute.[37] It was proposed that this fundamental flaw cannot be cured.[38] Austrian doctrine and the courts thus limited the possibly unjust effects of that provision by confirming that the parties themselves and their representatives can never serve as arbitrators (even if no party raised a timely objection).[39]

Now, Section 611(2) no. 4 ZPO provides that an award is to be set aside if 'the **16-030** constitution or composition of the arbitral tribunal violated a provision of this chapter or a permissible agreement of the parties'. It is difficult to accept that the participation of a biased arbitrator would violate 'a provision of this chapter or a permissible agreement of the parties' if the parties, in full knowledge of the disqualifying circumstances, have failed to avail themselves of the appropriate remedies within the appropriate timeframe, as provided by the statute or the agreed institutional rules.

However, with Sections 588(2) (last sentence) and 589(2) ZPO, the 2006 reform not **16-031** only introduced provisions emphasizing the party's responsibility in making appropriate choices with respect to the constitution of the tribunal, it also introduced, or at least confirmed, the notion of a *procedural ordre public*.[40] Section 611(2) no. 5 ZPO

---

35. OGH, 30 September 1925, 3 Ob 740/25, SZ 7/295.
36. H.W. Fasching, *Schiedsgericht und Schiedsverfahren im österreichischen und im internationalen Recht* (Vienna, Manz, 1973), p. 62.
37. H.W. Fasching, *Schiedsgericht und Schiedsverfahren im österreichischen und im internationalen Recht* (Vienna, Manz, 1973), p. 62.
38. H.W. Fasching, *Schiedsgericht und Schiedsverfahren im österreichischen und im internationalen Recht* (Vienna, Manz, 1973), pp. 62 *et seq.* with further reference. *See also* W.H. Rechberger and M. Rami, 'Ablehnung von Schiedsrichtern durch die Parteien' [1999] wbl, 103 with further reference.
39. W.H. Rechberger and M. Rami, 'Ablehnung von Schiedsrichtern durch die Parteien' [1999] wbl, 103 with further reference. *See.*, however, BGH, 3 July 1975, III ZR 78/73 in BGHZ 65, 59, JZ 1976, 245, 247 (with annotation by *Schlosser*), in which the challenge of an arbitrator was rejected, even though the arbitrator was the legal representative, only because that arbitrator reached a decision against the party that appointed him and whose representative he was. As *Rechberger/Rami* point out correctly, it must be irrelevant which decision the arbitrator reached in the end. The arbitrator deciding against 'his party' to demonstrate his 'independence' is just as biased as the arbitrator who is favorably inclined. Indeed, the purpose of the rules of arbitrators' independence is also to achieve an abstraction from the circumstances of the individual case, so as to safeguard the integrity of the arbitral process. *See* W.H. Rechberger and M. Rami, 'Ablehnung von Schiedsrichtern durch die Parteien' [1999] wbl, 103, 105.
40. F.T. Schwarz and H. Ortner, 'Procedural Ordre Public and the Internationalization of Public Policy in Arbitration' in *Austrian Arbitration Yearbook 2008*, C. Klausegger *et al.* (eds) (Vienna, Manz, 2008).

provides that an award must be set aside if 'the arbitral proceedings were conducted in a way that is in conflict with public policy.'

16-032 It is conceivable to argue that some rare and particularly egregious cases of bias – such as the examples given in the IBA Non-Waivable Red List[41] or Section 19 JN[42] – make the participation of an arbitrator unacceptable from the perspective of *procedural ordre public*. This would in particular include instances where an arbitrator essentially decides upon his or her own case. An argument based on Section 611(2) no. 5 ZPO would further posit that the public interest in maintaining and protecting the *procedural ordre public* superseded a party's failure to bring a challenge within the timeframes provided in Section 589 ZPO and Article 16, respectively.

16-033 Based on public policy considerations, such instances of severe bias are arguably not at the parties' disposition: even where parties choose not to bring a challenge, such cases of severe bias could be argued to be intolerable from the perspective of a state (who may indeed be required to give effect to minimum standards of fair trial and to provide for oversight through its own state courts). If that were true, then a party's choice not to bring a timely challenge (or to participate in the nomination of an arbitrator who is known to that party to be severely biased) would not preclude a setting aside of the award under Section 611(2) no. 5 ZPO.

16-034 On the other hand, it bears emphasis that a violation of the *procedural ordre public* (as opposed to a violation of the *substantive ordre public* under Section 611(2) no. 7 ZPO) will not be considered *ex officio*.[43] Indeed, the Austrian legislature has made a – perhaps decisive – distinction between the treatment of *procedural* and *substantive ordre public* in the context of setting aside proceedings. While the court must take the *substantive ordre public* into account *ex officio*,[44] the matter of *procedural ordre public* is considered by the court only upon application by a party.

16-035 A violation of the *procedural ordre public* is therefore not treated as outside the parties' disposition – a party can choose whether to raise such a violation or not. Being firmly grounded within the sphere of party autonomy, however, such choices are then also a party's responsibility. By leaving it to the aggrieved party to rely on the *procedural ordre public*, the Austrian legislature has put the enforcement of the procedural public order back into the parties' hands. What is at the parties' disposition, however, can also be waived by the parties. When a party acquiesces in the nomination of an arbitrator who is biased even for severe reasons, or knowingly chooses not to bring a timely challenge against a severely biased arbitrator, the resulting violation of the *procedural ordre public* would not be imposed on this party, but would be the result of its own choices.

---

41. IBA Conflict Guidelines, **Annex 17**.
42. *See* **Article 7**, at para. 102.
43. *See* Section 611(3) ZPO.
44. Section 611(3) ZPO.

Moreover, if the legislature explicitly excludes a remedy against the court decision **16-036** under Section 589(3) ZPO, it is hard to imagine that it intended to provide the parties with a subsequent remedy although the party had failed to initiate a challenge, or file an appeal, in the first place.

Although these principles have yet to be examined by the courts, the better view **16-037** appears to be, therefore, that Section 588(2) and Section 589 ZPO should not be undermined by allowing the party to later opt out of its own choices under the disguise of a *procedural ordre public* violation.[45] As a result, the most reasonable construction of Section 588(2) (last sentence) and Section 589(2) ZPO (as well as Article 16) is that the parties have the opportunity to initiate a challenge against a purportedly biased arbitrator *only* within the timeframe prescribed by the law. As a matter of principle, therefore, a party that fails to bring a timely challenge under the ZPO or Article 16, if applicable, is deemed to have waived its right to apply for the setting aside of the award.

It is conceivable, however, that a party becomes aware of disqualifying circum- **16-038** stances only after the award is issued. Grounds for disqualification not known to a party, neither at the time of nomination nor during the entire arbitration, may then be relied upon in setting aside proceedings pursuant to Section 611(2) nc. 4 ZPO, or, where such grounds form part of the *procedural ordre public*, pursuant to Section 611(2) no. 5 ZPO.

Any such application must be made within three months from the receipt of the **16-039** award, pursuant to Section 611(4) ZPO. This is a final deadline, which, in the interest of legal certainty, is meant to preclude any further action against the award.[46] It has been suggested, however, that other courts, for example in the context of enforcement proceedings, could take *ordre public* considerations into account, and thus effectively address cases of severe bias, beyond the three month period.[47] This suggestion is based on Section 613 ZPO which provides that '[i]f a court or another authority determines in another proceeding, for instance in an enforcement proceeding, that there is a reason for setting aside under Section 611(2) nos 7 and 8 ZPO, then the award shall be disregarded in this proceeding.' It is true that the application of Section 613 ZPO is not linked to any time period, so that courts or authority can disregard an award for an indefinite period of time. However, Section 613 ZPO expressly refers to the grounds for setting aside pre- scribed in Section 611(2) nos 7 and 8 ZPO, which regulate non-arbitrability and

---

45. F. T. Schwarz and H. Ortner, 'Procedural Ordre Public and the Internationalization of Public Policy in Arbitration' in *Austrian Arbitration Yearbook 2008*, C. Klausegger *et al.* (eds) (Vienna, Manz, 2008).
46. M. Platte in *Arbitration Law of Austria: Practice and Procedure*, S. Riegler, A. Petsche, A. Fremuth-Wolf, M. Platte and C. Liebscher (eds) (Huntington, Juris Publishing, 2007), Section 588, pp. 263 *et seq.*
47. M. Platte in *Arbitration Law of Austria: Practice and Procedure*, S. Riegler, A. Petsche, A. Fremuth-Wolf, M. Platte and C. Liebscher (eds) (Huntington, Juris Publishing, 2007), Section 588, pp. 263 *et seq.*

violations of the *substantive ordre public*. The participation of a severely biased arbitrator, however, constitutes, if at all, a violation of the *procedural ordre public*, so that Section 613 ZPO is not applicable to such cases.

III.   THE BOARD'S DECISION ON THE CHALLENGE

> **Article 16(3): Should the challenged arbitrator not withdraw from his office, the Board shall decide upon the challenge on the basis of the particulars in the challenging motion and the evidence attached thereto. Before the Board makes its decision, the Secretary General must obtain the comments of the arbitrator challenged and of the other parties. The Board can also request comments from other persons.**

16-040 Under the Vienna Rules, the power to decide upon a challenge is vested with the Board. Although Article 16(3) refers only to the Board's power to decide upon the merits of a challenge, the Board is also the proper forum to decide on the admissibility of the challenge under Article 16(2).

A.   Opportunity for Voluntary Withdrawal

16-041 As Article 16(3) makes clear, and as discussed above,[48] the arbitrator must be given the opportunity to voluntarily withdraw before the Board can proceed to decide on the challenge. If disqualifying circumstances actually exist, the arbitrator is obliged to do so. But even where no such reasons exist, an arbitrator exposed to a challenge may wish to consider whether a withdrawal would help the dynamics on the tribunal, or otherwise preserve the acceptance of the process. To protect an arbitrator in such circumstances, Section 590(3) ZPO now provides that the withdrawal 'does not imply acceptance of the validity of any ground' suggestive of the lack of impartiality or independence.

16-042 As also discussed, if the challenge is brought at the start of the arbitration, then an arbitrator's withdrawal cannot considerably disrupt the proceedings. However, if there are no objectively disqualifying circumstances, an arbitrator has a duty to remain in office to discharge his or her judicial function to both parties, maintaining the appointing party's right to have an arbitrator of its choosing hear the case, and avoiding the delay and obstruction of having to appoint a replacement.[49] For challenges launched at later stages of the proceeding, these considerations may well compel the arbitrator not to withdraw if he thinks the challenge is unjustified.[50]

---

48. *See* **Article 16**, at para. 016.
49. *See* **Article 7**, at para. 053.
50. *See* **Article 7**, paras. 053 *et seq.*

B.   DECISION-MAKING

When deciding on the merits of the challenge, the Board *must* take into account the **16-043** position of, and the evidence submitted by, the challenging party, and it *must* consider the position of the challenged arbitrator. In contrast to its predecessor provision of Article 11 of the Vienna Rules 2001,[51] the Board *must* now also hear all other parties before reaching a decision. This is a welcome confirmation of what constituted the VIAC's practice in any event. From a due process perspective, both parties to the arbitration should be heard because a challenge interferes with a party's right to have the dispute decided by an arbitrator of its choosing. As discussed in greater detail elsewhere, a party's right to participate in the constitution and appointment of the tribunal is considered a fundamental procedural right in arbitration.[52]

In addition, the Board still has the power – but under the terms of Article 16(3) not the **16-044** obligation – to hear other persons as well (such as the co-arbitrators, where applicable). As a matter of principle, however, the VIAC does not conduct any oral hearing before it decides on the challenge. As a result, the Board's decision is reached based on a summary proceeding, with evidence, by way of documents or conceivably witness statements or affidavits, and submissions being made in writing. However, if it were appropriate under the particular circumstances of a case, it ought to be in the Board's discretion to hear the parties, or to hear witnesses, orally as well.

Although it is not obliged to do so under the wording of Article 16, the Board **16-045** provides reasoned decisions in practice. This was always helpful to increase the acceptance of the Board's decision in the eyes of the parties, but has gained even more importance now with the introduction of a direct appeal mechanism against the Board's decision, discussed below. To be in a position to review the Board's decision, the state court will be aided by the reasons that the Board has given for rejecting the challenge.

In addition, the VIAC should seriously consider, as other institutions are in the **16-046** process of doing, to publish its decisions on challenges in anonymous form. Users of arbitration would benefit greatly from a body of precedent which would generally enhance the accountability of the institution and the transparency of the overall process. It would also provide useful guidance to arbitrators, and to counsel, in assessing the merits of future challenges.

C.   REMEDIES BEFORE THE STATE COURTS

Section 589(3) ZPO now provides: **16-047**

If a challenge under any procedure agreed upon by the parties or under the procedure of subs. 2 of this section is not successful, the challenging party may

---

51.   Vienna Rules 2001, **Annex 2a**.
52.   *See* **Article 14**, at para. 001.

request the court to decide on the challenge within four weeks after having received notice of the decision rejecting the challenge. No remedies are permitted against this decision. While such a request is pending, the arbitral tribunal, including the challenged arbitrator, may continue the arbitral proceedings and make an award.

16-048 This provision introduces a level of mandatory[53] control by the state courts[54] with regard to any decision taken by the VIAC under Article 16 (or by an arbitral tribunal under Section 589(2) ZPO) that rejects a challenge to an arbitrator.

16-049 The challenging party must bring its appeal within four weeks after having received the Board's decision rejecting the challenge. If a party fails to file its appeal in time, it is deemed to have waived its objections against the challenged arbitrator. Clearly, the legislature expressed its desire, by virtue of Section 589(3) ZPO, to bring finality and certainty to any challenge at as early a stage in the proceedings as possible.

16-050 The nature of the court proceedings is difficult to describe. In substance, the application to the court is a *de facto* appeal. Procedurally, it is an application in its own right (as there is no appellate hierarchy between the VIAC and the Austrian courts), and Section 589(3) ZPO requires the court simply to 'decide on the challenge'. However, the substantive nature of the application as an appeal mechanism arguably has import on the scope of arguments available to the challenging party before the court. On that view, the challenging party can only rely on factual grounds that it has advanced in its challenge to the VIAC. New factual grounds would constitute a new ground for challenge, which would have to be brought to the VIAC first, before it can be heard by the Austrian court under Section 589(3) ZPO. On the other hand, considerations of procedural efficiency might advocate for having the challenge of an arbitrator comprehensively resolved, in order to avoid further proceedings and to proceed with the arbitration without further disruption.

16-051 The court's decision under Section 589(3) ZPO is final and binding. Accordingly, a party that has failed to timely 'appeal' against the tribunal's decision, or that is now unsuccessful before the court, is not permitted to apply for the setting aside of the award on the same grounds (*see*, again, the discussion of waiver at **Article 16**, at paras. 026 *et seq*).[55]

16-052 Section 589(3) ZPO thus corrects what was perceived as a major shortcoming of the regime applicable under the fZPO. Under that regime, the tribunal's (or the VIAC's) decision rejecting a challenge was *not* subject to recourse before the courts. Rather, an aggrieved party was required to wait until the end of

---

53. *See* Explanatory Notes to Section 589 ZPO.
54. Jurisdiction is determined under Sections 615 and 616 ZPO.
55. *See* Explanatory Notes to Section 589 ZPO; C. Liebscher, *The Austrian Arbitration Act 2006: Text and Notes* (The Hague, Kluwer Law International, 2006), Annotated Text to Section 589(3) ZPO.

the proceeding and raise the issue of impartiality at the *vacatur* stage. The situation under the fZPO was for obvious reasons not satisfying, as it forced parties to endure an arbitration with a biased arbitrator, potentially wasting the expense and time of an entire proceeding, before it could properly raise the issue with the courts.[56]

At the same time, Section 589(3) ZPO leaves it to the arbitrators' discretion to **16-053** continue the arbitration and to make an award, with the participation of the arbitrator, while such the appeal is pending before the courts. This is intended to counter delaying tactics by parties, similar to Section 1037(3) German ZPO.[57] If the court regards the challenge of the arbitrator as justified, the arbitral award can be set aside under Section 611(2) no. 4 ZPO.[58]

By contrast, a successful challenge, whether before the tribunal under Section 589(2) **16-054** ZPO or under institutional rules, is not subject to appeal to the state courts. Although an erroneous decision that allows a challenge where no disqualifying circumstances exist infringes the appointing party's right to have an arbitrator of its choosing, the legislature decided, on balance, in the interest of speed. If a challenge is successful, the prevailing consideration is to move the arbitration forward, including by appointing a substitute arbitrator,[59] as expeditiously as possible, rather than delaying the final resolution by permitting further proceedings on appeal.

IV. CONTINUATION OF THE PROCEEDINGS DURING THE CHALLENGE

Article 16(4): An arbitrator challenged may continue the proceedings, notwithstanding the challenging motion. However, an award may not be rendered until after the final and binding decision of the Board.

Both the Vienna Rules and the ZPO provide for the possibility to continue the **16-055** arbitration while the challenge is pending with the VIAC and the Austrian courts, respectively. These provisions are designed to off-set adverse effects of obstructive and ultimately unsuccessful challenges on the expeditious conduct of the arbitration.

Article 11(5) of the Vienna Rules 2001[60] provided, in fact, that while the decision **16-056** on the challenge is pending before the Board, the challenged arbitrator, whether as

---

56. W.H. Rechberger and M. Rami, 'Ablehnung von Schiedsrichtern durch die Parteien' [1999] wbl, 103, 104.
57. K.H. Schwab and G. Walter (eds), *Schiedsgerichtsbarkeit* (7th edn, Munich, C.H. Beck, 2005), ch. 14, para. 26; R. Geimer in *Zöller – Zivilprozessordnung*, R. Zöller *et al.* (eds) (26th edn, Cologne, Verlag Dr. Otto Schmidt, 2007), Section 1037, para. 5.
58. R. Geimer in *Zöller – Zivilprozessordnung*, R. Zöller *et al.* (eds) (26th edn, Cologne, Verlag Dr. Otto Schmidt, 2007), Section 1059, paras. 42 *et seq.*
59. *See* **Article 18**, at paras. 001 *et seq.*
60. Vienna Rules 2001, **Annex 2a**.

sole arbitrator or as part of a tribunal, *must* continue with the proceedings. Article 16(4) now gives the arbitrator the possibility to continue the arbitration, without obliging him to do so. This discretion follows Section 589(3) ZPO, which also provides that 'the arbitral tribunal, including the challenged arbitrator, may continue the arbitral proceedings'. As discussed elsewhere,[61] arbitrators are required to conduct the arbitration with appropriate expedition. That does not mean, however, that the arbitrators cannot take the challenge into account when fixing the procedural timetable or undertaking further procedural steps. Rather, the arbitrators are free to schedule the further steps of the arbitration as is most appropriate under the circumstances, seeking to advance the arbitration while at the same time avoiding wasted costs, should the challenge be successful.

16-057 There is, however, an important difference between the continuation of proceeding while a challenge is pending before the Board under Article 16, and a challenge pending before the courts under Section 589(3) ZPO. In the first case, while the challenge is pending before the Board under Article 16, no award may be issued. This provision reflects common-sense; a decision on the challenge should logically precede the arbitrator's final decision on the merits. In contrast, a further appeal to the state court does not prevent the full progress of the arbitration. Section 589(3) ZPO expressly provides that '[w]hile such a request is pending [before the court], the arbitral tribunal, including the challenged arbitrator, may continue the arbitral proceedings and *make an award*'. As a result of the Vienna Rules and Austrian law, the arbitration can therefore proceed (if the arbitrator deems this appropriate) throughout the challenge before the VIAC Board *and* the appeal before the state court to a final award, further enhancing the speedy resolution of the parties' dispute.

---

61. *See* **Article 7**, at paras. 059 *et seq.*

Article 17

Early Termination of the Mandate of Arbitrators

	Para.			Para.
I. Reasons for Early Termination	1		4. Removal by the Board	12
A. Introduction	1	II.	Request to Remove the	
B. Grounds of Termination	4		Arbitrator	13
1. Agreement on Termination	5		A. Grounds for Removal	14
2. Voluntary Withdrawal from			B. Procedure	17
Office	7		C. *Ex Officio* Removal	19
3. Successful Challenge	11		D. Court Review	21

I.   REASONS FOR EARLY TERMINATION

Article 17(1): The mandate of an arbitrator terminates when
(a) the parties agree on the termination
(b) the arbitrator withdraws from office
(c) a challenging motion is granted
(d) the arbitrator is removed from his office by the Board.

A.   INTRODUCTION

The arbitrators' mandate typically ends, and they become *functus officio*, when **17-001**
they render a final award and conclude the arbitration. At most, they retain residual
jurisdiction for clarifications of the award under **Article 29** and Section 610 ZPO.
However, there are instances when an arbitrator's mandate is terminated before he
or she can issue a final award. These instances are addressed in Article 17.

Article 17 was added as a reaction to the new Austrian Arbitration Act, and in **17-002**
particular Section 590 ZPO. Section 590 ZPO specifically provides that the

mandate of an arbitrator terminates when the parties agree on the termination, or when the arbitrator withdraws from office. In addition, Section 590 ZPO allows parties 'to agree on a procedure regarding the termination of the arbitrator mandate', which was meant to allow parties to delegate the decision on the termination of an arbitrator's mandate to an arbitral institution. However, Section 590 ZPO also provides that this decision is subject to court review.

17-003 Article 17 therefore implements the circumstances under which an arbitrator mandate terminates under Section 590 ZPO within the framework of the Vienna Rules, and provides for a removal procedure, which is subject to mandatory review by the Austrian courts pursuing to Section 590 ZPO.[1]

B.   Grounds of Termination

17-004 Section 590 ZPO provides essentially for two grounds for the termination of an arbitrators mandate. First, an arbitrator's mandate terminates when the parties agree on the termination, and second, when the arbitrator withdraws from office. By way of clarification, and taking into account the specific procedure set forth in Article 17(2), Article 17(1) clarifies that a successful challenge or a removal of the arbitrator by the Board also terminates the mandate of the arbitrator.

1.   Agreement on Termination

17-005 Both Section 590(1) ZPO and Article 17(1)(a) provide in unison that the arbitrator's mandate expires if the parties agree on the termination. Just as with the constitution of the tribunal, and a subsequent challenge of the arbitrators mandate under **Article 16**, the parties are the masters of the procedure. At any time of the proceeding, they can agree to terminate the mandate of an arbitrator, irrespective of whether that arbitrator serves as a co-arbitrator, sole arbitrator, or chairman of the tribunal. This principle is also reflected in Section 589(2) ZPO, according to which an arbitrator can be removed, without a formal challenge procedure, if the other party so agrees. If the parties are in agreement regarding the unsuitability of an arbitrator, the arbitrator is required to resign.[2]

17-006 In practice, parties will be hesitant to agree on the termination of an arbitrator's mandate, in particular if the proceedings are substantially progressed. The termination of an arbitrator's mandate at an advanced stage of the proceedings runs the risk of significant delay and obstruction, including the risk that the proceedings will have to be repeated in part or altogether.[3] Also, the arbitrator forced to resign will generally claim fees and costs incurred up to the time of the parties' agreement. If the parties want to avoid being exposed to such a claim for fees by the

1.   *See* **Article 17**, at paras. 021 *et seq.*
2.   *See* **Article 16**, at para. 018.
3.   *See* **Article 18**, at paras. 007 *et seq.*

arbitrator, they will consider challenging the arbitrator for bias or applying to the Board to have the arbitrator removed. This is because the termination of an arbitrator's mandate as the result of fault on the arbitrator's part results in the arbitrator's loss of his claim for compensation.[4]

2. Voluntary Withdrawal from Office

The voluntary withdrawal of an arbitrator has already been discussed in the context **17-007** of a challenge under **Article 16**, or Section 589 ZPO.[5] Section 590(1) ZPO clarifies that, if the arbitrator himself chooses to withdraw from office, his mandate is terminated.

As also discussed, it must be examined on a case by case basis whether or not the **17-008** voluntary withdrawal of the arbitrator is justified. If an arbitrator becomes aware of disqualifying circumstances, he or she is under an obligation to withdraw.[6] Also, a withdrawal at the beginning of the proceedings – perhaps because of the dynamics on the tribunal or the arbitrator's realization that, for personal, scheduling or other reasons he is not best suited to serve in this case – will typically not disrupt the proceedings.

It has been argued that Section 590(1) ZPO is a mandatory provision and that, in **17-009** providing for the voluntary withdrawal, it installs a mandatory and 'unlimited right of withdrawal'.[7] However, Section 590(1) ZPO merely provides that the mandate ends with the withdrawal. As a result, the arbitrator cannot be forced to stay in office against his or her will. This does not mean that every withdrawal is justified, or that the arbitrator has a right to withdraw as against the parties.[8] Indeed, as discussed in detail, an arbitrator has a general duty to remain in office to discharge his or her judicial function to both parties, maintaining the appointing parties' right to have an arbitrator of their choosing hear the case and avoiding the delay and obstruction of having to appoint a replacement.[9] These considerations may well compel the arbitrator not to withdraw, so not to be in violation of his contractual duty to render an award,[10] and possibly incur liability under Section 594(4) ZPO.[11]

---

4. *See* **Article 7**, at para. 148.
5. *See* **Article 16**, at paras. 016 *et seq.*
6. *See* **Article 7**, at para. 053; *see also* IBA Conflict Guidelines, **Annex 17** and **Article 7**, at paras. 004 and 027.
7. A. Reiner, *Das neue österreichische Schiedsrecht/The new Austrian Arbitration Law* (Vienna, LexisNexis, 2006), Section 590, note 90.
8. Indeed, the legislative materials make clear that a withdrawal, even if it terminates the mandate, does not release the arbitrator from his contractual obligations *vis-à-vis* the parties. *See* Explanatory Notes to Section 590.
9. *See* **Article 7**, at paras. 052 *et seq.*
10. *See* **Article 7**, at para. 053. Others argue, although without substantiation, that an arbitrator does not have to show good cause for resigning. *See* J. Power, *The Austrian Arbitration Act – A Practitioner's Guide to Sections 577-618 of the Austrian Code of Civil Procedure* (Vienna, Manz, 2006), Section 590, para. 2 with further references.
11. *See* **Article 8**, at para. 008 *et seq.*

17-010 To facilitate the withdrawal, and to protect an arbitrator in justified circum-stances,[12] Section 590(3) ZPO provides that the withdrawal 'does not imply accep-tance of the validity of any ground' suggestive of the lack of impartiality or independence, or enumerated in Section 590(2) ZPO. In other words, voluntary withdrawal is held not to imply an admission by the arbitrator that he is either biased or unable to discharge his duties, or in delay of doing so. However, this merely creates a statutory presumption that the withdrawal was justified; as any *praesumptio iuris*, it is for the aggrieved party to show that the withdrawal was in fact not justified in the circumstances. As discussed, the withdrawal is effective whether it is justified or not, but if the reasons for the withdrawal are insufficient, the arbitrator may be liable pursuant to Section 594(4) ZPO.[13]

3.   Successful Challenge

17-011 Article 17 now clarifies what applies as a matter of course, that a successful challenge under **Article 16** or Section 589 ZPO also leads to the immediate ter-mination of the arbitrator's mandate. In such a case, the termination is effective as soon as the challenged arbitrator is served with the Board's decision (or the subsequent decision of a state court under Section 589(3) ZPO).

4.   Removal by the Board

17-012 Article 17(1)(d) provides that the mandate of the arbitrator is terminated if the arbitrator is removed from his office by the Board. This refers to the particular procedure regulated by Article 17(2), discussed further below. Again, the termi-nation of the arbitrator's mandate is, as a *contrarius actus* to the appointment by the Board, effective with the receipt by the arbitrator of the Board's decision to remove him.

II.   REQUEST TO REMOVE THE ARBITRATOR

> **Article 17(2): Any party may request the termination of the mandate of an arbitrator if the latter's incapacitation is not merely temporary, if he otherwise fails to perform his duties or unduly delays the proceedings. The request must be submitted to the Secretariat. The Board shall decide upon the request after hearing the arbitrator in question. If it is clear that incapacitation is not merely temporary, the Board may terminate the arbitrator's mandate even without a request from a party.**

---

12.   A. Reiner, *Das neue österreichische Schiedsrecht/The new Austrian Arbitration Law* (Vienna, LexisNexis, 2006), Section 590, note 91.

13.   *See* **Article 8**, at paras. 008 *et seq*. *See also* C. Liebscher, *The Austrian Arbitration Act 2006: Text and Notes* (The Hague, Kluwer Law International, 2006), Annotated Text to Section 590(1) ZPO.

As a threshold issue, any request by one party that an arbitrator be removed from **17-013** office presupposes that there was neither an agreement between the parties on the termination, nor a voluntary withdrawal by the arbitrator. In such cases, a party may request the Board to decide on the termination of the mandate on two principal grounds.

A.   GROUNDS FOR REMOVAL

First, a request can be based on the non-temporary incapacitation of the arbitrator. **17-014** Notably, the Vienna Rules do not require that the arbitrator must be permanently incapacitated, such as through death or other permanent circumstances. Of course, the Vienna Rules leave out what level of incapacitation exceeds an acceptable temporary unavailability of the arbitrator. This cannot be determined in the abstract, but will depend both on the nature of the case, the surrounding circumstances and the extent of the incapacitation. For example, the hospitalization of an arbitrator for a limited period of time will usually not justify the termination of a mandate. However, in circumstances where the parties have agreed on a fast-track procedure which is intended to serve important business objectives, a two-month hospitalization could frustrate the entire arbitral process and may therefore exceed the acceptable level of incapacitation. Any request to the Board will therefore be well advised to specify in detail why the expected period of incapacitation is not acceptable in the circumstances of the case. Notably, the temporary incapacitation of an arbitrator may well not be the arbitrator's fault. Rather, it describes an objective state in which the arbitrator is unable to perform his duties.

Second, a party may request the termination of an arbitrator's mandate if the **17-015** arbitrator 'otherwise fails to perform his duties or unduly delays the proceedings'. This category refers to cases where the arbitrator fails to perform his function in accordance with his duties.[14] It therefore refers to cases in which the arbitrator does not react to the parties' requests or is otherwise unwilling to progress the arbitration with due expedition. It also allows an arbitrator who his unduly delayed in rendering an award to be removed.

However, this scenario raises difficult issues in terms of procedural efficiencies. **17-016** For example, removing a sole arbitrator who has not rendered a final award for an extended period of time after the closing of the oral hearing, may have short-term benefits, but must result pursuant to **Article 18**, in the appointment of a substitute arbitrator who will at a minimum have to read into the file. In fact-intensive cases, or in case of the removed arbitrator's file being inconclusive, the new arbitrator may very well decide to rehear witnesses or otherwise repeat at least phases of the proceedings, which of course leads to further delays. Institutions are therefore hesitant to remove an arbitrator for reasons of delay at a final stage, for fear of causing yet greater disruption to the process by virtue of the removal.

---

14.   For descriptions of the arbitrators duties, *see* **Article 7**, at paras. 049 *et seq.*

B.   PROCEDURE

17-017 The request must be submitted to the Secretary General. The request must be in writing and state the reasons that justify the removal in the eyes of the applicant party.

17-018 Article 17 provides that the Board shall decide upon the request after hearing the arbitrator in question; however, due process considerations should compel the Board to hear the opposing party as well. As discussed previously, it is a fundamental right of a party to participate in a constitution of the tribunal and to have an arbitrator of its choosing decide the dispute.[15] Removing an arbitrator without hearing the party who nominated that arbitrator in the first place infringes substantially upon that right.

C.   *EX OFFICIO* REMOVAL

17-019 In cases of non-temporary incapacitation, the Board has the power to remove an arbitrator *ex officio*, without the application of a party to that effect. It is striking that the Vienna Rules do not provide for that same *ex officio* authority of the Board for cases where arbitrators fail to perform their duties or otherwise delay the proceedings. It is debatable whether, in the interest of the integrity of the arbitral process, that distinction is in fact justified. On the one hand, the actual incapacitation of an arbitrator is, as discussed, an objective criterion, which is relatively easy for the Board to determine. In contrast, what constitutes delay is more likely than not in the eyes of the beholder. The judgment incorporated in the Vienna Rules therefore is that cases of delay must be so severe that they prompt an application from the parties, whereas cases of incapacitation are *per se* so disruptive that they justify an *ex officio* intervention by the Board.

17-020 While that consideration has its merits, it is not entirely clear why the Board should not at least have the possibility of exercising an *ex officio* authority also with respect to cases of delay. For the reasons outlined above, the Board would exercise that authority perhaps in a more restrained manner, but could do so to protect the particular proceedings as well as the arbitral process in general, if the circumstances of the case so demanded.

D.   COURT REVIEW

17-021 Section 590(2) ZPO now provides for a mandatory review by the courts of any decision by the VIAC or another arbitral institution 'that does not result in the termination of the arbitrators mandate'. The review process envisaged by Section

---

15. *See* **Article 14**, at para. 001 and **Article 15**, at para. 033.

590(2) ZPO mirrors the court review established for the challenge of arbitrators for lack of impartiality or independence or agreed requirements. In both cases, a decision (by the tribunal or the VIAC) that leads to the removal of the arbitrator is not subject to appeal before the state courts. However, a decision (by the tribunal or the VIAC) that rejects either the challenge or the request of a party to terminate the arbitrator's mandate is subject to mandatory court review pursuant to Section 590(2) ZPO.

Specifically, Section 590(2) ZPO provides that   **17-022**

> any party may request the court to decide on the termination of the mandate where an arbitrator either becomes unable to perform his functions or fails to act within a reasonable period of time and (1) the arbitrator does not withdraw from office, (2) the parties cannot agree on his termination or (3) the procedure agreed upon by the parties does not result in the termination of the arbitrators mandate. This decision shall not be subject to appeal.

As with the procedure under Article 17(2), any request to the state courts is **17-023** premised, first of all, on the fact that the arbitrator did not voluntarily withdraw from office, and that the parties were unable to agree on his termination. If these two conditions are not met, parties can apply to the state courts to have the arbitrator removed. In *ad hoc* arbitration (and unlike a challenge for alleged bias), the removal is decided by the courts in the first instance, and not by the tribunal.[16]

However, if the parties have agreed, as they do by incorporating the Vienna Rules **17-024** into their arbitration agreement, on a specific procedure for the removal of an arbitrator, than they have to go through with this procedure first and await its results. If the result is such that the arbitrator is not removed, which in the context of the Vienna Rules means that the Board refuses to terminate the arbitrator's mandate under Article 17(2), then this negative decision of the VIAC is subject to review by the state courts.

In deciding on the request to remove the arbitrator, the courts will have to follow a **17-025** similar rationale as the one expressed in Article 17(2). Section 590 ZPO allows a request on the termination of the mandate 'when an arbitrator either becomes unable to perform his functions or fails to act within a reasonable period of time'. In essence, this mirrors the two categories of grounds for removal expressed in Article 17(2) – the objective incapacitation (is 'unable'), which in the case of Section 590 ZPO is not linked to a temporary element, on the one hand, and the arbitrator's subjective 'fail[ure] to act' within a reasonable period of time, therefore leading to a delay in the arbitration, on the other hand.

---

16. A. Reiner, *Das neue österreichische Schiedsrecht/The new Austrian Arbitration Law* (Vienna, LexisNexis, 2006), Section 590, note 89.

17-026 Interestingly, Section 590(2) ZPO does not provide a time limit within which an appeal against the decision of the Board must be filed with state courts.[17] This is an unfortunate, and apparently inadvertent, *lacuna*. For obvious reasons, the arbitral process will benefit from having certainty about the arbitrator's status as quickly as possible, and unreasonable delays should not be permitted. Given the parallel systemic structure of an appeal under Section 590 ZPO and an appeal against the dismissal of a challenge of an allegedly biased arbitrator under Section 589 ZPO, the four week appeal period of Section 589(3) ZPO should arguably be applicable by analogy for court review under Section 590 ZPO as well.

17-027 In any event, Section 590 ZPO makes clear that no appeal is available to review the state court's decision. Grounds for removal rejected by the Board, as subsequently confirmed by the courts, cannot later be raised in setting aside proceedings under Section 611 ZPO. The possibility to request court review once is sufficient to protect the interests of the parties and the integrity of the arbitral process.[18]

---

17. *Platte* suggests that the appeal must be brought 'within a reasonable period of time', as if that were a factor under Section 590 ZPO. *See* M. Platte in *Arbitration Law of Austria: Practice and Procedure*, S. Riegler, A. Petsche, A. Fremuth-Wolf, M. Platte and C. Liebscher (eds) (Huntington, Juris Publishing, 2007), Section 590, p. 283. This misreads the text of the statute. An arbitrator can be removed if he 'fails to act within a reasonable period of time'; this does not refer to the time within which an appeal must be filed.

18. Some authors argue that the grounds for removal can be invoked in setting aside proceedings, despite an unsuccessful appeal to the state courts under Section 590 ZPO, if they constitute a violation of *procedural ordre public*. *See* J. Power, *The Austrian Arbitration Act – A Practitioner's Guide to Sections 577-618 of the Austrian Code of Civil Procedure* (Vienna, Manz, 2006), Section 590, para. 5. This is not convincing. As discussed in detail at **Article 16**, at para. 034, a violation of the *procedural ordre public* (as opposed to a violation of the *substantive ordre public* under Section 611(2) no. 7 ZPO) will not be considered *ex officio*. Rather, the Austrian legislature has made the decisive judgment that issues of *procedural ordre public* are considered by the court only upon application by a party. A violation of the *procedural ordre public* is therefore not treated as outside the parties' disposition – a party can choose whether to raise such a violation or not. Being firmly grounded within the sphere of party autonomy, however, such choices are then also a party's responsibility. By leaving it to the aggrieved party to rely on the *procedural ordre public*, the Austrian legislature has put the enforcement of the procedural public order back into the parties' hands. What is at the parties' disposition, however, can also be waived by the parties. When a party acquiesces in the nomination of an arbitrator who is biased even for severe reasons, or knowingly chooses not to bring a timely challenge against a severely biased arbitrator, the resulting violation of the *procedural ordre public* would not be imposed on this party, but would be the result of its own choices. Moreover, if the legislature explicitly excludes a remedy against the court decision under Section 590(3) ZPO (as under Section 589(3) ZPO), it is hard to imagine, and difficult to justify, that it intended to provide the parties with a subsequent remedy although the party had failed to succeed on appeal in the first place. *See also* F.T. Schwarz and H. Ortner, 'Procedural Ordre Public and the Internationalization of Public Policy in Arbitration' in *Austrian Arbitration Yearbook 2008*, C. Klausegger *et al.* (eds) (Vienna, Manz, 2008).

Article 18

Consequences of Challenge or Early Termination of Mandate

	Para.		Para.
I. Appointing a Replacement Arbitrator 1		II. Repeating Previous Stages of the Procedure 7	

I. APPOINTING A REPLACEMENT ARBITRATOR

Article 18(1): If the challenge of an arbitrator has been allowed, if his mandate has been terminated, if he has resigned his mandate or has died, then,
(a) If that arbitrator is a sole arbitrator, the parties – or,
(b) If that arbitrator is the Chairman, the remaining arbitrators – or
(c) If that arbitrator has been nominated by a party or has been appointed for a party, the party that nominated him or for which he was appointed
shall be requested to nominate a new arbitrator within thirty days – by mutual consent in the cases covered by subparagraphs a) and b) of the present paragraph – and to indicate his name and address. If no such indication is received within that period, the new arbitrator shall be appointed by the Board. If a new arbitrator nominated has also been successfully challenged, the right to nominate a new arbitrator shall lapse and the new arbitrator shall be appointed by the Board.

Article 18 addresses the consequences of the successful challenge of an arbitrator **18-001** or the early termination of his or her mandate. It rests on, and must be read together with, **Articles 16** and **17.**

18-002 Specifically, Article 18(1) provides for a mechanism to appoint a new arbitrator to replace the arbitrator who has been successfully challenged or whose mandate has been formally terminated.[1] As a result, truncated tribunals, where only two of the three members of the panel proceed to an award, are not envisaged under the Vienna Rules. Where an arbitrator becomes unwilling or unable to fulfil his or her mandate he will be removed under **Article 17** and then replaced under Article 18. However, where an arbitrator is simply unwilling to sign the award, the signatures of the majority are sufficient.[2] Indeed, the Vienna Rules specifically provide for majority decisions.[3]

18-003 Article 18(1) applies, on its terms, 'if the challenge of the arbitrator has been allowed, if his mandate has been terminated, or if he has resigned his mandate or has died.' This description is confusing. It suggests that a successful challenge, the termination of the arbitrator's mandate, his resignation, or his death (or any other incapacitation) are all systemically different grounds. However, all of these grounds fall within the definition of 'termination' as provided by **Article 17(1)**.[4] As discussed, that provision already defines the termination of the arbitrator's mandate as (a) the parties' agreement on termination, (b) the arbitrator voluntary withdrawing from office; (c) a successful challenge; and (d) the removal of the arbitrator by the Board. As a result, Article 18(1) should simply be read to mean 'if an arbitrator's mandate has been terminated within the meaning of **Article 17(1)**.' Indeed, the corresponding provision of Section 591(1) ZPO provides:

> When arbitrator's mandate terminates early, a substitute arbitrator shall be appointed. Such appointment should be made in accordance with the rules that were applicable to appointment of the arbitrator who is being replaced.[5]

---

1. As a matter of course, Article 18 does not apply while a challenge or termination request is pending. *See* M. Platte in *Arbitration Law of Austria: Practice and Procedure*, S. Riegler, A. Petsche, A. Fremuth-Wolf, M. Platte and C. Liebscher (eds) (Huntington, Juris Publishing, 2007), Section 591, p. 290. On the other hand, it is argued that the replacement may occur at any stage of the proceedings until the arbitration is formally terminated under **Article 25**, even if the proceedings have been closed pursuant to **Article 20(8)**. *See* C. Liebscher in *Arbitration Law of Austria: Practice and Procedure*, S. Riegler, A. Petsche, A. Fremuth-Wolf, M. Platte and C. Liebscher (eds) (Huntington, Juris Publishing, 2007), p. 640.
2. *See* **Article 27**, at para. 014.
3. *See* **Article 26**, at paras. 014 *et seq.*
4. *See* **Article 17**, at paras. 004 *et seq.*
5. *See also* the similar provisions of, and attending commentary to, Article 15 UNCITRAL Model Law and Section 1039 German ZPO. A literal reading of Section 591 ZPO suggests that it is mandatory, preventing the parties from agreeing a different appointment mechanism for the appointment of the substitute arbitrator. *See* A. Reiner, *Das neue österreichische Schiedsrecht/ The new Austrian Arbitration Law* (Vienna, LexisNexis, 2006), Section 591, note 92. However, it is difficult to understand why parties should be allowed to agree on the mechanism for the original tribunal (as they undoubtedly are: *see* **Article 14**, at para. 001), but not on the mechanism for selecting replacement arbitrators. Party autonomy is a fundemtal principle of arbitration, including with respect to the constitution of the tribunal. *See* J. Power, *The Austrian Arbitration Act – A Practitioner's Guide to Sections 577-618 of the Austrian Code of Civil Procedure* (Vienna,

Accordingly, Article 18(1) proceeds to provide an appointing mechanism to **18-004** replace the arbitrator who has been successfully challenged or whose mandate has been terminated. In doing so, Article 18(1) mirrors the appointment mechanisms provided for party nominated sole arbitrators, party nominated co-arbitrators and presiding arbitrators in **Article 14**.[6] Thus, the parties are required to reconvene and jointly agree on a sole arbitrator; whereas the presiding arbitrator will be replaced by the joint nomination of the two co-arbitrators. If a party nominated co-arbitrator has been removed, the party that has made that appointment in the first place can nominate a replacement. As Article 18(1) makes specifically clear, the Secretary General will request the parties, or the co-arbitrators, to make the replacement to nominate a replacement within thirty-day period.[7] Where no such nomination is received within those 30 days, the Board will appoint the replacement. The considerations discussed in the context of **Article 14** apply *mutatis mutandis*.

Article 18 does not address the situation where more than one arbitrator is removed **18-005** at the same time. It is conceivable, for example, that, perhaps for illicit links between them, a party-nominated arbitrator and the presiding arbitrator are both successfully challenged and removed for the same reasons and at the same time. In such a case, the replacement mechanism of Article 18(1) would not work. The presiding arbitrator could not be appointed by the two co-arbitrators, precisely because one of them has been removed as well. There are two conceivable solutions for such a situation. First, Article 18(1) could be interpreted to require, within 30 days, the party who made the original appointment of the removed co-arbitrator, to nominate a replacement, and once this replacement nomination has been made, for the replacement arbitrator and the other co-arbitrator to jointly nominate the chairman. Obviously, such as solution carries a high degree of delay. The preferable approach might therefore be for the Board to appoint all replacements at the outset, in cases where the solution of the mechanism proposed by Article 18(1) is not possible.

The final provision of Article 18(1) stipulates that, if the arbitrator that has been **18-006** nominated or appointed as a replacement is also successfully challenged, the party that out those arbitrators forward looses the right to make a third nomination. Rather, in such cases, the Board itself will directly proceed to make an appointment. Notably, the solution is restricted to the case of a successful challenge. Therefore, it does not apply to the other reasons for terminating the arbitrator's mandate. This is justified because a party who repeatedly appoints arbitrators that

---

Manz, 2006), Section 587, para. 1; G. Zeiler, *Schiedsverfahren* (Vienna/Graz, Neuer Wissenschaftlicher Verlage, 2006), Section 587, p. 130. Indeed, Section 591 arguably refers back to the 'rules' the parties had originally agreed, confirming the principle of party autonomy.

6. *See* **Article 14**, at paras. 032 *et seq.* for party nominated sole arbitrators, at paras. 051 *et seq.* for party nominated co-arbitrators and at paras. 057 *et seq.* for presiding arbitrators.

7. Although the Secretary General is not explicitly mentioned in Article 18, his authority and power derives from **Article 5(2)** and **Article 14**.

fail to meet the required standards of impartiality and independence can no longer be trusted to make a nomination in accordance with the Vienna Rules. To expedite the process, and to ensure compliance with those standards of impartiality and independence, the right of appointment is therefore transferred to the Board.

II.   REPEATING PREVIOUS STAGES OF THE PROCEDURE

Article 18(2): If the challenge of an arbitrator has been allowed, if his mandate has been terminated, if he has resigned his mandate or has died, the new sole arbitrator (newly constituted arbitral tribunal) shall determine, after obtaining the comments of the parties, whether and, if so, to what extent, previous procedural stages are to be repeated.

18-007 Where a new arbitrator joins an existing proceeding, perhaps at advanced stage of the arbitration, difficult questions of procedure arise. Obviously, the new arbitrator will not have had the benefits of the same experience that the other arbitrators by that time will have accumulated. In particular, where evidence has already been taken, this may diminish the new arbitrator's ability to form a judgment on the merits of the dispute.

18-008 For this reason, the newly constituted arbitral tribunal (or, as the case may be, the newly appointed sole arbitrator) has the power, after consultation with the parties but at its own discretion, to repeat all or part of the proceedings. Article 18(2) is consistent with section 591(2) ZPO which reads:

unless otherwise agreed by the parties, the arbitral tribunal may continue the proceeding on the basis of results of the proceedings up to that point, in particular the existing minutes of the hearing as well as any other records.

18-009 Section 591 ZPO, just like Article 18(2), gives the arbitral tribunal (but also the sole arbitrator) the discretion to either continue the proceeding and rely on the existing record, or repeat previous procedural steps. Whether the tribunal decides to do so, will depend on a variety of factors, such as costs, efficiency, the fairness of decision making and the stage of the proceedings. Where a case turns, for example, on the oral evidence of witnesses, and hence the personal impression that the arbitrators must have of the witnesses, it may make sense (and may indeed be compelled by considerations of due process) to repeat the evidentiary hearing. Conversely, where the case turns on issues of law that can be decided on the basis of the parties' written submissions, the repetition of previous procedural steps may turn out to be unnecessary. Where an arbitrator has been successfully challenged, perhaps even after having participated in certain decisions, the proceedings and the tribunal's deliberations may be tainted, also calling for repetition of previously undertaken procedural steps.

18-010 Article 18(2) and Section 591(2) ZPO differ in one respect. Section 591(2) ZPO is prefaced by the words 'unless otherwise agreed by the parties'. Accordingly, the parties can override the arbitrators' discretion and agree either that the proceedings (or parts of it) should be repeated, or else exclude any repetition. By agreeing to the Vienna Rules, the parties adopt a different approach. Here, Article 18(2) only requires the arbitrators to consult with the parties, but does not give the parties the authority to reach agreement; the matter therefore seems to be at the disposal of the arbitrators. In many ways, this makes sense. The arbitrators (including the recently appointed replacement) are required to make an award, and must be comfortable doing so – it should be for them to decide whether or not to repeat certain parts or all of the proceedings. Also, arbitrators could argue that they have accepted their mandate on the basis of the Vienna Rules which vests that discretion with them and only requires them to consult with the parties. Still, where both parties reach agreement on how to proceed, the arbitrators will often follow that agreement.

The replaced arbitrator may receive some remuneration for his services, depending **18-011** on his contribution to the proceedings.[8] This will depend on the reason for the termination and replacement: if the replaced arbitrator's mandate has been terminated because of a successful challenge, or because the arbitrator obstructed or otherwise failed to perform his or her duties, he or she may have lost the right to remuneration.[9] Whether a split of the fees is between the replaced arbitrator and the replacement arbitrator is appropriate will also depend on the circumstances, including on whether the proceedings are repeated in large part or entirely or not.[10]

---

8. C. Liebscher in *Arbitration Law of Austria: Practice and Procedure*, S. Riegler, A. Petsche, A. Fremuth-Wolf, M. Platte and C. Liebscher (eds) (Huntington, Juris Publishing, 2007), p. 640.
9. *See* **Article 7**, at para. 148 and **Article 17**, at para. 006.
10. When the proceedings as a whole are terminated early, the Secretary General may reduce the arbitrators' fees as it appears just corresponding to the stage reached in the proceedings. *See* **Article 36(1)**, at paras. 006 *et seq.*

Article 19

Jurisdiction of the Arbitral Tribunal

		Para.			Para.
I.	Objection to Jurisdiction	1	B.	Decision by the Arbitrator(s)	19
	A. Introduction	1	C.	Court Review	21
	B. Timely Pleading	6	D.	Cost Decisions	30
	C. Admission of Delayed		III.	The Doctrine of Separability	34
	Objections	11	A.	International Recognition	35
	D. Different Treatment of Formal		B.	Presumption of Separability	36
	and Substantive Defects of the		C.	The Separability Doctrine in
	Arbitration Agreement	14		Austrian Law	40
II.	Kompetenz-Kompetenz	15	D.	Limits of the Separability
	A. Introduction	15		Doctrine	44

I. OBJECTION TO JURISDICTION

Article 19(1): A plea that the arbitral tribunal does not have jurisdiction shall be raised not later than the first pleading in the matter. A party is not precluded from raising such a plea by the fact that he has appointed, or participated in the appointment of an arbitrator. A plea that the arbitral tribunal is exceeding the scope of its authority shall be raised as soon as the matter alleged to be beyond the scope of its authority is raised during the arbitral proceedings. In both cases a later plea shall not be permitted; if the arbitral tribunal however considers the delay justified, the plea can be admitted.

A. INTRODUCTION

The tribunal's jurisdiction depends on the existence of a valid arbitration agree- **19-001** ment between the parties that covers in scope the arbitrable dispute before them.

The requirements for a valid arbitration agreement under Austrian law have been examined in detail in the context of **Article 1** and **Article 2**.

19-002 It is generally in the interest of the parties and the arbitral tribunal to establish as quickly as possible if the dispute at bar has been properly referred to arbitration. This is a matter of procedural efficiency. Most arbitration rules, encouraged by the vast majority of modern arbitration laws and international instruments, require the respondent to raise any objections as to jurisdiction at the first opportunity in the arbitration proceedings, or else be barred from raising it at all.[1]

19-003 As already discussed,[2] it was possible under the previous Austrian arbitration law for a respondent to fully arbitrate the merits of a case without ever raising an objection to the tribunal's jurisdiction (or indeed for the claimant to rely on an arbitration agreement), just to turn around, when the case is lost, to apply to the courts to have the award set aside because the arbitration agreement suffered from some defects, formal or otherwise, resulting in a lack of jurisdiction.[3] In addition, even where an objection was raised, and resolved of by the tribunal, the tribunal's decision on jurisdiction was not separately subject to court review. Rather, parties had to wait for the final award to be issued and then apply to the courts to have that award be set aside for lack of jurisdiction.

19-004 For obvious reasons, this regime was highly unsatisfying and presented one of the major weaknesses of the former Austrian arbitration law. It has now been expressly abandoned both under the new ZPO and the Vienna Rules, although even previously parties acting within the scope of the European Convention were barred from raising jurisdictional objections other than at the first opportunity in the proceedings. Specifically, Article V of European Convention[4] provides that:

> (1) [T]he party which intends to raise a plea as to the arbitrator's jurisdiction based on the fact that the arbitration agreement was either non-existent or null and void or had lapsed shall do so during the arbitration proceedings, not later than the delivery of its statement of claim or defence relating to the substance of the dispute; those based on the fact that an arbitrator has exceeded his terms of reference shall be raised during the arbitration proceedings as soon as the question on which the arbitrator is alleged to have no jurisdiction is raised

---

1. *See e.g.*, Article 23(2) LCIA Rules: 'A plea by a Respondent that the Arbitral Tribunal does not have jurisdiction shall be treated as having been irrevocably waived unless it is raised not later than the statement of defence.' Other arbitration rules extend the obligation to make a plea as soon as possible to further objections, *e.g.*, Article 15(3) AAA/ICDR Rules requires that not only the jurisdiction of the tribunal has to be objected at the time of the statement of defense, but also the 'arbitrability of a claim or counterclaim no later than the filing of the statement of defense' and the tribunal is allowed to permit such objections 'only until the first act of procedure is taken on the merits of the case'.
2. *See* **Article 1**, at para. 060.
3. *See*, *e.g.*, OGH, 26 January 2000, 7 Ob 368/98p.
4. Article V European Convention, **Annex 10**.

during the arbitral procedure. Where the delay in raising the plea is due to a cause which the arbitrator deems justified, the arbitrator shall declare the plea admissible.

(2) Pleas to the jurisdiction referred to in paragraph 1 above that have not been raised during the time limits there referred to, may not be entered either during a subsequent stage of the arbitral proceedings where they are pleas left to the sole discretion of the parties under the law applicable by the arbitrator, or during subsequent court proceedings concerning the substance or the enforcement of the award where such pleas are left to the discretion of the parties under the rule of conflict of the court seized of the substance of the dispute or the enforcement of the award. The arbitrator's decision on the delay in raising the plea, will, however, be subject to judicial control.

With Section 592 ZPO and Article 19, the legal environment in Austria now **19-005** follows the rules provided by the European Convention and Article 16 of the UNCITRAL Model Law.

B.   TIMELY PLEADING

Article 19 of the Vienna Rules contains an express obligation for a party to assert **19-006** the lack of the tribunal's jurisdiction 'not later than the first pleading in the matter'. It follows closely the provision of Section 592 ZPO which reads:

(1) The arbitral tribunal may rule on its own jurisdiction. The ruling can be made together with the ruling on the case or by separate award.

(2) A plea that the arbitral tribunal does not have jurisdiction shall be raised not later than the first pleading in the matter. A party is not precluded from raising such a plea by the fact that he has appointed, or participated in the appointment of, an arbitrator. A plea that the arbitral tribunal is exceeding the scope of its authority shall be raised as soon as the matter alleged to be beyond the scope of its authority is raised during the arbitral proceedings. In both cases, a later raising of the plea is prohibited; if the delay, however, is justified in the opinion of the arbitral tribunal, the plea may subsequently be admitted.

(3) Even while a claim for the setting aside of an award with which the arbitral tribunal affirmed its jurisdiction is still pending before the court, the arbitral tribunal may continue the arbitral proceedings and make an award.

In the context of the Vienna Rules, this will typically (but not necessarily) be the **19-007** memorandum in reply as the first written submission envisaged for the respondent.[5]

---

5. The question if and when the arbitral tribunal should consider its jurisdiction *ex officio* has been addressed at **Article 1**, at para. 140.

19-008 In order to facilitate the constitution of the arbitral tribunal, however, 'a party is not precluded from raising such a plea by the fact that he has appointed, or participated in the appointment of, an arbitrator'.[6] In practice, parties who object to the tribunal's jurisdiction but wish to defend against the merits as a matter of caution (as they may be well advised to do), will typically subject every procedural submission, or argument on the merits, to the caveat that it is 'without prejudice to the jurisdictional objection'.

19-009 The obligation to raise a timely objection applies to all instances of lack of jurisdiction, and Article 19 and Section 592 ZPO are structured accordingly. Where the respondent takes the position that there is no arbitration agreement at all, or that it suffers from a fatal defect, he must raise this objection at the outset. However, the tribunal has also no jurisdiction to resolve disputes that fall outside the scope of an existing and valid arbitration agreement. Article 19, in line with Section 592(2) ZPO, therefore introduces the additional obligation to raise an objection to the arbitral tribunal exceeding the scope of its authority 'as soon as the matter alleged to be beyond the scope of its authority is raised during the arbitral proceedings'. Both the authentic German version of the Vienna Rules and Section 592 ZPO indicate that the phrase 'raised during the arbitral proceedings' means that the matter potentially exceeding the tribunal's authority is made the subject of an application on the merits (*'zum Gegenstand eines Sachantrages erhoben'*), by amending a claim or introducing new claims.[7] This has the consequence that there is no duty to raise an objection if a party merely brings forward a procedural issue or offers evidence for a certain issue.[8]

19-010 A failure to raise the appropriate jurisdictional objection at the first available opportunity therefore has serious consequences. In both cases (i.e. lack of jurisdiction and excess of authority), the Vienna Rules provide that a party failing to raise a timely objection is deprived of the right to assert it at a later stage. Under this concept, the failure to raise a timely objection has not only consequences for the arbitration itself, but also precludes a party from asserting a belated jurisdictional objection in subsequent state court proceedings, including the setting aside of an award.[9]

---

6. Article 23(2) LCIA Rules seems to adopt a similar approach as it reads: 'A plea by a Respondent that the Arbitral Tribunal does not have jurisdiction shall be treated as having been irrevocably waived unless it is raised not later than the statement of defense.' *See also* Article 1(3) Czech Rules and Article 1(7) Hungarian Rules. Other arbitration rules extend the obligation to make a plea to further objections, *e.g.*, Article 15(3) AAA/ICDR Rules requires that not only the jurisdiction of the tribunal has to be objected at the time of the statement of defense, but also the 'arbitrability of a claim or counterclaim no later than the filing of the statement of defense' and the tribunal is allowed to permit such objections 'only until the first act of procedure is taken on the merits of the case'.

7. A. Reiner, *Das neue österreichische Schiedsrecht/The new Austrian Arbitration Law* (Vienna, LexisNexis, 2006), Section 592, note 96.

8. *See* Explanatory Notes to Section 592 ZPO.

9. *See* in a similar vein J. Power, *The Austrian Arbitration Act – A Practitioner's Guide to Sections 577-618 of the Austrian Code of Civil Procedure* (Vienna, Manz, 2006), Section 592, para. 9.

C.   ADMISSION OF DELAYED OBJECTIONS

As discussed, a failure to raise the appropriate jurisdictional objection at the first **19-011**
available opportunity has serious consequences. To mitigate these consequences
where appropriate, Article 19 vests the tribunal with the discretionary authority to
admit a belated objection, if the defaulting party can show good cause for the delay,
in other words, where the delay was justified.

This power is also provided for by Section 592(2) ZPO, which in turn was modelled **19-012**
after Article V(1) of the European Convention[10] which provides that '[w]here the
delay in raising the plea is due to a cause which the arbitrator deems justified, the
arbitrator shall declare the plea admissible'. Thus, any decision by the tribunal will
have to set out reasons and a strict test will have to be applied in this context, in
order not to frustrate the purpose of Article 19 and open the door to dilatory tactics
by obstructive parties.

Where the European Convention is directly applicable, the decision by the arbi- **19-013**
trators to not admit a delayed objection is considered to be reviewable by the
courts.[11] Whether the same power under the ZPO is a discretionary power of
the arbitral tribunal that is subject to review by the courts is disputed.[12]

D.   DIFFERENT TREATMENT OF FORMAL AND SUBSTANTIVE DEFECTS OF
                THE ARBITRATION AGREEMENT

Moreover, an objection to formal defects of the arbitration agreement must, pur- **19-014**
suant to Section 583(3) ZPO, always be raised with the first submission on the
merits, failing which the formal defect is cured.[13] Given this express statutory

---

10. *See* Article V(1) European Convention, **Annex 10**.
11. 'If the court reaches the conclusion, contrary to that of the arbitrators, that the plea should have
     been admitted, its powers to decide on the question of jurisdiction are unfettered by the con-
     ditions imposed by Article V(2). Conversely, if the arbitrator declared the pleading admissible,
     Article V(2) curbs the supervisory powers of courts over the questions of jurisdiction. Its
     provisions should be combined with those of Article V of the NY Convention which says
     nothing of the circumstances in which a party can be stopped from invoking the arbitrator's
     competence.' *See* D.T. Hascher, 'The European Convention on International Commercial Arbi-
     tration of 1961' (1990) XV YB Comm Arb, 624, 642.
12. *Fremuth-Wolf* considers it a right of the domestic courts to review the decision of the arbitral
     tribunal. *See* A. Fremuth-Wolf in *Arbitration Law of Austria: Practice and Procedure*,
     S. Riegler, A. Petsche, A. Fremuth-Wolf, M. Platte and C. Liebscher (eds) (Huntington, Juris
     Publishing, 2007), Section 592, p. 304.
13. Section 583(3) ZPO provides: 'A defect of form of the arbitration agreement shall be cured in
     the arbitration proceedings by entering an appearance in the case, if a notification of the defect is
     not made earlier or at the latest together with entering an appearance.'

provision, the tribunal has arguably no authority to admit objections to the form of the arbitration agreement at a later stage.[14]

II.   *KOMPETENZ-KOMPETENZ*

Article 19(2): The sole arbitrator (arbitral tribunal) shall rule on its own jurisdiction. The ruling can be made together with the ruling on the case or by separate arbitral award.

A.   INTRODUCTION

19-015 The authority of the arbitrators to consider and decide disputes regarding their own jurisdiction, including disputes over the existence, validity, legality and scope of the parties' arbitration agreement, is usually referred to as the arbitrator's *Kompetenz-Kompetenz* (or 'competence-competence').[15] It provides that international arbitral tribunals have the power to consider and to decide disputes concerning their own jurisdiction.[16]

19-016 The principle of competence-competence is widely acknowledged.[17] Article V(3) of the European Convention expressly provides, e.g. that '[s]ubject to any subsequent judicial control provided for under the *lex fori*, the arbitrator whose jurisdiction is called in question shall be entitled to proceed with the arbitration, to rule on his own jurisdiction and to decide upon the existence or the validity of the arbitration agreement or of the contract of which the agreement forms part'.[18] Similarly, Article 16(1) of the UNCITRAL Model Law (titled 'Competence of arbitral tribunal to rule on its jurisdiction') expressly vests arbitrators with the

---

14. A. Reiner, *Das neue österreichische Schiedsrecht/The new Austrian Arbitration Law* (Vienna, LexisNexis, 2006), Section 592, note 97.
15. The different terminology that is used to describe an arbitral tribunal's jurisdiction to decide on its own jurisdiction is discussed below.
16. F.B. Weigand in *Practitioner's Handbook on International Arbitration*, F.B. Weigand (ed.) (Munich, C.H. Beck, 2002), p. 71.
17. Article 23 LCIA Rules; Article 15 AAA/ICDR Rules; Article 21 UNCITRAL Rules; Article 21 Swiss Rules and Article 2 Polish Rules. Note an interesting approach under Article 23 Czech Rules, where '[t]he board of the Arbitration Court shall have the power to decide on issues of jurisdiction. To this end, the arbitrators, if already appointed or, otherwise, the Secretary, shall present the records of the case to the Board with a short report in each case, whenever a decision on the jurisdiction of the Arbitration Court is to be taken in view of an objection to the juris-diction taken by a party or in view of an objection to the jurisdiction taken by a party or in view of the doubts of the Secretary or the arbitrators, or their opinion that the Arbitration Court lacks the necessary jurisdiction.'
18. Article V(3) European Convention, **Annex 10**. *See* D.T. Hascher, 'The European Convention on International Commercial Arbitration 1961' (1995) XX YB Comm Arb, 1006, 1024.

authority to consider challenges to their own jurisdiction, including challenges to the arbitration agreement.[19]

The principle of competence-competence is central to the arbitral process. **19-017** Disputes over the formation, validity or scope of arbitration agreements all raise questions of the tribunal's jurisdiction.[20] Conceptually, any decision by the tribunal that no valid arbitration agreement exists would include at the same time a corollary finding that the tribunal lacked jurisdiction in the first place, precisely because the arbitration agreement – the basis for the tribunal's jurisdiction – was found not to exist. The doctrine of competence-competence overcomes the conceptual problems arising out of any decision by the arbitrator on his own jurisdiction.[21] It allows arbitrators to decide on all jurisdictional issues, and thus avoids the effect that jurisdictional objections have to be litigated in state courts.

In its purest form, the recognition of the tribunal's authority to determine its own **19-018** jurisdiction would result in such a decision having binding effect for state courts of law.[22] However, the modern notion of competence-competence subjects the power of the tribunal to rule on its own jurisdiction to later court review.[23] Due to this reservation of the final decision for the state courts, it would be more appropriate to replace the term of competence-competence by 'preliminary competence' of the arbitral tribunal to rule on its own jurisdiction.[24]

---

19. *See also* Report of the Secretary General, *Analytical Commentary on Draft Text of a Model Law on International Commercial Arbitration*, A/CN.9/264, 37, <http://www.uncitral.org> ('Article 16 adopts the important principle that it is initially and primarily for the arbitral tribunal itself to determine whether it has jurisdiction, subject to ultimate court control (. . .)'); H.M. Holtzmann and J.E. Neuhaus, *A Guide to the UNCITRAL Model Law on International Commercial Arbitration: Legislative History and Commentary* (The Hague, Kluwer Law and Taxation Publishers, 1989), pp. 478, 479.

20. G.B. Born, *International Commercial Arbitration – Commentary and Materials* (2rd edn, The Hague, Kluwer Law International, 2001), p. 6.

21. J. Lew, L. Mistelis and S. Kröll, *Comparative International Commercial Arbitration* (The Hague, Kluwer Law International, 2003), para. 14-13.

22. F.B. Weigand in *Practitioner's Handbook on International Arbitration*, F.B. Weigand (ed.) (Munich, C.H. Beck, 2002), p. 71.

23. G.B. Born, *International Commercial Arbitration – Commentary and Materials* (2nd edn, The Hague, Kluwer Law International, 2001), p. 6; F.B. Weigand in *Practitioner's Handbook on International Arbitration*, F.B. Weigand (ed.) (Munich, C.H. Beck, 2002), pp. 71 *et seq.* In similar vein K.H. Schwab and G. Walter (eds), *Schiedsgerichtsbarkeit* (7th edn, Munich, C.H. Beck, 2005), ch. 6, paras. 9 *et seq.*

24. F.B. Weigand in *Practitioner's Handbook on International Arbitration*, F.B. Weigand (ed.) (Munich, C.H. Beck, 2002), pp. 71 *et seq.* Recently confirmed by the German *Bundesgerichtshof*, 13 January 2005, III ZR 265/03, NJW 2005, 1125, which basically confirmed the doctrine under German law that 'the parties will no longer be authorized to exclude the competence of the German courts' and that 'the arbitrator's decision on his competence is always provisional.' *See* K.P. Berger, 'The New German Arbitration Law in International Perspective' (2000) 26 Forum Int'l, 1, 9; K.-H. Böckstiegel, 'An Introduction to the New German Arbitration Act Based on the UNCITRAL Model Law' (1998) 14(1) Arb Int'l, 19, 25. *See also* S. Kröll, 'Recourse Against

B.   DECISION BY THE ARBITRATOR(S)

19-019 The concept that, at least in the first instance, the arbitrator shall rule on its own jurisdiction is not new to Austrian arbitration law.[25] But Article 19(2), like Section 592 ZPO, now expressly provides that the decision on jurisdiction can be made either jointly with the ruling on the merits or by a separate arbitral award. Article 19(2), is intended to encourage an arbitral tribunal to decide on its own jurisdiction early in the proceedings. It is certainly in the parties' best interest to receive a decision on the arbitrator's jurisdiction at the earliest stage possible. However, if the jurisdictional question is factually and legally detached from any decision on the merits, this sometimes results in fact in a bifurcation of the proceedings. Whilst this might be perfectly legitimate in some cases, the question of jurisdiction may in other cases be so intertwined with a decision on the merits that a separate finding would not be justified (e.g. when it is disputed whether an assignment of a claim was valid and thus whether the assignee rightfully obtained its rights arising out of an arbitration agreement, also contained in the contract at bar).[26] However, it has deliberately been left to the discretion of the arbitral tribunal whether to render a decision on jurisdiction during the proceedings or with the final award, as the circumstances of the case demand.[27]

19-020 In any case, Section 592 ZPO obliges the arbitrator(s) to decide on jurisdiction in the form of an award, and not in the form of a procedural order.[28] Although Article 19 contains no such requirement, the better view will require arbitrators in proceedings sited in Austria to render their decision in the form of an award precisely to allow the review of their decision under Section 611 ZPO.[29]

C.   COURT REVIEW

19-021 Under former doctrine[30] and jurisprudence, jurisdictional rulings by arbitrators were not considered to be challengeable in separate proceedings.[31] A tribunal's

---

Negative Decisions on Jurisdiction' (2004) 20(1) Arb Int'l, 55; J.P. Lachmann, *Handbuch für die Schiedsgerichtspraxis* (3rd edn, Cologne, Verlag Dr. Otto Schmidt, 2008), pp. 187 *et seq.*

25. *See* W.H. Rechberger and W. Melis in *Kommentar zur ZPO*, W.H. Rechberger (ed.) (2nd edn, Vienna/New York, Springer, 2000), Section 577, para. 13.
26. P. Oberhammer, *Entwurf eines neuen Schiedsverfahrensrechts* (Vienna, Manz, 2002), pp. 77 *et seq.*
27. B. Kloiber and H. Haller in *Das neue Schiedsrecht – Schiedsrechts-Änderungsgesetz 2006*, B. Kloiber, P. Oberhammer, W.H. Rechberger and H. Haller (eds) (Vienna, Manz, 2006), p. 33.
28. J. Power, *The Austrian Arbitration Act – A Practitioner's Guide to Sections 577-618 of the Austrian Code of Civil Procedure* (Vienna, Manz, 2006), Section 592, para. 4.
29. In case of doubt a party can, given sufficient legal interest in such decision, make an application to the state court for the determination of the existence or non-existence of an award in accordance with Section 612 ZPO.
30. *See* H.W. Fasching, *Schiedsgericht und Schiedsverfahren im österreichischen und im internationalen Recht* (Vienna, Manz, 1973), p. 125.
31. The Austrian *Oberster Gerichtshof* ruled: 'Pursuant to the nature of an arbitral award as a decision by private parties equivalent to a judgement of a state court, arbitral award can only

affirmation of its jurisdiction could only be challenged with the final award, requiring parties to proceed with the entire arbitration before obtaining judicial clarification. Negative decisions on jurisdiction were considered not to be challengeable at all, absent an express statutory basis.[32]

Legal practice in Austria tried to redress this situation by admitting an independent **19-022** declaratory action (*Feststellungsklage*) on the validity of the arbitration agreement.[33] That was considered to be permissible even during pending arbitration proceedings.[34] However, this approach raises questions of its own, and, in opening state court litigation as an alternative forum at any time, is not reconcilable with the notion of competence-competence.

When considering whether to follow the UNCITRAL Model Law or the German **19-023** ZPO in terms of judicial court review, it was felt that both models provided inappropriate guidance. Although German scholars had developed the original *Kompetenz-Kompetenz* doctrine – which in its original meaning was intended to vest arbitrators with the ultimate jurisdiction to determine their own jurisdiction, without subsequent court review[35] – Germany since abandoned this approach and adopted a *sui generis* system of court review that differs significantly from the UNCITRAL Model Law.[36] Not only is 'the arbitrator's decision on his competence always provisional,'[37] Germany also introduced a complex system of interlocutory

be understood as an arbitral tribunal's decision on the merits that, at least in part, deals exhaustively with the parties' substantive motion'. *See* OGH, 25 June 1992, 7 Ob 545/92, case note by K. Heller, 'Die Anfechtung von Teil- und Zwischenschiedssprüchen in Österreich' [1994] IPRax, 142; partly confirmed in OGH, 26 January 2005, 7 Ob 314/04 h.

32. P. Oberhammer in *Das neue Schiedsrecht – Schiedsrechts-Änderungsgesetz 2006*, E. Kloiber, P. Oberhammer, W.H. Rechberger and H. Haller (eds) (Vienna, Manz, 2006), p. 123.

33. F. Mänhardt, 'Feststellungsgerichtsbarkeit bei inländischen Schiedsverfahren – Eine Regelungslücke?' [1989] AnwBl, 397; C. Aschauer, 'Keine Klage auf Feststellung der Unzuständigkeit des Schiedsgerichts bei anhängigem Schiedsverfahren' [2003] wbl, 413; P. Oberhammer, *Entwurf eines neuen Schiedsverfahrensrechts* (Vienna, Manz, 2002), p. 58.

34. The Austrian *Oberster Gerichtshof* has taken differing positions over time. In OGH, 23 October 1928, 3 Ob 648/28, SZ 10/ 303, such a claim was permitted during pending arbitration proceedings. In OGH, 19 June 1934, 2 Ob 506, 507, ZBl 1934/371 it was denied and in OGH, 2 October 1935, 3 Ob 572/35, SZ 17/131 permitted.

35. P. Schlosser, *Das Recht der internationalen privaten Schiedsgerichtsbarkeit* (2nd edn, Tübingen, Mohr Siebeck, 1989), para. 556; K.P. Berger, 'Germany Adopts the UNCITRAL Model Law' (1998) 1 Int'l Arb L Rev, 121, 122.

36. German judicial authority thus far arguably confirms this view. *See* BGH, 13 January 2005, III ZR 265/03, NJW 2005, 1125; *see also* BGH, 23 February 2006, III ZB 50/05, SchiedsVZ 2006, 161, 164.

37. K.P. Berger, 'The New German Arbitration Law in International Perspective' (2000) 26 Forum Int'l, 1, 9; *see also* K.-H. Böckstiegel, 'An Introduction to the New German Arbitration Act Based on the UNCITRAL Model Law' (1998) 14(1) Arb Int'l, 19, 25; W.J. Habscheid, 'Zur Kompetenz-Kompetenz nach dem neuen Schiedsrecht', in *Festschrift für Peter Schlosser zum 70.*

court review, which, to an extent depending on the stage of the proceedings, in general allows for judicial intervention on jurisdictional matters at any time.[38]

19-024 Specifically, Section 1032(2) German ZPO provides that '[p]rior to the constitution of the arbitral tribunal, an application may be made to the court to determine whether or not arbitration is admissible'.[39] After constitution of the tribunal, Section 1032(1) German ZPO allows a party to initiate court proceedings relating to the same subject matter that is before the tribunal, and, if the other party objects to the jurisdiction of the court by invoking the arbitration agreement, requires the court to decide on the existence of a valid arbitration agreement. The court's decision is binding on the parties as well as the arbitral tribunal.[40] Positive jurisdictional awards can be reviewed by the courts under Section 1040(3) German ZPO on a *de novo* basis.[41]

Geburstag, B. Bachmann, S. Breidenbach, D. Coester-Waltjen, B. Hess, A. Nelle, C. Wolf (eds) (Tübingen, Mohr Siebeck, 2005) p. 247; J. Münch, *Münchener Kommentar zur Zivilprozessordnung*, G. Lüke and P. Wax (eds) (2nd edn, Munich, C.H. Beck 2001), Section 1040, para. 26 (arbitration agreement providing for Kompetenz-Kompetenz 'ineffective because it violates mandatory law'); S. Kröll, 'Recourse Against Negative Decisions on Jurisdiction' (2004) 20(1) Arb Int'l, 55; J.P. Lachmann, *Handbuch für die Schiedsgerichtspraxis* (3rd edn, Cologne, Verlag Dr. Otto Schmidt, 2008), pp. 187 *et seq*. *Contra* A.S. Rau, 'The Arbitrability Question Itself' (1999) 10 Am Rev Int'l Arb, 287, 349 ('I confess I am hard put to understand why the Model Law should be thought to have any bearing whatever on this question').

38. *See* P. Schlosser in *Kommentar zur Zivilprozessordnung*, F. Stein, C. Berger and J. Martin (eds) (22nd edn, Tübingen, Mohr Siebeck, 2002), Section 1040, para. 2 (Contributors do not necessarily have the 'first word' on jurisdictional issues under the new German legislation).

39. Section 1032(2) German ZPO, BGH, 13 January 2005, III ZR 265/03, NJW 2005, 1125 (where party challenges validity of arbitration agreement, German court may consider challenge on interlocutory basis); J.P. Lachmann, *Handbuch für die Schiedsgerichtspraxis* (3rd edn, Cologne, Verlag Dr. Otto Schmidt, 2008), pp. 182 *et seq*.; K. Lionnet and A. Lionnet, *Handbuch der internationalen und nationalen Schiedsgerichtsbarkeit* (3rd edn, Stuttgart, Richard Boorberg Verlag, 2005), pp. 188 *et seq*.; G. Wagner in *Practitioner's Handbook on International Arbitration*, F.B. Weigand (ed.) (Munich, C.H. Beck, 2002), p. 710; R. Geimer in *Zöller – Zivilprozessordnung*, R. Zöller *et al.* (eds) (26th edn, Cologne, Verlag Dr. Otto Schmidt, 2007), Section 1032, para. 23. It appears clear that a court may decide any jurisdictional matter as an interlocutory matter, without waiting for arbitral consideration of the issue.

40. See, *e.g.*, K. Lionnet and A. Lionnet, *Handbuch der internationalen und nationalen Schiedsgerichtsbarkeit* (3rd edn, Stuttgart, Richard Boorberg Verlag, 2005), pp. 186 *et seq*.; G. Wagner in *Practitioner's Handbook on International Arbitration*, F.B. Weigand (ed.) (Munich, C.H. Beck, 2002), p. 708; R. Geimer in *Zöller – Zivilprozessordnung*, R. Zöller *et al.* (eds) (26th edn, Cologne, Verlag Dr. Otto Schmidt, 2007), Section 1032, para. 14.

41. G. Wagner in *Practitioner's Handbook on International Arbitration*, F.B. Weigand (ed.) (Munich, C.H. Beck, 2002), p. 705; R. Geimer in *Zöller – Zivilprozessordnung*, R. Zöller *et al.* (eds) (26th edn, Cologne, Verlag Dr. Otto Schmidt, 2007), Section 1040, para 1.

Unfortunately, the wording of the UNCITRAL Model Law also contains ambi- **19-025**
guities regarding the court's power to review a negative jurisdictional decision of
the arbitral tribunal. This has led the German *Bundesgerichtshof* to hold that there
is no possibility of judicial review of a negative jurisdictional award.[42]

The Working Group on the new Austrian arbitration law considered whether or not **19-026**
to include a provision similar to Section 1032 German ZPO, that would, prior to the
constitution of the arbitral tribunal, enable an application to the court to determine
the admissibility of the arbitration proceeding.[43] In the end, such a procedure was
not adopted. Instead, the tribunal's partial award on jurisdiction can now be challenged under Section 611(2) no. 1 ZPO. Declaratory judgements to determine the
existence or non-existence of an arbitration agreement are thus inadmissible,
whether before or during the arbitration proceedings.[44]

More specifically, and in order to provide a uniform system of review for all **19-027**
jurisdictional decisions, Section 611(2) no. 1 ZPO now provides that awards on
jurisdiction are challengeable either on the grounds that 'a valid arbitration agreement does not exist' or 'the arbitral tribunal denies its jurisdiction despite the
existence of a valid arbitration agreement'. That means that both decisions that
affirm and decisions that reject jurisdiction are subject to appeal under Section 611
ZPO. Austria's now harmonized approach to both affirmative and negative
jurisdictional decisions brings it in line with other UNCITRAL Model Law

42. That decision is supported by the absence of express language in the UNCITRAL Model Law
    that would provide a basis for annulling a negative jurisdictional determination. *See* G.B. Born,
    International Commercial Arbitration – Commentary and Materials (3rd edn, The Hague,
    Kluwer Law International, forthcoming), ch. 6 criticizing in detail BGH, 6 June 2002, III ZB
    44/01, SchiedsVZ 2003, 39; *see also* Hanseatisches OLG Hamburg, 30 August 2002, Case 11
    Sch 02/00, head note available under <http://www.dis-arb.de>; S. Kröll, 'Recourse Against
    Negative Decisions on Jurisdiction' (2004) 20(1) Arb Int'l, 55; *see also* A. Samuel, *Jurisdic-
    tional Problems in International Commercial Arbitration* (Zürich, Schulthess Polygraphischer
    Verlag, 1989), p. 218; A. Dimolitsa, 'Separability and Kompetenz-Kompetenz' (1999) 9 ICCA
    Congress Series (Paris), 217, 232.
43. P. Oberhammer, *Entwurf eines neuen Schiedsverfahrensrechts* (Vienna, Manz, 2002), pp. 57
    et seq.
44. This follows from Section 578 ZPO which limits the court intervention to those matters (explic-
    itly) provided for in the arbitration Act. *See* A. Reiner, *Das neue österreichische Schiedsrecht/
    The new Austrian Arbitration Law* (Vienna, LexisNexis, 2006), Section 578, note 9; C. Liebscher,
    The Austrian Arbitration Act 2006: Text and Notes (The Hague, Kluwer Law International,
    2006), Annotated Text to Section 578 ZPO.

jurisdictions, as well as legislation in other important legal systems (including Switzerland,[45] France,[46] England,[47] the United States[48] and Italy[49]).

19-028 While an appeal on a partial award on jurisdiction is pending with the courts, the tribunal may, if it deems it appropriate, nevertheless continue the proceedings and, according to Section 592(3) ZPO, even render an award in the matter.[50] In case the state court subsequently decides that the tribunal lacked jurisdiction, the arbitral proceedings will be considered terminated (provided that a final award had not yet been rendered).[51] In case an incompetent tribunal has not stayed the proceedings and rendered a final award, this award will be subject to setting aside under Section 611(2) no. 1 and, arguably nos 3 or 5.[52]

19-029 If the question of the jurisdiction of an arbitral tribunal with seat in Austria has already been determined by a legally binding court decision or a foreign court

45. Article 190(2)(b) Swiss IPRG ('Action for setting aside the award may only be initiated (. . .) (b) where the arbitral tribunal has wrongly declared itself to have or not to have jurisdiction'); M. Müller, *Die Zuständigkeit des Schiedsgerichts* (Bern, Haupt, 1997), p. 141; B. Berger and F. Kellerhals, *Internationale und interne Schiedsgerichtsbarkeit in der Schweiz* (Bern/Vienna, Stämpfli Verlag/Manz, 2006), para. 674; W. Wenger and C. Müller in *International Arbitration in Switzerland*, H. Honsell *et al.* (eds) (Basel/The Hague, Kluwer Law International, 2000), Article 186, para. 50.

46. Cour d'Appel de Paris, 26 October 1995, *Société Nationale des Chemins de Fer Tunisiens v. Société Voith*, [1997] Rev Arb, 553.

47. Section 67(1)(a) English Arbitration Act, 1996 (judicial power to set aside 'any award of the arbitral tribunal as to its substantive jurisdiction'); D. Sutton, J. Gill and M. Gearing, *Russell on Arbitration* (22nd edn, London, Sweet & Maxwell, 2003), paras. 5-078, 8-031.

48. *See China Minmetals Materials Imp. & Exp. Co., Ltd. v. Chi Mei Corp.*, 334 F.3d 274, 288 (3rd Cir. 2003) (without distinguishing between positive and negative jurisdictional awards, observing that under at least one 'brand of competence-competence' doctrine, 'the arbitrators' jurisdictional decision is subject to judicial review at any time before, after, or during arbitration proceedings, as was traditionally the case under English law'); J.J. Barceló, 'Who Decides the Arbitrator's Jurisdiction? Separability and Competence-Competence in Transnational Perspective' (2003) 36 Vand J Transnat'l L, 1115.

49. M. Rubbino-Sammartano in *Practitioner's Handbook on International Arbitration*, F.B. Weigand (ed.) (Munich, C.H. Beck, 2002), p. 839.

50. For an overview of possible scenarios and the effect of the arbitral tribunals' decision on the arbitral award, *see* A. Fremuth-Wolf in *Arbitration Law of Austria: Practice and Procedure*, S. Riegler, A. Petsche, A. Fremuth-Wolf, M. Platte and C. Liebscher (eds) (Huntington, Juris Publishing, 2007), Section 592, p. 305.

51. Even though Section 618 ZPO does not explicitly refer to this scenario to be a ground for termination of the arbitral proceedings, no other solution would be justifiable. *See also* A. Fremuth-Wolf in *Arbitration Law of Austria: Practice and Procedure*, S. Riegler, A. Petsche, A. Fremuth-Wolf, M. Platte and C. Liebscher (eds) (Huntington, Juris Publishing, 2007), Section 592, p. 305.

52. *See also* A. Fremuth-Wolf in *Arbitration Law of Austria: Practice and Procedure*, S. Riegler, A. Petsche, A. Fremuth-Wolf, M. Platte and C. Liebscher (eds) (Huntington, Juris Publishing, 2007), Section 592, p. 305.

decision that is to be recognized in Austria, such decision shall be respected by the arbitral tribunal. If the arbitral tribunal decides to ignore such decision, the arbitral award rendered contrary to this decision, might be challengeable as being contrary to public policy.[53]

D.   Cost Decisions

In addition, Section 609(2) ZPO puts an end to the debate if an arbitral tribunal is in **19-030** fact entitled to render a decision on costs if it denies its jurisdiction to decide the dispute. The statute now expressly provides:

> Upon the application of the Respondent, the arbitral tribunal may also decide upon the obligation of the plaintiff to reimburse the costs of the proceedings, if it has declared itself as not competent on the grounds that there is no arbitration agreement.

Arguably, the same must apply where the arbitral tribunal has dismissed the claim **19-031** on other jurisdictional grounds, including because it was not constituted in accordance with the parties' agreement or in accordance with applicable law.[54]

Finally, where a tribunal denies jurisdiction, the Austrian courts are obliged under **19-032** Section 584(2) ZPO to accept the claim. This provision protects the claimant from being left without a forum for legal recourse.

However, Section 584(2) ZPO also provides, once the claimant brings its claim to **19-033** the court, it also waives its right to challenge the tribunal's award denying jurisdiction under Section 611 ZPO. Thus, when confronted with an award denying jurisdiction the claimant can either challenge this award or bring its claim to the courts who cannot reject it on the basis that an arbitration agreement exists.

III.   THE DOCTRINE OF SEPARABILITY

The examination of the tribunal's jurisdiction is closely connected with the 'doc- **19-034** trine of separability' of the arbitration agreement, which is therefore addressed

---

53.   *See* A. Fremuth-Wolf in *Arbitration Law of Austria: Practice and Procedure*, S. Riegler, A. Petsche, A. Fremuth-Wolf, M. Platte and C. Liebscher (eds) (Huntington, Juris Publishing, 2007), Section 592, p. 299; J. Power, *The Austrian Arbitration Act – A Practitioner's Guide to Sections 577-618 of the Austrian Code of Civil Procedure* (Vienna, Manz, 2006), Section 592, para. 1; B. Kloiber and H. Haller in *Das neue Schiedsrecht – Schiedsrechts-Änderungsgesetz 2006*, B. Kloiber P. Oberhammer, W.H. Rechberger and H. Haller (eds) (Vienna, Manz, 2006), pp. 32 *et seq.*; Explanatory Notes to Section 592 ZPO; *see also* the discussion under **Article 27**, at paras. 054 and 060.
54.   A. Reiner, *Das neue österreichische Schiedsrecht/The new Austrian Arbitration Law* (Vienna, LexisNexis, 2006), Section 609, note 179.

here, in the context of Article 19. This doctrine refers to the principle that an arbitration agreement is at the outset treated as separate from the underlying contract in which it is contained, or to which it refers. Treating the arbitration agreement as an agreement separate from the underlying contract has significant consequences. It recognizes that different substantive legal rules may be applicable to the arbitration agreement as opposed to the underlying contract.[55] It also accepts the possibility that the arbitration agreement is valid, although the parties' underlying contract is invalid, void or illegal. These effects of the separability doctrine 'play vital roles in ensuring the efficacy of the international arbitral process'.[56]

A.   INTERNATIONAL RECOGNITION

19-035 In international doctrine, the principle of separability is widely acknowledged. Article 16(1) of the UNCITRAL Model Law provides that 'an arbitration clause which forms part of the contract shall be treated as an agreement independent of the other terms of the contract,' and both Article II and Article V(1)(a) of the European Convention[57] treat arbitration agreements as distinct agreements that, at least implicitly, exist separately from the parties' underlying contracts.[58] Article V(3) of the European Convention authorizes arbitrators to examine the 'existence or the validity of the arbitration agreement *or* of the contract of which the agreement forms part,'[59] and Article VI(2) of the European Convention provides for specific choice-of-law rules for arbitration agreements.[60] In Austria, the separate nature of the arbitration agreement is dogmatically justified because unlike commercial agreements, an arbitration agreement is considered to be a procedural agreement arising directly out of the ZPO as opposed to private law.[61] This, too, reinforces the distinct character of arbitration agreements and separates them from the private law contracts in which they are contained. Today, the separability doctrine is recognized in statute or case law in most modern jurisdictions, including in Austria's neighbouring legal systems Germany and Switzerland.[62]

---

55. *See* **Article 2**, at paras. 033 *et seq.*
56. G.B. Born, *International Commercial Arbitration – Commentary and Materials* (3rd edn, The Hague, Kluwer Law International, forthcoming), ch. 3.
57. Article II and V(1)(a) European Convention, **Annex 10**.
58. G.B. Born, *International Commercial Arbitration – Commentary and Materials* (3rd edn, The Hague, Kluwer Law Internatinal, forthcoming), ch. 3.
59. Article V(3) European Convention, **Annex 10**.
60. Article VI(2) European Convention, **Annex 10**.
61. *See* **Article 1**, at para. 059 with further references.
62. K.H. Schwab and G. Walter (eds), *Schiedsgerichtsbarkeit* (7th edn, Munich, C.H. Beck, 2005), ch. 4, paras. 16 *et seq.*; R. Geimer in *Zöller – Zivilprozessordnung*, R. Zöller *et al.* (eds) (26th edn, Cologne, Verlag Dr. Otto Schmidt, 2007), Section 1029, para. 1; B. Berger and F. Kellerhals, *Internationale und interne Schiedsgerichtsbarkeit in der Schweiz* (Bern/Vienna, Stämpfli Verlag/ Manz, 2006), para. 604.

B.   PRESUMPTION OF SEPARABILITY

Properly analyzed, the separability issue is a conceptual instrument to examine the **19-036**
parties' consent to arbitrate where (or rather, *even* where) the validity of their main
contractual relationship is in doubt. In other words, assuming that the main contract
between the parties is invalid, or void, would the parties prefer to have the dispute
about this issue be decided in arbitration, or before state courts? *Born* therefore
suggests that the principle of separability could better be described as a 'presumption of separability'.[63]

In international commerce, it is justified to assume that parties would have **19-037**
intended to resolve all of their disputes through arbitration, rather than submitting
certain disputes, such as disputes about the validity of the main contract, to the state
courts. Thus, commercial parties should be presumed to intend that an arbitration
agreement remains valid and binding even though the underlying contract is
claimed (or subsequently found) to be invalid, void, illegal, or that it has been
terminated.[64] Commercial parties typically want to maximize legal certainty, and
will prefer that all of their disputes are resolved in the same forum.[65]

By contrast, denying the presumption of separability would invite obstructive **19-038**
parties to avoid arbitration simply by declaring that the main contract, which
contains the arbitration clause, is void. The risk to then have to litigate the validity
of the underlying contract not in arbitration, but in a potentially inhospitable state
court forum, with attending risks of delay and potentially partisan decisions, is
unacceptable in the context of international trade. No reasonable commercial party
can be presumed to desire such effects.

---

63. G.B. Born, *International Commercial Arbitration – Commentary and Materials* (3rd edn, The
    Hague Kluwer Law International, forthcoming), ch. 3.
64. *See* U.K. Department of Trade and Industry Consultation Document on Proposed Clauses and
    Schedules for an Arbitration Bill, reprinted in (1994) 10(2) Arb Int'l, 189, 227 ('Whatever
    degree of legal fiction underlying the doctrine, it is not generally considered possible for
    international arbitration to operate effectively in jurisdictions where the doctrine is precluded
    (. . .) [I]nternational consensus on autonomy has now grown very broad.'). *See also* P. Mayer,
    'Les limites de la séparabilité de la clause compromissoire' [1997] Rev Arb, 359, 362 ('[T]he
    choice-of-law clause escapes the nullity of the contract because it is its very purpose to specify
    the applicable law according to which the judge or arbitrator will decide whether the contract is
    void. And for the same reason, the arbitration clause must be respected if it implies the parties'
    will to confide the question of whether the contract is valid or void to an arbitrator.').
65. BGH, 27 February 1970, VII ZR 68/68 in BGHZ 53, 315, (1990) 6(1) Arb Int'l, 79, 85 ('Above
    all, however, the parties to an arbitration agreement will as a rule wish to avoid the unpleasant
    consequences of separate jurisdiction.'); *Fiona Trust & Holding Corp. v. Privalov* [2007]
    UKHL 40 ('golden rule that if the parties wish to have issues as to the validity of their contract
    decided by one tribunal and issues as to its meaning or performance decided by another, they
    must say so expressly').

19-039 For the same reasons, the separability doctrine is a matter of the substantive validity of the agreement to arbitrate, and not, or only indirectly,[66] an issue of competence-competence. Properly viewed, the separability doctrine applies in the context of the parties' intentions regarding their agreement to arbitrate – and does not concern the legislative choice to allow a tribunal to determine its own jurisdiction. In other words, the separability doctrine allows for the presumption that the parties intended to arbitrate disputes even where the underlying contract is invalid, whereas the competence-competence doctrine merely provides that it is in the first instance for the arbitral tribunal to decide on all jurisdictional matters. Thus, separability is a matter of substance; competence-competence a matter of procedure.

C.   THE SEPARABILITY DOCTRINE IN AUSTRIAN LAW

19-040 Although the new ZPO closely follows the UNCITRAL Model Law, the autonomy of the arbitration agreement was not expressly included within the statute.[67] The Working Group decided against a statutory definition of separability – not because this principle has no application in Austrian law, but because the approach adopted by the UNCITRAL Model Law was considered to be 'grossly simplified.'[68]

19-041 The Working Group accepted that the existing case law in Austria would suffice to ensure that the invalidity of an arbitration agreement does not automatically lead to the invalidity of the main contract. As to the effect of an (allegedly) invalid main contract on the arbitration agreement, the Working Group stressed that this question depended on the hypothetical intention of the parties.[69]

19-042 Austrian law is therefore in line with the approach outlined above, which views the separability doctrine as a conceptual instrument to examine the parties' consent to arbitrate even where the validity of their main contractual relationship is in doubt. Although widely accepted by Austrian scholars,[70] the doctrine of separability has

---

66. G.B. Born, *International Commercial Arbitration – Commentary and Materials* (3rd edn, The Hague, Kluwer Law International, forthcoming), ch. 3.

67. A. Reiner, 'SchiedsRÄG 2006: Wissenswertes zum neuen österreichischen Schiedsrecht' [2006] ecolex, 468.

68. P. Oberhammer, *Entwurf eines neuen Schiedsverfahrensrechts* (Vienna, Manz, 2002), p. 75.

69. P. Oberhammer, *Entwurf eines neuen Schiedsverfahrensrechts* (Vienna, Manz, 2002), p. 75; P. Oberhammer in *Das neue Schiedsrecht – Schiedsrechts-Änderungsgesetz 2006*, B. Kloiber, P. Oberhammer, W.H. Rechberger and H. Haller (eds) (Vienna, Manz, 2006), pp. 233 *et seq.*

70. W.H. Rechberger and W. Melis in *Kommentar zur ZPO*, W.H. Rechberger (ed.) (2nd edn, Vienna/New York, Springer, 2000), Section 577, para. 16; H.W. Fasching, *Schiedsgericht und Schiedsverfahren im österreichischen und im internationalen Recht* (Vienna, Manz, 1973), p. 30; G. Backhausen, *Schiedsgerichtsbarkeit unter besonderer Berücksichtigung des Schiedsvertragsrechts* (Vienna, Manz, 1990), p. 98; C. Liebscher and A. Schmid in *Practitioner's Handbook on International Arbitration*, F.B. Weigand (ed.) (Munich, C.H., Beck, 2002), p. 546.

therefore been only applied on a case by case basis by the courts,[71] following the hypothetical intention of the parties. In most cases, the Austrian *Oberster Gerichtshof* confirmed on that basis that the invalidity or voidness of the main contract does not automatically entail the invalidity or voidness of the arbitration agreement.[72] Indeed, an arbitration agreement that refers to 'all disputes arising out of or in connection with the contract' was held not only to cover disputes concerning damages for breach of contract, but also the validity, recession or termination of the main contract.[73]

Thus, Austrian law approaches the issue of separability as a matter of contract **19-043** interpretation. Which disputes are covered by an arbitration agreement, must be determined on the basis of the scope of the arbitration agreement and interpreted in accordance with the intention of the parties.[74] Rather than the actual intention of the parties, one will have to examine what reasonable parties would have wanted in the circumstances, and thus focus on objectively reasonable expectations and intentions of commercial parties in the circumstances of the case. As discussed above, there is a powerful presumption that commercial parties have a strong preference for having all of their disputes decided in a single forum.

D.   LIMITS OF THE SEPARABILITY DOCTRINE

At the same time, it is inaccurate to describe the arbitration clause as 'autonomous' **19-044** or 'independent' from the parties' underlying contract. The parties cannot be presumed to want to arbitrate without reference to a specific legal relationship; and indeed, an agreement to arbitrate in the abstract raises issues of validity itself.[75]

Indeed, if the separability doctrine, or presumption, is correctly viewed as a **19-045** function of the substantive validity of the arbitration agreement, its limits are obvious: where the parties have not agreed to arbitrate in the first place, and the arbitration agreement itself has never been validly formed, the validity of the underlying contract becomes irrelevant. This means, however, that in certain cases the parties' lack of consent to enter into an agreement can extend to the arbitration clause contained therein. In these cases, the separability doctrine cannot cure the lack of consent of the parties. In the words of *Mayer*, '[t]he scenario in

---

71. For an overview *see* G. Zeiler, *Schiedsverfahren* (Vienna/Graz, Neuer Wissenschaftlicher Verlag, 2006), Section 581, pp. 68 *et seq.*; A. Fremuth-Wolf in *Arbitration Law of Austria: Practice and Procedure*, S. Riegler, A. Petsche, A. Fremuth-Wolf, M. Platte and C. Liebscher (eds) (Huntington, Juris Publishing, 2007), Section 592, p. 299 and the list of translated cases under Section 592, pp. 307 *et seq.*
72. OGH, 10 October 1962, 1 Ob 215/62.
73. OGH, 17 April 1996, 7 Ob 2097/96z.
74. OGH, 21 April 2004, 9 Ob 39/04g.
75. *See* **Article 1**, at paras. 048 *et seq.*

which an arbitration clause most clearly would not be severed, and hence would be invalid, is where the assent of one of the Parties is lacking. If the person to whom the offer is made does not accept it, then no contract has been formed, and the arbitration clause contained in the offer has not been agreed to any more than any of the other clauses, for there was no specific mutual agreement with respect to that clause.'[76]

19-046 Authorities agree that the separability doctrine cannot provide any basis for the arbitrators' jurisdiction where the main contract is inexistent for lack of consent, and the arbitration agreement therefore without any object.[77] Some suggest that 'where the question is not whether the principal agreement was or is valid, but whether it was actually concluded, there is room to challenge the authority of the arbitral tribunal to determine that question.[78] There is a distinction between the nullity of a contract – *ab initio* or, certainly *ex post facto* – and its never having existed at all.'[79] Similar limitations of the separability principle is also recognized by institutional rules. Article 6(4) of the ICC Rules, for example, provides that 'the Arbitral Tribunal shall not cease to have jurisdiction by reason of any claim that the contract (. . .) is non-existent'. As leading commentaries in the field confirm, however, the term 'non-existent' in this provision should be read as 'ceased to

---

76. P. Mayer, 'The Limits of Severability of the Arbitration Clause' (1999) 9 ICCA Congress Series (Paris), 264; P. Schlosser, 'Der Grad der Unabhängigkeit einer Schiedsvereinbarung vom Hauptvertrag' in *Law of International Business and Dispute Settlement in the 21st Century in Liber Amicorum K.-H. Böckstiegel*, R. Briner *et al.* (eds) (Cologne, Carl Heymanns Verlag, 2001), pp. 704, 706.

77. P. Sanders, 'L'autonomie de la clause compromissoire' in *Hommage à Frédéric Eisemann, Une initiative de la Chambre de Commerce International, Liber Amicorum* (Paris, ICC, 1978), pp. 31, 33; P. Jolidon, *Commentaire au Concordat Suisse sur l'Arbitrage* (Bern, Stämpfli Verlag, 1984), p. 139; P. Schlosser, *Das Recht der internationalen privaten Schiedsgerichtsbarkeit* (2nd edn, Tübingen, Mohr Siebeck, 1989), para. 393.

78. Note, however, this passage confuses separability with the principle of competence-competence. The lack of consent may extend to the arbitration clause, but it remains for the arbitral tribunal to determine, in the first instance, if that was so.

79. S. Schwebel, *International Arbitration: Three Salient Problems* (Cambridge, Grotius Publications Limited, 1987), p. 11. Courts and commentators make distinction between contracts that are 'voidable' and contracts that are 'void *ab initio*', applying the separability to the former but not the latter category. *See also* W.W. Park, 'An Arbitrator's Jurisdiction to Determine Jurisdiction' (2006) ICCA Congress hand-out, p. 94. *Park* distinguishes between '*ab initio* invalidity' of the arbitration agreement (in particular, cases in which the validity is put into question because of consensual defects), on the one hand, and 'events subsequent to signature' (comprising, amongst others, invalidity due to procedural events such as assignment, waiver of the right to arbitrate, failure to observe statutory or contractual time limits or undue delay in pursuing a claim), on the other hand. The case, in which no arbitration agreement has been signed, clearly relates to the category of '*ab initio*' invalidity of the arbitration agreement.

exist' and the provision does not apply where a contract, given the lack of the parties' consent, never existed at all.[80]

A similar line of argument is followed by Austrian decisions. Thus, an arbitration **19-047** clause built into a contractual relationship will cease to exist when the parties dissolve the entire agreement by way of consensus. This legal consequence will also apply when there is a unilateral dissolution of the main contract if the other party subsequently consents to the dissolution.[81]

Other Austrian decisions hold that, where the parties' lack of consent extends to the **19-048** entire contract, the arbitration agreement, as an ancillary agreement, shares the fate of the main contract and can no longer be considered applicable.[82] This is perhaps too simplistic. While it is accepted that in light of the relationship between the underlying contract and the arbitration agreement, there will be cases where defects in one affect the other, it will remain necessary for the courts to consider the specific factual allegations with respect to the agreement to arbitrate that are presented in the individual case. The crucial question remains whether there are factual allegations that the parties did not validly consent *specifically to the arbitration clause* – as distinct from the underlying contract – and whether there are alleged legal defects *specifically affecting the arbitration clause*.[83] The question posed by a US court – '[S]omething can be severed only from something else that exists. How can the Court "sever" an arbitration clause from a non-existent [contract]?'[84] – is therefore not self-evident. If there is a separate factual pattern that demonstrates consent to arbitrate – even where the consent for the main contract was lacking from the outset – a separate agreement to arbitrate is conceivable.

Austrian law recognizes a presumption that in doubt, the consent lacks only with **19-049** respect to the main contract but not the arbitration agreement.[85] Thus, if parties rescind part of a contract, but make no declaration with regards to the arbitration

---

80. A. Redfern, M. Hunter, N. Blackaby and C. Partasides, *Law and Practice of International Commercial Arbitration* (4th edn, London, Sweet & Maxwell, 2004), paras. 5-43 *et seq.* ('Although many institutional rules and national laws draft their separability rules to preserve the validity of arbitration clauses that are part of "non-existent" contracts (*see* Article 6(4) ICC Rules; Article 23(1) LCIA Rules; Section 7 English Arbitration Act), this non-existence cannot mean "never existed", but must mean "ceased to exist". If a contract has ceased to exist by the time of the arbitration, an arbitral tribunal still has the platform on which it may stand. If the contract never existed at all, then there was never an agreement. So the arbitral tribunal can have no valid existence, authority or jurisdiction.')
81. OGH, 16 January 2001, 4 Ob 330/00h; *see also* further OGH, 29 April 2003, 1 Ob 22/03x; OGH, 10 April 2003, 8 Ob 24/03t; OGH, 29 August 2002, 6 Ob 155/02s; OGH, 18 April 1985, 7 Ob 551/85.
82. OGH, 16 June 1982, 1 Ob 628/82.
83. G.B. Born, *International Commercial Arbitration – Commentary and Materials* (3rd edn, The Hague, Kluwer Law International, forthcoming), ch. 3.
84. *Pollux Marine Agencies v. Louis Dreyfus Corp.*, 455 F. Supp. 211, 219 (S.D.N.Y. 1978).
85. *See* **Article 19**, at para. 042.

agreement contained therein, the latter will remain effective for the part of the contract that remains in place.[86] If the main contract was initially valid and the disputes arise from a (unilateral) dismissal or termination of this contract, an arbitration agreement calling 'for all disputes arising out of this contract' remains also applicable for such disputes.[87] Even if the contract was allegedly void *ab initio*, the jurisdiction of an arbitral tribunal remains intact as long as the arbitration agreement itself was validly concluded.

---

86. OGH, 28 June 1977, 4 Ob 523/77, JBl 1979, 42.
87. G. Zeiler, *Schiedsverfahren* (Vienna/Graz, Neuer Wissenschaftlicher Verlag, 2006), Section 581, p. 70.

Article 20

The Conduct of the Proceedings

	Para.
I. Basic Principles of Arbitral Proceedings	1
A. Introduction	1
B. Conflicting Premises	5
C. The Right to Fair and Equal Treatment	15
1. Fair Treatment in International Arbitration	16
2. Fair Treatment in Austrian Arbitration Law	18
3. Fair Treatment Under the Vienna Rules	28
D. The Right to Be Heard	29
1. Basis for the Right to Be Heard in Austrian Law	33
2. Scope of the Right to Be Heard	37
2.1. Factual Assertions	38
2.2. Facts in the Public Domain	42
2.3. Legal Issues	43
2.4. Issues Raised by the Arbitrators *Ex Officio*	47
3. The Restrictive Approach Under Austrian Jurisprudence	49
4. Recent Criticism of the Austrian *Oberster Gerichtshof*	58
5. The Impact of the 2006 Reform on the Previous Case Law	62
6. Causality	67

	Para.
7. Limits to the Right to Be Heard	70
7.1. Evidentiary Cut-Off Date	71
7.2. 'Reasonable Opportunity'	76
7.3. Irrelevant Evidence	79
7.4. Appropriate Time Limits	81
E. Controlling the Conduct of the Arbitration	82
1. The Arbitrators' Discretion and the Parties' Agreement	85
1.1. The Primacy of the Parties' Agreement	86
1.2. The Arbitrator's Discretion	93
2. Managing the Conduct of the Arbitration	101
2.1. The Preliminary Hearing	103
2.2. Selected Issues of Case Management	112
(i) Procedural Timetable	113
(ii) Taking of Evidence	114
(iii) Identifying the Relevant Issues	115
(iv) Bifurcation or Other Segmentation of Proceedings	117

II.   The Language of the Arbitration 120
III. Written Submissions and the Right
      to an Oral Hearing 129
      A. The Right to an Oral
         Hearing 129
      B. Written Submissions in
         Arbitration 133
      C. The Right to Comment 141
IV.   The Oral Hearing 145
      A. Introduction 145
      B. Fixing the Hearing Date and
         Notifying the Parties 148
      C. Privacy of the Hearing
         (and Confidentiality of
         Arbitration) 152
         1. The Privacy of the
            Hearing 153
         2. The Confidentiality of
            Arbitration 156
      D. The Record of the
         Hearing 168
V.   The Taking of Evidence 171
      A. Introduction 171
      B. The Arbitrators' Right
         (or Duty) to Establish the Relevant
         Facts 178
         1. The Arbitrator's Duty to
            Establish the Facts Under the
            fZPO 181

      2. The Arbitrator's Right to
         Establish the Facts Under the
         ZPO 183
   C. Witness Testimony 193
      1. Written Witness Testimony 199
      2. Oral Witness Testimony 207
      3. Witness Preparation 216
   D. Documentary Evidence 224
      1. Document Disclosure in
         Common Law and Civil Law
         Litigation 227
      2. Document Disclosure in
         International Arbitration 238
   E. Court Intervention To Assist the
      Taking of Evidence 250
VI. *Ex Parte* Proceedings 257
   A. Introduction 257
   B. No Decision by Default 259
   C. Right to Proceed with One Party
      Alone 269
VII. The Obligation to Object Against
     Procedural Irregularities 272
   A. Objecting Against Procedural
      Irregularities Under the Vienna
      Rules 272
   B. Objecting Against
      Procedural Irregularities Under
      Austrian Law 279
VIII. Closing the Proceedings 288

I.   BASIC PRINCIPLES OF ARBITRAL PROCEEDINGS

Article 20(1): In the context of the Vienna Rules and the agreements between the parties, the sole arbitrator (arbitral tribunal) may conduct the arbitration proceedings at his (its) absolute discretion; the principle of equal treatment of the parties shall apply, the right to be heard being ensured at every stage of the proceedings. However, subject to advance notice, the sole arbitrator (arbitral tribunal) is entitled to declare that pleadings and the presentation of documentary evidence shall be admissible only up to a certain stage of the proceedings.

A.   INTRODUCTION

20-001 International commercial arbitration provides for the final resolution of disputes through neutral and non-governmental decision makers. These decision makers – the arbitrators – are usually,[1] just like state courts, expected to determine the facts

---

1. For a discussion of resolving disputes on the basis of equity or as *amiables compositeurs*, *see* **Article 24**, at paras. 048 *et seq.*

underlying the parties' dispute on the basis of the evidence put before them, and to apply those facts to the governing substantive law. Unlike state courts, however, an arbitral tribunal will usually neither be able nor required to rely on a 'code of civil procedure' or a set of developed case law providing extensive rules of procedure.[2] Indeed, most national arbitration laws, and most institutional arbitration rules, do not contain detailed provisions regulating the conduct of the proceedings, including, for example, the preparation and presentation of documents, the presentation of testimony of witnesses of fact or experts, the actual conduct of evidentiary hearings, or the exchange of written submissions.

It is, therefore, for the parties, or, if they cannot agree, for the arbitral tribunal, to determine the rules of procedure. Indeed, the procedural flexibility that attends this process is usually hailed as one of the hallmarks of arbitration. In an international setting, this process is informed by the varying legal backgrounds and cultural expectations of the parties, their counsel and the arbitrators involved, and thus requires an understanding of the often significantly different approaches taken by lawyers around the world. In international arbitration, counsel and arbitrators need to be able to bridge those differences in order to conduct proceedings in a neutral and fair manner. **20-002**

In the determination of a suitable procedure for their arbitration, the parties and the arbitrators are limited by the mandatory provisions of the applicable arbitration law, and the applicable procedural rules (such as the Vienna Rules) if their application was agreed.[3] While neither law nor rules will provide a detailed regime for the conduct of the proceedings, they will establish a minimum threshold aimed at ensuring the fair, equitable and efficient conduct of the proceedings. **20-003**

It is for the parties and the arbitrators to fill the gaps left by the law and the applicable institutional rules. This chapter therefore first examines the mandatory provisions of Austrian law as they impact on the conduct of any arbitration whose seat is in Austria. Secondly, this chapter addresses the provisions of Article 20 regarding the conduct of arbitration proceedings. Thirdly, it describes (as well as it can be determined) the current practice in international arbitration with a view to assist arbitration practitioners to fill the gaps left open by the law and the rules applicable to the dispute. **20-004**

---

2. As discussed at the outset, one has to distinguish between applicable procedural law and applicable procedural rules. The focus of this chapter is on the procedural rules regarding to the conduct of the proceeding, and will cover Austrian arbitration law (as the procedural law applicable to an arbitration sited in Austria) only insofar as is mandatory provisions impact on the parties' (or the arbitrators') freedom to determine the procedural rules of the dispute at hand.
3. *See* **Article 2**, at paras. 045 *et seq.*

B.   Conflicting Premises

20-005 Any international arbitral proceeding has to reconcile competing undercurrents that subject the arbitral process to significant tensions. These tensions need to be identified and addressed if the dispute at bar is to be resolved both in fairness and with efficiency.

20-006 First, there is an inherent tension between the autonomy of the parties that characterizes the arbitral process, on the one hand, and the judicial monopoly vested with the state, on the other hand. It is an axiomatic benefit of arbitration that allows the parties the freedom to structure and conduct their dispute in the manner that they consider to suit their particular circumstances.[4] The parties' autonomy is acknowledged in modern legislation, but limited by the state's claim (and responsibility) to ensure that basic tenets of fairness and the rule of law are upheld before vesting a private award with the enforceability otherwise reserved for state court judgments.[5]

20-007 Second, and in close connection with these considerations, some schools seek to isolate the arbitral process, as a *sui generis* form of dispute resolution, from the impact of national laws, and most specifically from the import of the law of the seat of the arbitration, whereas others view international arbitration as not international at all, but as firmly rooted in the legal system in which it takes place.[6] For arbitration to have legally recognized effects, including its validation as an exceptional system of dispute resolution in alternative to the state courts, it requires a statutory basis in the law.[7] The discussion, as well as the impact of the seat of the arbitration under Austrian law, is discussed in more detail in the context of **Article 2.**

20-008 A third and characteristic tension in international commercial arbitration arises from the clash of different legal cultures imported into the process by the parties, their counsel and the arbitrators. Specifically, the legal traditions prevailing in the Anglo-American system and the Continental-European system, respectively, can differ significantly with respect to what is understood as the proper conduct of the arbitral process.[8] This gap between the two major legal systems is oftentimes referred to as the 'common law – civil law divide' in international arbitration, an issue that, despite efforts at harmonization, periodically resurfaces in the discussion.[9]

20-009 Some of the differences between the systems are perceived, some are real and impact on a number of immediately-relevant aspects of the arbitral process: whether the

4. *See* **Article 9**, at para. 092.
5. *See* **Article 20**, at paras. 086 *et seq.* and 098 *et seq.*
6. K. Lionnet and A. Lionnet, *Handbuch der internationalen und nationalen Schiedsgerichtsbarkeit* (3rd edn, Stuttgart, Richard Bloorberg Verlag, 2005), p. 98.
7. K. Heller, *Der Verfassungsrechtliche Rahmen der Privaten Internationalen Schiedsgerichtsbarkeit* (Vienna, Manz, 1996), p. 3.
8. S. Elsing, 'Internationale Schiedsgerichte als Mittler zwischen den prozessualen Rechtskulturen' Supplement 7 to (2002) 46 BB, 19.
9. S. Elsing and J.M. Townsend, 'Bridging the Common Law – Civil Law Divide in Arbitration' (2002) 18(1) Arb Int'l, 59.

arbitration should be conducted in an adversarial or inquisitorial style; whether documents should be disclosed to the other side or not, or whether discovery requests should even be entertained; whether witnesses and experts should provide their testimony only orally or through written statements; whether and how cross-examination of witnesses through counsel should be conducted; and so forth. Arbitrators need to be acutely aware of the differences in approach. Given the different perceptions of what is 'fair', arbitrators need to be mediating between those differences to ensure that the parties' legitimate expectations of procedural fairness are met.[10]

Fourth, international arbitration is exposed to both a desire for flexibility, on the one **20-010** hand, and for predictability and legal certainty, on the other.[11] Of course, only a flexible approach to procedural issues does justice to the principle of party autonomy, and ensures a fair and balanced procedure that accommodates the expectations of parties from different legal cultures. On the other hand, granting the arbitrators unfettered discretion can severely undermine the predictability of the process for the parties and could conceivably endanger the integrity of the process.[12]

Recent years have seen a certain trend towards harmonization and codification. As **20-011** arbitration has established itself as the primary dispute resolution mechanism for international trade, certain commonly-accepted standards have started to evolve, possibly reflecting an internationally-harmonized approach to procedural issues. On the specific issue of the taking of evidence, the International Bar Association Rules on the Taking Evidence in International Commercial Arbitration (IBA Rules)[13] are the most prominent example of this internationalization. The IBA Rules were drafted by a working group comprised of both common law and civil law experts. They will apply to international commercial arbitration proceedings if the parties agree or the tribunal so orders, thereby supplementing applicable national laws or institutional or *ad hoc* rules. The IBA Rules have made a great contribution towards reconciling fundamental differences in legal tradition regarding evidentiary rules. Although it is difficult to assess how frequently the IBA Rules are actually adopted by parties, it is fair to say that they have had a considerable influence on the practice of taking evidence in international commercial arbitration.[14] Thus, parties and arbitrators are increasingly willing to employ in arbitration elements of a procedural system other than their own. Evidentiary solutions offered by the IBA Rules will be discussed in the appropriate context below.

---

10. S. Elsing, 'Internationale Schiedsgerichte als Mittler zwischen den prozessualen Rechtskulturen', Supplement 7 to (2002) 46 BB, 19.
11. K. Lionnet and A. Lionnet, *Handbuch der internationalen und nationalen Schiedsgerichtsbarkeit* (3rd edn, Stuttgart, Richard Bloorberg Verlag, 2005), pp. 98, 99.
12. K. Lionnet and A. Lionnet, *Handbuch der internationalen und nationalen Schiedsgerichtsbarkeit* (3rd edn, Stuttgart, Richard Bloorberg Verlag, 2005), p. 99.
13. IBA Rules, **Annex 16**.
14. W. Miles and F.T. Schwarz, 'Taking of Evidence in International Commercial Arbitration' in *International Comparative Legal Guide to International Arbitration 2004* (London, Global Legal Group, 2003).

20-012 Fifth, arbitration is required to reconcile the parties' desire to have their dispute resolved expeditiously, with a minimum of cost and resources expended, with the principle of a fair proceeding that affords both sides a reasonable opportunity to present their case. Indeed, most modern arbitration rules recognize that the duty of fairness and diligence coexist with the arbitrator's obligation to ensure efficient proceedings and to prevent unnecessary delay.[15]

20-013 With regards to the above, it is sometimes said that large Anglo-American law firms have turned international arbitration proceedings into offshore American style litigation.[16] This view has some merits, but is too simplistic. The reality is that over the last decades, arbitration has developed into the primary tool for cross-border dispute resolution. With the exceptional growth of arbitration as the preferred method of dispute resolution in international trade, disputes have become bigger and more complex and they involve higher stakes. In the circumstances, it is not surprising that parties are less inclined to view arbitration as a gentlemen's game, but would insist on employing all the weaponry available in more litigious *fora*. Where much is at stake, neither parties nor their lawyers can be blamed for a measure of zeal in pursuing their interests.

20-014 Yet the increasing cost and delay attending international arbitration is a matter of increasing concern.[17] This is less of an issue of having to reconcile different legal cultures, but more of an unwillingness to realize the full potential that is offered by the inherent flexibility of the arbitral process. Indeed, the increasing codification of arbitral procedure runs the risk of impeding the arbitrator's ability to customize the conduct of the arbitration. Rather than following an established practice, whether this practice is influenced by common-law or civil-law traditions, parties, counsel, and arbitrators should borrow freely from both systems whatever is best suited to ensure an affective and fair resolution of the particular dispute. What is suitable in one case, may result in delay in the other. As practitioners who arbitrate across borders and legal systems will readily testify, both civil law and the common law traditions offer procedural benefits. It is imperative, therefore, that arbitrators and parties retain 'an open mindedness toward different legal procedures and rules', and create a procedural framework for resolving the dispute that accommodates the legitimate expectations of parties from different legal systems in order to fully utilize the benefits of arbitration in each case.[18]

---

15. A. Philip, 'The Duties of an Arbitrator' in *The Leading Arbitrators' Guide to International Arbitration*, L.W. Newman and R.D. Hill (eds) (Huntington, Juris Publishing, 2004), p. 74; *see also* **Article 7**, at paras. 059 *et seq.*
16. H. van Houtte, 'Counsel – Witness Relations and Professional Misconduct in Civil Law Systems' (2003) 19(4) Arb Int'l, 459.
17. P. Hobeck, V. Mahnken and M. Koebke, 'Schiedsgerichtsbarkeit im internationalen Anlagenbau – Ein Auslaufmodell?' [2007] SchiedsVZ, 225, 229.
18. D. Bishop and L. Reed, 'Practical Guidelines for Interviewing, Selecting and Challenging Party-Appointed Arbitrators in International Commercial Arbitration' (1998) 14(4) Arb Int'l, 395, 400.

C.   THE RIGHT TO FAIR AND EQUAL TREATMENT

The right to a fair proceeding is a fundamental procedural guarantee, which forms **20-015**
part of the *procedural ordre public*.[19] It includes the principle of equality between
the parties, and the right of the parties to have a reasonable and fair opportunity to
present their case. This 'right to be heard' will be addressed separately in the next
sub-section.

1.   Fair Treatment in International Arbitration

The notion of due process and fair trial is an accepted and fundamental feature **20-016**
acknowledged in all major jurisdictions and international instruments.[20] It is perceived to form part of 'natural justice',[21] and seeks to avoid serious procedural
irregularities[22] that constitute 'a serious departure from a fundamental rule of
due procedure'[23] or from 'obvious'[24] general principles of 'international due

---

19. F.T. Schwarz and H. Ortner, 'Procedural Ordre Public and the Internationalization of Public
     Policy in Arbitration' in *Austrian Arbitration Yearbook 2008*, C. Klausegger *et al.* (eds) (Vienna,
     Manz, 2008); F. Mantilla-Serrano, 'Towards a Transnational Procedural Public Policy' (2004)
     20(4) Arb Int'l, 333, 342.
20. For an overview of the issue, *see* F.T. Schwarz and H. Ortner, 'Procedural Ordre Public and the
     Internationalization of Public Policy in Arbitration' in *Austrian Arbitration Yearbook 2008*,
     C. Klausegger *et al.* (eds) (Vienna, Manz, 2008).
21. This wording is not used in any of the jurisdictions under consideration here, but can be found,
     for example, in Australia, New Zealand and Zimbabwe which have enacted modified versions of
     the UNCITRAL Model Law providing that, 'for the avoidance of doubt and without limiting
     the generality of Articles 34 and 36 (of the Model Law), an award is contrary to public policy if
     (. . .) a breach of the rules of natural justice occurred (. . .)'. *See* International Law Association,
     London Conference (2000) 'Interim ILA Report on Public Policy as a Bar to Enforcement of
     International Awards', reprinted in (2003) 19(2) Arb Int'l, 217, 238; F. Mantilla-Serrano,
     'Towards a Transnational Procedural Public Policy' (2004) 20(4) Arb Int'l, 333, 346, too, refers
     to 'other elements of natural justice and due process' as a catch-all clause for procedural public
     policy in an international context.
22. A. Yakovlev, 'International Commercial Arbitration Proceedings and Russian Courts' (1996)
     13(1) J Int'l Arb, 37; International Law Association, London Conference (2000) 'Interim ILA
     Report on Public Policy as a Bar to Enforcement of International Arbitration', reprinted in
     (2003) 19(2) Arb Int'l, 217.
23. According to the ground for annulment stated in Article 52(d) ICSID Convention. J. Lew,
     L. Mistelis and S. Kröll, *Comparative International Commercial Arbitration* (The Hague,
     Kluwer Law International, 2003), para. 25-33 state that '[m]atters of natural justice or legality
     are often matters of (. . .) procedure.' S.M. Schwebel and S.G. Lahne, 'Public Policy' (1986) 3
     ICCA Congress Series (New York), 205, 217 state this public policy ground only refers to an
     'egregious departure from the due process or law'. *See also* International Law Association, New
     Delhi Conference (2002) 'Final ILA Report on Public Policy as a Bar to Enforcement of
     International Arbitral Awards', reprinted in (2003) 19(2) Arb Int'l, 249.
24. S.M. Schwebel and S.G. Lahne, 'Public Policy' (1986) 3 ICCA Congress Series (New York),
     205, 216.

process'.[25] As such, equal and fair treatment of the parties[26] is part of due process, together with the principle of fair notice (of both appointment of arbitrators and conduct of the proceedings) and a fair opportunity to present one's case.[27] Together, these essential values have been said to represent 'foundation pillars of any judicial procedure',[28] form part of the 'procedural *magna carta* of arbitration'[29] and have been termed 'basic principles that inform transnational procedural public policy'.[30] This is an accepted standard in international arbitration. Article 15(1) of the UNCITRAL Rules provides, for example, that '[s]ubject to these Rules, the arbitral tribunal may conduct the arbitration in such manner as it considers appropriate, provided that the parties are treated with equality and that at any stage of the proceedings each party is given a full opportunity of presenting his case.'[31] Similar provisions are contained in the ICC, LCIA, and AAA/ICDR Rules, all of which grant the tribunal power to determine the arbitral procedures[32] subject to providing the parties' with fair and equal treatment.[33] Similarly, the ICC and

---

25. P. Lalive, 'Transnational (or Truly International) Public Policy and International Arbitration' (1986) 3 ICCA Congress Series (New York), 257, 299 states that the concept of due process and its components equality of the parties and the principle *audiatur et altera pars* (or 'principle of contradiction') is 'undoubtedly a part of transnational public policy, as is demonstrated, on the one hand, by the remarkable harmony between national decisions and internal practices (or, in other words, by the coincidence of the concepts of domestic international public policy) and, on the other hand, their recognition by the practice of international jurisdictions or commissions'.

26. J. Lew, L. Mistelis and S. Kröll, *Comparative International Commercial Arbitration* (The Hague, Kluwer Law International, 2003), para. 25-36.

27. K.P. Berger, *International Economic Arbitration* (Boston, Kluwer Law International, 1993), p. 663; J. Lew, L. Mistelis and S. Kröll, *Comparative International Commercial Arbitration* (The Hague, Kluwer Law International, 2003), para. 25-36 ('minimum standards').

28. A. Reiner, 'Schiedsverfahren und rechtliches Gehör' [2003] ZfRV, 52, 52 *et seq.*

29. J. Lew, L. Mistelis and S. Kröll, *Comparative International Commercial Arbitration* (The Hague, Kluwer Law International, 2003), para. 5-68 describe this element as one of the two most 'fundamental standards of international arbitration', the 'constitutional cornerstones of arbitration proceedings', forming part of the procedural 'magna carta of arbitration': (i) due process and fair hearing; and (ii) independence and impartiality of arbitrators.

30. F. Mantilla-Serrano, 'Towards a Transnational Procedural Public Policy' (2004) 20(4) Arb Int'l, 333, 341.

31. Article 15(1) UNCITRAL Rules; *see* H. Bagner, 'Enforcement of International Commercial Contracts by Arbitration: Recent Developments' (1982) 14(3) Case W Res J Int'l L, 573, 577 (Article 15(1) is 'heart' of UNCITRAL Rules). The initial qualification of Article 15(1) refers to the mandatory procedural protections contained elsewhere in the Rules. This includes the parties' right to an opportunity to present their cases and to equal treatment. As noted elsewhere, the UNCITRAL Rules guarantee the parties the right to require a hearing (Article 15(2)), select the arbitral seat (Article 16(1)), and select the language of the arbitration (Article 17(1)).

32. Article 15(1) ICC Rules; Article 14(2) LCIA Rules and Article 16(1) AAA/ICDR Rules.

33. Article 15(2) ICC Rules; Article 14(1)(i) LCIA Rules and Article 16(1) AAA/ICDR Rules ('the parties [shall be] treated with equality and (. . .) each party [shall have] the right to be heard and (. . .) given a fair opportunity to present its case.').

LCIA Rules require that each party be afforded 'the right to be heard' and a 'fair opportunity to present its case.'[34]

In Europe, the pivotal significance of fair treatment is linked to Article 6 ECHR.[35] **20-017** Court decisions in a number of European countries have acknowledged the relevance of this provision for arbitral proceedings. The Swiss *Bundesgericht*, for example, held, although Article 6 ECHR does not directly apply in arbitration proceedings, the arbitral tribunal must nevertheless respect fundamental rules of due process.[36] The same attitude was echoed in England following the coming into force of the Humans Rights Act 1998, which incorporated the ECHR into English law,[37] famous by stating that '[t]he tentacles of the Human Rights Act 1998 reach into some unexpected places. The Commercial Court, even, when exercising its supervisory rule as regards arbitration, is not immune.'[38] Commentary has tried to distill those elements of Article 6 ECHR which represent indispensable procedural guarantees also in arbitral proceedings,[39] again particularly emphasizing the right to be heard and to fair and equal treatment. Under that standard of equality and fairness, each party must have been afforded an appropriate opportunity to present its case including its evidence, and to do so in circumstances which would not constitute a significant disadvantage *vis-à-vis* the opposing party.[40]

2.   Fair Treatment in Austrian Arbitration Law

The pivotal significance of these central concepts is also reflected in Austrian **20-018** arbitration law. Although under the previous legal regime, Section 587(1) fZPO did not expressly provide for the fair and equal treatment of the parties, it has always been uncontroversial that the principle of equal treatment is part of the Austrian *procedural ordre public* as a mandatory principle of the 'administration

---

34. Article 15(2) ICC Rules and Article 14(1)(i) LCIA Rules; *see also* Article 16(1) AAA/ICDR Rules and **Article 20(1)**.

35. Convention for the Protection of Human Rights and Fundamental Freedoms (Rome, November 4, 1950), (1955) 213 United Nations Treaty Series 221, as amended. Article 6(1) reads: 'In the determination of his civil rights and obligations or of any criminal charge against him, everyone is entitled to a fair and public hearing within a reasonable time by an independent and impartial tribunal established by law.'

36. BGer, 11 June 2001, BGE 127 III 429, (2001) 19(3) Bull ASA, 566; A. Redfern, M. Hunter, N. Blackaby and C. Partasides, *Law and Practice of International Commercial Arbitration* (4th edn, London, Sweet & Maxwell, 2004), para. 9-24.

37. A. Redfern, M. Hunter, N. Blackaby and C. Partasides, *Law and Practice of International Commercial Arbitration* (4th edn, London, Sweet & Maxwell, 2004), para. 9-24.

38. *Mousaka Inc. v Golden Seagull Maritime Inc. and Another* [2001] 2 Lloyd's Rep. 657 Q.B. (Comm.).

39. *See* especially A. Reiner, 'Schiedsverfahren und rechtliches Gehör' [2003] ZfRV, 52, 60 *et seq.*; C. Liebscher, *The Healthy Award* (The Hague, Kluwer Law International, 2003), pp 101 *et seq.*

40. EHR Court, 27 October 1993, *Dombo Beheer B.V.v the Netherlands*, App. 14448/88, ÖJZ 1994, 464.

of justice'.[41] Specifically, such a rule was implied into Austrian procedural law by virtue of the Austrian constitution and Article 6 ECHR.[42] Thus, the right to equal and fair treatment was considered mandatory.[43]

20-019 Section 594 ZPO now contains the express provision that the 'parties must be treated fairly'. Section 594(2) ZPO resembles Article 18 UNCITRAL Model Law und Section 1042(1) German ZPO, referring to the parties' right to 'be given full opportunity of presenting his case'. In contrast to the UNCITRAL Model Law, however, which states that 'the parties shall be treated with equality', the Austrian wording is broader, stating that '[t]he parties shall be treated fairly'. The fundamental principles of the right to be heard[44] as well as fair and equal[45] treatment[46] of the parties are protected by constituting grounds for setting aside an award.

20-020 Under the principle of fair treatment, arbitrators are required to ensure that there has been a fair and even-handed approach to the presentation of the argument and the taking of evidence from both parties; including that both parties' are given the opportunity to address each others' case.[47] Some have argued that the right to a fair treatment could also require the arbitrators to hold an oral hearing in 'special circumstances',[48] in particular where the decision would be based on 'the personal

---

41. C. Liebscher and A. Schmid in *Practitioner's Handbook on International Arbitration*, F.B. Weigand (ed.) (Munich, C.H. Beck, 2002), p. 557.
42. C. Liebscher and A. Schmid in *Practitioner's Handbook on International Arbitration*, F.B. Weigand (ed.) (Munich, C.H. Beck, 2002), p. 558 with further annotations.
43. H.W. Fasching, *Schiedsgericht und Schiedsverfahren im österreichischen und im internationalen Recht* (Vienna, Manz, 1973), p. 103.
44. For an overview of the 'right to be heard' in Austrian arbitration law, *see* G. Zeiler, *Schiedsverfahren* (Vienna/Graz, Neuer Wissenschaftlicher Verlag, 2006), Section 594, pp. 198 *et seq.*
45. A. Reiner, *Das neue österreichische Schiedsrecht/The New Austrian Arbitration Law* (Vienna, LexisNexis, 2006), Section 594, note 112.
46. For Austrian case law discussing 'fair treatment', *see* M. Platte in *Arbitration Law of Austria: Practice and Procedure*, S. Riegler, A. Petsche, A. Fremuth-Wolf, M. Platte and C. Liebscher (eds) (Huntington, Juris Publishing, 2007), Section 594, pp. 335 *et seq.*
47. *See also* E. Gaillard and J. Savage (eds) *Fouchard Gaillard Goldman On International Commercial Arbitration* (The Hague, Kluwer Law International, 1999), paras. 1638 *et seq.*; S.M. Schwebel and S.G. Lahne, 'Public Policy' (1986) 3 ICCA Congress Series (New York), 205, 220. In a German decision, the court found a violation of public policy in a case where the sole arbitrator held no oral hearings and decided on basis of the submitted documents, but did not forward a letter from the American firm (which won the arbitration) before the decision to the German firm. In addition the arbitrator gave no weight to the contradicting letter submitted by a German Ministry on behalf of the German firm. The *Oberlandesgericht Hamburg* (Hamburg Court of Appeal) denied enforcement of the award and said that the actions of this arbitrator presented the '*extreme case*' 'where a party had not been able to present his case in an arbitration abroad', that violated 'the basic principles of the German legal order'. *See* S.M. Schwebel and S.G. Lahne, 'Public Policy' (1987) 3 ICCA Congress Series (New York) 205, 219 *et seq.*
48. A. Reiner, 'Schiedsverfahren und rechtliches Gehör' [2003] ZfRV, 52, 60 *et seq.*

behaviour of a party',[49] or a 'direct assessment of the evidence'[50] appears mandated.[51]

In substituting the UNCITRAL Model Law's reference to 'equality' for a broader **20-021** notion of 'fairness', the ZPO acknowledges that equal treatment does not automatically guarantee fair treatment.[52] Indeed, the Working Group specifically noted that 'fairness' is a broad term beyond equality; it includes the requirement of equal treatment, yet prevents a purely formalistic approach to what is understood as 'equal'.[53] The Austrian legislature notes in the explanatory materials as well that formal equality is only one aspect of a comprehensive fair legal protection as it is guaranteed in Article 6(1) ECHR[54] as the governing standard for Austrian law[55] (discussed further below). The legislature thus made a conscious decision to deviate from the UNCITRAL Model Law, whose Article 18 only states that 'the parties shall be treated with equality'.

This is an important differentiation because some scholars, particularly in common **20-022** law jurisdictions, argue that the parties must be 'equally armed'.[56] The reference to 'fairness' in Section 594(2) ZPO makes clear, however, that this cannot mean a merely 'formal equality' (with respect, for example, to affording both sides automatically equal time limits or hearing time).[57] In contrast the broader Austrian formulation ('[t]he parties shall be treated fairly')[58] acknowledges that equal

---

49. EHR Commission, 2 October 1990, *Muyldermans v Belgium*, App. 12217/86, <http://www.echr.coe.int>.
50. EHR Court, 29 October 1991, *Jan-Ake Andersson v Sweden*, App. 11274/84, ÖJZ 1992, 304.
51. A. Reiner, *Das neue österreichische Schiedsrecht/The new Austrian Arbitration Law* (Vienna, LexisNexis, 2006), Section 598, note 124.
52. *See* M. Platte in *Arbitration Law of Austria: Practice and Procedure*, S. Riegler, A. Petsche, A. Fremuth-Wolf, M. Platte and C. Liebscher (eds) (Huntington, Juris Publishing, 2007), Section 594, p. 334; A. Reiner, 'Schiedsverfahren und rechtliches Gehör' [2003] ZfRV, 52, 60 *et seq.*
53. P. Oberhammer, *Entwurf eines neuen Schiedsverfahrensrechts* (Vienna, Manz, 2002), p. 92. Indeed, equally bad treatment is not good enough. *See* A. Philip, 'The Duties of an Arbitrator', in *The Leading Arbitrators' Guide to International Arbitration*, L.W. Newman and R.D. Hill (ed.) (Huntington, Juris Publishing, 2004), p. 75.
54. *See* P. Oberhammer, *Entwurf eines neuen Schiedsverfahrensrechts* (Vienna, Manz, 2002), p. 92.
55. M. Platte in *Arbitration Law of Austria: Practice and Procedure*, S. Riegler, A. Petsche, A. Fremuth-Wolf, M. Platte and C. Liebscher (eds) (Huntington, Juris Publishing, 2007), Section 594, pp. 334 *et seq.*
56. J.F. Poudret and S. Besson, *Comparative Law of International Arbitration* (2nd edn, London, Sweet & Maxwell, 2007), para. 816; U. Haas in *Practitioner's Handbook on International Arbitration*, F.B. Weigand (ed.) (Munich, C.H. Beck, 2002), pp. 399, 522.
57. P. Oberhammer, *Entwurf eines neuen Schiedsverfahrensrechts* (Vienna, Manz, 2002), p. 92. For a different view, *see* J. Power, *The Austrian Arbitration Act – A Practitioner's Guide to Sections 577-618 of the Austrian Code of Civil Procedure* (Vienna, Manz, 2006), Section 594, para. 4.
58. The original draft of the UNCITRAL Rules provided that the parties were required to be treated with 'absolute equality'. The reference to 'absolute' equality was deleted in the final draft in order to avoid suggestions that mechanical standards were applicable. *See* Report of the Secretary-General on the

treatment does not automatically guarantee fair treatment. Fair treatment also does not mean that both parties have actually participated in equal measure in the proceedings. If a party has been given a fair opportunity to participate, but chooses not to do so, it cannot later complain.[59]

20-023 The Working Group drafting the new Austrian arbitration law also suggested that the term 'fair' is directly taken from Article 6 ECHR (which is part of the Austrian legal order and on par with the Austrian constitution). This approach is reflected in Section 594(2) ZPO, as eventually adopted.[60] In its explanatory remarks, the legislature made clear[61] that both procedural guarantees, the right to be heard and fair treatment, are directly derived from Article 6(1) ECHR as interpreted by the pertinent case law of the EHR Court. It has been said, therefore, that this provision 'lays down the fundamental principles of arbitral procedure under the [Austrian Arbitration Act 2006]' and that they 'may be considered the overriding principles of the Arbitration Act 2006 as a whole'.[62] This is in line with the intention of

---

Preliminary Draft Set of Arbitration Rules, Preliminary Draft Set of Arbitration Rules for an Optional Use in *Ad Hoc* Arbitration Relating to International Trade, UNCITRAL 8th Session, UN Doc A/CN.9/97 (1974), (1975) VI UNCITRAL YB 163, 172-73; and Report of the UNCITRAL, 8th Session, Summary of Discussion of the Preliminary Draft, UN Doc. A/10017, para. 99 (1975), (1975) VI UNCITRAL YB 24, 35 ('In this context, the comment was made that what was important was not the imposition of an obligation to observe the principle of equal treatment, since in certain circumstances (such as where the parties made conflicting requests to an arbitral tribunal) such treatment was impossible; the real need was to stress that both parties should receive fair treatment. It was suggested, however, that the best course might be to modify the paragraph so as to impose an obligation on the arbitrators to treat the parties both with equality and fairness.').

59.   For France, *see* Cour de Cassation, 1re Ch. Civ., 7 January 1992, *Siemens AG/BKMI Indus-trienanlagen GmbH v. Dutco Construction Company*, (1993) XVIII YB Comm Arb, 140 *et seq.*; for Switzerland *see* BGer, 12 February 1958, BGE 84 I 56, 60 *et seq.*; BGer, 3 May 1967, BGE 93 I 265, 272; for Germany *see* BGH, 19 December 1968, VII ZR 83/66 in BGHZ 51, 255, 258; BGH, 26 January, 1989, XZR 23/87, JZ 1989, 588, 589; LG Hamburg, 10 December 1985, 23 0 147/85, (1987) XII YB Comm Arb, 487, 488; BGH, 15 May 1986, III ZR 192/84, RIW 1986, 816, 817 *et seq.* For a comparative survey of decisions based on Article 6 ECHR, *see* A. Reiner, 'Schiedsverfahren und rechtliches Gehör' [2003] ZfRV 52, 64.

60.   *See* M. Platte in *Arbitration Law of Austria: Practice and Procedure*, S. Riegler, A. Petsche, A. Fremuth-Wolf, M. Platte and C. Liebscher (eds) (Huntington, Juris Publishing, 2007), Section 594, p. 334.

61.   This is made explicit in the explanatory remarks of the legislator. *See also* P. Oberhammer, *Entwurf eines neuen Schiedsverfahrensrechts* (Vienna, Manz, 2002), p. 92, who notes that the term 'fair' has been taken over 'directly from Article 6(1) ECHR, which forms part of Austria's constitutional law and is, thus, no foreign matter in Austrian law'; J. Power, *The Austrian Arbitration Act – A Practitioner's Guide to Sections 577-618 of the Austrian Code of Civil Procedure* (Vienna, Manz, 2006), Section 594(2), para. 4; G. Zeiler, *Schiedsverfahren* (Vienna/ Graz, Neuer Wissenschaftlicher Verlag, 2006), Section 594, p. 198.

62.   J. Power, *The Austrian Arbitration Act – A Practitioner's Guide to Sections 577-618 of the Austrian Code of Civil Procedure* (Vienna, Manz, 2006), Section 594, para.4; *see* A. von Saucken, *Die Reform des österreichischen Schiedsverfahrensrechts auf der Basis des*

the drafters of the UNCITRAL Model Law that these principles apply to arbitral proceedings in general.[63] The *ratio* for establishing this link with Article 6 ECHR was to incorporate the extensive case law and literature interpreting and giving precise shape to these broad principles,[64] providing a maximal degree of legal certainty regarding this broad fundamental maxim of procedural law.[65]

In reality, the express reference to Article 6 ECHR is a welcome clarification, but does not present an actual change in the legal regime applying to arbitrations. Article 6 ECHR has formed an inherent part of Austrian constitutional law for decades,[66] and it is a familiar feature of the Austrian legal system.[67] An infringement of fair treatment thus constitutes a ground for challenging an arbitral award on the basis of Section 611(2) nos 2 and 4 ZPO, as well as the procedural public policy provision of Section 611(2) no. 5.   **20-024**

Notably, some authors still deny the applicability of the ECHR to arbitration. First, they argue that an arbitral tribunal is no 'tribunal' in the sense of Article 6 ECHR.[68]   **20-025**

UNCITRAL-Modellgesetzes über die Internationale Handelsschiedsgerichtsbarkeit (Frankfurt, Verlag Peter Lang, 2004), p. 203.

63. *See* H.M. Holtzmann and J.E. Neuhaus, *A Guide to the UNCITRAL Model Law on Commercial Arbitration: Legislative History and Commentary* (London, Kluwer Law and Taxation, 1989), Article 18, p. 552.

64. W.H. Rechberger and W. Melis in *Kommentar zur ZPO*, W H. Rechberger (ed.) (3rd edn, Vienna/New York, Springer, 2006), Section 594, para. 4; A. Reiner, 'Schiedsverfahren und rechtliches Gehör' [2003] ZfRV, 52; M. Platte in *Arbitration Law of Austria: Practice and Procedure*, S. Riegler, A. Petsche, A. Fremuth-Wolf, M. Platte and C. Liebscher (eds) (Huntington, Juris Publishing, 2007), Section 594, pp. 334 *et seq.*

65. The Austrian case law regarding the old Austrian provisions, too, are still valid in this respect; W.H. Rechberger and W. Melis in *Kommentar zur ZPO*, W.H. Rechberger (ed) (3rd edn, Vienna/New York, Springer, 2006), Section 594, para. 4. For case law *see* M. Platte in *Arbitration Law of Austria: Practice and Procedure*, S. Riegler, A. Petsche, A. Fremuth-Wolf, M. Platte and C. Liebscher (eds) (Huntington, Juris Publishing, 2007), Section 594, pp. 335 *et seq.*

66. For a more comprehensive discussion, *see, e.g.*, A. Reiner, 'Schiedsverfahren und rechtliches Gehör' [2003] ZfRV, 52; C. Liebscher, *The Healthy Award* (The Hague, Kluwer Law International, 2003), pp. 65 *et seq.*

67. *See* A. Reiner, 'Schiedsverfahren und rechtliches Gehör' [2003] ZfRV 52, 60 *et seq.*

68. According to the majority view and the decisions of the EHR Court, voluntary arbitral tribunals are not considered 'tribunals established by law' in the sense of Article 6 ECHR. The fact that they carry out judicial functions does not suffice, as, although they are constituted and operate within a legal framework, their establishment and a large part of the organization of the proceedings is not (only) grounded in statutory or case law, but based on the parties' agreement or discretionary decisions of the arbitral tribunal. In contrast, in cases of compulsory arbitration imposed by the state Article 6 ECHR is directly applicable (EHR Court, 8 July 1986, *Lithgow and others v United Kingdom*, App. 9006/80, 9262/81, 9263/81, 9265/81, 9266/81, 9313/81 and 9405/81, (1986) 8 EHRR 329; EHR Court, 25 October 1984, *Bramelid and Malmström v Sweden*, App. 8588/79 and 8589/79, (1986) 14 EHRR 116). To constitute a tribunal in the sense of Article 6 ECHR, two requirements must be met: (i) The tribunal must have a power to decide matters 'on the basis of rules of law and after proceedings conducted in a prescribed

At least under the new ZPO, this is no longer convincing. As discussed, the Austrian legislature has specifically mentioned the ECHR as an influence on the drafting of Section 594 ZPO, specifically in order to incorporate core elements of Article 6 ECHR into the Austrian arbitration law, and to make its guarantees available to parties in arbitration. More generally, however, Article 6 ECHR not only obligates Austria as a matter of public international law, but also forms part of its constitutional system. As a result, Austrian state courts are compelled to safeguard these guarantees when exerting their control over arbitral proceedings, including in procedures for setting aside an award.[69] When doing so, they are required to apply the principle of 'interpretation in conformity with the constitution' which necessitates an interpretation of the procedural public policy clause of Section 611(2) no. 5 ZPO in accordance with the procedural guarantees of Article 6 ECHR, to the extent they represent indispensable guarantees.

---

matter' (*see, e.g.*, EHR Court, 27 August 1991, *Demicoli v Malta*, App. 13057/87, (1992) 14 EHRR 47, at para. 39, with further references). (ii) Secondly, it must be 'established by law', which, in principle, means independence from the executive (P. van Dijk and G. van Hoof, *Theory and Practice of the European Convention on Human Rights* (4th edn, Antwerpen/ Oxford, Intersentia, 2006), pp. 623 *et seq.*). Cour d'Appel de Paris, 15 Septemebr 1998, *Cubic Defence Systems v Chambre de Commerce International*, [1999], Rev Arb, 103 with note by *Lalive*, and the French *Cour de Cassation's* decision in the same case two years later [2001] Rev Arb 511 with note by *Clay*, in which the French courts found that, as an arbitral institution, the ICC International Court of Arbitration was not a 'judicial body' within the meaning of Article 6 ECHR. (A. Redfern, M. Hunter, N. Blackaby and C. Partasides, *Law and Practice of International Commercial Arbitration* (4th edn, London, Sweet & Maxwell, 2004), para. 9-24). *See also* the discussion in C. Liebscher, *The Healthy Award* (The Hague, Kluwer Law International, 2003), pp. 73 *et seq.* with further references.

69. This is in line with the decisions of the EHR Court: *See* the discussion of the *Nordström, Schiebler, Jacob Boss Söhne* and *Souvaniemi* decisions in C. Liebscher, *The Healthy Award* (The Hague, Kluwer Law International, 2003), pp. 75 *et seq.* For example, in *Nordström* (27 November 1996, *L.M. Nordström-Janzon and A.M. Nordström-Lehtinen v the Netherlands*, App. 28101/95, <http://www.echr.coe.int>) the EHR Commission, although acknowledging that 'each Contracting State may in principle decide itself on which grounds an arbitral award should be quashed', did not deviate from the well established principle that the EHR Court has the final word as to whether the results achieved are in conformity with the ECHR. In *Schiebler* (EHR Commission 2 December 1991, *Heinz Schiebler v Germany*, App. 18805/91, <http://www.echr.coe.int>) the EHR Commission made clear that the fact that a party voluntarily enters into an arbitration agreement does not mean that the 'state's responsibility is completely excluded (. . .) as the arbitration award had to be recognized by the [national] courts and be given executory effect by them. The courts thereby exercised a certain control and guarantee as to the fairness and correctness of the arbitration proceedings.' The same position was taken in *Jakob Boss Söhne* (EHR Commission, 2 December 1991, *Jakob Boss Söhne KG v Germany*, App. 18479/91, <http://www.echr.coe.int>). *See also* A. Redfern, M. Hunter, N. Blackaby and C. Partasides, *Law and Practice of International Commercial Arbitration* (4th edn, London, Sweet & Maxwell, 2004), para. 9-25. Compare, *e.g.*, J. Lew, L. Mistelis and S. Kröll, *Comparative International Commercial Arbitration* (The Hague, Kluwer Law International, 2003), para. 5-65 and A. Reiner, 'Schiedsverfahren und rechtliches Gehör' [2003] ZfRV, 52, 62.

Some authors also argue that certain rights under the ECHR cannot be applied to **20-026** arbitration due to different characteristics in the process. For example, it is said that the right to a public trial is waived by the parties when they agree to resort to arbitration.[70] Given the privacy of hearings in arbitration (also under Article 20(4), discussed below), this is true. Indeed, as examined in the discussion of the right to be heard, the special nature of arbitration has to be taken into account when assessing the arbitral process against the standard of Article 6 ECHR. Given the parties' deliberate choice to subject themselves to a private process of dispute resolution, not every procedural guarantee applicable in state court proceedings can be mirrored with precision. However, arbitration 'surely is not intended to be a blanket waiver'[71] of fundamental guarantees like that to a 'fair hearing',[72] which, conceptually, are not at the parties' disposition.[73] Finally, some authors argue that it is not completely certain in which direction the EHR Court will further develop the guarantees of Article 6 ECHR.[74] This argument is circular. General provisions referring to concepts of fairness by their very nature entail an element of indetermination.

In short, the application of the core values enshrined in the ECHR to arbitrations in **20-027** Austria can no longer be seriously disputed. However, what will be open to the determination of the courts is the precise manner in which the procedural guarantees of Article 6 ECHR, originally indeed designed for state court proceedings, are applied to arbitration as a consensual dispute resolution mechanism.

3. Fair Treatment Under the Vienna Rules

Article 20(1) (just like its predecessor provision of Article 14(1) of the Vienna **20-028** Rules 2001)[75] provides that 'the principle of equal treatment of the parties shall apply (...) at every stage of the proceedings.' As a textual matter, Article 20(1), in referring to equality rather than fairness, does not reflect the deliberate legislative choice made in Section 594 ZPO, as discussed above. However, there is no doubt that the Vienna Rules, being systemically rooted in the Austrian legal

---

70. *See e.g.*, A. Redfern, M. Hunter, N. Blackaby and C. Partasides, *Law and Practice of International Commercial Arbitration* (4th edn, London, Sweet & Maxwell, 2004), para. 9-24, stating that 'an agreement to arbitrate constitutes a valid waiver of Article 6 in that arbitration provides no entitlement to a public hearing and an arbitral tribunal is not within the meaning of Article 6, considered a "tribunal established by law"'.
71. A. Redfern, M. Hunter, N. Blackaby and C. Partasides, *Law and Practice of International Commercial Arbitration* (4th edn, London, Sweet & Maxwell, 2004), para. 9-25.
72. *See* G. Petrochilos, *Procedural Law in International Arbitration* (Oxford, OUP, 2004), para. 4.51.
73. Note, however, the Section 611(2) no. 5 ZPO is only taken into account by the courts in setting aside proceedings if this ground is raised by a party and not, unlike violations of the *substantive ordre public*, on an *ex officio* basis.
74. P. Oberhammer, *Entwurf eines neuen Schiedsverfahrensrechts* (Vienna, Manz, 2002), p. 134.
75. Vienna Rules 2001, **Annex 2a**.

system, do not refer to a formal concept of equality between the parties, but intend to ensure that both parties are treated fairly throughout the proceedings.[76] Thus, the considerations set forth above apply in full to arbitrations under the Vienna Rules (and indeed, for arbitrations with their seat in Austria, the mandatory provision of Section 594 ZPO is not at the disposal of the parties or the arbitrators).

D.   THE RIGHT TO BE HEARD

20-029 As discussed, the right to fair treatment includes the right to be heard.[77] Although a part of due process, it has gained substantial prominence as an independent procedural guarantee. According to Article V(1)(b) of the New York Convention,[78] enforcement of the foreign award may be refused if the party against whom the award is invoked 'was not given proper notice of the appointment of the arbitrator or of the arbitration proceedings or was otherwise unable to present its case'. Under that definition, the right to be heard requires, first of all, that a party is put on notice that the arbitration exists. Naturally, the initial step of any arbitration is notification of its commencement; the other party's receipt of such a notification is the most basic prerequisite to be able to make use of its right to be heard and, therefore, universally accepted to be crucial to its being bound by any subsequent award.[79] In order for the notice procedures employed not to be defective, in terms of due process, they must be reasonably calculated to apprise the respondent that proceedings had been instituted against him and to afford respondent the opportunity to defend.[80] This is discussed in the context of **Article 9**.[81]

20-030 Further, a party must be given the opportunity to participate in the constitution of the tribunal, pursuant to the arbitration agreement and applicable law. This is

---

76. *See also* C. Liebscher in *Arbitration Law of Austria: Practice and Procedure*, S. Riegler, A. Petsche, A. Fremuth-Wolf, M. Platte and C. Liebscher (ed.) (Huntington, Juris Publishing, 2007), p. 642.
77. The Janus-faced nature of these procedural guarantees is also reflected in decisions of the EHR Commission and the EHR Court; just compare EHR Court, 27 October 1993, *Dombo Beheer B.V. v the Netherlands*, App.14448/88, ÖJZ 1994, 464, stating that each party must have a fair and equal opportunity to present their case.
78. NY Convention, **Annex 11**.
79. In the international context courts will look to the substance of whether notice was actually received, rather than to whether the technical service requirement of its domestic law were met. *See* S.M. Schwebel and S.G. Lahne, 'Public Policy' (1986) 3 ICCA Congress Series (New York) 205, 217; J. Lew, L. Mistelis and S. Kröll, *Comparative International Commercial Arbitration* (The Hague, Kluwer Law International, 2003), para. 25-36.
80. S.M. Schwebel and S.G. Lahne, 'Public Policy' (1986) 3 ICCA Congress Series (New York) 205, 218.
81. *See also* **Article 9**, at paras. 053 *et seq.*

examined in the context of **Article 14**, and, for proceedings involving multiple parties in **Article 15**.

Finally, all parties to an arbitration must be afforded the opportunity 'to present **20-031** [their] case'. Given the import of the New York Convention[82] it is undisputed that the right to be heard is a fundamental procedural safeguard. It constitutes, together with the right to fair and equal treatment, the core of due process. The parties' right to be heard impacts on, and must be observed at, all levels of an arbitration, including the parties' factual and legal submissions, the language of the proceedings, the taking of evidence and the results of the evidentiary process, and the challenge, if any, to the final award. The right to be heard is, therefore, a prominent feature under the Vienna Rules. Article 20(1) provides that 'the right to be heard [must be] ensured at every stage of the proceedings'. It also provides that evidentiary cut-off dates can only be imposed by the arbitrators with advance notice to the parties. Article 20(3) provides that an oral hearing must take place if one party requests it,[83] and that 'the parties must be given the opportunity to take note of, and comment on, the motions and pleadings of the other parties and the result of the evidentiary proceedings';[84] and under Article 20(8), the tribunal must ask the parties, before closing the proceedings, whether they 'have any further proof to offer, witnesses to be heard or submissions to make', in order to ascertain if the parties had 'an adequate opportunity' to present their case.[85] All of these provisions are intended to safeguard the parties' right to be heard – that is, to have a reasonable opportunity to present their case.[86]

While the principle is undisputed, its precise application still causes controversy, **20-032** and imposes difficult problems in individual cases, as does the challenge of an award on the basis that the right to be heard had been violated. Indeed, Austrian courts have traditionally applied an interpretation of the right to be heard that, in effect, is rather restrictive in comparison with international practice. This is the subject of the discussion below.

1.   Basis for the Right to Be Heard in Austrian Law

In Austrian arbitration law, the right to be heard is recognized, and protected, in **20-033** several ways. Previously, Section 595(1) no. 2 fZPO provided that:

> [T]he arbitral award is to be annulled (. . .) where the party seeking annulment of the arbitral award was not afforded the right to be heard in the proceedings before the arbitrators, or where such party, insofar as it requires a statutory

---

82. NY Convention, **Annex 11**.
83. *See* **Article 20**, at paras. 129 *et seq.*; *see also* Section 598 ZPO.
84. *See* **Article 20**, at paras. 141 *et seq.*; *see also* Sections 594(2) and 599 ZPO.
85. *See* **Article 20**, at paras. 288 *et seq.*; *see also* Section 594(2) ZPO.
86. *See* **Article 20**, at paras. 076 *et seq.*; *see also* Section 594(2) ZPO.

representative, was not represented by such person in those proceedings, unless the representation in the latter case was subsequently duly authorized.

20-034 Now, Section 594(2) ZPO provides, different from the UNCITRAL Model Law,[87] that '[e]ach party has the right to be heard'.[88] In order to facilitate this right, Section 598 ZPO (similar to Article 20(3)) requires the arbitrators to hold an oral hearing if one party so requests;[89] Section 599(2) ZPO requires that '[t]he parties are to be timely informed of every hearing and of every meeting of the arbitral tribunal for the purpose of taking of evidence';[90] and Section 599(3) ZPO requires that '[a]ll written submissions, written documents and other communications which are submitted to the arbitral tribunal by a party are to be brought to the attention of the other party. Expert opinions and other evidence to which the arbitral tribunal may refer in its decision are to be brought to the attention of both parties.'[91]

20-035 In addition, a violation of the right to be heard is codified as a ground for setting aside the award. Section 611(2) no. 2 ZPO states that '[a]n arbitral award shall be set aside if (. . .) a party was not given proper notice of the appointment of an arbitrator or of the arbitral proceedings or was unable for other reasons to *present his means of attack and defence*.'[92] Unlike Section 594(2) ZPO, but following Article 34(2)(a)(ii) UNCITRAL Model Law and Section 1059(2) no. 1b) German ZPO, this provision does not refer to the 'right to be heard' as such, but provides a narrative description of what that right entails:[93] (i) a failure to be notified of the appointment of an arbitrator; (ii) a failure to be notified of the arbitral proceedings altogether; or (iii) a failure for other reasons to present one's case.[94]

20-036 It is striking that Section 594(2) ZPO expressly refers to the broader concept of the 'right to be heard', apparently because that term (*'rechtliches Gehör'*) as applied in

---

87. Article 18 UNCITRAL Model Law refers to each parties' 'full opportunity of presenting the case'.

88. The parties' right to be represented by persons of their choosing under Section 594(3) ZPO can also be viewed as an expression of the parties' right to be heard in the sense that proper representation by counsel is an important safeguard to ensure a reasonable opportunity to present one's case. *See* **Article 23**, at paras. 001 *et seq.*

89. *See* **Article 20**, at paras. 129 *et seq.*

90. *See* **Article 20**, at para. 151.

91. *See* **Article 20**, at paras. 141 *et seq.*

92. So, the provision first explicitly states two particularly serious violations of the right to be heard, followed by a general clause. *See* W.H. Rechberger and W. Melis in *Kommentar zur ZPO*, W.H. Rechberger (ed.) (3rd edn, Vienna/New York, Springer, 2006), Section 611, para. 5; M. Wiebecke, 'Anfechtungsverfahren' in *Schiedsgerichtsbarkeit*, H. Torggler (ed.) (Vienna, Nomos/Verlag Österreich/Schulthess, 2007) p. 230.

93. P. Oberhammer, *Entwurf eines neuen Schiedsverfahrensrechts* (Vienna, Manz, 2002), p. 132; B. Kloiber and H. Haller in *Das neue Schiedsrecht – Schiedsrechts-Änderungsgesetz 2006*, B. Kloiber, P. Oberhammer, W.H. Rechberger and H. Haller (Vienna, Manz, 2006), pp. 11, 58; W.H. Rechberger and W. Melis in *Kommentar zur ZPO*, W.H. Rechberger (ed.) (3rd edn, Vienna/New York, Springer, 2006), Section 611, para. 5.

94. *See* **Article 27**, at paras. 046 *et seq.*

the context of Article 6 ECHR already forms an established part of the Austrian legal order,[95] yet Section 611 ZPO (governing the challenge of an award) refers to the arguably narrower concept of a party not being permitted to presenting its case. While authors argue, understandably, for a consistent standard for both arbitral procedure and the challenge of an award, it is in fact that somewhat restrictive description of the right to be heard as the parties' right to present their case[96] that reflects the narrow approach that has traditionally been adopted by the Austrian *Oberster Gerichtshof*.[97] However, grave violations of the right to be heard, in that they constitute a failure to observe due process as recognized in Article 6 ECHR, may also give rise to a challenge under Section 611(2) no. 5 ZPO (*procedural order public*).[98]

2. Scope of the Right to Be Heard

There is no dispute that the right to be heard extends to all factual elements of a case. This is discussed below, together with some more controversial issues, such as the right to be heard on the substantive law, and on the arbitrator's authority to raise legal issues on their own. **20-037**

2.1. Factual Assertions

A party must be given the opportunity 'to present its case' by making factual assertions, and offering evidence.[99] It must also be afforded the opportunity to 'present its case' in reply, and thus respond to the factual allegations asserted by the other side.[100] As a result, the tribunal is not permitted to base its award on evidence or factual assertions on which the parties have had no opportunity to comment. **20-038**

---

95. P. Oberhammer, *Entwurf eines neuen Schiedsverfahrensrechts* (Vienna, Manz, 2002), p. 92.
96. P. Oberhammer, *Entwurf eines neuen Schiedsverfahrensrechts* (Vienna, Manz, 2002), p. 132. *Riegler* criticizes this formulation as 'an unfortunate and ambiguous wording', as every violation of the 'right to be heard' in its legal sense certainly constitutes a reason for setting aside (even though this might indeed not encompass the every-day use of the expression), and, thus, the only relevant question must be to determine the scope of the right to be heard. *See* S. Riegler in *Arbitration Law of Austria: Practice and Procedure*, S. Riegler, A. Petsche, A. Fremuth-Wolf, M. Platte and C. Liebscher (eds) (Huntington, Juris Publishing, 2007), Section 611, pp. 523 *et seq. See also* Explanatory Notes to Section 611.
97. OGH, 27 October 1926, Ob III 768, ZBl 1927/60; OGH, 6 September 1990, 6 Ob 572/90; OGH, 5 May 1998, 3 Ob 2372/96m; OGH, 1 September 1999, 9 Ob 120/99h.
98. S. Riegler in *Arbitration Law of Austria: Practice and Procedure*, S. Riegler, A. Petsche, A. Fremuth-Wolf, M. Platte and C. Liebscher (eds) (Huntington, Juris Publishing, 2007), Section 611, p. 523. A. Reiner, *Das neue österreichische Schiedsrecht/The new Austrian Arbitration Law* (Vienna, LexisNexis, 2006), Section 611, note 196 argues that these grounds of setting aside are not to be understood in their strict literal sense, but rather in the sense of an infringement of the basic precept established in Section 594(2) ZPO that the parties should be treated fairly and that each party should be accorded the 'right to be heard'.
99. OGH, 13 January 1955, 2 Ob 422/54, JBl 1955, 503; OGH, 6 September 1990, 6 Ob 572/90.
100. OGH, 27 November 1991, 3 Ob 1091/91; OGH, 24 September 1931, 7 Ob 623/81, EvBl 1982/77.

20-039 Under Austrian procedural arbitration law, the right to be heard (Section 594(2) ZPO) must be given primary importance also when determining the facts and taking evidence. Pursuant to Section 594(2), 611(2) no. 2 ZPO and arguably 611(2) no. 5 ZPO, this constitutes a mandatory requirement and gives effect to the unassailable right to the equal and impartial treatment of the parties.[101]

20-040 In relation to the taking of evidence, this means that the parties must be afforded ample opportunity to comment on all facts and presented evidence on which the arbitral tribunal intends to base its decision.[102] According to *Fasching*, this imposes on the arbitral tribunal an obligation to confront the parties with any amendment to the facts.[103] Accordingly, the parties must also be permitted to participate in the taking of evidence by the arbitrators or by the ordinary courts by way of inter-court assistance (*Rechtshilfe*).[104]

20-041 One aspect which remains problematic is old case law (which *Fasching* seemingly continues to accept) holding that a hearing granted orally does not require the presence of all arbitrators[105] and there are no grounds for challenge if, for example, the third arbitrator (*Obmann*) of the arbitral tribunal, without hearing the parties, decides the case on the basis of the representations of the two arbitrators who heard the parties.[106] *Fasching* justifies this by reference to the fact that the rules governing the arbitral proceedings do not explicitly prescribe the immediacy (*Unmittelbarkeit*) of the proceedings[107] and some support this view on the basis of Section 602 ZPO which permits that only some of the arbitrators are present when a court takes the evidence in aid of arbitration.[108] However, these views are problematic where the taking of evidence is concerned. The parties should have the opportunity to present their case and the evidence to all arbitrators who participate

---

101. H.W. *Fasching, Schiedsgericht und Schiedsverfahren im österreichischen und im internationalen Recht* (Vienna, Manz, 1973), p. 103.

102. OGH, 6 September 1990, 6 Ob 572/90.

103. H.W. Fasching, *Schiedsgericht und Schiedsverfahren im österreichischen und im internationalen Recht* (Vienna, Manz, 1973), p. 102; *see also* OGH, 24 September 1981, 7 Ob 623/81, EvBl 1982/77. Even more problematic is the decision of the Austrian *Oberster Gerichtshof* in 2 Ob 199/61, where it was held that a change of the facts during the course of a hearing must be notified to the other party even if the party did not attend the hearing. *See* OGH, 12 May 1962, 2 Ob 199/61, EvBl 1961/387.

104. *See* **Article 2**, at paras. 055 *et seq.*

105. H.W. Fasching, *Schiedsgericht und Schiedsverfahren im österreichischen und im internationalen Recht* (Vienna, Manz, 1973), 103 with reference to OGH, 13 January 1955, 2 Ob 422/54, JBl 1955, 503.

106. H.W. Fasching, *Schiedsgericht und Schiedsverfahren im österreichischen und im internationalen Recht* (Vienna, Manz, 1973), p. 103 with reference to OGH, 19 November 1929, 1 Ob 1045/29, GH. 1930, 41.

107. H.W. Fasching, *Schiedsgericht und Schiedsverfahren im österreichischen und im internationalen Recht* (Vienna, Manz, 1973), p. 104.

108. M. Platte in *Arbitration Law of Austria: Practice and Procedure*, S. Riegler, A. Petsche, A. Fremuth-Wolf, M. Platte and C. Liebscher (eds) (Huntington, Juris Publishing, 2007), Section 599, p. 378.

in the making of a decision – that is, the entire tribunal. This position is not affected by Section 602 ZPO, where the taking of evidence is done by a court on behalf of the tribunal – this does not mean that certain members can generally withdraw from the taking of evidence. Indeed, all arbitrators owe a duty to render an award; and in order to perform this duty in a meaningful way, it seems problematic if they were absent from the taking of evidence. Unless both parties agree, therefore, it should be the entire tribunal to which the facts of the case, and the evidentiary record, is presented. Even more so, arbitrators are not entitled to delegate their judiciary function, including in the context of taking the evidence and establishing the facts, to third parties.[109]

2.2. Facts in the Public Domain

As regards facts in the public domain, there is Swiss precedent that no evidence **20-042** needs to be taken on such points, and the right to be heard cannot conceivably be violated.[110] This view may be problematic if the factual matrix relevant to the case goes beyond what is publicly known. In case of doubt, the parties should be heard on the application of such facts in the context of their case.

2.3. Legal Issues

It has traditionally been controversial whether the right to be heard should also be **20-043** extended to include the application of the law. Conceptually, in Austria as in other civil law jurisdictions, the law was perceived as something the court knows and applies *ex officio*, and not something that is susceptible to being pleaded (*iura novit curia*).[111] Notably, this position has changed in Austrian civil procedure over the last years. Under a recent reform, Austrian courts are now obliged to 'discuss the parties' factual and legal submissions with them.' The court is generally only permitted to base its decision on legal considerations, which a party has deemed irrelevant, if those considerations that were discussed with the parties and the parties were given the opportunity to make a submission.[112] It appears, therefore, that Austrian civil procedure has caught up with what is accepted practice in international arbitration,[113] where the parties clearly are entitled to make submissions, and be heard, on points of law as well. This result seems also mandated by Article 20(3) which requires that 'the parties must be given the opportunity to take note of, and comment on, the motions and pleadings of the other parties', which as

---

109. *See* **Article 7**, at para. 010; *see also* OGH, 13 January 1955, 2 Ob 422/54, JBl 1955, 503.
110. BGer, 22 February 1999, *B AS (Turkey) and C AS (Turkey) v. A S.p.A. (Italy)*, (1999) 17 (4) Bull ASA, 537.
111. OGH, 10 January 1991, 7 Ob 667/90, SZ 64/1; *see also* BGH, 8 October 1959, VII ZR 87/58, NJW 1959, 2213.
112. Section 182(a) ZPO; OGH, 25 May 2005, 7 Ob 83/05i; OGH, 8 June 2005, 7 Ob 105/05z.
113. A. Reiner, 'Schiedsverfahren und rechtliches Gehör' [2003] ZfRV, 52.

a textual matter does not seem restricted to only factual allegations, but appears to include legal pleadings and arguments as well.

20-044 However, it is acknowledged even under Article 6 ECHR that this does not extend to all legal questions which the arbitrators deem relevant for the case.[114] Thus, courts in Germany have regularly held that, based on the principle *iura novit curia*, 'the arbitrators are, within the scope of the right to be heard, not required to disclose their legal views to the parties and to invite them to comment'.[115] Similarly, the Austrian *Oberster Gerichtshof* has held in its decision 7 Ob 667/90, 10 January 1991, that 'in civil matters courts are not required to advise the parties that they make submissions on all legal issues which according to the courts' view apply in the individual case'.[116]

20-045 As *Reiner* points out, this may very well be problematic.[117] In a decision of the German *Bundesgerichtshof*[118] an arbitrator obtained legal opinions which he shared with his co-arbitrators in the course of the deliberations. The Court of Appeal upheld the subsequent award and stated that the obtaining of legal opinions is in essence no different than the thorough studying of literature and case law. German jurisprudence even admitted that 'an arbitrator is aided by a legal advisor in the course of the deliberations. The arbitrators had heard the parties on their legal views; it was not necessary to hear the parties on the legal views of the jurists.' The German *Bundesgerichtshof* confirmed this decision. This approach is not shared in all civil law jurisdictions, however. French courts, for example, have decided that the right to be heard is violated if a damages claim is based on tort in the award, although in the course of the proceeding the only legal basis discussed was a breach of contract.[119]

20-046 In international arbitration, a strict approach raises significant issues of legal culture. In common law systems, like England or the United States, counsel legitimately expect that an arbitrator will not reach a decision without hearing the parties on all relevant legal issues.[120] It is therefore advisable for arbitrators to set out the ground rules of their decision making, and discuss openly with the parties at the beginning of the arbitration how legal matters will be addressed. Practically, arbitrators will often have to apply substantive laws different from their own legal qualifications, and will therefore not rely on *iura novit curia* to decide the dispute.

---

114. EHR Commission, 7 February 1968, *X. & Co. (England) Ltd v Germany*, App. 3147/67, <http://www.echr.coe.int>.
115. BGH, 8 October 1959, VII ZR 87/58, NJW 1959, 2213; BGH, 12 July 1990, III ZR 174/89, NJW 1990, 3210.
116. OGH, 10 January 1991, 7 Ob 667/90, SZ 64/1.
117. A. Reiner, 'Schiedsverfahren und rechtliches Gehör' [2003] ZfRV, 52, 67 *et seq.*
118. BGH, 22 May 1957, V ZR 236/56, ZZP 71 (1958) 427 *et seq.*
119. Cour d' Appel de Paris, 25 November 1997, *Société VRV v Pharmachim*, [1998] Rev Arb, 684.
120. S. Mustill and C. Boyd, *Commercial Arbitration* (2nd edn, London and Edinburgh, Butterworths, 1989), p. 312.

2.4.   *Issues Raised by the Arbitrators* Ex Officio

Arbitrators may have to apply legal standards that have not been specifically raised **20-047** by the parties. This follows from the arbitrators' obligation to render an award that is not subject to setting aside under the public policy reservation of Section 611(2) no. 8 ZPO,[121] because the award is irreconcilable with the 'basic principles of the Austrian legal system'.[122] Such fundamental policies or values can come from Austrian constitutional law, criminal law, civil law, administrative law, or EU law.[123] Thus, arbitrators may have an obligation, irrespective of the law chosen by the parties, to apply certain regulatory rules or laws that aim to protect the public order (*loie de police*), such as currency and exchange regulations; competition law; restrictions on real estate transfer; or trade law ('*Eingriffsnormen*', 'protective rules'),[124] at least insofar as they are part of the Austrian *ordre public*.[125] Under Article 7 of the Rome Convention, there is no clear rule whether such provisions need to be taken into account *ex officio*, even if the parties do not rely on them.[126] On the one hand, it is argued that international arbitrators who have no connection to the arbitral *situs*, unlike judges, do not perform a judicial function in the name of or on behalf of a state – their mandate is one of resolving the parties' disputes, not of policing the parties.[127] Also, if arbitrators apply legal rules that have not been pleaded by the parties they may go beyond the scope of their mandate.[128] On the other hand, it is now firmly established, for example, that EU competition law as provided by Articles 81 and 82 EC Treaty constitutes part of the European *ordre public*, because of their fundamental importance for the functioning of the internal

---

121. It will typically be the public policy of the *situs* state that impacts on the parties' choice of law, through that state's *vacatur* provisions. *See* G.B. Born, *International Commercial Arbitration – Commentary and Materials* (2nd edn, The Hague, Kluwer Law International, 2001), p. 559.
122. OGH, 23 February 1998, 3 Ob 115/95.
123. *See* also **Article 24**, at para. 028 and **Article 27**, at paras. 060 *et seq*.
124. For the sake of clarity, public order in this context is not the same as *ordre public* which refers, as explained above, to the fundamental principles of the international or Austrian legal order.
125. *See* **Article 24**, at para. 027 *et seq*.
126. Article 7(1) of the Rome Convention provides: 'When applying under this Convention the law of a country, effect *may* be given to the mandatory rules of the law of another country with which the situation has a close connection, if and in so far as, under the law of the latter country, those rules must be applied whatever the law applicable to the contract. In considering whether to give effect to these mandatory rules, regard shall be had to their nature and purpose and to the consequences of their application or non-application.'
127. J. Lew, L. Mistelis and S. Kröll, *Comparative International Commercial Arbitration* (The Hague, Kluwer Law International, 2003), para. 17-53; B. Wortmann, 'Choice of Law by Arbitrators: The Applicable Conflict of Laws System' (1998) 14(2) Arb Int'l, 106.
128. *See* the Dutch Supreme Court Decision following Hoge Raad (Supreme Court of the Netherlands), 21 March 1997, *Eco Swiss China Time Ltd. v. Benetton International NV* (1998) XXIII YB Comm Arb, 180.

market.[129] Similar public policy concerns are raised with respect to certain areas of criminal law, such as drug trafficking, prostitution, arms trading, money laundering and other such activities that violate the *ordre public*,[130] and cannot easily be disregarded by the arbitrators. If the arbitrators consider the application of legal principles that have not been raised by the parties, they must invite the parties' comments before proceeding to an award on the basis of these considerations.

20-048 In that sense, the right to be heard is closely linked with the principle that the arbitral tribunal should not surprise the parties.[131] The German *Bundesgerichtshof's* decision of 10 October 1951,[132] is illustrative in this regard. There, the arbitral tribunal invited the parties to attend a hearing. The invitation contained the statement that if the parties would not appear before a tribunal, the tribunal would base its decision on existing materials. However, the arbitral tribunal then also summoned a witness to appear at this oral hearing without informing one of the parties. Consequently, when the uninformed party did not appear at the hearing and yet the witness was heard, the award was later set aside by the German *Bundesgerichtshof*. In that case, the tribunal had created expectations (that the hearing would not involve witness testimony) which it then did not meet by relying on witness testimony which one party had no opportunity to challenge. Accordingly, the German *Bundesgerichtshof* held in its decision of 28 May 1963[133] that the arbitral tribunal must not induce the parties to refrain to comment on certain aspects of the case, if the tribunal deems those facts relevant at a later stage.[134]

3.   The Restrictive Approach Under Austrian Jurisprudence

20-049 The Austrian courts have traditionally recognized that the parties must be able to present to the arbitrators all elements of their case.[135] A party must be made aware of any changes in the factual allegations of the other side, and must be given the opportunity to comment on such changed factual assertions.[136]

---

129. *See*, famously, ECJ, 1 June 1999, Case No. C-126/97, *Eco Swiss China Time Ltd v Benetton International NV*, [1999] ECR I-3055. *See* also **Article 7**, at para. 054.
130. For a detailed discussion, *see* R.H. Kreindler, *Strafrechtsrelevante und andere anstößige Verträge als Gegenstand von Schiedsverfahren* (Frankfurt/Main, Recht und Wirtschaft, 2005).
131. *See, e.g.*, BGer, 22 February 1999, *B AS (Turkey) and C AS (Turkey) v. A S.p.A. (Italy)*, (1999) 17(4) Bull ASA, 537; BGH, 11 November 1982, III ZR 77/81, NJW 1983, 867.
132. BGH, 10 October 1951, II ZR 99/51 in BGHZ 3, 215.
133. BGH, 28 May 1963, VII ZR 222/61, WM 1963, 944.
134. *See also* Cour de Justice de Genève, 1 June 1984, (1984) 2(3) Bull ASA, 200.
135. For a general discussion, *see* C. Liebscher, *The Healthy Award* (The Hague, Kluwer Law International, 2003), p. 244; H.W. Fasching, *Lehrbuch des österreichischen Zivilprozeßrechts* (2nd edn, Vienna, Manz, 1990), para. 2207; W.H. Rechberger and W. Melis in *Kommentar zur ZPO*, W.H. Rechberger (ed.) (3rd edn, Vienna/New York, Springer, 2006), Section 594, para. 4; A. Reiner, 'Schiedsverfahren und rechtliches Gehör' [2003] ZfRV 52, 52 *et seq.*
136. C. Liebscher, *The Healthy Award* (The Hague, Kluwer Law International, 2003), p. 244.

Austrian courts have regularly set aside awards if these principles had been **20-050**
violated in the course of the arbitral proceeding.[137] As early as 1899, the
Austrian *Oberster Gerichtshof* vacated an award where a sole arbitrator delegated
the taking of evidence to others without affording the parties of the arbitration the
opportunity to present their case to him.[138]

However, there is an equally long standing line of cases that arbitrators do not **20-051**
violate the parties' right to be heard if they disregard evidentiary applications or if
they establish the facts insufficiently.[139] This position dates back to cases from
1926[140] and 1934.[141] In the earlier case, a party challenged an award arguing,
amongst other things, that the arbitrators had falsely claimed in the award that
they had asked the parties to submit certain evidence and that in any event, such
evidence has been offered by the claimant but that the arbitrators had refused to
allow such evidence into the record. The *Oberlandesgericht Wien* (Vienna Court of
Appeal) held that the 'deficient procedural instructions in the arbitration do
not justify the setting aside of the award', remarking, in evident dislike of arbitration, that 'they form one of the dangers of this form of proceeding'. On appeal,
the Austrian *Oberster Gerichtshof*, in effect, confirmed this finding. It held that
procedural deficiencies – such as the arbitrators' failure to take or admit evidence –
do not justify the setting aside of the award, because a violation of procedural rules
and the resulting failure to establish the relevant facts are not expressly mentioned
in Section 595 ZPO as a ground for a challenge. This rationale was confirmed
in 1934.[142]

Although the Austrian courts have long accepted arbitration as a proper alternative **20-052**
to the judicial system, the reasoning applied in these early cases resonates in
modern case law. In 3 Ob 1091/91, 27 November 1991, a party relied on
Article V(b) New York Convention[143] and argued that the arbitral tribunal had
issued an award without taking into account certain documentary evidence and
without hearing certain witnesses that the party had offered. This was said to
constitute a violation of the right to be heard. On revision, the Austrian
Oberster Gerichtshof held:

> The refusal to enforce [an award] under Article 5 lit b of the [New York
> Convention] requires that the party, against who a foreign award is invoked,
> was not given proper notice of the appointment of the arbitrator or of

---

137. *See* A. Reiner, 'Schiedsverfahren und rechtliches Gehör' [2003] ZfRV, 52; C. Liebscher, *The Healthy Award* (The Hague, Kluwer Law International, 2003), p. 244.
138. C. Liebscher, *The Healthy Award* (The Hague, Kluwer Law International, 2003), p. 244.
139. W.H. Rechberger and W. Melis in *Kommentar zur ZPO*, W.H. Rechberger (ed.) (2nd edn, Vienna/New York, Springer, 2000), Section 595, para. 6.
140. OGH, 27 October 1926, Ob II 768, ZBl 1927/60, 141.
141. OGH, 20 November 1934, 3 Ob 735/34, Rsp 1935, 11.
142. OGH, 20 November 1934, 3 Ob 735/34, Rsp 1935, 11; *see also* A. Reiner, 'Schiedsverfahren und rechtliches Gehör' [2003] ZfRV, 52, 57 *et seq.*
143. NY Convention, **Annex 11**.

the arbitration proceedings or was otherwise unable to present its case. This in turn requires a violation of both parties' right to be heard (. . .) and this corresponds materially to the ground for a challenge set forth in Section 595 no. 2 1st case ZPO. Through its claim that the foreign tribunal had issued the arbitral award after four hearings and the production of voluminous documentary evidence without taking this documentary evidence into consideration and without hearing witnesses, the aggrieved party does not demonstrate the basis for refusal [discussed above], but merely objects against procedural irregularities. An irregularity of the award, because the tribunal has disregarded evidentiary applications or has insufficiently established the facts of the case, is not the same as a violation of the right to be heard (. . .) Even if according to more recent case law the right to be heard is impeded as soon as the decision is based on facts and evidence on which the parties were not afforded the opportunity to respond (see also Article 6 ECHR), the aggrieved party [in this case] limits itself to claiming that its case (. . .) was not sufficiently taken into account. This is not equal to the ground for refusal [discussed above], which is constituted if the party could not present its case in the first place[144]

20-053 This reasoning was followed in subsequent cases. In a decision of 24 July 1997, the Austrian *Oberster Gerichtshof* held, again with reference to the New York Convention, that the right to be heard is only violated,

> if the party was unable to present its case. The right to be heard is not violated on the other hand if a party's submissions were only sufficiently taken into account (. . .) it does not fall on the grounds for setting aside an award pursuant to Section 595 (1) no. 6 ZPO if the arbitrators have disregarded the factual or legal submissions of the claimant.[145]

20-054 Similar decisions were reached recently.[146] Thus, a violation of the right to be heard is not established if a party had the opportunity to make a submission, but this submission was not considered in the final award. According to the position of the Austrian *Oberster Gerichtshof*, the right to be heard is therefore only violated if there was no opportunity 'at all' for a party to present its case on all factual assertions and the evidence, neither orally nor in writing. The position that a party must have been deprived of any possibility to present its case goes back to 1955, when the Austrian *Oberster Gerichtshof* held:

> The right to be heard requires that, wherever the need arises in the proceedings, both parties are afforded the opportunity to submit to the arbitrators everything that they deem relevant, to participate in the taking of evidence or to comment on the results of any evidentiary hearing.[147]

---

144. OGH, 27 November 1991, 3 Ob 1091/91.
145. OGH, 24 July 1997, 6 Ob 186/97i.
146. *See, e.g.,* OGH, 6 September 1990, 6 Ob 572/90; OGH, 5 May 1998, 3 Ob 2372/96m.
147. OGH, 13 January 1955, 2 Ob 422/54, JBl 1955, 503.

However, the Austrian *Oberster Gerichtshof* also held that an award can only be set **20-055**
aside under Section 595(1) no. 2 fZPO if

> the right to be heard was not afforded to the claimant at all (*überhaupt nicht*).
> The incompleteness of the relevant facts or the insufficient discussion of
> legally relevant facts does not constitute the basis for the challenge. (. . .)
> The award is not subject to setting aside because the arbitrator has ignored
> evidentiary applications or because he did not otherwise establish the relevant
> facts appropriately and/or according to the guidance set forth in the arbitration
> agreement. An error in the [arbitrator's] determination of the relevant facts is
> not the same as the violation of the right to be heard.[148]

In this case, the Austrian *Oberster Gerichtshof* not only took the position that the **20-056**
arbitrators' total disregard for evidentiary applications is irrelevant, but that, for a
challenge of the award under (then) Section 595 no. 2 fZPO to be successful, the
aggrieved party must not have been afforded the right to be heard 'at all'. In a later
decision, the Austrian *Oberster Gerichtshof* explained:

> A party must not be generally deprived of the opportunity to make factual and
> legal submissions, including, of course, through its legal representative. The
> form and scope of the determination [of the case], however, are at the tribu-
> nal's discretion. It is sufficient to afford [the parties] the opportunity to submit
> its position on the dispute along with claims and evidentiary applications.
> The award is only subject to a challenge if the aggrieved party has not
> been afforded the right to be heard at all. An incomplete determination of
> the facts or an insufficient discussion of the legally-relevant facts do not justify
> the challenge.[149]

This strict reasoning has essentially been applied to this date,[150] but more recent **20-057**
decisions, in light of the ECHR, suggest a somewhat moderated approach. Thus, the
Austrian *Oberster Gerichtshof* has recognized that Article 6 ECHR requires that
the parties have the opportunity to comment on all facts and evidentiary issues that
are relevant for the final decision.[151] The Austrian *Oberster Gerichtshof* has therefore accepted that the right to be heard 'requires that both parties, as often as the
proceedings require, are afforded the opportunity, to submit to the arbitrators everything that they deem relevant, to participate in the taking of evidence and to comment
the results of those evidentiary proceedings'.[152] The Austrian *Oberster Gerichtshof*
also held that 'it is a fundamental principle of the right to be heard that the opposing
party is notified of every change of the relevant facts, and is afforded the opportunity

---

148. OGH, 13 January 1955, 2 Ob 422/54, JBl 1955, 503.
149. OGH, 6 September 1990, 6 Ob 572/90.
150. For a recent and very comprehensive analysis of Austrian case law in this respect, *see*
A. Reiner, 'Schiedsverfahren und rechtliches Gehör' [2003] ZfRV, 52, 57 *et seq*.
151. OGH, 27 November 1991, 3 Ob 1091/91.
152. OGH, 13 January 1955, 2 Ob 422/54, JBl 1955, 503.

to comment thereon'.[153] In that sense, not being heard 'at all' does not mean that the party has been excluded from the proceedings altogether, but that it has not been heard 'at all' with regard to a specific factual allegation (or a specific piece of evidence) that is relevant for the arbitrators' decision.

4.   Recent Criticism of the Austrian *Oberster Gerichtshof*

20-058 The position of the Austrian *Oberster Gerichtshof* has attracted considerable criticism from Austrian scholars, who argue that this standard falls short of Article 6 ECHR and of legal systems that are typically closely aligned with Austria, such as Germany and Switzerland. The most comprehensive and persuasive analysis criticizing existing Austrian case law (albeit under the regime prior to the 2006 reform) was levelled by *Reiner*.[154]

20-059 According to *Reiner*, there is no reason to define the right to be heard in arbitration in a manner that is less strict than the one in proceedings before the state courts. A lower quality standard is said neither to follow from the statute nor to meet the parties' legitimate expectations. *Reiner* thus confronts the Austrian *Oberster Gerichtshof's obiter* that a more narrow approach in arbitration is justified because of the fundamentally different nature of arbitration when compared to litigation before the state courts:

> There is a significant difference between the state courts on the one hand, which are bound by strict procedural rules and which decisions are typically subject to appeal, and arbitral tribunals on the other hand, against which decisions an ordinary appeal is not admissible and which can proceed, as far as the organization of the proceeding is concerned, in a far more flexible fashion when compared to the state courts. For that reason a challenge is possible only if there was a very substantial violation of fundamental principles of an orderly proceeding.[155]

20-060 In response, it is argued that the arbitrators' significant discretion in conducting the proceeding, their reasoning and their decision on the merits are not subject to appeal (save for *ordre public* violations). This is said to be all the more reason to require scrupulous and strict compliance with the right to be heard. As *Reiner* pointedly argues, the parties do not expect model proceedings without the possibility of appeal, but proceedings with uncompromised compliance with the right to be heard as a fundamental procedural safeguard.[156] Only because of this compliance, the parties would willingly give up their right to appeal an award on the merits.

---

153. OGH, 24 September 1981, 7 Ob 623/81, EvBl 1982/77.
154. A. Reiner, 'Schiedsverfahren und rechtliches Gehör' [2003] ZfRV, 52, 57 *et seq.*
155. OGH, 6 September 1990, 6 Ob 572/90; *see also* OGH, 18 April 1985, 7 Ob 551/85.
156. A. Reiner, 'Schiedsverfahren und rechtliches Gehör' [2003] ZfRV, 52, 59.

Reiner therefore argues that parties must not only be allowed to 'present their case' **20-061** if that presentation is then ignored; rather, the parties have a right that the arbitrators take into account, and consider in the reasons of the award, what the parties have argued. *Reiner's* position is in fact supported by the ECHR and pertinent case law. Under Article 6 ECHR, the right to be heard in a fair trial includes an appropriate assessment of the parties submissions, and the evidence they offered. Thus, the Commission decided in *Fouquet v. France* that the right to be heard is violated if an essential part of the evidence is misunderstood or disregarded, which would also violate the parties' right to have the proceeding conducted fairly within the meaning of Article 6(1) ECHR.[157] This result is confirmed by a comparative analysis. In Germany, the *Bundesgerichtshof* has held that 'the right to be heard is not satisfied merely by affording the parties the opportunity to present whatever they deem relevant. The court must also take their submissions into account and consider them.'[158] Similarly, the Swiss *Bundesgericht* held on 25 April 1995 that 'flowing from the parties' right to make submissions is their right to be heard with respect to legally relevant submissions.[159] Thus, the decision maker must evaluate all arguments, evidence that has been offered by the parties in the course of the proceeding, insofar as those are relevant for resolving the dispute. However, a formal breach of this principle can consist in the court inadvertently not dealing with certain submissions or misinterpreting them.'[160] Such case law suggests, contrary to precedent of the Austrian *Oberster Gerichtshof*, that ignoring relevant submissions can justify the setting aside of the awards.

5.   The Impact of the 2006 Reform on the Previous Case Law

The right to be heard as prescribed by Section 594 ZPO is also sanctioned, if it is **20-062** violated, as a ground for setting aside under Section 611(2) no. 2 ZPO and arguably under Section 611 (2) no. 5 ZPO.[161] The legislative process leading to the new law contains both arguments in favour of a restrictive approach (as previously adopted by the Austrian courts) and a more extensive approach, taking into account case law under Article 6 ECHR.

On the one hand, the legislator deliberately did not refer to a general 'right to be **20-063** heard' in Section 611(2) no. 2 ZPO, but chose to refer to the right to be notified of the arbitration and the constitution of the tribunal, and to 'otherwise present' one's case.

---

157. EHR Commission, 12 October 1994, *Fouquet v France*, App. 20398/92, <http://www.echr. coe.int> and EHR Court 31 January 1996, *Fouquet v France*, App.20398/92, (1996) 22 EHRR 279.
158. BGH, 14 May 1992, III ZR 169/90, NJW 1992, 2299.
159. BGer, 25 April 1995, BGE 121 III 331, 333.
160. *See also* BGer, 24 March 1997, *T AG v. H Company*, (1997) 15(2) Bull ASA, 316; BGer, 17 February 1999, *G. AG (Switzerland) v. TAS (Turkey)*, (2000) 18(2) Bull ASA, 311; BGer, 22 February 1999, BGE 4P.277.1998, (1999) 17(4) Bull ASA, 537.
161. F.T. Schwarz and H. Ortner, 'Procedural Ordre Public and the Internationalization of Public Policy in Arbitration' in *Austrian Arbitration Yearbook 2008*, C. Klausegger *et al.* (eds) (Vienna, Manz, 2008).

Indeed, it has been argued that a violation of the right 'to present one's case' only covers violations whose severity is equivalent to the two first instances – that a party 'was not given proper notice of the appointment of the arbitrator or of the arbitration proceedings' – explicitly mentioned in Section 611(2) no. 2 ZPO.[162]

20-064 On the other hand, the significance of the right to be heard under Article 6 ECHR is fully accepted in modern Austrian law. The fundamental principle of the right to be heard[163] is enshrined in Section 594(2) ZPO.[164] It has been said that this provision 'lays down the fundamental principles of arbitral procedure under the [Austrian Arbitration Act 2006]' and that it 'may be considered the overriding principles of the Arbitration Act 2006 as a whole'.[165] Indeed, in its explanatory remarks concerning Section 594 ZPO, the legislature made clear[166] that both procedural guarantees, the right to be heard and fair treatment, are derived from Article 6(1) ECHR as interpreted by the pertinent case law of the European Court of Human Rights. This is in line with the intention of the drafters of the UNCITRAL Model Law that these principles apply to arbitral proceedings.[167] Thus, the *ratio* for

---

162. W.H. Rechberger and W. Melis in *Kommentar zur ZPO*, W.H. Rechberger (ed.) (3rd edn, Vienna/New York, Springer, 2006), Section 611, para. 5.

163. For an overview of the 'right to be heard' in Austrian arbitration law, *see* G. Zeiler, *Schiedsverfahren* (Vienna/Graz, Neuer Wissenschaftlicher Verlag, 2006), Section 594, pp. 198 *et seq.*

164. 594(2) ZPO resembles Article 18 UNCITRAL Model Law und Section 1042(1) German ZPO. It reads: 'The parties shall be treated fairly. Each party shall be granted the right to be heard.' The UNCITRAL Model Law states that 'each party shall be given full opportunity of presenting his case'. The wording of Section 594(2) ZPO (Each party shall be granted the right to be heard') incorporates this thought using a formulation which is in line with the Austrian legal tradition (as well as Section 1042 (2) German ZPO). In contrast to the UNCITRAL Model Law, which states that 'the parties shall be treated with equality', the Austrian wording is broader, stating that '[t]he parties shall be treated fairly', acknowledging that equal treatment does not automatically guarantee fair treatment. *See* M. Platte in *Arbitration Law of Austria: Practice and Procedure*, S. Riegler, A. Petsche, A. Fremuth-Wolf, M. Platte and C. Liebscher (eds) (Huntington, Juris Publishing, 2007), Section 594, p. 334; A. Reiner, 'Schiedsverfahren und rechtliches Gehör' [2003] ZfRV, 52, fn. 2.

165. J. Power, *The Austrian Arbitration Act – A practitioner's Guide to Sections 577-619 of the Austrian Code of Civil Procedure* (Vienna, Manz, 2006), Section 594, para. 4; *see* A. von Saucken, *Die Reform des österreichischen Schiedsverfahrensrechts auf der Basis des UNCITRAL-Modellgesetzes über die Internationale Handelsschiedsgerichtsbarkeit* (Frankfurt, Verlag Peter Lang, 2004), p. 203.

166. This is made explicit in the explanatory remarks of the legislator. *See also* P. Oberhammer, *Entwurf eines neuen Schiedsverfahrensrechts* (Vienna, Manz, 2002), p. 92, who notes that the term 'fair' has been taken over 'directly from Article 6(1) ECHR, which forms part of Austria's constitutional law and is, thus, no foreign matter in Austrian law'. *See also* J. Power, *The Austrian Arbitration Act – A Practitioner's Guide to Sections 577-618 of the Austrian Code of Civil Procedure* (Vienna, Manz, 2006), Section 594, para.4; G. Zeiler, *Schiedsverfahren* (Vienna/Graz, Neuer Wissenschaftlicher Verlag, 2006), Section 594, p. 198.

167. *See* H.M. Holtzmann and J.E. Neuhaus, *A Guide to the UNCITRAL Model Law on Commercial Arbitration: Legislative History and Commentary* (London, Kluwer Law and Taxation, 1989), Article 18, p. 552.

establishing an express link with Article 6 ECHR was to incorporate by reference the extensive case law and literature interpreting and giving precise shape to these broad principles,[168] in order to provide a maximal degree of legal certainty regarding this broad fundamental maxim of procedural law.[169]

However, Article 6 ECHR should not be abused to undermine the special nature of **20-065** arbitration; it cannot be applied in the context of arbitration without taking into account the specific characteristics of the arbitral process.[170] Specifically, an overreaching application of the right to be heard may be at odds with the principle that there is no *revision au fonds* of arbitral awards.[171] For example, criticizing the tribunal for not sufficiently having considered all of the parties' arguments comes close to criticizing the tribunal's reasoning and thus, the substance of their award. Substantive scrutiny of an arbitral award, however, is to be limited to grave violations amounting to infringements of substantive public policy. In similar vein, the Swiss *Bundesgericht* clarified a mistake of the tribunal in considering not all of the parties' arguments only constitutes a relevant breach of law if

> the parties are deprived of the opportunity to participate in the proceeding, or to influence it and to make their position part of it, in that their right to be heard is the factor undermined by virtue of the inadvertent mistake (. . .) The formal breach of law is not constituted by the arbitrators deciding the dispute submitted to them incorrectly, but rather through the fact that the party was unable to submit its position in the proceeding, so that it was not sufficiently taken into account in the 'decision making' process. In that context, it is irrelevant whether the arbitrators do not take factual elements into account at all or whether they misinterpret it. What is relevant is that a party has suffered a disadvantage in the

---

168. W.H. Rechberger and W. Melis in *Kommentar zur ZPO*, W.H. Rechberger (ed.) (3rd edn, Vienna/New York, Springer, 2006), Section 594, para. 4; A. Reiner, 'Schiedsverfahren und rechtliches Gehör' [2003] ZfRV, 52; M. Platte in *Arbitration Law of Austria: Practice and Procedure*, S. Riegler, A. Petsche, A. Fremuth-Wolf, M. Platte and C. Liebscher (eds) (Huntington, Juris Publishing, 2007), Section 594, pp. 334 *et seq.*

169. The Austrian case law regarding the fZPO, too, is arguably still valid in this respect. *See* W.H. Rechberger and W. Melis in *Kommentar zur ZPO*, W.H. Rechberger (ed.) (3rd edn, Vienna/New York, Springer, 2006), Section 594, para. 4. For Case law *see* M. Platte in *Arbitration Law of Austria: Practice and Procedure*, S. Riegler, A. Petsche, A. Fremuth-Wolf, M. Platte and C. Liebscher (eds) (Huntington, Juris Publishing, 2007), Section 594, pp. 335 *et seq.*

170. F.T. Schwarz and H. Ortner, 'Procedural Ordre Public and the Internationalization of Public Policy in Arbitration' in *Austrian Arbitration Yearbook 2008*, C. Klausegger *et al.* (eds) (Vienna, Manz, 2008).

171. Compare W.H. Rechberger, 'Die Widersprüchlichkeit eines Schiedsspruchs als Aufhebungsgrund nach österreichischem Recht' [2006] SchiedsVZ, 169, 174, with further references. *See also* Explanatory Notes to Section 611 which emphasize that not every violation of the right to be heard constitutes grounds for setting aside and N. Pitkowitz 'Setting Aside Arbitral Awards Under The New Austrian Arbitration Act' in *Austrian Arbitration Yearbook 2007*, C. Klausegger *et al.* (eds) (Vienna, Manz, 2007), at least on p. 241.

proceeding and that its right to participate has been deprived of value to such an extent that, as a result, it is prejudiced just as much as if it would not have been afforded an opportunity to be heard with respect to a relevant question in the first place.[172]

20-066 This states the law accurately. The parties are protected against substantive mistakes of the arbitrators only to the extent they violate the *substantive ordre public* (at the seat of the arbitration or the enforcement state); this includes the arbitrator misinterpreting or even disregarding the parties' arguments. Procedurally, such mistakes are only relevant if they reach the level of constituting a fundamental flaw in the process that denies (or comes close to denying) a party a fair opportunity to present its case.

6.   Causality

20-067 It is also debatable if a violation of the right to be heard must always result in the successful challenge of the award, or only if the violation has resulted in an adverse decision for the party whose right to be heard was violated. In other words, is the right to be heard absolute, or must the aggrieved party demonstrate that, had the right to be heard been complied with, the proceedings had resulted in a different, more favourable award.

20-068 This issue is not specifically addressed in the ZPO. It has been suggested that the grounds for challenging an arbitral award are functionally comparable to the grounds applicable to the annulment of court judgments under Sections 477 *et seq.* ZPO. Under that provision, no causality is required, so that, by way of analogy, no causality should be required for the challenge of arbitral awards.[173] Indeed, insofar as the right to be heard is part of the *procedural ordre public*, a violation of which is grounds for setting aside under Section 611(2) no. 5 ZPO, a requirement of causality appears systemically inconsistent. The purpose of *ordre public* is not only to protect a party, but the integrity of the overall process.[174]

20-069 The Austrian courts have followed that rationale. In its decision of 24 September 1981,[175] the Austrian *Oberster Gerichtshof* set aside an award because certain documents had not been made available to one of the parties. The Austrian *Oberster Gerichtshof* did not require a showing that the party who was unable to comment on the document was actually disadvantaged in a manner that resulted

---

172. BGer, 10 September 2001, BGE 127 III 576, 579 *et seq.* With the caveat of course that such an error in law would not also constitute a violation of the applicable *ordre public*.
173. C. Liebscher, *The Healthy Award* (The Hague, Kluwer Law International, 2003), p. 148. Note that for some grounds, however, Section 611 ZPO expressly requires causality.
174. Note, however, that Section 611(2) no. 5 ZPO must be raised by a party, and is not to be taken into account by the court *ex officio*.
175. OGH, 24 September 1981, 7 Ob 623/81, EvBl 1982/77.

in an award unfavourable to it, but held in general terms 'that it cannot be excluded that the plaintiff's comments would have influenced the relevant facts'. This position is in line with other major civil law jurisdictions. The Swiss *Bundesgericht* rejected the requirements of a causality between the violation of the right to be heard and the subsequent award,[176] as did the German *Bundesgerichtshof.*[177] A similar position is also taken by *Fouchard/Gaillard/ Goldman* with respect to the New York Convention[178] in that a violation of the right to be heard is sufficient for a challenge in and of itself without placing further burden on the aggrieved party to demonstrate that without such violation such party would have obtained a more favourable result.[179]

---

176. In its decision of 25 April 1995, BGE 121 III 331, 334 *et seq* the Swiss *Bundesgericht* held that 'the entitlement to be heard is of a formal nature. Its violation results, irrespective of the parties' chances to succeed in the proceeding, in the setting aside of the challenged award. This is particularly true for the setting aside proceeding in international arbitration, where the factual determinations and legal considerations of the tribunal can only be re-assist by the courts within the very limited scope of Article 190 (2) IPRG so that the *Bundesgericht* hardly has the opportunity to supplement the facts as they have established by the tribunal or to correct them in order to heal the violation of the right to be heard. The position that the violation of the right to be heard is a formal breach of the law is also not undermined by the argument that such a violation is irrelevant if it does not go against the applicable ordre public (...) this principle, which originally was derived from substantive law, is not applicable in the area of formal procedural guarantees, because the relevance of those guarantees lies not in ensuring that, subject to the appeal before the higher instances, a correct resolution of the dispute on the merits, but lies rather in guaranteeing to the parties an unbiased evaluation of the claims and submissions that have been put to the courts in accordance with the applicable procedural rules.'

177. In its decision of 10 October 1951, II ZR 99/51 in BGHZ 3, 215 in a case where the challenging party was not informed during the arbitration of the testimony taken from a witness and was not afforded the opportunity to comment thereon, the German *Bundesgerichtshof* held that 'the position that in order for a challenge according to Section 1041 no. 4 [German] ZPO to be successful, an award must be based in the violation of the right to be heard, or that proof is required that such violation has influenced the award cannot be followed. The award does not need to be based in the violation of the principle of the right to be heard. This follows from the nature of the matter, because it is difficult to exclude the possibility that the arbitral award would have been a different one if all parties had been heard properly. Rather, it must suffice that the violation of the right to be heard could have aggrieved the losing party.' *Similar*, BGH, 8 October 1959, VII ZR 87/58, NJW 1959, 2213. *See also* W. Voit. in *Kommentar zur Zivilprozessordnung*, H.J. Musielak (ed.) (5th edn, Munich, Verlag Franz Vahlen, 2008), Section 1059, para 27, '[it is only] required that the violation *could* have affected the award, however the requirements are minor'.

178. NY Convention, **Annex 11**.

179. E. Gaillard and J. Savage (eds), *Fouchard Gaillard Goldman On International Commercial Arbitration* (The Hague, Kluwer Law International, 1999), para. 1699.

7.   Limits to the Right to Be Heard

20-070 The parties' right to be heard may be in conflict with the efficiency of the proceed-ings.[180] Indeed, a party may invoke the right to be heard as a dilatory tactic, requesting or making submissions at every conceivable opportunity, and then some more. The right to be heard is not a *cart blanche* for parties to offer ever expanding factual allegations or legal arguments. Thus, it is recognized that the right to be heard has important limitations that allow the arbitrator to conduct the proceedings efficiently.

7.1.   *Evidentiary Cut-Off Date*

20-071 Article 20(1) entitles the arbitrators 'subject to advance notice (. . .) to declare that pleadings and the presentation of documentary evidence shall be admissible only up to a certain stage of the proceedings.'[181] The authority to cut-off the parties' presentation of their case seems to extend, as a textual matter, only to 'pleadings and documentary evidence', but witness statements and expert reports, and indeed any kind of submission, should be included.[182]

20-072 Notably, arbitrators can only set a cut-off date after having first notified this to the parties. This is intended to avoid surprise decisions. The parties should know in advance that they can submit evidence only until a certain point of the proceedings, so that they can arrange the presentation of their case accordingly. It is good practice for the arbitrators to discuss this at the start of the proceeding, such as in a preliminary hearing,[183] or in a provisional timetable.[184]

20-073 After the cut-off date, the parties are in principle not entitled to offer any additional evidence or raise new factual assertions. Some arbitrators will also cut-off the presentation of new legal arguments, in order to streamline the presentation of the case. Concerned with due process, many arbitrators do not provide for an absolute cut-off date, but order that no new evidence may be submitted unless with express leave of the tribunal and good cause shown.

20-074 The instrument of a cut-off date is now accepted in international arbitration, and expressly provided by many of the major institutional rules.[185]

---

180. The Vienna Rules consistently protect the parties against the delay of the proceedings. *See, e.g.,* **Article 11(3)**, **Article 11(4)**, **Article 14(2)**, **Article 14(4)**, **Article 15(4)**, **Article 16(2)** and **Article 17(2)**.
181. *See* **Article 20(1)**, at paras. 111 *et seq.*
182. *See also* C. Liebscher in *Arbitration Law of Austria: Practice and Procedure*, S. Riegler, A. Petsche, A. Fremuth-Wolf, M. Platte and C. Liebscher (eds) (Huntington, Juris Publishing, 2007), p. 642.
183. *See* **Article 20**, at paras. 103 *et seq.*
184. *See* **Article 20**, at para. 113.
185. *See, e.g.,* Article 22(1) ICC Rules: 'When it is satisfied that the parties have had a reasonable opportunity to present their case, the Arbitral Tribunal shall declare the proceedings closed. Thereafter, no further submission or argument may be made, or evidence produced, unless

It has also been suggested that, because (then) Article 14(1)[186] refers to the lim- **20-075**
itation of submissions and evidence by a certain 'stage' of the proceedings, the
arbitral tribunal is not permitted to set a cut-off date (but rather, may set a cut-off
'stage').[187] This interpretation is impractical and unconvincing. The tribunal's cut-
off right was included in Article 20(1) by way of clarification, and not to introduce
a right that the tribunal otherwise would not have. Parties cannot be allowed to
occupy the floor 'until they are satisfied' – some parties would never leave.
Counsel are to be given 'reasonable opportunity' to put in their evidence and to
persuade the arbitrators, but it is for the tribunal to determine the extent of what is
'reasonable.'[188] Thus, the arbitral tribunal must be guided by the purpose of Article
20(1) to ensure both due process and the efficiency of the arbitral proceedings.
With that purpose in mind, the tribunal has free discretion to set a cut-off date for
all, or parts, of the parties' submissions or offered evidence, or indeed to order
similar measures as the circumstances of the case may require. This authority has
been recognized by the Austrian courts,[189] and is now confirmed by Section 599(1)
ZPO which permits the arbitrators generally to determine the permissibility of
evidence.[190]

7.2. 'Reasonable Opportunity'

The right to be heard refers to a reasonable opportunity to present one's case. As **20-076**
discussed, it is for the tribunal to determine the extent of what is 'reasonable'.[191] In
addition, it bears emphasis that the party must only be afforded an opportunity; the
arbitrators are not required to wait until a party actually avails itself of the right to
be heard. Thus, a party who simply disregards the opportunities given to it by the

---

    requested or authorized by the Arbitral Tribunal'. Article 29(1) UNCITRAL Rules: 'The
    arbitral tribunal may inquire of the parties if they have any further proof to offer or witnesses
    to be heard or submissions to make and, if there are none, it may declare the hearings closed'.
    Article 24(1) AAA/ICDR Rules: 'After asking the parties if they have any further testimony or
    evidentiary submissions and upon receiving negative replies or if satisfied that the record is
    complete, the tribunal may declare the hearings closed.'
186. A provision of the Vienna Rules 2001 identical in relevant part to Article 20(1), **Annex 2a**.
187. M. Aden, *Internationale Handelsschiedsgerichtsbarkeit* (2nd edn, Munich, C.H. Beck, 2003),
    p. 543. *Aden* also suggests that the tribunal divide the proceedings into several 'stages', such as
    a stage of affirmative submission, reply submission, witness evidence and expert evidence.
188. J. Paulsson, 'The Timely Arbitrator: Reflections on the Böckstiegel Method' in *Law of
    International Business and Dispute Settlement in the 21st Century, Liber Amicorum K.-H.
    Böckstiegel*, R. Briner, L. Y. Fortier, K. P. Berger and J. Bredow (eds) (Cologne/Berlin/Bonn/
    Munich, Carl Heymanns Verlag, 2001), p. 608.
189. OGH, 31 March 2005, 3 Ob 35/05a.
190. *See* **Article 20**, at paras. 184 *et seq.*
191. *See* also J. Paulsson, 'The Timely Arbitrator: Reflections on the Böckstiegel Method' in *Law of
    International Business and Dispute Settlement in the 21st Century, Liber Amicorum K.-H.
    Böckstiegel*, R. Briner, L. Y. Fortier, K. P. Berger and J. Bredow (eds) (Cologne/Berlin/Bonn/
    Munich, Carl Heymanns Verlag, 2001), p. 608.

tribunal to present its case, can later not complain that its right to be heard has been violated.[192]

20-077 Indeed, Article 20(6) provides that 'if one party does not take part in the proceedings, the case must be heard with the other party alone'. Although this provision prevents a decision by default,[193] it does entitle the arbitrator to proceed with the arbitration with one party alone, if the other side, despite having been given notice of the proceedings and the hearing, chooses not to exercise its right to present its case.

20-078 Similarly, the right to be heard is not violated if a witness does not appear before a tribunal after having been summoned upon the application of the party and the arbitral tribunal does not procure the appearance of the witness through the state courts *ex officio*.[194] The arbitral tribunal will also be typically entitled to limit the scope of the evidence taken, for example hearing only four of ten witnesses offered by a party, without violating the party's right to be heard.[195]

7.3.   *Irrelevant Evidence*

20-079 Another important limitation of the right to be heard is the principle of relevance and materiality. A party is not entitled, in the guise of its right to be heard, to make factual assertions or produce evidence that is irrelevant or immaterial to the dispute. Although the Vienna Rules are silent on this point, this is an accepted principle in international arbitration.[196] Specifically, Article 9(2) of the IBA Rules provides an accepted standard of best practice in this regard:

> The Arbitral Tribunal shall, at the request of a Party or on its own motion, exclude from evidence or production any document, statement, oral testimony

---

192. OGH, 24 July 1997, 6 Ob 186/97i. Similarly, the right to be heard is not, according to case law, infringed by ignoring motions for the admission of evidence or an incomplete finding of facts, but merely if the arbitrators base their decision on facts or evidence on which the parties were unable to comment. *See* OGH, 27 November 1991, 3 Ob 1091/91; OGH, 6 September 1990, 6 Ob 572/90.
193. *See* **Article 20**, at paras. 259 *et seq.*
194. BGer, 25 July 1997, BGE 4P.221.1996, (2000) 18(1) Bull ASA, 96; *See* **Article 20**, at para. 192.
195. *Reiner* recommends that in such a case that the parties are heard on which of the ten witnesses shall be ordered to appear before the tribunal. *See* A. Reiner, 'Schiedsverfahren und rechtliches Gehöhr' [2003] ZfRV, 52, 64.
196. W. Voit in *Kommentar zur Zivilprozessordnung*, H.-J. Musielak (6th edn, Munich, Verlag Franz Vahlen, 2008), Section 1042, para. 21; M. Platte in *Arbitration Law of Austria: Practice and Procedure*, S. Riegler, A. Petsche, A. Fremuth-Wolf, M. Platte and H. Haller (eds) (Huntington, Juris Publishing, 2007), Section 594, p. 337; A. Reiner, 'Schiedsverfahren und rechtliches Gehör' [2003] ZfRV, 52. Article 25(6) UNCITRAL Rules: 'The arbitral tribunal shall determine the admissibility, relevance, materiality and weight of the evidence offered.' Article 22(1)(f) LCIA Rules'(. . .) the Arbitral Tibunal shall have the power (. . .) to decide whether or not to apply strict rules of evidence (or any other rules) as to the admissibility, relevance or weight of any material tendered by a party on any matter of fact or expert opinion'. Article 16(3) AAA/ICDR Rules: 'The tribunal may in its discretion direct the order of proof, bifurcate proceedings,

or inspection for any of the following reasons: (a) lack of sufficient relevance or materiality.[197]

Thus, the right to be heard is not violated if the arbitrators, either *ex officio* or **20-080** upon the request of a party, exclude or dismiss factual allegations or evidence that fail to make a material contribution to the resolution of the case. Dogmatically, it has been said that the right to be heard is 'objectively limited in scope by the subject matter of the arbitration and the facts necessary to make an award'.[198] As a result, factual allegations or evidence that do not bear on the subject matter of the arbitration, or are irrelevant to reach a final decision in the case, can be rejected without fear of violating the parties' right to be heard.[199]

7.4.   *Appropriate Time Limits*

Which time limits are appropriate depends on the individual case. Again, parties **20-081** must be given a reasonable opportunity to state their argument, which is standard for the arbitrators to determine. In doing so, they will take into account the particular circumstances of the case, the complexity of the matter and of the evidence, the economic or strategic importance of the dispute as well as, appropriately, local circumstances, such as problems of communication, the need for translations, religious or state holidays, traditional vacation times or other difficulties which may arise from the circumstances or the cultural or economic status of the parties.[200]

E.   CONTROLLING THE CONDUCT OF THE ARBITRATION

Arbitration is also torn between the discretion of the arbitrators to conduct the **20-082** proceedings as they see fit, as expressly recognized under Article 20, and the agreement of the parties that creates, and limits, the arbitrators' jurisdiction in the first place. Who is really in control of the arbitration: the arbitrators or the parties?

While arbitration is undoubtedly a consensual process based on the parties' agree- **20-083** ment to resolve their disputes through a contractually-imposed, essentially private mechanism, parties sometimes feel that despite their agreement 'arbitrations

---

exclude cumulative or irrelevant testimony or other evidence, and direct the parties to focus their presentations on issues the decision of which could dispose of all or part of the case.'

197. IBA Rules, **Annex 16**.
198. H.W. Fasching, *Schiedsgericht und Schiedsverfahren im österreichischen und im internationalen Recht* (Vienna, Manz, 1973), p. 103. (The right to be heard 'is objectively limited as to the scope of the subject matter of the arbitral proceedings and maturity (*Spruchreife*).')
199. *See, e.g.*, BGer, 6 September 1996, (1997) 15(2) Bull ASA, 291, 306; BGH, 28 May 1963, VII ZR 222/61, WM 1963, 944.
200. A. Reiner, 'Schiedsverfahren und rechtliches Gehör' [2003] ZfRV, 52, 53; *see also* **Article 13**, at paras. 001 *et seq.*

take on almost a *Dickensian* life of their own and escape their control'.[201] Some arbitrators, in contrast, take the view that they should control the arbitration to the exclusion of counsel, who are perceived to be out of touch with their clients.[202]

20-084 The following section examines the relationship between the agreement of the parties on procedural issues and the discretion of the arbitrator. Then, it addresses instruments to structure, and manage, the arbitral process in accordance with the parties' expectations and their desire for a flexible proceeding that suits the circumstances of the individual case.

1.   The Arbitrators' Discretion and the Parties' Agreement

20-085 The relationship between the arbitrators' discretion and the parties' agreement in determining the conduct of the arbitration is one of the tensions underpinning the arbitral process.[203] Generally, the supremacy of the parties' agreement is acknowledged under Austrian law, the Vienna Rules, and international instruments and practice. However, there may be certain instances when the arbitrators are called to protect the integrity of the process, which may compel them to act against the parties' agreement.

1.1.   The Primacy of the Parties' Agreement

20-086 Article 20(1) of the Vienna Rules confers upon the arbitrators the power to determine the conduct of the proceedings at their 'absolute discretion'. The word 'absolute' suggests a power that the arbitrator does not really have – as Article 20(1) itself makes clear, the arbitrators' discretion must be exercised 'in the context of the Vienna Rules' and 'the agreements between the parties'. Similarly, the authentic German version of Article 20 places the arbitrators' discretion within the 'framework' ('*im Rahmen*') of the Vienna Rules and the parties' agreements. Article 20(1) therefore appears to establish a hierarchy that limits the arbitrators' discretion to matters that are not otherwise agreed between the parties. This suggests that it is primarily for the parties to determine the procedure of the arbitration, either directly or with reference to the Vienna Rules. Only absent such agreement, it is for the arbitrators to determine the conduct of the proceeding.

20-087 In this determination, the arbitrators indeed enjoy free discretion, and are limited only by applicable mandatory law.[204] In *ad hoc* arbitration conducted under Austrian law, there is an argument that the arbitrators exercise their procedural

---

201. T.H. Webster, 'Party Control in International Arbitration' (2003) 19(2) Arb Int'l, 119.
202. T.H. Webster, 'Party Control in International Arbitration' (2003) 19(2) Arb Int'l, 119 and fn 1.
203. *See* **Article 20**, at para. 010.
204. *See* M. Aden, *Internationale Handelsschiedsgerichtsbarkeit* (2nd edn, Munich, C.H. Beck, 2003), p. 542.

discretion subject to both mandatory and non-mandatory law.[205] The argument accepts that neither the parties nor the arbitrators can deviate from mandatory provisions of the *lex arbitri*, and then postulates that only the parties can deviate from non-mandatory provisions of the arbitration law (which indeed often provide 'unless the *parties* provide otherwise' or wording to similar effect). In that sense, arbitrators are restricted by the law (whether mandatory or not) and the parties' agreement. Under the Vienna Rules (or any other set of institutional rules) the situation is arguably different. Here, the parties have 'provided otherwise' (and thus derogated from the non-mandatory provisions of the *lex arbitri*) precisely by referring to the institutional rules. In this context, the broader discretion granted by Article 20(1) – which is *only* limited by the parties' agreement – overrides any further non-mandatory restrictions that would otherwise apply. In such situations, the arbitrators' discretion is arguably limited only by applicable mandatory arbitration law and the parties' agreement, but not by any non-mandatory provisions that regulate the conduct of the proceeding.

The hierarchy in favour of the parties' agreement over the arbitrators' discretion, however, is firmly recognized as a basic principle of the arbitral process.[206] Thus, Section 594(1) ZPO provides that '[s]ubject to the mandatory provisions of this section, the parties are free to determine the rules of procedure', and that only '[f]ailing such agreement, the arbitral tribunal shall, subject to the provisions of this chapter, conduct the arbitration in the manner that it considers appropriate'.[207] Similarly, the European Convention provides in Article IV(1)(b)(iii) that parties shall be free 'to lay down the procedure to be followed by the arbitrators',[208] **20-088**

---

205. Explanatory Notes to Section 594; M. Platte in *Arbitration Law of Austria: Practice and Procedure*, S. Riegler, A. Petsche, A. Fremuth-Wolf, M. Platte and C. Liebscher (eds) (Huntington, Juris Publishing, 2007), Section 594, pp. 332 *et seq.*

206. The 1923 Geneva Protocol required in its Article 2 that 'the arbitral procedure, including the constitution of the arbitral tribunal shall be governed by the will of the parties and by the law of the country in whose territory the arbitration takes place'. As discussed above, this provision was understood as requiring compliance with the procedural law of the arbitral seat.

207. Section 594(1) ZPO expressly authorizes the parties to agree on 'the rules of procedure', which is not only meant to refer to (institutional) arbitration rules (which are expressly mentioned separately), but also to civil procedure rules. Thus, if the parties wanted to replicate court proceedings, or use certain rules applicable to state court litigation, they would be free to do so under Austrian law. *See* **Article 2**, at paras. 041 *et seq. See also* M. Platte in *Arbitration Law of Austria: Practice and Procedure*, S. Riegler, A. Petsche, A. Fremuth-Wolf, M. Platte and C. Liebscher (eds) (Huntington, Juris Publishing, 2007), Section 594, p. 333.

208. Article IV(1)(b)(iii) European Convention, **Annex 10**. As discussed below, Article IV(4)(d) also provides that, where the parties have not agreed upon the arbitral procedure, the arbitral tribunal shall determine the arbitral rules. Like Article V(1)(d) of the NY Convention, Article IX(1)(d) of the European Convention provides for the non-recognition of arbitral awards if the procedure followed by the tribunal departed from that agreed by the parties. *See* D.T. Hascher, 'European Convention on International Arbitration (1961)' (1995) XX YB Comm Arb, 1006, 1017 *et seq.*; E. Gaillard and J. Savage (eds), *Fouchard Gaillard Goldman On International*

and Article V(1)(d) of the New York Convention permits a state to refuse the recognition or enforcement of an award on the basis that 'the arbitral procedure was not in accordance with the agreement of the parties'.[209] The same hierarchy is also reflected, as in Article 20, in other institutional rules. Article 15(1) of the ICC Rules provides 'that the proceedings before the Arbitral Tribunal shall be governed by these Rules, and, where these Rules are silent, by any rules which the parties or, failing them, the Arbitral Tribunal may settle on'.[210] The LCIA Rules state that '[t]he parties may agree on the conduct of their arbitral proceedings and they are enourcaged to do so, consistent with the Arbitral Tribunal's general duties all the times (. . .) Unless agreed otherwise by the parties (. . .) the Arbitral Tribunal shall have the widest discretion to discharge its duties allowed under such law(s) or rules of law as the Arbitral Tribunal may determine to be applicable'.[211]

20-089 This view also does most justice to the consensual nature of arbitration, which unlike any state court procedure, cannot be imposed on one of the parties. It is based on the agreement of both parties to have recourse to arbitration in case of emerging disputes.[212] The parties decide on the kind of arbitration to be put in place, whether it is *ad hoc* or to be administered by an institution, and on which procedural rules will be applied.[213] Thus, almost all modern legal systems leave it to the parties to agree upon the form of the procedure, only subject to mandatory provisions at the *situs*.[214]

20-090 Indeed, parties choose arbitration specifically because they enjoy the freedom to agree upon a procedure that is flexible and efficient and customized to fit their

---

Commercial Arbitration (The Hague, Kluwer Law International, 1999), paras. 759, 1184; L.J. Bouchez, 'The Prospects for International Arbitration: Disputes Between States and Private Enterprises' (1991) 8(1) J Int'l Arb, 81, 96.

209. Article V(1)(d) NY Convention, **Annex 11**.

210. Article 11 ICC Rules.

211. Article 14 LCIA Rules. Rule 20(2) of the ICSID Arbitration Rules is also explicit in affirming the parties' procedural autonomy: 'In the conduct of the proceeding, *the Tribunal shall apply any agreement between the parties on procedural matters,* except as otherwise provided in the Convention or the Administrative and Financial Regulations.'

212. P. Schlosser, *Das Recht der internationalen privaten Schiedsgerichtsbarkeit* (2nd edn, Tübingen, Mohr Siebeck, 1989), para. 630. For restrictions of party autonomy under mandatory law, *see, e.g.*, A. Reiner, *Das neue österreichische Schiedsrecht/The new Austrian Arbitration Law* (Vienna, LexisNexis, 2006), Section 598, note 124.

213. 'The choice of arbitration is a first joint exercise over control of the procedure (. . .)'. *See* T.H. Webster, 'Party Control in International Arbitration' (2003) 19(2) Arb Int'l, 120.

214. P. Schlosser, *Das Recht der internationalen privaten Schiedsgerichtsbarkeit* (2nd edn, Tübingen, Mohr Siebeck, 1989), para. 631.

individual case,[215] and that avoids the formalities of state court litigation.[216] As one author comments:

> Parties have opted for arbitration in preference to litigation in national courts in part because of the flexibility as compared to the dichotomy of national systems. By focusing on exactly what rules they are agreeing to, parties can ensure that they maintain basic control over the ground rules. After such rules have been chosen – and the dispute has arisen – the parties can best influence, if not control, the proceedings by focusing on the stage of proceedings and the possibilities at each stage.[217]

As another commentator pointedly argues, there is therefore no room for arbitral **20-091** dictators; and no arbitration tribunal functions by divine right. Rather, in any consensual arbitration, an arbitrator's primary qualification derives from his or her appointment, directly or indirectly, by the parties. Arbitrators must therefore necessarily acknowledge the parties, and their supreme agreement, as their creators.[218]

Some authors argue that the supremacy of the parties is such that the parties can **20-092** even agree to override previous procedural orders by the tribunal.[219] This seems to go too far. A procedural order, once issued, is binding on both parties and can as such not be revoked. However, it is conceivable that, where the order has not been fully effectuated, the parties agree on an alternative procedural avenue which the tribunal will then be compelled to follow. As discussed in greater detail below, if the tribunal proceeds against the parties' procedural agreement, the parties must object without delay.[220]

1.2.   The Arbitrator's Discretion

Yet some authors argue that at the end it is the arbitrator who controls, and should **20-093** control the process. According to some, the parties expect 'that arbitration like any

---

215. J. Crawford, 'Advocacy Before the International Court of Justice and Other International Tribunals in State-to-State Cases' in *The Art of Advocacy in International Arbitration*, R. Bishop (ed.) (Huntington, Juris Publishing, 2004) pp. 11 *et seq.* (describing historic use of 'combination of full written and oral phases').
216. G. Petrochilos, *Procedural Law in International Arbitration* (Oxford, OUP, 2004), p. 84; R. Pietrowski, 'Evidence in International Arbitration' (2006) 22(3) Arb Int'l, 373, 374.
217. T.H. Webster, 'Party Control in International Arbitration' (2003) 19(2) Arb Int'l, 119, 142.
218. V.V. Veeder, 'Whose Arbitration is it Anyway: The Parties or the Arbitration Tribunal – An Interesting Question?' in *The Leading Arbitrators' Guide to International Arbitration*, L.W. Newman and R.D. Hill (ed.) (Huntington, Juris Publishing, 2004), p. 347.
219. M. Platte in *Arbitration Law of Austria: Practice and Procedure*, S. Riegler, A. Petsche, A. Fremuth-Wolf, M. Platte and C. Liebscher (eds) (Huntington, Juris Publishing, 2007), Section 594, p. 333.
220. *See* **Article 20**, at paras. 272 *et seq.* and Section 579 ZPO.

form of dispute resolution results in a gradual shifting of control away from the parties and to the tribunal for what is after all the adjudication of a dispute'.[221]

20-094 In practice, the issue does not too often become relevant. Where parties act professionally and retain the ability to agree on procedural matters, their agreement will in most cases be sensible and reflect their procedural needs. In such cases, arbitrators will feel comfortable to follow a procedure that has the consent of both parties.[222] On the other hand, once parties have entered the litigious phase of their relationship, they are often unable to agree on procedural issues, either for fear of agreeing to a disadvantageous compromise that somehow favours the other side, or out of principle or spite. In such cases, it is of course for the arbitrators to determine procedural matters at their discretion. Where the parties cannot agree, institutional rules, including the Vienna Rules in Article 20(1), typically provide only a rudimentary framework with considerable gaps which the arbitrators need to fill.[223]

20-095 Indeed, this discretion of the arbitrator is a hallmark of the arbitral process, and the necessary corollary of party autonomy, with the parties vesting the arbitrator with the authority to determine the procedure when they are unable to do so.[224] This is recognized by major international instruments,[225] and pervades most national laws,[226] and institutional rules.[227]

---

221. T.H. Webster, 'Party Control in International Arbitration' (2003) 19(2) Arb Int'l, 142.
222. Indeed, arbitrators often will, and should, thrive to obtain the parties' consent on procedural matters. A proceeding that finds the agreement of both sides will set the basis for an award that is acceptable to the parties irrespective of the outcome.
223. *See* **Article 20**, at paras. 082 *et seq.*
224. *See* **Article 20**, at paras. 085 *et seq.* This was and remains the case in state-to-state arbitrations. *See* Institut de Droit International, 'Projet de règlement pour la procedure arbitrale internationale' (Session de La Haye, 1875), Article 15 reprinted in W.E. Darby, *International Tribunals: A Collection Of The Various Schemes Which Have Been Propounded, And Of Instances Since 1815 (1897)* (Whitefish, Kessinger Publishing, 2008); International Law Commission, *Memorandum on Arbitral Procedure, Prepared by the Secretariat*, Doc. A/ CN.4/35, (1950) II YB ILC, 157, 165-66, 171-74 ('where such rules are lacking in the compromise, it has been customary for tribunals to adopt their own rules'); K.S. Carlston, *The Process of International Arbitration* (New York, Columbia UP, 1946), p. 204 ('We may therefore regard it as established that whether so expressed or not in the protocol, commissions have an inherent right to establish rules governing the method of presentation and the consideration of cases submitted to them').
225. Article IV(4)(d) of the European Convention provides that, where the parties have not agreed upon arbitral procedures, the tribunal may 'establish directly or by reference to the rules and statutes of a permanent arbitral institution the rules of procedure to be followed by the arbitrators.' **Annex 10**.
226. Section 594(1) ZPO; Section 1042(4) German ZPO; Article 182(2) Swiss IPRG; Article 19(2) UNCITRAL Model Law.
227. **Article 20(1)**; Article 15(1) ICC Rules: 'The proceedings before the Arbitral Tribunal shall be governed by these Rules and, where these Rules are silent, by any rules which the parties or, failing them, the Arbitral Tribunal may settle on, whether or not reference is thereby made to the rules of procedure of a national law to be applied to the arbitration.' Article 14(2) LCIA

However, there may be cases in which the parties agree on a procedural issue in a **20-096** way that appears unacceptable to the arbitrator. For example, parties may (in theory) agree on a document-only procedure, although the case turns on the recollection of witnesses. In such a case, the arbitrator will find it difficult to dispense with witness testimony altogether, and proceed to an award only on the basis of documentary evidence. Or, a party represented by experienced counsel is able to induce its less experienced counter-part into an agreement that it grossly advantageous to one side, but not the other. Does the arbitrator have to accept the parties' agreement under all circumstances, or can he impose his own view on the parties?[228] A number of commentators suggest that the arbitrator should take control:

> I would advocate the existence of (. . .) a right for the arbitrator to lead – even lead firmly, when necessary – in establishing the arbitral procedures over the heads of counsel on both sides. The arbitrator does not have a judge's power to regulate procedures unilaterally, nor should he or she forget that party auton- omy may be the most important arbitral principle of all. The scope for per- suasion by the arbitrator before making a ruling is large, and the need to impose procedures should thus be rare. But it is possible – at least for one with a common law background – to imagine situations in which counsel for both sides may slide toward extended and acrimonious evidentiary procedures that could be shortened or avoided by an arbitrator who was prepared to 'just say no'.[229]

While this has force, it has been said that the debate is not advanced by tales of **20-097** warfare between lawyer and arbitrator: both are asserting different applications of the same principle that it remains the parties' dispute and the parties' arbitration.[230]

Rules: 'Unless otherwise agreed by the parties under Article 14(1), the Arbitral Tribunal shall have the widest discretion to discharge its duties allowed under such law(s) or rules of law as the Arbitral Tribunal may determine to be applicable.' Article 16(1) AAA/ICDR Rules: 'Subject to these rules, the tribunal may conduct the arbitration in whatever manner it considers appropriate, provided that the parties are treated with equality and that each party hast the right to be heard and is given a fair opportunity to present its case.'

228. *See* generally V.V. Veeder, 'Whose Arbitration is it Anyway: The Parties or the Arbitration Tribunal – An Interesting Question?' in *The Leading Arbitrators' Guide to International Arbi- tration*, L.W. Newman and R.D. Hill (ed.) (Huntington, Juris Publishing, 2004), p. 351; J.H. Carter, 'The Rights and Duties of the Arbitrator: Six Aspects of the Rule of Reasonableness' (1995) ICC Ct Bull Special Supplement: The Status of the Arbitrator, 24, 31; M. Littman, 'The Arbitration Act 1996: The Parties' Right to Agree Procedure' (1997) 13(3) Arb Int'l, 269; C. Partasides, 'Sections 33 and 34 of the English Arbitration Act 1996: A Potential Conflict' (1997) 13(4) Arb Int'l, 417; K. Rokison, ' . . . Pastures New' (1998) 14(4) Arb Int'l, 361.
229. J.H. Carter, 'The Rights and Duties of the Arbitrator: Six Aspects of the Rule of Reason- ableness' (1995) ICC Ct Bull Special Supplement: The Status of the Arbitrator, 24, 31; K. Rokison, ' . . . Pastures New' (1998) 14(4) Arb Int'l, 361, 366-67.
230. V.V. Veeder, 'Whose Aribtration is it Anyway: The Parties or the Arbitration Tribunal – An Interesting Question?' in *The Leading Arbitrators' Guide to International Arbitration*, L.W. Newman and R.D. Hill (ed.) (Huntington, Juris Publishing, 2004), pp. 347, 348.

Others argue, therefore, that the better view gives preference to the parties' agreement to arbitrate, including with regard to procedural aspects of the arbitration.[231] Of course, this view has the consensual nature of arbitration for it. An international arbitration tribunal is not a state court. A court has public duties beyond the disputant parties; and in his own person, a state judge maintains an independent status and dignity. It has also been said, in common law countries in particular, the courts are public law makers; and their decisions are needed for the contemporary development of the law, unlike the individual awards of commercial arbitrators, which often go unpublished and are not infrequently confidential.[232] For all of these reasons, the contractual view of arbitration plainly deems the arbitrator bound to the terms not only of the parties' arbitration agreement, but also to the parties' subsequent agreements on procedural issues.[233]

20-098 Under any view, however, there are two cases in which the arbitrator is entitled to refuse to implement the parties' procedural arrangements. First, an arbitrator may be entitled to resign 'if the parties reach unforeseen post-appointment procedural agreements that are oppressive or unreasonable for the arbitrator'.[234] Of course, the arbitrator will have to carefully consider if the resignation (which, in particular at a late stage in the proceedings is a drastic step that can potentially disrupt the proceedings and result in significant additional cost to the parties) is justified, bearing in mind his obligation to render an award.[235] However, an arbitrator should not be

---

231. G.B. Born, *International Commercial Arbitration – Commentary and Materials* (3rd edn, The Hague, Kluwer Law International, forthcoming), ch. 14.

232. V.V. Veeder, 'Whose Aribtration is it Anyway: The Parties or the Arbitration Tribunal – An Interesting Question?' in *The Leading Arbitrators' Guide to International Arbitration*, L.W. Newman and R.D. Hill (eds) (Huntington, Juris Publishing, 2004), p. 348.

233. The UNCITRAL and AAA/ICDR Rules arguably compromise the parties' otherwise prevailing autonomy, instead granting the arbitrators power to determine the arbitral procedure, even in the face of subsequent agreements between the parties on specific procedural matters. Article 15(1) UNCITRAL Arbitration Rules and Article 16 AAA/ICDR Rules. In principle, the parties should be free to compromise their procedural autonomy (this being an element of such autonomy). *See also Award in PCA Case of 5 February 2001, Larsen v. The Hawaiian Kingdom* (2002) 119 ILR, 566, 579-80 ('In accordance with Article 32 of the UNCITRAL Rules, and with the general principles of arbitral procedure, it is for the Tribunal to determine which issues need to be dealt with and in what order.(. . .) If the parties are not content with the submission of the dispute to arbitration under the UNCITRAL Rules and under the auspices of the Permanent Court of Arbitration, they may no doubt, by agreement notified to the Permanent Court, terminate the arbitration. What they cannot do, in the Tribunal's view, is by agreement to change the essential basis on which the Tribunal itself is constituted, or require the Tribunal to act other than in accordance with the applicable law.'). Other institutional rules appear to give greater weight to the parties' procedural agreements, arguably granting them priority over the tribunal's rulings. Article 15(1) ICC Rules ('any rules which the parties, *or failing them*, the Arbitral Tribunal may settle on'); Article 19(1) and Article 19(2) UNCITRAL Model Law and Rule 20(2) ICSID Arbitration Rules.

234. G.B. Born, *International Commercial Arbitration – Commentary and Materials* (3rd edn, The Hague, Kluwer Law International, forthcoming), ch. 14.

235. *See* **Article 7**, at paras. 052 *et seq.* and **Article 8**, at paras. 008 *et seq.*

forced to implement procedures that he considers improper, or that he is unable to follow.

Second, parties cannot compel the arbitrator to follow agreed procedures that **20-099** violate mandatory rules of fairness and equality, that restrict one party's opportunity to be heard,[236] or that otherwise disregard mandatory law at the seat of the arbitration. Not only are the mandatory procedural guarantees not at the parties' disposal, arbitrators also have a duty to both parties to act judicially, to provide a fair resolution of the dispute referred to them and to render an award in compliance with the mandatory law of the seat of the arbitration.[237]

In practice, arbitrators will make their best effort to serve the parties and to adhere **20-100** to their procedural arrangements and preferences. Where the parties enter into problematic procedural arrangements, skilled arbitrators will be able (and have every right to attempt) to dissuade the parties from such unreasonable or inefficient procedures. Oftentimes, however, parties and their counsel will be willing to accommodate the arbitrator and find a suitable compromise, in order not to alienate the arbitrator.

2. Managing the Conduct of the Arbitration

Arguably, international arbitrations ensure a higher degree of due process, and in **20-101** particular the right to be heard, when compared to proceedings before state courts. Specifically, arbitration provides for a stronger involvement of the parties in procedural issues; for long term and advance planning of the proceeding; efficient management of the proceedings that involves the parties; for, in international practice, more extended taking of evidence (and in particular witness testimony when compared to civil law courts); and where necessary, for a more elaborate discussion of legal issues. These elements are all joined by a high degree of flexibility, allowing the arbitrators to take the case and the parties' procedural preferences into account. This is a hallmark of international arbitration:

> [U]nlike the position in court, when both the parties and the tribunal are governed by fixed procedural rules which will be generally adversarial in character, in arbitrations the mutual functions of the parties' lawyers and the tribunal tend to be complementary and co-operational, at least on the surface. Although coming from different cultures and legal philosophies, they must work, and to some extent live, together from the beginning to the end of each case, with intermittent hearings in hotels or other locations which may cover periods of weeks, interspersed with periods of correspondence. During this process they must largely fashion their own procedure. They must perforce get to know and show respect for each other, and make

---

236. *See, e.g.*, A. Reiner, *Das neue österreichische Schiedsrecht/The new Austrian Arbitration Law* (Vienna, LexisNexis, 2006), Section 598, note 124.
237. *See* **Article 7**, at paras. 049 *et seq.*

allowances for different points of view, with both the lawyers and the tribunal constantly trying to ensure as much harmony as circumstances may permit.[238]

20-102 With such flexibility comes considerable responsibility. In order to realize the benefits of arbitration, arbitrators and parties need to communicate, and exchange their views on, both procedure and substance. The arbitrator will not simply disregard the legitimate expectations of the parties, will avoid procedural (let alone substantive) surprises, and will thrive to provide a fair mechanism tailored to suit the parties' dispute.

2.1. The Preliminary Hearing

20-103 As aptly put by a renowned arbitration practitioner, it is a curious feature of the legal process, 'and in particular its arbitral manifestation, that work tends to expand to exceed available time. This is what the timely arbitrator must prevent'.[239] To the extent the arbitral process is more flexible than highly-regulated proceedings before state courts, it also requires a higher degree of organization both from the parties and the arbitrators. At the beginning of the arbitral process, therefore, arbitrators and parties must find a way to synchronize, where possible, their individual expectations and arrive at a consensus, or at least a common understanding, of the procedure that will follow.

20-104 Skilled arbitrators will therefore establish the ground rules that will govern the proceeding at the very outset of the arbitration, and will do so in significant detail. This is usually done through a preliminary (or 'preparatory' or 'case management') hearing. Indeed, in modern practice, most arbitrators insist on such an early meeting to discuss the organization of the proceedings.[240]

20-105 Prior to conducting the preliminary hearing, the tribunal needs to resolve whether to hold the meeting in person, or remotely (over the telephone, or through video-link). A hearing in person will help to develope a personal rapport between the parties' counsel and the arbitrators, and to establish a constructive dynamic

---

238. M. Kerr, 'Concord and Conflict in International Arbitration' (1997) 13(2) Arb Int'l, 121, 125.
239. J. Paulsson, 'The Timely Arbitrator: Reflections on the Böckstiegel Method' in *Law of International Business and Dispute Settlement in the 21st Century, Liber Amicorum K.-H. Böckstiegel*, R. Briner, L.Y. Fortier, K.P. Berger and J. Bredow (eds) (Cologne/Berlin/Bonn/Munich, Carl Heymanns Verlag, 2001), p. 607.
240. A. Redfern, M. Hunter, N. Blackaby and C. Partasides, *Law and Practice of International Commercial Arbitration* (4th edn, London, Sweet & Maxwell, 2004), paras. 6-27 *et seq.* (discussion of preliminary meetings and their role and importance). *See also* Report of the Secretary-General on the Revised Draft Set of Arbitration Rules, UNCITRAL, 9th Session, Addendum 1 (Commentary), UN Doc. A/CN.9/112/Add. 1 (1975), (1976) VII UNCITRAL YB 166, 175 (Article 25(3) of the UNCITRAL Rules 'deals with certain preparatory measures for hearings that the arbitrators must take in order to ensure that the hearings run smoothly').

between the arbitrators themselves (who may not have met in person before). From the tribunal's perspective, it may also be helpful to see the parties, rather than hearing them over the phone. Some underlying tensions, or procedural disagreements, can be better resolved in person. Indeed, some arbitrators insist that a party representative attend the preliminary hearing. This is thought to assist the tribunal in establishing a procedure that truly complies with the parties' wishes, rather than being taken hostage by the parties' lawyers and their own agenda.

Despite the significant advantages of a preliminary hearing in person, important **20-106** reasons may counsel for conducting this hearing over the phone. Most importantly, having the arbitrators, the parties and their counsel convene for a relatively short hearing will often involve considerable expense that must be carefully weighed against the attending benefits. Indeed, where videolink facilities can be used, they may approximate the benefits of a meeting in person. In cases of doubt, arbitrators may wish to solicit the parties' views on how the preliminary hearing should be conducted.

What is important, in the end, is that a preliminary hearing is held. Unlike in state **20-107** court litigation, no pre-conceived procedure exists. Thus, the preliminary hearing gives the arbitrators and the parties a forum to discuss their procedural expectations, identify agreements as well as differences in opinions, and establish the timetable for the proceeding. Most importantly, if properly done, the preliminary hearing will ensure that both parties know how and when exactly they are expected to present their case. This in itself is an important feature of procedural fairness. Indeed, where the parties come from different legal traditions with different expectations, or where they (or their counsel) are perhaps less experienced in international arbitration, the preliminary hearing becomes essential to ensure a fair and efficient process free from misunderstandings and procedural surprises.

As for international instruments, the 1996 UNCITRAL Notes on Organizing **20-108** Arbitral Proceedings (UNCITRAL Notes)[241] provide useful guidance. Some of the suggestions contained in the UNCITRAL Notes are somewhat controversial, however. For example, the Notes suggest that the tribunal may in appropriate circumstances issue procedural orders without first consulting the parties,[242] although in practice the parties will expect to be consulted on all procedural matter of any importance. If nothing else, however, the UNCITRAL Notes provide a helpful list of issues that the arbitrators and the parties may want to address.

---

241. UNCITRAL Notes, **Annex 15**.
242. UNCITRAL Notes, para. 7. When a tribunal is deciding whether to consult the parties on procedural matters, the UNCITRAL Notes suggest that the nature of the issue in question is relevant, as is whether consultation would be beneficial in improving procedural predictability or the atmosphere. **Annex 15**.

20-109 Among other things, the UNCITRAL Notes recommend that the following points be considered:

  a) adoption of procedural rules;[243]
  b) language, translations and costs;[244]
  c) seat of the arbitration and location of hearings;[245]
  d) administrative matters and appointment of a secretary;[246]
  e) deposits for costs and arbitrators' fees;[247]
  f) communications and confidentiality;[248]
  g) timetable for written submissions, evidence (documentary and physical), witness testimony (fact and expert) and hearing;[249]
  h) hearing procedures;[250]
  i) possible settlement issues;[251] and
  j) issue definition.[252]

20-110 In institutional arbitration, some of these issues are pre-determined. For example, the Vienna Rules provide for the seat of arbitration (if there is no agreement by the parties in the first place);[253] arbitrator remuneration and cost deposits;[254] means of communication[255] (although the preliminary hearing should still record the parties' proper address of service and may provide for additional specifications for how, and how many,[256] submissions and communications are being exchanged between the parties and the tribunal); and other issues. Yet some crucial procedural issues – such as the form and content of written submissions, document production, witness testimony and other forms of taking the evidence – are not addressed at all, and should be discussed at the preliminary hearing for the reasons outlined above.

---

243. UNCITRAL Notes, paras. 14-16, **Annex 15**.
244. UNCITRAL Notes, paras. 17-20, **Annex 15**.
245. UNCITRAL Notes, paras. 21-23, **Annex 15**.
246. UNCITRAL Notes, paras. 24-27, **Annex 15**.
247. UNCITRAL Notes, paras. 28-30, **Annex 15**.
248. UNCITRAL Notes, paras. 31-37, **Annex 15**.
249. UNCITRAL Notes, paras. 38-42, 48-49, 55-58, 60-68, 74-77, **Annex 15**.
250. UNCITRAL Notes, paras. 74-85, **Annex 15**.
251. UNCITRAL Notes, para. 47, **Annex 15**.
252. UNCITRAL Notes, paras. 43-46, **Annex 15**.
253. *See* **Article 2**, at paras. 004 *et seq.*
254. *See* **Article 34**, at paras. 007 *et seq.* and 019 *et seq.*
255. *See* **Article 13**, at paras. 015 *et seq.*
256. Arbitrators are well advised to regulate what submissions are permitted and to discourage 'unsolicited' submissions. As *Born* notes, 'the adversarial process can sometimes provoke intemperate and unnecessary correspondence by counsel (of all nationalities). A firm hand by the tribunal often helps reduce much wasted cost and emotion, while not interfering with the parties' ability to present their respective cases'. *See* G.B. Born, *International Commercial Arbitration – Commentary and Materials* (3rd edn, The Hague, Kluwer Law International, forthcoming), ch. 14.

Procedurally, the tribunal will aim at reaching consensus with the parties. A pro- **20-111** cedure built on joint agreement is the best basis for an arbitration perceived as successful by all parties irrespective of the outcome on the merits. Where no consensus can be established, at least a common understanding of the ground rules must be developed. For this reason, it is also good practice to record the consensus (or the tribunal's decision) on the procedural issues discussed during the preliminary hearing in a 'Procedural Order No. 1' or similar instruments.

2.2. Selected Issues of Case Management

Tribunals will be well advised to provide the parties with an agenda for the **20-112** preliminary hearing which will often include many of the points identified above pursuant to the UNCITRAL Notes. Some of the possible (or recommended) items for such an agenda warrant additional comments.

(i) Procedural Timetable

At the first procedural or preparatory hearing, with everyone's calendar available, **20-113** the arbitrators and the parties are also well advised to establish a procedural time-table (or schedule) for the arbitration. Determining the schedule for written sub-missions, documents production and the oral hearing at the outset of the case allows for better planning and clarifies expectations. Again, the tribunal will seek to establish a schedule, ideally with the parties agreeing to many of the procedural steps, that is both efficient and fair, and that suits the particular require-ments of the case. The parties should also be put on notice that they will be held to the schedule by the tribunal, and that extensions will only be granted exceptionally upon a showing of good cause.[257]

(ii) Taking of Evidence

The tribunal may also wish to discuss in some detail with the parties how evi- **20-114** dence will be taken. Different methods in adducing witness testimony and allow-ing documentary evidence into the proceeding are discussed below,[258] but whatever methods are preferred or chosen, they should be discussed in advance so that the parties and their counsel are aware of how they are expected to present their case. This discussion should include expert testimony, both of a factual or technical and of a legal nature.[259]

---

257. *See* D. Caron, L. Caplan and M. Pellonpaa, *The UNCITRAL Arbitration Rules: A Commentary* (Oxford, OUP, 2006) pp. 520, 522 ('Legitimate reasons for an extension may include illness of counsel, communications problem, or unexpected problems in gathering evidence to be sub-mitted in support of the written witness statement in question.' Refusal to accept late-filed submission may be appropriate if no explanation is offered, previous requests for extension were already denied or the opposing party will suffer prejudice).
258. *See* **Article 20**, at paras. 193 *et seq.* and 224 *et seq.*
259. *See* **Article 21**, at paras. 001 *et seq.*

(iii)   Identifying the Relevant Issues

20-115 The sooner the parties and the tribunal identify the relevant issues upon which the case turns, the better they are able to provide for a focused procedure that affirmatively addresses these issues. As is contemplated in the ICC Rules,[260] there are significant advantages, in terms of procedural efficiency, to identify the relevant factual and legal issues at the outset of the arbitration.

20-116 In some cases, counsel will be reluctant (for good reasons) to agree on a final list of issues, and thus to being locked into a particular position too early in the process, for fear that the other side's case may still be a moving target. Thus, while a list of issues is helpful, parties need to retain a measure of freedom to plead and develop their case in subsequent written submissions.[261] In other cases, it may be useful for the tribunal, after having received the parties' full pleadings but before the oral hearing, to identify what it believes the relevant issues are. This ensures that the parties have a full opportunity to address not only the relevant issues, but also to correct, where necessary, the tribunal's views on what is relevant.[262]

(iv)   Bifurcation or Other Segmentation of Proceedings

20-117 In the process of identifying issues, the tribunal and the parties may find that certain issues are of a preliminary or prejudicial nature, and should be addressed first, in order to avoid the waste of resources. Thus, the tribunal may be inclined to dispose of jurisdictional objections (unless they are intertwined with the merits of the case) before entering into the merits; or to rule on liability in principle before addressing the quantum.[263] This process of splitting the arbitration into logical phases (which, because of raising distinct factual or legal questions, deserve separate treatment) is often referred to as bifurcation (or, where it results in more than two phases, segmentation). It entails significant procedural efficiencies: where jurisdiction is denied, no effort to establish the merits of the case (often at great cost) is necessary. Where liability is denied, difficult issues of damage quantification can be avoided; where liability is affirmed, too, no resources have been wasted.[264]

20-118 Bifurcation is within the arbitrators' discretionary power to order, although in practice the parties will often agree on whether or not to bifurcate the arbitration. Of course, where arbitrations are segmented into different phases, particular care should be given to defining the phases with precision, so that the parties know exactly what they are expected to address in each phase.

---

260. Article 18 ICC Rules.
261. *See* the discussion of amending a claim under **Article 11**, at paras. 029 *et seq.*
262. M. Hunter, 'The Procedural Powers of Arbitrators Under the English 1996 Act' (1997) 13(4) Arb Int'l, 345, 352; H.M. Holtzmann, 'Fact-Finding by the Iran-U.S. Claims Tribunal' in *Fact-Finding Before International Tribunals*, R.B. Lillich (ed.) (Ardsley-on-Hudson, Translational Publishers, 1992), p. 106.
263. For a separate award on jurisdiction, *see* **Article 19**, at paras. 019 *et seq.*
264. In practice, the parties may also be able to settle the case once the issue of liability has been resolved.

With arbitration under increasing criticism for being overly costly and time con- **20-119**
suming,[265] it can be expected that segmentation will further develop as a procedural
instrument. This can include, for example, summary judgments (or, in civil law
jurisdictions, failure to state a legally-cognizable claim which would attract the relief
that is sought even if all facts alleged by the claimant were considered to be true);[266]
issues of time bar and Statute of Limitations; or arbitrability and the like.

II.   THE LANGUAGE OF THE ARBITRATION

**Article 20(2): Immediately after transmission of the files to the sole arbi-
trator (arbitral tribunal), the latter shall determine the language or languages of the proceedings, taking into consideration all circumstances, in
particular, the language of the contract. In such matters, he (it) is bound
by any agreement between the parties. The sole arbitrator (arbitral tribunal) can order that a translation be submitted of all documents that are
not drafted in that language (those languages).**

While the fZPO was silent on the matter of language, Section 596 ZPO now **20-120**
expressly allows the parties to agree on the language or languages of the arbitration, including by reference to institutional rules,[267] failing which the language will be determined by the arbitrators. As a result, the Austrian courts
will not involve themselves with the determination of the language of the arbitration. The Austrian *Oberster Gerichtshof* dismissed a plaintiffs' application to
have the language of the arbitration established by the courts through injunctive
relief, because the Austrian courts are only entitled to interfere the arbitral process
only where specifically so empowered by the statute.[268]

Section 596 ZPO follows Article 22 UNCITRAL Model Law, which in addition **20-121**
grants the arbitrators the power to request translations of documents. This
provision was not included in Section 596 ZPO, because it was perceived to
apply as a matter of course.[269]

---

265. *See e.g.*, Report from the ICC Commission on Arbitration, 'Techniques for Controlling Time
and Costs in Arbitration' (2007) ICC Publication No. 843.
266. Compare the concept of *mangelnde Schlüssigkeit* under Austrian law. *See* P.D. Ehrenhaft,
'Effective International Commercial Arbitration' (1977) 9 L & P Int'l Bus, 1191.
267. C. Liebscher, *The Austrian Arbitration Act 2006: Text and Notes* (The Hague, Kluwer Law
International, 2006), Annotated Text to Section 596 ZPO.
268. OGH, 12 April 1994, 4 Ob 1542/94; *see* Section 578 ZPO.
269. P. Oberhammer, *Entwurf eines neuen Schiedsverfahrensrechts* (Vienna, Manz, 2002), p. 96. In
order to safeguard the parties' right to be heard, arbitrators will typically order that all documents be translated into the language of the arbitration, as agreed or as determined, in order to
avoid the risk of a party claiming that it was unable to understand, and thus unable to properly
address, the evidence before the tribunal. *See also* M. Platte in *Arbitration Law of Austria:
Practice and Procedure*, S. Riegler, A. Petsche, A. Fremuth-Wolf, M. Platte and C. Liebscher
(eds) (Huntington, Juris Publishing, 2007), Section 596, p. 352.

20-122 Article 20(2) mirrors this approach,[270] which also reflects the international practice for parties to agree in the arbitration agreement on a particular language in which the arbitration shall be conducted (such an agreement being highly advisable in any event). Article 20(2) recognizes the binding effect of such an agreement.[271] Where the parties have not specified the language of the arbitration, it is for the arbitrators (not the institution) to determine it. As a procedural order, this decision is not subject to review by the Austrian courts.[272]

20-123 As the wording 'immediately after transmission of the files' suggests, the identification (or determination) of the language of the arbitration should be amongst the first acts of the arbitrators. This is in any event the only practicable solution, for without a determination of the appropriate language at the outset, a meaningful conduct of the arbitration would not be possible and the right to be heard potentially be impeded.

20-124 The determination of the applicable language is at the arbitrators discretion. The arbitrators must base their decision on 'all circumstances, in particular, the language of the contract'. Under this approach, the language of the contract appears to be the most important factor in establishing the language of the arbitration. As a matter of practice, this will often be sensible, as the main contract and related documentation will typically be at the core of the dispute. By choosing a particular language for the main contract, the parties have indicated that they are comfortable to conduct business with each other in that language. However, the language of the contract is not solely determinative; arbitrators must recognize 'all circumstances' which indicate that a language other than the language of the contract is more preferable in the individual case, such as the parties' nationality, the language of their previous correspondence, the language (if known) of likely witnesses and documentary evidence (as well as attending costs of translation) and all other considerations bearing on the fairness and efficacy of the proceedings. The parties may be heard on which language should govern the arbitration, but the arbitrators do not seem to be required under Article 20(2) to solicit the parties' views.[273]

20-125 Article 20(2) permits the arbitrator to determine the language or '*languages*' of the arbitration. Indeed, in some (perhaps exceptional) cases it may be appropriate to conduct the arbitration in more than one language. In practice, it is not uncommon to require the parties to make submission in one language but to allow them to

---

270. M. Aden, *Internationale Handelschiedsgerichtsbarkeit* (2nd edn, Munich, C.H. Beck, 2003), p. 544.
271. H.W. Fasching, *Schiedsgericht und Schiedsverfahren im österreichischen und im internationalen Recht* (Vienna, Manz, 1973), p. 105.
272. OGH, 12 April 1994, 4 Ob 1542/94.
273. For a different view, *see* C. Liebscher in *Arbitration Law of Austria: Practice and Procedure*, S. Riegler, A. Petsche, A. Fremuth-Wolf, M. Platte and C. Liebscher (eds) (Huntington, Juris Publishing, 2007), p. 643.

produce documents or witness statements in other languages without having to provide a translation.

If the arbitrators determine the language of the arbitration contrary to the parties' agreement, the aggrieved party would have to demonstrate that the resulting procedural irregularity had an adverse effect on the outcome of the proceeding. Arguably, such a determination constitutes only an ordinary procedural deficiency (*einfacher Verfahrensmangel*).[274] This demonstration of causality may be difficult in practice. Arbitrators could effectively ignore the parties' choice of language without sanction.[275] As *Fasching* points out, however, the arbitrators' determination of the procedural language is limited by the parties' right to be heard.[276] The choice of language must not result in impeding the parties' ability to properly present their case, including by imposing prohibitive costs.[277] **20-126**

Pursuant to Article 20(7) (and Section 579 ZPO), the aggrieved party needs to object against the determination of the arbitral language against the parties' agreement at the first opportunity. However, the determination of a language that would impede the parties' right to be heard arguably remains a ground for setting aside the award even without an objection, since the right to be heard is based on Section 594(2) ZPO and hence, a mandatory provision.[278] **20-127**

The language of the arbitration – i.e. the language used in the arbitration between the tribunal and the parties – is not identical to the language of correspondence between the parties (and presumably the arbitrators), on the one hand, and the VIAC, on the other hand. Whatever the language of the arbitration, correspondence with the bodies of the VIAC must be in English or German.[279] **20-128**

III.   WRITTEN SUBMISSIONS AND THE RIGHT
           TO AN ORAL HEARING

Article 20(3): The proceedings may be oral or only in writing. Oral hearings shall take place at the request of one party or if the sole arbitrator (arbitral tribunal) to whom (which) the case has been referred considers it necessary. In any case, the parties must be given the opportunity to take

---

274. *See* C. Hausmaninger in *Zivilprozeßgesetze, V/2*, H.W. Fasching (ed.) (2nd, Vienna, Manz, 2007), Section 597, para. 56.
275. M. Aden, *Internationale Handelsschiedsgerichtsbarkeit* (2nd edn, Munich, C.H. Beck, 2003), p. 545.
276. H.W. Fasching, *Schiedsgericht und Schiedsverfahren im österreichischen und im internationalen Recht* (Vienna, Manz, 1973), p. 105. In domestic arbitrations, German may arguably be the only permissible language, unless the parties expressly agree otherwise.
277. H.W. Fasching, *Schiedsgericht und Schiedsverfahren im österreichischen und im internationalen Recht* (Vienna, Manz, 1973), p. 105.
278. *See* **Article 20**, at para. 028.
279. *See* **Article 6**, at paras. 001 *et seq.*

note of, and comment on, the motions and pleadings of the other parties and the result of the evidentiary proceedings.

A.   The Right to an Oral Hearing

20-129 The fZPO did not contain any provisions regarding the oral or written conduct of the arbitration. According to the Austrian *Oberster Gerichtshof*, it was therefore for the arbitrators to 'decide at their discretion' if they 'want to hear the parties at the same time or consecutively, orally or in writing',[280] insofar as the issue was not 'determined by the applicable procedural rules on the basis of which the arbitration was conducted'.[281] Thus, the parties' right to be heard was, in principle, not violated if the party was just heard in writing, although this depends on the individual case.[282]

20-130 The arbitrators' discretionary power to hold an oral hearing, or not, is confirmed in Article 20(3). However, one party alone can also request that an oral hearing be held. In similar vein, Section 598 ZPO, which in turn is based on Article 24(1) of the UNCITRAL Model Law, provides in relevant part that the 'arbitral tribunal decides whether to hold oral hearings or whether the proceedings should be conducted in writing', but that 'if so requested by a party, the arbitral tribunal shall hold an oral hearing at an appropriate stage of the proceedings'.[283]

20-131 However, Section 598 ZPO expressly allows the parties to provide otherwise. Thus, the arbitrators cannot hold an oral hearing against the parties' express agreement to the contrary, even if the arbitrators deem such hearing necessary.[284] This was a deliberate decision by the drafting committee, which recognized that the conduct of the proceeding is in principle at the parties' disposition, in particular with respect of whether or not an oral hearing should be held.[285] Although this can raise delicate questions (if the arbitrator considers, for example, that he cannot arrive at a decision without having heard the parties or certain witnesses), this position reflects international practice.[286] Also, in some cases, the arbitrator will

---

280. OGH, 6 September 1990, 6 Ob 572/90. This followed a longstanding line of cases, *see* OGH, 26 February 1901, Nr. 2164, GIUNF 1304; OGH, 9 June 1937, 3 Ob 402/37, EvBl 1937, 722.
281. OGH, 27 November 1991, 3 Ob 1091/91.
282. A. Reiner, *Das neue österreichische Schiedsrecht/The new Austrian Arbitration Law* (Vienna, LexisNexis, 2006), Section 598, note 124.
283. Where the proceeding have been bifurcated (*e.g.*, into issues of liability and quantum), and thus consists of more than one stage, more than one oral hearing might be appropriate, and indeed, can be requested by a party under Section 598 ZPO. *See also* A. Reiner, *Das neue österreichische Schiedsrecht/The new Austrian Arbitration Law* (Vienna, LexisNexis, 2006), Section 598, note 126.
284. P. Oberhammer, *Entwurf eines neuen Schiedsverfahrensrechts* (Vienna, Manz, 2002), p. 101.
285. P. Oberhammer, *Entwurf eines neuen Schiedsverfahrensrechts* (Vienna, Manz, 2002), p. 101.
286. *See, e.g.*, Article 19(1) LCIA Rules: 'Any party which expresses a desire to that effect has the right to be heard orally before the Arbitral Tribunal on the merits of the dispute, unless

have to schedule an oral hearing in order to comply with Article 6 ECHR, where the circumstances of the case demand, for example because the case heavily turns on witness testimony and a fair resolution is not conceivable without hearing the witnesses in person.[287] Also, a request by a party to have an oral hearing does not mean that the entire proceeding have to be conducted orally, but only that in the course of the proceedings, a hearing takes place.[288] However, where the arbitration is segmented into different phases (for example, on jurisdiction, liability and quantum), one oral hearing for each phase should be conducted if so requested by one of the parties, particularly where witness or expert testimony is involved.[289]

By reference to the Vienna Rules, the parties have of course agreed to the application of Article 20(3), and thus, on the arbitrators' discretion in the matter Article 20(3), on its face, appears to give arbitrators the opportunity to conduct an oral hearing against the parties' declared intention. However, as discussed,[290] Article 20(3) must be read in connection with Article 20(1), which places the arbitrators' powers to conduct the arbitration at their discretion 'in the context of the parties' agreement'. In principle, therefore, the Vienna Rules require that arbitrators should not conduct an oral hearing against the parties' express agreement. Austrian law, if it applies, goes even further. Section 598 ZPO expressly provides for an oral hearing only if 'the parties have not excluded' it.[291] If the arbitrators consider that they cannot fulfill their mandate under such circumstances, they will have to consider to resign.[292] In addition, there may be certain (arguably rare)[293]   **20-132**

---

the parties have agreed in writing on documents-only arbitration.' Article 28 DIS Rules: 'Subject to agreement by the parties, the arbitral tribunal shall decide whether to hold oral hearings or whether the proceedings shall be conducted on the basis of documents and other materials. Unless the parties have agreed that no hearing shall be held, the arbitral tribunal shall hold such hearings at an appropriate stage of the proceedings, if so requested by a party.'

287. See **Article 20**, at paras. 029 *et seq.*; *see also* A. Reiner, *Das neue österreichische Schiedsrecht/ The new Austrian Arbitration Law* (Vienna, LexisNexis, 2006), Section 598, note 124.

288. C. Liebscher, *The Austrian Arbitration Act 2006: Text and Notes* (The Hague, Kluwer Law International, 2006), Annotated Text to Section 598 ZPO.

289. See **Article 21**, at paras. 001 *et seq.*

290. See **Article 20**, at paras. 086 *et seq.*

291. Section 598 ZPO: 'Unless the parties have otherwise agreed, the arbitral tribunal shall decide whether to hold oral hearings or whether the proceedings shall be conducted in writing. Where the parties *have not excluded* an oral hearing, the arbitral tribunal shall, upon motion of a party, hold an oral hearing at an appropriate stage of the proceedings.'

292. If the exclusion of a hearing was not evident from the arbitration agreement, and the parties deviate only later from the discretion afforded to arbitrators under Article 20(3), arbitrators have a good argument to resign because the procedure subsequently agreed by the parties deviates from the conditions on which the arbitrators accepted their mandate. *See also* **Article 20**, at para. 098.

293. In most cases, the parties will be able to properly present their case (within the meaning of Section 611(2) no. 2 ZPO, by addressing the evidence in writing. However, where

circumstances where a party may not be able to properly present its case without an oral hearing, which would then violate its right to be heard;[294] in such cases, the parties' procedural agreement does not bind the arbitrator.[295] As discussed, it is conceivable that certain cases turn on witness testimony which must be presented orally to the arbitrator to be properly assessed for its evidentiary value. Indeed, in international arbitration, and certainly in any case of importance, an oral hearing is the rule. Arbitrators should advise the parties at an early stage of the proceeding if, in their view, an oral hearing is unnecessary.[296]

B.   WRITTEN SUBMISSIONS IN ARBITRATION

20-133 As discussed, it is not mandatory in arbitration that an oral hearing is conducted. Some arbitrations proceed only through the exchange of written submissions, or on a 'document only' basis. Even where an oral hearing takes place, there is a clear trend in current arbitration practice to focus heavily on written materials, in order to avoid the costs and inefficiencies of having to bring the parties, witnesses, experts, and their lawyers, often all from different countries, together for a lengthy meeting in person. Written submissions are therefore of central importance in international arbitration.[297]

---

witness testimony is used, an oral hearing often appears necessary. Indeed, as discussed at **Article 20**, at paras. 202 *et seq.*, the use of written witness statements is not intended to eliminate the need for cross-examination, but indeed reinforces the opposing party's right to test the recollection that has been put to it in writing. In practice, however, this will not be an issue: all that party has to do is ask the arbitrator to conduct an oral hearing, and the arbitrator will have to comply.

294. H.W. Fasching, *Schiedsgericht und Schiedsverfahren im österreichischen und im internationalen Recht* (Vienna, Manz 1973), p. 105.

295. A. Reiner, *Das neue österreichische Schiedsrecht/The new Austrian Arbitration Law* (Vienna, LexisNexis, 2006), Section 598, note 124; A. Petsche in *Arbitration Law of Austria: Practice and Procedure*, S. Riegler, A. Petsche, A. Fremuth-Wolf, M. Platte and C. Liebscher (eds) (Huntington, Juris Publishing, 2007), Section 598, p. 371; H.W. Fasching, *Schiedsgericht und Schiedsverfahren im österreichischen und im internationalen Recht* (Vienna, Manz, 1973), p. 102; *see also* at **Article 20**, at para. 099.

296. As to case management and the right to be heard, *see* **Article 20**, at paras. 101 *et seq.*

297. D. Caron, L. Caplan and M. Pellonpaa, *The UNCITRAL Arbitration Rules: A Commentary* (Oxford, OUP Oxford, 2006), p. 392 ('In an overwhelming majority of cases, the arbitral procedure begins with an exchange of written submissions. Written pleadings are often given primary emphasis throughout the proceedings, with a short oral hearing or no hearing at all.'); J. Crawford, 'Advocacy Before the International Court of Justice and Other International Tribunals in State-to-State Cases' in *The Art of Advocacy in International Arbitration*, R. Bishop (ed.) (Huntington, Juris Publishing, 2004), pp. 11, 28.

The parties will normally file further written submissions with the tribunal,[298] in **20-134** addition to the statement of claims and the memorandum in reply.[299] The purpose of these submissions is to prepare the case to the fullest extent possible, in order to reduce the need for, and ultimately the length of, any oral hearing.

In order to afford each side a proper opportunity to present its own case as well **20-135** as respond to the other side's and to minimize the need for lengthy oral pleadings, written submissions will typically contain a detailed description of the factual allegations and will elaborate in detail on the applicable substantive law. The pre-hearing written submissions should therefore set forth the claimant's (and the respondent's) entire case, and not be confined to notice-style skeletal pleadings used in some (mostly common law) jurisdictions.[300] Similarly, it is good practice to direct the parties to attach *all* evidence on which they rely (such as documents, written witness statements, expert reports[301]) to their main written submissions (which are often referred to as 'memorials')[302] as well as

---

298. *See* the Report of the Secretary-General on the Revised Draft Set of Arbitration Rules, UNCITRAL, 9th Session, Addendum 1 (Commentary), UN Doc. A/CN.9/112/Add. 1 (1975), (1976) VII UNCITRAL YB 166, 173 (1976) (under Article 19(2), the respondent's defence is 'without prejudice to his right to present additional or substitute documents at a later stage in the arbitral proceeding'); D. Caron, L. Caplan and M Pellonpaa, *The UNCITRAL Arbitration Rules: A Commentary* (Oxford, OUP, 2006), p. 498 ('In most international arbitrations, further written submissions are likely to be useful, unless the case is disposed of on jurisdictional or other preliminary grounds. Provision should therefore usually be made for a second round of written pleadings, consisting of a reply (replique) by the claimant to the statement of defence (and any counterclaim) and a rejoinder (duplique) to this by the respondent.'); W. Wilberforce, 'Written Briefs and Oral Advocacy' (1989) 5(4) Arb Int'l, 348.
299. *See* **Article 9**, at paras. 044 *et seq.* and **Article 10**, at paras. 015 *et seq.*
300. R. Briner, 'Domestic Arbitration: Practice in Continental Europe and its Lessons for Arbitration in England' (1997) 13(2) Arb Int'l, 155, 161. *See also* the principles outlined in Iran-US Claims Tribunal, 1 December 1987, *Arthur Young & Co. v. The Islamic Republic of Iran*, Award No. 338-484-1, (1987) 17 Iran-US CTR 245, 253-254 ('[T]he arbitrating parties are obliged to present their claim or defence, in principle, as early as possible and appropriate under the circumstances in each case. Compliance with this obligation is indispensable, in the tribunal's view, to ensure an orderly conduct of the arbitral proceedings and equal treatment of the parties'). International Court of Justice, Practice Direction VII (7 February 2002) ('[P]leading are intended not only to reply to the submissions and arguments of the other party, but also, and above all, to present clearly the submission and argument of the party which is filing the pleadings').
301. *See* **Article 20**, at paras. 199 *et seq.* and 224 *et seq.* Although witness statements are sometimes submitted separately, after the written submissions, this practice is increasingly disfavoured, as it involves an additional step which necessarily draws out the schedule of the arbitration.
302. There are a wide variety of terms used to describe written submissions in arbitration; to a limited extent, institutional rules provide names for some submissions (such as the ICC's 'Request for Arbitration), but often this is not the case. Examples of commonly-used titles include 'statement of claim', 'statement of case', 'brief', 'points of claim', 'memorial', and so forth. There is no precise definition of these terms, and the label attached to a particular

legal materials (such as expert opinions, copies of statutory provisions and judicial authorities).[303]

20-136 In larger arbitrations, written submissions can require several months to prepare, will be hundreds of pages long (not including exhibits, which will entail thousands of additional pages or more) and will be very comprehensive, detailed documents. In smaller arbitrations, or where parties for their own valid reasons prefer efficiency and speed over predictability, written submissions can be much shorter and follow a rapid sequence.

20-137 Sometimes, written briefs are submitted not sequentially, but simultaneously by both parties. This is often done to expedite the arbitration even further, but has the disadvantage, since written briefs are exchanged on the same day, that neither party can properly respond to the other side's case. Thus, the parties' arguments may pass each other like ships in the night without ever truly engaging each other's case. This is particularly problematic from the respondent's perspective, who may argue that he has no sufficient opportunity to present his defence.[304] Sequential pre-hearing written filings are almost invariably preferable, with the claimant making the first submission.[305]

20-138 Where written submissions are sequenced, as they most often are, both parties will often claim the right to the last word. In civil law systems, the respondent is traditionally entitled to the last say,[306] whereas the common law tradition appears

---

submission is usually not important. In general, a 'memorial', 'complaint', a 'statement of case', and a 'brief' are fairly detailed documents submitted after the process of issue definition has largely concluded and factual development has commenced.

303. In international arbitration, where the arbitrators may well come from legal systems different from the applicable law, it is important that the parties plead the law (which is then necessarily foreign to some or all of the arbitrators) with particular care and detail, including by submitting legal authorities – such as case law and commentary – translated into the language of the arbitration, or as otherwise directed by the tribunal.

304. V. Mani, *International Adjudication: Procedural Aspects* (The Hague, Martinus Nijhoff Publishers, 1980), p. 107 stating that 'where the plaintiff-defendant relationship is discernible simultaneous presentation is illogical in that it requires the defendants to produce a complete defence without knowing fully in advance of the arguments of the claimant'.

305. In some arbitrations, a mixed approach is adopted. Even where pre-hearing memorials are submitted in an alternating order by the claimant and the respondent, respectively, post-hearing briefs will be submitted by both parties on the same day.

306. R. Briner, 'Domestic Arbitration: Practice in Continental Europe and its Lessons for Arbitration in England' (1997) 13(2) Arb Int'l, 155, 161; D. Caron, L. Caplan and M. Pellonpaa, *The UNCITRAL Arbitration Rules: A Commentary* (Oxford, OUP, 2006), p. 503 (Iran-US Claims tribunal practice evolved towards permitting the respondent to have the last word); Iran-US Claims Tribunal, 15 September 1993, *Foremost Tehran Inc. v. The Islamic Republic of Iran*, (1993) 3 Iran-US CTR 361, 362 ('While the filing by claimants of their Memorial on the Merits prior to the Hearing may be an advantage to the respondents in that it informs them in detail of claimants' contentions and arguments and may be of assistance to the tribunal in analyzing the case, nevertheless it cannot be accepted without providing the respondents an equal opportunity to make a written submission.').

to afford the claimant the final word.[307] For this reason, too, the simultaneous exchange of final post-hearing submissions is favoured by many arbitrators. Indeed, instead of, or in addition to, oral closing arguments, written submissions are often also submitted after the hearing (so-called 'post-hearing briefs'). These present the parties with the opportunity to summarize their case and apply the facts, as established in their view by the evidence taken throughout the arbitration and specifically at the oral hearing, to the law.

Of course, each party will have its own tactical expectations with respect to the **20-139** order and timing of written submissions, 'with each party seeking the maximum opportunity to present its case in an effective manner (and, less constructively, the most limited opportunity for its counter-party to do so)'.[308] Arbitrators (and this should ultimately guide counsel in presenting their case) will expect written briefs that are clear, accessible, measured in tone, avoid overstatement both in terms of rhetoric and substance,[309] and generally provide maximum assistance to the arbitrators in reaching their decision.[310]

The precise content, form and timing of written submissions is for the arbitrators and **20-140** the parties to discuss at the outset of the arbitration so that everyone involved knows exactly what to expect,[311] and can be tailored to the specific requirements of the proceedings at bar. Where a party fails to detail its case as directed (for example, by lacking adequate specificity), the arbitrators can request it to make a further submission, with the resulting delays being sanctioned through costs orders,[312] or otherwise (such as dismissing a claim for procedural non-compliance).[313]

---

307. A. Redfern, M. Hunter, N. Blackaby and C. Partasides, *Law and Practice of International Commercial Arbitration* (4th edn, London, Sweet & Maxwell, 2004), para. 6-118.
308. G.B. Born, *International Commercial Arbitration – Commentary and Materials* (3rd edn, The Hague, Kluwer Law International, forthcoming), ch. 14.
309. J. Crawford, 'Advocacy Before the International Court of Justice and Other International Tribunals in State-to-State Cases' in *The Art of Advocacy in International Arbitration*, R. Bishop (ed.) (Huntington, Juris Publishing, 2004), pp. 11, 30 stating that '[written submissions] need not to pour abuse on the other side or to use language which is overblown or unsustainable' and that 'the written pleadings should not be excessively argumentative, nor should they be academic or pedantic in their presentation'.
310. J. Crawford, 'Advocacy Before the International Court of Justice and Other International Tribunals in State-to-State Cases' in *The Art of Advocacy in International Arbitration*, R. Bishop (ed.) (Huntington, Juris Publishing, 2004), pp. 11, 30 ('A feature of the written pleadings is that they can be and often are read and reread by the tribunal.')
311. D. Caron, L. Caplan and M. Pellonpaa, *The UNCITRAL Arbitration Rules: A Commentary* (Oxford, OUP, 2006), p. 502 recommending that '[w]hatever the approach taken, the arbitral tribunal must always state clearly what kind of submission it expects'.
312. D. Caron, L. Caplan and M. Pellonpaa, *The UNCITRAL Arbitration Rules: A Commentary* (Oxford, OUP, 2006), p. 397 ('It is accepted, both in theory and in practice, that a claimant who has submitted a defective statement of claim may cure the shortcomings by submitting supplementary information.').
313. D. Caron, L. Caplan and M. Pellonpaa, *The UNCITRAL Arbitration Rules: A Commentary* (Oxford, OUP, 2006), p. 398 (Defects in statement of claim 'only rarely justify the termination of the proceedings under Article 28').

C.   THE RIGHT TO COMMENT

20-141 Article 20(3) provides in closing that, whether the arbitration is conducted on a
'document only' basis or whether it involves an oral hearing, 'the parties must be
given the opportunity to take note of, and comment on, the motions and pleadings
of the other parties and the result of the evidentiary proceedings'. This reinforces
the importance of the parties' right to be heard, as established by Article 20(1).[314]
As discussed in detail above, it would violate the parties' right to present their case
if they were excluded from commenting on the other side's submissions or on the
evidence that has been taken.[315] In similar vein, Section 599(3) ZPO provides:

> All written submissions, written documents and other communications which
> are submitted to the arbitral tribunal by a party are to be brought to the atten-
> tion of the other party. Expert opinions and other evidence to which the arbitral
> tribunal may refer in its decision are to be brought to the attention of both
> parties.

20-142 Section 599(3) ZPO requires, first of all, that every submission by one party
(whether it be a procedural submission, letter, communication, or any filing
with regard to the merits) is shared with the other side. Most arbitrators provide
in the initial directions to the parties that all correspondence to the tribunal has to be
simultaneously copied to the other party. This provides the greatest degree of
transparency, in that the other party receives the correspondence at the same
time as the tribunal, and is thereby put in a position to comment immediately if
necessary. Section 599(3) ZPO also requires that any evidence to which the tribunal refers in its decision to be shared with *both* parties.[316] This refers to evidence
that the tribunal is taking at its own volition, as any other evidence when submitted
by one party must be communicated to the other side in any event.

20-143 In that sense, arbitration provides for greater party involvement when compared to
litigation before the Austrian courts, where the parties are usually not asked to
comment on content or credibility of the witness testimony after the witnesses have
testified. This would be unacceptable in international arbitration. Only after
witness testimony is taken, it is possible to assess which facts have indeed been
established, and to connect those facts with the law.[317] Hence, parties should be
afforded the opportunity to comment on the evidentiary process. This can be done
orally at the end of the hearing. However, in international practice, and certainly in

---

314. *See* **Article 20**, at paras. 029 *et seq.*
315. This has always been the position under Austrian law. *See* OGH, 27 November 1991, 3 Ob
     1091/91.
316. This seems to include any evidence which is featured in the award, even if the tribunal does not
     really rely on this evidence to reach a decision. This is perhaps an overstatement. It should
     arguably be sufficient for the parties' to have had an opportunity to comment on the evidence
     on which the tribunal actually relies.
317. A. Reiner, 'Schiedsverfahren und rechtliches Gehör' [2003] ZfRV, 52, 56.

more complex matters, parties are often afforded the opportunity to submit post-hearing briefs in which they summarize their case and address the evidence that has been taken before, providing the tribunal with a final, often comprehensive view of their case that applies the law to the facts as they have been established in the eyes of the parties.

Given the mandatory character of Section 599(3) ZPO, some authors argue that **20-144** the appointment of a neutral confidentiality advisor, as envisaged for example by Article 20(7) of the ICC Rules[318] or Articles 3(7)[319] and 9(3)[320] of the IBA Rules, is not possible, rather, all information in the arbitration needs to be disclosed to both parties.[321] However, Section 599(3) ZPO may still leave some room for such measures, if carefully managed and, ideally, agreed with the parties. If, for example, confidential information is disclosed by one party to a neutral confidentiality advisor *before* it is submitted to the tribunal, it does not seem to be 'submitted to the arbitral tribunal' within the meaning of Section 599(3) ZPO and therefore needs not be immediately disclosed to the other side. Only what that neutral advisory determines should be disclosed to the tribunal must obviously be shared with the other side. The ultimate purpose of Section 599(3) ZPO is to ensure that the tribunal does not rely in its decision on any evidence on which the parties had no opportunity to comment beforehand. Confidentiality mechanisms should be structured to achieve that purpose.

IV.   THE ORAL HEARING

Article 20(4): The date of oral hearings shall be fixed by the sole arbitrator or the Chairman of the arbitral tribunal. Hearings shall be private. A record of at least the results of the hearings shall be made, which the sole arbitrator or the Chairman of the arbitral tribunal shall sign.

---

318. Article 20(7) ICC Rules: 'The Arbitral Tribunal may take measures for protecting trade secrets and confidential information.'
319. Article 3(7) IBA Rules: '(. . .) In that event, the Arbitral Tribunal may, after consultation with the Parties, appoint an independent and impartial expert, bound to confidentiality, to review any such document and to report on the objection. To the extent that the objection is upheld by the arbitral tribunal, the expert shall not disclose to the arbitral tribunal and to the other Parties the contents of the document reviewed.' **Annex 16**.
320. Article 9(3) IBA Rules: 'The Arbitral Tribunal may, where appropriate, make necessary arrangements to permit evidence to be considered subject to suitable confidentiality protection.' **Annex 16**.
321. M. Platte in *Arbitration Law of Austria: Practice and Procedure*, S. Riegler, A. Petsche, A. Fremuth-Wolf, M. Platte and C. Liebscher (eds) (Huntington, Juris Publishing, 2007), Section 599, p. 378; A. Reiner, *Das neue österreichische Schiedsrecht/The new Austrian Arbitration Law* (Vienna, LexisNexis, 2006), Section 599, note 128.

A.   INTRODUCTION

20-145 The first rule for a successful and productive hearing that assists the arbitrators in resolving the dispute before them is early preparation. The tribunal (or very often the presiding arbitrator) should consult with the parties to understand how the parties intend to present their case and to explain to the parties the tribunal's expectations in that regard.[322]

20-146 Recently, a style attributed to Professor *Böckstiegel* has found an increasing following. According to the *Böckstiegel*-method, the tribunal establishes a few firm rules but then allows the parties to proceed as they please within these boundaries.[323] Specifically, the tribunal allocates the same amount of time to both parties, who are entirely free to use their time at the hearing for opening or closing presentations or direct or cross-examination. Time is charged against the party which is using it.[324] The diligent arbitrator will, in consultation with the parties, determine the total amount of time appropriate under the circumstances on the basis of what has emerged in the written pleadings.[325] He will also be an active referee determined to prevent the plundering of the adversary's time-bank through unresponsive digressions.[326] Some time should also be set aside in advance for questions by the arbitrators. This is preferable to members of the tribunal interrupting the flow of the parties' carefully prepared presentations, but does of course not hinder the arbitrators to seek clarifications or confirmations that need, and should indeed be, addressed immediately.[327]

---

322.   J. Paulsson, 'The Timely Arbitrator: Reflections on the Böckstiegel Method' in *Law of International Business and Dispute Settlement in the 21st Century, Liber Amicorum K.-H. Böckstiegel*, R. Briner, L. Y. Fortier, K. P. Berger and J. Bredow (eds) (Cologne/Berlin/Bonn/Munich, Carl Heymanns Verlag, 2001), p. 608.

323.   J. Paulsson, 'The Timely Arbitrator: Reflections on the Böckstiegel Method' in *Law of International Business and Dispute Settlement in the 21st Century, Liber Amicorum K.-H. Böckstiegel*, R. Briner, L. Y. Fortier, K. P. Berger and J. Bredow (eds) (Cologne/Berlin/Bonn/Munich, Carl Heymanns Verlag, 2001), p. 608.

324.   Thus, although a witness is presented by party A, time is charged against party B to the extent that B occupies the witness in cross-examination. *See* J. Paulsson, 'The Timely Arbitrator: Reflections on the Böckstiegel Method' in *Law of International Business and Dispute Settlement in the 21st Century, Liber Amicorum K.-H. Böckstiegel*, R. Briner, L. Y. Fortier, K. P. Berger and J. Bredow (eds) (Cologne/Berlin/Bonn/Munich, Carl Heymanns Verlag, 2001), p. 611.

325.   J. Paulsson, 'The Timely Arbitrator: Reflections on the Böckstiegel Method' in *Law of International Business and Dispute Settlement in the 21st Century, Liber Amicorum K.-H. Böckstiegel*, R. Briner, L. Y. Fortier, K. P. Berger and J. Bredow (eds) (Cologne/Berlin/Bonn/Munich, Carl Heymanns Verlag, 2001), p. 613.

326.   Therefore, the arbitrators should be quick to reprimand evasive witnesses and frivolous procedural interventions by counsel. *See* J. Paulsson, 'The Timely Arbitrator: Reflections on the Böckstiegel Method' in *Law of International Business and Dispute Settlement in the 21st Century, Liber Amicorum K.-H. Böckstiegel*, R. Briner, L. Y. Fortier, K. P. Berger and J. Bredow (eds) (Cologne/Berlin/Bonn/Munich, Carl Heymanns Verlag, 2001), pp. 613 *et seq.*

327.   J. Paulsson, 'The Timely Arbitrator: Reflections on the Böckstiegel Method' in *Law of International Business and Dispute Settlement in the 21st Century, Liber Amicorum*

While a pre-determined schedule allows counsel a fair and equal opportunity to **20-147** prepare for the hearing, such schedule should of course never be considered to be written in stone. Deviation should – and if considerations of due process so require, must – be allowed to preserve the flexibility rightly cherished in international arbitration.

B.   FIXING THE HEARING DATE AND NOTIFYING THE PARTIES

Under Article 20(4), it is for the arbitrators to fix the date of the hearing. As a **20-148** matter of course, they need to take into account the availability of the parties and their counsel. However, were parties fail to cooperate in the scheduling of the oral hearing for tactical reasons, arbitrators have the power to fix a hearing date and proceed with the hearing without the defaulting party, provided that this party has been properly informed. In that regard, Article 20(4) is the corollary to the provision of Article 20(6) which regulates default proceedings.

As a matter of practice, it is advisable to fix the hearing as far in advance as **20-149** possible, in particular so that the parties can ensure the attendance of witnesses and experts. On procedural management, *see* **Article 20(1)**, at paras. 101 *et seq.*

In case of an arbitral tribunal, Article 20(4) expressly provides that the hearing **20-150** date is fixed by the chairman. This does not pre-empt the tribunal from adopting a different internal organization by requiring that procedural measures are taken only upon the decision of the tribunal *in toto*. In any event, the chairman generally takes any procedural measures on behalf of, and for, the collective tribunal.[328]

It is a fundamental aspect of the right to be heard for parties to be notified of any **20-151** hearing (whether on the law or the facts), as well as of any other meeting dedicated to the taking of evidence. Thus, the mandatory provision of Section 599(2) ZPO stipulates that '[t]he parties are to be timely informed of every hearing and of every meeting of the arbitral tribunal for the purpose of taking of evidence'. Section 599(2) ZPO requires the timely notification, which is designed to effectuate the parties' right to be heard in a meaningful way: the parties need to be notified reasonably in advance of the hearing, in order to allow for their prepared participation. As discussed, arbitrators will often fix the date of the oral hearing at the very outset of the arbitration.[329]

K.-H. *Böckstiegel*, R. Briner, L. Y. Fortier, K. P. Berger and J. Bredow (eds) (Cologne/Berlin/ Bonn/Munich, Carl Heymanns Verlag, 2001), p. 609.

328. M. Aden, *Internationale Handelsschiedsgerichtsbarkeit* (2nd edn, Munich, C.H. Beck, 2003), p. 546. *See* also discussion under **Article 26**, at paras. 034 *et seq.*

329. *See* **Article 20**, at para. 113.

C. PRIVACY OF THE HEARING (AND CONFIDENTIALITY OF ARBITRATION)

20-152 Under Austrian law and the Vienna Rules, arbitral hearings are, in principle, private. The issue of confidentiality is, however, less clear, both in the international debate as well as in Austrian doctrine. A discussion of both issues is set out below.

1. The Privacy of the Hearing

20-153 The fZPO was silent on the matter of privacy, and so is the new ZPO. According to traditional Austrian doctrine, the arbitral process as such is private,[330] meaning that the 'public' (i.e. third parties) are excluded from attending and participating at procedural meetings, hearings and the taking of evidence. Although there is no express statutory provision to this effect, the privacy of the arbitral process results from the contractual relationship between the parties, and between the parties and the arbitrators. Third parties lacking this privity of contract also lack the right to participate in the proceeding.

20-154 There is no dispute, therefore, that arbitration hearings are conducted in private.[331] Some scholars have argued under the old law, however, that the privacy of the process is at the discretion of the arbitrators, and that the arbitrators could order under Article 587(1) fZPO (what is now Section 594(1) ZPO) that the arbitration be conducted in public.[332] This would go against the contractual nature of arbitration. Whether to open their hearings to the public is, at least in principle, an issue for the parties to decide; and unless both parties agree on public hearings, arbitrators cannot grant access to parties who are not parties to the arbitration agreement.[333]

20-155 This debate is mute in the context of Vienna Rules. Article 20(4) expressly provides that 'hearings shall be private'. This language ('shall') suggests that the 'privacy' of the hearing is not at the arbitrators' disposition. Of course, if both parties expressly agree that the hearing should be open to the general public or certain third parties, then such agreement should override the seemingly-mandatory language of Article 20(4). This provision, read together with Article 20(1), makes clear

---

330. H.W. Fasching, *Schiedsgericht und Schiedsverfahren im österreichischen und im internationalen Recht* (Vienna, Manz, 1973), p. 104.
331. C. Liebscher and A. Schmidt in *Practitioner's Handbook on International Arbitration*, F.B. Weigand (ed.) (Munich, C.H. Beck, 2002), p. 577.
332. H.W. Fasching, *Schiedsgericht und Schiedsverfahren im österreichischen und im internationalen Recht* (Vienna, Manz, 1973), p. 104.
333. Arbitrators are therefore well advised to exercise their discretion to allow the public conduct of the arbitration only in the rarest of circumstances. Such circumstances maybe the public nature of, or public interest in, the arbitration, as has lately been suggested with respect to investment treaty disputes. *See* N. Blackaby, 'Public Interest and Investment Treaty Arbitration' (2004) I(1) TDM. However, for the joinder of interested third parties and non-signatories, *see* also **Article 15**, at paras. 074 *et seq.*

on the other hand that one party alone cannot request the public conduct of the hearing.

2.   The Confidentiality of Arbitration

A related question concerns the confidentiality of the arbitral process as such. This **20-156** question – whether, and, if so, to what extent arbitration is confidential – is still disputed. The traditional view has held that arbitration is a private and therefore necessarily confidential means of dispute resolution.[334] Confidentiality can, of course, be based on an express confidentiality agreement contained in a separate contract; or in the main contract defining the parties' relationship; or in the arbitration agreement; or in the institutional rules; or else, as the case may be in an ICC arbitration, in the terms of reference, or indeed a comparable procedural instrument.

The issue becomes more difficult in the absence of a confidentiality agreement. In **20-157** view of the certainty with which the promoters of confidentiality claimed (and claim) the existence of a principled obligation to that effect, it is perhaps surprising that there is no basis for a principle of confidentiality in most national arbitration laws. Others rely on this silence of national laws to claim that it only demonstrates that confidentiality applies to arbitration as a matter of course.

Absent clear provisions in applicable law or agreement, parties on occasion invoke **20-158** a 'generally accepted principle of confidentiality of arbitral proceedings'. In international practice, however, the notion of confidentiality has been somewhat corroded by a series of national court decisions. In the notorious *Esso* case, the High Court of Australia held that confidentiality was not 'an essential attribute of private arbitration imposing an obligation on each party not to disclose the proceedings or documents and information provided in and for the purpose of arbitration'.[335] In Europe, the Swedish Supreme Court has held in an equally famous decision that 'a party to arbitration proceedings cannot be deemed to be bound by a duty of confidentiality, unless the parties have concluded an agreement concerning this'.[336]

Some jurisdictions still imply, at least as a matter of principle, a confidentiality **20-159** obligation into the parties' agreement to arbitrate. In England, confidentiality in arbitration was endorsed in principle in *Dollinger-Baker v. Merret and another*

---

334. J. Power, *The Austrian Arbitration Act – A Practitioner's Guide to Sections 577-618 of the Austrian Code of Civil Procedure* (Vienna, Manz, 2006), Section 616, para. 3; W. Voit in *Kommentar zur Zivilprozessordnung*, H.-J. Musielak (6th edn. Munich, Verlag Franz Vahlen, 2008), Section 1042, paras. 11, 13.

335. *Esso Australia Resources Ltd. And others v. The Honorable Sidney James Howard and others* (1995) 11(3) Arb Int'l, 235, 246 *et seq.* (High Court of Australia).

336. Swedish Supreme Court, 27 October 2000, *AI Trade Finance Inc. v. Bulgarian Foreign Trade Bank Ltd.* (2001) XXVI YB Comm Arb, 291-298.

because of 'the very nature of arbitration'.[337] English courts have also held that a party to an arbitration is subject to an *implied* obligation of confidence which 'arises as the nature of the contract itself implicitly requires'.[338] A party must therefore not make use of material generated in an arbitration other than for the purposes of this arbitration. In a recent decision of the Privy Council, this approach was criticized as '[i]t runs the risk of failing to distinguish between different types of confidentiality which attach to different types of document'.[339]

20-160   The English law approach of perception of confidentiality as an obligation that is implied, if not expressly contained in the parties' arbitration agreement, may have some appeal under many national laws of contract, including under continental European systems. Whether that is so, is a question of contract interpretation under the substantive law applicable to the parties' agreement, and an approach that has been accepted by courts.[340] It is at least conceivable that the circumstances of the parties' contract suggest that the parties perceived that disputes arising out of their contractual relationship to be confidential. Confidentiality could also be applied as an (international) trade practice in certain industries, although this seems as a general rule increasingly unlikely in light of the sceptical view taken towards confidentiality by courts and commentators in many jurisdictions. In any event, it will often be extremely difficult in practice to mark the precise boundaries of an implied duty of confidentiality, even where such duty could in principle be assumed.[341]

20-161   Even where confidentiality obligations can be implied as a matter of principle, their scope might be difficult to determine, and several exceptions will typically apply. As regards the scope, one needs to distinguish very carefully which aspect of arbitration exactly is supposedly confidential, with potentially different analyses attending. Consider for example the existence of the arbitration as such: in some industries or cases, it may be implied that even the existence of the dispute should be kept from the public, but this is often far from certain (and hence too uncertain to constitute an implied confidentiality obligation). A different analysis will apply to submissions, documents or evidence that the parties exchange in the course of the arbitration: oftentimes, it can be assumed that the parties will not want to share such documents with the general public. Yet distinct issues are raised with respect

---

337. As cited by N. Rawding and K. Seeger, 'Aegis v. European Re and the Confidentiality of Arbitration Awards' (2003) 19(4) Arb Int'l, 483.
338. N. Rawding and K. Seeger, 'Aegis v. European Re and the Confidentiality of Arbitration Awards' (2003) 19(4) Arb Int'l, 483.
339. *Associated Electric and Gas Insurance Services Ltd. v. European Reinsurance Co. of Zurich*, [2003] I WLR 1041, (Privy Council).
340. *See* A. Fremuth-Wolf in *Arbitration Law of Austria: Practice and Procedure*, S. Riegler, A. Petsche, A. Fremuth-Wolf, M. Platte and C. Liebscher (eds) (Hunington, Juris Publishing, 2007), pp. 670 *et seq.*
341. N. Rawding and K. Seeger, 'Aegis v. European Re and the Confidentiality of Arbitration Awards' (2003) 19(4) Arb Int'l, 485.

to the award: should it be kept confidential in all circumstances, or can the parties rely on it in public?

It is also evident that confidentiality obligations, even where they exist, are not **20-162** absolute but subject to exceptions. A party may, for example, be under an obligation to disclose the existence of an arbitration under applicable securities laws,[342] even where it is bound by a confidentiality agreement. Similarly, it is difficult to prevent a party from relying on the award in subsequent proceedings (for example for the purposes of enforcement) even where the proceedings are public. However, the *Cour d'Appel de Paris* (Paris Court of Appeal) held that a challenge of an award brought in bad faith 'allowed public debate of facts that should remain confidential', and that arbitration required 'the utmost discretion when settling private disagreements as it had been agreed by the parties'. This decision has been heavily criticized.[343] The English courts have held recently that, under certain circumstances, the confidentiality of arbitration could extend to court proceedings in connection with arbitration: 'The parties' agreement to arbitrate and their failure to apply for a public hearing indicated a desire for confidentiality that should be given effect. Publication of the court's judgement which would reveal matters in dispute in the arbitration 'runs counter to the principle of confidentiality' in arbitration. Other factors, notably the commercial and political nature of the dispute, weighed against publication, particularly in the absence of 'issues of law or of wider interest'.[344] Where confidentiality is agreed, it makes indeed sense to

---

342. J. Paulsson and N. Rawding, 'The Trouble with Confidentiality' (1995) 11(3) Arb Int'l, 303, 311.

343. J. Paulsson and N. Rawding, 'The Trouble with Confidentiality' (1995) 11(3) Arb Int'l, 303, 312 rejecting the court's finding because 'it does not give authority for either of these premises i.e. that the "nature" of arbitration intrinsically calls for confidentiality and that the parties had so "agreed" and since it does not articulate any limits to the extent of the duty of confidentiality'.

344. *Department of Economics Policy Development of the City of Moscow v. Bankers Trust Co and International industrial Bank*, Unreported, Cooke J., [2003] Q.B. (Comm.) in [2003] 6(5) Int'l Arb L Rev, N-45, note by *S.R. Shackleton*. On 25 March 2004 the Court of Appeal held that a judgment of the High Court declining an application under s68 Arbitration Act 1996 should remain private as it contained confidential and sensitive information. Following arbitration, IIB and BT applied under s68 of the Arbitration Act 1996 to set aside the arbitrator's award for serious irregularity. The challenges before the High Court were heard in private and the resulting judgment was published only to the parties. The Appellant (Moscow), then applied to publish the Court's judgment relating to the s68 application. In the meantime, a brief and factually neutral summary was mistakenly published by Lawtel on its web-site. No confidential facts were disclosed and it was removed once the error was discovered. The High Court determined that the judgment should remain private because it contained sensitive matters of great confidentiality. Moscow appealed that decision to the Court of Appeal and sought permission to publicize the Lawtel summary. The Court held that whilst the 'starting point' for arbitration claims brought under s68 of the Act and CPR Part 62.10 is that the hearing should be conducted in private (meaning in secret), there could not be a blanket protection of non-publication in all cases. If a question of publication is raised, the judge's task is to weigh

extended it to related court proceedings. In Austria, Section 616(2) ZPO therefore provides that 'upon request of a party, the public may also be excluded where a justified interest in doing so can be shown'.

20-163 In any event, parties can hardly be prevented to use an award, even if they have concluded an express confidentiality agreement, to enforce their claims.[345] Recognizing the multiple exceptions to confidentiality, Article 30(1) LCIA Rules provides, for example, that:

> Unless the parties expressly agree in writing to the contrary, the parties undertake as a general principle to keep confidential all awards in their arbitration, together with all materials in the proceedings created for the purpose of the arbitration and all other documents produced by another party in the proceedings not otherwise in the public domain – save and to the extent that disclosure may be required of party by legal duty, to protect or pursue a legal right or to enforce or challenge an award in bona fide legal proceedings before a state court or other judicial authority.

20-164 Providing for more exceptions than a solid basis for confidentiality, this provision shows that, in today's legal environment, comprehensive confidentiality provisions will be difficult to establish, or to formulate. For these reasons, many institutional arbitration rules do not even require the parties to keep the proceedings confidential. In the case of the ICC Rules, which to date do not contain such a confidentiality obligation, the ICC drafting committee has, in fact, specifically rejected the notion of a principle of confidentiality,[346] although parties and

---

the factors in favor of publicity against the desirability of preserving the confidentiality of the original arbitration. The 'spectrum' as to the confidentiality of an arbitration runs from the arbitration hearing at one end to an order following a reasoned judgment under s68 at the other. The Court held that the judgment relating to the s68 application contained an account of highly sensitive political and commercial issues and therefore concluded that the judgment should remain private. In respect of the Lawtel summary, the Court stated that as the summary did not contain sensitive or confidential information and had already entered the public domain, general publication of the Lawtel summary could be given. *Department of Economic Development of the City of Moscow and the Government of Moscow v. Bankers Trust Company and International Industrial Bank*, [2004] EWCA Civ 314 (Court of Appeal).

345. *Associated Electric and Gas Insurance Services Ltd. v. European Reinsurance Co. of Zurich*, [2003] I WLR 1041 (Privy Council); *see also* N. Rawding and K. Seeger, 'Aegis v. European Re and the Confidentiality of Arbitration Awards' (2003) 19(4) Arb Int'l, 483, 485 *et seq.*

346. Y. Derains and E.A. Schwartz, *A Guide to the New ICC Rules of Arbitration* (The Hague, Kluwer Law International, 1998), pp. 12, 13 ('A provision has been added (Article 20.7) explicitly authorizing the Arbitral Tribunal to "take measures for protecting trade secrets and confidential information." However, the ICC rejected the option of including in the New Rules a general provision requiring the parties to respect the confidentiality of the arbitration. In this regard, the ICC Rules, like many other arbitration rules, have never explicitly obligated the participants in an arbitration (. . .) to protect the confidentiality of the proceedings. Although the confidentiality of arbitration is often assumed, a number of recent court cases (. . .) have demonstrated that this cannot be taken for granted in all places and

arbitrators often set out a specific confidentiality agreement in the terms of reference. For the same hesitations, the UNCITRAL committee on arbitration currently considering a revision of the UNCITRAL Rules has rejected the inclusion of an express confidentiality provision.

In Austria, the parties can determine whether or not they want the award to be **20-165** published.[347] Absent such agreement, the arbitrators' (or the arbitral institutions') right to publish an award is viewed sceptically; in practice, only two awards issued under the auspices of the VIAC have been published to date.[348] In recent years, the majority of commentators appear to reject the notion of a general principle of confidentiality,[349] although some remain vigorous defenders of what traditionally has been perceived as one of arbitration's major virtues.[350]

It appears, therefore, that the purported principle of confidentiality raises signif- **20-166** icant uncertainties. The parties in an arbitration are therefore well advised to include a confidentiality provision that fits their circumstances in their arbitration agreement, if they indeed desire the confidentiality of their arbitration. However, the notion of an implied confidentiality provision should not be too easily disregarded; it must be assessed from the contractual framework in existence between the parties, under whatever substantive law (and attending rules of contract interpretation) are applicable.

Where the parties have agreed to arbitrate under the Vienna Rules, there may be an **20-167** argument that a more general confidentiality obligation (beyond the narrow notion of the privacy of the hearing) is implied. Such an argument would be based on the general preference for confidentiality that is reflected in several provisions of the Vienna Rules, and thus can be read to imply a general notion of confidentiality into the arbitration agreement. For example, **Articles 3** and **5** require the Board and the Secretary General to keep all arbitrations (including the existence of proceedings)

---

circumstances and that, in the absence of an express agreement to this effect, the parties do not necessarily have an absolute obligation to respect the confidentiality of the arbitration. (. . .) [I]t was decided not to propose a general confidentiality provision and, hence, to leave the matter, as it presently is, for the parties (. . .) to deal with.').

347. See **Article 30**, at para. 003.
348. C. Liebscher and A. Schmid in *Practitioner's Handbook on International Arbitration*, F.B. Weiland (ed.) (Munich, C.H. Beck, 2002), p. 578. These awards are discussed in greater detail at **Article 30**.
349. *See, e.g.*, J. Paulsson and N. Rawding, 'The Trouble with Confidentiality' (1995) 11(3) Arb Int'l, 303, 304 ('May the mere existence of the dispute be published without the consent of both parties? (. . .) Such disclosures may be unavoidable and harmless.'); H. Smit, 'Confidentiality in Arbitration' (1995) 11(3) Arb Int'l, 340; J. Lew, 'Expert Report of Dr. Julian D.M. Lew (in Esso/BHP v. Plowman)' (1995) 11(3) Arb Int'l, 283; H. Bagner, 'Confidentiality-A Fundamental Principle in International Commercial Arbitration?' (2001) 18(2) J Int'l Arb, 248.
350. E. Gaillard and J. Savage (eds), *Fouchard Gaillard Goldman On International Commercial Arbitration* (The Hague, Kluwer Law International, 1999), para. 384 ('There has never been a general tradition of confidentiality').

confidential; the same is true for the arbitrators under **Article 7**. Similarly, the Board can publish awards only in anonymous format.[351] Although all of these provisions are not directly aimed at the parties, they create an environment of confidentiality which may be argued to inform the overall process under the Vienna Rules.

D.   THE RECORD OF THE HEARING

20-168 Article 20(4) also provides that a 'record of at least the results of the hearings shall be made, which the arbitrator or the Chairman of the arbitral tribunal shall sign'. Again, the language strongly indicates that this provision is mandatory. It sets a minimum standard ('at least'), from which the arbitrators must not deviate. Much speaks in favour of the position, however, that parties can provide otherwise, and thus exclude the requirement of any record, through their express agreement. In any event, it is clear that arbitrators can impose, and the parties can agree on, stricter recording requirements, including verbatim court reporting.

20-169 The minimum requirement to record *'the results'* of the hearing may strike Anglo-American users of the Vienna Rules as unusual. The concept is taken from Austrian civil procedure (*Ergebnisprotokoll*), in which the parties' oral pleadings and the testimony are only summarized for the record. In Austria, *verbatim* minutes are known in criminal proceedings, but rarely used – although possible on the request of a party – in civil or commercial matters.[352] In international arbitration, however, the record is usually taken *verbatim*, at least if evidence is taken or if the merits of the case are discussed.[353] Although the costs of hiring a court reporter, who records and transcribes the hearing, will be prohibitive in small matters, *verbatim* minutes are highly recommendable, in particular as such services are becoming increasingly available on the European continent. A *verbatim* transcript provides a complete and objective record of the parties' oral submissions, the oral evidence taken at the hearing, of all questions put to the witnesses and of their answers. Such a record is preferable to summary minutes taken at the hearing at a time when the real issues, or a party's reason to ask a particular question, may not yet be clear to the arbitrators. In providing a complete and accurate record of the hearing to which the parties and the arbitrators can return after the events, a *verbatim* transcript also facilitates the parties' right to be heard.[354] A *verbatim* record can also provide a useful, and indeed perhaps necessary, tool should a party later want to challenge the award.[355] Other

---

351. *See* **Article 30**, at paras. 001 *et seq.*
352. In most instances, the judge records the minutes in a summary fashion (*Resumeprotokoll*).
353. Because of cost implications, *verbatim* minutes of procedural hearings are rare.
354. A. Reiner, 'Schiedsverfahren und rechtliches Gehör' [2003] ZfRV, 52, 56.
355. H.W. Fasching, *Schiedsgericht und Schiedsverfahren im österreichischen und im internationalen Recht* (Vienna, Manz, 1973), p. 105.

methods to establish a record of the arbitration, such as tape recordings or dictated minutes, are, of course, also permissible.[356]

It has been argued that the written record of the hearing is, unlike a court record,[357] **20-170** a private document (*Privaturkunde*) with such evidentiary value as is attached to it under applicable law and that the written record is a joint document of the arbitral tribunal, even if signed only by the chairman.[358] The better view is that the written record is a joint document of the arbitrators *and the parties*; a document is deemed to be a 'joint' document in respect of those persons in whose interest the document was drafted or whose respective legal relationship is evidenced in the document.[359] The characterization as a 'joint document' (*gemeinsame Urkunde*) is relevant under Austrian civil procedure, and hence for subsequent court proceedings, because a party is obligated to produce a 'joint' document of the parties by way of disclosure, whereas disclosure of other documents is severely restricted.[360] In practice, parties are often given the opportunity to comment on the accuracy of the transcript or other record of the hearing.[361]

V. THE TAKING OF EVIDENCE

Article 20(5): If the sole arbitrator (arbitral tribunal) considers it necessary, he (it) may on his (its) own initiative collect evidence, and in particular may question parties or witnesses, may request the parties to submit documents and visual evidence and may call in experts. If costs are incurred through the evidentiary proceedings and in particular through the appointment of experts, the procedure under Article 35 shall be followed.

A. INTRODUCTION

The taking of evidence in arbitration is often the crucial element of the contentious **20-171** process. In international arbitration, the taking of evidence is subject to significant tensions, discussed above, of different legal cultures, distinct expectations of the

---

356. C. Liebscher and A. Schmid, in *Practitioner's Handbook on International Arbitration*, F.B. Weigand (ed.) (Munich, C.H. Beck, 2002), p. 563.
357. H.W. Fasching, *Schiedsgericht und Schiedsverfahren im österreichischen und im internationalen Recht* (Vienna, Manz, 1973), p. 105.
358. M. Aden, *Internationale Handelsschiedsgerichtsbarkeit* (2nd edn, Munich, C.H. Beck, 2003), p. 546.
359. *See* **Article 22**, at paras. 118 *et seq.*
360. Section 304(1) no. 3 ZPO.
361. C. Liebscher in *Arbitration Law of Austria: Practice and Procedure*, S. Riegler, A. Petsche, A. Fremuth-Wolf, M. Platte and C. Liebscher (eds) (Huntington, Juris Publishing, 2007), p. 643.

parties and the arbitrators, and requirements of speed, efficiency, flexibility and fairness. Different views, in different legal cultures, extend from the conduct of witness testimony and the method of examination to compelled document production, disclosure or discovery.

20-172 The taking of evidence in arbitration can therefore take many forms. It will depend to a lesser extent on applicable law (as most arbitration laws are silent on the precise conduct of the arbitration) and more importantly on the parties' procedural agreements and the inclinations of the tribunal who in most cases will enjoy considerable latitude in conducting the taking of evidence.[362] Further, the assistance available from the state courts, either at the seat of the arbitration or elsewhere, can have an impact on the efficient taking of evidence in arbitration.[363]

20-173 It is, then, for the parties, or, if they cannot agree, for the arbitral tribunal to determine the rules of evidence that apply to the arbitration. This process is informed by the legal background and cultural expectations of the parties, their counsel and the arbitrators involved, and thus requires an understanding of the often significantly different approaches taken by lawyers around the world. In international arbitration, counsel and arbitrators need to be able to bridge those differences in order to conduct proceedings in a neutral and equitable manner.

20-174 In recent years, as arbitration has established itself as the primary dispute resolution mechanism for international trade, certain commonly-accepted standards have evolved that reflect an internationally-harmonized approach to procedural issues. As far as the taking of evidence is concerned, the most prominent example are the Rules on the Taking Evidence in International Commercial Arbitration adopted by the International Bar Association (IBA Rules).[364] The IBA Rules were drafted by a working group comprised of both common law and civil law experts with a view to making them acceptable to lawyers from both systems. They will apply to international commercial arbitrations if the parties agree or the tribunal so orders, thereby supplementing applicable national laws or institutional or *ad hoc* rules.

20-175 The IBA Rules were an ambitious undertaking, in that they had to overcome fundamental cultural differences regarding evidentiary rules. While it is difficult to assess how frequently the IBA Rules are actually adopted by parties, it is fair to say that they have had a considerable influence on the practice of taking evidence in international commercial arbitration. Thus, parties and arbitrators are increasingly willing to employ in arbitration elements of a procedural system other than their own. Oftentimes, they are not adopted as a set of rules in the strict sense, but many arbitrators indicate at the outset of the arbitration that they will be guided by them in evidentiary matters.

---

362. *See* **Article 20**, at paras. 082 *et seq.*
363. G.B. Born, *International Commercial Arbitration – Commentary and Materials* (2nd edn, The Hague, Kluwer Law International, 2001), p. 469.
364. *See* IBA Rules, **Annex 16**.

Despite this trend of harmonization, differences remain. Parties, counsel and arbi- **20-176** trators from common law jurisdictions are still accustomed to, and might prefer, proceedings that are more distinctly adversarial in nature. In such a system, the role of the judge is to apply detailed and often complex rules of evidence to determine the relevance and admissibility of documents and testimonial evidence tendered by each party. Evidence put forward by one party in support of its case may be subject to a legal challenge by the opposing party. In such a case, it is the judge's role to act as referee and to determine whether or not evidence offered by a party is admitted. However, the judge has no independent capacity to identify or obtain additional evidence and must come to a decision based on the admissible evidence put before him by the parties. In civil law countries, by contrast, the judge will usually assume a far more inquisitorial role. He will often take an active part in assessing the relevance of the evidence offered by the parties, and in conducting the hearing and questioning of the witnesses. In conclusion, it remains highly important for arbitration practitioners to understand the differences inherent in the evidentiary rules under civil law and common law, respectively. Such understanding is vital in preparing for, and adequately dealing with, the frictions that may arise as a result of these different approaches. Indeed, so prepared, arbitration practitioners will be able to anticipate each other's expectations, perceptions and, perhaps, the conduct of the parties, their counsel and the tribunal members in the arbitration.

This chapter examines the standard of taking of evidence in arbitration under **20-177** Austrian law and the Vienna Rules; examines the discretionary powers available to the arbitrators; and then proceeds to a discussion of the civil law and common law approaches relating to obtaining and using documentary evidence; preparation of witness statements; and the examination of witnesses, with a view towards suggesting a best practice in international arbitration. The use of expert evidence is discussed separately in the context of **Article 21**.

B.   THE ARBITRATORS' RIGHT (OR DUTY) TO ESTABLISH
         THE RELEVANT FACTS

Article 20(5) affords the arbitrators maximum discretion in establishing the facts **20-178** and taking evidence as they deem appropriate. It provides that '[i]f the sole arbi- trator (arbitral tribunal) considers it necessary, he (it) may on his (its) own initiative collect evidence, and in particular may question parties or witnesses, may request the parties to submit documents and visual evidence and may call in experts'. The arbitrators' evidentiary discretion extends to all forms of evidence, and list certain forms only by way of example ('in particular'). Article 20(5) reflects international practice.[365] The arbitrators' evidentiary discretion also allows

---

365. As far as institutional rules are concerned, many rules leave it to the arbitrators' discretion to ascertain the relevant facts beyond the parties' submissions. *See, e.g.*, Article 20 ICC Rules; Article 22(1)(c) LCIA Rules and Article 16 AAA/ICDR Rules: 'The tribunal may in its dis- cretion direct the order of proof (. . .)'. Article 19 AAA/ICDR Rules: 'At any time during the

them to weigh the evidence, and to attach to it the evidentiary value they deem appropriate.[366] Where a party fails without satisfactory explanation to produce any document despite being ordered to do so by the tribunal, the tribunal may make adverse inferences in the context of its evidentiary discretion.[367]

20-179 The arbitrators' evidentiary discretion stipulated in Article 20(5) is an extension of the general discretionary powers established under Article 20(1), and confirmed by Section 599(1) ZPO, which provides that '[t]he arbitral tribunal is authorized to decide upon the permissibility of the taking of evidence, to conduct such taking of evidence, and to freely evaluate such evidence'.

20-180 The particular wording of Article 20(5) raises the question, however, if the parties can limit the arbitrators' discretion (as they can under Article 20(1)),[368] or whether the arbitrators' discretion to take the evidence he or she considers appropriate cannot be limited by the parties' agreement. On a contractual level, the Vienna Rules are an extension of the parties' agreement to arbitrate, in which the Rules are incorporated by reference. As discussed, therefore, the parties can agree to limit the arbitrators' evidentiary authority; and conceptually, it is difficult to see why a different analysis should apply to Article 20(5).

**1.   The Arbitrator's Duty to Establish the Facts
          Under the fZPO**

20-181 Of course, irrespective of the structure of the Vienna Rules, the parties could not by agreement limit the arbitrators' evidentiary authority if that authority were

---

proceedings, the tribunal may order parties to produce other documents, exhibits or other evidence it deems necessary or appropriate.' Article 22 AAA/ICDR Rules: 'The tribunal may appoint one or more independent experts to report to it, in writing, on specific issues designated by the tribunal and communicated to the parties' *See also* Articles 3(9) *et seq.* of the IBA Rules: 'The arbitral tribunal, at any time before the arbitration is concluded, may request a Party to produce to the arbitral tribunal and to the other Parties any documents that it believes to be relevant and material to the outcome of the case. A Party may object to such a request based on any of the reasons set forth in Article 9(2). If a Party raises such an objection, the Arbitral tribunal shall decide whether to order the production of such documents based upon the considerations set forth in Article 3(6) and, if the Arbitral tribunal considers it appropriate, through the use of the procedures set forth in Article 3(7).' and 3(10): 'Within the time ordered by the arbitral tribunal, the Parties may submit to the arbitral tribunal and to the other Parties any additional documents which they believe have become relevant and material as a consequence of the issues raised in documents, Witness Statements or Expert Reports submitted or produced by another Party or in other submissions of the Parties.' **Annex 16.**

366. *See, e.g.*, Article 9 of the IBA Rules: 'The Arbitral Tribunal shall determine the admissibility, relevance, materiality and weight of evidence.' **Annex 16.**

367. This is not a concept alien to Austrian law. For state court litigation in Austria, *see* Section 307(2) ZPO. For arbitration, *see* **Article 20**, at paras. 192 and 241 *et seq.* and Article 9 of the IBA Rules: '[T]he arbitral tribunal may infer that such document would be adverse to the interests of that Party.' **Annex 16.**

368. *See* **Article 20**, at paras. 086 *et seq.*

mandated by the *lex arbitri* at the seat of the arbitration. For example, Section 587(1) fZPO provided, *inter alia*, that the tribunal 'has to ascertain the facts underpinning the dispute (...) before issuing an award'. Section 587(1) fZPO was a mandatory provision of Austrian arbitration law,[369] and applied, *mutatis mutandis*, to both partial and final awards.[370] Conceptually, the tribunal was considered under an obligation to ascertain the factual basis of the dispute at a minimum to the extent that is necessary to make a decision (*Spruchreife* – 'maturity to render a decision').[371] Although this was understood to be an obligation imposed on the arbitrators, a decision rendered before the required 'maturity' of the case is established was not subject to challenge under Section 595 fZPO, unless the incomplete assessment of the facts resulted in a violation of the *ordre public* (Section 595 no. 6 fZPO) or of the parties' right to be heard.[372] Thus, if the arbitrators would arrive at a provisional determination of the facts that deviates from both parties' submissions, the arbitrators were required to put that determination to the parties before deciding the case. This ensured (and still ensures) that the parties have the opportunity to comment on the arbitrators' views of the facts.[373]

As a result, Section 587(1) fZPO introduced a strong inquisitorial element into **20-182** Austrian arbitral proceedings (*Untersuchungsgrundsatz*).[374] This deviated from the general principle of Austrian civil procedure providing for the parties' ability to define the scope of the argument (*Verhandlungsmaxime*).[375] The arbitral tribunal was obliged to ascertain the facts of the case on their own volition (*ex officio*),[376]

---

369. H.W. Fasching, *Schiedsgericht und Schiedsverfahren im österreichischen und im internationalen Recht* (Vienna, Manz, 1973), p. 103.
370. H.W. Fasching, *Schiedsgericht und Schiedsverfahren im österreichischen und im internationalen Recht* (Vienna, Manz, 1973), p. 104.
371. H.W. Fasching, *Schiedsgericht und Schiedsverfahren im österreichischen und im internationalen Recht* (Vienna, Manz, 1973), p. 103. 'Maturity exists when all evidences have been taken and further motions to take evidences have not been filed.' *See* C Fritz, 'Die Vorteilhaftigkeit von Schiedsgerichtsvereinbarungen im Gesellschaftsrecht' [1997] SWK, W 13.
372. H.W. Fasching, *Schiedsgericht und Schiedsverfahren im österreichischen und im internationalen Recht* (Vienna, Manz, 1973), p. 103.
373. This is not necessary, on the other hand, if the arbitrators adopt one party's version of the facts, as the other party will already have had the opportunity to present its case on that version of the facts.
374. C. Liebscher and A. Schmid in *Practitioner's Handbook on International Arbitration*, F.B. Weigand (ed.) (Munich, C.H. Beck, 2002), p. 560; G. Backhausen, *Schiedsgerichtsbarkeit unter besonderer Berücksichtigung des Schiedsvertragsrechts* (Vienna, Manz, 1990), pp. 151 et seq., H.W. Fasching, *Schiedsgericht und Schiedsverfahren im österreichischen und im internationalen Recht* (Vienna, Manz, 1973), p. 106. A different view is argued by F. Matscher, 'Probleme der Schiedsgerichtsbarkeit im österreichischen Recht' [1975] JBl, 412, 452, 462 et seq.
375. H.W. Fasching, *Schiedsgericht und Schiedsverfahren im österreichischen und im internationalen Recht* (Vienna, Manz, 1973), p. 106.
376. *See also* Article 27 DIS Rules.

without being bound by the parties' submissions or by the evidence offered.[377]

2.   The Arbitrator's Right to Establish the Facts Under the ZPO

20-183 According to some scholars, the regime under the fZPO had peculiar consequences. *Fasching* argued, for example, that an agreement that a party must make relevant submissions at the earliest possible opportunity with the automatic penalty of preclusion (*Vereinbarung der Eventualmaxime*) should not be permitted,[378] because it undermines the arbitrator's duty to establish all relevant facts. This was doubtful even at the time. Arbitrators were not prohibited under Austrian law to attach the effect of preclusion to their procedural orders. Specifically, the tribunal was always (and still is) allowed to order that certain evidence be offered, or submissions be made, by a certain date, or else not be admitted into the record,[379] as also reflected in the 'cut-off' date permitted in Article 20(1).[380] Any preclusion of evidence or submissions is, of course, limited by the parties' right to be heard and their right to fair and equal treatment.[381] In particular, the arbitrators must notify the parties in advance that evidence or submissions will be precluded if they fail to meet a certain deadline.

20-184 In any event, Section 587(1) fZPO is no longer relevant. The new Austrian arbitration law does not contain a provision requiring an inquisitorial approach.[382] However, Section 599(1) ZPO provides that

> [t]he arbitral tribunal is authorized to decide upon the permissibility of the taking of evidence, to conduct such taking of evidence, and to freely evaluate such evidence.

20-185 Section 599(2) ZPO proceeds to reinforce the parties' right to be heard, by requiring the arbitrators to notify both parties every time of any step involving the taking

---

377. Evidence contracts, which entitle a third party to decide procedural facts binding the arbitral tribunal, shall therefore be invalid; OGH, 30 October 1913, R. VI, 316/13, GlUNF 6631.

378. H.W. Fasching, *Schiedsgericht und Schiedsverfahren im österreichischen und im internationalen Recht* (Vienna, Manz, 1973), p. 104.

379. H.W. Fasching, *Schiedsgericht und Schiedsverfahren im österreichischen und im internationalen Recht* (Vienna, Manz, 1973), p. 104; W.H. Rechberger and W. Melis in *Kommentar zur ZPO*, W.H. Rechberger (ed.) (2nd edn, Vienna/New York, Springer, 2000), Section 587, para. 3.

380. *See* the discussion of cut-off dates in **Article 20**, at paras. 071 *et seq.*

381. H.W. Fasching, *Schiedsgericht und Schiedsverfahren im österreichischen und im internationalen Recht* (Vienna, Manz, 1973), p. 104.

382. The discretionary approach adopted in **Article 20(5)** reflects international standards. *See* **Article 20**, at para. 178. However, not all rules follow suit. Article 27 DIS Rules, *e.g.*, seems to impose an inquisitorial *obligation* on the arbitrators to ascertain the facts of the case.

of evidence. These are mandatory provisions,[383] and extreme errors in ascertaining the relevant facts can conceivably give rise to a challenge as a violation of the Austrian *procedural ordre public.*[384]

Although no longer giving the arbitrators an affirmative mandate to inquire into the **20-186** facts, Section 599(1) ZPO is designed to give the arbitrators a broad evidentiary authority. Thus, arbitrators are entitled to refuse evidence on the basis that it is irrelevant, or not material to the case, or that there are other reasons that make the evidence not admissible. Arbitrators are also entitled to decide that evidence is not permissible because its submission is delayed (for example, because the tribunal, while giving the parties sufficient advance notice, provided for a cut-off date),[385] and they can weigh the evidence freely as they deem appropriate. According to the legislative materials, this provision is particularly addressed at common law users of arbitration in Austria, who might expect from the adversarial process in their home jurisdictions that the tribunal has to take whatever evidence the parties offer;[386] Section 599(1) ZPO makes clear that arbitrators have the right to decide on the admissibility (in terms of relevance or otherwise) of the evidence before it is actually taken.

Arbitrators are also authorized to 'conduct (. . .) such taking of evidence'. The use **20-187** of the word 'such' seems to indicate that the arbitrators are free to conduct the taking only of the evidence that they have declared admissible (or to which they have not objected). In and of itself, the provision is unclear, therefore, as to whether the arbitrators are in principle entitled to ask *ex officio* for evidence irrespective of the evidence that the parties have offered, as they can under Article 20(5). Given the wide discretion of arbitrators to conduct the proceeding, such power should generally be assumed. Indeed, given the mandatory character of Section 599(1) ZPO and its systemic purpose to give the arbitrators control over the evidentiary process, it is unlikely that the parties could under Austrian law limit by joint agreement the arbitrators' discretion to take on their own volition the evidence they deem appropriate.[387]

In practice, an agreement to restrict the arbitrators' evidentiary authority will be **20-188** rare, and the arbitrators will typically be able to fully avail themselves of the power granted by Article 20(5). Section 599(1) ZPO is mandatory only in that it provides

---

383. C. Liebscher, *The Austrian Arbitration Act 2006: Text and Notes* (The Hague, Kluwer Law International, 2006), Annotated Text to Section 599(1) ZPO.
384. P. Oberhammer, *Entwurf eines neuen Schiesdvefahrensrechts* (Vienna, Manz, 2002), p. 93; *see also* F.T. Schwarz and H. Ortner, 'Procedural Ordre Public and the Internationalization of Public Policy in Arbitration' in *Austrian Arbitration Yearbook 2008*, C. Klausegger *et al.* (eds) (Vienna, Manz, 2008).
385. *See* **Article 20**, at paras. 071 *et seq.*
386. Explanatory Notes to Section 599 ZPO.
387. The counter-argument follows perhaps from Section 598 ZPO which allows the parties to exclude an oral hearing (without which some taking of evidence is not possible).

a minimum standard from which the parties cannot derogate. Thus, the arbitrators' authority to limit the taking of evidence cannot be restricted. At the same time, the parties are free to give the arbitrators greater evidentiary authority. Thus, even if such power were not considered as being conferred onto the arbitrators under Section 599(1) ZPO, the parties are certainly free to agree, as they do by reference to the Vienna Rules, to empower the arbitrators '[i]f [they] consider it necessary, (. . .) on [their] own initiative [to] collect evidence'. Thus, the arbitrators will be allowed to draw into the discussion of the case facts that have not been alleged by the parties, and to ask that evidence be presented that has not been offered by the parties, if the arbitrators deem such facts or evidence relevant to deciding the dispute. Similarly, the arbitrators do not have to take the parties' admissions or concessions for granted, unless there is a procedural agreement by the parties to that effect.[388]

20-189 As discussed, the power of arbitrators to obtain evidence at their volition reflects international practice. Article 4(11) of the IBA Rules provides, for example, that '[t]he Arbitral Tribunal may, at any time before the arbitration is concluded, order any Party to provide, or to use its best efforts to provide, the appearance for testimony at an Evidentiary Hearing of any person, including one whose testimony has not yet been offered'.[389] Thus, while in arbitration witnesses of fact are, in principle, the parties' responsibility, arbitrators can request under the IBA Rules that a witness who has not been called by the parties appear at the evidentiary hearing if the arbitrators consider it useful to put questions to such a witness.[390] The IBA Rules also permit the arbitrators to appoint, after consultation with the parties, an independent expert.[391] Similarly, Article 3(9) of the IBA Rules[392] allows the arbitrators, 'at any time before the arbitration is concluded, [to] request a Party to produce to the Arbitral Tribunal and to the other Parties any documents that it believes to be relevant and material to the outcome of the case'.[393]

20-190 It is again a different question whether arbitrators want to exercise the discretion afforded under Article 20(5) to its full extent. As discussed, arbitrators should be mindful of the tradition particularly in common law countries where proceedings are strictly adversarial in nature, and where parties expect the decision-maker to come to a decision based on the admissible evidence put before him by the parties, rather than to participate in the evidentiary process by identifying or obtaining

---

388. H.W. Fasching, *Schiedsgericht und Schiedsverfahren im österreichischen und im internationalen Recht* (Vienna, Manz, 1973), p. 106.
389. Article 4(11) IBA Rules, **Annex 16**.
390. IBA Working Party, 'Commentary on the new IBA Rules of Evidence' in *Beweiserhebung in internationalen Schiedsverfahren*, K.-H. Böckstiegel (ed.) (Cologne, Karl Heymanns Verlag, 2001), p. 160.
391. Article 6 IBA Rules, **Annex 16**.
392. IBA Rules, **Annex 16**.
393. However, objections to such a request are possible. *See* **Article 20**, at para. 244.

additional evidence. The problem is most acute where the arbitrators engage facts that the parties specifically want to keep outside the dispute, because of confidentiality concerns or strategic reasons. From that perspective, too, it has been accepted that the parties can restrain the inquisitorial role of the arbitrators by limiting, through agreement,[394] their jurisdiction to hear and ascertain facts only insofar as those facts have been alleged, submitted or otherwise made relevant by the parties. Arguably, the arbitrators themselves can limit the scope of their mandate in this respect by procedural order.[395] As also discussed elsewhere, however, the arbitrators retain discretion to ascertain facts insofar as they are required to enforce provisions of public order in order to arrive at an enforceable award.[396]

The arbitrators' freedom to ascertain the relevant facts also impacts the legal **20-191** evaluation of the relief requested by the parties. The Austrian *Oberster Gerichtshof* held that arbitrators could, under Section 587(1) fZPO, grant the relief requested by a party on any legal basis, even if not expressly pleaded, as long as it is founded on the established facts of the case.[397] This should hold true under the new arbitration law as well.[398] It must be noted again, however, that the arbitrators' freedom to do so has its limit in due process considerations. Specifically, if the arbitrators intend to apply a legal rule different than a rule specifically relied on by the parties, they should give the parties a timely opportunity to comment.

In Austria, as elsewhere, the arbitrators can order the parties to produce documents **20-192** or witnesses, but they are not permitted to force parties to do so or compel witnesses to appear.[399] If the arbitrators want to compel a party or witness to comply with the tribunal's evidentiary orders, the arbitrators need to apply to the Austrian (or any other) courts for judicial assistance.[400] Given the delays often associated with judicial assistance, in particular in a cross-border scenario, arbitrators will often be content, however, to draw adverse inferences from a party's refusal to produce a particular piece of evidence.[401]

---

394. Such an agreement can be part of the arbitration agreement, or can be concluded later. It has to comply with formal requirements the applicable law imposes on arbitration agreements in general. See H.W. Fasching, *Schiedsgericht und Schiedsverfahren im österreichischen und im internationalen Recht* (Vienna, Manz, 1973), p. 106.
395. H.W. Fasching, *Schiedsgericht und Schiedsverfahren im österreichischen und im internationalen Recht* (Vienna, Manz, 1973), p. 106.
396. *See* **Article 20**, at para. 099; **Article 7**, at paras. 052 *et seq.* and **Article 24**, at paras. 027 *et seq.*
397. OGH, 14 December 1927, 1 Ob 1187/27, SZ 9/303; *see also* W.H. Rechberger and W. Melis in *Kommentar zur ZPO*, W.H. Rechberger (ed.) (2nd edn, Vienna/New York, Springer, 2000), Section 587, para. 3.
398. *See* **Article 24**, at paras. 030 *et seq.*
399. C. Liebscher and A. Schmid in *Practitioner's Handbook on International Arbitration*, F.B. Weigand (ed.) (Munich, C.H. Beck, 2002), p. 564.
400. *See* **Article 20**, at paras. 250 *et seq.*
401. *See* Article 9 IBA Rules, **Annex 16**.

C.   WITNESS TESTIMONY

20-193 For the reasons outlined in the context of Article 20(3) above, parties in international commercial arbitration will often place heavy emphasis on documentary evidence in support of their case. Nonetheless, witness testimony remains an important form of evidence in international arbitration.

20-194 As with most arbitration laws, the ZPO does not contain provisions regulating specifically the witness testimony taken in international arbitration. Any person can in principle be called as a witness. Different to the practice in civil law litigation, including in the Austrian courts,[402] the parties themselves can give witness testimony, and usually no distinction is made between the testimony of a proper party and witnesses.[403] This is in line with international practice.[404] It is for the arbitrators to exercise their discretion as to whether the testimony of a witness is relevant, whether it should therefore be taken, and what weight should be given to it.[405] The arbitrators' discretion is limited only by the requirement to hear the parties and to treat them fairly and equally.[406]

20-195 The lack of regulation in arbitration law or institutional rules makes the taking of witness testimony, together with the issue of document disclosure, a contested question, where cultural and legal traditions can clash. First, there remain substantial jurisdictional differences as to the importance of witnesses in arbitration which are informed by the role conferred to witnesses in national litigation. In many continental jurisdictions, witnesses are perceived as being of 'secondary importance';[407] indeed, procedural regimes based on the Code Napoleon may, in civil matters, not permit at all the use of witnesses to contradict documentary evidence.[408] In common law jurisdictions, on the other hand, witness testimony stands at the core of the taking of evidence, and, by way of a careful and considered process of examination and cross-examination through the parties' respective counsel, is perceived as a reliable tool to adduce the 'truth' behind a case, also in commercial matters. Second, and to some extent reflecting these divergent views

---

402. *See* Section 373 ZPO.
403. C. Liebscher and A. Schmid in *Practitioner's Handbook on International Arbitration*, F.B. Weigand (ed.) (Munich, C.H. Beck, 2002), p. 562.
404. *See also* Article 4 IBA Rules, which provides: '2. Any person may present evidence as a witness, including a Party or a Party's officer, employee or other representative. 3. It shall not be improper for a Party, its officers, employees, legal advisors or other representatives to interview its witnesses or potential witnesses.' **Annex 16**.
405. C. Liebscher and A. Schmid in *Practitioner's Handbook on International Arbitration*, F.B. Weigand (ed.) (Munich, C.H. Beck, 2002), p. 562.
406. *See* **Article 20**, at paras. 015 *et seq.* and 029 *et seq.*
407. H. van Houtte, 'Counsel – Witness Relations and Professional Misconduct in Civil Law Systems' (2003) 19(4) Arb Int'l, 457, 458 with further references.
408. H. van Houtte, 'Counsel – Witness Relations and Professional Misconduct in Civil Law Systems' (2003) 19(4) Arb Int'l, 457, 458 with further references.

of the nature and value of witness testimony, there is debate as to whether and what extent witnesses may be approached, interviewed or 'prepared' by counsel prior to their giving written or oral testimony. While in most continental countries (e.g. Austria,[409] Germany, the Netherlands, Sweden) counsel is not expressly prohibited from approaching and interviewing prospective witnesses,[410] in some countries (e.g. Belgium, France, Italy and Switzerland) professional rules still prevent counsel from doing so.[411] In the UK and the U.S., in contrast, the thorough preparation of witnesses is considered an essential duty of counsel, and is perceived, again, to facilitate the fair and just resolution of the dispute. Indeed, US lawyers could incur a professional negligence claim if they allowed an unprepared witness to testify.

Third, there are significantly different traditions as to how a witness is questioned **20-196** at the oral hearing. In civil law jurisdictions, the questioning is done predominantly by the judge, and not by the lawyers; in some jurisdictions, counsel can put questions to the witness only by putting them before the judge who may decide to pass them on to the witness.[412] In common law jurisdictions, it is counsel's primary responsibility, as an expression of the adversarial process, to adduce witness testimony through the play and counter-play of direct testimony and cross-examination.[413]

In today's practice of international arbitration, the common law approach to **20-197** witness testimony appears to have prevailed, and it is used more and more even in domestic arbitrations on the European Continent. This is particularly reflected by a substantial reliance on witness testimony in many cases;[414] by the advent of the written witness statement (as borrowed from English practice); by an increasing acceptance of contacts between counsel and witness in international arbitration; and by the use of cross-examination techniques also by civil law practitioners.[415] Thus, it has been said that

> continental arbitrators, rooted in the inquisitorial tradition, have discovered the benefits of adversarial questioning. That allows many of them to

---

409. However, Austrian rules of professional ethics require the lawyer to avoid any 'appearance of influence' on the witness.
410. H. van Houtte, 'Counsel – Witness Relations and Professional Misconduct in Civil Law Systems' (2003) 19(4) Arb Int'l, 457, 458 with further references.
411. H. van Houtte, 'Counsel – Witness Relations and Professional Misconduct in Civil Law Systems' (2003) 19(4) Arb Int'l, 457, 458 with further references.
412. H. van Houtte, 'Counsel – Witness Relations and Professional Misconduct in Civil Law Systems' (2003) 19(4) Arb Int'l, 457, 458 with further references.
413. For a discussion of the terminology, *see* **Article 20**, at para. 208.
414. H. van Houtte, 'Counsel – Witness Relations and Professional Misconduct in Civil Law Systems' (2003) 19(4) Arb Int'l, 457, 459, 460.
415. H. van Houtte, 'Counsel – Witness Relations and Professional Misconduct in Civil Law Systems' (2003) 19(4) Arb Int'l, 457, 459, 460.

combine the best of the continental European tradition with Anglo-American approaches.[416]

20-198 The following discusses Austrian doctrine and case law, if any, as far as important aspects of witness testimony is concerned. In addition, however, the international practice regarding witness testimony is set out, as well as it can be determined, in an attempt to resolve some of the tensions identified above.

1.   Written Witness Testimony

20-199 Written witness statements come from Anglo-American litigation procedure; even there, they are a relatively new instrument.[417] In state court proceedings in civil law jurisdictions, written witness statements are practically unheard of. The witness is nominated in the written submissions of the party that intends to rely on that witness's testimony and, if it is admitted by the court as relevant evidence, the witness must usually appear at the hearing to give his evidence orally.

20-200 In international commercial arbitration, the written witness statement has established itself as an accepted form of witness testimony.[418] The advantages of having a witness put his or her testimony in writing in advance of an oral hearing are obvious. In international business between parties from different regions of the world, it can be extremely expensive and time consuming to arrange for all witnesses to appear before the tribunal and testify orally. Where the oral testimony can be reduced, in part or entirely, to cross-examination, because the witnesses' affirmative story has been put in writing in advance of the hearing, obvious benefits in terms of cost and efficiency follow. Although this is now accepted practice, in some cases it may still be appropriate to place more emphasis on oral testimony, whether in addition or in place of written statements.

20-201 From the perspective of Austrian law, it has already been discussed that the principles of immediacy (*Unmittelbarkeit*) and of oral presentation (*Mündlichkeit*), which mandate oral testimony in court proceedings, do not apply in arbitration.[419]

---

416. H. van Houtte, 'Counsel – Witness Relations and Professional Misconduct in Civil Law Systems' (2003) 19(4) Arb Int'l, 457, 460.

417. W. Miles and F.T. Schwarz, 'Taking of Evidence in International Commercial Arbitration' in *International Comparative Legal Guide to International Arbitration 2004* (London, Global Legal Group, 2003). Traditionally, witnesses would be expected to attend the hearing and, at the hearing, would present their evidence in full in the course of an oral examination-in-chief by counsel for the party seeking to rely on that evidence. Counsel for the opposing party would be entitled to cross-examine the witness and, following cross-examination, the original party's counsel would be entitled to re-examine. The judge would not be expected to have an active role in independently questioning the witness.

418. W. Miles and F.T. Schwarz, 'Taking of Evidence in International Commercial Arbitration' in *International Comparative Legal Guide to International Arbitration 2004* (London, Global Legal Group, 2003).

419. *See* **Article 20**, at paras. 129 *et seq.*

Written witness statements are therefore permissible under Austrian law.[420]

However, there are important caveats attached to the use of written witness state- **20-202** ments. Most importantly, a written statement should not stand as evidence without the opposing party having had the opportunity to test the accuracy of the witnesses' written account in cross-examination (*see* in detail immediately below). Written testimony is intended to introduce procedural efficiencies by eliminating, or at least reducing, the need for the witness to present his affirmative case orally. This also facilitates the parties' right to be heard – where witness statements are attached to the parties' written submissions, as is usually the case. parties are put on notice of the other side's evidence well in advance of the hearing, affording it more ample opportunity to prepare for the hearing. However, the written witness statement does not replace the other side's right to address, and challenge, the witness at the hearing. It is therefore a matter of fairness that, where written witness statements are used, the witness must appear at the oral hearing to face the other party's questions. If the witness is not produced at the hearing, the tribunal may disregard the written statement.[421]

These considerations are reflected, as a matter of international practice, in the IBA **20-203** Rules, which provide in Article 4:

> The Arbitral Tribunal may order each Party to submit within a specified time to the Arbitral Tribunal and to the other Parties a written statement by each witness on whose testimony it relies, except for those witnesses whose testimony is sought pursuant to Article 4(10) (the 'Witness Statement'). If Evidentiary Hearings are organized on separate issues (such as liability and damages), the Arbitral Tribunal or the Parties by agreement may schedule the submission of Witness Statements separately for each Evidentiary Hearing.[422]

Parties may be ordered to submit written statements within a particular period of **20-204** time. Such witness statements must include a number of details including a full description of the witness and his or her present and past relationship with any of the parties, a description of his or her background, qualifications, training and experience (if relevant and material to the dispute or the contents of the statement), a full and detailed description of the facts, the source of the witness's information as to those facts, an affirmation of truth and the signature of the

---

420. C. Liebscher and A. Schmid in *Practitioner's Handbook on International Arbitration*, F.B. Weigand (ed.) (Munich, C.H. Beck, 2002), p. 563.

421. *See* Article 4(8) IBA Rules: 'If a witness who has submitted a Witness Statement does not appear without a valid reason for testimony at an Evidentary Hearing, except by agreement of the Parties, the Arbitral Tribunla shall disregard that Witness Statement unless, in exceptional circumstances, the Arbitral Tribunal determines otherwise.' **Annex 16**.

422. IBA Rules, **Annex 16**.

witness as well as its date and place. In this regard, Article 5 of the IBA Rules recommends:

> Each Witness Statement shall contain:
>
> (a) the full name and address of the witness, his or her present and past relationship (if any) with any of the Parties, and a description of his or her background, qualifications, training and experience, if such a description may be relevant and material to the dispute or to the contents of the statement;
> (b) a full and detailed description of the facts, and the source of the witness's information as to those facts, sufficient to serve as that witness's evidence in the matter in dispute;
> (c) an affirmation of the truth of the statement; and
> (d) the signature of the witness and its date and place.[423]

20-205 Despite the IBA's efforts to set a harmonized standard, the fact remains that practitioners from civil law jurisdictions, at least those less experienced in international arbitration, will be less familiar, and perhaps less comfortable with written witness statements. As written witness statements are now widely used in international commercial arbitration, it is important to be aware of the issues faced by lawyers from different legal systems and to ensure that adequate safeguards are in place to avoid any procedural disadvantage to one party.[424]

20-206 At the same time, parties should bear in mind that the evidentiary value members of a tribunal will be prepared to give to written witness statements may well be determined by their cultural and legal background.[425] Excessive length of the witness statement should be avoided, as well as needless repetition. A witness statement should not simply repeat a party's pleadings, which sometimes occurs when counsel, rather than the witness, does the drafting. Counsel can legitimately assist the witness in the preparation of the statement to avoid lack of clarity, repetition and irrelevance;[426] but the substance of the statement must in any case come from the witness. A 'lawyer's statement' will have little or no credibility.[427]

---

423. IBA Rules, **Annex 16**.
424. W. Miles and F.T. Schwarz, 'Taking of Evidence in International Commercial Arbitration' in *International Comparative Legal Guide to International Arbitration 2004* (London, Global Legal Group, 2003).
425. W. Miles and F.T. Schwarz, 'Taking of Evidence in International Commercial Arbitration' in *International Comparative Legal Guide to International Arbitration 2004* (London, Global Legal Group, 2003).
426. *See* **Article 20**, at paras. 216 *et seq.*
427. M. Bühler and C. Dorgan, 'Witness Testimony Pursuant to the 1999 IBA Rules of Evidence in International Commercial Arbitration – Novel or Tested Standards?' (2001) 17(1) J Int'l Arb, 14.

2. Oral Witness Testimony

The oral examination of a witness is conducted very differently in the Anglo- **20-207** American tradition, on the one hand, and the legal tradition in European and other civil law countries, on the other hand. Before the Austrian courts, witness examination is, first and foremost, undertaken by the judge.

In the Anglo-American tradition, the parties' representatives assume a far more **20-208** active role. Oral witness testimony in common law jurisdictions comprises three basic phases (which in the U.S. are preceded by a pre-trial phase, which includes the so-called deposition of witnesses).[428] First, in the direct examination (or examination-in-chief), the witness is examined by the representative of the party which has nominated the witness. The direct examination is used, often skilfully, to have the witness tell a compelling story of the full factual affirmative case that the party which has named the witness wants to communicate to the tribunal. In cross-examination, however, the witnesses' story is put to the test by the opposing party's counsel. This can be, and often is, a process of considerable intensity where skilful counsel will expose any weakness and inconsistency in the witnesses' direct testimony. Cross-examination is also used to adduce the factual evidence to support the opposing party's case. Finally, the witness is released back into the hands of the party representative who has nominated the witness for re-direct examination, which, as the hope may be, serves to repair the damage

---

428. It is sometimes debated whether it is permissible in arbitration to depose witnesses in the U.S. meaning of the word. In a U.S. style deposition, a witness is questioned by opposing party's counsel, in the presence of the counsel of the party that nominated him (and perhaps also with his own counsel present). The judge is not present at the deposition; it is an exercise conducted between the lawyers who will typically arrange for a *verbatim* transcript of the deposition. The deposition, being part of pre-trial discovery, is intended to allow the parties to establish the relevant facts *before* actually trying the case. If the case proceeds to trial, the witness is later examined in front of the jury. However, if the witness contradicts his earlier statements, the witness can be confronted with the deposition record. *Liebscher/Schmid* argue that depositions are not permissible under Austrian law because at evidentiary hearings, at least one arbitrator has to be present. *See* C. Liebscher and A. Schmid in *Practitioner's Handbook on International Arbitration*, F.B. Weigand (ed.) (Munich, C.H. Beck, 2002), p. 562. That suggestion is debatable. As *Liebscher/Schmid* state elsewhere, the principle of immediacy (*Unmittelbarkeit*) does not apply in arbitration. *See* C. Liebscher and A. Schmid in F.B. Weigand, *Practitioner's Handbook on International Arbitration*, F.B. Weigand (eds) (Munich, C.H. Beck, 2002), p. 562; *see also* **Article 20**, at para. 201. In any event, if the parties agree on deposing a witness in advance of a hearing and then submit the written record of the deposition to the arbitrators, the arbitrators are free to assess such record at least as documentary evidence, and to attach such probative value to the deposition record as they deem appropriate (*freie Beweiswürdigung*). On the other hand, it must be noted that pre-trial discovery, including deposition of witnesses, is a lengthy and cost-intensive process. Unless both parties expressly agree on conducting depositions, the arbitrators are well advised to consider more efficient means of adducing witness testimony, in particular through the submission of written witness statement and cross-examination.

inflicted during cross-examination. The judge's role during this process will typically be minimal.

20-209 In civil law jurisdictions, the judge will usually assume a more inquisitorial role and thus, 'test' the credibility of witness testimony and elicit from the witness those facts that the judge himself requires in order to determine the case. Counsel for both parties have the right to pose additional questions to the witness, usually after the judge has finished the examination. It has also been suggested that witness testimony in civil law countries is considered less reliable than documentary evidence, particularly if the documents are contemporaneous. Therefore, although witness testimony is considered important, and at times critical, to the outcome of a case, strong documentary support often determines the success of a party in civil law litigation.

20-210 In international arbitration, the Anglo-American approach appears to dominate. Austrian law – which does not regulate the method of examining witnesses in arbitration – certainly does not prohibit such examination techniques.[429] Rather, the arbitrators can determine the method of examination at their discretion, including by not allowing questions from the party representatives that the arbitrators deem irrelevant.

20-211 As far as the relationship between written and oral witness testimony is concerned, it has been suggested that 'one could draw the conclusion that the parties have no right to subsequently orally examine [a] witness who gave a written statement'.[430] While sometimes witnesses may limit their testimony to a written statement,[431] this is misconceived as a general conclusion. The written statement is intended to replace the often lengthy direct examination. It is a recommendable practice in that it saves valuable time at the oral hearing. It also gives the opposing party advance notice of the witnesses' testimony, thus facilitating the parties' right to be heard. Thus, the role of examination-in-chief has become largely superseded by the written witness statement, although some direct examination is usually permitted. In any event, however, the opposing party will want, and should be given the opportunity, to subject the witness to intensive cross-examination, in order to provide an effective check and balance to the (written) testimony in chief.[432] The tribunal will usually permit the cross-examination and re-examination of witnesses in particular if the testimony in chief was substituted by a written witness statement.[433]

---

429. C. Liebscher and A. Schmid in *Practitioner's Handbook on International Arbitration*, F.B. Weigand (ed.) (Munich, C.H. Beck, 2002), p. 563.
430. C. Liebscher and A. Schmid in *Practitioner's Handbook on International Arbitration*, F.B. Weigand (ed.) (Munich, C.H. Beck, 2002), p. 563.
431. *See, e.g.*, Article 25(5) UNCITRAL Rules.
432. W. Miles and F.T. Schwarz, 'Taking of Evidence in International Commercial Arbitration' in *International Comparative Legal Guide to International Arbitration 2004* (London, Global Legal Group, 2003).
433. W. Miles and F.T. Schwarz, 'Taking of Evidence in International Commercial Arbitration' in *International Comparative Legal Guide to International Arbitration 2004* (London, Global Legal Group, 2003).

As discussed, the written witness statement is not substitute for, and instead necessitates, the other party's right to challenge the witness at the hearing. It is therefore a matter of fairness that, where written witness statements are used, the witness must appear at the oral hearing to face the other party's questions. If the witness is not produced at the hearing, the tribunal may disregard the written statement. Reflecting that practice, the IBA Rules provide in Article 4(7) that '[e]ach witness who has submitted a Witness Statement shall appear for testimony an Evidentiary Hearing, unless the parties agree otherwise'.[434] In their Commentary on the IBA Rules, the Working Party who had drafted the rules recognized that '[a]s a general principle, (...) witnesses who have submitted a written statement have to be available for oral questioning at a hearing, especially when their testimony has been contested'.[435] Indeed, Article 4(8) of the IBA Rules provides in the event that a witness – after having submitted a written statement – does not appear at a hearing without a valid reason, except by agreement of the parties, the arbitral tribunal is to disregard that witness's statement unless exceptional circumstances justify this failure to attend:[436]

> If a witness who has submitted a Witness Statement does not appear without a valid reason for testimony at an Evidentiary Hearing, except by agreement of the Parties, the Arbitral Tribunal shall disregard that Witness Statement unless, in exceptional circumstances, the Arbitral Tribunal determines otherwise.[437]

The practice of cross-examination remains a foreign concept to many civil law **20-212** practitioners who expect the judge to assume the active role of inquisitor,[438] and civil law practitioners not trained in the skills of cross-examination may find themselves at a disadvantaged position *vis-à-vis* their common law counterparts. Also, in the common law tradition, there are elaborate rules on what form questions have to be put in (e.g. leading questions are not allowed in direct examination, but permitted in cross examination).

---

434. IBA Rules, **Annex 16**.
435. IBA Working Party, 'Commentary on the new IBA Rules of Evidence' in *Beweiserhebung in internationalen Schiedsverfahren*, K.-H. Böckstiegel (ed.) (Cologne, Carl Heymanns Verlag, 2001), p. 160.
436. IBA Working Party, 'Commentary on the new IBA Rules of Evidence' in *Beweiserhebung in internationalen Schiedsverfahren*, K.-H. Böckstiegel (ed.) (Cologne, Carl Heymanns Verlag, 2001), p. 161.
437. Article 4(8) IBA Rules, **Annex 16**.
438. W. Miles and F.T. Schwarz, 'Taking of Evidence in International Commercial Arbitration' in *International Comparative Legal Guide to International Arbitration 2004* (London, Global Legal Group, 2003); C. Liebscher and A. Schmid in *Practitioner's Handbook on International Arbitration*, F.B. Weigand (ed.) (Munich, C.H. Beck, 2002), p. 563.

20-213 This has caused some commentators to question whether employing certain examination techniques could violate procedural fairness, especially when one party and its counsel comes from a jurisdiction where such techniques are not used. This argument is, as a legal matter, not persuasive. When parties agree to arbitration, they accept a dispute resolution mechanism that is flexible and allows for different procedural instruments to be employed. Indeed, it would be unfair to prevent common law counsel from conducting cross-examination only because the other side has chosen counsel who is not familiar with the technique. In practice, however, an experienced tribunal will be very mindful of difference experiences and backgrounds of the parties' counsel. In seeking to level the playing field between the parties' representatives, arbitrators will at the very least discuss the procedure to be applied with the parties at the outset of the case, ideally well before the evidentiary hearing.[439]

20-214 Of course, arbitrators or parties are not limited to adopting examination techniques from existing national regimes. As international arbitration develops, new techniques and mechanisms have been developed specifically for the arbitral process. In recent years, for example, the concept of 'witness conferencing' or 'hot tubbing' has gained some acceptance.[440] Under that concept, a number of witnesses from both parties are questioned at the same time on a particular subject. As witnesses can immediately react to each other's testimony, and challenge each other's account, witness conferencing, if properly managed by the arbitrators, can be very effective, especially with expert witnesses.

20-215 By virtue of Section 588 fZPO, the arbitrators were prevented from taking an oath from a witness. If the arbitrators wanted to hear the sworn testimony of a witness, they were required to apply for the assistance of the Austrian courts.[441] This is still so.

3.   Witness Preparation

20-216 It is practice in international commercial arbitration that witnesses are interviewed by counsel prior to giving written or oral examination – an approach adopted from

---

439. W. Miles and F.T. Schwarz, 'Taking of Evidence in International Commercial Arbitration' in *International Comparative Legal Guide to International Arbitration 2004* (London, Global Legal Group, 2003); For a discussion of case management, *see* **Article 20**, at paras. 101 *et seq.*

440. W. Peter, 'Witness Conferencing' (2002) 18(1) Arb Int'l, 47. In this method, all witnesses of fact and, where applicable, experts are heard at the same time. Thus, witnesses are immediately confronted with each other which is supposed to facilitate fast fact finding. Witness conferencing certainly requires strict management by the tribunal, and discipline by counsel, but is said to be particularly effective in technical, fact intensive disputes.

441. C. Liebscher and A. Schmid in *Practitioner's Handbook on International Arbitration*, F.B. Weigand (ed.) (Munich, C.H. Beck, 2002), pp. 563, 564. Today, this is regulated under Section 602 ZPO. *See* J. Power, *The Austrian Arbitration Act – A Practitioner's Guide to Sections 577-618 of the Austrian Code of Civil Procedure* (Vienna, Manz, 2006), Section 602, para. 2.

the Anglo-American tradition. Indeed, it is standard practice in most common law jurisdictions for counsel to carefully interview witnesses prior to their giving testimony, and it may be negligent for counsel not to do so.[442]

This process does not involve 'coaching' a witness, but for counsel to understand **20-217** the precise nature of the evidence that a witness is to give at the hearing and to prepare accordingly.[443] Where the witness cannot remember at all, or cannot recall events accurately, contemporaneous documents may be used to refresh the witnesses' recollection. Of course, ethical rules in common law jurisdictions prevent counsel from influencing a witness into making a statement that does not conform with the witnesses' true memory.[444]

With the advent of the written witness statement in English courts and subsequently **20-218** in international arbitration,[445] it is also common for counsel to assist a witness to draft his or her written witness statement. In England, the Solicitors' Code of Conduct 2007 permits a solicitor to interview and take statements from any witness or prospective witness at any stage in the proceedings. It is also accepted practice that counsel explains to the witness what sort of questions to expect. This process is sometimes referred to as 'witness preparation' or 'familiarization'.

In all jurisdictions that provide for prior contacts between counsel and witnesses, **20-219** however, it is also made clear that counsel must not manipulate the witness's testimony in any way. The Solicitors' Code of Conduct 2007 also states, for example, that a solicitor must not deceive the court by 'tampering with evidence or seeking to persuade witness to change their evidence'.[446]

With that important caveat, contacts between counsel and witnesses are accepted **20-220** in international arbitration,[447] including increasingly by civil law practitioners, who, for real or perceived reasons, have viewed such contacts more sceptically than their common law counterparts. The international practice is now reflected in the IBA Rules, which expressly allow for contacts between a counsel and a witness. Article 4(3) of the IBA Rules[448] provides: 'It shall not be improper for a Party, its

---

442. W. Miles and F.T. Schwarz, 'Taking of Evidence in International Commercial Arbitration' in *International Comparative Legal Guide to International Arbitration 2004* (London, Global Legal Group, 2003).

443. W. Miles and F.T. Schwarz, 'Taking of Evidence in International Commercial Arbitration' in *International Comparative Legal Guide to International Arbitration 2004* (London, Global Legal Group, 2003).

444. *See, e.g.*, Solicitors Regulation Authority, Solicitors' Code of Conduct, Rule, 11.01, 12(e) which determines that a solicitor must not deceive the court by 'attempting to influence a witness, when taking a statement from the witness, with regard to the content of their statement'.

445. *See* **Article 20**, at paras. 199 *et seq.*

446. *See* Solicitors Regulation Authority, Solicitors' Code of Conduct, Rule 11.01, 12(f).

447. W.L. Craig, W.W. Park and J. Paulsson, *International Commerce Arbitration* (3rd edn, New York, Oceana Publications, 2000), p. 441.

448. IBA Rules, **Annex 16**.

officers, employees, legal advisors or other representatives to interview its witnesses or potential witnesses.' Contacting the other side's witnesses is not addressed in the IBA Rules, and raises even greater problems.[449]

20-221   In any event, it must be pointed out that neither international practice nor the IBA Rules can supersede professional or ethical rules applicable to counsel. In the European Union, the CCBE Code of Conduct states in Article 4(1) that '[a] lawyer who appears or takes part in a case before a court or tribunal in a Member State must comply with the rules of conduct applied before that court or tribunal'. Although some have argued that professional prohibitions on contacting, interviewing or preparing prospective or actual witnesses which are applicable in litigation before national courts are not necessarily applicable in international arbitration,[450] Article 5(4) of the CCBE Code of Conduct provides that '[t]he rules governing a lawyer's relationship with the courts apply also to his relations with arbitrators'.[451] Arguable, therefore, Austrian professional standards (should) apply to European lawyers taking part in an arbitration sited in Austria, in addition to the professional rules of their home bar.[452]

20-222   The professional rules for Austrian lawyers require in Article 8 *Standesrichtlinien*, that an Austrian lawyer 'must refrain from any behavior *which creates the appearance of influencing* the witness'.[453] It must be doubted, however, that a practice endorsed by the IBA – *see* Article 4(3) IBA Rules[454] – can as such (that is, absent further aggravating circumstances) create an improper appearance. It is therefore accepted in Austria that a party (or its counsel) may in principle approach, meet with and interview a prospective or current witness; only an attempt to induce the witness to give false (or, as the case may be, deliberately misleading) evidence may result in criminal liability for fraud.[455]

20-223   Finally, while it indeed appears to be an accepted practice in international arbitration that counsel will interview and prepare a witness prior to his testimony, this increasingly raises issues of equality between the parties. An arbitration

---

449. H. van Houtte, 'Counsel – Witness Relations and Professional Misconduct in Civil Law System' (2003) 19(4) Arb Int'l, 457, 461-462.
450. H. van Houtte, 'Counsel – Witness Relations and Professional Misconduct in Civil Law Systems' (2003) 19(4) Arb Int'l, 457, 461 with further references.
451. The CCBE is the Consultative Committee of the European Bars. *See* H. van Houtte, 'Counsel – Witness Relations and Professional Misconduct in Civil Law Systems' (2003) 19(4) Arb Int'l 457, 462-463.
452. H. van Houtte, 'Counsel – Witness Relations and Professional Misconduct in Civil Law Systems' (2003) 19(4) Arb Int'l 457, 461 with further references.
453. Code of Practice (*Standesrichtlinien*); *see* C. Liebscher and A. Schmid in *Practitioner's Handbook on International Arbitration*, F.B. Weigand (ed.) (Munich, C.H. Beck, 2002), p. 563.
454. IBA Rules, **Annex 16**.
455. C. Liebscher and A. Schmid in *Practitioner's Handbook on International Arbitration*, F.B. Weigand (ed.) (Munich, C.H. Beck, 2002), p. 562.

practitioner from civil law jurisdictions, who feels reluctant to prepare the witness because he feels required under ethical and professional rules applicable to litigation not to meet with the witness to prepare the testimony, might be at a competitive disadvantage *vis-à-vis* his common law counterpart. Such competitive inequality could be aggravated if the civil law practitioner were inexperienced in the usages of international expectations, resulting in a distorted expectation as to what the process entails. The principle of equal treatment, however, requires that both parties apply the same standard; a competitive disadvantage stemming from (real or perceived) differences in applicable professional rules is unfair.[456] Thus, the issue of contacts between counsel and witnesses ought to be addressed and resolved at the earliest opportunity to ensure a level playing field.[457]

D.   DOCUMENTARY EVIDENCE

In many arbitrations, the production of documentary evidence plays a central role. **20-224** First, arbitral proceedings are, by their nature, less formal than court proceedings; witnesses, in particular, may not be under oath as they are when giving oral evidence in a common law court. As a result of this, coupled with the different philosophies regarding the role of witness evidence, tribunals often place greater reliance on documentary than testimonial evidence, in particular where contemporaneous documents are offered. Secondly, recent international practice in commercial arbitration typically involves the presentation of a party's case in full and in writing from the outset. The emphasis on written submissions puts documentary evidence at the forefront of a party's case.[458] Thirdly, documents will often be a less time consuming and less expensive form of adducing evidence than witnesses testimony.

The importance of the role of documents in international commercial arbitration is **20-225** therefore universally acknowledged. Given recent advances in technology, it is also uncontroversial that 'documents' include any written or printed material capable of being made evidence; the definition of a document must extend well beyond conventional 'paper documents' and will cover a wide range of media including email, computer records, tape recordings, television, film and photographs.[459]

However, the taking of documentary evidence is often subject of great controversy **20-226** between the parties. Specifically, the extent of 'document discovery' and hence, a

---

456. H. van Houtte, 'Counsel – Witness Relations and Professional Misconduct in Civil Law Systems' (2003) 19(4) Arb Int'l, 457, 461.
457. *De lege ferenda*, this issue appears ripe for harmonization at least on the European Union level.
458. W. Miles and F.T. Schwarz, 'Taking of Evidence in International Commercial Arbitration' in *International Comparative Legal Guide to International Arbitration 2004* (London, Global Legal Group, 2003).
459. W. Miles and F.T. Schwarz, 'Taking of Evidence in International Commercial Arbitration' in *International Comparative Legal Guide to International Arbitration 2004* (London, Global Legal Group, 2003).

party's obligation to produce documents to the other side or the tribunal that are harmful to its own case, are heavily disputed, both in practice and in academic writing.[460] The discussion below examines the different approaches taken by common law and civil law practitioners and their application under Austrian law, and attempts to provide guidance on how these approaches could be reconciled.

1.   Document Disclosure in Common Law and Civil Law Litigation

20-227 The core principle of the *adverserial* system in the Anglo-American tradition is the equality of the parties. No party shall win a legal dispute because it is better informed about the facts; conversely, no party must gain what is perceived to be an unfair advantage by concealing evidence that is harmful to its case. Thus, before the trial, the parties conduct extensive fact finding, in which process they are obliged to cooperate with each other. Document disclosure under common law systems therefore typically means the disclosure of all relevant documents. That is, a party is not permitted simply to produce the documents that support its case – rather, it must produce every single relevant and admissible document in its possession, including documents that may harm its case. Failure to comply with a disclosure order in litigation proceedings may lead to severe sanctions.

20-228 In the U.S., this process is termed *pre-trial discovery*, a term that has achieved notorious fame on the European continent. As the word suggests, 'discovery' allows for interrogative investigation by one party into the existence of documents in another party's possession, custody or control, so to enable the investigating party to uncover materials in the possession of the opposing party as evidence in its own case. U.S. litigants are therefore entitled to seek 'discovery' not only of documents directly relevant to the dispute but of any document that is 'calculated to lead to the discovery of admissible evidence'. The scope of discoverable documents is thus very broad and the obligations on a party subject to a discovery application are strict. In England, a more restricted regime applies as a result of the reforms of Lord Woolf in 1999. Tellingly, the Woolf Reform does not use the U.S. term '*discovery*', but refers to the narrower phrase of 'disclosure and inspection of documents'. Depending on the complexity and the amount of the dispute, different litigation tracks provide for different levels of disclosure which reduces the scope of document production in certain categories of civil proceedings. The reform was certainly intended to lessen the burden of disclosure for parties in English litigation proceedings. However, it did not alter the underlying principle

---

460. For a recent – and fairly sceptical – civil law analysis of Anglo-American methods of adducing evidence in international arbitration, *see* F. Schäffler, *Zulässigkeit und Zweckmässigkeit der Anwendung angloamerikanischer Beweismethoden in deutschen und internationalen Schiedsverfahren* (Munich, Sellier European Law Publisher, 2003).

that a party must disclose relevant documents irrespective of whether they are helpful or harmful to its case.[461]

By contrast, continental European systems have traditionally held a deep **20-229** discontent against the production of documents in civil and commercial cases. In civil law jurisdictions, parties are required to present to the court at the commencement of the proceedings (or promptly thereafter) all the facts necessary to support, as a matter of law, the relief they are requesting. It is the party's own obligation to produce all relevant evidence to corroborate the allegations it is putting forward. It is not necessary for a party to disclose to the opposing party documents that are harmful to its own case or to respond to broad or searching requests for documents.[462]

This approach to document production is rooted in core principles of civil law **20-230** litigation. In Germany and Austria, the courts have no power to inquire *ex officio* into the facts underlying the parties' dispute. Rather, the courts are bound to accept the limits set by the parties' submissions (*Verhandlungsmaxime*). Thus, the factual scope of the dispute is defined by the parties' submissions; the court is confined to the 'relative reality' created by the parties' submissions, which may be different from the objective truth. (As a result, it is actually misleading to say that continental European civil procedure is inquisitorial, rather than adversarial – labels that, in any event, mean different things to different people).[463] The principle of *Verhandlungsmaxime* clearly limits any inquisitorial elements civil procedure is often said to have in Germany or Austria.

In any event, the *Verhandlungsmaxime* has fundamental import on the way **20-231** evidence is taken and presented in civil litigation in Germany and Austria. It leaves the presentation of evidence to the party who carries the burden of proof regarding a particular issue in the dispute, and causes reluctance on the part of the courts to interfere with the party's presentation of that evidence. The *Verhandlungsmaxime* also strictly precludes fishing expeditions as they are known in U.S. discovery, as it would necessarily go beyond the scope of the parties' submissions. As the German *Bundesgerichtshof* has held, 'the taking of evidence by the court needs to be based in the parties' disputed factual submission and must not attempt to establish other facts that go beyond the parties' submissions'.[464] In the context of document production, this principle has been interpreted as preventing the courts from

---

461. W. Miles and F.T. Schwarz, 'Taking of Evidence in International Commercial Arbitration' in *International Comparative Legal Guide to International Arbitration 2004* (London, Global Legal Group, 2003).

462. J. Zekoll and J. Bolt, 'Die Pflicht zur Vorlage von Urkunden im Zivilprozess – Amerikanische Verhältnisse in Deutschland' [2002] NJW, 3129, 3129; BGH, 11 June 1990, II ZR 159/89, NJW 1990, 3151.

463. F. Schäffler, *Zulässigkeit und Zweckmässigkeit der Anwendung angloamerikanischer Beweismethoden in deutschen und internationalen Schiedsverfahren* (Munich, Sellier European Law Publisher, 2003), p. 7.

464. BGH, 11 July 2000, X ZR 126/98, NJW 2000, 3488, 3490.

ordering the disclosure of documents on the basis of a party's unsubstantiated submission, lacking concrete reference to specific documents, in order to establish facts potentially relevant to the proceedings (*Ausforschungsverbot*).[465]

20-232   On the other hand, many civil law jurisdictions do allow for limited disclosure requests. Under Section 303 ZPO, for example, a party asserting that a relevant document is in the hands of the opposing party can request the court to order the opposing party to produce the document. The requesting party has to describe the content of the document as accurately as possible and has to describe the facts which are to be evidenced through the document. The opposing party is then obligated to produce the document if the opposing party itself referred to the document in its submissions;[466] if the opposing party is obliged to produce the document as a matter of applicable statutory rules of civil law;[467] or if the document is a 'joint' document of the parties.[468] A document is deemed to be a 'joint' document in respect to those persons in whose interest the document was drafted or whose respective legal relationship is evidenced in the document. 'Joint' documents include correspondence in the course of the parties' negotiations.[469] Under certain circumstances, however, a party is entitled to refuse the production of a document.[470] Also, under certain circumstances the court has the power to question, under oath, the party obliged to produce a document as to whether this party has the document, or knows where it is, or has destroyed it.[471]

20-233   However, and importantly, the court cannot compel a party to produce a document. Rather, it may, after having considered the totality of the evidence before it, draw adverse inferences from the party's refusal to disclose a document upon the court's request.[472]

20-234   With respect to the disclosure of documents by third parties, the court can order a third party to produce a document under the third party's control, if the third party is obligated to produce the document under statutory rules of civil law or if the document is a 'joint' document between the third party and the party requesting the document.[473] If these conditions are disputed, the party requesting the document has to file a separate claim against the third party, requesting an order that the document be released to it.[474]

---

465.   J. Zekoll and J. Bolt, 'Die Pflicht zur Vorlage von Urkunden im Zivilprozess – Amerikanische Verhältnisse in Deutschland?' [2002] NJW 3129, 3130.
466.   Section 304(1) no. 1 ZPO.
467.   Section 304(1) no. 2 ZPO.
468.   Section 304(1) no. 3 ZPO.
469.   Section 304(2) ZPO.
470.   Section 305 ZPO. This includes, most importantly, refusal on the basis of attorney-client privilege.
471.   Section 307(1) ZPO.
472.   Section 307(2) ZPO.
473.   Section 308(1) ZPO.
474.   Section 309(1) ZPO.

If anything, there is a trend in civil law jurisdictions to allow for broader document **20-235** production than traditionally had been the case. In a recent reform, for example, the German disclosure rules were substantially revised,[475] strengthening the parties' right to request documents that are in the opposition's possession under Sections 420 *et seq.* German ZPO.[476] Specifically, a party discharges its burden of proof not only by producing a document, but also by requesting[477] the court to order the opposing party to supply the document.[478] Similarly to the position in Austria, the opposing party is obliged to provide the document to the court if it is either committed to do so under statutory rules of civil (or commercial) law[479] or if the opposing party itself has referred to this document in the course of its submissions.[480] While the courts will still prevent unspecified fishing expeditions,[481] the court will order the production of the document by the opposing party.[482] In this case, the ordered party is also obligated to perform a thorough and diligent search for the document.[483] If the opposing party refuses to produce the document, the court can, after consideration of the evidence before it, assume that the assertions made by the requesting party as to the nature and content of the document are true.[484]

The court's power to order document disclosure has been further increased through **20-236** the new provision of Section 142 German ZPO. Here, the court *may* order that a party produce a document under its control, to which a party has referred. In other words, both parties, irrespective of whether they are carrying the burden of proof on the issue that is to be evidenced by the document, can be required to disclose it. The decision is in the discretion of the court.[485] Again, the court cannot force a party to disclose a document under Section 142 German ZPO. Rather, if a party resists the production of a document on which it needs to rely on to support its claim, it will fail to meet the burden of proof it carries in that respect, and its claim

---

475. Revision of the German ZPO, 27 July 2001, BGBl I, No. 40, 1887.
476. Section 420 German ZPO.
477. The request for a disclosure order to the opposing party has to be highly specific. It has to contain (i) detailed information regarding the name of the document, (ii) the facts to be evidenced by the documents, (iii) a description of the content of the document, as complete as possible, (iv) a description of the circumstances that support the assumption that the document is under the control of the opposing party and (v) the description for the bases, on which the opposing party is obligated to provide the document at issue (*see* Section 424 German ZPO).
478. Section 421 ZPO.
479. Section 422 ZPO. By way of example, a shareholders has a statutory right to access the books of the company.
480. Section 423 ZPO.
481. A. Baumbach, W. Lauterbach, J. Albers and P. Hartmann (eds), *Zivilprozessordnung*, (66th edn, Munich, C.H. Beck, 2008), Section 424, para. 1.
482. Section 425 ZPO.
483. Section 426 ZPO.
484. Section 427 ZPO.
485. It '*may*' be so ordered. *See* A. Baumbach, W. Lauterbach, J. Albers and P. Hartmann, *Zivilprozessordnung* (66th edn, Munich, C.H. Beck, 2008), Section 142, para. 5.

(or defence) will likely be dismissed. If the party that does not carry the burden of proof on the issue evidenced by a document resists its production, the court may in its discretion[486] assume that the claims the other party made with respect to the document are true.[487] German courts now also hold the power to request third parties to produce documents that are relevant to the proceedings at issue, also under Section 142 German ZPO.

20-237 At the very least, an analysis of Austrian and German disclosure provisions demonstrates that the civil law approach carries its own checks and balances.[488] First, the judge in civil law jurisdictions will place substantial emphasis on the rules relating to burden of proof. Second, while the court does not usually have the authority to impose sanctions on a party that refuses to comply with a production order, the court may draw appropriate (adverse) inferences from a party's refusal to produce the required evidence.

2.   Document Disclosure in International Arbitration

20-238 Anglo-American style disclosure, on the other hand, although in complex cases almost inevitably increasing cost and nuisance, should not too readily be disregarded by continental European lawyers. There is merit to the concept that, for a fair result to be achieved, both parties should have equal access to the evidence relevant to the case, and should therefore be required to make documents more broadly available to each other. Conversely, defining the scope of a dispute solely by the parties' submissions (as required by the *Verhandlungsmaxime*[489]), and, thus, creating only 'relative truth' runs the risk of producing unfair results that do not serve justice. Indeed, German courts have occasionally supported the production of documents and requested greater cooperation of the party not carrying the burden of proof in the interest of procedural fairness.[490]

20-239 There is growing recognition that neither approach, applied in an isolated fashion, will do justice to the nature of international arbitration. For example, U.S. courts have recently held that unmodified discovery is not appropriate in international arbitration proceedings:

> Parties to a private arbitration agreement forgo certain procedural rights attendant to formal litigation in return for a more efficient and cost-effective resolution of

---

486. Under German law, the court is in principle, unless expressly provided otherwise by relevant statute, not bound by rules of evidence. It decides on the admissibility and the probative value of evidence on the basis of a free and discretionary consideration of the evidence (*Freie Beweiswürdigung*, Section 286 ZPO).

487. Section 427 German ZPO.

488. W. Miles and F.T. Schwarz, 'Taking of Evidence in International Commercial Arbitration' in *International Comparative Legal Guide to International Arbitration 2004* (London, Global Legal Group, 2003).

489. *See* **Article 20**, at paras. 182 and 230 *et seq.*

490. P. Schlosser, 'Die lange deutsche Reise in die prozessuale Moderne' [1991] JZ, 599; BGH, 11 June 1990, II ZR 159/89, NJW 1990, 3151.

their disputes (. . .) A hallmark of arbitration – and a necessary precursor to is efficient operation – is a limited discovery process.[491]

The same considerations hold true from the other hand of the spectrum. By agree- **20-240** ing to arbitration, parties opt out of the strict rules of national civil procedure into a more flexible dispute resolution mechanism that can include an appropriate measure of document production. Of course, parties are free to exclude the production of documents altogether should they so wish.

Recent practice in international commercial arbitration goes some way toward rec- **20-241** onciling the differences between common and civil law procedure. Typically, both parties will set out their case in full and, attached to their written submissions, will produce all the documentary evidence in support of their case. Subsequently, the parties often agree on, or the tribunal will determine that there be, the opportunity for the parties to request documents from each other, including documents that are harmful to one's own case. If a party refuses to produce a document, the tribunal will, upon application, order the production of a document under certain circumstances. Specifically, as a concession to civil law systems, disclosure will be ordered only if the document request was sufficiently specific, and the requested documents are, in the view of the tribunal, relevant and material to the outcome of the case. If a party refuses to produce a document (and no other avenues are available under the applicable arbitration law), the tribunal will usually be permitted to draw appropriate adverse inferences with respect to the documents in question.

This practice is, in general terms, reflected in the IBA Rules. Article 3 IBA **20-242** Rules[492] provides:

1. Within the time ordered by the Arbitral Tribunal, each Party shall submit to the Arbitral Tribunal and to the other Parties all documents available to it on which it relies, including public documents and those in the public domain, except for any documents that have already been submitted by another Party.
2. Within the time ordered by the Arbitral Tribunal, any Party may submit to the Arbitral Tribunal a Request to Produce.

A request for production of documents under the IBA Rules must contain a descrip- **20-243** tion of a particular document or a category of documents, with sufficient particularity to enable it to be identified, as well as a description of how the document is relevant and a statement that the document is not in the possession of the party making the request and why it believes it is in the possession of the party to whom the request is made. Crucially, requests to produce must relate to narrow and specific documents (or categories of documents) and explain why these documents are relevant and material for the outcome of the case:[493]

---

491. *Comsat Corporation v. National Science Foundation*, 190 F.3d 269 (4th. Cir. 1999).
492. IBA Rules, **Annex 16**.
493. Article 3(3) IBA Rules, **Annex 16**.

A Request to Produce shall contain:

(a) (i) a description of a requested document sufficient to identify it, or (ii) a description in sufficient detail (including subject matter) of a narrow and specific requested category of documents that are reasonably believed to exist;

(b) a description of how the documents requested are relevant and material to the outcome of the case; and

(c) a statement that the documents requested are not in the possession, custody or control of the requesting Party, and of the reason why that Party assumes the documents requested to be in the possession, custody or control of the other Party.

20-244 The decision of the tribunal whether or not to order disclosure will be based on the relevance and materiality of the documents. Article 3(6) of the IBA Rules[494] provides, accordingly, that '[t]he Arbitral Tribunal (. . .) may order the Party to whom such Request is addressed to produce to the Arbitral Tribunal and to the other Parties those requested documents in its possession, custody or control as to which the Arbitral Tribunal determines that (i) the issues that the requesting Party wishes to prove are relevant and material to the outcome of the case, and (ii) none of the reasons for objection set forth in Article 9(2)[495] apply.' As this provision makes clear, the IBA Rules also recognize certain grounds for objecting against a request for document production. These are:

(a) lack of sufficient relevance or materiality;

(b) legal impediment or privilege under the legal or ethical rules determined by the Arbitral Tribunal to be applicable;

(c) unreasonable burden to produce the requested evidence;

(d) loss or destruction of the document that has been reasonably shown to have occurred;

(e) grounds of commercial or technical confidentiality that the Arbitral Tribunal determines to be compelling;

(f) grounds of special political or institutional sensitivity (including evidence that has been classified as secret by a government or a public international institution) that the Arbitral Tribunal determines to be compelling; or

(g) considerations of fairness or equality of the Parties that the Arbitral Tribunal determines to be compelling.

20-245 It may be, of course, that certain objections (for example, that the document contains business confidences or privileged information) can only be assessed by reviewing it – when of course, the review by the tribunal is exactly what the objecting party seeks to prevent. For such cases, Article 3(7) of the IBA Rules permit the tribunal 'after consultation with the Parties, [to] appoint an independent

---

494. IBA Rules, **Annex 16**.
495. IBA Rules, **Annex 16**.

and impartial expert, bound to confidentiality, to review any such document and to report on the objection. To the extent that the objection is upheld by the Arbitral Tribunal, the expert shall not disclose to the Arbitral Tribunal and to the other Parties the contents of the document reviewed.'[496]

Any document ordered to be produced will be confidential to the tribunal and the **20-246** parties. In the event that a party fails to produce a document when ordered to do so under the IBA Rules, the tribunal is entitled to draw negative inferences in respect of that document. Distinctly 'inquisitorial' civil law elements have found their way into the IBA Rules as well, permitting the tribunal, for example, to order *ex officio* the production of a document from the parties, if the tribunal deems that document to be material for the outcome of the case.[497]

With the focus appropriately on materiality and relevance, the German discussion **20-247** regarding the relationship between the constitutional[498] *Ausforschungsverbot*[499] and document disclosure, particularly in cases in which the parties did not expressly agree on using such methods of taking evidence, but were so ordered by the arbitral tribunal,[500] becomes less problematic.[501] The German *Bundesgerichtshof*

---

496. IBA Rules, **Annex 16**.
497. *See* **Article 20**, at paras. 183 *et seq.*
498. Article 2(1) German GG.
499. Other fundamental procedural principles – like the right to be heard, impartiality of the arbitral procedure or a fair trial – are in principle not endangered merely because Anglo-American methods of taking evidence are applied. Just compare Section 68(2) of the English Arbitration Act. Another issue raised in the literature is whether the application of Anglo-American methods of taking evidence (like depositions and interrogatories, discovery, the hearing of witnesses by way of examination in chief, cross-examination and re-examination etc.) in proceedings in which only one party is familiar with and trained in these kinds of techniques would not yield an unfair advantage for this party and, thus, violate the right to be treated fairly and equally. German commentary, again, is divided on the question. With F. Schäffler, *Zulässigkeit und Zweckmässigkeit der Anwendung angloamerikanischer Beweismethoden in deutschen und internationalen Schiedsverfahren* (Munich, Sellier European Law Publisher, 2003), p. 96 advocating the setting aside of an award in such cases in extreme circumstances only, in which a number of criteria are cumulatively met.
500. As the constitutional protection of the sanctity of the personal sphere of freedom can in principle be waived by the parties, an explicit agreement by the parties of arbitral proceedings to employ techniques of taking evidence which would otherwise invade this protected sphere is viewed to be unproblematic. *See* F. Schäffler, *Zulässigkeit und Zweckmässigkeit der Anwendung angloamerikansicher Beweismethoden in deutschen und internationalen Schiedsverfahren* (Munich, Sellier European Law Publisher, 2003), p. 96.
501. *See* F.T. Schwarz and H. Ortner, 'Procedural Ordre Public and the Internationalization of Public Policy in Arbitration' in *Austrian Arbitration Yearbook 2008*, C. Klausegger *et al.* (eds) (Vienna, Manz, 2008); F. Schäffler, *Zulässigkeit und Zweckmässigkeit der Anwendung angloamerikansicher Beweismethoden in deutschen und internationalen Schiedsverfahren* (Munich, Sellier European Law Publisher, 2003), pp. 81 *et seq.* with further references.

takes the view that the mere abstract possibility of an evidentiary fishing expedition is not enough to violate procedural public policy.[502]

20-248 In any event, the distinction, drawn by some authors,[503] between the parties having agreed on such methods and the tribunal imposing such methods cannot be decisive. Internationally active businesses are capable of responsibly providing for their legal affairs. They have the possibility to exclude the application of Anglo-American methods of taking evidence in their arbitration agreements *ex ante* if they wish. If they do not, the law imputes the knowledge and awareness to them that the arbitrator will be in a position to employ such methods at his discretion (and many institutional rules, incorporated into the parties' agreement to arbitrate, give the arbitrator such rights).[504] Indeed, as certain evidentiary methods become internationally accepted, parties will be deemed to have accepted these methods implicitly by not having taken the necessary precaution to prevent their application. This is sufficient to defuse the concerns which usually are brought forward, especially those related to the competitive procedural disadvantage of one party being less experienced than the other in using such evidentiary methods.[505] Moreover, document disclosure is frequently employed in England whose courts apply procedural standards conforming with the ECHR. A outright rejection of document production would therefore be difficult to sustain in international arbitration.[506]

20-249 In conclusion, prevailing practice places particular emphasis on the specificity, the relevance and the materiality of the documents that a party wishes to obtain from the other side, thus preventing U.S. style fishing expeditions, but allow for document production where procedural fairness so requires. However, where parties dislike even the restricted document production envisaged under the IBA Rules (and prevailing international practice), they are of course free to avail themselves of the flexibility of arbitration to restrict document production, or to exclude it

---

502. Rather a close scrutiny of each case is necessary to determine whether *in concreto* the result of the application of foreign law violates fundamental principles of German law and the value of judicial establishment of truth. *See* BGH, 4 June 1992, IX ZR 149/91, ZZP 106 (1993), 87, 88.

503. See F. Schäffler, *Zulässigkeit und Zweckmässigkeit der Anwendung angloamerikansicher Beweismethoden in deutschen und internationalen Schiedsverfahren* (Munich, Sellier European Law Publisher, 2003), pp. 81 *et seq.*

504. *See* **Article 20**, at paras. 179 and 186 *et seq.* and Section 599(1) ZPO.

505. V. Triebel and J. Zons, 'Discovery of Documents in international Schiedsverfahren – Theorie und Praxis', Supplement 7 to (2002) BB, 26; P. Schlosser, *Das Recht der interntionalen privaten Schiedsgerichtsbarkeit* (2nd edn, Tübingen, Mohr Siebeck, 1989) para. 636; F. Schäffler, *Zulässigkeit und Zweckmässigkeit der Anwendung angloamerikansicher Beweismethoden in deutschen und internationalen Schiedsverfahren* (Munich, Sellier European Law Publisher, 2003), pp. 76, 90.

506. F.T. Schwarz and H. Ortner, 'Procedural Ordre Public and the Internationalization of Public Policy in Arbitration' in *Austrian Arbitration Yearbook 2008*, C. Klausegger *et al.* (eds) (Vienna, Manz, 2008).

altogether, either in their arbitration agreement[507] or in subsequent procedural agreements.

E. COURT INTERVENTION TO ASSIST THE TAKING OF EVIDENCE

It reflects a modern trend in legislation regulating international arbitration to **20-250** restrict the interference of the courts at the seat of the arbitration to a minimum. Protecting the arbitral process from the interference of the courts is fundamentally important to give meaningful effect to the parties' agreement to arbitrate. As discussed,[508] this principle is fully incorporated in Section 578 ZPO which states:

> The court may only become active in matters governed by this section if this section so provides.

This provision prevents courts from interfering in any way with the arbitral process **20-251** outside the scope of the fourth section of the Austrian ZPO (entitled 'Arbitration Procedure')[509] unless there is a specific statutory basis in Austrian arbitration law that would expressly allow the courts to intervene.

One of these instances is Section 602 ZPO which permits courts, subject to the **20-252** control of the tribunal, to assist the arbitral process. This provision is also applicable if the seat of the arbitral tribunal is not within Austria or has not yet been determined, so that Austrian courts will assist arbitral tribunals both seated within and outside the territory of Austria.[510] Section 602 ZPO provides:

> The arbitral tribunal, arbitrators who have been accordingly authorized by the arbitral tribunal, or a party with the approval of the arbitral tribunal, may request from a court the performance of judicial acts for which the arbitral tribunal has no authorization. The judicial assistance may also consist of the court requesting a foreign court or a public agency to conduct such acts. Section 37, paragraphs 2 to 5 and Sections 38, 39 and 40 JN shall apply accordingly, provided that the arbitral tribunal and the parties to the arbitral proceedings shall have the right to appeal in accordance with Section 40 JN. The arbitral tribunal or an arbitrator mandated by the arbitral tribunal and the parties may participate in the taking of evidence

---

507. When excluding document production in their arbitration agreement, parties should exercise some caution. It is often difficult to anticipate at the time of entering into the arbitration agreement whether the availability of document production will be tactically advantageous or not in future disputes.
508. *See* **Article 2**, at paras. 051 *et seq.*
509. *See* C. Liebscher, *The Austrian Arbitration Act 2006: Text and Notes* (The Hague, Kluwer Law International, 2006), Annotated Text to Section 578 ZPO.
510. *See* Section 577(2) ZPO. In principle that was already possible before the enactment of the new ZPO. *See* P. Oberhammer, *Entwurf eines neuen Schiedsverfahrensrechts* (Vienna, Manz, 2002), p. 106.

by the court and may pose questions. Section 289 of this law shall apply accordingly.

20-253 This provision has already been discussed in the context of **Article 2**.[511] For cases in which an arbitral tribunal is asked to perform judicial acts that are by virtue of their nature reserved for the state courts, typically because these acts involve some measure of executive force that the arbitral tribunal is naturally not authorized to apply (such as summoning unwilling witnesses), or because the judicial act would concern third parties that are not privy to the arbitration agreement and therefore outside the tribunal's jurisdictional reach. Notably, Section 602 ZPO does not restrict the available measures with which the state court can assist the arbitration; it will depend on the circumstances of the case how the courts can aid the tribunal in the administration of justice.[512] As discussed above, Section 602 ZPO is not limited to evidentiary acts, but extends to any judicial assistance.[513]

20-254 Judicial assistance may also involve the Austrian court formally requesting the assistance of a foreign court or a public agency under international agreements and diplomatic protocol, by *letters rogatory* or similar instruments.[514] Further, the provisions are applicable even where the seat of the arbitration is not in Austria, with the aim of making Austrian courts available to assist tribunals seated elsewhere, where this is appropriate.

20-255 By referring to Section 289 ZPO (governing the taking of evidence before the Austrian courts) it is ensured that the court assisting the arbitration does not perform the evidentiary task by itself, but that the arbitrators and the parties are invited to attend when the court takes the evidence,[515] and that they have a right to assist the judge to put certain questions to witnesses and experts.[516] Some argue that examination by the parties (or their counsels) is only allowed with permission granted by the judge,[517] while others would permit the arbitrators and the parties

---

511. *See* **Article 2**, at paras. 055 *et seq.*
512. Arguing for a broad scope of available measures: A. Petsche in *Arbitration Law of Austria: Practice and Procedure*, S. Riegler, A. Petsche, A. Fremuth-Wolf, M. Platte and C. Liebscher (eds) (Huntington, Juris Publishing, 2007), Section 602, p. 403.
513. *See* **Article 2**, at paras. 055 *et seq.*
514. Bi- and multilateral treaties govern the relationship between the state courts. With the introduction of Council Regulation No. 1206/2001 of 28 May 2001 on cooperation between the courts of the Member States in the taking of evidence in civil or commercial matters, transnational legal assistance between state courts has increasingly become more effective. For an overview on the impact, *see* N.A. Schoibl, 'Europäische Rechtshilfe bei der Beweisaufnahme in Zivil – und Handelssachen durch ordentliche Gerichte für Schiedsgerichte' in *Festschrift für W. H. Rechberger zum 60. Geburtstag*, L. Bittner, T. Klicka, G. Kodek and P. Oberhammer (eds) (Vienna/New York, Springer, 2005), pp. 513 *et seq.*
515. C. Liebscher, *The Austrian Arbitration Act 2006: Text and Notes* (The Hague, Kluwer Law International, 2003), Annotated Text to Section 602 ZPO.
516. Section 289(2) ZPO.
517. C. Klausegger, 'Legal Assistance by Austrian Courts in International Arbitration Proceedings' in *Austrian Arbitration Yearbook 2007*, C. Klausegger *et al.* (eds) (Vienna, Manz, 2007), p. 294.

to ask questions to any witness summoned under this provision.[518] This is the better view – the court only provides the official framework by summoning the witness (or taking other compulsory evidentiary steps or measures), but it is the court who is assisting; the taking of evidence firmly rests with the tribunal and the parties.[519]

Indeed, the right to request judicial assistance is controlled by the arbitral tribunal. **20-256** Section 602 ZPO vests this right with '[t]he arbitral tribunal' or individual 'arbitrators who have been accordingly authorized by the arbitral tribunal' or 'a party with the approval of the arbitral tribunal'. At the end, it is therefore for the tribunal to decide, on its own account, whether to seek judicial assistance. In that regard, Section 602 ZPO fits well with the systemic concept of Article 20(5). It also reflects established international practice. For example, the IBA Rules provide in Article 3(8) that '[i]f a Party wishes to obtain the production of documents from a person or organization who is not a Party to the arbitration and from whom the Party cannot obtain the documents on its own, the Party may, within the time ordered by the Arbitral Tribunal, ask it to take whatever steps are legally available to obtain the requested documents. The Party shall identify the documents in sufficient detail and state why such documents are relevant and material to the outcome of the case. The Arbitral Tribunal shall decide on this request and shall take the necessary steps if in its discretion it determines that the documents would be relevant and material'.[520] Again, it is the arbitral tribunal that is ultimately in control of seeking judicial assistance in the taking of evidence. It is therefore an important principle that such procedures may only be used with the permission of the tribunal or the agreement of the parties. Circumventing the arbitration agreement and the tribunal's control of the arbitration by soliciting the assistance of courts without, or even against, the tribunal's permission undermines the arbitral process, and should not be permissible.[521]

---

518. A. Reiner, *Das neue österreichische Schiedsrecht/The new Austrian Arbitration Law* (Vienna, LexisNexis, 2006), Section 602, note 143.

519. Arguing to give at least the tribunal an unlimited right to examine the witness summoned by the court: A. Petsche in *Arbitration Law of Austria: Practice and Procedure*, S. Riegler, A. Petsche, A. Fremuth-Wolf, M. Platte and C. Liebscher (eds) (Huntington, Juris Publishing, 2007), Section 602, p. 405.

520. IBA Rules, **Annex 16**.

521. Recently, there have been cases where parties resident in the U.S. have been subjected to discovery by the U.S. courts allegedly in aid of arbitration, under 28 U.S.C. Section 1782. *See In re Roz Trading Ltd*, 469 F Supp. 2d, 1221 (N.D. Ga. 2006) (granting a party to an arbitration proceeding in Austria the right to take evidence from a non-party based in the US in aid of that proceeding); *In re Hallmark Capital Corp.*, 534 F.Supp.2d 951 (D.Minn. 2007) (permiting the taking of evidence from a non-party located in the United States for use in Israeli arbitration proceedings). Insofar as this occurs outside the arbitral process, without the agreement of both parties or without directions from the tribunal, it can constitute a violation of the agreement to arbitrate. Indeed, it is doubtful if such a broad reading of Section 1782 (which is supposed to assist foreign tribunals, not circumvent them) is appropriate. *See* F.T. Schwarz and K. Beale, 'Disclosure In Aid Of Foreign Arbitration Under U.S. Law' (forthcoming).

VI.   *EX PARTE* PROCEEDINGS

Article 20(6): If one party does not take part in the proceedings, the case must be heard with the other party alone.

A.   Introduction

20-257 Article 20(6) addresses a situation in which one party fails to participate in the proceedings, although it is put on proper notice of the proceedings and invited to participate in all procedural steps. This failure has two consequences. First, the arbitrator is entitled to proceed with the case to an award even with only one party taking part in the proceedings, and indeed must do so. Second, however, the arbitrator is not entitled under such circumstances to simply proceed to a default award against the party that fails to participate. Rather, the arbitrator has to 'hear' the case in full, and decide it on the basis of the evidence before him.

20-258 In practice, it will often be the respondent who, either from the outset of the arbitration or at some stage, decides not to participate in the arbitration. It bears emphasis, however, that Article 20(6) addresses all cases where 'a party' fails to take part in the proceedings, which includes the default of the claimant as well. Indeed, once the statement of claims is served on the respondent under **Article 10**, the respondent may have a legitimate legal interest to have the case decided and dismissed with prejudice, by an award.

B.   No Decision by Default

20-259 Some national law systems allow for automatic default judgments in state court litigation. Where a party does not take part in the proceedings, although it is put on proper notice of the proceedings and invited to participate in all procedural steps, the judge can in certain circumstances either assume that the other side's allegations are true, or else automatically enter a judgment against the defaulting party.

20-260 Automatic default judgments do not sit well with the consensual nature of arbitration. Most arbitration regimes, both in national laws and institutional rules, are therefore very reluctant to give the arbitrator the authority to proceed to a default award, and in most cases exclude that authority.[522] Article 20(6) thus provides that '[i]f one party does not take part in the proceedings, the case must be heard with the other party alone'. The emphasis is on the case having to be 'heard' with the other

---

522. According to Section 396 ZPO a decision by default can be rendered a) if a party does not file its statement of defense on time or b) if a party fails to appear in a hearing before participating in the proceeding by submitting orally on the merits. However, the Austrian courts can only do so if a party applies for a decision by default, but are not allowed to become active *ex officio*.

side alone, rather than being decided in any automatic way against the defaulting party. In this regard, the Vienna Rules reflect international practice.[523]

This result is in any event mandated by Austrian law. Under the old regime, Section **20-261** 587(2) fZPO provided that 'if a party fails to participate in the arbitration, the tribunal must conduct the arbitration with the other party alone'. Under the prevailing opinion of Austrian legal doctrine, Section 587(2) fZPO did not permit the arbitrators to sanction a parties' failure to participate in the proceedings by issuing a default award. Similarly, the arbitrators were not permitted to assume, based on a party's refusal to participate, that the other party's submissions were true.[524] This prohibition of awards 'by default' was considered a mandatory provision, that is not at the parties' – or the arbitrators' – disposition.[525] A violation of this prohibition subjected the award to a challenge under Section 595(1) no. 2 fZPO.[526]

In the authentic German version of the statutory text, the term participation used **20-262** in Section 587(2) fZPO referred to the Austrian concept of *Einlassung*. A party 'participates' in a proceeding in the legal sense of this term as soon as it responds to the merits of the complaint launched against it.[527] However, the prohibition imposed by Section 587(2) fZPO was to apply as well where a party participated in the proceedings at the outset, but at some later stage decided not to participate anymore.

The prohibition of default judgments is repeated, although in somewhat relaxed **20-263** form, in the new Section 600 ZPO which provides that

(1) If the claimant fails to file his statement of claim in accordance with Section 597, paragraph 1 of this law, the arbitral tribunal shall terminate the proceedings.

---

523. Article 21(2) ICC Rules: 'If any of the parties, altough duly summoned, fails to appear without valid excuse, the arbitral tribunal shall have the power to proceed with the hearing.' Article 23(2) AAA/ICDR Rules: 'If a party, duly notified under these rules, fails to appear at a hearing without showing sufficient cause for such failure, as determined by the tribunal, the tribunal may proceed with the arbitration.' Article 28(2) Swiss Rules: 'If one of the parties, duly notified under these Rules, fails to appear at a hearing, without showing sufficient cause for such failure, the arbitral tribunal may proceed with the arbitration.' Article 28(2) UNCITRAL Rules: 'If one of the parties, duly notified under these Rules, fails to appear at a hearing, without showing sufficient cause for such failure, the arbitral tribunal may proceed with the arbitration'.

524. H.W. Fasching, *Schiedsgericht und Schiedsverfahren im österreichischen und im internationalen Recht* (Vienna, Manz, 1973), p. 104.

525. H.W. Fasching, *Schiedsgericht und Schiedsverfahren im österreichischen und im internationalen Recht* (Vienna, Manz, 1973), p. 104.

526. C. Liebscher and A. Schmid in *Practitioner's Handbook on International Arbitration*, F.B. Weigand (ed.) (Munich, C.H. Beck, 2002), p. 561.

527. W.H. Rechberger and T. Klicka in *Kommentar zur ZPO*, W.H. Rechberger (ed.) (3rd edn, Vienna/NewYork, Springer, 2006), Section 239, para. 1.

(2) If the respondent fails to respond in accordance with Section 597, paragraph 1 of this law during the agreed or determined period of time, the arbitral tribunal shall, unless the parties have agreed otherwise, continue the proceedings without treating such failure in itself as an admission of the claimant's allegations. The same shall apply where a party has failed to perform any other procedural act. The arbitral tribunal may continue the proceedings and may make an award on the basis of the evidence taken. If a failure to perform a procedural act has been excused to the arbitral tribunal's satisfaction, it may then be performed by the party.

20-264 Section 600 ZPO distinguishes between the claimant's and the respondent's default in submitting the statement of claim and the response, respectively, and then also contains provisions addressed at both parties with respect to their 'other procedural act[s]'.

20-265 As regards the claimant, his failure to submit a statement of claim within the meaning of Section 597(1) ZPO results in the termination of the arbitration by the arbitrators. This provision is only applicable in *ad hoc* proceedings under Austrian law, where the arbitration is initiated through a request to constitute the tribunal,[528] following which the claimant is required to file a statement of claim either as directed by the tribunal or within the timeframe agreed by the parties.[529] In arbitration under the Vienna Rules, this provision has no application. The arbitration is started when a statement of claims is received by the VIAC.[530] Hence, a failure to submit a statement of claims does not result in the termination of the arbitration – rather, the arbitration simply does not commence.

20-266 The termination resulting from the claimant's failure to submit a statement of claim is without prejudice, so that the claimant can file the claim again. Authors have criticized the lack of an express authorization in Section 600(1) ZPO that allows the arbitrators to allow a belated statement of claim for good cause, but such authority can in fact be inferred from the arbitrators' general power to conduct the arbitration at their discretion.[531] Although the legislature appears to have considered a decision on the claimant's default in filing a statement of claim a waste of resources, an extension may be appropriate where the delay in submitting the statement of claims is for good reason, or can otherwise be excused, and the claimant risks disproportionately adverse consequences.[532] Other authors note that

---

528. *See* Section 587(4) ZPO.
529. *See* **Article 9**, at para. 015.
530. *See* **Article 9**, at para. 015.
531. *See* **Article 20**, at paras. 093 *et seq.*; *see also* A. Reiner, *Das neue österreichische Schiedsrecht/ The new Austrian Arbitration Law* (Vienna, LexisNexis, 2006), Section 600, note 129.
532. For example, the claimant may not be able to re-commence the arbitration if the claims are subject to Statute of Limitations restrictions. *See also* A. Reiner, *Das neue österreichische Schiedsrecht/ The new Austrian Arbitration Law* (Vienna, LexisNexis, 2006), Section 600, note 129.

it would be unfair to grant the respondent the possibility of an extension (as Section 600(2) ZPO does), but not the claimant.[533] This has some force; on the other hand, the claimant is in a better position at the outset to judge when to initiate the arbitration in the first place, and should therefore in principle be ready to file the statement of claim when so directed by the tribunal. In that sense, the respondent will typically be more exposed to time pressures.

As to the respondent, the principal position under Section 600(2) ZPO (which is **20-267** based on the UNCITRAL Model Law[534] as well as the German ZPO[535]) remains that despite the respondent's default, the arbitration is to be continued, and no (automatically adverse) default judgment is rendered against the respondent. The respondent's failure to respond shall, by express statutory order, not be treated as an admission of the claim and the allegations advanced by the claimant.

The same is true with respect to both claimant and respondent as regards 'any other **20-268** procedural act' apart from the statement of claims and the response.[536] Thus, any decision rendered without the defaulting party's participation in the proceedings must take into account the defaulting party's previous submissions, and all evidence put before the arbitrators, and any additional evidence that the arbitrators may wish to take. Specifically, arbitrators are prevented from assuming that the non-defaulting party's submissions are true merely on the basis of the default. The Working Group correctly pointed out that the question whether or not a default at a certain stage of the proceeding indicates an admission is not an issue of procedural discretion, but an issue of probative value. As a matter of principle, the arbitrators are free to weigh the evidence, and attach the appropriate probative value to it (*freie Beweiswürdigung*). A rule that penalizes a default with an adverse decision is, of course, not a rule of evidence, but a rule of procedure.[537] Rather, under Section 600 ZPO, the arbitrators will freely evaluate the probative effect of the default, if any – in certain cases, they will be able to draw adverse inferences from a party's failure to participate or to offer evidence;[538] but they are not permitted to automatically take one side's allegation as proved because the other side defaulted. As discussed above, the ZPO does not require arbitrators to establish the relevant

---

533. M. Platte, in *Arbitration Law of Austria: Practice and Procedure*, S. Riegler, A. Petsche, A. Fremuth-Wolf, M. Platte and C. Liebscher (eds) (Huntington, Juris Publishing, 2007), Section 600, p. 385.

534. Article 25 UNCITRAL Model Law; *see* P. Oberhammer in *Das neue Schiedsrecht – Schiedsrechtsänderungsgesetz 2006*, B. Kloiber, P. Oberhammer, W.H. Rechberger and H. Haller (eds) (Vienna, Manz, 2006), p. 273.

535. Section 1048 German ZPO; *see* P. Oberhammer in *Das neue Schiedsrecht – Schiedsrechtsänderungsgesetz 2006*, B. Kloiber, P. Oberhammer, W.H. Rechberger and H. Haller (eds) (Vienna, Manz, 2006), p. 273.

536. Section 600(2) ZPO.

537. P. Oberhammer, *Entwurf eines neuen Schiedsverfahrensrechts* (Vienna, Manz, 2002), p. 104.

538. *See* in similar vein C. Liebscher in *Arbitration Law of Austria: Practice and Procedure*, S. Riegler, A. Petsche, A. Fremuth-Wolf, M. Platte and C. Liebscher (eds) (Huntington, Juris Publishing, 2007), p. 643.

facts of the case on their own volition, certainly not to extent previously required.[539] Also, Section 600 ZPO is not drafted as a mandatory provision: the parties may provide otherwise, and may thus provide for an award by default.[540]

C.   RIGHT TO PROCEED WITH ONE PARTY ALONE

20-269 Although arbitrators are not entitled to proceed to an automatic award by default, Article 20(6) and Section 600 ZPO have an obvious affirmative element as well: the arbitrator is permitted to proceed to an award on the merits. Indeed, given his duty to render an award, he is under an obligation to do so.[541] Otherwise, obstructive parties could sabotage the arbitration simply by deciding not to take part in it.

20-270 However, proceeding with a case without one of the parties is uncomfortable for the arbitrators. They will be mindful to notify the defaulting party of all procedural steps that are being undertaken, and to continue to invite the defaulting party to submit submissions and to attend any hearing, so that the defaulting party cannot later claim that it's right to be heard was violated. In any event, a strict test will have to be applied to late submissions; the true test is whether the defaulting party's right to present its case would be violated if the belated procedural step would not be admitted. Generally, it will be good practice for arbitrators to notify both parties that they intend proceed to an award by default; under the Vienna Rules, they are obliged to do so.[542] This gives the defaulting party the opportunity to at least request that its delay be excused.

---

539.   *See* **Article 20**, at paras. 183 *et seq.*

540.   P. Oberhammer, *Entwurf eines neuen Schiedsverfahrensrechts* (Vienna, Manz, 2002), p. 103. It is unclear, however, why this agreement *must* be express, as a matter of law (*see* M. Platte in *Arbitration Law of Austria: Practice and Procedure*, S. Riegler, A. Petsche, A. Fremuth-Wolf, M. Platte and C. Liebscher (eds) (Huntington, Juris Publishing, 2007), Section 600, p. 388), although implied agreement on default awards will be difficult to prove. *Platte* also argues that, even where the tribunal is authorized to make a default award as per the parties' agreement, 'even then the arbitral tribunal may not merely take the claimant's allegations as true'. If that were correct, an award by default would not have any meaningful application. The better view therefore is to give priority to the parties' autonomy: if the parties agree that the respondent's, or indeed any party's failure to make submissions, leads to procedural sanctions (such as treating silence as admission), then the parties' agreement should be given effect. Indeed, although Section 600(1) ZPO is silent on the matter with respect to statements of claim, Section 600(2) ZPO applies to procedural acts of both parties.

541.   *See* **Article 7**, at paras. 052 *et seq.* In that sense, 'may proceed' in Section 600 ZPO should be read as 'must proceed'. *See* also M. Platte in *Arbitration Law of Austria: Practice and Procedure*, S. Riegler, A. Petsche, A. Fremuth-Wolf, M. Platte and C. Liebscher (eds) (Huntington, Juris Publishing, 2007), Section 600, p. 386.

542.   *See* **Article 20(8)**, at paras. 088 *et seq.*

Indeed, under the mandatory provisions of Section 600 ZPO,[543] the arbitrators are **20-271** entitled to allow a defaulting party to do later what it had failed to do if 'the default is sufficiently justified'. Article 20(6) does not contain a similar provision, but allowing late submissions or evidence falls in the general discretion of the arbitrator (unless it is expressly excluded by the parties' agreement).

VII. THE OBLIGATION TO OBJECT AGAINST PROCEDURAL IRREGULARITIES

Article 20(7): If a violation by the sole arbitrator (arbitral tribunal) of a provision of these arbitration rules or of other provisions applicable to the proceedings comes to the notice of a party, that party must immediately enter an objection otherwise the party will be barred from entering an objection against that defect.

A. OBJECTING AGAINST PROCEDURAL IRREGULARITIES UNDER THE VIENNA RULES

Article 20(7) requires parties to object at the earliest opportunity against any **20-272** transgression by the arbitrators against the Vienna Rules, or the parties' agreement, or any other provision (presumably of the *lex arbitri*) that is applicable to the proceedings. Although Article 20(7) does not expressly say so, it is clear from a systemic analysis and from Austrian law (as further discussed below) that a party failing to enter an immediate objection forfeits its right to later rely on that procedural error, including in proceedings to challenge the award.

Provisions similar to Article 20(7) are not unfamiliar in international arbitration **20-273** rules. For example, Article 30 UNCITRAL Rules states:

> A party who knows that any provision of, or requirement under, these Rules has not been complied with and yet proceeds with the arbitration without promptly stating his objection to such non-compliance, shall be deemed to have waived his right to object.

As a result, case law and doctrine on Article 30 UNCITRAL Rules can be instruc- **20-274** tive for the interpretation of Article 20(7), although there remains at least one important difference.

---

543. This provision is mandatory because, in order to safeguard the parties' right to be heard, arbitrators must be in a position to admit late submissions or evidence where the circumstances so demand. *See also* J. Power, *The Austrian Arbitration Act – A Practitioner's Guide to Sections 577-618 of the Austrian Code of Civil Procedure* (Vienna, Manz, 2006), Section 600, para. 5.

20-275 First, Article 20(7) applies only to a party that is aware of the procedural violation. The same is true for Article 30 UNCITRAL Rules, which apply to a party '*who knows*'. This standard was chosen deliberately; the preliminary draft contained a provision for constructive waiver, where a party fails to promptly object and should have known about the non-compliance.[544]

20-276 Second, Article 20(7) requires a party to enter an '*immediate*' objection against a violation of the Vienna Rules or otherwise applicable procedure. Article 30 UNCITRAL Rules, on the other hand, uses the term '*promptly*', which is perhaps more appropriate. The requirement to file an '*immediate*' objection should not be interpreted too formalistically. The objective of the provision is to ensure efficient proceedings by cutting of procedural objections that could have been raised at an earlier stage, as in the famous case of *Cook Indus. Inc. v. Iran*,[545] where a party requested a retranslation of documents one and a half years after their original filing (which was denied).[546] At the same time, a party must be given the necessary time to consider whether to raise the objection without falling foul of the *immediacy* requirement. Weighing the efficiency of the process against the party's right to a considered arbitration strategy, the party should be required to react promptly (but not strictly immediately).

20-277 Although some authors criticize that it is unclear to whom the objection should be addressed,[547] it is quite evident that the objection should be directed at the entity responsible for the alleged procedural irregularity. In most cases, this will be the tribunal. Only where the Vienna Rules vest a specific authority with the institution (for example in cost matters), complaints should be addressed to the Secretary General or to the Board.[548]

20-278 Third, the consequences attached to a failure to object are serious. Article 30 UNCITRAL Rules provides that a party failing to object promptly '*shall be deemed to have waived his right to object*'. Similarly, Article 20(7) is designed to prevent a party from challenging the final award on the basis of the arbitrators' non-compliance with applicable procedural rules, where that same party did not promptly object, but rather 'saved' its objections for the setting aside procedure.[549]

---

544. J.J. van Hof, *Commentary on the UNCITRAL Arbitration Rules. The application by the Iran-U.S. Claims Tribunal* (The Hague, Kluwer Law International, 1991), p. 207.
545. Order in Iran-US Claims Tribunal Case No. 393, 6 September 1986, *Cook Indus. Inc. v. Iran* (unpublished).
546. J.J. van Hof, *Commentary on the UNCITRAL Arbitration Rules. The application by the Iran-U.S. Claims Tribunal* (The Hague, Kluwer Law International, 1991), p. 209.
547. M. Aden, *Internationale Handelsschiedsgerichtsbarkeit* (2nd edn, Munich, C.H. Beck, 2003), p. 547.
548. *See also* A. Reiner, *Das neue österreichische Schiedsrecht/The new Austrian Arbitration Law* (Vienna, LexisNexis, 2006), Section 579, note 10.
549. P. Sanders, *The Work of UNCITRAL on Arbitration and Conciliation* (The Hague, Kluwer Law International, 2001), p. 14.

Following the same rationale, a party that fails to raise a timely objection 'will be barred' from doing so at a later stage.

B. OBJECTING AGAINST PROCEDURAL IRREGULARITIES UNDER AUSTRIAN LAW

Article 20(7) (like Article 30 UNCITRAL Rules), being incorporated by reference **20-279** into the arbitration clause, forms part of the parties' agreement, and can consequently be derogated by the parties. Also, being a purely contractual provision, a party's failure to object against mandatory procedural principles, such as the right to be heard, cannot override applicable mandatory law, and thus does not result in waiving that party's right to assert such violation in the setting aside procedure.

In addition, following the 2006 reform, Section 579 ZPO contains a separate and **20-280** independent requirement for a party to object against procedural irregularities. It provides:

> If the arbitral tribunal has not complied with a procedural provision of this section from which the parties may derogate, or with an agreed procedural requirement of the arbitral proceedings, a party shall be deemed to have waived its right to object if it does not object without undue delay after learning of the defect, or within the designated time limit.

Section 579 ZPO, similar to Article 20(7), requires an immediate objection; again, **20-281** this should not be interpreted as a prohibitively strict standard.[550] The purpose of this provisions, and other provisions like it, clearly is to prevent undue delay, not to cut-off a party's procedural right without a reasonable opportunity to articulate its concerns.[551] The period to raise an objection starts when a party knows of the violation (rather than from when it should have known).[552] Under its general procedural discretion, the tribunal retains the right to admit belated objections, both under Article 20(7) and Section 579 ZPO. Although this does not follow from the text of either provision, it appears to have been the understanding of the legislature;[553] and indeed, arbitrators should not be prevented from correcting procedural mistakes while they still can do so. Similarly, however, the courts retain the independent right to assess, for example in setting aside proceedings, whether

---

550. *See*, however, A. Fremuth-Wolf in *Arbitration Law of Austria: Practice and Procedure*, S. Riegler, A. Petsche, A. Fremuth-Wolf, M. Platte and C. Liebscher (eds) (Huntington, Juris Publishing, 2007), Section 579, p. 32.
551. *See* A. Reiner, *Das neue österreichische Schiedsrecht/The new Austrian Arbitration Law* (Vienna, LexisNexis, 2006), Section 579, note 12.
552. A. Reiner, *Das neue österreichische Schiedsrecht/The new Austrian Arbitration Law* (Vienna, LexisNexis, 2006), Section 579, note 13.
553. Explanatory Notes to Section 579.

the objection was raised in a timely fashion or not, without being bound by the tribunal's determination.[554]

20-282 Section 579 ZPO requires a party to object only against a 'procedural provision of [the arbitration law] from which the parties may derogate, or (...) an agreed procedural requirement of the arbitral proceedings'. Some authors argue that Section 579 ZPO (and presumably Article 20(7)) also require a party to object if a tribunal acts in conflict with its own previous procedural orders.[555] Section 579 ZPO is modelled on (although not identical to) Article 4 of the UNCITRAL Model Law.[556] In both cases, objection against violations of mandatory procedural law was on purpose not required, as the consequence of having waived one's mandatory procedural right was considered too severe. Even where no objections against violations of mandatory law are made, therefore, parties retain the right to raise these violations subsequently, including, where appropriate, in setting aside proceedings.

20-283 With respect to the UNCITRAL Model Law, it is stated that '[i]n the form in which it was first considered by the [UNCITRAL] Working Group, a party which failed to make a timely objection to non-compliance with 'any provision of, or requirement under, this Law' was deemed to have waived his right to object. There was some support for deleting the draft article as inappropriate in an arbitration law as distinguished from arbitration rules. The prevailing view was, however, to retain a waiver rule but to exclude from its operation failure to object to non-compliance with mandatory provisions of the model law. A party thus retained its right to invoke such non-compliance at any time even if it had not objected to it earlier.'[557]

---

554. This is the position under German law, and hence, in a comparable legal framework. *See* A. Fremuth-Wolf in *Arbitration Law of Austria: Practice and Procedure*, S. Riegler, A. Petsche, A. Fremuth-Wolf, M. Platte and C. Liebscher (eds) (Huntington, Juris Publishing, 2007), Section 579, p. 37 with further reference.

555. A. Fremuth-Wolf in *Arbitration Law of Austria: Practice and Procedure*, S. Riegler, A. Petsche, A. Fremuth-Wolf, M. Platte and C. Liebscher (eds) (Huntington, Juris Publishing, 2007), Section 579, p. 35.

556. Article 4 of the UNCITRAL Model Law provides: 'A party who knows that any provision of this Law from which the parties may derogate or any requirement under the arbitration agreement has not been complied with and yet proceeds with the arbitration without stating his objection to such non-compliance without undue delay or, if a time -limit is provided therefore, within such period of time, shall be deemed to have waived his right to object.'

557. A. Broches, *Commentary on the UNCITRAL Model Law on International Commercial Arbitration* (Deventer/Boston, Kluwer Law and Taxation Publishers, 1990), p. 27, who continues to note that '[w]hen the Working Group considered a new draft at its next and final session, a minority continued to oppose a waiver provision both because waiver was considered too rigorous a sanction and, more generally, because questions of waiver and estoppel were better left to be decided by arbitrators and judges. Divergent views were also expressed as to the scope of the provision. Some considered that the waiver should operate without limitation, that is, to mandatory and non-mandatory provisions alike. Others would exclude only fundamental procedural defects, such as violation of public policy or non-arbitrability. The prevailing view

A similar analysis has been put forward by *Sanders*.[558] Despite its apparent relevance to deter parties from delaying proceedings[559] or avoid honouring an award by raising objections on points of which they were aware and could have raised at an earlier stage,[560] there is little case law on Article 4 of the UNCITRAL Model Law.[561]

With respect to Section 579 ZPO, which is modelled on Article 4 UNCITRAL **20-284** Model Law, the Austrian Working Group states that 'the loss of the right to object shall not occur in cases of violations of mandatory provisions of this chapter; a "waiver" of mandatory provisions shall not be reached by way of preclusion.'[562] Mandatory provisions however are not expressly listed in the arbitration law. As a

---

was, however, to retain the limitation to non-mandatory provisions. The Working Group also considered the separate question whether the waiver provision would have effect only in the arbitral proceedings or whether its effect would or should extend to judicial proceedings when a party founds a request for setting aside on non-compliance by its opponent with provisions of the model law or requirements of the arbitration agreement, or relies on them as a ground for contesting recognition and enforcement of the award. The majority view was that it extended to judicial proceedings as well. The written observations on the Working Group draft by governments and interested organizations largely repeated arguments which were covered in the Working Group discussions. The discussions in the Commission led to two changes in the Working Group draft, both intended to soften its provisions. That draft had sanctioned a party's failure to object to non-compliance which he knew or "ought to have known". The commission decided to exclude imputed knowledge and deleted the quoted words. The Working Group draft also sanctioned failure to object "without delay" and the commission softened this to "without undue delay," when it was found that no time period would be appropriate for all instances. The Commission did not accept a proposal to deal with the question of waiver only in those provisions in regard to which a waiver rule was regarded as essential and confirmed the view of the Working Group that a general waiver rule, which should however not affect mandatory provisions, should be maintained in order to help the arbitration process function efficiently and in good faith. The Commission also confirmed the Working Groups view that the effect of a waiver under Article 4 was not limited to the arbitral proceedings but extended to subsequent court proceedings in the context of Articles 34 and 36 and its Report so states. It also records the comments made in the discussion to the effect that where an arbitral tribunal has ruled that a party was deemed to have waived its right to object, the Article 6 court or the 'competent court', as the case may be, could come to a different conclusion in its review of the arbitral procedure pursuant to Article 34, or provided the proceedings were conducted under this Law, Article 36.'

558. P. Sanders, *The Work of UNCITRAL on Arbitration and Conciliation* (The Hague, Kluwer Law International, 2001), p. 28.
559. B. Harris, R. Planterose and J. Tecks, *The Arbitration Act 1996* (3rd edn, Oxford, Blackwell, 2003), p. 354.
560. M. Mustill and S.C. Boyd, *Commercial Arbitration, 2001 Companion* (2nd edn, Butterworths, London, 2001), Appendix 1, p. 444.
561. H.C. Alvarez, N. Kaplan, D. Rivkin, *Model Law Decisions, Cases applying the UNCITRAL Model Law on International Commercial Arbitration (1985-2001)* (The Hague, Kluwer Law International, 2003), p. 27.
562. Explanatory Notes to Section 579.

general rule, non-mandatory provisions can be identified by the phrasing 'unless otherwise agreed by the parties'.[563]

20-285 Section 579 ZPO raises a number of questions. First, its relationship to Article 20(7) is not entirely clear. Specifically, Article 20(7) requires an objection against violations of 'any provision of, or requirement under, these Rules', whereas Section 579 ZPO appears to go further, including not only an 'an agreed procedural requirement of the arbitral proceedings' (such as procedural requirements under the Vienna Rules), but, as discussed, any violation of 'a procedural provision of this section from which the parties may derogate', that is, any non-mandatory provision of Austrian arbitration law. There are, therefore, two separate levels of which the parties' need to be aware in order to preserve, and exercise, their right to object: first, objections against violations of any procedural agreements (including violations of the Vienna Rules), and second, violations of non-mandatory Austrian arbitration law.[564] Where parties fail to promptly object, they cannot raise a procedural complaint subsequently, and are prevented from relying on the procedural violation in setting aside proceedings.

20-286 However, it has been noted that the scope of Section 579 ZPO in the ambit of Section 611 ZPO is limited. Section 611 ZPO provides the exclusive grounds for setting aside an award, and it defines those grounds narrowly. A violation of even mandatory procedural provisions does usually not lead to the setting aside of an award, unless it concerns the composition or constitution of the tribunal[565] or rises to the level of a violation of the *procedural ordre public*.[566] In this regard, Austrian law contains some peculiar tensions. On the one hand, Section 579 ZPO does not extend to violations of mandatory law – as a result, a mere failure to object against the violation of such mandatory provisions does not result in a waiver of the objection.[567] On the other hand, it is clear from Section 611(2) no. 5 ZPO that even the most egregious violations of a procedural nature – namely those violating the *procedural ordre public* – can be waived by a party simply by not raising them in setting aside proceedings.[568] In that sense, it would have been systemically more

---

563. C. Liebscher, *The Austrian Arbitration Act 2006: Text and Notes* (The Hague, Kluwer Law International, 2006), Annotated Text to Section 579 ZPO; A. Fremuth-Wolf in *Arbitration Law in Austria: Practice and Procedure*, S. Riegler, A. Petsche, A. Fremuth-Wolf, M. Platte and C. Liebscher (Juris Publishing, Huntington/New York, 2007), Section 579, p. 33.

564. Non-mandatory provisions typically include wording such as 'unless the parties agree otherwise' or similar text indicating the parties' freedom to deviate from the statute. *See* A. Fremuth-Wolf in *Arbitration Law of Austria: Practice and Procedure*, S. Riegler, A. Petsche, A. Fremuth-Wolf, M. Platte and C. Liebscher (eds) (Huntington, Juris Publishing, 2007), Section 579, p. 33 (with an attempted list of provisions); C. Liebscher, *The Austrian Arbitration Act 2006: Text and Notes* (The Hague, Kluwer Law International, 2006), Annotated Text to Section 579 ZPO.

565. Section 611(2) no. 4 ZPO. *See* **Article 27**, at paras. 051 *et seq.*

566. Section 611(2) no. 5 ZPO. *See* **Article 27**, at paras. 054 *et seq.*

567. Explanatory Notes to Section 579.

568. *See* F.T. Schwarz and H. Ortner, 'Procedural Ordre Public and the Internationalization of Public Policy in Arbitration' in *Austrian Arbitration Yearbook 2008*, C. Klausegger *et al.*

consistent to either extend Section 579 ZPO to mandatory provisions, making it the parties' responsibility to monitor compliance with both their agreement and the applicable *lex arbitri* (including its mandatory provisions) throughout the arbitration (as opposed to the setting aside proceedings when they need to raise such violations at the latest) – or in the alternative, if greater emphasis is being placed on giving the state courts supervisory powers to preserve the integrity of the arbitral process irrespective of the parties' individual grievances, make violations of the *procedural ordre public* a ground for setting aside which the courts can consider *ex officio*, and not only upon a party's application. As matters stand now, parties appear to be able to preserve violations of mandatory law (by not raising an objection under Section 579 ZPO in the proceedings) and wait until the final award is issued. Parties can then raise violations of the mandatory law, if they rise to the level of procedural public policy violations, in the setting aside proceedings or not, depending on whether the ultimate outcome is favourable to them. In that regard, Austrian law (as the law in other jurisdictions) still has potential to be structured more efficiently.

Adding to the complexity, some procedural or other deficiencies are not subject to **20-287** Section 579 ZPO, and follow different rules, for example: Section 583(3) ZPO (regarding formal flaws in the arbitration agreement which are deemed cured if a party proceeds without objection to the merits);[569] Section 588(2) ZPO (regarding the challenge of an arbitrator by the party who participated in his nomination),[570] Sections 589(2) and (3) ZPO (providing for certain time limits for the challenge of arbitrators and recourse to the courts);[571] and Section 592(2) ZPO (regarding objections against the arbitrators' jurisdiction which must be raised at the first opportunity before entering the merits).[572] These provisions are not only relevant in that they specify particular rules (*leges speciales*) for certain issues; they also define, and narrow, the scope of what constitutes a procedural matter under Section 579 ZPO. For example, an issue falling under Section 592 ZPO regarding the tribunal's jurisdiction is therefore not an issue of procedure within the meaning of Section 579 ZPO.[573]

(eds) (Vienna, Manz, 2008). *See* **Article 16**, at paras. 026 *et seq.* for a discussion of the issue of waiver in the context of arbitrator bias.

569. *See* **Article 1**, at paras. 081 *et seq.*
570. *See* **Article 16**, at paras. 005 *et seq.*
571. *See* **Article 16**, at paras. 019 and 047 *et seq. See also* Section 601(3) ZPO regarding the challenge of tribunal-appointed experts.
572. *See* **Article 19**, at paras. 006 *et seq.*
573. For this reason, *Reiner* argues convincingly that the incorrect constitution of the tribunal (*e.g.*, one instead of three arbitrators) is a jurisdictional issue to be addressed under, and within the framework of, Section 592 ZPO; and not a procedural issue to be raised under Section 579 ZPO. *See* A. Reiner, *Das neue österreichische Schiedsrecht/The new Austrian Arbitration Law* (Vienna, LexisNexis, 2006), Section 579, note 11.

VIII.   CLOSING THE PROCEEDINGS

Article 20(8): The sole arbitrator (arbitral tribunal) must ask the parties whether they have any further proof to offer, witnesses to be heard or submissions to make. As soon as the sole arbitrator (arbitral tribunal) is convinced that the parties have had an adequate opportunity for such purposes, the sole arbitrator (arbitral tribunal) must declare the proceedings closed.

20-288 Article 20(8) requires the arbitrator to formally close the proceedings. The purpose of this provision is to protect the parties' right to be heard and to prevent surprise decisions. Thus, before proceeding to an award, the arbitrators need to declare their intention to close the proceedings and must ask the parties whether they have any last submissions to make or evidence to offer. Although Article 20(8) only refers to witnesses, the provision is drafted broadly enough to include all forms of evidence, including expert testimony.[574]

20-289 Article 20(8) must be read in the context of the arbitrators' discretion to conduct the proceedings and, specifically, to allow evidence only until a certain point in time.[575] It does therefore not give parties an unrestricted right to add evidence at the eleventh hour, much less after any cut-off date of which the parties had previously been notified. Rather, if parties want to offer last-minute evidence, the arbitrator can make an informed decision whether to admit this evidence, or to close the proceedings as intended.

20-290 Article 20(8) also reemphasizes the arbitrator's duty to conduct the arbitration expeditiously.[576] As soon as the arbitrator is convinced that the relevant facts are established, and that the parties have had a reasonable opportunity to present their case,[577] he should not prolong the arbitration unnecessarily but must close the proceedings.

---

574. C. Liebscher in *Arbitration Law of Austria: Practice and Procedure*, S. Riegler, A. Petsche, A. Fremuth-Wolf, M. Platte and C. Liebscher (eds) (Huntington, Juris Publishing, 2007), p. 643.
575. *See* **Article 20**, at paras. 071 *et seq.*
576. *See* **Article 7**, at paras. 059 *et seq.*
577. *See* **Article 20**, at paras. 076 *et seq.*

Article 21

Experts and Expert Witnesses

	Para.		Para.
I. Introduction	1	III. Experts Appointed by the Tribunal	7
II. Experts in International Arbitration	3	IV. Experts Appointed by the Parties	15

Article 21: Article 16 shall apply accordingly to the challenging of experts appointed by the sole arbitrator (arbitral tribunal). However, the sole arbitrator (arbitral tribunal) shall decide on the challenge.

I.   INTRODUCTION

Experts and expert witnesses are a regular feature of international arbitration. Parties put forward, and arbitrators appoint, experts on factual matters, be it on any kind of technical issue, to quantify damages, or to valuate companies. as well as experts of law, more often on substance but sometimes also on procedure. **21-001**

Article 21 addresses only a small aspect of the work of experts: the standard of impartiality and independence of experts appointed by the tribunal, and the mechanism to remove such experts if they are biased. In addition, however, Austrian law now contains a series of provisions with respect to expert evidence in arbitration that need to be taken into account. All of this is examined below. **21-002**

II.   EXPERTS IN INTERNATIONAL ARBITRATION

In common law countries, parties generally submit expert evidence in a form similar to evidence from witnesses of fact. The appointment of experts by the **21-003** courts is the exception. Common law practitioners will accept, however, that the role of an expert witness is to provide objective and neutral evidence. Accordingly, the expert witness is expected to be independent of the parties. Therefore, it is less common for common law counsel to assist in the preparation of expert witness reports to the same extent that counsel would assist in the preparation of written statements by witnesses of fact. If counsel were to do so, there would be a risk that the credibility of the so-called independent expert be seriously undermined. Nonetheless, it is accepted in common law jurisdictions that the independent expert witness's role is to assist the party that calls him or her to prove its own case.

21-004 In civil law systems on the other hand, it is most common for the judge, after consulting the parties on appropriate candidates, to appoint the required expert, who then assumes the role of expert adviser to the court itself, as opposed to being an expert witness for one or the other of the parties. That practice is consistent with the judge's role of fact finder in the dispute resolution process.

21-005 In international commercial arbitration, and also under the IBA Rules on the Taking of Evidence in International Commercial Arbitration (IBA Rules),[1] both practices are common. In international construction disputes, tribunals sometimes order the party-appointed experts to meet separately before the hearing, in order to establish a set of agreed technical facts and issues. Occasionally, a tribunal may require its own expert to attend such a meeting or, alternatively, report to the tribunal in respect of those issues the party-appointed experts were unable to agree on.

21-006 However, in international arbitration, there is perhaps an increasing trend away from tribunal-appointed experts; leaving it to the parties to offer the expert evidence they deem necessary to prove their case. Of course, how expert evidence is adduced in an arbitration, and how the tribunal intends to establish the applicable law, should be discussed with the parties at the outset of the arbitration.[2] In that discussion, arbitrators may wish to establish precise terms of reference that define the mandate of the expert, in particular if the expert is appointed by the tribunal.[3]

III.   EXPERTS APPOINTED BY THE TRIBUNAL

21-007 Expert evidence can be adduced through experts put forward and prepared by each party or by an expert appointed by the tribunal, or both. Most national arbitration

---

1. *See* IBA Rules, **Annex 16**.
2. For the benefits of an organizational conference in arbitration, *see* **Article 20**, at paras. 103 *et seq.*
3. Article 27(2) UNCITRAL Rules; D. Caron, L. Caplan and M. Pellonpaa, *The UNCITRAL Arbitration Rules: A Commentary* (Oxford, OUP, 2006), pp. 670 *et seq.*; M. Straus, 'The Practice of the Iran-United States Claims Tribunal in Receiving Evidence from Parties and from Experts' (1986) 3(3) J Int'l Arb 65-67.

laws[4] and institutional arbitration rules[5] specifically authorize tribunals to appoint an expert if they deem it appropriate.[6] In Austria, Section 601(1) ZPO expressly provides that

> [u]nless otherwise agreed by the parties, the arbitral tribunal may 1. appoint one or more experts to report to it on specific issues to be determined by the arbitral tribunal; 2. require the parties to give the expert any relevant information or to produce, or to provide access to, any relevant documents or goods or other property for inspection by the expert.

Thus, arbitrators are not only authorized to appoint experts at their own initiative, Section 601(1) ZPO also establishes a duty of the parties to co-operate with the expert by providing all relevant documentation and materials that the expert requires to discharge his or her mandate.[7] Arbitrators will generally welcome recommendations from the parties concerning possible experts.[8] **21-008**

This authority can be excluded by the parties; parties can therefore agree, for cost or other reasons, not to have tribunal-appointed experts at all, or not to have the tribunal appoint a particular expert.[9] Notably, however, **Article 20(5)** (which is incorporated into the parties' agreement to arbitrate by reference to the Vienna Rules) gives the arbitrators a similar authority by providing that, '[i]f the sole arbitrator (arbitral tribunal) considers it necessary, he (it) may on his (its) own initiative collect evidence, and in particular may (. . .) call in experts'.[10] Absent an express agreement that excludes the arbitrator's authority to appoint an expert, both the Vienna Rules and Austrian law confer this authority on the arbitrators. Under the Vienna Rules, the arbitrators have to ensure, however, if necessary in consultation with the Secretary General, that the deposit covers the expected costs of the expert before making the appointment.[11] **21-009**

---

4. Article 26(1) UNCITRAL Model Law, for example, authorizes an arbitral tribunal to appoint 'one or more experts to report to it on specific issues to be determined by the arbitral tribunal'.
5. Article 27 UNCITRAL Rules; Article 20(4) ICC Rules; Article 22 AAA/ICDR Rules and Article 21 LCIA Rules.
6. For general guidance, *see also* Article 6 IBA Rules, **Annex 16**.
7. For site inspections, *see* Article 7 IBA Rules, **Annex 16**; *see also* D. Caron, L. Caplan and M. Pellonpaa, The UNCITRAL Arbitration Rules: A Commentary (Oxford, OUP, 2005), p. 672; *Award in ICC Case No. 6497 of 1994*, (1999) XXIV YB Comm Arb, 71, 77-78.
8. R. Allison and H.M. Holtzmann, 'The Tribunal's Use of Experts' in *The Iran-United States Claims Tribunal and the Process of International Claims Resolution*, D. Caron and J. Crook (eds) (Ardsley-on-Hudson, Transnational Publishers, 2000), p. 271; M. Straus, 'The Practice of the Iran-United States Claims Tribunal in Receiving Evidence from Parties and from Experts' (1986) 3(3) J Int'l Arb, 57, 65-67.
9. A. Reiner, *Das neue österreichische Schiedsrecht/The new Austrian Arbitration Law* (Vienna, LexisNexis, 2006), Section 594, note 113.
10. *See also* **Article 20**, at paras. 178 *et seq.*
11. *See* **Article 35**, at paras. 003 and 005.

21-010 Where the tribunal has appointed an expert, Section 601(2) ZPO stipulates that

> [u]nless otherwise agreed by the parties, if a party so requests or if the arbitral tribunal considers it necessary, the expert shall, after delivering his report, participate in an oral hearing. In the hearing, the parties shall have the opportunity to put questions to him.[12]

21-011 This is, again, not a mandatory provision; the parties can agree not to hear an expert at the oral hearing. However, absent such agreement, each party has the right to call an expert appointed by the tribunal to appear at the hearing, in order to test the accuracy of the expert report in cross-examination. Systemically, this makes sense. Just like with written witness statements, parties need to be given the opportunity to challenge the expert directly should they so wish.[13] Parties can also bring expert advisers as part of their team to assist them in formulating appropriate questions to the expert.[14] Some authors suggest that the parties should provide the tribunal, the expert and the other side[15] with an advance list of questions they intend to put to the expert at the hearing;[16] this is said to avoid surprise questions (thereby avoiding any violation of the right to be heard), to put arbitrators in the position to strike questions for lack of relevance,[17] and to allow the expert to prepare properly.[18] There may be cases where this is appropriate for these reasons; but generally, these purposes can be achieved without an advance list of questions, which may, if applied in a strict manner, unduly limit the parties' right to cross-examination and to react to the developments at the oral hearing. Indeed, the expert will have to be prepared to answer any question within the scope and subject matter of his expert report; and the tribunal will be able to rule on the spot on the relevance of any questions put to the expert by the parties. Where a list of questions is appropriate, however, and where the parties' input should be sought, is when the expert is appointed in the first place, and his mandate as well as the scope and subject matter of his report defined. In that context, it is appropriate that the tribunal consult with the parties on the proper specifications to be directed at the tribunal-appointed expert.

---

12. This provisions corresponds in essence to Article 26(2) UNCITRAL Model Law and Section 1049(2) German ZPO.
13. *See also* **Article 20**, at para. 211; *see also* Articles 5(4), 5(5) and 6(6) IBA Rules, **Annex 16**.
14. A. Reiner, *Das neue österreichische Schiedsrecht/The new Austrian Arbitration Law* (Vienna, LexisNexis, 2006), Section 601, note 135.
15. *See* Section 599(3) ZPO.
16. A. Reiner, *Das neue österreichische Schiedsrecht/The new Austrian Arbitration Law* (Vienna, LexisNexis, 2006), Section 601, note 135; M. Platte in *Arbitration Law of Austria: Practice and Procedure*, S. Riegler, A. Petsche, A. Fremuth-Wolf, M. Platte and C. Liebscher (eds) (Huntington, Juris Publishing, 2007), Section 601, p. 394.
17. *See* **Article 20**, at para. 079 and Section 599(1) ZPO.
18. A. Reiner, *Das neue österreichische Schiedsrecht/The new Austrian Arbitration Law* (Vienna, LexisNexis, 2006), Section 601, note 135; M. Platte in *Arbitration Law of Austria: Practice and Procedure*, S. Riegler, A. Petsche, A. Fremuth-Wolf, M. Platte and C. Liebscher (eds) (Huntington, Juris Publishing, 2007), Section 601, p. 394.

Arbitrators are also free to instruct experts, whether tribunal-or party-appointed, to **21-012** meet with each other in advance of the hearing, in an attempt to reach agreement on certain issues, and factual assumptions, to the degree possible, and to record such agreement in preparation for the oral hearing.[19]

From the perspective of the parties, the role of the expert appointed by the tribunal **21-013** is crucial, as he or she will often have significant influence on the tribunal's decision-making. Indeed, it is important that the arbitrators do not delegate their responsibility for deciding the dispute to the expert.[20] In any event, both Article 21 and Section 601(3) ZPO require the tribunal-appointed expert to be as independent of the parties, and as impartial, as the arbitrators themselves. Specifically, Section 601(3) ZPO provides that 'Sections 588 [setting the standard of impartiality, independence and disclosure for arbitrators] and 589(1) and (2) ZPO [providing for the challenge of arbitrators] of this law shall apply accordingly to the expert appointed by the arbitral tribunal'; while Article 21 refers to **Article 16**.

Tribunal-appointed experts can therefore be challenged like arbitrators, under the **21-014** standards applicable in the context of **Articles 7** and **16**,[21] and pursuant to the mechanism established in **Article 16**.[22] However, it is the tribunal (and not the VIAC Board) who decides on this issue; and the tribunal's decision is not subject to appeal to the state court.[23] This is systemically correct, as the tribunal should retain ultimate control of evidentiary matters; the exercise of its evidentiary authority is only subject to control of the state courts under the standard imposed by Section 611 ZPO.[24] It is also intended to avoid the delays that would attend the possibility for parties to challenge expert appointments not only before the tribunal, but also before the court.[25] It has been suggested that Section 590 ZPO (equivalent to **Article 17**) should apply *per analogiam*, giving the arbitrators the right to terminate the expert's mandate if the expert is no longer able to discharge his function.[26] The arbitrators' authority to do so follows already from their

---

19. *See, e.g.,* Article 5(3) IBA Rules, **Annex 16**.
20. Iran-US Claims Tribunal, 14 August 1987, *Starrett Housing Corp. v. The Government of the Islamic Republic of Iran, Award No. 314-24-1* (1987) 16 Iran-US CTR 112, 197 ('It is fundamental that an arbitral tribunal cannot delegate to [the expert] the duty of deciding the case.').
21. *See* **Article 7**, at paras. 092 *et seq.,* **Article 16**, at paras. 003 *et seq.*
22. *See* **Article 16**, at paras. 013 *et seq.*
23. Section 601(3) ZPO does on purpose not refer to Section 589(3) ZPO.
24. *Liebscher* suggests that the participation of a biased expert appointed by the tribunal might give rise to a challenge for violation of *procedural ordre public,* but it will have to be an extreme case of bias that justifies the setting aside of an award. It is also debatable whether a party would have to show that the expert's bias was the reason for the decision by the tribunal. *See* C. Liebscher, *The Austrian Arbitration Act 2006: Text and Notes* (The Hague, Kluwer Law International, 2006), Annotated Text to Section 601(3) ZPO.
25. P. Oberhammer, *Entwurf eines neuen Schiedsverfahrensrechts* (Vienna, Manz, 2002), p. 105.
26. *See* **Article 17**, at paras. 013 *et seq.*

general control of the taking of evidence,[27] zand from the discretion they enjoy in conducting the arbitration.[28]

IV.   EXPERTS APPOINTED BY THE PARTIES

21-015 Most national arbitration laws and institutional rules also permit parties, as a general matter, to present expert evidence from their own party-appointed experts.[29] Indeed, Section 601(2) ZPO provides that '[i]n the hearing, the parties shall have the opportunity (. . .) to present their own expert witnesses in order to testify on the points at issue',[30] and Section 601(4) ZPO states that '[u]nless otherwise agreed by the parties, each party has the right to produce reports from its own experts'. In that case, unless excluded by agreement of the parties, the party-appointed expert can also be called by either party (or by the tribunal) to appear at the oral hearing and to be subjected to examination.[31] Section 601(4) ZPO was specifically included (adding to the text of the UNCITRAL Model Law) in recognition that the use of party-appointed experts is increasingly common in international arbitration, even though it does not follow with the tradition in civil law systems, including in Austria.[32] Contrary to the text of Section 601(2) ZPO which could be read to suggest that parties can produce experts as late as the hearing, advance notice to the tribunal and the other side will be generally appropriate, in order to ensure that the other side has sufficient opportunity to prepare its case and to preserve that party's right to be heard.[33] Indeed, arbitrators will usually include specific deadlines for the submission of expert opinions in the timetable for the arbitration and include the modalities for those reports in their procedural directions.

21-016 Notably, both Austrian law and the Vienna Rules require only tribunal-appointed arbitrators – and not the experts put forward by the parties – to follow the same standard of impartiality and independence that applies to arbitrators. In common law jurisdictions, party-nominated experts are also expected to be independent and

---

27. *See* **Article 20**, at paras. 171 *et seq.*
28. *See* **Article 20**, at paras. 093 *et seq.*
29. Article 23(1) UNCITRAL Model Law (parties' general right to submit evidence); Article 5(1) IBA Rules, **Annex 16** and Article 15(2) UNCITRAL Rules.
30. It is unclear if this is a mandatory provision or not, as the 'unless the parties agree otherwise' is only contained in the first sentence of that paragraph, and seems to refer only to whether an expert has to appear at a hearing. This could sensibly be interpreted to mean that, once an expert has to appear at a hearing, the parties cannot exclude each other's right to put questions to the expert.
31. *See also* Articles 5(4) and 5(5) IBA Rules, **Annex 16**.
32. P. Oberhammer, *Entwurf eines neuen Schiedsverfahrensrechts* (Vienna, Manz, 2002), p. 106.
33. A. Reiner, *Das neue österreichische Schiedsrecht/The new Austrian Arbitration Law* (Vienna, LexisNexis, 2006), Section 601, note 135.

impartial,[34] but in international practice, this is ultimately an issue of evidentiary value and credibility.[35] Experts give an informed opinion on a subject, and where they just advocate a party's case, they are likely to loose credibility in the eyes of the tribunal. Of course, the expert's relationship to a party or its counsel;[36] his remuneration;[37] the methodology applied by the expert; and the expert's interaction with counsel in preparing the expert report or opinion can all be subjects for cross-examination.

As discussed, it is a common law tradition for parties to present 'their' expert **21-017** witnesses,[38] a tradition built on the notion of a fully adversarial system. Civil law arbitrators, by contrast, have historically been more sceptical about the benefits and costs of party-nominated expert witnesses,[39] as a result from their state court experiences where *Privatgutachten* – that is, expert opinions put forward by the parties – carry limited evidentiary value. Thus, civil law arbitrators, if they are more traditionally-minded,[40] may still tend to favour the appointment of experts that follow the tribunal's and not the parties' instructions.

However, as also discussed, the trend in international arbitration is clearly towards **21-018** party-appointed expert witnesses. At a minimum, arbitrators will be very hesitant to deny parties the opportunity to present 'their' own expert evidence if they so wish. Also, tribunals are increasingly sensitive towards the additional cost incurred by tribunal-appointed experts (at least where they are appointed in addition to experts put forward by the parties), and will not necessarily follow the request of one party alone.[41] Again, it is important that, whatever course is chosen, the

---

34. Article 4 Protocol for the Use of Party-Appointed Expert Witnesses in International Arbitration of the Chartered Institute of Arbitrators.
35. *See* Section 599(1) ZPO, as discussed at **Article 20**, at paras. 184 *et seq.*
36. *See* Article 5(2)(a) IBA Rules, **Annex 16**.
37. There are cases, reportedly, where experts are remunerated on a success fee basis, which is difficult to square with an entirely objective approach.
38. A. Redfern, M. Hunter, N. Blackaby and C. Partasides, *Law and Practice of International Commercial Arbitration* (4th edn, London, Sweet & Maxwell, 2004), paras. 6-90, 6-94; R.H. Kreindler, 'Benefiting From Oral Testimony of Expert Witnesses' in *Arbitration and Oral Evidence* [2004] ICC Dossier, 87; D. Caron, L. Caplan and M. Pellonpaa, *The UNCITRAL Arbitration Rules: A Commentary* (Oxford, OUP, 2006), p. 676 ('UNCITRAL's support for the use of party-appointed experts at any time and in any manner necessary is unambiguous.').
39. V. Triebel, 'An Outline of the Swiss/German Rules of Civil Procedure and Practice Relating to Evidence' (1982) 47 Arbitration, 221, 226.
40. *See* G.B. Born, *International Commercial Arbitration – Commentary and Materials* (The Hague, Kluwer Law International, forthcoming), ch. 14.
41. H.M. Holtzmann, 'Fact-Finding by the Iran-US Claims Tribunal' in *Fact-Finding Before International Tribunals*, R. Lillich (ed.) (Ardsley-on-Hudson, Transnational Publishers, 1992), p. 123; M. Strauss, 'The Practice of the Iran-United States Claims Tribunal in Receiving Evidence from Parties and from Experts' (1986) 3(3) J Int'l Arb, 57; G. White, *The Use of Experts by International Tribunals* (Syracuse, Syracuse University Press, 1965).

tribunal and the parties discuss the form, content, and timing of expert evidence at the beginning of the proceeding.

21-019 The trend away from tribunal-appointed experts is even more pronounced with regards to experts of law. There, the substantive law, although being often 'foreign' to one or more of the arbitrators, is increasingly treated as part of the parties' argument that will be the subject of the parties' submissions and oral pleadings – and less as a quasi-fact that the parties somehow have to prove. Accordingly, legal experts are less frequently appointed by the tribunal and more employed as assisting the parties. This increasingly means that legal experts do not appear as expert witnesses in the classical sense, but more and more as special advisers to the parties who assist the parties in preparing and presenting their legal argument.

21-020 Under traditional Austrian doctrine, the judge has to ascertain the law *ex officio*. As far as foreign law is concerned, this would advocate for the arbitrator *ex officio* to appoint an expert in that legal field. Some Austrian commentators stress indeed that the burden of ascertaining the law must not be shifted to the parties,[42] and seem to suggest that, because foreign law is not a fact that needs to be proven by the parties, legal issues are not susceptible to expert evidence at all.[43] Even where the principle of *iura novit curia* does not apply in any technical sense in arbitration, it is of course the arbitrator who is ultimately responsible to apply the law properly to the facts of the case; but arbitration offers sufficient flexibility to ascertain the law in a number of appropriate ways. Modern practice suggests that the law should be pleaded by the parties, if necessary with the help of legal experts from the relevant field, rather than being made the subject of (perhaps inherently subjective) legal opinions that often are of limited assistance to the arbitrator. Again, it is vital that it is discussed at the outset how the applicable law is ascertained.[44]

---

42. C. Liebscher and A. Schmid in *Practitioner's Handbook on International Arbitration*, F.B. Weigand (edn) (Munich, C.H. Beck, 2002), p. 571.
43. M. Platte in *Arbitration Law of Austria: Practice and Procedure*, S. Riegler, A. Petsche, A. Fremuth-Wolf, M. Platte and C. Liebscher (eds) (Huntington, Juris Publishing, 2007), Section 601, p. 393.
44. *See also* **Article 24**, at paras. 001 *et seq.*

Article 22

Interim Measures of Protection

		Para.
I.	The Tribunal's Power to Grant Interim Relief	1
	A. Introduction	1
	B. The Tribunal's Authority to Grant Interim Relief	7
	1. Interim Measures in Austrian Doctrine Before the 2006 Reform	8
	2. The Basis for Interim Relief Under the ZPO	18
	3. The Basis for Interim Relief Under the Vienna Rules	24
	C. Procedural Preconditions for Interim Relief	26
	1. Power by Default	27
	2. Order Upon Application by a Party	30
	3. No *Ex Parte* Relief	32
	4. As Between the Parties	38
	5. Security	40
	6. Contractual Obligation to Comply	41
	D. Substantive Preconditions for Interim Relief	46
	1. Necessary Relief with Respect to the Subject Matter of the Arbitration	52
	2. Frustration of Final Award	60
	3. Irreparable Harm	63
	4. No Pre-Judgment of the Case	67

		Para.
	5. *Prima Facie* Establishment of the Applicant's Case	69
	6. Urgency	70
	7. Balancing the Parties' Interests	72
	8. Standard of Proof	74
	9. Interim Relief Despite Jurisdictional Objection	76
	10. Deviating from the Substantive Requirements of Section 593(1) ZPO and Article 22	79
	11. Modifying and Terminating Interim Measures	81
	E. Categories of Interim Relief	83
	1. Orders Ensuring Enforcement of the Final Award and Preventing Irreparable Harm	85
	2. Orders Protecting the *Status Quo*	88
	3. Orders Preventing the Aggravation of the Dispute	90
	4. Orders Protecting the Taking of Evidence	92
	5. Orders Regulating a Relationship	95
	6. Orders Involving the Tribunal	100
	7. Orders for Security of Costs	101

		Para.				Para.
II.	Formal Considerations......................	108	VII.	Enforcing Arbitral Interim		
III.	Reasoned Order	111		Measures in Austria........................	131
	A. Requirements	111		1.	Jurisdictional Basis..............	133
	B. Order or Award	113		2.	Procedure	140
IV.	Record of the Order	117		3.	Adapting Foreign Relief to	
V.	Confirmation of Enforceability.........	119			the Austrian System	141
VI.	Parallel Jurisdiction of the State			4.	Grounds to Refuse	
	Courts.....................	122			Enforcement.......................	145
	A. Interim Measures by State Courts	122		5.	Grounds to Set Aside the	
	B. Duty to Inform the Tribunal and				Enforcement.......................	153
	the VIAC	128				

I.   THE TRIBUNAL'S POWER TO GRANT INTERIM RELIEF

Article 22(1): Unless otherwise agreed by the parties, the sole arbitrator (arbitral tribunal) may, at the request of a party order any party, after hearing such party, to take such interim measure of protection as the sole arbitrator (arbitral tribunal) may consider necessary in respect of the subject matter of the dispute, as otherwise the enforcement of the claim would be frustrated or considerably impeded or there is a danger of irreparable harm. The sole arbitrator (arbitral tribunal) may require any party to provide appropriate security in connection with such measure. The parties are obliged to comply with such orders, whether or not they are enforceable by State courts.

A.   INTRODUCTION

22-001 Interim measures are an important instrument to protect the parties' interests not only in state court litigation, but also in international arbitration. Until a final decision is reached – that is, in the time passing from when the tribunal is constituted to the time the final award is rendered – the parties' rights are regularly subject to significant risks. Evidence may be corrupted; assets may be dissipated; the subject matter of the arbitration may be placed beyond reach; irreparable harm may be inflicted on a party; and the parties' relationship may further deteriorate during the course of the arbitration, harming their joint ventures.[1]

22-002 Thus, interim measures are and should be available to ensure that the parties' rights are safeguarded and to prevent a party from frustrating the effective enforcement of the final award. Contemporary international arbitration law and practice indeed recognize the broad power of international arbitrators to order interim or protective

---

1. J. Lew, L. Mistelis and S. Kröll, *Comparative International Commercial Arbitration* (The Hague, Kluwer Law International, 2003), para. 23-1.

measures. This power is recognized in the UNCITRAL Model Law,[2] almost all modern arbitration statutes,[3] leading institutional rules for international arbitration,[4] arbitral awards and national court decisions,[5] and academic commentary.[6] In light of this uniform body of authority, a distinguished English commentator observed in 1992 that:

> There can be no doubt that the procedural power to grant provisional or protective measures reflects a general principle of law, and that principle nowadays is based on the need to prevent the judgment of the court from being prejudiced or frustrated by actions of the parties. That general principle of law is reflected in the practice of national courts, administrative bodies, arbitral tribunals, and international courts.[7]

The foregoing consensus rests on a simple, commonsense premise: in order for the **22-003** international arbitral processes to function in a fair and effective manner, it is essential that an arbitral tribunal possess broad powers to safeguard the parties' rights and its own remedial authority during the pendency of the arbitration. Unless the arbitral tribunal is able to grant provisional measures, its ability to provide effective final relief may be frustrated, one party may suffer grave damage or the parties' dispute may be unnecessarily exacerbated.

Traditionally, however, legislatures have been reluctant to vest arbitrators with the **22-004** power to grant interim measures.[8] Historically, in Austria, the majority opinion in academic doctrine appeared hostile to permitting arbitrators to grant interim relief.[9] Yet more recently, prevailing opinion has given way to the pressures of the practical requirements of arbitral practice. Indeed, the change in perception as to interim relief in arbitration gives testimony to the impressive development of arbitration, within a relatively short period of time, from an alternative means of dispute resolution to the prevailing standard in settling international disputes:

> Traditionally, only national courts were empowered to grant interim or conservatory measures. The power to grant such measures was thought

---

2. Article 17 UNCITRAL Model Law.
3. Section 39 English Arbitration Act 1996; Sections 1041 and 1063(3) German ZPO; Article 1696 Belgian Judicial Code 1998 and Article 183(1) Swiss IPRG.
4. Article 23 ICC Rules; Article 25 LCIA Rules; Article 26 UNCITRAL Rules and Article 21 AAA/ ICDR Rules.
5. See **Article 22**, at paras. 085 *et seq.*
6. See Y. Derains and E.A. Schwartz, *A Guide to the ICC Rules of Arbitration* (2nd edn, The Hague, Kluwer Law International, 2005), pp. 294-296 and K.P. Berger, *International Economic Arbitration* (Boston, Kluwer Law International, 1993), pp. 331-342.
7. L. Collins, 'Provisional and Protective Measures in International Litigation' (1992) 234 Recueil des Cours, 9, 234-236.
8. J. Lew, L. Mistelis and S. Kröll, *Comparative International Commercial Arbitration* (The Hague, Kluwer Law International, 2003), para. 23-10.
9. C. Hausmaninger, *Die einstweilige Verfügung im schiedsgerichtlichen Verfahren* (Vienna/New York, Springer, 1989), p. 1.

to be a prerogative of the courts because of public policy considerations. The national courts' power was supported by the perceived problems of enforcing provisional measures issued by an arbitral tribunal, and the fact that an arbitral tribunal did not have the power to enforce its orders or award for these measures. However, in recent years, increasingly, national courts have come to see their role as supportive of the international arbitration process. This role owes much to the fact that arbitration as a dispute resolution mechanism has demonstrated its reliability.(...) The difficulty of direct enforcement has not been an obstacle to the development of the new supportive role of the courts, whose coercive powers are not necessarily required to ensure the effectiveness of interim and conservatory measures. In some respects, the fact that arbitral tribunals can draw adverse conclusions from failure to comply with their decisions concerning these measures encourages voluntary compliance with such orders. In any event, a measure for interim or conservatory relief can, if necessary, be enforced through competent judicial authorities.[10]

22-005 The Vienna Rules in their current form expressly grant the arbitrators the authority to order interim measures of protection in the course of the arbitral proceedings. This chapter examines the approach to interim relief in arbitration taken by traditional Austrian doctrine; the regime adopted under the Vienna Rules; some practice pointers regarding prerequisites for, and categories of, arbitral interim relief in international arbitration; the enforcement of interim measures of protection; and, finally, the issue of security. The relationship between interim relief granted by arbitrators, on the one hand, and by courts, on the other hand, is discussed still further below in the context of **Article 22(6)**, at paras. 122 *et seq.*

22-006 As a preliminary remark on terminology, it should be noted that generally speaking the terms 'interim relief', 'measures of interim relief', 'provisional measures', 'provisional measures and injunctions', 'protective measures',[11] 'provisional remedies', 'interim measures of protection',[12] 'conservatory measures',[13] 'interim measures',[14] and 'interim and conservatory measures',[15] 'prejudgment or pre-award relief' refer to the same concept, and are often used interchangeably[16] by arbitrators and counsel, depending on their legal and cultural

---

10. J. Lew, 'Commentary on Interim and Conservatory Measures in ICC Arbitration Cases' (2000) 11(1) ICC Ct Bull, 23, 24 *et seq.*
11. *See* Article 183 Swiss IPRG.
12. *See* Article 26 UNCITRAL Rules and **Article 22**.
13. *See* Article 23 ICC Rules.
14. *See* Article 21 AAA/ICDR Rules.
15. *See* Article 25 LCIA Rules.
16. E. Gaillard and J. Savage (eds), *Fouchard Gaillard Goldman On International Commercial Arbitration* (The Hague, Kluwer Law International, 1999), para. 1303.

background.[17] Strictly speaking, irrespective of the term used and as further discussed below, it is possible to characterize different categories of 'interim measures', according to their nature and purpose.[18] Some commentators duly noted that these categories are not closed,[19] and that no classification can be exclusive.

B.   THE TRIBUNAL'S AUTHORITY TO GRANT INTERIM RELIEF

The Vienna Rules 1991 did not contain an express authorization of the tribunal to **22-007** grant interim measures of protection.[20] The issue of 'interim jurisdiction' under the Vienna Rules was, therefore, subject to some considerable debate, which was accentuated in Austria by a statutory situation traditionally hostile to interim relief in arbitration. Under the fZPO, arbitrators, who unlike state courts lack *imperium*, were considered to be prevented from imposing measures of force on the parties, which, for a long time, was said to include interim measures of protection. This position, however, has never been persuasive; it is, in any event, superseded by modern developments of arbitral law and practice.[21]

1.   **Interim Measures in Austrian Doctrine Before the 2006 Reform**

The arbitrators' power to grant interim measures of protection is typically con- **22-008** sidered a matter of procedure, and hence, subject to the applicable *lex arbitri*.[22] Notably, however, arbitrators frequently do not apply any specific law when determining that they have the power to grant interim relief, or rather refer to the place where the interim measure is likely to be enforced.[23]

---

17.   For example, French arbitrators and counsel may have a tendency to have recourse to the term 'provisional measures'; US attorneys to 'provisional relief'; Anglo-Commonwealth lawyers to 'interim relief' and Austrian lawyers to 'interim measures'.
18.   E. Gaillard and J. Savage (eds), *Fouchard Gaillard Goldman On International Commercial Arbitration* (The Hague, Kluwer Law International, 1999), para. 1303.
19.   *See* A. Redfern, M. Hunter, N. Blackaby and C. Partasides, *Law and Practice of International Commercial Arbitration* (4th edn, London, Sweet & Maxwell, 2004), para. 7-23.
20.   Article 14(2) Vienna Rules 1991 entitles the arbitrator to instruct the parties to produce documents. This can be regarded as the authorization to order certain interim relief. This does not, of course, constitute a general authorization.
21.   However, both the Greek and Italian Codes of Civil Procedure provide that the arbitral tribunal may *not* have the necessary powers to grant interim relief. *See* Article 889 Greek Code of Civil Procedure and Article 818 Italian Code of Civil Procedure.
22.   G.B. Born, *International Commercial Arbitration – Commentary and Materials* (2nd edn, The Hague, Kluwer Law International, 2001), p. 922.
23.   J. Lew, L. Mistelis and S. Kröll, *Comparative International Commercial Arbitration* (The Hague, Kluwer Law International, 2003), para. 23-9; J. Lew, 'Commentary on Interim and Conservatory Measures in ICC Arbitration Cases' (2000) 11(1) ICC Ct Bull, 23, 25.

22-009 In Austria, there has been considerable debate whether, as a matter of law, arbitrators may order measures of interim relief. This debate roots in Section 588 fZPO, which provides that:

> The Arbitrators may not take under oath the testimony of the parties, of witnesses and of experts, who appear voluntarily before them. They may not use enforcement measures or set fines against the parties or other persons.

22-010 Under traditional Austrian doctrine[24] and case law,[25] the granting of interim relief has been considered subject to the exclusive jurisdiction of the state courts. Given their lack of enforcement powers, arbitrators were supposedly not able to grant injunctions, which, in the Austrian system, are part of enforcement law, rather than being part of civil procedure.[26] Interim measures were thus perceived as enforcement measures, which arbitrators, pursuant to the second sentence of Section 588 fZPO, were not permitted to enact.[27] In other words, interim relief was said not to engage the merits of a case, but to ensure, through its essentially protective nature, the enforceability of the final award. This, however, is said to be for the state courts to address pursuant to Sections 379 *et seq.* EO.[28] In traditional Austrian doctrine, it was maintained, therefore, that measures of interim relief granted by arbitrators in Austria in spite of Section 588 fZPO are invalid and not enforceable.[29] The invalidity of such measures applies by operation of law, and cannot be waived through the parties' agreement.[30]

22-011 This view dominated Austrian doctrine for a long time. Only *Schönherr* argued,[31] adopting the position of some German authors,[32] that arbitrators could grant

---

24. H.W. Fasching, *Schiedsgericht und Schiedsverfahren im österreichischen und im internationalen Recht* (Vienna, Manz, 1973), p. 22; H.W. Fasching, *Lehrbuch des österreichischen Zivilprozeßrechts* (2nd edn, Vienna, Manz, 1990), paras. 2177, 2181; F. Matscher, 'Probleme der Schiedsgerichtsbarkeit im österreichischem Recht' [1975] JBl, 412, 452.

25. See OGH, 7 June 1977, 4 Ob 350/77.

26. W.H. Rechberger and W. Melis in *Kommentar zur ZPO*, W.H. Rechberger (ed.) (2nd edn, Vienna/New York, 2000), Section 577, para. 14.

27. F. Matscher, 'Probleme der Schiedsgerichtsbarkeit im österreichischem Recht' [1975] JBl, 412, 452.

28. See K.H. Schwab, 'Einstweiliger Rechtsschutz und Schiedsgerichtsbarkeit' in *Festschrift für Fritz Baur*, W. Grunsky (ed.) (Tübingen, Mohr Siebeck, 1981), pp. 627, 638 *et seq.*

29. H.W. Fasching, *Schiedsgericht und Schiedsverfahren im österreichischen und im internationalen Recht* (Vienna, Manz, 1973), p. 111.

30. F. Schönherr, 'Streitigkeiten aus dem Gesellschaftsverhältnis und Schiedsgericht' [1980] Ges RZ, 184.

31. F. Schönherr, 'Streitigkeiten aus dem Gesellschaftsverhältnis und Schiedsgericht' [1980] Ges RZ, 184.

32. W.F. Lindacher, 'Schiedsgerichtliche Kompetenz zur vorläufigen Entziehung der Geschäftsführungs – und Vertretungsbefugnis für Personengesellschaften' [1979] ZGR, 201; F. Baur, *Neuere Probleme der privaten Schiedsgerichtsbarkeit* (Berlin/New York, de Gruyter, 1980), pp. 22 *et seq.* Although at the time prevailing opinion in Germany went the other way. See P. Schlosser,

interim measures of protection. However, some authors had doubts.³³ *Schönherr* required that the parties expressly exclude the jurisdiction of the state courts to issue interim orders, and confer interim jurisdiction to the arbitrators.

The traditional argument prohibits the arbitrators to *enforce* as well as *order* **22-012** interim measures of protection.³⁴ This was never persuasive. Even if one accepts the uncontroversial proposition, as the fZPO indeed indicates, that arbitrators have judicial authority, but no enforcement powers,³⁵ it seems that traditional doctrine confuses the *order* of interim relief with its *enforcement*, perhaps unduly guided by the systematic position which interim relief assumes in the Austrian statute.³⁶ It is hard to dispute that, under Section 577 fZPO, arbitrators lacked enforcement powers, which, of course, also prevents them from enforcing their own awards. However, it is equally hard to dispute that, by virtue of an arbitration agreement, the parties submit their dispute to the jurisdiction of the arbitrators. As a result, the arbitrators have the power to issue decisions which are binding as against the parties.

Granting interim relief is, in and of itself, not an imposition of force. Conceptually, **22-013** if one accepts that arbitrators have jurisdiction and authority to dispose through their award finally of a case on the merits, one ought to accept that, included within this authority, arbitrators have jurisdiction to decide the issues before them on an interim basis. Just like with an award, the imposition of force – *enforcement* – may well be reserved for the state courts – but just like with awards, this is less a question of jurisdiction in the course of the arbitration that one of enforcement *after* the tribunal has rendered its decision.

Das Recht der internationalen privaten Schiedsgerichtsbarkeit (2nd edn, Tübingen, Mohr Siebeck, 1989), para. 404; K. H. Schwab, 'Einstweiliger Rechtsschutz und Schiedsgerichtsbarkeit' in *Festschrift für Fritz Baur*, W. Grunsky (ed.) (Tübingen, Mohr Siebeck, 1981), pp. 627 *et seq.* with further reference; P. Schlosser, 'Einstweiliger Rechtsschutz durch staatliche Gerichte im Dienste der Schiedsgerichtsbarkeit' [1986] ZZP 241; as did the courts: *see* BGH, 7 Oktober 1953, II ZR 170/52, ZZP 71 (1958), 423, 436.

33. With this in mind H.W. Fasching, *Schiedsgericht und Schiedsverfahren im österreichischen und im internationlen Recht* (Vienna, Manz, 1973), p. 22; H.W. Fasching, *Lehrbuch des österreichischen Zivilprozeßrechts* (2nd edn, Vienna, Manz, 1990), para. 2177; F. Matscher, 'Probleme der Schiedsgerichtsbarkeit im österreichischem Recht' [1975] JBl, 412, 452, 455; C. Hausmaninger, *Die einstweilige Verfügung im schiedsgerichtlichen Verfahren* (Vienna/New York, Springer, 1989), pp. 22 *et seq.*; differentiating W.H. Rechberger and W. Melis in *Kommentar zur ZPO*, W.H. Rechberger (ed.) (2nd edn, Vienna/New York, 2000), Section 577, para. 14.

34. F. Matscher, 'Probleme der Schiedsgerichtsbarkeit im österreichischem Recht' [1975] JBl, 412, 452, 455.

35. H.W. Fasching, *Lehrbuch des österreichischen Zivilprozeßrechts* (2nd edn, Vienna, Manz, 1990), para. 107.

36. Indeed, *Zeiler* has shown recently that this doctrine was even based on an incorrect reading of the case law. *See* G. Zeiler, *Schiedsverfahren* (Vienna/Graz, Neuer Wissenschaftlicher Verlag, 2006), Section 593, p. 177.

22-014 This result is reinforced by the broad discretion that arbitrators enjoy in conducting the proceedings. Arguably, arbitrators did not *need* an express authorization permitting them to order interim relief, as this could be considered part of their overall procedural power under Section 587 fZPO.[37] As mentioned above, if arbitrators have the authority to decide finally a dispute, they ought to have the authority to order measures that preserve the *status quo* until they reach a final decision, so that their eventual award will not be frustrated.

22-015 In this respect, the arbitrators' competence to issue an award is conceptually not entirely different from their competence to issue a decision on an interim basis. Whether award or interim order, the question of enforceability comes second, and is distinct from the question of jurisdiction. In still other words, whether award or interim order, the question of who issues an award or order is entirely distinct from the question of who enforces that award or order. Any judicial request[38] for a party to effect a certain performance[39] (*richterliche Anordnung zu bestimmter Leistung*) contains an *instruction* (*Verfügungsebene*), which is separate from, and distinct of, its enforcement. Any judgement requesting the defendant party to pay a certain amount to the plaintiff, is first and foremost an instruction for the defendant to pay. Only if the defendant fails to comply with this instruction voluntarily will the courts lend their force to implement the instruction. This concept can equally be applied to interim measures ordered, but not enforced, by arbitrators.[40]

22-016 Quite to the contrary, it is argued that the arbitration agreement gives the arbitrators *all* the powers necessary to resolve the parties' dispute.[41] This must imply all such interim measures that are necessary to preserve the arbitrators' power to provide effective final relief to the party and to ensure that the final award can be effectively enforced. The correlation between the arbitrators' general subject-matter jurisdiction and their power to grant interim relief is stressed, for example, in Article 25(1) LCIA Rules which provides that arbitrators can order any provisional relief, 'which the Arbitral Tribunal would have the power to grant in an award'. The underlying rational for this convincing approach is that the arbitrators' jurisdiction to *determine* the parties' dispute is defined by the arbitration agreement – and if this determination falls within the scope of the arbitration agreement, it is quite irrelevant, in terms of jurisdiction, whether the determination is made in a final award or in an interim order.

---

37. Section 587 fZPO: 'The proceeding is determined (. . .) at the arbitratiors' own discretion.'
38. That does not only apply to *arbitral* judicial requests.
39. Declaratory judgment/constitutive judgment.
40. P. Oberhammer, *Entwurf eines neuen Schiedsverfahrensrechts* (Vienna, Manz, 2002), p. 82; G. Zeiler, *Schiedsverfahren* (Vienna/Graz, Neuer Wissenschaftlicher Verlag, 2006), Section 593, pp. 175 *et seq.*
41. J. Lew, L. Mistelis and S. Kröll, *Comparative International Commercial Arbitration* (The Hague, Kluwer Law International, 2003), para. 23-30.

In sum, Section 577 fZPO did in principle[42] not restrict the Tribunal's power to **22-017**
grant interim measures of protection; rather, it prevents the arbitrators to *enforce*
such orders themselves. Although this view was not shared by traditional Austrian
doctrine,[43] more recent writings do support this position.[44]

2. The Basis for Interim Relief Under the ZPO

Conceptually, commentators have identified three different categories in legisla- **22-018**
tion giving power to arbitrators to grant interim relief. First, laws that confer, by
default, broad power to the arbitrators, subject to the parties' agreement to the
contrary; second, somewhat restricted power, limited to certain types of interim
relief, unless the parties choose to broaden the arbitrators' authority through their
agreement; and third, laws that do not vest any such powers with the arbitrators, but
allow the parties to make arrangements in the arbitration agreement.[45]

The UNCITRAL Model Law falls in the first category, giving arbitrators the power **22-019**
to grant interim relief in broad terms. Article 17 UNCITRAL Model Law provides
in relevant part:

(1) Unless otherwise agreed by the parties, the arbitral tribunal may, at the
request of a party, grant interim measures.

(2) An interim measure is any temoporary measure whether in the form of an
award or in another form, by which, at any time prior to the issuance of the
award by which the dispute is finally decided, the arbitral tribunal orders a
party to
(a) Maintain or restore the status quo pending determination of the
dispute

---

42. There may be some categories of interim relief that do require the use of coercive powers, such as
attachments. *See* J. Lew, 'Commentary on Interim and Conservatory Measures in ICC Arbitration
Cases' (2000) 11(1) ICC Ct Bull, 23, 25. Indeed, depending on the nature of the interim relief, the
distinction between the order and its enforcement may be blurred. *See* P. Oberhammer, *Entwurf
eines neuen Schiedsverfahrensrechts* (Vienna, Manz, 2002), p. 82.

43. H.W. Fasching, *Schiedsgericht und Schiedsverfahren im österreichischem und im internationlen Recht* (Vienna, Manz, 1973), p. 20; W.H. Rechberger and W. Melis in *Kommentar zur ZPO*,
W.H. Rechberger (ed.) (2nd edn, Vienna/New York, Springer, 2000), Section 577, para. 14; F.
Matscher, 'Probleme der Schiedsgerichtsbarkeit im österreichischen Recht' [1975] JBl, 412,
452, 455.

44. A. Reiner, *Handbuch der ICC-Schiedsgerichtsbarkeit* (Vienna, Manz, 1989), p. 221; K. Hempel,
'Einstweiliger Rechtsschutz durch Schiedsgerichte – Cui Bono?' in *Festschrift Rudolf
Welser zum 65. Geburtstag*, C. Fischer-Czermak, A. Kletecka, M. Schauer and W. Zankl
(eds) (Vienna, Manz, 2004), p. 275. For the most in-depth analysis, *see* C. Hausmaninger,
Die einstweilige Verfügung im schiedsgerichtlichen Verfahren (Vienna/New York, Springer,
1989).

45. *See* J. Lew, L. Mistelis and S. Kröll, *Comparative International Commercial Arbitration* (The
Hague, Kluwer Law International, 2003), paras. 23-15 *et seq.* with examples.

   (b) Take action that would prevent, or refrain from taking action that is likely to cause, current or imminent harm or prejudice to the arbitral process itself;
   (c) Provide a means preserving assets out of which a subsequent award may be satisfied; or
   (d) Preserve evidence that may be relevant and material to the resolution of the dispute.

22-020 This approach was followed in systems close to the Austrian legal order, notably in Germany with Section 1041 German ZPO[46] and in Switzerland with Article 183 Swiss IPRG.[47]

22-021 The second category of legislation whereby unless otherwise agreed by the parties, the law only allows certain types of interim relief is exemplified in the English Arbitration Act 1996.[48] The third category of legislation where laws do not vest any such powers with the arbitrators, but allow the parties to make arrangements in the arbitration agreement, can be found, for example, in the US or French laws.[49]

22-022 The new ZPO follows the broad approach adopted in the UNCITRAL Model Law. As the lack of a statutory authorization of arbitrators to order interim measures of protection has been one of the most significant misgivings of arbitration in Austria,

---

46.   Section 1041 German ZPO provides that: '(1) Unless otherwise agreed by the parties, the arbitral tribunal may, at the request of a party, order such interim measures of protection as the arbitral tribunal may consider necessary in respect of the subject-matter of the dispute. The arbitral tribunal may require any party to provide appropriate security in connection with such measure.'
47.   Article 183 Swiss IPRG provides that: '1. Unless the parties have agreed otherwise, the arbitral tribunal may, at the request of a party, order provisional or protective measures.'
48.   Section 38 English Arbitration Act 1996 provides that: '(4) The tribunal may give directions in relation to any property which is the subject of the proceedings or as to which any question arises in the proceedings, and which is owned by or is in the possession of a party to the proceedings (a) for the inspection, photographing, preservation, custody or detention of the property by the tribunal, an expert or a party, or (b) ordering that samples be taken from, or any observation be made of or experiment conducted upon, the property. (. . .) (6) The tribunal may give directions to a party for the preservation for the purposes of the proceedings of any evidence in his custody or control.' For all other types of interim relief which do not fall within the above-mentioned definition under Section 38(4) and (6), the agreement of the parties is required. Section 39(1) English Arbitration Act 1996 provides that 'the parties are free to agree that the tribunal shall have power to order on a provisional basis any relief which it would have power to grant in a final award'.
49.   The French New Code of Civil Procedure and the US FAA and Uniform Arbitration Act are silent on the arbitrator's powers to order provisional measures. For French law, *see* M. de Boisséson, *Le droit Français de l'arbitrage interne et international* (Paris, GLN-éditions, 1990), pp. 749 *et seq.*; for US law *see* G.B. Born, *International Commercial Arbitration – Commentary and Materials* (2nd edn, The Hague, Kluwer Law International, 2001), pp. 924 *et seq.*

this clarification brings Austrian law in line with accepted practice in international arbitration. Section 593(1) ZPO now provides:

> Unless otherwise agreed by the parties, the arbitral tribunal may, at the request of a party, order such provisional or protective measures against another party, after hearing such party, as the arbitral tribunal may consider necessary in respect of the subject matter of the dispute, as otherwise the enforcement of the claim would be frustrated or considerably impeded or there is a danger that irreparable damage will occur. The arbitral tribunal may require any party to provide appropriate security in connection with such measure.

The Working Group drafting the new law specifically took issue with the formerly **22-023** prevailing view in Austrian doctrine against arbitral interim relief and accepted that the lack of power regarding the *enforcement* of interim measures does as such not imply a lack of *jurisdiction* to *order* such protective measures.[50] As a matter of practice, the Working Group considered it necessary to ensure that the scope of legal protection available to parties in arbitration is equivalent to the scope of protection afforded by state courts.[51] At the same time, as discussed in more detail further below, Section 585 ZPO clarifies that parties still may apply for interim measures to the state courts, which may be able in certain circumstances to provide injunctive relief quicker and more effectively.[52] In addition, as also discussed further below, Section 593 ZPO provides for the enforcement of interim orders issued by arbitrators through the state courts in aid of arbitration.[53] As such, a tribunal's power to order interim measures of protection can no longer be disputed under Austrian law.

3.   The Basis for Interim Relief Under the Vienna Rules

Facing the increasing pressure of international practice, some arbitrators were **22-024** (even under the Vienna Rules 1991) willing to assume jurisdiction with regard to interim measures of protection that would preserve their authority to effectively decide the dispute on the merits.[54] With the adoption of Article 14a of the Vienna Rules 2001,[55] arbitrators were expressly authorized to 'order the interim measures

---

50. P. Oberhammer, *Entwurf eines neuen Schiedsverfahrensrechts* (Vienna, Manz, 2002), p. 82.
51. P. Oberhammer, *Entwurf eines neuen Schiedsverfahrensrechts* (Vienna, Manz, 2002), p. 82.
52. *See* **Article 22**, at paras. 122 *et seq.*
53. *See* **Article 22**, at paras. 131 *et seq.*
54. *Order in VIAC Case No. SCH- 4750 of 2004* (unpublished). This was also frequently the case under the 1988 ICC Rules, which contained no express provision granting arbitrators the power to order interim measures of protection. *See* J. Lew, L. Mistelis and S. Kröll, *Comparative International Commercial Arbitration* (The Hague, Kluwer Law International, 2003), para. 23-30 with further reference.
55. *See* Article 14a Vienna Rules 2001, **Annex 2a**. Although it can be assumed that the decision to amend the Vienna Rules in this instance was not a unanimous decision by the Board.

of protection that he (it) considers to be appropriate, on application by one party'. Article 14a was closely modeled after Article 23 ICC Rules 1998. Like with Article 23 ICC Rules, there was no suggestion when Article 14a was adopted that it was changing existing practice under the Vienna Rules. Rather, it made explicit what was already understood.

22-025 Now, the regime governing interim relief under the Vienna Rules has been modified again, with the adoption of Article 22(1), which mirrors, in almost identical terms, Section 593(1) ZPO.

C.   PROCEDURAL PRECONDITIONS FOR INTERIM RELIEF

22-026 Given the nearly identical language of Section 593(1) ZPO and Article 22(1) as regards the tribunal's authorization to issue interim relief, both provisions are discussed, element by element, below. This section focuses on the procedural framework in which the provisions operate, while the next section looks at the substantive requirements arbitrators should observe when considering an interim measure of protection.

1.   **Power by Default**

22-027 Section 593(1) ZPO and Article 22 authorize the arbitrators to order interim measures of protection 'unless the parties have agreed otherwise'. Thus, Austrian law and the Vienna Rules take the position that the tribunal's authority to grant interim relief applies automatically by default operation of the law – that is, unless the parties specifically decide to exclude it. Rather than requiring a specific agreement to confer the authority to grant interim relief on the arbitrators, therefore, the parties must expressly 'opt out' should they wish to limit the arbitrators' powers.

22-028 The predecessor provisions of Article 22 (Article 14a of the Vienna Rules 2001[56]) contained the additional jurisdictional requirement that the file must have been transmitted to the arbitrators. As discussed in the context of **Article 12**,[57] the file is transmitted after the initial submissions are filed, the tribunal is constituted and the entire deposit has been paid.[58] Only with the transmission of the file to the arbitrators is the arbitration properly commenced. Thus, even though Article 22 does not say so expressly, arbitrators can only order interim measures of protection once the file has been transmitted to them pursuant to **Article 12**.

22-029 Unlike state courts which have judges available to deal with interim applications on an *ad hoc* basis, this is a natural deficit of arbitral tribunals: They need to be

---

56. Vienna Rules 2001, **Annex 2a**.
57. *See* **Article 12**, at paras. 004 *et seq.*
58. *See* **Article 12**, at paras. 004 *et seq.*

constituted (which can take some time), before they become fully operational. Notably, therefore, other arbitral institutions offer mechanisms for granting interim relief at an earlier stage. For example, the ICC Pre-Arbitral Referee procedure,[59] the 'WIPO Emergency Relief Rules'[60] and in particular Articles 42a–42o of the new Netherlands Arbitration Institute Rules offer an alternative to the inability of arbitrators to act prior to the formation of the tribunal.[61] If both the ICC Pre-Arbitral Referee procedure and the 'WIPO Emergency Relief Rules' require a separate agreement of the parties, – which is always difficult to secure when a dispute arises – the mere consent of the parties to the NAI Rules empowers any party to have recourse to summary arbitration proceedings and request the NAI to appoint a single arbitrator for the purpose of granting provisional measures.[62] Article 37 AAA/ICDR Rules entitles the parties to appoint an emergency arbitrator, who will hear requests for emergency relief that may be necessary prior to the formation of the entire arbitration panel.

2. Order Upon Application by a Party

It was also debated amongst the members of the Working Group if the arbitrators' **22-030** power to grant interim relief should be subject to a party's application for such measures, or if arbitrators should be able to order interim measures *ex officio*. In the end, an *ex officio* authority was considered inappropriate.[63]

The arbitrators' power to order interim measures therefore requires an application **22-031** by a party.[64] Under Article 22 (as under Section 593 ZPO), the arbitrators lack the jurisdiction to grant interim relief at their own initiative. This approach is the prevailing one in modern arbitration, and has also been adopted in Section 1041 German ZPO, on the basis of Article 17 UNCITRAL Model Law.[65] As a result, arbitrators also cannot order interim measures that exceed the measures requested in the party's application.

---

59. *See* E. Gaillard and P. Pinsolle, 'The ICC Pre-Arbitral Referee: First Practical Experiences' (2004) 20(1) Arb Int'l, 1, 13.
60. J. Lew, L. Mistelis and S. Kröll, *Comparative International Commercial Arbitration* (The Hague, Kluwer Law International, 2003), para. 23-33.
61. *See* A. Redfern, M. Hunter, N. Blackaby and C. Partasides, *Law and Practice of International Commercial Arbitration* (4th edn, London, Sweet & Maxwell, 2004), para. 7-14.
62. Article 42a(4) NAI Rules provides that the summary arbitration proceedings procedure applies 'if the place of arbitration is situated within the Netherlands'.
63. P. Oberhammer, *Entwurf eines neuen Schiedsverfahrensrechts* (Vienna, Manz, 2002), p. 84.
64. G. Zeiler, *Schiedsverfahren* (Vienna/Graz, Neuer Wissenschaftlicher Verlag, 2006), Section 593, p. 181.
65. *See also* Article 23 ICC Rules; Article 25 LCIA Rules; Article 21 AAA/ICDR Rules and Article 20 DIS Rules. By contrast, under Rule 39(3) ICSID Arbitration Rules, arbitrators can recommend provisional measures on their own initiative or recommend measures other than those specified in a request.

3.   No *Ex Parte* Relief

22-032 The consensual nature of arbitration may impose a further restriction on arbitrators as that does not limit state courts: Whether to grant interim relief *ex parte* – that is, without hearing the other side first.[66] On the one hand, the principle of *auditur et altera pars* is a core principle of arbitration. Arbitrators, therefore, typically wish to consider the evidence and hear the arguments of the parties before reaching any conclusions which may affect the parties' rights. On the other hand, hearing the other side before ordering interim relief may frustrate the relief that is sought – the time inevitably spent on hearing both sides gives the other party the opportunity to dissipate assets, corrupt the evidence or rid itself of the subject-matter of the dispute.[67]

22-033 Traditionally, international arbitrators have been overall hostile to granting interim relief *ex parte*.[68] It is argued that *ex parte* relief violates the consensual nature of arbitration and the party's unalterable right to be heard. *Ex parte* relief, where it is necessary, is for the state courts to grant. It has also been pointed out that the different, more restrictive treatment in arbitration is justified because parties lack the right to appeal in arbitration that they enjoy before the state courts.[69]

22-034 On the other hand, arbitrators enjoy a greater flexibility than state courts. They can easily change their interim orders when the circumstances change as well. It is therefore not entirely inconceivable that, in exceptional cases, arbitrators order interim relief *ex parte*, and then give the party subjected to the order the immediate opportunity to respond, which could lead to a reassessment of the interim order by the arbitrators.[70] In practice, some creative solutions are available to arbitrators to resolve the tension between hearing the parties and granting effective interim relief. For example, arbitrators can invite the opposing party to comment on the application of interim relief, yet, with this invitation, express the *expectation* that,

---

66. Most arbitration rules are silent on the issue. Rule 39(4) ICSID Arbitration Rules provides that '[t]he Tribunal shall only recommend provisional measures, or modify or revoke its recommendations, after giving each party an opportunity of presenting its observations'.

67. *See* F. Baur, *Neuere Probleme der privaten Schiedsgerichtsbarkeit* (Berlin/New York, de Gruyter, 1980), p. 24; K.H. Schwab, 'Einstweiliger Rechtsschutz und Schiedsgerichtsbarkeit' in *Festschrift für Fritz Baur*, W. Grunsky (ed.) (Tübingen, Mohr Siebeck, 1981) p. 642.

68. *See* B. Goldman, 'Provisional Measures in International Arbitration' (1993) Int'l Bus LJ 3, 6; *see* in general A. Redfern, M. Hunter, N. Blackaby and C. Partasides, *Law and Practice of International Commercial Arbitration* (4th edn, London, Sweet & Maxwell, 2004), para. 7-17. For a commentator supporting the possibility of arbitrators granting *ex parte* interim measures of protections, *see* K.P. Berger, *International Economic Arbitration* (Boston, Kluwer Law International, 1993), p. 337.

69. H.C. Scheef, *Der einstweilige Rechtsschutz und die Stellung der Schiedsrichter bei dem Abschluss von Schiedsvergleichen nach dem deutschen und englischen Schiedsverfahrensrecht: Eine rechtsvergleichende Untersuchung* (Frankfurt/Main, Peter Lang Verlag, 2000), p. 37.

70. J. Lew, L. Mistelis and S. Kröll, *Comparative International Commercial Arbitration* (The Hague, Kluwer Law International, 2003), para. 23-70; J.P. Lachmann, *Handbuch für die Schiedsgerichtspraxis* (3rd edn, Cologne, Verlag Dr. Otto Schmidt, 2008), p. 687.

pending the interim proceeding, the opposing party will not do anything to frustrate a future interim order, let alone a final award.[71] In view of the arbitrators' authority (including its authority to draw adverse inferences), a polite expression of an expectation will in many cases suffice as an incentive for the opposing party to preserve the *status quo*.

A proposal for the possibility of granting arbitrators authority to order interim **22-035** measures on an *ex parte* basis has been discussed in the framework of the UNCITRAL Working Commission on Interim Measures of Protection since 2001.[72] Some commentators were strongly opposed to this proposal on the ground that it would be a breach of due process,[73] whilst other commentators liken the debate to a tempest in a teapot, since this proposal 'would only take effect on adoption by a state and most leading arbitral venues have recently renewed their laws without including such a power'.[74] On 4 December 2006, the UNCITRAL Model Law Working Group adopted the amended version of the Model Law on International Commercial Arbitration, including a completely revised Chapter VI. A. on interim measures and the newly-introduced category of preliminary orders.[75]

---

71. The basis for this expectation would be the parties' arbitration agreement. A good faith performance of an agreement to arbitrate must imply the obligation not to frustrate the arbitral process and the effective enforcement of a future award.
72. The UNCITRAL Working Commission was initially set up in 2001 to update the Model Law and solve, *inter alia*, the difficulties encountered by successful requesting parties to enforce orders or 'awards' for provisional measures.
73. *See* H. van Houtte, 'Ten Reasons Against A Proposal For Ex Parte Interim Measures of Protection in Arbitration' (2004) 20(1) Arb Int'l, 85, 89; for a contrary view *see* J.E. Castello 'Ex Parte Measures -a view in favour' (2003) 8 LCIA Newsletter, 16.
74. *See* A. Redfern, M. Hunter, N. Blackaby and C. Partasides, *Law and Practice of International Commercial Arbitration* (4th edn, London, Sweet & Maxwell, 2004), para. 7-17.
75. Chapter IV A., of the 2006 UNCITRAL Model Law, concerning interim measures and preliminary orders, reads as follows:
Article 17A. Conditions for granting interim measures
(1) The party requesting an interim measure under Article 17(2)(a), (b) and (c) shall satisfy the arbitral tribunal that:
(a) Harm not adequately reparable by an award of damages is likely to result if the measure is not ordered, and such harm substantially outweighs the harm that is likely to result to the party against whom the measure is directed if the measure is granted; and
(b) There is a reasonable possibility that the requesting party will succeed on the merits of the claim. The determination on this possibility shall not affect the discretion of the arbitral tribunal in making any subsequent determination.
(2) With regard to a request for an interim measure under Article 17(2)(d), the requirements in paragraphs (1)(a) and (b) of this article shall apply only to the extent the arbitral tribunal considers appropriate.
Article 17B. Applications for preliminary orders and conditions for granting preliminary orders
(1) Unless otherwise agreed by the parties, a party may, without notice to any other party, make a request for an interim measure together with an application for a preliminary order directing a party not to frustrate the purpose of the interim measure requested.

While the tribunal is still required to hear the other party before it issues an interim measure, Article 17B UNCITRAL Model Law now explicitly provides, together with a request for interim measures, a party can request a preliminary order directing a party not to frustrate the purpose of the interim measure 'without notice to any other party.'[76] The tribunal may grant such an order 'provided it considers that the prior disclosure of the request for the interim measure to the party against whom it is directed risks frustrating the purpose of the measure.'[77] However, the preliminary order stays effective only for a period of twenty days.[78] Moreover, as soon as the tribunal has made a determination in respect of an application for a preliminary order, it shall communicate both the preliminary order and the request for the interim measure to the opposing party who is then heard.[79] As a result, the preliminary order, as an *ex parte* measure, is only intended to cover the short time between the application and the decision of the tribunal on the proper interim measure. Still, commentary remains critical about the new stipulations, bringing forward that *ex parte* relief has no real application where an arbitral tribunal cannot issue immediately-effective coercive relief, e.g. attachment or garnishment of bank accounts.[80]

---

(2) The arbitral tribunal may grant a preliminary order provided it considers that prior disclosure of the request for the interim measure to the party against whom it is directed risks frustrating the purpose of the measure.

(3) The conditions defined under Article 17A apply to any preliminary order, provided that the harm to be assessed under Article 17A(1)(a), is the harm likely to result from the order being granted or not.

Article 17C. Specific regime for preliminary orders

(1) Immediately after the arbitral tribunal has made a determination in respect of an application for a preliminary order, the arbitral tribunal shall give notice to all parties of the request for the interim measure, the application for the preliminary order, the preliminary order, if any, and all other communications, including by indicating the content of any oral communication, between any party and the arbitral tribunal in relation thereto.

(2) At the same time, the arbitral tribunal shall give an opportunity to any party against whom a preliminary order is directed to present its case at the earliest practicable time.

(3) The arbitral tribunal shall decide promptly on any objection to the preliminary order.

(4) A preliminary order shall expire after twenty days from the date on which it was issued by the arbitral tribunal. However, the arbitral tribunal may issue an interim measure adopting or modifying the preliminary order, after the party against whom the preliminary order is directed has been given notice and an opportunity to present its case.

(5) A preliminary order shall be binding on the parties but shall not be subject to enforcement by a court. Such a preliminary order does not constitute an award.

76. Article 17B(1) UNCITRAL Model Law.
77. Article 17B(2) UNCITRAL Model Law.
78. Article 17C(4) UNCITRAL Model Law.
79. Article 17C UNCITRAL Model Law.
80. G.B. Born, *International Commercial Arbitration – Commentary and Materials* (3rd edn, The Hague, Kluwer Law International, forthcoming), ch. 16.

The discussions by UNCITRAL concerning unilateral interim measures of arbitral **22-036** tribunals also informed the debate in the ZPO Working Group.[81] The Working Group aimed at ensuring legal protection in arbitration that is functionally equivalent to the legal protection in state court litigation. However, it was also said that the authorization of arbitral tribunals to execute *ex parte* interim measures may cause intricate problems concerning subsequent regulations. For example, an order to give the respondent the opportunity of being heard subsequently (that is, after the order of interim measures), an objection might be granted to the respondent, either before the tribunal or the enforcement courts. However, it was said that the result would be a complex 'side by side' of objection suits in front of the arbitral tribunal and execution proceedings in front of the state courts. Finally, it was doubted whether need for genuine *ex parte* interim relief in arbitration was real, when parties always had, and still retain, recourse to the state court for urgent measures of protection.[82]

Against this background, the Working Group and ultimately the Austrian legisla- **22-037** ture decided against *ex parte* measures in arbitration.[83] Thus, unlike Section 1041(1) German ZPO, Section 593(1) ZPO expressly requires that arbitrators can issue an order of interim relief only 'after having heard [the] other party'. Although the text of Section 593(1) ZPO does not immediately suggest this ('unless the parties agree otherwise'), party autonomy does not extend to this aspect of interim relief: The prohibition on *ex parte* measures is supposed to be mandatory,[84] and the legislature ensured that interim relief granted on an *ex parte* basis by a tribunal would not be enforceable through Austrian state courts. Thus, Section 593(4) ZPO prevents the enforcement of interim measures if the order of the tribunal suffers from a defect which in the case of an award would represent a reason for setting aside under Section 611(2) ZPO (or in the case of foreign award would entitle the Austrian courts to refuse enforcement). As regards *ex parte* measures of interim relief, this provision therefore prevents enforcement of the interim measure if the party subjected to the measure has been denied the opportunity to be heard.

4.   As Between the Parties

It is axiomatic in international arbitration that awards are binding only as between **22-038** the parties of the arbitration agreement.[85] This must hold true for interim orders as

---

81.   P. Oberhammer, *Entwurf eines neuen Schiedsverfahrensrechts* (Vienna, Manz, 2002), pp. 83 *et seq.*
82.   *See* **Article 22**, at paras. 122 *et seq.* and the discussion of Section 585 ZPO.
83.   For a more detailed discussion, *see* **Article 22**, at paras. 032 *et seq.*
84.   Explanatory Notes to Section 593 ZPO.
85.   G.B. Born, *International Commercial Arbitration – Commentary and Materials* (2nd edn, The Hague, Kluwer Law International, 2001), p. 925; K. Hempel, 'Einstweiliger Rechtsschutz durch Schiedsgerichte – Cui Bono?' in *Festschrift Rudolf Welser zum 65. Geburtstag*, C. Fischer-Czermak, A. Kletecka, M. Schauer and W. Zankl (eds) (Vienna, Manz, 2004), p. 273.

well. Recognizing that principle, Article 14a(1) of the Vienna Rules 2001[86] provided expressly with respect to interim relief that 'only the parties are bound by such measures'. In practice, this is an important limitation that may impair the effectiveness of interim relief granted by arbitrators; state courts may be able to grant further-reaching relief that affect third parties as well.

22-039   Article 22 does no longer contain such an express language, but it is clear from the text of this provision that any interim measure can typically only be directed at the parties to the arbitration. As a matter of course, the tribunal assumes jurisdiction only from, and within the scope of, the arbitration agreement, and on the terms of the mandate put before it, so that it has no power to address itself to third parties in any binding manner.

5.   Security

22-040   Article 22 and Section 593(1) ZPO also entitle arbitrators to 'require any party to provide appropriate security in connection with such measure'. The obvious purpose of this provision is to protect the interests of the party that is subjected to interim measures. Any security ordered should therefore not exceed the potential damages caused to that party if, at a later stage, the interim measures are found to be unjustified.[87]

6.   Contractual Obligation to Comply

22-041   Article 22 goes further than Section 593(1) ZPO in establishing that '[t]he parties are obliged to comply with such orders [of interim relief], whether or not they are enforceable by State courts'. Similar wording was already contained in Article 14a of the Vienna Rules 2001.[88] Then, the drafters of the Vienna Rules had some difficult tensions to resolve in light of the resistance of Austrian doctrine against interim relief in arbitration. While having to recognize that Austrian courts would most likely follow the majority position in academic writing and deny arbitrators the power to grant interim measures, the drafters sought to bring the Vienna Rules in line with international practice and other institutional rules. The drafters assumed, quite correctly, that rules that lacked a provision entitling arbitrators to issue interim orders would be at a competitive disadvantage compared to rules that did contain such provisions.

22-042   Although the immediate enforceability of interim measures ordered by tribunals in the Austrian state courts is now ensured by Section 593(3) ZPO[89], this approach still makes sense. After all, interim measures ordered by tribunals under the Vienna Rules may be enforced in countries that do not recognize as

---

86.   Vienna Rules 2001, **Annex 2a**.
87.   J. Lew, L. Mistelis and S. Kröll, *Comparative International Commercial Arbitration* (The Hague, Kluwer Law International, 2003), para. 23-80.
88.   Vienna Rules 2001, **Annex 2a**.
89.   *See* **Article 22**, at paras. 131 *et seq.*

such, or only under more limited circumstances, the enforceability of such relief. For such cases, the provison that '[t]he parties are obliged to comply with such [interim] orders, whether or not they are enforceable by state courts' establishes (or confirms) a contractual obligation of the party subjected to an order of interim protection to comply. Like any contractual obligation (in this case incorporated by reference to the Vienna Rules into the parties' agreement to arbitrate) it gives rise to a claim for performance, or, alternatively, damages arising from the procrastinated execution or non-execution of the order, as well as an order of costs.

In addition, the possibility of the tribunal drawing negative inference from a party's **22-043** refusal to comply will often be sufficient to ensure that the latter follows voluntarily with the order. First, arbitrators are not prevented from setting forth certain consequences attaching to the parties' failure to voluntarily comply with the interim order, such as punitive payments for parties that refuse to follow the tribunal's payments.[90] According to *Rechberger/Melis*:

> Some Arbitration Rules of institutional arbitration courts as well as the UNCITRAL Rules provide the Tribunal with the power to order preliminary or protective measures. Since such orders are not enforceable in Austria, the Tribunal may provide in their award for the consequences of non-compliance with their orders.[91]

Such provisions could include damages. It is argued that the tribunal retains juris- **22-044** diction to determine any claim of damages by the party against whom unjustified measures were ordered.[92] Indeed, resolving non-compliance through an award of (perhaps liquidated) damages may be particularly appropriate under the Vienna Rules, because interim orders are, as discussed, construed as contractual obligations of the parties. Although it may be difficult, in practice, for arbitrators to order consequences that are effectively supporting the interim relief order,[93] creative

---

90. W.H. Rechberger and W. Melis in *Kommentar zur ZPO*, W.H. Rechberger (ed.) (2nd edn, Vienna/New York, Springer, 2000), Section 577 ZPO, para. 14; G. Zeiler, *Schiedsverfahren* (Vienna/Graz, Neuer Wissenschaftlicher Verlag, 2006), Section 593, p. 184 with further reference to German doctrine.

91. W.H. Rechberger and W. Melis in *Kommentar zur ZPO*, W.H. Rechberger (ed.) (2nd edn, Vienna/New York, Springer, 2000), Section 577 ZPO, para. 14. *See also Karrer* who considers that '[p]arties may include penalty clauses, they presumably do this for legitimate reasons, and penalty clauses are normally enforced in international commercial arbitration'. *See* P. Karrer, 'Interim Measures Issued by Arbitral Tribunals and the Courts: Less Theory, Please' (2000) 10 ICCA Congress Series (New Delhi), 97, 98.

92. J. Lew, L. Mistelis and S. Kröll, *Comparative International Commercial Arbitration* (The Hague, Kluwer Law International, 2003), para. 23-80; for more detail, *see* **Article 22**, at para. 138.

93. If, for example, the tribunal orders a freeze of certain assets, and the addressee party of that order nevertheless transfers its assets to another entity, an additional claim for damages may be of little value to the aggrieved party.

arbitrators may choose such consequences in their interim orders that provide an effective deterrent for potentially non-compliant parties.

22-045 Finally, through their judicial function, arbitrators enjoy a natural authority. If they issue an order, the parties are well advised to comply with this order whether it is enforceable or not. Sophisticated parties will understand that, if they refuse to follow the tribunal's instructions, their credibility will suffer.[94] In addition, they may incur additional costs.[95] Arbitrators can reinforce their natural authority by monitoring compliance with their orders, and by issuing reminders to disobedient parties.[96] If nothing helps, arbitrators may draw adverse inferences from a party's non-compliance with the tribunal's interim order, if so appropriate under the circumstances; or they may take a party's non-compliance into account when assessing the damages and/ or allocating the costs of the arbitration in their final award. However, some commentators argue that adverse inferences should be strictly limited to questions of proof: The arbitral tribunal should be only allowed to draw adverse inference in case of failure to preserve evidence against its order, or from the failure to produce evidence available to a party, and not in case of other forms of non-cooperation.[97]

D.   SUBSTANTIVE PRECONDITIONS FOR INTERIM RELIEF

22-046 Interim measures are a recognized instrument in state court litigation in all developed jurisdictions. Their primary purpose appears to be to preserve the *status quo* and protect the rights of a party pending the final outcome of the dispute.

22-047 In the United Kingdom, for example, an interim injunction is defined as 'a court order prohibiting a person from doing something or requiring a person to do something',[98] being 'a provisional remedy to preserve the subject matter of controversy pending trial'.[99] Thus, an injunction will

> apply only until the final hearing or final determination by the court of the rights of the parties; and accordingly it issues in a form that requires that, in the

---

94. K. Hempel, 'Einstweiliger Rechtsschutz durch Schiedsgerichte – Cui Bono?' in *Festschrift Rudolf Welser zum 65. Geburtstag*, C. Fischer-Czermak, A. Kletecka, M. Schauer and W. Zankl (eds) (Vienna, Manz, 2004), p. 276.

95. For example, Article 21(4) AAA/ICDR Rules provides that '[t]he tribunal may in its discretion apportion costs associated with applications for interim relief in any interim award or in the final award'.

96. J. Lew, 'Commentary on Interim and Conservatory Measures in ICC Arbitration Cases' (2000) 11(1) ICC Ct Bull, 28.

97. *See* P. Karrer, 'Interim Measures Issued by Arbitral Tribunals and the Courts: Less Theory, Please' (2000) 10 ICCA Congress Series (New Delhi), 97, 103.

98. White Book 2004, Civil Procedure Vol 1, Lord Justice Brooke (ed.) (London, Sweet & Maxwell, 2004), Section A, CPR 25.1.9 and Glossary, G1.1.

99. H.C. Black, *Black's Law Dictionary* (6th edn, St. Paul, West Publishing Co, 1990), definition of 'injunction', temporary injunction.

absence of a subsequent order to the contrary, it should continue up to but not beyond the final hearing of the proceedings. The two matters with which the court is concerned in granting an injunction of this kind are, first the maintenance of a position that will most easily enable justice to be done when its final order is made, and secondly, an interim regulation of the acts of the parties that is, in other respects, the most just and convenient in all the circumstances.[100]

In the United States, courts may issue so-called preliminary injunctions[101] to **22-048** preserve the *status quo* prior to the trial[102] and to protect the plaintiff against untoward harm while the proceedings are going forward.[103] German law recognizes on the one hand measures aiming at the protection of monetary claims (*Arrest*, Section 916 German ZPO) and on the other hand *both* security measures (*Sicherungsverfügung*, Section 935 German ZPO, protecting one party's substantive claim) and injunctive measures (*Regelungsverfügung*, Section 940 German ZPO, provisionally regulating a legal relationship). Similarly, in Austria, relief can consist of security measures (Sections 379 and 381 no. 1 EO) and injunctive measures (Section 381 no. 2 EO). Interim measures are also an established instrument of EU law,[104] as set out, *inter alia*, in Articles 278 (ex-Article 242), 279 (ex-Article 243) and 299 (ex-Article 256) EC Treaty, which preserve the *status quo* during the pending trial.[105]

National laws, it appears, regularly spell out the circumstances that must exist and **22-049** the prerequisites that must be met before the courts can grant interim or conservatory measures. In international arbitration, however, no clear guidelines appear to exist as to the types of relief available or under which circumstances they should be granted.[106] As a recent ICC Report on interim measures summarizes:

> Arbitration practice has moved a long way in recent years. It is now beyond question that arbitrators have the power to grant interim and conservatory

---

100. I.C.F. Spry, *The Principles of Equitable Remedies* (6th edn, LBC Information Services, 2001), p. 446.

101. Federal Civil Judicial Procedure and Rules, 2004 Edition, Rules of Civil Procedure, Rule 65, Advisory Committee Notes, 1937 Adoption, Note to Subdivisions (a) and (b).

102. *See* <http://definitions.uslegal.com/p/preliminary-injunction>, definition of 'preliminary injunction'.

103. M. Rosenberg, J.B. Weinstein, H. Smit and L. Korn, *Elements of Civil Procedure Cases and Materials* (3rd edn, Mineola, Foundation Press, 1976), p. 168.

104. G.C. Rodriguez Iglesias, 'Der EuGH und die Gerichte der Mitgliedsstaaten – Komponenten der richterlichen Gewalt in der Europäischen Union' [2000] NJW, 1889, 1893.

105. H. Krück in *Kommentar zum EU-/EG-Vertrag, IV*, H. Gröben, J. Thiesing and C.-D. Ehlermann (eds) (5th edn, Baden-Baden, Nomos-Verlag, 1997), Articles 135, 186 para. 2; *see also* ECJ, 18 November 1998, *Van Uden Maritime BV, Trading as Van Uden Africa Line v. Kommanditgesellschaft in Firma Deco-Line*, Case No. 391/95, [1998] ECR I 07091, para. 37.

106. J. Lew, 'Commentary on Interim and Conservatory Measures in ICC Arbitration Cases' (2000) 11(1) ICC Ct Bull, 23, 26.

measures. The only question is the circumstances in which arbitrators should issue such measures.[107]

22-050 Conceptually, arbitrators can choose one of two alternative legal standards. First, unless the parties have agreed otherwise, arbitrators can either make use of the law applicable to the arbitration (or another national law they deem applicable).[108] In Germany, for example, some commentators advocate that arbitrators should apply the standards set by civil procedure for interim applications before the state courts.[109] Second, arbitrators can approach the issue of interim relief without reference to any applicable law, literally relying on any practical standards they deem appropriate – and many institutional rules encourage them to do so.[110] It has been argued that the first approach – for the arbitrators to rely on a national law – is safer (presumably because national laws provide well-established, reliable regimes for interim measures) but yet less preferable, because the inevitable diversity in requests for interim measures necessarily results in perhaps arbitrary reliance on various national laws, and hence, in inconsistency.[111] The second approach – determining the issue of whether to grant relief without reference to any national law – would appear to be more common, evidencing the growing trend of harmonization of standards in international arbitration.[112]

22-051 In Austria, the Working Group considered it inappropriate to attempt a general statutory definition of interim measures in arbitration, for fear that any such attempt could be misused to argue *e contrario* that, what the law does not expressly allow, arbitrators cannot order.[113] Yet the Austrian legislature, and subsequently the drafters of the Vienna Rules, provide a number of substantive principles that would guide the arbitrators in determining whether or not to grant interim relief. These principles are discussed below; with some additional factors for arbitrators to consider as a matter of practice in order to determine whether or not interim measures are appropriate.[114]

---

107. J. Lew, 'Commentary on Interim and Conservatory Measures in ICC Arbitration Cases' (2000) 11(1) ICC Ct Bull, 23, 30.
108. In practice, it seems that arbitrators may only grant provisional relief once they are satisfied that the national arbitration law applicable to the arbitration proceedings, the *lex arbitri* and, sometimes, the law of the enforcement jurisdiction allow them to do so. *See* G.B. Born, *International Commercial Arbitration – Commentary and Materials* (2nd edn, The Hague, Kluwer Law International, 2001), p. 922.
109. R. A. Schütze, *Schiedsgericht und Schiedsverfahren* (4th edn, Munich, Beck, 2007), para. 257.
110. *See, e.g.*, Article 23 ICC Rules. Article 14a(1) Vienna Rules 2001 also did not provide specific criteria that arbitrators needed to apply; rather, it simply conferred upon the arbitrators the power to order those interim measures that they '*consider[ed] to be appropriate*'. **Annex 2a**.
111. J. Lew, 'Commentary on Interim and Conservatory Measures in ICC Arbitration Cases' (2000) 11(1) ICC Ct Bull, 23, 26, 27.
112. J. Lew, 'Commentary on Interim and Conservatory Measures in ICC Arbitration Cases' (2000) 11(1) ICC Ct Bull 23, 26, 27.
113. P. Oberhammer, *Entwurf eines neuen Schiedsverfahrensrechts* (Vienna, Manz, 2002), p. 82.
114. *See, e.g.*, the requirements in the United States of 'a clear showing by party seeking the extraordinary remedy of probable success upon a trial on the merits, likely irreparable injury

| 1. | **Necessary Relief with Respect to the Subject Matter of the Arbitration** |

Section 593(1) ZPO and Article 22 give the arbitrators authority to 'order such **22-052** interim measures of protection against another party as the arbitral tribunal may consider *necessary in connection with the subject-matter of the dispute*'. Compared to, for example, Article 14a of the Vienna Rules 2001, which simply authorized arbitrators to '*order the interim measures of protection that [they] consider to be appropriate*',[115] Article 22 and Section 593(1) ZPO seem to limit the arbitrators' power in at least two important respects.

First, arbitrators cannot order simply what they deem is 'appropriate', but only **22-053** what is 'necessary'. As a matter of discretion, this appears to be a narrower term.[116] When arbitrators are allowed to order 'appropriate' interim relief, the arbitrators' discretion as to the kind of interim relief they are permitted to grant, or what prerequisites an application for interim measures must meet in order to be granted, is far-reaching. By contrast, the use of the term 'necessary' indicates, at least more expressly, an element of proportionality that must guide the arbitrators' decision. Only what is necessary (in other words: not more than is necessary) to achieve the purpose of interim relief, should be ordered.

Further, Section 593(1) ZPO and Article 22 restrict arbitrators to order interim **22-054** measures that they deem necessary 'in respect of the subject-matter of the dispute'. This follows the examples of Article 26 UNCITRAL Rules[117] and Section 1041(1) German ZPO, but falls behind what the Working Group had originally proposed. Indeed, the Working Group did not want to limit the arbitrators' power to grant interim measures with regard to the 'subject-matter of the litigation', but proposed specifically to extend it to issues which are related to the subject-matter of the litigation or the proceeding, but which are not subject-matter of the litigation in a technical sense.[118] The Working Group felt that arbitrators should, in principle, enjoy some flexibility to also order such measures that do not concern the subject-matter of the dispute as such, but that are relevant and necessary to protect the

---

to him unless the injunction is granted, or if his showing of probable success is limited but he raised substantial and difficult issues meriting further inquiry, that the harm to him overweighs the injury to others if it is denied which have influenced arbitral practice significantly'. *See* H.C. Black, *Black's Law Dictionary* (6th edn, St. Paul, West Publishing Co, 1990).

115. Vienna Rules 2001, **Annex 2a**; *see also* Article 9 ICC Rules: '(..) the Arbitral Tribunal may, at the request of a party, order any interim or conservatory measure it deems appropriate.'
116. *See also* Article 20(1) DIS Rules, which provides that: 'Unless otherwise agreed by the parties, the arbitral tribunal may, at the request of a party, order any interim measure of protection as the arbitral tribunal may consider necessary in respect of the subject-matter of the dispute.'
117. *See also* Article 20(1) DIS Rules, which provides that: 'Unless otherwise agreed by the parties, the arbitral tribunal may, at the request of a party, order any interim measure of protection as the arbitral tribunal may consider necessary in respect of the subject-matter of the dispute.'
118. P. Oberhammer in *Das neue Schiedsrecht – Schiedsrechts-Änderungsgesetz 2006*, B. Kloiber, P. Oberhammer, W.H. Rechberger and H. Haller (eds) (Vienna, Manz, 2006), p. 245.

integrity and efficiency of the arbitral process and the enforceability of a final award.[119]

22-055 Yet this should still be possible even where the law allows interim relief only '*in respect of the subject-matter of the dispute*'. On the one hand, the arbitrator's power to grant interim measures is limited and defined by the scope of the underlying arbitration agreement.[120] The arbitrators' jurisdiction to resolve the parties' dispute is ultimately defined by the arbitration agreement, which ought to limit also what arbitrators can order in terms of interim relief.[121] Conversely, if there is no valid arbitration agreement and the arbitrators therefore lack jurisdiction to hear the parties' case, they also lack jurisdiction to order interim relief. Indeed, interim measures based on a decision that exceeds the arbitrators' jurisdiction are not enforceable.[122]

22-056 On the other hand, the arbitrators are also limited jurisdictionally by the specific mandate they receive. Even if covered by the arbitration agreement, the arbitrators cannot order relief that exceeds their mandate as defined by the parties' requests, or else risk deciding *ultra petita*. Arguably, therefore, protective measures not issued 'in respect of' the subject-matter of the dispute fall outside the arbitrators' jurisdiction to grant interim relief.[123] In some way, this is stating the obvious: the arbitrators' power to grant interim relief cannot exceed their general subject-matter jurisdiction.

22-057 However, it would be equally inappropriate, and ultimately frustrate the purpose of interim relief in arbitration, if the substantive requirement that interim relief is ordered '*in respect of the subject-matter of the dispute*' be read to unduly limit the arbitrators' authority. Rather, any interim relief that preserves or protects the tribunal's remedial power with respect to the merits of the case is still '*in respect of the subject-matter of the dispute*'. Thus, interim relief aimed at protecting the *status quo* pending a final award; at protecting the taking of evidence; at providing security for the costs of the respondent; or at requiring or prohibiting a specific conduct from or by one of the parties,[124] is still permissible in order to preserve the

---

119. P. Oberhammer, *Entwurf eines neuen Schiedsverfahrensrechts* (Vienna, Manz, 2002), p. 82.

120. *See* **Article 22**, at para. 039.

121. *See* I. Goldrein, *Commercial Litigation: Pre-Emptive Remedies* (4th edn, London, Sweet & Maxwell, 2003), A1-017, which explains that an interim injunction is not itself a cause of action but 'ancillary to a substantive cause of action'.

122. *See* **Article 22**, at paras. 145 *et seq.*

123. J. Lew, L. Mistelis and S. Kröll, *Comparative International Commercial Arbitration* (The Hague, Kluwer Law International, 2003), para. 23-26. *See also* Article 25(1) LCIA Rules, which, at the outset, limits the arbitrators' power to grant interim relief even further by specifying in some detail to certain categories of interim relief. In the final paragraph of the provision, arbitrators are given the broader power to 'order on a provisional basis, subject to final determination in an award, any relief which the Arbitral Tribunal would have power to grant in an award'.

124. For a detailed discussion of various categories of interim relief in arbitration, *see* **Article 22**, at paras. 083 *et seq.*

tribunal's authority to effectively grant relief on the merits, and is hence ordered, 'in respect to the subject-matter of the dispute'.

This reading is supported, as a textual matter, by Section 593(1) ZPO itself which **22-058** clarifies that relief is necessary if 'otherwise the enforcement of the claim would be frustrated or considerably impeded'. As discussed in more detail further below, interim relief therefore appears to aim at ensuring the *effective* enforcement of a future (final) award. In that regard, the arbitrators' jurisdiction to grant interim relief is a necessary corollary to their general subject-matter jurisdiction to finally resolve the parties' dispute – and measures preserving that subject-matter juris-diction and the tribunal's authority to grant effective relief of the merits are within the ambit of Section 593(1) ZPO and Article 22.

The Working Group had also proposed to include the clarification in Section **22-059** 593(1) ZPO that 'the power of the arbitral tribunal referred to in the 5th subchapter of this chapter shall remain unaffected'. This referred to the arbitrators' power to conduct the arbitration proceedings freely and at their discretion, subject of course, to due process considerations.[125] There is indeed some potential overlap between the power to order interim measures and the power to determine the procedural aspects of the arbitration in particular with respect to the taking of evidence, which may be relevant in the context of enforcing such orders and/or seeking the assis-tance of the Austrian courts in support of arbitration.[126] Although not included in the wording of Section 593(1) ZPO as eventually adopted, it is clear that the arbitrators' general discretion to conduct the proceedings remains unaffected.[127]

2. Frustration of Final Award

As discussed, Section 593(1) ZPO authorizes the arbitrators to issue 'necessary' **22-060** interim relief. But necessary to what end? Section 593(1) ZPO defines the purpose of interim relief in two ways. Relief is necessary if 'otherwise the enforcement of the claim would be frustrated or considerably impeded'. As discussed, this entitles the tribunal to preserve or protect, by way of interim measures, its ultimate reme-dial power with respect to the merits of the case.

Section 593(1) ZPO refers to the 'enforcement of the claim' (that is, the main claim **22-061** on the merits) and makes thereby clear that it is concerned with affording the claimant *effective* relief in a future (final) award, rather than relief on paper that is without use in practice because it has been frustrated in the meantime. Thus, interim relief aims at protecting the *status quo* pending a final award – it seeks to avoid any aggravation of the parties' dispute, and change of the state that may

---

125. *See* the detailed discussion in the context of **Article 20**, at paras. 086 *et seq.*
126. P. Oberhammer, *Entwurf eines neuen Schiedsverfahrensrechts* (Vienna, Manz, 2002), p. 84. A typical example of a potentially hybrid order is an order instructing the parties to produce certain documents in the course of document disclosure.
127. *See* **Article 20**, at paras. 093 *et seq.*

further impede the claimant's rights and thus frustrate the tribunal's remedial authority until the tribunal can decide on the merits.[128] Where assets are dissipated before a final award, an award in the claimant's favour will be of little use.

22-062 Notably, Section 593(1) ZPO and Article 22 do not require that the enforcement of the claim is altogether frustrated (i.e., no longer possible) but for measures of interim relief; rather, it is sufficient that the enforcement of the claim is 'considerably impeded'. This includes any considerable difficulties in the enforcement of the claim *strictu sensu* (e.g. the respondent makes it considerably more difficult for the claimant to access the respondent's assets), but also any considerable difficulties arising from the respondent's conduct in establishing the merits of the claim in the first place. For example, interim relief is appropriate to preserve evidence that is at risk of being corrupted unless the tribunal intervened, if the loss of that evidence would make it considerably more difficult for the tribunal to ascertain the merits of the claim. Again, the ultimate test is whether the interim measure of protection is necessary to preserve the tribunal's remedial authority to effectively grant relief on the merits.

3.   Irreparable Harm

22-063 Section 593(1) ZPO also permits interim measures of relief if 'there is a danger that irreparable damage will occur'. This requirement is an alternative to the risk of frustration to a final award. Thus, the applicant has to show that absent the requested interim measure *either* the enforcement of the final award would be frustrated or considerably impeded *or* there is a risk of irreparable harm.

22-064 The crux of this requirement is that on the literal reading, the harm needs to be 'irreparable'. Where the harm is purely monetary, it is not irreparable but can be remedied through an award of damages. The idea is, therefore, to refuse interim measures unless harm comes to the applicant that cannot be redressed by awarding damages.

22-065 This is a rather strict requirement. International practice seems to prefer a test of adequacy, rather than a test of irreparability. Article 17(3)(a) of the UNCITRAL Model Law, with amendments as adopted in 2006, for example, refers to '[h]arm not *adequately reparable* by an award of damage [which] is likely to result if the measure is not ordered', and in Interim Award in Case No. 8786, an ICC arbitral tribunal[129] stated that 'the Arbitral Tribunal may only order provisional measures if the requesting party has substantiated the threat of *a not easily reparable*

---

128. J. Power, *The Austrian Arbitration Act – A Practitioner's Guide to Sections 577-618 of the Austrian Code of Civil Procedure* (Vienna, Manz, 2006), Section 593, at para. 7; K.H. Schwab and G. Walter (eds), *Schiedsgerichtsbarkeit* (7th edn, Munich, C.H. Beck, 2005), ch. 17a, para. 6.
129. *Interim Award in ICC Case No. 8786 of 1996*, (2000) 11(1) ICC Ct Bull, 81, 83. Of course, an ICC tribunal is authorized to order the interim relief it deems 'appropriate', without being bound by the requirements spelled out in **Article 22**.

prejudice'. It has been observed, therefore, that interim measures are appropriate where the claimant is exposed to damage which would be 'substantial (but not necessarily "irreparable" as known in common law doctrine)'.[130]

It is argued, therefore, that the requirement of 'irreparable' harm should not be **22-066** construed in the literal sense of the word. In commercial reality, arbitrators ought to take into account that some wrongs cannot be sufficiently, adequately or without prohibitive difficulty compensated through damages.[131] In the context of Article 22 and Section 593(1) ZPO, the requirement if 'irreparability' is also somewhat cushioned by the alternative requirement: An applicant may not be able to show that absent the interim measure, the harm will be irreparable in the literal sense (if the requirement were to be read that way) – but it may be more easily able to make a *prima facie* case that not granting the interim measure would 'considerably impede' the enforcement of its claim. This seems to be a less stringent test: A certain action may not cause irreparable harm *strictu sensu*, but may still make considerably more difficult the ultimate enforcement of the claim. Indeed, given the relaxed standard of 'considerable impediment' (rather than outright frustration), a teleological rather than purely textual interpretation of Section 593(1) ZPO could conceivably justify a somewhat relaxed reading of 'irreparable' as well.

4.   No Pre-Judgment of the Case

A tribunal will always wish to leave the parties the opportunity for their full cases **22-067** to be heard. Interim relief, which is often requested at the early stages of an arbitration, presents a particular problem in that respect: arbitrators may be forced to make a decision before having been fully briefed on the merits of the case. Where a party applies for interim relief, arbitrators therefore often face a *prima facie* dilemma:[132]

> Interim and conservatory measures are aimed at protecting parties' rights pending the final resolution of the dispute. Although the major issue is whether such exceptional interim relief is necessary, arbitrators will in some cases need to consider and take a view on part of the substantive dispute. Whilst wishing to protect a situation so the award can be effective and meaningful, they will

---

130. K.P. Berger, *International Economic Arbitration* (Boston, Kluwer Law International, 1993), p. 336; *see also Interim Award in ICC Case No. 8786 of 1996*, (2000) 11(1) ICC Ct Bull, 81; *Interim Award in ICC Case No. 7692 of 1995*, (2000) 11(1) ICC Ct Bull, 62 (referring to 'sufficient likelihood or danger').
131. J. Lew, L. Mistelis and S. Kröll, *Comparative International Commercial Arbitration* (The Hague, Kluwer Law International, 2003), para. 23-65.
132. *See* J. Lew, 'Commentary on Interim and Conservatory Measures in ICC Arbitration Cases' (2000) 11(1) ICC Ct Bull, 23, 25.

also be reluctant to show their thinking in advance of when all the evidence and argument has not been considered.[133]

22-068 Although not expressly mentioned in Section 593(1) ZPO or Article 22, it is therefore generally accepted that an interim injunction should 'regulate the position of the parties pending trial whilst avoiding a decision on issues which could only be resolved at trial'.[134] In dealing with a request for an interim measure, therefore, an arbitral tribunal must, like a state court, refrain from pre-judging the merits of the case.[135] Accordingly, an arbitral tribunal will be hesitant to grant an interim measure where the request essentially covers what it is asked to resolve in the substantive arbitration. The underlying principle is that if relief is sought on both an interim and a permanent basis, only the latter will, in principle, be granted.[136]

| 5. | ***Prima Facie* Establishment of the Applicant's Case** |

22-069 Understandably, it is often considered unfair that a party which ultimately loses the principle case should be able to obtain interim relief, potentially inflicting harm on the eventually winning party. It is argued, therefore, that arbitrators should look at whether the applicant for the interim measure has established a *prima facie* case,[137] although the threshold for meeting this *prima facie* requirement should not be set too highly.[138] As discussed above, arbitrators are well advised not to make an interim order that prejudges the principle case; nor will they wish to make any determination with regard to the parties' dispute without having had the full opportunity to hear the evidence and consider the parties' arguments. Hence, rather than require the applicant to affirmatively establish his case, arbitrators may wish to

---

133. *See* J. Lew, 'Commentary on Interim and Conservatory Measures in ICC Arbitration Cases' (2000) 11(1) ICC Ct Bull, 23, 25.

134. I. Goldrein, *Commercial Litigation: Pre-Emptive Remedies* (4th edn, London, Sweet & Maxwell, 2003), A1-003.

135. A. Baumbach, W. Lauterbach, J. Albers and P. Hartmann (eds) *Zivilprozessordnung*, (66th edn, Munich, C.H. Beck, 2008), Introduction to Section 916 para. 5; *see also* Article 17A UNCITRAL Model Law '(1) The party requesting an interim measure under Article 17(2)(a), (b) and (c) shall satisfy the arbitral tribunal that: (a) (. . .); and (b) There is a reasonable possibility that the requesting party will succeed on the merits of the claim. The determination on this possibility shall not affect the discretion of the arbitral tribunal in making any subsequent determination.'

136. *See Partial Award in ICC Case No. 8113 of 1995*, (2000) XXV YB Comm Arb 324; Iran-US Claims Tribunal, 22 February 1985, *Behring International, Inc. v. Iranian Air Force*, (1985) 8 Iran-US CTR, 44; Iran-US Claims Tribunal, 10 December 1986, *United Technologies International, Inc. v. Iran*, (1986) 13 Iran-US CTR, 254; *see also* J.J. van Hof, *Commentary on the UNCITRAL Arbitration Rules – The application by the Iran-U.S. Tribunal* (The Hague, Kluwer Law International, 1991), pp. 179 *et seq.*

137. *Award in NAI Case No. 2212*, 28 July 1999, (2001) XXVI YB Comm Arb, 198, 204 *et seq.*

138. *See also* J. Lew, L. Mistelis and S. Kröll, *Comparative International Commercial Arbitration* (The Hague, Kluwer Law International, 2003), para. 23-62.

look at the question from the other end, determining whether 'it is clear that the underlying claim is not groundless on the merits'.[139]

6. Urgency

The need for 'urgent' or 'prompt' relief is also frequently identified as one of **22-070** the criteria relevant to the exercise of a tribunal's discretion to grant provisional measures. In principle, if a party can await the final resolution of a dispute, logically there is no reason to grant the interim measure requested, provided no irreparable damage will be caused to the property and the rights of the parties can ultimately be upheld by a damages award.[140]

Although urgency is no express requirement of Section 593(1) ZPO or Article 22, it **22-071** is implied. Where the frustration of the claim is speculative, and no real, actual or impending 'danger' of harm can be shown, the request for interim measures lacks urgency in that the requesting party's position does not seem to require immediate protection. A request that is not urgent is therefore not 'necessary' within the meaning of Section 593(1) ZPO or Article 22.

7. Balancing the Parties' Interests

It is also argued that arbitrators should grant interim relief only exceptionally, **22-072** under limited and restricted circumstances. It is feared that interim measures may unduly prejudge the principal dispute; may inflict harm on the party that is subjected to such measures that is difficult or impossible to repair; and may be used as strategic, dilatory or obstructive tools by parties seeking to disrupt the arbitral process.[141]

Given the consensual nature and the flexibility arbitrators enjoy in granting interim **22-073** measures of protection, it is therefore often argued that arbitrators should 'undertake a balancing of the interests with respect of the requested relief'.[142] In effect, interim measures shift risks associated with the dispute from the party applying for such measures to the other side for the duration of the principal proceedings.[143] It has been suggested that the 'possible injury caused by the requested interim

---

139. *Interim Award in NAI Case No. 1694*, 12 December 1996, (1998) XXIII YB Comm Arb, 97.
140. *Interim Award in NAI Case No. 1694*, 12 December 1996, (1998) XXIII YB Comm Arb, 97; M. Wirth, 'Interim or Preventive Measures in Support of International Arbitration in Switzerland' (2000) 18(1) Bull ASA, 31, 37 (referring to 'reasonable probability' of 'impending injury').
141. J. Lew, L. Mistelis and S. Kröll, *Comparative International Commercial Arbitration* (The Hague, Kluwer Law International, 2003), para. 23-24; *see also* K.P. Berger, *International Economic Arbitration* (Boston, Kluwer Law International, 1993), p. 336.
142. *Interim Award in NAI Case No. 1694*, 12 December 1996, (1998) XXIII YB Comm Arb, 97.
143. J. Lew, L. Mistelis and S. Kröll, *Comparative International Commercial Arbitration* (The Hague, Kluwer Law International, 2003), para. 23-2.

measure must not be out of proportion with the advantage which the claimant hopes to derive from it'.[144] Similarly, Article 17A UNCITRAL Model Law, with amendments as adopted in 2006, provides that '[t]he party requesting the interim measure (. . .) shall satisfy the arbitral tribunal that: (a) Harm not adequately reparable by an award of damages is likely to result if the measure is not ordered, and such harm substantially outweighs the harm that is likely to result to the party against whom the measure is directed if the measure is granted'. Although not expressly mentioned in Section 593(1) ZPO or Article 22, the arbitrators can balance the parties' interests in their decision.[145] Where necessary to do so, they can also order the requesting party to post security for any damage that is feared to arise to the other side from the interim measure.[146]

8.   Standard of Proof

22-074   There is some doubt as to what standard of proof arbitrators should apply to an application for interim relief. Obviously, arbitrators will be disinclined to grant interim relief based on nothing more than unsupported allegations. Indeed, the higher the stakes; the more drastic the potential impact of the proposed interim measures; and the more uncertain the success of the applicant in the principal case, the more will arbitrators expect in terms of evidence.

22-075   As a principle, however, and not unlike state court proceedings, the tribunal will at least expect *prima facie* evidence supporting the request for an order of interim measures.[147]

9.   Interim Relief Despite Jurisdictional Objection

22-076   Interim relief applications are often made in arbitration in which the tribunal's jurisdiction is contested. In such cases, the respondent, who denies that the tribunal has jurisdiction to hear the claim, will often argue that the tribunal also lacks jurisdiction to order interim relief. Indeed, the tribunal's power to make any disposition binding on the parties depends on its jurisdiction under the parties' arbitration agreement.

---

144.   K.P. Berger, *International Economic Arbitration* (Boston, Kluwer Law International, 1993), p. 337.
145.   *See also* G. Zeiler, *Schiedsverfahren* (Vienna/Graz, Neuer Wissenschaftlicher Verlag, 2006), Section 593, p. 184.
146.   *See* **Article 22**, at para. 040.
147.   *See* P. Angst, W. Jakusch and F. Mohr, *EO-Exekutionsordnung*, (14th edn, Vienna, Manz, 2004), Section 389, item 54. *See also Interim Award in ICC Case No. 8786 of 1996*, (2000) 11(1) ICC Ct Bull, 81, 83 *et seq.* where the tribunal concluded that 'the defendant has failed to sufficiently substantiate with *prima facie* evidence that any delay in the adjudication of the main claim would lead to a not easily reparable prejudice and that provisional protective measures in the present arbitration are therefore urgently needed'.

However, the uncertainty regarding the tribunal's jurisdictional authority must be **22-077** weighed against the urgency underlying the request for interim measures seeking to prevent irreparable harm or the frustration of the claim. On balance, it is therefore accepted that an arbitral tribunal has the power to order provisional relief notwithstanding the existence of a jurisdictional objection on the part of the party against whom such relief is sought, at least if there is a *prima facie* showing of jurisdiction.[148] Similarly, an arbitral tribunal has the power to require that a party, who disputes jurisdiction, complies with its procedural and disclosure orders under **Article 20**.

This result is consistent with the principle of *Kompetenz-Kompetenz* as specifically **22-078** adopted by the Vienna Rules[149] and Austrian law.[150] Even if the respondent challenges the existence or validity of the parties' agreement to arbitrate, the tribunal has the power to rule on its own jurisdiction. Until it makes such a ruling, it has the ancillary power to preserve its mandate and ensure the enforceability of the claim on the merits.

10.   Deviating from the Substantive Requirements of Section 593(1) ZPO and Article 22

Section 593(1) ZPO provides that '[u]nless otherwise agreed by the parties, the **22-079** arbitral tribunal may (. . .) order (. . .) provisional or protective measures against

---

148. ICJ, 10 May 1984, Order in Military and Paramilitary Activities in and against Nicaragua, *Nicaragua v. United States*, (1984) ICJ Reports 169, 179: 'On a request for provisional measures, the Court need not, before deciding whether or not to indicate them, finally satisfy itself that it has jurisdiction on the merits of the case, or, as the case may be, that an objection taken to jurisdiction is well-founded, yet it ought not to indicate such measures unless the provisions invoked by the Applicant appear, *prima facie*, to afford a basis on which the jurisdiction of the Court might be founded'. *Award of Iran-United States Claims Tribunal*, 7 June 1984, *Bendone-Derossi Int'l v. Iislamic Rebulic of Iran, Award No. ITM 40-375-1*, (1984) 6 Iran-US CTR, 130, 131-33, declining to order provisional measure because 'the Tribunal is not at present satisfied that it appears, prima facie, that there exists a basis on which it can exercise jurisdiction'. *Award of Iran-United States Claims Tribunal*, 11 November 1985, *The United States of America, on behalf of and and for the benefit of Tadjer-Cohen Assoc. v. Islamic Republic of Iran, Award No. ITM 52-12118-3*, (1985) 9 Iran-US CTR, 302-304-5: 'The Tribunal is satisfied that there is at least a prima facie showing that it has jurisdiction over the substantive claim pending before it. Such preliminary determination is, however, without prejudice to the Tribunal's final decision on jurisdiction (. . .).'; D. Caron, L. Caplan and M. Pellonpaa, *The UNCITRAL Arbitration Rules: A Commentary* (Oxford, OUP, 2006), pp. 536-37 ('although the tribunal may not order interim measures in the absence of jurisdiction over the merits of the case, considerations of urgency dictate that a prima facie showing of jurisdiction is sufficient at the stage that interim measures are requested').
149. *See* **Article 19(2)**: 'The sole arbitrator (arbitral tribunal) shall rule on its own jurisdiction. The ruling can be made together with the ruling on the case or by separate arbitral award.'.
150. Section 592(1) ZPO: 'The arbitral tribunal shall rule on its own jurisdiction. The decision may be made together with the decision on the merits or by separate arbitral award.

another party'. It is evident that the parties can by agreement exclude the arbitrators' power to order interim measures of protection.[151] Perhaps less evidently, Section 593(1) ZPO should also entitle the parties to deviate by agreement from the requirements for interim relief spelled out in that provision.[152] For example, parties are still free to give the arbitrators wider discretion to order any interim relief that the arbitrators deem appropriate, rather than only interim relief that is necessary to prevent the frustration of the claim or irreparable harm. Parties can also limit the arbitrators' authority to grant interim relief, either by specifying particular requirements or by excluding certain categories of interim measures.[153]

22-080 Similarly, the parties can exclude or modify the arbitrators' authority to order interim measures within the framework of the Vienna Rules. Any such agreement would generally not give rise to the sanction of **Article 9(6)**,[154] except if it were incompatible with the institutional structure of the VIAC.[155]

| 11. | **Modifying and Terminating Interim Measures** |

22-081 Although a decision on an interim measure, once issued by the arbitral tribunal, cannot, in principle, be appealed as such, the tribunal has the power to revise or revoke its previous decision on interim measures where the circumstances under which the measure was granted have changed.[156] As discussed further below, this is now expressly recognized in Austria in Section 593(6) no. 2 ZPO which provides that, upon application, the Austrian courts will no longer enforce an arbitral interim measure where the tribunal has modified the interim measure it had originally ordered, or where it has repealed it altogether.

22-082 Arbitral tribunals are in principle under an obligation to set aside an interim measure ordered during the arbitration, once the arbitration is terminated under Section 608 ZPO (or at least once the award has been enforced).[157] Indeed, this obligation survives the termination of the arbitrators' mandate and applies to tribunals that are otherwise *functus officio*; according to the express terms of Section 608(3) ZPO, '[t]he mandate of the arbitral tribunal terminates with the

---

151. See **Article 22**, at para. 027.
152. See also A. Reiner, *Das neue österreichische Schiedsrecht/The new Austrian Arbitration Law* (Vienna, LexisNexis, 2006), Section 593, note 100.
153. J. Power, *The Austrian Arbitration Act – A Practitioner's Guide to Sections 577-618 of the Austrian Code of Civil Procedure* (Vienna, Manz, 2006), Section 593, para. 3.
154. See **Article 9**, at paras. 088 *et seq.*
155. It would be doubtful, *e.g.*, if the parties could delegate the power to order interim measures to the VIAC Board or the Secretary General who could hardly be forced to accept that function.
156. J. Lew, 'Commentary on Interim and Conservatory Measures in ICC Arbitration Cases' (2000) 11(1) ICC Ct Bull, 23, 28.
157. For a more detailed discussion, *see* **Article 25**, at paras. 024 *et seq.*

termination of the arbitral proceedings, subject [*inter alia*] to the obligation to set aside an ordered provisional or protective measure'.[158]

E.   CATEGORIES OF INTERIM RELIEF

Pursuant to Article 22 and Section 593(1) ZPO, an arbitral tribunal is empowered **22-083** to take any interim measure that is 'necessary' to ensure that the claim remains enforceable without considerable difficulty and irreparable harm is prevented pending the final outcome of the arbitration. Although this standard will inform the kind of interim relief the tribunal will grant, it does not provide specific guidance to arbitrators or parties as to what relief exactly is available. That uncertainty is, again, the necessary corollary of the flexibility and freedom arbitrators enjoy in providing effective relief to the parties that is customized to the circumstances of the case. As *Derains/Schwartz* explain in their treatise on the ICC Rules: '[t]he expression "interim or conservatory measures" has not been defined, thus permitting the Arbitral Tribunal to construe those words as broadly as may be appropriate in each case'. As a result, '[t]he variety of conservatory and interim measures encountered in connection with international arbitration proceedings is enormous'.[159] In Austria, the Working Group specifically refused to attempt a general statutory definition of interim measures in arbitration, in order to permit arbitrators to order the kind of relief necessary in the specific circumstances of the case. It was indeed feared that any statutory definition could be misused with the argument *e contrario* that, what the law does not expressly allow, arbitrators cannot order.[160]

There are certain categories of interim relief typically granted by arbitrators in **22-084** international arbitration that can be observed. These categories are discussed below; they are in no way exclusive and may significantly overlap.[161]

---

158. *See* **Article 25**, at para. 025.
159. Y. Derains and E.A. Schwartz, *A Guide to the ICC Rules of Arbitration* (2nd edn, The Hague, Kluwer Law International, 2005), pp. 296 *et seq.*; for Germany *see* K.H. Schwab and G. Walter (eds), *Schiedsgerichtsbarkeit* (7th edn, Munich, C.H. Beck, 2005), ch. 17a, paras. 6 *et seq.*; P. Schlosser in *Kommentar zur Zivilprozessordnung*, F. Stein and M. Jonas (eds) (22nd edn, Tübingen, Mohr Siebeck, 2002), Section 1041, paras. 2 *et seq*; for Article 17 UNCITRAL Model Law *see* A. Broches, *Commentary on the UNCITRAL Model Law on International Commercial Arbitration* (Deventer/Boston, Kluwer Law and Taxation Publishers, 1990), Article 17, pp. 91 *et seq.*
160. P. Oberhammer, *Entwurf eines neuen Schiedsverfahrensrechts* (Vienna, Manz, 2002), p. 82.
161. *See* J. Lew, 'Commentary on Interim and Conservatory Measures in ICC Arbitration Cases' (2000) 11(1) ICC Ct Bull, 23, 29; A. Redfern, M. Hunter, N. Blackaby and C. Partasides, *Law and Practice of International Commercial Arbitration* (4th edn, London, Sweet & Maxwell, 2004), para. 7-23.

1.   **Orders Ensuring Enforcement of the Final Award and
              Preventing Irreparable Harm**

22-085 For obvious reasons, any order is appropriate that seeks to realize the express
purpose of Section 593(1) ZPO and Article 22 by ensuring that the claim remains
enforceable (at least without considerable impediment) and irreparable harm is
prevented pending the final outcome of the arbitration. This is, of course, the core
function of interim relief; the desire to ensure the enforceability of the final award
constitutes an accepted principle in international arbitration. The tribunal's authority in such cases 'is based on the need to prevent the judgment of the court from
being prejudiced or frustrated by the actions of the parties'.[162] It rests on the
proposition that no party should be permitted unilaterally to take steps during
the course of the arbitral process which interfere with the arbitral tribunal's authority to render effective, final relief at the conclusion of the arbitral proceedings.[163]
This includes the main claim on the merits, as well as any ancillary claim sufficiently connected with the subject matter of the dispute (such as the costs of
arbitration).[164]

22-086 In ICC Case No. 3896 of 1982, for example, the tribunal declared that: 'the parties
must abstain from all measures that might have a negative effect on the execution
of the decision to be made (. . .)'.[165] In ICC Case No. 6632, the tribunal referred to
the 'general principle according to which the parties ought to take such reasonable
steps as are necessary to render the arbitration proceedings effective. It also means
that the arbitrators can order measures to prevent the breach of this principle.'[166]
Also recognized as a general principle in international arbitration (and expressly
endorsed by Section 395(1) ZPO and Article 22) is the tribunal's authority to enjoin
conduct likely to cause irreparable harm concerning the subject matter of the
dispute (such as, for example, the calling of bank guarantees provided for in a

---

162. L. Collins, 'Provisional and Protective Measures in International Litigation' (1992) 234
      Recueil des Cours, 9, 234.
163. *Bond* characterizes this principle as one of the principal purposes of conservatory and
      provisional measures; it ensures 'that the very purpose of the litigation is not frustrated
      while awaiting the pronouncement and enforcement of a final decision on the merits'. *See*
      S. Bond, 'The Nature of Conservatory and Provisional Measures' in *Conservatory and
      Provisional Measures in International Arbitration* (1993) ICC Pub No. 519, 9.
164. *See* P. Vcelouch, 'Interim and Protective Measures' in *Austrian Arbitration Yearbook 2007*,
      C. Klausegger *et al.* (eds) (Vienna, Manz, 2007), p. 178; P. Oberhammer, *Entwurf eines neuen
      Schiedsverfahrensrechts* (Vienna, Manz, 2002), p. 84; for security of costs, *see* **Article 22**,
      at paras. 101 *et seq.*
165. *Award in ICC Case No. 3896 of 1982*, (1983) JDI, 914, 917; *see also* S. Jarvin and Y. Derains,
      Collection of ICC Arbitral Awards, 1974-1985 (Deventer, Kluwer Law and Taxation Pub-
      lisher, 1997), pp. 161 *et seq.*
166. A. Reiner, 'Les mesures provisoires et conservatoires et l'Arbitrage international, notamment
      l'Arbitrage CCI' (1998) JDI, 890.

construction contract where the call would be contrary to the provisions of the contact).[167]

In order to achieve these purposes, arbitrators may order a party both to refrain **22-087** from a certain conduct, or to conduct itself in a certain way. While prohibitory injunction requires a party not to perform certain specified acts,[168] a mandatory interim injunction is 'directed to the performance of specified acts so as to restore an antecedent position',[169] if the *status quo* had been changed before interim relief could be requested or granted.

2.   Orders Protecting the *Status Quo*

The preservation of the contractual *status quo ante* is another one of the principal **22-088** objectives of interim measures. The prime example of interim protection consists of 'measures that serve to preserve the *status quo* until the final decision on the merits is rendered (preservation order)'.[170]

Preserving the *status quo* directly facilitates the purpose of interim relief as pre- **22-089** scribed by Section 593(1) ZPO and Article 22. By maintaining the state of affairs and preventing any change, the arbitrators ensure that they will ultimately be able to afford effective relief. Indeed, one of the most frequent forms of interim relief in international arbitration therefore consists of '[p]rotective orders maintaining the status quo: Their purpose is to prevent factual changes that would undermine the enforceability of the eventual award'.[171] Arbitral tribunals have frequently adopted this approach, explaining that '[p]rovisional measures, as a rule, aim at avoiding or preventing a modification of the state of facts or law of the subject matter of the dispute which could render more difficult or impossible later performance',[172] or (without prejudice to the merits) 'to protect the subject matter of the dispute and to regulate the conduct of and the relations between the parties as partners in disagreement, pending resolution of their dispute'.[173]

---

167. W.L. Craig, W.W. Park and J. Paulsson, *International Chamber of Commerce Arbitration* (2nd edn, New York, Oceana Publications, 1990), pp. 417 *et seq.*
168. For example, an order not to sell the shares in dispute.
169. I. Goldrein, *Commercial Litigation: Pre-Emptive Remedies* (4th edn, London, Sweet & Maxwell, 2003), A1-003.
170. K.P. Berger, *International Economic Arbitration* (Boston, Kluwer Law International, 1993), p. 339; *see also* W.L. Craig, W.W. Park and J. Paulsson, *International Chamber of Commerce Arbitration* (3rd edn, New York, Oceana Publications, 1990), p. 137.
171. M. Wirth, 'Interim or Preventive Measures in Support of International Arbitration in Switzerland' (2000) 18(1) Bull ASA, 31, 33.
172. Order made in 1989 by an arbitral tribunal composed of Rolando Forni, Pierre Heyer and Gabrielle Kaufmann-Kohler (1994) 12(1) Bull ASA, 142, 144.
173. *Award in ICC Case No. 8879 of 1998*, (2000) 11(1) ICC Ct Bull, 84, 89.

3.   **Orders Preventing the Aggravation of the Dispute**

22-090 Related to the preservation of the *status quo* is the legitimate desire to confine the
dispute, and thus prevent that it is aggravated by the parties' actions during the
ongoing arbitration. Any such aggravation is *prima facie* likely to make the resolution of the dispute, and hence the arbitrators' mandate with regard to the subject
matter of the case, more difficult. The principle has been stated authoritatively by
the Permanent Court of International Justice in the case of *The Electricity Company
of Sofia and Bulgaria*:

> Parties to a case must abstain from any measure capable of exercising a prej-
> udicial effect in regard to the execution of the decision to be given and, in
> general, not allow any step of any kind to be taken which might aggravate or
> extend the dispute.[174]

22-091 Similarly, in *Amco v. Indonesia* an ICSID tribunal referred to 'the good and fair
practical rule, according to which both parties to a legal dispute should refrain (. . .)
to do anything that could aggravate or exacerbate the same, thus rendering its solution possibly more difficult'.[175] Such measures are covered by Section 593(1) ZPO
and Article 22 because they protect the arbitrators' mandate with respect to the
subject matter of the arbitration and ensure that the resolution and enforcement of
the claim on the merits is not considerably impeded.

4.   **Orders Protecting the Taking of Evidence**

22-092 Preserving physical evidence from destruction or dissipation at an early stage of
arbitration proceedings until a record is made often appears essential in arbitration.
For example, it may be crucial for arbitrators to determine the quality of a
consignment of goods before they are sold or perish. Similarly, an inspection by

---

174. PCIJ, 5 December 1939, *The Electricity Company of Sofia and Bulgaria*, [1939] 79 Ser. A/B
      194, 199.
175. C. H. Schreuer, 'Commentary on the ICSID Convention, Articl 47' (1998) 13 ICSID Rev 1,
      208, 240. In ICC Case No. 3896, the tribunal declared that the parties 'shall not commit any act
      of whatever nature, that might aggravate or extend the dispute'. *See Award in ICC Case No.
      3896 of 1982* (1983) JDI, 914-919, with notes by *Jarvin*, p. 917; *see also* S. Jarvin and
      Y. Derains, *Collection of ICC Arbitral Awards, 1974-1985* (Deventer, Kluwer Law Taxation
      Publisher, 1990), pp. 161 *et seq.* The principle is confirmed by an order made in 1993 in ICC
      Case No. 7388: 'As held by several ICC awards, provisional measures may be ordered not only
      in order to prevent irreparable damage but also to avoid aggravation of the dispute submitted to
      arbitration'. *See* A. Reiner, 'Les mesures provisoires et conservatoires et L'Arbitrage
      international, notamment l'Arbitrage CCI' (1998) JDI, 853, 889, fn. 82. In ICC Case No.
      4156 of 1983, the tribunal declared that provisional or conservatory measures 'might be
      necessary to avoid that the material or contractual situation of the parties deteriorates during
      the course of the proceedings'. *See* S. Jarvin and Y. Derains, *Collection of ICC Arbitral
      Awards, 1974-1985* (Deventer, Kluwer Law Taxation Publisher, 1990), pp. 515, 517.

the arbitrators or an expert of a warehouse or an airport terminal may be urgently needed before the property is further damaged by flood or other events.

It is widely admitted that arbitral tribunals can take the necessary measures of **22-093** protection to preserve evidence under most laws or rules.[176] These measures are either expressly referred to in specific provisions[177] or encompassed within general provisions.

Such measures are also permissible under Austrian law. Preserving evidence rel- **22-094** evant to the 'subject matter of the dispute' goes to the core of the arbitrators' mandate and it ensures that the claim remains enforceable without considerable impediment within the meaning of Section 593(1) ZPO and Article 22.[178] In addition,[179] Section 594(1)ZPO and **Article 20** give the arbitrators wide ranging discretion to conduct the proceedings,[180] including specifically with respect to the taking of evidence.[181] Insofar as the preservation or production of evidence is concerned, the tribunal is entitled to direct appropriate orders at the parties under those provisions as well. As discussed elsewhere, however, arbitrators generally do not have the power to compel witnesses under the control of the parties, or third parties witnesses, to attend a hearing and testify or to produce documents. Arbitrators may need the assistance of the relevant state court of the seat of arbitration in the taking of evidence.[182]

---

176. *See* A. Redfern, M. Hunter, N. Blackaby and C. Partasides, *Law and Practice of International Commercial Arbitration* (4th edn, London, Sweet & Maxwell, 2004), paras. 7-24 *et seq.*; *see also* J. Lew, L. Mistelis and S. Kröll, *Comparative International Commercial Arbitration* (The Hague, Kluwer Law International, 2003), para. 23-37; W.L. Craig, W.W. Park and J. Paulsson, *International Chamber of Commerce Arbitration* (3rd edn, New York, Oceana Publications, 2000), para. 26-05.

177. Section 38(4) English Arbitration Act; Article 21(1) AAA/ICDR; Article 26(1) UNCITRAL Rules and Article 25(1)(b) LCIA Rules.

178. *See also* Article 26(1) UNCITRAL Rules: 'At the request of either party, the arbitral tribunal may take any interim measures it deems necessary in respect of the subject matter of the dispute, including measures for the conservation of the goods forming the subject-matter in dispute, such as ordering their deposit with a third person or the sale of perishable goods.'

179. **Article 20** accords the arbitrators the authority to issue procedural orders separate from the authority to order interim relief under Article 22. This distinction has procedural consequences. For example, as regards procedural orders under **Article 20**, the tribunal does not always have to hear both parties before making the order, whereas there is no *ex parte* relief available under Article 22 (and Section 593 ZPO). *See* Explanatory Notes to Section 593 ZPO; C. Liebscher, *The Austrian Arbitration Act 2006: Text and Notes* (The Hague, Kluwer Law International, 2006), Annotated Text to Section 593 ZPO.

180. *See* **Article 20**, at paras. 093 *et seq.*

181. *See* **Article 20**, at paras. 171 *et seq.*

182. *See* **Article 20**, at paras. 250 *et seq.*; Article 27 UNCITRAL Model Law; Article 184(2) Swiss IPRG 1987; Sections 2(3) and 43 English Arbitration Act; Section 7 US FAA; *see* A. Redfern, M. Hunter, N. Blackaby and C. Partasides, *Law and Practice of International Commercial Arbitration* (4th edn, London, Sweet & Maxwell, 2004), para. 7-24.

5.   **Orders Regulating a Relationship**

22-095 International authority also recognizes that provisional relief may be appropriate to require parties to continue performance of their contractual relations until their dispute about those relations has been finally decided. This power is a specific application of the more general principle that the arbitral tribunal may direct that the parties to preserve the *status quo* (here: continue their contractual obligations until a final determination of the dispute by the tribunal) and not take steps during the pendency of the arbitration to aggravate their dispute. *Bond* describes the powers of international arbitrators as including 'interim specific performance of the contract (as when, for example, in a dispute relating to the termination of a charter party, the court prohibits any use of the vessel not in accordance with the charter)'.[183] Similarly, it has been argued that '[i]f it is justified by the protection of the interest in issue, the arbitrator may even order *the provisional performance of the parties' obligations until the matter has been decided* (...)'.[184] This may be particularly appropriate in cases (such as construction contracts) involving long-term cooperation or mutual obligations between the parties.[185]

22-096 In an ICC case between X and Y, a Swiss tribunal considered two applications. The application made by Y requested the tribunal to order 'that the parties could continue to rely on the terms of the contract of 1 November (...) until the matter be decided or agreed by them'.[186] In contrast, the application of X requested that the order a modified regime between the parties during the arbitration. The tribunal rejected the application of X and granted that of Y, concluding that 'the relationship between the parties are governed by the contract of 1 November' and ordering that the parties abide by the terms thereof for a specified time limit.[187]

22-097 In a similar ICC case, the tribunal held that it was 'essential, until the final award on all the claims and counter-claims, that the contractual provisions agreed between

---

183. S. Bond, 'The Nature of Conservatory and Provisional Measures' in *Conservatory and Provisional Measures in International Arbitration* (1993) ICC Pub. No. 519, 8, 11.

184. P. Lalive, J.F. Poudret and C. Reymond, *Le droit de l'arbitrage interne et international en Suisse* (Lausanne, Payot, 1989), p. 364, note 7.

185. P. Lalive, J.F. Poudret and C. Reymond, *Le droit de l'arbitrage interne et international en Suisse* (Lausanne, Payot, 1989), p. 364, note 7.

186. Order made in 1989 by an arbitral tribunal composed of Rolando Forni, Pierre Heyer and Gabrielle Kaufmann-Kohler, (1994) 12(1) Bull ASA, 142. In particular, Y requested an order that '(...) X [the principal Claimant in the arbitration] continue to be bound by its contractual obligations, in particular to provide Y with technical and scientific assistance as provided by Article 3, both with respect to present products and future products or products in course of development'.

187. Order made in 1989 by an arbitral tribunal composed of Rolando Forni, Pierre Heyer and Gabrielle Kaufmann-Kohler, (1994) 12(1) Bull ASA, 145.

the parties keep producing all their effects'.[188] Suspension of the performance of these obligations was admitted only as an exception.

In another ICC case, a tribunal sitting in Geneva and proceeding under the Swiss **22-098** Private International Law Act had to consider a case where the termination of a license was in issue. One of the parties had terminated the contract, effective 31 December 1989, and the other party challenged the termination. Because the Terms of Reference were signed only in September 1989, the tribunal could not render a decision on the license's termination before the date it would have come to an end if the termination had been valid. The tribunal issued an order for provisional measures in November 1989, ordering that the parties' relations continue to be governed by the contract until December 1990, by which time it expected to have made its decision on the validity of the termination.[189]

An ICSID tribunal invited the parties before it 'to abstain from all measures **22-099** incompatible with the maintenance of the contract and to assure that measures already taken in the future have no effects contrary to this maintenance'.[190] And in another ICC case, the tribunal held:

> In the present case, A requests the arbitral tribunal to place the parties again in the position in which, with respect to the guarantees, they were at commencement of the arbitration. The arbitral tribunal observed already that B did not comply with the contract in calling the guarantees before the drawing up of the final account, while A was prepared to prolong the guarantees. Ordering that the parties be placed again in the position in which they were at the beginning of the proceedings and that they remain in this position until the final award is a conservatory measure in the wider sense which finds its place among the measures which the arbitrator may order on the basis of Article 183 SLPIL. It is all the more necessary when the contractual equilibrium, as the parties had intended it, must be restored. Limited to the duration of the arbitration, the measure does not prejudge the merits.[191]

6.   Orders Involving the Tribunal

Arbitral tribunals may grant orders for provisional measures directing a party to **22-100** pay a sum of money in an escrow account controlled by the arbitral tribunal. The arbitral tribunal is then in a position to use the proceeds in the escrow account to make payments to a party either as agreed by the parties or as the result of a partial

---

188. E.A. Schwartz, 'The Practices and Experience of the ICC Court' in *Conservatory and Provisional Measures in International Arbitration* (1993) ICC Pub. No. 519, 45, 51.
189. *ICC Case No. 6508 of 1990*, (1995) JDI, 1022-1031, with comments by *Derains*.
190. *Decision No. 22 in ICSID Arbitration of 1972*, (1994) 12(1) Bull ASA, 148, 152.
191. Order rendered in *ICC Case No. 7388 of 1993*, quoted by A. Reiner, 'Les mesures provisoires et conservatoires et l'Arbitrage international, notamment l'Arbitrage CCI' (1998) JDI, 853, 886.

or final award. For example, in an ICC case relating to a construction project in Africa, the arbitral tribunal granted an interim order directing the employer to pay promissory notes (which represented instalment payments on the price) into an escrow account controlled by the tribunal.[192] A similar order was granted in another ICC arbitration with its seat in Switzerland.[193]

7. Orders for Security of Costs

22-101 A particular form of interim relief is security for costs, whereby typically the respondent requests that the claimant provides certain funds (or a bank guarantee) as security for the costs incurred by the respondent in defending against the claimant's claim. This is a familiar concept in state court litigation.[194]

22-102 In principle, Section 593(1) ZPO should cover order for the security of costs,[195] because they are an ancillary measure that protects the ultimate enforcement of the respondent's claim on the merits for dismissal and costs, and hence, is sufficiently related to the subject matters of the dispute.[196] However, in international commercial arbitration, arbitrators and commentators alike seem to be very cautious in granting security for costs applications.[197] This caution is well placed.

22-103 First, the respondent's application for security of costs is often underpinned by a suggestion that the claimant's claim is without substance and frivolous, and that the respondent should therefore not be burdened by having to outlay any costs in connection with the arbitration. Arbitrators will, however, for good reasons be

---

192. *See* W.L. Craig, W.W. Park and J. Paulsson, *International Chamber of Commerce Arbitration* (3rd edn, New York, Oceana Publications, 2000), paras. 462 *et seq.*
193. *Partial Award in ICC Case No. 3896 of 1982*, (1983) JDI, 914; (1985) X YB Comm Arb, 47.
194. *See, e.g.*, Section 57 ZPO; Section 110 German ZPO; Articles 102 and 103 ZPO GE; Part 25.12 of the Civil Procedure Rules 1998 of England and Wales.
195. *See also* A. Reiner, *Das neue österreichische Schiedsrecht/The new Austrian Arbitration Law* (Vienna, LexisNexis, 2006), Section 593, note 101.
196. The tribunal is generally entitled to order interim measures that are sufficiently connected with the subject matter of the dispute. *See* P. Vcelouch, 'Interim and Protective Measures' in *Austrian Arbitration Yearbook 2007*, C. Klausegger *et al.* (eds) (Vienna, Manz, 2007), p. 178; P. Oberhammer, *Entwurf eines neuen Schiedsverfahrensrechts* (Vienna, Manz, 2002), p. 84. For a different view regarding security for costs, *see* M. Platte in *Arbitration Law of Austria: Practice and Procedure*, S. Riegler, A. Petsche, A. Fremuth-Wolf, M. Platte and C. Liebscher (eds) (Huntington, Juris Publishing, 2007), Section 593, p. 321 with reference to B. Kloiber, 'Vorläufige oder sichernde Massnahmen durch Schiedsgerichte' [2006] Zak, 247.
197. *See* A. Redfern, M. Hunter, N. Blackaby and C. Partasides, *Law and Practice of International Commercial Arbitration* (4th edn, London, Sweet & Maxwell, 2004), para. 7-39; B. Berger, 'Prozesskostensicherheit (cautio iudicatum solvi) im Schiedsverfahren' (2004) 22(1) Bull ASA, 4; E.R. Leahy and C.J. Bianchi, 'The Changing Face of International Arbitration' (2000) 17(4) J Int'l Arb, 19; M. Wirth, 'Interim or Preventive Measures in Support of International Arbitration in Switzerland' (2000) 18(1) Bull ASA, 31; *see also* M. Bühler, 'Costs in ICC Arbitration: A Practitioner's View' (1993) 3 Am Rev Int'l Arb, 146.

hesitant to prejudge the case by accepting that assertion before having heard the parties' full arguments and before having taken the evidence.

Second, the provisions found in national litigation rules cannot be considered **22-104** helpful or appropriate guidance in the context of international arbitration.[198] Section 57(1) ZPO, for example, requires a 'foreign' plaintiff to provide securities of costs to the (Austrian) defendant simply upon the defendant's request. The rationale behind these provisions of national law is to protect the defendant, who has no choice but to defend itself, against being unable to recover the costs of a successful defence from a 'foreign' party over which the defendant's home courts have no jurisdiction.[199] In international arbitration, however, parties will typically come from different jurisdictions so that one of the parties will almost invariably be 'foreign' in respect to the other, and they voluntarily concluded an arbitration agreement. To provide for securities of costs in all these cases, based on the 'foreign' status of one of the parties alone, would not reflect the international character that interim measures necessarily have in cross-border arbitration.[200] Indeed, some modern arbitration laws therefore specifically provide that the tribunal, in considering an application for security of costs, shall not take into account that the claimant is a corporation incorporated in a 'foreign' country.[201]

Moreover, the enforcement risks that historically applied in national litigation with **22-105** respect to foreign litigants are today, at least as far as international arbitration is concerned, largely off-set by the application of the New York Convention. Thus, where the New York Convention or other treaties ensuring enforcement apply, the parties' interest in effective enforcement against 'foreign' entities is sufficiently safeguarded, and the additional grant of security of costs, as a rule, redundant.[202] Where the arbitration involves parties without such protection, on the other hand, an application for security of costs may be justified.

A third basis for security of costs often is the assertion that the claimant lacks assets **22-106** or business income sufficient to satisfy a future claim for costs by the respondent. Again, this assertion typically seems to be treated with caution in international practice. Commentators seem to require a high standard of proof for the respondent to 'show convincingly that the Claimant will almost certainly be unable to meet an

---

198. *See* J. Lew, L. Mistelis and S. Kröll, *Comparative International Commercial Arbitration* (The Hague, Kluwer Law International, 2003), para. 15-19.
199. B. Berger, 'Prozesskostensicherheit (cautio iudicatum solvi) im Schiedsverfahren' (2004) 22(1) Bull ASA, 4.
200. M. Wirth, 'Interim or Preventive Measures in Support of International Arbitration in Switzerland' (2000) 18(1) Bull ASA, 31.
201. *See, e.g.*, Section 38(3) English Arbitration Act.
202. Indeed, Section 57 ZPO does not apply if the decision of the court awarding costs to the defendant is enforceable in the plaintiff's state of residence, pursuant to, for example, international agreements.

award of costs against it'.[203] Some cases suggest that the claimant's precarious financial situation does not justify security of costs if that situation was known to the respondent when the parties concluded the arbitration agreement.[204] Arbitrators also need to make sure that an application for security of costs is not used by the respondent to shift the financial burden of the arbitration entirely to the claimant. As a matter of principle, the parties should be expected to share the costs of the arbitration in equal measure.[205]

22-107 Finally, security of costs can curb the claimant's access to justice, insofar as they make the claimant's pursuit of his claim contingent on the provision of security. This can also present an issue under Article 6 ECHR.[206]

II.   FORMAL CONSIDERATIONS

Article 22(2): Measures referred to in paragraph (1) are to be ordered in writing and a signed copy is to be served on each party. In arbitral proceedings with more than one arbitrator the signature of the presiding arbitrator or, if he is prevented, the signature of another arbitrator shall suffice, provided that the presiding arbitrator or another arbitrator records on the order the reason preventing the signature.

22-108 Section 593(2) ZPO provides for some formal requirements with respect to interim orders, in terms almost identical to Article 22(2).[207] If a national law allows for the enforceability of interim measures in arbitration, it appears reasonable for that law also to determine some minimum formal requirements. In Austria, these are based on the formal requirements applicable to final awards.[208] In particular, interim orders need to be in writing as well.[209]

22-109 However, contrary to the provisions regulating the final award, the signature of the chairperson, in the case of a tribunal, is considered sufficient. This is not intended to dispense of the requisite majority of arbitrators approving the interim order, but

---

203. *See also* A. Redfern, M. Hunter, N. Blackaby and C. Partasides, *Law and Practice of International Commercial Arbitration* (3rd edn, London, Sweet & Maxwell, 1999), para. 7-32.
204. *Final Award in ICC Case No. 7047 of 1994*, (1997) 8(1) ICC Ct Bull, 62; *see also* O. Sandrock, 'The Cautio Judicatum Solvi in Arbitration Proceedings' (1997) 14(2) J Int'l Arb, 17.
205. *See, e.g.*, **Article 34(2)**, at paras. 024 *et seq.*
206. N. Rubins, 'In God We Trust, All Others Pay Cash: Security for Costs in International Arbitration' (2000) Am Rev Int'l Arb, 307, 320.
207. Section 593(1) ZPO provides: 'Such measures shall be issued in writing. In an arbitration with more than one arbitrator, the signature of the chairperson or, in the event of its hindrance, the signature of another arbitrator, shall suffice, provided that the chairperson or the other arbitrator makes a note on the decision as to what hindrance prevented the signing from taking place. Section 606(2), (3), (5), (6) apply *mutatis mutandis*.'
208. P. Oberhammer, *Entwurf eines neuen Schiedsverfahrensrechts* (Vienna, Manz, 2002), p. 85.
209. *See* **Article 27**, at paras. 001 *et seq.*

merely ensures to avoid the awkward situation where the typically urgent measures cannot be formally adopted because some arbitrators are unable to provide their signature expeditiously.[210] In international arbitration, where arbitrators may be at very different locations, this solution appears commendable.

The interim order becomes effective upon being served on the parties, in analogy to **Article 27(5)**.[211]

22-110

III.   REASONED ORDER

> **Article 22(3): Unless the parties have agreed otherwise, the measures are to be substantiated. The measure must include the date on when it was ordered and the place of arbitration. The measure shall be deemed to have been ordered on that date and at that place.**

A.   REQUIREMENTS

Article 22(3) and Section 593(3) ZPO draw from Section 606 ZPO regulating the formal requirements for interim orders. Just with awards, it is required that interim orders need to be reasoned (or 'substantiated', as the English version of the Vienna Rules states).[212] It is arguable, however, that a less stringent threshold should apply to interim orders, which, are they to be meaningful, need to be discharged in an expedited fashion which naturally leaves less time for the tribunal to provide very detailed reasons for their decision.

22-111

Further, it is required that the measure contains the date of the order and reference the place of the arbitration (as the distinction between national and foreign interim measures can be relevant for the enforcement of the order in Austria).[213]

22-112

B.   ORDER OR AWARD

Both the ZPO and the Vienna Rules refer to 'interim measures', leaving it open as a matter of terminology whether such measures are issued as orders or as awards. Some authors have argued that under Austrian law, interim measures are viewed as orders that follow, in terms of form and other requirements, the rules of awards.[214]

22-113

---

210. P. Oberhammer, *Entwurf eines neuen Schiedsverfahrensrechts* (Vienna, Manz, 2002), p. 86.
211. *See* **Article 27**, at paras. 019 *et seq.* **Article 27(5)** provides that '[a]wards become effective as against the parties on service of the copies'.
212. G. Zeiler, *Schiedsverfahren* (Vienna/Graz, Neuer Wissenschaftlicher Verlag, 2006), Section 593, p. 186.
213. *See* **Article 22**, at paras. 131 *et seq.*
214. A. Reiner, *Das neue österreichische Schiedsrecht/The new Austrian Arbitration Law* (Vienna, LexisNexis, 2006), Section 593, note 102; J. Power, *The Austrian Arbitration Act – A*

Clearly, interim measures are not awards in the sense of Section 606 ZPO (which applies only *mutatis mutandis*), and cannot be challenged under Section 611 ZPO; the courts will simply refuse enforcement in Austria where grounds for setting aside under Sections 611 *et seq.* ZPO exist. Others have correctly pointed out that interim measures are not procedural orders either,[215] which follow their own rules.[216] As a result, tribunals may wish to state whether their direction constitutes a procedural order or an interim measure in the sense of Section 593 ZPO that is subject to enforcement.[217]

22-114 Thus, interim measures appear to be a *sui generis* instrument under Section 593 ZPO. However, this should not mean that tribunals are necessarily prevented from giving an interim measure the form of an award.[218] This question is potentially relevant for the enforcement of interim measures elsewhere. Of course, with Section 593 ZPO providing an express basis for the enforcement of arbitral interim measures in Austria, this question is moot as a matter of Austrian law. However, interim measures issued by tribunals seated in Austria may have to be enforced elsewhere, where no such express basis for enforcement exists. In those jurisdictions, arbitrators need also determine if they grant interim relief in form of an order or an award.[219]

22-115 The main distinction between an award and an order is that an award is enforceable pursuant to the terms of the New York Convention, whereas there is at present no such international enforcement regime for the enforcement of orders.[220] However, the New York Convention requires awards to be 'final' for them to be enforced.

Practitioner's Guide to Sections 577-618 of the Austrian Code of Civil Procedure (Vienna, Manz, 2006), Section 593, para. 12.

215. M. Platte in *Arbitration Law of Austria: Practice and Procedure*, S. Riegler, A. Petsche, A. Fremuth-Wolf, M. Platte and C. Liebscher (eds) (Huntington, Juris Publishing, 2007), Section 593, p. 318.

216. *See* **Article 20**, at paras. 001 *et seq.*

217. **Article 20** accords the arbitrators the authority to issue procedural orders separate from the authority to order interim relief under Article 22. This distinction has procedural consequences. For example, as regards procedural orders under **Article 20**, the tribunal does not always have to hear both parties before making the order, whereas there is no *ex parte* relief available under Article 22 (and Section 593 ZPO). *See* Explanatory Notes to Section 593 ZPO; C. Liebscher, *The Austrian Arbitration Act 2006: Text and Notes* (The Hague, Kluwer Law International, 2006), Annotated Text to Section 593 ZPO.

218. Indeed, the Working Group specifically did not want to exclude that possibility. *See* P. Oberhammer, *Entwurf eines neuen Schiedsverfahrensrechts* (Vienna, Manz, 2002), p. 87; *see also* A. Reiner, *Das neue österreichische Schiedsrecht/The new Austrian Arbitration Law* (Vienna, LexisNexis, 2006), Section 593, note 103.

219. Article 23(1) ICC Rules, for example, expressly entitles the arbitrators to choose the form of their decision, although they must give the reasons for their decision in both cases.

220. J. Lew, 'Commentary on Interim and Conservatory Measures in ICC Arbitration Cases' (2000) 11(1) ICC Ct Bull, 23, 28. Orders may be enforceable pursuant to national laws, however.

An interim award ordering provisional measures of protection will often not finally dispose of a relevant part of the parties' dispute. Rather, it is, by definition, provisional in nature, and therefore not '*final*' within the meaning of the New York Convention.[221] In Austria, the Working Group considered that tribunals should not be prevented from issuing interim measures in the form of an award, although it recognized that the enforceability of interim measures ordered in the form of an (interim) award under the New York Convention is questionable.[222]

In practice, requests for interim measures typically do not specify the form of the measure sought. Indeed, parties will be anxious to obtain the tribunal's order, whatever form it takes.[223] Also, in cases of urgency, tribunals have rendered their decision on interim measures initially in the form of an order, but subsequently incorporated it into an award, to meet concerns over speed and enforceability.[224]   **22-116**

IV.   RECORD OF THE ORDER

Article 22(4): The measures and the records on the serving are joint documents of the parties and the sole arbitrator (arbitral tribunal). The sole arbitrator (arbitral tribunal) shall discuss with the parties the possibility of depositing the measure and the records on the serving.

Interim measures by the tribunal are important documents, and a proper record of these orders must be kept. Article 22 mirrors the suggestion made in Section 593(2) ZPO in conjunction with Section 606(5) according to which the order along with the record of service on the parties (which is relevant for the order taking effect) is 'deposited'. In arbitration administered by the VIAC, the order and the record of service can easily and safely be deposited with the Secretary General. Indeed, this is the prescribed solution for awards.[225]   **22-117**

Both according to Article 22 and Section 593(2) ZPO in conjunction with Section 606(5), the interim order, and documents certifying its delivery, are 'joint documents' of the parties and the arbitrators as a matter of Austrian procedural law. The characterization as a 'joint document' ('*gemeinsame Urkunde*') is relevant under Austrian civil procedure, and hence for subsequent court proceedings, because a party is obligated to produce a 'joint' document of the parties by way of disclosure,[226] whereas disclosure of other documents is severely restricted.   **22-118**

---

221. See *Resort Condominiums International Inc (USA) v. Ray Bolwell and Resort Condominiums (Australasia) Pty Ltd*, 118 ALR 655 (Supreme Court of Queensland).
222. P. Oberhammer, *Entwurf eines neuen Schiedsverfahrensrechts* (Vienna, Manz, 2002), p. 83.
223. J. Lew, 'Commentary on Interim and Conservatory Measures in ICC Arbitration Cases' (2000) 11(1) ICC Ct Bull, 28.
224. J. Lew, 'Commentary on Interim and Conservatory Measures in ICC Arbitration Cases' (2000) 11(1) ICC Ct Bull, 23, 28, with further reference.
225. See **Article 27**, at paras. 019 *et seq.*
226. Section 304(1) no. 3 ZPO.

V.   CONFIRMATION OF ENFORCEABILITY

Article 22(5): The sole arbitrator (the presiding arbitrator) or, if he is prevented, another arbitrator, shall upon the motion of a party, confirm the unappealability and enforceability of the measure on a copy of the measure.

22-119   Article 22(5) and Section 593(5) ZPO both provide the presiding arbitrator to confirm that the interim measure is enforceable and not subject to appeal. In essence, this confirmation reflects the tribunal's understanding that it has indeed intended to issue a binding order of interim relief. A similar provision exists with respect to arbitral awards.[227]

22-120   If the confirmation is urgently needed, and the presiding arbitrator indisposed, another member of the tribunal can give this confirmation. However, this is a procedural safeguard to expedite such confirmations. It does not entitle an individual arbitrator to confirm the enforceability of the order if this does not reflect the understanding of the entire tribunal.

22-121   The confirmation is to be given 'upon the application of a party', although there is no reason why the tribunal should not be able to confirm the enforceability *ex officio* when it issues the interim measure to the parties, in order to expedite its enforcement. Certainly, a party can request the confirmation together with its request for the interim measure.

VI.   PARALLEL JURISDICTION OF THE STATE COURTS

Article 22(6): This provision does not prevent the parties from applying to any competent State organ for interim measures of protection. Such an application to a State organ for ordering such measures or for the enforcement of measures ordered by the sole arbitrator (arbitral tribunal) shall not constitute an infringement or waiver of the arbitration agreement and shall not affect the powers of the sole arbitrator (arbitral tribunal). The Secretariat and the sole arbitrator (arbitral tribunal) must be immediately informed of any such application as well as of all measures ordered by the State organ.

A.   Interim Measures by State Courts

22-122   Arbitral tribunals are often a preferable forum to decide upon applications for interim measures when compared to state courts. While state courts may be able to react more swiftly to such applications with judges being available on an *ad hoc* basis, arbitral tribunals, once constituted, will typically be more familiar

---

227.   *See* **Article 27**, at paras. 022 *et seq.*

with the factual and legal background of the case at hand, be in a better position to judge the merits of the applicant's case (which, is often considered a prerequisite for granting interim relief at least as a *prima facie* matter); may be better able to assess the impact of the interim relief, if granted, on the case; and may be better equipped to differentiate between applications for interim relief submitted in good faith to protect a party's legitimate interests from applications that merely serve dilatory, tactical or obstructive purposes.[228]

However, despite the great effort legislatures and practitioners have made in devel- **22-123** oping standards for interim measures in arbitration that allow for fast and effective relief, there may well be cases where the state courts may be more effective, and more expedient, in providing the relief the parties require. The *lex arbitri*, or the law at the place of enforcement, may still be hostile to arbitral interim measures; the tribunal is not yet constituted; or the arbitrators in the individual case are, regrettably, acting slower than the parties have a right to expect. In all of these cases, recourse to state courts will be preferable for parties seeking fast relief.

Recognizing this, major arbitration rules typically permit the parties to apply to the **22-124** state courts for interim measures in spite of the parties' existing arbitration agreement.[229] Article 22(6) provides, specifically, that the parties are not prevented 'from applying to any competent State organ for interim measures of protection' and that such an application to a state court 'shall not constitute an infringement or waiver of the arbitration agreement' or otherwise affect the powers of the tribunal. By way of clarification, Article 22(6) confirms that an application to the state courts 'for the enforcement of measures ordered by the sole arbitrator (arbitral tribunal)' shall also not waive a parties' rights under the arbitration agreement.

This is now expressly confirmed by Section 585 ZPO, a mandatory[230] provision **22-125** which states that '[i]t is not incompatible with an arbitration agreement for a party to request from a court, before or during arbitral proceedings, an interim measure of protection and for a court to grant such measure'. In other words, under the Vienna Rules (and Austrian law generally),[231] a party cannot oppose an application for interim measures in the state courts on the basis that the courts lack jurisdiction because of the existing arbitration agreement, as it can with respect to the merits of

---

228. K.P. Berger, *International Economic Arbitration* (Boston, Kluwer Law International, 1993), p. 348; J. Lew, L. Mistelis and S. Kröll, *Comparative International Commercial Arbitration* (The Hague, Kluwer Law International, 2003), para. 23-14.
229. *See* Article 23(2) ICC Rules; Article 25(3) LCIA Rules; Article 21(3) AAA/ICDR Rules and Article 20(2) DIS Rules.
230. Explanatory Notes to Section 585; C. Liebscher, *The Austrian Arbitration Act 2006: Text and Notes* (The Hague, Kluwer Law International, 2006), Annotated Text to Section 585 ZPO.
231. Even before the 2006 reform, Austrian courts assumed jurisdiction to grant interim relief where the main claim was subject to an arbitration agreement. *See* OGH, 12 September 1996, 6 Ob 2148/96t; and M. Platte in *Arbitration Law of Austria: Practice and Procedure*, S. Riegler, A. Petsche, A. Fremuth-Wolf, M. Platte and C. Liebscher (eds) (Huntington, Juris Publishing,

the parties' dispute.[232] Similarly, a party cannot argue that the other side has waived its right to arbitrate by applying for interim measures to some state courts, whether in Austria or elsewhere.[233] Thus, Article 22(6) and Section 585(6) ZPO establish a true concurrent jurisdiction between state courts and arbitral tribunals. While the legislative goal of Section 585 ZPO is commendable, it is not easy to see why the provision had to be mandatory, thus preventing the parties to exclude state court jurisdiction for interim measures if they so wished (and as they are entitled to do with regards to the merits.) *Oberhammer* argues that the exclusion of access to the state courts for the purposes of interim relief would fall foul of Article 6 ECHR at least in cases where the tribunal is unable to provide the same effective relief as the state courts can.[234] In light of Section 593 ZPO, this argument is doubtful because the parties are sufficiently protected, at least from the perspective of Austrian law (if applicable),[235] to have arbitral interim measures fully enforced by the courts. In such circumstances, the parties should be entitled to waive access to the state courts by agreement (either directly or by reference to institutional rules), at least once the tribunal is constituted and operational and thus able to grant

---

2007), Section 585, pp. 213, 214 with an overview of court decisions under the law prior to the 2006 reform.

232. See **Article 1**, at paras. 085 *et seq*. and **Article 9**, at paras. 030 *et seq*.

233. Section 585 ZPO states that it is compatible with the arbitration agreement for a party to apply for interim measures to 'a court', without specifying whether this court is in Austria or abroad. *See* P. Oberhammer, *Entwurf eines neuen Schiedsverfahrensrechts* (Vienna, Manz, 2002), pp. 59 *et seq*., explaining that this was meant to introduce as general a rule of Austrian law as possible, that should specifically cover requests for interim measures to, or granted from, foreign courts. Of course, for arbitral tribunals seated elsewhere, the question of interim relief by the state courts, and the parties' autonomy to determine these issues, may be subject to a *lex arbitri* at the seat of the arbitration that contains different provisions. *See* K. Hempel, 'Einstweiliger Rechtsschutz durch Schiedsgerichte – Cui Bono?' in *Festschrift Rudolf Welser zum 65. Geburtstag*, C. Fischer-Czermak, A. Kletecka, M. Schauer and W. Zankl (eds) (Vienna, Manz, 2004), p. 281.

234. P. Oberhammer, *Entwurf eines neuen Schiedsverfahrensrechts* (Vienna, Manz, 2002), p. 60, a view shared by J. Power, *The Austrian Arbitration Act – A Practitioner's Guide to Sections 577-618 of the Austrian Code of Civil Procedure* (Vienna, Manz, 2006), Section 585, para. 3; G. Zeiler, 'Erstmals einstweilige Massnahmen im Schiedsverfahren?' [2006] SchiedsVZ 79, 81 and P. Vcelouch, 'Interim and Protective Measures' in *Austrian Arbitration Yearbook 2007*, C. Klausegger *et al*. (eds) (Vienna, Manz, 2007), p. 175 who notes, however, that in light of some German case law, the opposite view is conceivable. He ultimately supports the position against waiving access to state courts on the basis that there is no indication in the text of the statute to differentiate in terms of chronology between a stage before and a stage after the tribunal's constitution. But that position is circular: a lack of textual basis does not prevent an interpretation that achieves the purpose of the provision and protects the parties, yet at once respects overriding principles such as party autonomy.

235. *Hempel* argues with some force that it is for the *lex arbitri* at the seat of the arbitration to determine whether the parties can opt out of the state court system. *See* K. Hempel, 'Einstweiliger Rechtsschutz durch Schiedsgerichte – Cui Bono?' in *Festschrift Rudolf Welser*

effective relief.[236] This view is also more consistent with the (now recognized) true parallelism of state courts and arbitral tribunal in terms of interim relief.[237] This necessarily presumes that the parties have real choice of forum which in turn means that they should be able to exclude one forum by agreement.

By direction of Section 577(2) ZPO, Section 585 ZPO applies both to arbitration **22-126** with their seat in Austria and abroad. Austrian courts can therefore not refuse interim measures in aid of arbitration if the arbitration has its seat outside Austria.

It is arguable that once the arbitral tribunal is constituted, a party should primarily **22-127** petition the arbitral tribunal for interim measures, and only 'in appropriate circumstances'[238] or 'in exceptional cases'[239] petition the state courts, reflecting the general consensus that the role of state courts is subsidiary to, and supportive of, arbitration.[240] However, no such preference is expressed in Article 22(6) and Section 585 ZPO, leaving it to the parties to decide which course to take.[241]

B.   DUTY TO INFORM THE TRIBUNAL AND THE VIAC

Article 22(6) further provides that a party's application to the state courts for **22-128** interim measures '*shall not affect the powers of the sole arbitrator (arbitral tribunal)*'. This has two immediate consequences. First, this provision reinforces the principle that the arbitrators fully retain their jurisdiction over the parties' dispute, and their pertinent powers under the Vienna Rules, despite an interim application to the state courts. Second, and more specifically, even if an application for interim measures is pending before state courts, arbitrators retain the power to grant appropriate interim relief upon the application of one party.

The resulting problem of potentially diverging interim decisions by the state court, **22-129** on the one hand, and the arbitrators, on the other hand, is mitigated by the parties' obligation under Article 22(6) to inform the tribunal of any developments in the proceedings before the state courts. Specifically, Article 22(6) requires the parties to 'immediately inform' '[t]he Secretariat and the sole arbitrator (arbitral tribunal)

---

zum 65. Geburtstag, C. Fischer-Czermak, A. Kletecka, M. Schauer and W. Zankl (eds) (Vienna, Manz, 2004), p. 281.

236. A. Reiner, *Das neue österreichische Schiedsrecht/The new Austrian Arbitration Law* (Vienna, LexisNexis, 2006), Section 593, notes 65 *et seq.*
237. P. Oberhammer, *Entwurf eines neuen Schiedsverfahrensrechts* (Vienna, Manz, 2002), p. 60.
238. *See, e.g.,* Article 23(2) ICC Rules.
239. *See, e.g.,* Article 25(3) LCIA Rules.
240. *See* Article 44(5) English Arbitration Act; *see also* J. Lew, L. Mistelis and S. Kröll, *Comparative International Commercial Arbitration* (The Hague, Kluwer Law International, 2003), paras. 23-120 *et seq.*
241. If it is accepted that Section 585 ZPO is mandatory, any agreement (whether directly or by reference to institutional rules) that restricts access to the Austrian courts for the purposes of

(...) of any such application [for interim measures] as well as of all measures ordered by the State organ'.[242]

22-130 As a practice pointer, it is often useful for arbitrators, in the appropriate circumstances, to remind the parties of their obligation to keep the Secretariat and the arbitrators informed; in the 'heat of battle', this obligation is sometimes forgotten.

VII.   ENFORCING ARBITRAL INTERIM MEASURES IN AUSTRIA

22-131 The enforcement of interim measures ordered by arbitral tribunals raises particular questions in and of itself.[243] As a matter of course, arbitrators lack jurisdiction and power to enforce their own interim measures of protection. In many jurisdictions, the parties are therefore directed to the courts to apply for the enforcement of interim measures they have obtained from the arbitrators. Others suggest that interim measures of protection should be issued in the form of an award, in order to secure the benefits of international recognition and enforcement under the New York Convention; but this approach has difficulties of its own.[244]

22-132 In the discussion below, particular emphasis is given to the enforcement of interim relief granted by arbitral tribunals through the Austrian courts, following the very modern regime provided by the new ZPO that anticipates, and perhaps even sets, several current trends in international arbitration.

1.   Jurisdictional Basis

22-133 The prevailing opinion in international arbitration appears to be that interim orders cannot be enforced by arbitral tribunals; and that they cannot be enforced by state courts as if they were awards without an express basis in the law.[245] In Austria, it was argued by some that arbitrators could apply to the courts to order injunctive relief or to enforce the arbitrators' interim order in support of the arbitration,[246] on the basis of

---

interim measures would be ineffective. *See* G. Zeiler, *Schiedsverfahren* (Vienna/Graz, Neuer Wissenschaftlicher Verlag, 2006), Section 585, p. 117.

242. A similar rule was contained in the predecessor provision of Article 14a(2) of the Vienna Rules 2001, **Annex 2a**. *See also* Article 23(2) ICC Rules and Article 25(3) LCIA Rules.

243. J. Lew, L. Mistelis and S. Kröll, *Comparative International Commercial Arbitration* (The Hague, Kluwer Law International, 2003), para. 23-5.

244. *See* **Article 22**, at paras. 113 *et seq.*

245. *See* **Article 22**, at para. 135.

246. A. Reiner, *Handbuch der ICC-Schiedsgerichtsbarkeit* (Vienna, Manz, 1989), pp. 218 *et seq.* Recognizing the difficulties inherent in the traditional position of Austrian doctrine, he explained that 'Article 588 ZPO prevents the arbitrator from "using measures of force or imposing penalties" against the parties (...). Interim measures are neither measures of

Section 589 fZPO which provided that '[j]udicial measures, which are deemed necessary by the tribunal and which the tribunal is not entitled to undertake itself, are undertaken by the competent State Court upon the tribunal's request'.

Following the 2006 reform, Section 593 ZPO adopts a statutory regime that allows **22-134** the enforcement of interim measures granted by arbitrators in domestic and international proceedings through the Austrian state courts. This regime antici- pates, and was inspired by, the current UNCITRAL discussions regarding a reform of interim relief,[247] and expands upon the less detailed regime under Section 1041 German ZPO. It provides a truly modern enforcement mechanism that will hope- fully be replicated elsewhere.

Section 593(3) ZPO provides in relevant part that: **22-135**

> Upon the application of a party, the district court where the opponent of the endangered party has its seat, domicile or habitual place of residence in Austria at the time of the first filing of the plea – or otherwise the district court in whose area the measure of enforcement for the preliminary injunction shall take place – shall enforce such measure. (. . .).

In other words, the competent Austrian state court has authority, and is obliged, to **22-136** enforce interim measures granted by arbitrators.[248] Because this provision applies both to arbitration seated in Austria and seated abroad, Austrian courts will now enforce arbitral interim measures ordered by tribunals seated in Austria, as well as such measures ordered by tribunals seated elsewhere provided that the enforce- ment measure takes place in Austria, if the party against whom the interim measure has been ordered resides in Austria, or if the enforcement action should take place in Austria, for example, if assets are located here. With one sweeping strive, the Austrian legislature has therefore opted to accord arbitral measures, whether domestic or from abroad, full enforceability in Austria.

However, although the question was discussed intensively by the Working Group, **22-137** the courts have not be given jurisdiction to order the applicant party to provide security. This power rests with the tribunal only.[249] Such authority may, however, still be implied.[250]

---

force nor penalties. The arbitrator can order interim relief, but he cannot enforce it. He can apply to the state courts to effect enforcement on his behalf pursuant to Section 589 ZPO (. . .)'.

247. P. Oberhammer, *Entwurf eines neuen Schiedsverfahrensrechts* (Vienna, Manz, 2002), pp. 81 *et seq.*; J. Power, *The Austrian Arbitration Act – A Practitioner's Guide to Sections 577-618 of the Austrian Code of Civil Procedure* (Vienna, Manz, 2006), Section 593, para. 1.

248. This competent Austrian court is determined by reference to Section 387(2) EO which subjects the interim matter to the same court that would be competent to order an interim injunction in those cases in which no state proceeding is pending on the main issue.

249. *See* **Article 22**, at para. 040.

250. P. Oberhammer in *Das neue Schiedsrecht – Schiedsrechtsänderungsgesetz 2006*, B. Kloiber, P. Oberhammer, W.H. Rechberger and H. Haller (eds) (Vienna, Manz, 2006), p. 247.

22-138 Section 593(5) ZPO also expressly provides that the Austrian enforcement courts have no jurisdiction to award damages for unjustified interim relief (as they would under Section 394 EO[251] in state court proceedings). There is a credible argument that this legislative choice should be interpreted to mean that such damages are not for the state courts to adjudicate, but for the arbitral tribunal.[252] However, some authors are sceptical about arbitrators' jurisdiction to award such damages, and propose that this is a separate claim to be brought before competent state courts (other than the enforcement court).[253] This view is highly impractical and presumes an interpretation of the arbitration agreement that suggests that the parties intended to artificially refer certain claims to arbitration, and other claims arising out of their relationship to state court litigation. It also presumes, equally impractically, that the parties accorded the arbitrators the power to issue interim relief, but not the power to adjudicate the consequences of the relief so granted.[254] In modern commerce, the better assumption (unless there is evidence to the contrary) is that, by agreeing to arbitrate, the parties intended to bring all claims arising out of their contractual relationship before one forum, including specifically all claims for damages. After all, damages incurred from unjustified interim measures (provided that all substantive requirements for a damages claim are met) arise directly out of, or are at least ancillary to, the parties' contractual relationship that is subject to an arbitration agreement. Thus, depending on the interpretation of the arbitration agreement, the power to award consequential damages may well be with the arbitral tribunal.[255]

---

251. Section 593(5) ZPO: If the claim protected by the interim measure is not awarded, then the opposing party may be entitled to a claim for damages. Pursuant to Section 394 EO, the courts are not competent to decide on damage claims in the proceeding for the enforcement of the interim measure.

252. Note, however, that in Germany, there is an express statutory provision that confers such power on the tribunal: Section 1041(4) German ZPO. The choice of the Austrian legislature not to include a similar provision in the Austrian ZPO would advocate against this position.

253. M. Platte in *Arbitration Law of Austria: Practice and Procedure*, S. Riegler, A. Petsche, A. Fremuth-Wolf, M. Platte and C. Liebscher (eds) (Huntington, Juris Publishing, 2007), Section 593, p. 326; B. Kloiber, 'Vorläufige oder sichernde Massnahmen durch Schiedsgerichte' [2006] Zak, 247, 249; B. Kloiber and H. Haller in *Das Neue Schiedsrecht – Schiedsrechts-Änderungsgesetz 2006*, B. Kloiber, P. Oberhammer, W.H. Rechberger and H. Haller (eds) (Vienna, Manz, 2006), p. 36.

254. P. Vcelouch, 'Interim and Protective Measures' in *Austrian Arbitration Yearbook 2007*, C. Klausegger *et al.* (eds) (Vienna, Manz, 2007), p. 177.

255. In agreement: A. von Saucken, *Die Reform des österreichischen Schiedsverfahrensrechts auf der Basis des UNCITRAL-Modellgesetzes über die Internationale Handelsschiedsgerichtsbarkeit* (Frankfurt, Verlag Peter Lang, 2004), p. 198; P. Vcelouch, 'Interim and Protective Measures' in *Austrian Arbitration Yearbook 2007*, C. Klausegger *et al.* (eds) (Vienna, Manz, 2007), p. 177.

Given that Section 593(1) ZPO provides for arbitral interim measures 'until the **22-139** parties provide otherwise', some authors have questioned whether the parties can accept the tribunal's power to grant interim relief but restrict by agreement the possibility that such measures are enforced through the Austrian courts.[256] Although different arguments exist for and against this proposition,[257] the overriding principle of party autonomy should in principle permit parties to restrict the enforceability of arbitral measures by agreement; it is, of course, not easy to see in practice why parties would wish to do so.

2.   Procedure

As a procedural matter, Section 593(5) ZPO provides that, when ordering the **22-140** enforcement of the arbitral interim measure, '[t]he court may hear the opposing party prior to making its decision on the enforcement'.[258] In other words, the Austrian courts can enforce the measure without necessarily having to hear the party subjected to it (except where, as discussed below, the relief ordered by the arbitral tribunal is adapted or modified); after all, that party must have been heard on the measure when it was made by the tribunal.[259] However, '[i]f the opposing party was not heard prior to the making of the decision, it can lodge an objection against the order of enforcement (. . .)' pursuant to Section 397 EO,[260] within 14 days. Whenever the opposing party is heard, it can only rely on the specific grounds provided by Section 593(4) ZPO, discussed further below.[261]

3.   Adapting Foreign Relief to the Austrian System

Section 593(3) ZPO proceeds to address the issue of how an Austrian court is to **22-141** enforce a measure granted by a foreign tribunal that is conceptually alien to Austrian law. This problem is real in practice, as foreign tribunals will typically not be able to concern themselves with the details of all national enforcements laws potentially relevant to the enforcement of their interim orders. Thus, Section 593(3) ZPO provides that, where measures are unknown to Austrian law, the

---

256. P. Vcelouch, 'Interim and Protective Measures' in *Austrian Arbitration Yearbook 2007*, C. Klausegger *et al.* (eds) (Vienna, Manz, 2007), p. 171.
257. P. Vcelouch, 'Interim and Protective Measures' in *Austrian Arbitration Yearbook 2007*, C. Klausegger *et al.* (eds) (Vienna, Manz, 2007), p. 171.
258. Section 593(5) ZPO: The *ex parte* enforcement of a measure by a court is possible; however, if the measure is modified by the court, then it is mandatory that the opposing party be heard.
259. *See* **Article 22**, at paras. 032 *et seq.*; Explanatory Notes to Section 593 ZPO.
260. Section 593(5) ZPO: In the objection, the opposing party can assert the reasons for setting aside specified in Section 593(4) after the approval of the enforcement, provided that the party was not heard by the court before the approval.
261. *See* **Article 22**, at paras. 145 *et seq.*

court of enforcement can, upon application by a party,[262] adapt the measure to ensure that its purpose is achieved:[263]

> Where the measure provides for a measure of protection unknown to Austrian law, the court can, upon application and hearing of the opposing party, execute the measure of protection of Austrian law that comes closest to the measure of the arbitral tribunal. In this case, the court, upon request, can also modify the measure of the arbitral tribunal in order to safeguard the realization of its purpose.

22-142 As a result, the process of adapting interim measures is structured in two phases (which can overlap in practice).[264] First, if the arbitrators have ordered a particular measure that is alien to Austrian enforcement law, the Austrian court can simply substitute that measure with a measure of Austrian enforcement law that approximates, in terms of effect, the ordered measure as closely as possible. Second, the Austrian court may, again upon application, redraft the interim measure ordered by the arbitrators, thereby ensuring that at least its purpose is realized as effectively as possible. It was the intention of the Working Group that in both cases, the state court would not be able to go beyond the measures ordered by the arbitrators, by having to approximate the measure and by achieving its purpose as closely as possible.[265]

22-143 The statute does not appear to express a clear hierarchy between the two methods. The guiding principle ought to be to do whatever approximates the measure most closely as it was originally ordered. As mentioned, however, both alternatives apply only upon application by a party. This application is meant to include a specific submission by the party as to which measure of Austrian enforcement law would be an appropriate substitute, or, respectively, which Austrian measure would most effectively realize the purpose of the arbitral injunction.[266] In this context, the Working Group appears to expect the parties to sufficiently familiarize themselves with the particularities of Austrian enforcement law.[267]

22-144 If the state court wants to order means of protection different from the one mentioned by the arbitral tribunal or if it wants to redraft the arbitral interim measure it has to hear the respondent in advance ('upon (. . .) hearing of the opposing party').

---

262. P. Oberhammer, *Entwurf eines neuen Schiedsverfahrensrechts* (Vienna, Manz, 2002), p. 87 (arguing that the court cannot be reasonably expected to look out *ex officio* for the party's interest of what sort of measure is appropriate in the circumstances); *see also* G. Zeiler, *Schiedsverfahren* (Vienna/Graz, Neuer Wissenschaftlicher Verlag, 2006), Section 593, p. 190.
263. *See also* Section 1041(2) German ZPO which contains a similar regulation.
264. P. Oberhammer, *Entwurf eines neuen Schiedsverfahrensrechts* (Vienna, Manz, 2002), p. 86.
265. P. Oberhammer, *Entwurf eines neuen Schiedsverfahrensrechts* (Vienna, Manz, 2002), p. 87.
266. P. Oberhammer, *Entwurf eines neuen Schiedsverfahrensrechts* (Vienna, Manz, 2002), p. 87.
267. In practice, this will require the parties usually to retain local counsel. As this is typically the case in enforcement proceedings anyway, the additional burden imposed on the parties does not appear to be excessive.

The opposing party must therefore be given the opportunity to defend itself against an improper adaptation of the arbitral interim measure. Although this might affect the efficacy of the measure in cases of urgency (as it no longer permits the immediate decision of execution with the possibility of subsequent objection), it has to be taken into consideration that the state court in this case is already significantly favouring the applicant whose interim measure is being enforced.

4. Grounds to Refuse Enforcement

Section 593(4) ZPO then goes on to provide for certain instances in which the **22-145** Austrian courts must ('shall') refuse to enforce an arbitral interim measure:

> The court shall refuse to enforce a measure under paragraph 1 of this section if
>
>   1. the seat of the arbitral tribunal is in Austria and the measure suffers from a defect which would constitute a reason for setting aside an Austrian award under Sections 611(2), 617(6) and (7) or 618 of this law;
>
>   2. the seat of the arbitral tribunal is not in Austria and the measure suffers from a defect which would constitute cause for refusal of recognition or enforcement in the case of a foreign award;
>
>   3. the enforcement of the measure would be incompatible with an Austrian court measure which was either applied for or made earlier, or with a foreign court measure which was made earlier and which is to be recognised;
>
>   4. the measure provides for a measure of protection unknown in Austrian law and no appropriate measure of protection as provided by Austrian law was applied for.

Section 593(4) ZPO entitles (and indeed obligates *ex officio*: 'shall') the Austrian **22-146** courts to refuse enforcement in certain instances. In this regard, Section 593(4) nos 1 and 2 ZPO distinguishes between national and foreign interim measures, reflecting the (different) legal standards applicable to domestic awards (made in Austria) and those made abroad (and enforced in Austria). Thus, interim measures issued by tribunals seated in Austria will not be enforced if they suffer from a defect that, if they were an award, would justify their setting aside under Sections 611 *et seq.* ZPO. By contrast, interim measures issued by tribunals seated abroad will not be enforced if they suffer from a defect that, if they were an award, would justify their non-enforcement under the New York Convention or any else applicable enforcement treaty. In the end, this imports the same considerations that apply to awards to the validity and enforcement of arbitral interim measures.

Section 593(4) no. 3 ZPO is concerned with avoiding the enforcement of con- **22-147** flicting court decisions. Thus, if an Austrian court has already seized jurisdiction in the matter because an interim measure has been applied for, or has already been granted, and that matter is incompatible with a subsequent measure ordered by an arbitral tribunal (whether seated in Austria or abroad), the Austrian courts will refuse the enforcement of the arbitral measure. This is to preserve the integrity of the Austrian legal system. Austrian courts should not be instrumentalized to enforce a measure that is in conflict with their own previous orders. This provision is inspired by considerations of *lis pendens*, so that the order must be between the same parties and regarding the same subject matter (indeed, arguably, in aid of the same arbitration). It is sufficient, however, that the application for the interim measure has been made to the Austrian court: a pending application raises sufficient concerns of conflict.

22-148 Of course, while such an application is pending before a state court, the tribunal retains full jurisdiction to order interim relief under Section 593(1) ZPO and Article 22; but the tribunal needs to avoid ordering an interim measure that is incompatible with the one that has been applied for before the Austrian court. In some sense, this provision does establish an (if only practical) preference for interim measures to be ordered by state courts. This reinforces the rationale of Article 22(6) requiring the parties to inform the tribunal and the Secretariat of all interim measures that they have applied from, or that have been granted by, the state courts.

22-149 Section 593(4) no. 3 ZPO captures a second scenario as well: An interim order made by a foreign court. This is also concerned with preserving the integrity of the Austrian legal system, but is distinct from cases regarding interim orders by Austrian courts. First, for interim orders issuing from foreign courts it is required that these orders have already been made (as opposed to merely having been applied for), because an order that has only been applied for before a foreign court does not seem to pose a systemic threat to the Austrian legal order. Second, and reinforcing this consideration, a foreign court order is only relevant for the purposes of Section 593(4) no. 3 ZPO if it needs to be recognized in Austria under international obligations or otherwise applicable. If that is not so, a risk of conflicting decisions within the Austrian legal system does not materialize.

22-150 In any event, it will be subject of some debate what makes two orders 'incompatible' with each other in the sense of Section 593(4) no. 3 ZPO. The legislative materials suggest that '[i]n each case, the requested [arbitral] measure will have to be contrasted against a measure applied for earlier [from the court] in terms of content and effect'.[268] According to the Working Group, the provision is intended to avoid that 'parallel measures come into being by way of abuse of law which in content and purpose correspond but differ slightly as a textual matter'.[269] If the Austrian courts have denied a measure, they should therefore in principle not be compelled to subsequently enforce that measure if so ordered by a tribunal.[270]

---

268. Explanatory Notes to Section 593.
269. P. Oberhammer, *Entwurf eines neuen Schiedsverfahrensrechts* (Vienna, Manz, 2002), p. 89.
270. P. Oberhammer, *Entwurf eines neuen Schiedsverfahrensrechts* (Vienna, Manz, 2002), p. 89.

However, it may not always be abusive for a party to apply to the tribunal after a **22-151**
court has denied a measure (at least if the circumstances have changed in the
meantime);[271] of course, the denial by another court of tribunal may in any
event hold persuasive authority. If a court in Austria cr elsewhere rejects the
application for interim measure for jurisdictional reasons, this should certainly
not prevent the parties to apply again to the tribunal.[272] It has also been suggested
that, once a party has applied for an interim measure to the Austrian courts, the
tribunal may no longer grant an interim measure with respect to the same subject
matter 'regardless of whether the application of before the [Austrian] court was
successful'.[273] This arguably takes matters too far. It not only ignores that Austrian
law expressly recognizes that tribunals and courts have parallel jurisdiction for
interim measures on the same subject matter,[274] but also misconstrues the purpose
of Section 593(4) ZPO which is only concerned with avoiding the enforcement of
conflicting decisions. The better view is therefore that, once a party has applied to
the Austrian court, the tribunal retains full jurisdiction to issue an interim measure
on the same subject matter – which runs the risk, however, of not being enforceable
(and that only in Austria) if the tribunal's measure is incompatible with the
measure ordered by the Austrian court. If the Austrian court denies the application
for an interim measure, the tribunal will probably look closely at that decision, but,
in particular in the face of circumstances that were not addressed by the court, also
retains the jurisdiction to issue its own interim measure. In similar vein, if the court
grants an interim measure, the tribunal can still grant its own measure, if so
requested, on the same subject matter; as long as the arbitral measure is not
incompatible with state court measure, both measures should be enforceable
alongside each other. This may make sense where the measures have similar effect,
but differ in scope, and hence provide different levels of protection to the requesting party.[275]

---

271. *See also* A. Reiner, *Das neue österreichische Schiedsrecht/The new Austrian Arbitration Law*
(Vienna, LexisNexis, 2006), Section 593, note 108, although the Explanatory Notes state that,
if a measure has been denied by the state court, the same measure cannot be enforced if
subsequently ordered by the tribunal. However, the overall purpose of Section 593 ZPO is
to avoid that conflicting measures are enforced at the same time, not to constitute an overly
broad rule of res judicata. Thus, if a measure is rejected by the state court, but the applicant
party can, in particular on the basis of new arguments that were not addressed by the state court
or on the basis of changed circumstances, persuade a tribunal to order a similar measure, this
arbitral measure should be enforced.
272. Explanatory Notes to Section 593 ZPO.
273. M. Platte in *Arbitration Law of Austria: Practice and Procedure*, S. Riegler, A. Petsche,
A. Fremuth-Wolf, M. Platte and C. Liebscher (eds) (Huntington, Juris Publishing, 2007),
Section 593, p. 320.
274. *See* Section 585 ZPO as discussed at **Article 22**, at paras. 122 *et seq.*
275. P. Vcelouch, 'Interim and Protective Measures' in *Austrian Arbitration Yearbook 2007*,
C. Klausegger *et al.* (eds) (Vienna, Manz, 2007), p. 172; for a similar approach in Germany,
see H. J. Schroth, 'Einstweiliger Rechtsschutz im deutschen Schiedsverfahren' [2003]
SchiedsVZ 102, 106.

22-152 It also bears emphasis that Section 593(4) ZPO is only concerned with arbitral measures in conflict with court measures; it does not address incompatible orders issued by another arbitral tribunal (even though that order would also be enforceable in Austria under Section 593(1) ZPO. This appears to leave parties the possibility to first apply to the tribunal, and, when their application was unsuccessful or the measure ordered deemed insufficient, subsequently apply to the state courts[276] – the state courts seem to retain full parallel jurisdiction to issue their own interim measure, whether those are incompatible with the tribunal's order or not. However, this may run into separate issues under Austrian law.[277]

5.   Grounds to Set Aside the Enforcement

22-153 Section 593(6) ZPO recognizes that circumstances may change, or the basis for the enforcement may fall away, after the court has granted the enforcement of arbitral interim measures. It provides:

> Upon request the court shall set aside the enforcement if
> 1. the term of the measure as set by the arbitral tribunal has expired;
> 2. the arbitral tribunal has limited the scope of or set aside the measure;
> 3. a case as referred to in Section 399(1) nos 1 – 4 EO is present; provided that such a circumstance has not already been unsuccessfully asserted before the arbitral tribunal and there are no obstacles to the recognition (paragraph 4) of the respective decision of the arbitral tribunal;
> 4. a security as referred to in paragraph 1 of this section was provided, which makes the enforcement unnecessary.

22-154 Section 593(6) ZPO allows the opposing party to request the courts to repeal the measure in the certain circumstances. Notably, the court has no right to consider these circumstances *ex officio*, but only upon application by a party.

22-155 First, if the tribunal has ordered that the measure shall take effect only for a limited specified period of time, there is no basis to enforce the measure beyond that period. Second, although a decision on an interim measure, once issued by the arbitral tribunal, cannot, in principle, be appealed, the tribunal has the power to revise or revoke its previous decision on interim measures where the circumstances

---

276. *See also* J. Power, *The Austrian Arbitration Act – A Practitioner's Guide to Sections 577-618 of the Austrian Code of Civil Procedure* (Vienna, Manz, 2006), Section 593, para. 21.

277. P. Vcelouch, 'Interim and Protective Measures' in *Austrian Arbitration Yearbook 2007*, C. Klausegger *et al.* (eds) (Vienna, Manz, 2007), p. 172, arguing that an existing arbitral measure that sufficiently protects the interests of the applicant party could lead to a lack of legal interest, with the result that the courts are prevented from issuing a measure on the same subject; noting however that there appears case law that rejects this notion. *See* OGH, 15 December 1993, 3 Ob 505/94.

under which the measure was granted have changed.[278] Section 593(6) no. 2 ZPO expressly recognizes that the tribunal retains the power to modify the interim measure it had ordered, or to repeal it altogether – in which case the opposing party can ask the courts that the measure be no longer enforced.

Under Section 593(6) no. 3 ZPO, the opposing party can ask the Austrian court to **22-156** take into account, even where the tribunal is silent, that the circumstances have changed since measure was ordered. The provision refers to Section 399 (1) nos 1-4 EO, which make it possible to set aside or limit the interim measure if a lesser measure is sufficient; if the protection is no longer necessary due to a change in circumstances; if the opposing party provides a sufficient security; or if the protected claim has expired or been denied with final and binding effect. In these circumstances, the opposing party can request that the state court not to wait for the tribunal to modify or repeal the interim measure but rather itself decides to no longer enforce it. Again, however Section 593(6) no. 3 ZPO recognizes the primacy of the tribunal: Where these arguments have been made before the tribunal, and the tribunal decided to keep the measure in place regardless, the court cannot refuse enforcement of the arbitral measure (except for the reasons given in Section 593(4) ZPO).

As regards Section 593(6) no. 4 ZPO and as discussed above, the tribunal has the **22-157** power under Section 593(1) ZPO to order either party to post security in the context of interim measures. Security will be required from the applicant party to cover any damages arising from the interim measure, should the ultimate claim be dismissed. However, the tribunal can also require the opposing party to post security.[279] If that security makes the measure redundant, the opposing party can ask the Austrian courts not to enforce the interim measure.

---

278. J. Lew, 'Commentary on Interim and Conservatory Measures in ICC Arbitration Cases' (2000) 11(1) ICC Ct Bulletin, 23, 28.
279. J. Power, *The Austrian Arbitration Act – A Practitioner's Guide to Sections 577-618 of the Austrian Code of Civil Procedure* (Vienna, Manz, 2006), Section 593, para. 11.

Article 23

Authorized Agents

	Para.		Para.
I. Introduction	1	III. Authorization	9
II. Free Choice of Party Representative	4		

Article 23: The parties shall have the right to be represented or advised by persons of their choice in the proceedings before the sole arbitrator (arbitral tribunal).

I.   INTRODUCTION

Some jurisdictions place restrictions on who can appear on behalf of the parties in an arbitration proceeding held within its borders, and impose constraints by way of professional or ethical obligations.[1] Indeed, some countries consider the use of foreign counsel as unauthorized practice of law; in these countries, the law requires that the representative be a member of its local bar association. Yet other countries require a local member of its state bar to assist the party's chosen representative, if that representative is a foreign counsel.[2] Any such rule affects non-lawyers and foreign lawyers alike.   **23-001**

The principal reason for limiting the choice of party representatives was explained by the Singapore High Court in 1988 in *Turner (East Asia) Pte Ltd. v. Builders*   **23-002**

---

1. G.B. Born, *International Commercial Arbitration – Commentary and Materials* (2nd edn, The Hague, Kluwer Law International, 2001), p. 514.
2. G.B. Born, *International Commercial Arbitration – Commentary and Materials* (2nd edn, The Hague, Kluwer Law International, 2001), p. 520.

Federal (Hong Kong) Ltd. and Joseph Gartner & Co. (FR Germany)[3] justifying the preclusion of foreign lawyers from international arbitrations conducted in Singapore by the need to protect the public from the provision of legal services by unqualified persons.[4] Not surprisingly, this decision was broadly criticized by the international community and the restrictions were eventually repealed.[5]

23-003   Indeed, the clear trend is towards allowing foreign counsel (as well as non-lawyers) to appear in arbitration, even in jurisdictions which were traditionally restrictive.[6] As countries compete for the role (or image) as a leading business centre, there has been growing recognition that measures protecting the local bar from foreign competition will deter users of international arbitration to choose such countries as the seat of arbitration.[7] It seems that the approach taken major arbitration institutions in allowing lawyers and non-lawyers alike to represent parties in an arbitration, irrespective of their nationality or connection to a local bar, is now the prevailing approach in modern doctrine.[8]

---

3. High Court of Singapore, 30 March 1988, *Turner (East Asia) Pte Ltd (Singapore) v. Builders Federal (Hong Kong) Ltd (Hong Kong) and Josef Gartner & Co (FR Germany)* [1988] 2 Malaysian LJ, 280-287.
4. Other traditionally restrictive jurisdictions include China, Malaysia and Canada and, until 2002, the States of California and New York. *See Birbrower, Montalbano, Condon & Frank, P.C. v. Superior Court of Santa Clara County*, 949 P. 2d 1 (Cal. 1998); *Williamson v. John D. Quinn Construction Corp.*, 537 F. Supp. 613 (S.D.N.Y 1982); in both cases the court held that lawyers having advised and represented their parties in arbitration trials could not recover fees for the services performed, because of lack of local qualification.
5. In June 2004, remaining restrictions on the representation by foreign advocates were eliminated in Singapore.
6. M. Polkinghorne, 'More Changes in Singapore: Appearance Rights of Foreign Counsel' (2005) 22(1) J Int'l Arb, 75; M. Polkinghorne and D. Fitzgerald, 'Arbitration in Southeast Asia: Hong Kong, Singapore and Thailand Compared' (2001) 18(1) J Int'l Arb, 101.
7. J. Lew, L. Mistelis and S. Kröll, *Comparative International Commercial Arbitration* (The Hague, Kluwer Law International, 2003), paras. 21-69 *et seq.* (citing Supreme Court of Malaysia, 2 January 1990, *Government of Malaysia v. Zublin-Muhibbah Joint Venture, consisting of Ed Zublin AG (FR Germany) and Muhibbah Engineering (M) Sdn Bhd. (Malaysia)* (1991) XVI YB Comm Arb, 166; High Court of Singapore, 30 March 1988, *Turner (East Asia) Pte Ltd (Singapore) v. Builders Federal (Hong Kong) Ltd (Hong Kong) and Josef Gartner & Co (FR Germany)* (1988) 5(3) J Int'l Arb, 139; (1988) 3(4) Mealey's Int'l Arb Rep, 6-9 and C1-C26; (1989) XIV YB Comm Arb, 224, overruled by the Legal Profession (Amendment No 2) Act 1991). *See also Birbrower, Montalbano, Condon & Frank P.C. v. The Superior Court of Santa Clara County*, 949 P. 2d 1 (Cal 1998) (holding that to practice law in California the lawyer must be a member of the local bar; and noting the Civil Procedural Code of the state of California, Section 1297.11, as the exception which allows for parties to choose their representatives in international commercial arbitration regardless of state bar membership).
8. J. Lew, L. Mistelis and S. Kröll, *Comparative International Commercial Arbitration* (The Hague, Kluwer Law International, 2003), para. 21-73 (citing in France *see* Cour de Cassation, 1re Ch. Civ., 19 June 1979, *SARL Primor v. Société d'Exploitation Industrielle de Bétaigne* [1979] Rev Arb, 487; *see also* D.W. Rivkin, 'Restriction on Foreign Counsel in International Arbitrations'

II.   FREE CHOICE OF PARTY REPRESENTATIVE

Article 23 adopts, with only slight changes, former Article 15.[9] A similar provision **23-004** can also be found in Section 594(3) ZPO which provides that '[t]he parties may be represented or advised by persons of their own choosing. This right cannot be excluded or restricted'.

Given the express language of Section 594(3) ZPO, this provision is undoubtedly of **23-005** a mandatory nature, preventing the parties to exclude certain persons or groups of persons from representation.[10] It has been suggested that a violation of Section 594(3) ZPO may give rise to a challenge of the award as contrary to the Austrian *procedural ordre public*.[11] Not every violation of mandatory law, however, violates the fundamental values of the Austrian legal system. Therefore, applying the *procedural ordre public* reservation under Section 611(2) no. 5 ZPO cautiously and reserving it for the most fundamental procedural errors, it will depend on the circumstances of the case, and the existence of specific aggravating factors, whether an agreement to exclude certain persons or group of persons from representing the parties constitutes an *ordre public* violation. Where due process, fair and equal treatment of the parties, and the right to be heard are adversely affected, this may indeed be conceivable.

In any event, the Vienna Rules and Austrian law, adopting a liberal regime with **23-006** regards to the parties' representatives, afford the parties the right to be represented by persons of their choice. Indeed, while the leading arbitration institutions use slightly different wording to provide for a party's right representation, they all either express-ly or impliedly permit the parties to choose their representation freely.[12] The parties' right to choose their representatives typically extends to non-lawyers. The LCIA

(1991) XVI YB Comm Arb, 402. The survey identified in the early 1990's Singapore, Turkey, Japan, Portugal and Yugoslavia as arbitration venues which do not allow for foreign legal counsels. In almost all these countries the practice or law has changed).

9.   Vienna Rules 2001, **Annex 2a**.
10. P. Oberhammer, *Entwurf eines neuen Schiedsverfahrensrechts* (Vienna, Manz, 2002), p. 93; J. Power, *The Austrian Arbitration Act – A Practitioner's Guide to Sections 577-618 of the Austrian Code of Civil Procedure* (Vienna, Manz, 2006), Section 594, para 5. By contrast, Section 1042 German ZPO merely provides that lawyers cannot be excluded from being party representatives. *Reiner* points out that there is no justification for preventing the parties (as Section 594(3) ZPO does) in general terms from agreeing that only lawyers may appear as representatives in the arbitration. *See* A. Reiner, *Das neue österreichische Schiedsrecht/The new Austrian Arbitration Law* (Vienna, LexisNexis, 2006), Section 594, note 113. (This view is correct; but, of course, if the parties prefer to be represented by lawyers, as they may well do, they will appoint lawyers in any event.)
11. J. Power, *The Austrian Arbitration Act – A Practitioner's Guide to Sections 577-618 of the Austrian Code of Civil Procedure* (Vienna, Manz, 2006), Section 594, para. 5, with reference to Section 611(2) no. 5 ZPO.
12. J. Lew, L. Mistelis and S. Kröll, *Comparative International Commercial Arbitration* (The Hague, Kluwer Law International, 2003), para. 21-67 (explaining that the 'silence of the other rules should not be read as a tacit exclusion of non-lawyers' citing T. Tateishi, 'Recent

Rules state in Article 18, for example, that a party may be 'represented by legal practitioners *or any other representatives.*' The ICC Rules state that the parties 'may appear in person or through duly authorized representatives.'[13] Similarly, the UNCITRAL Rules allow a party to be presented by *'persons of their choice.'*[14] Within the framework of institutional rules, the right to free choice of counsel should extend not only to representation *'before the tribunal'* as the Vienna Rules suggest, but also to representation *vis-à-vis* the VIAC.

23-007 The wording of Article 23 (and Section 594(3) ZPO) provides the parties with great flexibility in choosing their representatives. Specifically, it does not require that the representatives have any legal background or set of qualifications.[15] Apparently by way of additional clarification, Article 23 provides that the parties may not only be represented, but also *advised* by persons of their choice.[16] An attorney may, or may not, have both capacities;[17] an adviser does not need a power of attorney, whereas a representative will typically need the power of attorney to appear before the tribunal with binding effect on the party he represents, in particular if that party is not present.[18] Indeed, some particular consequences attach only to the status of representatives.[19] However, since 'advisers' are specifically mentioned in Article 23, the parties may ask for a reimbursement of costs relating to advisers and representatives alike if those costs were appropriate within the meaning of **Article 32(b)**.[20]

23-008 Whatever the meaning of the distinction between representatives and advisers, it is clear that the parties are free to appoint representatives (or advisers) of their choosing without regard to specific qualifications. As a result, non-lawyers can be appointed as party representatives (or advisers) as well. Indeed, while the parties will typically choose to be represented by a lawyer,[21] the liberal regime set forth in the Vienna Rules and other institutional rules indicates that engineers or businessmen can represent the parties as well, including for the purposes of putting forward

---

Japanese Case Law in Relation to International Arbitrations' (2000) 17(4) J Int'l Arb, 66; D.W. Rivkin, 'Keeping Lawyers out of International Arbitration' (1990) Int'l Fin L Rev, 11).

13. Article 21(4) ICC Rules.
14. Article 4 UNCITRAL Rules.
15. J. Lew, L. Mistelis and S. Kröll, *Comparative International Commercial Arbitration* (The Hague, Kluwer Law International, 2003), para. 21-66.
16. *See also* Article 21(4) ICC Rules and Y. Derains and E.A. Schwartz, *A Guide to the ICC Rules of Arbitration* (2nd edn, The Hague, Kluwer Law International, 2005), p. 291.
17. Y. Derains and E.A. Schwartz, *A Guide to the ICC Rules of Arbitration* (2nd edn, The Hague, Kluwer Law International, 2005), p. 291.
18. Y. Derains and E.A. Schwartz, *A Guide to the ICC Rules of Arbitration* (2nd edn, The Hague, Kluwer Law International, 2005), p. 291.
19. *See* in particular **Article 13(3)**, at paras. 048 *et seq.*, regarding service to a representative.
20. *See* **Article 32(b)**, at para. 003.
21. A. Redfern, M. Hunter, N. Blackaby and C. Partasides, *Law and Practice of International Commercial Arbitration* (4th edn, London, Sweet & Maxwell, 2004), para. 6-108.

oral argument and examining witnesses. It may be appropriate to include non-lawyers with particular technical or other professional expertise in one's representation, depending on the nature of the case.[22] From a policy perspective, arbitration should certainly allow for the flexibility to accommodate forms of representations that would be unusual, or excluded, in state court litigation.

III.   AUTHORIZATION

International rules also typically provide that parties advance some proof of the **23-009** authority granted to their representatives.[23] The Vienna Rules do not specify the manner of authorization. Indeed, the Vienna Rules do not require (or even refer to) a power of attorney, much less one in writing. A written power of attorney may be required by the law applicable to the representation.[24] An Austrian attorney can rely on an oral power of attorney under Section 8 RAO, both for the representation of a party in the arbitration.[25]

In practice, many parties attach the appropriate power of attorney with their state- **23-010** ment of claims or the memorandum in reply, respectively. Usually, this is regularly requested from the Secretary General at the outset.[26] From the arbitrators' perspective, it is good practice to require such proof in any event, in order to confirm the representative's authority to represent that party, thus ensuring that a representative's submission in the arbitration is binding on the represented party. Indeed, a party that participates in the arbitration through a 'representative' lacking a power of attorney may be found not to have participated at all, potentially raising concerns for the enforceability of the award. It is therefore advisable that arbitrators ensure, upon application but also *ex officio* where appropriate, that a proper relationship of representation exists before accepting declarations and submissions of purported representatives in the proceedings.

---

22. A. Redfern, M. Hunter, N. Blackaby and C. Partasides, *Law and Practice of International Commercial Arbitration* (4th edn, London, Sweet & Maxwell, 2004), para. 6-107.
23. Under Article 4 UNCITRAL Rules, *e.g.*, the names and addresses of party representatives must be communicated in writing to the other party; such communication must specify whether the appointment is being made for purposes of representation or assistance.
24. C. Liebscher in *Institutionelle Schiedsgerichtsbarkeit*, R.A. Schütze (ed.) (Cologne, Carl Heymanns Verlag, 2006), p. 293.
25. OGH, 22 August 1928, 4 Ob 243/28, Rsp 1928/349, 194.
26. See **Article 9**, at para. 068.

Article 24

Applicable Law and Equity

		Para.				Para.
I.	The Substantive Law Applicable to				2.3. Tronc Commun and Other	
	the Dispute	1			Special Choice-of-Law	
	A. Introduction	1			Clauses	25
	B. Choice of Law by the				3. Restrictions on the Parties'	
	Parties	4			Autonomous Choice	27
	1. The Choice of a National				4. No *Renvoi*	35
	Law	7	II.	Determination of the Applicable Law		
	2. The Choice of Other Legal			by the Arbitrators		36
	Rules	9		A. Conceptual Approach		36
	2.1. General Principles			B. 'The Law' *v.* 'Rules of Law'		44
	of Law and *Lex*			C. 'Incorrect' Determination by		
	Mercatoria	11		the Arbitrators		46
	2.2. Trade Usages	20	III.	Equity-based Decisions		48

I.   THE SUBSTANTIVE LAW APPLICABLE TO THE DISPUTE

Article 24(1): The sole arbitrator (arbitral tribunal) shall decide the dispute in accordance with such legislation or rules of law as are chosen by the parties as applicable. Any choice of law or legal system of a given state shall be construed, unless otherwise expressed by the parties, as directly referring to the substantive law of that state and not to its conflict-of-law rules.

A.   INTRODUCTION

Article 24 addresses the issue of the law governing the substantive issues in dis- **24-001** pute, frequently referred to as the 'applicable law', the 'governing law', the 'substantive law' or the 'proper law of the contract'.[1] Article 24 does not address other conceivably relevant laws, such as the law governing the parties' capacity to conclude an arbitration agreement;[2] the law applicable to the arbitration agreement and its performance;[3] the law governing the arbitral proceedings (*lex arbitri*);[4] or the law(s) governing the recognition and enforcement of awards.[5]

24-002 In practice, it is often said that the substantive law, or its determination, plays a secondary role in arbitration, where arbitrators tend to focus on the terms of the commercial contracts between the parties and their interpretation. Where the parties are sophisticated commercial entities, and their agreements detailed, this may be true to some extent.[6] But of course, agreements, to have recognized consequences, do not exist in a legal vacuum. Rather, it is the substantive law that determines the validity of the contract, its interpretation; its performance; and the consequences attached to its breach.[7] Indeed, subsequent changes in the applicable law may modify or dissolve the contractual bonds defined by the parties.[8]

24-003 The determination of the applicable substantive law is also important since arbitrators, absent agreement by the parties, are in principle not entitled under Article 24(3) to base their decision on equity, but must base it in law. The discussion below is structured along the classic steps that any determination of the applicable law should follow: Is there a choice of law by the parties? If so, are there any applicable restrictions on that choice? Absent a choice, how should the arbitrators determine the applicable law?[9]

B.   CHOICE OF LAW BY THE PARTIES

24-004 In most international commercial contracts, parties will make an express choice as to the law governing their agreement. Such a choice of law is uniformly recognized

---

1. For the terminology, *see* A. Redfern, M. Hunter, N. Blackaby and C. Partasides, *Law and Practice of International Commercial Arbitration* (4th edn, London, Sweet & Maxwell, 2004), para. 2-04.
2. *See* **Article 1**, at paras. 033 *et seq.*
3. *See* **Article 2**, at paras. 032 *et seq.*
4. *See* **Article 2**, at paras. 037 *et seq.*
5. *See* **Article 2**, at paras. 069 *et seq.*
6. K.H. Böckstiegel, 'Perspectives of Future Development in International Arbitration' in *The Leading Arbitrator's Guide to International Arbitration*, L.W. Newman and R.D. Hill (eds) (Huntington, Juris Publishing, 2004), p. 505.
7. A. Redfern, M. Hunter, N. Blackaby and C. Partasides, *Law and Practice of International Commercial Arbitration* (4th edn, London, Sweet & Maxwell, 2004), para. 2-31.
8. A. Redfern, M. Hunter, N. Blackaby and C. Partasides, *Law and Practice of International Commercial Arbitration* (4th edn, London, Swet & Maxwell, 2004), para. 2-32 with reference to currency laws and resulting investment disputes in Czechoslovakia.
9. For a more elaborate three-step method, *see also* J. Lew, L. Mistelis and S. Kröll, *Comparative International Commercial Arbitration* (The Hague, Kluwer Law International, 2003), para. 17-78. This method is not entirely applicable under the Vienna Rules which imposes its own structure on the arbitrators' determination of the applicable law.

by major international conventions, most notably the Rome Convention within the European Union.[10] National laws (including Austrian law), as well as all major institutional arbitration rules[11], are also typically allowing for the parties' choice of law as a fundamental expression of party autonomy.[12] Today, this autonomy is recognized to the extent that the parties can modify their choice, or introduce a new chosen law, after they have entered into their original agreement, including when their dispute arises.[13] Indeed, some commentators argue that party autonomy with respect to the parties' choice of law

> operates as a right in itself. The rule has a special transnational or universal character and has binding effect because it has been agreed to and adopted by the parties. Unquestionably, party autonomy is the most prominent and widely accepted international conflict of laws rule. These national conflict of laws systems recognize that contracting parties do express their view as to the law to govern their contractual relations, and the national laws have no reason to ignore and very limited rights to interfere with the expressed will of the parties.[14]

In Austria, the fZPO did not address the matter for international arbitrations. **24-005** However, Austria, which is a signatory to the Rome Convention, has recognized the parties' autonomy to choose an applicable substantive law under Sections 11, 19 and 35 IPRG. In addition, Section 603 ZPO now provides:

> The arbitrators shall decide the dispute in accordance with the law or the rules of law which have been agreed by the parties.

---

10. In Austria: *Europäisches Vertragsstatutübereinkommen*, BGBl III No. 166/1998 and BGBl III No. 208/1998. The Convention is – according to *Giuliano Lagarde* – 'a uniform measure of private international law which will replace the rules of private international law in force in each of the Contracting States, with regard to the subject matter which it covers and subject to any other convention to which the Contracting States are party'. *See* D. Czernich and H. Heiss, *EVÜ: Das Europäische Schuldvertragsübereinkommen* (Vienna, LexisNexis, 1999), paras. 15 *et seq.*; D. Czernich and H. Heiss, 'Das Europäische Schuldvertragsübereinkommen: Neues internationales Vertragsrecht für Österreich' [1998] ÖJZ, 681.
11. *See* J. Lew, *Applicable Law in International Commercial Arbitration* (The Hague, Kluwer Law International, 1978), p. 75.
12. J. Lew, L. Mistelis and S. Kröll, *Comparative International Commercial Arbitration* (The Hague, Kluwer Law International, 2003), para. 17-8 with further references.
13. *See* Article 3 Rome Convention; apparently confirming this position: P. Oberhammer, *Entwurf eines neuen Schiedsverfahrensrechts* (Vienna, Manz, 2002), p. 111.
14. J. Lew, L. Mistelis and S. Kröll, *Comparative International Commercial Arbitration* (The Hague, Kluwer Law International, 2003), para. 17-10. *See also* E. Gaillard and J. Savage (eds), *Fouchard Gaillard Goldman On International Commercial Arbitration* (The Hague, Kluwer Law International, 1999), paras. 1421, 1430 with further references; M. Rubino-Sammartano, *International Arbitration – Law and Practice* (2nd edn, The Hague, Kluwer Law International, 2001), pp. 417 *et seq.*; L. Collins (gen. eds), *Dicey, Morris and Collins On The Conflict of Laws* (14th edn, London, Sweet & Maxwell, 2006), para. 32; E.F. Scoles, P. Hay, P. Borchers and S.C. Symeonides, *Conflict of Laws* (4th edn, London, Thomson, 2004), pp. 947 *et seq.*

24-006 This provisions effectively follows Article 28(1) of the UNCITRAL Model Law and Section 1051(1) German ZPO.

1. The Choice of a National Law

24-007 As discussed, most parties in cross-border transactions include a choice-of-law clause in their commercial agreements. Parties typically choose a law that they (or their lawyers) are familiar with; that is accessible; that is sophisticated and reliable in the relevant field; that is suitable to govern international contracts;[15] and that will likely remain stable over time.[16] Arbitrators need to be aware that, under Article 3(1) of the Rome Convention, the parties' choice of law need not be express – such choice can also be *implied* if the parties have 'demonstrated with reasonable certainty' that a certain law was chosen by them. On the other hand, arbitrators should not infer an implied choice of law where the parties were lacking a clear intention to make such a choice.[17]

24-008 The choice of a law incorporates all rules of a legal system 'with the hierarchy of sources as valid in that system [including] references to statutes, case law, scholarly writings and customs, with the authority they are vested with in that legal system.'[18] Thus, the choice of the national law of an EU member state also incorporates applicable EU law.

---

15. Laws that, by way of currency and trade regulations and restrictions, do not permit the free exchange of goods across borders may, for example, not be the best laws for international contracts. *See* A. Redfern, M. Hunter, N. Blackaby and C. Partasides, *Law and Practice of International Commercial Arbitration* (4th edn, London, Sweet & Maxwell, 2004), para. 2-42.

16. This is a particular concern in contracts with states or state parties, where the state legislature can change a law that turns out to be unfavorable to it. Parties try to preempt such adverse changes by 'freezing clauses' (which agree on the law as of a given date) or 'stabilization clauses' (by which the state undertakes not to make adverse changes without the consent of the other party). For a discussion of such clauses and their problems, *see* E. Gaillard, 'The Role of the Arbitrator in Determining the Applicable Law' in *The Leading Arbitrator's Guide to International Arbitration*, L.W. Newman and R.D. Hill (eds) (Huntington, Juris Publishing, 2004), p. 185; A. Redfern, M. Hunter, N. Blackaby and C. Partasides, *Law and Practice of International Commercial Arbitration* (4th edn, London, Sweet & Maxwell, 2004), para. 2-44, with further references, and paras. 2-48 *et seq.*

17. *See* M. Giuliano and P. Lagarde, 'Report on the Convention on the law applicable to contractual obligations' *Journal Officiel No. C 282, 31 October 1980*, 1, 17. Arbitrators seem to have implied a choice of law, for example, when parties argued their case on the basis of the same law. *See* J. Lew, L. Mistelis and S. Kröll, *Comparative International Commercial Arbitration* (The Hague, Kluwer Law International, 2003), para. 17-16.

18. J. Lew, L. Mistelis and S. Kröll, *Comparative International Commercial Arbitration* (The Hague, Kluwer Law International, 2003), para. 18-24.

2.   The Choice of Other Legal Rules

Parties sometimes choose legal sources other than national laws, such as 'general **24-009** principles' of law, transnational law, *lex mercatoria* or trade usages. It is widely accepted that parties can in principle do so.[19] However, former Article 16 appeared to limit the parties' ability to refer to other 'rules of law' as opposed to a national law in the strict sense.[20]

This restrictive approach has now been abandoned in favor of the more liberal rule **24-010** in Article 24(1) which allows the parties to choose a law or 'rules of law' to govern the substance of their dispute. Similarly, Section 603(1) ZPO provides that the arbitrators must decide the parties' dispute in accordance with the laws or 'rules of law' ('*Rechtsvorschriften oder Rechtsregeln*') on which the parties have agreed. The term 'rules of law' was added specifically to allow the parties greater flexibility to choose a normative framework other than a precisely-delineated national law and to 'leave the door wide open for party autonomy.'[21] The drafters intended that this term would also cover internationally recognized legal principles, including the UNIDROIT Principles of International Commercial Contracts (UNIDROIT Principles).[22] This solution is appropriate. There are strong reasons to permit the parties to agree on whatever normative framework they deem appropriate. Indeed, if parties are free to agree that the arbitrators decide in equity, there is no reason to prevent them from submitting their dispute to legal rules other than national laws.[23] In this regard, party autonomy should reign supreme.[24]

2.1.   *General Principles of Law and* Lex Mercatoria

Parties sometimes agree on the application of 'general principles of law.' In **24-011** practical terms, this is not without problems because such references may lack the specificity required to solve particular legal issues. If a reference to 'general principles of law' is desired, it may therefore be preferable to agree on such principles as a concurrent body of rules complementing a national law.[25]

---

19. J. Lew, L. Mistelis and S. Kröll, *Comparative International Commercial Arbitration* (The Hague, Kluwer Law International, 2003), para. 17-18.
20. Article 16 Vienna Rules 2001 provided that the tribunal must apply '*the law* that the parties have designated as applicable.' **Annex 2a**. This is in contrast to other provisions which appear to give the parties greater flexibility. Article 17(1) ICC Rules, for example, provides that 'the parties shall be free to agree upon the *rules of law* to be applied by the Arbitral Tribunal to the merits of the dispute'.
21. P. Oberhammer, *Entwurf eines neuen Schiedsverfahrensrechts* (Vienna, Manz, 2002), p. 109.
22. P. Oberhammer, *Entwurf eines neuen Schiedsverfahrensrechts* (Vienna, Manz, 2002), p. 109.
23. P. Oberhammer, *Entwurf eines neuen Schiedsverfahrensrechts* (Vienna, Manz, 2002), p. 109.
24. For legitimate restrictions on party autonomy, *see* **Article 24**, at paras. 027 *et seq.*
25. Concurrent choices may also be another way to protect a party when contracting with a state, by agreeing to that state's law unless it is contrary to general principles of international law.

24-012 One such possible source of legal rules, at least to some, is the so-called *lex mercatoria* as a set of rules and practices developed and recognized by the international business communities. It appears rooted, in part, in Article 38(a) of the Statute of the International Court of Justice, complemented 'by the general and constant usage of international trade.'[26] The emergence of INCOTERMS, ICC Code of Practices, and the UNIDROIT Principles have been said to evidence the development of such uniform international standards[27] and international conventions such as the UN Convention on Contracts for the International Sale of Goods and are seen as a source of transnational rules as well.[28]

24-013 Scholarly writings in the field sought to establish a list of rules that form part of *lex mercatoria*. Such rules include such fundamental principles as *pacta sunt servanda; clausula rebus sic stantibus; culpa in contrahendo;* performance of a contract in good faith; illegal purpose may void a contract; and others.[29]

24-014 Early proponents of *lex mercatoria* were the late Professors *Goldman*[30] and *Fouchard*, and the concept seems to have attracted considerable attention from the international arbitration community.[31] Austrian and German scholars have been mostly reserved.[32] The Austrian *Oberster Gerichtshof*, however, appears to have accepted the concept of *lex mercatoria* in a decision which at the time attracted only limited attention in Austria,[33] but which has been the subject of

---

See A. Redfern, M. Hunter, N. Blackaby and C. Partasides, *Law and Practice of International Commercial Arbitration* (4th edn, London, Sweet & Maxwell, 2004), paras. 2-47 *et seq.*

26. B. Goldman, 'Lex Mercatoria' (1983) 3 *Forum Internationale*, 21. For a definition of *lex mercatoria, see also* B. Goldman, 'The Applicable Law: General Principles of Law' in *Contemporary Problems in International Arbitration*, J. Lew (ed.) (The Hague, Kluwer Law International, 1987), p. 113.
27. *See* recently D. Brödermann, 'Die erweiterten UNIDROIT Prinzipien 2004' [2004] RIW, 721.
28. J. Lew, L. Mistelis and S. Kröll, *Comparative International Commercial Arbitration* (The Hague, Kluwer Law International, 2003), para. 18-55, note 61, with further references.
29. For such lists, *see* J. Lew, L. Mistelis and S. Kröll, *Comparative International Commercial Arbitration* (The Hague, Kluwer Law International, 2003), para. 18-57; O. Lando, 'The Lex Mercatoria and International Commercial Arbitration' (1985) 34(4) ICLQ, 747; M.J. Mustill, 'The New Lex Mercatoria: the First Twenty-five Years' in *Liber amicorum for Lord Wilberforce*, M. Boss and I. Brownlie (eds) (Oxford, Clarendon Press, 1987), pp. 149-183.
30. B. Goldman, 'Lex Mercatoria' (1983) 3 *Forum Internationale*.
31. *See* P. Lalive, 'Transnational (or Truly International) Public Policy and International Arbitration' (1986) 3 ICCA Congress Series (New York), 258; E. Gaillard, 'Transnational Rules in International Arbitration' (1993) ICC Pub No. 480/4, 19-36.
32. F.A. Mann, 'The Proper Law in the Conflict of Laws' (1987) 36(3) ICLQ, 437. Critics point out that 'general principles' are not sufficiently particular to be applied to and provide real solutions for specific problems.
33. *See*, however, the detailed, albeit skeptical, analysis by E.-M. Bajons, 'Zur Nationalität internationaler Schiedssachen – Der Fall "Norsolor" vor den österreichischen Gerichten'

widespread international commentary:[34] the case of *Norsolor SA v. Pabalk Ticaret*.[35]

The *Norsolor* case arose from an ICC arbitration sited in Vienna. The claimant in **24-015** the arbitration had terminated an agency agreement with the defendant, and was seeking damages. Absent a choice of law by the parties, the tribunal did not determine the applicable law by reference to appropriate conflict of laws rules, but referred instead to *lex mercatoria* and the principle of good faith: 'Faced with the difficulty of choosing a national law the application of which is sufficiently compelling, the tribunal considered it appropriate, given the international nature of the agreement, to leave aside any compelling reference to a specific legislation, be it Turkish or French, and to apply the international *lex mercatoria*. One of the principles which inspires the latter is that of the good faith which must preside over the formation and the performance of contracts.'[36] On that basis, the tribunal found that the defendant was to blame for the termination of the agency agreement. The defendant in the arbitration challenged the award in the Austrian courts, alleging, first, that the tribunal, by referring to *lex mercatoria*, and relying on the principle of good faith had violated provisions of Austrian mandatory law and *ordre public*.[37]

The Austrian *Oberster Gerichtshof* upheld the award, demonstrating that Austrian **24-016** courts will interpret the grounds for setting aside an award under Section 611 ZPO (Section 595 fZPO) narrowly. The Austrian *Oberster Gerichtshof* held, first, that 'the tribunal had refused to apply conflicts of laws rules of a national law and instead relied, referring to the "*lex mercatoria*", on the principle of good faith ("*Treu und Glauben*") when resolving the issue of whether the claimant was liable to the defendant for damages resulting from the claimant's termination of the agency agreement. In doing so, the tribunal applied an inherent principle of private law orders, which cannot conceivably go against mandatory legal rules of the relevant jurisdictions in this case.' Thus, the Austrian *Oberster Gerichtshof* found that the award did not violate Austrian mandatory rules or *ordre public*.

---

in *Festschrift für Winfried Kralik zum 65. Geburtstag*, W.H. Rechberger und R. Welser (eds) (Vienna, Manz, 1986), pp. 3, 22 *et seq*.; *see also* W. Melis, Case note to OGH, 18 November 1982, 8 Ob 520/82 (1984) IX YB Comm Arb, 159, 162 *et seq*.; I. Seidl-Hohenveldern, Case note to OGH, 18 November 1982, 8 Ob 520/82, (1983) JDI, 645.

34. B. Goldman, 'Une bataille judiciaire autour de la lex mercatoria – L'affaire Norsolor' [1983] Rev Arb, 379; P. Schlosser, Case note to OGH, 18 November 1982, 8 Ob 520/82 [1983] KTS, 666; B. von Hoffmann, 'Lex Mercatoria vor internationalen Schiedsgerichten' [1984] IPRax, 106; M.J. Mustill, 'Transnational Arbitration and English Law' (1984) 37 *Current Legal Problems*, 133.

35. OGH, 18 November 1982, 8 Ob 520/82.

36. As cited by the French *Cour de Cassation* in proceedings relating to the enforcement of the *Norsolor* award in France, 9 October 1984, (1986) XI YB Comm Arb, 484.

37. The lower courts had already held that a violation of arbitral rules regarding the timing or length of the proceedings does not constitute a ground for challenge under Section 595(1) no. 3 fZPO (which concerns mandatory provisions regarding the constitution and decision-making of the tribunal). These findings were confirmed by the Austrian *Oberster Gerichtshof*.

24-017 Having found the claimant liable on that basis, the arbitrators had assessed the quantum of the liability according to equity. Under the then applicable ICC Rules, the arbitrators' power to decide in equity ought to have been expressly authorized by the parties in the terms of reference. This did not happen, and the award was challenged on this ground as well. The Austrian *Oberster Gerichtshof* held, however, that 'the question of whether the arbitral tribunal was permitted to decide in equity or if it should have quantified damages in a detailed analysis, is a question pertaining to the structure and effects of the procedure, and as such not be ground for setting aside the award under [then] Section 595 no. 6 fZPO[38] [dealing with mandatory provisions and *ordre public*].' The claimant also argued that by deciding in equity without express authorization, the arbitrators went beyond the scope of their jurisdiction and decided *ultra petita.*[39] The Austrian *Oberster Gerichtshof* rejected this argument as well because the decision on damages as such was covered by the scope of the arbitration agreement and because the decision on damages also did not exceed the parties' applications.

24-018 This decision has been heavily criticized by *Bajons* because, in her view, the Austrian *Oberster Gerichtshof* arguments essentially remove arbitral decisions from *any* effective control by the courts, opening the door for the application of arbitrary or indeed no legal standards by arbitrators. According to *Bajons*, the supposed 'standard' imposed by the *lex mercatoria* and by principles such as good faith is insufficient because such principles require a concrete manifestation in the normative rules of a national law.[40] *Seidl-Hohenveldern*, on the other hand, welcomed the decision, arguing that an award based on legal principles is an award in law. German scholars have been critical[41], and the German *Bundesgerichtshof* set aside an award in 1988, holding that the award was not reasoned as it did not reveal which law the arbitrators applied.[42] *Melis* pointed out that the impact of the decision in *Norsolor* should not be overstated. The Austrian *Oberster Gerichtshof* merely held that a decision based on general legal principles and/or equity does not (necessarily) violate mandatory law; the Austrian *Oberster Gerichtshof* did, however, not address, let alone set out to define, the legal nature of *lex mercatoria.*[43]

24-019 The decision in *Norsolor SA*, and the commentary it attracted, are children of their time. From today's perspective, *Melis'* analysis is ultimately most on point. The decision in *Norsolor SA* did little to clarify the nature of *lex mercatoria*.

---

38. Note: This provision at the time did not contain the reference to Section 35 IPRG and was therefore arguably broader.
39. Section 595 no. 5 in the then applicable version of the ZPO.
40. E.-M. Bajons, 'Zur Nationalität internationaler Schiedssachen – Der Fall, "Norsolor" vor den österreichischen Gerichten' in *Festschrift für Winfried Kralik zum 65. Geburtstag*, W.H. Rechberger und R. Welser (eds) (Vienna, Manz, 1986), pp. 24-27.
41. *See* G. Walter and B. von Hoffmann, 'Lex Mercatoria vor internationalen Schiedsgerichten' [1984] IPRax, 106.
42. BGH, 3 May 1988, X ZR 99/86, ZfRV 1989, 149.
43. W. Melis, Case note to OGH, 18 November 1982, 8 Ob 520/82 (1984) IX YB Comm Arb, 159, 163.

The decision in *Norsolor SA* is more remarkable for its courageous support of arbitration. Arbitration was in the 1980s not the predominant method of international dispute resolution that it is today, and many commentators must have felt uncomfortable with acknowledging the equality of arbitration and the courts. Indeed, even well-argued and very persuasive commentaries such as from *Bajons* reveal a great discomfort that arbitration may slip out of the control of the courts, which effectively betrays a distrust in arbitration itself. Yet by focusing on the nature of *lex mercatoria* and the fundamental importance of determining and applying the 'correct' law, these commentaries neglect the critical question if the *result* in *Norsolor SA* was such that it would have warranted setting aside the award. As the Austrian *Oberster Gerichtshof* explained, 'no-one even argued that the application of equity led to a violation of mandatory substantive law.'[44] Thus, the real value of the *Norsolor SA* decision is in its application of a modern *result-based* standard, which places trust in the arbitral process and affords it the desired flexibility: if the decision as such does not violate the *ordre public*, it is ultimately of less importance by application of what legal rules the arbitrators arrive at that decision. This approach appears to be in line with modern doctrine that courts must not review the merits of the arbitrators' decision on the merits, save in exceptional circumstances where the *ordre public* warrants otherwise.

2.2.   Trade Usages

Neither Article 24 nor Section 603 ZPO expressly refer to trade usages.[45] However, **24-020** by allowing the parties to agree on the application of 'rules of law', accepted trade usages are relevant.[46] Indeed, it appears that the legislature did not adopt the provision of Article 28(4) UNCITRAL Model Law (which expressly requires the arbitrators to take account of trade usages and of the parties' contract) simply because it was thought that doing so would be 'stating the obvious.'[47]

International arbitration rules frequently require arbitrators to take account of **24-021** relevant trade usage.[48] In such cases, trade usages are perceived to form an integral

---

44. OGH, 18 November 1982, 8 Ob 502/82.
45. Trade usages refer to the Austrian (and German) legal term *Handelsbrauch*. This must not be confused with the Austrian term *Usance* which frequently means general terms of business.
46. Indeed, the extension to rules of law was specifically included to allow the application of, *e.g.*, the UNIDROIT Principles. *See* P. Oberhammer, *Entwurf eines neuen Schiedsverfahrensrechts* (Vienna, Manz, 2002), p. 109. For a discussion of the term 'rules of law', *see* **Article 24**, at paras. 010, 020 and 045.
47. P. Oberhammer, *Entwurf eines neuen Schiedsverfahrensrechts* (Vienna, Manz, 2002), p. 111. *See also* A. Reiner, 'The 2001 Version of the Vienna Rules' (2001) 18(6) J Int'l Arb, 661, 665; C. Liebscher in *Institutionelle Schiedsgerichtsbarkeit*, R.A. Schütze (ed.) (Cologne. Carl Heymanns Verlag, 2006), p. 294.
48. *See, e.g.*, Article 17(2) ICC Rules: 'In all cases the Arbitral Tribunal shall take account of the provisions of the contract and the relevant trade usages'. And Article 33(3) UNCITRAL Rules: 'In all cases the arbitral tribunal shall decide in accordance with the terms of the contract and shall take into account the usages of the trade applicable to the transaction'.

part of the contract, providing insight as to the parties' intentions.[49] The relevant trade usages will be typically established by evidence provided by the parties, unless perhaps the arbitrators are specialists in the field.[50] The ICC as an institution has been prominent in attempting to establish a commonly understood meaning for expressions that are in frequent use in international trade contracts.[51] The ICC materials are often quoted to determine trade usage, but the dispositive factor is the extent to which the industry accepts and practices the custom in question. It has also been suggested that parties do not necessarily have to be consciously aware of the trade usage; it is enough if trade usage itself justifies an expectation that such custom and usage in the trade will be observed.[52]

24-022 Trade usage has on occasion even been contended to provide the basis for arbitration. In *New Moon Shipping Co. v. MAN B&W Diesel AG* for example, the court held that arbitration did rise to the level of trade usage between the two parties over the course of their business relationship. Here, a manufacturer sent purchase order confirmations containing an arbitration clause to the buyer in each business transaction. The buyer either signed and returned the forms or retained them without objection. Over time the buyer submitted to arbitration in every situation where it received a purchase order confirmation.[53]

24-023 Some commentators argue that accepted trade standards should be applied in preference to the rules of national law.[54] Such preference is based on the assumption that trade usages are closer to the commercial realities and thus will more accurately

---

49. *See* J. Lew, *Applicable Law in International Commercial Arbitration* (The Hague, Kluwer Law International, 1978), p. 465.
50. A. Redfern, M. Hunter, N. Blackaby and C. Partasides, *Law and Practice of International Commercial Arbitration* (4th edn, London, Sweet & Maxwell, 2004), para. 2-70. Similarly, in Austria, trade usages are treated as an issue of fact that needs to be proven unless it is notorious, *i.e.*, widely-accepted and known to the court. *See* E.A. Kramer in *Kommentar zum HGB, 1*, M. Straube (ed.) (3rd edn, Vienna Manz, 2003), Section 346, para. 30.
51. 'Incoterms 2000' (1999) ICC Pub No. 560, cited in A. Redfern, M. Hunter, N. Blackaby and C. Partasides, *Law and Practice of International Commercial Arbitration* (4th edn, London, Sweet & Maxwell, 2004), para. 2-70; J. Lew, *Applicable Law in International Commercial Arbitration* (The Hague, Kluwer Law International, 1978), p. 455 ('They (. . .) are today extensively used in international trade and recognized and uniformly interpreted throughout the world.'); *see also* Uniform Customs and Practice for Documentary Credits, (1983) ICC Pub No. 400 (generalizing banking practices).
52. McKinney's consolidated laws of New York, Book 62 1/5, Uniform Commercial Code (St. Pauls, Thomson West, 2006), Section 1-205(2).
53. *New Moon Shipping Co. v. MAN B&W Diesel AG*, 121 F.3d 24 (2nd Cir. 1997). By contrast, *in Avedon Engineering*, the defendant proposed arbitration which was customarily used in the textile industry and introduced two trade codes and an affidavit by a textile merchant in support of this proposal. The court found this evidence to be insufficient to show (as matter of New York law) that arbitration was customary. *See Avedon Engineering, Inc. v. Seatex*, 126 F.3d 1279 (10th Cir. 1997).
54. J. Lew, L. Mistelis and S. Kröll, *Comparative International Commercial Arbitration* (The Hague, Kluwer Law International, 2003), para. 18-4.

reflect the intentions and expectations of the contracting parties.[55] Finally, under the assumption that the arbitrator has no *lex fori*,[56] trade usage will be subject only to international public policy and the policy of the state in which enforcement is most likely to be sought.[57]

While trade usages indeed are practicable instruments in resolving commercial dis- **24-024** putes, they should be given the weight they have in the context of the applicable substantive law.[58] Recognizing this, Article 17(2) of the ICC Rules requires the arbitrators to apply trade usages, but merely to 'take account of the provisions of the contract and the relevant trade usages.' Similarly, as a matter of Austrian substantive law, Section 346 UGB requires that trade usages need to be taken into account to determine the meaning and effect of conduct as between commercial entities. Under that provision, trade usage is applied to interpret and, under certain circumstances, to complement the parties' agreements.[59]

2.3. Tronc Commun and Other Special Choice-of-Law Clauses

Another suggested possibility is the choice of a combination of laws, or principles **24-025** of laws, under the doctrine of *tronc commun*.[60] Here, the choice of law clause provides for the application of legal principles common to two (or more) national laws. In the famous *Channel Tunnel* arbitration, for example, the parties provided that their contract 'in all respects be governed by and interpreted in accordance with the principles common to both English law and French law, and in the absence of such common principles by such general principles of international trade law as have been applied by national and international tribunals.'[61] While the courts upheld this choice of 'law', it is obvious that any such choice can require considerable efforts to determine what, if any, common principles exist between the two referred laws. In practice, therefore, the choice of a single commercially-sophisticated and reliable national law will generally be more preferable.

---

55. J. Lew, *Applicable Law in International Commercial Arbitration* (The Hague, Kluwer Law International, 1978), p. 443.
56. *See* **Article 2**, at para. 028.
57. J. Lew, *Applicable Law in International Commercial Arbitration* (The Hague, Kluwer Law International, 1978), p. 440.
58. In Austria, trade usages cannot override mandatory commercial law. *See* E.A. Kramer in *Kommentar zum HGB, 1*, M. Straube (ed.) (3rd edn, Vienna Manz, 2003), Section 346, para. 20.
59. E.A. Kramer in *Kommentar zum HGB, 1*, M. Straube (ed.) (3rd edn, Vienna Manz, 2003), Section 346, paras. 1, 5, 17 *et seq*. The reference to trade practices as an interpretative instrument continues under the new *Unternehmensgesetzbuch* (UGB) that replaced the *Handelsgesetzbuch* (HGB) as of 1 January 2007. The amendment of Section 346 only regards the subjective scope of the provision, which is now addressed at companies. *See* M. Schauer in *Reform-Kommentar UGB*, S. Bydlinski *et al.* (eds) (Vienna, Manz, 2007), Section 346, para. 1.
60. *See* M. Rubino-Sammartano, 'The Channel Tunnel and the Tronc Commun Doctrine' (1993) 10(3) J Int'l Arb, 59.
61. *Channel Tunnel Group Ltd. v. Balfour Beatty Construction Ltd.* (1992) 1 Q.B., 656 (Comm.).

24-026 Parties may also agree on a 'floating choice' whereby a particular law, from a pool of two or more alternatives, becomes applicable depending in which jurisdiction the claim is brought. So-called 'saving clauses' typically refer to two national laws and provide that the law under which the claim is preserved shall apply. Such saving clauses have been upheld by the Austrian *Oberster Gerichtshof.*[62] Parties, or arbitrators, have also been known to distinguish between different parts of a single contract, applying different laws to each part (*dépeçage*).[63]

3. Restrictions on the Parties' Autonomous Choice

24-027 If the parties have chosen the applicable law, arbitrators should refrain, as a matter of principle, from second-guessing the parties' choice.[64] However, the parties' freedom to apply a law of their choosing may indeed be limited by good faith considerations and public policy.[65] Consequently, a choice of law for the purpose of tax evasion could be found invalid,[66] as could the distribution of profits from drug dealing; smuggling; slavery or prostitution; money laundering; the supply of weapons to terrorists or enemy states; or indeed any transaction designed to circumvent or evade criminal sanctions.[67] On the other hand, public policy claims should not be allowed to easily override the parties' choice of law.[68]

---

62. OGH, 23 February 1998, *Kajo-Erzeugnisse Essenzen GmbH v. DO Zdravilisce Radenska* (1999) XXIVa YB Comm Arb, 919.

63. J. Lew, L. Mistelis and S. Kröll, *Comparative International Commercial Arbitration* (The Hague, Kluwer Law International, 2003), para. 17-20, with further references.

64. For a detailed discussion of various unsatisfactory theories of the arbitrator-substituted application of laws, *see* E. Gaillard and J. Savage (eds), *Fouchard Gaillard Goldman On International Commercial Arbitration* (The Hague, Kluwer Law International, 1999), paras. 1511 *et seq.*

65. *See, e.g.*, Article 7 Rome Convention on the law applicable to Contractual Obligations.

66. A. Redfern, M. Hunter, N. Blackaby and C. Partasides, *Law and Practice of International Commercial Arbitration* (4th edn, London, Sweet & Maxwell, 2004), para. 2-37.

67. *See* references in J. Lew, L. Mistelis and S. Kröll, *Comparative International Commercial Arbitration* (The Hague, Kluwer Law International, 2003), para. 17-36.

68. *See Caterpillar Financial Services Corporation v. SNC Passion* [2004] EWHC, 569 Q.B. (Comm.) and case note in [2004] 4(5) Arb L Monthly, 11 *et seq.* In this case, the defendant (a French company) had entered into a credit agreement with the claimant (a Delaware company) through the claimant's UK office. When the defendant defaulted, he raised the defense in the arbitration that the credit agreement was void under domestic French law, because credit agreements, in order to be valid, require that the lender is an authorized credit institution under French regulatory law. Thus, the defendant argued that under Article 3(3) of the Rome Convention the parties' choice of English law did not prevent the nullity of the credit agreement. *J. Cooke* held that the contract was sufficiently international under the circumstances, so that there was no reason to assume that the parties had isolated an otherwise domestic French contract from French law for the purpose of evading French banking regulations.

The position in Austrian doctrine is based on Section 595(1) no. 6 fZPO (now **24-028**
Section 611(2) no. 8 ZPO).[69] Under this public policy reservation, an award will be
set aside if it is irreconcilable with the 'basic principles of the Austrian legal
system,' that is, if the award 'would be entirely incompatible with the Austrian
legal order and such incompatibility were obvious'[70] or if an award causes an
'unacceptable infringement of the fundamental policies of the Austrian legal
system'.[71] Such fundamental policies or values can come from Austrian constitutional law, criminal law, civil law, administrative law, or EU law.[72]

Section 595(1) no. 6 fZPO also permitted *vacatur* if the award were to violate **24-029**
provisions of mandatory Austrian law that cannot be opted out of under Austrian
choice of law rules pursuant to Section 35 IPRG.[73] The relevant 'provisions of
mandatory law' under Section 35 IPRG are limited to consumer contracts, some
lease contracts, and employment contracts.[74] It has been inferred from these limited
grounds for *vacatur* that, apart from the public policy restrictions and the matters
covered by Section 35 IPRG, Austrian Private International Law allows parties to
deviate from mandatory provisions of Austrian law.[75] Thus, arbitrators in an arbitration in Austria could ignore the parties' choice of law insofar such choice violated
Austrian (or international) public policy or those mandatory provisions of Austrian
law cemented in Section 35 IPRG. Under Section 611(2) no. 8 ZPO, this ground for

---

69. It will typically be the public policy of the *situs* state that impacts on the parties' choice of law,
    through that state's *vacatur* provisions. *See* G.B. Born, *International Commercial Arbitration –
    Commentary and Materials* (2nd edn, The Hague, Kluwer Law International, 2001), p. 559.
70. OGH, 23 February 1998, 3 Ob 115/95.
71. C. Liebscher, *The Healthy Award* (The Hague, Kluwer Law International, 2003), pp. 310-311,
    with reference to OGH, 8 June 2000, 2 Ob 158/00z.
72. *See* the discussion under **Article 20**, at para. 047.
73. H.W. Fasching, *Schiedsgericht und Schiedsverfahren im österreichischen und im internatio-
    nalen Recht* (Vienna, Manz, 1973), p. 108.
74. OGH, 31 August 1995, 3 Ob 566/95; C. Liebscher, *The Healthy Award* (The Hague, Kluwer
    Law International, 2003), p. 311, with further references.
75. C. Liebscher, *The Healthy Award* (The Hague, Kluwer Law International, 2003), p. 311, with
    further references. It should also be noted that, when the parties have chosen a particular law, the
    reference to mandatory provisions of another law seems arbitrary and will frustrate the parties'
    choice. Such a reference should therefore be adopted only when justified because of public
    policy concerns. *See* the famous example in *Hilmarton*, in which the arbitrators voided a con-
    tract governed by Swiss law because mandatory Algerian law prohibited the use of agents. The
    award was later set aside by the Geneva courts in Cour de Justice de Genève, 17 November
    1989, *Hilmarton v. OTV*, (1994) XIX YB Comm Arb, 214, on the basis that the use of
    intermediaries does not violate Swiss public policy. The *vacatur* decision was confirmed by
    the Swiss *Bundesgericht* (BGer, 17 April 1990, *Hilmarton v. OTV*, [1993] Rev Arb, 342; (1994)
    XIX YB Comm Arb, 214, 220). *But see Westinghouse Elec. Corp. v. Republic of Philippines* 951
    F.2d 1414 (3rd Cir. 1991), (1992) 7(1) Mealey's Int'l Arb Rep, B-1 *et seq.*; *Award in ICC Case
    No. 7047 of 1994 Westacre Investments Inc. v. Jugoimport – SPDR Holding Co. Ltd. & others*,
    (1995) 13(2) Bull ASA, 301, confirmed by the Swiss *Bundesgericht*, 30 December 1994, *F. and
    U. v. W Inc.*, (1995) 13(2) Bull ASA, 217.

vacatur is now limited to public policy only, without additional reference to certain provisions of mandatory law.[76]

24-030 A related issue is whether arbitrators, irrespective of the law chosen by the parties, have to apply certain regulatory rules or laws that aim to protect the public order (*loie de police*), such as currency and exchange regulations; competition law; restrictions on real estate transfer; or trade law (*Eingriffsnormen*, 'protective rules').[77] These *Eingriffsnormen* can apply because they are part of the substantive law; or part of the *ordre public* of the arbitral *situs*; or, relevant if enforcement is resisted, part of the law at the place of enforcement.

24-031 The most difficult situation for arbitrators arises, however, if the parties fail to raise the application of such legal rules during the arbitration. Because of the public policy nature of such rules, there is some debate if arbitrators have to apply such provisions *ex officio*, even if the parties do not rely on them. Under Article 7 of the Rome Convention, there is no clear rule whether such provisions need to be taken into account.[78] On the one hand, international arbitrators that have no connection to the arbitral *situs*, unlike judges, do not perform a judicial function in the name of or on behalf of a state – their mandate is one of resolving the parties' disputes, not of policing the parties.[79] Also, if arbitrators apply legal rules that have not been pleaded by the parties they may go beyond the scope of their mandate.[80] The problem of *ultra petita* may be even more pronounced if the parties *agree* that these provisions, e.g. of EU competition law, are not applicable in their case.

24-032 On the other hand, disregard of such *Eingriffsnormen* may lead to *vacatur* if they form part of the *ordre public*, and some laws may expose the arbitrators themselves to sanctions if ignored. It is now firmly established, for example, that EU competition law as provided by Articles 81 and 82 EC Treaty constitutes part of the European *ordre public*, because of their fundamental importance for the functioning of the internal market.[81] Similar public policy concerns are raised with respect

---

76. *See* the discussion under **Article 27**, at para. 061.
77. For the sake of clarity, public order in this context is not the same as *ordre public* which refers, as explained above, to the fundamental principles of the international or Austrian legal order.
78. Article 7 Rome Convention provides: 'When applying under this Convention the law of a country, effect may be given to the mandatory rules of the law of another country with which the situation has a close connection, if and in so far as, under the law of the latter country, those rules must be applied whatever the law applicable to the contract. In considering whether to give effect to these mandatory rules, regard shall be had to their nature and purpose and to the consequences of their application or non-application.'
79. J. Lew, L. Mistelis and S. Kröll, *Comparative International Commercial Arbitration* (The Hague, Kluwer Law International, 2003), para. 17-53. B. Wortmann, 'Choice of Law by Arbitrators: The Applicable Conflict of Laws System' (1998) 14(2) Arb Int'l, 97, 106-107.
80. *See* Hoge Raad (Supreme Court of the Netherlands), 21 March 1997, *Eco Swiss China Time Ltd. v. Benetton International NV* (1998) XXIII YB Comm Arb, 180.
81. *See*, famously, ECJ, 1 June 1999, Case No. C-126/97, *Eco Swiss China Time Ltd v. Benetton International NV*, [1999] ECR I-3055.

to certain areas of criminal law, such as drug trafficking, prostitution, arms trading, money laundering and other such activities that violate the *ordre public*.[82]

In such circumstances, arbitrators arguably have a mandate to ensure that their **24-033** award is not subject to setting aside.[83] In addition, under the principle of *ius novit curia*, arbitral tribunals have the duty to assess *ex officio* the legal consequences attaching to the facts (as pleaded or as found) without being bound by the legal position of the parties.[84] Hence, at least where there is some indication in the file, arbitrators will want to raise grave public policy issues even though the parties have not relied on them. The *ordre public* relevant to the arbitrators' assessment in this context is, first and foremost, the *ordre public* at the place of arbitration (which would govern any subsequent challenge to the award).[85] This may include the additional layer of the *international ordre public* as relevant from a national perspective.[86] It has been suggested, however, that consideration of an international or foreign *ordre public* should not be overreaching; there must be a relevant connection to the parties and the dispute at bar.[87]

---

82. For a detailed discussion, *see* R. H. Kreindler, *Strafrechtsrelevante und andere anstößige Verträge als Gegenstand von Schiedsverfahren* (Frankfurt/Main, Recht und Wirtschaft, 2005).
83. BGH, 5 May 1986, III 2 R 233/84 in BGHZ 98, 32-40.
84. BGer, 2 March 2001, *Bank Saint Petersburg PLC v. ATA Insaat Sanayi ve Ticaret Ltd.*, (2001) 19(3) Bull ASA, 531.
85. BGH, 5 May 1986, III 2 R 233/84 in BGHZ 98, 32-40. The obvious difficulty is for arbitrators not to appear to assist one party by introducing new legal issues that benefit one party at the expense of the other.
86. *See* F.T. Schwarz and H. Ortner, 'Procedural Ordre Public and the Internationalization of Public Policy in Arbitration' in *Austrian Arbitration Yearbook* 2008, C. Klausegger *et al* (eds) (Vienna, Manz, 2008); BGer, 28 March 2001, *Beverly Overseas SA v. Privredna Banka Zagreb d.d.*, (2001) 19(4) Bull ASA, 807, 814 *et seq.* finding a violation of the Swiss *ordre public* as a result of activities violating the international *ordre public* where 'the violation concerns foreign rules of a permanent nature which in the community of states have such importance that their violation is capable of disrupting our own legal order. The violated foreign law must serve the protection of individual interests as well as those of human society that are of fundamental and lifesaving importance, or it must concern legal rights which, according to the general ethical understanding, weigh more than the parties autonomy to freely conclude their contracts (which, were it the only determinative factor, would result in the contract being valid in our country).'
87. *Award in ICC Case No. 9333 of 1998*, (2001) 19(4) Bull ASA, 757, 773 holding that '[e]ven if one supposes that (i) the [U.S. Federal Corrupt Practices Act] is a mandatory law and (ii) the arbitrator admits that such a law can be applied notwithstanding the choice of another substantive law, the powerful and legitimate interests of the United States in the application of this law must also be shown. Serious doubts can in this matter result from the fact that the FCPA does not primarily aim to protect the fundamental public policy of the United States, but rather has the purpose to restore the confidence of the public in the integrity of American corporations whose reputation has been tarnished by a series of high profile corporate scandals.'

24-034 Thus, arbitrators cannot simply delegate their judicial powers to the state courts where matters of public policy or criminal law are concerned. As 'the arbitrability of a dispute is not excluded by the sole fact that rules of public policy are applicable to the dispute, [arbitrators] have the power to draw the civil consequences of an illicit behaviour under the profile of rules of public policy which can be directly applicable to the legal relationships at hand.'[88] In cases where public policy issues are at stake, therefore, there is indeed a strong case for arbitrators to raise such issues *ex officio*.[89] In these cases, it is vital of course that both parties are given sufficient opportunity to address these points before the arbitrators reach a decision on them.[90]

4.   No *Renvoi*

24-035 A choice of law is usually construed to refer to a substantive law without *renvoi*, so that the conflicts of laws rules of the chosen law are excluded.[91] While the fZPO did not address this question, this is now confirmed by Section 603(1) ZPO. Article 24(1) contains identical language. The wording of Article 24 (and Section 603 ZPO) appears to suggest that the parties' agreement on *renvoi* must be express.

II.   DETERMINATION OF THE APPLICABLE LAW
           BY THE ARBITRATORS

Article 24(2): Failing any designation by the parties, the sole arbitrator (arbitral tribunal) shall apply the rules of law considered by him (it) as appropriate.

A.   Conceptual Approach

24-036 Under Article 24(2), the tribunal determines the applicable law on the basis of what it 'considers appropriate'. This is a marked change from the previous version of the Vienna Rules. Former Article 16(1)[92] (following Article 28(2) of the UNCITRAL Model Law) adopted a form of *voie indirecte* that required the application of a set

---

88. Cour d'Appel de Paris, 19 May 1993, *Sté Labinal v. Stés Mors et Westland Aerospace*, [1993] Rev Arb, 645.
89. For EC competition law, this is certainly the case if the award is likely to be enforced in a Member State of the European Union. *See*, famously, ECJ, 1 June 1999, Case No. C-126/97, *Eco Swiss China Time Ltd v. Benetton International NV*, [1999] ECR I-3055.
90. The parties' right to be heard ought to include legal issues as well; arbitrators must not issue surprise decisions.
91. *See, e.g.*, Article 28(1) UNCITRAL Model Law; *see also* Section 11(1) IPRG.
92. Vienna Rules 2001, **Annex 2a**.

of conflict rules rather than the direct application of a law.[93] In that, former Article 16(1) differed from the entirely discretionary approach taken, e.g. by Article 17(1) of the ICC Rules, which, absent the parties' agreement, left it to the tribunal to apply any substantive law that it considers 'appropria:e;' or the determinative approach of Article 23(2) DIS Rules which requires arbitrators to 'apply the law of the State with which the subject-matter of the proceedings is most closely connected'.

Although former Article 16(1)[94] was somewhat limited when compared with **24-037** other rules, it was already a welcome deviation from the principle of *qui indicem forum elegit ius* which seeks to automatically link the choice of a forum (here: the seat of the arbitration) to the choice of law. Under such principle, absent an express or implied choice by the parties, a dispute sited in Austria would be governed by substantive Austrian law. That view will more often than not fail to persuade in international arbitration, where the parties enjoy a greater degree of flexibility to distinguish between the substance and the procedure of a dispute.[95] Indeed:

> As international arbitration has an independent, non-national and transnational character varying from case to case, so too the applicable laws and the choice of law methodologies also differ in every case. The existence of the arbitration in every instance is the result of the exercise of party autonomy. The choice of law process should reflect that same party autonomy.[96]

An approach automatically linking the parties' choice of *situs* to a (perceived) **24-038** choice of law will typically not do justice to the parties' autonomy in international arbitration.[97] As a leading commentary states, it would be 'inappropriate to local-ize legal issues arising out of an international contract'.[98] At most, the parties' choice of forum can, if the circumstances permit, be construed as a connecting factor[99] or as an indication that the parties have made an implied choice of law.[100]

---

93. *See* Article VII European Convention, which adopts a similar approach. **Annex 10**.

94. Vienna Rules 2001, **Annex 2a**.

95. A. Redfern, M. Hunter, N. Blackaby and C. Partasides, *Law and Practice of International Commercial Arbitration* (4th edn, London, Sweet & Maxwell, 2004), para. 2-78.

96. J. Lew, L. Mistelis and S. Kröll, *Comparative International Commercial Arbitration* (The Hague, Kluwer Law International, 2003), para. 17-4.

97. The choice of an Austrian *situs* is construed by the Austrian courts, with some force, as a choice of Austrian law with respect to the validity and interpretation of the arbitration agreement.

98. J. Lew, L. Mistelis and S. Kröll, *Comparative International Commercial Arbitration* (The Hague, Kluwer Law International, 2003), para. 17-42.

99. J. Lew, L. Mistelis and S. Kröll, *Comparative International Commercial Arbitration* (The Hague, Kluwer Law International, 2003), para. 17-15.

100. Lord Morris in *Compagnie d'Armément Maritime v. Compagnie Tunisienne de Navigation SA* [1971] A.C. 572, 588 (House of Lords).

24-039 At the same time, former Article 16(1)[101] did not provide any guidance to the tribunal as to which body of law should provide the applicable choice of law rules.[102] The ZPO (prior to its 2006 reform) was also entirely silent on the issue of the law applicable in (international) arbitrations. According to the traditional view in Austria, the national law of the country of the seat of the arbitration provided the relevant choice of law rules.[103] For an arbitration sited in Austria, therefore, arbitrators could be considered as having to apply the law determined by Austrian conflict of laws rules, as codified in the Private International Law Act (*Internationales Privatrechtsgesetz –* IPRG) or the Rome Convention.[104] This has also been the traditional position in international arbitration.[105] This concept attracted considerable criticism. It was argued that arbitrators, unlike judges, do not perform a judicial function in the name of or on behalf of a state and should therefore not be bound by the conflict of laws rules applicable at the arbitral *situs*.[106]

24-040 Indeed, as with the principle of *qui indicem forum elegit ius* (albeit to a lesser extent), it was not quite clear why Austrian law, and be it only through its conflict of laws rules, should bear in any way on the merits of an international dispute merely by virtue of the fact that the parties have chosen Austria as a neutral venue. Indeed, former Article 16 liberated the arbitrators from that traditional restriction: it did *not* refer to the rules of conflict of the arbitral *situs*. Thus, arbitrators could determine that the conflict of laws rules of the *situs* are the most appropriate under the circumstances; however, they could also choose, if they thought it appropriate, other conflict of laws rules, such as the conflict of laws rules of the place where the underlying contract was concluded; of the place that has the closest connection to the dispute; or possibly even general principles of conflict laws. Some commentators also advocated the 'cumulative-application' approach, where arbitrators

---

101. Vienna Rules 2001, **Annex 2a**.
102. *See, e.g.*, Article 23(2) DIS Rules which contains its own choice of law rule by requiring the application of the law that has the closest connection to the dispute. This conforms with Article 28 EGBGB. *See* M. Aden, *Internationale Handelsschiedsgerichtsbarkeit* (2nd edn, Munich, C.H. Beck, 2003), p. 553.
103. H. W. Fasching, *Schiedsgericht und Schiedsverfahren im österreichischen und im internationalen Recht* (Vienna, Manz, 1973), p. 108. More recent commentary suggests, however, that arbitrators may directly refer to applicable law, without going through a choice of law analysis. *See* A. Reiner, 'Die internationale Schiedsgerichtsbarkeit nach österreichischem und französischem Recht' [1986] ZfRV, 162, 210 *et seq*.
104. Note, however, that bilateral treaties may have to be taken into account as well.
105. F.A. Mann, 'Lex Facit Arbitrum' in *International Arbitration – Liber Amicorum for Martin Domke*, Pieter Sanders (ed.) (The Hague, Martinus Nijhof, 1967), p. 167. *See also Award in ICC Case No. 5460 of 1987, Austrian franchisor v. South African franchisee*, (1988) XIII YB Comm Arb, 104.
106. J. Lew, L. Mistelis and S. Kröll, *Comparative International Commercial Arbitration* (The Hague, Kluwer Law International, 2003), para. 17-53; B. Wortmann, 'Choice of Law by Arbitrators: The Applicable Conflict of Laws System' (1998) 14(2) Arb Int'l, 97, 106-107.

look at the conflict of laws rules of all jurisdictions relevant to the dispute, to assess if all the different rules point to the same applicable law. The limits of this approach are obvious, but if the various conflict rules result in one applicable law, the arbitrator's choice will obviously satisfy all parties, ensuring a truly international, yet predictable outcome.[107]

Another approach is taken by Section 1051 German ZPO which calls for the **24-041** application of the substantive law that has the closest connection to the dispute.[108] While this *prima facie* does not require the arbitrators to undertake a conflict of laws analysis, it provides little guidance as to how the closest connection ought to be established. For practical purposes, it re-introduces a conflict of laws determination through the backdoor.[109]

It appears that the reference to conflict of laws rules, as a means to determine the **24-042** applicable law, has in recent years been largely abandoned in international practice and doctrine,[110] to allow the arbitrators, through the *voie directe* method, to apply whatever law they deem appropriate, without having to choose and apply conflict of laws rules first.

This approach of *voie directe* has now been adopted by a significant number of **24-043** modern arbitral rules[111] and also by Section 603(2) ZPO. Unrestricted *voie directe* leaves the arbitrators with the greatest possible discretion.[112] It allows them to skip the often difficult search for the applicable conflict of laws rules and go directly to the legal system they desire to apply. In that regard, the requirement to apply the substantive law the arbitrators deem 'appropriate' is intended to guide their discretion towards objective criteria[113] – not by applying a proper set of conflict rules taken from a national law, but by applying instead more freely internationally-accepted conflict principles.[114] Thus, arbitrators should 'look for the common intentions of the parties, and use the connecting factors generally used in doctrine

---

107. *See also* J. Lew, L. Mistelis and S. Kröll, *Comparative International Commercial Arbitration* (The Hague, Kluwer Law International, 2003), para. 17-64.
108. *See also* Article 187(1) Swiss IPRG.
109. P. Oberhammer, *Entwurf eines neuen Schiedsverfahrensrechts* (Vienna, Manz, 2002), p. 110.
110. G.B. Born, *International Commercial Arbitration – Commentary and Materials* (2nd edn, The Hague, Kluwer Law International, 2001), pp. 529-530 with further references; P. Oberhammer, *Entwurf eines neuen Schiedsverfahrensrechts* (Vienna, Manz, 2002), p. 110.
111. *See, e.g.*, Article 17(1) ICC Rules; Article 22(3) LCIA Rules and Article 28(1) AAA/ICDR Rules.
112. Note that, for example, Section 1051(2) German ZPO requires arbitrators to apply the national law with the strongest connection to the subject matter of the dispute. This is also a direct application of the law without a preceding conflict of laws analysis; a restricted *voie directe*.
113. J. Power, *The Austrian Arbitration Act – A Practitioner's Guide to Sections 577-618 of the Austrian Code of Civil Procedure* (Vienna, Manz, 2006), Section 603, para. 6.
114. Indeed, in having to determine the *appropriate* law, arbitrators will typically be guided by general principles of conflict rules. *See* P. Oberhammer, *Entwurf eines neuen Schiedsverfahrensrechts* (Vienna, Manz, 2002), pp. 109-110.

and in case law, [and to] disregard national peculiarities',[115] such as the law of the place where the parties reside, where the underlying contract was concluded, where performance has to be effected, or which has more generally the closest connection to the dispute. While critics note that *voie directe* lacks the predictability and legal certainty that conflict of laws rules offer,[116] *voie directe* enhances the flexibility of the arbitral process and furthers its de-nationalization. On balance, therefore, it is to be preferred.

B.   'THE LAW' *v.* 'RULES OF LAW'

24-044 As with the parties' choice, the question again arises if arbitrators need to determine the application of a 'law', or if they can also apply other more loosely defined 'legal rules' or principles. It appears that under Article 24(2), arbitrators are allowed to apply any body of rules and not only a law in the proper sense. This is so, arguably, because Article 24(2) permits arbitrators 'to apply rules of law'. However, a different approach has been adopted under the supposedly mandatory provision of Section 603(2) ZPO;[117] it appears to be a deliberate (if unfortunate) choice of the Austrian legislature to limit the arbitrators' discretion in this respect.[118]

24-045 Other modern arbitral rules appear to give arbitrators similar flexibility. Notably, Article 17(1) ICC Rules also entitles the arbitrators to apply 'the rules of law' which they deem appropriate. As discussed, the change in Article 17(1) ICC Rules from an application of 'the law' to 'rules of law' has been deliberate.[119] The use of the term 'rules of law' was intended, based on the discussion leading to Article 28 UNCITRAL Model Law, to refer to a normative framework broader than 'the law,' permitting the arbitrators to apply only a part – that is, certain rules – of a national law; or rules of law other than those of a single state, including perhaps general principles of law and *lex mercatoria*.[120] This may therefore be a point worth revisiting in Austrian law: since the results of the different possible approaches

---

115. A. Redfern, M. Hunter, N. Blackaby and C. Partasides, *Law and Practice of International Commercial Arbitration* (4th edn, London, Sweet & Maxwell, 2004), para. 2-80.

116. G.B. Born, *International Commercial Arbitration – Commentary and Materials* (2nd edn, The Hague, Kluwer Law International, 2001), p. 531.

117. Section 603(2) ZPO: 'Failing any designation by the parties, the arbitral tribunal shall apply the law that it considers appropriate,' but not the 'rules of law' (*Rechtsregeln*) on which the parties can agree.

118. Explanatory Notes to Section 603(1); B. Kloiber and H. Haller in *Das Neue Schiedsrecht – Schiedsrechts-Änderungsgesetz 2006*, B. Kloiber, P. Oberhammer, W.H. Rechberger and H. Haller (eds) (Vienna, Manz, 2006), p. 47.

119. Y. Derains and E.A. Schwartz, *A Guide to the ICC Rules of Arbitration* (2nd edn, The Hague, Kluwer Law International, 2005), p. 234.

120. A. Redfern, M. Hunter, N. Blackaby and C. Partasides, *Law and Practice of International Commercial Arbitration* (4th edn, London, Sweet & Maxwell, 2004), para. 2-72; Y. Derains and E.A. Schwartz, *A Guide to the ICC Rules of Arbitration* (2nd edn, The Hague, Kluwer Law International, 2005), p. 238.

will often not differ, the approach conferring the greatest flexibility on the arbitral process should be preferable.[121]

C.   'INCORRECT' DETERMINATION BY THE ARBITRATORS

The question of what consequences attach to a false determination of applicable **24-046** substantive law by the tribunal is largely moot under the Vienna Rules. First, it is difficult to argue that the arbitrators have applied the 'wrong' law when Article 24(2) gives the arbitrators broad discretionary powers to determine the applicable law they deem 'appropriate.' The exercise of such a discretion can as such hardly result in the incorrect determination of an applicable law.

Second, Section 611(2) no. 8 ZPO permits *vacatur* only if an award is irreconcilable **24-047** with the 'basic principles of the Austrian legal system.' Just as – within the limits of public policy – an erroneous interpretation or application of the law is irrelevant, the 'wrong' determination of the applicable substantive law is irrelevant too.[122] Indeed, the Austrian *Oberster Gerichtshof* has upheld an award for these reasons, even where the arbitrators decided without reference to the law merely 'in equity', without being authorized to do so by the parties.[123]

III.   EQUITY-BASED DECISIONS

Article 24(3): The sole arbitrator (arbitral tribunal) may decide on equity only if the parties have expressly authorized him (it) to do so.

Article 24(3) restricts the tribunal's power to decide on the basis of equity; the **24-048** tribunal can do so only if it is authorized by the parties, which requirement follows both Section 603(3) ZPO and international practice. Article 24(3) and Section 603(3) ZPO to be particularly strict in that they require that the authorization must be 'express', but not necessarily in writing. This rule follows the traditional view in Austria, which always required the express agreement of the parties if the decision was to be based on rules other than the applicable law[124] and corresponds

---

121. P. Oberhammer, *Entwurf eines neuen Schiedsverfahrensrechts* (Vienna, Manz, 2002), p. 110.
122. P. Oberhammer in *Das neue Schiedsrecht – Schiedsrechts-Änderungsgesetz 2006*, B. Kloiber, P. Oberhammer, W.H. Rechberger and H. Haller (eds) (Vienna, Manz, 2006), p. 133; *see also* M. Aden, *Internationale Handelsschiedsgerichtsbarkeit* (2nd edn, Munich, C.H. Beck, 2003), pp. 64, 554.
123. OGH, 18 November 1982, 8 Ob 520/82.
124. H.W. Fasching, *Schiedsgericht und Schiedsverfahren im österreichischen und im internationalen Recht* (Vienna, Manz, 1973), p. 108.

to Article 28(3) UNCITRAL Model Law. The authorization can be given at any time before the tribunal's decision.[125]

24-049 Article 24(2) corresponds closely to Article 17(3) of the ICC Rules, which requires the parties' express authorization for the tribunal to decide *ex aequo et bono* or as an *amiable compositeur*.[126] The reference to 'amiable compositeur' is left away in both Article 24(3) and Section 603(3) ZPO, presumably because that term has no roots in Austrian legal tradition.[127]

24-050 As discussed above, the Austrian *Oberster Gerichtshof* has held in *Norsolor SA* that, even where there is no express agreement of the parties authorizing the arbitrators to decide in equity, the arbitrator's exercise of their fair and equitable discretion does not constitute grounds for challenging the award, as long as this does not lead to violations of the *ordre public* and the arbitrators' decision falls within their jurisdiction, as defined by the arbitration agreement.[128] It will be open to debate if the newly introduced ground for setting aside an award for violation of the Austrian *procedural ordre public* will lead to a different result.[129]

24-051 The term 'in equity' corresponds to the legal concept of '*Billigkeit*' which is familiar to Austrian law. From an international perspective, however, it is not entirely clear what it means for an arbitrator to decide 'in equity.' As *Redfern/Hunter* point out, this could mean that arbitrators shall in principle apply the law,

---

125. P. Oberhammer, *Entwurf eines neuen Schiedsverfahrensrechts* (Vienna, Manz, 2002), p. 111.
126. Given the near identical nature of the two provisions it appears justified to refer to ICC-based case law and commentary on that provision.
127. P. Oberhammer, *Entwurf eines neuen Schiedsverfahrensrechts* (Vienna, Manz, 2002), p. 110.
128. OGH, 18 November 1982, 8 Ob 520/82. It is debatable if the introduction of Section 603(3) ZPO and the modifications of the grounds for challenging an award in Section 611 ZPO will change the position reached in *Norsolor*. Section 611(2) no. 5 ZPO provides for vacatur if the 'arbitral proceedings were conducted in a manner that violates the *ordre public*'. Different to the current position which focuses on the *substantive ordre public*, this provision introduces a new ground for challenge that takes account of the *procedural ordre public* as well. This is; however, much more limited than the solution adopted by the UNCITRAL Model Law or the German ZPO, which provides for setting aside if there were procedural errors that had an effect on the award (which according to the German *Bundesgerichtshof* includes a decision in equity without the parties' authorization). It is doubtful if the application of equity, absent aggravating circumstances, will constitute a violation of the *procedural ordre public*, in particular if the result of an application of equity does not violate *substantive ordre public*. On the other hand, it cannot be entirely excluded that the new ground of Section 611(2) no. 5 ZPO may apply in cases where the application of equity, absent an express authorization by the parties, is wholly arbitrary under the circumstances. This will require some clarification from the Austrian courts. *See* **Article 27**, at paras. 054-055.
129. *See* F.T. Schwarz and H. Ortner, 'Procedural Ordre Public and the Internationalization of Public Policy in Arbitration' in *Austrian Arbitration Yearbook 2008*, C. Klausegger *et al.* (Vienna, Manz, 2008); J. Power, *The Austrian Arbitration Act – A Practitioner's Guide to Sections 577-618 of the Austrian Code of Civil Procedure* (Vienna, Manz, 2006), Section 604, para. 7.

but may ignore purely formalistic rules; or that they may apply the law but may ignore rules the tribunal determines to be particularly unfair in the circumstances of the case; or that arbitrators should decide according to general principles of law, such as good faith; or, finally, that arbitrators may ignore the law completely, deciding the case at their discretion.[130] Such discretion may have limits, as a decision *contra legem* may violate basic notions of justice. Even if the parties agree on a decision 'in equity', it may be problematic from a public policy perspective to lend the courts' power of enforcement to an award that is completely outside basic legal principles.[131] Indeed, as discussed, an award 'in equity' that violates public policy is subject to setting aside.[132] In practice, most arbitrators make a decision 'in equity' by looking at the contractual provisions as the most immediate embodiment of the law between the parties, and by then making sure that no provision of the contract (or applicable law) operates unfairly under the circumstances of the case.[133]

---

130. A. Redfern, M. Hunter, N. Blackaby and C. Partasides, *Law and Practice of International Commercial Arbitration* (4th edn, London, Sweet & Maxwell, 2004), para. 2-73.

131. *See*, however, Y. Derains and E.A. Schwartz, *A Guide to the ICC Rules of Arbitration* (2nd edn, The Hague, Kluwer Law International, 2005), p. 245, whose description of the term amiable compositeur seems to suggest that a commercial 'business solution' may override legal concerns.

132. *See also* C. Liebscher and A. Schmid in *Practitioner's Handbook on International Arbitration*, F.B. Weigand (ed.) (Munich, C.H. Beck, 2002), p. 572.

133. Y. Derains and E. A. Schwartz, *A Guide to the ICC Rules of Arbitration* (2nd edn, The Hague, Kluwer Law International, 2005), p. 245.

Article 25

Termination of the Proceedings

		Para.			Para.
I.	Introduction	1	C.	Impossibility to Continue Proceedings	14
II.	Termination by Award	3	D.	Failure to File the Claim	22
III.	Termination by Settlement	6	V.	Consequences of Termination	24
IV.	Termination by Order	8	A.	Functus Officio	25
	A. Withdrawal of Claim	10	B.	Ongoing Obligations of the Tribunal	26
	B. Agreement on Termination	12			

Article 25: The proceedings are terminated by

(a) the rendering of an award,

(b) the conclusion of a settlement,

(c) an order of the sole arbitrator (arbitral tribunal) where

> **(aa) the claimant withdraws his claim, unless the respondent objects thereto and the sole arbitrator (arbitral tribunal) recognizes a legitimate interest on his part in obtaining a final settlement of the dispute;**
>
> **(bb) the parties agree on the termination of the proceedings and communicate this to the sole arbitrator (arbitral tribunal);**
>
> **(cc) the sole arbitrator (arbitral tribunal) finds that the continuation of the proceedings has become impossible, in particular when the parties to the proceedings do not continue the arbitral proceedings despite written notification from the sole arbitrator (arbitral tribunal), in which it refers to the possibility of terminating the proceedings.**

I.   INTRODUCTION

25-001 Article 25 has the purpose of bringing formality and structure to the end of arbitral proceedings. The termination of the proceedings has important procedural consequences: the arbitrators receive their remuneration,[1] their mandate expires, the tribunal becomes *functus officio* and, with certain exceptions discussed further below, is no longer available to the parties. For these reasons, it is reasonable to outline the conditions under which the proceedings can be formally terminated. Article 25 is without prejudice to terminating the arbitrators' mandate early, if they are no longer able to discharge their office or for the other circumstances that have been discussed in the context of **Article 17**.

25-002 Article 25 follows the mandatory provision of Section 608 ZPO,[2] and replaces the old system under the Vienna Rules which did not address the termination of the proceedings, and only provided for the deletion of a case from the list of pending cases in certain circumstances. This is no longer possible; under the new Vienna Rules and Austrian law, an arbitration is terminated either by an award or by settlement, or else by procedural order, in the circumstances discussed below.

II.   TERMINATION BY AWARD

25-003 The quintessential case of terminating the proceeding is by rendering an award on the merits. Article 25 refers only to the rendering of 'an award', but what is meant is an award on the merits that disposes of the entire relief requested by the parties, and thus completely discharges the arbitrators' mandate to make a decision on the claims that have been put before them. The award must comply with the requirements of Section 606 ZPO to effect the termination of the proceedings.[3] Where the proceedings have been split into several phases (e.g. on liability and damages),[4] only an award disposing of all claims before the tribunal leads to the termination of the proceedings and the exhaustion of the arbitrators' mandate.[5] Of course, the same is true for an award in which the tribunal denies its jurisdiction for the claims before it.[6]

---

1. *See* **Article 36**, at paras. 006 *et seq.*
2. S. Riegler in *Arbitration Law of Austria: Practice and Procedure*, S. Riegler, A. Petsche, A. Fremuth-Wolf, M. Platte and C. Liebscher (eds) (Huntington, Juris Publishing, 2007), Section 608, p. 471 with further reference.
3. J. Power, *The Austrian Arbitration Act – A Practitioners' Guide to Sections 577-618 of the Austrian Code of Civil Procedure* (Vienna, Manz, 2006), Section 608, para. 2 with reference to German doctrine. For those requirements, *see* **Article 27**, at paras. 001 *et seq.*, 010 *et seq.* and 017 *et seq.*
4. *See* **Article 20**, at paras. 117 *et seq.*
5. This includes all claims that are legitimately before the tribunal, such as the claims originally asserted and also claims subsequently introduced, and admitted, by way of amendment. It does not mean, however, that the parties are entitled to introduce new claims *ad infinitum* to keep the arbitration alive. For late claims and amendments, *see* **Article 11**, at paras. 029 *et seq.*
6. A. Reiner, *Das neue österreichische Schiedsrecht/The new Austrian Arbitration Law* (Vienna, LexisNexis, 2006), Section 608, note 164; S. Riegler in *Arbitration Law of Austria: Practice and*

As discussed elsewhere, arbitrators need to put the parties on notice that they are closing the proceedings before issuing an award.[7]

Article 25 requires that an award must be 'rendered', but this should include **25-004** awards rendered following the tribunal's substantive determination of the dispute as well as awards rendered by consent of the parties. Section 608(1) ZPO is clearer in this regard, providing that '[t]he arbitral proceedings are terminated by the award on the merits [or] by an award by consent'.

It has been argued that a court decision may also terminate the arbitration, if, for **25-005** example, a court sets aside the tribunal's award confirming its jurisdiction.[8] The argument appears to be that, in this case too, there is nothing left for the tribunal to decide, and there is no reason to keep the arbitration pending, with all the effects this has, until the tribunal terminates the proceedings by order. However, there are also merits to requiring an order in these circumstances, in particular to give the parties instant access to a decision on costs from the tribunal and to allow the tribunal to address other outstanding issues.[9]

III.   TERMINATION BY SETTLEMENT

If the parties settle their dispute, there is obviously no need to proceed with the **25-006** arbitration (unless the settlement resolves only part of the dispute, and some claims continue to be pending before the tribunal).[10] According to the terms of Article 25, a settlement will in and of itself terminate the proceedings; it is not required that the settlement is recorded by way of procedural order or award[11] (although the parties have the possibility to request that this is done in a consent award, usually for purposes of enforcement).[12]

Procedure, S. Riegler, A. Petsche, A. Fremuth-Wolf, M. Platte and C. Liebscher (eds) (Huntington, Juris Publishing, 2007), Section 608, p. 471. A different view is taken by J. Power, *The Austrian Arbitration Act – A Practitioners' Guide to Sections 577-618 of the Austrian Code of Civil Procedure* (Vienna, Manz, 2006), Section 608, para. 2, who argues that under the text of Section 608 ZPO, proceedings are only terminated by an award on the merits, and not by an award on jurisdiction. This interpretation makes no sense with the purpose of Section 608(1) ZPO; where the tribunal has completely discharged its function by award, there is no room for further proceedings.

7. *See* **Article 20**, at para. 288.

8. S. Riegler in *Arbitration Law of Austria: Practice and Procedure*, S. Riegler, A. Petsche, A. Fremuth-Wolf, M. Platte and C. Liebscher (eds) (Huntington, Juris Publishing, 2007), Section 608, p. 472.

9. It will depend on the nature of the jurisdictional issue whether the tribunal has no jurisdictional authority at all, or whether it retains some authority with respect to some of the claims before it.

10. A. Reiner, *Das neue österreichische Schiedsrecht/The new Austrian Arbitration Law* (Vienna, LexisNexis, 2006), Section 608, note 165.

11. S. Riegler in *Arbitration Law of Austria: Practice and Procedure*, S. Riegler, A. Petsche, A. Fremuth-Wolf, M. Platte and C. Liebscher (eds) (Huntington, Juris Publishing, 2007), Section 608, p. 472.

12. *See* **Article 28**, at paras. 001 *et seq.*

25-007 Although (unlike Article 25(c)(bb)), it is not expressly required, the parties will obviously have to communicate (and should provide a copy of) the settlement to the tribunal and the VIAC for the termination of the arbitration to take effect.

IV.   TERMINATION BY ORDER

25-008 There are circumstances, however, when an arbitration does not end with a resolution of the merits of the case, either by award or voluntary settlement. Under Article 25 (and the mandatory provision of Sections 608(1) and (2) ZPO), these cases must be addressed by order of the tribunal; and only upon such order are the proceedings deemed terminated. On the other hand, where these circumstances exist, the tribunal appears to be under an obligation to terminate the proceedings.[13] Similarly, it is argued that the enumeration contained in Article 25 of the three instances for termination by order are exhaustive, so that the tribunal is not permitted to order the termination of the arbitration if none of these instances exists.

25-009 As discussed further below, such orders are only procedural in nature. Orders issued under this provision are not subject to appeal before the Austrian state courts.[14] They do not dispose of the merits of the parties' dispute and have themselves no *res judicata* effect.[15] As a result, the order as such does not prevent the parties from reasserting their claim.[16]

A.   WITHDRAWAL OF CLAIM

25-010 A claimant may wish, for whatever reason, to withdraw the claim.[17] Without a claim, there is nothing for the tribunal to decide and the arbitration should end.

---

13. Section 608(2) ZPO provides that in these circumstances, '[t]he arbitral tribunal *shall* terminate the arbitral proceedings'.
14. Explanatory Notes to Section 608 ZPO. This also follows from Section 578 ZPO which allows courts to interfere with the arbitration only on the basis of an express statutory authorization. Such authorization is lacking with regard to orders made pursuant to Section 608 ZPO. *See also* J. Power, *The Austrian Arbitration Act – A Practitioners' Guide to Sections 577-618 of the Austrian Code of Civil Procedure* (Vienna, Manz, 2006), Section 608, para 3.
15. S. Riegler in *Arbitration Law of Austria: Practice and Procedure*, S. Riegler, A. Petsche, A. Fremuth-Wolf, M. Platte and C. Liebscher (eds) (Huntington, Juris Publishing, 2007), Section 608, p. 473.
16. J. Power, *The Austrian Arbitration Act – A Practitioners' Guide to Sections 577-618 of the Austrian Code of Civil Procedure* (Vienna, Manz, 2006), Section 608, para 3. Of course, a party who has withdrawn a claim with prejudice will typically be barred from reasserting that claim for that reason.
17. Similar considerations must apply to counter-claimants and their counter-claims.

Thus, when a claim is withdrawn, rendering the proceedings redundant, the tribunal is in principle obliged to issue an order terminating the proceedings.[18]

However, Article 25 recognizes, as does the identical provision of Section 608(2) **25-011** no. 2 ZPO, that the respondent has 'a legitimate interest on his part in obtaining a final settlement of the dispute'. In particular, where the claimant withdraws the claim without prejudice (that is, reserving the right to reassert the claim at some later point in time), the respondent, in particular if it already has had to expend significant resources in its defence,[19] may legitimately wish to have the matter settled once and for all.[20] Article 25 gives the tribunal the authority to recognize such a legitimate interest and to essentially refuse the claimant's withdrawal of its claim unless it is made with prejudice.

B.   AGREEMENT ON TERMINATION

Where the parties settle their case on the merits, the arbitration is terminated **25-012** according to Article 25(b). However, parties may wish not to settle the merits of their dispute but nevertheless agree not to proceed with the arbitration. In such a case, where their agreement to no longer arbitrate is purely procedural rather than based on an agreement that resolves the substance of the dispute, they can apply to the tribunal for a procedural order terminating the arbitration. The parties should in this case also agree on the allocation of costs between them. Not doing so would pose significant difficulties for the tribunal.[21]

---

18. Some authors argue that the withdrawal as such is sufficient to terminate the proceedings. *See* S. Riegler in *Arbitration Law of Austria: Practice and Procedure*, S. Riegler, A. Petsche, A. Fremuth-Wolf, M. Platte and C. Liebscher (eds) (Huntington, Juris Publishing, 2007), Section 608, p. 474. This goes against the express text of Section 608 ZPO which provides that the arbitration is terminated by order of the tribunal, and not by the withdrawal itself. Section 608 ZPO is drafted to give the respondent the opportunity to object against the withdrawal, and to afford the tribunal the opportunity to consider whether the withdrawal should in fact terminate the proceedings.
19. K.H. Schwab and G. Walter (eds), *Schiedsgerichtsbarkeit* (7th edn, Munich, C.H. Beck, 2005), ch. 23a, para. 6. The stage of the proceedings is therefore one of the factors to take into account as to whether the respondent has a legitimate interest in a decision on the merits. The tribunal is generally under an obligation to take all circumstances of the case into consideration. *See* J. Power, *The Austrian Arbitration Act – A Practitioners' Guide to Sections 577-618 of the Austrian Code of Civil Procedure* (Vienna, Manz, 2006), Section 608, para. 5.
20. By contrast, if the claim is withdrawn with prejudice and the dispute on that point finally resolved, the respondent's legitimate interest in a decision by the tribunal is removed. *See also* A. Reiner, *Das neue österreichische Schiedsrecht/The new Austrian Arbitration Law* (Vienna, LexisNexis, 2006), Section 608, note 169.
21. Under Section 609 ZPO, the tribunal normally allocates the costs by taking into account the outcome of the case on the merits. Where the parties have agreed procedurally to terminate the arbitration, the outcome of the merits is of course unknown.

25-013 Both Article 25 and the identical provision of Section 608(2) no. 3 ZPO require both parties to jointly communicate their procedural agreement to the tribunal; therefore, before issuing an order under this provision the tribunal should have ensured that it has indeed the consent of all parties to terminate the arbitration. Where a party wants the tribunal to rule on costs, it needs to make a request together with its communication that the arbitration is terminated by joint agreement.[22]

C.   IMPOSSIBILITY TO CONTINUE PROCEEDINGS

25-014 Finally, Article 25 and the identical provision of Section 608(2) no. 4 ZPO now give the arbitrators the possibility to terminate the proceedings *ex officio*, without request from the parties. This possibility is reserved for cases where it is in the circumstances no longer possible for the arbitrators to continue with the proceedings.[23]

25-015 Any kind of impossibility entitles the arbitrators to such measure. In such cases, the arbitrators are not required to remain at the parties' disposal forever; they cannot be expected to reserve the time and resources necessary for conducting the arbitration, and perhaps to even turn down other engagements, when the parties show no interest in pursuing the case.

25-016 Article 25, if only by way of example ('in particular'), singles out a specific scenario which perhaps is most relevant in practice: that both parties fail to proceed with the arbitration. This refers to both parties. If the claimant fails to duly proceed with the case, the respondent can still insist on a decision dismissing or rejecting the claim (once the statement of claims has been served). If, on the other hand, only the respondent remains silent, the tribunal can proceed to a hearing, and ultimately to an award, against the defaulting party.[24]

25-017 Before the arbitrators can order the proceedings terminated, the arbitrators need to notify the parties, in writing, that they consider the possibility of terminating the arbitration under this provision. Only if the parties remain inactive after such notification, an order can be issued. Although the requirement of a written advance notice seems to apply, as a textual matter only to cases of inactivity of the parties, arbitrators will generally be required to give advance notice of their intention to terminate the proceedings, depending on the circumstances of the impossibility to continue the arbitration. Whatever prevents the arbitration from proceeding, it seems to be the purpose of this provision for the arbitrators to make an attempt

---

22. *See* Section 609(1) ZPO and **Article 31**, at paras. 001 *et seq*. The potential consequences of a settlement with regard to stamp duties are discussed in **Article 28**, at para. 005.
23. Explanatory Notes to Section 608 ZPO; P. Oberhammer, *Entwurf eines neuen Schiedsverfahrensrechts* (Vienna, Manz, 2002), p. 122.
24. *See* **Article 20**, at paras. 257 *et seq*.

to overcome it. Indeed, the arbitrators will have to apply a strict standard to whether it is impossible to continue the arbitration and may in principle prefer to simply suspend it, in particular if the impossibility is in reality only temporary or if one of the parties can offer a legitimate justification for why it has been inactive for a particular period of time.[25] This strict standard is also justified in light of the legislature's decision to grant arbitrators the power to terminate arbitration only if it is 'impossible' to continue them; not merely, as the UNCITRAL Model Law would have suggested in Article 32(2)(c), if the continuation has become 'unnecessary'. The Austrian legislature specifically wanted to remove from the arbitrator's discretion any judgment on whether the pursuit of a claim is necessary.[26]

In *ad hoc* proceedings, the parties' failure to pay the arbitrators' advance on costs **25-018** may also entitle the arbitrators to terminate the proceedings.[27] Under the Vienna Rules, however, the file is only transmitted to the arbitrators if and when the entire deposit on costs has been paid (either by each party in equal share, or entirely by the claimant if the respondent defaults).[28]

Another example for impossibility discussed in the literature includes the case that **25-019** the statement of claims cannot be served on the respondent and the claimant is unable to provide a correct address for delivery.[29] Under the Vienna Rules, however, the proceedings before the arbitrators are not even commenced and the file not even transmitted to the tribunal before the respondent has been served with the statement of claims.[30]

The parties' failure to advance costs that would be necessary for the taking of **25-020** evidence is not sufficient to establish impossibility within the meaning of

---

25. A. Reiner, *Das neue österreichische Schiedsrecht/The new Austrian Arbitration Law* (Vienna, LexisNexis, 2006), Section 608, note 172, arguing that a termination even without prejudice can have serious consequences for applicable statutes of limitations. War or emergencies may therefore lead to suspension, rather than termination. A different opinion is expressed in Germany by P. Schlosser in *Kommentar zur Zivilprozessordnung*, F. Stein and M. Jonas (eds) (22nd edn, Tübingen, Mohr, 2002) Section 1056, note 6.
26. P. Oberhammer, *Entwurf eines neuen Schiedsverfahrensrechts* (Vienna, Manz, 2002), p. 121.
27. S. Riegler in *Arbitration Law of Austria: Practice and Procedure*, S. Riegler, A. Petsche, A. Fremuth-Wolf, M. Platte and C. Liebscher (eds) (Huntington, Juris Publishing, 2007), Section 608, p. 476.
28. *See* **Article 34**, at para. 026. In such cases, the claimant may have an immediate claim for reimbursement against the respondent, *see* **Article 34**, at paras. 035 *et seq.* The consequences of both parties' failure to pay the deposit against the expected costs of the arbitration are discussed under **Article 34(4)**, at para. 033.
29. P. Oberhammer, *Entwurf eines neuen Schiedsverfahrensrechts* (Vienna, Manz, 2002), p. 122. In that case, the arbitrators have to send the notification that they intend to terminate the proceedings only to the claimant.
30. Note, however, that the arbitration becomes pending as soon as the statement of claims is received by the VIAC. *See* **Article 9**, at para. 015.

Section 608 ZPO.[31] Here, the arbitrators will have to weigh that failure as an evidentiary matter.

25-021 The Explanatory Notes also suggest that Section 608(2) no. 4 ZPO may apply to cases where the arbitrators cannot reach a decision on the merits so that the arbitration becomes frustrated. This is dubious:[32] the provisions regarding majority decisions sufficiently guarantee that a decision can be reached without a majority.[33] Indeed, if an arbitrator refuses, or becomes unable, to participate in the decision-making of the tribunal, he can also be removed from office.[34]

D.   FAILURE TO FILE THE CLAIM

25-022 For *ad hoc* proceedings, Section 608(2) ZPO entitles the tribunal to terminate the arbitration by order if 'the claimant fails to file his claim in accordance with Section 597(1) [ZPO]'.[35] This is because in *ad hoc* arbitration, the proceedings are not initiated with a statement of claims but rather with a notice of arbitration and the request to appoint an arbitrator.[36] As a result, the claimant may have formally initiated the arbitration but never have filed a claim. In such cases, an order of the tribunal is required to terminate the proceedings. Notably, the respondent's conceivably legitimate interest to obtain a binding resolution of the dispute is not recognized at this stage.

25-023 In any event, this provision has no real application in proceedings under the Vienna Rules. Here, the arbitration is initiated by a statement of claims. Thus, if the claimant did not file its claim, the arbitration would not commence in the first place, and no order of termination is ever required.

V.   CONSEQUENCES OF TERMINATION

25-024 With the termination of the proceedings under Article 25 (and Section 608(3) ZPO), the case is closed. The arbitration is therefore no longer pending within

---

31. S. Riegler in *Arbitration Law of Austria: Practice and Procedure*, S. Riegler, A. Petsche, A. Fremuth-Wolf, M. Platte and C. Liebscher (eds) (Huntington, Juris Publishing, 2007), Section 608, p. 476.
32. A. Reiner, *Das neue österreichische Schiedsrecht/The new Austrian Arbitration Law* (Vienna, LexisNexis, 2006), Section 608, note 174.
33. S. Riegler in *Arbitration Law of Austria: Practice and Procedure*, S. Riegler, A. Petsche, A. Fremuth-Wolf, M. Platte and C. Liebscher (eds) (Huntington, Juris Publishing, 2007), Section 608, p. 477 with reference to Section 604 ZPO.
34. *See* **Article 17**, at para. 012.
35. *See also* Section 600(1) ZPO which provides: 'Where the claimant fails to submit the statement of claim in accordance with Section 597 (1), the arbitral tribunal shall terminate the proceedings.'
36. *See* **Article 9**, at para. 045.

the meaning of Section 584 ZPO;[37] the Statute of Limitations may no longer be interrupted, depending on the provisions of the applicable substantive law.[38] Some authors suggest that the date of the award, the settlement or the order are determinative for the purposes of the termination of the proceedings.[39] This finds support in Section 606(3) ZPO, according to which the award is deemed rendered on the date specified in the award.[40] However, **Article 27(5)** provides that '[a]wards become effective as against the parties on service of the copies'. Similarly, the period for filing a request with the state courts to set aside an award starts only with receipt of the award by the parties.[41] Therefore, it seems systemically difficult to impose effects on the parties before the order or award has even been served on them.

A.   FUNCTUS OFFICIO

Further, the termination of the arbitration leads to the automatic expiration of the arbitrators' mandate. Section 608(3) ZPO provides expressly that '[t]he mandate of the arbitral tribunal terminates with the termination of the arbitral proceedings'. As a result, once the arbitration is terminated and the arbitrators' mandate has expired, the arbitrators become *functus officio*, i.e. loose their power to decide on matters of procedure or substance against the parties (save for the specific matters discussed below). It can therefore be argued under Austrian law (and absent a statutory authorization to the contrary) that if the dispute becomes again alive – for example, because an award is set aside and the dispute referred back to arbitration, or a claim that was withdrawn without prejudice, resulting in the termination of the arbitration, is subsequently reasserted – a new tribunal might have to be constituted.[42] **25-025**

B.   ONGOING OBLIGATIONS OF THE TRIBUNAL

However, even where their mandate is otherwise exhausted, there are certain duties that the arbitrators may still have to fulfil. Section 608(3) ZPO provides that the termination of the tribunal's mandate is 'subject to the provisions of Section 606, **25-026**

---

37. *See* **Article 9**, at paras. 015 *et seq.*
38. *See* **Article 9**, at paras. 016 *et seq*; C. Liebscher, *The Austrian Arbitration Act 2006: Text and Notes* (The Hague, Kluwer Law International, 2006), Annotated Text to Section 608(2) ZPO.
39. S. Riegler in *Arbitration Law of Austria: Practice and Procedure*, S. Riegler, A. Petsche, A. Fremuth-Wolf, M. Platte and C. Liebscher (eds) (Huntington, Juris Publishing, 2007), Section 608, p. 473.
40. *See* **Article 27**, at paras. 010 *et seq.*
41. Section 611(4) ZPO; *see* **Article 27**, at para. 021.
42. Explanatory Notes to Section 608; P. Oberhammer, *Entwurf eines neuen Schiedsverfahrensrechts* (Vienna, Manz, 2002), p. 123. This does not mean, subject to considerations of impartiality, that the parties cannot nominate the same arbitrators again.

paragraphs (4) to (6), Section 609, paragraph (5), and Section 610 of this law, as well as to the obligation to set aside an ordered provisional or protective measure'. Thus, even where its mandate is terminated, the tribunal must deliver the award;[43] deposit the award;[44] confirm the enforceability of the award;[45] correct clerical errors and interpret the award;[46] issue an additional award under the circumstances of Section 610 ZPO;[47] set aside an interim measure issued in the course of the proceedings;[48] and determine the costs of the arbitration and allocate these costs between the parties.[49]

---

43. *See* **Article 27**, at paras. 019 *et seq.*
44. *See* **Article 27**, at paras. 019 *et seq.*
45. *See* **Article 27**, at paras. 022 *et seq.*
46. *See* **Article 29**, at paras. 001 *et seq.*
47. *See* **Article 29**, at paras. 015 *et seq.*
48. *See* **Article 22**, at para. 082.
49. *See* **Article 31**, at paras. 001 *et seq.*

Article 26

Decision Making of the Arbitral Tribunal

		Para.				Para.
I.	Quorum	1		D.	The Tribunal's	
	A. Introduction	1			Deliberations	21
	B. Quorum Requirements Under			E.	Dissenting Opinions	24
	Austrian Law	3	II.	Procedural Decisions		34
	C. Quorum Requirements Under the					
	Vienna Rules	14				

I.   QUORUM

Article 26(1): Any award or any other decision of the arbitral tribunal shall be made by a majority of all its members. If no majority of votes is obtained, the presiding arbitrator shall decide alone.

A.   INTRODUCTION

Ideally, decisions in the arbitral process are made unanimously amongst the arbitrators. Unanimity creates confidence in the process and enhances the credibility attached to the award. The parties are more likely to accept the decision of the tribunal, favourable or not, if it has been reached on common grounds. **26-001**

Previous versions of the Vienna Rules had not contained an express quorum requirement regarding the decision-making of the arbitral tribunal. The resulting uncertainty was compounded by the unconventional approach of the former Austrian arbitration law to this question. It allowed any party to apply to the courts for a declaration that the arbitration agreement is rescinded or of no effect in the particular case 'if the necessary majority for taking a decision, or where there are **26-002** only two arbitrators, unanimity cannot be reached'.[1] If, on the other hand, more than two arbitrators were appointed to the decision-making, the award had to be rendered by an absolute majority of the votes.[2] The former legislation allowed the parties only to agree on stricter requirements, but not to ease any of the statutory voting rules.[3] Now, and as discussed in detail below, both the Vienna Rules and Austrian law have been substantially amended to provide for a more practicable solution.

B.   QUORUM REQUIREMENTS UNDER AUSTRIAN LAW

26-003 The 2006 reform sought to address the previously existing uncertainty with respect to voting requirements for decisions of the tribunal. Section 604(1) ZPO now provides (absent a deviating agreement by the parties):

> In arbitral proceedings with more than one arbitrator, any decision of the arbitral tribunal shall be made by a majority of all its members. Questions of procedure may be decided by the presiding arbitrator alone if so authorized by the parties or by all members of the arbitral tribunal.

This provision is based on Article 29 UNCITRAL Model Law and sets out the basic rule for the decision-making by requiring a majority vote for any decision of the tribunal. It applies whenever the place of arbitration is within Austria.[4]

26-004 The initial draft of the ZPO, as proposed by the Working Group, had suggested the additional proviso that, where a majority cannot be obtained amongst the arbitrators, the chairman alone carries the decisive vote (unless the parties agree otherwise). The Working Group argued that this power of the chairman would help avoiding a deadlock in the arbitrators' decision-making process: if the co-arbitrators know that absent majority, the chairman will decide alone, they will be more inclined to build a majority in order to give at least some weight to their own position and not effectively cancel their entire vote by delegating the decision-making solely to the chairman.[5]

---

1. Section 591(2) fZPO.
2. Section 590 fZPO. *See* C. Liebscher and A. Schmid in *Practitioner's Handbook on International Arbitration*, F.B. Weigand (ed.) (Munich, C.H. Beck, 2002), pp. 568 *et seq.*
3. H.W. Fasching, *Schiedsgericht und Schiedsverfahren im österreichischen und im internationalen Recht* (Vienna, Manz, 1973), p. 120.
4. Section 577 ZPO: The provisions of this part apply only if the seat of the arbitration is in Austria.
5. Section 604 draft provision of the ZPO: 'Unless otherwise agreed by the parties: 1. In arbitration proceedings with more than one arbitrator, any decision of the arbitral tribunal shall be made by a majority of its members. If such majority can not be reached, the chairman alone is authorized to decide. Questions of procedure may be decided by the chairman alone, if so authorized by the parties or all members of the arbitral tribunal.'

The Working Group's proposal was modelled on Article 25 ICC Rules.[6] However, **26-005**
as practical as this solution might seem, it is not without controversy. It is argued
that this solution deprives the other members of the arbitral tribunal of 'appropriate
influence' on the decisions taken. Also, it is suggested that contested issues might
in fact receive fuller consideration if the tribunal is forced to reach a majority
decision, rather than falling back, perhaps too easily, on the presiding arbitrator's
power to decide alone in case of deadlock.[7]

Ultimately, Section 604 ZPO provides for a majority decision without affording the **26-006**
chairman a decisive vote. As a result, if the tribunal is unable to reach a majority
decision on a certain issue, only limited options exist. The parties could conceivably request the tribunal to issue an order for termination of the proceedings
because their continuation has become impossible.[8] However, this solution is
obviously impractical, would waste the effort and expense conceivably of an entire
arbitration, and possibly force arbitrators into half-hearted compromises in order to
avoid a deadlock scenario.[9]

Section 604 ZPO is prefaced by the unambiguous phrase 'unless otherwise agreed **26-007**
by the parties' and thus acknowledges that this is a non-mandatory provision. As a
result, the parties are entitled to make deviating arrangements, including by agreeing on the application of the Vienna Rules. Although the wording does not indicate
any restriction, the Explanatory Notes suggest that the parties' autonomy in this
respect is limited; parties are supposedly able to agree only on stricter voting
requirements because 'a provision that affords the decisive vote to the minority
is absurd; and the allocation of decisive votes would disguise an unlawfully

---

6. Article 25 ICC Rules reads as follows: '(1) When the Arbitral Tribunal is composed of more than
   one arbitrator, an Award is given by a majority decision. If there be no majority, the Award shall
   be made by the chairman of the Arbitral Tribunal alone. (2) The Award shall state the reasons
   upon which it is based. (3) The Award shall be deemed to be made at the place of the arbitration
   and on the date stated therein.' *See* P. Oberhammer, *Entwurf eines neuen Schiedsverfahrensrechts* (Vienna, Manz, 2002), pp. 111 *et seq.*
7. H.M. Holtzmann and J.E. Neuhaus, *A Guide To The UNCITRAL Model Law On International
   Commercial Arbitration: Legislative History and Commentary* (The Hague, Kluwer Law
   International, 1989), pp. 808 *et seq.* Furthermore, it was noted that cases of actual deadlock
   were rare and the provision is in any event non-mandatory. The parties can always agree to
   provide for the presiding arbitrator to cast the deciding vote or for some other form of voting.
8. Section 608(2) no. 4 ZPO: 'The arbitral tribunal shall terminate the arbitral proceedings when it
   finds that the continuation of the proceedings has become impossible, in particular, because the
   parties active in the proceedings to that point do not continue the arbitral proceedings despite
   written notification by the arbitral tribunal which refers to the possibility of terminating the
   arbitral proceedings.'
9. The RAKTA arbitration illustrates how deadlock may arise in such a way that the presiding
   arbitrator would have to sacrifice principle in order to render an award under the UNCITRAL
   Rules. RAKTA, ICC 1703/1971, summarized in W.L. Craig, W.W. Park and J. Paulsson,
   International Chamber of Commerce Arbitration (3rd edn, New York, Oceana Publications,
   2000), p. 370.

constituted tribunal.'[10] This reasoning could be understandable if the parties agreed on an entirely arbitrary decision-making process based on chance rather than reason. However, a decision-making process that allows the chairman to decide alone, if otherwise no decision can be reached, is not arbitrary. It avoids dead-lock; and entrusts the presiding arbitrator, who is by definition most removed from the parties and hence enjoys the highest perception of neutrality. Thus, provisions like Article 26(1) (discussed in detail below) comply with Section 604 ZPO.[11] Indeed, parties very rarely include specific arrangements for decision-making in the arbitration agreement other than incorporating by reference provisions in institutional rules dealing with the decision-making process on the tribunal.

26-008 The approach adopted in Section 604(1) ZPO – providing for a majority decision, without affording the chairman a decisive vote – is characterized by an inherent risk. A partisan arbitrator could sabotage the tribunal's decision-making simply by refusing to participate in the tribunal's deliberations or votes. To address this and other cases of 'truncated' arbitral tribunals, Section 604(2) ZPO proceeds to provide:

> Unless otherwise agreed by the parties, the following shall apply: (. . .) If one or more arbitrators do not participate in a vote without justified reason, the other arbitrators may decide without them. In this case, the necessary majority shall be calculated by reference to the total number of all arbitrators participating and not participating. In the case of taking votes for an award, the parties must first be informed of the intention to proceed in this manner. With regard to other decisions, the parties must be informed about the failure to participate in the vote after such vote.

26-009 As a result, if an arbitrator refuses to participate in the decision-making the other (two) arbitrators can proceed without him. As a matter of quorum, the non-participating arbitrator is counted as if present. If the two participating arbitrators share the same view, they have therefore established a majority of two against one. If they are unable to find a common view amongst them, the two participating arbitrators have formed no majority, and no decision can be rendered. Notably, Section 604(2) ZPO also applies '[i]f one *or more arbitrators* do not participate in a vote without justified reason.' Where a tribunal consists of five arbitrators (or any larger odd number), this makes sense. In a three panel tribunal, the non-participation of two arbitrators raises the question if a majority is possible at all.

26-010 As a matter of course, Section 604(2) ZPO allows an arbitrator to be excluded from the vote only if his non-participation is not reasonably justified. The right of an arbitrator to participate in the deliberations and the attending voting is fundamental to the arbitral process; it also impacts the parties' right to have their dispute decided

---

10. Explanatory Notes to Section 604.
11. *See* J. Power, *The Austrian Arbitration Act – A Practitioner's Guide to Sections 577-618 of the Austrian Code of Civil Procedure* (Vienna, Manz, 2006), Section 604, para. 3.

by a fully-functioning panel of three arbitrators (where they have so agreed). The absence of justified reasons must be obvious; and the opportunity for the defaulting arbitrator to cast his vote must be adequate. On the other hand, Section 604(2) ZPO gives the arbitrators an effective tool against delaying tactics on the part of an arbitrator so inclined.

Whether it is justified to proceed to a vote without the defaulting arbitrator is for the **26-011** remaining arbitrators to determine. However, in order to control their right to do so, the remaining arbitrators need to first notify the parties that they intend to proceed to an award without all members of the tribunal. This notification serves two purposes: First, the parties should be given the opportunity to demonstrate that the absence of the defaulting arbitrator is, for reasons previously unknown to the remaining arbitrators, in fact justified; or to call on the defaulting arbitrator to participate in the vote, or else to terminate the arbitrator's mandate in accordance with Section 590 ZPO. Second, such advance notice affords the parties the opportunity to agree on a different decision-making process, such as vesting the presiding arbitrator with the power to cast a decisive vote. Only where the arbitrators' decision relates to a procedural order (rather than an award), the parties need only be notified after the vote has been taken. This is intended to permit the remaining arbitrators to make procedural determination swiftly.

It is still a contested issue among legal authorities in Austria whether or not the **26-012** failure of the remaining arbitrators to comply with the requirements and procedure set out in Section 604(2) ZPO gives rise to a successful challenge under Section 611(2) nos 4 and 5 ZPO.

Section 604(2) ZPO has no reasonable application in arbitrations under the Vienna **26-013** Rules. Rather than providing for a fall-back solution for truncated tribunals, the defaulting arbitrator's mandate would be terminated under the procedure of **Article 17**[12] and with the consequences contemplated by **Article 18**.[13]

C.   Quorum Requirements Under the Vienna Rules

The Vienna Rules now for the first time expressly address the decision-making of **26-014** the tribunal, in reaction to the introduction of Section 604 ZPO. Article 26 provides for the principle of a majority quorum in the decision-making process. However, following the approach of Article 25 of the ICC Rules and in contrast to Section 604(1) ZPO, if no majority of votes is obtained, the presiding arbitrator's vote alone will be decisive.[14]

As discussed above, the possibility for the chairman to render an award alone **26-015** where it is impossible to rally a majority is an effective device which deters the

---

12. *See* **Article 17**, at paras. 013 *et seq.*
13. *See* **Article 18**, at paras. 001 *et seq.*
14. *See* **Article 26**, at paras. 003 *et seq.*

co-arbitrators from dead-lock. This approach reinforces the chairman's position as independent and discourages partisan conduct on the part of the co-arbitrators (who know that the chairman is not required to agree with either one of them in order to issue an award). This, in turn, serves to strengthen the position of the presiding arbitrator and promote the integrity of decision-making under the Vienna Rules.[15]

26-016 Former Article 18(2) gave only an indirect indication that majority votes were admissible by stating that 'the signatures of the majority of the arbitrators shall suffice'. Article 18(2) of the 2001 version of the Vienna Rules[16] has been transformed into **Article 27(3)** which provides:

> All copies of awards must be signed by the arbitrators. The signatures of the majority of the arbitrators shall suffice if the award contains a statement that one arbitrator refuses to sign or that his signature is prevented by an obstacle which cannot be overcome within a reasonable period of time. If the award is made by a majority decision, mention thereof shall be made in the award at the request of the arbitrator who is in a minority.[17]

26-017 However, this does not account for the new quorum requirement provided in Article 26: under this provision, the signature of the chairman alone must suffice where a decisive vote is cast in case of deadlock.[18]

26-018 In practice, awards rendered by the chairman alone are rare. This, in fact, may prove the value of permitting the presiding arbitrator to decide an issue alone, as if acting as sole arbitrator. Knowledge that unreasonable positions will not yield any tactical benefit dissuades partisan conduct on the part of the co-arbitrators. Conversely, the presiding arbitrator need not compromise his views and join with the least unreasonable of the co-arbitrators in order to form a majority.[19]

26-019 However, the tribunal can be expected to at least endeavour to reach common grounds for its decision. The language of Article 26 suggests that, as a rule, 'the decision shall be made by the majority' of the arbitrators. The power of the presiding arbitrator to cast the decisive vote is therefore only a fall-back to prevent dead-lock. Hence, before the presiding arbitrator will go forward with the sole decision-making in accordance with Article 26(1), the tribunal will have attempted to identify the lowest common denominator of consensus amongst the arbitrators,

---

15. *See* Y. Derains and E.A. Schwartz, *A Guide to the ICC Rules of Arbitration* (2nd edn, The Hague, Kluwer Law International, 2005), p. 306.
16. Vienna Rules 2001, **Annex 2a**.
17. *See* **Article 27(3)**, at paras. 014 *et seq.*
18. *See* **Article 27**, at para. 016.
19. *See* J. Paulsson and G. Petrochilos, 'Revision of the UNCITRAL Arbitration Rules' (Paris, 2006), <http://www.uncitral.org/pdf/english/news/arbrules_report.pdf>.

and then make the informed decision that an award cannot be rendered on that basis. Practice shows that real, insurmountable dissent between all three members of the tribunal is relatively rare. Save for partisan arbitrators who advocate 'their' party's position and lack any interest in genuine decision-making, discontent within the decision-making is often the result of unvoiced expectations, differing backgrounds and varying experience on the part of the arbitrators, rather than genuine disagreement on substance. It is the skill and art of chairmanship to negotiate those different expectations, without compromising the result mandated by the applicable law. In the end, the power of the presiding arbitrator to cast the decisive vote should be exercised with caution.

Unlike Section 604(2) ZPO, Article 26 does not require the arbitrators to notify the **26-020** parties in advance before the chairman can cast a decisive vote.[20] Thus, in case the presiding arbitrator intends to render a decision on his own, he will not be obliged to inform the parties beforehand, although it can be expected that for any decision rendered under on Article 26(1) by the chairman alone, he will set forth the basis for this conclusion in the award.

D.   THE TRIBUNAL'S DELIBERATIONS

Whether the award is made unanimously, by majority vote or by the chairman **26-021** alone, it must, as a rule, be preceded by deliberations among all of the members of the arbitral tribunal. Article 26 requires the arbitrators to make a reasonable good-faith effort to achieve a majority – but they do not have to compromise their professional conscience to form a majority in every case.[21]

The need for deliberations is sometimes even considered to constitute a require- **26-022** ment of international public policy.[22] The role of each arbitrator in deliberation is important. Usually, there will be meetings among the three members of the tribunal to discuss certain issues. Deliberations which always involve all three arbitrators are preferable as they ensure that all arbitrators have an equal voice in the discussions. If one member is not available to participate in person, then the chairman will have to ensure that the arbitrator is apprised of the deliberation and given the

---

20. *See* P. Oberhammer, *Entwurf eines neuen Schiedsverfahrensrechts* (Vienna, Manz, 2002), pp. 112 *et seq.*; C. Stippl and V. Öhlberger, 'Rendering of the Award by Multipartite Arbitral Tribunals' in *Austrian Arbitration Yearbook 2008*, C. Klausegger *et al.* (eds) (Vienna, Manz, 2008), pp. 371 *et seq.*; S. Riegler in *Arbitration Law of Austria: Practice and Procedure*, S. Riegler, A. Petsche, A. Fremuth-Wolf, M. Platte and C. Liebscher (eds) (Huntington, Juris Publishing, 2007), Section 604, pp. 424 *et seq.*

21. *See also* J. Paulsson and G. Petrochilos, 'Revision of the UNCITRAL Arbitration Rules'(Paris, 2006), <http://www.uncitral.org/pdf/english/news/arbrules_report.pdf>.

22. Y. Derains and E.A. Schwartz, *A Guide to the ICC Rules of Arbitration* (2nd edn, The Hague, Kluwer Law International, 2005), p. 307.

opportunity to express his opinion prior to any decision being taken.[23] In practice, there is active interchange amongst the arbitrators, often per e-mail or in telephone conferences and in personal meetings.[24] A draft of important decisions, whether on substance or procedure, is circulated by the presiding arbitrator to the co-arbitrators for comments.

26-023 There are no formal requirements as to the way these deliberations will have to take place. The Austrian *Oberster Gerichtshof* recently confirmed for an ICC arbitration that the arbitral tribunal enjoys broad discretion to determine the manner of deliberations. Although a clear preference has been expressed towards a personal meeting, it was acknowledged that ICC arbitral tribunals may also deliberate via telephone or video conferencing, provided that this is in accordance with the law at the seat of the arbitration.[25] The same is true for arbitration under the Vienna Rules, with the seat of the arbitration in Austria.

E.   DISSENTING OPINIONS

26-024 It is increasingly common that in case a unanimous decision cannot be reached in the panel, some arbitrators express their discontent with the decision, so not to be associated with the reasoning or even parts or all of the dispositive segment of the award.

26-025 Such an expression of disagreement is usually referred to as a *dissenting opinion*. This is as such not a term of art in arbitration, and can take many forms. Some arbitrators articulate this in the form of a separate decision, an addendum or an annex to the award or even by separate letter to the parties.[26] Any opinion deviating from the common decision of the tribunal can be seen as a dissenting one.

---

23. M. Bühler and T. Webster, *Handbook of ICC Arbitration: Commentary, Precedents, Materials* (London, Sweet & Maxwell, 2005), p. 309.
24. *See* **Article 13**, at para. 022.
25. OGH, 26 April 2006, 3 Ob 211/05h.
26. The tendency can be observed in more recent ICC statistics according to which in 2006 a total of 293 awards were rendered. Twenty-three of these awards failed to reach unanimity. *See* 2006 Statistical Report (2007) 18(1) ICC Ct Bull, 5; *see also* Y. Derains and E.A. Schwartz, *A Guide to the ICC Rules of Arbitration* (2nd edn, The Hague, Kluwer Law International, 2005), p. 308. For further discussion on dissenting opinions in international arbitration, *see* 'Final Report on Dissenting and Separate Opinions' of the ICC Commission Working Party on this subject (M. Hunter, Chairman) (1991) 2(1) ICC Ct Bull, 32; *see also* A. Redfern, 'The 2003 Freshfields Lecture – Dissenting Opinions in International Commercial Arbitration: The Good, the Bad and the Ugly' (2004) 20(3) Arb Int'l, 223.

Dissenting opinions are a gift from common law jurisdictions.[27] In a legal system **26-026** based on case law and precedent, dissenting opinions are perceived to contribute to the development of law.[28] It is argued that dissenters elevate the quality of and intellectual rigor of a decision, inciting each judge or arbitrator to consider more carefully the content of his decision. In common law systems, the ability to render a dissenting opinion is also considered a hallmark of the independence and impartiality of a judge or arbitrator.[29]

In civil law jurisdictions, on the other hand, the members of a court decide in **26-027** principle anonymously, on behalf of the judicial panel on which they serve (rather than in an individual capacity) and with their internal deliberations usually being kept confidential.[30] The civil law debate on dissenting opinions thus focuses on whether the deliberations which lead to an arbitral award should be published at all. It is feared, first, that they may inhibit the open discussion amongst the members of the tribunal which is protected by the secrecy of the deliberations (which ought not to be breached by a separate, public opinion disagreeing with the reasons ultimately adopted by the majority). Secondly, it is argued that dissenting opinions may cast doubts on the correctness or validity of the award made by the majority. In the context specifically of arbitration, it is also said that they do not serve to advance the development of the law, because there is no doctrine of precedence in arbitration, there is, in general, no appeal on the merits against the award, and there is no broader publication of the tribunal's decision on the merits.[31] In the words of *Redfern*,

> there is a simple, practical argument against dissenting opinions, which would seem to carry the most weight of all. The purpose of an arbitration is to arrive at a decision. It is the decision which matters; and it matters not as a guide to the opinions of a particular arbitrator, or as an indication of the future development of the law, but because it resolves the particular dispute that divides the parties; and it resolves that dispute as part of a private, not public, dispute resolution process that the parties themselves have chosen.[32]

---

27. A. Redfern, 'The 2003 Freshfields Lecture – Dissenting Opinions in International Commercial Arbitration: The Good, the Bad and the Ugly' (2004) 20(3) Arb Int'l, 223, 224.
28. A. Redfern, M. Hunter, N. Blackaby and C. Partasides, *Law and Practice of International Commercial Arbitration* (4th edn, London, Sweet & Maxwell, 2004), para. 8-82.
29. *See* C. Stippl and V. Öhlberger, 'Rendering of the Award by Multipartite Arbitral Tribunals' in *Austrian Arbitration Yearbook 2008*, C. Klausegger *et al.* (eds) (Vienna, Manz, 2008), pp. 371 *et seq.*
30. J. Laffranque, 'Dissenting opinion and Judical Independence' (2003) Juridica International VIII, 163.
31. A. Redfern, M. Hunter, N. Blackaby and C. Partasides, *Law and Practice of International Commercial Arbitration* (4th edn, London, Sweet & Maxwell, 2004), para. 8-82.
32. A. Redfern, 'The 2003 Freshfields – Lecture Dissenting Opinions in International Commercial Arbitration: The Good, the Bad and the Ugly' (2004) 20(3) Arb Int'l, 223, 224. *See also* the

26-028 In some civil law jurisdictions it is therefore argued that dissenting opinions – although not expressly prohibited by national law – are violating the secrecy of deliberations and are, thus, inadmissible.[33] In Germany, for example, the publication of dissenting opinions is not explicitly regulated in German arbitration law and still a contested issue.[34]

26-029 The new Austrian ZPO has not taken an express position regarding the dissenting opinion and their admissibility. However, it clearly permits the majority vote on an award, as addressed in Section 604(1) ZPO, and, also a separate decision-making by a truncated tribunal, as addressed by Section 604(2) ZPO.[35] Most notably, Section 606(2) ZPO requires the presiding arbitrator to provide the reasons in the award for any missing signature of members of the tribunal. Arguably, this can be seen as an admitting dissenting opinions by implication.

26-030 Recently, the Austrian *Oberster Gerichtshof* dealt with a dissenting opinion in an arbitration award in the context of enforcement proceedings.[36] In its ruling, the Austrian *Oberster Gerichtshof* explicitly acknowledged that dissenting opinions are permissible under the ICC Rules. However, it clarified that a dissenting opinion was not to be considered as part of the award and therefore not necessarily needed to be produced in the enforcement proceedings.

---

cases cited in the Report on the revision of the UNCITRAL Arbitration Rules by *Paulsson/Petrochilos*: <http://www.uncitral.org/pdf/english/news/arbrules_report.pdf>. It was reported that the Iran-US Claims Tribunal saw several cases of jigsaw majorities being formed on an issue-by-issue basis, resulting in narrowly decided and worded awards followed by forceful dissenting/concurring opinions by the Iranian and US judges.

33. *See* C. Stippl and V. Öhlberger, 'Rendering of the Award by Multipartite Arbitral Tribunals' in *Austrian Arbitration Yearbook 2008*, C. Klausegger *et al.* (eds) (Vienna, Manz, 2006), pp. 371 *et seq.* with reference to France.

34. Some legal authorities deny the right of an arbitrator to publish a dissenting opinion as this might violate the confidentiality of deliberations. *See, e.g.,* R. Geimer in *Zöller – Zivilprozessordnung*, R. Zöller *et al.* (eds) (26th edn, Cologne, Verlag Dr. Otto Schmidt, 2007), Section 1052, para. 5 with reference to BGH, 23 January 1963, VZR 132/55, NJW 1957, 1592; R.A. Schütze, *Schiedsgericht und Schiedsverfahren* (4th edn, Munich, C.H. Beck, 2007), para. 222; R.A. Schütze, 'Dissenting Opinions im Schiedsverfahren' in *Festschrift für Hideo Nakamura zum 70. Geburtstag*, A. Heldrich and T. Uchida (eds) (Tokyo, Seibundo, 1996), pp. 525, 535. Opposing: K.P. Berger, *Internationale Wirtschaftsschiedsgerichtsbarkeit* (Berlin/New York, de Gruyter, 1992), pp. 425 *et seq.*; H. Raeschke-Kessler and K.P. Berger, *Recht und Praxis des Schiedsverfahrens* (3rd edn, Cologne, RWS Verlag, 1999), para. 204; P. Schlosser, *Das Recht der internationalen privaten Schiedsgerichtsbarkeit* (2nd edn, Tübingen, Mohr Siebeck, 1989), para. 691. *Schlosser* argues that a published dissenting opinion is admissible and even a violation of the confidentiality of deliberation would not allow to challenge the arbitral award.

35. *See* also **Article 17**, **Article 18** and **Article 27**.

36. OGH, 26 April 2006, 3 Ob 211/05h.

Arbitration rules do usually not address the question of permissibility of dissenting **26-031** opinions.[37] The Vienna Rules neither expressly permit nor discourage the rendering of dissenting opinions. **Article 27(3)** only makes indirect reference to that possibility in that the arbitrator can request that an express statement be included in the award that it was the result of a majority decision.[38] The general view in international arbitration is that even under laws where no express reference is made to dissenting opinions, they may still be delivered.[39] Hence, provided that the *lex arbitri* does not provide anything to the contrary, it is ultimately permissible to express a dissenting opinion to a decision of an arbitral tribunal under the Vienna Rules.[40]

It is important, however, that the dissenting opinion does not undermine the **26-032** secrecy of the tribunal's deliberations. The scope of that secrecy is narrower in arbitration proceedings than it is in court proceedings. In litigation before the Austrian courts, the secrecy of deliberations covers both the deliberations and the voting;[41] no secrecy of voting applies to arbitral tribunals.[42]

The tribunal's deliberations, however, must remain confidential. This enables the **26-033** arbitrators to express their views frankly without risking that their arguments will be disclosed involuntarily; the authority of the award is safeguarded *vis-à-vis* the parties; and the arbitrators' duties of collegiality, impartiality and diligence are not undermined.[43] The secrecy of deliberations in its stricter meaning, as applicable in Austrian arbitration proceedings, will therefore be violated if an arbitrator in a dissenting opinion reveals the actual substance of the deliberations by, for example, citing specific statements made during the deliberations which were not revealed to the parties in the award; or disclosing the process by which each arbitrator shaped his view. Conversely, there is no violation of the secrecy of deliberations if a dissenting opinion is limited to an alternative statement on

---

37. Exceptions can be found *e.g.* in Article 43(4) CIETAC Rules and Article 48(4) ICSID Convention.

38. See **Article 27**, at para. 015.

39. J. Lew, L. Mistelis and S. Kröll, *Comparative International Commercial Arbitration* (The Hague, Kluwer Law International, 2003), paras. 24-47.

40. *See also* C. Liebscher in *Institutionelle Schiedsgerichtsbarkeit*, R.A. Schütze (ed.) (Cologne, Carl Heymanns Verlag, 2006), pp. 255, 299; A. Reiner, 'The 2001 Version of the Vienna Rules' (2001) 18(6) J Int'l Arb, 661, 666.

41. For Austrian civil proceedings, the secrecy of deliberations is regulated in Section 413 ZPO which provides that '[t]he deliberation and voting of judges is not public'. However, an infringement of that principle is generally considered to amount only to a mere misdemeanor (*Ordnungswidrigkeit*), which does not lead to any procedural consequences, in particular, not to grave defect in the resulting judgment. *See* M. Bydlinski in *Kommentar zu den Zivilprozeßgesetzen, III*, H.W. Fasching (ed.) (2nd end, Vienna, Manz, 2004), Section 413 para. 1.

42. *See* Section 606 ZPO; *see also* **Article 27**, at paras. 014 *et seq.*

43. C. Stippl and V. Öhlberger 'Rendering of the Award by Multipartite Arbitral Tribunals' in *Austrian Arbitration Yearbook 2008*, C. Klausegger *et al.* (eds) (Vienna, Manz, 2008), pp. 371 *et seq.*

issues of fact or law that disagrees with the reasoning or the conclusion of the majority.[44]

II.   PROCEDURAL DECISIONS

Article 26(2): Questions of procedure may be decided by the presiding arbitrator alone if so authorized by the arbitral tribunal, with reservation to possible amendments by the arbitral tribunal.

26-034 In certain circumstances, procedural decisions are suitable to be decided by the chairman alone. This provision is intended to expedite the process, by dispensing the need for consultation on issues that are routine and uncontroversial.

26-035 The notion of 'questions of procedure' must therefore be interpreted narrowly and denotes exclusively questions that affect the course of the proceedings. This includes, for example, the determination of the language(s) of the arbitration proceedings;[45] logistical arrangements for the hearing; or determining the order in which witnesses testify.[46] By contrast, decisions determining the tribunal's jurisdiction; the applicable substantive law; or the grant of interim relief are not of a purely procedural nature and must be rendered by the tribunal *in toto*.[47] In cases of doubt, the entire tribunal should be involved.

26-036 In order for the chairman to be able to exercise this power, he requires an authorization from the arbitral tribunal. This concept is widely accepted by other prominent arbitral institutions.[48] The authorization is granted by *all* members of the arbitral tribunal (and not by the other members of the tribunal alone); thus requiring the presiding arbitrator's consent to this authority. Although an implied consent is conceivable, this authorization should be recorded in writing, preferably at the organisational conference in order to solicit the parties' comments on this issue.[49] If such power is granted to the chairman, it is then typically (and should be)

---

44. C. Stippl and V. Öhlberger 'Rendering of the Award by Multipartite Arbitral Tribunals' in *Austrian Arbitration Yearbook 2008*, C. Klausegger *et al.* (eds) (Vienna, Manz, 2008), pp. 271 *et seq.*

45. C. Liebscher, *The Austrian Arbitration Act 2006: Text and Notes* (The Hague, Kluwer Law Interantional, 2006), Annotated Text to Section 604 ZPO.

46. H. Thomas and H. Putzo, *Zivilprozessordnung – Kommentar* (26th edn, Munich, C.H. Beck, 2004), Section 1052, para. 4; R. Geimer in *Zöller – Zivilprozessordnung*, R. Zöller *et al.* (eds) (26th edn, Cologne, Verlag Dr. Otto Schmidt, 2007), Section 1052, para. 7.

47. J. Power, *The Austrian Arbitration Act – A Practitioner's Guide to Sections 577-618 of the Austrian Code of Civil Procedure* (Vienna, Manz, 2006), Section 604, para. 4.

48. Article 25(1) ICC Rules and Article 26(3) LCIA Rules.

49. *See* **Article 20**, at paras. 103 *et seq.*

recorded in the first procedural order communicated to the parties that sets out the procedural parameters of the arbitration.[50]

The chairman's power to issue procedural orders on his own, once granted, remains **26-037** subject to the reservation of possible subsequent amendments by the arbitral tribunal. Thus, even if the co-arbitrators have authorized such rulings, they maintain the power to insist on a plenary vote, or to revoke this authority at any stage.[51] A majority decision is sufficient to do so; although in practice, the chairman will be well advised to consider voluntarily giving up this authority if only one other member of the tribunal so desires. The parties can also by agreement exclude such a power, or remove it from the chairman at a later stage.

---

50. *See* **Article 20**, at para. 111.
51. This has also been argued under the framework of the UNCITRAL Rules. *See* I.I. Dore, *The UNCITRAL Framework for Arbitration in Contemporary Perspective* (London, Graham & Trotman/Martinus Nijhoff, 1993), p. 33.

Article 27

The Award

		Para.
I.	The Reasoned Award in Writing....	1
II.	Statement of Date and Arbitral Seat	10
III.	Signed Award	14
IV.	Confirmation by the VIAC	17
V.	Service and Effect of the Award....	19
VI.	Confirmation of Finality and Enforceability	22
VII.	Partial and Interim Awards	24
VIII.	Implementing the Award	29
IX.	Recourse Against an Award in the Austrian Courts..............................	32
	A. Jurisdiction and Proceedings....	33
	B. Grounds for Setting Aside an Arbitral Award.........................	39
	1. Jurisdictional Issues.............	42
	2. Violation of the Right to be Heard..................................	46

		Para.
	3. Decision *Ultra Petita*	48
	4. Deficient Formation or Composition of the Arbitral Tribunal...........................	51
	5. *Procedural Ordre Public*	54
	6. Reopening of Court Proceedings....................	56
	7. Lack of Arbitrability	58
	8. *Substantive Ordre Public*	60
	C. Consequences of Setting Aside Proceedings ...._......	62
	D. Declaration that an Award Does or Does Not Exist...............__......	64
	E. Enforcement of Foreign Awards ...._......	65

I. THE REASONED AWARD IN WRITING

Article 27(1): Awards shall be drawn up in writing. The grounds upon which the award is based must be stated, unless all parties, either in the arbitration agreement or in the oral proceedings, have agreed that no grounds are to be stated.

27-001 At a minimum, an award must be rendered in writing and signed by the arbitrators in the prescribed way.[1] If the decision does not satisfy those basic formal requirements, it is classified as a 'non-award' that lacks any legal effects.[2]

27-002 Today, most modern international arbitration rules require a reason to be given in the award; and it is required by law in most jurisdictions.[3] For example, the UNCITRAL Rules state: 'The arbitral tribunal shall state the reasons upon which the award is based, unless the parties have agreed that no reasons are to be given.'[4] Article 27(1) is therefore in line with international practice.

27-003 Setting forth the reasons for the tribunal's decisions has many benefits. It demonstrates that the tribunal has given full consideration to the parties' submissions and arguments. Some say that a reasoned award, which ensures that the tribunal addresses the parties' arguments in full, is a necessary corollary to the parties' right to be heard.[5] A well reasoned award that takes account of both sides' positions may in any event increase acceptance and, hence, the likelihood that the parties will voluntarily abide by the tribunal's decision.[6]

27-004 Some awards will be as brief as stating which party's evidence the tribunal accepted, while others will be a detailed account of all the evidence and arguments put forward, leading to a reasoned conclusion on the facts and the law.[7] At a minimum, the award should contain the name of the parties; the members of the tribunal; a discussion of the claims advanced, and a dispositive part that states with particularity the declaration that has been requested, or the order of performance directed against one or more parties. Arbitrators will often be influenced by the drafting style and structure of judicial decisions in their home jurisdictions.

---

1. *See* **Article 27**, at paras. 014 *et seq.*
2. Explanatory Notes to Section 611 ZPO. *See* also **Article 27**, at para. 014.
3. A. Redfern, M. Hunter, N. Blackaby and C. Partasides, *Law and Practice of International Commercial Arbitration* (4th edn, London, Sweet & Maxwell, 2004), paras. 8-65 *et seq.;* J. Lew, L. Mistelis and S. Kröll, *Comparative International Commercial Arbitration* (The Hague, Kluwer Law International, 2003), paras. 24-64 *et seq.; see, e.g.*, Article 43(2) CIETAC Rules; Article 25(2) ICC Rules; Rule 47(1)(i) ICSID Arbitration Rules; Article 32(3) Swiss Rules and Article 36(1) SCC Rules.
4. Article 32(3) UNCITRAL Rules; *see, e.g.*, Article 26(1) LCIA Rules: 'The Arbitral Tribunal shall make its award in writing and, unless all parties agree in writing otherwise, shall state the reasons upon which its award is based.' Article 27(2) AAA/ICDR Rules: 'The tribunal shall state the reasons upon which the award is based, unless the parties have agreed that no reasons need be given.'
5. *See* **Article 20**, at para. 061.
6. Y. Derains and E.A. Schwartz, *A Guide to the ICC Rules of Arbitration* (2nd edn, The Hague, Kluwer Law International, 2005), p. 309 citing M. Fontaine, 'Drafting the Award: A Perspective From A Civil Law Jurist' (1994) 5(1) ICC Ct Bull, 30.
7. A. Redfern, M. Hunter, N. Blackaby and C. Partasides, *Law and Practice of International Commercial Arbitration* (4th edn, London, Sweet & Maxwell, 2004), para. 8-65.

There are no set guidelines on how specific or detailed the reasons need to be,[8] and **27-005** unlike the ICC Court, the VIAC does not (officially) scrutinize the award for a consistent and compelling reasoning.[9] This raises the issue of whether an award that is badly reasoned, or that contains no reasons at all, can be challenged. Although national arbitration (and institutional) rules typically require that the award be 'reasoned', it is usually held, including in Austria,[10] that failure to give reasons is no valid ground for refusal of enforcement of an international award.[11] Similarly, the prevailing view is that assessment of evidence in the reasons is in the discretion of the tribunal and will usually not amount to a ground for challenge of an award.[12] Consequently, in cases in which the reasons given for an award are contrary to the facts, or even fundamentally irrational, it is generally regarded that this *per se* is not a sufficient ground for refusing enforcement

---

8. J. Lew, L. Mistelis and S. Kröll, *Comparative International Commercial Arbitration* (The Hague, Kluwer Law International, 2003), para. 24-69.

9. A. Redfern, M. Hunter, N. Blackaby and C. Partasides, *Law and Practice of International Commercial Arbitration* (4th edn, London, Sweet & Maxwell, 2004), para. 8-64.

10. J. Power, *The Austrian Arbitration Act – A Practitioner's Guide to Sections 577-518 of the Austrian Code of Civil Procedure* (Vienna, Manz, 2006), Section 606, paras. 3, 4. This is different from German law, where failure to comply with the German ZPO can be a ground for setting aside the award. *See* Section 1059(2) no. 1(d) German ZPO.

11. For French law *see* J.F. Poudret and S. Besson, *Comparative Law of International Arbitration* (2nd edn, London, Sweet & Maxwell, 2007), para. 816 with further references; *compare also* the decision of Cour d'Appel de Reims, 23 July 1981, *Denis Coakley Ltd. v. Sté. Michel Reverdy*, (1984) IX YB Comm Arb, 400, 402, where the court came to the conclusion with regard to an English (GAFTA – Grain and Feed Trade Association) award that '[a]n absence of reasons in conformity with the foreign law chosen by the parties is not, as such, contrary to French international public policy'. *See also* P. Mayer, 'Note – Cour d'Appel de Paris (1re Ch. Suppl.), 28 Novembre 1989; Cour d'Appel de Paris (1re Ch. Suppl.), 8 Mars 1990' [1990] Rev Arb, 675, 680. For Switzerland *see* BGer, 21 August 1990, *I. v C. SA and IHK-Schiedsgericht*, BGE 116 II 373; BGer, 12 December 1975, *Provenda S.A. v Alimenta S.A. et Genève, Cour de justic*, BGE 101 Ia 521, 526 *et seq.*; BGer, 11 November 1959, *Vegetable Oil Products Cy c v. Sieur Elmassian*, [1960] Rev Arb, 105, 106; G. Walter, 'Das Schiedsverfahren im deutsch-italienischem Rechtsverkehr' [1982] RIW, 693, 702. Also under English law, an arbitrator is not required to give reasons for an award. *See* R. Merkin, *Arbitration Act 1996* (3rd edn, London, LLP, 2005), pp. 140 *et seq.*; S.M. Schwebel and S.G. Lahne, 'Public Policy' (1986) 3 ICCA Congress Series (New York), 205, 224. For German court decisions compare LG Berlin, 4 December 1964, 81 OH 8/64, KTS 1966, 182, 184. *See also* International Law Association, London Conference (2000), Interim ILA Report on Public Policy as a Bar to Enforcement of International Arbitral Awards, reprinted in (2003) 19(2) Arb Int'l 217; S.M. Schwebel and S.G. Lahne, 'Public Policy' (1986) 3 ICCA Congress Series (New York), 205, 224 *et seq.*; U. Haas in *Practitioner's Handbook on International Arbitration*, F.B. Weigand (ed.) (Munich, C.H. Beck, 2002), p. 523.

12. J. Lew, L. Mistelis and S. Kröll, *Comparative International Commercial Arbitration* (The Hague, Kluwer Law International, 2003), para. 25-37 with further references.

on grounds of public policy.[13] From a substantive perspective, an award is to be set aside if the decision violates public policy:[14] but the decisive element for such a public policy violation is the dispositive part of the award, not its reasons. It is the result expressed in the dispositiv part of the award, not the rationale underline the award's reasoning, that must comply with substantive public policy.[15]

27-006 Some authors argue, and court decisions have held, that it might constitute an infringement of procedural public policy if the reasons given in the award contain serious contradictions.[16] However, on the basis of the strong majority view that an award with no reasons at all does not violate procedural public policy, it seems preferable to consider awards with contradictory reasons as not violating public policy either.[17] An award whose reasons do not make sense should not be treated worse than an award with no reasons at all.[18] This majority view in European doctrine should also be applied in the context of the procedural public policy provision in Section 611(2) no. 5 ZPO.[19] A possible exception could be awards where the reasoning appears so arbitrary that, as a matter of procedure, it is evident that the parties have been denied fair treatment.

---

13. International Law Association, London Conference (2000), Interim ILA Report on Public Policy as a Bar to Enforcement of International Arbitral Awards, reprinted in (2003) 19(2) Arb Int'l, 217.
14. Section 611(2) no. 8.
15. *See* also **Article 24**, at para. 019.
16. F.T. Schwarz and H. Ortner, 'Procedural Ordre Public and the Internationalization of Public Policy in Arbitration' in *Austrian Arbitration Yearbook 2008*, C. Klausegger *et al.* (eds) (Vienna, Manz, 2008). *See* U. Haas in *Practitioner's Handbook on International Arbitration*, F.B. Weigand (ed.) (Munich, C.H. Beck, 2002), p. 523 with further references.
17. The Swiss *Bundesgericht* made this very clear in its decision of 14 November 1990, *E. AG v. K. Ltd and IHK-Schiedsgericht Zürich*, (1992) XVII YB Comm Arb, 279, 284, when it stated that even an arbitral award which was (according to the allegations of the respondent) 'illogical, nonsensical, inexplicable, arbitrary, untenable, completely incorrect, inequitable, absurd, abstruse, boundlessly unenlightened, unreasonable, in violation of common sense, (. . .)' would not violate public policy *per se*, because 'only the result and not the individual considerations of the arbitral judgment can be attacked as incompatible with public policy'.
18. *See also, e.g.*, Cour d'Appel de Paris, 23 October 1997, *IAIGC-Inter-Arab Investment Guarantee Corporation(Kuwait) v. Ball – Banque Arab et Internationale d'Investissements SA (France)* (1988) XXIII YB Comm Arb, 644, 652 *et seq.*
19. F.T. Schwarz and H. Ortner, 'Procedural Ordre Public and the Internationalization of Public Policy in Arbitration' in *Austrian Arbitration Yearbook 2008*, C. Klausegger *et al.* (eds) (Vienna, Manz, 2008). However, S. Riegler in *Arbitration Law of Austria: Practice and Procedure*, S. Riegler, A. Petsche, A. Fremuth-Wolf, M. Platte and C. Liebscher (eds) (Huntington, Juris Publishing, 2007), Section 611, p. 525 argues that in cases in which decisions that appear arbitrary do not state any reasons, even though the parties agreed on the tribunal to state such reasons, procedural public policy might be violated, referring to OGH, 4 December 1931, 3 Ob 847, JBl 1932/306.

Problems of a different kind arise if the operative provisions of the award are **27-007** contradictory so that the meaning and effects of the arbitral award itself, and not merely of its reasons, cannot be determined.[20] From an Austrian perspective, it has been argued that such an award can be set aside for public policy reasons;[21] a classification which appears in line with the view in Germany.[22] It is argued that the legislature has made clear that it considers the inconsistency of a state court decision to be a major defect representing a cause for an annulment of judgments under Section 477(1) no. 9 ZPO – which is the most severe sanction available under Austrian civil procedure. As the same ground is not explicitly mentioned under Section 611(2) ZPO, the only way to achieve an equivalent legal result for the setting aside of an award is a subsumption under the general procedural public policy clause.[23] Otherwise, this problem is argued to 'fall through the (legislative) grid' in arbitral proceedings resulting in a baseless differentiation and a 'perverseness of party autonomy'.[24] To justify this result further, a second argument relies on the right to have a recourse to a court (*Justizgewährungsanspruch*) – which again brings into play Article 6 ECHR.[25] If an award whose operative provisions are so contradictory as to render it senseless could not be set aside, an arbitral tribunal issuing such an award would violate this constitutional right, because such an award would have *res judicata* effect,[26] preventing the parties from commencing proceedings afresh in front of an arbitral tribunal or a state court in the same matter. At the same time, the parties would be left in the rain with an entirely useless and unenforceable award. As a result, he considers 'a certain parallelism of sanctions against court decisions and awards' necessary'.[27]

---

20. *See also* BGer, 14 November 1990, *E. AG v. K. Ltd. and IHK-Schiedsgericht Zürich*, (1992) XVII YB Comm Arb, 279.
21. W.H. Rechberger, 'Die Widersprüchlichkeit eines Schiedsspruchs als Aufhebungsgrund nach österreichischem Recht' [2006] SchiedsVZ 169, 175.
22. *See* K.H. Schwab and G. Walter (eds), *Schiedsgerichtsbarkeit* (7th edn, Munich, C.H. Beck, 2005), ch. 24, paras. 35, 41 *et seq.*; W. Voit in *Kommentar zur Zivilprozeßordnung*, H.J. Musielak (ed.) (6th edn, Munich, Verlag Franz Vahlen, 2008), Section 1059, para. 26.
23. W.H. Rechberger, 'Die Widersprüchlichkeit eines Schiedsspruchs als Aufhebungsgrund nach österreichischem Recht' [2006] SchiedsVZ, 169, 175, admits that, in principle, a subsumption under the substantive public policy clause of no. 8 would be conceivable but favors a categorization as a violation of *procedural ordre public*, again with a view to the classification of the legal remedy in the case of court decisions.
24. W.H. Rechberger, 'Die Widersprüchlichkeit eines Schiedsspruchs als Aufhebungsgrund nach österreichischem Recht' [2006] SchiedsVZ, 169, 175.
25. W.H. Rechberger, 'Die Widersprüchlichkeit eines Schiedsspruchs als Aufhebungsgrund nach österreichischem Recht' [2006] SchiedsVZ, 169, 175; H.W. Fasching, *Lehrbuch des österreichischen Zivilprozßsrechts* (2nd edn, Vienna, Manz, 1990), para. 9.
26. W.H. Rechberger, 'Die Widersprüchlichkeit eines Schiedsspruchs als Aufhebungsgrund nach österreichischem Recht' [2006] SchiedsVZ, 169, 172.
27. W.H. Rechberger, 'Die Widersprüchlichkeit eines Schiedsspruchs als Aufhebungsgrund nach österreichischem Recht' [2006] SchiedsVZ, 169, 175.

27-008 These arguments are largely based on an interpretative approach based on systemic principles of Austrian law and the consistency of values within the Austrian legal order.[28] It is questionable if this intra-systematic approach which heavily relies on the peculiarities of the Austrian legal order is appropriate for cases of an international nature.[29] Insofar as contradictory awards violate Article 6 ECHR, this may be the case. By contrast, reliance on Section 477(1) no. 9 ZPO (applicable to Austrian state court proceedings) may be inappropriate precisely because the Austrian legislature decided not to include a pendant for Section 477(1) no. 9 ZPO in the grounds for setting aside an award under Section 611 ZPO: the list of grounds for setting aside an award is generally deemed exhaustive.[30] Indeed, the parties are sufficiently protected by the result-based standard of substantive public policy. If an award results in a violation of substantive public policy, it will be set aside pursuant to Section 611(2) no. 8 ZPO. If the award does not violate the substantive public policy, it will be maintained – and in that case, it matters little on what basis or reasons the tribunal arrived at its decision.[31]

27-009 Both under Article 27 and Section 606 ZPO, the parties may agree, in any event, that the award does not have to state any reasons. Where such an agreement is reached, it should be read to constitute an implied waiver not to challenge the award on this ground. On the other hand, absent such an agreement, where the award does not contain reasons and the parties have not reached such an agreement, either party can request the tribunal to 'explain' the award according to Section 610(1) no. 2 ZPO and **Article 29(1)(b)**.[32]

II.   STATEMENT OF DATE AND ARBITRAL SEAT

Article 27(2): The award shall state the date on which it was made and the place of arbitration (Article 2).

27-010 Article 27(2) contains the simple instruction for the arbitrators to expressly include the date the award was made (which is usually the date the award is signed by the presiding arbitrator) and place (that is, the legal seat) of the arbitration within the meaning of **Article 2**.[33] Usually, these express statements are made at the end

---

28. See F. Bydlinski, *Juristische Methodenlehre und Rechtsbegriff* (2nd edn, Springer, NewYork/ Vienna, 1991), pp. 442 *et seq.*
29. F.T. Schwarz and H. Ortner, 'Procedural Ordre Public and the Internationalization of Public Policy in Arbitration' in *Austrian Arbitration Yearbook 2008*, C. Klausegger *et al.* (eds) (Vienna, Manz, 2008).
30. S. Riegler in *Arbitration Law of Austria: Practice and Procedure*, S. Riegler, A. Petsche, A. Fremuth-Wolf, M. Platte and C. Liebscher (eds) (Huntington, Juris Publishing, 2007), Section 606, p. 450.
31. *See* also **Article 24**, at para. 019.
32. *See* also **Article 29**, at paras. 004 *et seq.*
33. *See* **Article 2**, at paras. 004 *et seq.*

of the award, next to the arbitrators' signatures. Failure to include those statements is not, however, listed in Section 611 ZPO as a ground for setting aside the award.

Section 606(3) ZPO states that 'the award shall be deemed to have been made on **27-011** that day and at that place.' Section 606(3) ZPO therefore sets forth the legal fiction that, no matter what actually happened, the award is rendered at the time and place that is stated in the award. This is consistent with the notion that the legal seat of the arbitration is a legal fiction in the first place, which is detached from the actual, physical location of the tribunal or of some or all procedural acts.[34] That fiction is relevant, of course, to determine whether the award is 'domestic' for the purposes of setting aside and enforcement, and, where the seat is in Austria, triggers the application of Austrian arbitration law.[35]

If the tribunal states a different seat in the award than the seat that was agreed by the **27-012** parties (or determined under applicable rules), this could have significant consequences for the parties, who may then have to challenge the award at the perhaps inhospitable courts of a 'seat' that was forced upon them. While some authors argue that the fiction of Section 606(3) ZPO is 'irrefutable',[36] the better view therefore is to disregard the arbitrators' false statement of the seat of the arbitration for the purposes of setting aside proceedings, if the parties can demonstrate the existence of a different, prior agreement on the seat. This reading seems in line with the text of Article 27(2) that expressly refers to **Article 2**, thus recognizing that the arbitrators are not free to state any seat, but only the seat that has been determined in accordance with **Article 2**, and thus pursuant to the parties' agreement.[37] Indeed, where the parties fail to agree on a seat, the seat of the arbitration is deemed to be in Vienna,[38] again limiting the arbitrators' freedom to state otherwise.

Under Section 606(3) ZPO, a similar legal fiction extends to the date of the award. **27-013** This is relevant for the deadline under **Article 29(3)** which permits the arbitrators to correct clerical errors within thirty days from the award.[39] The more important time period for filing a setting aside motion with the courts starts to run with the receipt of the award by the party bringing the challenge.

---

34. See **Article 2**, at paras. 010 *et seq*; A. Reiner, *Das neue österreichische Schiedsrecht/The new Austrian Arbitration Law* (Vienna, LexisNexis, 2006), Section 606, note 157.
35. See **Article 2**, at para. 002.
36. J. Power, *The Austrian Arbitration Act – A Practitioner's Guide to Sections 577-618 of the Austrian Code of Civil Procedure* (Vienna, Manz, 2006), Section 606, para. 6 with further reference.
37. See **Article 2**, at paras. 004 *et seq*.
38. See **Article 2**, at para. 006.
39. See **Article 29**, at paras. 013 *et seq*.

III.   SIGNED AWARD

Article 27(3): All copies of awards must be signed by the arbitrators. The signatures of the majority of the arbitrators shall suffice if the award contains a statement that one arbitrator refuses to sign or that his signature is prevented by an obstacle which cannot be overcome within a reasonable period of time. If the award is made by a majority decision, mention thereof shall be made in the award at the request of the arbitrator who is in a minority.

27-014   The Vienna Rules require that all three arbitrators sign the award. If one arbitrator fails to sign the award, the signatures of the majority is sufficient, it must be accompanied by the reason for the absence of the signature.[40] The signatures of the arbitrators in accordance with the law or applicable agreement constitute a mandatory form requirement.[41] If the decision does not satisfy that requirement, it is classified as a 'non-award' that lacks any legal effects.[42] However, the parties are free to agree on specific arrangements for the arbitrators' signatures.[43]

27-015   Article 27(3) recognizes that the reasons for only the majority signing the award can be manifold. First, an arbitrator can simply refuse to give his or her signature to the award, usually because there is disagreement as to the reasons or the result. In such a case, where the award is adopted by majority decision, the arbitrator who refuses to sign can request that the award notes expressly that it is issued against his or her vote. Second, however, it may be that one of the arbitrators is unable – for reasons that cannot be easily overcome[44] – to sign the award. In such a case, the award should not be delayed. Again, the award must contain a reference to the circumstances that prevented that arbitrator from signing.

27-016   Article 27(3) also makes clear that the majority must sign the award. An award signed only by one arbitrator, even if that arbitrator is the presiding arbitrator, does as a textual matter not appear valid under the Vienna Rules. This is problematic in light of Article 26(1) which affords the presiding arbitrator the decisive vote in those cases where no majority can be achieved. If Article 26(1) is to be given effect, the signature of the presiding arbitrator who cast the decisive vote should be sufficient for rendering a formally valid award. Otherwise, the other arbitrators could prevent an award from being rendered simply by refusing to give their signature, thereby frustrating in effect the presiding arbitrator's authority to cast

---

40.   Article 26(1) AAA/ICDR Rules and Article 32(4) UNCITRAL Rules.
41.   *See* **Article 27**, at para. 001.
42.   Explanatory Notes to Section 611 ZPO.
43.   Section 606(1) ZPO.
44.   This requirement is not contained in Section 606(1) ZPO which merely refers to an obstacle. However, the provisions should only be applied to cases where the obstacle cannot be overcome within a reasonable period of time. A. Reiner, *Das neue österreichische Schiedsrecht/The new Austrian Arbitration Law* (Vienna, LexisNexis, 2006), Section 606, note 156.

the decisive vote. A systemic interpretation of the Vienna Rules would therefore allow the presiding arbitrator, in cases of Article 26(1), to sign by himself where the other two arbitrators refuse to do so. In such a case, the award should detail the circumstances that led to the presiding arbitrator signing alone. Some authors argue against such a solution because Section 606(1) ZPO supposedly allows the parties only to impose stricter requirements that those imposed by law; the better view is to give priority to party autonomy: if the parties are satisfied with, and thus agree on, a particular form requirement, there is little policy reason to intervene with that agreement.[45] There is also case law under the former arbitration law suggesting that, where only the missing signature prevents the award from becoming effective, a party can apply to the courts to direct the arbitrator to give his or her signature to the award.[46]

IV.   CONFIRMATION BY THE VIAC

Article 27(4): Awards are confirmed on all copies as awards of the Centre by the signature of the Secretary General and the stamp of the Centre. By this it is confirmed that the award is an award of the International Arbitral Centre of the Austrian Federal Economic Chamber and that it was made and signed by (an) arbitrator(s) chosen or appointed in accordance with these Rules of Arbitration.

Article 27(4) provides, simply, that the VIAC will apply its official seal to all **27-017** copies of the award, signed by the Secretary General. This official imprimatur is designed to facilitate the recognition of awards rendered under the Vienna Rules elsewhere; and indeed, awards issued under the auspices of respectable institutions are said to have a higher chance both of voluntary compliance and enforcement by foreign courts. The signature of the Secretary General and the application of the VIAC's seal does not only confirm the provenance of the award but also confirms that the award was rendered and signed by arbitrators whose appointment occurred validly under the Vienna Rules.

Article 27(4) does not specify how many copies of an award will be produced by **27-018** the VIAC. However, it is standing practice to produce one copy for each party and for each arbitrator, which at least one copy remaining in the VIAC's archives for future reference. This is confirmed by a reading of Article 27(5), discussed below.

---

45. S. Riegler in *Arbitration Law of Austria: Practice and Procedure*, S. Riegler, A. Petsche, A. Fremuth-Wolf, M. Platte and C. Liebscher (eds) (Huntington, Juris Publishing, 2007), Section 606, p. 448 with further reference.
46. OGH, 29 January 1970, 1 Ob 252/69; OGH, 10 July 2001, 4 Ob 156/01x.

V.   SERVICE AND EFFECT OF THE AWARD

Article 27(5): The award shall be served on the parties by the Secretary General. Awards become effective as against the parties on service of the copies. One copy of the award and the records on the serving shall be deposited with the Secretariat of the Centre.

27-019   The parties are being served with a copy of the award that has been duly signed by the arbitrators (pursuant to Article 27(3)) and sealed and signed by the Secretary General (pursuant to Article 27(4)). Service is effected not through the arbitrators, but through the VIAC. Section 606(4) ZPO provides that 'a copy signed by the arbitrators in accordance with paragraph 1 of this Section shall be delivered to each party'. Service by email is therefore neither possible,[47] unless perhaps with a secure electronic signature,[48] and in any event not advisable.[49] Typically, the award will be served by courier or registered mail, in order to provide for a proper record of service.

27-020   Article 27(5) also provides that, with receipt of their copy, the award becomes 'effective' against the parties. Under Section 607 ZPO, this means that, with receipt of the award, the award has the effect of a final judgment[50] between the parties.[51] As a result, the award constitutes *res judicata* between the parties. Also, the award, whether partial or final, is immediately enforceable, unless the award itself prescribes a grace period,[52] or an appellate arbitral procedure.[53] A motion of

---

47. A. Reiner, *Das neue österreichische Schiedsrecht/The new Austrian Arbitration Law* (Vienna, LexisNexis, 2006), Section 606, note 158. Referring to the possibility of an electronic signature, *see* J. Power, *The Austrian Arbitration Act – A Practitioner's Guide to Sections 577-618 of the Austrian Code of Civil Procedure* (Vienna, Manz, 2006), Section 606, para. 7.

48. P. Oberhammer, *Entwurf eines neuen Schiedsverfahrensrechts* (Vienna, Manz, 2002), p. 117.

49. A signed hardcopy will often be required for international enforcement. *See* P. Oberhammer, *Entwurf eines neuen Schiedsverfahrensrechts* (Vienna, Manz, 2002), p. 117.

50. Section 607 ZPO. This is not the case, however, if the parties have agreed on an appellate mechanism, such as an appellate tribunal, and that appellate procedure has not been concluded. *See* C. Liebscher, *The Austrian Arbitration Act 2006: Text and Notes* (The Hague, Kluwer Law International, 2006), Annotated Text to Section 607 ZPO.

51. For a discussion of the words 'between the parties', *see* P. Oberhammer, *Entwurf eines neuen Schiedsverfahrensrechts* (Vienna, Manz, 2002), p. 119. However, it has been pointed out that the words 'between the parties' should not be construed to mean 'only' between the parties. Whether, and to what extent, third parties can be bound by an award is still disputed. It is difficult to see how an award extends in effect to parties that have not participated in the proceedings, or that are not even bound by the arbitration agreement. This would go against the consensual nature of arbitration. *See also* **Article 15**, at para. 018.

52. OGH, 24 September 1981, 7 Ob 623/81, EvBl 1982/77.

53. Section 607 ZPO applies only to domestic Austrian awards. Foreign awards need to go through an *exequatur* process before they can be enforced. *See* **Article 27**, at paras. 023 and 066.

setting aside is an extraordinary remedy, and not a proper appeal, and does therefore not prevent the award from being enforced until it is set aside.[54]

In any event, the date of service is relevant for any order specified in the award; and **27-021** for any statutory time period to challenge the award.[55] For this reason, the VIAC will not only keep a copy of the award,[56] but also a record of its service on the parties. For *ad hoc* arbitrations, Section 606(5) ZPO provides that '[t]he award and the documentation on its service are joint documents of the parties and the arbitrators. The arbitral tribunal shall discuss with the parties a possible safekeeping of the award and the documentation on its service'. The qualification of the award and the records of service as joint documents apply to arbitrations under the Vienna Rules as well.[57]

VI.   CONFIRMATION OF FINALITY AND ENFORCEABILITY

Article 27(6): The sole arbitrator (Chairman of the arbitral tribunal, or, if he is prevented, another arbitrator) shall confirm on all copies at the request of a party the finality and enforceability of the award.

Article 27(6) permits the parties to request the sole arbitrator, or the presiding **27-022** arbitrator in case of an arbitral tribunal, to confirm that the award is final and enforceable.[58] Where the presiding arbitrator is prevented from doing so, another arbitrator can issue that confirmation.[59]

As discussed, the award is final and enforceable under Austrian law as soon as it is **27-023** served on the parties; at such point, it has 'effect of a final and binding court judgment' as between the parties.[60] A domestic award is therefore immediately and *ipso iure* enforceable on its terms.[61] A subsequent challenge does not hinder

---

54. Explanatory Notes to Section 607 ZPO. It is possible, under certain circumstances and usually in connection with the provision of security, to apply for a suspension of enforcement while a setting aside motion is pending. *See* Sections 42 *et seq.* EO.
55. *See* **Article 27**, at para. 013.
56. *See also* Article 36(1) DIS Rules.
57. For a discussion of the notion of 'joint documents', *see* **Article 20**, at para. 170.
58. This does not hinder the Austrian courts and authorities to disregard the award in the narrow circumstances of Section 613 ZPO, if the award was rendered on a non-arbitrable subject matter (*see* **Article 1**, at para. 138) or in violation of the *substantive ordre public*. *See* **Article 27**, at para. 060; A. Reiner, *Das neue österreichische Schiedsrecht/The new Austrian Arbitration Law* (Vienna, LexisNexis, 2006), Section 606, note 162.
59. *See also* Section 606(6) ZPO; A. Reiner, *Das neue österreichische Schiedsrecht/The new Austrian Arbitration Law* (Vienna, LexisNexis, 2006), Section 606, note 161. For insufficient confirmation *see* OGH, 3 March 1925, SZ 7/252 and OGH 25 September 1924, Rsp 1915, 108 (although those decisions appear overly strict from today's perspective).
60. Section 607 ZPO.
61. *See* Section 1 no. 16 EO.

the enforcement of the award unless and until the award is successfully set aside.[62] Foreign awards need to be recognized in an *exequatur* proceeding before they can be enforced in Austria.[63]

VII. PARTIAL AND INTERIM AWARDS

Article 27(7): Partial and interim awards may be issued.

27-024 Most arbitration institutions expressly allow the tribunal to make partial and/or interim awards.[64] The Vienna Rules now contain an express authorization to do so.

27-025 There is still some confusion with respect to the terminology of those kinds of awards. Indeed, the ZPO does not define the term 'award'.[65] A final award disposes of all the issues on the merits, jurisdiction and costs raised in the arbitration in a final and binding manner[66] – it resolves and thus concludes the dispute.[67] Final awards in the traditional sense customarily are *functus officio* and end the arbitration proceedings.[68] As long as there are outstanding issues to be resolved, a decision is not a final award.

27-026 However, the distinction between partial and interim awards is more difficult; the terms seem to be used interchangeably. *Lew/Mistelis/Kröll* suggest that for reasons of clarity an interim award should be limited to awards that do not settle a separate part of the proceedings, such as making an order for interim relief in the form of an interim award.[69] Thus, the term 'interim' award seems to have a preliminary connotation. Because of its transient nature, this type of award cannot be equated with a final award and cannot be declared enforceable at court.[70] Indeed, the

---

62. Explanatory Notes to Section 607. *See* also C. Liebscher, *The Austrian Arbitration Act 2006: Text and Notes* (The Hague, Kluwer Law International, 2006), Annotated Text to Section 607 ZPO; S. Riegler in *Arbitration Law of Austria: Practice and Procedure*, S. Riegler, A. Petsche, A. Fremuth-Wolf, M. Platte and C. Liebscher (eds) (Huntington, Juris Publishing, 2007), Section 611, p. 545; A. Reiner, *Das neue österreichische Schiedsrecht/The new Austrian Arbitration Law* (Vienna, LexisNexis, 2006), Section 607, note 163.
63. *See* **Article 27**, at para. 066 and Section 614 ZPO.
64. Article 2(iii) ICC Rules; Article 32(1) UNCITRAL Rules; Article 26(7) LCIA Rules and Article 27(7) AAA/ICDR Rules.
65. C. Liebscher, *The Austrian Arbitration Act 2006: Text and Notes* (The Hague, Kluwer Law International, 2006), Annotated Text to Section 606.
66. J. Power, *The Austrian Arbitration Act – A Practitioner's Guide to Sections 577-618 of the Austrian Code of Civil Procedure* (Vienna, Manz, 2006), Section 606, para. 1 with further reference.
67. *See* **Article 25**, at para. 025 on the termination of the arbitrators' mandate.
68. A. Redfern, M. Hunter, N. Blackaby and C. Partasides, *Law and Practice of International Commercial Arbitration* (4th edn, London, Sweet & Maxwell, 2004), paras. 8-02 *et seq.*
69. J. Lew, L. Mistelis and S. Kröll, *Comparative International Commercial Arbitration* (The Hague, Kluwer Law International, 2003), para. 24-24.
70. O. Glossner, 'National Report: Federal Republic of Germany' (1979) IV YB Comm Arb 60, 71.

Austrian *Oberster Gerichtshof* has held under the former arbitration law that an interim award (*Zwischenschiedsspruch*) could not be challenged separately from the final award, because it does not finally determine an issue.[71] It is also unclear whether such an award would also be enforceable under the New York Convention.[72]

On the other hand, a partial award would be a final ruling on a distinct issue, such as an award on jurisdiction,[73] liability,[74] applicable law[75] or quantification of damages. Thus, a partial award would resolve *one* issue *finally*, but would not resolve all issues before the tribunal. It is advisable for the tribunal to designate such a partial award as such. Such partial awards can be enforced because they are resolving a substantive part of the dispute with finality.

27-027

However, the finality and resulting enforceability of an award is not a matter of terminology or label, but of substance. An award may be (wrongly) termed 'interim', but may still contain a final determination of a substantive issue. On that basis, courts have even treated procedural orders as awards.[76] In *Braspetro Oil Services Company v. The Management and Implementation Authority of the Great Man-Made River Project*, the arbitral tribunal issued what they termed as an order, but the Court of Appeals set this decision aside. It held that the tribunal had effectively issued an award, not a procedural order, because it settled a substantive

27-028

---

71. J. Lew, L. Mistelis and S. Kröll, *Comparative International Commercial Arbitration* (The Hague, Kluwer Law International, 2003), para. 24-28 citing OGH, 25 June 1992, 7 Ob 545/92, (1997) XXII YB Comm Arb, 619; *see also* OGH, 14 June 2005, 2 Ob 136/05x (due to its non-final character an interim award may not be challenged in the absence of an agreement to that effect). *Contra* R. Riegler in *Arbitration Law of Austria: Practice and Procedure*, S. Riegler, A. Petsche, A. Fremuth-Wolf, M. Platte and C. Liebscher (Huntington, Juris Publishing, 2007), Section 611, p. 514; A. Reiner, *Das neue österreichische Schiedsrecht/The new Austrian Arbitration Law* (Vienna, LexisNexis, 2006), Section 611, note 190 *et seq.*

72. This issue is highly disputed. For the prevailing opinion of non-enforceability of such interim awards *see* J. Lew, L. Mistelis and C. Kröll, *Comparative International Commercial Arbitration* (The Hague, Kluwer Law International, 2003), paras. 24-27 *et seq.* Born argues for the enforceability of certain interim awards. See G.B. Born, *International Commercial Arbitration – Commentary and Materials* (3rd edn, The Hague, Kluwer Law International, forthcoming), ch. 16, 22.

73. J. Lew, L. Mistelis and S. Kröll, *Comparative International Commercial Arbitration* (The Hague, Kluwer Law International, 2003), para. 24-19; *see, e.g., Partial Award in ICC Case No. 4402 of 1983*, (1984) IX YB Comm Arb, 138.

74. J. Lew, L. Mistelis and S. Kröll, *Comparative International Commercial Arbitration* (The Hague, Kluwer Law International, 2003), para. 24-19; *see, e.g.*, Partial Award in Ad Hoc Arbitration, 5 February 1988, *Wintershall AG et al v. Government of Qatar*, (1989) 28 ILM, 798.

75. J. Lew, L. Mistelis and S. Kröll, *Comparative International Commercial Arbitration* (The Hague, Kluwer Law International, 2003), para. 24-19; *see, e.g., Partial Award in ICC Case No 8113 of 1995*, (2000) XXV YB Comm Arb, 324.

76. J. Lew, L. Mistelis and S. Kröll, *Comparative International Commercial Arbitration* (The Hague, Kluwer Law International, 2003), paras. 24-03 *et seq.*

issue; and should therefore have submitted it to the ICC Court for scrutiny.[77] Similarly, the US Court of Appeals for the 7th Circuit held that 'the content of a decision – not its nomenclature – determines finality' and that despite the tribunal's designation as an 'order' instead of an 'award' it was the intent to create a final decision as to that part of the case.[78] 'A ruling on a discrete, time-sensitive issue may be final and ripe for confirmation even though other claims remain to be addressed by arbitrators.'[79] In that sense, all awards are final if '(subject to the possibility of challenge in the courts) they dispose of one or more issues in dispute between the parties'.[80] An 'interim' award that determines, or denies, the tribunal's jurisdiction is a final decision on that issue.

VIII.   IMPLEMENTING THE AWARD

Article 27(8): By their agreement to the Vienna Rules, the parties undertake to implement the award.

27-029   As soon as the award is issued, it is final and binding on the parties. Indeed, it is still said that a majority of awards are performed voluntarily.[81]

27-030   To reinforce the principle of compliance, most arbitration institutions contain provisions similar to Article 27(8) that require the parties to carry out the award without delay.[82] Such provisions are of a contractual nature, in that the parties incorporate those provisions by reference to the arbitral rules into their arbitration agreement. Some jurisdictions provide that, by virtue of such undertakings, parties can in advance limit or restrict the right to challenge the award in the courts.[83] In Austria, such an advance waiver is said not to be admissible;[84] a party is only permitted to waive recourse against the award after the award has been rendered. As a result, Article 27(8) does not restrict a party's right to apply to the Austrian courts under Section 611 ZPO, if the seat of the arbitration was in Austria.[85]

77. Cour' d'Appel de Paris, 1 July 1999, *Braspetro Oil Services Company – Brasoil (Cayman) v. The Management and Implementation Authority of the Great Man-Made River Project (Libya)* (1999)14(8) Mealey's IAR (1999), XXIVa YB Comm Arb, 296-302.
78. *Publicis Commun. v. True North Communs. Inc.*, 206 F.3d 725, 729, 731 (7th Cir. 2000).
79. *Publicis Commun. v. True North Communs. Inc.*, 206 F.3d 725, 729 (7th Cir. 2000).
80. A. Redfern, M. Hunter, N. Blackaby and C. Partasides, *Law and Practice of International Commercial Arbitration* (4th edn, London, Sweet & Maxwell, 2004), para. 8-39.
81. A. Redfern, M. Hunter, N. Blackaby and C. Partasides, *Law and Practice of International Commercial Arbitration* (4th edn, London, Sweet & Maxwell, 2004), para. 10-01.
82. Article 32(2) UNCITRAL Rules; Article 27(1) AAA/ICDR Rules; Article 28(6) ICC Rules and Article 26(9) LCIA Rules.
83. *See e.g.*, Articles 190 and 192 Swiss IPRG; Section 69(1) English Arbitration Act 1996 and Section 51 Swedish Arbitration Act
84. *See* **Article 27**, at para. 041.
85. However, under the old law, Article 27(8) could be understood as a waiver with respect to Section 595(1) no. 7 and Section 598(2) fZPO.

However, irrespective of the right to challenge the award under Section 611 **27-031**
ZPO, the contractual provision remains. As a result, a party that levies an unjustified challenge, runs the risk of breaching its obligation under Article 27(8) to
implement the award, conceivably giving rise to additional claims for resulting
damages.

IX.   RECOURSE AGAINST AN AWARD IN THE AUSTRIAN
           COURTS

Under Austrian law, the grounds of setting aside an award are narrowed and strictly **27-032**
confined to a minimum of judicial control. Yet the supervision exercised by the
courts under Section 611 ZPO is still the most important influence that Austria as
the host country to an arbitration can exercise on the arbitral process. The following
discussion provides a brief overview of the jurisdiction and applicable procedures;
considers the grounds for setting aside an award; and examines the effect of such a
challenge on the parties and the proceedings under Austrian law. As discussed,
Section 611 ZPO only applies to awards rendered in proceedings that had their seat
in Austria. Recourse against foreign arbitral awards is available only in the context
of resisting enforcement in *exequatur* proceedings.[86]

A.   JURISDICTION AND PROCEEDINGS

For the action for setting aside an award, as well as the action for a declaration of **27-033**
the existence or non-existence of an award, and for proceedings pertaining to
matters addressed in the third chapter of the ZPO, the regional court[87] having
jurisdiction over civil law matters that was specified in the arbitration agreement
or whose jurisdiction was agreed upon in accordance with Section 104 JN, or,
failing such specification or agreement, the regional court where the arbitral tribunal has its seat, shall have jurisdiction.[88] This jurisdiction exists regardless of the
value in dispute.[89] In practice, the vast majority of arbitral tribunals have their seat
in Vienna. Thus, the *Handelsgericht Wien* (Commercial Court of Vienna) and, for

---

86. *See* **Article 2**, at paras. 069 *et seq.*
87. The regional courts are uniformly envisioned as the courts of first instance. At these courts, as
    well as at the courts of appeal that have jurisdiction over appeals, arbitration matters should be
    respectively assigned to individual departments. *See* C. Liebscher, *The Austrian Arbitration Act
    2006: Text and Notes* (The Hague, Kluwer Law International, 2006), Annotated Text to Section
    615 ZPO.
88. Section 615(1) ZPO. The court that has jurisdiction over the enforcement of provisional and
    protective measures is the district court where the opposing party has its seat, domicile, or usual
    place of residence, or the district court in whose district the measure is to be enforced.
89. Section 615 ZPO.

appeals, the *Oberlandesgericht Wien* (Vienna Court of Appeal) will hear most cases.[90] Indeed, if the seat of the arbitral tribunal has not yet been determined, or if, in the case of Section 612 ZPO, it is not within Austria, then the *Handelsgericht Wien* shall also have jurisdiction.

27-034 If the legal matter in dispute underlying the award is a matter of commercial law within the meaning of Section 51 JN, then the regional court shall act as a commercial court. In Vienna, this is again the specialized *Handelsgericht Wien*.[91]

27-035 The proceedings regarding an action for setting aside an award and an action for a declaration of the existence or non-existence of an award are governed by the general provisions of the ZPO.[92] Upon application of a party, the public can be excluded if a justified interest in doing so is shown.[93]

27-036 Proceedings regarding an action for setting aside an award are subject to a three-stage judicial process, allowing for appeal (where decisions are made by a panel of three judges) and, in certain circumstances, the Austrian *Oberster Gerichtshof* (where decisions are usually made by a panel of five judges).[94]

27-037 The action for setting aside an arbitral award must be filed within the non-extendable period of three months from receipt of the award.[95] Under the new regime, partial awards, in particular those dealing with the tribunal's jurisdiction, are now challengeable as well.[96] If an award is challenged for reasons of 'reopening a case' (Section 611(2) no. 6 ZPO), the time limit to file such action

---

90. C. Liebscher, *The Austrian Arbitration Act 2006: Text and Notes* (The Hague, Kluwer Law International, 2006), Annotated Text to Section 615(1) ZPO.

91. The *Handelsgericht Wien* or the regional courts, in exercise of their jurisdiction in commercial law matters, generally have jurisdiction over the proceeding to set aside an award when the underlying dispute is a transaction related to a business and the statement of claims was directed against a business entity registered in the commercial register. Pursuant to Section 1(2) UGB, a business is any organization of commercial activity created on a permanent basis, even if it is non-profit. Labour law matters within the meaning of Section 50(1) no. 1 ASGG, the regional courts acting as labour and social courts shall have jurisdiction; in Vienna the *Gericht für Arbeits- und Sozialsachen Wien* (Labour and Social Court of Vienna) shall have jurisdiction. *See* C. Liebscher, *The Austrian Arbitration Act 2006: Text and Notes* (The Hague, Kluwer Law International, 2006), Annotated Text to Section 615 ZPO.

92. C. Liebscher, *The Austrian Arbitration Act 2006: Text and Notes* (The Hague, Kluwer Law International, 2006), Annotated Text to Section 616(1) ZPO.

93. Section 616(2) ZPO.

94. C. Liebscher, *The Austrian Arbitration Act 2006: Text and Notes* (The Hague, Kluwer Law International, 2006), Annotated Text to Section 616(1) ZPO.

95. Section 611(4) ZPO. For a discussion of this time period in the context of corrections or interpretations of awards, *see* **Article 29**, at paras. 001 *et seq.*

96. *See in detail* **Article 19**, at paras. 026 *et seq.*

is calculated according to the provisions on the application for the proceedings to be reopened.[97]

If the parties fail to observe the deadline for bringing an action for setting aside, **27-038** they are precluded from doing so later;[98] grounds for setting aside (save for substantive public policy and arbitrability issues which can be considered by the courts *ex officio*)[99] are considered to be cured. However, it is possible under Austrian procedural law to ask to be reinstated into a procedural deadline if the observance of that deadline was prevented by unforeseeable or unavoidable events. Under the fZPO, this was considered possible with respect to the deadline to apply for setting aside an arbitration award;[100] and is arguably possible under the new regime as well.[101]

B.   GROUNDS FOR SETTING ASIDE AN ARBITRAL AWARD

The action for setting aside an award is a claim to alter a procedural state (*pro-* **27-039** *zessuale Rechtsgestaltungsklage*). Here, it is the existence of the award (a legally recognized state with specified effects)[102] that is being challenged.

So-called non-awards need not to be set aside.[103] These are awards that are **27-040** 'ineffective by operation of law'[104] because they fail to satisfy the minimum

---

97.   The action for setting aside based on reasons for reopening pursuant to Section 530(1) nos 1-5 ZPO must be brought within four weeks after the day when the final criminal court judgment or the order of discontinuance of the criminal proceedings becomes final and binding. After the expiration of ten years, however, an action for setting aside based on these grounds can no longer be brought. *See* C. Liebscher, *The Austrian Arbitration Act 2006: Text and Notes* (The Hague, Kluwer Law International, 2006), Annotated Text to Section 611(4) ZPO. Another opinion is that of *Schumacher* who argues also a three months time limit in such cases. *See* H. Schumacher, 'Ein Schiedsspruch – und was nun?' [2006] SchiedsVZ, 70, 75.

98.   They can then only suggest an official examination within the scope of Section 613 ZPO. *See* C. Liebscher, *The Austrian Arbitration Act 2006: Text and Notes* (The Hague, Kluwer Law International, 2006), Annotated Text to Section 611(1) ZPO.

99.   Section 611(2) nos 7 and 8 ZPO.

100. W.H. Rechberger and W. Melis in *Kommentar zur ZPO*, W.H. Rechberger (ed.) (3rd edn, Vienna/New York, Springer, 2006), Section 611, para. 11; *also* OGH, 7 October 1996, 3 Ob 2360/96x.

101. J. Power, *The Austrian Arbitration Act – A Practitioner's Guide to Sections 577-618 of the Austrian Code of Civil Procedure* (Vienna, Manz, 2006), Section 611, para. 42.

102. *See* Section 607 ZPO and **Article 27**, at para. 020.

103. *See* **Article 27**, at para. 064. Section 612 ZPO provides: 'An application may be made for the determination of the existence or non-existence of an award if the applicant has a legal interest therein.' This does, however, not extend the time limit for setting aside the arbitration award.

104. H.W. Fasching, *Schiedsgericht und Schiedsverfahren im österreichischen und im internationalen Recht* (Vienna, Manz, 1973), pp. 135 *et seq.*

requirements for an award under the law, such as an award that is not made in writing and signed by the arbitrators in the prescribed way;[105] if the decision was rendered by persons not even appointed as arbitrators;[106] or apparently if there was no request for an arbitral decision by the parties.[107] As discussed below, an award rendered on a non-arbitral matter is still an award and must be challenged.[108]

27-041 Section 611 ZPO contains an exhaustive list of the grounds for setting aside an arbitration award in Austria. It mirrors the provisions under Article 34 of the UNCITRAL Model Law and Article V of the New York Convention.[109] An important distinction is made between those grounds which are only considered upon application – Section 611(2) nos 1-6 ZPO – and those considered *ex officio* – Section 611(2) nos 7[110] and 8[111] ZPO.[112] The statutory grounds for setting aside an award are not waivable by the parties in advance.[113] The following discussion sets forth an overview of the statutory grounds for setting aside awards in Austria, highlighting in particular those provisions that were newly introduced with the 2006 reform.[114]

1.   Jurisdictional Issues

27-042 An award shall be set aside if a valid arbitration agreement does not exist (Section 611(2) no. 1 case 1 ZPO). This provision, in essence, corresponds with former Section 595(1) no. 1 ZPO, and is the ground for setting aside an award most frequently invoked before the Austrian courts.[115] It covers any case of lack of

---

105. OGH, 13 January 2004, 5 Ob 123/03d.
106. However, if the appointment was made in violation of applicable law or the parties' agreement, the decision still constitutes an award and must be challenged under Section 611(2) no. 4 ZPO.
107. S. Riegler in *Arbitration Law of Austria: Practice and Procedure*, S. Riegler, A. Petsche, A. Fremuth-Wolf, M. Platte and C. Liebscher (eds) (Huntington, Juris Publishing, 2007), Section 606, p. 446 with further reference.
108. *See also* **Article 1**, at paras. 135 *et seq*.
109. NY Convention, **Annex 11**.
110. This provision addresses lack of arbitrability under Austrian law.
111. This provision addresses a violation of the *substantive ordre public*.
112. W.H. Rechberger and W. Melis in *Kommentar zur ZPO*, W.H. Rechberger (ed.) (3rd edn, Vienna/New York, Springer, 2006), Section 611, para. 3.
113. This was explicitly regulated in Section 598 fZPO. The new ZPO does not address this issue. However, this has already been argued for the new regime by W.H. Rechberger and W. Melis in *Kommentar zur ZPO*, W.H. Rechberger (ed.) (3rd edn, Vienna/New York, Springer, 2006), Section 611, para. 3; G. Zeiler, *Schiedsverfahren* (Vienna/Graz, Neuer Wissenschaftlicher Verlag, 2006), Section 611, p. 275.
114. These grounds correspond completely to the UNCITRAL Model Law and the NY Convention.
115. OGH, 24 July 1997, 6 Ob 186/97i; OGH, 24 September 1981, 7 Ob 623/81, EvBl 1982/77; OGH, 10 October 1962, 1 Ob 215/62; OGH, 11 September 1957, 2 Ob 382/57; OGH, 21 January 1953, 1 Ob 1044/52; OGH, 6 September 1990, 6 Ob 572/90; OGH, 20 September 1961, 6 Ob 305/61; OGH, 26 April 2006, 7 Ob 236/05i.

jurisdiction arbitration agreement for the dispute at bar,[116] including *inter alia* a formally invalid arbitration agreement,[117] and cases of incapacity to enter into arbitration agreements.

Awards that deny jurisdiction even though a valid arbitration agreement exists can **27-043** also be challenged under this provision. Indeed, there was no possibility under the former legislation to set aside an award that dealt only with the tribunal's juris- diction. This was considered an interim decision of the tribunal and as such not capable of being set aside.[118] Consequently, an arbitral tribunal's affirmative decision on jurisdiction was only subject to challenge after the final award on the merits had been rendered. An arbitral tribunal's decision declining jurisdiction was not subject to challenge at all.[119]

Section 611(2) no. 1 case 2 ZPO now provides that an award shall be set aside if **27-044** the arbitral tribunal has denied its jurisdiction despite the existence of a valid arbitration agreement. The new regime is intended to encourage arbitral tribu- nals to decide on their own jurisdiction in a separate decision early in the proceedings in the interest of both time and cost efficiency.[120] In any case, the application for setting aside an award on that specific ground can only be requested for reasons that were already raised before the arbitral tribunal. New grounds cannot be raised for the first time in the setting aside proceedings. The national court, however, is not bound by evidence or findings of the arbitral tribunal; but the arbitral tribunal is in turn bound by the findings of law of the national court that a valid arbitration clause exists and that the tribunal has to decide on the merits of the matter.[121]

An award will also be set aside if a party was under some incapacity to validly **27-045** conclude the arbitration agreement under the law which was personally relevant to that party (Section 611(2) no. 1 case 3 ZPO). This provision corresponds with

---

116. J. Power, *The Austrian Arbitration Act – A Practitioner's Guide to Sections 577-618 of the Austrian Code of Civil Procedure* (Vienna, Manz, 2006), Section 611, para. 13.

117. W.H. Rechberger and W. Melis in *Kommentar zur ZPO*, W H. Rechberger (ed.) (3rd edn, Vienna/New York, Springer, 2006), Section 611, para. 4. Note, however, that according to Section 583(3) ZPO, '[a] defect of form of the arbitration agreement shall be cured in the arbitration proceedings by entering an appearance in the case, if a notification of the defect is not made earlier or at the latest together with entering an appearance'.

118. W.H. Rechberger and W. Melis in *Kommentar zur ZPO*, W.H. Rechberger (ed.) (2nd edn, Vienna/New York, Springer, 2000), Section 595, para. 2.

119. *See* OGH, 21 February 1922, 2 OB 17/22, SZ 4/23.

120. J. Power, *The Austrian Arbitration Act – A Practitioner's Guide to Sections 577-618 of the Austrian Code of Civil Procedure* (Vienna, Manz, 2006), Section 611, para. 8.

121. A. Reiner, *Das neue österreichische Schiedsrecht/The new Austrian Arbitration Law* (Vienna, LexisNexis, 2006), Section 611, notes 193 *et seq.*

former Section 595(1) no. 1 ZPO and is in line with Section 12 in conjunction with Sections 9 and 10 IPRG, whereas the party's capacity to enter into an arbitration agreement is determined by its personal legal status.[122] In order to rely on Section 611(2) no. 1 ZPO, a party must have objected against the tribunal's jurisdiction at the first opportunity in the proceedings.[123]

2.   Violation of the Right to be Heard

27-046 An award shall be set aside if a party was not given proper notice of the appointment of an arbitrator or of the arbitral proceedings, or if it was unable for another reason to adequately present its case (Section 611(2) no. 2 ZPO). This provision protects the fundamental right to be heard in arbitration. Section 595(2) fZPO similarly applied to cases where a party 'was unable to present its case in the proceedings before the arbitrators', although it included an additional express reference to a violation of the right to be heard being violated if a person has no legal representation in the arbitration even though the representation is required by statute. Although the wording of the two provisions (former and new) is therefore not identical, the legislative materials clarify that the meaning is intended to remain unchanged.[124] The extensive Austrian jurisprudence available under the fZPO will therefore still have significant import under the new regime.[125]

27-047 Section 611(2) no. 2 ZPO must be understood in conjunction with Section 594(2) ZPO, which states that the party should be treated fairly and that each party should be accorded to the right to be heard.[126] This is discussed in detail in the context of **Article 20**.[127]

3.   Decision *Ultra Petita*

27-048 An award shall be set aside if 'the award deals with a dispute not falling within the terms of the arbitration agreement, or contains decisions on matters beyond the scope of the arbitration agreement or beyond the claims of the parties' (Section 611(2) no. 3 ZPO). This provision corresponds with former Section 595 no. 5 ZPO,

---

122. *See also* **Article 1**, at para. 033.
123. *See* **Article 19**, at paras. 006 *et seq.*
124. *See* Explanatory Notes to Section 611 ZPO.
125. OGH, 24 July 1997, 6 Ob 186/97i; OGH, 24 September 1981, 7 Ob 623/81, EvBl 1982/77; OGH, 27 November 1991, 3 Ob 1091/91; OGH, 1 December 1954, 3 Ob 689, 690/54; OGH, 12 May 1961, 2 Ob 199/61, EvBl 1961/387; OGH, 6 September 1990, 6 Ob 572/90; OGH, 20 September 1961, 6 Ob 305/61; OGH, 26 April 2006, 7 Ob 236/05i.
126. This is only accorded if the arbitral tribunal actually looked into and deals with the case presented by each of the parties. *See* A. Reiner, *Das neue österreichische Schiedsrecht/The new Austrian Arbitration Law* (Vienna, LexisNexis, 2006), Section 611, note 196.
127. *See* **Article 20**, at paras. 029 *et seq.*

but is drafted more concisely.[128] *Ultra petita* decisions can either be decisions which are not covered by the scope of the arbitration agreement,[129] or decisions exceeding the scope of the parties' request for relief.[130] In essence, the prohibition of *ultra petita* reinforces jurisdictional principles; both the arbitration agreement and the parties' request for relief define the tribunal's jurisdiction and specific mandate, and the tribunal must not go beyond the limits so delineated.

Notably, a party is only entitled to rely on Section 611(2) no. 3 ZPO if it has objected **27-049** against the tribunal's transgression at the first opportunity in the proceedings.[131]

However, an award does not exceed the arbitral tribunal's authority if the tribunal **27-050** decides *ex aequo et bono* without authorization from the parties, as required by Section 603(3) ZPO.[132] Also, if the jurisdictional defect concerns only a distinct part of the award, only that part of the award will be set aside.[133]

4. Deficient Formation or Composition of the Arbitral Tribunal

An arbitral award shall be set aside if the formation or composition of the arbitral **27-051** tribunal is not in accordance with a provisions of the ZPO or with an admissible agreement of the parties (Section 611(2) no. 4 ZPO).[134] This is narrower than Section 595(1) no. 3 fZPO which provided for setting aside for several procedural issues,[135] including the lack of the tribunal's signature on the arbitral award.[136] Procedural deficiencies are no longer grounds for setting aside unless they reach the level of constituting a violation of the *procedural ordre public* (discussed below).[137]

This ground includes lack of impartiality and independence.[138] It is not required **27-052** that the defective composition could have had an effect on the outcome of the

---

128. P. Oberhammer, *Entwurf eines neuen Schiedsverfahrensrechts* (Vienna, Manz, 2002), p. 133.
129. LGZ Vienna, 8 June 1967, 44 Cg 67/67, ArbSlg 8434.
130. OGH, 24 January 1968, 1 Ob 297/67, EvBl 1968/345; OGH, 15 December 1971, 5 Ob 208/71; OGH, 18 November 1982, 8 Ob 520/82.
131. *See* **Article 19**, at paras. 006.
132. *See* **Article 24**, at paras. 015 *et seq.* At least this was ruled under the former arbitration law. *See* OGH, 18 November 1982, 8 Ob 520/82; OGH, 14 December 1927, 1 Ob 1187/27. SZ 9/303.
133. OGH, 1 December 1954, 3 Ob 689, 690/54.
134. Section 611(2) no. 4 ZPO. However, if doubts as to the impartiality or independence of an arbitrator become known only after the expiration of the three-month period for the bringing of an action for setting aside (Section 611(4) ZPO), then they may no longer be asserted.
135. OGH, 15 December 1971, 5 Ob 208/71; OGH, 7 June 1990, 7 Ob 584/90; OGH, 26 April 2006, 7 Ob 236/05i.
136. OGH, 15 December 1971, 5 Ob 208/71.
137. W.H. Rechberger and W. Melis in *Kommentar zur ZPO*, W.H. Rechberger (ed.) (3rd edn, Vienna/New York, Springer, 2006), Section 611, para. 7.
138. C. Liebscher, *The Austrian Arbitration Act 2006: Text and Notes* (The Hague, Kluwer Law International, 2006), Annotated Text to Section 611 ZPO.

arbitration. For a detailed discussion of lack impartiality and independence, and its procedural ramifications, *see* **Article 7** and **Article 16**.

27-053 A party who has the knowledge that the formation or composition of the arbitral tribunal is not in accordance with a provision or agreement of the parties must object as soon as possible, or else is deemed precluded from challenging the award for this reason.[139]

5.   *Procedural Ordre Public*

27-054 An arbitral award will be set aside if the arbitral procedure was not carried out in accordance with the basic values of the Austrian legal system. This refers to the *procedural ordre public* (Section 611(2) no. 5 ZPO).[140] According to Austrian jurisprudence under the former legislation, the notion of public policy was understood in principle only to encompass breaches of *substantive ordre public*, but not violations of a procedural nature.[141] Until now, therefore, judicial scrutiny of the awards with respect to procedural issues was essentially confined to violations of the right to be heard.[142]

27-055 Section 611(2) no. 5 ZPO now expressly refers to the *procedural ordre public*, which is comprised of the most basic and fundamental procedural protection available under Austrian law.[143] Some authors consider such violation to exist if an award is rendered without conducting any evidentiary proceeding; or where the arbitral tribunal, automatically or without any justification, assumes the disputed assertions of one party to be true;[144] or where the dispositive part of the award is seriously inconsistent.[145] Some also argue that the grounds for setting aside an

---

139. *See* also **Article 20**, at paras. 272 *et seq.*

140. For a general discussion of this provision, *see* F.T. Schwarz and H. Ortner, 'Procedural Ordre Public and the Internationalization of Public Policy in Arbitration' in *Austrian Arbitration Yearbook 2008*, C. Klausegger, *et al.* (eds) (Vienna, Manz, 2008).

141. In OGH, 20 May 1931, 2 Ob 529/31, SZ 13/131 the Austrian *Oberster Gerichtshof* decided that Section 595 no. 6 fZPO (*ordre public* provision) only encompasses breaches of substantive law. In the same year on 4 December 1931 it was decided that an award without any reasons does not violate such *ordre public* (OGH, 4 December 1931, 3 Ob 847, ZBl 1932/306). This was confirmed in OGH, 13 June 1933, 3 Ob 419/33, Rsp 1933/234; OGH, 1 December 1954, 3 Ob 689, 690/54 and in OGH, 18 January 1982, 8 Ob 520/82, GesRZ 1983, 102.

142. J. Power, *The Austrian Arbitration Act – A Practitioner's Guide to Sections 577-618 of the Austrian Code of Civil Procedure* (Vienna, Manz, 2006), Section 611, para. 28.

143. OGH, 31 August 1995, 3 Ob 566/95; OGH, 5 May 1998, 3 Ob 2372/96m; OGH, 26 January 2005, 3 Ob 221/04b.

144. P. Oberhammer, *Entwurf eines neuen Schiedsverfahrensrechts* (Vienna, Manz, 2002), p. 134.

145. *See* W.H. Rechberger, 'Die Widersprüchlichkeit eines Schiedsspruchs als Aufhebungsgrund nach österreichischem Recht' [2006] SchiedsVZ 169, 175. *See* also, for a more detailed discussion of this issue, **Article 27**, at paras. 007 *et seq* with further references.

arbitral award under Section 611(1) no. 2 ZPO simultaneously satisfy the criteria for no. 5.[146]

6.   Reopening of Court Proceedings

An arbitral award will also be set aside if 'the requirements have been met accord-   **27-056**
ing to which a judgement of a court can be appealed under Section 530(1) nos 1-5 ZPO via an application for the proceedings to be reopened' (Section 611(2) no. 6 ZPO). This refers to the possibility of reopening court proceedings based on criminal offences such as falsification of documents, suppression of documents, or perjury.[147] Section 611(2) no. 6 ZPO, does not, however, refer to Section 530(1) nos 6 and 7 ZPO, addressing the discovery of new facts or evidence.[148]

The limitation period for filing an action to set aside an award on this ground does   **27-057**
not commence at the time the arbitral award is served on the party, but as of the date

---

146.   *See* A. Reiner, *Das neue österreichische Schiedsrecht/The new Austrian Arbitration Law* (Vienna, LexisNexis, 2006), Section 611, note 200. *See* also **Article 20**, at paras. 024, 036 and 062.

147.   *See* Section 530(1) nos 1-5 ZPO: Application to re-open a case: A case concluded by a judgment can be re-opened on application of a party, 1. if a document on which the judgment was based was completely or partially forged; 2. if a witness or expert of the opposing party has given false testimony during his examination and the judgment is based on this testimony; 3. if the judgment was given as a result of an act punishable at law, whether as wilful misrepresentation (Section 108 StGB), embezzlement (Section 134 StGB), fraud (Section 146 StGB), forgery of documents (Section 223 StGB), forgery of documents especially protected by the law (as defined in Section 224 StGB), forgery of public seals (Section 225 StGB), indirect false recording or certification (Section 228 StGB), suppression of documents (Section 229 StGB), or of displacement of boundary marks (Section 230 StGB), on the part of the representative of the party, or of the opposing party or its representative; 4. if the judge has been guilty of criminal negligence of his official duties to the prejudice of the applicant in giving judgment or in a previous decision relating to the case on which the judgment is based and 5. if a decision by a criminal court on which the judgment is based has been set aside by a subsequent final judgment. Note that this ground of setting aside an arbitration award has rarely been granted under the former jurisprudence. A false witness statement before an arbitral tribunal has so far not been considered a criminal offence. *See* OGH, 9 June 1937, 3 Ob 402/37, Rsp 1937/204, 162; OGH, 1 December 1954, 3 Ob 689, 690/54; *also* more recently OGH, 26 January 2005, 3 Ob 221/04b.

148.   *See* Section 530 (1) nos 6-7 ZPO: Application to re-open a case: 6. if the applicant discovers the existence of, or is placed in a position to use a previous judgment concerning the same claim or the same legal relationship which is already final and which determines the rights of and between the parties of the case to be re-opened; or 7. if the applicant has discovered or is placed in a position to use new facts or evidence which would have resulted in a more favourable decision for the applicant on the merits, if they had been presented in the previous hearing. (2) The re-opening of the case under figures 6 and 7 is only permissible if the applicant was unable without fault on his part to assert the finality of the judgment or the new facts or evidence before the end of the oral hearing after which the judgment of the First Instance was given. *See* OGH, 9 June 1937, 3 Ob 402/37, Rsp 1937/204, 162; OGH, 1 December 1954, 3 Ob 689, 690/54; *see also* C. Liebscher, *The Austrian Arbitration Act 2006: Text and Notes* (The Hague, Kluwer Law International, 2006), Annotated Text to Section 611 ZPO.

the criminal judgment confirming the incriminating offence has become final; the applicable period is four weeks from that date.[149] In any event, after ten years such criminal offences can no longer be raised as a basis for setting aside.[150]

7.   **Lack of Arbitrability**

27-058 An arbitral award shall be set aside *ex officio* if 'the subject-matter of the dispute is not arbitrable under Austrian law' (Section 611(2) no. 7 ZPO). For a detailed discussion of arbitrability, *see* **Article 1**, at paras. 105 *et seq.*

27-059 Under the fZPO and attending case law, the legal consequence of an arbitral award on a non-arbitrable subject matter was the nullity of the award.[151] Under the new provision of Section 611(2) no. 7 ZPO, such an award is not null and void but must be set aside by courts *ex officio*.[152] Indeed, even where such an award is not challenged by the parties, it shall nonetheless be disregarded by the Austrian courts and authorities.[153]

8.   *Substantive Ordre Public*

27-060 An arbitral award shall be set aside *ex officio* if 'it is in conflict with basic values of the Austrian legal system (*ordre public*)' (Section 611(2) no. 8 ZPO). Again, in case the parties decide not to challenge such an award, it shall, nonetheless, be disregarded by a court or another authority pursuant to Section 613 ZPO.[154]

27-061 This ground for setting aside protects the most fundamental values of the Austrian legal system.[155] Not every mandatory provision of Austrian law rises to this level of *ordre public*.[156] This provision corresponds to Section 595(1) no. 6 fZPO, with previous case law still having significant import. In determining whether an

---

149. A. Reiner, *Das neue österreichische Schiedsrecht/The new Austrian Arbitration Law* (Vienna, LexisNexis, 2006), Section 611, note 201.
150. *See* Section 611(4) ZPO, last sentence and Section 534(3) ZPO.
151. OGH, 13 January 2004, 5 Ob 123/03d; *see* discussion under **Article 1**, at paras. 135 *et seq.*
152. W.H. Rechberger and W. Melis in *Kommentar zur ZPO*, W.H. Rechberger (ed.) (3rd edn, Vienna/New York, Springer, 2006) Section 611, para. 10.
153. *See* Section 613 ZPO which reads: 'Should a court or an administrative authority find in other proceedings, for instance in enforcement proceedings, that grounds for setting aside in accordance with Section 611(2) nos 7 and 8 exist, then the arbitral tribunal award shall not be relevant in those proceedings.'
154. *See* Section 613 ZPO.
155. OGH, 9 February 1955, 3 Ob 37/55; OGH, 18 November 1982, 8 Ob 520/82; OGH, 7 June 1990, 7 Ob 584/90; OGH, 31 August 1995, 3 Ob 566/95; OGH, 5 May 1998, 3 Ob 2372/96m; OGH, 26 January 2005, 3 Ob 221/04b; OGH, 18 September 1991, 1 Ob 582/91; OGH, 5 April 1966, 8 Ob 92/66; OGH, 27 October 1960, 5 Ob 341/60; OGH, 26 April 2006, 7 Ob 236/05i.
156. C. Liebscher, *The Austrian Arbitration Act 2006: Text and Notes* (The Hague, Kluwer Law International, 2006), Annotated Text to Section 611(2) no. 8 ZPO.

ordre public violation occurred, the court is not bound by the findings of facts of the arbitral tribunal.[157] However, the court will ultimately only look at the result of the award, as specified in the award's dispositive part.[158]

C.   CONSEQUENCES OF SETTING ASIDE PROCEEDINGS

The setting aside of an award has no influence on the effectiveness of the under- **27-062** lying arbitration agreement.[159] However, if an award on the same subject matter has already been set aside twice in a final and binding way, and if a further award on the same subject matter is to be set aside, then the court, upon the application of a party, shall declare the arbitration agreement invalid with respect to that subject matter.[160]

If an award has been set aside, its legal existence is destroyed. It no longer has the **27-063** effect of a final and binding court judgment between the parties, as Section 607 ZPO provides for awards, and will no longer be enforceable in Austria, and perhaps even elsewhere.[161] Further, Section 613 ZPO introduces an obligation for any court (or another authority) to disregard an arbitral award if it determines grounds to exist for setting aside the award under Section 611(2) no. 7 (objective arbitrability) and no. 8 ZPO (*ordre public*), but only in the proceedings at issue.[162] Some authors argue that this provision should also apply to arbitral settlements as they will not fall under the setting aside regime of an arbitral award.[163]

D.   DECLARATION THAT AN AWARD DOES OR DOES NOT EXIST

Section 612 ZPO has been newly introduced to the Austrian arbitration law. An **27-064** application may be made to the state court for the determination of the existence or non-existence of an award if the applicant has a legal interest therein. Hence, the disputed right or claim must directly impact the applicant's legal status; a mere

---

157. A. Reiner, *Das neue österreichische Schiedsrecht/The new Austrian Arbitration Law* (Vienna, LexisNexis, 2006), Section 611, note 204.
158. *See* **Article 24**, at para. 019.
159. Section 611(5) ZPO.
160. Section 611(5) ZPO.
161. *See* A. Redfern, M. Hunter, N. Blackaby and C. Partasides, *Law and Practice of International Commercial Arbitration* (4th edn, London, Sweet & Maxwell, 2004), para. 9-02.
162. W.H. Rechberger and W. Melis in *Kommentar zur ZPO*, W.H. Rechberger (ed.) (3rd edn, Vienna/New York, Springer, 2006), Section 613, para. 1.
163. A. Reiner, *Das neue österreichische Schiedsrecht/The new Austrian Arbitration Law* (Vienna, LexisNexis, 2006), Section 613, note 214; W.H. Rechberger and W. Melis in *Kommentar zur ZPO*, W.H. Rechberger (ed.) (3rd edn, Vienna/New York, Springer, 2006), Section 613, para. 2.

economic interest does not suffice to afford standing.[164] The question of whether or not an arbitral award has been rendered can be of significant relevance in cases where the legal nature of a decision of an arbitral tribunal is unclear or disputable.[165] The application is not subject to a statutory time period and may be brought as a subsidiary motion in conjunction with an action for setting aside an award.[166] This provision also applies in cases where the seat of the arbitral tribunal is not within Austria.[167] Its practical relevance is doubtful at best.[168]

E.   ENFORCEMENT OF FOREIGN AWARDS

27-065 Domestic Austrian arbitration awards do not require any *exequatur* to be enforceable in Austria; such awards constitute an enforceable legal title.[169] An arbitral award is considered to be 'national' if the place of arbitration is seated in Austria.[170] The place stated in the award is deemed to have been the seat of the arbitration for this purpose.[171]

27-066 As foreign awards do not fall under the challenge regime of Section 611 ZPO, they do need to be declared enforceable in an *exequatur* proceeding in accordance with the provisions of the Austrian Enforcement Act (*Exekutionsordnung* – EO).[172] However, the Austrian Enforcement Act is largely superseded by the substantial provisions of international conventions dealing with recognition and enforcement

---

164. J. Power, *The Austrian Arbitration Act – A Practitioner's Guide to Sections 577- 618 of the Austrian Code of Civil Procedure* (Vienna, Manz, 2006), Section 612, para. 2.

165. *See, e.g.*, the distinction between an expert's opinion and an arbitral award **Article 1**, at para. 098.

166. P. Oberhammer, *Entwurf eines neuen Schiedsverfahrensrechts* (Vienna, Manz, 2002), p. 142. Note that the time limits for setting aside an award remain unaltered.

167. Section 577(2) ZPO.

168. *Reiner* rightly points out that in such cases the real issue is whether the arbitral award is capable of being recognized and enforced; procedural questions which are not dealt with under Section 612 ZPO. *See* A. Reiner, *Das neue österreichische Schiedsrecht/The new Austrian Arbitration Law* (Vienna, LexisNexis, 2006), Section 612, note 210.

169. P. Angst, W. Jakusch and H. Pimmer, *Exekutionsordnung* (14th edn, Vienna, Manz, 2006), Section 1 no. 16; *see also* OGH, 24 May 2002, 3 Ob 18/02x.

170. *See* Section 577 ZPO.

171. Section 606(3) ZPO.

172. Unless otherwise provided in international law or in legal acts of the European Union, Section 614 ZPO. According to W.H. Rechberger and W. Melis in *Kommentar zur ZPO*, W.H. Rechberger (ed.) (3rd edn, Vienna/New York, Springer, 2006), Section 614, para. 2, the last part of this sentence is meant to cover future regulations of this issue by the EC. The recognition of the foreign arbitral award takes effect *ipso jure*, however, not its enforcement. *See* G. Zeiler, *Schiedsverfahren* (Vienna/Graz, Neuer Wissenschaftlicher Verlag, 2006), Section 614, p. 288. The *exequatur* proceedings are vital to afford such foreign awards legal effect. *See* OGH, 28 April 1931, 2 Ob 388, ZBl 1931/222.

of arbitral awards, most notably the New York Convention.[173] The formal requirements can be fulfilled either by compliance with the provisions of the New York Convention[174] or by fulfilling both standards established under Austrian law and under the law applicable to the arbitration agreement.[175] The latter shall only apply if these provisions are more favourable than the New York Convention.

Section 614 ZPO, reflecting an international trend of liberalization, states that **27-067** presentation of the original arbitration agreement or a certified copy thereof[176] is only necessary if requested by the court. This should facilitate the enforcement where no written arbitration agreement exists, for example when one party has impliedly accepted the arbitral tribunal's jurisdiction by not expressing any objections.[177] The existence of the arbitration agreement still needs be proven, of course, if the opposing party raises an objections against the tribunal's jurisdiction at the enforcement state.[178]

173. Note also pertaining provisions under the European Convention, **Annex 10**.
174. NY Convention, **Annex 11**.
175. This ZPO draft initially sought to unify the form requirements and to expressly exclude the application of the NY Convention. *See* P. Oberhammer, *Entwurf eines neuen Schiedsverfahrensrechts* (Vienna, Manz, 2002). The final version actually introduced a more restrictive approach for foreign awards. *See* J. Power, *The Austrian Arbitration Act – A Practitioner's Guide to Sections 577-618 of the Austrian Code of Civil Procedure* (Vienna, Manz, 2006), Section 614, para. 4. A foreign arbitral award may also be declared partially enforceable. *See* A. Reiner, *Das neue österreichische Schiedsrecht/The new Austrian Arbitration Law* (Vienna, LexisNexis, 2006), Section 614, note 219 with reference to OGH, 26 January 1995, 3 Ob 221/ 04b.
176. As required by Article IV 1(b) of the NY Convention, **Annex 11**.
177. *See* **Article 19**, at paras. 001 *et seq.*
178. P. Oberhammer in *Das Neue Schiedsrecht – Schiedsrechts-Änderungsgesetz 2006*, B. Kloiber, P. Oberhammer, W.H. Rechberger and H. Haller (eds) (Vienna, Manz, 2006), p. 343.

Article 28

Settlement and Consent Award

Article 28: The Parties can request that a record is drawn up on a settlement they have concluded or that an award *(on agreed terms)* be made thereof.

In arbitration, parties often agree to settle their dispute before the tribunal reaches a final award on the merits. In such a case, Article 28 confirms that parties can have the settlement recorded by the tribunal. In such a case, the parties effectively withdraw their claims,[1] and notify the tribunal that a settlement has been reached.[2] The tribunal will include that notification in the record of the arbitration, resulting in the termination of the proceedings according to **Article 25** and Section 608(1) ZPO.[3] This will likewise terminate the tribunal's mandate.[4] **28-001**

Article 28 further affords the parties an alternative mechanism, allowing them to have the settlement by formalized through a so-called 'consent award' (or 'award by consent' or 'award on agreed terms'). Such consent awards can also record a partial settlement, with the arbitration proceeding on the remaining issues.[5] Most arbitral rules provide, in one form or the other, for consent awards. The UNCITRAL Rules allow for the settlement to be recorded by an order or an **28-002**

---

1. Y. Derains and E.A. Schwartz, *A Guide to the ICC Rules of Arbitration* (2nd edn, The Hague, Kluwer Law International, 2005), p. 311.
2. A. Redfern, M. Hunter, N. Blackaby and C. Partasides, *Law and Practice of International Commercial Arbitration* (4th edn, London, Sweet & Maxwell, 2004), para. 8-50.
3. *See* **Article 25**, at paras. 006 *et seq.*
4. *See* **Article 25**, at para. 025.
5. Y. Derains and E.A. Schwartz, *A Guide to the ICC Rules of Arbitration* (2nd edn, The Hague, Kluwer Law International, 2005), p. 312. *See, e.g., Award in ICC Case No. 4761 of 1984* in S. Jarvin, Y. Derains and J.-J. Arnaldez, *Collection of ICC Arbitral Awards 1986-1990* (Deventer, Kluwer Law and Taxation Publishers, 1994), p. 298 *et seq.*

award if the parties so request,[6] and most institutional rules allow for the instrument of an award by consent.[7]

28-003 Both possibilities are also afforded by Section 605 ZPO, which reads:

> If, during arbitral proceedings, the parties settle the dispute, and if the parties are able to agree on a settlement of the matter in dispute, they can apply for

> 1. the arbitral tribunal to draw up a record of the settlement, provided that the contents of the settlement are not in conflict with the basic values of the Austrian legal system (*ordre public*); it shall be sufficient if the record of the settlement is signed by the parties and the presiding arbitrator;
> 2. the arbitral tribunal to record the settlement in the form of an award on agreed terms, provided that the contents of the settlement are not in conflict with the basic values of the Austrian legal system (*ordre public*). Such an award is to be made in accordance with Section 606 of this act and has the same effect as any other award on the merits of the case.

28-004 Notably, Section 605 ZPO clarifies that the parties must be capable, as a matter of applicable law, to settle the dispute.[8] Section 605 ZPO also provides for both a recorded settlement and a consent award that neither instrument must violate the Austrian *ordre public*.

28-005 There are several reasons why the parties might want their settlement agreement in the form of an award.[9] First, consent awards are generally considered to be enforceable as any other form of final award.[10] Indeed, while recorded arbitral settlements constitute an enforceable title comparable to settlements concluded in court under Austrian law[11] and perhaps under some bilateral agreements,[12] they are not considered to benefit from international enforceability under the New York

---

6. Article 34(1) UNCITRAL Rules.
7. Article 26 ICC Rules; Article 26(8) LCIA Rules and Article 29(1) AAA/ICDR Rules.
8. Notably, Section 605 ZPO applies a narrower standard than the definition of arbitrability under Section 582 ZPO (which includes matters both capable of settlement **and** of an economic nature). Conceptually, therefore, not all matters that are arbitrable can also be the subject matter of an arbitral settlement or a consent award. *See* Explanatory Notes to Section 605 ZPO. For examples, taken from Austrian law, *see* S. Riegler in *Arbitration Law of Austria: Practice and Procedure*, S. Riegler, A. Petsche, A. Fremuth-Wolf, M. Platte and C. Liebscher (eds) (Huntington, Juris Publishing, 2007), Section 605, p. 434.
9. A. Redfern, M. Hunter, N. Blackaby and C. Partasides, *Law and Practice of International Commercial Arbitration* (4th edn, London, Sweet & Maxwell, 2004), para. 8-48.
10. A. Redfern, M. Hunter, N. Blackaby and C. Partasides, *Law and Practice of International Commercial Arbitration* (4th edn, London, Sweet & Maxwell, 2004), para. 8-48.
11. *See* Section 1 No. 16 EO; C. Liebscher, *The Austrian Arbitration Act 2006: Text and Notes* (The Hague, Kluwer Law International, 2006), Annotated Text to Section 605 ZPO.
12. For Austria-Germany, *see* BGBl No. 105/1960 and for Austria-Switzerland BGBl No. 125/1962. On 5 July 2004, the *Bayerische Oberste Landesgericht* (Bavarian Highest Regional Court)

Convention.[13] Indeed, Section 605 ZPO expressly provides that an award by consent 'has the same effects as any other award on the merits'. Such an award by consent is therefore fully enforceable, both in Austria and under the New York Convention,[14] if it is worded to include an enforceable order.[15] Second, it is often beneficial to have a definite, tangible 'result' such as an award issued by the arbitral tribunal (albeit with the parties' consent) which can be passed on to the appropriate authority for implementation.[16] Whether an award by consent may avoid otherwise applicable stamp duties and taxes that apply to settlements under Austrian law, is still disputed.[17] In this case, the consultation with an Austrian tax adviser is therefore always recommendable.

Article 28 leaves open whether the tribunal is under an obligation to issue a consent **28-006** award if the parties so request. It is evident that a consent award requires the joint

---

therefore held that a settlement agreement concluded before an arbitral tribunal but not recorded in the form of an award on agreed terms was to be recognized and enforced in Germany. Although the settlement agreement was recorded in the minutes of the arbitral proceedings, and therefore did not fall within the scope of the NY Convention the court pointed out that the NY Convention does not affect the validity of other conventions concerning the recognition and enforcement of arbitral awards. It held that pursuant to a bilateral agreement between Germany and Austria, settlement agreements concluded before an arbitral tribunal are to be considered as arbitral awards. Thus, the court held that the settlement agreement could be recognized and enforced as if it were an arbitral award on agreed terms. *See* BayObLG, 4 July 2004, 4 Z Sch 009/04, 4 Z Sch 9/04, SchiedsVZ 2004, 316.

13. J. Lew, L. Mistelis and S. Kröll, *Comparative International Commercial Arbitration* (The Hague, Kluwer Law International, 2003), para. 24-31. *See, e.g., United States v. Sperry Corp. et al.*, 493 U.S. 52 (U.S. S. Ct. 1989).
14. *See* Section 1 no. 16 EO; C. Liebscher, *The Austrian Arbitration Act 2006: Text and Notes* (The Hague, Kluwer Law International, 2006), Annotated Text to Section 605 ZPO.
15. A. Reiner, *Das neue österreichische Schiedsrecht/The new Austrian Arbitration Law* (Vienna, LexisNexis, 2006), Section 605, note 152.
16. A. Redfern, M. Hunter, N. Blackaby and C. Partasides, *Law and Practice of International Commercial Arbitration* (4th edn, London, Sweet & Maxwell, 2004), para. 8-45.
17. The execution of a settlement agreement not concluded before state courts may trigger the application of Austrian stamp duty law (*Gebührengesetz* – GebG). An award by consent could arguably be seen as a form of settlement, in which case stamp duties may apply. Whether arbitral tribunals can be considered to equal state courts proceedings has been discussed in Austrian literature (*See, e.g.,* W.-D. Arnold, *Rechtsgebühren* (8th edn, Vienna, WUV, 2006), Section 33 TP 20, para. 9); and it has also been pointed out that an award by consent has the same effects under Section 607 ZPO as a judgment, advocating against the application of settlement stamp duties. *See* S. Riegler in *Arbitration Law of Austria: Practice and Procedure*, S. Riegler, A. Petsche, A. Fremuth-Wolf, M. Platte and C. Liebscher (eds) (Huntington, Juris Publishing, 2007), Section 605, p. 436. Austrian tax authorities, however, have taken the position that arbitral tribunals do not qualify as state courts for stamp duty purposes. *See* Austrian Federal Ministry of Finance, General Stamp Duty Guideline 2007, para 998. Therefore, settlements concluded before an arbitral tribunal may be considered dutiable transactions pursuant to Section 33 TP 20 GebG.

request of the parties.[18] Even then, it is difficult to justify that the tribunal has no discretion at all to refuse issuing a consent award (after all bearing the signatures of the arbitrators). For the ICC Rules, *Redfern/Hunter* point out that the wording of Article 26 ('if so requested by the parties' and 'if the arbitral tribunal agrees to do so') indicate that the tribunal is not obliged to make a consent award.[19] As a textual matter, the Vienna Rules do not allow the arbitrators any express choice in the matter, stating that '[t]he Parties can request that a record is drawn up on a settlement they have concluded or that an award (*on agreed terms*) be made thereof'.[20] Section 605 ZPO, on the other hand, merely provides that the parties 'may request' a consent award, without stating that the arbitrators must issue it. It seems clear from the wording of Section 605 ZPO that the arbitrators do not have to (and indeed must refuse to) record a settlement, or issue a consent award, if this would violate Austrian *ordre* public,[21] or on a subject matter that the parties cannot settle. Moreover, although the tribunal will generally accommodate the parties' request to obtain a consent award, there may well be circumstances where the tribunal may be reluctant to do so; for instance if the proposed award was illegal or fraudulent, or contrary to relevant laws.[22]

28-007 A consent award that violates public policy can be set aside according to Section 611(2) no. 8 ZPO, and a consent award on a non-arbitrable subject matter can be set aside according to Section 611(2) no. 7 ZPO. However, there is no specific provision in Section 611 ZPO that would provide for the setting aside of an award on a matter that is incapable of being settled under applicable law (as long as it is still arbitrable). Some authors suggest that Section 611(2) no. 7 ZPO on non-arbitrability should be extended to such cases by analogy.[23] However, given the extraordinary character of setting aside proceedings, and the legislative intention to provide for an exclusive, narrow list of grounds,[24]

---

18. Given the effects of a consent award, which are identical to an award issued on the merits by the tribunal, arbitrators will be very hesitant to issue a consent award were only one party so requests and the other one is silent. Where agreement exists between the parties on a consent award, it should cause no difficulty to clearly evidence that agreement to the tribunal.

19. A. Redfern, M. Hunter, N. Blackaby and C. Partasides, *Law and Practice of International Commercial Arbitration* (4th edn, London, Sweet & Maxwell, 2004), paras. 8-49 *et seq.*

20. *See, e.g.*, Article 65(b) WIPO Arbitration Rules. *But see*, J. Lew, L. Mistelis and S. Kröll, *Comparative International Commercial Arbitration* (The Hague, Kluwer Law International, 2003), para. 24-29, arguing that tribunals always have this discretion whether or not expressly granted in the rules.

21. A. Reiner, *Das neue österreichische Schiedsrecht/The new Austrian Arbitration Law* (Vienna, LexisNexis, 2006), Section 605, note 153.

22. Y. Derains and E.A. Schwartz, *A Guide to the ICC Rules of Arbitration* (2nd edn, The Hague, Kluwer Law International, 2005), p. 311.

23. S. Riegler in *Arbitration Law of Austria: Practice and Procedure*, S. Riegler, A. Petsche, A. Fremuth-Wolf, M. Platte and C. Liebscher (eds) (Huntington, Juris Publishing, 2007), Section 605, p. 435.

24. Explanatory Notes to Section 611.

extending setting aside to cases not expressly mentioned in Section 611 ZPO is problematic.

Mere recorded settlements do in principle not constitute awards, and should there- **28-008** fore not be subject to challenge. However, it has been suggested that arbitral settlements are subject to Sections 612 and 613 ZPO.[25] Also, like any settlement, they may be subject to claims under applicable substantive law that they were not validly concluded for formal or substantive reasons, e.g., that the settlement was concluded under duress.[26]

Consent awards have to comply with the form requirements that apply to all **28-009** awards.[27] As regards the requirement of a 'reasoned' award, it will generally be sufficient for the tribunal to state that the award was based on a settlement between the parties.[28] Where the parties do not request a consent award, but merely record their settlement, it is sufficient for that record to be signed by the presiding arbitrator and the parties.[29]

Article 29 on the correction, interpretation and supplementation of awards applies **28-010** to consent awards as well. The rendering of the consent award has, however, no consequences for the calculation for the arbitrators' fees which are set as if they had rendered an award on the merits. However, where the consent award is issued early, before evidence has been taken and an oral hearing has taken place, it is arguable that the arbitrators' fees should be reduced in line with the VIAC's practice for merit awards.

---

25. S. Riegler in *Arbitration Law of Austria: Practice and Procedure*, S. Riegler, A. Petsche, A. Fremuth-Wolf, M. Platte and C. Liebscher (eds) (Huntington, Juris Publishing, 2007), Section 605, p. 436.
26. J. Power, *The Austrian Arbitration Act – A Practitioner's Guide to Sections 577-618 of the Austrian Code of Civil Procedure* (Vienna, Manz, 2006), Section 605 ZPO, para. 4 with further reference.
27. *See* Section 605 ZPO which expressly provides that the consent award 'shall be made in accordance with section 606 [ZPO].'
28. A. Reiner, *Das neue österreichische Schiedsrecht/The new Austrian Arbitration Law* (Vienna, LexisNexis, 2006), Section 605, note 153; Y. Derains and E.A. Schwartz, *A Guide to the ICC Rules of Arbitration* (2nd edn, The Hague, Kluwer Law International, 2005), p. 312
29. *See* Section 605 ZPO, first alternative, last sentence. This form requirement is considered to be a mandatory minimum standard, however.

Article 29

Correction and Interpretation of Awards

	Para.			Para.
I.	Application for Correction,		III.	*Ex Officio* Correction 13
	Interpretation or Supplementation of		IV.	Application for Correction,
	the Award 1			Interpretation or Supplementation of
II.	Decision by the Tribunal 8			the Award 15

I. APPLICATION FOR CORRECTION, INTERPRETATION OR SUPPLEMENTATION OF THE AWARD

Article 29(1): Each party may within 30 days of receipt of the award file with the Secretariat the following applications to the sole arbitrator (arbitral tribunal):

(a) to correct in the award any errors in computation, any clerical or typographical errors or any errors of similar nature;

(b) if so agreed by the parties, to interpret certain parts of the award;

(c) to make an additional award as to claims presented in the arbitral proceedings but omitted from the award.

Despite the tribunal's best efforts, the award may contain inadvertent mistakes, or **29-001** be not entirely clear to the parties in certain points. Where the arbitrators make serious errors, the award may be subject to setting aside under the grounds specified by Section 611 ZPO, provided that arbitration proceedings were seated in Austria. However, many mistakes are far less serious and can be easily corrected. Article 29 provides a mechanism to do so, in line with similar provisions in all major arbitral rules,[1] and following in essence the concept of

---

1. *See, e.g.,* Article 29 ICC Rules; Article 27(1) LCIA Rules; Article 37(1) DIS Rules and Article 30 AAA/ICDR Rules.

the mandatory[2] provision of Section 610(1) ZPO.[3] It is argued that this provision applies to all forms of awards, whether on the merits, on jurisdiction or on costs; whether partial, interim or final; or even on agreed terms.[4]

29-002 Article 29(1)(a) and Section 610(1) no. 1 ZPO in near-identical terms allow for the correction of certain minor errors. These include 'errors in computation', such as errors in the calculation of the quantum or, particularly relevant in practice, errors in the calculation of the interest awarded. Such errors would typically not rise to the level of a public policy violation, and there would be no remedy to correct them but for Article 29(1). Of course, where a party asks the tribunal to reconsider, or revisit, its quantification of damages, or other such monetary claims, in the guise of a request to correct a supposedly 'computational' error, the tribunal will reject the request under Article 29(2). Article 29(1) is not meant to open the door to substantive review of the award, but merely seeks to ensure that inadvertent errors of calculation can be corrected.[5]

29-003 This reading is confirmed by the description of other errors that are susceptible for correction.[6] Thus, parties can ask to correct typographical mistakes and mistakes of a clerical nature (such as obvious errors in otherwise undisputed dates), or 'errors of a similar nature'. Again, a coherent reading of this provision will limit its application to minor inadvertent mistakes in the award, rather than subjecting the award to another quasi-appellate round of substantive review. Minor mistakes of the nature described in Article 29 (and Section 610 ZPO) can be corrected; but the tribunal's award as such can no longer be altered.[7]

29-004 Article 29(1) also allows the parties to request that the tribunal 'interpret certain parts of the award' that have remained unclear and that, as a result, will perhaps hinder the voluntary implementation of the award by the parties.[8] Under that

2. The time-limit of Section 610(1) ZPO is not mandatory.
3. *See* also Article 33 UNCITRAL Model Law.
4. S. Riegler in *Arbitration Law of Austria: Practice and Procedure*, S. Riegler, A. Petsche, A. Fremuth-Wolf, M. Platte and C. Liebscher (eds) (Huntington, Juris Publishing, 2007), Section 610, p. 499. In case of doubt, parties can also request a declaration whether an award exists. *See* Section 612 ZPO and **Article 27**, at paras. 064 *et seq.*
5. In similar vein for the ICC rules, *see* M. Bühler and T. Webster, *Handbook of ICC Arbitration; Commentary, Precedents, Materials* (London, Sweet & Maxwell, 2005), p. 346.
6. Indeed, the authentic German version of Section 610 ZPO refers to *'Rechen-, Schreib- und Druckfehler'*, all uniformly mistakes of a minor order.
7. C. Liebscher, *The Austrian Arbitration Act 2006: Text and Notes* (The Hague, Kluwer Law International, 2006), Annotated Text to Section 610 ZPO. *Rechberger* argues, therefore, that inconsistencies in the award are not subject to correction. *See* W.H Rechberger, 'Die Widersprüchlickeit eines Schiedsspruches als Aufhebungsgrund nach österreichischem Recht' [2006] SchiedsVZ 2006, 169, 172.
8. As a general matter, the dispositive findings of the award can be interpreted by making use of the reasons given in the award. *See* OGH, 31 March 2005, 3 Ob 259/04s as cited by S. Riegler in *Arbitration Law of Austria: Practice and Procedure*, S. Riegler, A. Petsche, A. Fremuth-Wolf, M. Platte and C. Liebscher (eds) (Huntington, Juris Publishing, 2007), Section 610, p. 500.

provision, the tribunal can be asked to interpret any part of the award, whether from the reasons or the dispositive holdings. As discussed below, the interpretation is itself issued in the form of an award and indeed forms part of the award it sets out to interpret. As such, the interpretation is binding on the parties.

Section 610(1) no. 2 ZPO provides in near-identical terms that, upon joint request **29-005** from the parties, the tribunal can 'explain' the award, or parts of it. Section 610(1) no. 2 ZPO is said to deliberately use the term 'explain' rather 'interpret'. However, there is no real semantic or normative difference between those words.[9] The authentic German version of Section 610 ZPO uses the term *'erläutern'* which can be translated both as 'explain' and 'interpret'. Whatever the terminology, it is clear that Section 610 ZPO seeks to afford the tribunal with the opportunity, if so requested by the parties, to clarify inadvertent ambiguities in the award. As the legislative materials make clear, this was intended to avoid setting aside proceedings where an explanation from the tribunal suffices to clarify existing ambiguities in the award;[10] it is not intended, however, to provide the parties or the arbitrators with an instrument to modify the award.[11]

Finally, the tribunal may have intended to issue its final award, but in fact have **29-006** failed to dispose of all claims put before it. As discussed elsewhere, the tribunal owes the parties a decision on all claims that are brought (and admitted) in the proceedings.[12] Where certain claims are left undecided, the award so rendered is not finally resolving the dispute; the tribunal has not exhausted its mandate.[13] In such a case, a party can apply to the tribunal to have those omitted claims decided as well.

Requests under Article 29(1) must be made within thirty days from the receipt of **29-007** the original award.[14] For corrections of the award and the resolution of additional claims, the application by one party is sufficient. However, Article 29(1)(b) and Section 610 (1) no. 2 ZPO require a joint request by all parties for an interpretation of the award.[15]

---

9. A. Reiner, *Das neue österreichische Schiedsrecht/The new Austrian Arbitration Law* (Vienna, LexisNexis, 2006), Section 610, note 182.
10. Explanatory Notes to Section 610 ZPO.
11. Explanatory Notes to Section 610 ZPO.
12. *See* **Article 7**, at para. 055.
13. *See* **Article 25**, at para. 025 and Section 608 ZPO.
14. Section 610(1) ZPO requires such requests to be made 'within four weeks.' However, Section 610(1) ZPO also expressly allows the parties to agree on a different time period. If it is not clear whether the initial decision was an award at all, parties may be well advised to file in parallel a request under Section 612 ZPO. In such cases of doubt, the parties should still file an application for correction in parallel, within the 30 day time limit from receipt of the document.
15. Such an agreement can also be contained in the arbitration agreement, in which case a unilateral request is sufficient.

II.   DECISION BY THE TRIBUNAL

**Article 29(2): The decision on such an application is made by the sole
arbitrator (arbitral tribunal). Prior to making a decision upon such an
application, the other party is to be heard. The sole arbitrator (arbitral
tribunal) shall determine a time period for that purpose, which should not
exceed 30 days.**

29-008   Once a request is made, the tribunal will (and has to)[16] decide on its admissibility
and merits. The tribunal's additional work on this matters is still covered by its
original fee. The tribunal is entitled to reject the application if it is made after the
30 day deadline specified in Article 29(1) or, in *ad hoc* proceedings, the four week
deadline specified in Section 610(1) ZPO. Before reaching a decision, the tribunal
has to hear the other party; the opportunity for written comment will usually be
sufficient. The other party 'should' under Article 29(2) not be allowed more than
thirty days to take a position on the request, but this is only a guideline for the
tribunal expressing a desire on the part of the VIAC to expedite those issues. The
arbitrators are free to set a shorter or a longer deadline if they deem so appropriate
under the circumstances. If the arbitrators refuse to grant the request under Article
29, there is, according to the Explanatory Notes, no recourse to the courts.[17]

29-009   If the tribunal admits a request for correction of typographical or clerical errors
because it was filed in time, the tribunal will be able to decide expeditiously
whether such corrections should be made. However, if the tribunal has failed to
address all claims put before it, and one party requests an additional award addressing such claims, the tribunal may take longer to arrive at a supplemental decision.
One would assume that evidence and submissions with respect to those claims have
already been taken, or else the parties would have objected to the closing of the
proceedings under Article 20(7) in the first place, seeking to prevent the tribunal
from closing the proceedings when not all evidence has been taken. However, to
the extent that the tribunal considers that it needs to hear the parties again on certain
points, it is entitled to reopen the proceedings with regard to the claims it has
omitted from the award. Of course, the tribunal cannot revisit, or deviate from,
issues already addressed in the original award.[18] On the other hand, the adjudication of previously unaddressed claims may have an impact on the overall allocation
of the costs between the parties, which also needs to be addressed in the supplementary award.[19]

---

16.   The obligation to address requests for correction, interpretation or the rendering of an additional
award survives the expiration of the arbitrator's mandate with the issuance of the final award.
See **Article 25**, at para. 026.
17.   Explanatory Notes to Section 610.
18.   OGH, 13 March 1955, 2 Ob 422/54, JBl 1955, 503.
19.   S. Riegler in *Arbitration Law of Austria: Practice and Procedure*, S. Riegler, A. Petsche,
A. Fremuth-Wolf, M. Platte and C. Liebscher (eds) (Huntington, Juris Publishing, 2007),
Section 610, p. 502.

Pursuant to Article 29(1) and Section 610(1) no. 2 ZPO, the tribunal can give an **29-010** interpretation of its own award only if all parties so agree.

Section 610(3) ZPO deviates from Article 29 in one important aspect. It provides **29-011** that:

> The arbitral tribunal shall decide upon the correction or interpretation of the award within four weeks and upon an additional award within eight weeks.

As a textual matter, these deadlines appear to be mandatory ('shall'). However, the **29-012** legislative materials make clear that those deadlines serve only as guidance to the arbitrators, and have no mandatory character.[20] Their violation is therefore without direct consequences, save perhaps for assessing undue delays in the performance of the arbitrator under **Article 17(2)** and Section 590(2) ZPO.[21]

III.   *EX OFFICIO* CORRECTION

Article 29(3): The sole arbitrator (arbitral tribunal) may correct any error of the type referred to in paragraph (1) a) of this Article on its own initiative within 30 days of the date of the award.

Like many arbitral rules,[22] Article 29(3) permits the arbitrators to correct typo- **29-013** graphical or clerical errors on its own volition, without the request by a party. This *ex officio* authority applies only to errors under Article 29(1)(a). Thus, the tribunal has no *ex officio* authority to issue an interpretation of its own award (which requires a joint request of both parties), nor to address additional claims that it had failed to address in its original award. An identical approach is adopted by Section 610(4) ZPO.

Notably, Article 29(3) does not require the tribunal to hear the parties. This makes **29-014** sense, in that Article 29(3) only applies to minor clerical errors and does not affect the substance of the award.[23]

---

20. Explanatory Notes to Section 610 ZPO, which expressly refer to the possibility of taking new evidence in the context of a supplementary award.
21. *See* Explanatory Notes to Section 610 and **Article 17**, at para. 015.
22. *See, e.g.*, Article 29(1) ICC Rules: 'On its own initiative, the Arbitral Tribunal may correct a clerical, computational or typographical error, or any errors of similar nature contained in an Award, provided such correction is submitted for approval to the Court within 30 days of the date of such Award.' Article 27(2) LCIA Rules: 'The Arbitral Tribunal may likewise correct any error of the nature described in Article 27(1) on its own initiative within 30 days of the date of the award, to the same effect.' Article 37(4) DIS Rules: 'The arbitral tribunal may also make a correction to the award on its own initiative.'
23. Note that for corrections made upon request of a party, the other party must be heard even where the correction relates to such a minor error. *See* **Article 29**, at para. 008.

IV.   APPLICATION FOR CORRECTION, INTERPRETATION
                       OR SUPPLEMENTATION OF THE AWARD

Article 29(4): The provisions of Article 27 paragraphs 1 to 6 shall apply to the correction, interpretation or making of an additional award. The interpretation or correction shall be part of the arbitral award.

29-015   Article 29(4) clarifies that the tribunal must make its correction or interpretation of the previous award again in the form of an award.[24] This award must comply with all the formal requirements expressed in **Article 27(1) to (6)**. Although not expressly mentioned here, this new award is also subject to the provisions on decision-making as provided in **Article 26**. As a practical matter, a correction can be made as a separate award (stating in the dispositive section that the original award is corrected in points x, y and z) or it can reissue the original award in corrected form.[25] An interpretation will usually take the form of a stand-alone document.

29-016   In any event if the tribunal issues a correction or interpretation, the new award is deemed an integral part of the previous award, both pursuant to Article 29(4) and Section 610(5) ZPO. This raises interesting issues for the approriate time to file a setting aside application with the Austrian courts (which must be done three months from receipt of the award). One school of thought (which has the legislative materials[26] and policy considerations of legal certainty and predictability for it) relies on the provision that corrections or interpretations, even if made in the form of an award, are deemed by operation of law to form part of the original award.[27] On that basis, the period for a setting aside application is supposed to run from the receipt of the original award, irrespective of the subsequent correction or interpretation.[28]

29-017   However, another school of thought would argue that, precisely because the correction or interpretation forms part of the original award, the original award is not complete until the correction or interpretation is handed down by the tribunal (or until a request for correction or interpretation is denied). Under that school of thought, the timelimit for setting aside proceedings would only start to run until the correction or interpretation (or the rejection of the tribunal of such requests) are received by the parties and the original award becomes complete. Until this issue is

---

24. *See* also Explanatory Notes to Section 610 ZPO.
25. In that case, the tribunal will usually request the parties to return the original award that was previously issued.
26. Explanatory Notes to Section 610 ZPO.
27. A separate challenge to the interpretation or correction, even if made in the form of an award, is therefore not contemplated. For a different view, see A. Reiner, Das *neue österreichische Schiedsrecht/The new Austrian Arbitration Law* (Vienna, LexisNexis, 2006), Section 610, note 189, who raises the interesting issue of a possible lack of jurisdiction if the tribunal issues an interpretation of the award without joint request.
28. S. Riegler in *Arbitration Law of Austria: Practice and Procedure*, S. Riegler, A. Petsche, A. Fremuth-Wolf, M. Platte and C. Liebscher (eds) (Huntington, Juris Publishing, 2007), Section 610, pp. 503 *et seq.*

clarified by the courts, parties should consider as a matter of caution to file a setting aside motion within three months from the receipt of the original award (alone or in parallel with a motion under Article 29).

If the tribunal decided to address additional claims it has omitted from its previous **29-018** decisions, it will also have to address those claims (and attending cost conseqeunces)[29] in the form of an award. However, that award is simply an additional award in its own right (rather than an integral part of the previous award).[30] As a result, it must be challenged separately under Section 611 ZPO, with its own separate and independent deadline.

---

29. A. Reiner, *Das neue österreichische Schiedsrecht/The new Austrian Arbitration Law* (Vienna, LexisNexis, 2006), Section 610, note 189.
30. C. Liebscher, *The Austrian Arbitration Act 2006: Text and Notes* (The Hague, Kluwer Law International, 2006), Annotated Text to Section 610 ZPO.

Article 30

Publishing Awards and Decisions

		Para.			Para.
I.	Publishing Awards	1	III.	Publishing Decisions of the VIAC	6
II.	Publishing Procedural Orders	5			

Article 30: The Board is entitled to publish an award in legal journals or in its own publications in anonymous form, unless publication is objected to by at least one party within thirty days after service of the copy of the award on it.

I.   PUBLISHING AWARDS

There is an increasing desire in international commercial arbitration to make decisions accessible to the public. This trend has many good reasons for it. First, published awards, both on the merits and perhaps even more so on matters of jurisdiction, arbitrability and procedure, would establish a body of precedent which, although not binding *strictu sensu*, would provide guidance to future arbitrators and help establish a uniform application of arbitration law and matters of international commerce.[1]   **30-001**

Traditionalists suggest that the idea of publishing arbitral decisions does not sit easily with the confidential nature of arbitration and the resulting arbitral awards. As discussed elsewhere,[2] however, many commentators appear to have rejected the   **30-002**

---

1. E. Gaillard and J. Savage (eds), *Fouchard Gaillard Goldman On International Commercial Arbitration* (The Hague, Kluwer Law International, 1999), para. 383.
2. *See* **Article 20**, at paras. 156 *et seq.*

notion of a general principle of confidentiality in recent years,[3] although some remain as vigorous defenders of what traditionally has been perceived as one of arbitration's major virtues.[4] Yet confidentiality, even if it were accepted as an overarching principle in arbitration,[5] is not absolute; and it must be distinguished from the privacy of the hearing.[6] Confidentiality is usually not breached by the publication of the reasons of an award on an anonymous basis. Such publication satisfies the general interests of legal practice; the users of arbitration ought to have access to how the rules are applied.

30-003 In many fields, arbitral awards are therefore increasingly made available to the public, in most cases without disclosing the name of the parties. The general concept in other arbitration rules is that the award may be published only with the prior consent of the parties.[7] In Austria, as elsewhere, it is for the parties to determine whether or not they want the award to be published.[8] The Vienna Rules differ slightly from this concept, in that Article 30 assumes such a consent unless 'at least one party' objects against the publication. A party has to do so within thirty days, but does not need to give reasons for its objection. Objections after the thirty day period appear to be irrelevant (although VIAC will, in practice, take any late objection into consideration and will be cautious to publish an award against the will of a party, no matter the timing of the objection). Clearly, if both parties agree, they should be able to prevent the publication on the basis of a joint objection, even where the thirty day period has expired: Article 30 has force only by virtue of the parties' agreement, and can be derogated by the parties as well.

30-004 The decision to publish an award is one of the VIAC, and not the arbitrators. If an arbitrator intends to publish the award, as a rule, he or she will have to seek the prior consent of all parties involved.[9] Arbitrators have no valid claim to intellectual

---

3. *See, e.g.*, J. Paulsson and N. Rawding, 'The Trouble with Confidentiality' (1995) 11(3) Arb Int'l, 304. ('May the mere existence of the dispute be published without the consent of both parties? (. . .) Such disclosures may be unavoidable and harmless.'). *See also* H. Smit, 'Confidentiality in Arbitration' (1995) 11(3) Arb Int'l, 340; J. Lew, 'Expert Report of Dr. Julian D.M. Lew (in Esso/ BHP v. Plowman)' (1995) 11(3) Arb Int'l, 283; H. Bagner, 'Confidentiality-A Fundamental Principle in International Commercial Arbitration?' (2001) 18(2) J Int'l Arb, 248.

4. E. Gaillard and J. Savage (eds), *Fouchard Gaillard Goldman On International Commercial Arbitration* (The Hague, Kluwer Law International, 1999), para. 384 ('There has never been a general tradition of confidentiality').

5. *See* **Article 20**, at para. 162.

6. *See* **Article 20**, at paras. 153 *et seq.*

7. Article 30(3) LCIA Rules; Article 42 DIS Rules and Article 27(4) AAA/ICDR Rules. *See*, however, Article 48(4) ICSID Arbitration Rules: 'The Centre shall not publish the award without the consent of the parties. The Centre shall, however, promptly include in its publications excerpts of the legal reasoning of the Tribunal.'

8. C. Liebscher and A. Schmid in *Practitioner's Handbook on International Arbitration*, F.B. Weigand (ed.) (Munich, C.H. Beck, 2002), p. 577.

9. F. Meyer-Hauser, *Anwaltsgeheimnis und Schiedsgericht*, (Zürich, Schulthess, 2004), paras. 235 *et seq.*

property rights over their awards (save perhaps for being named as arbitrator).[10] However, it is accepted that arbitrators can discuss their decisions, in anonymous and abstract form, in journals and specialized publications, just like any other abstract legal problem. In practice, the VIAC has, perhaps regrettably, to date made rare use of its authority to publish arbitral awards: only two awards issued under the auspices of the VIAC have been published to date, with several further awards to be published soon.[11]

II. PUBLISHING PROCEDURAL ORDERS

The reasons that advocate for the publication of awards also support the publication **30-005** of procedural orders which would arguably, *a majore ad minorem*, be permitted under Article 30 as well. If anything, procedural issues directly relevant to the conduct of arbitration under the Vienna Rules and Austrian arbitration law are even more immediately relevant to users of arbitration than substantive decisions under any variety of applicable law, and hence even more deserving of publication than awards on the merits. It would greatly benefit the process and rule of law if users of arbitration – arbitrators, counsel and parties alike – could rely on a developing body of precedent providing guidance on how the Vienna Rules are applied in practice and how procedural issues are resolved.

III. PUBLISHING DECISIONS OF THE VIAC

Under the Vienna Rules, the Board is regularly called upon to make decisions that **30-006** have potentially a severe impact on the arbitration, such as decisions on the removal of a biased arbitrator,[12] on the early termination of the arbitrator's mandate[13] or the refusal by the VIAC to carry out the proceedings under **Article 9(6)**.[14] As discussed elsewhere,[15] and although it is not obliged to do so under the wording of the Vienna Rules, the Board typically provides reasoned decisions to the parties.[16] This was always helpful to increase the acceptance of the Board's decision in the eyes of the parties, but has gained even more importance now that, for example, decision rejecting an application to disqualify an arbitrator for lack of impartiality

---

10. E. Gaillard and J. Savage (eds), *Fouchard, Gaillard Goldman On International Commercial Arbitration* (The Hague, Kluwer Law International, 1999), para. 384.
11. C. Liebscher and A. Schmid in *Practitioner's Handbook on International Arbitration*, F.B. Weigand (ed.) (Munich, C.H. Beck, 2002), p. 578. These awards are discussed in greater detail under **Article 9**, at para. 96.
12. *See* **Article 16**, at paras. 040 *et seq.*
13. *See* **Article 18**, at para. 006.
14. *See* **Article 9**, at paras. 088 *et seq.*
15. *See* **Article 16**, at para. 045.
16. *See* **Article 3**, at para. 013.

or independence, can be appealed before the courts.[17] To be in a position to review the Board's decision, the state court will be aided by the reasons that the Board has given for rejecting the challenge.

30-007 For similar reasons, however, the VIAC should seriously consider, as other institutions are in the process of doing,[18] to publish its decisions on challenges in anonymous form. In addition to other arguments for increased institutional transparency, a body of publicly available precedent would advance the uniform application of the relevant standards of impartiality and independence.[19] Users of arbitration would benefit greatly from a body of precedent which would enhance the accountability of the institution and the transparency of the overall process. It would also provide useful guidance to arbitrators, and to counsel, in assessing the merits of future challenges or other matters typically arising in institutional arbitration.

---

17. *See* **Article 16**, at paras. 047 *et seq.*
18. G. Nicholas and C. Partasides, 'LCIA Court Decisions on Challenges to Arbitrators: A Proposal to Publish' (2007) 23(1) Arb Int'l, 1.
19. For a persuasive argument in favour of transparency, *see* G. Nicholas and C. Partasides, 'LCIA Court Decisions on Challenges to Arbitrators: A Proposal to Publish' (2007) 23 Arb Int'l, 1.

Article 31

The Award on Costs

		Para.			Para.
I.	Introduction	1	B. The Austrian Approach		42
II.	Determining the Costs of the Arbitration	3	1. Traditional Method of Cost Allocation in Austria		43
III.	Determining the Costs of the Parties	7	2. The Modern Austrian Approach to Cost Allocation in Arbitration		47
	A. Legal Basis	9	V. Determining the Costs Absent		
	B. Determining What Costs Were 'Reasonable'	17	Jurisdiction on the Merits		50
	C. Other Outlay Related to Arbitration Proceedings	29	VI. Procedural Considerations		53
IV.	Allocating the Costs Between the Parties	34	A. Procedure		54
			B. Request for Costs		56
	A. International Trends	36	C. Timing of Cost Decision		58
			D. Form of Cost Decision		60

Article 31: When the arbitral proceedings are terminated, the sole arbitrator (arbitral tribunal) shall, upon application of a party, state in the award on the merits or by separate award: the costs of arbitration fixed by the Secretary General in accordance with Article 34 paragraph 1; shall determine the amount of costs of the parties; and shall state who should bear the costs of the proceedings or the proportion in which the costs of the proceedings are to be shared.

I.   INTRODUCTION

The following section deals mainly with the rules concerning the determination **31-001** and allocation of the party costs of the parties and the arbitration. It examines the duties that arise for the arbitrator(s) in stating the costs in the award on the merits or by separate award, as fixed by the Secretary General and discusses the different concepts and methods used when calculating the amount and allocating the costs of the proceedings. Particular emphasis is not only placed on the relevant rules under Austrian law but, insofar as is practical and necessary, also international standards, and individual cases that in practice often cause debate.

31-002   Although not required under the Vienna Rules, it is recommended for arbitrators to provide reasoning for their costs decision. In fact, this is in line with international practice and Austrian Law. Arbitrators are required to make the cost determination in an award. Whether this is done in the award on the merits, or a separate award, it must comply with all the requirements that Austrian law and the Vienna Rules impose on an award. In particular, cost decisions must be reasoned. As Article 31 makes clear, the arbitrators' cost determination involves three different aspects. First, the arbitrators simply state the administrative costs of the arbitration (that is, the fees for the arbitrators and the VIAC). This does not involve any judicial act on the arbitrators' part, as those costs are determined by the Secretary General under **Article 34(1)**. Second, however, the arbitrators determine the amount of the costs of the parties, most importantly the cost of legal representation, that is reimbursable. In doing so, arbitrators will look at what costs where reasonable incurred in the pursuit of the parties' case. Third, and finally, the arbitrators decide which party, and to what extent, will carry those costs. The determination of the costs of the arbitration proceedings is dealt with in **Article 34(1)** and **Article 36** in greater detail.

II.   DETERMINING THE COSTS OF THE ARBITRATION

31-003   The parties have a right to a decision that contains a determination of costs.[1] This is supported by Article 31 that clearly provides for an obligation of the arbitrators ('*shall state*') to include the costs of arbitration determined by the Secretary General in an award.

31-004   Following the definition of **Article 32(a)**, the *costs of the arbitration* consist of the outlay of the Centre (administrative costs), the arbitrators' fees, plus any value added tax and cash outlay. That definition limits the authority of the Secretary General to fix any further costs that might arise during the arbitration proceedings.[2] Thus, it is for the arbitrators to determine the amount and the legal costs of the parties, and allocate these costs appropriately.

31-005   As regards the costs of the arbitration, however, it is the arbitrator's express obligation to include the costs determined by the Secretary General.[3] For this reason,

---

1. *See also* OGH, 22 March 1995, 7 Ob 647/94.
2. *See* **Article 34**, at para. 003.
3. *See* **Article 34**, at paras. 001 *et seq.*

each arbitrator, with his or her declaration of independence, expressly undertakes to observe the costs provision under the Vienna Rules and acknowledges any costs decision made by the Secretary General as binding upon him or her.[4]

Even if the arbitral tribunal disagrees with the method of determining costs or the **31-006** quantity thereof, it cannot veto or amend the Secretary General's cost decision under the Vienna Rules. Although relatively rare, differences sometimes arise in practice when arbitrators do not keep proper documentation of their cash outlays[5] or oppose the Secretary General's view that the case is not *difficult* enough to justify an increase of the arbitrator's fees.[6]

III. DETERMINING THE COSTS OF THE PARTIES

The time where arbitration proceedings were favoured as an alternative to court **31-007** litigation merely due to cost reasons has come to an end.[7] International arbitration cases by their very nature usually involve complex facts and advanced legal considerations. The preparation of the case, the examination of witnesses in different countries, the requests for different legal opinions in various jurisdictions, the implications on pending court proceedings, and the considerations as to enforceability are just a few indications of the complexity and particularity of international commercial arbitration. Additionally, the tactics employed by some parties in order to torpedo the proceedings become increasingly sophisticated and can as a consequence, increase the cost of arbitration.[8]

When entrusted with the ultimate cost decision, arbitrators face a difficult task. **31-008** There exists no universally valid and recognized system of cost determination. National arbitration laws vary, as do arbitration rules.[9] The lack of a uniform method for resolving claims for costs and fees has resulted in similarly situated parties receiving vastly different awards on costs. At best, this unpredictability makes a case more difficult to settle; at worst, it undermines the legitimacy of the arbitral process.[10] Additionally, arbitrators are to a certain degree responsible for exercising cost control in the arbitral process, particularly through the efficient

---

4. *See* Arbitrator's Declaration of Acceptance, Statement of Independence and Undertaking to Observe Rules on Costs, **Annex 4**.
5. *See* **Article 36(9)**, at paras. 035 *et seq.*
6. *See* **Article 36(6)**, at paras. 028 *et seq.*
7. *See also* F.B. Weigand in *Practitioner's Handbook on International Arbitration*, F.B. Weigand (ed.) (Munich, C.H. Beck, 2002), p. 16.
8. J.Y. Gotanda, 'Awarding Costs and Attorneys' Fees in International Commercial Arbitrations' (1999) 21(1) Mich J Int'l L, 1.
9. M.E. Schneider, 'Lean Arbitration: Cost Control and Efficiency Through Progressive Identification of Issues and Separate Pricing of Arbitration Services' (1994) 10(2) Arb Int'l, 119.
10. J.Y. Gotanda, 'Awarding Costs and attorneys' Fees in International Commercial Arbitrations' (1999) 21(1) Mich J Int'l L, 1, 4.

management of the arbitration.[11] In the end, both, arbitrators and parties share a common responsibility to keep the costs of the proceedings reasonable and in proportion to the nature and complexity of the dispute.

A.   LEGAL BASIS

31-009 The Vienna Rules, as most institutionalized arbitration rules, do not suggest which law to apply in determining the amount and allocation of the costs of the parties. However, most arbitration rules make it clear that the arbitrators will have to follow the prior agreement of the parties.[12] Although the Vienna Rules are entirely silent on this issue, there remains no doubt that arbitrators, in allocating and determining costs, will take into account any prior agreement between the parties.[13] This can be, for example, by reference to a particular legal rule, a basic principle[14] or even a set of rules specifically addressing costs issues.[15]

---

11. *Schneider* considers the complexity of the case as one of the foremost reasons of increased costs. This can be seen when 'classical' international commercial proceedings are compared to arbitrations at commodity exchanges as GAFTA, as these proceedings, although often involving considerable amounts, are resolved relatively swiftly and costly. Possible reasoning is that most cases relate to a number of standard situations which arise out of specimen contracts with a dispute taking place amongst a group of traders who engage in repeated business interactions. Typical international commercial arbitration *proceedings differ:* 'The disputes relate to often complex factual and legal situations which differ largely from one case to another. Standard forms of contract, where they are used, are often those prepared by one of the parties alone; collective standard conditions which exist in some industries ate often employed in versions modified by a particular user or adapted to a particular case. The law applicable to the dispute differs from case to case and frequently the choice of law forms one of the issues to be decided.' *See* M.E. Schneider, 'Lean Arbitration: Cost Control and Efficiency Through Progressive Identification of Issues and Separate Pricing of Arbitration Services' (1994) 10(2) Arb Int'l, 119; *see also* K. Wilson, 'Saving Costs In International Arbitration' (1990) 6(2) Arb Int'l, 151.
12. *See* J. Power and C.W. Konrad, 'Costs in International Arbitration, A Comparative Overview of Civil and Common Law Doctrines' in *Austrian Arbitration Yearbook 2007*, C. Klausegger *et al.* (eds) (Vienna, Manz, 2007), pp. 261 *et seq.*
13. Without explicit reference to the Vienna Rules, this is considered to be a general obligation. *See* J. Lew, L. Mistelis and S. Kröll, *Comparative International Commercial Arbitration* (The Hague, Kluwer Law International, 2003), para. 24-86; M.L. Smith, 'Costs of International Commercial Arbitration' in *American Arbitration Association Handbook on International Arbitration and ADR*, T.E. Carbonneau and J.A. Jaeggi (eds) (Huntington, Juris Publishing, 2006), p. 133; J.Y. Gotanda, 'Awarding Costs and Attorneys' Fees in International Commercial Arbitrations' (1999) 21(1) Mich J Int'l L, 1, 13.
14. Such as the costs follow the event.
15. Such as the Austrian Attorney Tariff Act (*Rechtsanwaltstarifgesetz* – RATG 1969), BGBl No. 189/1969 last amended by BGBl I No. 90/2008.

In case the issue of costs has been clearly agreed between the parties and no further **31-010** evidentiary difficulties arise for the arbitral tribunal, this will in principle not pose a problem. However, absent such clarity, the arbitrators will have to weigh to what extent the determination of a prior agreement on costs between the parties distracts further, disproportionate resources and causes yet further costs to the parties.[16] If the parties have reached respective agreements, those will have to be measured against the threshold of **Article 9(6)**.[17] Lacking such agreements, which will usually be the case, there remains the question which law the arbitral tribunal should apply or follow when making its costs decision.

Different opinions are expressed in international doctrine. According to *Schlosser*, **31-011** in state court proceedings costs are never determined according to the law applicable to the decision on the merits but always according to *lex fori*. A similar rule is argued to apply in international arbitration proceedings, as it is too cumbersome and complicated for the arbitral tribunal to consult rules of foreign law.[18]

Redfern/Hunter argue that 'any specific provision of the *lex arbitri* concerning costs **31-012** must be taken into account'.[19] Some question whether it would be too much for an arbitral tribunal to scrutinize in detail national jurisprudence dealing with cost decisions,[20] and others consider it more appropriate to apply the prevailing rules at the place where the parties' counsels have their place of residence 'since counsel selected by the parties will calculate their fees in accordance with their own national practices, which will not necessarily be those of the place of arbitration'.[21]

The question of the applicable law in costs determination has potentially far reach- **31-013** ing consequences. In Europe, it is undisputed that the arbitrators are entitled to decide on costs. Many national arbitration laws and most of the institutional arbitration rules expressly confer on the arbitrators the authority to do so. U.S. law, however, requires an express authorization of the arbitrators, such that even a general clause authorizing the arbitral tribunal to determine the costs of arbitration is no legal basis for declaring that the winning party may recover its costs.[22]

---

16. *Bydlinski*, in respect to state court proceedings, developed the principle of simplification and proportionality of costs. *See* M. Bydlinski, *Der Kostenersatz im Zivilprozess* (Vienna, Manz, 1992), p. 39. This strict view can, however, be debatable in international commercial arbitration proceedings, as it can happen that the costs expenditure exceed the principal claim.
17. *See* **Article 9(6)**, at paras. 088 *et seq.*
18. P. Schlosser, *Das Recht der internationalen privaten Schiedsgerichtsbarkeit* (2nd edn Tübingen, Mohr Siebeck, 1989), para. 704.
19. A. Redfern, M. Hunter, N. Blackaby and C. Partasides, *Law and Practice of International Commercial Arbitration* (4th edn, London, Sweet & Maxwell, 2004), para. 8-92.
20. J.P. Lachmann, *Handbuch für die Schiedsgerichtspraxis* (3rd edn, Cologne, Verlag Dr. Otto Schmidt, 2008), p. 281.
21. M. Bühler and S. Jarvin in *Practitioner's Handbook on International Arbitration*, F.B. Weigand (ed.) (Munich, C.H. Beck, 2002), p. 297.
22. P. Schlosser, *Das Recht der internationalen privaten Schiedsgerichtsbarkeit* (2nd edn, Tübingen, Mohr Siebeck, 1989), para. 700.

This rule is understood to mean that a tribunal in an U.S. arbitration has the power to award party representation costs to a prevailing party only if the parties' contract, a specific statute or the arbitration rules so allow. Accordingly, the courts have regularly vacated arbitral cost awards for want of authority to award legal fees. Consequently, the arbitration agreement becomes of central importance since courts will uphold a cost award for attorneys' fees only if the arbitration clause expressly contemplates a 'fee-shifting'.[23] Practice shows that arbitration agreements regularly fail to address this issue (properly). In these situations, arbitrators have used their discretion to resolve claims for costs and fees by relying on the applicable national law, the arbitral rules governing the dispute, or principles of fairness and reasonableness. These differing approaches are sometimes difficult to apply and, 'typically result in inconsistent or arbitrary awards.'[24] With respect to the ICC Rules, it has been said:

> Unless otherwise agreed, the arbitrators do not have to follow the judicial rules or practices on cost allocation applicable at the place of arbitration, but it seems that many arbitrators yield to such practices. The merits of this approach are difficult to evaluate – certainly for the parties this represents some practical disadvantages: The lack of a yardstick governing the exercise of this discretion in ICC Rules is combined with the fact that the allocation of costs between the parties in ICC Awards is rarely expressed in great detail. This means that it is not only difficult to predict how the costs may be allocated in a particular case, but also to explain the allocation thereafter.[25]

Most countries consider the decision on costs and fees to be a matter of procedural law. The key rationale for awarding costs to a party is that

> a claimant who is forced to resort to court action to enforce his claim against a reluctant debtor is entitled to recover the full value of the claim and should not be expected to be satisfied with a lesser amount because of the necessity of suing.

In essence, this is a perception of costs akin to consequential damages.[26]

---

23. M. Bühler, 'Awarding Costs in International Commercial Arbitration: an Overview' (2004) 22(2) Bull ASA, 249, 257.
24. 'Some tribunals do not apply a particular law to claim for costs and fees, but instead rely on principles of fairness and reasonableness. The advantage of applying principles of fairness is that it allows arbitrators to tailor awards of costs and fees to the circumstances of each case. However, this flexibility makes it possible that awards will vary substantially from case to case because individual perceptions of what is fair and reasonable can differ significantly.' *See* J.Y. Gotanda, 'Awarding Costs and Attorneys' Fees in International Commercial Arbitrations' (1999) 21(1) Mich J Int'l L, 1, 13.
25. M. Bühler and S. Jarvin in *Practitioner's Handbook on International Arbitration*, F.B. Weigand (ed.) (Munich, C.H. Beck, 2002), p. 300.
26. M Bühler, 'Awarding Costs in International Commercial Arbitration: an Overview' (2004) 22(2) Bull ASA, 249, 251.

While the former arbitration law contained no specific provision on costs, the new **31-014**
arbitration law introduced Section 609 ZPO, a provision explicitly dealing with
costs issues in arbitration proceedings:

(1) If the arbitral proceedings are terminated, the arbitral tribunal shall decide
upon the obligation to reimburse the costs of the proceedings, provided that
the parties have not agreed otherwise. The arbitral tribunal shall, at its
discretion, take into consideration the circumstances of the individual
case, in particular the outcome of the proceedings. The obligation to reimburse may include any and all reasonable costs appropriate for bringing or
defending against the action. In the case referred to in Section 608(2) no. 3
of this act, such a decision shall only be made where a party applies for such
a decision together with the notification upon the agreement to terminate
the proceedings.

(2) Upon the application of the respondent, the arbitral tribunal may also
decide upon the obligation of the plaintiff to reimburse the costs of the
proceedings, if it has declared itself as not competent on the grounds that
there is not arbitration agreement.

(3) Together with the decision upon the liability to pay the costs, the arbitral
tribunal shall, as far as this is already possible and the costs are not set off
against each other, determine the amount of costs to be reimbursed.

(4) In any case, the decision upon liability to pay the costs and the determination of the amount shall be made in the form of an award pursuant to
Section 606 of this act.

(5) If no decision was made upon the liability to pay the costs, or if the
amount to be reimbursed was not determined, or if it was only possible
to determine this after termination of the arbitral proceedings, then the
decision thereupon shall be made in a separate award.

The pertinent provisions of this section are discussed below where appropriate. **31-015**
However, this section achieves two important clarifications. First, for the arbitrators to determine the costs of the arbitration, a specific agreement of the parties is
no longer required. The parties can exclude that power, but if they do not, the
arbitrators can proceed to determine the costs of the arbitration. Second, Section
609 ZPO follows the modern trend in arbitral legislation to liberate cost determination from stringent rules of national procedure. The arbitrators can, at their
discretion, determine what costs are reasonable and therefore recoverable, and
how these costs shall be allocated between the parties.

In summary, practice shows that different approaches are adopted on a case by case **31-016**
basis.[27] Many tribunals tend to award the costs of legal representation without even

---

27. For a comprehensive overview as to how costs in international arbitration are influenced by
domestic court systems and considered by arbitral tribunals in the CEE and SEE regions. *See*
G.J. Horvath, C.W. Konrad and J. Power, *Costs in International Arbitration – A Central and
Southern Eastern European Perspective* (Vienna, Linde, 2008).

discussing questions of applicable law,[28] and Section 609 ZPO, with its discretionary standard, permits them to do so in arbitrations seated in Austria. However, any cost decision has, as a matter of course, to follow the principle of economic efficiency as, '[f]ailure to take into consideration the commercial reality of legal costs may lead to a failure to do justice'.[29]

B.   DETERMINING WHAT COSTS WERE 'REASONABLE'

31-017 As to the amount of costs to be reimbursed, most arbitration rules follow the concept of reasonability[30] or necessity:[31] The winning party is entitled to recover any reasonable costs that were necessary for the pursuit of its rights. Some rules exceptionally limit the power of the arbitral tribunal to apportion costs[32] or even fix a certain maximum in advance.[33]

---

28. G.B. Born, *International Commercial Arbitration – Commentary and Materials* (2nd edn, The Hague, Kluwer Law International, 2001), p. 911.
29. M.L. Smith, 'Costs of International Commercial Arbitration' in *American Arbitration Association Handbook on International Arbitration and ADR*, T.E. Corbonneau and J.A. Jaeggi (eds) (Huntington, Juris Publishing, 2006), p. 132.
30. Article 31(1) ICC Rules in cost of arbitration: '[R]easonable legal and other costs incurred by the parties'. Article 28(3) LCIA Rules: 'The Arbitral Tribunal shall determine and fix the amount of each item comprising such costs on such *reasonable basis* as it thinks fit.' Article 9 Regulation on the Arbitration Fees, Costs and Expenses of the Parties attached to Hungarian Rules speaks of '*justified expenses* of the parties'. Section 1(5) Principles Governing the costs of Arbitral Proceedings attached to the Czech Rules calls for '*The proper expenditures of the parties (proper costs)* shall be the expenditures incurred by the parties in connection with defending their interests (travelling costs, fees of their counsels, etc.).' Article 31 AAA/ ICDR Rules: 'The tribunal shall fix the costs of arbitration in its award. The tribunal may apportion such costs among the parties if it determines that such *apportionment is reasonable, taking into account the circumstances of the case.*' Article 40(2) UNCITRAL Rules: 'With respect to the costs of legal representation and assistance (. . .) the arbitral tribunal, taking into account the circumstances of the case, shall be free to determine which party shall bear such costs or may apportion such costs between the parties if it determines that apportionment is *reasonable.*'
31. Article 35(1) DIS Rules: 'Unless otherwise agreed by the parties, the arbitral tribunal shall also decide in the arbitral award which party is to bear the costs of the arbitral proceedings, including those costs incurred by the parties and which were necessary for the proper pursuit of their claim or defence.'
32. As for example Article 59 CIETAC Rules, on a percentage basis: 'The arbitration tribunal has the power to rule in the arbitral award that the losing party shall pay the winning party as compensation a portion of the expenses reasonably incurred by the winning party in dealing with the case. The amount of such compensation shall not in any case exceed 10% of the total amount awarded to the winning party.'
33. As can be found in Section 43 Polish Rules, where an award shall, *inter alia*, include, 'a decision on the obligation to reimburse costs of the proceedings and representation by a single counsel in proportion to the work input, up to the maximum amount of half of the arbitration fee in the case,

Article 31 of the 1991 Vienna Rules indicated that 'the arbitrators shall decide on **31-018** the proportions in which the costs as well as the costs duly incurred by the parties in respect of legal representation and further expenses for due prosecution of legal claims shall be borne by the parties'. That description of the parties' costs has been eliminated with the amendment in 2001. Now, the Vienna Rules contain a reference to the parties' costs via **Article 32(b)**, which defines the costs of the parties as the '*appropriate expenses* of the parties for their representation and *other outlay* related to the arbitration proceedings'. Further guidance is not provided. What is 'appropriate' in the sense of this provision is ultimately a matter of the arbitrator's discretion. However, Section 609(1) ZPO provides some additional guidance, providing that those costs are reimbursable that were 'reasonable [and] appropriate for bringing or defending against the action.' This introduces a measure of objectivity by focusing on the goal of procedural success. Arguably, this also includes an element of proportionality.

In practice, given the inherent imprecision of those standards, the difficulties that **31-019** occur in assessing 'appropriate' expenses for the parties' representation are manifold. There might be, for example, situations where the use of several co-counsel by one party is perfectly legitimate whereas in other cases it might be considered excessive. Difficulties arise also when counsel from different legal traditions claim costs that are in other jurisdictions considered as legally problematic, such as contingency or success fees.[34] As *Bühler/Jarvin* have put it, no hard and fast rules govern how the amount of 'appropriate' expenses should be calculated. These authors suggest:

> The simplest method is to award a global sum. Generally, this will be a flat rate sum, a breakdown of which is not provided by the arbitrators. Under the standard of 'reasonable legal and other costs', this sum will not necessarily cover the actual costs incurred by the parties. The fact that a party has paid the fees and expenses of its counsel can be viewed as a first indication of their reasonableness. However, since each party is free to manage its litigation resources as it sees fit, the issue is whether it is reasonable to place the financial burden of that party's decision on to the other side.[35]

Wehrli, on the other hand, proposes to list the costs in specific categories, basically **31-020** differentiating between those with and those lacking supporting documents or a

---

however not exceeding *PLN 100,000* or its equivalent in other currency calculated in accordance with the average rate of the Polish currency against other currencies as announced by the National Bank of Poland on the date preceding the award.'

34. *See* J. Power and C.W. Konrad, 'Costs in International Arbitration, A Comparative Overview of Civil and Common Law Doctrines' in *Austrian Arbitration Yearbook 2008*, C. Klausegger *et al.* (eds) (Vienna, Manz, 2008), p. 412.

35. M. Bühler and S. Jarvin in *Practitioner's Handbook on International Arbitration*, F.B. Weigand (ed.) (Munich, C.H. Beck, 2002), p. 299.

specific billing period. As a practical solution he suggests to pass those lists to the other side's counsel and leave the arbitral tribunal to decide only on those positions that are disputed by the other party.[36]

31-021 The question of which costs are appropriate has differing answers in various jurisdictions.[37] Often it is the amount in dispute that is decisive; sometimes it is the complexity of the case. *Bühler/Jarvin* additionally would consider the amount of separate claims and counter-claims or the need to mobilize independent resources, such as on foreign law. They suggest:

> By comparing the costs of one party with the costs of the other party, the Arbitral Tribunal may also get some sense of the reasonableness. However, a party having the burden of proof with respect to evidence that may be largely located out of its hands, possibly in a distant country, is likely to incur higher costs than its opponent. There may be other reasons why the costs of one side are much higher than those of the other and nevertheless reasonable.[38]

31-022 *Redfern/Hunter*[39] refer to a number of Iran-US Claims Tribunal awards which on costs issues followed the test of reasonableness established by *Howard M. Holtzmann* in an award in the US-Iran claims tribunal.[40] *Holtzmann* posed the following questions. Firstly, were such costs claimed in the arbitration? Secondly, was employing lawyers necessary in this case? Thirdly, are the amounts of such costs reasonable? And fourthly, are there circumstances in this case that make it reasonable to apportion such costs? He further argued:

> A test of reasonableness is not, however, an invitation to mere subjectivity. Objective tests of reasonableness of lawyers' fees are well known. Such tests typically assign weight primarily to the time spent and complexity of the case.

---

36. D. Wehrli, 'Zu Höhe und Umfang erstattungsfähiger Parteikosten' in *DIS-Materialien, Kosten im Schiedsverfahren – Tagungsbeiträge* (Cologne, 2005), p. 62.
37. In the US, many courts determine the amount of reasonable attorneys fees using the lodestar figure, which is the number of hours reasonably spent on the matter multiplied by a reasonable hour rate. *See* J.Y. Gotanda, 'Awarding Costs and Attorneys' Fees in International Commercial Arbitrations' (1999) 21(1) Mich J Int'l L, 1, 46. According to *Black's Law Dictionary* reasonable amount of attorney's fees in a given case, usually calculated by multiplying a reasonable number of hours worked by the prevailing hourly rate in the community for similar work, and often considering such additional factors as the degree of skill and difficulty involved in the case, the degree of its urgency, its novelty, and the like. Most statutes that authorize an award of attorney's fees use the 'lodestar method' for computing the award. *See* B.A. Garner, *Black's Law Dictionary* (8th edn, St. Pauls, Thomson West, 2004), definition of 'lodestar'.
38. M. Bühler and S. Jarvin in *Practitioner's Handbook on International Arbitration*, F.B. Weigand (ed.) (Munich, C.H. Beck, 2002), p. 299.
39. A. Redfern, M. Hunter, N. Blackaby and C. Partasides, *Law and Practice of International Commercial Arbitration* (4th edn, London, Sweet & Maxwell, 2004), para. 8-91.
40. *See* Iran-US Claims Tribunal, 27 June 1985, *Sylvania Technical Systems, Inc. v. The Government of the Islamic Republic of Iran*, as reported in (1986) XI YB Comm Arb, 290, 302.

In modern practice, the amount of time required to be spent is often a gauge of the extent of the complexities involved. Where the Tribunal is presented with copies of bills for services, or other appropriate evidence, indicating the time spent, the hourly billing rate, and a general description of the professional services rendered, its task need be neither onerous nor mysterious. The range of typical hourly billing rates is generally known and, as evidence before the Tribunal in various cases including this one indicates, it does not greatly differ between the United States and countries of Western Europe, where both Claimants and Respondents before the Tribunal typically hire their outside counsel. Just how much time any lawyer reasonably needs to accomplish a task can be measured by the number of issues involved in a case and the amount of evidence requiring analysis and presentation. While legal fees are not to be calculated on the basis of the pounds of paper involved, the Tribunal by the end of a case is able to have a fair idea, on the basis of the submissions made by both sides, of the approximate extent of the effort that was reasonably required.[41]

This has considerable force. As arbitration proceedings do not regularly follow a **31-023** fixed schedule and the issue of costs determination imports a strong subjective element, statements on such important issues such as cost determination obviously must remain vague and open for interpretation. Some authors consider, very generally, that the costs 'must be incurred in activities that are normal and necessary for the arbitration'[42] whilst others notice that arbitral tribunals suggest a 'broadbrush' approach in assessing the amount to be paid.[43]

From an Austrian perspective, the new arbitration law introduced a specific **31-024** provision dealing with cost determination and allocation. Section 609(1) ZPO provides in relevant part:

> The arbitral tribunal shall, at its discretion, take into consideration the circumstances of the individual case, in particular the outcome of the proceedings. The obligation to reimburse may include any and all reasonable costs appropriate for bringing or defending against the action.

---

41. *See* Iran-US Claims Tribunal, 27 June 1985, *Sylvania Technical Systems, Inc. v. The Government of the Islamic Republic of Iran*, as reported in (1986) XI YB Comm Arb, 290, 302.
42. J.Y. Gotanda, 'Awarding Costs and Attorneys' Fees in International Commercial Arbitrations' (1999) 21(1) Mich J Int'l L, 1, 45.
43. A. Redfern, M. Hunter, N. Blackaby and C. Partasides, *Law and Practice of International Commercial Arbitration* (4th edn, London, Sweet & Maxwell, 2004), para. 8-96. In another case, *Final Award in ICC Case No. 8486 of 1996* (1999) XXIVa YB Comm Arb, 162, 173, an arbitral tribunal argued that: 'The normality of the legal costs is defined according to the general principles of the law on the costs of arbitration. It is decisive to this aim whether the legal costs are objectively necessary and adequate with respect to the factual and legal complexity of the case, including the presumable time spent (for the proceedings).'

31-025 This provision, which follows Section 1057 German ZPO,[44] is based on Section 41 ZPO as well as Section 78 AußStrG.[45] Following these provisions, only those costs are considered reimbursable that were *necessary* for the *adequate* pursuit of the claim. 'Adequate' means a procedural act that is able to realize the procedural aim of the party, while 'necessary' means an act whose purpose cannot be achieved by lesser effort.[46] 'Reasonableness', however, is still the key criterion when it comes to determination of costs in arbitration. According to the concept of 'reasonableness', costs are typically considered reasonable where the party's actions in creating such costs support it in proving its cause of action. Furthermore, although this raises significant difficulties in practice, it has been argued that the party claiming costs must show that the results of each action could not have been achieved by lesser efforts or funds.[47]

31-026 Initially, the legislature contemplated not adopting even these basic principles for cost determination as this would, in its opinion, 'contradict the approach of more flexibility in the arbitration proceeding, and could alienate parties from different legal backgrounds that oppose to the continental European law of costs disbursement'.[48] It is understood that Section 609 ZPO provision allows the arbitrators – detached from national law – to adopt a flexible approach in their costs determination.[49] Notably, however, Section 609 ZPO requires the arbitral tribunal to determine the amount of costs, rather than merely quota ruling.[50]

---

44. Section 1057 German ZPO reads: '(1) Unless the parties agree otherwise, the arbitral tribunal shall allocate, by means of an arbitral award, the costs of the arbitration as between the parties, including those incurred by the parties necessary for the proper pursuit of their claim or defence. It shall do so at its discretion and take into consideration the circumstances of the case, in particular the outcome of the proceedings.
   (2) To the extent that the costs of the arbitral proceedings have been fixed, the arbitral tribunal shall also decide on the amount to be borne by each party. If the costs have not been fixed or if they can only be fixed once the arbitral proceedings have been terminated, the decision shall be taken by means of a separate award.'

45. *See* J. Power, *The Austrian Arbitration Act – A Practitioner's Guide to Sections 577-618 of the Austrian Code of Civil Procedure* (Vienna, Manz, 2006), Section 609, para. 3.

46. R. Fucik in *Kommentar zur ZPO*, W.H. Rechberger (ed.) (3rd edn, Vienna/New York, Springer, 2006), Section 41 ZPO, para. 5.

47. J. Power, *The Austrian Arbitration Act – A Practitioner's Guide to Sections 577-618 of the Austrian Code of Civil Procedure* (Vienna, Manz, 2006), Section 609, para. 3.

48. *See* draft to Explanatory Notes to Section 609 ZPO.

49. *See* P. Oberhammer, *Entwurf eines neuen Schiedsverfahrensrechts* (Vienna, Manz, 2002), p. 125. Note that the initial draft also contained the indication that: 'As to which costs are to be viewed as appropriate, the arbitral tribunal shall determine this at is own discretion in consideration of the circumstances of the individual cases and without granting a hearing of evidence'. This has not been adopted in the new law.

50. Section 609(3) ZPO: 'Together with the decision upon the liability to pay the costs, the arbitral tribunal shall, as far as this is already possible and the costs are not set off against each other, determine the amount of costs to be reimbursed.'

Because of the particular nature of arbitration, it seems unlikely that an arbitral **31-027**
tribunal would decline to award a party its representation costs simply because
the attorney's fees are higher than those which are usually applied for in
litigation proceedings at the place of the arbitration.[51] The Austrian ZPO
contains no mandatory provisions on attorneys' costs.[52] In practice, these
costs are determined either on an hourly rate or in accordance with the
Attorney Tariff Act (*Rechtsanwaltstarifgesetz* – RATG). The Attorney Tariff
Act contains cost scales, depending on the amount in dispute, for typical
procedural actions (e.g. filing of a claim, written submissions, trial hearings).
This set of rules is also relevant for determining an advocate's fee if there is no
specific agreement between the advocate and the client. However, if the
Attorney Tariff Act does not contain any provisions for specific actions, in
the absence of an agreement, lawyers are usually entitled to an 'appropriate
amount' of fees. The appropriateness is usually determined by the Autonomous
Fee Guidelines for Attorneys (*Autonome Honorar-Richtlinien* – AHR) of the
General Assembly of the Austrian Bar '*Rechtsanwaltskammertag*' in its version of 10 October 2005, which provides for calculation formulae in almost
all kinds of proceedings and which in turn refer to the Attorney Tariff Act's
cost scales in most cases. The Autonomous Fee Guidelines for Attorneys
are not official Austrian 'law' but are guidelines developed by the Austrian
Bar Association.[53]

Different expectations can exist as to how detailed a party should be obliged to **31-028**
itemize the actual costs that it incurred. While this will be relatively easy in
case of expert fees or costs of translators, practical difficulties can arise in case
of payment for third parties, such as witness expenses[54] or travel costs. This
issue should be clarified with the tribunal and the parties at the beginning of
the proceedings. It is noteworthy to emphasize that under the former Austrian
arbitration law the costs determination of the arbitral tribunal legally only
affected the parties to the proceedings. The arbitral tribunal was entitled to
determine the costs of a third party, such as an expert or a witness, but only

---

51. K.P. Berger, *Internationale Wirtschaftsschiedsgerichtsbarkeit* (Berlin/New York, de Gruyter, 1992), p. 431.
52. C. Liebscher and A. Schmid in *Practitioner's Handbook on International Arbitration*, F.B. Weigand (ed.) (Munich, C.H. Beck, 2002), p. 577.
53. E. Feil and F. Wenning, *Anwaltsrecht* (4th edn, Vienna, Linde Verlag, 2006), Section 1 RATG, para. 2.
54. It is, in any way, questionable how far witnesses expenses should in general be reimbursed or be recoverable in an arbitration proceeding. These costs may require different treatment, so that such costs are borne by the party calling the witness or by the party in whose favour the witness gives evidence. Similar considerations apply to interpreters and translation costs. *See* M. Bühler and S. Jarvin in *Practitioner's Handbook on International Arbitration*, F.B. Weigand (ed.) (Munich, C.H. Beck, 2002), p. 300.

with legal effect amongst the parties to the arbitration.[55] Neither the parties to the arbitration could (exclusively) base their potential claim against the third party on the arbitration award or *vice versa*.

C.   OTHER OUTLAY RELATED TO ARBITRATION PROCEEDINGS

31-029 The amendment in 2001 of the Vienna Rules already extended the arbitrator's authority to determine not only the appropriate expenses of the parties' representation but also to determine *other outlay related to the arbitration proceedings*.[56] That is done, as with the costs of representation, by an indirect reference through the definition of **Article 32(b)**. There, reference is made to certain actions entailing costs, such as the appointment of experts, interpreters or translators, verbatim records, visual inspections, or relocation of the proceedings according to **Article 35**. All these costs occur due to procedural steps taken by the arbitrators *'for the benefit of'* or *'on behalf of'* the parties.[57] Besides, as indicated by the wording 'in particular', there expenditures can occur that are outlays not caused by procedural decisions of the tribunal, but by the parties themselves. Most of such can be seen as 'appropriate expenses of the parties'.

31-030 However, the distinction between 'appropriate expenses for representation' and 'other outlay related to the arbitration proceedings' is essential, notwithstanding that the authority to determine both now lies with the arbitral tribunal. Strictly interpreted, the subjective element of appropriateness only covers the expenses of the parties for their representation and not other outlays incurred – this follows the wording of **Article 32(b)**. Consequently, this would mean that, lacking a test of appropriateness, any cash outlay would have to be considered reimbursable. This provision requires a broader reading. Hence, both the expenses of the parties for their representation and other outlays incurred in the proceedings are determined by the discretion of the arbitrators and, therefore, all under the *test of appropriateness*.

31-031 Besides the costs explicitly mentioned in **Article 35**, parties, sometimes influenced by their different legal backgrounds, often claim other costs such as executive costs of in-house counsel. These costs are sometimes referred to as 'executive time', which have traditionally been viewed as part of the normal costs of running a department or business enterprise. No general practice as to the treatment of costs

---

55. H.W. Fasching, *Schiedsgericht und Schiedsverfahren im österreichischein und im internationalen Recht* (Vienna, Manz, 1973), p. 129; C. Liebscher and A. Schmid in *Practitioner's Handbook on International Arbitration*, F.B. Weigand (ed.) (Munich, C.H. Beck, 2002), p. 577 with reference to OGH 30 October 1995, ZfRV 1986, 141.
56. An authority initially entrusted to the Secretary. Article 23(1) Vienna Rules 1991 read: 'The costs of arbitration (administrative costs, arbitrators' fees, cash outlay on such as experts' fees, travelling and subsistence expenses of arbitrators and experts, rental amounts, costs of minuting, interpretation and translation) shall be fixed by the Secretary.'
57. *See also* **Article 35**, at paras. 001 *et seq*.

in international commercial arbitration can be discerned.[58] However, the view that these costs should be considered recoverable has gained increased acceptance by academics and in arbitral practice alike.[59] From an Austrian perspective, there are no regulations on the costs of in-house lawyers; the Vienna Rules are also silent on this issue.[60] However, **Article 23** has introduced the right of the parties to be advised – in addition to the regular representation – by persons of their choice. This can be seen as opening the Vienna Rules to other forms of reimbursement than for 'classic' party representation.

Difficulties arise when party counsel claim contingency fees or similar success fee based agreements concluded with their clients. In some jurisdictions, including in Austria, a *pactum de quota litis* is considered impermissible.[61] In any event, it is doubtful at best if such arrangements constitute 'adequate' or 'necessary' costs in the sense discussed above. Frequently, parties also claim costs that are (directly or indirectly) connected to the arbitration proceedings rather than arising out of the arbitration as such.[62] To some authors the costs of previous litigation are not costs of the arbitral proceedings as parties will be reimbursed for these costs by the applicable costs decision in that previous state court litigation.[63] However, there are circumstances, be it because the costs decision in the court proceeding did not cover the whole claim for costs or be it perhaps because there was no cost disbursement in that particular type of proceeding, that could justify a claim for compensation for costs in the subsequent arbitration proceedings. Arbitral tribunals tend to take a rather restrictive approach on this issue.[64]

31-032

---

58. A. Redfern, M. Hunter, N. Blackaby and C. Partasides, *Law and Practice of International Commercial Arbitration* (4th edn, London, Sweet & Maxwell, 2004), para. 8-88.

59. M. Bühler, 'Awarding Costs in International Commercial Arbitration: an Overview' (2004) 22(2) Bull ASA, 249, 275.

60. *See* J. Power and C.W. Konrad, 'Costs in International Arbitration, A Comparative Overview of Civil and Common Law Doctrines' *in Austrian Arbitration Yearbook 2008*, C. Klausegger *et al.* (eds) (Vienna, Manz, 2008), p. 414; C. Liebscher and A. Schmid in *Practitioner's Handbook on International Arbitration*, F.B. Weigand (ed.) (Munich, C.H. Beck, 2002), p. 577. *Oberhammer* noted in the initial draft to Section 609 ZPO that it was considered to include a demonstrable list of reimbursable costs. Thereby, it was intended to express in particular that those costs reimbursable in arbitration proceedings can exceed those costs in court proceedings, by considering, for example, costs for in-house counsel in legal departments. *See* P. Oberhammer, *Entwurf eines neuen Schiedsverfahrensrechts* (Vienna, Manz, 2002), p. 125.

61. *See* Section 879 ABGB. Note that the agreement on success fee is, under specific circumstances permissible, the differentiation is difficult to make. *See* J. Power and C.W. Konrad, 'Costs in International Arbitration, A Comparative Overview of Civil and Common Law Doctrines' in *Austrian Arbitration Yearbook 2008*, C. Klausegger *et al.* (eds) (Vienna, Manz, 2008), p. 412.

62. For example, like prior court proceedings on the question of competency, assistance by state courts, or costs occurred by an appointing authority.

63. R. Trittmann and C. Duve in *Practitioner's Handbook on International Arbitration* F.B. Weigand (ed.) (Munich, C.H. Beck, 2002), p. 367, with explicit reference to the exclusive character of Article 38 UNCITRAL Rules.

64. In the *Award in ICC Case No. 5946 of 1990*, (1991) XVI YB Comm Arb, 97, 112, the Arbitral Tribunal refused to grant legal fees in connection with court proceedings as 'Claimant has

31-033 The authority of the arbitral tribunal to fix the costs to be reimbursed (in the form of an arbitral award) in Section 609(3) ZPO has also not changed prior law which provided that every party upon whom an arbitral tribunal (and not the arbitral institution) has imposed their own fees may have the courts review them. Whilst pursuant to Section 607 ZPO an arbitral award has the effect, as between the parties, of a legally effective court judgement, it does not have such an effect as between the parties and the arbitrators.[65] An arbitral tribunal may, however, decide how such costs will be reimbursed where the amount of such costs is agreed between the parties or remains undisputed.[66]

IV.   ALLOCATING THE COSTS BETWEEN THE PARTIES

31-034 It is sometimes argued that one major disadvantage of arbitration proceedings is the unpredictability of the cost decision. The expectation as to which costs will be considered reasonable and in that sense recoverable differ widely and are, as discussed, based largely on the parties' different background and legal culture. Once these costs have been determined, it remains for the arbitrators to allocate these costs amongst the parties, thereby ultimately assessing the parties' cost exposure in the proceedings. Unpredictability might be even worse in matters of allocation, as different practices exist and arbitral tribunals can and have reached different conclusions on this issue based on the same facts and law.

31-035 This calls for establishing a widely accepted principle for the allocation of costs. It is argued here that in international commercial arbitration, arbitrators should, as a rule, allocate costs in a manner which reflects the parties' relative success and failure in the arbitration, unless special circumstances warrant an exception or the parties otherwise agree.[67] This is discussed below.

---

violated the arbitration clause in the Agreement by bringing suit before the United States Federal District Court in New York rather than instituting arbitration proceedings (. . .) in the light of the clear arbitration clause contained in the agreement, the refusal of claimant to submit the dispute to arbitration must be considered sufficiently frivolous and unreasonable to warrant of attorneys fees against it'. In the *Award in ICC Case No. 6268 of 1990*, (1991) XVI YB Comm Arb, 119, 125 *et seq.*, the Arbitral Tribunal argued that 'we do not read Art 20 to encompass legal costs incurred in judicial proceedings ancillary to the arbitration. The only theory on which seller might recover the costs would be as damages for breach of the agreement to arbitrate. However, seller has not advanced such a theory or attempted to present evidence in support of it'.

65. *See* A. Reiner, *Das neue österreichische Schiedsrecht/The new Austrian Arbitration Law* (Vienna, LexisNexis, 2006), Section 610, note 180.

66. J. Power, *The Austrian Arbitration Act – A Practitioner's Guide to Sections 577-618 of the Austrian Code of Civil Procedure* (Vienna, Manz, 2006), Section 609, para. 3.

67. M. Bühler, 'Awarding Costs in International Commercial Arbitration: an Overview' (2004) 22(2) Bull ASA, 249, 268.

A.   INTERNATIONAL TRENDS

Article 31 authorizes the arbitrators, after having determined the amount of costs, **31-036** to 'state who should bear the costs of the proceedings or the proportion in which the costs of the proceedings are to be shared'. It thereby entrusts the arbitrators with absolute discretion, which to a greater or lesser extent can be found in the rules of other arbitral institutions.[68]

In international practice, there are a great variety of ways in which costs are **31-037** allocated and of factors that are likely to influence this allocation. The primary principle seems to be, however, that costs follow the event. This seems internationally recognized and, by some commentators, considered as a *general principle of international law* and *prevailing practice in the international arena*,[69] for others it is axiomatic in most jurisdictions.[70] It encourages claimants 'to proceed more cautiously and to proceed only with higher quality claims'[71] and honours the most decisive factor in relation to the allocation of procedural costs, that is, the outcome of the proceedings.[72]

On the one hand, a claimant succeeding in all of its claims can usually expect that **31-038** the unsuccessful respondent will be ordered to pay the procedural costs of the arbitration in full. On the other hand, the respondent can expect the claimant to be burdened with the costs where the claim is dismissed or the arbitral tribunal found not to be competent.[73] Where neither party is completely successful, it is practice to allocate the costs proportionate to the outcome of the substantive issues in the proceedings. That principle can be found in many arbitration rules.[74] In those

---

68. *See* **Article 31**, at para. 017.
69. J.Y. Gotanda, 'Awarding Costs and Attorneys' Fees in International Commercial Arbitrations' (1999) 21(1) Mich J Int'l L, 1, 34; *also* J.Y. Gotanda, *Supplemental Damages in Private International Law* (The Hague, Kluwer Law International, 1998), pp. 173-192.
70. M.L. Smith, 'Costs in International Commercial Arbitration' in *American Arbitration Association Handbook on International Arbitration and ADR*, T.E. Carbonneau and J.A. Jaeggi (eds) (Huntington, Juris Publishing, 2006), p. 127.
71. J.Y. Gotanda, 'Awarding Costs and Attorneys' Fees in International Commercial Arbitrations' (1999) 21(1) Mich J Int'l L, 1, 46.
72. Although the rule that 'costs follow the event' has a longstanding tradition in Europe, a comparative analysis of cost practices in European civil procedure rules reveals a picture of 'confusing variety and complexity'. Not only is the 'costs follow the event' rule subject to a wide range of different qualifications, but even the understanding of who 'won' the case may not be the same depending on which national civil procedure is applied. *See* M. Bühler, 'Awarding Costs in International Commercial Arbitration: an Overview' (2004) 22(2) Bull ASA, 249, 252.
73. Cost decision in case of lack of jurisdiction, *see* **Article 31**, at paras. 050 *et seq.*
74. Article 28(4) LCIA Rules; similar in Article 35(2) DIS Rules 'In principle, the unsuccessful party shall bear the costs of the arbitral proceedings. The arbitral tribunal may, taking into consideration the circumstances of the case, and in particular where each party is partly successful and partly unsuccessful, order each party to bear his own costs or apportion the costs between the parties.' Article 3 Decision on Costs attached to Croatian Rules reflects 'the success

arbitration laws and rules, which expressly provide that costs follow the event, however, this principle is by no means made absolute. It is invariably subject to the broad exception that the arbitrator, in the exercise of his discretion, may depart from the presumption if the circumstances of the case so require.[75]

31-039 When looking at the outcome, it may be insufficient to take a mathematical view by comparing the amount claimed and the amount awarded. For a claimant to succeed on the issue of liability may be major achievement, and may have required significant resources to obtain. Likewise, the scope of work of an arbitral tribunal would not necessarily have been reduced if the claimant had only pursued the strict minimum of its entitlement. On the other hand, the gross exaggeration of a claim may have led to additional work for the arbitral tribunal. The failure, or successful outcome, on an issue on which a large amount of time and effort were spent may also be taken into account.[76]

31-040 The allocation of costs is sometimes also made entirely irrespective of the outcome of the proceedings. This particularly happens where the (counter-) claims raised and set-off(s) declared make it practically impossible to analyze how much of the costs incurred relate to the specific procedural action. The simplest approach for such cases is that each party pays its own legal costs.

31-041 An emerging trend, when allocating costs between the parties, is to recognize the parties' attitude during the proceedings.[77] When delaying tactics are employed, proceedings may get very lengthy and expensive, and cost awards seem an appropriate instrument to sanction uncooperative behaviour by either party.[78]

---

in the proceedings and other relevant circumstances'. Same in Article 44(1) Slovenian Rules. Different in Section 12 attached to the Czech Rules: 'As a rule, each party shall bear itself the costs incurred by it. If good cause is shown a partial coverage of these costs by the other party may be adjudicated to such party, having incurred same.'

75. M. Bühler, 'Awarding Costs in International Commercial Arbitration: an Overview' (2004) 22(2) Bull ASA, 249, 265.
76. J.Y. Gotanda, 'Awarding Costs and Attorneys' Fees in International Commercial Arbitrations' (1999) 21(1) Mich J Int'l L, 1, 46.
77. J. Lew, L. Mistelis and S. Kröll, *Comparative International Commercial Arbitration* (The Hague, Kluwer Law International, 2003), para. 24-79.
78. *See, e.g., Award in ICC Case No. 8486 of 1996*, (1999) XXIVa YB Comm Arb, 162, 171, where the tribunal held that the defendant lost its counter-claim and claimant's claim was granted only in part. The award states: 'Nonetheless, the costs of the arbitration shall be borne totally by the defendant. According to the general principles of international arbitration law, the arbitral tribunal must take into account for its decision on costs not only the result of the proceedings but also the behaviour of the parties during the proceedings. According to good faith, the parties to an international arbitration must in particular facilitate the proceedings and abstain from all delaying tactics. The behaviour of the defendant during the entire proceedings did not comply with these requirements in any way. The defendant made none of the advance payments on costs which are required for the proceedings. Further, not only did it file its counterclaim belatedly, that is, only after the first draft of the Terms of Reference; it also refuses to sign the Terms of Reference (. . .).'

Cost allocation may therefore sanction a party whose conduct prior or during the arbitration has added unnecessary cost and delay to the proceedings, or take into account the amicable and professional cooperation of parties in the resolution of the dispute.[79] This approach can in fact be found in some arbitration rules in the CEE region.[80] An interesting study, undertaken by the ICC Court's Secretariat in 1991, can be found in *Derains/Schwartz*, assessing over a period of two years costs decisions in ICC arbitration cases.[81] The results of this study reflect to a great extent the approaches as discussed above.

B.   THE AUSTRIAN APPROACH

As with all matters touching upon the powers of the arbitral tribunal, any specific **31-042** provision of the *lex arbitri* concerning costs must be considered by the arbitral tribunal.[82] The practice of national courts in awarding costs, by contrast, has no

---

79. M. Bühler and S. Jarvin in *Practitioner's Handbook on International Arbitration*, F.B. Weigand (ed.) (Munich, C.H. Beck, 2002), p. 300. In the *Award in ICC Case No. 6955 of 1993*, (1999) XXIVa YB Comm Arb, 107, 139, the Arbitral Tribunal has quite directly addressed this issue as follows: 'The tribunal is reluctant to award costs in favour of either party. Not only has the claimant in this case not fully succeeded, but the dispute in this instance is one that could have been handled in a more commercially effective manner (. . .). Neither party has contributed in any way to lessening the number or complexity of the issues to be resolved by the tribunal on the contrary, each has contributed to inflate this arbitration in particular by raising numerous procedural matters. Therefore, the tribunal has no difficulty in deciding that each party shall bear an equal share of the costs of the arbitration, including all the costs relating to the sampling and the testing in this arbitration; likewise, each party shall bear the legal costs, including lawyers' fees that it has in occurred in its defence.'

80. Article 13 Rules Governing the Costs of Arbitration Proceedings before the Court of Arbitration of the Slovak Chamber of Commerce and Industry: 'The Court of Arbitration may derogate (. . .) and hold a party liable for the expenses that have been unnecessarily incurred by the opposing party as a result of the former party's ineffective or unnecessary acts. These acts shall include any act that has caused unnecessary expenses for the other party because it was not necessary, in particular expenses caused by unreasonable delays in the proceedings.' *See also* Section 13 Principles attached to Czech Rules: '(. . .), the Arbitration Court shall be free to impose a duty to pay the costs of the party incurred by it in vain as result of unnecessary of reckless steps by that party. Such unnecessary or reckless steps shall mean steps causing unnecessary costs to the other party in connection with taking steps in the proceedings that were unnecessary, particularly by circumstances leading to unjustified prolongation of the proceedings.' And Article 10 Regulation attached to the Hungarian Rules: '(. . .) the Arbitration Court may prescribe for a party to pay such surplus costs which have been caused by his inexpedient or unjustified acts or procedural acts carried out in bad faith. In this category are, among others, procedural acts, which cause surplus costs due to the taking of measures proving to be unnecessary (*e.g.*, causing a delay of the proceedings unjustified by the circumstances of the case).'

81. *See* Y. Derains and E.A. Schwartz, *A Guide to the ICC Rules of Arbitration* (2nd edn, The Hague, Kluwer Law International, 2005), p. 417.

82. A. Redfern, M. Hunter, N. Blackaby and C. Partasides, *Law and Practice of International Commercial Arbitration* (4th edn, London, Sweet & Maxwell, 2004), para. 8-97.

legally-binding impact on the way in which an international arbitral tribunal should exercise the discretion granted in the cost decision. National practices may, however, have a more subtle impact on the treatment of costs: arbitrators are not always immune to the influence of their own domestic civil procedures, or national arbitral practice and, in reality, tend to follow their approach.[83] In that respect, the following section deals with the method of cost allocation in Austria, as it was practised traditionally, and the proceeds to examine the impact of the new Austrian arbitration law.

1.   Traditional Method of Cost Allocation in Austria

31-043 Under Austrian arbitration law prior to the 2006 reform, there was no provision on the allocation of costs of the arbitration. Austrian scholarship, however, has argued that the provisions on legal costs under Sections 41 *et seq.* ZPO shall be applied by analogy in so far as the parties did not agree otherwise.[84] Leaving aside the general reluctance to apply by analogy provisions of state court litigation to international arbitration,[85] under these provisions, the calculation and determination of costs incurred during legal proceedings is made according to the principle of absolute liability (*Prinzip der Erfolgshaftung*). This principle states that the allocation of costs depends on the ultimate success of a party in the proceedings, rather than the success of a party with respect to particular issues. Hence, reimbursement of the full costs is granted to the respondent even if only one of its objections proves successful or, *vice versa*, if only one ground for the claimant's claim has been found valid, leading to a success on the merits. If the claimant succeeds on basis of an alternative claim (*Eventualbegehren*), it shall obtain full reimbursement calculated on the basis of this claim alone. The same applies if the respondent is successful only due to a counter-claim raised in the equal amount as the amount of the claim.[86] These principles follow the rationale that the person whose position proves to be justified and who therefore rightly commenced the proceedings shall not suffer any disadvantage due to the costs incurred even if some of its arguments failed.[87]

31-044 The application of these principles will be difficult where the success or defeat of either party cannot be ascertained with precision. Monetary claims, in particular, are sometimes only partially successful. Section 43 ZPO sets forth certain basic principles applicable to such situations.[88] First, it requires that each party shall be

---

83. M. Bühler, 'Awarding Costs in International Commercial Arbitration: an Overview' (2004) 22(2) Bull ASA, 249, 257.
84. C. Liebscher and A. Schmid in *Practitioner's Handbook on International Arbitration*, F.B. Weigand (ed.) (Munich, C.H. Beck, 2002), p. 574.
85. *See* **Article 2**, at para. 017.
86. R. Fucik in *Kommentar zur ZPO*, W.H. Rechberger (ed.) (3rd edn, Vienna/New York, Springer, 2006), Section 41 ZPO, para. 1.
87. M. Bydlinski, *Der Kostenersatz im Zivilprozess* (Vienna, Manz, 1992), p. 39.
88. Freely translated – Section 43 ZPO: '(1) In the event each party succeeds and partly fails in an action, the expenses shall be set off against each other or proportionally split between the parties.

burdened with at least a portion of the legal costs. Second, it provides for exceptions, in which parties may receive full reimbursement in spite of partial loss of the claim. In the event each party partly succeeds and partly fails with its claim, the costs shall be set off against each other or be split in proportion between the parties. Setting-off of the costs means that neither party is entitled to recover the full amount of its expenses. When the costs are divided, this can be in figures or in percentages. If, for example, the claimant is successful on three quarters regarding his initial claim, he will be entitled to three quarters of his costs, but shall indemnify the respondent of one quarter of respondent's costs. Consequently, this means, after setting off those claims, that claimant is entitled to receive disbursement of half of his costs.

An exception from the principle of absolute liability can be found when a party is **31-045** liable for intentionally making allegations or submitting evidence at a late stage, thus delaying the resolution of the dispute. In such cases the successful party shall nevertheless be burdened with the full costs of proceedings. However, even a successful claimant must indemnify the respondent for his expenses if the respondent had immediately admitted the claim after receipt of the statement of claims and his behaviour was generally not responsible for the initiation of the proceedings.[89]

If Sections 41 *et seq.* ZPO are applicable, the unsuccessful party must, in principle, **31-046** compensate the other party for costs of the arbitral procedure, costs of representation, as well as certain expenses. In a recent decision, the Austrian *Oberster Gerichtshof* held also that Section 54(a) ZPO is applicable to costs which have been awarded to one party. According to this provision, the losing party is liable to pay default interest, from the date of the decision on costs, if the party has not paid the awarded costs before the decision became enforceable. Therefore, because this applies by automatic operation of law, the enforceable legal title does not have to state the default interest.[90]

The recoverable fraction can be expressed in figures or as percentage. Court fees and other public fees regulated by federal law payable by a party, costs for official acts performed outside the court, witnesses', experts', interpreters', translators' and assessors' fees, costs for the required official statements as well as a trustees' costs defrayed by a party following Section 10, shall be awarded proportionally to the fraction corresponding to the extend of this party's success in the action. (2) However, in the event each party partly succeeds and partly fails in an action, the Court may order one party to indemnify the opposing party and his intervener for the full costs of the proceedings, if the opposing party is unsuccessful in the action regarding only a relatively trivial part of his claim, the assertion of which has moreover not caused any particular costs, or if the determination of the amount of the opposing party's claim was dependant on judicial discretion, ascertainment by an expert or a reciprocal clearing settlement.'

89. W.H. Rechberger and P.A. Simotta, *Das österreichischen Zivilprozeßrechts* (6th edn, Vienna, Manz, 2003), para. 299.
90. C. Liebscher and A. Schmid in *Practitioner's Handbook on International Arbitration*, F.B. Weigand (eds) (Munich, C.H. Beck, 2002), p. 574 with reference to OGH, 16 December 1998, 3 Ob 287/98x.

2.   The Modern Austrian Approach to Cost Allocation
              in Arbitration

31-047 As discussed elsewhere, this treatise advocates an approach to arbitration that draws a distinction between Austria's arbitration law (contained in Sections 577 ZPO *et seq.*) and provisions of the ZPO dealing with state court proceedings. As a result it generally resists an analogous application of the ZPO's remaining provisions where the arbitration law is silent.[91] This is true for cost matters as well, in particular following the 2006 reform. Section 609 ZPO now states that, when allocating the costs between the parties,

> [t]he arbitral tribunal shall, at its discretion, take into consideration the circumstances of the individual case, in particular the outcome of the proceedings.

31-048 Although this provision emphasizes the tribunal's discretion in making its cost decision, it also introduces, for the first time under Austrian arbitration law, some express guidance for the arbitrators. This provision sets out that 'the circumstances of the individual case, in particular the outcome of the proceedings' shall be taken into consideration. This does not come as a surprise. As discussed elsewhere, this approach reflects international trends both in academic writing and arbitral practice. As *Bühler* concludes, arbitrators enjoy significantly greater discretion in determining, and allocating, the costs of the arbitration that state court judges can apply:

> [F]irst, the cost rules followed in national courts at the place of arbitration are not binding on the tribunal (unless so agreed by the parties). Second, both the lex arbitri and the applicable arbitration rules will be confined, if at all, to the basic principles as to the treatment of costs. Third, arbitrators will have a wide discretion when deciding cost matters.[92]

31-049 These conclusions are convincing. They show that national law as applicable to the courts has no real legal influence on the cost determination. National law applies only through the arbitration-specific provisions of the *lex arbitri*. In Austria, this is Section 609 ZPO which in fact confirms the arbitrator's discretion in cost matters.

V.   DETERMINING THE COSTS ABSENT JURISDICTION
              ON THE MERITS

31-050 Historically, the question was raised of whether and to what extent the arbitral tribunal may determine the amount and the allocation of costs in the event it

---

91. Where the Austrian arbitration law is silent, the arbitrators' discretion should be guided by international practice, the parties' expectations, and the circumstances of the individual case. *See* **Article 2**, at paras. 037 *et seq.* and **Article 20**, at paras. 015 *et seq.*
92. M. Bühler, 'Awarding Costs in International Commercial Arbitration: an Overview' (2004) 22(2) Bull ASA, 249, 255.

finds that it does not have jurisdiction over the dispute. According to *Fasching*, institutionalized arbitration rules like the Vienna Rules, that deal with compensation for costs, could only be applied if the arbitral tribunal has jurisdiction.[93] As a result, if the tribunal found that it had no jurisdiction, it was argued that it could not rule on the costs attending the jurisdictional phase. *Habscheid* even argued that rules on cost allocation such as in the Austrian ZPO, which authorizes national courts to rule on the costs also in case of lacking jurisdiction, should only apply in arbitration proceedings if the parties have expressly agreed on such compensation or the applicable arbitration rules expressly provide for it. Lacking such express authorization, the arbitral tribunal was said to have no power to rule on the costs attending the dispute on jurisdiction. According to *Habscheid*, such a ruling would have caused an act of *ultra petita*, and hence be challengeable, or would not have received recognition at the enforcement stage (although it would not affect the right to claim such costs in state court proceedings).[94] This position was doubtful even under the old law. It makes no commercial sense to suggest that parties intend to defer cost decisions to the state courts, forcing them into yet another legal proceeding in a forum less familiar with the history of the parties' dispute and their procedural conduct. Only where no arbitration agreement exists, could the state courts be competent to decide on costs. However, if one takes the principle of competence-competence seriously, permitting the tribunal to decide on its own jurisdiction, it is difficult to deny the tribunal to rule on the costs attending this determination. In the more recent German doctrine, the perception that the arbitral tribunal can rule on costs even where it finds that it lacks jurisdiction, has prevailed,[95]and the German *Bundesgerichtshof* has confirmed this position in the recent past.[96]

The Vienna Rules, like most arbitration rules, do not contain an express provision **31-051** on this issue.[97] Austrian law, however, has now removed any speculation in this

---

93. *See* H.W. Fasching, *Schiedsgericht und Schiedsverfahren im österreichischen und im internationalen Recht* (Vienna, Manz, 1973), p. 129 with the comment that an arbitration award could only grant compensation for expenses of proceedings if the parties have expressly agreed to that in the arbitration agreement or in a subsequent written agreement.

94. W.J. Habscheid 'Der Kostenersatzanspruch des Beklagten bei Unzuständigkeitsausspruch des Schiedsgerichtes' in *Festgabe für Hans W. Fasching zum 70. Geburtstag*, W. Jelinek, P. Böhm, A. Konecny, W. Buchegger (eds) (Vienna, Manz, 1993), p. 394; *see also* P. Schlosser. *Das Recht der internationalen privaten Schiedsgerichtsbarkeit* (2nd edn, Tübingen, Mohr Siebeck, 1989), para. 705; H. Thomas and H. Putzo, *Zivilprozeßordnung* (26th edn, Munich, C.H. Beck, 2003), Section 1057, para. 9; K.H. Schwab and G. Walter (eds), *Schiedsgerichtsbarkeit* (7th edn, Munich, C.H. Beck, 2005), ch. 33, paras. 3 *et seq.*

95. J.P. Lachmann, *Handbuch für die Schiedsgerichtspraxis* (3rd edn, Cologne, Verlag Dr. Otto Schmidt, 2008), p. 462; H. Raeschke-Kessler and K.-P. Berger, *Recht und Praxis des Schiedsverfahrens* (3rd edn, Cologne, RWS Verlag, 1999), para. 889; R. Geimer in *Zöller – Zivilprozeßordnung*, R. Zöller *et al.* (eds) (26th edn, Cologne, Verlag Dr. Otto Schmidt, 2007), Section 1057, para. 3.

96. BGH, 6 June 2002, III ZB 44/01, SchiedsVZ 2003, 39.

97. *See, e.g.*, Article 3 Rules Governing the Costs of Arbitration Proceedings before the Court of Arbitration of the Slovak Chamber of Commerce and Industry provides an exceptional

respect and explicitly addresses this situation in Section 609(2) ZPO. It stipulates that

> [u]pon the application of the respondent, the arbitral tribunal may also decide upon the obligation of the plaintiff to reimburse the costs of the proceedings, if it has declared itself as not competent on the grounds that there is no arbitration agreement.

31-052 This covers at least the most common case where the claimant files a claim and the arbitral tribunal, by virtue of its competence-competence, rules that it has no jurisdiction. In this respect, the new provision is a welcome clarification. It remains, however, problematic as the wording of this provision seems to only refer to the situation where 'there is no arbitration agreement'. This is somewhat unsatisfactory as there are numerous other reasons for why an arbitral tribunal may decline its jurisdiction, for example, for lack of objective arbitrability. Based on an argument *ad minorem*, any denial of jurisdiction should entitle the arbitral tribunal to rule on costs issues,[98] also in proceedings under the Vienna Rules. In any case, it may be advisable for an arbitral tribunal, if the plea of lack of jurisdiction is raised, to seek to obtain the parties' express written consent that the tribunal may assess costs even if it should decline jurisdiction on the merits.

VI.   PROCEDURAL CONSIDERATIONS

31-053 The Vienna Rules do not contain specific procedural rules which the arbitrators must follow in arriving at a cost decision. In light of **Article 20**, this procedure will typically be a matter of the arbitrators' discretion. The following section briefly examines some practical questions as to when and how an arbitral tribunal should deal with the cost decision and which form needs to be applied under the Vienna Rules and Austrian arbitration law.

---

provision concerning the objection against the arbitral tribunal's jurisdiction: 'The party who files an objection to the jurisdiction of arbitrators or of the Court of Arbitration shall pay 60 % of the registration fee calculated according to the Schedule of Fees. If the fee is not paid within the specified period, the objection to the jurisdiction shall not be considered. If the objection to the jurisdiction is granted, the Court of Arbitration shall reimburse the party the fee paid according to paragraph 1. If the objection to the jurisdiction is dismissed after an oral hearing before the Presiding Board, the registration fee paid according to paragraph 1 shall not be reimbursed. If the objection to the jurisdiction is dismissed without an oral hearing before the Presiding Board, the Court of Arbitration shall reimburse the party one half of the fee paid according to paragraph 1'.

98.   *See also* A. Reiner, *Das neue österreichische Schiedsrecht/The new Austrian Arbitration Law* (Vienna, LexisNexis, 2006), Section 610, note 179.

A.   PROCEDURE

Sometimes, and it is indeed advisable to do so, an arbitration tribunal deals with the **31-054** scope of costs and the basis of its decision at a preliminary or organisational hearing. Inevitably, the authority of the tribunal to award costs is always subject to the agreement of the parties.[99] Hence, if the parties have, besides the application of the Vienna Rules, agreed upon a certain procedure for the determination of costs, this would have to be followed.[100] In any case, the arbitral tribunal has to ensure that the principle of equal treatment of the parties is observed[101] and, arguably, the right to be heard is ensured.[102] Indeed, it is international arbitration practice that the parties receive an opportunity to comment on the other parties' cost application,[103] usually in final or post hearing briefs.

In order to accord each party its right to be heard, practical problems could arise in **31-055** particular when specific costs (justified or not) cannot yet be fully substantiated.[104] It will depend on the individual case if the arbitral tribunal will declare its consent to grant an extension of time for a party to specify further or additional claims for costs. In practice, it is noticeable that some parties only then 'dare' to claim full costs after receipt of the other party's claim for costs by submitting unrequested 'additional' or 'post hearing' cost claims. In this case, also, it will to a large extent depend on the individual case if the arbitral tribunal considers such behaviour permissible, or the additional claim justified, even when the original time limit to claim costs has already expired.

B.   REQUEST FOR COSTS

In this context it is debatable whether the arbitral tribunal shall have the right, or **31-056** even the obligation, to grant costs if a party has not explicitly applied for them. Under the former Austrian arbitration law, the Austrian *Oberster Gerichtshof* held in an *obiter dictum* that 'arbitrators are only allowed to grant costs if there is a joint application of the parties'.[105] Section 609 ZPO, however, does not require a separate application or motion to the arbitral tribunal for such decision. **Article 32(b)** refers to the 'expenses' and 'other outlays' of the parties. This only indicates that

---

99.   J. Lew, L. Mistelis and S. Kröll, *Comparative International Commercial Arbitration* (The Hague, Kluwer Law International, 2003), para. 24-79.
100.   It is advisable for the arbitrators to carefully scrutinize the arbitration agreement before accepting the mandate.
101.   *See* **Article 20**, at paras. 016 *et seq.*
102.   *See* **Article 20**, at paras. 029 *et seq.*
103.   A. Reiner, 'Schiedsverfahren und rechtliches Gehör' [2003] ZfRV, 52.
104.   The proper documentation of in-house costs that have occurred in the course of and due to the arbitration proceedings can be time-consuming and require often more preparation then the filing of counsel fees which are mostly prepared by specific computer software.
105.   *See* OGH, 1 October 1952, 1 Ob 803/52.

the costs must *realiter* have been incurred during the proceedings. On the other hand, Article 31 explicitly demands 'an application' made by the parties. As a practical matter, the amount of costs claimed must be made known, and explained, to the arbitral tribunal.[106] In summary, under the Vienna Rules, a claim for costs in order to be taken into consideration by an arbitral tribunal must have been applied for by the party to be granted.

31-057 It is therefore questionable whether the tribunal has to satisfy itself the costs so claimed were actually incurred, or if it can or should be satisfied with a mere allegation. That will depend on several factors, including on the amount and kind of costs claimed,[107] and whether the quantum of costs is contested by the other side. In case of doubts, the arbitral tribunal is entitled to investigate and request further proof.[108]

C.   Timing of Cost Decision

31-058 Article 31 provides that the determination of costs can either be done as part of the final award on the merits or by separate award. Some arbitral tribunals, for various reasons, prefer to grant a final award on the merits first, and the proceed to a cost determination a an additional and separate award.

31-059 As far as the costs of arbitration are concerned, this could arguably contradict **Article 34(1)** which provides for the Secretary General to determine these costs at the end of the proceedings, apparently leaving no room for any earlier decision of the arbitrators. As far as the outlay of the Centre and the arbitrators fees are concerned, such decision is therefore, also for practical reasons, reserved to the end of the proceedings.[109] This is not so if the parties, for example by changing their legal representation during the course of the proceedings or after accomplishment of certain stages in the proceedings, request an earlier decision on costs of legal representation. Of course, any such early decision will in most cases only determine the amount of legal costs, but will not yet allocate that amount between the parties. Indeed, the possibility to render a separate award on costs was inserted

---

106. A. Reiner, *Das neue österreichische Schiedsrecht/The new Austrian Arbitration Law* (Vienna, LexisNexis, 2006), Section 610, note 176.
107. Legal costs claimed in accordance with fixed statutory tariffs must arguably not be proven.
108. According to *Bühler/Jarvin*, 'the Arbitral Tribunal must verify whether these costs have been properly incurred and at the same time. Parties should also be asked to submit a statement from their Financial Director confirming that the amount of costs claimed has actually been incurred and paid by that party.' *See* M. Bühler and S. Jarvin in *Practitioner's Handbook on International Arbitration*, F.B. Weigand (ed.) (Munich, C.H. Beck, 2002), pp. 297 *et seq.* According to *Gotanda*, 'the party seeking an award of costs and fees must provide sufficient proof to substantiate its claim'. *See* J.Y. Gotanda, 'Awarding Costs and Attorneys' Fees in International Commercial Arbitrations' (1999) 21(1) Mich J Int'l L, 1, 46.
109. To the question of a payment on account on arbitrator's fee, *see* **Article 34**, at para. 014.

to enable and encourage the arbitral tribunal to decide on the merits of the case and *delay* the costs decision, and not to make an earlier decision on costs.[110]

D.   FORM OF COST DECISION

The decision on costs is made by award. Article 31 does not indicate a different **31-060** form, and Section 609(4) ZPO expressly stipulates that 'in any case, the decision upon the liability to pay the costs and the determination of the amount shall be made in the form of an award'. This will also apply in case the arbitration proceedings were settled or terminated according to **Article 25**.

Although not explicitly regulated under the Vienna Rules, it is required for arbi- **31-061** trators to provide a reasoned award for their costs decision. This follows the concept that arbitration awards under the Vienna Rules must state the grounds upon which the award is based, unless all parties, either in the arbitration agreement or in the oral proceedings, have agreed otherwise.[111] As the cost decision forms either an integral part of the award or is made in a separate award, it is governed by this requirement.[112]

---

110.   *See also* Section 609(5) ZPO: 'If no decision was made upon the liability to pay the costs, or if the amount to be reimbursed was not determined, or if it was only possible to determine this after termination of the arbitral proceedings, then the decision thereupon shall be made in a separate award.'
111.   *See* **Article 27(1)**, at paras. 001 *et seq.*, and Section 609(4) ZPO.
112.   P. Oberhammer, *Entwurf eines neuen Schiedsverfahrensrechts* (Vienna, Manz, 2004), p. 126; *see also* **Article 27**, at para. 004.

Article 32
Categories of Costs

Article 32: The costs of the proceedings consist of the following elements:

(a) The costs of arbitration, that is to say, the outlay of the Centre (administrative costs), arbitrators' fees plus any value added tax and cash outlay (such as travel and subsistence expenses of arbitrators, costs of service of documents, rent, costs of simple minuting); and

(b) The costs of the parties, that is to say, the appropriate expenses of the parties for their representation and other outlay related to the arbitration proceedings, in particular, the costs specified in Article 35 paragraph 1.

Article 32 serves as an explanatory note to **Article 31**, and must be read together **32-001** with that provision. Article 32 draws a distinction between, and sets out to define, the costs of the arbitration and the costs of the parties.

The costs of the arbitration are the administrative costs of the proceedings. The **32-002** amount of those administrative costs is determined by the Secretary General as an administrative responsibility according to **Article 34**[1] (but stated, and then allocated as between the parties, by the arbitrators in their final decision according to **Article 31**).[2] In setting those costs, the Secretary General has to follow the requirements and the procedures set out at various stages in the Vienna Rules. Whenever the exercise of discretion is permissible in this context, the parties and the arbitrators, as a rule, should be granted the right to be heard and express their comments.[3]

---

1. *See* **Article 34**, at para. 003.
2. *See* **Article 31**, at paras. 001 *et seq*.
3. *See* **Article 31**, at para. 055.

32-003 The costs of the parties can be described only in general terms. They consist in particular of the 'appropriate' expenses of the parties incurred to pay for their legal representation and other outlays related to the proceedings. Consistent with other institutional rules, the Vienna Rules were drafted so as to provide the arbitrators with the widest possible discretion to determine these costs. What constitutes 'appropriate' expenses (and thus expenses that are recoverable) is discussed in the context of **Article 31**.[4]

---

4. *See* **Article 31**, at paras. 017 *et seq.*

Article 33

The Registration Fee

		Para.			Para.
I.	Payment and Purpose	1	III.	Deduction From Deposit	7
II.	Increase in Multiparty Arbitrations	6	IV.	Failure to Pay the Registration Fee ...	9

I.   PAYMENT AND PURPOSE

Article 33(1): On filing the claim (counter-claim), the Claimant (Counter-claimant) shall pay into the account of the Centre, free of charges, a registration fee in the amount stated. That fee is intended to cover the costs up to the submission of the files to the sole arbitrator (arbitral tribunal). If higher outlay is incurred, an additional sum may be prescribed.

The registration fee is a fixed, non-refundable sum, amounting at present to **33-001** €2,000.00, which is designed to cover the initial administrative costs of the VIAC between the filing of the statement of claims and the submission of the files to the arbitrators. The collection of an registration fee reflects the general practice of other arbitral institutions.[1] Article 4(4) and Appendix III Article 1 of the ICC Rules provides for advance payment for administrative expenses amounting to US $2,500.00. Schedule of Fees and Costs, 1(a) of the LCIA Rules contains a similar system, providing for an amount of £1,500.00. The AAA/ICDR Rules and

---

1.   *See also* Article 4(4) ICC Rules and Appendix III Article 1(1) to ICC Rules; Article 1(1)(f) LCIA Rules and item 1(a) of Schedule of Fees and Costs of LCIA Rules; Article 7(1) DIS Rules and Article 11(1) DIS Rules and 'Administrative Fees' of AAA/ICDR Rules.

DIS Rules deviate from this approach; they calculate the administration[2] or initial fees[3] with reference to the amount in dispute as quantified by the claimant.

33-002 Clarifying what had remained an ambiguous provision in the 2001 amendment of the Vienna Rules, Article 33(1) now provides in clear terms that the claimant must pay the registration fee (free of any charges) into the Centre's account at the time of the filing of the claim. The claimant (or, as the case may be, the counter-claimant) assumes the risk of a delay in transfer, or of other defects. However, it bears emphasis that **Article 9** mentions neither the registration fee nor a proof of its payment as mandatory requirements for the valid submission of the statements of claims. It can therefore be assumed that missing or delayed transfer of the registration fee does not prevent the claim from becoming 'pending' within the meaning of **Article 9** of the Vienna Rules.[4] In practice, the Secretary General will, immediately after receipt of the statement of claims, request the registration fee to be paid before processing the claim any further. Time extensions are usually granted in accordance with **Article 13**.[5]

33-003 The fee is intended to cover the administrative costs of the VIAC arising until the submission of the files to the sole arbitrator (arbitral tribunal). Under this explicit designation, the VIAC is not permitted to use the registration fee for any other purpose.

33-004 Occasionally, the delivery of the statement of claims calls for higher expenditures, for example when a large number of parties, resident perhaps in remote places, have to be notified. In such cases, an additional sum may be prescribed if higher outlay is actually incurred, and the VIAC will only process a statement of claims if its costs are covered. Additional fees will not follow a pre-defined sum, but will reflect anticipated actual costs. The increased registration fee will fall onto the claimant.[6]

33-005 Indeed, following the wording of this provision, the registration fee is to be paid exclusively by the claimant ('claimant or counter-claimant respectively shall pay into account'). In some instances, however, the respondent may have a vital interest that the claim is delivered to it. Arguably, it should make no difference whether the claimant, the respondent or even a third party pays the registration fee. Of course, where the claimant or counter-claimant fails to effect the payment, the

---

2. Article 7(1) DIS Rules: 'Upon filing the statement of claim, the claimant shall pay to the DIS the administrative fee (. . .)' and Article 11(1) DIS Rules: 'Upon filing a counterclaim, the respondent shall pay to the DIS the administrative fee (. . .)' in connection with item 15) Appendix to Section 40. sub. 5, which bases the DIS administrative fee on the amount in dispute.
3. Administrative Fees of AAA/ICDR Rules: 'An initial filing fee is payable in full by a filing party when a claim, counterclaim or additional claim is filed.' This fee shall be billed in accordance with the schedule of costs, which is based of the amount of claim.
4. *See* **Article 9**, at paras. 015 *et seq.*
5. *See* **Article 13**, at paras. 009 *et seq.*
6. *See* **Article 10**, at para. 008.

Secretary General is neither obliged to notify the respondent about a claim lodged against it, nor is the VIAC entitled to demand from the respondent that it pays the registration fee.[7]

II. INCREASE IN MULTIPARTY ARBITRATIONS

Article 33(2): If there are more than two parties to the proceedings, the registration fee shall be increased by 10% for each additional party.

The registration fee under Article 33(1) covers proceedings with one claimant and one respondent. However, pursuant to Article 33(2), the registration fee increases by incremental steps of 10% for each additional party, whether on the claimant's or the respondent's side. There is no limit to additional increases;[8] subsequent increases in the arbitration of the number of parties also lead to an increase of the registration fee, as parties not originally named but later added incur administrative costs for the VIAC as well. By contrast, a reduction in the number of the parties will, in analogous application of **Article 36(8)**, only be considered when (validly) made before the transmission of the files to the arbitrators. Should the actual costs exceed the 10% flat increase per additional party, an additional fee can be prescribed in accordance with Article 33(1). All of these issues constitute administrative matters of the VIAC, and therefore fall within the sole authority of the Secretary General.[9]

33-006

III. DEDUCTION FROM DEPOSIT

Article 33(3): The registration fee shall not be repayable. The registration fee, as well as any additional amount required in accordance with paragraph 1 of the present Article shall be deducted from the Claimant's (Counter-claimant's) share of the deposit against costs of arbitration.

The registration fee constitutes a non-refundable part of the deposit of costs and, in consequence, forms part of the costs of the arbitration as defined in **Article 32(a)**. The registration fee is deducted from the Claimant's share of the deposit at the due date of the deposit of costs under **Article 34(2)**.[10]

33-007

---

7. *See* **Article 9**, at para. 086.
8. A similar provision can be found in the Appendix to Article 40 DIS Rules, sub. 5, item 11. It provides that in the case that more than two parties are involved in the arbitral proceedings, the administrative fee, which shall be paid on filing the statement of claim or counter-claim (according to Article 7 and Article 11 DIS Rules), increases by 20% for each additional party.
9. *See* **Article 5**, at paras. 007 *et seq.*
10. In the (rare but conceivable) case the registration fee was paid by the respondent, this payment, in analogical application of Article 33(3), must be deducted from the respondent's share of the cost deposit.

33-008 Should proceedings ultimately fail to commence (for instance because the parties have reached an agreement before the file was transmitted to the arbitrators), the registration fee will still not be refunded. It is difficult to conceive circumstances where a statement of claims has been filed but not caused any administrative effort of the VIAC. Parties have, for example, unsuccessfully claimed the refund of a registration fee for a counter-claim that was immediately withdrawn after filing. It is standing practice of the present Secretary General to apply Article 33(3) strictly on its terms, and to consider the registration fee as non-refundable even in such cases. This seems to correspond to the practice of other international arbitral institutions.[11]

IV.   FAILURE TO PAY THE REGISTRATION FEE

Article 33(4): The claim (counter-claim) shall be treated only after the registration fee is fully paid.

33-009 The former version of the Vienna Rules provided that the claim (counter-claim) was to be deleted from the list of pending cases if the claimant failed to pay the registration fee, despite an additional request from the VIAC.[12] As discussed, the deletion from the list of pending cases no longer constitutes a sanction under the 2006 version of the Vienna Rules.[13]

33-010 Now, the failure to pay the prescribed registration fee simply results in the claim not being administered.[14] Extension will be granted in accordance with **Article 13**, but if the registration fee remains unpaid within the deadline set by the Secretary General, the claim will not be processed. In this case, the claimant will receive a notification that the VIAC will not treat the case any further.

33-011 It is not entirely obvious what consequences the claimant's failure to pay the registration case (and the resulting non-treatment of the claim) has with respect to the pendency of the dispute and the statute of limitation.[15] On the one hand, Article 33(4) does not provide, as a textual matter, that claims will be dismissed, or even that they will not be treated at all in the future – it merely provides that they will be treated *after* payment of the registration fee, whenever that may be.

---

11. *See also* Appendix III Article 1(1) to ICC Rules; Schedule of Fees and Costs to LCIA Rules, item 1 (a).
12. Article 22(4) Vienna Rules 2001, **Annex 2a**.
13. *See* **Article 9**, at para. 085.
14. The practice of VIAC complies well with the general practice of other arbitral institutions where the non-payment of the registration fee leads to similar sanctions such as in Article 4(4) ICC Rules: '[T]he file shall be closed.' Or Article 1(1) LCIA Rules: '[T]he Request shall be treated as not having been received by the Registrar and the arbitration as not having been commenced.' Or Article 7(2) DIS Rules: '[T]he proceedings are terminated.' And Article 11(2) DIS Rules: '[T]he counterclaim is deemed not to have been filed.'
15. *See* **Article 9**, at paras. 086 and 087.

Moreover, as discussed earlier, the payment of the registration fee is not a mandatory requirement under **Article 9** for the proper submission of a statement of claims. In practice, however, the Secretary General simply makes no service of the statement of claims to the respondent until the registration fee is paid in full. It is conceivable for a claimant to argue, therefore, that despite the failure to pay the registration fee, the claim has been properly brought and remains pending, with the statute of limitation being interrupted. This, of course, will depend on the law applicable to this particular question.[16]

The opposite view would argue that Article 33 implies the punctual payment of the registration fee, and that a claimant who fails to pay this fee despite requests from the Secretary General, has neither brought its claim in compliance with the Vienna Rules nor pursued its claim with the determination that is necessary to interrupt the statute of limitations. Under that theory, the payment of the registration fee after the initial time limit has elapsed would not be sufficient for the further treatment of the claim. Rather, the claim would be considered to have been withdrawn without prejudice; it would have to be re-filed.[17] **33-012**

---

16. *See* **Article 9**, at paras. 016 *et seq*.
17. Similar in Article 4(4) ICC Rules: '(. . .) the file shall be closed without prejudice to the right of the claimant to submit the same claims at a later date in another Request.' *See also* Article 7 DIS Rules: '(. . .) the proceedings are terminated without prejudice to the claimant's right to reintroduce the same claim.'

Article 34

The Determination of the Costs of the Arbitration and the Deposit

		Para.			Para.
I.	Determining the Costs of the Arbitration	1		B. Payment of the Deposit Against Costs	24
	A. Introduction	1	III.	The Claimant's Failure to Pay the Deposit	29
	B. Authority to Determine the Costs of the Arbitration	3	IV.	The Respondent's Failure to Pay the Deposit	32
	1. Administrative Costs	4		A. Procedural Consequences	33
	2. The Arbitrator's Fees	7		B. Remedy Against Non-Payment	35
	C. Procedure for Determining the Costs of the Arbitration	15	V.	Increase of the Amount in Dispute	56
II.	The Amount of the Deposit Against Costs	19	VI.	Additional Expenses	59
	A. Calculation of the Amount of the Deposit	19			

I. DETERMINING THE COSTS OF THE ARBITRATION

Article 34(1): The costs of arbitration shall be determined by the Secretary General at the end of the proceedings.

A. INTRODUCTION

Article 34(1) refers, by way of introduction, to the Secretary General's power to determine the costs of the arbitration,[1] which are defined in **Article 32** and

34-001

---

1. The Secretary General determines only the amount of the costs of the arbitration, but it is for the arbitrators to state that amount in the award and also allocate that amount as between the parties. *See* **Article 31**, at para. 005.

addressed in detail in **Article 36**. Article 34(2) to (6) then proceeds to cover the separate issue of the scope and treatment of the deposit of costs.

34-002 Systemically, Article 34(1) should therefore be moved to **Article 36**, where it properly belongs. Regardless, the discussion below follows the structure of the Vienna Rules as currently set out, and thus examines first the legal basis for the Secretary General's authority to determine the costs of the arbitration proceedings. In doing so, it offers some guidance for arbitrators as to how and when they ought to contact the VIAC directly to discuss their fees. The discussion then proceeds to address in some detail the deposit on costs, placing particular emphasis on the respondent's failure to pay its share of the deposit – an issue of considerable practical importance.

B.   AUTHORITY TO DETERMINE THE COSTS OF THE ARBITRATION

34-003 The exclusion of personal financial interests from the decision-making process is considered to be a fundamental principle of objective and independent administration of justice. The Vienna Rules seek to achieve this objective by placing the determination of costs not with the arbitral tribunal, but with an organ of the VIAC.[2] As Article 34(1) makes clear, the costs of the arbitration (including the deposit) are calculated and then finally determined by the Secretary General. They include, in particular, the administrative costs of the VIAC as well as the arbitrators' fees. The calculated amount by the Secretary General is then stated by the arbitrators in the final award,[3] who have no authority to question the amount, but can make a decision in the final award as to which party, if at all, has to carry these costs in whole or in part.[4]

1.   Administrative Costs

34-004 The VIAC is entitled to costs covering the expenses incurred in administering the arbitration. It therefore charges a registration fee to cover the initial costs,[5] as well as administrative costs. These administration costs cover any expenditure following the transmission of the file to the arbitrators. Like the arbitrator's fees, these costs are determined in accordance with Annex 1 to the VIAC Rules. This appendix sets the administrative costs at a minimum of €3,000.00, increasing in direct proportion to the amount in dispute and the number of parties to the proceedings.[6]

---

2. H.W. Fasching, 'Kostenvorschüsse zur Einleitung schiedsgerichtlicher Verfahren' [1993] JBl, 545.
3. *See* **Article 31**, at para. 003.
4. *See* **Article 31**, at paras. 034 *et seq.*
5. See **Article 33**, at paras. 001 *et seq.*
6. *See* **Article 36(2)**, at para. 011.

The administrative costs are intended to cover all expenses and work done by the **34-005** VIAC for the arbitration, but they are fixed according to the schedule in Annex 1. Unlike in other arbitration rules,[7] the VIAC has no authority to claim additional costs or request further payments beyond Annex 1, irrespective of the ultimate length or complexity of the proceedings. By the same token, however, the parties are not entitled to any reduction of these costs even where perhaps justified by the circumstances. In particular, once the file has been transmitted to the arbitrators, there is no reduction of the administrative costs even where the arbitration proceedings are terminated prior to an award (although there may be a reduction in the arbitrator's fees).[8] As most of VIAC's administrative work is actually performed at the very beginning of the proceedings, a termination at a later stage of the proceedings would arguably not justify a reduction in administrative costs.

The administrative costs form part of the deposit of costs; they will be finally **34-006** determined by the Secretary General at the end of the proceedings (in order to take any changes in the amount of dispute into account).

2. The Arbitrator's Fees

Under Austrian law, an arbitrator is entitled to reasonable remuneration pursuant to **34-007** Sections 1151(1) and 1152 ABGB. This entitlement arises by default, without specific agreement, as it is assumed that the arbitrator will not act for free.[9]

The claim for the arbitrator's fees is based upon a private agreement between the **34-008** parties and the arbitrators. Arbitrators are not entitled to determine the amount of their own fees by award.[10] No-one can be a judge in their own affairs. If arbitrators were to determine their own fees by award, such an award would be unenforceable in relevant part; the determination of costs would be considered as *pro non scripto*.[11] Arbitrators therefore have to resort to the state courts to enforce a claim for fees against the parties. In *ad hoc* arbitration, arbitrators will for that

---

7. *See, e.g.*, Article 2(5) Appendix III to ICC Rules: 'In exceptional circumstances, the Court may fix the administrative expenses at a lower or higher figure than that which would result from the application of such scale, provided that such expenses shall normally not exceed the maximum amount of scale. Further, the Court may require the payment of administrative expenses in addition to those provided in the scale of administrative expenses as a condition to holding an arbitration in abeyance at the request of the parties or of one of them with the acquiescence of the other.'

8. *See* **Article 36**, at paras. 033 and 034.

9. C. Liebscher and A. Schmid in *Practitioner's Handbook on International Arbitration*, F.B. Weigand (ed.) (Munich, C.H. Beck, 2002), p. 554.

10. OGH, 18 November 1925, 25 Ob III 872, ZBl 1926, 391; OGH, 1 June 1926, Ob I 443/26, SZ 8/ 179; OGH, 8 July 1931, 4 Ob 362/31, Rsp 1932, 11.

11. H.W. Fasching, *Schiedsgericht und Schiedsverfahren im österreichischen und im internationalen Recht* (Vienna, Manz, 1973), p. 75.

reason typically assume their work only once the fees have been agreed and advanced in full by the parties.[12]

34-009 Where an arbitration institution such as the VIAC is involved, the Vienna Rules have been interpreted to provide that a third party, namely the Secretary General, has been entrusted by the parties to determine these costs. To some degree it might be debatable if the process under the Vienna Rules is in fact a real determination in the true sense of the word as such costs are in fact fixed in advance according to the applicable fee schedule. However, there are still subjective elements which leave the cost determination to the discretion of the Secretary General.[13] The Austrian *Oberster Gerichtshof* ruled that the costs determined by the Secretary General under the Vienna Rules are recoverable and thus confirmed by implication that the system for determining costs established under the Vienna Rules conforms to both Austrian legal doctrine and existing jurisprudence.[14]

34-010 Arbitrator's fees under the Vienna Rules are fixed with reference to the amount in dispute and are assessed in accordance with a digressive costs schedule.[15] The rates quoted in the schedule of arbitrators' fees are the fees for sole arbitrators. They shall be raised to two-and-a-half times the amounts quoted if an arbitral tribunal is appointed and to up to three times if a case is particularly difficult.[16]

34-011 In the case of an arbitral tribunal, the arbitrators are in principle free to agree on a fee allocation amongst themselves. Absent such agreement, the VIAC applies a distribution of 40% for the presiding arbitrator and of 30% for each co-arbitrator off the total fee for the tribunal. Practice on this point varies under other arbitration rules.[17]

34-012 If the arbitrators have agreed on a particular apportionment, they must communicate it to the Secretary General together with the last unsettled account for cash outlays, upon termination of the proceedings at the latest. This deadline is not stipulated in the Vienna Rules, but forms part of the guidelines provided to the arbitrators together with the files of the case.[18]

---

12. Once the fees have been advanced in full, the arbitrators can of course allocate the cost burden as between the parties in a final award on costs.
13. *See* **Articles 36(5)**, at paras. 023 *et seq.* and **36(6)**, at paras. 028 *et seq.*
14. OGH, 26 June 1991, 3 Ob 70/91. Referring to the former version of the Vienna Rules, the Austrian *Oberster Gerichtshof* concluded that the arbitrators' costs are costs necessary to pursue a claim according to Section 41 ZPO and thus recoverable.
15. *See* **Article 36**, at paras. 002 *et seq.*
16. *See* **Article 36(6)**, at paras. 028 *et seq.*
17. Article 1 Appendix II to SCC Rules fixes the fee due to the co-arbitrator as 60% of the total fee paid to the Chairman. The DIS Rules contain an express division of the fees in the schedule of costs, generally by adding 30% to the fees for the chairman. The Hungarian Rules also provide for the presiding arbitrator to receive 30% more than the other arbitrators. Article 39(3) Swiss Rules provides that 'the Chairman shall receive between 40% and 50% and each co-arbitrator between 25% and 30% of the total fees, in view of the time and efforts spent by each arbitrator.'
18. *See* Guidelines for Arbitrators, **Annex 5**.

The arbitrators' fees are paid, usually at the time of delivery of the award to the **34-013** parties, to the account that each arbitrator has identified upon his or her nomination. The time limit of thirty days for a potential application for correction or interpretation of the award in accordance with **Article 29** is not suspending the payment.[19]

The Vienna Rules do not provide for advance payments of arbitrators' fees. In **34-014** the past, however, in proceedings of very substantial length or complexity, the Secretary General has upon their request exceptionally granted an advance on fees to the arbitrators. The advance on fees is also complicated by the need to calculate the VAT payable on arbitrator's fees.[20] Whether and how an arbitrator could claim payment in case of a successful challenge (**Article 16**) or an early termination of the mandate (**Article 17**) is discussed below.[21]

C.   PROCEDURE FOR DETERMINING THE COSTS OF THE ARBITRATION

The determination of the amount of the costs of arbitration is addressed in some **34-015** detail in the context of **Article 36**. Procedurally, the authority to determine the costs of the arbitration is clearly entrusted to the Secretary General, who fixes those costs when 'the arbitral proceedings are terminated'. The former version of this provision referred to the 'end of the proceedings'. This textual amendment was made to adopt the wording of Section 608 ZPO (providing for specific means to end an arbitral proceeding) and to bring it in line with **Article 25** of the Vienna Rules 2006.[22]

Whilst the consequences of any such termination of proceedings will be determined **34-016** by the applicable substantive law,[23] **Article 31** imposes an obligation on the arbitrators to notify the Secretary General of the anticipated termination (to the extent the arbitrators are not themselves surprised by an unexpected agreement between parties providing for the early termination of the proceedings). If the arbitrators decide to reopen the proceedings, the determination of costs will have to be stayed.

In practical terms, such advance notice allows the Secretary General to complete **34-017** the cost determination in advance; and clarify possibly open issues with an impact on the determination of costs, such as whether the case concerns a series of individual claims,[24] or whether a party's claim was 'obviously undervalued'.[25] Hence, arbitrators should as a matter of courtesy inform the Secretary General when the deliberations or the drafting of the final award have commenced. Where

---

19. *See* **Article 29**, at paras. 001 *et seq.*
20. *See* **Article 36(10)**, at para. 044.
21. *See* **Article 36**, at paras. 006 *et seq.*
22. *See* **Article 25**, at paras. 001 *et seq.*
23. *See* C. Liebscher, *The Austrian Arbitration Act 2006: Text and Notes* (The Hague, Kluwer Law International, 2006), Annotated Text to Section 608(2) ZPO.
24. *See* **Article 36(4)**, at paras. 019 *et seq.*
25. *See* **Article 36(5)**, at paras. 023 *et seq.*

the proceedings are before an arbitral tribunal, the task of communicating with the Secretary General with respect to cost matters falls usually to the chairman.[26] At this point, the arbitrators should ensure that all of their expenses and cash outlays are communicated to the Secretariat.

34-018 The arbitrators will submit the final draft of the award to the Secretariat and leave the determination of the final costs of the arbitration open for the Secretary General to complete. If the parties are to share the procedural costs as a percentage of total costs rather than as a numerical amount, this should be communicated to the Secretary General accordingly. In practice, the Secretary General provides the arbitrators with a spreadsheet detailing all the costs of the arbitration. Upon request, this calculation has in the past also been provided to the parties. Although a reasoned decision is not provided, the current Secretary General has not hesitated to explain his decision where appropriate.

II. THE AMOUNT OF THE DEPOSIT AGAINST COSTS

Article 34(2): The Secretary General shall fix the amount of the deposit against the expected costs of arbitration. That deposit shall be paid in equal shares by the parties before transmission of the files to the sole arbitrator (arbitral tribunal) and within thirty days after service of the payment request.

A. Calculation of the Amount of the Deposit

34-019 Article 34(2) obliges the Secretary General to fix the amount of the deposit against the expected costs of arbitration. Following **Article 32**, these costs comprise the administrative costs of the VIAC, the arbitrators' fees, plus any value added tax and the expected cash outlay.[27] Both the administrative costs and the arbitrators' fees are calculated with reference to the amount in dispute, as set out in the schedule in Annex 1 to the Vienna Rules, and vary with the number of arbitrators.[28] For this reason, the statement of claims must contain, *inter alia*, the amount in dispute,[29] and the number of arbitrators requested.[30] These particulars enable the Secretary General to calculate the amount in dispute on a preliminary basis. The VIAC has recently installed a cost calculation on its website (www.wko.at/arbitration) which enables the parties to calculate the anticipated costs. If the parties fail to furnish such information, the Secretary General can request further clarifications, notwithstanding the consequences for a defective statement of claims pursuant to **Article 9(5)**. If such request is not satisfactorily complied with, the Secretary

---

26. *See* **Article 26(2)**, at para. 034.
27. *See* **Article 32**, at para. 003.
28. *See* **Article 36(1)**, at para. 028.
29. Unless the claims are not related exclusively to a specific sum of money.
30. *See* **Article 9**, at para. 062.

General can exercise his discretion under **Article 36(5)** and deviate from the statements of the parties in determining the amount in dispute.[31]

For arbitral tribunals, it is the practice of the VIAC's current Secretary General to **34-020** calculate the rates of the arbitrator's fees according to **Article 36(7)** by tripling the amount.[32] If there are more than two parties to the proceedings, the rates for the administrative costs and the arbitrator's fees are automatically increased by 10% for each additional party.[33] The amount of expected cash outlays is typically estimated on the basis of a minimum of three days of hearings and attending travel expenses. Where the parties have already nominated their respective arbitrator, travel expenses for a foreign arbitrator will be more accurately considered.[34] The amount of VAT on the arbitrators' fees will be calculated on the basis of the information provided by the arbitrators.[35]

If it is obvious that the parties' statements as to costs and related data are incorrect, **34-021** the Secretary General's calculations may deviate from that of the parties. As a matter of caution, the Secretary General will usually endeavour to ensure that there is proper cost coverage from the outset of the proceedings. If during the course of the proceedings, it is necessary to increase the deposit – for example, due to an increase in the amount in dispute or the exhaustion of cash outlays – Article 34(5) and (6) enables the Secretary General to request further payment, as discussed in greater detail below.[36]

If the Secretary General has, in the eyes of a party, incorrectly calculated the **34-022** deposit of costs, that party is in practice free to approach the Secretary General and submit a reasoned request for reconsideration. If the Secretary General refuses to reconsider his calculation, it should be permissible for a party to request the arbitral tribunal to approach the Secretary General as the arbitrators might possibly have a different understanding of the financial impact of the particular case.

The deposit on costs is intended to cover the expected costs of the arbitration. **34-023** Legally, it does not serve to secure any claims the parties might have against each other, or against the VIAC or the arbitrators. This can be viewed as the main difference between security for procedural costs under Sections 57 *et seq.* ZPO (*aktorische Kaution*) and the security in enforcement proceedings.[37]

---

31. *See* **Article 36(5)**, at paras. 023 *et seq.*
32. This does not indicate that the requirements under this Article are effectively fulfilled, as the Secretary General is not bound by this decision.
33. *See* **Article 36(2)**, at paras. 028 *et seq.*
34. Note, however, that such additional expenses caused by the nomination of a foreign lawyer will be equally borne by both parties, irrespective of the other party's nomination. This is different under Article 43(1) Slovenian Rules or Article 8(4) (Regulation on the Arbitration Fees, Costs and Expenses of the Parties) attached to the Hungarian Rules.
35. *See* **Article 36(10)**, at para. 044.
36. *See* **Article 34**, at para. 057 and 061.
37. Claimant's deposit (*aktorische Kaution*) is a concept that derives under Austrian civil procedure. If a foreigner acts as claimant before an Austrian court, he might be obliged to secure the

Consequently, consent from the other party is not necessary in the event of a refund of surplus by the VIAC, following the final determination of costs. Hence, it would generally not be possible to successfully attempt execution proceedings against deposits temporarily entrusted to the VIAC to be held in its accounts.[38]

B.   PAYMENT OF THE DEPOSIT AGAINST COSTS

34-024 After the deposit of costs has been calculated, the parties are each requested to pay within thirty days equal shares of the deposit into a specified VIAC account.

34-025 Article 34(2) could be understood to require a *per capita* division of the amount in multi-party proceedings. Under that approach, an arbitration involving one claimant against three respondents would result in a ¼ share for each party. This does not, however, conform to the VIAC's practice. Rather, the amount is divided into equal halves for the claimant's and the respondent's side, respectively. In a multi-party scenario, each half is the further subdivided within the respective group. In the example of one claimant against three respondents, the claimant would be requested to pay one half of the deposit, and each respondent one third of the remaining half. Notwithstanding such division, the parties on each side remain jointly and severably liable for 'their' half.

34-026 Under Article 34(2), the Secretary General will not transfer the file to the arbitrators before payment has been received in full into the VIAC's bank account. Partial payments or payments to other accounts, such as accounts of the arbitrators, are not permitted. In the past, and relying on the text of Article 34(2) which requires actual payment, the VIAC has also not accepted bank guarantees or any other form of security.

34-027 A refund of an excess or yet unused deposit *during* the arbitration proceedings is in principle not permissible as this would run counter to the duty to maintain the operability and independence of the arbitral tribunal.[39] Any unusual surplus of the deposit will, independent from the outcome of the proceedings, be returned to each

---

defendant's procedural costs. *See* A. Klauser and G. Kodek, *JN-ZPO* (16th edn, Vienna, Manz, 2006), Section 57; R. Fucik in *Kommentar zur ZPO*, W.H. Rechberger (ed.) (3rd edn, Vienna/ New York, Springer, 2006), Section 57, p. 572. A separate application is necessary. *See* W.H. Rechberger and P.A. Simotta, *Grundriss des österreichischen Zivilprozessrecht* (6th edn, Vienna, Manz, 2003), para. 303. However, this does not apply to EU-citizens. *See* N. Schoibl in *Kommentar zu den Zivilprozeßgesetzen II/1*, H.W. Fasching (ed.) (2nd edn, Vienna, Manz, 2002), Section 57 ZPO, paras. 27 *et seq.*

38. H.W. Fasching, 'Kostenvorschüsse zur Einleitung schiedsgerichtlicher Verfahren' [1993] JBl 545, 549.

39. *See* H.W. Fasching, 'Kostenvorschüsse zur Einleitung schiedsgerichtlicher Verfahren' [1993] JBl, 545, 556.

party when the Secretary General determines the final costs of the arbitration and clears the file at the end of the proceedings.[40]

As the payments of the deposit on costs usually remain in the VIAC's accounts for a considerable period of time, questions regarding title to the interest accrued have arisen. Like other prominent institutions,[41] the VIAC uses the revenue from interest as an additional source of income, justifying that practice with the relatively static administrative fee schedule which typically remains unaltered for several years.   **34-028**

III.   THE CLAIMANT'S FAILURE TO PAY THE DEPOSIT

Article 34(3): If the share of the Claimant (Counter-claimant) is not received within the time-limit, despite prolongation thereof, the claim (counter-claim) shall not be treated any further. The Secretary General shall inform the parties thereof.

By agreeing to the application of the Vienna Rules, the parties are required to honour the payment obligations arising from the proceedings. As discussed, the relation between the VIAC and the arbitrators can be seen as an agreement of agency.[42] As a result of this legal characterization, the VIAC has the right to refuse to provide its services as long as the parties are in breach of their payment obligations.[43] The earlier version of this provision thus sanctioned non-payment of the deposit with the deletion from the list of the pending cases. This sanction has been abandoned by the latest amendment of the Vienna Rules.[44] If the claimant's (or counter-claimant's) share is not received in full, the claim or the counter-claim will simply 'not be treated any further'.[45]   **34-029**

As a result, the Secretary General is in fact obligated to desist from further administration of the counter-claim if the claimant fails to pay its share of the deposit.   **34-030**

---

40. *See* **Article 27**, at para. 019.
41. *See* Y. Derains and E.A. *Schwartz, A Guide to the ICC Rules of Arbitration* (2nd edn, The Hague, Kluwer Law International, 2005), p. 352.
42. *See* **Article 1**, at paras. 026 *et seq.*
43. H.W. Fasching, 'Kostenvorschüsse zur Einleitung schiedsgerichtlicher Verfahren' [1993] JBl 545, 549.
44. *See* **Article 9**, at para. 085.
45. For the consequences on the Statute of Limitations, *see* **Article 9**, at paras. 016 *et seq.* Procedurally, the practice of arbitral institutions differs. *See, e.g.*, Article 30(4) ICC Rules, where '(...) after consultation with the Arbitral tribunal, the Secretary General may direct the Arbitral tribunal to suspend its work and set a time limit, which must be not less than 15 days, on the expiry of which the relevant claims, or counterclaims, shall be considered as withdrawn'. Similarly under Article 24(4) LCIA Rules: 'Failure by a claimant or counterclaiming party to provide promptly and in full the required deposit may be treated by the LCIA Court and the Arbitral Tribunal as a withdrawal of the claim or counterclaim respectively.' *See also*

Before the parties are so notified, the claimant will be granted additional time for payment, usually 15 days. This extension, together with information regarding the consequences of non-compliance, will be notified to the claimant in writing. Upon lapse of such additional time, all parties will receive a notification that the claim or counter-claim will not be treated any further. The Vienna Rules no longer express-ly indicate that the claim or counter-claim can be resubmitted at a later stage;[46] this, however, is in principle permissible.[47]

34-031 As a textual matter, Article 34(3) requires the receipt of the deposit, without specifying by whom the deposit must be paid. It follows from Article 34(3) that it is in principle the claimant's burden to pay the deposit, and to pay it in whole for a defaulting respondent.[48] It is conceivable, however, that the respondent has a vested interest in a decision by the arbitral tribunal. In such a case, as long as the claim is not unconditionally withdrawn by the claimant, it should be permis-sible for the respondent to pay the share of a defaulting claimant. Also, if one of several claimants defaults on the deposit, the other claimants can step in and make the payment in its place, in order for the arbitration to proceed analogous to Article 34(4).

IV. THE RESPONDENT'S FAILURE TO PAY THE DEPOSIT

Article 34(4): If the share of the Respondent (Counter-Respondent) is not received within the time-limit set, the Secretary General shall inform the Claimant (Counter-claimant) thereof and shall request him to pay the outstanding share of the deposit within thirty days of receipt of the pay-ment request. If that amount is not received within the time-limit, the claim (counter-claim) shall not be treated any further. The Secretary General shall inform the parties thereof.

34-032 As it is the claimant who seeks legal recourse in the first place, it is arguable that it alone should bear the burden of the deposit.[49] This is, however, not the practice under most arbitration rules,[50] and for good reason. Arbitration, as a consensual

---

Article 7(2) DIS Rules where '(. . .) the proceedings are terminated (. . .)' or also suspended, as under Article 33(3) AAA/ICDR Rules.

46. This was expressly so in the 1991 version of this provision.

47. For the consequences on the Statute of Limitations, *see* **Article 9**, at paras. 016 *et seq.* and **Article 33**, at para. 011.

48. *See*, however, **Article 34(4)**, at paras. 032 *et seq.*

49. This is the case in some state court litigation systems, including in Austria, where the claimant alone must advance the fees of the court.

50. The same concept is found in Article 30(3) ICC Rules. DIS Rules differentiate between the provisional advance (Article 7(1)) and advance on costs of the arbitral tribunal (Article 25). Whereas the former must be paid by the claimant, the latter is subdivided between the parties. Article 24(1) LCIA takes a different approach as it leaves the division to the Court's discretion 'in such proportions as it thinks appropriate'.

mechanism of dispute resolution based on the parties' joint agreement to arbitrate, imposes equal obligations on both parties to allow the arbitration to proceed, including by financing the proceedings as agreed. Like other rules,[51] the Vienna Rules therefore provide in Article 34(2) that the deposit 'shall be paid in equal share by both parties', thus imposing in no uncertain terms an obligation on both the claimant *and* the respondent to pay the deposit fixed by the Secretary General. Yet in practice, respondents frequently default on that obligation regardless, be it in order to force the claimant out of spite to finance the arbitration alone, be it for more legitimate reasons. The respondent's failure to pay its share of the cost deposit is addressed below, both from a procedural level and from the perspective of possible additional remedies.

A.   PROCEDURAL CONSEQUENCES

If the respondent fails to pay its share of the deposit, Article 34(4) provides an **34-033** express procedural consequence designed to permit the arbitration to proceed. Specifically, if the respondent defaults, the claimant receives a request from the Secretary General to pay the outstanding amount within thirty days. This request also notes that, if the outstanding share is not received in full, the claim or counterclaim shall not be dealt with further, pursuant to Article 34(3). Extensions of time may be granted upon request. In order to expedite the proceedings, the claimant is of course not required to wait until the thirty-day limit lapses. Indeed, if it is obvious from the respondent's conduct that it will not pay, it is permissible for the claimant to immediately pay the respondent's shares.

Article 34(4) leaves it to the discretion and control of the claimant to decide **34-034** whether or not to continue the proceedings. This makes sense. The claimant should be entitled to control the fate of the arbitration at this early stage, and should be enabled to progress the case against a recalcitrant respondent. However, the fallback procedure provided in Article 34(4) in case of default payment does not give the respondent or counter-respondent the right to simply ignore its payment obligations.

B.   REMEDY AGAINST NON-PAYMENT

The parties' obligation to comply with the request received by the Secretary **34-035** General derives from the general contractual nature of the Vienna Rules. By explicit reference to this set of rules, the parties have incorporated the Vienna Rules into their arbitration agreement.[52] Given the respondent's unambiguous

---

51. *See, e.g.*, Article 30(3) ICC Rules.
52. *See also* the interpretation of the Vienna Rules under **Article 1**, at paras. 157 *et seq.*

promise, by reference to Article 34(2), to 'pay an equal share of the deposit', the claimant may well seek a decision of the arbitral tribunal ordering such payment. This approach is based on the premise that, since both parties have contractually agreed on the application of the Vienna Rules, they are obliged to honour any payment required under that set of rules.

34-036 This issue was expressly addressed by the Working Group, which proposed, in its draft Section 598 ZPO, to include a specific provision to address the advance on costs. The Working Group's proposal provided, *inter alia*, that '[i]f a party does not pay the advance on costs demanded of it, then the other party may pay the entire advance on costs. In such a case, the party may make a request to the arbitral tribunal that the opposing party be requested by an award to reimburse its portion to the party.' Although this provision was also included in the original governmental draft of the amended arbitration law, it was not incorporated in the ZPO as ultimately adopted. This is unfortunate, as it allows a degree of uncertainty to persist.

34-037 Under the previous Austrian arbitration law, it had been held that as long as the arbitration proceedings continued, the claimant could not claim his additional deposit in the national court. A claim in the state courts was only possible if the arbitration was terminated without an award being rendered;[53] similarly, it was held that a decision on costs by the arbitral tribunal can also include the amount of deposit,[54] but cannot be claimed in separate state court proceedings.[55] The respondents' payment obligation was described as a separate claim for reimbursement against the party which was jointly liable under the arbitration agreement.[56]

34-038 In a recent decision, the Austrian *Oberster Gerichtshof* held that an award of an arbitral tribunal granting the claimant the right to claim payment of the respondent's share is a partial award and, therefore not open to challenge under the former arbitration law.[57] The Austrian *Oberster Gerichtshof* has also recognized an award ordering the payment of a cost deposit when it reviewed a decision by a tribunal seated in Switzerland granting one party a right of recourse after that party had paid the other party's portion of the deposit on costs. The Austrian *Oberster Gerichtshof* found that the decision conformed with Austrian public policy and indeed held that it was 'thoroughly reasonable' for an arbitral tribunal to issue an award redressing a party's default of its obligation to pay its share of the deposit.[58]

---

53. M. Roth, 'Tendenzen im internationalen Kostenrecht – erläutert am Beispiel eines neuen österreichischen Schiedsverfahrensrecht' [2004] SchiedsVZ, 65, 67.
54. OGH, 18 December 2002, 7 Ob 265/02z.
55. OGH, 2 October 2003, 6 Ob 41/03b.
56. H.W. Fasching, 'Kostenvorschüsse zur Einleitung schiedsgerichtlicher Verfahren' [1993] JBl, 545, 551.
57. OGH, 8 March 2006, 7 Ob 252/05t.
58. *See* OGH, 30 October 1985, 3 Ob 89/85.

As this decision dealt with the enforcement of a foreign award in Austria, the **34-039** question whether an arbitral tribunal is in fact entitled to make such a decision through an interim award has not been directly answered (much less under the new Austrian arbitration law).

There are good reasons, however, as for why a claimant should in principle be **34-040** entitled to request the tribunal, once constituted, to direct the respondent to pay its share of the deposit. As discussed, the respondent's contractual obligation to arbitrate under the Vienna Rules includes an express obligation in Article 34(2) to pay a share of the deposit on costs set by the VIAC at the beginning of the arbitration. Article 34(2) is, by its terms, mandatory (*'shall'*), and it is unambiguous in directing both parties to pay the deposit *'in equal shares'*.

A comparison with other institutional rules bears this out. Virtually all institutional **34-041** rules contain a provision requiring both parties to pay an equal share of the advance on the costs of the arbitration. For example, Article 30(3) of the ICC Rules also requires the deposit (referred to under the ICC Rules as an 'advance on costs') to be paid 'in equal shares' by claimants and respondents.[59] Similarly, the UNCITRAL Rules provide at Article 41 that the arbitral tribunal 'may request each party to deposit an equal amount as an advance for the costs' of the arbitration.[60] Article 30 of the ICC Rules is virtually identical to, and served as a model for, Article 34(2) of the Vienna Rules. For Article 30 of the ICC Rules, *Craig/Park/Paulsson* state that the '[r]espondent parties *have the same obligation to pay the advance on costs* as do claimant parties. *By agreeing to ICC arbitration the parties have bound themselves to abide by the Rules. This clearly includes the payment of advances on costs, which is the obligation of both parties.'*[61] Commentaries therefore conclude that *'the defaulting party's refusal to pay its advance* would ordinarily constitute a *breach of contract* since by agreeing to arbitration under the ICC Rules it has

---

59. *See* Article 30(3) ICC Rules: 'The advance on costs fixed by the Court shall be payable in equal shares by the Claimant and the Respondent (...).'
60. Article 41(1) UNCITRAL Rules. *See also* Article 41(1) Swiss Rules: 'The arbitral tribunal, on its establishment, shall request each party to deposit an equal amount as an advance for the costs.' Article 26(2) SIAC Rules: 'The Registrar shall fix the advances or deposits on costs of the arbitration to cover the fees and expenses of the Tribunal and the Centre. Unless the Registrar directs otherwise, such advances and deposits shall be payable by the parties in equal shares.' Article 45(3) SCC Rules: 'Each party shall pay half of the Advance on Costs, unless separate advances are determined.' Article 24(1) LCIA Rules: 'The LCIA Court may direct the parties, in such proportions as it thinks appropriate, to make one or several interim or final payments on account of the costs of the arbitration.'
61. W.L. Craig, W.W. Park and J. Paulsson, *International Chamber of Commerce Arbitration* (3rd edn, New York, Oceana Publications, 2000), p. 263; *see also* Y. Derains and E.A Schwartz, *A Guide to the ICC Rules of Arbitration* (2nd edn, The Hague, Kluwer Law International, 2005), p. 343 ('The parties are nevertheless generally considered, under Article 30(3), to have an obligation, during the course of the arbitration, to share equally in the payment of the advance fixed by the Court (...).').

agreed to respect its provisions regarding advances on costs.'[62] The same analysis applies under Article 34(2) of the Vienna Rules.

34-042 Published arbitral awards addressing the issue also endorse this view. In one of the first ICC awards to address this question, the tribunal reasoned that the rule requiring each party to pay a share of the advance 'imposes upon each party a contractual obligation to pay half of the advance on costs'.[63] Other arbitral tribunals have since echoed that reasoning.[64] For example, in ICC Case No. 11330, the tribunal concluded that 'the parties in arbitrations conducted under the ICC Rules have a mutually binding obligation to pay the advance on costs as determined by the ICC Court, based on Article 30(3) ICC Rules which – by reference – forms part of the parties' agreement to arbitrate under such Rules. Accordingly, in the instant case [non-defaulting party]'s request is, in principle, well founded',[65] and that therefore 'it is appropriate, in view of the contractually independent and autonomous character of the parties' obligation, to render its decision in the form of a partial or interim award rather than as an order only (. . .)'.[66] Similarly, in ICC Case No. 10526, the tribunal rendered a partial award holding that the obligation to pay half of the advance was a 'contractual obligation', and that '[a] decision of the arbitral tribunal on this issue (. . .) has to take the form of a partial award'.[67]

---

62. W.L. Craig, W.W. Park and J. Paulsson, *International Chamber of Commerce Arbitration* (3rd edn, New York, Oceana Publications, 2000), p. 267, *see also* E. Gaillard and J. Savage (eds), *Fouchard Gaillard Goldman On International Commercial Arbitration* (The Hague, Kluwer Law International, 1999), para. 1254 ('The costs of the arbitration are generally advanced by the parties in equal shares. However, the party in whose interest it is to resort to arbitration may have to pay the entire advance where the other party fails to put forward its share. In that case, the party advancing the costs will ask the arbitral tribunal to order the defaulting party, in the final award or even in a partial award confined to that issue, to pay its share because, by agreeing to refer disputes to arbitration, the defaulting party had undertaken to do so.').

63. *Interim Award in ICC Case No. 7289*, 2 September 1996, [2002] Rev Arb, 1001, 1005.

64. *See, e.g., Partial Award in ICC Case No. 11330*, 17 June 2002, cited and quoted in M. Secomb, 'Awards and Orders Dealing with the Advance on Costs in ICC Arbitration: Theoretical Questions and Practical Problems' (2003) 14(1) ICC Ct Bull, 59, 66 ('[T]he Arbitral Tribunal concludes that *the parties in arbitrations conducted under the ICC Rules have a mutually binding obligation to pay the advance on costs as determined by the ICC Court, based on Article 30-3 ICC Rules which* – by reference – *forms part of the parties' agreement to arbitration under such Rules'*). *See also Partial Award in ICC Case No. 10526*, 2 December 2000, [2001] JDI, 1179, 1182 ('*[T]he obligation to pay half of the advance, as provided by the Rules, must be regarded as a contractual obligation*, and any dispute relating thereto is a 'dispute arising of the present contract' within the meaning of the arbitration clause').

65. *Partial Award in ICC Case No. 11330*, 17 June 2002, cited and quoted in M. Secomb, 'Awards and Orders Dealing with the Advance on Costs in ICC Arbitration: Theoretical Questions and Practical Problems' (2003) 14(1) ICC Ct Bull, 59, 63.

66. *Partial Award in ICC Case No. 11330*, 17 June 2002, cited and quoted in M. Secomb, 'Awards and Orders Dealing with the Advance on Costs in ICC Arbitration: Theoretical Questions and Practical Problems' (2003) 14(1) ICC Ct Bull, 59, 67.

67. *See Partial Award in ICC Case No. 10526 (Switzerland)*, 27 March 2001, [2002] Rev Arb, 1035, 1039 ('The claim of the plaintiff who had to pay the entire deposit in no way constitutes (. . .)

Indeed, the principle that each party has a contractual obligation to pay a share of **34-043** the deposit on costs is not unique to arbitrations conducted under institutional rules which codify such a payment requirement. Rather, it can convincingly be argued that this obligation is a term implied into any arbitration agreement as a matter of good faith. It is fundamental to any arbitration agreement that the parties are obliged to cooperate in the arbitral process, including by cooperating in constituting and compensating the tribunal.[68] *Reiner* therefore concludes for Austrian law that 'the arbitration agreement and the parties' duties of co-operation and advancing the proceedings (. . .) mean that the parties have a substantive legal obligation to pay their share of the prepayment on costs, in the absence of an agreement to the contrary'.[69]

International authorities confirm that by agreeing to subject their disputes to arbi- **34-044** tration, parties agree to act, and to arbitrate, in good faith.[70] Therefore, courts have

---

a provisional or conservative measure. It tends to the enforcement of a contractual obligation which will expire only with the reimbursement to the plaintiff of the sums paid by him on behalf of the respondent. On this point, the arbitral Tribunal's decision is neither provisional, nor conservative; it merely aims at ensuring the respect of the engagements resulting from the arbitration clause that have been breached by the respondent. (. . .) *A decision of the arbitral tribunal on this issue definitely decides a dispute relating to a contractual claim. Consequently, it has to take the form of a partial award and not of an interim measure.*').

68. International Law Commission, *Draft on Arbitral Procedure Prepared by the International Law Commission at its Fourth Session, 1952*, UN DOC. A/CN.4/59, Article 1(3), (1952) 2 YB ILC 59, 60 ('The undertaking [to arbitrate] constitutes a legal obligation which must be carried out in good faith, whatever the nature of the agreement from which results'); *Bremer Vulkan Schiffbau und Maschinenfabrik v. South India Shipping Corp.* [1981] 1 All E.R. 289, 299, 301 (House of Lords) ('[T]he obligation is, in my view, mutual: *it obliges each party to cooperate with the other in taking appropriate steps to keep the procedure in the arbitration moving,* whether he happens to be the claimant or the respondent in the particular dispute (. . .). [I]t is in my view a necessary implication from their having agreed that the arbitrator shall resolve their dispute that both parties, respondent as well as claimant, are under a mutual obligation to one another to join in applying to the arbitrator for appropriate directions to put an end to the delay.'). *See also* BGer, 10 May 1982, BGE 108 Ia 197, 201 ('One of the aims of arbitration is to come to a fast resolution of the disputes submitted to it. The parties who agree to arbitration are bound by the rules of good faith to avoid any conduct which might delay without absolute necessity the normal conduct of the arbitral proceedings.').

69. *Reiner* mentions this point in the context of security for costs and interim measures. After dealing with these issues, he then turns to the parties' substantive obligation to pay the advance on costs. ('Furthermore, the arbitration agreement and the parties' duties of co-operation and advancing the proceedings (the German courts have expressly found this duty in German law BGHZ 55, 344) mean that the parties have a substantive legal obligation to pay their share of the prepayment on costs, in the absence of an agreement on the contrary. As a general rule, this is a matter to be ruled on by the arbitral tribunal by arbitral award (and not by the national courts, *see* in this regard, OGH 28.6.2000, 6 Ob 143/00y)'). *See* A. Reiner, *Das neue österreichische Schiedsrecht/The new Austrian Arbitration Law* (Vienna, LexisNexis, 2006), Section 593, note 101.

70. *See* M. Bühler, 'Non-payment of the advance on costs by the respondent party: is there really a remedy?' (2006) 24(2) Bull ASA, 290, 291 *et seq.* ('This implicit obligation is said to stem from

consistently recognized that parties are obligated to pay all advances necessary to initiate and further the arbitral proceedings, as an obligation implied into the agreement to arbitrate in good faith.[71] The obligation to pay a share of the deposit on costs is therefore said to constitute an implied obligation under any arbitration agreement.[72] One commentator has observed for Article 30 of the ICC Rules:

> The parties' obligation under Article 30(3) of the Rules of Arbitration is not just an obligation towards the Court. It forms part of the arbitration agreement. The parties cannot agree to refer their dispute to arbitration and at the same time retain the freedom not to do whatever needs to be done to make arbitration possible, as they would then be in breach of their obligation to act in good faith. In fact, although this obligation is specifically laid down in Article 30(3) of the ICC Rules, it is inherent in any arbitration agreement.[73]

34-045 If this duty, which is express in the context of Article 34(2), is breached, it should like any breach give rise to a remedy. This remedy could be an arbitral award containing a payment order, against the respondent, as for any other payment that is

---

the parties' procedural duty of good faith which requests both parties to further the proceedings and abstain from any actions designed to hamper the arbitration.').

71. *See, e.g.*, AG Düsseldorf, 17 June 2003, 36 C 19607/02, SchiedsVZ, 2003, 240, ('The duty to pay the advance on costs set by the sole arbitrator belongs to the enforceable duties of co-operation and facilitation (good faith duties)'). *See also* OGH, 30 October 1985, 3 Ob 89/85 ('Austrian law affords to the arbitrators the right to a reasonable costs advance with respect to their fees (. . .). The imposition of a duty to pay a costs advance not only on the Plaintiff in the arbitration but also on the Defendant, is a reflection of the fact that both parties, by entering into the arbitration agreement, jointly sought the intervention of arbitrators and are thus jointly and severally liable for their fees. In order to achieve this equal allocation of the risk between both parties, it appears thoroughly reasonable to create a procedure in the event that one party should fail to perform its duty, as is governed in Section 247 of the Zurich Code of Civil Procedure.'). *See also* BGer, 8 December 2003, BGE 4P. 173.2003, (2005) 23(1) Bull ASA 119, 125 (rejecting challenge to enforcement of award issued by ICC tribunal seated in England ordering respondent to reimburse claimant for 50 percent of advance on costs).

72. One leading commentator has explained that 'the parties' obligation to act in good faith to contribute to the organization and furtherance of the arbitration results from [the arbitration agreement]. This means that the arbitration agreement, in addition to the principal obligation to arbitrate the dispute, gives rise to implicit rights and obligations to an extent necessary to perform the agreement. It appears to us that the general obligation to further the advancement of the arbitration results in the parties' reciprocal duty to cover the fees of the arbitration, not only when the final award is executed, which is self-evident, but already by abiding to the arbitrator's demand [to make such payment] as the proceedings progress and as determined by the arbitrator himself.' *See* C. Reymond, 'Note sur l'avance des frais de l'arbitrage et sa repartition' in *Etudes de procedure et d'arbitrage en l'honneur de Jean-Francois Poudret*, J. Haldy, J.-M. Rapp and P. Ferrari (eds) (Lausanne, Stämpfli Verlag, 1999), p. 498.

73. I. Fadlallah, 'Payment of the Advance to Cover Costs in ICC Arbitration: the parties' Reciprocal Obligations' (2003) 14(1) ICC Ct Bull, 53, 55.

due but remains unsatisfied.[74] This solution is indeed suggested by considerable international authority. For example, *Craig/Park/Paulsson* observe:

> All the conditions for an interim award seem fulfilled: immediate harm has been done to the non-defaulting party, the breach of the contractual obligation raises simple issues, the amount of damages are known and the claim is for a liquidated amount. The fact that the final determination of who shall pay the costs of the arbitration will only be known at the time of the final award is irrelevant: the breach of the obligation to pay the advance on costs is final and irrevocable and the damages to the paying party are known (...).[75]

Similarly, *Fouchard/Gaillard/Goldman* state that: **34-046**

> The costs of the arbitration are generally advanced by the parties in equal shares. However, the party in whose interest it is to resort to arbitration may have to pay the entire advance where the other party fails to put forward its share. In that case, the party advancing the costs will ask the arbitral tribunal to order the defaulting party, in the final award or even in a partial award confined to that issue, to pay its share because, by agreeing to refer disputes to arbitration, the defaulting party had undertaken to do so.[76]

---

74. Indeed, **Article 34(2)** specifically provides in relevant part that the 'deposit shall be paid in equal shares by the parties (...) within thirty days after service of the payment request', making it easy to calculate a due date.
75. W.L Craig, W.W. Park and J. Paulsson, *International Chamber of Commerce Arbitration* (3rd edn, New York, Oceana Publications, 2000), p. 268; *see also* I. Fadlallah, 'Payment of the Advance to Cover Costs in ICC Arbitration: The parties' Reciprocal Obligations' (2003) 14(1) ICC Ct Bull, 53, 56 *et seq.* ('A party's obligation to pay its share of the advance on costs is extinguished by payment. To make it dependent upon the final award on costs would be to ignore its very purpose as an advance. The decision is a final decision on this obligation which, by its very nature, paves the way for the final award. *A partial award is therefore required, not an order, since the decision does not concern a procedural matter but extinguishes the contractual obligation to pay the advance. Accordingly, it is in no way an interim measure and is not subject to the conditions applying to such measures.*'). *See also* C. Reymond, 'Note sur l'avance des frais de l'arbitrage et sa repartition' in *Etudes de procedure et d'arbitrage en l'honneur de Jean-François Poudret*, J. Haldy, J.-M. Rapp and P. Ferrari (eds) (Lausanne, Stämpfli Verlag, 1999), p. 502 ('If it is admitted that *the parties' duty to reciprocally contribute to the payment of the advance on costs demanded by the arbitrator results from the arbitration agreement, it must also be admitted that the breach of this obligation justifies such a [partial award].*'). For commentary on Swiss Rules, *see also* M. Stacher in *Swiss Rules of International Arbitration*, T. Zuberbühler, C. Müller and P. Habegger (eds) (Zürich, Schulthess Verlag, 2005), Article 41, para. 20 ('A decision of the arbitral tribunal to this effect is not an interim measure, but an award.').
76. E. Gaillard and J. Savage (eds), *Fouchard Gaillard Goldman On International Commercial Arbitration* (The Hague, Kluwer Law International, 1999), para. 1254. For Swiss law, *see also* W. Wenger and C. Müller in *International Arbitration in Switzerland*, H. Honsell *et al.* (eds)

34-047 In Austria, *Reiner* states in similar terms that 'the parties have a substantive legal obligation to pay their share of the prepayment on costs, in the absence of an agreement to the contrary. As a general rule, this is a matter to be ruled on by the arbitral tribunal by arbitral award (and not by the national courts (. . .).)'.[77] Of course, in rendering such an award, the tribunal retains its authority under Section 609 ZPO to re-allocate these costs between the parties once the arbitration is concluded, taking into account, in particular, the outcome of the proceedings.

34-048 Although modern Austrian doctrine, supported by substantial international authority, endorses the notion of a partial award directing a defaulting respondent to pay its share of the cost deposit, there is a more traditional view in Austria that opposes that approach. Thus, some Austrian authors rehearse, perhaps without much independent reflection, the strict view of *Fasching*, first formulated in 1973, that an arbitration agreement is of a purely procedural nature that does not give rise to substantive obligations, or sanctions.[78] Under that theory, the obligation to pay the cost deposit is of a merely procedural nature and distinct from a substantive payment obligation. As a procedural obligation, it supposedly falls outside the scope of the arbitration agreement. Whilst its historic merits are understandable, this view raises substantial policy concerns and finds little support in modern doctrine.

34-049 First, as a policy matter, it is quite unsatisfactory to suggest that the respondent could agree to arbitrate under the Vienna Rules, and therefore by reference accept Article 34(2) and its express obligation to pay an equal share of the deposit, but then not be held to this promise. A solution that postulates a breach of contract without sanction leaves much to wish for.

34-050 Second, it is argued that the Vienna Rules itself provide the immediate consequence for the respondent's failure to pay its share of the deposit, by requesting the claimant to pay the full deposit alone,[79] again as a purely procedural matter. It is undisputed that Article 34(4) of the Vienna Rules provides a procedural fallback mechanism.[80] Where a recalcitrant party refuses to meet its obligation to pay its

---

(Basel/The Hague, Kluwer Law International, 2000), Article 178, para. 71 ('A claimant who has an interest that the arbitral proceedings be conducted is also entitled to pay that part of the advance on the costs of the proceedings which the other party refuses to pay *and* – if it has paid the whole amount in order to accelerate the arbitral proceedings – *to recovery of such costs* irrespective of whether the agreement to arbitrate or the applicable arbitration rules contain any provisions on this point. *An arbitration agreement contains the implicit obligation that each party make an advance payment towards the prospective costs of the arbitral proceedings in the amount ordered by the arbitral tribunal (. . .).*').

77. A. Reiner, *Das neue österreichische Schiedsrecht/The new Austrian Arbitration Law* (Vienna, LexisNexis, 2006), Section 593, note 101.

78. H.W. Fasching, 'Kostenvorschüsse zur Einleitung schiedsgerichtlicher Verfahren' [1993] JBl, 545, 549, 511; W. Hahnkamper in *Schiedsgerichtsbarkeit*, H. Torggler (ed.) (Vienna, Verlag Österreich, 2007), pp. 129 *et seq.*

79. See **Article 34**, at para. 033.

80. 'If the share of the Respondent (Counter-Respondent) is not received within the time-limit set, the Secretary General shall inform the claimant (Counter-Claimant) thereof and shall request

share of the deposit, the Vienna Rules permit the other, non-defaulting party to pay the deposit in full so that the arbitrators can be secured and the arbitration can proceed.[81] Any other solution would allow the respondent to bring the arbitration to a standstill simply by defaulting on its payment obligation. This is because **Article 12** provides that the 'Secretary General shall transmit the files to the arbitral tribunal as soon as the deposit for costs has been paid (Article 34). The proceedings before the sole arbitrator (arbitral tribunal) shall thereby commence.' Without the procedural possibility of advancing the defaulting respondent's share, therefore, the arbitration would not even commence and the claimant would be left without a tribunal from which to obtain relief, based simply on the refusal on the part of the respondent to comply with its obligation to pay its share of the deposit.

However, the existence of a procedural fallback mechanism that allows the non-defaulting party to constitute the tribunal and commence the arbitral proceedings even where the other party has breached its obligation to arbitrate in good faith in no way justifies or excuses that breach. There is no suggestion in the Vienna Rules or elsewhere that the fallback procedure in Article 34(4) relieves the defaulting party of its express obligation under Article 34(2) that the 'deposit shall be paid in equal shares by the parties'. Article 34(4) is, by its terms, a procedural mechanism that allows the arbitration to proceed despite the defaulting party's breach of its payment obligation. As *Reiner* has summarized, '[t]he possibility of allowing the plaintiff to make payment in place of the defaulting defendant is not offered in the latter's interest, and does not release the defendant from its contractual obligation to pay its share of the advance'.[82] Indeed, tribunals constituted under the Vienna Rules 2006 have adopted this approach and assumed jurisdiction to compel the respondent to pay its share of the deposit.[83] **34-051**

A comparison with the ICC Rules is again instructive. Article 30(3) of the ICC Rules is virtually identical to Article 34(4) of the Vienna Rules in allowing the non-defaulting party 'to pay the whole of the advance on costs (. . .) should the other party fail to pay its share'.[84] Notwithstanding this fallback procedure, the Secretary General of the ICC Court of Arbitration has clarified that '*it is not an accepted practice* (. . .) for a party to refuse to pay all or part of its share of the advance on costs and to leave it to the other party to pay for the defaulting party'.[85] One of the **34-052**

---

him to pay the outstanding share of the deposit within thirty days of receipt of the payment request. If that amount is not received within the time-limit, the claim (counter-claim) shall not be treated any further. The Secretary General shall inform the parties thereof.'

81. This provision is identical to similar mechanisms contained in all leading institutional arbitration rules. *See* Article 30(3) ICC Rules; Article 41(4) UNCITRAL Rules; Article 41(4) Swiss Rules; Article 45(4) SCC Rules and Article 24(3) LCIA Rules.

82. A. Reiner, 'Les mesures provisoires et conservatoires et l'Arbitrage international, notamment l'Arbitrage CCI' (1998) JDI, 853, 891.

83. *See Order in VIAC Case No. SCH-5004 of 2008* (unpublished).

84. *See* Article 30(3) ICC Rules: 'The advance on costs fixed by the Court shall be payable in equal shares by the Claimant and the Respondent.'

85. W.L. Craig, W.W. Park and J. Paulsson, *International Chamber of Commerce Arbitration* (3rd edn, New York, Oceana Publications, 2000), pp. 263 *et seq.*

earliest ICC awards to address the fallback provision in the ICC Rules observed that this provision is 'merely an expedient intended to facilitate the continuation of the proceedings' and '[i]t does not remove the substantive obligation that lies on each party in ICC arbitration, as a result of the contractual undertaking they make towards each other, to have to participate equally in the payment of the advance on costs'.[86] Published awards addressing this issue confirm this approach and have, accordingly, awarded reimbursement to the non-defaulting party.[87]

34-053 Third, the position of *Fasching* and others, in resting on the procedural nature of arbitration agreements, assumes its own conclusion. That an arbitration agreement is a procedural instrument does not mean that substantive rules are inapplicable. To the contrary, modern doctrine is unanimous in accepting that, to the extent procedural law is silent, an arbitration agreement (even if viewed as a purely procedural instrument) follows substantive rules of contract law.[88] There is no reason, therefore, not to apply substantive rules of contract law on the parties' promise to pay equal shares of the deposit. As a result, once the obligation to pay the deposit is due, it should be capable of being enforced like any other payment obligation, including by affording the claimant a right to reimbursement for any amounts already paid on behalf of a defaulting respondent.[89]

34-054 Fourth, and finally, even if one accepted the purely procedural character of the obligation to share in equal measure in the payment of the deposit, to the exclusion of any substantive rules of contract law, this would not automatically lead to the loss of any remedy for the claimant. For example, a party's obligation to disclose certain documents is clearly of a procedural nature. No-one would suggest that this obligation falls outside the scope of the arbitration agreement, or that the tribunal would otherwise lack the authority to address the matter. To the contrary, the tribunal is the master, under **Article 20**, of all procedural matters and could, if

---

86. *See Interim Award in ICC Case No. 7289*, 2 September 1996, [2002] Rev Arb, 1001-1007.
87. *See Award in ICC Case No. 10169*, 10 September 1999; *Partial Award in ICC Case No. 1186*, 20 December 2002 and *Partial Award in ICC Case 11392*, 25 October 2002, cited and quoted in M. Secomb, 'Awards and Orders Dealing with the Advance on Costs in ICC Arbitration: Theoretical Questions and Practical Problems' (2003) 14(1) ICC Ct Bull, 65 *et seq*.
88. S. Riegler in *Arbitration Law of Austria: Practice and Procedure*, S. Riegler, A. Petsche, A. Fremuth-Wolf, M. Platte and C. Liebscher (eds) (Huntington, Juris Publishing, 2007), Section 609, p. 483 ('The arbitration agreement is seen as a "procedural agreement" (and not as a "substantive agreement") by both legal literature and case law in Austria. Its main effect is to deviate from court proceedings, which is seen as a procedural effect. *This however does not mean that only procedural rules are applicable to arbitration agreements.* Only where procedural law expressly provides (e.g. with respect to form and effect of the arbitration agreement, subjective and objective arbitrability), its rules prevail; *where it is silent* (e.g. general validity, conclusion and termination of contracts, interpretation etc.) *the respective rules of substantive law on contracts may apply.*'). *See also* W.H. Rechberger and W. Melis in *Kommentar zur ZPO*, W.H. Rechberger (ed.) (3rd edn, Vienna/New York, Springer, 2006), Section 581, para. 5.
89. For example, Section 1042 ABGB provides that a person who 'makes a payment on someone else's behalf, which that person was obliged to do under the law, has a claim for reimbursement'.

the procedural school were followed, address the respondent's failure to pay its share of the deposit by procedural order.

In short, there is widespread acceptance in international practice of remedies **34-055** addressing a respondent's default on the deposit. However, there are circumstances in which a respondent will legitimately question the obligation under Article 34(2). Most importantly, a respondent denying that an arbitration agreement has been concluded or that it applies to the dispute at issue will refer to its lack of consent to arbitrate under the Vienna Rules. Where no arbitration agreement has been concluded, or where the arbitration agreement does not apply the obligation under Article 34(2) to pay an equal share of the deposit has not been assumed. Where such defences are raised, arbitrators will be hesitant to make an award before having heard the parties, and indeed before having denied on jurisdiction.

V.   INCREASE OF THE AMOUNT IN DISPUTE

Article 34(5): If it should be necessary in the course of the proceedings to increase the deposit against costs because of an increase in the amount in dispute, a procedure analogous to that provided for in paragraphs 2 to 4 of the present Article shall be adopted. Until payment of the additional deposit, the amplification of the claim that led to the increase of the amount in dispute shall not be taken into account in the arbitral proceedings.

The administrative costs and the arbitrators' fees depend on the amount in dispute. **34-056** As a result, the arbitrators must inform the Secretary General of any subsequent increase in the amount in dispute. This can occur if the claim is amended, if a counter-claim is introduced, a set-off defence raised, or another party with separate claims joined to the proceeding. As a textual matter, the Vienna Rules only refer to 'the amplification of the claim'; in reality, any of these procedural acts can lead to an increase in the amount in dispute. Any such increase falls within Article 34(5), although a clarification in the text of the provision would be welcome.

An increase of the amount in dispute will lead to a recalculation of the deposit and, **34-057** if necessary, to a request for an additional deposit to the party which has caused the increase.[90] The time limit for additional payment will be thirty days; extensions are usually granted. Under the practice of the current Secretary General, this further request for a deposit, like the initial deposit, will be divided between the parties. The reference to an analogous procedure under Article 34(2) to (4) enables the Secretary General to proceed in line with these provisions, in particular in case of default by either party. Hence, as discussed above, in case the opposing party has an interest in the procedural action that increased the amount, it should be allowed to honour the other parties' payment obligation.

---

90. A reduction of the amount in dispute shall only be taken into consideration if such reduction occurred before the transmission of the files to the arbitrators. *See* **Article 36(8)**, at paras. 033 and 034.

34-058 The second sentence of Article 34(5) introduces an additional obligation on the arbitrators. Until payment of the additional deposit has been received in full, the arbitrators must not engage the claim (or other procedural act) that caused the increase of the amount in dispute. This could cause difficulties in the practical handling of the proceedings, as the facts and issues of the case are sometimes not clearly divisible. Properly interpreted, Article 34(5) does not necessarily prevent the arbitrators from proceeding with the case, but the arbitrators must at least refuse to address this claim in the award. In case an increase of the amount in dispute is anticipated, the arbitrators should inform both the Secretary General and the parties.

VI.   ADDITIONAL EXPENSES

Article 34(6): If it should be necessary in the course of the proceedings to increase the deposit against costs because the amount fixed for cash outlay on determining the deposit is not sufficient, a procedure analogous to that provided for in paragraphs 2 to 4 of the present Article shall be adopted.

34-059 Cash outlays are determined according to actual expenditure.[91] The authority for the initial determination of the cash outlays lies with the Secretary General. This provision confirms that this authority remains with the Secretary General throughout the course of the proceedings. It also establishes an obligation for the Secretary General to monitor the financial status of the file. In complex matters, additional expenditures, not foreseen at the outset of the arbitration and therefore not included in the initial deposit, may easily be incurred.

34-060 Whilst the non-payment of an additional deposit under Article 34(5) attracts the express sanction of non-treatment, no express sanction is provided by Article 34(6). The reference to the adoption of a procedure analogous to Article 34(2) to (4) indicates that the parties will again be requested to share in the additional cash outlay. In case of non-payment, the opposing party will be requested to step in provisionally. In case neither party follows the payment request, the Secretary General will inform the arbitrators about the lack of funds to cover additional expenditures. The arbitrators will then have to decide which conclusion to draw from the parties' conduct and decide on the impact of the arbitration proceedings.

34-061 This is in line with **Article 35**, as it is for the arbitrators to determine the consequences of any failure to pay such further deposits to cover additional expenditures.[92] However, Article 34(6) has deliberately been allowed to remain in existence and forms a fallback option for arbitrators to secure the payment of the cash outlays. In such cases, depending on the directions given, the Secretary General may be entrusted with auxiliary work of the arbitral tribunal.[93]

---

91. *See* **Article 36(9)**, at para. 040.
92. *See* **Article 35(3)**, at paras. 008 *et seq.*
93. *See* **Article 35(1)**, at para. 003.

Article 35

Further Costs of Procedure

	Para.		Para.
I. Cost Cover for All Procedural Actions	1	III. Failure to Pay Additional Cost Deposits	8
II. Budgeting Expenditures	4	IV. Liability for Procedural Costs	13

I.   COST COVER FOR ALL PROCEDURAL ACTIONS

Article 35(1): If the sole arbitrator (arbitral tribunal) considers certain actions entailing costs, such as the appointment of experts, interpreters or translators, making verbatim records of the proceedings, a visual inspection, or relocation of the proceedings, to be necessary, he (it) must make arrangements to cover the expected costs and inform the Secretary General thereof.

Article 35 was in terms introduced with the 2001 amendment of the Vienna Rules,[1] and was adopted in its entirety in the Vienna Rules 2006. It ensures that the costs of the arbitration are sufficiently covered at every stage of the proceedings. It also imposes an obligation on the arbitrators to monitor the financial status of the case – an obligation that exists in parallel to the Secretary General's obligation to monitor expenditures under **Article 34(6)**. The VIAC emphasizes the importance of this provision by requiring each arbitrator to separately acknowledge the wording of Article 35(1) together with signing the declaration of acceptance and independence at the beginning of the proceedings.[2] **35-001**

---

1. Article 23a Vienna Rules 2001, **Annex 2a**.
2. *See* Arbitrator's Declaration of Acceptance, Statement of Independence and Undertaking to Observe Rules on Costs, **Annex 4**; *see also* Guidelines for Arbitrators, **Annex 5**.

35-002 The enumeration of procedural actions in Article 35(1) is illustrative, listing examples of actions that typically incur additional costs. However, arbitrators need to monitor *all* costs incurred throughout the arbitration, whether arising from acts listed in Article 35(1) or not. It also makes no difference if the procedural acts that will incur costs have been requested by the parties or if they are conducted *ex officio* by the arbitral tribunal.

35-003 Article 35(1) requires the arbitrators to schedule specific procedural acts only if the costs incurred by conducting these acts are covered by the deposit already on hold. To fulfil this function, arbitrators will have to liaise closely with the Secretary General who runs a separate account for each arbitration. If the costs for procedural actions are covered by the initial deposit of costs as calculated by the Secretary General, no further action needs to be taken. If the existing deposit does not suffice, Article 35(1) requires the arbitrators to arrange financial cover ('*must make arrangements*'). To that end, arbitrators can either exercise their procedural discretion under **Article 20** and issue a procedural order, setting time limits within which payments for the contemplated procedural acts have to be affected; or else they can seek the assistance of the Secretary General to request an additional deposit pursuant to **Article 34(6)**. In that case, the arbitrators have to inform the Secretary General about the nature of the procedural action and the amount that needs to be collected.[3]

II.   BUDGETING EXPENDITURES

> **Article 35(2): The sole arbitrator (arbitral tribunal) may undertake procedural steps in accordance with paragraph 1 of the present Article only if adequate cover for the expected costs exists.**

35-004 The Vienna Rules entrust to the arbitrators full discretion in conducting their case; **Article 20** entitles them to establish the facts of the case as they deem appropriate to fulfil their judicial mandate. This does not permit the arbitrators to disregard economic reality. Inexperienced arbitrators, eager perhaps to meticulously investigate the facts of their case, have been known to instruct experts, or obtain verbatim records of hearings, without any consideration of whether the associated costs were actually necessary or covered by the existing deposit. Where costs are outstanding at the end of the proceedings, parties anticipating an adverse outcome may be reluctant to comply with any additional payment order, shifting the burden and ultimately the risk of recovery solely to the other party.

35-005 Reinforcing the principles set out by Article 35(1), Article 35(2) imposes a strict obligation on the arbitrators to undertake procedural steps only if adequate cover for such costs exists. As a textual matter, the adequacy of the cover appears to be at the sole discretion of the arbitrators; hence, other security than cash payment could

---

3. *See* **Article 34(6)**, at para. 061.

be acceptable. Given the practice of the VIAC as regards the initial deposit, additional cash deposit is, however, preferable.[4]

While the obligation for arbitrators to arrange for adequate cover for any **35-006** procedural act is clear, Article 35(2) does not shift the ultimate financial responsibility to the arbitrators. If the arbitrators happen to undertake procedural actions without providing for adequate financial cover, the parties will still remain financially accountable for those actions. This is the result of Article 35(4) which authorizes the arbitrators to undertake any such commitments in the name and for the account of the parties.[5]

In order to comply with Article 35(2), arbitrators are again well advised to avail **35-007** themselves of the services offered by the VIAC. The Secretary General will not only keep a separate account for the case, but will assist in collecting additional cash deposits and otherwise assist the arbitrators in monitoring the financial status and progress of the file.

III.   FAILURE TO PAY ADDITIONAL COST DEPOSITS

Article 35(3): The sole arbitrator (arbitral tribunal) shall decide what consequences for the proceedings arise from the failure to pay a prescribed deposit against costs.

If the initial deposit is not paid in full, the file is not transmitted to the arbitrators **35-008** and the claim will not be treated any further.[6] Equally, if the amount in dispute subsequently increases, or if additional claims are added that increase the amount in dispute or if additional parties are joined that affect the calculation of the administrative fees and the fees of the arbitrators, an additional deposit is calculated; it must be paid in full, lest the additional or amended claim will not be treated in the arbitration.[7]

It follows from the provisions of Article 35(1) and (2) that the same is true with **35-009** respect to procedural acts. If the costs they incur are not sufficiently covered by the existing deposit, and the additional deposit is not paid in full, the arbitrators are not entitled to conduct those procedural acts.

However, as an evidentiary matter, this may have consequences for the proceed- **35-010** ings and the establishment of the facts of the case. If the travel costs necessary to conduct a site inspection are not funded, the site inspection will not be conducted. If the tribunal intends to appoint an expert, but the deposit for the associated costs is

---

4. *See* **Article 36**, at paras. 001 *et seq.*
5. *See* **Article 35(4)**, at paras. 013 *et seq.*
6. *See* **Article 34**, at paras. 032 *et seq.*
7. *See* **Article 34**, at paras. 056 *et seq.*

not paid in full, the instruction cannot proceed. In all of these cases, the tribunal's ability to establish that facts of the case is affected.

35-011 A failure to pay a cost deposit for evidentiary acts may also have consequences for a party's discharge of its burden of proof. If a party has, for example, applied for a visual inspection of a site and is not willing to cover the expected travel costs of the arbitrators, this can, in the exercise of the arbitrators' discretion, be construed as having failed to offer proof in the first place. If the arbitrators consider a party's failure to pay the cost deposit as obstructive, perhaps as a deliberate decision to prevent crucial evidence from being taken, it is also conceivable that the arbitrators draw adverse inferences from such refusal to fund the costs of an evidentiary measure.[8] In such a case, the arbitrators may wish to draw the parties' attention to the fact that such behaviour could yield negative consequences.

35-012 For this reason, Article 35(3) clarifies that the tribunal has the authority to determine the consequences of such cost default for the proceedings. Although Article 35(3) is a welcome clarification, this power already derives from the principle of procedural discretion as expressed in **Article 20**.[9]

IV.   LIABILITY FOR PROCEDURAL COSTS

> **Article 35(4): All commitments related to the procedural steps mentioned in paragraph 1 of the present Article shall be undertaken by the sole arbitrator (arbitral tribunal) in the name and for the account of the parties.**

35-013 This provision contains an express power for the arbitrators to incur liability for the costs associated with any procedural act on behalf of the parties. As a result, the parties – and not the arbitrators – are liable for any cost incurred. This applies to any procedural act, not merely the examples given in Article 35(1).[10] Costs incurred for such procedural acts, and financed by the parties through additional deposits, constitute appropriate expenditures related to the arbitration, and will therefore be recoverable under **Article 31**.[11]

35-014 However, it bears emphasis, again, that the arbitrators may undertake procedural actions only adequate financial cover exists. It could be argued, therefore, that the arbitrators are permitted to actually make use of their authority to commit the parties only to the extent that the parties have honoured the request to pay a deposit. In other words, if the arbitrators instruct an expert without securing financial cover, the parties would be liable for the costs incurred under Article 35(4) – but the arbitrators would have exceeded their authority *vis-à-vis* the parties. The consequences of such

---

8. *See* **Article 20**, at paras. 171 *et seq.*
9. *See* **Article 20**, at paras. 001 *et seq.*
10. As discussed, the list in **Article 35(1)** is illustrative, not exclusive.
11. *See* **Article 31**, at paras. 017 *et seq.*

an excess use of authority as between the arbitrators and the parties would have to be examined under the substantive law applicable to the arbitrators' contract.[12]

Unless otherwise agreed, the procedural act will be undertaken in the name and for **35-015** the account of *all* the parties to the arbitration. For purposes of VAT, it is essential that the arbitrators do not order services in their own name.[13] Absent any deviating agreements, the arbitrators should arrange for each party, upon request, to receive a proper invoice of the service divided *per capita*.

---

12. For restrictions placed on the arbitrators' liability, *see also* **Article 8**, at paras. 025 *et seq.*
13. *See* C. W. Konrad and H. Gurtner, *Die Umsatzsteuer im Schiedsverfahren* (Cologne/Munich, Carl Heymanns Verlag, 2008).

Article 36

Calculating the Costs of Arbitration

		Para.			Para.
I.	Determination of Arbitration		IV.	Separate Calculations	19
	Costs	1	V.	Partial Claim and Undervaluation	23
	A. Introduction	1	VI.	Raise of Fees	28
	B. The Schedule of Arbitration		VII.	Comprehensive Cost	
	Costs	2		Determination	32
	C. Early Termination of the		VIII.	Reduction of the Amount in	
	Proceedings	6		Dispute	33
II.	Multi-Party Proceedings	11	IX.	Determination of Cash Outlays	35
III.	Declaration of Set-Off	12	X.	Value Added Tax	41

I.   DETERMINATION OF ARBITRATION COSTS

Article 36(1): The administrative costs of the Centre and the arbitrators' fees shall be fixed on the basis of the amount in dispute, according to the schedule of arbitration costs attached to these Rules (Annex 1). Where the proceedings are terminated early, the Secretary General may reduce the arbitrators' fees as it appears just corresponding to the stage reached in the proceedings.

A.   Introduction

The authority to determine the costs of the arbitration proceedings lies exclusively **36-001** with the Secretary General. This corresponds with Austrian arbitration law, which does not permit the arbitrators to create for themselves a valid title to their costs in an award. The costs depend on the amount in dispute. In principle, their calculation follows the schedule of arbitration costs, which can be found in Annex I attached to the Rules. There are, however, various additional factors that can influence the cost determination. Although the system adopted by the Vienna Rules is transparent and reliable, there are certain situations where the Secretary General has sole discretion to determine some aspects of the costs. All of this is discussed below, with the emphasis on the VIAC's standard practice.

B.   THE SCHEDULE OF ARBITRATION COSTS

36-002 The administrative costs of the VIAC and the arbitrators' fees depend on the amount in dispute – an approach that is also adopted in other prominent arbitration rules.[1] The currently applicable costs schedule was last amended on 30 November 2000 and took effect on 1 January 2001. It contains a table of progressive costs which divides the amount in dispute into different sections. Each section specifies a minimum basis for evaluating costs and adds a percentage based amount on top. The minimum administrative charge is €3,000.00, the maximum is €20,500.00 plus 0.01% of any amount in excess of €10,000,000.00. The minimum arbitrator's fee is €1,000.00 or 6% of the amount in dispute. The maximum basis is €174,500.00 plus 0,01% of any amount in excess of €100,000,000.00.

36-003 The amount in dispute is the principal basis for the determination of costs. Apart from Article 36(6), the amount of costs is almost completely independent from the time or resources consumed by a particular proceeding. There is no reduction of the fees or the administrative costs in the event the arbitration is concluded in a relatively swift or straightforward manner, nor any increase for particularly lengthy or complex cases. Likewise, the amount of time spent on a particular case by the individual arbitrator will influence the decision on costs, only in the case of an early termination of the proceedings, as discussed below.[2]

36-004 The Vienna Rules conceptually do not provide for parties and the arbitrators to contractually exclude the application of the fee structure or agree on alternative arrangements. In this, the Vienna Rules are not significantly different from the Rules of other institutionalized arbitration proceedings.

36-005 Further, it could also be argued that, as with Article 2(4) Appendix III to the ICC Rules, separate fee arrangements between the parties and the arbitrator would be considered contrary to the Rules. Whilst this could presumably reach the threshold

---

1. Article 2(1) Appendix III and Article 31 ICC Rules; Article 40(5) DIS Rules; Article 9 (The Decision on Costs) attached to Croatian Rules; Article 2(3) (Principles Governing the Costs of Arbitral Proceedings) attached to Czech Rules; Article 3 (Regulation on the Arbitration Fees, Costs and Expenses of the Parties) attached to Hungarian Rules; Article 9 (Rules Governing the Costs of Arbitration Proceedings) attached to the Slovak Rules. Note a different approach in Article 4(a) (Schedule of Fees and Costs) attached to LCIA Rules and Article 32 AAA/ICDR Rules primarily on an hourly rate basis.
2. *See* **Article 36**, at paras. 006 *et seq.*

established under **Article 9(6)**, it would directly affect the contractual relation of the arbitrators *vis-à-vis* the parties.[3] Agreement to the Vienna Rules arguably leads to the implicit conclusion that the parties have simultaneously accepted the remuneration system specified therein. Any agreement to the contrary would have to be brought to the arbitrator's attention and would require his or her full consent prior to the acceptance of the mandate.

C.   EARLY TERMINATION OF THE PROCEEDINGS

The schedule of costs provided in the Vienna Rules is intended to cover the full **36-006** range and length of arbitral proceedings. As a corollary, an early termination of the proceedings must have some financial impact on the cost determination.[4] The second sentence of Article 36(1) explicitly addresses this issue. It permits the Secretary General, where the arbitration has been terminated early, to reduce the arbitrator's fees depending on the stage reached in the proceedings.[5] It does not, however, penalize arbitrators for reaching a swift decision. In other words, an arbitration, which was conducted efficiently and therefore 'terminated early' by a final award, will not lead to a reduction in the costs of the arbitration.

The former version of the Vienna Rules[6] empowered the Secretary General to **36-007** determine the arbitrators' fees at the *appropriate levels*. Under the new Article 36, this authority remains with the Secretary General who now exercises this power at his equitable discretion (*nach billigem Ermessen*).

The determination of costs thus depends on the phase the proceedings have reached. It **36-008** is the standing practice of the Secretary General to distinguish between three different phases. The first phase starts with the transmission of the files to the arbitrators and includes the tribunal's first procedural orders. The second phase covers the conduct of the proceedings, including in particular the oral hearings and the taking of evidence. The third and final phase is comprised of the arbitrators' rendering of the award.

Of course, there is a significant degree of variation; this form of classification into **36-009** stages merely serves as a guideline rather than a fixed model for calculation. In order to determine the different stages in the proceedings in a manner that gives sufficient consideration to the specific context of the arbitration, the Secretary General might approach the arbitrators and/or the parties and ask for further comments. In doing so, the Secretary General acts at his sole equitable discretion and is not bound by any unilateral or joint declaration by the parties and/or the arbitrators.

---

3. *See* **Article 8**, at 011 *et seq.*
4. Article 2(6) Appendix III to ICC Rules; Article 28(5) LCIA Rules; *see* also Article 40(3) DIS Rules: 'If proceedings are terminated prematurely, the arbitral tribunal may at its equitable discretion reduce the fees in accordance with the progress of the proceedings.'
5. *See* **Article 25**, at paras. 001 *et seq.*
6. Article 24(1) Vienna Rules 2001, **Annex 2a**.

The final decision on the calculation of costs will contain reasons and is transmitted to the arbitrators and the parties alike.

36-010 It may be noted that this paragraph only addresses the calculation of the arbitrator's fees. The former version, dealing with an early termination of the proceedings, also permitted a reduction of the administrative costs of the Centre. This was deliberately abandoned through the last amendment in order to adapt the wording to the standard practice of the Secretary General. As discussed earlier, the VIAC takes the position that most of the administrative work is effectively done at the beginning of the proceedings in the period preceding the transmission of the files to the arbitrators. Since an early termination would therefore not influence its workload, a reduction of costs on this ground has hitherto rarely occurred.[7]

II.   MULTI-PARTY PROCEEDINGS

Article 36(2): If there are more than two parties to the proceedings, the rates for the administrative costs of the Centre and the arbitrators' fees contained in the schedules attached to these Rules shall be increased by 10% for each additional party.

36-011 The involvement of more than two parties will normally result in increased workload for the VIAC and the arbitrators. Therefore, Article 36(2) provides for the increase of 10 % in both the administrative costs[8] and the arbitrator's fees for each additional party. A decrease in the number of parties involved in the arbitration will only lead to a decrease of the costs if it occurred prior to the transmission of the file to the arbitrators.[9] By contrast, an increase in the number of parties at any stage of the proceedings will result in an increase of the applicable rates. Somewhat surprisingly and in contrast with other institutional rules,[10] the Vienna Rules do not contain a cap on the increase in fees caused by the addition of parties, theoretically allowing for an unlimited increase of the fees. Arbitrators might therefore be inclined to allow the inclusion of other parties in their proceedings, for example where the parties have made an application for joinder of proceedings or the extension of their claim to third parties. As there is no preliminary authority controlling the arbitrators' decision on this issue, there exists a potential conflict with the principle under Austrian law prohibiting arbitrators from determining their own costs.[11] This principle must equally be true for an increase of their fees.[12]

---

7. *See* **Article 34**, at paras. 007 *et seq.*
8. *See* **Article 33(2)**, at para. 006. for the increase of the registration fee.
9. *See* **Article 36**, at paras. 033 *et seq.*
10. Item 11) Appendix to Section 40 sub. 5 attached to DIS Rules: 'If more than two parties are involved in the arbitral proceedings, the amounts of the arbitrators' fees pursuant to this schedule are increased by 20% for each additional party. The arbitrators' fees are increased by no more than 50% in total.'
11. *See* **Article 34**, at para. 008.
12. *See* **Article 34**, at para. 010.

Since the increase in the number of parties depends solely upon a party's application and is not a decision that can be made *suo motu* by the arbitrators, it can be argued that this process is in line with that principle. However, where a party intends to increase the number of the initial parties to the proceedings during the arbitration, the arbitrators should draw the parties' attention to the increase in fees that would arise as a result of this procedural action. As such an application will also immediately result in an increase of the deposit of costs, the arbitrators will have to inform the Secretary General accordingly.[13]

III.   DECLARATION OF SET-OFF

Article 36(3): The arbitration costs for claims that are submitted to offset against the claim (counter-claims) and that are in fact and in law of no connection with the cause of action (principle claims), are to be calculated separately and paid as like counter-claims. Article 34 shall apply accordingly to determine the deposits. Counter-claims are not to be dealt with in the proceedings concerning the principle claims until the additional deposits have been fully paid.

General considerations arising out of the defence of set-off in arbitration proceedings are discussed under **Article 11**.[14] This section surveys the financial impact of a claim for set-off on the costs of the arbitration. **36-012**

Article 36(3) was inserted through the last amendment of the Vienna Rules in 2006. It reflects the VIAC's previous practice of including set-off declarations in the calculation of the arbitration costs. The idea behind this approach is that a set-off defence can easily introduce new facts into the proceedings which are capable of increasing the arbitrators' workload, sometimes even in excess of the main claim.[15] Such work is not recognized in the initial calculation of the arbitration costs and would otherwise be unaccounted for. **36-013**

In the past, parties have tried to circumvent the financial burden of a counter-claim by first declaring their claim against the claimant in the form of a defence of set-off and then relying on the absence of any provision for calculating the costs of a set-off in the Vienna Rules. It was then argued that the Vienna Rules in such a case provide for no extra cost calculation. The Secretary General, absent an express provision under the former version of the Vienna Rules, usually addressed this situation by invoking (then) Article 24(4) and argued that this would in fact amount to a separate claim which would justify the calculation of additional fees as **36-014**

---

13. *See* paragraph 4 for the influence on calculating the arbitrators fees.
14. *See* **Article 11**, at paras. 043 *et seq.*
15. This seems equally recognized in other arbitration rules. *See, e.g.*, Article 30(5) ICC Rules; Article 4 (Tariff of Fees) attached to Polish Rules and Article 5 on the Arbitration Fees attached to Hungarian Rules.

foreseen by that provision.[16] This result was often criticized and led to dissatisfaction amongst parties as the Rules appeared to be silent on the point. This area of ambiguity was believed to limit the parties' ability to plan their litigation strategy accordingly.

36-015 Leaving aside the question of whether such criticism was justified or not, the perceived uncertainty has now been sufficiently clarified. The Secretary General is expressly entitled to include a defence of set-off in the calculation of the costs of the arbitration. His discretion is, however, limited by two principal factors. Firstly, the computation of the extra costs, in terms of procedure and calculation, has to strictly follow the regime established for the deposit of costs, as discussed under **Article 34**.[17] Secondly, for additional fees to apply, the set-off raised must not have any connection in fact or in law with the claim or counter-claim against which it is raised. The English translation of this paragraph incorrectly limits its application to cases where the set-off and the main claim are unconnected in fact *and* in law. By contrast, the authentic German version provides that the claims should have no connection in fact *or* in law. In both cases, the set-off leads to additional work for the arbitrators 'justifying' the calculation of the additional fees.

36-016 The application of this provision requires a narrow reading, however. The mere fact that the same parties are involved in a commercial dispute and, as the case may be, are covered by the same arbitration agreement is obviously not enough to create a connection of facts to the case. Similarly, the fact that, for example, all claims raised are of a contractual nature is not sufficient to create a legal connection either. It is submitted that it must be clear that there is no connection between the two or more claims at issue.

36-017 The question of whether there is a connection between these claims or not is a question that goes deep into the merits of the case. Such a determination would, however, go beyond the authority entrusted to the Secretary General as an administrative organ of the VIAC. The corollary would be that the Secretary General would be dependent upon the evaluation of the arbitrators on this issue. That, however, would contradict **Article 5(3)**, which leaves the Secretary General in the direction of his activities free from any directives.[18] Additionally, granting the arbitrators a right to impose their view on the cost calculation could conflict with the principle that the arbitrators are not to determine their own fees.[19] Hence, this determination is ultimately in the sole discretion of the Secretary General, unfettered by any joint or separate declaration made by the arbitrators or the parties.

---

16. Article 24(4) Vienna Rules 2001: 'The Secretary may deviate from the statements of the parties in fixing the amount in dispute if the parties have made only a partial claim or request by the parties whose purpose was not the payment of sums in money was obviously undervalued.' **Annex 2a**.
17. *See* **Article 34**, at paras. 019 *et seq.*
18. *See* **Article 5(3)**, at paras. 020 *et seq.*
19. *See* **Article 34(1)**, at paras. 007 *et seq.*

Where it is anticipated that a separate calculation will be required and such separate **36-018** calculation was not requested by the arbitrators, an invitation should be issued to the arbitrators and the parties to comment on the requirement of such separate calculation. It is worth noting that the question of whether the set-off should be included in the arbitration costs is completely different from the question of whether such a defence should be admitted in the proceedings. This lies in the sole direction of the arbitrator.[20] The discretion of the arbitrators is, however, limited by the fact that they ought not to deal with the set-off defence until the additional deposit has been paid. The translation of Article 36(3) is again misleading as it makes a surprising reference to counter-claims in its last sentence. Whilst this statement is certainly correct for counter-claims, which are thoroughly covered by **Article 11**, the authentic German version makes it clear that this provision is meant to refer to set-off defences (*Gegenforderungen*). It could be argued that the sanction of 'not dealing' with the set-off presupposes its admissibility in the proceedings. The better view is, however, that even the principal question of admissibility has to be stayed until the full payment of the prescribed deposit has been received. Consequently, the arbitrators have an obligation to inform the parties unequivocally that their set-off will not be dealt within the interim.

IV. SEPARATE CALCULATIONS

> **Article 36(4): In the case of proceedings conducted concerning a number of individual claims or counter-claims, which are both in fact and in law of no connection, the Secretary General may at any stage of the proceedings make a separate calculation of the costs of arbitration according to the amounts in dispute in respect of the individual claims.**

The 1991 version of the Vienna Rules already contained a similar provision. **36-019** In the past it primarily served to enable the Secretary General to address the financial coverage of set-off defences and counter-claims raised in the arbitration proceedings. Although, the financial impact of these procedural acts is now expressly addressed in Article 36(3), there remain circumstances for its application.

The wording refers to *proceedings*. Hence, one might be led to assume that this **36-020** provision would apply in a scenario involving at least two proceedings. Rather, the reference to issues that are mutually unconnected in fact and in law is not made with regard to different arbitration proceedings but to individual claims or counter-claims. Hence, even when a multitude of individual claims is raised in a single proceeding, such claims are generally covered by the scope of this provision.

The English translation of this paragraph incorrectly limits its application to cases **36-021** which are mutually unconnected in fact *and* in law. The authentic German version

---

20. *See* **Article 11**, at paras. 043 *et seq.*

provides that the claims are required to be mutually unconnected in fact *or* in law. In either case a separate calculation of the costs of the arbitration is mandated. Conversely, where individual claims share either a factual or legal connection with the main claim, this would not justify a separate calculation. This provision and its application require a narrow reading. The absence of a connection between the various claims raised in the proceedings must be apparent on its face. Thus, for example, when various claims in the same arbitration proceedings are emanating from completely different projects, they are clearly unconnected. The possible separation of each claim in different phases of the arbitration, addressing distinct evidence and legal arguments, indicates that the various claims are 'separate' within the meaning of Article 36(4).

36-022   In its current form, the provision empowers the Secretary General to determine the costs on a separate basis at any stage of the proceeding. Hence, such power of separate determination could be exercised when the Secretary General calculates the amount of deposit,[21] or requests an additional payment due to an increase of the amount in dispute during the proceedings.[22] Where a separate calculation is anticipated, it is standing practice for the Secretary General to invite the arbitrators and the parties for their comments on such separate calculations. The exact figure of the separate calculation must be made available at this juncture. The Secretary General is not bound by any joint or separate declaration made by the arbitrators and/or the parties, as this authority is entrusted to him to be exercised at his sole discretion. The final decision will usually contain reasons and will be provided to the parties and the arbitrators.[23]

V.   PARTIAL CLAIM AND UNDERVALUATION

Article 36(5): The Secretary General may deviate from the statements of the parties in fixing the amount in dispute if the parties have made only a partial claim or if a request by the parties whose purpose was not the payment of sums of money was obviously undervalued.

36-023   Tactical and financial reasons often lead parties to submit only partial claims to the arbitration proceeding, thereby reserving the further expansion of the claim. Whilst it is perfectly legitimate to only pursue parts of a claim, this may result in an unjustified calculation of the amount in dispute. At least on liability (although not necessarily on quantum), the work entrusted to the arbitrators will eventually be the same as if the full amount at stake had been requested. The same is true for claims which purpose is not the payment of a particular sum of money, such as declaratory judgements or applications for an injunction. Given that the costs system under the Vienna Rules is solely determined by the amount in dispute, it

---

21.   *See* **Article 34(2)**, at paras. 019 *et seq.*
22.   *See* **Article 34(5)**, at paras. 056 *et seq.*
23.   *See* **Article 5**, at para. 026.

is essential that these non-monetary claims also be appropriately valued. If this evaluation is not included in the statement of claim, it can be requested from the claimant at a later stage.[24] It is to be noted that the undervaluation must be obvious from the facts of the case; a mere suspicion as to any undervaluation would not justify a deviation.

In the usual course of the proceedings, it is the arbitrators who will inform the **36-024** Secretary General regarding a partial claim or an undervaluation which is apparent on the face of the record. Although this is not mandatory, arbitrators usually file a separate request to the Secretary General to depart from the parties' statement as to the value of the claims. In the event of such a request being filed, the reasoning behind the request must be set forth and a proposal must be provided for an amount that would, in the arbitrators' considered opinion, reflect the real value of the dispute. The Secretary General will then intervene if and to the extent this issue has already been discussed with the parties. As the ultimate decision on any differing amount in dispute directly affects the parties to the arbitration, it is essential that all parties involved be granted a right to comment.

Of course, it is also possible for the respondent to have an interest in rectifying the **36-025** amount in dispute. Hence, if a respondent feels aggrieved by the amount claimed by claimant, it can direct a complaint to the Secretary General, with courtesy copy to the arbitrators.

The decision of the Secretary General will contain reasons and be provided to the **36-026** arbitrators and the parties. Where the amount in dispute is increased for the purposes of cost calculation, the parties may still need to properly amend their prayers for relief to reflect any changes in the relevant amount, in order to allow the arbitrators to take the new amount into account in their award and avoid a case of *ultra petita*.

The authority to deviate from the amount in dispute fixed by the parties entitles the **36-027** Secretary General to not only arrive at a basis for the arbitrator's fees but also purposes of the administrative costs of the VIAC. This might give rise to some debate as it could create the impression that the VIAC might have an interest in increasing the amount in dispute. As discussed earlier in the context of the arbitrators' fees, it is a principle of Austrian law that one should not be entitled to determine one's own costs (or, for that matter, rule on specific factors which have a bearing on such cost determinations, such as findings as to the amount in dispute). However, as the Secretary General gains no personal benefit from an increase in the administrative costs, this arrangement does ultimately not violate the general principle that one should not be entitled to determine one's own costs. Even so, an appearance of an institutional interest remains; and the Secretary General may have to exercise caution in increasing the amount in dispute only in

---

24. *See* **Article 9(3)**, at paras. 059 *et seq.*

cases where it is 'obviously undervalued', also to avoid the impression that the institution too easily intends to increase the basis for its income.

VI.   RAISE OF FEES

Article 36(6): The rates quoted in the schedule of arbitrators' fees are the fees for sole arbitrators. In any case they shall be raised to two-and-a-half times the amounts quoted if an arbitral tribunal is appointed and to up to three times the rates stated in the event of the particular difficulty of a case.

36-028 The schedule of arbitration costs is calculated on the assumption that the matters is to be decided by a sole arbitrator. This amount is automatically increased by two-and-a-half times the original amount in the event of a three member tribunal being nominated. Cases of 'particular difficulty' may also qualify for a three-fold increase but this necessarily involves an element of discretion.

36-029 In deciding whether a particular case justifies an increase in the rates, the present Secretary General looks at several criteria, including the length of the arbitration, the amount of time spent on hearings,[25] the length of an arbitration, the application of a foreign legal system, the taking of evidence at another place than the seat of the arbitration, the number of witnesses and experts, or the number and difficulty of procedural questions and applications the tribunal has to address in addition to the merits.[26] Whether or not these factors justify an increase of the fee, will depend on the circumstances of the case.

36-030 There are cases where the length of the arbitration may be attributable to improper time management of the arbitral tribunal. Some cases might involve the application of the laws of a legal system with whom only some of the arbitrators are familiar. Other cases might only require a short inspection of an onsite location rather than a long evidentiary proceeding. At the end, any increase of the applicable fee is a matter of discretion for the Secretary General.[27]

36-031 The 'particular difficulty' of the case is often unknown at the outset for the proceedings, except possibly to the parties concerned. However, as a matter of a caution, the Secretary General usually calculates the deposit of costs on a three-fold basis, as a subsequent request to the parties regarding an increase in fees could cause otherwise avoidable difficulties in the course of the proceedings.[28] Arbitrators usually receive no advance information regarding the decision on

---

25. More than 10 working days spent at hearings are in practice considered to indicate complexity.
26. Given Article 36(7), raising the fee under Article 36(6) is the only way to compensate arbitrators for procedurally complex proceedings.
27. It is common practice of the current secretary general to substantiate and explain his decisions. *See* **Article 5**, at para. 026.
28. *See* **Article 34**, at para. 020.

costs, although this has been done in some cases. In the normal course, however, the arbitrators will only learn of the cost determination when they receive the relevant note requesting them to include the amount in the award.[29] Hence, if the arbitrators feel that the particular case justifies an increase in their fees under this provision, they should approach the Secretary General at the earliest opportunity. The ultimate decision of the Secretary General will contain reasons which will be made known to the parties and the arbitrators separately at the end of the proceedings. Although sole arbitrators may well experience the same difficulties discussed above, indeed without being able to avail themselves of the assistance of co-arbitrators, the provision applies to arbitral tribunals only and not to the fees for a sole arbitrator.

VII.   COMPREHENSIVE COST DETERMINATION

Article 36(7): The tariffs specified in the schedule for arbitrator's fees include any and all partial and interim decisions, such as awards on jurisdiction, partial awards, decisions on the challenge of arbitrators, interim measures of protection, other decisions and orders that manage the proceedings.

This paragraph was inserted by means of the latest amendment to the Vienna Rules. **36-032** It essentially serves as clarification on two levels. First, it indirectly confirms that the proceedings under the Vienna Rules allow for no other remuneration scheme than that established in the Schedule of Annex I. In particular, contrary to what is sometimes argued, it does not permit for the specific amount of time spent by an individual arbitrator to be taken into consideration. Second, it reiterates that a determination of fees in accordance with the fee scale of Appendix I is final, and intended to compensate the arbitrators fully for all their obligations and duties under the Vienna Rules.

VIII.   REDUCTION OF THE AMOUNT IN DISPUTE

Article 36(8): Reductions of the amount in dispute shall be taken into consideration in calculating the arbitrators' fees and administrative costs only if they were made before transmission of the files to the sole arbitrator (arbitral tribunal).

Occasionally, only after the first exchange of written submissions, parties **36-033** sometimes realize how weak or strong their respective position may appear in impending proceedings. Claimants occasionally reduce the initial amount claimed whereas respondent parties, presumably after the first hearing of the witnesses,

---

29. *See* **Article 36**, at paras. 001 *et seq.*

may well be persuaded to admit parts of the claim. All these situations inevitably affect the amount in dispute.

36-034 However, in order to prevent parties from using the amount of their claim as a tactical instrument in the proceedings, Article 36(8) deems the amount in dispute to be frozen as soon as the file has been handed over to the arbitrators in accordance with **Article 12**. No reasons for a reduction of the amount will be taken into consideration by the Secretary General after this point in time.[30] Any increase in the amount will be addressed by **Article 34(4)**.

IX.   DETERMINATION OF CASH OUTLAYS

Article 36(9): Cash outlays shall be determined according to the actual expenditure.

36-035 Arbitrators must be entitled to reimbursement for cash outlays incurred in the course of the proceedings. This approach is quite common under other arbitration rules.[31] The provisional deposit on costs paid by the parties includes an amount reserved for such outlays.[32] This amount is calculated by the Secretary General and is based on the VIAC's other experiences.

36-036 Arbitrators' cash outlays, such as travel and accommodation costs, will generally only be reimbursed upon receipt of invoices, tickets, hotel bills, etc. If the arbitrators fail(s) to provide such evidence, reimbursement may not be possible.

36-037 First class train tickets and business class airline tickets are usually reimbursable. The *per diem* rate for non-resident arbitrators is generally €100.00. If overnight-stays are necessary a maximum amount of €350.00 (per diem and overnight-stay) will be reimbursed if hotel bills are produced. If no hotel bills are produced a maximum amount of €300.00 (per diem and overnight-stay) will be paid. Taxi fares will be reimbursed upon receipt of the bills. If an arbitrator uses his/her own car, the official Austrian mileage allowance (currently €0.376 per kilometre) will apply, not to exceed, however, the business class airfare for the same distance.

36-038 As arbitrators are presumed to have access to a certain level of administrative infrastructure, usually no reimbursement is made for expenses regarding the use of legal data services or for the purchase of legal literature. However, if an arbitrator offers to use his or her own facilities, e.g. a hearing room in his or her law firm, secretaries, etc., he is usually granted a reimbursement equalling the amount that would be charged if the premises would have to be rented or personnel hired.

---

30. As to the exact time at which the file is considered to be transmitted to the arbitrators, *see* **Article 12**, at para. 002.
31. *See, e.g.*, Article 4(d) (Schedule of Fees and Costs) attached to LCIA Rules; Rule 50 AAA Commercial Arbitration Rules and Article 31(a) AAA/ICDR Rules.
32. *See* **Article 34(2)**, at para. 020.

As the position of an Administrative Secretary is unfamiliar to the Vienna Rules, additional reimbursement will not ordinarily be provided for an administrative secretary.[33]

In addition, photocopies may be charged at €0.30 per copy while facsimiles are **36-039** charged at €0.50 for local facsimiles and €1.00 for all other facsimiles. Separate proof of photocopies and facsimiles is generally not required. Arbitrators are not entitled to claim cash outlays for e-mails. Unless otherwise instructed, cash outlays will be refunded in Euros into the account designated by the arbitrator or by bank cheque (to non-Austrian arbitrators only).

In order to ensure that sufficient funds for the reimbursement of cash outlays are **36-040** provided, the VIAC generally requests the arbitrators to state their expenses immediately when particular expenditures have been made. Where the cash outlays do not further cover the expenditures, both the arbitrators, under **Article 35**, and the Secretary General, under **Article 34(6)**, are required to secure adequate coverage.

X.   VALUE ADDED TAX

Article 36(10): The tariffs specified in the schedule for arbitrator's fees do not include value added tax, to which the arbitrator's fees may be subject. Those arbitrators whose fees are subject to value added tax shall inform the Secretary of the prospective amount of value added tax upon taking up office.

Arbitral institutions have traditionally been reluctant to interfere with the question **36-041** of applicable tax levies on arbitrator's fees.[34] The Vienna Rules have now taken an express position on this point, and permit arbitrators to claim VAT on their fees and also oblige the Secretary General to administer the collection of VAT.

This discussion arises out of a decision of the ECJ handed down on 16 September **36-042** 1997, Rs C-145/96, *Bernd von Hofmann*, ruling that services rendered as arbitrators are not services usually or normally rendered in the course of a lawyer's profession, as far as their treatment for VAT issues are concerned. With respect to their place of performance, such services fall within the general provision of

---

33. *See* **Article 7**, at para. 158. Typically, the administrative secretary is to be compensated out of the arbitrators' fees, although voluntary arrangements with the parties for additional compensations are conceivable.

34. Article 25 DIS Rules provides: 'In fixing the advance, the arbitrators' total fees and the anticipated reimbursements as well as any applicable value added tax may be taken into consideration (...)'. Article 2(9) Appendix III to ICC Rules provides: '[A]mounts paid to the arbitrator do not include any possible value added taxes (VAT) or other taxes or charges and imposts applicable to the arbitrator's fees. Parties have a duty to pay any such taxes or charges; however, the recovery of any such charges or taxes is a matter solely between the arbitrator and the parties'.

Article 9(1) Sixth Council Directive 77/388/EEC of 17 May 1977 on the harmonization of the laws of the Member States relating to turnover taxes. Austrian law has implemented the ECJ jurisprudence; services rendered as arbitrator are not to be considered under Section 3a (10) no. 3 UStG 1994, but rather Section 3a (12) UStG 1994.[35] Consequently, services by arbitrators who have their place of business or permanent establishment in Austria are – independent of the seat or actual place of the arbitration – for VAT purposes deemed to be rendered from the seat of the arbitrator's business.[36]

36-043   Under Austrian tax law the amount to which the 20% VAT rate is applicable is the amount effectively received by the arbitrators, such as the arbitrator's fees and cash outlays. If the parties follow the Secretary General's request and pay the amount of deposit of costs to the VIAC, the arbitrators have effectively not received the payment, hence VAT will arguably not be applicable at this stage. This result can vary where a payment on accounts is granted or cash outlays are disbursed during the proceedings. Parties to the arbitration proceedings are generally entitled to receive a proper invoice of the arbitrators' fees at the end of the proceedings, as they might be entitled to reclaim the VAT paid.[37] The issue of VAT payment and refund should ideally be addressed at the beginning of the proceedings, preferably in concert with the parties.

36-044   The Secretary General, when calculating the deposit of costs for the particular arbitration proceedings, will have to calculate the VAT on the arbitrator's fees according to the figures transmitted to him by the arbitrators. To do so, the Secretary General will first have to inform the arbitrators about the prospective amount in dispute. A change in the VAT percentage would result in a new calculation of the deposit of costs according to **Article 34(5)**. Hence, arbitrators are advised to provide the correct VAT amount applicable to their fees, if any, at the outset of the proceedings.

---

35. *See* P. Kolacny and L. Mayr, *Umsatzsteuergesetz 1994* (2nd edn, Vienna, Manz, 1997), Section 3a, note 33; M. Scheiner, P. Kolacny and E. Caganek, *Kommentar zur Mehrwertsteuer – UStG 1994* (Vienna, Verlag Orac, 2003), Section 3a(9) and (10), para. 191.

36. *See* C. W. Konrad and H. Gurtner, *Die Umsatzsteuer im Schiedsverfahren* (Cologne/Munich, Carl Heymanns Verlag, 2008), p. 15.

37. For a detailed discussion on how, to whom and when such invoice should be delivered *see* C.W. Konrad and H. Gurtner, *Die Umsatzsteuer im Schiedsverfahren* (Cologne/Munich, Carl Heymanns Verlag, 2008).

Article 37

Transitional Provisions

	Para.		Para.
I. Introduction	1	III. The Application of Future Versions of the Vienna Rules	7
II. The Application of Austrian Arbitration Law	4		

Article 37: This version of the Vienna Rules shall apply to all proceedings in which the claim was filed after 30th June, 2006.

I.   INTRODUCTION

Transitional provisions bind parties that have submitted to the institution's rules to submit to the most recent version of the relevant rules – usually at the commencement of an arbitration – of the chosen institution. English courts have determined, for example, that when an institution's rules have been specified in an arbitration agreement, it is the most recent version of the rules as at the date of the statement of claim to which the parties are deemed to have submitted, unless the arbitration agreement provides for a specific version of the institution's rules.[1] As a policy matter, it is believed that it is generally desirable to give the parties the benefit of the most up-to-date rules.   **37-001**

Article 37 provides that the 2006 version of the Vienna Rules applies in all proceedings in which the claim was filed, in accordance with **Article 9**, after 30 June 2006 (deliberately coinciding with the introduction of the new arbitration law contained in the ZPO). Under **Article 9**, the arbitration is commenced with the   **37-002**

---

1. *Offshore International S.A. v. Banco Central S.A.* [1976] 2 Lloyd's Rep. 402, Q.B. (Comm.) and *Bunge SA v. Kruse* [1979] 1 Lloyd's Rep. 279, Q.B. (Comm.).

receipt of the statement of claim by the VIAC. As a result, the proceedings commence; the arbitration is pending with all the associated effects of *lis pendens.*[2]

37-003 It should be possible for the parties to agree that they want to arbitrate under an earlier version of the Vienna Rules. However, in such a case, the parties' agreement needs to cross the threshold of **Article 9(6)**. Where previous versions of the rule provide for a different role of the institution, and thus prevent the VIAC or its organs to comply with its functions as provided by the Vienna Rules 2006, the VIAC may well refuse to administer the case.[3]

II.   THE APPLICATION OF AUSTRIAN ARBITRATION LAW

37-004 Article VII of the act introducing the new arbitration law contained in Sections 577 *et seq.* ZPO contains similar transitional provisions, which are mandatory. It reads:

(1) This Act shall come into effect on 1 July 2006.
(2) The provisions that have been in force so far shall apply to arbitral proceedings which have been commenced prior to 1 July 2006.
(3) The validity of arbitration agreements that have been concluded prior to 1 July 2006 shall be governed by the provisions in force so far.
(4) The federal minister of justice shall be competent for the enforcement of this Act.

37-005 As a result, the new ZPO applies to proceedings commenced on or after 1 July 2006. However, the provisions make also clear that arbitration agreements concluded before that date will continue to be governed by the former ZPO effective prior to the 2006 reform, and will thus, *inter alia*, have to follow the old form requirements.[4] However, even where a formal deficiency in the agreement exist, a party in an arbitration commenced after 1 July 2006 must enter an objection against the form, or else be bared from raising it later.[5] Section 583(3) ZPO forms part of arbitral procedure, and hence must be applied to all arbitrations commenced on or after 1 July 2006, irrespective of when the arbitration agreement was concluded.[6]

37-006 The legislative materials also make clear that associated court proceedings – e.g., for the assistance of state courts;[7] the substitute appointment of arbitrators; for

---

2. *See* **Article 9**, at paras. 015 and 023 *et seq.*
3. *See* **Article 9**, at paras. 088 *et seq.*
4. *See* **Article 1**, at paras. 053 and 061 *et seq.* For the impact on arbitrability, *see* **Article 1**, at paras. 105 *et seq.*
5. *See* **Article 1**, at paras. 079 *et seq.*
6. M. Platte and A. Fremuth-Wolf in *Arbitration Law of Austria: Practice and Procedure*, S. Riegler, A. Petsche, A. Fremuth-Wolf, M. Platte and C. Liebscher (eds) (Huntington, Juris Publishing, 2007), Article VII, p. 605.
7. For a different view, *see* A. Reiner, *Das neue österreichische Schiedsrecht/The new Austrian Arbitration Law* (Vienna, LexisNexis, 2006), Article VII, note 245, whose interpretation of the

setting aside an award; or for the declaration of a non-award – follow the law applicable to the arbitral proceedings.[8] As a result, for arbitrations commenced prior to 1 July 2006, recourse to the Austrian courts is available only under the former ZPO (even if the court proceedings are initiated after 30 June 2006).[9] For arbitrations commenced on or after 1 July 2006, by contrast, recourse to the Austrian courts is available only under the new ZPO. Thus, Sections 612 and 613 ZPO (provisions that previously did not exist) are only available with respect to awards resulting from arbitrations commenced after 1 July 2006. Section 614 ZPO on the enforcement of foreign awards applies to all enforcement actions filed on or after 1 July 2006, irrespective of when the arbitration was commenced.[10]

III.	THE APPLICATION OF FUTURE VERSIONS OF THE VIENNA RULES

Article 37 sets out that the most recent VIAC Rules (which came into effect on 1 **37-007** July 2006) shall apply to all proceedings in which the claim was filed after 30 June 2006. Article 37 must be read together with **Article 1(2)** that states: 'If the parties have agreed to the jurisdiction of the Centre, these arbitration rules ("Vienna Rules") shall thereby apply in the version valid at the time of commencement of the proceedings.' This recognizes that arbitral rules are not static. Transitional provisions such as this enable institutions to update and modernize their rules in response to legal developments and other developments, often allowing for a faster and more efficient arbitral process.

This is illustrated by the famous case of *Jurong Engineering Ltd v. Black & Veatch* **37-008** *Singapore*.[11] In line with those considerations, a review of the main institution

---

law is arbitration-friendly, and therefore has good policy considerations for it, but does not seem to be covered by the text of Article VII or the legislative materials.

8. Explanatory Notes to Article VII.
9. A. Reiner, *Das neue österreichische Schiedsrecht/The new Austrian Arbitration Law* (Vienna, LexisNexis, 2006), Section VII, note 241; M. Platte and A. Fremuth-Wolf in *Arbitration Law of Austria: Practice and Procedure*, S. Riegler, A. Petsche, A. Fremuth-Wolf, M. Platte and C. Liebscher (eds) (Huntington, Juris Publishing, 2007), Article VII, p. 604.
10. A. Reiner, *Das neue österreichische Schiedsrecht/The new Austrian Arbitration Law* (Vienna, LexisNexis, 2006), Article VII, note 244.
11. High Court of Singapore, 26 November 2003, *Jurong Engineering Ltd. v. Black & Veatch Singapore PTE LTD*, [2004] 1 SLR 333. There, the parties had agreed in the arbitration agreement to submit to SIAC Rules. However, at the commencement of the arbitration, SIAC had two sets of rules: (i) the International Rules; and (ii) the Domestic Rules. The parties agreed that theirs was a domestic arbitration, but they were not in agreement over which set of SIAC Rules they had agreed to submit to. The relevant provision in the arbitration agreement read: '[A]ny arbitration will be conducted (. . .) in accordance with the rules of arbitration promulgated by [SIAC].' One party argued that they could only have agreed to the rules in place at the time of the arbitration agreement, as the domestic rules did not exist then. However, it was held that once

rules indicates that transitional provisions are much the same across the arbitration institutions and that they reflect the approach adopted by various domestic courts. In the introduction to the LCIA Rules, for example, the transitional provision states that the parties shall be taken to have agreed to such amended rules as the LCIA may have adopted since the date of the relevant arbitration agreement and before the commencement of the arbitration. Article 6(1) of the most recent ICC Rules provides that parties have agreed, by virtue of submitting to ICC Rules, to submit to the ICC Rules in force on the date of the commencement of the arbitration proceeding. Parties are free to agree to submit to the ICC Rules in force at the date of the arbitration agreement. This should be stated explicitly in the arbitration agreement. Other rules equally refer to the date of commencement of the arbitrator as relevant to determine the applicable version of the institutional rules.[12]

37-009 However, the indiscriminate or automatic application of those rules that are valid at the commencement of the arbitration is not without problems. Parties may have agreed in the arbitration clause to refer the dispute to arbitration with a particular set of (then existing) rules in mind. Subsequent changes, which would then apply under Articles 37 and 1, may contain new provisions that are surprising or indeed undesirable from the parties' perspective.[13] As the intention of the parties is an important factor in arbitration as a consensual process, this can present an issue (although by accepting the Vienna Rules, the parties have specifically accepted Articles 1 and 37 and thus waived in advance any objection against subsequently introduced modifications of the Vienna Rules). For arbitration

---

parties had agreed to adopt the rules of a particular arbitral institution, without specifying a particular set of rules, the applicable rules would be those current at the time of submission to arbitration, regardless of whether the rules were newly amended or an entirely different set of rules. It appears, in short, that national courts are generally keen to respect the application of the new rules valid at the commencement of the arbitration over the rules in force at the time of the arbitration agreement.

12. Article 1 AAA/ICDR Rules states that where parties have provided for AAA/ICDR Rules in the arbitration agreement without designating particular rules, then the most recent version at the date of commencement of the arbitration shall be the applicable version. Article 1(3) of the Swiss Rules indicates that the most recent rules will apply to all proceedings commenced on or after 1 January 2004 which is when the Swiss Rules came into force.

13. Compare, *e.g.*, the discussion surrounding the recent introduction of the new Swiss Rules which contain a highly controversial and currently untested rule by way of Article 21(5). Article 21(5) Swiss Rules introduces an important innovation in conferring jurisdiction upon the tribunal to hear a set-off defence even when the relationship out of which this defence is said to arise is not within the scope of the arbitration agreement or is the object of another arbitration agreement or choice of forum clause. Article 21(5) Swiss Rules states that:

> [T]he arbitral tribunal shall have jurisdiction to hear a set-off defence even when the relationship out of which this defence is said to arise is not within the scope of the arbitration clause or is the subject of another arbitration agreement or forum- selection clause

It is fair to say that a provision like this will catch many parties by surprise. Is it then fair to say that those parties have agreed to the application of this provision by agreeing to transitional rules?

agreements concluded prior to the 2006 reform, Article 25 of the Vienna Rules gave the parties the choice to specify which version of the rules they wanted to apply.

There is little discussion in international doctrine of what constitutes a fundamentally or radically different rule.[14] Yet there are indications that institutional rules cannot through the transitional provision definitively determine the intention of the parties at the time of the arbitration agreement. Also, the intention of the parties may well be for the arbitrators to determine, and not for the institution.[15]   **37-010**

---

14. Interim Award in ICC Case 2671 of 1976, *Mobil Oil Indonesia v. Asamera Oil (Indonesia) Ltd*, (1976) NY Law Journal, 10, col. 4.; *Mobil Oil Indonesia Inc. v Asamera Oil (Indonesia) Ltd.* 392 N.Y.S.2d 614, 616 (N.Y. App. Div. 1977); *see also, Award in ICC Case No. 5622 of 1992*, (1997)8(1) ICC Ct Bull, 52. An ICC arbitration arising from an arbitration agreement signed in 1980 was commenced under the ICC Rules in force as of 1975 (1975 Rules). The Terms of Reference were also signed under the 1975 Rules. An award was rendered in August 1988 (post the introduction of the 1988 Rules) and subsequently annulled by the Swiss Courts in 1989. In November 1990, a new sole arbitrator was appointed by the ICC Court, in the same case, under the 1988 Rules. The arbitration was continued on the basis of Article 2(12) of the 1988 Rules which specifies that where an arbitrator is replaced, the arbitral tribunal shall determine if and to what extent prior proceedings shall again take place. Under the 1975 Rules it was not clear that such a power existed.

 In this case, the parties had not explicitly provided for the 1975 Rules in the arbitration agreement, but the 1975 Rules had been applied to the initial arbitration and the 1975 Rules were cited in the Terms of Reference.

 One of the questions to be determined by the sole arbitrator, upon the objections raised by the defendant, contending that a new request for arbitration had to be filed after the annulment, was the determination of which version – the 1975 Rules or the 1988 Rules – would apply to the second/continued arbitration. An interim award was handed down in 1992. In his interim award, the arbitrator considered that the 1988 Rules applied to the second/continued arbitration. His reasoning, from the summary in the ICC Bulletin, was that Article 2(12) of the 1988 Rules (the current Article 12(4) in the 1998 Rules) was not so radical that the parties would not have agreed to it when agreeing the arbitration agreement. The sole arbitrator also explained that the 1988 Rules were generally not radically different from the 1975 Rules. He appears to have remained silent however as to what he thought the effect would have been had he considered the 1988 Rules to be radically different from the 1975 Rules.

15. *Mobil Oil Indonesia Inc. v. Asamera Oil (Indonesia) Ltd.* 392 N.Y.S.2d 614, 616 (N.Y. App. Div. 1977).

Annexes

I.   Vienna International Arbitration Centre (VIAC) Rules and Forms

1a   International Arbitral Centre of the Austrian Federal Economic
     Chamber Rules of Arbitration 2006 (Vienna Rules 2006)

1b   Internationales Schiedsgericht der Wirtschaftskammer Österreich
     Schiedsordnung 2006 (Wiener Regeln 2006)

2a   International Arbitral Centre of the Austrian Federal Economic
     Chamber Rules of Arbitration 2001 (Vienna Rules 2001)

2b   Internationales Schiedsgericht der Wirtschaftskammer Österreich
     Schiedsordnung 2001 (Wiener Regeln 2001)

3a   International Arbitral Centre of the Austrian Federal Economic
     Chamber Conciliation Rules 2006

3b   Internationales Schiedsgericht der Wirtschaftskammer Österreich
     Schlichtungsordnung 2006

4   Arbitrator's Declaration of Acceptance, Statement of Independence and
     Undertaking to Observe Rules on Costs

5   Guidelines for Arbitrators

6   Account Details

7   Schiedsgerichtsordnung für die Ständigen Schiedsgerichte der
     Wirtschaftskammern 2006

II.   Austrian Arbitration Legislation

8a   Code of Civil Procedure, Fourth Section: Arbitration (Austrian
     Arbitration Act 2006)

8b   Zivilprozessordnung, Vierter Abschnitt: Schiedsverfahren

9a   Former Code of Civil Procedure

9b   Zivilprozessordnung (in der Fassung vor der
     Schiedsrechtsänderungsreform 2006, 'Alte Fassung')

III. International Conventions
10 European Convention on International Commercial Arbitration 1961 (European Convention)
11 Convention on the Recognition and Enforcement of Foreign Arbitral Awards 1958 (New York Convention)
12 List of Bilateral Agreements Concluded by Austria That Refer to Arbitration
13 List of Multilateral Agreements Concluded by Austria That Refer to Arbitration
14 List of Bilateral Investment Treaties Concluded Between Austria and Other Countries

IV. Guidelines and Reports
15 UNCITRAL Notes on Organizing Arbitral Proceedings 1996 (UNCITRAL Notes)
16 IBA Rules on the Taking of Evidence in International Commercial Arbitration (IBA Rules of Evidence)
17 IBA Guidelines on Conflict of Interest in International Commercial Arbitration (IBA Conflict Guidelines)
18 IBA Rules of Ethics for International Arbitrators (IBA Rules of Ethics)

Annex 1a

International Arbitral Centre of the Austrian Federal Economic Chamber Rules of Arbitration 2006 (Vienna Rules 2006)*

GENERAL PROVISIONS

THE INSTITUTION

Article 1

1. The International Arbitral Centre of the Austrian Federal Economic Chamber in Vienna (the Vienna International Arbitral Centre – 'the Centre') shall make arrangements for the settlement by arbitration of disputes in which not all contracting parties that concluded the arbitration agreement had their place of business or their normal residence in Austria at the time of conclusion of that agreement.

The jurisdiction of the Centre can also be agreed by parties whose place of business or normal residence is in Austria for the settlement of disputes of an international character.

2. If the parties have agreed to the jurisdiction of the Centre, these arbitration rules ('Vienna Rules') shall thereby apply in the version valid at the time of commencement of the proceedings.

---

* Translation from the German original, which is the authentic text. Adopted by the Extended Board of the Austrian Federal Economic Chamber on 3 May 2006, with effect from 1 July 2006. Reprinted with kind permission of the Vienna International Arbitration Centre (VIAC).

3. If parties which had their place of business or normal residence in Austria at the time of conclusion of the arbitration agreement have agreed that their disputes should be finally settled by a sole arbitrator or an arbitral tribunal to be appointed according to the Vienna Rules, and if the dispute is not international in character, the Permanent Arbitral Tribunal of the Vienna Economic Chamber, or, if another venue in Austria has been agreed, of the regional economic chamber in whose territorial jurisdiction the agreed venue is situated, shall be competent to make arrangements for settlement by arbitration. The latter tribunal shall conduct the proceedings in accordance with the rules of arbitration for the Permanent Arbitral Tribunals of the regional economic chambers.

PLACE OF ARBITRATION

Article 2

Unless the parties have agreed otherwise

- a. the place of arbitration shall be Vienna
- b. the sole arbitrator (arbitral tribunal) may conduct procedural acts at any place where he deems appropriate.

The arbitral tribunal may in any case meet at any place to consult in any way.

ORGANIZATION

THE BOARD

Article 3

1. The Board of the Centre shall have at least five members. They shall be appointed for a period of office of five years by the Extended Board of the Austrian Federal Economic Chamber by recommendation of the President of the Centre and can be reappointed. If there is no new appointment by the time of the expiration of a period of office, the members of the Board shall remain in office until a new Board is appointed. If a member of the Board is permanently incapacitated during his period of office (for instance, by resignation or death), a substitute member can be appointed for the remainder of the period of office of the serving Board.

2. The members of the Board shall elect one of their number to act as President for the duration of their term of office. Where the President is prevented, the member who is oldest by age shall take over his tasks.

3. The meetings of the Board are convened by the President, and presided over by the President or in his absence, by the most senior member by age present who is eligible to vote. The Board can validly take decisions if more than half of its

members are present. It shall take decisions by a simple majority of the members present who are eligible to vote (see paragraph 4). In the event of a tie in voting, the Chairman shall have a casting vote.

4. Members of the Board who are parties to particular arbitration proceedings in any capacity whatsoever shall be excluded from decisions pertaining to those proceedings, however they are to be counted for the presence quorum.

5. Decisions may be made by correspondence. In this case the President shall submit a written proposal to the members and shall set a time limit for voting by correspondence. Paragraph 3, sub-sections 3 and 4 shall apply accordingly. Each member has the right to request a meeting regarding the written proposal.

6. The members of the Board must perform their duties to the best of their ability; they are independent and are not subject to any directives in that respect. They are bound to secrecy on all matters coming to their notice in the course of their duties.

INTERNATIONAL ADVISORY BOARD

Article 4

The International Advisory Board consists of international arbitration experts who may be invited by the respective Board of the Centre for the duration of its period of office. Its purpose is to discuss factual issues of immediate interest.

THE SECRETARY GENERAL

Article 5

1. The Secretary General of the Centre shall be appointed by the Extended Board of the Austrian Federal Economic Chamber for a period of office of five years by recommendation of the Board of the Arbitral Centre; he can be reappointed. The third sentence of Article 3 paragraph 1, shall apply by analogy.

2. The Secretary General shall direct the activities of the Secretariat and shall perform the administrative tasks of the Centre insofar as they are not reserved to the Board of the Centre.

3. The Secretary General must perform his duties to the best of his ability and is not subject to any directives in that respect. He is bound to secrecy on all matters coming to his notice in the course of his duties.

4. If the Secretary General is unable to perform his duties or if he is permanently incapacitated, a member of the Board of the Centre, appointed by that Board, shall perform the relevant functions until a Secretary General is appointed.

LANGUAGES OF CORRESPONDENCE

Article 6

Correspondence by the Parties with the Board and the Secretary General shall be conducted in German or English.

ARBITRATORS

Article 7

1. The parties shall be free to appoint the arbitrators. Any person having legal capacity – irrespective of nationality – may be an arbitrator, provided the parties have not agreed upon any special additional qualification requirements.

2. The requirements for the appointment as arbitrator are:

   a. A written statement as to his impartiality and independence in accordance with paragraph 5. The Secretary General shall transmit to the parties a copy of the form in which the sole arbitrator (all members of the arbitral tribunal) has (have) confirmed his (its) impartiality and independence.
   b. A written statement to submit to these Rules of Arbitration including to the provisions on the costs of the proceedings.

3. A member of the Board may act only as Chairman of an arbitral tribunal or sole arbitrator.

4. The arbitrators must perform their duties in complete independence and impartiality, to the best of their ability, and are not subject to any directives in that respect. They are bound to secrecy in respect of all matters coming to their notice in the course of their duties.

5. When a person is approached in connection with his possible appointment as arbitrator, he shall disclose any circumstances likely to give rise to doubts as to his impartiality or independence or that are in conflict with the agreement of the parties. An arbitrator, from the time of his appointment and throughout the arbitral proceedings, shall without delay disclose any such circumstances to the parties unless they have already been informed of them by him.

LIABILITY

Article 8

Liability of the arbitrators, the Secretary General, the Board and its members and the Austrian Federal Economic Chamber and its employees for any act or omission in relation to arbitration proceedings, insofar as such liability may be admissible by law, shall be excluded.

ARBITRAL PROCEEDINGS

COMMENCEMENT OF THE PROCEEDINGS

Article 9

1. Arbitral proceedings are commenced when a statement of claims is filed with the Secretariat. The proceedings become pending on receipt of the statement of claims by the Secretariat.

2. One copy of the statement of claims together with enclosures must be submitted for each Respondent, each arbitrator and the Secretariat.

3. The statement of claims must include:

   a. The designation of the parties and their addresses;
   b. A specific statement of claims and the particulars and supporting documents on which the claims are based;
   c. The amount in dispute at the time of submission of the statement of claims, unless the claims are not related exclusively to a specific sum of money;
   d. Particulars regarding the number of arbitrators in accordance with Article 14;
   e. If a decision by three arbitrators is requested, the nomination of an arbitrator and the address of that person.

4. A copy of the agreement specifying the jurisdiction of the Arbitral Centre must be attached to the statement of claims.

5. If the statement of claims does not comply with the provisions of paragraph 3 of the present Article or if copies of documents or enclosures are missing, the Secretary General shall request the Claimant to remedy the defect or to submit the necessary documents or enclosures. The Claimant is to be informed that until the defects have been remedied, the claim shall not be processed.

6. The Board can refuse to carry out proceedings if the parties have designated the International Arbitral Centre of the Austrian Federal Economic Chamber in the arbitration agreement but have made agreements that deviate from the Vienna Rules.

MEMORANDUM IN REPLY

Article 10

1. If the claim is not to be dealt with under Article 9 paragraphs 5 and 6, the Secretary General shall make service to the Respondent of the statement of claims and one copy each of the rules of arbitration and shall invite the Respondent to submit a memorandum in reply within a period of thirty days, in the number of copies required under Article 9 paragraph 2.

2. The memorandum in reply must include:

    a. A reply to the pleadings in the statement of claims;
    b. Particulars regarding the number of arbitrators in accordance with Article 14;
    c. Indication of the name and address of an arbitrator, if a decision by an arbitral tribunal is requested or if a decision by three arbitrators has been agreed upon in the arbitration agreement.

COUNTER-CLAIMS

Article 11

1. Claims by the Respondent against the Claimant that are based on an arbitration agreement which constitutes the jurisdiction of the International Arbitral Centre of the Austrian Federal Economic Chamber can be raised as counter-claims up to the time of closure of the evidentiary proceedings.

2. Counter-claims must be submitted to the Secretariat of the Centre and must be forwarded by the latter to the sole arbitrator (arbitral tribunal) for further action after the deposit against costs has been paid.

3. If the claim designated as a counter-claim is not based on an arbitration agreement which constitutes the jurisdiction of the International Arbitral Centre of the Austrian Federal Economic Chamber, if the parties are not identical, or if the submission of a counter-claim after transmission of the files to the sole arbitrator (arbitral tribunal) would lead to a substantial delay in the main proceedings, the sole arbitrator (arbitral tribunal) must return the claim to the Secretariat to be dealt with in separate proceedings.

4. The sole arbitrator (arbitral tribunal) must give the Counter-Respondent to an admissible counter-claim the opportunity to submit a memorandum in reply in writing and must set a time-limit for that purpose.

TRANSMITTING OF THE FILE TO THE SOLE ARBITRATOR (ARBITRAL TRIBUNAL)

Article 12

The Secretary General shall transmit the files to the sole arbitrator (arbitral tribunal) as soon as a statement of claims (counter-claim) has been received in due form, the sole arbitrator (all members of the arbitral tribunal) has (have) confirmed acceptance of the mandate and his (its) objectivity, using a form issued by the Centre (Article 7 paragraph 2), and the deposit for costs has been paid (Article 34). The proceedings before the sole arbitrator (arbitral tribunal) shall thereby commence.

TIME-LIMITS, SERVICE AND COMMUNICATIONS

Article 13

1. A time-limit shall be deemed to have been observed if the document is dispatched as provided under paragraph 2 of the present Article on the last day of the period set. Time-limits can be prolonged by the Secretary General on sufficient grounds; after the transmission of the files to the sole arbitrator (arbitral tribunal), the sole arbitrator (arbitral tribunal) shall be competent to prolong time-limits (except in the cases covered by Article 34 paragraphs 5 and 6).

2. Communications shall be considered as having been validly served if they are forwarded by registered letter, courier service, telefax or by other means of communication that guarantee evidence of transmission to the address most recently notified in writing to the sole arbitrator (arbitral tribunal) by the addressee as the address for service, or if the document to be served has been demonstrably transmitted.

3. As soon as a party has appointed a representative, service to the most recently indicated address of that representative shall be considered as having been made to the party represented.

NOMINATION AND APPOINTMENT OF ARBITRATORS

Article 14

1. The parties can agree that their dispute is to be decided either by a sole arbitrator or by an arbitral tribunal that shall consist of three arbitrators.

2. When no such agreement has been made and the parties do not agree on the number of arbitrators, the Board shall determine whether the dispute is to be decided by a sole arbitrator or by an arbitral tribunal. In that context, the Board

shall take into consideration in particular the difficulty of the case, the magnitude of the amount in dispute and the interest of the parties in a rapid and cost-effective decision.

3. The parties shall be notified of the decision of the Board pursuant to paragraph 2 of the present Article; in the event that proceedings before a sole arbitrator are decided upon, the parties shall be requested to agree on a sole arbitrator and to indicate that person's name and address within thirty days after service of the request. If no such indication is made within that period, the sole arbitrator shall be appointed by the Board.

4. If the dispute is to be decided by an arbitral tribunal, the party that has not yet nominated an arbitrator shall be requested to indicate the name and address of an arbitrator within thirty days after service of the request. If the party has not appointed an arbitrator within that time-limit, the arbitrator shall be appointed by the Board.

5. If the dispute is to be decided by an arbitral tribunal, the arbitrators nominated by the parties or appointed by the Board shall be requested to agree on a Chairman and to indicate his name and address within thirty days after service of the request. If no such indication is made within that period, the Chairman shall be appointed by the Board.

6. The parties are bound by their nomination of arbitrators as soon as the identity of the arbitrator nominated has been made known to the other party.

MULTIPARTY PROCEEDINGS

Article 15

1. A claim against two or more Respondents shall be admissible only if the Centre has jurisdiction for all of the Respondents, and, in the case of proceedings before an arbitral tribunal, if all Claimants have nominated the same arbitrator, and:

   a. If the applicable law positively provides that the claim is to be directed against several persons; or
   b. If all Respondents are by the applicable law in legal accord or are bound by the same facts or are joint and severally bound; or
   c. If the admissibility of multiparty proceedings has been agreed upon; or
   d. If all Respondents submit to multiparty proceedings and, in the case of proceedings before an arbitral tribunal, all Respondents nominate the same arbitrator; or
   e. If one or more of the Respondents on whom the claim was served fails or fail to provide the particulars mentioned in Article 10 paragraph 2, (b) and (c) within the thirty-day time-limit (Article 10 paragraph 1).

2. Where a claim against a number of Respondents cannot be served on all Respondents, the arbitral proceedings shall, upon application of the Claimant (the Claimants), be continued against those Respondents on whom the claim was served. The claim against those Respondents to which the claim could not be served shall be subject to separate proceedings.

3. If multiparty proceedings are admissible, the Respondents must agree among themselves whether they wish to have the dispute decided by one arbitrator or by three arbitrators, and, if a decision by three arbitrators is desired, must jointly nominate an arbitrator.

4. In the case covered by paragraph 3 of the present Article, if there is no agreement among the Respondents concerning the number of arbitrators, the Respondents shall be requested by the Secretary General to provide evidence of such agreement within thirty days after service of the request.

5. If no evidence of agreement on the number of arbitrators is presented within the period mentioned in paragraph 4 of the present article, the Board shall determine whether the dispute is to be decided by one arbitrator or by an arbitral tribunal.

6. If the Respondents have agreed that the dispute is to be decided by an arbitral tribunal, but without nominating an arbitrator, they shall be requested by the Secretary General to indicate the name and address of an arbitrator within thirty days after service of the request.

7. If no arbitrator is jointly nominated within the period mentioned in paragraph 6 of the present Article and if the dispute is to be decided by an arbitral tribunal, the Board shall appoint the arbitrator for the defaulting Respondents.

8. In cases other than those mentioned in paragraph 1 of the present Article, the consolidation of two or more disputes shall be admissible only if the same arbitrators have been appointed in all the disputes that are to be consolidated and if all parties and the sole arbitrator (arbitral tribunal) agree.

9. The decision whether multiparty proceedings, as per paragraph 1 of this Article, are admissible, shall be taken by the sole arbitrator (the arbitral tribunal) upon application of one of the Respondents. If the admissibility of multiparty proceedings is denied, the arbitral proceedings return to the stage they were in for the Respondents before the sole arbitrator (the arbitral tribunal) was appointed.

CHALLENGE OF ARBITRATORS

Article 16

1. An arbitrator may be challenged only if circumstances exist that give rise to justifiable doubts as to his impartiality or independence, or that are in conflict with the agreement of the parties. A party may challenge an arbitrator appointed by him,

or in whose appointment he participated, only for reasons of which he becomes aware after the participation in the appointment or after the appointment has been made.

2. If a party challenges an arbitrator, it must without delay inform the Secretary General thereof, stating the grounds for the challenge.

3. Should the challenged arbitrator not withdraw from his office, the Board shall decide upon the challenge on the basis of the particulars in the challenging motion and the evidence attached thereto. Before the Board makes its decision, the Secretary General must obtain the comments of the arbitrator challenged and of the other parties. The Board can also request comments from other persons.

4. An arbitrator challenged may continue the proceedings, notwithstanding the challenging motion. However, an award may not be rendered until after the final and binding decision of the Board.

EARLY TERMINATION OF THE MANDATE OF ARBITRATORS

Article 17

1. The mandate of an arbitrator terminates when

   a. the parties agree on the termination,
   b. the arbitrator withdraws from office,
   c. a challenging motion is granted,
   d. the arbitrator is removed from his office by the Board.

2. Any party may request the termination of the mandate of an arbitrator if the latter's incapacitation is not merely temporary, if he otherwise fails to perform his duties or unduly delays the proceedings. The request must be submitted to the Secretariat. The Board shall decide upon the request after hearing the arbitrator in question. If it is clear that incapacitation is not merely temporary, the Board may terminate the arbitrator's mandate even without a request from a party.

CONSEQUENCES OF CHALLENGE OR EARLY TERMINATION OF MANDATE

Article 18

1. If the challenge of an arbitrator has been allowed, if his mandate has been terminated, if he has resigned his mandate or has died, then,

   a. If that arbitrator is a sole arbitrator, the parties – or,
   b. If that arbitrator is the Chairman, the remaining arbitrators – or
   c. If that arbitrator has been nominated by a party or has been appointed for a party, the party that nominated him or for which he was appointed

shall be requested to nominate a new arbitrator within thirty days – by mutual consent in the cases covered by subparagraphs a) and b) of the present paragraph – and to indicate his name and address. If no such indication is received within that period, the new arbitrator shall be appointed by the Board. If a new arbitrator nominated has also been successfully challenged, the right to nominate a new arbitrator shall lapse and the new arbitrator shall be appointed by the Board.

2. If the challenge of an arbitrator has been allowed, if his mandate has been terminated, if he has resigned his mandate or has died, the new sole arbitrator (newly constituted arbitral tribunal) shall determine, after obtaining the comments of the parties, whether and, if so, to what extent, previous procedural stages are to be repeated.

JURISDICTION OF THE ARBITRAL TRIBUNAL

Article 19

1. A plea that the arbitral tribunal does not have jurisdiction shall be raised not later than the first pleading in the matter. A party is not precluded from raising such a plea by the fact that he has appointed, or participated in the appointment of an arbitrator. A plea that the arbitral tribunal is exceeding the scope of its authority shall be raised as soon as the matter alleged to be beyond the scope of its authority is raised during the arbitral proceedings. In both cases a later plea shall not be permitted; if the arbitral tribunal however considers the delay justified, the plea can be admitted.

2. The sole arbitrator (arbitral tribunal) shall rule on its own jurisdiction. The ruling can be made together with the ruling on the case or by separate arbitral award.

CONDUCT OF THE PROCEEDINGS

Article 20

1. In the context of the Vienna Rules and the agreements between the parties, the sole arbitrator (arbitral tribunal) may conduct the arbitration proceedings at his (its) absolute discretion; the principle of equal treatment of the parties shall apply, the right to be heard being ensured at every stage of the proceedings. However, subject to advance notice, the sole arbitrator (arbitral tribunal) is entitled to declare that pleadings and the presentation of documentary evidence shall be admissible only up to a certain stage of the proceedings.

2. Immediately after transmission of the files to the sole arbitrator (arbitral tribunal), the latter shall determine the language or languages of the proceedings, taking into consideration all circumstances, in particular, the language of the contract.

In such matters, he (it) is bound by any agreement between the parties. The sole arbitrator (arbitral tribunal) can order that a translation be submitted of all documents that are not drafted in that language (those languages).

3. The proceedings may be oral or only in writing. Oral hearings shall take place at the request of one party or if the sole arbitrator (arbitral tribunal) to whom (which) the case has been referred considers it necessary. In any case, the parties must be given the opportunity to take note of, and comment on, the motions and pleadings of the other parties and the result of the evidentiary proceedings.

4. The date of oral hearings shall be fixed by the sole arbitrator or the Chairman of the arbitral tribunal. Hearings shall be private. A record of at least the results of the hearings shall be made, which the sole arbitrator or the Chairman of the arbitral tribunal shall sign.

5. If the sole arbitrator (arbitral tribunal) considers it necessary, he (it) may on his (its) own initiative collect evidence, and in particular may question parties or witnesses, may request the parties to submit documents and visual evidence and may call in experts. If costs are incurred through the evidentiary proceedings and in particular through the appointment of experts, the procedure under Article 35 shall be followed.

6. If one party does not take part in the proceedings, the case must be heard with the other party alone.

7. If a violation by the sole arbitrator (arbitral tribunal) of a provision of these arbitration rules or of other provisions applicable to the proceedings comes to the notice of a party, that party must immediately enter an objection otherwise the party will be barred from entering an objection against that defect.

8. The sole arbitrator (arbitral tribunal) must ask the parties whether they have any further proof to offer, witnesses to be heard or submissions to make. As soon as the sole arbitrator (arbitral tribunal) is convinced that the parties have had an adequate opportunity for such purposes, the sole arbitrator (arbitral tribunal) must declare the proceedings closed.

CHALLENGE OF EXPERTS

Article 21

Article 16 shall apply accordingly to the challenging of experts appointed by the sole arbitrator (arbitral tribunal). However, the sole arbitrator (arbitral tribunal) shall decide on the challenge.

INTERIM MEASURES OF PROTECTION

Article 22

1. Unless otherwise agreed by the parties, the sole arbitrator (arbitral tribunal) may, at the request of a party order any party, after hearing such party, to take such interim measure of protection as the sole arbitrator (arbitral tribunal) may consider necessary in respect of the subject matter of the dispute, as otherwise the enforcement of the claim would be frustrated or considerably impeded or there is a danger of irreparable harm. The sole arbitrator (arbitral tribunal) may require any party to provide appropriate security in connection with such measure. The parties are obliged to comply with such orders, whether or not they are enforceable by State courts.

2. Measures referred to in paragraph (1) are to be ordered in writing and a signed copy is to be served on each party. In arbitral proceedings with more than one arbitrator the signature of the presiding arbitrator or, if he is prevented, the signature of another arbitrator shall suffice, provided that the presiding arbitrator or another arbitrator records on the order the reason preventing the signature.

3. Unless the parties have agreed otherwise, the measures are to be substantiated. The measure must include the date on when it was ordered and the place of arbitration. The measure shall be deemed to have been ordered on that date and at that place.

4. The measures and the records on the serving are joint documents of the parties and the sole arbitrator (arbitral tribunal). The sole arbitrator (arbitral tribunal) shall discuss with the parties the possibility of depositing the measure and the records on the serving.

5. The sole arbitrator (the presiding arbitrator) or, if he is prevented, another arbitrator, shall upon the motion of a party, confirm the unappealability and enforceability of the measure on a copy of the measure.

6. This provision does not prevent the parties from applying to any competent State organ for interim measures of protection. Such an application to a State organ for ordering such measures or for the enforcement of measures ordered by the sole arbitrator (arbitral tribunal) shall not constitute an infringement or waiver of the arbitration agreement and shall not affect the powers of the sole arbitrator (arbitral tribunal). The Secretariat and the sole arbitrator (arbitral tribunal) must be immediately informed of any such application as well as of all measures ordered by the State organ.

AUTHORIZED AGENTS

Article 23

The parties shall have the right to be represented or advised by persons of their choice in the proceedings before the sole arbitrator (arbitral tribunal).

APPLICABLE LAW, EQUITY

Article 24

1. The sole arbitrator (arbitral tribunal) shall decide the dispute in accordance with such legislation or rules of law as are chosen by the parties as applicable. Any choice of law or legal system of a given state shall be construed, unless otherwise expressed by the parties, as directly referring to the substantive law of that state and not to its conflict-of-law rules.

2. Failing any designation by the parties, the sole arbitrator (arbitral tribunal) shall apply the rules of law considered by him (it) as appropriate.

3. The sole arbitrator (arbitral tribunal) may decide on equity only if the parties have expressly authorized him (it) to do so.

TERMINATION

Article 25

The proceedings are terminated by

- a. the rendering of an award,
- b. the conclusion of a settlement,
- c. an order of the sole arbitrator (arbitral tribunal) where
  - aa. the claimant withdraws his claim, unless the respondent objects thereto and the sole arbitrator (arbitral tribunal) recognizes a legitimate interest on his part in obtaining a final settlement of the dispute;
  - bb. the parties agree on the termination of the proceedings and communicate this to the sole arbitrator (arbitral tribunal);
  - cc. the sole arbitrator (arbitral tribunal) finds that the continuation of the proceedings has become impossible, in particular when the parties to the proceedings do not continue the arbitral proceedings despite written notification from the sole arbitrator (arbitral tribunal), in which it refers to the possibility of terminating the proceedings.

DECISION MAKING OF THE ARBITRAL TRIBUNAL

Article 26

1. Any award or any other decision of the arbitral tribunal shall be made by a majority of all its members. If no majority of votes is obtained, the presiding arbitrator shall decide alone.

2. Questions of procedure may be decided by the presiding arbitrator alone if so authorized by the arbitral tribunal, with reservation to possible amendments by the arbitral tribunal.

THE AWARD

Article 27

1. Awards shall be drawn up in writing. The grounds upon which the award is based must be stated, unless all parties, either in the arbitration agreement or in the oral proceedings, have agreed that no grounds are to be stated.

2. The award shall state the date on which it was made and the place of arbitration (Article 2).

3. All copies of awards must be signed by the arbitrators. The signatures of the majority of the arbitrators shall suffice if the award contains a statement that one arbitrator refuses to sign or that his signature is prevented by an obstacle which cannot be overcome within a reasonable period of time. If the award is made by a majority decision, mention thereof shall be made in the award at the request of the arbitrator who is in a minority.

4. Awards are confirmed on all copies as awards of the Centre by the signature of the Secretary General and the stamp of the Centre. By this it is confirmed that the award is an award of the International Arbitral Centre of the Austrian Federal Economic Chamber and that it was made and signed by (an) arbitrator(s) chosen or appointed in accordance with these Rules of Arbitration.

5. The award shall be served on the parties by the Secretary General. Awards become effective as against the parties on service of the copies. One copy of the award and the records on the serving shall be deposited with the Secretariat of the Centre.

6. The sole arbitrator (Chairman of the arbitral tribunal, or, if he is prevented, another arbitrator) shall confirm on all copies at the request of a party the finality and enforceability of the award.

7. Partial and interim awards may be issued.

8. By their agreement to the Vienna Rules, the parties undertake to implement the award.

SETTLEMENT

Article 28

The Parties can request that a record is drawn up on a settlement they have concluded or that an award *(on agreed terms)* be made thereof.

CORRECTION AND INTERPRETATION OF AWARD; ADDITIONAL AWARD

Article 29

1. Each party may within 30 days of receipt of the award file with the Secretariat the following applications to the sole arbitrator (arbitral tribunal):

   a. to correct in the award any errors in computation, any clerical or typo-graphical errors or any errors of similar nature;
   b. if so agreed by the parties, to interpret certain parts of the award;
   c. to make an additional award as to claims presented in the arbitral proceedings but omitted from the award.

2. The decision on such an application is made by the sole arbitrator (arbitral tribunal). Prior to making a decision upon such an application, the other party is to be heard. The sole arbitrator (arbitral tribunal) shall determine a time period for that purpose, which should not exceed 30 days.

3. The sole arbitrator (arbitral tribunal) may correct any error of the type referred to in paragraph (1) a) of this Article on its own initiative within 30 days of the date of the award.

4. The provisions of Article 27 paragraphs 1 to 6 shall apply to the correction, interpretation or making of an additional award. The interpretation or correction shall be part of the arbitral award.

PUBLISHING OF AWARDS

Article 30

The Board is entitled to publish an award in legal journals or in its own publications in anonymous form, unless publication is objected to by at least one party within thirty days after service of the copy of the award on it.

DETERMINATION OF COSTS

Article 31

When the arbitral proceedings are terminated, the sole arbitrator (arbitral tribunal) shall, upon application of a party, state in the award on the merits or by separate award: the costs of arbitration fixed by the Secretary General in accordance with Article 34 paragraph 1; shall determine the amount of costs of the parties; and shall state who should bear the costs of the proceedings or the proportion in which the costs of the proceedings are to be shared.

COSTS OF THE PROCEEDINGS

Article 32

The costs of the proceedings consist of the following elements:

a. The costs of arbitration, that is to say, the outlay of the Centre (administrative costs), arbitrators' fees plus any value added tax and cash outlay (such as travel and subsistence expenses of arbitrators, costs of service of documents, rent, costs of simple minuting); and

b. The costs of the parties, that is to say, the appropriate expenses of the parties for their representation and other outlay related to the arbitration proceedings, in particular, the costs specified in Article 35 paragraph 1.

REGISTRATION FEE

Article 33

1. On filing the claim (counter-claim), the Claimant (Counter-claimant) shall pay into the account of the Centre, free of charges, a registration fee in the amount stated. That fee is intended to cover the costs up to the submission of the files to the sole arbitrator (arbitral tribunal). If higher outlay is incurred, an additional sum may be prescribed.

2. If there are more than two parties to the proceedings, the registration fee shall be increased by 10% for each additional party.

3. The registration fee shall not be repayable. The registration fee, as well as any additional amount required in accordance with paragraph 1 of the present Article shall be deducted from the Claimant's (Counter-claimant's) share of the deposit against costs of arbitration.

4. The claim (counter-claim) shall be treated only after the registration fee is fully paid.

Costs of Arbitration and Deposit

Article 34

1. The costs of arbitration shall be determined by the Secretary General at the end of the proceedings.

2. The Secretary General shall fix the amount of the deposit against the expected costs of arbitration. That deposit shall be paid in equal shares by the parties before transmission of the files to the sole arbitrator (arbitral tribunal) and within thirty days after service of the payment request.

3. If the share of the Claimant (Counter-claimant) is not received within the time-limit, despite prolongation thereof, the claim (counter-claim) shall not be treated any further. The Secretary General shall inform the parties thereof.

4. If the share of the Respondent (Counter-Respondent) is not received within the time-limit set, the Secretary General shall inform the Claimant (Counter-claimant) thereof and shall request him to pay the outstanding share of the deposit within thirty days of receipt of the payment request. If that amount is not received within the time-limit, the claim (counter-claim) shall not be treated any further. The Secretary General shall inform the parties thereof.

5. If it should be necessary in the course of the proceedings to increase the deposit against costs because of an increase in the amount in dispute, a procedure analogous to that provided for in paragraphs 2 to 4 of the present Article shall be adopted. Until payment of the additional deposit, the amplification of the claim that led to the increase of the amount in dispute shall not be taken into account in the arbitral proceedings.

6. If it should be necessary in the course of the proceedings to increase the deposit against costs because the amount fixed for cash outlay on determining the deposit is not sufficient, a procedure analogous to that provided for in paragraphs 2 to 4 of the present Article shall be adopted.

Further Costs of Procedure

Article 35

1. If the sole arbitrator (arbitral tribunal) considers certain action entailing costs, such as the appointment of experts, interpreters or translators, making verbatim records of the proceedings, a visual inspection, or relocation of the proceedings, to be necessary, he (it) must make arrangements to cover the expected costs and inform the Secretary General thereof.

2. The sole arbitrator (arbitral tribunal) may undertake procedural steps in accordance with paragraph 1 of the present Article only if adequate cover for the expected costs exists.

3. The sole arbitrator (arbitral tribunal) shall decide what consequences for the proceedings arise from the failure to pay a prescribed deposit against costs.

4. All commitments related to the procedural steps mentioned in paragraph 1 of the present Article shall be undertaken by the sole arbitrator (arbitral tribunal) in the name and for the account of the parties.

CALCULATION OF THE COSTS OF ARBITRATION

Article 36

1. The administrative costs of the Centre and the arbitrators' fees shall be fixed on the basis of the amount in dispute, according to the schedule of arbitration costs attached to these Rules (Annex 1). Where the proceedings are terminated early, the Secretary General may reduce the arbitrator's fees as it appears just corresponding to the stage reached in the proceedings.

2. If there are more than two parties to proceedings, the rates for the administrative costs of the Centre and the arbitrators' fees contained in the schedules attached to these Rules shall be increased by 10% for each additional party.

3. The arbitration costs for claims that are submitted to offset against the claims (counter-claims) and that are in fact and in law of no connection with the cause of action (principle claims), are to be calculated separately and paid as like counter-claims. Article 34 shall apply accordingly to determine the deposits. Counter-claims are not to be dealt with in the proceedings concerning the principle claims until the additional deposits have been fully paid.

4. In the case of proceedings conducted concerning a number of individual claims or counter-claims, which are both in fact and in law of no connection, the Secretary General may at any stage of the proceedings make a separate calculation of the costs of arbitration according to the amounts in dispute in respect of the individual claims.

5. The Secretary General may deviate from the statements of the parties in fixing the amount in dispute if the parties have made only a partial claim or if a request by the parties whose purpose was not the payment of sums of money was obviously undervalued.

6. The rates quoted in the schedule of arbitrators' fees are the fees for sole arbitrators. In any case they shall be raised to two-and-a-half times the amounts quoted if an arbitral tribunal is appointed and to up to three times the rates stated in the event of the particular difficulty of a case.

7. The tariffs specified in the schedule for arbitrator's fees include any and all partial and interim decisions, such as awards on jurisdiction, partial awards, decisions on the challenge of arbitrators, interim measures of protection, other decisions and orders that manage the proceedings.

8. Reductions of the amount in dispute shall be taken into consideration in calculating the arbitrators' fees and administrative costs only if they were made before transmission of the files to the sole arbitrator (arbitral tribunal).

9. Cash outlays shall be determined according to the actual expenditure.

10. The tariffs specified in the schedule for arbitrator's fees do not include value added tax, to which the arbitrator's fees may be subject. Those arbitrators whose fees are subject to value added tax shall inform the Secretary General of the prospective amount of value added tax upon taking up office.

TRANSITIONAL PROVISION

Article 37

This version of the Vienna Rules shall apply to all proceedings in which the claim was filed after 30th June, 2006.

SCHEDULE OF ARBITRATION COSTS

Registration Fee: EUR 2,000[1]

Administrative Charges[2]

| Amount in dispute in EUR | | Rate in EUR |
From	To	
0	100.000	3.000
100.001	200.000	3.000 + 1,5 % of excess over 100.000
200.001	500.000	4.500 + 1,0 % of excess over 200.000
500.001	1.000.000	7.500 + 0,7 % of excess over 500.000
1.000.001	2.000.000	11.000 + 0,4 % of excess over 1.000.000
2.000.001	5.000.000	15.000 + 0,1 % of excess over 2.000.000
5.000.001	10.000.000	18.000 + 0,05 % of excess over 5.000.000
over 10.000.000		20.500 + 0,01 % of excess over 10.000.000

1. See Article 33 paragraph 1.
2. See Article 36 paragraph 1.

Fees for sole arbitrators[3]

| Amount in dispute in EUR | | Rate in EUR |
From	To	
0	100.000	6 % – minimum fee 1.000
100.001	200.000	6.000 + 3 % of excess over 100.000
200.001	500.000	9.000 + 2,5 % of excess over 200.000
500.001	1.000.000	16.500 + 2 % of excess over 500.000
1.000.001	2.000.000	26.500 + 1 % of excess over 1.000.000
2.000.001	5.000.000	36.500 + 0,6 % of excess over 2.000.000
5.000.001	10.000.000	54.500 + 0,4 % of excess over 5.000.000
10.000.001	20.000.000	74.500 + 0,2 % of excess over 10.000.000
20.000.001	100.000.000	94.500 + 0,1 % of excess over 20.000.000
over 100.000.000		174.500 + 0,01 % of excess over 100.000.000

3. See Article 36 paragraph 6.

Annex 1b

Internationales Schiedsgericht der Wirtschaftskammer Österreich Schiedsordnung 2006 (Wiener Regeln 2006)*

ALLGEMEINE BESTIMMUNGEN

DIE INSTITUTION

Artikel 1

1. Das Internationale Schiedsgericht der Wirtschaftskammer Österreich in Wien (Wiener Internationales Schiedsgericht, im folgenden 'Schiedsgericht' genannt) trägt Vorsorge für die schiedsgerichtliche Erledigung von Streitigkeiten, bei denen nicht alle Vertragsparteien, welche die Schiedsvereinbarung geschlossen haben, zum Zeitpunkt des Abschlusses dieser Vereinbarung ihren Sitz oder gewöhnlichen Aufenthalt in Österreich hatten.

Dieses Schiedsgericht kann auch von Parteien mit Sitz oder gewöhnlichem Aufenthalt in Österreich für die Erledigung von Streitigkeiten internationalen Charakters vereinbart werden.

2. Haben die Parteien die Zuständigkeit des Schiedsgerichts vereinbart, so gilt damit die Anwendung dieser Schiedsordnung (im folgenden 'Wiener Regeln') in der bei Einleitung des Schiedsverfahrens geltenden Fassung als vereinbart.

---

* Vom erweiterten Präsidium der Wirtschaftskammer Österreich am 3. Mai 2006 mit Wirkung von 1. Juni 2006 beschlossen. Mit freundlicher Genehmigung des Internationalen Schiedsgerichtes der Wirtschaftskammer Österreich abgedruckt.

3. Haben Parteien, die zum Zeitpunkt des Abschlusses der Schiedsvereinbarung ihren Sitz oder gewöhnlichen Aufenthalt in Österreich hatten, vereinbart, dass ihre Streitigkeiten von einem Schiedsrichter oder einem Schiedsrichtersenat, der nach den Wiener Regeln zu ernennen ist, endgültig entschieden werden soll, und hat die Streitsache keinen internationalen Charakter, so ist das Ständige Schiedsgericht der Wirtschaftskammer Wien oder, wenn ein anderer Schiedsort in Österreich vereinbart wurde, jener Wirtschaftskammer, in deren örtlichen Zuständigkeitsbereich der vereinbarte Schiedsort fällt, zur Vorsorge für die schiedsrichterliche Erledigung zuständig. Dieses führt das Verfahren nach der Schiedsgerichtsordnung für die Ständigen Schiedsgerichte der Wirtschaftskammern.

SCHIEDSORT

Artikel 2

Sofern die Parteien nichts anderes vereinbart haben,

    a. ist der Sitz des Schiedsgerichts Wien;
    b. kann der Schiedsrichter (Schiedsrichtersenat) an jedem ihm geeignet erscheinenden Ort Verfahrenshandlungen vornehmen.

Dem Schiedsrichtersenat steht es jedenfalls frei, an jedem beliebigen Ort auf jede beliebige Weise zu beraten.

ORGANISATION

DAS PRÄSIDIUM

Artikel 3

1. Das Präsidium des Schiedsgerichts hat mindestens fünf Mitglieder. Sie werden vom erweiterten Präsidium der Wirtschaftskammer Österreich auf Vorschlag des Präsidenten des Schiedsgerichts für eine Funktionsperiode von fünf Jahren bestellt; Wiederbestellung ist zulässig. Erfolgt bis zum Ablauf einer Funktionsperiode keine Neubestellung, so behalten die Mitglieder des Präsidiums ihre Funktion bis zur Neubestellung. Fällt ein Mitglied des Präsidiums während der Funktionsperiode auf Dauer aus (etwa durch Rücktritt oder Tod), so kann eine Nachbestellung für den Rest der Funktionsperiode des im Amt befindlichen Präsidiums erfolgen.

2. Die Mitglieder des Präsidiums wählen aus ihrer Mitte für die Dauer der Funktionsperiode einen Präsidenten. Im Falle seiner Verhinderung werden seine Aufgaben von dem an Lebensjahren ältesten Mitglied wahrgenommen.

3. Die Sitzungen des Präsidiums werden vom Präsidenten einberufen und von ihm oder in seiner Stellvertretung von dem an Lebensjahren ältesten anwesenden und stimmberechtigten Mitglied geleitet. Das Präsidium ist beschlussfähig, wenn mehr als die Hälfte seiner Mitglieder anwesend ist. Es entscheidet mit einfacher Mehrheit der anwesenden stimmberechtigten (siehe Abs 4) Mitglieder. Bei Stimmengleichheit entscheidet die Stimme des Sitzungsleiters.

4. Mitglieder des Präsidiums, die in irgendeiner Eigenschaft an einem Schiedsverfahren beteiligt sind, sind bei Entscheidungen, die dieses Verfahren betreffen, nicht stimmberechtigt, sind aber auf das Anwesenheitserfordernis anzurechnen.

5. Entscheidungen auf schriftlichem Wege sind zulässig. In diesem Fall übermittelt der Präsident den Mitgliedern einen schriftlichen Beschlussvorschlag und setzt eine Frist zur schriftlichen Stimmabgabe. Abs 3 dritter und vierter Satz sind sinngemäß anzuwenden. Jedes Mitglied hat aber das Recht, über den Beschlussvorschlag eine Sitzung zu verlangen.

6. Die Mitglieder des Präsidiums haben ihr Amt nach bestem Wissen und Gewissen auszuüben und sind in der Ausübung ihrer Funktion unabhängig und an keine Weisungen gebunden. Sie sind über alles, was ihnen in dieser Funktion bekannt geworden ist, zur Verschwiegenheit verpflichtet.

INTERNATIONALER BEIRAT

Artikel 4

Der Internationale Beirat besteht aus Fachleuten der Internationalen Schiedsgerichtsbarkeit, die das jeweilige Präsidium für die Dauer seiner Amtsperiode einladen kann. Er dient der Erörterung aktueller Sachfragen.

DER GENERALSEKRETÄR

Artikel 5

1. Der Generalsekretär des Schiedsgerichts wird auf Vorschlag des Präsidiums des Schiedsgerichts vom Vorstand der Wirtschaftskammer Österreich für eine Funktionsperiode von fünf Jahren bestellt. Wiederbestellung ist zulässig. Art 3 Abs 1 zweiter Satz gilt analog.

2. Der Generalsekretär leitet das Sekretariat und erledigt die administrativen Angelegenheiten des Schiedsgerichts, soweit sie nicht dem Präsidium vorbehalten sind.

3. Der Generalsekretär hat sein Amt nach bestem Wissen und Gewissen auszuüben und ist dabei an keine Weisungen gebunden. Er ist über alles, was ihm in dieser Funktion bekannt geworden ist, zur Verschwiegenheit verpflichtet.

4. Ist der Generalsekretär an der Ausübung seines Amtes verhindert oder fällt er auf Dauer aus, so übt ein vom Präsidium betrautes Mitglied desselben dessen Funktionen bis zur Bestellung eines Generalsekretärs aus.

KORRESPONDENZSPRACHEN

Artikel 6

Der Schriftverkehr der Parteien mit dem Präsidium und dem Generalsekretär hat in deutscher oder englischer Sprache zu erfolgen.

DIE SCHIEDSRICHTER

Artikel 7

1. Den Parteien steht die Bestimmung der Schiedsrichter frei. Schiedsrichter kann – ungeachtet der Staatsbürgerschaft – jede geschäftsfähige Person sein, soweit die Parteien keine besonderen zusätzlichen Qualifikationserfordernisse vereinbart haben.

2. Voraussetzungen für die Bestellung als Schiedsrichter sind:

    a. die schriftliche Erklärung über seine Unparteilichkeit und Unabhängigkeit nach Abs 5. Der Generalsekretär leitet eine Kopie des Vordrucks, auf welchem der Schiedsrichter (die Mitglieder des Schiedsrichtersenates) ihre Unbefangenheit bestätigt haben, an die Parteien weiter.

    b. Die schriftliche Unterwerfung unter die Vorschriften dieser Schiedsordnung einschließlich der Bestimmungen über die Verfahrenskosten.

3. Mitglieder des Präsidiums dürfen nur die Funktion des Vorsitzenden eines Schiedsrichtersenates oder eines Einzelschiedsrichters annehmen.

4. Die Schiedsrichter haben ihr Amt in voller Unabhängigkeit und Unparteilichkeit nach bestem Wissen und Gewissen auszuüben und sind dabei an keine Weisungen gebunden. Sie sind über alles, was ihnen in dieser Funktion bekannt geworden ist, zur Verschwiegenheit verpflichtet.

5. Will eine Person ein Schiedsrichteramt übernehmen, so hat sie alle Umstände offen zu legen, die Zweifel an ihrer Unparteilichkeit oder Unabhängigkeit wecken können oder der Parteienvereinbarung widersprechen. Ein Schiedsrichter hat vom Zeitpunkt seiner Bestellung an und während des Schiedsverfahrens den Parteien unverzüglich solche Umstände offen zu legen, wenn er sie ihnen nicht schon vorher mitgeteilt hat.

HAFTUNG

Artikel 8

Die Haftung der Schiedsrichter, des Generalsekretärs, des Präsidiums und seiner Mitglieder und der Wirtschaftskammer Österreich und ihrer Beschäftigten für jedwede Handlung oder Unterlassung im Zusammenhang mit dem Schiedsverfahren ist, soweit gesetzlich zulässig, ausgeschlossen.

DAS SCHIEDSVERFAHREN

EINLEITUNG

Artikel 9

1. Das Schiedsverfahren wird durch Einreichung einer Klage beim Sekretariat eingeleitet. Mit Einlangen der Klage im Sekretariat ist das Verfahren anhängig.

2. Für jeden Beklagten, jeden Schiedsrichter und das Sekretariat ist je eine Klagsausfertigung samt Beilagen einzureichen.

3. Die Klage hat zu enthalten:

   a. die Bezeichnung der Parteien und ihre Anschriften;
   b. ein bestimmtes Begehren, die tatsächlichen Angaben, auf die es sich stützt, und die beantragten Beweise;
   c. den Wert des Streitgegenstandes zum Zeitpunkt der Einbringung der Klage, wenn das Klagebegehren nicht ausschließlich auf eine bestimmte Geldsumme gerichtet ist;
   d. Angaben zur Zahl der Schiedsrichter gemäß Art 14;
   e. die Benennung eines Schiedsrichters mit Angabe der Anschrift, wenn eine Entscheidung durch drei Schiedsrichter beantragt wird.

4. Der Klage ist eine Kopie jener Vereinbarung anzuschließen, aus der sich die Zuständigkeit des Schiedsgerichts ergibt.

5. Entspricht die Klage nicht dem Abs 3 oder fehlen Ausfertigungen oder Beilagen, so fordert der Generalsekretär den Kläger zur Verbesserung oder Ergänzung auf. Der Kläger ist dabei zu informieren, dass bis zur Verbesserung oder Ergänzung der Klage diese nicht weiter behandelt wird.

6. Das Präsidium kann die Durchführung des Verfahrens verweigern, wenn die Parteien in der Schiedsvereinbarung zwar das Internationale Schiedsgericht der Wirtschaftskammer Österreich bezeichnen, aber von den Wiener Regeln abweichende Vereinbarungen getroffen haben.

KLAGEBEANTWORTUNG

Artikel 10

1. Ist die Klage nicht gemäß Art 9 Abs 5 und 6 zu behandeln, so stellt der Generalsekretär der beklagten Partei die Klage sowie ein Exemplar der Schiedsordnung zu und fordert sie auf, binnen 30 Tagen eine Klagebeantwortung in der nach Art 9 Abs 2 erforderlichen Zahl von Ausfertigungen einzubringen.

2. Die Klagebeantwortung hat zu enthalten:

   a. eine Äußerung zum Vorbringen in der Klage,
   b. Angaben zur Zahl der Schiedsrichter gemäß Art 14,
   c. die Benennung eines Schiedsrichters unter Angabe seiner Anschrift, wenn die Entscheidung durch einen Schiedsrichtersenat beantragt wird oder in der Schiedsvereinbarung die Entscheidung durch drei Schiedsrichter vereinbart ist.

WIDERKLAGE

Artikel 11

1. Klagen der beklagten Partei gegen den Kläger, die auf einer Schiedsvereinbarung beruhen, die die Zuständigkeit des Internationalen Schiedsgerichts der Wirtschaftskammer Österreich begründet, können bis zum Schluss des Beweisverfahrens als Widerklage erhoben werden.

2. Widerklagen sind beim Sekretariat des Schiedsgerichts einzubringen und von diesem nach Erlag des Kostenvorschusses dem Schiedsrichter (Schiedsrichtersenat) zur weiteren Behandlung zuzuleiten.

3. Beruht die als Widerklage bezeichnete Klage nicht auf einer Schiedsvereinbarung, die die Zuständigkeit des Internationalen Schiedsgerichts der Wirtschaftskammer Österreich begründet, oder besteht keine Parteienidentität oder würde eine nach Übergabe der Unterlagen zum Fall an den Schiedsrichter (den Schiedsrichtersenat) eingebrachte Widerklage zu einer erheblichen Verzögerung des Hauptverfahrens führen, so hat der Schiedsrichter (Schiedsrichtersenat) diese Klage dem Sekretariat zur Behandlung in einem gesonderten Verfahren zurückzustellen.

4. Der Schiedsrichter (Schiedsrichtersenat) hat dem Widerbeklagten einer zulässigen Widerklage Gelegenheit zur Erstattung einer schriftlichen Klagebeantwortung zu geben und hiefür eine Frist zu setzen.

FALLÜBERGABE AN DEN SCHIEDSRICHTER (SCHIEDSRICHTERSENAT)

Artikel 12

Der Generalsekretär übersendet die Unterlagen zum Fall dem Schiedsrichter (Schiedsrichtersenat), sobald eine mangelfreie Klage (Widerklage) vorliegt, der Schiedsrichter (sämtliche Mitglieder des Schiedsrichtersenates) die Übernahme des Auftrages und ihre Unbefangenheit auf einem Vordruck des Schiedsgerichts bestätigt haben (Art 7 Abs 2) und der Kostenvorschuss vollständig bezahlt ist (Art 34). Damit beginnt das Verfahren vor dem Schiedsrichter (Schiedsrichtersenat).

FRISTEN, ZUSTELLUNGEN UND MITTEILUNGEN

Artikel 13

1. Eine Frist ist gewahrt, wenn das Schriftstück am letzten Tag der Frist in einer in Abs 2 vorgesehenen Weise versendet wird. Fristen können vom Generalsekretär aus berücksichtigungswürdigen Gründen verlängert werden; nach der Übergabe der Unterlagen zum Fall an den Schiedsrichter (Schiedsrichtersenat) ist dafür der Schiedsrichter (Schiedsrichtersenat) zuständig (ausgenommen die Fälle des Art 34 Abs 5 und 6).

2. Zustellungen gelten als ordnungsgemäß durchgeführt, wenn sie mittels eingeschriebenen Briefes, Kurierdienstes, Telefax oder durch andere Formen der Nachrichtenübermittlung, die einen Nachweis der Übermittlung sicherstellen, an jene Anschrift erfolgt sind, die der Adressat des Schriftstückes zuletzt dem Schiedsgericht bzw. dem Schiedsrichter (Schiedsrichtersenat) schriftlich als Zustelladresse bekannt gegeben hat, oder wenn das zuzustellende Schriftstück dem Adressaten ausgehändigt wurde.

3. Sobald eine Partei einen Vertreter bestellt hat, gelten Zustellungen an die zuletzt bekannt gegebene Anschrift dieses Vertreters als an die vertretene Partei erfolgt.

BENENNUNG UND BESTELLUNG VON SCHIEDSRICHTERN

Artikel 14

1. Die Parteien können vereinbaren, dass ihr Rechtsstreit von einem Schiedsrichter oder von einem aus drei Schiedsrichtern bestehenden Schiedsrichtersenat entschieden werden soll.

2. Liegt eine solche Vereinbarung nicht vor und einigen sich die Parteien nicht auf die Zahl der Schiedsrichter, so bestimmt das Präsidium, ob der Rechtsstreit von einem Schiedsrichter oder einem Schiedsrichtersenat zu entscheiden ist. Hiebei berücksichtigt das Präsidium insbesondere die Schwierigkeit des Falles, die Höhe

des Streitwertes und das Interesse der Parteien an einer raschen und kostengünstigen Entscheidung.

3. Die Entscheidung des Präsidiums nach Abs 2 wird den Parteien mit der Aufforderung mitgeteilt, sich in den Fällen, in denen auf ein Verfahren vor einem Schiedsrichter entschieden wurde, binnen 30 Tagen ab Zustellung der Aufforderung auf einen Schiedsrichter zu einigen und dessen Namen und Adresse bekannt zu geben. Erfolgt innerhalb dieser Frist keine solche Mitteilung, so wird der Schiedsrichter vom Präsidium bestellt.

4. Ist der Rechtsstreit von einem Schiedsrichtersenat zu entscheiden, so wird die Partei, die noch keinen Schiedsrichter benannt hat, aufgefordert, binnen 30 Tagen ab Zustellung der Aufforderung den Namen und die Adresse eines Schiedsrichters bekannt zu geben. Wenn die Partei innerhalb dieser Frist keinen Schiedsrichter benennt, so wird dieser vom Präsidium bestellt.

5. Ist der Rechtsstreit von einem Schiedsrichtersenat zu entscheiden, so werden die von den Parteien benannten oder vom Präsidium bestellten Schiedsrichter aufgefordert, sich binnen 30 Tagen ab Zustellung der Aufforderung auf einen Vorsitzenden zu einigen und dessen Namen und Adresse bekannt zu geben. Erfolgt innerhalb dieser Frist keine solche Mitteilung, so wird der Vorsitzende vom Präsidium bestellt.

6. Die Parteien sind an ihre Schiedsrichterbenennung gebunden, sobald der benannte Schiedsrichter der Gegenpartei bekannt gegeben wurde.

Mehrparteienverfahren

Artikel 15

1. Eine Schiedsklage gegen zwei oder mehrere Beklagte ist nur zulässig, sofern das Schiedsgericht für alle Beklagten zuständig ist, bei einem Verfahren vor einem Schiedsrichtersenat alle Kläger denselben Schiedsrichter benennen und

   a. die Klage nach dem anzuwendenden Recht zwingend gegen mehrere Personen zu richten ist oder
   b. die beklagten Parteien nach dem anzuwendenden Recht in Rechtsgemeinschaft stehen oder aus demselben tatsächlichen Grund oder solidarisch verpflichtet sind, oder
   c. wenn die Zulässigkeit eines Mehrparteienverfahrens vereinbart ist oder
   d. alle Beklagten sich auf ein Mehrparteienverfahren einlassen und bei einem Verfahren vor einem Schiedsrichtersenat alle Beklagten denselben Schiedsrichter benennen oder
   e. einer oder mehrere der Beklagten, denen die Klage zugestellt wurde, innerhalb der 30-tägigen Frist (Art 10 Abs 1) die in Art 10 Abs 2 lit b und c bezeichneten Angaben nicht erstatten.

2. Kann eine gegen mehrere Beklagte gerichtete Klage nicht allen Beklagten zugestellt werden, so ist das Schiedsverfahren auf Antrag des Klägers (der Kläger) gegen jene Beklagten, denen die Klage zugestellt wurde, fortzusetzen. Die Klage gegen jene Beklagten, denen die Klage nicht zugestellt werden konnte, ist in einem gesonderten Verfahren zu behandeln.

3. Ist ein Mehrparteienverfahren zulässig, so haben sich die Beklagten untereinander zu einigen, ob sie den Rechtsstreit von einem oder von drei Schiedsrichtern entschieden haben wollen, und, falls eine Entscheidung durch drei Schiedsrichter gewünscht wird, gemeinsam einen Schiedsrichter zu berennen.

4. Sollte im Falle des Abs 3 eine Einigung der Beklagten über die Zahl der Schiedsrichter nicht vorliegen, so werden sie vom Generalsekretär aufgefordert, binnen 30 Tagen ab Zustellung der Aufforderung eine solche Einigung nachzuweisen.

5. Erfolgt innerhalb der in Abs 4 genannten Frist kein Nachweis der Einigung auf die Zahl der Schiedsrichter, so bestimmt das Präsidium, ob der Rechtsstreit von einem Schiedsrichter oder von einem Schiedsrichtersenat zu entscheiden ist.

6. Haben sich die Beklagten darauf geeinigt, dass der Rechtsstreit von einem Schiedsrichtersenat zu entscheiden ist, ohne einen Schiedsrichter zu benennen, so werden sie vom Generalsekretär aufgefordert, binnen 30 Tagen ab Zustellung der Aufforderung den Namen und die Adresse eines Schiedsrichters bekannt zugeben.

7. Erfolgt innerhalb der in Abs 6 genannten Frist keine Benennung eines gemeinsamen Schiedsrichters und ist der Streitfall von einem Schiedsrichtersenat zu entscheiden, so bestellt das Präsidium den Schiedsrichter für die säumigen Beklagten.

8. In anderen als den in Abs 1 genannten Fällen ist die Verbindung zweier oder mehrerer Rechtssachen nur zulässig, wenn in allen zu verbindenden Rechtssachen dieselben Schiedsrichter bestellt wurden und alle Parteien und der Schiedsrichter (Schiedsrichtersenat) zustimmen.

9. Die Entscheidung, ob ein Mehrparteienverfahren gemäß Abs 1 zulässig ist, trifft über Antrag einer der beklagten Parteien der Einzelschiedsrichter (Schiedsrichtersenat). Falls dieser die Zulässigkeit des Mehrparteienverfahrens verneint, tritt das Schiedsverfahren in jenen Stand zurück, den es vor der Bestellung des Einzelschiedsrichters (des Schiedsrichters für die beklagten Parteien) hatte.

ABLEHNUNG VON SCHIEDSRICHTERN

Artikel 16

1. Ein Schiedsrichter kann nur abgelehnt werden, wenn Umstände vorliegen, die berechtigte Zweifel an seiner Unparteilichkeit oder Unabhängigkeit wecken, oder wenn er die zwischen den Parteien vereinbarten Voraussetzungen nicht erfüllt.

Eine Partei kann einen Schiedsrichter, den sie bestellt hat oder an dessen Bestellung sie mitgewirkt hat, nur aus Gründen ablehnen, die ihr erst nach der Bestellung oder Mitwirkung daran bekannt geworden sind.

2. Lehnt eine Partei einen Schiedsrichter ab, so hat sie dies unverzüglich unter Angabe des Ablehnungsgrundes dem Sekretariat bekannt zu geben.

3. Tritt der abgelehnte Schiedsrichter nicht zurück, so entscheidet über die Ablehnung das Präsidium aufgrund der Angaben im Ablehnungsantrag und der diesem beigeschlossenen Beweismittel. Der Generalsekretär hat vor der Entscheidung des Präsidiums die Stellungnahme des abgelehnten Schiedsrichters und der anderen Partei(en) einzuholen. Das Präsidium kann auch andere Personen zur Stellungnahme auffordern.

4. Ein abgelehnter Schiedsrichter kann das Verfahren ungeachtet des Ablehnungsantrages fortführen. Ein Schiedsspruch darf jedoch erst nach Rechtskraft der Entscheidung des Präsidiums gefällt werden.

Vorzeitige Beendigung des Schiedsrichteramtes

Artikel 17

1. Das Amt eines Schiedsrichters endet, wenn

    a. die Parteien dies vereinbaren,
    b. der Schiedsrichter zurücktritt,
    c. einem Ablehnungsantrag stattgegeben wird oder
    d. der Schiedsrichter vom Präsidium seines Amtes enthoben wird.

2. Jede Partei kann die Enthebung eines Schiedsrichters beantragen, wenn er nicht nur vorübergehend verhindert ist, sonst seiner Aufgabe nicht nachkommt oder das Verfahren ungebührlich verzögert. Der Antrag ist beim Sekretariat einzubringen. Über ihn entscheidet nach Anhörung des betroffenen Schiedsrichters das Präsidium. Ist offensichtlich, dass die Verhinderung nicht nur vorübergehend ist, so kann das Präsidium die Enthebung auch ohne Antrag einer Partei verfügen.

Folgen der vorzeitigen Beendigung des Schiedsrichteramtes

Artikel 18

1. Wurde der Ablehnung eines Schiedsrichters stattgegeben, wurde er seines Amtes enthoben, hat er dieses niedergelegt oder ist er gestorben, so werden,

    a. wenn es sich um einen Einzelschiedsrichter handelt, die Parteien
    b. wenn es sich um den Vorsitzenden eines Schiedsrichtersenates handelt, die verbleibenden Schiedsrichter und

c. wenn es sich um einen von einer Partei benannten oder für eine Partei bestellten Schiedsrichter handelt, die Partei, die ihn benannt hat oder für die er bestellt wurde,

aufgefordert, binnen 30 Tagen einen Ersatzschiedsrichter – in den Fällen gemäß lit a und b einvernehmlich – zu benennen und dessen Namen und Adresse bekannt zu geben. Erfolgt innerhalb dieser Frist keine solche Mitteilung, so wird der Ersatzschiedsrichter vom Präsidium bestellt. Wurde auch ein benannter Ersatzschiedsrichter erfolgreich abgelehnt, so erlischt das Ersatzbenennungsrecht und der Ersatzschiedsrichter wird vom Präsidium bestellt

2. Wurde der Ablehnung eines Schiedsrichters stattgegeben, wurde er seines Amtes enthoben, hat er dieses niedergelegt oder ist er gestorben, so bestimmt der neue Schiedsrichter (neu zusammengesetzte Schiedsrichtersenat) nach Einholung einer Stellungnahme der Parteien, ob und in welchem Umfang vorausgegangene Verfahrensabschnitte zu wiederholen sind.

ZUSTÄNDIGKEIT DES SCHIEDSGERICHTS

Artikel 19

1. Die Einrede der Unzuständigkeit des Schiedsgerichts ist spätestens mit dem ersten Vorbringen zur Sache zu erheben. Von der Erhebung dieser Einrede ist eine Partei nicht dadurch ausgeschlossen, dass sie einen Schiedsrichter bestellt oder an der Bestellung eines Schiedsrichters mitgewirkt hat. Die Einrede, eine Angelegenheit überschreite die Befugnisse des Schiedsgerichts, ist zu erheben, sobald diese zum Gegenstand eines Sachantrags erhoben wird. In beiden Fällen ist eine spätere Erhebung der Einrede ausgeschlossen; wird die Versäumung jedoch nach Überzeugung des Schiedsgerichts genügend entschuldigt, so kann die Einrede nachgeholt werden.

2. Der Schiedsrichter (Schiedsrichtersenat) entscheidet selbst über seine Zuständigkeit. Die Entscheidung kann mit der Entscheidung in der Sache getroffen werden, aber auch vorher gesondert in einem eigenen Schiedsspruch.

DURCHFÜHRUNG DES VERFAHRENS

Artikel 20

1. Im Rahmen der Wiener Regeln und der Vereinbarungen der Parteien kann der Schiedsrichter (Schiedsrichtersenat) das Schiedsverfahren nach freiem Ermessen durchführen; es gilt der Grundsatz der Gleichbehandlung der Parteien unter Wahrung des rechtlichen Gehörs in jedem Stadium des Verfahrens. Der Schiedsrichter (Schiedsrichtersenat) ist jedoch berechtigt, nach Vorankündigung

Vorbringen und die Vorlage von Beweisurkunden nur bis zu einem bestimmten Verfahrensstadium für zulässig zu erklären.

2. Unverzüglich nach Übergabe der Unterlagen zum Fall an den Schiedsrichter (Schiedsrichtersenat) hat dieser die Sprache oder die Sprachen des Verfahrens unter Berücksichtigung aller Umstände, insbesondere der Sprache des Vertrages, zu bestimmen. Hiebei ist er an eine allfällige Vereinbarung der Parteien gebunden. Der Schiedsrichter (Schiedsrichtersenat) kann anordnen, dass von allen Urkunden, die nicht in dieser Sprache (diesen Sprachen) abgefasst sind, eine Übersetzung vorgelegt werde.

3. Das Verfahren kann mündlich oder schriftlich durchgeführt werden. Eine mündliche Verhandlung hat auf Antrag einer Partei oder, wenn es der mit der Entscheidung betraute Schiedsrichter (Schiedsrichtersenat) für erforderlich hält, statt zu finden. Den Parteien ist jedenfalls Gelegenheit zu geben, von den Anträgen und den Vorbringen der anderen Parteien und dem Ergebnis der Beweisaufnahmen Kenntnis zu nehmen und sich dazu zu äußern.

4. Die mündliche Verhandlung wird von dem Schiedsrichter oder dem Vorsitzenden des Schiedsrichtersenates anberaumt. Sie ist nicht öffentlich. Über die Verhandlung ist zumindest ein Ergebnisprotokoll anzufertigen, das der Schiedsrichter bzw. der Vorsitzende des Schiedsrichtersenates zu unterfertigen hat.

5. Der Schiedsrichter (Schiedsrichtersenat) kann, wenn er es für erforderlich hält, von sich aus Beweise erheben, insbesondere Parteien oder Zeugen vernehmen, die Parteien zur Vorlage von Urkunden und Augenscheinsgegenständen auffordern und Sachverständige beiziehen. Sind mit der Beweisaufnahme, insbesondere mit der Sachverständigenbestellung Kosten verbunden, ist nach Art 35 vorzugehen.

6. Beteiligt sich eine Partei nicht am Verfahren, so ist mit der anderen Partei allein zu verhandeln.

7. Erlangt eine Partei Kenntnis von einer Verletzung einer Bestimmung dieser Schiedsordnung oder sonstiger auf das Verfahren anwendbarer Bestimmungen durch den Schiedsrichter (Schiedsrichtersenat), so hat sie dies unverzüglich zu rügen, widrigenfalls die Partei den behaupteten Mangel nicht mehr geltend machen kann.

8. Der Schiedsrichter (Schiedsrichtersenat) hat die Parteien zu befragen, ob sie noch weitere Beweise anzubieten, Zeugen vernehmen zu lassen oder Erklärungen abzugeben haben. Sobald nach Überzeugung des Schiedsrichters (Schiedsrichtersenates) die Parteien dazu ausreichend Gelegenheit hatten, hat der Schiedsrichter (Schiedsrichtersenat) das Verfahren für geschlossen zu erklären. Der Schiedsrichter (Schiedsrichtersenat) kann das Verfahren jederzeit wieder eröffnen.

ABLEHNUNG VON SACHVERSTÄNDIGEN

Artikel 21

Auf die Ablehnung von Sachverständigen, die vom Schiedsrichter (Schiedsrichtersenat) bestellt wurden, ist Art 16 sinngemäß anzuwenden. Über die Ablehnung entscheidet jedoch der Schiedsrichter (Schiedsrichtersenat).

SICHERNDE UND VORLÄUFIGE MASSNAHMEN

Artikel 22

1. Haben die Parteien nichts anderes vereinbart, so kann der Schiedsrichter (Schiedsrichtersenat) auf Antrag einer Partei vorläufige oder sichernde Maßnahmen gegen eine andere Partei nach deren Anhörung anordnen, die er in Bezug auf den Streitgegenstand für erforderlich hält, weil sonst die Durchsetzung des Anspruchs vereitelt oder erheblich erschwert werden würde oder ein unwiederbringlicher Schaden droht. Der Schiedsrichter (Schiedsrichtersenat) kann von jeder Partei im Zusammenhang mit einer solchen Maßnahme angemessene Sicherheit fordern. Die Parteien sind verpflichtet, solche Anordnungen zu befolgen, ungeachtet ob diese von staatlichen Gerichten vollstreckbar sind.

2. Maßnahmen nach Abs 1 sind schriftlich anzuordnen; jeder Partei ist ein unterfertigtes Exemplar der Anordnung zuzustellen. In Schiedsverfahren mit mehr als einem Schiedsrichter genügt die Unterschrift des Vorsitzenden oder im Falle seiner Verhinderung eines anderen Schiedsrichters, sofern der Vorsitzende oder der andere Schiedsrichter auf der Anordnung vermerkt, welches Hindernis der Unterfertigung entgegensteht.

3. Haben die Parteien nichts anderes vereinbart, sind die Maßnahmen zu begründen. Es sind der Tag, an dem sie erlassen wurden und der Sitz des Schiedsgerichts anzugeben. Die Maßnahme gilt als an diesem Tag und an diesem Ort erlassen.

4. Die Maßnahmen und die Urkunden über deren Zustellung sind gemeinschaftliche Urkunden der Parteien und des Schiedsrichters (Schiedsrichtersenates). Der Schiedsrichter (Schiedsrichtersenat) hat mit den Parteien eine allfällige Verwahrung der Maßnahme sowie der Urkunden über deren Zustellung zu erörtern.

5. Der Schiedsrichter (der Vorsitzende des Schiedsrichtersenates, im Falle seiner Verhinderung ein anderer Schiedsrichter) hat auf Verlangen einer Partei die Rechtskraft und Vollstreckbarkeit der Maßnahme auf einem Exemplar der Maßnahme zu bestätigen.

6. Diese Bestimmung hindert die Parteien nicht, bei jedem zuständigen staatlichen Organ sichernde und vorläufige Maßnahmen zu beantragen. Ein solcher Antrag an

ein staatliches Organ auf Anordnung solcher Maßnahmen oder auf Vollziehung vom Schiedsrichter (Schiedsrichtersenat) angeordneter Maßnahmen stellt keinen Verstoß gegen oder Verzicht auf die Schiedsvereinbarung dar und lässt die dem Schiedsrichter (Schiedsrichtersenat) zustehenden Befugnisse unberührt. Ein solcher Antrag sowie alle durch das staatliche Organ angeordneten Maßnahmen sind unverzüglich dem Sekretariat und dem Schiedsrichter (Schiedsrichtersenat) mitzuteilen.

BEVOLLMÄCHTIGTE

Artikel 23

Die Parteien können sich im Verfahren vor dem Schiedsgericht durch Personen ihrer Wahl vertreten oder beraten lassen.

ANWENDBARES RECHT, BILLIGKEIT

Artikel 24

1. Der Schiedsrichter (Schiedsrichtersenat) hat die Streitigkeit in Übereinstimmung mit den Rechtsvorschriften oder Rechtsregeln zu entscheiden, die von den Parteien vereinbart worden sind. Die Vereinbarung des Rechts oder der Rechtsordnung eines bestimmten Staates ist, sofern die Parteien nicht ausdrücklich etwas anderes vereinbart haben, als unmittelbare Verweisung auf das materielle Recht dieses Staates und nicht auf sein Kollisionsrecht zu verstehen.

2. Haben die Parteien die anzuwendenden Rechtsvorschriften oder Rechtsregeln nicht bestimmt, so hat der Schiedsrichter (Schiedsrichtersenat) jene Rechtsvorschriften anzuwenden, die er für angemessen erachtet.

3. Der Schiedsrichter (Schiedsrichtersenat) hat nur dann nach Billigkeit zu entscheiden, wenn die Parteien ihn ausdrücklich dazu ermächtigt haben.

BEENDIGUNG

Artikel 25

Das Verfahren wird beendet mit:

    a. der Erlassung des Schiedsspruches,
    b. dem Abschluss eines Schiedsvergleiches,
    c. Beschluss des Schiedsrichters (Schiedsrichtersenats), wenn

aa. der Kläger seine Klage zurücknimmt, es sei denn, dass der Beklagte dem widerspricht und der Schiedsrichter (Schiedsrichtersenat) ein berechtigtes Interesse des Beklagten an der endgültigen Beilegung der Streitigkeit anerkennt;

bb. die Parteien die Beendigung des Verfahrens vereinbaren und dies dem Schiedsrichter (Schiedsrichtersenat) mitteilen;

cc. ihm die Fortsetzung des Verfahrens unmöglich geworden ist, insbesondere weil die bisher im Verfahren tätigen Parteien trotz schriftlicher Aufforderung des Schiedsrichters (Schiedsrichtersenats), mit welcher dieser auf die Möglichkeit einer Beendigung des Schiedsverfahrens hinweist, das Schiedsverfahren nicht weiter betreiben.

ENTSCHEIDUNGEN IM SCHIEDSRICHTERSENAT

Artikel 26

1. Im Schiedsrichtersenat ist jeder Schiedsspruch oder jede andere Entscheidung mit Stimmenmehrheit zu erlassen. Kommt keine Stimmenmehrheit zustande, so entscheidet der Vorsitzende allein.

2. Soweit es sich um Verfahrensfragen handelt, kann der Vorsitzende des Schiedsgerichts, wenn der Schiedsrichtersenat ihn dazu ermächtigt, vorbehaltlich einer etwaigen Änderung durch den Schiedsrichtersenat, allein entscheiden.

SCHIEDSSPRUCH

Artikel 27

1. Schiedssprüche ergehen schriftlich. Sie sind zu begründen, sofern nicht alle Parteien entweder im Schiedsvertrag oder in der mündlichen Verhandlung auf eine Begründung verzichtet haben.

2. Im Schiedsspruch sind der Tag, an dem er erlassen wurde, und der Sitz des Schiedsgerichts anzugeben (Art 2).

3. Schiedssprüche sind auf allen Ausfertigungen von den Schiedsrichtern zu unterschreiben. Die Unterschrift der Mehrheit der Schiedsrichter genügt, wenn im Schiedsspruch vermerkt wird, dass ein Schiedsrichter die Unterschrift verweigert oder dass der Unterzeichnung durch ihn ein Hindernis entgegensteht, das nicht in angemessener Frist überwunden werden kann. Wird der Schiedsspruch mit Stimmenmehrheit gefällt, so muss dies auf Wunsch des überstimmten Schiedsrichters im Schiedsspruch angeführt werden.

4. Schiedssprüche werden auf allen Ausfertigungen mit der Unterschrift des Generalsekretärs und dem Stempel des Schiedsgerichts versehen. Damit wird

bestätigt, dass es sich um einen Schiedsspruch des Internationalen Schiedsgerichts der Wirtschaftskammer Österreich handelt und dass dieser von dem (den) gemäß der Schiedsordnung gewählten oder bestellten Schiedsrichter(n) erlassen und unterschrieben wurde.

5. Der Schiedsspruch wird vom Generalsekretär den Parteien zugestellt. Den Parteien gegenüber werden Schiedssprüche mit der Zustellung der Ausfertigungen wirksam. Eine Ausfertigung des Schiedsspruches wird beim Sekretariat des Schiedsgerichts hinterlegt, wo auch die Urkunden über die Zustellung verwahrt werden.

6. Der Schiedsrichter (Vorsitzende des Schiedsrichtersenates, im Falle seiner Verhinderung ein anderer Schiedsrichter) hat auf Verlangen einer Partei Rechtskraft und Vollstreckbarkeit des Schiedsspruches auf sämtlichen Ausfertigungen zu bestätigen.

7. Die Erlassung von Teil- und Zwischenschiedssprüchen ist zulässig.

8. Durch die Vereinbarung der Wiener Regeln haben sich die Parteien verpflichtet, den Schiedsspruch zu erfüllen.

VERGLEICH

Artikel 28

Die Parteien können verlangen, dass der Inhalt eines von ihnen geschlossenen Vergleiches protokolliert oder darüber ein Schiedsspruch erlassen wird.

BERICHTIGUNG, ERLÄUTERUNG UND ERGÄNZUNG DES SCHIEDSSPRUCHS

Artikel 29

1. Jede Partei kann innerhalb von 30 Tagen ab Empfang des Schiedsspruchs beim Sekretariat folgende Anträge an den Schiedsrichter (Schiedsrichtersenat) einbringen:

   a. Rechen-, Schreib- und Druckfehler oder Fehler ähnlicher Art im Schiedsspruch zu berichtigen;
   b. bestimmte Teile des Schiedsspruchs zu erläutern, sofern die Parteien dies ausdrücklich vereinbart haben;
   c. einen ergänzenden Schiedsspruch über Ansprüche zu erlassen, die im Schiedsverfahren zwar geltend gemacht, im Schiedsspruch aber nicht erledigt worden sind.

2. Die Entscheidung über einen solchen Antrag trifft der Schiedsrichter (Schiedsrichtersenat). Vor der Entscheidung ist die andere Partei zu hören. Der

Schiedsrichter (Schiedsrichtersenat) setzt hiefür eine Frist, die 30 Tage nicht überschreiten soll.

3. Die Berichtigungen gemäß Abs 1 lit a kann der Schiedsrichter (Schiedsrichtersenat) binnen 30 Tagen ab dem Datum des Schiedsspruchs auch ohne Antrag vornehmen.

4. Artikel 27 Abs 1 bis 6 sind auf die Berichtigung, Erläuterung oder Ergänzung des Schiedsspruchs anzuwenden. Die Berichtigung und die Erläuterung sind Bestandteile des Schiedsspruchs.

VERÖFFENTLICHUNG VON SCHIEDSSPRÜCHEN

Artikel 30

Das Präsidium ist berechtigt, einen Schiedsspruch in juristischen Fachzeitschriften oder in eigenen Publikationen in anonymisierter Form zu veröffentlichen, wenn nicht zumindest eine Partei der Veröffentlichung innerhalb einer Frist von 30 Tagen ab Zustellung der Mitteilung der beabsichtigten Veröffentlichung an sie widerspricht.

KOSTENBESTIMMUNG

Artikel 31

Wird das Schiedsverfahren beendet, hat der Schiedsrichter (Schiedsrichtersenat) auf Antrag einer Partei im Schiedsspruch über die Hauptsache oder in einem gesonderten Schiedsspruch die vom Generalsekretär gemäß Art 34 Abs 1 bestimmten Schiedsgerichtskosten anzuführen, die Höhe der Parteienkosten zu bestimmen und festzulegen, wer die Verfahrenskosten zu tragen hat oder in welchem Verhältnis diese Verfahrenskosten verteilt werden.

VERFAHRENSKOSTEN

Artikel 32

Die Verfahrenskosten setzen sich aus folgenden Teilen zusammen:

a. den Schiedsgerichtskosten, das sind die Auslagen des Schiedsgerichts (Verwaltungskosten), die Honorare der Schiedsrichter zuzüglich allfälliger Umsatzsteuer und die Barauslagen (wie Reise- und Aufenthaltskosten von Schiedsrichtern, Kosten der Zustellung, Mieten, Protokollierungskosten) und

b. den Parteienkosten, das sind die angemessenen Aufwendungen der Parteien für ihre Vertretung und andere Auslagen im Zusammenhang mit dem Schiedsverfahren, insbesondere die in Art 35 Abs 1 genannten Kosten.

EINSCHREIBEGEBÜHR

Artikel 33

1. Die klagende (widerklagende) Partei hat mit Überreichung der Klage (Widerklage) eine Einschreibegebühr in der angegebenen Höhe auf das Konto des Schiedsgerichts spesenfrei zu entrichten. Diese Gebühr dient zur Deckung der Auslagen bis zur Übergabe der Unterlagen zum Fall an den Schiedsrichter (den Schiedsrichtersenat). Sollten höhere Auslagen entstehen, kann ein zusätzlicher Betrag vorgeschrieben werden.

2. Sind an dem Schiedsverfahren mehr als zwei Parteien beteiligt, so erhöht sich die Einschreibegebühr um 10 % für jede zusätzliche Partei.

3. Die Einschreibegebühr wird nicht zurückgezahlt. Die Einschreibegebühr sowie ein allfälliger zusätzlicher Betrag nach Abs 1 werden in den Kostenvorschuss des Klägers (Widerklägers) für die Schiedsgerichtskosten (Art 34 Abs 2) eingerechnet.

4. Die Behandlung der Klage (Widerklage) erfolgt erst nach vollständiger Bezahlung der Einschreibegebühr.

SCHIEDSGERICHTSKOSTEN UND KOSTENVORSCHUSS

Artikel 34

1. Die Schiedsgerichtskosten werden vom Generalsekretär am Ende des Verfahrens bestimmt.

2. Der Generalsekretär setzt den Kostenvorschuss für die voraussichtlichen Schiedsgerichtskosten fest. Dieser ist vor Übergabe der Unterlagen zum Fall an den Schiedsrichter (Schiedsrichtersenat) von den Parteien binnen 30 Tagen ab Zustellung der Aufforderung zu gleichen Teilen zu erlegen.

3. Langt der auf den Kläger (Widerkläger) entfallende Anteil trotz Nachfristsetzung nicht innerhalb der gesetzten Frist ein, so wird die Klage (Widerklage) nicht weiter behandelt. Der Generalsekretär hat dies den Parteien mitzuteilen.

4. Langt der auf den Beklagten (Widerbeklagten) entfallende Anteil nicht innerhalb der gesetzten Frist ein, so teilt der Generalsekretär dies dem Kläger (Widerkläger) mit und fordert ihn auf, den fehlenden Teil des Vorschusses binnen 30 Tagen ab Erhalt der Aufforderung zu bezahlen. Langt dieser Betrag nicht

innerhalb der gesetzten Frist ein, so wird die Klage (Widerklage) nicht weiter behandelt. Der Generalsekretär hat dies den Parteien mitzuteilen.

5. Wird im Laufe des Verfahrens wegen einer Erhöhung des Streitwertes eine Erhöhung des Kostenvorschusses erforderlich, so ist analog den Bestimmungen der Abs 2 bis 4 vorzugehen. Bis zum Erlag des zusätzlichen Vorschusses ist die Klagsausdehnung, die zur Erhöhung des Streitwertes geführt hat, im Schiedsverfahren nicht zu berücksichtigen.

6. Wird im Laufe des Verfahrens eine Erhöhung des Kostenvorschusses erforderlich, weil der bei seiner Festsetzung veranschlagte Betrag für Barauslagen nicht ausreicht, so ist analog den Bestimmungen der Abs 2 bis 4 vorzugehen.

WEITERE VERFAHRENSKOSTEN

Artikel 35

1. Hält der Schiedsrichter (Schiedsrichtersenat) die Durchführung von bestimmten, mit Kosten verbundenen Verfahrensschritten, wie die Bestellung von Sachverständigen, Dolmetschern oder Übersetzern, die wörtliche Aufzeichnung des Verhandlungsverlaufes, die Abhaltung eines Lokalaugenscheines oder die Verlegung des Verhandlungsortes, für erforderlich, so hat er für die Deckung der voraussichtlichen Kosten zu sorgen und den Generalsekretär darüber zu informieren.

2. Der Schiedsrichter (Schiedsrichtersenat) darf Verfahrensschritte gemäß Abs 1 erst vornehmen, wenn eine ausreichende Deckung für die voraussichtlichen Kosten vorhanden ist.

3. Der Schiedsrichter (Schiedsrichtersenat) entscheidet, welche Folgen sich aus der Nichtentrichtung eines etwa vorgeschriebenen Kostenvorschusses für das Verfahren ergeben.

4. Alle Aufträge im Zusammenhang mit den in Abs 1 genannten Verfahrensschritten erteilt der Schiedsrichter (Schiedsrichtersenat) im Namen und auf Rechnung der Parteien.

BERECHNUNG DER SCHIEDSGERICHTSKOSTEN

Artikel 36

1. Die Verwaltungskosten des Schiedsgerichts und die Schiedsrichterhonorare werden aufgrund des Streitwertes nach der Tabelle der Verfahrenskosten (Anhang 1) berechnet. Bei vorzeitiger Beendigung des Verfahrens kann der Generalsekretär die Schiedsrichterhonorare entsprechend dem Verfahrensstand nach billigem Ermessen ermäßigen.

2. Sind an einem Verfahren mehr als zwei Parteien beteiligt, so erhöhen sich die in den der Schiedsordnung beigefügten Tabellen enthaltenen Sätze für Verwaltungskosten und Schiedsrichterhonorare um 10 % für jede zusätzliche Partei.

3. Für Forderungen, die im Wege der Aufrechnung gegen Klagsansprüche eingewendet werden (Gegenforderungen) und die mit den Klagsansprüchen (Hauptforderungen) in keinem rechtlichen oder tatsächlichen Zusammenhang stehen, sind so wie für Widerklagen die gesondert berechneten Schiedsgerichtskosten zu entrichten. Für die Vorschreibung von Kostenvorschüssen ist Art 34 sinngemäß anzuwenden. Bis zum vollständigen Erlag der zusätzlichen Kostenvorschüsse sind die Gegenforderungen im Verfahren über die Hauptforderungen nicht zu behandeln.

4. Bei Verfahren, die über eine Mehrzahl von einzelnen Ansprüchen geführt werden, die untereinander in keinem rechtlichen oder tatsächlichen Zusammenhang stehen, kann der Generalsekretär in jedem Stadium des Verfahrens für die Schiedsgerichtskosten eine gesonderte Berechnung nach den Streitwerten der einzelnen Ansprüche vornehmen.

5. Der Generalsekretär kann den Streitwert abweichend von den Angaben der Parteien festlegen, wenn die Parteien nur einen Teilbetrag einer Forderung eingeklagt haben oder wenn ein nicht auf Zahlung von Geldbeträgen gerichtetes Begehren von den Parteien offenkundig unterbewertet wurde.

6. Die in der Tabelle für Schiedsrichterhonorare angegebenen Sätze sind die Honorare für Einzelschiedsrichter. Sie erhöhen sich bei einem Schiedsrichtersenat jedenfalls auf das Zweieinhalbfache, bei besonderer Schwierigkeit des Falles bis zum Dreifachen des angegebenen Satzes.

7. Die in der Tabelle für Schiedsrichterhonorare angegebenen Sätze vergüten auch alle Teil- und Zwischenentscheidungen, wie z.B. Schiedssprüche über die Zuständigkeit, Teilschiedssprüche, Entscheidungen über die Ablehnung von Sachverständigen, Anordnung sichernder und vorläufiger Maßnahmen, sonstige Entscheidungen und verfahrensleitende Verfügungen.

8. Herabsetzungen des Streitwertes sind bei der Berechnung der Schiedsrichterhonorare und Verwaltungskosten nur zu berücksichtigen, wenn sie vor Übergabe der Unterlagen zum Fall an den Schiedsrichter (Schiedsrichtersenat) vorgenommen wurden.

9. Barauslagen werden nach dem tatsächlichen Aufwand bestimmt.

10. Die in der Tabelle für Schiedsrichterhonorare angegebenen Sätze enthalten keine Umsatzsteuer, die möglicherweise auf die Schiedsrichterhonorare anfällt. Die Schiedsrichter, deren Honorare Gegenstand von Umsatzsteuer sind, haben dem Generalsekretär bei Amtsübernahme die voraussichtliche Höhe der Umsatzsteuer bekannt zu geben.

Artikel 37

Diese Fassung der Wiener Regeln gilt für alle Verfahren, bei denen die Klage nach dem 30. 6.2006 eingebracht wurde.

TABELLE DER VERFAHRENSKOSTEN

Einschreibegebühr EUR 2.000[1]

Verwaltungskosten[2]

Streitwert in EUR		Tarif in EUR
Von	Bis	
0	100.000	3.000
100.001	200.000	3.000 + 1,5 % des 100.000 übersteigenden Betrags
200.001	500.000	4.500 + 1,0 % des 200.000 übersteigenden Betrags
500.001	1.000.000	7.500 + 0,7 % des 500.000 übersteigenden Betrags
1.000.001	2.000.000	11.000 + 0,4 % des 1.000.000 übersteigenden Betrags
2.000.001	5.000.000	15.000 + 0,1 % des 2.000.000 übersteigenden Betrags
5.000.001	10.000.000	18.000 + 0,05 % des 5.000.000 übersteigenden Betrags
Über 10.000.000		20.500 + 0,01 % des 10.000.000 übersteigenden Betrags

Honorare für Einzelschiedsrichter[3]

---

1. Siehe Artikel 33 Abs. 1.
2. Siehe Artikel 36 Abs. 1.
3. Siehe Artikel 36 Abs. 6.

| Streitwert in EUR | | Tarif in EUR |
Von	Bis	
0	100.000	6 % mindestens 1.000
100.001	200.000	6.000 + 3 % des 100.000 übersteigenden Betrags
200.001	500.000	9.000 + 2,5 % des 200.000 übersteigenden Betrags
500.001	1.000.000	16.500 + 2 % des 500.000 übersteigenden Betrags
1.000.001	2.000.000	26.500 + 1 % des 1.000.000 übersteigenden Betrags
2.000.001	5.000.000	36.500 + 0,6 % des 2.000.000 übersteigenden Betrags
5.000.001	10.000.000	54.500 + 0,4 % des 5.000.000 übersteigenden Betrags
10.000.001	20.000.000	74.500 + 0,2 % des 10.000.000 übersteigenden Betrags
20.000.001	100.000.000	94.500 + 0,1 % des 20.000.000 übersteigenden Betrags
über 100.000.000		174.500 + 0,01 % des 100.000.000 übersteigenden Betrags

Annex 2a

International Arbitral Centre of the Austrian Federal Economic Chamber Rules of Arbitration 2001 (Vienna Rules 2001)*

GENERAL PROVISIONS

THE INSTITUTION

Article 1

1. The International Arbitral Centre of the Austrian Federal Economic Chamber in Vienna (the Vienna International Arbitral Centre – 'the Centre') shall make arrangements for the settlement by arbitration of disputes in which not all contracting parties that concluded the arbitration agreement had their place of business or their normal residence in Austria at the time of conclusion of that agreement.

The jurisdiction of the Centre can also be agreed by parties whose place of business or normal residence is in Austria for the settlement of disputes of an international character.

2. If the parties have agreed to the jurisdiction of the Centre, these arbitration rules ('Vienna Rules') shall thereby apply in the version valid at the time of commencement of the proceedings.

---

* Translation from the German original, which is the authentic text. Adopted by the General Assembly of the Austrian Federal Economic Chamber on 30 November 2000, with effect from 1 January 2001. Reprinted with kind permission of the Vienna International Arbitration Centre (VIAC).

3. If parties which had their place of business or normal residence in Austria at the time of conclusion of the arbitration agreement have agreed that their disputes should be finally settled by a sole arbitrator or an arbitral tribunal to be appointed according to the Vienna Rules, and if the dispute is not international in character, the Permanent Arbitral Tribunal of the Vienna Economic Chamber, or, if another venue in Austria has been agreed, of the regional economic chamber in whose territorial jurisdiction the agreed venue is situated, shall be competent to make arrangements for settlement by arbitration. The latter tribunal shall conduct the proceedings in accordance with the rules of arbitration for the Permanent Arbitral Tribunals of the regional economic chambers.

Article 2

Arbitration proceedings shall be conducted at the seat of the Centre in Vienna. Nevertheless, the parties can agree that the proceedings be conducted elsewhere.

ORGANIZATION

THE BOARD

Article 3

1. The Board of the Centre shall have at least five members. They shall be appointed for a period of office of five years by the Board of the Austrian Federal Economic Chamber and can be reappointed. If there is no new appointment by the time of the expiration of a period of office, the members of the Board shall remain in office until a new Board is appointed. If a member of the Board is permanently incapacitated during his period of office (for instance, by resignation or death), a substitute member can be appointed for the remainder of the period of office of the serving Board.

2. The members of the Board shall elect one of their number to act as Chairman for the duration of their term of office.

3. The meetings of the Board are presided over by the Chairman, or in his absence, by the most senior member present. The Board can validly take decisions if more than half of its members are present. It shall take decisions by a simple majority of the members present. In the event of a tie in voting, the Chairman shall have a casting vote.

4. Decisions may be made by correspondence. The Board shall determine the relevant rules.

5. Members of the Board who are parties to particular arbitration proceedings in any capacity whatsoever shall be excluded from decisions pertaining to those proceedings.

6. The members of the Board must perform their duties to the best of their ability; they are independent and are not subject to any directives in that respect. They are bound to secrecy on all matters coming to their notice in the course of their duties.

THE SECRETARY

Article 4

1. The Secretary of the Centre shall be appointed by the Board of the Austrian Federal Economic Chamber for a period of office of five years at the proposal of the Board of the Arbitral Centre; he can be reappointed. The third sentence of Article 3 paragraph 1, shall apply by analogy.

2. The Secretary shall direct the activities of the Secretariat and shall perform the administrative tasks of the Centre insofar as they are not reserved to the Board of the Centre.

3. The Secretary must perform his duties to the best of his ability and is not subject to any directives in that respect. He is bound to secrecy on all matters coming to his notice in the course of his duties.

4. If the Secretary is unable to perform his duties or if he is permanently incapacitated, a member of the Board of the Centre, appointed by that Board, shall perform the relevant functions until a Secretary is appointed.

LANGUAGES OF CORRESPONDENCE

Article 4a

Correspondence by the Parties with the Board and the Secretary shall be conducted in German or English.

ARBITRATORS

Article 5

1. The parties shall be free to appoint the arbitrators. Any person having legal capacity – irrespective of nationality – may be an arbitrator.

2. The Board of the Centre shall draw up a list of arbitrators every three years, to be valid for three calendar years in each case. Inclusion in the list of arbitrators shall not be a prerequisite for appointment as an arbitrator.

3. A member of the Board may act only as Chairman of an arbitral tribunal or sole arbitrator.

4. The arbitrators must perform their duties in complete independence and impartiality, to the best of their ability, and are not subject to any directives in that respect. They are bound to secrecy in respect of all matters coming to their notice in the course of their duties.

5. Liability of the arbitrators, the Secretary, the Board and its members and of the Austrian Federal Economic Chamber and its employees for any act or omission related to the arbitration proceedings, insofar as such liability may be admissible by law, shall be excluded.

ARBITRAL PROCEEDINGS

Commencement of the Proceedings

Article 6

1. Arbitral proceedings are commenced when a statement of claims is filed with the Secretariat. The proceedings become pending on receipt of the statement of claims by the Secretariat.

2. One copy of the statement of claims together with enclosures must be submitted for each Defendant, each arbitrator and the Secretariat.

3. The statement of claims must include:

    a. The designation of the parties and their addresses;
    b. A specific statement of claims and the particulars and supporting documents on which the claims are based;
    c. The amount in dispute at the time of submission of the statement of claims, unless the claims are not related exclusively to a specific sum of money;
    d. Particulars regarding the number of arbitrators in accordance with Article 9;
    e. If a decision by three arbitrators is requested, the nomination of an arbitrator and the address of that person.

4. A copy of the agreement specifying the jurisdiction of the Arbitral Centre must be attached to the statement of claims.

5. If the statement of claims does not comply with the provisions of paragraph 3 of the present Article or if copies of documents or enclosures are missing, the Secretary shall request the Claimant to remedy the defect or to submit the necessary documents or enclosures, setting a time-limit. If the defects are not remedied within the time-limit(s), the claim shall be deleted from the list of pending proceedings.

6. The Board can return the statement of claims to the Claimant as not suitable for further action if the parties have designated the International Arbitral Centre of the Austrian Federal Economic Chamber in the arbitration agreement but have made agreements that conflict with the Vienna Rules.

MEMORANDUM IN REPLY

Article 7

1. If the claim is not to be dealt with under Article 6 paragraphs 5 and 6, the Secretary shall make service to the Defendant of the statement of claims and one copy each of the rules of arbitration and the list of arbitrators and shall invite the Defendant to submit a memorandum in reply within a period of thirty days, in the number of copies required under Article 6 paragraph 2.

2. The memorandum in reply must include:

  a. A reply to the pleadings in the statement of claims;
  b. Particulars regarding the number of arbitrators in accordance with Article 9;
  c. Indication of the name and address of an arbitrator, if a decision by an arbitral tribunal is requested or if a decision by three arbitrators has been agreed upon in the arbitration agreement.

3. The Secretary shall transmit the files to the sole arbitrator (arbitral tribunal) as soon as: a statement of claims has been received in due form, the sole arbitrator (all members of the arbitral tribunal) has (have) confirmed acceptance of the mandate and his (their) objectivity, using a form issued by the Centre, and the deposit against costs has been paid (Article 23). The proceedings before the sole arbitrator (arbitral tribunal) shall thereby commence. The Secretary shall transmit to the parties a copy of the form on which the sole arbitrator (the members of the arbitral tribunal) has (have) confirmed his (their) objectivity.

COUNTER-CLAIMS

Article 7a

1. Claims by the Defendant against the Claimant that are based on the same arbitration agreement can be raised as counter-claims up to the time of closure of the evidentiary proceedings.

2. Counter-claims must be submitted to the Secretariat of the Centre and must be forwarded by the latter to the sole arbitrator (arbitral tribunal) for further action after the deposit against costs has been paid.

3. If the claim designated as a counter-claim is not based on the same arbitration agreement, if the parties are not identical, or if the submission of a counter-claim after transmission of the files to the sole arbitrator (arbitral tribunal) would lead to a substantial delay in the main proceedings, the sole arbitrator (arbitral tribunal) must return the claim to the Secretariat to be dealt with in separate proceedings.

4. The sole arbitrator (arbitral tribunal) must give the Counter-defendant to an admissible counter-claim the opportunity to submit a memorandum in reply in writing and must set a time-limit for that purpose.

TIME-LIMITS, SERVICE AND COMMUNICATIONS

Article 8

1. A time-limit shall be deemed to have been observed if the document is dispatched as provided under paragraph 2 of the present Article on the last day of the period set. Time-limits can be prolonged by the Secretariat on sufficient grounds; after the transmission of the files to the sole arbitrator (arbitral tribunal), the sole arbitrator (arbitral tribunal) shall be competent to prolong time-limits (except in the cases covered by Article 23 paragraphs 5 and 6).

2. Communications shall be considered as having been validly served if they are forwarded by registered letter, courier service, or telefax to the address most recently notified in writing to the sole arbitrator (arbitral tribunal) by the addressee as the address for service, or if the document to be served has been demonstrably transmitted.

3. As soon as a party has appointed a representative, service to the most recently indicated address of that representative shall be considered as having been made to the party represented.

NOMINATION AND APPOINTMENT OF ARBITRATORS

Article 9

1. The parties can agree that their dispute is to be decided either by a sole arbitrator or by an arbitral tribunal. Arbitral tribunals shall consist of three arbitrators.

2. When no such agreement has been made and the parties do not agree on the number of arbitrators, the Board shall determine whether the dispute is to be decided by a sole arbitrator or by an arbitral tribunal. In that context, the Board shall take into consideration in particular the difficulty of the case, the magnitude of the amount in dispute and the interest of the parties in a rapid and cost-effective decision.

3. The parties shall be notified of the decision of the Board pursuant to paragraph 2 of the present Article; in the event that proceedings before a sole arbitrator are decided upon, the parties shall be requested to agree on a sole arbitrator and to indicate that person's name and address within thirty days after service of the request. If no such indication is made within that period, the sole arbitrator shall be appointed by the Board.

4. If the dispute is to be decided by an arbitral tribunal, the party that has not yet nominated an arbitrator shall be requested to indicate the name and address of an arbitrator within thirty days after service of the request. If the Claimant has not appointed an arbitrator within that time-limit and does not expressly leave the appointment to the Board, the case must be deleted from the list of pending cases. However, if the Defendant fails to appoint an arbitrator within that time-limit, the arbitrator shall be appointed by the Board.

5. If the dispute is to be decided by an arbitral tribunal, the arbitrators nominated by the parties or appointed by the Board shall be requested to agree on a Chairman and to indicate his name and address within thirty days after service of the request. If no such indication is made within that period, the Chairman shall be appointed by the Board.

6. The parties are bound by their nomination of arbitrators as soon as the identity of the arbitrator nominated has been made known to the other party.

MULTIPARTY PROCEEDINGS

Article 10

1. A claim against two or more Defendants shall be admissible only if the Centre has jurisdiction for all of the Defendants, and, in the case of proceedings before an arbitral tribunal, if all Claimants have nominated the same arbitrator, and:

   a. If the applicable law positively provides that the claim is to be directed against several persons; or
   b. If all parties are bound by the same arbitration agreement; or
   c. If the admissibility of multiparty proceedings has been agreed upon; or
   d. If all Defendants submit to multiparty proceedings and, in the case of proceedings before an arbitral tribunal, all Defendants nominate the same arbitrator; or
   e. If one or more of the Defendants on whom the claim was served fails or fail to provide the particulars mentioned in Article 7 paragraph 2, b) and c) within the thirty-day time-limit (Article 7 paragraph 1).

2. Where a claim against a number of Defendants cannot be served on all Defendants, the proceedings shall be continued against those Defendants on whom the claim was served only if the Claimant declares within a period set by

the Secretary that he withdraws the claim against those Defendants on whom the claim could not be served. If no such declaration is made within the period set by the Secretary or if a claim cannot be served within one year of filing the claim, the claim must be deleted from the list of pending cases.

3. If an agreement exists concerning the admissibility of multiparty proceedings, the Defendants must agree among themselves whether they wish to have the dispute decided by one arbitrator or by three arbitrators, and, if a decision by three arbitrators is desired, must jointly nominate an arbitrator.

4. In the case covered by paragraph 3 of the present Article, if there is no agreement among the Defendants concerning the number of arbitrators, the Defendants shall be requested by the Secretary to provide evidence of such agreement within thirty days after service of the request.

5. If no evidence of agreement on the number of arbitrators is presented within the period mentioned in paragraph 4 of the present article, the Board shall determine whether the dispute is to be decided by one arbitrator or by an arbitral tribunal.

6. If the Defendants have agreed that the dispute is to be decided by an arbitral tribunal, but without nominating an arbitrator, they shall be requested by the Secretary to indicate the name and address of an arbitrator within thirty days after service of the request.

7. If no arbitrator is jointly nominated within the period mentioned in paragraph 6 of the present Article and if the dispute is to be decided by an arbitral tribunal, the Board shall appoint the arbitrator for the defaulting Defendants.

8. In cases other than those mentioned in paragraph 1 of the present Article, the consolidation of two or more disputes shall be admissible only if the same arbitrators have been appointed in all the disputes that are to be consolidated and if all parties and the sole arbitrator (arbitral tribunal) agree.

CHALLENGE OF ARBITRATORS

Article 11

1. An arbitrator may be challenged if there are sufficient grounds for doubting his independence or impartiality.

2. If a party challenges an arbitrator, it must inform the Secretary thereof, stating the grounds for the challenge.

3. A challenge is inadmissible if the party making the challenge has taken part in the proceedings notwithstanding the knowledge which it already had or ought to have had of the grounds of challenge relied upon, or if the party making the challenge notified the grounds of challenge with undue delay.

4. The Board shall decide upon the challenge on the basis of the particulars in the challenging motion and the evidence attached thereto. Before the Board makes its decision, the Secretary must obtain the comments of the arbitrator challenged. The Board can also request comments from other persons.

5. An arbitrator challenged must continue the proceedings, notwithstanding the challenging motion, until the time of service of the Board's decision regarding the challenging motion. However, an award may not be rendered until after the Board has made its decision.

TERMINATION OF THE MANDATE OF ARBITRATORS

Article 12

Any party may request the termination of the mandate of an arbitrator if the latter's incapacitation is not merely temporary, if he otherwise fails to perform his duties or unduly delays the proceedings. The request must be submitted to the Secretariat. The Board shall decide upon the request after hearing the arbitrator in question. If it is clear that incapacitation is not merely temporary, the Board may terminate the arbitrator's mandate even without a request from a party.

CONSEQUENCES OF CHALLENGE OR TERMINATION OF MANDATE

Article 13

1. If the challenge of an arbitrator has been allowed, if his mandate has been terminated, if he has resigned his mandate or has died, then,

   a. If that arbitrator is a sole arbitrator, the parties – or,
   b. If that arbitrator is the Chairman, the remaining arbitrators – or
   c. If that arbitrator has been nominated by a party or has been appointed for a party, the party that nominated him or for which he was appointed

shall be requested to nominate a new arbitrator within thirty days – by mutual consent in the cases covered by subparagraphs a) and b) of the present paragraph – and to indicate his name and address. If no such indication is received within that period, the new arbitrator shall be appointed by the Board. If a new arbitrator nominated has also been successfully challenged, the right to nominate a new arbitrator shall lapse and the new arbitrator shall be appointed by the Board.

2. If the challenge of an arbitrator has been allowed, if his mandate has been terminated, if he has resigned his mandate or has died, the new sole arbitrator (newly constituted arbitral tribunal) shall determine, after obtaining the comments of the parties, whether and, if so, to what extent, previous procedural stages are to be repeated.

CONDUCT OF THE PROCEEDINGS

Article 14

1. In the context of the Vienna Rules and the agreements between the parties, the sole arbitrator (arbitral tribunal) may conduct the arbitration proceedings at his (its) absolute discretion; the principle of equal treatment of the parties shall apply, the right to be heard being ensured at every stage of the proceedings. However, subject to advance notice, the sole arbitrator (arbitral tribunal) is entitled to declare that pleadings and the presentation of documentary evidence shall be admissible only up to a certain stage of the proceedings.

2. Immediately after transmission of the files to the sole arbitrator (arbitral tribunal), the latter shall determine the language or languages of the proceedings, taking into consideration all circumstances, in particular, the language of the contract. In such matters, he (it) is bound by any agreement between the parties. The sole arbitrator (arbitral tribunal) can order that an appropriate translation be submitted of all documents that are not drafted in that language (those languages).

3. The proceedings may be oral or only in writing. Oral proceedings shall take place at the request of one party or if the sole arbitrator (arbitral tribunal) to whom (which) the case has been referred considers it necessary. In any case, the parties must be given the opportunity to take note of, and comment on, the motions and pleadings of the other parties and the result of the evidentiary proceedings.

4. The date of oral hearings shall be fixed by the sole arbitrator or the Chairman of the arbitral tribunal. Hearings shall be private. A record of at least the results of the hearings shall be made, which the arbitrator or the Chairman of the arbitral tribunal shall sign.

5. If the sole arbitrator (arbitral tribunal) considers it necessary, he (it) may on his (its) own initiative collect evidence, and in particular may question parties or witnesses, may request the parties to submit documents and visual evidence and may call in experts. If costs are incurred through the evidentiary proceedings and in particular through the appointment of experts, the procedure under Article 23 a shall be followed.

6. If one party does not take part in the proceedings, the case must be heard with the other party alone.

7. If a violation by the sole arbitrator (arbitral tribunal) of a provision of these arbitration rules or of other provisions applicable to the proceedings comes to the notice of a party, that party must immediately enter an objection.

8. The sole arbitrator (arbitral tribunal) must ask the parties whether they have any further proof to offer, witnesses to be heard or submissions to make. As soon as the sole arbitrator (arbitral tribunal) is convinced that the parties have had an adequate

opportunity for such purposes, the sole arbitrator (arbitral tribunal) must declare the proceedings closed.

INTERIM MEASURES OF PROTECTION

Article 14a

1. Unless the parties have agreed otherwise and as soon as the files have been transmitted to him (it), the sole arbitrator (arbitral tribunal) can order the interim measures of protection that he (it) considers to be appropriate, on application by one party. However, only the parties are bound by such measures. The parties are obliged to comply with such orders, whether or not they are enforceable by State courts. The sole arbitrator (arbitral tribunal) can make the ordering of such measures conditional on the provision of appropriate security by the requesting party.

2. This provision does not prevent the parties from applying to any competent State organ for interim measures of protection. Such an application to a State organ for ordering such measures or for the enforcement of measures ordered by the sole arbitrator (arbitral tribunal) shall not constitute an infringement or waiver of the arbitration agreement and shall not affect the powers of the sole arbitrator (arbitral tribunal). The Secretariat and the sole arbitrator (arbitral tribunal) must be immediately informed of any such application as well as of all measures ordered by the State organ.

AUTHORIZED AGENTS

Article 15

The parties shall have the right to be represented by authorized agents of their choice in the proceedings before the sole arbitrator (arbitral tribunal).

APPLICABLE LAW, EQUITY

Article 16

1. As to the substance of the case, the sole arbitrator (arbitral tribunal) shall apply the law that the parties have designated as applicable. Failing such designation by the parties, he (it) shall apply the law that is designated by the choice of law rules that he (it) considers to be applicable.

2. The sole arbitrator (arbitral tribunal) may base his (its) decisions on equity only if he (it) has been expressly empowered by the parties.

INTERRUPTION AND SUSPENSION OF PROCEEDINGS

Article 17

1. The parties must pursue the proceedings with due expedition. Interruption of the proceedings for indefinite or unduly long periods shall not be permitted, even at the joint request of the parties. If necessary after obtaining comments from the parties, the Board may delete from the list of pending cases the proceedings in which the parties have agreed on permanent suspension or which, without adequate grounds, are not pursued by the parties with due expedition. The pendency of the proceedings and the mandate of the arbitrators shall thereby be terminated.

2. If the decision of the sole arbitrator (arbitral tribunal) depends wholly or in part on the resolution of a preliminary question in the context of other proceedings before a court, an arbitral tribunal or an administrative authority, the sole arbitrator (arbitral tribunal) may interrupt his (its) proceedings until a final decision has been made on that preliminary question.

TERMINATION

Article 17a

The proceedings are terminated by:
   a. The rendering of an award;
   b. The conclusion of a settlement;
   c. The return of the claim under Article 6 paragraph 6;
   d. The deletion of the case from the list of pending cases for reasons that are determined by these Rules. Deletion is not inherently an obstacle to refiling of the claim.

THE AWARD

Article 18

1. Awards shall be drawn up in writing. The grounds upon which the award is based must be stated, unless all parties, either in the arbitration agreement or in the oral proceedings, have agreed that no grounds are to be stated.

2. All copies of awards must be signed by the arbitrators. The signatures of the majority of the arbitrators shall suffice if the award contains a statement that one arbitrator refuses to sign or that his signature is prevented by an obstacle which cannot be overcome within a reasonable period of time. If the award is made by a majority decision, mention thereof shall be made in the award at the request of the arbitrator who is in a minority.

3. Awards are confirmed on all copies as awards of the Centre by the signature of the Secretary and the stamp of the Centre and served on to the parties Awards become effective as against the parties on service of the copies.

4. One copy of the award shall be deposited with the Secretariat of the Centre.

5. The sole arbitrator (Chairman of the arbitral tribunal, or, if he is prevented, another arbitrator) shall confirm on all copies at the request of a party the finality and enforceability of the award.

6. Partial and interim awards may be issued.

7. By their agreement to the Vienna Rules, the parties undertake to implement the award.

8. The sole arbitrator (arbitral tribunal) shall at any time, either on request or on his (its) own initiative, correct clerical, typographical or computation errors as well as other obvious inaccuracies in the award or in the copies thereof.

9. The parties can demand that an award be issued concerning the content of a settlement concluded by them.

10. The Board is entitled to publish an award in legal journals or in its own publications, in anonymous form, unless publication is objected to by at least one party, within thirty days after service of the copy of the award on it.

DETERMINATION OF COSTS

Article 19

The sole arbitrator (arbitral tribunal) shall state in the award the costs of arbitration fixed by the Secretariat in accordance with Article 23 paragraph 1, shall determine the amount of costs of the parties, and shall state who should bear the costs of the proceedings or the proportion in which the costs of the proceedings are to be shared.

ENFORCEMENT

Article 20

If an award or a settlement is to be enforced, the Secretary may on request provide the prosecuting party, free of charge but without guarantee of correctness or completeness, with the information that is known to him regarding the law on enforcement and the enforcement practice of the State in which the award or settlement is to be enforced.

COSTS OF THE PROCEEDINGS

Article 21

The costs of the proceedings consist of the following elements:

a. The costs of arbitration, that is to say, the outlay of the Centre (administrative costs), arbitrators' fees and cash outlay (such as travel and subsistence expenses of arbitrators, costs of service of documents, rent, costs of simple minuting); and

b. The costs of the parties, that is to say, the appropriate expenses of the parties for their representation and other outlay related to the arbitration proceedings, in particular, the costs specified in Article 23 a paragraph 1.

REGISTRATION FEE

Article 22

1. On filing the claim (counter-claim), the Claimant (Counter-claimant) shall pay into the account of the Centre, free of charges, a registration fee in the amount stated. That fee is intended to cover the costs up to the submission of the files to the sole arbitrator (arbitral tribunal). If higher outlay is incurred, an additional sum may be prescribed.

2. If there are more than two parties to the proceedings, the registration fee shall be increased by 10% for each additional party.

3. The registration fee shall not be repayable. The registration fee, as well as any additional amount required in accordance with paragraph 1 of the present Article shall be deducted from the Claimant's (Counter-claimant's) share of the deposit against costs of arbitration.

4. If the registration fee is not deposited despite prolongation of the time-limit, the Secretary must delete the claim (counter-claim) from the list of pending cases.

Article 23

1. The costs of arbitration shall be determined by the Secretary at the end of the proceedings.

2. The Secretary shall fix the amount of the deposit against the expected costs of arbitration. That deposit shall be paid in equal shares by the parties before transmission of the files to the sole arbitrator (arbitral tribunal) and within thirty days after service of the payment request.

3. If the share of the Claimant (Counter-claimant) is not received within the time-limit, despite prolongation thereof, the Secretary shall delete the claim

or counter-claim from the list of pending cases of the Centre. He shall inform the parties thereof.

4. If the share of the Defendant (Counter-defendant) is not received within the time-limit set, the Secretary shall inform the Claimant (Counter-claimant) thereof and shall request him to pay the outstanding share of the deposit within thirty days of receipt of the payment request. If that amount is not received within the time-limit, the Secretary must delete the claim (counter-claim) from the list of pending cases of the Centre. He shall inform the parties thereof.

5. If it should be necessary in the course of the proceedings to increase the deposit against costs because of an increase in the amount in dispute, a procedure analogous to that provided for in paragraphs 2 to 4 of the present Article shall be adopted. Until payment of the additional deposit, the amplification of the claim that led to the increase of the amount in dispute shall not be taken into account in the arbitral proceedings.

6. If it should be necessary in the course of the proceedings to increase the deposit against costs because the amount fixed for cash outlay on determining the deposit is not sufficient, a procedure analogous to that provided for in paragraphs 2 to 4 of the present Article shall be adopted.

Article 23a

1. If the sole arbitrator (arbitral tribunal) considers certain action entailing costs, such as the appointment of experts, interpreters or translators, making verbatim records of the proceedings, a visual inspection, or relocation of the proceedings, to be necessary, he (it) must make arrangements to cover the expected costs.

2. The sole arbitrator (arbitral tribunal) may undertake procedural steps in accordance with paragraph 1 of the present Article only if adequate cover for the expected costs exists.

3. The sole arbitrator (arbitral tribunal) shall decide what consequences for the proceedings arise from the failure to pay a prescribed deposit against costs.

4. All commitments related to the procedural steps mentioned in paragraph 1 of the present Article shall be undertaken by the sole arbitrator (arbitral tribunal) for the account of the parties.

CALCULATION OF THE COSTS OF ARBITRATION

Article 24

1. The administrative costs of the Centre and the arbitrators' fees shall be fixed on the basis of the amount in dispute, according to the schedule of arbitration costs

attached to these Rules (Annex 1). If the arbitral proceedings are terminated other than by means of an arbitral award or a settlement, the Secretary shall determine the administrative costs of the Centre and the arbitrators' fees at the appropriate levels.

2. If there are more than two parties to proceedings, the rates for the administrative costs of the Centre and the arbitrators' fees contained in the schedules attached to these Rules shall be increased by 10% for each additional party.

3. In the case of proceedings conducted concerning a number of individual claims or counter-claims, the Secretary may at any stage of the proceedings make a separate calculation of the costs of arbitration according to the amounts in dispute in respect of the individual claims.

4. The Secretary may deviate from the statements of the parties in fixing the amount in dispute if the parties have made only a partial claim or if a request by the parties whose purpose was not the payment of sums of money was obviously undervalued.

5. The rates quoted in the schedule of arbitrators' fees are the fees for sole arbitrators. In any case they shall be raised to two-and-a-half times the amounts quoted if an arbitral tribunal is appointed and to up to three times the rates stated in the event of the particular difficulty of a case.

6. Reductions of the amount in dispute shall be taken into consideration in calculating the arbitrators' fees and administrative costs only if they were made before transmission of the files to the sole arbitrator (arbitral tribunal).

7. Cash outlays shall be determined according to the actual expenditure.

TRANSITIONAL PROVISIONS

Article 25

This version of the Vienna Rules shall apply to all proceedings in which the claim was filed after 31 December 2000. If the arbitration agreement was concluded before 1 January 2001, the parties may agree that the proceedings will be conducted according to the arbitration rules valid until that date; however, even in the event of such an agreement, the provisions of Articles 21 to 24 of the present version shall apply.

SCHEDULE OF ARBITRATION COSTS

Registration Fee: EUR 2,000[1]

Administrative Charges[2]

Amount in dispute in EUR		Rate in EUR
From	*To*	
0	100.000	3.000
100.001	200.000	3.000 + 1,5 % of excess over 100.000
200.001	500.000	4.500 + 1,0 % of excess over 200.000
500.001	1.000.000	7.500 + 0,7 % of excess over 500.000
1.000.001	2.000.000	11.000 + 0,4 % of excess over 1.000.000
2.000.001	5.000.000	15.000 + 0,1 % of excess over 2.000.000
5.000.001	10.000.000	18.000 + 0,05 % of excess over 5.000.000
over 10.000.000		20.500 + 0,01 % of excess over 10.000.000

Fees for sole arbitrators[3]

Amount in dispute in EUR		Rate in EUR
From	*To*	
0	100.000	6 % – minimum fee 1.000
100.001	200.000	6.000 + 3 % of excess over 100.000
200.001	500.000	9.000 + 2,5 % of excess over 200.000
500.001	1.000.000	16.500 + 2 % of excess over 500.000
1.000.001	2.000.000	26.500 + 1 % of excess over 1.000.000
2.000.001	5.000.000	36.500 + 0,6 % of excess over 2.000.000
5.000.001	10.000.000	54.500 + 0,4 % of excess over 5.000.000
10.000.001	20.000.000	74.500 + 0,2 % of excess over 10.000.000
20.000.001	100.000.000	94.500 + 0,1 % of excess over 20.000.000
over 100.000.000		174.500 + 0,01 % of excess over 100.000.000

---

1. See Article 22 paragraph 1.
2. See Article 24 paragraph 1.
3. See Article 24 paragraph 6.

Annex 2b

Internationales Schiedsgericht der Wirtschaftskammer Österreich Schiedsordnung 2001 (Wiener Regeln 2001)*

ALLGEMEINE BESTIMMUNGEN

DIE INSTITUTION

Artikel 1

1. Das Internationale Schiedsgericht der Wirtschaftskammer Österreich in Wien (Wiener Internationales Schiedsgericht, im folgenden 'Schiedsgericht' genannt) trägt Vorsorge für die schiedsgerichtliche Erledigung von Streitigkeiten, bei denen nicht alle Vertragsparteien, welche die Schiedsvereinbarung geschlossen haben, zum Zeitpunkt des Abschlusses dieser Vereinbarung ihren Sitz oder gewöhnlichen Aufenthalt in Österreich hatten.

Dieses Schiedsgericht kann auch von Parteien mit Sitz oder gewöhnlichem Aufenthalt in Österreich für die Erledigung von Streitigkeiten internationalen Charakters vereinbart werden.

2. Haben die Parteien die Zuständigkeit des Schiedsgerichts vereinbart, so gilt damit die Anwendung dieser Schiedsordnung (im folgenden 'Wiener Regeln') in der bei Einleitung des Schiedsverfahrens geltenden Fassung als vereinbart.

---

* Vom Kammertag der Wirtschaftskammer Österreich am 30. November 2000 mit Wirkung von 1. Januar 2001 beschlossen. Mit freundlicher Genehmigung des Internationalen Schiedsgerichtes der Wirtschaftskammer Österreich abgedruckt.

3. Haben Parteien, die zum Zeitpunkt des Abschlusses der Schiedsvereinbarung ihren Sitz oder gewöhnlichen Aufenthalt in Österreich hatten, vereinbart, dass ihre Streitigkeiten von einem Schiedsrichter oder einem Schiedsrichtersenat, der nach den Wiener Regeln zu ernennen ist, endgültig entschieden werden soll, und hat die Streitsache keinen internationalen Charakter, so ist das Ständige Schiedsgericht der Wirtschaftskammer Wien oder, wenn ein anderer Schiedsort in Österreich vereinbart wurde, jener Wirtschaftskammer, in deren örtlichen Zuständigkeitsbereich der vereinbarte Schiedsort fällt, zur Vorsorge für die schiedsrichterliche Erledigung zuständig. Dieses führt das Verfahren nach der Schiedsgerichtsordnung für die Ständigen Schiedsgerichte der Wirtschaftskammern.

Artikel 2

Schiedsverfahren finden am Sitz des Schiedsgerichts in Wien statt. Die Parteien können aber vereinbaren, dass das Verfahren an einem anderen Ort durchzuführen ist.

ORGANISATION

DAS PRÄSIDIUM

Artikel 3

1. Das Präsidium des Schiedsgerichts hat mindestens fünf Mitglieder. Sie werden vom Vorstand der Wirtschaftskammer Österreich für eine Funktionsperiode von fünf Jahren bestellt; Wiederbestellung ist zulässig. Erfolgt bis zum Ablauf einer Funktionsperiode keine Neubestellung, so behalten die Mitglieder des Präsidiums ihre Funktion bis zur Neubestellung. Fällt ein Mitglied des Präsidiums während der Funktionsperiode auf Dauer aus (etwa durch Rücktritt oder Tod), so kann eine Nachbestellung für den Rest der Funktionsperiode des im Amt befindlichen Präsidiums erfolgen.

2. Die Mitglieder des Präsidiums wählen aus ihrer Mitte für die Dauer der Funktionsperiode einen Obmann.

3. Die Sitzungen des Präsidiums werden vom Obmann, in seiner Stellvertretung von dem an Lebensjahren ältesten anwesenden Mitglied geleitet. Das Präsidium ist beschlussfähig, wenn mehr als die Hälfte seiner Mitglieder anwesend ist. Es entscheidet mit einfacher Mehrheit der anwesenden Mitglieder. Bei Stimmengleichheit entscheidet die Stimme des Sitzungsleiters.

4. Entscheidungen auf schriftlichem Wege sind zulässig. Das Präsidium bestimmt die Regeln hiefür.

5. Mitglieder des Präsidiums, die in irgendeiner Eigenschaft an einem Schiedsverfahren beteiligt sind, sind von den Entscheidungen, die dieses Verfahren betreffen, ausgeschlossen.

6. Die Mitglieder des Präsidiums haben ihr Amt nach bestem Wissen und Gewissen auszuüben und sind in der Ausübung ihrer Funktion unabhängig und an keine Weisungen gebunden. Sie sind über alles, was ihnen in dieser Funktion bekannt geworden ist, zur Verschwiegenheit verpflichtet.

DER SEKRETÄR

Artikel 4

1. Der Sekretär des Schiedsgerichts wird auf Vorschlag des Präsidiums des Schiedsgerichts vom Vorstand der Wirtschaftskammer Österreich für eine Funktionsperiode von fünf Jahren bestellt. Wiederbestellung ist zulässig. Art 3 Abs 1 zweiter Satz gilt analog.

2. Der Sekretär leitet das Sekretariat und erledigt die administrativen Angelegenheiten des Schiedsgerichts, soweit sie nicht dem Präsidium vorbehalten sind.

3. Der Sekretär hat sein Amt nach bestem Wissen und Gewissen auszuüben und ist dabei an keine Weisungen gebunden. Er ist über alles, was ihm in dieser Funktion bekannt geworden ist, zur Verschwiegenheit verpflichtet.

4. Ist der Sekretär an der Ausübung seines Amtes verhindert oder fällt er auf Dauer aus, so übt ein vom Präsidium betrautes Mitglied desselben dessen Funktionen bis zur Bestellung eines Sekretärs aus.

KORRESPONDENZSPRACHEN

Artikel 4a

Der Schriftverkehr der Parteien mit dem Präsidium und dem Sekretär hat in deutscher oder englischer Sprache zu erfolgen.

DIE SCHIEDSRICHTER

Artikel 5

1. Den Parteien steht die Bestimmung der Schiedsrichter frei. Schiedsrichter kann – ungeachtet der Staatsbürgerschaft – jede geschäftsfähige Person sein.

2. Das Präsidium des Schiedsgerichts erstellt für jeweils eine Periode von drei Kalenderjahren eine Schiedsrichterliste. Die Aufnahme in die Schiedsrichterliste ist nicht Voraussetzung für die Bestellung zum Schiedsrichter.

3. Mitglieder des Präsidiums dürfen nur die Funktion des Vorsitzenden eines Schiedsrichtersenates oder eines Einzelschiedsrichters annehmen.

4. Die Schiedsrichter haben ihr Amt in voller Unabhängigkeit und Unparteilichkeit nach bestem Wissen und Gewissen auszuüben und sind dabei an keine Weisungen gebunden. Sie sind über alles, was ihnen in dieser Funktion bekannt geworden ist, zur Verschwiegenheit verpflichtet.

5. Die Haftung der Schiedsrichter, des Sekretärs, des Präsidiums und seiner Mitglieder und der Wirtschaftskammer Österreich und ihrer Beschäftigten für jedwede Handlung oder Unterlassung im Zusammenhang mit dem Schiedsverfahren ist, soweit gesetzlich zulässig, ausgeschlossen.

DAS SCHIEDSVERFAHREN

Einleitung

Artikel 6

1. Das Schiedsverfahren wird durch Einreichung einer Klage beim Sekretariat eingeleitet. Mit Einlangen der Klage im Sekretariat ist das Verfahren anhängig.

2. Für jeden Beklagten, jeden Schiedsrichter und das Sekretariat ist je eine Klagsausfertigung samt Beilagen einzureichen.

3. Die Klage hat zu enthalten:

    a. die Bezeichnung der Parteien und ihre Anschriften;
    b. ein bestimmtes Begehren, die tatsächlichen Angaben, auf die es sich stützt, und die beantragten Beweise;
    c. den Wert des Streitgegenstandes zum Zeitpunkt der Einbringung der Klage, wenn das Klagebegehren nicht ausschließlich auf eine bestimmte Geldsumme gerichtet ist;
    d. Angaben zur Zahl der Schiedsrichter gemäß Art 9;
    e. die Benennung eines Schiedsrichters mit Angabe der Anschrift, wenn eine Entscheidung durch drei Schiedsrichter beantragt wird.

4. Der Klage ist eine Kopie jener Vereinbarung anzuschließen, aus der sich die Zuständigkeit des Schiedsgerichts ergibt.

5. Entspricht die Klage nicht dem Abs 3 oder fehlen Ausfertigungen oder Beilagen, so fordert der Sekretär den Kläger unter Setzung einer Frist zur Verbesserung oder Ergänzung auf. Werden die Mängel nicht innerhalb der gesetzten Frist(en) behoben, so ist die Klage von der Liste der anhängigen Fälle zu streichen.

6. Das Präsidium kann die Klage als nicht zur weiteren Behandlung geeignet an den Kläger zurückstellen, wenn die Parteien in der Schiedsvereinbarung zwar das Internationale Schiedsgericht der Wirtschaftskammer Österreich bezeichnen, aber Absprachen getroffen haben, die den Wiener Regeln widersprechen.

KLAGEBEANTWORTUNG

Artikel 7

1. Ist die Klage nicht gemäß Art 6 Abs 5 und 6 zu behandeln, so stellt der Sekretär der beklagten Partei die Klage sowie je ein Exemplar der Schiedsordnung und der Schiedsrichterliste zu und fordert sie auf, binnen 30 Tagen eine Klagebeantwortung in der nach Art 6 Abs 2 erforderlichen Zahl von Ausfertigungen einzubringen.

2. Die Klagebeantwortung hat zu enthalten:

    a. eine Äußerung zum Vorbringen in der Klage,
    b. Angaben zur Zahl der Schiedsrichter gemäß Art 9,
    c. die Benennung eines Schiedsrichters unter Angabe seiner Anschrift, wenn die Entscheidung durch einen Schiedsrichtersenat beantragt wird oder in der Schiedsvereinbarung die Entscheidung durch drei Schiedsrichter vereinbart ist.

3. Der Sekretär übersendet die Unterlagen zum Fall dem Schiedsrichter (dem Schiedsrichtersenat), sobald eine mangelfreie Klage vorliegt, der Schiedsrichter (sämtliche Mitglieder des Schiedsrichtersenates) die Übernahme des Auftrages und ihre Unbefangenheit auf einem Vordruck des Schiedsgerichts bestätigt haben und der Kostenvorschuss bezahlt ist (Art 23). Damit beginnt das Verfahren vor dem Schiedsrichter (Schiedsrichtersenat). Der Sekretär leitet eine Kopie des Vordrucks, auf welchem der Schiedsrichter (die Mitglieder des Schiedsrichtersenates) ihre Unbefangenheit bestätigt haben, an die Parteien weiter.

WIDERKLAGE

Artikel 7a

1. Klagen der beklagten Partei gegen den Kläger, die auf derselben Schiedsvereinbarung beruhen, können bis zum Schluss des Beweisverfahrens als Widerklage erhoben werden.

2. Widerklagen sind beim Sekretariat des Schiedsgerichts einzubringen und von diesem nach Erlag des Kostenvorschusses dem Schiedsrichter (Schiedsrichtersenat) zur weiteren Behandlung zuzuleiten.

3. Beruht die als Widerklage bezeichnete Klage nicht auf derselben Schiedsverein-
barung oder besteht keine Parteienidentität oder würde eine nach Übergabe der
Unterlagen zum Fall an den Schiedsrichter (den Schiedsrichtersenat) eingebrachte
Widerklage zu einer erheblichen Verzögerung des Hauptverfahrens führen, so hat der
Schiedsrichter (Schiedsrichtersenat) diese Klage dem Sekretariat zur Behandlung in
einem gesonderten Verfahren zurückzustellen.

4. Der Schiedsrichter (Schiedsrichtersenat) hat dem Widerbeklagten einer zulässigen Widerklage Gelegenheit zur Erstattung einer schriftlichen Klagebeantwortung
zu geben und hiefür eine Frist zu setzen.

FRISTEN, ZUSTELLUNGEN UND MITTEILUNGEN

Artikel 8

1. Eine Frist ist gewahrt, wenn das Schriftstück am letzten Tag der Frist in einer
in Abs 2 vorgesehenen Weise versendet wird. Fristen können vom Sekretär aus
berücksichtigungswürdigen Gründen verlängert werden; nach der Übergabe der
Unterlagen zum Fall an den Schiedsrichter (Schiedsrichtersenat) ist dafür der
Schiedsrichter (Schiedsrichtersenat) zuständig (ausgenommen die Fälle des Art
23 Abs 5 und 6).

2. Zustellungen gelten als ordnungsgemäß durchgeführt, wenn sie mittels einges-
chriebenen Briefes, Kurierdienstes oder Telefax an jene Anschrift erfolgt sind, die
der Adressat des Schriftstückes zuletzt dem Schiedsgericht bzw. dem
Schiedsrichter (Schiedsrichtersenat) schriftlich als Zustelladresse bekannt gegeben
hat, oder wenn das zuzustellende Schriftstück dem Adressaten ausgehändigt
wurde.

3. Sobald eine Partei einen Vertreter bestellt hat, gelten Zustellungen an die zuletzt
bekannt gegebene Anschrift dieses Vertreters als an die vertretene Partei erfolgt.

BENENNUNG UND BESTELLUNG VON SCHIEDSRICHTERN

Artikel 9

1. Die Parteien können vereinbaren, dass ihr Rechtsstreit von einem
Einzelschiedsrichter oder von einem Schiedsrichtersenat entschieden werden
soll. Schiedsrichtersenate bestehen aus drei Schiedsrichtern.

2. Liegt eine solche Vereinbarung nicht vor und einigen sich die Parteien nicht auf
die Zahl der Schiedsrichter, so bestimmt das Präsidium, ob der Rechtsstreit von
einem Einzelschiedsrichter oder einem Schiedsrichtersenat zu entscheiden ist.
Hiebei berücksichtigt das Präsidium insbesondere die Schwierigkeit des Falles,

die Höhe des Streitwertes und das Interesse der Parteien an einer raschen und kostengünstigen Entscheidung.

3. Die Entscheidung des Präsidiums nach Abs 2 wird den Parteien mit der Aufforderung mitgeteilt, sich in den Fällen, in denen auf ein Verfahren vor einem Einzelschiedsrichter entschieden wurde, binnen 30 Tagen ab Zustellung der Aufforderung auf einen Einzelschiedsrichter zu einigen und dessen Namen und Adresse bekannt zugeben. Erfolgt innerhalb dieser Frist keine solche Mitteilung, so wird der Einzelschiedsrichter vom Präsidium bestellt.

4. Ist der Rechtsstreit von einem Schiedsrichtersenat zu entscheiden, so wird die Partei, die noch keinen Schiedsrichter benannt hat, aufgefordert, binnen 30 Tagen ab Zustellung der Aufforderung den Namen und die Adresse eines Schiedsrichters bekannt zugeben. Wenn der Kläger innerhalb dieser Frist keinen Schiedsrichter bestellt und die Bestellung auch nicht ausdrücklich dem Präsidium überlässt, ist der Fall von der Liste der anhängigen Fälle zu streichen. Bestellt hingegen der Beklagte innerhalb dieser Frist keinen Schiedsrichter, so wird dieser vom Präsidium bestellt.

5. Ist der Rechtsstreit von einem Schiedsrichtersenat zu entscheiden, so werden die von den Parteien benannten oder vom Präsidium bestellten Schiedsrichter aufgefordert, sich binnen 30 Tagen ab Zustellung der Aufforderung auf einen Vorsitzenden zu einigen und dessen Namen und Adresse bekannt zugeben. Erfolgt innerhalb dieser Frist keine solche Mitteilung, so wird der Vorsitzende vom Präsidium bestellt.

6. Die Parteien sind an ihre Schiedsrichterbenennung gebunden, sobald der benannte Schiedsrichter der Gegenpartei bekannt gegeben wurde.

MEHRPARTEIENVERFAHREN

Artikel 10

1. Eine Schiedsklage gegen zwei oder mehrere Beklagte ist nur zulässig, sofern das Schiedsgericht für alle Beklagten zuständig ist, bei einem Verfahren vor einem Schiedsrichtersenat alle Kläger denselben Schiedsrichter benennen und

    a. die Klage nach dem anzuwendenden Recht zwingend gegen mehrere Personen zu richten ist oder

    b. alle Parteien durch dieselbe Schiedsvereinbarung gebunden sind oder

    c. wenn die Zulässigkeit eines Mehrparteienverfahrens vereinbart ist oder

    d. alle Beklagten sich auf ein Mehrparteienverfahren einlassen und bei einem Verfahren vor einem Schiedsrichtersenat alle Beklagten denselben Schiedsrichter benennen oder

e. einer oder mehrere der Beklagten, denen die Klage zugestellt wurde, innerhalb der 30-tägigen Frist (Art 7 Abs 1) die in Art 7 Abs 2 lit b und c bezeichneten Angaben nicht erstatten.

2. Kann eine gegen mehrere Beklagte gerichtete Klage nicht allen Beklagten zugestellt werden, so ist das Schiedsverfahren gegen jene Beklagten, denen die Klage zugestellt wurde, nur fortzusetzen, wenn der Kläger binnen einer vom Sekretär gesetzten Frist erklärt, die Klage gegen jene Beklagten, denen nicht zugestellt werden konnte, zurückzuziehen. Erfolgt innerhalb der vom Sekretär gesetzten Frist keine Äußerung oder kann eine Klage binnen einem Jahr ab Klagseinbringung nicht zugestellt werden, so ist die Klage von der Liste der anhängigen Fälle zu streichen.

3. Liegt eine Vereinbarung über die Zulässigkeit eines Mehrparteienverfahrens vor, so haben sich die Beklagten untereinander zu einigen, ob sie den Rechtsstreit von einem oder von drei Schiedsrichtern entschieden haben wollen, und, falls eine Entscheidung durch drei Schiedsrichter gewünscht wird, gemeinsam einen Schiedsrichter zu benennen.

4. Sollte im Falle des Abs 3 eine Einigung der Beklagten über die Zahl der Schiedsrichter nicht vorliegen, so werden sie vom Sekretär aufgefordert, binnen 30 Tagen ab Zustellung der Aufforderung eine solche Einigung nachzuweisen.

5. Erfolgt innerhalb der in Abs 4 genannten Frist kein Nachweis der Einigung auf die Zahl der Schiedsrichter, so bestimmt das Präsidium, ob der Rechtsstreit von einem Schiedsrichter oder von einem Schiedsrichtersenat zu entscheiden ist.

6. Haben sich die Beklagten darauf geeinigt, dass der Rechtsstreit von einem Schiedsrichtersenat zu entscheiden ist, ohne einen Schiedsrichter zu benennen, so werden sie vom Sekretär aufgefordert, binnen 30 Tagen ab Zustellung der Aufforderung den Namen und die Adresse eines Schiedsrichters bekannt zugeben.

7. Erfolgt innerhalb der in Abs 6 genannten Frist keine Benennung eines gemeinsamen Schiedsrichters und ist der Streitfall von einem Schiedsrichtersenat zu entscheiden, so bestellt das Präsidium den Schiedsrichter für die säumigen Beklagten.

8. In anderen als den in Abs 1 genannten Fällen ist die Verbindung zweier oder mehrerer Rechtssachen nur zulässig, wenn in allen zu verbindenden Rechtssachen dieselben Schiedsrichter bestellt wurden und alle Parteien und der Schiedsrichter (Schiedsrichtersenat) zustimmen.

ABLEHNUNG VON SCHIEDSRICHTERN

Artikel 11

1. Ein Schiedsrichter kann abgelehnt werden, wenn ein zureichender Grund vorliegt, seine Unabhängigkeit oder Unparteilichkeit in Zweifel zu ziehen.

2. Lehnt eine Partei einen Schiedsrichter ab, so hat sie dies unter Angabe des Ablehnungsgrundes dem Sekretariat bekannt zugeben.

3. Die Ablehnung ist unzulässig, wenn sich die ablehnende Partei in das Verfahren eingelassen hat, obwohl ihr der von ihr geltend gemachte Ablehnungsgrund schon vorher bekannt war oder bekannt sein musste, oder wenn die ablehnende Partei den Ablehnungsgrund mit ungebührlicher Verzögerung bekannt gegeben hat.

4. Über die Ablehnung entscheidet das Präsidium aufgrund der Angaben im Ablehnungsantrag und der diesem beigeschlossenen Beweismittel. Der Sekretär hat vor der Entscheidung des Präsidiums die Stellungnahme des abgelehnten Schiedsrichters einzuholen. Das Präsidium kann auch andere Personen zur Stellungnahme auffordern.

5. Ein abgelehnter Schiedsrichter hat das Verfahren ungeachtet des Ablehnungsantrages bis zur Zustellung der Entscheidung des Präsidiums über den Ablehnungsantrag fortzuführen. Ein Schiedsspruch darf jedoch erst nach der Entscheidung des Präsidiums gefällt werden.

ENTHEBUNG VON SCHIEDSRICHTERN

Artikel 12

Jede Partei kann die Enthebung eines Schiedsrichters beantragen, wenn er nicht nur vorübergehend verhindert ist, sonst seiner Aufgabe nicht nachkommt oder das Verfahren ungebührlich verzögert. Der Antrag ist beim Sekretariat einzubringen. Über ihn entscheidet nach Anhörung des betroffenen Schiedsrichters das Präsidium. Ist offensichtlich, dass die Verhinderung nicht nur vorübergehend ist, so kann das Präsidium die Enthebung auch ohne Antrag einer Partei verfügen.

FOLGEN DER ABLEHNUNG BEZIEHUNGSWEISE DER ENTHEBUNG

Artikel 13

1. Wurde der Ablehnung eines Schiedsrichters stattgegeben, wurde er seines Amtes enthoben, hat er dieses niedergelegt oder ist er gestorben, so werden,

a. wenn es sich um einen Einzelschiedsrichter handelt, die Parteien

   b. wenn es sich um den Vorsitzenden eines Schiedsrichtersenates handelt, die verbleibenden Schiedsrichter und

   c. wenn es sich um einen von einer Partei benannten oder für eine Partei bestellten Schiedsrichter handelt, die Partei, die ihn benannt hat oder für die er bestellt wurde,

aufgefordert, binnen 30 Tagen einen Ersatzschiedsrichter – in den Fällen gemäß lit a und b einvernehmlich – zu benennen und dessen Namen und Adresse bekannt zugeben. Erfolgt innerhalb dieser Frist keine solche Mitteilung, so wird der Ersatzschiedsrichter vom Präsidium bestellt. Wurde auch ein benannter Ersatzschiedsrichter erfolgreich abgelehnt, so erlischt das Ersatzbenennungsrecht und der Ersatzschiedsrichter wird vom Präsidium bestellt.

2. Wurde der Ablehnung eines Schiedsrichters stattgegeben, wurde er seines Amtes enthoben, hat er dieses niedergelegt oder ist er gestorben, so bestimmt der neue Schiedsrichter (neu zusammengesetzte Schiedsrichtersenat) nach Einholung einer Stellungnahme der Parteien, ob und in welchem Umfang vorausgegangene Verfahrensabschnitte zu wiederholen sind.

DURCHFÜHRUNG DES VERFAHRENS

Artikel 14

1. Im Rahmen der Wiener Regeln und der Vereinbarungen der Parteien kann der Schiedsrichter (Schiedsrichtersenat) das Schiedsverfahren nach freiem Ermessen durchführen; es gilt der Grundsatz der Gleichbehandlung der Parteien unter Wahrung des rechtlichen Gehörs in jedem Stadium des Verfahrens. Der Schiedsrichter (Schiedsrichtersenat) ist jedoch berechtigt, nach Vorankündigung Vorbringen und die Vorlage von Beweisurkunden nur bis zu einem bestimmten Verfahrensstadium für zulässig zu erklären.

2. Unverzüglich nach Übergabe der Unterlagen zum Fall an den Schiedsrichter (Schiedsrichtersenat) hat dieser die Sprache oder die Sprachen des Verfahrens unter Berücksichtigung aller Umstände, insbesondere der Sprache des Vertrages, zu bestimmen. Hiebei ist er an eine allfällige Vereinbarung der Parteien gebunden. Der Schiedsrichter (Schiedsrichtersenat) kann anordnen, dass von allen Urkunden, die nicht in dieser Sprache (diesen Sprachen) abgefasst sind, eine entsprechende Übersetzung vorgelegt werde.

3. Das Verfahren kann mündlich oder schriftlich durchgeführt werden. Eine mündliche Verhandlung findet auf Antrag einer Partei oder, wenn es der mit der Entscheidung betraute Schiedsrichter (Schiedsrichtersenat) für erforderlich hält, statt. Den Parteien ist jedenfalls Gelegenheit zu geben, von den Anträgen und den Vorbringen der anderen Parteien und dem Ergebnis der Beweisaufnahmen Kenntnis zu nehmen und sich dazu zu äußern.

4. Die mündliche Verhandlung wird von dem Schiedsrichter oder dem Vorsitzenden des Schiedsrichtersenates anberaumt. Sie ist nicht öffentlich. Über die Verhandlung ist zumindest ein Ergebnisprotokoll anzufertigen, das der Schiedsrichter bzw. der Vorsitzende des Schiedsrichtersenates zu unterfertigen hat.

5. Der Schiedsrichter (Schiedsrichtersenat) kann, wenn er es für erforderlich hält, von sich aus Beweise erheben, insbesondere Parteien oder Zeugen vernehmen, die Parteien zur Vorlage von Urkunden und Augenscheinsgegenständen auffordern und Sachverständige beiziehen. Sind mit der Beweisaufnahme, insbesondere mit der Sachverständigenbestellung Kosten verbunden, ist nach Art 23 a vorzugehen.

6. Beteiligt sich eine Partei nicht am Verfahren, so ist mit der anderen Partei allein zu verhandeln.

7. Erlangt eine Partei Kenntnis von einer Verletzung einer Bestimmung dieser Schiedsordnung oder sonstiger auf das Verfahren anwendbarer Bestimmungen durch den Schiedsrichter (Schiedsrichtersenat), so hat sie dies unverzüglich zu rügen.

8. Der Schiedsrichter (Schiedsrichtersenat) hat die Parteien zu befragen, ob sie noch weitere Beweise anzubieten, Zeugen vernehmen zu lassen oder Erklärungen abzugeben haben. Sobald nach Überzeugung des Schiedsrichters (Schiedsrichtersenates) die Parteien dazu ausreichend Gelegenheit hatten, hat der Schiedsrichter (Schiedsrichtersenat) das Verfahren für geschlossen zu erklären.

SICHERNDE UND VORLÄUFIGE MASSNAHMEN

Artikel 14a

1. Soweit die Parteien nichts anderes vereinbart haben, kann der Schiedsrichter (Schiedsrichtersenat), sobald ihm die Unterlagen zum Fall übermittelt worden sind, auf Antrag einer Partei ihm angemessen erscheinende sichernde und vorläufige Maßnahmen anordnen, an die jedoch nur die Parteien gebunden sind. Diese sind verpflichtet, solche Anordnungen zu befolgen, ungeachtet ob diese von staatlichen Gerichten vollstreckbar sind. Der Schiedsrichter (Schiedsrichtersenat) kann die Anordnung solcher Maßnahmen von der Stellung angemessener Sicherheiten durch die antragstellende Partei abhängig machen.

2. Diese Bestimmung hindert die Parteien nicht, bei jedem zuständigen staatlichen Organ sichernde und vorläufige Maßnahmen zu beantragen. Ein solcher Antrag an ein staatliches Organ auf Anordnung solcher Maßnahmen oder auf Vollziehung vom Schiedsrichter (Schiedsrichtersenat) angeordneter Maßnahmen stellt keinen Verstoß gegen oder Verzicht auf die Schiedsvereinbarung dar und lässt die dem Schiedsrichter (Schiedsrichtersenat) zustehenden Befugnisse unberührt. Ein solcher Antrag sowie alle durch das staatliche Organ angeordneten Maßnahmen sind

unverzüglich dem Sekretariat und dem Schiedsrichter (Schiedsrichtersenat) mitzuteilen.

BEVOLLMÄCHTIGTE

Artikel 15

Die Parteien können sich im Verfahren vor dem Schiedsgericht durch Bevollmächtigte ihrer Wahl vertreten lassen.

ANWENDBARES RECHT, BILLIGKEIT

Artikel 16

1. Der Schiedsrichter (Schiedsrichtersenat) hat in der Sache selbst das Recht anzuwenden, das die Parteien als maßgebend bezeichnet haben. Fehlt eine solche Bezeichnung durch die Parteien, so hat er jenes Recht anzuwenden, das von den Kollisionsnormen, die er für maßgeblich erachtet, bezeichnet wird.

2. Der Schiedsrichter (Schiedsrichtersenat) darf nur dann nach Billigkeit entscheiden, wenn er dazu ausdrücklich von den Parteien ermächtigt worden ist.

UNTERBRECHUNG UND RUHEN DES VERFAHRENS

Artikel 17

1. Die Parteien haben das Verfahren gehörig fortzusetzen. Unterbrechungen des Verfahrens für unbestimmte oder unangemessen lange Zeiträume sind auch auf gemeinsamen Parteienantrag nicht gestattet. Das Präsidium kann Verfahren, in denen die Parteien ewiges Ruhen des Verfahrens vereinbart haben oder die ohne ausreichende Begründung von den Parteien nicht gehörig fortgesetzt werden, allenfalls nach Einholung einer Stellungnahme der Parteien aus der Liste der anhängigen Fälle streichen; dadurch sind Verfahrensanhängigkeit und Mandat der Schiedsrichter beendet.

2. Hängt die Entscheidung des Schiedsrichters (Schiedsrichtersenates) ganz oder zum Teil von der Lösung einer Vorfrage in einem anderen Verfahren vor einem Gericht, einem Schiedsgericht oder einer Verwaltungsbehörde ab, so kann der Schiedsrichter (Schiedsrichtersenat) sein Verfahren bis zur rechtskräftigen Entscheidung dieser Vorfrage unterbrechen.

BEENDIGUNG

Artikel 17a

Das Verfahren wird beendet mit:

   a. der Erlassung des Schiedsspruches,
   b. dem Abschluss eines Schiedsvergleiches,
   c. der Zurückstellung der Klage nach Art 6 Abs 6,
   d. der Streichung des Falles aus der Liste anhängiger Fälle aus Gründen, die diese Regeln bestimmen; die Streichung an sich steht der Neueinbringung der Klage nicht entgegen.

SCHIEDSSPRUCH

Artikel 18

1. Schiedssprüche ergehen schriftlich. Sie sind zu begründen, sofern nicht alle Parteien entweder im Schiedsvertrag oder in der mündlichen Verhandlung auf eine Begründung verzichtet haben.

2. Schiedssprüche sind auf allen Ausfertigungen von den Schiedsrichtern zu unterschreiben. Die Unterschrift der Mehrheit der Schiedsrichter genügt, wenn im Schiedsspruch vermerkt wird, dass ein Schiedsrichter die Unterschrift verweigert oder dass der Unterzeichnung durch ihn ein Hindernis entgegensteht, das nicht in angemessener Frist überwunden werden kann. Wird der Schiedsspruch mit Stimmenmehrheit gefällt, so muss dies auf Wunsch des überstimmten Schiedsrichters im Schiedsspruch angeführt werden.

3. Schiedssprüche werden auf allen Ausfertigungen durch die Unterschrift des Sekretärs und den Stempel des Schiedsgerichts als Schiedssprüche des Schiedsgerichts bestätigt und den Parteien zugestellt. Den Parteien gegenüber werden Schiedssprüche mit der Zustellung der Ausfertigungen wirksam.

4. Eine Ausfertigung des Schiedsspruches wird beim Sekretariat des Schiedsgerichts hinterlegt.

5. Der Schiedsrichter (Vorsitzende des Schiedsrichtersenates, im Falle seiner Verhinderung ein anderer Schiedsrichter) hat auf Verlangen einer Partei Rechtskraft und Vollstreckbarkeit des Schiedsspruches auf sämtlichen Ausfertigungen zu bestätigen.

6. Die Erlassung von Teil- und Zwischenschiedssprüchen ist zulässig.

7. Durch die Vereinbarung der Wiener Regeln haben sich die Parteien verpflichtet, den Schiedsspruch zu erfüllen.

8. Schreib- oder Rechenfehler sowie andere offenbare Unrichtigkeiten im Schiedsspruch oder in dessen Ausfertigungen hat der Schiedsrichter (Schiedsrichtersenat) jederzeit auf Antrag oder von sich aus zu berichtigen.

9. Die Parteien können verlangen, dass über den Inhalt eines von ihnen geschlossenen Vergleiches ein Schiedsspruch erlassen wird.

10. Das Präsidium ist berechtigt, einen Schiedsspruch in juristischen Fachzeitschriften oder in eigenen Publikationen in anonymisierter Form zu veröffentlichen, wenn nicht zumindest eine Partei der Veröffentlichung innerhalb einer Frist von 30 Tagen ab Zustellung der Ausfertigung des Schiedsspruches an sie widerspricht.

Kostenbestimmung

Artikel 19

Der Schiedsrichter (Schiedsrichtersenat) hat im Schiedsspruch die vom Sekretär gemäß Art. 23 Abs 1 bestimmten Schiedsgerichtskosten anzuführen, die Höhe der Parteienkosten zu bestimmen und festzulegen, wer die Verfahrenskosten zu tragen hat oder in welchem Verhältnis diese Verfahrenskosten verteilt werden.

Vollstreckung

Artikel 20

Soll ein Schiedsspruch oder Schiedsvergleich vollstreckt werden, so kann der Sekretär die betreibende Partei auf Anfrage kostenlos, aber ohne Gewähr für Richtigkeit und Vollständigkeit, nach seinem Wissensstand über das Vollstreckungsrecht und die Vollstreckungspraxis des Staates, in dem der Schiedsspruch oder Schiedsvergleich vollstreckt werden soll, informieren.

Verfahrenskosten

Artikel 21

Die Verfahrenskosten setzen sich aus folgenden Teilen zusammen:

    a. den Schiedsgerichtskosten, das sind die Auslagen des Schiedsgerichts (Verwaltungskosten), die Honorare der Schiedsrichter und die Barauslagen (wie Reise- und Aufenthaltskosten von Schiedsrichtern, Kosten der Zustellung, Mieten, einfache Protokollierungskosten) und

b. den Parteienkosten, das sind die angemessenen Aufwendungen der Parteien für ihre Vertretung und andere Auslagen im Zusammenhang mit dem Schiedsverfahren, insbesondere die in Art 23 a Abs 1 genannten Kosten.

EINSCHREIBEGEBÜHR

Artikel 22

1. Die klagende (widerklagende) Partei hat mit Überreichung der Klage (Widerklage) eine Einschreibegebühr in der angegebenen Höhe auf das Konto des Schiedsgerichts spesenfrei zu entrichten. Diese Gebühr dient zur Deckung der Auslagen bis zur Übergabe der Unterlagen zum Fall an den Schiedsrichter (den Schiedsrichtersenat). Sollten höhere Auslagen entstehen, kann ein zusätzlicher Betrag vorgeschrieben werden.

2. Sind an dem Schiedsverfahren mehr als zwei Parteien beteiligt, so erhöht sich die Einschreibegebühr um 10 % für jede zusätzliche Partei.

3. Die Einschreibegebühr wird nicht zurückgezahlt. Die Einschreibegebühr sowie ein allfälliger zusätzlicher Betrag nach Abs 1 werden in den Kostenvorschuss des Klägers (Widerklägers) für die Schiedsgerichtskosten (Art 23 Abs 2) eingerechnet.

4. Wird die Einschreibegebühr trotz Nachfristsetzung nicht erlegt, so hat der Sekretär die Klage (Widerklage) von der Liste der anhängigen Fälle zu streichen.

Artikel 23

1. Die Schiedsgerichtskosten werden vom Sekretär am Ende des Verfahrens bestimmt.

2. Der Sekretär setzt den Kostenvorschuss für die voraussichtlichen Schiedsgerichtskosten fest. Dieser ist vor Übergabe der Unterlagen zum Fall an den Schiedsrichter (Schiedsrichtersenat) von den Parteien binnen 30 Tagen ab Zustellung der Aufforderung zu gleichen Teilen zu erlegen.

3. Langt der auf den Kläger (Widerkläger) entfallende Anteil trotz Nachfristsetzung nicht innerhalb der gesetzten Frist ein, so hat der Sekretär die Klage (Widerklage) von der Liste der anhängigen Fälle des Schiedsgerichts zu streichen. Er teilt dies den Parteien mit.

4. Langt der auf den Beklagten (Widerbeklagten) entfallende Anteil nicht innerhalb der gesetzten Frist ein, so teilt der Sekretär dies dem Kläger (Widerkläger) mit und fordert ihn auf, den fehlenden Teil des Vorschusses binnen 30 Tagen ab Erhalt der Aufforderung zu bezahlen. Langt dieser Betrag nicht innerhalb der gesetzten Frist ein, so hat der Sekretär die Klage (Widerklage) von der Liste der anhängigen Fälle des Schiedsgerichts zu streichen. Er teilt dies den Parteien mit.

5. Wird im Laufe des Verfahrens wegen einer Erhöhung des Streitwertes eine
Erhöhung des Kostenvorschusses erforderlich, so ist analog den Bestimmungen
der Abs 2 bis 4 vorzugehen. Bis zum Erlag des zusätzlichen Vorschusses ist
die Klagsausdehnung, die zur Erhöhung des Streitwertes geführt hat, im
Schiedsverfahren nicht zu berücksichtigen.

6. Wird im Laufe des Verfahrens eine Erhöhung des Kostenvorschusses erforderlich, weil der bei seiner Festsetzung veranschlagte Betrag für Barauslagen nicht
ausreicht, so ist analog den Bestimmungen der Abs 2 bis 4 vorzugehen.

Artikel 23a

1. Hält der Schiedsrichter (Schiedsrichtersenat) die Durchführung von bestimmten,
mit Kosten verbundenen Verfahrensschritten, wie die Bestellung von
Sachverständigen, Dolmetschern oder Übersetzern, die wörtliche Aufzeichnung
des Verhandlungsverlaufes, die Abhaltung eines Lokalaugenscheines oder die
Verlegung des Verhandlungsortes, für erforderlich, so hat er für die Deckung
der voraussichtlichen Kosten zu sorgen.

2. Der Schiedsrichter (Schiedsrichtersenat) darf Verfahrensschritte gemäß Abs 1
erst vornehmen, wenn eine ausreichende Deckung für die voraussichtlichen
Kosten vorhanden ist.

3. Der Schiedsrichter (Schiedsrichtersenat) entscheidet, welche Folgen sich aus der
Nichtentrichtung eines etwa vorgeschriebenen Kostenvorschusses für das
Verfahren ergeben.

4. Alle Aufträge im Zusammenhang mit den in Abs 1 genannten
Verfahrensschritten erteilt der Schiedsrichter (Schiedsrichtersenat) im Namen
der Parteien.

BERECHNUNG DER SCHIEDSGERICHTSKOSTEN

Artikel 24

1. Die Verwaltungskosten des Schiedsgerichts und die Schiedsrichterhonorare
werden aufgrund des Streitwertes nach der Tabelle der Verfahrenskosten
(Anhang 1) berechnet. Wird das Schiedsverfahren anders als durch
Schiedsspruch oder Schiedsvergleich beendet, so bestimmt der Sekretär die
Verwaltungskosten des Schiedsgerichts und die Schiedsrichterhonorare in ange-
messener Höhe.

2. Sind an einem Verfahren mehr als zwei Parteien beteiligt, so erhöhen sich die in
den der Schiedsordnung beigefügten Tabellen enthaltenen Sätze für
Verwaltungskosten und Schiedsrichterhonorare um 10 % für jede zusätzliche
Partei.

3. Bei Verfahren, die über eine Mehrzahl von einzelnen Ansprüchen oder Gegenansprüchen geführt werden, kann der Sekretär in jedem Stadium des Verfahrens für die Schiedsgerichtskosten eine gesonderte Berechnung nach den Streitwerten der einzelnen Ansprüche vornehmen.

4. Der Sekretär kann den Streitwert abweichend von den Angaben der Parteien festlegen, wenn die Parteien nur einen Teilbetrag einer Forderung eingeklagt haben oder wenn ein nicht auf Zahlung von Geldbeträgen gerichtetes Begehren von den Parteien offenkundig unterbewertet wurde.

5. Die in der Tabelle für Schiedsrichterhonorare angegebenen Sätze sind die Honorare für Einzelschiedsrichter. Sie erhöhen sich bei einem Schiedsrichtersenat jedenfalls auf das Zweieinhalbfache, bei besonderer Schwierigkeit des Falles bis zum Dreifachen des angegebenen Satzes.

6. Herabsetzungen des Streitwertes sind bei der Berechnung der Schiedsrichterhonorare und Verwaltungskosten nur zu berücksichtigen, wenn sie vor Übergabe der Unterlagen zum Fall an den Schiedsrichter (Schiedsrichtersenat) vorgenommen wurden.

7. Barauslagen werden nach dem tatsächlichen Aufwand bestimmt.

ÜBERGANGSBESTIMMUNG

Artikel 25

Diese Fassung der Wiener Regeln gilt für alle Verfahren, bei denen die Klage nach dem 31.12.2000 eingebracht wurde. Wurde die Schiedsvereinbarung vor dem 1.1.2001 abgeschlossen, können die Parteien vereinbaren, dass das Verfahren nach der bis dahin geltenden Schiedsordnung durchgeführt wird; auch im Falle einer solchen Vereinbarung gelten jedoch die Bestimmungen der Art 21 bis 24 in der vorliegenden Fassung.

TABELLE DER VERFAHRENSKOSTEN

Einschreibegebühr EUR 2.000[1]

Verwaltungskosten[2]

---

1. Siehe Artikel 22 Abs. 1.
2. Siehe Artikel 24 Abs. 1.

Streitwert in EUR		Tarif in EUR
Von	*Bis*	
0	100.000	3.000
100.001	200.000	3.000 + 1,5 % des 100.000 übersteigenden Betrags
200.001	500.000	4.500 + 1,0 % des 200.000 übersteigenden Betrags
500.001	1.000.000	7.500 + 0,7 % des 500.000 übersteigenden Betrags
1.000.001	2.000.000	11.000 + 0,4 % des 1.000.000 übersteigenden Betrags
2.000.001	5.000.000	15.000 + 0,1 % des 2.000.000 übersteigenden Betrags
5.000.001	10.000.000	18.000 + 0,05 % des 5.000.000 übersteigenden Betrags
Über 10.000.000		20.500 + 0,01 % des 10.000.000 übersteigenden Betrags

Honorare für Einzelschiedsrichter[3]

Streitwert in EUR		Tarif in EUR
Von	*Bis*	
0	100.000	6 % mindestens 1.000
100.001	200.000	6.000 + 3 % des 100.000 übersteigenden Betrags
200.001	500.000	9.000 + 2,5 % des 200.000 übersteigenden Betrags
500.001	1.000.000	16.500 + 2 % des 500.000 übersteigenden Betrags
1.000.001	2.000.000	26.500 + 1 % des 1.000.000 übersteigenden Betrags
2.000.001	5.000.000	36.500 + 0,6 % des 2.000.000 übersteigenden Betrags
5.000.001	10.000.000	54.500 + 0,4 % des 5.000.000 übersteigenden Betrags
10.000.001	20.000.000	74.500 + 0,2 % des 10.000.000 übersteigenden Betrags
20.000.001	100.000.000	94.500 + 0,1 % des 20.000.000 übersteigenden Betrags
über 100.000.000		174.500 + 0,01 % des 100.000.000 übersteigenden Betrags

---

3. Siehe Artikel 24 Abs. 6.

Annex 3a

International Arbitral Centre of the Austrian Federal Economic Chamber Conciliation Rules 2006*

Article 1

At the request of a party, conciliation proceedings can be conducted where the Centre has jurisdiction as to the subject matter. They are not subject to the existence of a valid arbitration agreement.

Article 2

The request for the opening of conciliation proceedings shall be filed with the Secretariat of the Centre. The latter shall invite the opposing party or parties to reply within thirty days after service of the request. If a party refuses to participate in the conciliation proceedings or does not reply within that period, the attempted conciliation shall be considered as having failed.

Article 3

When the opposing party or parties accepts/accept recourse to conciliation, the Board shall nominate one of its members or another qualified person to act as conciliator. The latter shall study the documents submitted by the parties, shall convene them to a hearing and shall then submit proposals for the amicable settlement of the dispute.

---

*   Translation from the German original, which is the authentic text. Reprinted with kind permission of the Vienna International Arbitration Centre (VIAC).

Article 4

If agreement is reached, that shall be the subject of a record signed by the parties and the conciliator. If a valid arbitration agreement exists, the Board shall appoint the conciliator as sole arbitrator, provided that all parties so request. The sole arbitrator must authenticate the agreement in the form of a settlement or, if the parties so wish, make an award on the basis of the agreement.

Article 5

If no agreement is reached, the conciliation shall be considered as having failed. Declarations made by the parties in the course of conciliation proceedings shall not bind them in later arbitration proceedings. Except under the conditions set forth in Article 4 of these Rules, the conciliator may not be appointed as an arbitrator in subsequent arbitration proceedings.

Article 6

The costs of the conciliation proceedings and those of any activity of the conciliator under the conditions set forth in Article 4 shall be set by the Secretary General at an appropriate share of the charges applicable for arbitration proceedings on the basis of the corresponding amount in dispute (Article 36 paragraph 1 of the Rules of Arbitration). The same shall apply to the deposits against costs to be set by the Secretary General.

Annex 3b

Internationales Schiedsgericht der Wirtschaftskammer Österreich Schlichtungsordnung 2006*

Artikel 1

Auf Antrag einer Partei kann im Rahmen der sachlichen Zuständigkeit des Schiedsgerichts ein Schlichtungsverfahren durchgeführt werden. Hiefür ist das Vorliegen einer gültigen Schiedsvereinbarung nicht erforderlich.

Artikel 2

Der Antrag auf Einleitung des Schlichtungsverfahrens ist beim Sekretariat des Schiedsgerichts einzubringen. Dieses fordert die Gegenpartei(en) auf, sich innerhalb einer Frist von 30 Tagen ab Zustellung zu äußern. Weigert sich eine Partei, an dem Schlichtungsverfahren teilzunehmen oder erfolgt innerhalb der gesetzten Frist keine Äußerung, so ist die Schlichtung gescheitert.

Artikel 3

Bei Einverständnis der Gegenpartei(en) mit der Durchführung eines Schlichtungsverfahrens bestimmt das Präsidium eines seiner Mitglieder oder eine andere geeignete Person zum Schlichter. Dieser prüft die von den Parteien vorgelegten Unterlagen, lädt sie zur Erörterung des Streitfalles und unterbreitet sodann Vorschläge zu dessen gütlicher Beilegung.

---

* Mit freundlicher Genehmigung des Internationalen Schiedsgerichtes der Wirtschaftskammer Österreich abgedruckt.

Artikel 4

Wird Einigung erzielt, so ist das Ergebnis in einem Protokoll festzuhalten, das von den Parteien und dem Schlichter zu unterschreiben ist. Bei Vorliegen einer gülti-gen Schiedsvereinbarung ernennt das Präsidium den Schlichter, wenn alle Parteien dies beantragen, zum Einzelschiedsrichter. Dieser hat die Einigung in Form eines Schiedsvergleichs zu beurkunden oder, wenn die Parteien dies wünschen, aufgrund der Einigung einen Schiedsspruch zu erlassen.

Artikel 5

Kommt keine Einigung zustande, so ist die Schlichtung gescheitert. Im Rahmen eines Schlichtungs-verfahrens von den Parteien abgegebene Erklärungen sind für ein folgendes Schiedsverfahren nicht bindend. Der Schlichter darf – außer im Falle des Artikel 4 – in einem folgenden Schiedsverfahren nicht Schiedsrichter sein.

Artikel 6

Die Kosten des Schlichtungsverfahrens und jene eines allfälligen Tätigwerdens des Schlichters nach Artikel 4 werden vom Generalsekretär mit einem angemessenen Teil der für ein Schiedsverfahren mit dem entsprechenden Streitwert geltenden Kosten (Art 36 Abs 1 der Schiedsordnung) festgesetzt. Gleiches gilt für die vom Generalsekretär aufzuerlegenden Kostenvorschüsse.

Annex 4

Arbitrator's Declaration of Acceptance, Statement of Independence and Undertaking to Observe Rules on Costs*

Name: _____   Case No: _____

ACCEPTANCE / REJECTION

I accept the appointment to act as arbitrator in these proceedings pursuant the Rules of Arbitration and Conciliation of the International Arbitral Centre of the Austrian Federal Economic Chamber dated 1 July 2006 (the 'Vienna Rules') and I submit to the provisions of the Vienna Rules. I take note of the [Guidelines for Arbitrators] dated July 2006.

I decline to act as arbitrator in these proceedings,

DECLARATION OF INDEPENDENCE

There are no circumstances known to me which would justify a challenge to my acting as arbitrator in these proceedings pursuant to Article 16 of the Vienna Rules.

There are no circumstances known to me which would justify a challenge to my acting as arbitrator in these proceedings pursuant to Article 16 of the Vienna Rules. However, I would like to disclose the following circumstances, which, from the perspective of the parties, could possibly call my independence into question (add an additional sheet if necessary):

_____

_____

_____

---

* Reprinted with kind permission of the Vienna International Arbitration Centre (VIAC).

UNDERTAKING TO OBSERVE RULES ON COSTS

I acknowledge that determinations as to costs advances, arbitrators' fees and administrative costs in these proceedings shall be made exclusively by the Secretary of the International Arbitral Centre of the Austrian Federal Economic Chamber pursuant to Articles 34 and 36 of the Vienna Rules and I recognise that such determinations shall be binding on me.

I acknowledge that as arbitrator in these proceedings, I may not take any action entailing costs, such as the appointment of experts, before I make arrangements to cover the expected costs.

Place and Date: _____   Signature: _____

Annex 5

Guidelines for Arbitrators*

In order to facilitate the co-operation with the arbitral centre's secretariat, you are kindly requested to observe the following recommendations based upon the secretariat's administrative practice. The secretariat will be at your disposal for any further questions.

CASE ADMINISTRATION

The Secretary General is the head of the secretariat. Within the secretariat a case manager is responsible for handling the file. Her name will be announced in due time. The case manager will assist you whenever you need the secretariat's support in administrative matters.

If the arbitrator (arbitral tribunal) considers certain action entailing costs, such as the appointment of experts, interpreters or translators, making verbatim records of the proceedings, a visual inspection or relocation of the proceedings, to be necessary, he (it) must make arrangements for the expected costs to be covered,

The arbitrator (arbitral tribunal) may only undertake procedural steps if adequate cover for the expected costs exist.

The arbitral centre does not assume liability for costs resulting from arbitrators' dispositions without being covered by parties' advance payments.

---

* Reprinted with kind permission of the Vienna International Arbitration Centre (VIAC).

VENUE OF HEARINGS

Hearings with parties and meetings of arbitrators may be held in Vienna either at the seat of the arbitral centre at the Austrian Federal Economic Chamber or at any other place outside the Chamber.

If court rooms or meeting rooms are required at the Chamber's premises, you are kindly requested to contact the case manager before fixing time and date of the meeting. Furthermore, we would also require information regarding the number of participants, the expected duration, the requested technical equipment, such as projectors, microphones, and other administrative services, such as minuting, etc.

We will, of course, do our best to provide for the necessary infrastructure. We kindly ask for your understanding that we cannot assume any liability, if we are not informed of your requirements in due time.

COPIES OF PROCEDURAL ORDERS

The secretariat will keep shadow files for all cases. Presiding arbitrators and sole arbitrators thus are kindly requested to submit copies of all its procedural orders, in particular copies of all summons, to the secretariat (in addition, the secretariat will order the parties to send copies of all submissions together with all enclosures directly to the secretariat).

MODIFICATIONS OF THE AMOUNT IN DISPUTE

The costs of arbitration are fixed by the Secretary General according to the rates as of the schedule attached to the rules of arbitration. They depend upon the amount in dispute. The provisorial deposit will be fixed by the Secretary General and will be calculated upon the amount in dispute of the claim (or counter-claim) as it is at the time of the transfer of files to the arbitrator (arbitral tribunal).'

To enable us to prescribe additional advance payments to the parties, you are kindly requested to inform the secretariat of any modifications of the amount in dispute immediately. Failing such information, the increased amount in dispute will not be considered for the determination of arbitrators' fees.

DETERMINATION OF THE COSTS OF ARBITRATION

Pursuant to the rules of arbitration the costs of arbitration shall be determined exclusively by the Secretary General.

Thus, presiding arbitrators and sole arbitrators are kindly requested to inform the secretariat of all cash outlays for which they have not yet been reimbursed, to enable the Secretary General to determine the costs of arbitration.

You are also kindly requested to contact the secretariat if, according to a settlement before the arbitral tribunal, the parties shall share the procedural costs not perceptually, but in amounts expressed in figures; this is to enable the Secretary General to determine the costs and to inform the arbitral tribunal accordingly.

ARBITRAL AWARDS

Presiding arbitrators and sole arbitrators are kindly requested to provide the secretariat with a signed copy of the arbitral award.

To provide for a standardized form of the award, the necessary number of copies shall be printed on the arbitral centre's stationery. The copies will be sewn, sealed and signed by the Secretary General. The award will be circulated among arbitrators for signature. Eventually, the secretariat will serve the award on the parties.

REIMBURSEMENT FOR CASH OUTLAYS

The provisorial deposit paid by the parties includes an amount reserved for cash outlays. This amount has been calculated by the Secretary General and is based on the experience gained from previous cases.

Arbitrators' cash outlays, such as travel and accommodation costs, will be refunded upon receipt of invoices, tickets, hotel bills, etc. Refundable are first class train tickets and business class airline tickets. The per diem rate for non-resident arbitrators is EUR 100. If overnight-stays are necessary a maximum amount of EUR 350 (per diem and overnight-stay) will be refunded if hotel bills are produced and without bills a maximum amount of EUR 300 (per diem and overnight-stay) will be paid. Taxi (Cab) fares will be refunded upon receipt of the bills. If an arbitrator uses his/her own car, the official Austrian mileage allowance (currently EUR 0.38 per kilometre) shall apply, however not exceeding the business class airfare for the same distance.

In addition, the following maximum rates for expenses shall apply:

photocopies: EUR 0,30 (per copy)
fax messages: EUR 0,50 (for local facsimiles)
                EUR 1,00 (for all other facsimiles)

The above rates include all taxes and charges.

As a certain administrative infrastructure is a prerequisite for an arbitrator, no refund shall be made for expenses regarding the use of legal data services, for the purchase of legal literature, etc.

To make sure that sufficient funds for the reimbursement of cash outlays are provided for, we kindly request arbitrators to state their expenses immediately if higher cash outlays have accrued, e.g. after hearings.

Unless instructed otherwise, cash outlays will be refunded in EURO currency into the account designated by the arbitrator or by bank cheque (foreign arbitrators only).

ARBITRATORS FEES

We kindly draw your attention to Articles 34 and 36 of our rules of arbitration.

Arbitrators are free to agree upon a key for the splitting of arbitrators' fees. If you don't inform the secretariat otherwise (at latest together with the last unsettled account for cash outlays at termination of the proceedings) arbitrators' fees will be split in the proportion of 40% for the presiding arbitrator and of 30% for each co-arbitrator.

Annex 6

Account Details*

To the
International Arbitral Centre of the
Austrian Federal Economic Chamber
Wiedner Hauptstraße 63
A-1045 Vienna

Re.: Case no. _____   **vs.**   _____

Dear Sirs,

My fee is subject to V.A.T.:   Yes   No

The tax rate is: .... %

The transfer of my arbitrator's fee and cash outlays shall be made

to the bank account no. ....

in the name of...

with ....

bank code number ....

IBAN...

BIC...

SWIFT..

Date: _____   Signature: _____

---

*   Reprinted with kind permission of the Vienna International Arbitration Centre (VIAC).

Annex 7

Schiedsgerichtsordnung für die Ständigen Schiedsgerichte der Wirtschaftskammern 2006*

ALLGEMEINE BESTIMMUNGEN

Artikel 1 – Die Institution

1. Bei den Landeskammern können gemäß § 139 Abs. 1 WKG, BGBl I 103/1998, Ständige Schiedsgerichte (Landeskammer-Schiedsgerichte) zur Erledigung von Streitigkeiten über Angelegenheiten der Wirtschaft eingerichtet werden.

2. Die Ständigen Schiedsgerichte der Landeskammern, im folgenden 'Schiedsgericht' genannt, tragen Vorsorge für die schiedsgerichtliche Erledigung von Streitigkeiten, bei denen alle Vertragsparteien, welche die Schiedsvereinbarung geschlossen haben, zum Zeitpunkt des Abschlusses dieser Vereinbarung ihren Sitz oder gewöhnlichen Aufenthalt in Österreich hatten.

Artikel 2 – Zuständigkeit

1. Die Zuständigkeit eines Landeskammer-Schiedsgerichts ist gegeben, wenn eine Schiedsvereinbarung vorliegt. Diese muss entweder in einem von den Parteien unterzeichneten Schriftstück oder in zwischen ihnen gewechselten Schreiben, Telefaxen, E-Mails oder anderen Formen der Nachrichtenübermittlung enthalten

---

* Beschlossen vom erweiterten Präsidium der Wirtschaftskammer Österreich am 3. Mai 2006 mit Wirkung von 1. Juni 2006. Mit freundlicher Genehmigung des Internationalen Schiedsgerichtes der Wirtschaftskammer Österreich abgedruckt.

sein, die einen Nachweis der Vereinbarung sicherstellen. Nimmt ein diesen Formerfordernissen entsprechender Vertrag auf ein Schriftstück Bezug, das eine Schiedsvereinbarung enthält, so begründet dies eine Schiedsvereinbarung, wenn die Bezugnahme dergestalt ist, dass sie diese Schiedsvereinbarung zu einem Bestandteil des Vertrages macht.

2. Hatten zum Zeitpunkt des Vertragsabschlusses nicht alle Parteien ihren Sitz oder gewöhnlichen Aufenthalt in Österreich, so ist das *Internationale Schiedsgericht der Wirtschaftskammer Österreich*, Wien (Bundeskammer-Schiedsgericht), zuständig, welches das Verfahren am Sitz des namentlich bezeichneten Landeskammer-Schiedsgerichts durchführt.

3. Haben die Parteien, wenn alle ihren Sitz oder gewöhnlichen Aufenthalt in Österreich haben, die Zuständigkeit des Schiedsgerichts einer österreichischen Wirtschaftskammer vereinbart, ohne diese namentlich zu bezeichnen, so ist

  a. jenes Landeskammer-Schiedsgericht zuständig, in dessen örtlichem Zuständigkeitsbereich die beklagte Partei ihren Sitz oder gewöhnlichen Aufenthalt hat;
  b. wenn mehrere Beklagte vorhanden sind, die ihren Sitz oder gewöhnlichen Aufenthalt nicht in demselben Bundesland haben, jenes Landeskammer-Schiedsgericht zuständig, in dessen örtlichem Zuständigkeitsbereich die Mehrzahl der beklagten Parteien ihren Sitz oder gewöhnlichen Aufenthalt haben;
  c. in allen anderen Fällen das Ständige Schiedsgericht der Wirtschaftskammer Wien zuständig.

4. Haben die Parteien, wenn wenigstens eine von ihnen ihren Sitz oder gewöhnlichen Aufenthalt außerhalb Österreichs hat, die Zuständigkeit des Schiedsgerichts einer österreichischen Wirtschaftskammer vereinbart, ohne diese namentlich zu bezeichnen, so ist das Bundeskammer-Schiedsgericht zuständig.

Artikel 3 – Der Sekretär

1. Die administrativen Agenden des Landeskammer-Schiedsgerichts werden von der Kammerdirektion erledigt, die entweder für alle anfallenden Streitfälle, oder für jeden Fall gesondert, einen rechtskundigen Angestellten als Sekretär bestellt.

2. Der Sekretär leitet das Sekretariat und erledigt die administrativen Angelegenheiten des Schiedsgerichts, soweit sie nicht dem Präsidenten der Landeskammer vorbehalten sind.

3. Der Sekretär hat sein Amt nach bestem Wissen und Gewissen auszuüben und ist dabei an keine Weisungen gebunden. Er ist über alles, was ihm in dieser Funktion bekannt geworden ist, zur Verschwiegenheit verpflichtet.

Artikel 4 – Korrespondenzsprachen

1. Der Schriftverkehr der Parteien mit dem Sekretär und den Schiedsrichtern hat in deutscher Sprache zu erfolgen.

2. Die Verfahrenssprache vor dem Schiedsgericht ist Deutsch.

Artikel 5 – Die Schiedsrichter, Liste

1. Als Schiedsrichter können voll geschäftsfähige natürliche Personen tätig sein, die über besondere Kenntnisse und Erfahrungen auf rechtlichem, wirtschaftlichem oder technischem Gebiet verfügen. Die österreichische Staatsbürgerschaft ist nicht erforderlich. Mangels anderer Parteienvereinbarung müssen Einzelschiedsrichter und Vorsitzende von Schiedsrichtersenaten ein juristisches Hochschulstudium absolviert haben. Die Parteien können zusätzliche Qualifikationserfordernisse vereinbaren.

2. Zum Schiedsrichteramt geeignete Personen können in eine *Schiedsrichterliste* eingetragen werden, die von der Kammerdirektion geführt wird. Über die Aufnahme in oder Streichung von der Liste entscheidet der Präsident der Landeskammer ohne Angabe von Gründen.

3. Die Aufnahme in die Schiedsrichterliste ist nicht Voraussetzung für die Ausübung des Schiedsrichteramtes. Die Parteien, die von ihnen benannten Schiedsrichter und der Präsident der Landeskammer können, soweit ihnen nach dieser Schiedsgerichtsordnung das Recht der Benennung oder Ernennung von Schiedsrichtern zusteht, jede Person benennen oder ernennen, die die in Abs. 1 genannten Voraussetzungen erfüllt.

4. Die Schiedsrichter haben ihr Amt in voller Unabhängigkeit und Unparteilichkeit nach bestem Wissen und Gewissen auszuüben und sind dabei an keine Weisungen gebunden. Sie sind über alles, was ihnen in dieser Funktion bekannt geworden ist, zur Verschwiegenheit verpflichtet.

5. Will eine Person ein Schiedsrichteramt übernehmen, so hat sie alle Umstände offen zu legen, die Zweifel an ihrer Unparteilichkeit oder Unabhängigkeit wecken können oder der Parteienvereinbarung widersprechen. Ein Schiedsrichter hat vom Zeitpunkt seiner Bestellung an und während des Schiedsverfahrens den Parteien unverzüglich solche Umstände offen zu legen, wenn er sie ihnen nicht schon vorher mitgeteilt hat.

Artikel 6 – Haftung

Die Haftung der Schiedsrichter, des Sekretärs, des Präsidenten der Landeskammer und seiner Stellvertreter und der Landeskammern und ihrer Beschäftigten für jedwede Handlung oder Unterlassung im Zusammenhang mit dem Schiedsverfahren ist, soweit gesetzlich zulässig, ausgeschlossen.

DAS SCHIEDSVERFAHREN

Artikel 7 – Einleitung / Klage

1. Das Schiedsverfahren wird durch Einreichung einer Klage beim Sekretariat eingeleitet. Mit Einlangen der Klage im Sekretariat ist das Verfahren anhängig.

2. Für jeden Beklagten, jeden Schiedsrichter und das Sekretariat ist je eine Klagsausfertigung samt Beilagen einzureichen.

3. Die Klage hat zu enthalten:

   a. die Bezeichnung der Parteien und ihre Anschriften;
   b. ein bestimmtes Begehren, die tatsächlichen Angaben, auf die es sich stützt, und die beantragten Beweise;
   c. den Wert des Streitgegenstandes zum Zeitpunkt der Einbringung der Klage, wenn das Klagebegehren nicht ausschließlich auf eine bestimmte Geldsumme gerichtet ist;
   d. Angaben zur Zahl der Schiedsrichter gemäß Art 12;
   e. die Benennung eines Schiedsrichters mit Angabe der Anschrift, wenn eine Entscheidung durch drei Schiedsrichter (Schiedsrichtersenat) beantragt wird.

4. Der Klage ist eine Kopie jener Vereinbarung anzuschließen, aus der sich die Zuständigkeit des Schiedsgerichts ergibt. Falls diese Vereinbarung nicht in deutscher Sprache gehalten ist, ist eine Übersetzung anzuschließen.

5. Entspricht die Klage nicht dem Abs. 3 oder fehlen Ausfertigungen oder Beilagen, so fordert der Sekretär den Kläger zur Verbesserung oder Ergänzung auf. Der Kläger ist dabei zu informieren, dass bis zur Verbesserung oder Ergänzung der Klage diese nicht weiter behandelt wird.

6. Der Präsident der Landeskammer kann die Durchführung des Verfahrens verweigern, wenn die Parteien in der Schiedsvereinbarung zwar ein Landeskammer-Schiedsgericht bezeichnen, aber von dieser Schiedsordnung abweichende Vereinbarungen getroffen haben.

Artikel 8 – Klagebeantwortung

1. Ist die Klage nicht gemäß Art 7 Abs. 5 und 6 zu behandeln, so stellt der Sekretär der beklagten Partei die Klage sowie ein Exemplar der Schiedsordnung zu und fordert sie auf, binnen 30 Tagen eine Klagebeantwortung in der nach Art 7 Abs. 2 erforderlichen Zahl von Ausfertigungen einzubringen.

2. Die Klagebeantwortung hat zu enthalten:

   a. eine Äußerung zum Vorbringen in der Klage,
   b. die Benennung eines Schiedsrichters unter Angabe seiner Anschrift, wenn die Entscheidung durch einen Schiedsrichtersenat zu erfolgen hat oder in

der Schiedsvereinbarung die Entscheidung durch drei Schiedsrichter vereinbart ist.

Artikel 9 – Widerklage

1. Klagen der beklagten Partei gegen den Kläger, die auf einer Schiedsvereinbarung beruhen, die die Zuständigkeit des Landeskammer-Schiedsgerichts begründet, können bis zum Schluss des Beweisverfahrens als Widerklage erhoben werden.

2. Widerklagen sind beim Sekretariat des Schiedsgerichts unter Beachtung der Bestimmungen des Art 7 Abs. 2 einzubringen und von diesem nach Erlag des Kostenvorschusses dem Schiedsrichter (Schiedsrichtersenat) zur weiteren Behandlung zuzuleiten.

3. Beruht die als Widerklage bezeichnete Klage nicht auf einer Schiedsvereinbarung, die die Zuständigkeit des Landeskammer-Schiedsgerichts begründet, oder besteht keine Parteienidentität oder würde eine nach Übergabe der Unterlagen zum Fall an den Schiedsrichter (den Schiedsrichtersenat) eingebrachte Widerklage zu einer erheblichen Verzögerung des Hauptverfahrens führen, so hat der Schiedsrichter (Schiedsrichtersenat) diese Klage dem Sekretariat zur Behandlung in einem gesonderten Verfahren zurückzustellen.

4. Der Schiedsrichter (Schiedsrichtersenat) hat dem Widerbeklagten einer zulässigen Widerklage Gelegenheit zur Erstattung einer schriftlichen Klagebeantwortung zu geben und hiefür eine Frist zu setzen.

Artikel 10 – Fallübergabe an den Schiedsrichter (Schiedsrichtersenat)

Der Sekretär übersendet die Unterlagen zum Fall dem Schiedsrichter (Schiedsrichtersenat), sobald eine mangelfreie Klage (Widerklage) vorliegt, der Schiedsrichter (sämtliche Mitglieder des Schiedsrichtersenates) die Übernahme des Auftrages und ihre Unbefangenheit (Art 5 Abs. 5) auf einem Vordruck des Schiedsgerichts bestätigt haben und der Kostenvorschuss vollständig bezahlt ist (Art 32). Damit beginnt das Verfahren vor dem Schiedsrichter (Schiedsrichtersenat).

Artikel 11 – Fristen, Zustellungen und Mitteilungen

1. Eine Frist ist gewahrt, wenn das Schriftstück am letzten Tag der Frist in einer in Abs. 2 vorgesehenen Weise versendet wird. Fristen können vom Sekretär aus berücksichtigungswürdigen Gründen verlängert werden; nach der Übergabe der Unterlagen zum Fall an den Schiedsrichter (Schiedsrichtersenat) ist dafür der Schiedsrichter (Schiedsrichtersenat) zuständig (ausgenommen die Fälle des Art 32 Abs. 5 und 6).

2. Zustellungen gelten als ordnungsgemäß durchgeführt, wenn sie mittels einges-chriebenen Briefes, Kurierdienstes, Telefax oder durch andere Formen der Nachrichtenübermittlung, die einen Nachweis der Übermittlung sicherstellen, an jene Anschrift erfolgt sind, die der Adressat des Schriftstückes zuletzt dem Schiedsgericht bzw. dem Schiedsrichter (Schiedsrichtersenat) schriftlich als Zustelladresse bekannt gegeben hat, oder wenn das zuzustellende Schriftstück dem Adressaten ausgehändigt wurde.

3. Sobald eine Partei einen Vertreter bestellt hat, gelten Zustellungen an die zuletzt bekannt gegebene Anschrift dieses Vertreters als an die vertretene Partei erfolgt.

Artikel 12 – Benennung und Bestellung von Schiedsrichtern

1. Die Parteien können vereinbaren, ob ihr Rechtsstreit von einem Einzelschiedsrichter oder einem aus drei Schiedsrichtern zusammengesetzten Schiedsrichtersenat entschieden werden soll.

2. Mangels anderer Parteienvereinbarung sind Streitfälle bis zu einem Streitwert von €100.000, – von einem Einzelschiedsrichter zu entscheiden.

3. Liegt eine solche Vereinbarung nicht vor und erfolgt seitens einer der Parteien keine Benennung eines Schiedsrichters gemäß Art 7 Abs. 3 lit. E. und Art 8 Abs. 2 lit. b., beschließt, wenn der Streitwert €100.000, – übersteigt, der Präsident der Landeskammer, ob der Rechtsstreit von einem oder drei Schiedsrichtern zu entscheiden ist.

4. Ist der Rechtsstreit von einem Einzelschiedsrichter zu entscheiden, werden die Parteien aufgefordert, sich binnen zehn Tagen ab Zustellung der Aufforderung auf eine gemäß Art 5 geeignete Person zu einigen.

5. Der Vorsitzende eines Schiedsrichtersenats wird von den Schiedsrichtern, die von den Parteien benannt bzw. vom Präsidenten der Landeskammer bestellt wurden, gewählt.

6. Machen die Parteien von ihrem Recht, einen Schiedsrichter gemäß Art 7 Abs. 3 lit. E. oder Art 8 Abs. 2 lit. b. zu benennen, keinen Gebrauch oder einigen sich die von den Parteien benannten Schiedsrichter binnen zehn Tagen ab Zustellung der Aufforderung nicht auf einen Vorsitzenden, wird der Schiedsrichter durch den Präsidenten der Landeskammer bestellt.

Artikel 13 – Mehrparteienverfahren

1. Eine Schiedsklage gegen zwei oder mehrere Beklagte ist nur zulässig, sofern das Schiedsgericht für alle Beklagten zuständig ist, bei einem Verfahren vor einem Schiedsrichtersenat alle Kläger denselben Schiedsrichter benennen und

    a. die Klage nach dem anzuwendenden Recht zwingend gegen mehrere Personen zu richten ist, oder

b. die beklagten Parteien nach dem anzuwendenden Recht in Rechtsgemeinschaft stehen oder aus demselben tatsächlichen Grund oder solidarisch verpflichtet sind, oder

c. wenn die Zulässigkeit eines Mehrparteienverfahrens vereinbart ist, oder

d. alle Beklagten sich auf ein Mehrparteienverfahren einlassen und bei einem Verfahren vor einem Schiedsrichtersenat alle Beklagten denselben Schiedsrichter benennen.

2. Kann eine gegen mehrere Beklagte gerichtete Klage nicht allen Beklagten zugestellt werden, so ist das Schiedsverfahren auf Antrag des Klägers (der Kläger) gegen jene Beklagten, denen die Klage zugestellt wurde, fortzusetzen. Die Klage gegen jene Beklagten, denen die Klage nicht zugestellt werden konnte, ist in einem gesonderten Verfahren zu behandeln.

3. Ist ein Mehrparteienverfahren zulässig und liegt keine Vereinbarung über die Zahl der Schiedsrichter vor, so haben sich die Beklagten untereinander zu einigen, ob sie den Rechtsstreit von einem oder von drei Schiedsrichtern entschieden haben wollen, und, falls eine Entscheidung durch drei Schiedsrichter gewünscht wird, gemeinsam einen Schiedsrichter zu benennen.

4. Sollte im Falle des Abs. 3 eine Einigung der Beklagten über die Zahl der Schiedsrichter nicht vorliegen, so wird bei Streitwerten von mehr als EUR 100.000, – ein Schiedsrichtersenat tätig. Bei Streitwerten unter EUR 100.000, – entscheidet ein Einzelschiedrichter.

5. Ist der Rechtsstreit von einem Schiedsrichtersenat zu entscheiden, und haben die Beklagten keinen gemeinsamen Schiedsrichter benannt, so werden sie vom Sekretär aufgefordert, binnen 14 Tagen ab Zustellung der Aufforderung den Namen und die Adresse eines Schiedsrichters bekannt zugeben.

6. Erfolgt innerhalb der in Abs. 5 genannten Frist keine Benennung eines gemeinsamen Schiedsrichters, so bestellt der Präsident der Landeskammer den Schiedsrichter für die säumigen Beklagten.

7. In anderen als den in Abs. 1 genannten Fällen ist die Verbindung zweier oder mehrerer Rechtssachen nur zulässig, wenn in allen zu verbindenden Rechtssachen dieselben Schiedsrichter bestellt wurden und alle Parteien und der Schiedsrichter (Schiedsrichtersenat) zustimmen.

8. Die Entscheidung, ob ein Mehrparteienverfahren gem. Abs. 1 zulässig ist, trifft über Antrag einer der beklagten Parteien der Einzelschiedsrichter (Schiedsrichtersenat). Falls dieser die Zulässigkeit des Mehrparteienverfahrens verneint, tritt das Schiedsverfahren in jenen Stand zurück, den es vor der Bestellung des Einzelschiedsrichters (des Schiedsrichters für die beklagten Parteien) hatte.

Artikel 14 – Ablehnung von Schiedsrichtern

1. Ein Schiedsrichter kann nur abgelehnt werden, wenn Umstände vorliegen, die berechtigte Zweifel an seiner Unparteilichkeit oder Unabhängigkeit wecken, oder wenn er die zwischen den Parteien vereinbarten Voraussetzungen nicht erfüllt. Eine Partei kann einen Schiedsrichter, den sie bestellt hat oder an dessen Bestellung sie mitgewirkt hat, nur aus Gründen ablehnen, die ihr erst nach der Bestellung oder Mitwirkung daran bekannt geworden sind.

2. Ein Schiedsrichter kann insbesondere abgelehnt werden:

   a. in Sachen, in denen er selbst Partei ist oder zu einer der Parteien im Verhältnis eines Mitberechtigten, Mitverpflichteten oder Regresspflichtigen steht;

   b. in Sachen seines Ehegatten oder solcher Personen, welche mit ihm in gerader Linie verwandt oder verschwägert sind oder mit welchen er in der Seitenlinie bis zum vierten Grad verwandt oder bis zum zweiten Grad verschwägert ist;

   c. in Sachen seiner Wahl- oder Pflegeeltern, Wahl- oder Pflegekinder, seiner Mündel oder Pflegebefohlenen;

   d. in Sachen, in welchen er als Bevollmächtigter einer der Parteien bestellt war oder bestellt ist oder in welchen er als Zeuge oder Sachverständiger vernommen wurde oder werden soll.

3. Lehnt eine Partei einen Schiedsrichter ab, so hat sie dies unverzüglich unter Angabe des Ablehnungsgrundes dem Sekretariat bekannt zugeben.

4. Tritt der abgelehnte Schiedsrichter nicht zurück, so entscheidet über die Ablehnung das Präsidium des Internationalen Schiedsgerichts der Wirtschaftskammer Österreich aufgrund der Angaben im Ablehnungsantrag und der diesem beigeschlossenen Beweismittel. Der Sekretär hat vor der Entscheidung des Präsidiums die Stellungnahme des abgelehnten Schiedsrichters und der anderen Partei(en) einzuholen. Das Präsidium kann auch andere Personen zur Stellungnahme auffordern.

5. Ein abgelehnter Schiedsrichter kann das Verfahren ungeachtet des Ablehnungsantrages fortführen. Ein Schiedsspruch darf jedoch erst nach Rechtskraft der Entscheidung des Präsidiums gefällt werden.

Artikel 15 – Vorzeitige Beendigung des Schiedsrichteramtes

1. Das Amt eines Schiedsrichters endet, wenn

   a. die Parteien dies vereinbaren,

   b. der Schiedsrichter zurücktritt,

   c. einem Ablehnungsantrag stattgegeben wird,

   d. der Schiedsrichter vom Präsidium seines Amtes enthoben wird oder

   e. der Schiedsrichter verstirbt.

2. Jede Partei kann die Enthebung eines Schiedsrichters beantragen, wenn er nicht nur vorübergehend verhindert ist, sonst seiner Aufgabe nicht nachkommt oder das Verfahren ungebührlich verzögert. Der Antrag ist beim Sekretariat einzubringen. Über ihn entscheidet nach Anhörung des betroffenen Schiedsrichters das Präsidium des Internationalen Schiedsgerichts der Wirtschaftskammer Österreich. Ist offensichtlich, dass die Verhinderung nicht nur vorübergehend ist, so kann das Präsidium des Internationalen Schiedsgerichts der Wirtschaftskammer Österreich die Enthebung auch ohne Antrag einer Partei, jedoch nach Verständigung durch den Sekretär, verfügen.

Artikel 16 – Folgen der vorzeitigen Beendigung des Schiedsrichteramtes

1. Wurde der Ablehnung eines Schiedsrichters stattgegeben, wurde er seines Amtes enthoben, hat er dieses niedergelegt oder ist er gestorben, so werden,

    a. wenn es sich um einen Einzelschiedsrichter handelt, die Parteien

    b. wenn es sich um den Vorsitzenden eines Schiedsrichtersenates handelt, die verbleibenden Schiedsrichter und

    c. wenn es sich um einen von einer Partei benannten oder für eine Partei bestellten Schiedsrichter handelt, die Partei, die ihn benannt hat oder für die er bestellt wurde,

aufgefordert, binnen 14 Tagen einen Ersatzschiedsrichter – in den Fällen gemäß lit a. und b. einvernehmlich – zu benennen und dessen Namen und Adresse bekannt zugeben. Erfolgt innerhalb dieser Frist keine solche Mitteilung, so wird der Ersatzschiedsrichter vom Präsidenten der Landeskammer bestellt. Wurde auch ein benannter Ersatzschiedsrichter erfolgreich abgelehnt, so erlischt das Ersatzbenennungsrecht und der Ersatzschiedsrichter wird vom Präsidenten der Landeskammer bestellt.

2. Wurde der Ablehnung eines Schiedsrichters stattgegeben, wurde er seines Amtes enthoben, hat er dieses niedergelegt oder ist er gestorben, so bestimmt der neue Schiedsrichter (neu zusammengesetzte Schiedsrichtersenat) nach Einholung einer Stellungnahme der Parteien, ob und in welchem Umfang vorausgegangene Verfahrensabschnitte zu wiederholen sind.

3. Schiedsrichter, die vor Abschluss des Verfahrens ausscheiden, verlieren ihren Honoraranspruch gemäß Art. 34. Der Sekretär hat in diesen Fällen Barauslagen, die dem Schiedsrichter nachweislich entstanden sind, aus den von den Parteien erlegten Kostenvorschüssen zu ersetzen.

Artikel 17 – Bestreitung der Zuständigkeit

1. Die Einrede der Unzuständigkeit des Schiedsgerichts ist spätestens mit dem ersten Vorbringen zur Sache zu erheben. Von der Erhebung dieser Einrede ist eine Partei nicht dadurch ausgeschlossen, dass sie einen Schiedsrichter bestellt

oder an der Bestellung eines Schiedsrichters mitgewirkt hat. Die Einrede, eine Angelegenheit überschreite die Befugnisse des Schiedsgerichts, ist zu erheben, sobald diese zum Gegenstand eines Sachantrags erhoben wird. In beiden Fällen ist eine spätere Erhebung der Einrede ausgeschlossen; wird die Versäumung jedoch nach Überzeugung des Schiedsgerichts genügend entschuldigt, so kann die Einrede nachgeholt werden.

2. Das Schiedsgericht (Einzelschiedsrichter oder Senat) entscheidet selbst über seine Zuständigkeit. Die Entscheidung kann mit der Entscheidung in der Sache getroffen werden, aber auch vorher gesondert in einem eigenen Schiedsspruch.

Artikel 18 – Durchführung des Verfahrens

1. Im Rahmen dieser Schiedsordnung und der Vereinbarungen der Parteien kann der Schiedsrichter (Schiedsrichtersenat) das Schiedsverfahren nach freiem Ermessen durchführen; es gilt der Grundsatz der Gleichbehandlung der Parteien unter Wahrung des rechtlichen Gehörs in jedem Stadium des Verfahrens. Der Schiedsrichter (Schiedsrichtersenat) ist jedoch berechtigt, nach Vorankündigung Vorbringen und die Vorlage von Beweisurkunden nur bis zu einem bestimmten Verfahrensstadium für zulässig zu erklären.

2. Der Schiedsrichter (Schiedsrichtersenat) kann anordnen, dass von allen Urkunden, die nicht in deutscher Sprache abgefasst sind, eine Übersetzung vorgelegt werde.

3. Das Verfahren kann mündlich oder schriftlich durchgeführt werden. Eine mündliche Verhandlung hat auf Antrag einer Partei oder, wenn es der mit der Entscheidung betraute Schiedsrichter (Schiedsrichtersenat) für erforderlich hält, statt zu finden. Den Parteien ist jedenfalls Gelegenheit zu geben, von den Anträgen und den Vorbringen der anderen Parteien und dem Ergebnis der Beweisaufnahmen Kenntnis zu nehmen und sich dazu zu äußern.

4. Die mündliche Verhandlung wird von dem Schiedsrichter oder dem Vorsitzenden des Schiedsrichtersenates anberaumt. Sie ist nicht öffentlich. Über die Verhandlung ist zumindest ein Ergebnisprotokoll anzufertigen, das der Schiedsrichter bzw. der Vorsitzende des Schiedsrichtersenates zu unterfertigen hat.

5. Der Schiedsrichter (Schiedsrichtersenat) kann, wenn er es für erforderlich hält, von sich aus Beweise erheben, insbesondere Parteien oder Zeugen vernehmen, die Parteien zur Vorlage von Urkunden und Augenscheinsgegenständen auffordern und Sachverständige beiziehen. Sind mit der Beweisaufnahme, insbesondere mit der Sachverständigenbestellung Kosten verbunden, ist nach Art 33 vorzugehen.

6. Beteiligt sich eine Partei nicht am Verfahren, so ist mit der anderen Partei allein zu verhandeln.

7. Erlangt eine Partei Kenntnis von einer Verletzung einer Bestimmung dieser Schiedsordnung oder sonstiger auf das Verfahren anwendbarer Bestimmungen

durch den Schiedsrichter (Schiedsrichtersenat), so hat sie dies unverzüglich zu rügen, widrigenfalls die Partei den behaupteten Mangel nicht mehr geltend machen kann.

8. Sobald nach Überzeugung des Schiedsrichters (Schiedsrichtersenates) die Parteien dazu ausreichend Gelegenheit hatten, hat der Schiedsrichter (Schiedsrichtersenat) das Verfahren für geschlossen zu erklären. Der Schiedsrichter (Schiedsrichtersenat) kann das Verfahren jederzeit wieder eröffnen.

9. Nach Fallübergabe an den Schiedsrichter (Schiedsrichtersenat) erfolgt der Verkehr zwischen den Parteien und dem Schiedsrichter (Schiedsrichtersenat) direkt. Die Parteien und der Schiedsrichter (Schiedsrichtersenat) haben den Sekretär über alle verfahrensrelevanten Vorgänge nachrichtlich zu informieren.

Artikel 19 – Ablehnung von Sachverständigen

Auf die Ablehnung von Sachverständigen ist Art. 14 sinngemäß anzuwenden. Über die Ablehnung entscheidet jedoch der Schiedsrichter (Schiedsrichtersenat).

Artikel 20 – Sichernde und vorläufige Maßnahmen

1. Haben die Parteien nichts anderes vereinbart, so kann der Schiedsrichter (Schiedsrichtersenat) auf Antrag einer Partei vorläufige oder sichernde Maßnahmen gegen eine andere Partei nach deren Anhörung anordnen, die es in Bezug auf den Streitgegenstand für erforderlich hält, weil sonst die Durchsetzung des Anspruchs vereitelt oder erheblich erschwert werden würde oder ein unwiederbringlicher Schaden droht. Der Schiedsrichter (Schiedsrichtersenat) kann von jeder Partei im Zusammenhang mit einer solchen Maßnahme angemessene Sicherheit fordern. Die Parteien sind verpflichtet, solche Anordnungen zu befolgen, ungeachtet ob diese von staatlichen Gerichten vollstreckbar sind.

2. Maßnahmen nach Abs 1 sind schriftlich anzuordnen; jeder Partei ist ein unterfertigtes Exemplar der Anordnung zuzustellen. In Schiedsverfahren mit mehr als einem Schiedsrichter genügt die Unterschrift des Vorsitzenden oder im Falle seiner Verhinderung eines anderen Schiedsrichters, sofern der Vorsitzende oder der andere Schiedsrichter auf der Anordnung vermerkt, welches Hindernis der Unterfertigung entgegensteht.

3. Haben die Parteien nichts anderes vereinbart, sind die Maßnahmen zu begründen. Es sind der Tag, an dem sie erlassen wurden und der Sitz des Schiedsgerichts anzugeben. Die Maßnahme gilt als an diesem Tag und an diesem Ort erlassen.

4. Die Maßnahmen und die Urkunden über deren Zustellung sind gemeinschaftliche Urkunden der Parteien und des Schiedsrichters (Schiedsrichtersenates). Der Schiedsrichter (Schiedsrichtersenat) hat mit den Parteien eine allfällige Verwahrung der Maßnahme sowie der Urkunden über deren Zustellung zu erörtern.

5. Der Schiedsrichter (der Vorsitzende des Schiedsrichtersenates, im Falle seiner Verhinderung ein anderer Schiedsrichter) hat auf Verlangen einer Partei die Rechtskraft und Vollstreckbarkeit der Maßnahme auf einem Exemplar der Maßnahme zu bestätigen.

6. Diese Bestimmung hindert die Parteien nicht, bei jedem zuständigen staatlichen Organ sichernde und vorläufige Maßnahmen zu beantragen. Ein solcher Antrag an ein staatliches Organ auf Anordnung solcher Maßnahmen oder auf Vollziehung vom Schiedsrichter (Schiedsrichtersenat) angeordneter Maßnahmen stellt keinen Verstoß gegen oder Verzicht auf die Schiedsvereinbarung dar und lässt die dem Schiedsrichter (Schiedsrichtersenat) zustehenden Befugnisse unberührt. Ein solcher Antrag sowie alle durch das staatliche Organ angeordneten Maßnahmen sind unverzüglich dem Sekretariat und dem Schiedsrichter (Schiedsrichtersenat) mitzuteilen.

Artikel 21 – Bevollmächtigte

Die Parteien können sich im Verfahren vor dem Schiedsgericht durch bevollmächtigte Personen ihrer Wahl vertreten oder beraten lassen.

Artikel 22 – Anwendbares Recht, Billigkeit

1. Die Schiedsrichter haben mangels anderer Parteienvereinbarung österreichisches materielles Recht anzuwenden. Sie können das Verfahren unter Berücksichtigung der Bestimmungen dieser Schiedsgerichtsordnung und zusätzlicher Parteienvereinbarungen nach freiem Ermessen gestalten.

2. Der Schiedsrichter (Schiedsrichtersenat) hat nur dann nach Billigkeit zu entscheiden, wenn die Parteien ihn ausdrücklich dazu ermächtigt haben.

Artikel 23 – Beendigung

Das Verfahren wird beendet mit:

    a. der Erlassung des Schiedsspruches,
    b. dem Abschluss eines Schiedsvergleiches,
    c. Beschluss des Schiedsrichters (Schiedsrichtersenats), wenn
       aa. der Kläger seine Klage zurücknimmt, es sei denn, dass der Beklagte dem widerspricht und der Schiedsrichter (Schiedsrichtersenat) ein berechtigtes Interesse des Beklagten an der endgültigen Beilegung der Streitigkeit anerkennt;
       bb. die Parteien die Beendigung des Verfahrens vereinbaren und dies dem Schiedsrichter (Schiedsrichtersenat) mitteilen;
       cc. ihm die Fortsetzung des Verfahrens unmöglich geworden ist, insbesondere weil die bisher im Verfahren tätigen Parteien trotz schriftlicher Aufforderung des Schiedsrichters (Schiedsrichtersenats), mit welcher dieses auf die Möglichkeit einer Beendigung des Schiedsverfahrens hinweist, das Schiedsverfahren nicht weiter betreiben.

Artikel 24 – Entscheidungen im Schiedsrichtersenat

Im Schiedsrichtersenat ist jeder Schiedsspruch oder jede andere Entscheidung des Schiedsgerichts mit Stimmenmehrheit zu erlassen. Kommt keine Stimmenmehrheit zustande, so entscheidet der Vorsitzende des Schiedsgerichts allein. Soweit es sich um Verfahrensfragen handelt, kann der Vorsitzende des Schiedsgerichts, wenn das Schiedsgericht ihn dazu ermächtigt, vorbehaltlich einer etwaigen Änderung durch das Schiedsgericht, allein entscheiden.

Artikel 25 – Schiedsspruch

1. Schiedssprüche ergehen schriftlich. Sie sind zu begründen, sofern nicht alle Parteien entweder im Schiedsvertrag oder in der mündlichen Verhandlung auf eine Begründung verzichtet haben.

2. Im Schiedsspruch sind der Tag, an dem er erlassen wurde, und der Sitz des Schiedsgerichts anzugeben.

3. Schiedssprüche sind auf allen Ausfertigungen von den Schiedsrichtern zu unterschreiben. Die Unterschrift der Mehrheit der Schiedsrichter genügt, wenn im Schiedsspruch vermerkt wird, dass ein Schiedsrichter die Unterschrift verweigert oder dass der Unterzeichnung durch ihn ein Hindernis entgegensteht, das nicht in angemessener Frist überwunden werden kann. Wird der Schiedsspruch mit Stimmenmehrheit gefällt, so muss dies auf Wunsch des überstimmten Schiedsrichters im Schiedsspruch angeführt werden.

4. Schiedssprüche werden auf allen Ausfertigungen mit der Unterschrift des Sekretärs und dem Stempel des Schiedsgerichts versehen. Damit wird bestätigt, dass es sich um einen Schiedsspruch des Schiedsgerichts der jeweiligen Landeskammer handelt und dass dieser von dem (den) gemäß der Schiedsordnung gewählten oder bestellten Schiedsrichter(n) erlassen und unterschrieben wurde.

5. Der Schiedsspruch wird vom Sekretär den Parteien zugestellt. Den Parteien gegenüber werden Schiedssprüche mit der Zustellung der Ausfertigungen wirksam. Eine Ausfertigung des Schiedsspruches wird beim Sekretariat des Schiedsgerichts hinterlegt, wo auch die Urkunden über die Zustellung verwahrt werden.

6. Der Schiedsrichter (Vorsitzende des Schiedsrichtersenates, im Falle seiner Verhinderung ein anderer Schiedsrichter) hat auf Verlangen einer Partei Rechtskraft und Vollstreckbarkeit des Schiedsspruches auf sämtlichen Ausfertigungen zu bestätigen.

7. Die Erlassung von Teil- und Zwischenschiedssprüchen ist zulässig.

8. Durch die Vereinbarung dieser Schiedsordnung haben sich die Parteien verpflichtet, den Schiedsspruch zu erfüllen.

Artikel 26 – Vergleich

Jede der Parteien kann verlangen, dass der Inhalt eines von ihnen geschlossenen Vergleiches protokolliert oder darüber ein Schiedsspruch erlassen wird.

Artikel 27 – Berichtigung, Erläuterung und Ergänzung des Schiedsspruchs

1. Jede Partei kann innerhalb von 30 Tagen ab Empfang des Schiedsspruchs beim Sekretariat folgende Anträge an das Schiedsgericht einbringen:

    a. Rechen-, Schreib- und Druckfehler oder Fehler ähnlicher Art im Schiedsspruch zu berichtigen;

    b. bestimmte Teile des Schiedsspruchs zu erläutern, sofern die Parteien dies ausdrücklich vereinbart haben;

    c. einen ergänzenden Schiedsspruch über Ansprüche zu erlassen, die im Schiedsverfahren zwar geltend gemacht, im Schiedsspruch aber nicht erledigt worden sind.

2. Die Entscheidung über einen solchen Antrag trifft der Schiedsrichter (Schiedsrichtersenat) Vor der Entscheidung ist die andere Partei zu hören. Der Schiedsrichter (Schiedsrichtersenat) setzt hiefür eine Frist, die 14 Tage nicht überschreiten soll.

3. Die Berichtigungen gem. Abs. 1 lit. a kann der Schiedsrichter (Schiedsrichtersenat) binnen 30 Tagen ab dem Datum des Schiedsspruchs auch ohne Antrag vornehmen.

4. Artikel 25 Abs. 1 bis 6 sind auf die Berichtigung, Erläuterung oder Ergänzung des Schiedsspruchs anzuwenden. Die Berichtigung und die Erläuterung sind Bestandteile des Schiedsspruchs.

Artikel 28 – Veröffentlichung von Schiedssprüchen

Der Sekretär ist berechtigt, einen Schiedsspruch in anonymisierter Form zu veröffentlichen, wenn nicht zumindest eine Partei der Veröffentlichung innerhalb einer Frist von 30 Tagen ab Zustellung der Mitteilung der beabsichtigten Veröffentlichung an sie widerspricht.

Artikel 29 – Kostenbestimmung

Wird das Schiedsverfahren beendet, hat der Schiedsrichter (Schiedsrichtersenat) auf Antrag einer Partei im Schiedsspruch die vom Sekretär gemäß Art. 32 Abs. 1 bestimmten Schiedsgerichtskosten anzuführen, die Höhe der Parteienkosten (Anwaltshonorare etc.) zu bestimmen und festzulegen, wer die Verfahrenskosten zu tragen hat.

Artikel 30 – Verfahrenskosten

Die *Verfahrenskosten* setzen sich aus folgenden Teilen zusammen:

a. den Schiedsgerichtskosten, das sind die Auslagen des Schiedsgerichts (Verwaltungskosten), die Honorare der Schiedsrichter und die Barauslagen (wie Reise- und Aufenthaltskosten von Schiedsrichtern, Kosten der Zustellung, Mieten, Protokollierungskosten) und

b. den Parteienkosten, das sind die angemessenen Aufwendungen der Parteien für ihre Vertretung und andere Auslagen im Zusammenhang mit dem Schiedsverfahren, insbesondere die in Art 33 Abs. 1 genannten Kosten. Für Auslagen von Zeugen und deren Verdienstentgang wird kein Ersatz geleistet.

Artikel 31 – Einschreibegebühr

1. Die klagende (widerklagende) Partei hat mit Überreichung der Klage (Widerklage) eine Einschreibegebühr in der angegebenen Höhe auf das Konto des Schiedsgerichts spesenfrei zu entrichten. Diese Gebühr dient zur Deckung der Auslagen bis zur Übergabe der Unterlagen zum Fall an den Schiedsrichter (den Schiedsrichtersenat). Sollten höhere Auslagen entstehen, kann ein zusätzlicher Betrag vorgeschrieben werden.

2. Sind an dem Schiedsverfahren mehr als zwei Parteien beteiligt, so erhöht sich die Einschreibegebühr um 10% für jede zusätzliche Partei.

3. Die Einschreibegebühr wird nicht zurückgezahlt.

4. Die Behandlung der Klage (Widerklage) erfolgt erst nach vollständiger Bezahlung der Einschreibegebühr.

Artikel 32 – Schiedsgerichtskosten und Kostenvorschuss

1. Die Schiedsgerichtskosten werden vom Sekretär am Ende des Verfahrens bestimmt.

2. Der Sekretär setzt den Kostenvorschuss für die voraussichtlichen Schiedsgerichtskosten fest. Dieser ist vor Übergabe der Unterlagen zum Fall an den Schiedsrichter (Schiedsrichtersenat) von den Parteien binnen 14 Tagen ab Zustellung der Aufforderung zu gleichen Teilen zu erlegen.

3. Langt der auf den Kläger (Widerkläger) entfallende Anteil trotz Nachfristsetzung nicht innerhalb der gesetzten Frist ein, so teilt der Sekretär dies dem Beklagten (Widerbeklagten) mit und fordert ihn auf, binnen 14 Tagen den fehlenden Teil des Vorschusses zu bezahlen. Langt dieser Betrag nicht innerhalb der gesetzten Frist ein, so wird die Klage (Widerklage) nicht weiter behandelt. Der Sekretär hat dies den Parteien mitzuteilen.

4. Langt der auf den Beklagten (Widerbeklagten) entfallende Anteil nicht innerhalb der gesetzten Frist ein, so teilt der Sekretär dies dem Kläger (Widerkläger) mit und fordert ihn auf, den fehlenden Teil des Vorschusses binnen 14 Tagen ab Erhalt der Aufforderung zu bezahlen. Langt dieser Betrag nicht innerhalb der gesetzten Frist ein, so wird die Klage (Widerklage) nicht weiter behandelt. Der Sekretär hat dies den Parteien mitzuteilen.

5. Wird im Laufe des Verfahrens wegen einer Erhöhung des Streitwertes eine Erhöhung des Kostenvorschusses erforderlich, so ist analog den Bestimmungen der Abs. 2 bis 4 vorzugehen. Bis zum Erlag des zusätzlichen Vorschusses ist die Klagsausdehnung, die zur Erhöhung des Streitwertes geführt hat, im Schiedsverfahren nicht zu berücksichtigen.

6. Wird im Laufe des Verfahrens eine Erhöhung des Kostenvorschusses erforderlich, weil der bei seiner Festsetzung veranschlagte Betrag für Barauslagen nicht ausreicht, so ist analog den Bestimmungen der Abs. 2 bis 4 vorzugehen.

7. Die Schiedsrichterhonorare gemäß dieser Schiedsordnung enthalten keine Umsatzsteuer. Die Parteien sind verpflichtet, die Umsatzsteuer auf Schiedsrichterhonorare zu tragen. Die Erstattung der Umsatzsteuer ist jedoch ausschließlich eine Angelegenheit zwischen den Parteien und dem (den) Schiedsrichter(n).

Artikel 33 – Weitere Verfahrenskosten

1. Hält der Schiedsrichter (Schiedsrichtersenat) die Durchführung von bestimmten, mit Kosten verbundenen Verfahrensschritten, wie die Bestellung von Sachverständigen, Dolmetschern oder Übersetzern, die wörtliche Aufzeichnung des Verhandlungsverlaufes, die Abhaltung eines Lokalaugenscheines oder die Verlegung des Verhandlungsortes, für erforderlich, so hat er für die Deckung der voraussichtlichen Kosten zu sorgen und den Sekretär darüber zu informieren.

2. Der Schiedsrichter (Schiedsrichtersenat) darf Verfahrensschritte gemäß Abs. 1 erst vornehmen, wenn eine ausreichende Deckung für die voraussichtlichen Kosten vorhanden ist.

3. Der Schiedsrichter (Schiedsrichtersenat) entscheidet, welche Folgen sich aus der Nichtentrichtung eines etwa vorgeschriebenen Kostenvorschusses für das Verfahren ergeben.

4. Alle Aufträge im Zusammenhang mit den in Abs. 1 genannten Verfahrensschritten erteilt der Schiedsrichter (Schiedsrichtersenat) im Namen und auf Rechnung der Parteien.

Artikel 34 – Berechnung der Schiedsgerichtskosten

1. Die Verwaltungskosten des Schiedsgerichts und die Schiedsrichterhonorare werden aufgrund des Streitwertes nach der Tabelle der Verfahrenskosten (Anhang) berechnet. Bei vorzeitiger Beendigung des Verfahrens kann der

Sekretär die Schiedsrichterhonorare entsprechend dem Verfahrensstand nach billigem Ermessen ermäßigen.

2. Für Forderungen, die im Wege der Aufrechnung gegen Klagsansprüche eingewendet werden (Gegenforderungen) und die mit den Klagsansprüchen (Hauptforderungen) in keinem rechtlichen oder tatsächlichen Zusammenhang stehen, sind so wie für Widerklagen die gesondert berechneten Schiedsgerichtskosten zu entrichten. Der Schiedsrichter (Schiedsrichtersenat) entscheidet, ob ein rechtlicher oder tatsächlicher Zusammenhang besteht, oder nicht. Für die Vorschreibung von Kostenvorschüssen ist Art 32 sinngemäß anzuwenden. Bis zum vollständigen Erlag der zusätzlichen Kostenvorschüsse sind die Gegenforderungen im Verfahren über die Hauptforderungen nicht zu behandeln.

3. Bei Verfahren, die über eine Mehrzahl von einzelnen Ansprüchen geführt werden, die untereinander in keinem rechtlichen oder tatsächlichen Zusammenhang stehen, kann der Sekretär in jedem Stadium des Verfahrens für die Schiedsgerichtskosten eine gesonderte Berechnung nach den Streitwerten der einzelnen Ansprüche vornehmen. Der Schiedsrichter (Schiedsrichtersenat) entscheidet, ob ein rechtlicher oder tatsächlicher Zusammenhang besteht, oder nicht.

4. Der Sekretär kann den Streitwert abweichend von den Angaben der Parteien festlegen, wenn die Parteien nur einen Teilbetrag einer Forderung eingeklagt haben oder wenn ein nicht auf Zahlung von Geldbeträgen gerichtetes Begehren von den Parteien offenkundig unterbewertet wurde.

5. Die in der Tabelle für Schiedsrichterhonorare angegebenen Sätze sind die Honorare für Einzelschiedsrichter. Sie können, wenn der Rechtsstreit von einem Schiedsrichtersenat entschieden wird, bis auf das Dreifache erhöht werden.

6. Die in der Tabelle für Schiedsrichterhonorare angegebenen Sätze vergüten auch alle Teil- und Zwischenentscheidungen, wie z.B. Schiedssprüche über die Zuständigkeit, Teilschiedssprüche, Entscheidungen über die Ablehnung von Sachverständigen, Anordnung sichernder und vorläufiger Maßnahmen, sonstige Entscheidungen und verfahrensleitende Verfügungen.

7. Herabsetzungen des Streitwertes sind bei der Berechnung der Schiedsrichterhonorare und Verwaltungskosten nur zu berücksichtigen, wenn sie vor Übergabe der Unterlagen zum Fall an den Schiedsrichter (Schiedsrichtersenat) vorgenommen wurden.

8. Barauslagen werden nach dem tatsächlichen Aufwand bestimmt.

Artikel 35 – Sprachliche Gleichbehandlung

Soweit in dieser Schiedsordnung personenbezogene Bezeichnungen nur in männlicher Form angeführt sind, beziehen sie sich auf Frauen und Männer in gleicher Weise. Bei der Anwendung auf bestimmte Personen ist die jeweils geschlechtsspezifische Form zu verwenden.

Artikel 36 – Übergangsbestimmung

Diese Fassung der Schieds- und Schlichtungsordnung gilt für alle Verfahren, bei denen die Klage nach dem 30.6.2006 eingebracht wurde.

ANHANG

EINSCHREIBEGEBÜHR   €200,–

VERWALTUNGSKOSTEN*

Streitwert in €	*Verwaltungskosten*
bis €35.000,–	€700,–
über €35.000,– bis €70.000,–	2%
über €70.000,– bis €350.000,–	1%
über €350.000,– bis €700.000,–	0.4%
über €700.000,– bis €1,400.000,–	0.2%
über €1,400.000,–	0.02%

SCHIEDSRICHTERHONORARE

Streitwert in €	*Honorar*
bis €35.000,–	10%, mind. €1.000,–
über €35.000,– bis €70.000,–	5%
über €70.000,– bis €350.000,–	4%
über €350.000,– bis €700.000,–	3%
über €700.000,– bis €1,400.000,–	2%
über €1,400.000,– bis €3,500.000,–	1%
über €3,500.000,–	0.2%

Die Verwaltungskosten und die Schiedsrichterhonorare werden auf Grund der obigen Tabelle gestaffelt berechnet und zusammengezählt.

---

* Die angegebenen Sätze beinhalten ausschließlich die Verwaltungskosten des Schiedsgerichts, nicht aber die Barauslagen der Schiedsrichter, Sachverständigenhonorare und -auslagen, Dolmetsch- und Übersetzungskosten, Protokollführungskosten und sonstige Auslagen.

Annex 8a

Code of Civil Procedure, Fourth Section: Arbitration (Austrian Arbitration Act 2006)*

FIRST CHAPTER – GENERAL PROVISIONS

SCOPE OF APPLICATION

Section 577

1. The provisions of this section shall apply if the seat of the arbitral tribunal is within Austria.

2. Sections 578, 580, 583, 584, 585, 593 paragraph 3 to 6, Sections 602, 612 and 614 are also applicable if the seat of the arbitral tribunal is not within Austria or has not yet been determined.

---

* Translation (©2006 Christoph Liebscher) from the German original, which is the authentic text. Reprinted with kind permission from Christoph Liebscher, The Austrian Arbitration Act 2006: Text and Notes (Kluwer Law International, 2006), p. 1-54.

    Article VII Transitional Provisions of the *Schiedsrechts-Änderungsgesetz* 2006 (authors' own translation) reads as follows:

Effective date, transitional and executive provisions:

(1) This Act shall come into effect on 1 July 2006.

(2) The provisions that have previously been in force shall apply to arbitral proceedings which have been commenced prior to 1 July 2006.

(3) The validity of arbitration agreements that have been concluded prior to 1 July 2006 shall be governed by the provisions previously in force.

(4) The federal minister of justice shall be competent for the enforcement of this Act.

3. As long as the seat of the arbitral tribunal has not yet been determined, Austrian courts shall be competent for those court functions specified in the third chapter if one of the parties has its seat, domicile or habitual residence within Austria.

4. The provisions of this section shall not be applicable to institutions according to the Association Act for the conciliation of disputes arising out of the association relationship.

COURT INTERVENTION

Section 578

The court may only become active in matters governed by this section if this section provides therefor.

WAIVER OF RIGHT TO OBJECT

Section 579

If the arbitral tribunal has not complied with a procedural provision of this section from which the parties may derogate, or with an agreed procedural requirement of the arbitral proceedings, a party shall be deemed to have waived its right to object if it does not object without undue delay after learning of the defect, or within the designated time limit.

RECEIPT OF WRITTEN COMMUNICATIONS

Section 580

1. Unless otherwise agreed by the parties, any written communication is deemed to have been received on the day upon which it is personally delivered to the addressee or to an authorized recipient or, if this was not possible, upon which it is delivered to the registered office, place of residence or habitual residence of the recipient.

2. If the addressee has knowledge of the arbitral proceedings, and if, despite reasonable investigation, his residence or the residence of an authorized recipient remains unknown, then any written communication is deemed to have been received, on the day on which a proper delivery was verifiably attempted at a location that was specified at the conclusion of the arbitration agreement or that the addressee subsequently gave to the other party or to the arbitral tribunal as the address and that has not yet been revoked by giving a new address.

3. Paragraphs 1 and 2 shall not apply to communications in court proceedings.

SECOND CHAPTER – ARBITRATION AGREEMENT

DEFINITION

Section 581

1. An arbitration agreement is an agreement by the parties to submit to arbitration all or certain disputes which have arisen or which may arise between them in respect of a defined legal relationship, whether contractual or not. The arbitration agreement may be concluded in the form of a separate agreement or as a clause within a contract.

2. The provisions of this section shall also apply accordingly to arbitral tribunals that are, in a manner permitted by law, set up by testamentary disposition or by other legal transactions that are not based on agreements of the parties, or that are provided for by articles of incorporation.

ARBITRABILITY

Section 582

1. Any claim involving an economic interest that lies within the jurisdiction of the courts of law can be the subject of an arbitration agreement. An arbitration agreement on claims which do not involve an economic interest shall be legally effective insofar as the parties are capable of concluding a settlement on the issue in dispute.

2. Claims involving family law, as well as all claims arising out of contracts that are even only partially subject to the Landlord and Tenant Act or the Limited-Profit Housing Act, including disputes about the conclusion, existence, termination, and legal classification of such contracts, and all claims involving condominium law, cannot be the subject of an arbitration agreement. Statutory provisions outside this section by virtue of which certain disputes may not be submitted to arbitration, or may be submitted to arbitration only under certain conditions, shall remain unaffected.

FORM OF THE ARBITRATION AGREEMENT

Section 583

1. The arbitration agreement must be contained either in a document signed by the parties or in letters, faxes, e-mails or other forms of communication exchanged between them that provide proof of the existence of the agreement.

2. When an agreement which fulfils the form requirements of paragraph 1 refers to a document which contains an arbitration agreement, it shall constitute an arbitration agreement if the reference is such that it makes the arbitration agreement part of the contract.

3. A defect of form of the arbitration agreement shall be cured in the arbitration proceedings by entering an appearance in the case, if a notification of the defect is not made earlier or at the latest together with entering an appearance.

ARBITRATION AGREEMENT AND SUBSTANTIVE CLAIM BEFORE COURT

Section 584

1. A court before which an action is brought in a matter which is the subject of an arbitration agreement shall reject the claim, provided that the respondent does not submit a pleading in the matter or does not orally plead before court without making an objection in this respect. This shall not apply if the court establishes that the arbitration agreement does not exist or is incapable of being performed. If such proceedings are still pending at a court, arbitration proceedings may nevertheless be commenced or continued and an award may be made.

2. Where an arbitral tribunal denies its competence for the matter in dispute on the grounds that there is no arbitration agreement for this matter or that such agreement cannot be executed, the court may not reject an action on this matter on the grounds that an arbitral tribunal is competent in the matter. The right of the claimant to make an application under Section 611 of this act to set aside the decision with which the arbitral tribunal denied its competence shall expire with the bringing of an action in court.

3. When an arbitration procedure is pending, no other legal dispute may be carried out before a court or an arbitral tribunal on the asserted claim. Any action brought on the grounds of the same claim is to be rejected. This shall not apply if an objection to the jurisdiction of the arbitral tribunal was raised to the arbitral tribunal at the latest together with entering an appearance in the case and a decision of the arbitral tribunal on this matter cannot be obtained within a reasonable period of time.

4. When an action is rejected by a court of law due to the jurisdiction of an arbitral tribunal or by an arbitral tribunal due to the jurisdiction of a court of law or of another arbitral tribunal, or when, in proceedings for the setting aside of an award, an award is set aside due to the lack of jurisdiction of the arbitral tribunal, the proceedings shall be deemed to be properly continued if the action is immediately brought before the court of law or arbitral tribunal.

5. A party that has invoked the existence of an arbitration agreement at an earlier stage in the proceedings can at a later stage not claim that such agreement does not exist, unless the relevant circumstances have since changed.

ARBITRATION AGREEMENT AND INTERIM MEASURES BY COURT

Section 585

It is not incompatible with an arbitration agreement for a party to request from a court, before or during arbitral proceedings, an interim measure of protection and for a court to grant such measure.

THIRD CHAPTER – FORMATION OF ARBITRAL TRIBUNAL

COMPOSITION OF ARBITRAL TRIBUNAL

Section 586

1. The parties are free to determine the number of arbitrators. However, if the parties have agreed on an even number of arbitrators, then these shall appoint a further person to be the presiding arbitrator.

2. Unless the parties have determined otherwise, three arbitrators are to be appointed.

APPOINTMENT OF ARBITRATORS

Section 587

1. The parties are free to agree on a procedure of appointing the arbitrator(s).

2. Failing an agreement on a procedure of appointing the arbitrator(s), the following shall apply:

   (1) In an arbitration with a sole arbitrator, if the parties are unable to agree on the arbitrator within four weeks of receipt of a written request to do so from one party to the other, the arbitrator shall be appointed, upon request of a party, by the court.
   (2) In an arbitration with three arbitrators, each party shall appoint one arbitrator. The two arbitrators thus appointed shall appoint the third arbitrator who shall preside over the arbitral tribunal.
   (3) In an arbitration with more than three arbitrators, each party shall appoint the same number of arbitrators, who shall appoint a further arbitrator, who shall preside over the arbitral tribunal.
   (4) If a party fails to appoint an arbitrator within four weeks of receipt of a written request to do so from the other party, or if the parties do not receive the notification regarding the third arbitrator appointed by the arbitrators within four weeks of their appointment, the appointment shall be made, upon the request of a party, by the court.

(5) A party is bound to its appointment of an arbitrator as soon as the other party has received the written notice of the appointment.

3. If, under an appointment procedure agreed upon by the parties,

(1) a party fails to act as required under such procedure or

(2) the parties or the arbitrators are unable to reach an agreement in compliance with such procedure or

(3) a third party fails to perform any function entrusted to it under such procedure within three months of receipt of a written notification to that respect,

then any party may request the court to take the necessary measure, unless the agreement on the appointment procedure provides other means for securing the appointment.

4. The written request for the appointment of an arbitrator must also state which claim is being asserted and which arbitration agreement the party is invoking.

5. If several parties who together must appoint one or more arbitrators cannot agree on the appointment(s) within four weeks of receipt of a written request to do so, then the arbitrator(s) shall be appointed by a court in response to a request by a party, unless the agreement on the appointment procedure provides other means for securing the appointment.

6. The arbitrator(s) shall also be appointed by a court upon the request of a party if its or their appointment cannot be made for reasons other than those specified in the previous paragraphs within four weeks of receipt of a written request to do so by one party to the other, or also if the appointment procedure for securing the appointment does not result in an appointment within an appropriate period of time.

7. If the appointment takes place prior to the first instance decision and a party proves this, then the application is to be dismissed.

8. The court, in appointing an arbitrator, shall have due regard to any qualifications required of the arbitrator by the agreement of the parties and to such considerations as are likely to secure the appointment of an independent and impartial arbitrator.

9. A decision with which an arbitrator is appointed shall not be subject to appeal.

GROUNDS FOR CHALLENGE

Section 588

1. When a person is approached in connection with a possible appointment as an arbitrator, this person shall disclose any circumstances likely to give rise to doubts as to their impartiality or independence, or that are in conflict with the agreement of the parties. An arbitrator, from the time of the appointment and throughout the

arbitral proceedings, shall without delay disclose any such circumstances to the parties unless the arbitrator has already informed them.

2. An arbitrator may be challenged only if circumstances exist that give rise to justifiable doubts as to his impartiality or independence, or if he does not possess qualifications agreed to by the parties. A party may challenge an arbitrator appointed by it, or in whose appointment it has participated, only for reasons of which it becomes aware after the appointment or its participation therein.

CHALLENGE PROCEDURE

Section 589

1. The parties are free to agree on a procedure for challenging an arbitrator, subject to the provisions of paragraph 3 of this section.

2. Failing such agreement, a party who challenges an arbitrator shall, within four weeks of becoming aware of the composition of the arbitral tribunal or after becoming aware of any circumstance referred to in Section 588, paragraph 2 of this act, send a written statement of the reasons for the challenge to the arbitral tribunal. Unless the challenged arbitrator withdraws from office or the other party agrees to the challenge, the arbitral tribunal, including the challenged arbitrator, shall decide on the challenge.

3. If a challenge under any procedure agreed upon by the parties or under the procedure of paragraph 2 of this section is not successful, the challenging party may, within four weeks of having received the decision rejecting the challenge, request the court to decide on the challenge. This decision shall not be subject to appeal. While such a request is pending, the arbitral tribunal, including the challenged arbitrator, may continue the arbitral proceedings and make an award.

EARLY TERMINATION OF THE ARBITRATOR'S MANDATE

Section 590

1. The mandate of an arbitrator terminates when the parties agree on the termination or when the arbitrator withdraws from office. Subject to the provisions of paragraph 2 of this section, the parties can agree on a procedure for the termination of the arbitrator mandate.

2. Any party may request the court to decide on the termination of the mandate when an arbitrator either becomes unable to perform his functions or fails to act within a reasonable period of time and

    (1) the arbitrator does not withdraw from office,
    (2) the parties cannot agree on his termination or

(3) the procedure agreed upon by the parties does not result in the termination of the arbitrator's mandate.

This decision shall not be subject to appeal.

3. If an arbitrator withdraws from office under paragraph 1 of this section or under Section 589, paragraph 2 of this act, or if a party agrees to the termination of the mandate of an arbitrator, this does not imply acceptance of the validity of any ground referred to in paragraph 2 of this section or in Section 588, paragraph 2 of this act.

APPOINTMENT OF SUBSTITUTE ARBITRATOR

Section 591

1. Where the mandate of an arbitrator terminates early, a substitute arbitrator shall be appointed according to the rules that were applicable to the appointment of the arbitrator being replaced.

2. Unless otherwise agreed by the parties, the arbitral tribunal may continue the proceedings using the results of the proceedings up to that point, in particular the record of the proceedings as well as any other existing documentation.

FOURTH CHAPTER – JURISDICTION OF ARBITRAL TRIBUNAL

COMPETENCE OF ARBITRAL TRIBUNAL TO RULE ON ITS OWN JURISDICTION

Section 592

1. The arbitral tribunal shall rule on its own jurisdiction. The ruling can be made together with the ruling on the case or it can be made in a separate award.

2. An objection to the jurisdiction of the arbitral tribunal shall be raised no later than the first pleading in the matter. A party is not precluded from raising such objection by the fact that it has appointed, or participated in the appointment of, an arbitrator. An objection that the arbitral tribunal is exceeding the scope of its authority shall be raised as soon as the matter alleged to be beyond the scope of its authority is raised during the arbitral proceedings. In either case, a later objection shall not be permitted; however, if the arbitral tribunal considers the delay justified, the objection can still be raised by the party.

3. Even while a request for the setting aside of an award with which the arbitral tribunal accepted its jurisdiction is still pending with the court, the arbitral tribunal may preliminarily continue the arbitral proceedings and even render an award.

ORDERING OF PROVISIONAL OR PROTECTIVE MEASURES

Section 593

1. Unless otherwise agreed by the parties, the arbitral tribunal may, at the request of a party, order such provisional or protective measures against another party, after hearing such party, as the arbitral tribunal may consider necessary in respect of the subject matter of the dispute, as otherwise the enforcement of the claim would be frustrated or considerably impeded or there is a danger that irreparable damage will occur. The arbitral tribunal may require any party to provide appropriate security in connection with such measure.

2. Measures referred to in paragraph 1 are to be ordered in writing; each party shall be served a signed copy of the order. In arbitral proceedings with more than one arbitrator the signature of the presiding arbitrator or, in case he is hindered, the signature of another arbitrator shall suffice, provided that the presiding arbitrator or another arbitrator records on the order the reason preventing the signature. Section 606, paragraphs 2, 3, 5 and 6 of this act shall apply accordingly.

3. Upon the application of a party, the district court where the opponent of the endangered party has its seat, domicile or habitual place of residence in Austria at the time of the first filing of the plea — or otherwise the district court in whose area the measure of enforcement for the preliminary injunction shall take place — shall enforce such measure. Where the measure provides for a measure of protection unknown to Austrian law, the court can, upon application and hearing of the opposing party, execute the measure of protection of Austrian law that comes closest to the measure of the arbitral tribunal. In this case, the court, upon request, can also modify the measure of the arbitral tribunal in order to safeguard the realization of its purpose.

4. The court shall refuse to enforce a measure under paragraph 1 of this section if

   (1) the seat of the arbitral tribunal is in Austria and the measure suffers from a defect which would constitute a reason for setting aside an Austrian award under Sections 611, paragraph 2, 617, paragraphs 5 and 7, or 618 of this act;
   (2) the seat of the arbitral tribunal is not in Austria and the measure suffers from a defect which would constitute cause for refusal of recognition or enforcement in the case of a foreign award;
   (3) the enforcement of the measure would be incompatible with an Austrian court measure which was either applied for or made earlier, or with a foreign court measure which was made earlier and which is to be recognised;
   (4) the measure provides for a measure of protection unknown in Austrian law and no appropriate measure of protection as provided by Austrian law was applied for.

5. The court may hear the opposing party prior to making its decision on the enforcement of the measure under paragraph 1 of this section. If the opposing party was not heard prior to the making of the decision, it can lodge an objection against the order of enforcement within the meaning of Section 397 of the

Enforcement Act. In both cases, the opposing party may merely argue that there is a ground for refusing the enforcement as referred to in paragraph 4 of this section. In these proceedings, the court is not competent to rule on claims for damages under Section 394 of the Enforcement Act.

6. Upon request the court shall set aside the enforcement if

(1) the term of the measure as set by the arbitral tribunal has expired;
(2) the arbitral tribunal has limited the scope of or set aside the measure;
(3) a case as referred to in Section 399, paragraph 1, numbers 1-4 of the Enforcement Act is present; provided that such a circumstance has not already been unsuccessfully asserted before the arbitral tribunal and there are no obstacles to the recognition (Paragraph 4) of the respective decision of the arbitral tribunal;
(4) a security as referred to in paragraph 1 of this section was provided, which makes the enforcement unnecessary.

FIFTH CHAPTER – CONDUCT OF ARBITRAL PROCEEDINGS

GENERAL PRINCIPLES

Section 594

1. Subject to the mandatory provisions of this section, the parties are free to determine the rules of procedure. The parties may thereby refer to other rules of procedure. Failing such agreement, the arbitral tribunal shall, subject to the provisions of this chapter, conduct the arbitration in the manner that it considers appropriate.

2. The parties shall be treated fairly. Each party has the right to be heard.

3. The parties may be represented or advised by persons of their own choosing. This right cannot be excluded or restricted.

4. An arbitrator who does not at all or who does not timely fulfil any obligation resulting from the acceptance of his appointment shall be liable to the parties for all damage caused by his culpable refusal or delay.

SEAT OF THE ARBITRAL TRIBUNAL

Section 595

1. The parties are free to agree on the seat of the arbitral tribunal. They may also allow the seat of the arbitral tribunal to be determined by an arbitral institution. Failing such agreement, the seat of the arbitral tribunal shall be determined by the arbitral tribunal having regard to the circumstances of the case, including the convenience of the seat for the parties.

2. Notwithstanding the provisions of paragraph 1 of this section, the arbitral tribunal may, unless otherwise agreed by the parties, meet at any place it considers appropriate for conducting proceedings, especially for deliberation, making decisions, conducting oral hearings and the taking of evidence.

LANGUAGE OF PROCEEDINGS

Section 596

The parties are free to agree on the language or languages to be used in the arbitral proceedings. Failing such agreement, the arbitral tribunal shall determine the language or languages to be used in the proceedings.

STATEMENTS OF CLAIM AND DEFENCE

Section 597

1. Within the period of time agreed by the parties or determined by the arbitral tribunal, the claimant shall state its claim and the facts supporting its claim, and the respondent shall respond thereto. The parties may submit with their statements all documents they consider to be relevant or may add a reference to the documents or other evidence they will submit.

2. Unless otherwise agreed by the parties, either party may amend or supplement its claim or pleadings during the course of the arbitral proceedings, unless the arbitral tribunal considers this inappropriate due to delay.

ORAL HEARINGS AND WRITTEN PROCEEDINGS

Section 598

Unless otherwise agreed by the parties, the arbitral tribunal shall decide whether to hold oral hearings, or whether the proceedings shall be conducted in writing. If the parties have not excluded an oral hearing, the arbitral tribunal shall, upon the motion of a party, hold an oral hearing at an appropriate stage of the proceedings.

PROCEEDINGS AND TAKING OF EVIDENCE

Section 599

1. The arbitral tribunal is authorized to decide upon the permissibility of the taking of evidence, to conduct such taking of evidence, and to freely evaluate such evidence.

2. The parties are to be timely informed of every hearing and of every meeting of the arbitral tribunal for the purpose of taking of evidence.

3. All written submissions, written documents and other communications which are submitted to the arbitral tribunal by a party are to be brought to the attention of the other party. Expert opinions and other evidence to which the arbitral tribunal may refer in its decision are to be brought to the attention of both parties.

FAILURE TO PERFORM PROCEDURAL ACTS

Section 600

1. If the claimant fails to file his statement of claim in accordance with Section 597, paragraph 1 of this act, the arbitral tribunal shall terminate the proceedings.

2. If the respondent fails to respond in accordance with Section 597, paragraph 1 of this act during the agreed or determined period of time, the arbitral tribunal shall, unless the parties have agreed otherwise, continue the proceedings without treating such failure in itself as an admission of the claimant's allegations. The same shall apply where a party has failed to perform any other procedural act. The arbitral tribunal may continue the proceedings and may make an award on the basis of the evidence taken. If a failure to perform a procedural act has been excused to the arbitral tribunal's satisfaction, it may then be performed by the party.

EXPERT APPOINTED BY ARBITRAL TRIBUNAL

Section 601

1. Unless otherwise agreed by the parties, the arbitral tribunal may

    (1) appoint one or more experts to report to it on specific issues to be determined by the arbitral tribunal;
    (2) require the parties to give the expert any relevant information or to produce, or to provide access to, any relevant documents or goods or other property for inspection by the expert.

2. Unless otherwise agreed by the parties, if a party so requests or if the arbitral tribunal considers it necessary, the expert shall, after delivering his report, participate in an oral hearing. In the hearing, the parties shall have the opportunity to put questions to him and to present their own expert witnesses in order to testify on the points at issue.

3. Sections 588 and 589, paragraphs 1 and 2 of this act shall apply accordingly to the expert appointed by the arbitral tribunal.

4. Unless otherwise agreed by the parties, each party has the right to produce reports from its own experts. Paragraph 2 of this section shall apply accordingly.

COURT ASSISTANCE

Section 602

The arbitral tribunal, arbitrators who have been accordingly authorized by the arbitral tribunal, or a party with the approval of the arbitral tribunal, may request from a court the performance of judicial acts for which the arbitral tribunal has no authorization. The judicial assistance may also consist of the court requesting a foreign court or a public agency to conduct such acts. Section 37, paragraphs 2 to 5 and Sections 38, 39 and 40 of the Judicature Act shall apply accordingly, provided that the arbitral tribunal and the parties to the arbitral proceedings shall have the right to appeal in accordance with Section 40 of the Judicature Act. The arbitral tribunal or an arbitrator mandated by the arbitral tribunal and the parties may participate in the taking of evidence by the court and may pose questions. Section 289 of this act shall apply accordingly.

SIXTH CHAPTER – AWARD AND TERMINATION OF PROCEEDINGS

LAW APPLICABLE TO SUBSTANCE OF DISPUTE

Section 603

1. The arbitral tribunal shall decide the dispute in accordance with the rules of law that have been chosen by the parties as applicable. Any designation of the law or legal system of a given state shall be construed, unless the parties have expressly agreed otherwise, as directly referring to the substantive law of that state and not to its conflict of laws rules.

2. Failing any designation by the parties, the arbitral tribunal shall apply the law that it considers appropriate.

3. The arbitral tribunal shall decide ex aequo et bono or as amiable compositeur only if the parties have expressly authorized it to do so.

DECISION MAKING BY PANEL OF ARBITRATORS

Section 604

Unless otherwise agreed by the parties, the following shall apply:

    (1) In arbitral proceedings with more than one arbitrator, any decision of the arbitral tribunal shall be made by a majority of all its members. Questions of procedure may be decided by the presiding arbitrator alone if so authorized by the parties or by all members of the arbitral tribunal.

(2) Where one or more arbitrators do not participate in a vote without justified reason, the other arbitrators may decide without them. In this case as well, the necessary majority of votes is to be calculated by the total of all participating and non-participating arbitrators. In the case of a vote on an award, the parties must receive prior information on the intention to proceed in this manner. With regard to other decisions, the parties are to be subsequently informed about the failure to participate in the voting.

SETTLEMENT

Section 605

If, during arbitral proceedings, the parties settle the dispute, and if the parties are able to agree on a settlement of the matter in dispute, they can apply for

(1) the arbitral tribunal to draw up a record of the settlement, provided that the contents of the settlement are not in conflict with the basic values of the Austrian legal system (ordre public); it shall be sufficient if the record of the settlement is signed by the parties and the presiding arbitrator;

(2) the arbitral tribunal to record the settlement in the form of an award on agreed terms, provided that the contents of the settlement are not in conflict with the basic values of the Austrian legal system (ordre public). Such an award is to be made in accordance with Section 606 of this act and has the same effect as any other award on the merits of the case.

AWARD

Section 606

1. The award shall be made in writing and shall be signed by the arbitrator or arbitrators. Unless otherwise agreed by the parties, in arbitral proceedings with more than one arbitrator, the signatures of the majority of all members of the arbitral tribunal shall suffice, provided that the reason for any omitted signature is stated on the award by the presiding or another arbitrator.

2. Unless the parties have agreed otherwise, the award shall state the reasons upon which it is based.

3. The award shall state the date on which it was made and the seat of the arbitral tribunal as determined in accordance with Section 595, paragraph 1 of this act. The award shall be deemed to have been made on that day and at that place.

4. After the award is made, a copy signed by the arbitrators in accordance with paragraph 1 of this section shall be delivered to each party.

5. The award and the documentation on its service are common documents of the parties and the arbitrators. The arbitral tribunal shall discuss with the parties a possible safekeeping of the award and the documentation on its service.

6. The president or another arbitrator in the event that he is prevented from acting, shall confirm the final and binding nature and the enforceability of the award on a copy of the award at the request of one of the parties.

7. By making the award, the underlying arbitration clause does not become ineffective.

EFFECTS OF THE AWARD

Section 607

The award has the effect of a final and binding court judgement between the parties.

TERMINATION OF PROCEEDINGS

Section 608

1. The arbitral proceedings are terminated by the award cn the merits, by an award by consent, or by an order of the arbitral tribunal in accordance with paragraph 2 of this section.

2. The arbitral tribunal shall terminate the arbitral proceedings when:

  (1) the claimant fails to file his claim in accordance with Section 597, paragraph 1;
  (2) the claimant withdraws his claim, unless the respondent objecᴛs thereto and the arbitral tribunal recognizes a legitimate interest on hᴉs part in obtaining a final settlement of the dispute;
  (3) the parties agree on the termination of the proceedings and communicate this to the arbitral tribunal;
  (4) the arbitral tribunal finds that the continuatioᴨ of the proceedings has become impossible, in particular when the parties active so far in the proceedings do not continue the arbitral proceedings despite a written request from the arbitral tribunal, in which it refers to the possibility of termination of the proceedings.

3. The mandate of the arbitral tribunal terminates wiᴛh the termination of the arbitral proceedings, subject to the provisions of Sectᴉons 606 paragraphs 4 to 6, 609 paragraph 5 and 610 of this act, as well as to the obligation to set aside an ordered provisional or protective measure.

Decision on Costs

Section 609

1. If the arbitral proceedings are terminated, the arbitral tribunal shall decide upon the obligation to reimburse the costs of the proceedings, provided that the parties have not agreed otherwise. The arbitral tribunal shall, at its discretion, take into consideration the circumstances of the individual case, in particular the outcome of the proceedings. The obligation to reimburse may include any and all reasonable costs appropriate for bringing or defending against the action. In the case referred to in Section 608, paragraph 2, number 3 of this act, such a decision shall only be made where a party applies for such a decision together with the notification upon the agreement to terminate the proceedings.

2. Upon the application of the respondent, the arbitral tribunal may also decide upon the obligation of the plaintiff to reimburse the costs of the proceedings, if it has declared itself as not competent on the grounds that there is no arbitration agreement.

3. Together with the decision upon the liability to pay the costs, the arbitral tribunal shall, as far as this is already possible and the costs are not set off against each other, determine the amount of costs to be reimbursed.

4. In any case, the decision upon the liability to pay the costs and the determination of the amount shall be made in the form of an award pursuant to Section 606 of this act.

5. If no decision was made upon the liability to pay the costs, or if the amount to be reimbursed was not determined, or if it was only possible to determine this after termination of the arbitral proceedings, then the decision thereupon shall be made in a separate award.

Correction, Interpretation and Amendment of the Award

Section 610

1. Unless another period of time has been agreed upon by the parties, each party may, within four weeks of receipt of the award, request the arbitral tribunal

(1) to correct in the award any errors in computation, any clerical or typographical errors or any errors of a similar nature;
(2) if so agreed by the parties, to give an interpretation of certain parts of the award;
(3) to make an additional award as to claims presented in the arbitral proceedings, but not dealt with in the award.

2. The application under paragraph 1 of this section shall be delivered to the other party. Prior to making a decision upon such an application, the other party is to be heard.

3. The arbitral tribunal shall decide upon the correction or interpretation of the award within four weeks and upon an additional award within eight weeks.

4. The arbitral tribunal may correct any error of the type referred to in paragraph 1, number 1 of this section on its own initiative within four weeks of the date of the award.

5. The provisions of Section 606 of this act shall apply to the correction, interpretation or making of an additional award. The interpretation or correction shall be part of the award.

SEVENTH CHAPTER – RECOURSE AGAINST AWARD

APPLICATION FOR SETTING ASIDE AN AWARD

Section 611

1. An appeal to a court against an award may be made only by means of an action for setting aside. This also applies to awards by which the arbitral tribunal has ruled on its jurisdiction.

2. An award shall be set aside if

    (1) a valid arbitration agreement does not exist, or if the arbitral tribunal denies its jurisdiction despite the existence of a valid arbitration agreement, or if a party was not capable of concluding a valid arbitration agreement under the law which was personally relevant to that party;

    (2) a party was not given proper notice of the appointment of an arbitrator or of the arbitral proceedings or for another reason was unable to adequately defend itself or challenge the claims of the opposing party;

    (3) the award deals with a dispute not falling within the terms of the arbitration agreement, or contains decisions on matters beyond the scope of the arbitration agreement or beyond the claims of the parties; however, if the defect concerns only a separable part of the award, then only that part of the award shall be set aside;

    (4) the formation or composition of the arbitral tribunal is not in accordance with a provision of this section or with an admissible agreement of the parties;

    (5) the arbitral procedure was not carried out in accordance with the basic values of the Austrian legal system (ordre public);

    (6) the requirements have been met according to which a judgement of a court can be appealed under Section 530, paragraph 1, numbers 1 to 5 via an application for the proceedings to be reopened;

    (7) the subject-matter of the dispute is not arbitrable under Austrian law;

    (8) the award is in conflict with basic values of the Austrian legal system (ordre public).

3. The reasons for setting aside stipulated in paragraph 2, numbers 7 and 8 are also to be considered by a court ex officio.

4. The action for setting aside must be brought within three months. The time period shall begin with the day on which the plaintiff received the award or the additional award. An application made in accordance with Section 610, paragraph 1, number 1 or 2 of this act shall not extend this time period. In the case of paragraph 2, number 6, the time period for bringing the action for setting aside shall be judged according to the provisions on the application for the proceedings to be reopened.

5. The setting aside of an award has no influence on the effectiveness of the underlying arbitration agreement. If an award on the same subject matter has already been set aside twice in a final and binding way, and if a further award on the same subject matter is to be set aside, then the court, upon the application of a party, shall concurrently declare the arbitration agreement invalid with respect to that subject matter.

DECLARATION THAT AN AWARD DOES OR DOES NOT EXIST

Section 612

An application may be made for the determination of the existence or non-existence of an award if the applicant has a legal interest therein.

CONSIDERATION OF REASONS FOR SETTING ASIDE IN OTHER PROCEEDINGS

Section 613

If a court or another authority determines in another proceeding, for instance in an enforcement proceeding, that there is a reason for setting aside under Section 611, paragraph 2, numbers 7 and 8, then the award shall be disregarded in this proceeding.

EIGHTH CHAPTER – RECOGNITION AND ORDER OF ENFORCEMENT OF FOREIGN AWARDS

Section 614

1. The recognition and order of enforcement of foreign awards shall be made in accordance with the provisions of the Enforcement Act, unless otherwise provided in international law or in legal acts of the European Union. The formal requirement for the arbitration agreement shall also be regarded as fulfilled if the arbitration

agreement complies both with the provisions of Section 583 of this act and with the formal requirements of the law applicable to the arbitration agreement.

2. The presentation of the original arbitration agreement or a certified copy thereof in accordance with Article IV paragraph 1 (b) of the New York (UN) Convention on the Recognition and Enforcement of Foreign Awards shall only be necessary if requested by the court.

NINTH CHAPTER – COURT PROCEEDINGS

JURISDICTION

Section 615

1. For the action for setting aside an award and for the action for a declaration of the existence or non-existence of an award, as well as for proceedings pertaining to matters addressed in the third chapter, the regional court having jurisdiction over civil law matters that was specified in the arbitration agreement or whose jurisdiction was agreed upon in accordance with Section 104 of the Judicature Act, or, failing such specification or agreement, the regional court in whose district the arbitral tribunal has its seat shall have jurisdiction in the first instance, regardless of the value in dispute. If the seat of the arbitral tribunal has not yet been determined, or if, in the case of Section 612, it is not within Austria, then the Commercial Court of Vienna shall have jurisdiction.

2. If the legal matter in dispute underlying the award is a matter of commercial law within the meaning of Section 51 of the Judicature Act, then, acting as commercial courts, the regional court shall have jurisdiction, in Vienna the Commercial Court of Vienna shall have jurisdiction; for labour law matters within the meaning of Section 50, paragraph 1 of the Labour and Social Court Act, the regional courts acting as labour and social courts shall have jurisdiction, in Vienna the Labour and Social Court of Vienna shall have jurisdiction.

PROCEEDINGS

Section 616

1. Proceedings regarding an action for setting aside an award and an action for a declaration of the existence or non-existence of an award shall be governed by the provisions of this act. Proceedings regarding matters addressed in the third chapter shall be governed by the general provisions of the Act on Non-Contentious Matters.

2. Upon the application of a party, the public can be excluded if a justified interest in excluding the public is shown.

TENTH CHAPTER – SPECIAL PROVISIONS

Section 617

1. Arbitration agreements between an entrepreneur and a consumer may validly be concluded only for disputes that have already arisen.

2. Arbitration agreements with the participation of a consumer must be contained in a document which has been personally signed by the consumer. This document may not contain any agreements other than those that refer to the arbitration proceedings.

3. For arbitration agreements between an entrepreneur and a consumer, the consumer must, prior to the conclusion of the arbitration agreement, be issued written legal information on the substantial differences between arbitration proceedings and proceedings before a court of law.

4. In arbitration agreements between entrepreneurs and consumers, the seat of the arbitral tribunal must be stipulated. The arbitral tribunal may only meet at a different place for an oral hearing or for the taking of evidence if the consumer has consented to this or if considerable difficulties stand in the way of the taking of evidence at the seat of the arbitral tribunal.

5. Where an arbitration agreement was concluded between an entrepreneur and a consumer, and where the consumer at the time of concluding the arbitration agreement or at the time when legal proceedings are instituted does not have his domicile, habitual place of residence or place of employment in that state where the arbitral tribunal has its seat, the arbitration agreement shall only be of relevance if the consumer invokes it.

6. An award shall also be set aside if, in arbitration proceedings in which a consumer is involved,

    (1) mandatory provisions of the law have been violated and these provisions of the law could not have been waived through the choice of law of the parties even in a case with international relevance, or

    (2) the requirements have been satisfied such that, pursuant to Section 530, paragraph 1, numbers 6 and 7, a judgement of a court of law could be appealed by means of an application for the proceedings to be reopened; in this case, the time period for the filing of the action for setting aside shall be judged under the respective provisions regarding the application for the proceedings to be reopened.

7. If the arbitration proceedings took place between an entrepreneur and a consumer, the award is also to be set aside if the consumer did not receive written legal information as stipulated in paragraph 3.

LABOUR LAW CASES

Section 618

Section 617, paragraphs 2 to 7 shall apply accordingly to arbitration proceedings in labour law matters within the meaning of Section 50, paragraph 1 of the Labour and Social Court Act.

Annex 8b

Zivilprozessordnung, Vierter Abschnitt: Schiedsverfahren*

ERSTER TITEL – ALLGEMEINE BESTIMMUNGEN

ANWENDUNGSBEREICH

§ 577

1. Die Bestimmungen dieses Abschnitts sind anzuwenden, wenn der Sitz des Schiedsgerichts in Österreich liegt.

2. §§ 578, 580, 583, 584, 585, 593 Abs. 3 bis 6, §§ 602, 612 und 614 sind auch anzuwenden, wenn der Sitz des Schiedsgerichts nicht in Österreich liegt oder noch nicht bestimmt ist.

3. Solange der Sitz des Schiedsgerichts noch nicht bestimmt ist, besteht die inländische Gerichtsbarkeit für die im dritten Titel genannten gerichtlichen Aufgaben, wenn eine der Parteien ihren Sitz, Wohnsitz oder gewöhnlichen Aufenthalt in Österreich hat.

---

*   Art. VII In-Kraft-Treten, Übergangsbestimmungen und Vollziehung des Schiedsrechts-Änderungsgesetz 2006:
    In-Kraft-Treten, Übergangsbestimmungen und Vollziehung:
    (1) Dieses Bundesgesetz tritt mit 1. Juli 2006 in Kraft.
    (2) Auf Schiedsverfahren, die noch vor dem 1. Juli 2006 eingeleitet wurden, sind die bisher geltenden Bestimmungen anzuwenden.
    (3) Die Wirksamkeit von Schiedsvereinbarungen, die vor dem 1. Juli 2006 geschlossen worden sind, richten sich nach den bisher geltenden Bestimmungen.
    (4) Mit der Vollziehung dieses Bundesgesetzes ist die Bundesministerin für Justiz betraut.

4. Die Bestimmungen dieses Abschnitts sind nicht auf Einrichtungen nach dem Vereinsgesetz zur Schlichtung von Streitigkeiten aus dem Vereinsverhältnis anwendbar.

GERICHTLICHE TÄTIGKEIT

§ 578

Das Gericht darf in den in diesem Abschnitt geregelten Angelegenheiten nur tätig werden, soweit dieser Abschnitt es vorsieht.

RÜGEPFLICHT

§ 579

Hat das Schiedsgericht einer Verfahrensbestimmung dieses Abschnitts, von der die Parteien abweichen können, oder einem vereinbarten Verfahrenserfordernis des Schiedsverfahrens nicht entsprochen, so kann eine Partei den Mangel später nicht mehr geltend machen, wenn sie ihn nicht unverzüglich ab Kenntnis oder innerhalb der dafür vorgesehenen Frist gerügt hat.

EMPFANG SCHRIFTLICHER MITTEILUNGEN

§ 580

1. Haben die Parteien nichts anderes vereinbart, so gilt eine schriftliche Mitteilung an dem Tag als empfangen, an dem sie dem Empfänger oder einer zum Empfang berechtigten Person persönlich ausgehändigt wurde oder, wenn dies nicht möglich war, an dem sie am Sitz, Wohnsitz oder gewöhnlichen Aufenthalt des Empfängers sonst übergeben wurde.

2. Hat der Empfänger Kenntnis vom Schiedsverfahren und ist er oder eine zum Empfang berechtigte Person trotz angemessener Nachforschungen unbekannten Aufenthalts, so gilt eine schriftliche Mitteilung an dem Tag als empfangen, an dem eine ordnungsgemäße Übermittlung nachweislich an einem Ort versucht wurde, der bei Abschluss der Schiedsvereinbarung oder in der Folge vom Empfänger der anderen Partei oder dem Schiedsgericht gegenüber als Adresse bekannt gegeben worden ist und bisher nicht unter Angabe einer neuen Adresse widerrufen wurde.

3. Abs. 1 und 2 gelten nicht für Mitteilungen in gerichtlichen Verfahren.

ZWEITER TITEL – SCHIEDSVEREINBARUNG

BEGRIFF

§ 581

1. Die Schiedsvereinbarung ist eine Vereinbarung der Parteien, alle oder einzelne Streitigkeiten, die zwischen ihnen in Bezug auf ein bestimmtes Rechtsverhältnis vertraglicher oder nichtvertraglicher Art entstanden sind oder künftig entstehen, der Entscheidung durch ein Schiedsgericht zu unterwerfen. Die Schiedsvereinbarung kann in Form einer selbständigen Vereinbarung oder in Form einer Klausel in einem Vertrag geschlossen werden.

2. Die Bestimmungen dieses Abschnitts sind auch auf Schiedsgerichte sinngemäß anzuwenden, die in gesetzlich zulässiger Weise durch letztwillige Verfügung oder andere nicht auf Vereinbarung der Parteien beruhende Rechtsgeschäfte oder durch Statuten angeordnet werden.

SCHIEDSFÄHIGKEIT

§ 582

1. Jeder vermögensrechtliche Anspruch, über den von den ordentlichen Gerichten zu entscheiden ist, kann Gegenstand einer Schiedsvereinbarung sein. Eine Schiedsvereinbarung über nicht vermögensrechtliche Ansprüche hat insofern rechtliche Wirkung, als die Parteien über den Gegenstand des Streits einen Vergleich abzuschließen fähig sind.

2. Familienrechtliche Ansprüche sowie alle Ansprüche aus Verträgen, die dem Mietrechtsgesetz oder dem Wohnungsgemeinnützigkeitsgesetz auch nur teilweise unterliegen, einschließlich der Streitigkeiten über die Eingehung, das Bestehen, die Auflösung und die rechtliche Einordnung solcher Verträge, und alle wohnungseigentumsrechtlichen Ansprüche können nicht Gegenstand einer Schiedsvereinbarung sein. Gesetzliche Vorschriften außerhalb dieses Abschnitts, nach denen Streitigkeiten einem Schiedsverfahren nicht oder nur unter bestimmten Voraussetzungen unterworfen werden dürfen, bleiben unberührt.

FORM DER SCHIEDSVEREINBARUNG

§ 583

1. Die Schiedsvereinbarung muss entweder in einem von den Parteien unterzeichneten Schriftstück oder in zwischen ihnen gewechselten Schreiben, Telefaxen, e-mails oder anderen Formen der Nachrichtenübermittlung enthalten sein, die einen Nachweis der Vereinbarung sicherstellen.

2. Nimmt ein den Formerfordernissen des Abs. 1 entsprechender Vertrag auf ein Schriftstück Bezug, das eine Schiedsvereinbarung enthält, so begründet dies eine Schiedsvereinbarung, wenn die Bezugnahme dergestalt ist, dass sie diese Schiedsvereinbarung zu einem Bestandteil des Vertrages macht.

3. Ein Formmangel der Schiedsvereinbarung wird im Schiedsverfahren durch Einlassung in die Sache geheilt, wenn er nicht spätestens zugleich mit der Einlassung gerügt wird.

SCHIEDSVEREINBARUNG UND KLAGE VOR GERICHT

§ 584

1. Wird vor einem Gericht Klage in einer Angelegenheit erhoben, die Gegenstand einer Schiedsvereinbarung ist, so hat das Gericht die Klage zurückzuweisen, sofern der Beklagte nicht zur Sache vorbringt oder mündlich verhandelt, ohne dies zu rügen. Dies gilt nicht, wenn das Gericht feststellt, dass die Schiedsvereinbarung nicht vorhanden oder undurchführbar ist. Ist ein solches Verfahren noch vor einem Gericht anhängig, so kann ein Schiedsverfahren dennoch eingeleitet oder fortgesetzt werden und ein Schiedsspruch ergehen.

2. Hat ein Schiedsgericht seine Zuständigkeit für den Gegenstand des Streits verneint, weil hierüber keine Schiedsvereinbarung vorhanden ist oder die Schiedsvereinbarung undurchführbar ist, so darf das Gericht eine Klage darüber nicht mit der Begründung zurückweisen, dass für die Angelegenheit ein Schiedsgericht zuständig ist. Mit der Erhebung der Klage bei Gericht erlischt das Recht des Klägers, nach § 611 eine Klage auf Aufhebung der Entscheidung zu erheben, mit welcher das Schiedsgericht seine Zuständigkeit verneint hat.

3. Ist ein Schiedsverfahren anhängig, so darf über den geltend gemachten Anspruch kein weiterer Rechtsstreit vor einem Gericht oder einem Schiedsgericht durchgeführt werden; eine wegen desselben Anspruches angebrachte Klage ist zurückzuweisen. Dies gilt nicht, wenn die Unzuständigkeit des Schiedsgerichts vor diesem spätestens mit der Einlassung in die Sache gerügt wurde und eine Entscheidung des Schiedsgerichtes hierüber in angemessener Dauer nicht zu erlangen ist.

4. Wird eine Klage von einem Gericht wegen Zuständigkeit eines Schiedsgerichtes oder von einem Schiedsgericht wegen Zuständigkeit eines Gerichtes oder eines anderen Schiedsgerichts zurückgewiesen oder wird in einem Aufhebungsverfahren ein Schiedsspruch wegen Unzuständigkeit des Schiedsgerichts aufgehoben, so gilt das Verfahren als gehörig fortgesetzt, wenn unverzüglich Klage vor dem Gericht oder Schiedsgericht erhoben wird.

5. Eine Partei, die sich zu einem früheren Zeitpunkt in einem Verfahren auf das Vorhandensein einer Schiedsvereinbarung berufen hat, kann später nicht mehr geltend machen, dass diese nicht vorliegt, es sei denn, die maßgebenden Umstände haben sich seither geändert.

SCHIEDSVEREINBARUNG UND EINSTWEILIGE GERICHTLICHE MAßNAHMEN

§ 585

Eine Schiedsvereinbarung schließt nicht aus, dass eine Partei vor oder während des Schiedsverfahrens bei einem Gericht eine vorläufige oder sichernde Maßnahme beantragt und dass das Gericht eine solche Maßnahme anordnet.

DRITTER TITEL – BILDUNG DES SCHIEDSGERICHTS

ZUSAMMENSETZUNG DES SCHIEDSGERICHTS

§ 586

1. Die Parteien können die Anzahl der Schiedsrichter frei vereinbaren. Haben die Parteien jedoch eine gerade Zahl von Schiedsrichtern vereinbart, so haben diese eine weitere Person als Vorsitzenden zu bestellen.

2. Haben die Parteien nichts anderes vereinbart, so sind drei Schiedsrichter zu bestellen.

BESTELLUNG DER SCHIEDSRICHTER

§ 587

1. Die Parteien können das Verfahren zur Bestellung des Schiedsrichters oder der Schiedsrichter frei vereinbaren.

2. Fehlt eine Vereinbarung über das Verfahren zur Bestellung, so gilt Folgendes:

 (1) In Schiedsverfahren mit einem Einzelschiedsrichter wird der Schiedsrichter, wenn sich die Parteien über seine Bestellung nicht binnen vier Wochen nach Empfang einer entsprechenden schriftlichen Aufforderung einer Partei durch die andere Partei einigen können, auf Antrag einer Partei durch das Gericht bestellt.

 (2) In Schiedsverfahren mit drei Schiedsrichtern bestellt jede Partei einen Schiedsrichter. Diese beiden Schiedsrichter bestellen den dritten Schiedsrichter, der als Vorsitzender des Schiedsgerichts tätig wird.

 (3) Wenn mehr als drei Schiedsrichter vorgesehen sind, hat jede Partei die gleiche Zahl an Schiedsrichtern zu bestellen. Diese bestellen einen weiteren Schiedsrichter, der als Vorsitzender des Schiedsgerichts tätig wird.

 (4) Hat eine Partei einen Schiedsrichter nicht binnen vier Wochen nach Empfang einer entsprechenden schriftlichen Aufforderung durch die andere Partei bestellt oder empfangen die Parteien nicht binnen vier Wochen nach der Bestellung der Schiedsrichter von diesen die Mitteilung über

den von ihnen zu bestellenden Schiedsrichter, so ist der Schiedsrichter auf Antrag einer Partei durch das Gericht zu bestellen.

(5) Eine Partei ist an die durch sie erfolgte Bestellung eines Schiedsrichters gebunden, sobald die andere Partei die schriftliche Mitteilung über die Bestellung empfangen hat.

3. Haben die Parteien ein Verfahren für die Bestellung vereinbart und

(1) handelt eine der Parteien nicht entsprechend diesem Verfahren oder
(2) können die Parteien oder die Schiedsrichter eine Einigung entsprechend diesem Verfahren nicht erzielen oder
(3) erfüllt ein Dritter eine ihm nach diesem Verfahren übertragene Aufgabe innerhalb von drei Monaten nach Empfang einer entsprechenden schriftlichen Mitteilung nicht,

so kann jede Partei bei Gericht die entsprechende Bestellung von Schiedsrichtern beantragen, sofern das vereinbarte Bestellungsverfahren zur Sicherung der Bestellung nichts anderes vorsieht.

4. Die schriftliche Aufforderung zur Bestellung eines Schiedsrichters hat auch Angaben darüber zu enthalten, welcher Anspruch geltend gemacht wird und auf welche Schiedsvereinbarung sich die Partei beruft.

5. Können sich mehrere Parteien, die gemeinsam einen oder mehrere Schiedsrichter zu bestellen haben, darüber nicht innerhalb von vier Wochen nach Empfang einer entsprechenden schriftlichen Mitteilung einigen, so ist der Schiedsrichter oder sind die Schiedsrichter auf Antrag einer Partei vom Gericht zu bestellen, sofern das vereinbarte Bestellungsverfahren zur Sicherung der Bestellung nichts anderes vorsieht.

6. Der Schiedsrichter oder die Schiedsrichter sind auf Antrag einer Partei vom Gericht auch zu bestellen, wenn seine oder ihre Bestellung aus anderen in den vorhergehenden Absätzen nicht geregelten Gründen nicht innerhalb von vier Wochen nach Empfang einer entsprechenden schriftlichen Mitteilung der einen an die andere Partei erfolgen kann oder auch das Bestellungsverfahren zur Sicherung der Bestellung nicht binnen angemessener Zeit zur Bestellung führt.

7. Wenn noch vor Entscheidung erster Instanz die Bestellung erfolgt und eine Partei dies nachweist, ist der Antrag abzuweisen.

8. Das Gericht hat bei der Bestellung eines Schiedsrichters alle nach der Parteivereinbarung für den Schiedsrichter vorgesehenen Voraussetzungen angemessen zu berücksichtigen und allen Gesichtspunkten Rechnung zu tragen, welche die Bestellung eines unabhängigen und unparteiischen Schiedsrichters sicherstellen.

9. Gegen eine Entscheidung, mit der ein Schiedsrichter bestellt wird, ist kein Rechtsmittel zulässig.

ABLEHNUNGSGRÜNDE

§ 588

1. Will eine Person ein Schiedsrichteramt übernehmen, so hat sie alle Umstände offen zu legen, die Zweifel an ihrer Unparteilichkeit oder Unabhängigkeit wecken können oder der Parteienvereinbarung widersprechen. Ein Schiedsrichter hat vom Zeitpunkt seiner Bestellung an und während des Schiedsverfahrens den Parteien unverzüglich solche Umstände offen zu legen, wenn er sie ihnen nicht schon vorher mitgeteilt hat.

2. Ein Schiedsrichter kann nur abgelehnt werden, wenn Umstände vorliegen, die berechtigte Zweifel an seiner Unparteilichkeit oder Unabhängigkeit wecken, oder wenn er die zwischen den Parteien vereinbarten Voraussetzungen nicht erfüllt. Eine Partei kann einen Schiedsrichter, den sie bestellt hat oder an dessen Bestellung sie mitgewirkt hat, nur aus Gründen ablehnen, die ihr erst nach der Bestellung oder Mitwirkung daran bekannt geworden sind.

ABLEHNUNGSVERFAHREN

§ 589

1. Die Parteien können vorbehaltlich des Abs. 3 ein Verfahren für die Ablehnung eines Schiedsrichters frei vereinbaren.

2. Fehlt eine solche Vereinbarung, so hat die Partei, die einen Schiedsrichter ablehnt, binnen vier Wochen, nachdem ihr die Zusammensetzung des Schiedsgerichts oder ein Umstand im Sinne von § 588 Abs. 2 bekannt geworden ist, dem Schiedsgericht schriftlich die Ablehnungsgründe darzulegen. Tritt der abgelehnte Schiedsrichter von seinem Amt nicht zurück oder stimmt die andere Partei der Ablehnung nicht zu, so entscheidet das Schiedsgericht einschließlich des abgelehnten Schiedsrichters über die Ablehnung.

3. Bleibt eine Ablehnung nach dem von den Parteien vereinbarten Verfahren oder nach dem in Abs. 2 vorgesehenen Verfahren erfolglos, so kann die ablehnende Partei binnen vier Wochen, nachdem ihr die Entscheidung, mit der die Ablehnung verweigert wurde, zugegangen ist, bei Gericht eine Entscheidung über die Ablehnung beantragen. Gegen diese Entscheidung ist kein Rechtsmittel zulässig. Während ein solcher Antrag anhängig ist, kann das Schiedsgericht einschließlich des abgelehnten Schiedsrichters das Schiedsverfahren fortsetzen und einen Schiedsspruch erlassen.

VORZEITIGE BEENDIGUNG DES SCHIEDSRICHTERAMTS

§ 590

1. Das Amt eines Schiedsrichters endet, wenn die Parteien dies vereinbaren oder wenn der Schiedsrichter zurücktritt. Vorbehaltlich des Abs. 2 können die

Parteien auch ein Verfahren für die Beendigung des Schiedsrichteramts vereinbaren.

2. Jede Partei kann bei Gericht eine Entscheidung über die Beendigung des Amtes beantragen, wenn der Schiedsrichter entweder außer Stande ist, seine Aufgaben zu erfüllen oder er diesen in angemessener Frist nicht nachkommt und

(1) der Schiedsrichter von seinem Amt nicht zurücktritt,
(2) sich die Parteien über dessen Beendigung nicht einigen können oder
(3) das von den Parteien vereinbarte Verfahren nicht zur Beendigung des Schiedsrichteramtes führt.

Gegen diese Entscheidung ist ein Rechtsmittel nicht zulässig.

3. Tritt ein Schiedsrichter nach Abs. 1 oder nach § 589 Abs. 2 zurück oder stimmt eine Partei der Beendigung des Amtes eines Schiedsrichters zu, so bedeutet das nicht die Anerkennung der in Abs. 2 oder § 588 Abs. 2 genannten Gründe.

BESTELLUNG EINES ERSATZSCHIEDSRICHTERS

§ 591

1. Endet das Amt eines Schiedsrichters vorzeitig, so ist ein Ersatzschiedsrichter zu bestellen. Die Bestellung erfolgt nach den Regeln, die auf die Bestellung des zu ersetzenden Schiedsrichters anzuwenden waren.

2. Haben die Parteien nichts anderes vereinbart, so kann das Schiedsgericht die Verhandlung unter Verwendung der bisherigen Verfahrensergebnisse, insbesondere des aufgenommenen Verhandlungsprotokolls und aller sonstigen Akten, fortsetzen.

VIERTER TITEL – ZUSTÄNDIGKEIT DES SCHIEDSGERICHTS

BEFUGNIS DES SCHIEDSGERICHTS ZUR ENTSCHEIDUNG ÜBER DIE EIGENE ZUSTÄNDIGKEIT

§ 592

1. Das Schiedsgericht entscheidet selbst über seine Zuständigkeit. Die Entscheidung kann mit der Entscheidung in der Sache getroffen werden, aber auch gesondert in einem eigenen Schiedsspruch.

2. Die Einrede der Unzuständigkeit des Schiedsgerichts ist spätestens mit dem ersten Vorbringen zur Sache zu erheben. Von der Erhebung dieser Einrede ist eine Partei nicht dadurch ausgeschlossen, dass sie einen Schiedsrichter bestellt oder an der Bestellung eines Schiedsrichters mitgewirkt hat. Die Einrede, eine Angelegenheit überschreite die Befugnisse des Schiedsgerichts, ist zu erheben, sobald diese zum Gegenstand eines Sachantrags erhoben wird. In beiden Fällen ist eine spätere Erhebung der Einrede ausgeschlossen; wird die Versäumung

jedoch nach Überzeugung des Schiedsgerichts genügend entschuldigt, so kann die Einrede nachgeholt werden.

3. Auch wenn eine Klage auf Aufhebung eines Schiedsspruches, mit welchem das Schiedsgericht seine Zuständigkeit bejaht hat, noch bei Gericht anhängig ist, kann das Schiedsgericht vorerst das Schiedsverfahren fortsetzen und auch einen Schiedsspruch fällen.

ANORDNUNG VORLÄUFIGER ODER SICHERNDER MASSNAHMEN

§ 593

1. Haben die Parteien nichts anderes vereinbart, so kann das Schiedsgericht auf Antrag einer Partei vorläufige oder sichernde Maßnahmen gegen eine andere Partei nach deren Anhörung anordnen, die es in Bezug auf den Streitgegenstand für erforderlich hält, weil sonst die Durchsetzung des Anspruchs vereitelt oder erheblich erschwert werden würde oder ein unwiederbringlicher Schaden droht. Das Schiedsgericht kann von jeder Partei im Zusammenhang mit einer solchen Maßnahme angemessene Sicherheit fordern.

2. Maßnahmen nach Abs. 1 sind schriftlich anzuordnen; jeder Partei ist ein unterfertigtes Exemplar der Anordnung zuzustellen. In Schiedsverfahren mit mehr als einem Schiedsrichter genügt die Unterschrift des Vorsitzenden oder im Falle seiner Verhinderung eines anderen Schiedsrichters, sofern der Vorsitzende oder der andere Schiedsrichter auf der Anordnung vermerkt, welches Hindernis der Unterfertigung entgegensteht. § 606 Abs. 2, 3, 5 und 6 gelten entsprechend.

3. Auf Antrag einer Partei hat das Bezirksgericht, bei dem der Gegner der gefährdeten Partei zur Zeit der ersten Antragstellung seinen Sitz, Wohnsitz oder gewöhnlichen Aufenthalt im Inland hat, sonst das Bezirksgericht, in dessen Sprengel die dem Vollzug der einstweiligen Verfügung dienende Handlung vorzunehmen ist, eine solche Maßnahme zu vollziehen. Sieht die Maßnahme ein dem inländischen Recht unbekanntes Sicherungsmittel vor, so kann das Gericht auf Antrag nach Anhörung des Antragsgegners jenes Sicherungsmittel des inländischen Rechts vollziehen, welches der Maßnahme des Schiedsgerichts am nächsten kommt. Dabei kann es die Maßnahme des Schiedsgerichts auf Antrag auch abweichend fassen, um die Verwirklichung ihres Zwecks zu gewährleisten.

4. Das Gericht hat die Vollziehung einer Maßnahme nach Abs. 1 abzulehnen, wenn

(1) der Sitz des Schiedsgerichts im Inland liegt und die Maßnahme an einem Mangel leidet, der bei einem inländischen Schiedsspruch einen Aufhebungsgrund nach § 611 Abs. 2, § 617 Abs. 6 und 7 oder § 618 darstellen würde;

(2) der Sitz des Schiedsgerichts nicht im Inland liegt und die Maßnahme an einem Mangel leidet, der bei einem ausländischen Schiedsspruch einen Grund für die Versagung der Anerkennung oder Vollstreckbarerklärung darstellen würde;

(3) die Vollziehung der Maßnahme mit einer früher beantragten oder erlassenen inländischen oder früher erlassenen und anzuerkennenden ausländischen gerichtlichen Maßnahme unvereinbar ist;

(4) die Maßnahme ein dem inländischen Recht unbekanntes Sicherungsmittel vorsieht und kein geeignetes Sicherungsmittel des inländischen Rechts beantragt wurde.

5. Das Gericht kann den Antragsgegner vor Entscheidung über die Vollziehung der Maßnahme nach Abs. 1 hören. Wenn der Antragsgegner vor der Beschlussfassung nicht gehört wurde, kann er gegen die Bewilligung der Vollziehung Widerspruch im Sinne von § 397 EO einlegen. In beiden Fällen kann der Antragsgegner nur geltend machen, dass ein Grund zur Versagung der Vollziehung nach Abs. 4 vorliegt. In diesem Verfahren ist das Gericht nicht befugt, gemäß § 394 EO über Schadenersatzansprüche zu entscheiden.

6. Das Gericht hat die Vollziehung auf Antrag aufzuheben, wenn

(1) die vom Schiedsgericht bestimmte Geltungsdauer der Maßnahme abgelaufen ist;

(2) das Schiedsgericht die Maßnahme eingeschränkt oder aufgehoben hat;

(3) ein Fall von § 399 Abs. 1 Z 1 bis 4 EO vorliegt, sofern ein solcher Umstand nicht bereits vor dem Schiedsgericht erfolglos geltend gemacht wurde und der diesbezüglichen Entscheidung des Schiedsgerichts keine Anerkennungshindernisse (Abs. 4) entgegenstehen;

(4) eine Sicherheit nach Abs. 1 geleistet wurde, welche die Vollziehung der Maßnahme entbehrlich macht.

FÜNFTER TITEL – DURCHFÜHRUNG DES SCHIEDSVERFAHRENS

ALLGEMEINES

§ 594

1. Vorbehaltlich der zwingenden Vorschriften dieses Abschnitts können die Parteien die Verfahrensgestaltung frei vereinbaren. Dabei können sie auch auf Verfahrensordnungen Bezug nehmen. Fehlt eine solche Vereinbarung, so hat das Schiedsgericht nach den Bestimmungen dieses Titels, darüber hinaus nach freiem Ermessen vorzugehen.

2. Die Parteien sind fair zu behandeln. Jeder Partei ist rechtliches Gehör zu gewähren.

3. Die Parteien können sich durch Personen ihrer Wahl vertreten oder beraten lassen. Dieses Recht kann nicht ausgeschlossen oder eingeschränkt werden.

4. Ein Schiedsrichter, welcher die durch Annahme der Bestellung übernommene Verpflichtung gar nicht oder nicht rechtzeitig erfüllt, haftet den Parteien für allen durch seine schuldhafte Weigerung oder Verzögerung verursachten Schaden.

SITZ DES SCHIEDSGERICHTS

§ 595

1. Die Parteien können den Sitz des Schiedsgerichts frei vereinbaren. Sie können die Bestimmung des Sitzes auch einer Schiedsinstitution überlassen. Fehlt eine solche Vereinbarung, so wird der Sitz des Schiedsgerichts vom Schiedsgericht bestimmt; dabei sind die Umstände des Falles einschließlich der Eignung des Ortes für die Parteien zu berücksichtigen.

2. Haben die Parteien nichts anderes vereinbart, so kann das Schiedsgericht ungeachtet des Abs. 1 an jedem ihm geeignet erscheinenden Ort Verfahrenshandlungen setzen, insbesondere zur Beratung, Beschlussfassung, mündlichen Verhandlung und zur Beweisaufnahme zusammentreten.

VERFAHRENSSPRACHE

§ 596

Die Parteien können die Sprache oder die Sprachen, die im Schiedsverfahren zu verwenden sind, vereinbaren. Fehlt eine solche Vereinbarung, so bestimmt hierüber das Schiedsgericht.

KLAGE UND KLAGEBEANTWORTUNG

§ 597

1. Innerhalb der von den Parteien vereinbarten oder vom Schiedsgericht bestimmten Frist hat der Kläger sein Begehren zu stellen und die Tatsachen, auf welche sich der Anspruch stützt, darzulegen sowie der Beklagte hiezu Stellung zu nehmen Die Parteien können dabei alle ihnen erheblich erscheinenden Beweismittel vorlegen oder weitere Beweismittel bezeichnen, derer sie sich bedienen wollen.

2. Haben die Parteien nichts anderes vereinbart, so können beide Parteien im Laufe des Verfahrens ihre Klage oder ihr Vorbringen ändern oder ergänzen, es sei denn, das Schiedsgericht lässt dies wegen Verspätung nicht zu.

MÜNDLICHE VERHANDLUNG UND SCHRIFTLICHES VERFAHREN

§ 598

Haben die Parteien nichts anderes vereinbart, so entscheidet das Schiedsgericht ob mündlich verhandelt oder ob das Verfahren schriftlich durchgeführt werden soll.

Haben die Parteien eine mündliche Verhandlung nicht ausgeschlossen, so hat das Schiedsgericht auf Antrag einer Partei eine solche in einem geeigneten Abschnitt des Verfahrens durchzuführen.

VERFAHREN UND BEWEISAUFNAHME

§ 599

1. Das Schiedsgericht ist berechtigt, über die Zulässigkeit einer Beweisaufnahme zu entscheiden, diese durchzuführen und ihr Ergebnis frei zu würdigen.

2. Die Parteien sind von jeder Verhandlung und von jedem Zusammentreffen des Schiedsgerichts zu Zwecken der Beweisaufnahme rechtzeitig in Kenntnis zu setzen.

3. Alle Schriftsätze, Schriftstücke und sonstigen Mitteilungen, die dem Schiedsgericht von einer Partei vorgelegt werden, sind der anderen Partei zur Kenntnis zu bringen. Gutachten und andere Beweismittel, auf die sich das Schiedsgericht bei seiner Entscheidung stützen kann, sind beiden Parteien zur Kenntnis zu bringen.

VERSÄUMUNG EINER VERFAHRENSHANDLUNG

§ 600

1. Versäumt es der Kläger, die Klage nach § 597 Abs. 1 einzubringen, so beendet das Schiedsgericht das Verfahren.

2. Versäumt es der Beklagte nach § 597 Abs. 1 binnen der vereinbarten oder aufgetragenen Frist Stellung zu nehmen, so setzt das Schiedsgericht, wenn die Parteien nichts anderes vereinbart haben, das Verfahren fort, ohne dass allein wegen der Versäumung das Vorbringen des Klägers für wahr zu halten ist. Gleiches gilt, wenn eine Partei eine andere Verfahrenshandlung versäumt. Das Schiedsgericht kann das Verfahren fortsetzen und eine Entscheidung auf Grund der aufgenommenen Beweise fällen. Wird die Versäumung nach Überzeugung des Schiedsgerichts genügend entschuldigt, so kann die versäumte Verfahrenshandlung nachgeholt werden.

VOM SCHIEDSGERICHT BESTELLTER SACHVERSTÄNDIGER

§ 601

1. Haben die Parteien nichts anderes vereinbart, so kann das Schiedsgericht

    (1) einen oder mehrere Sachverständige zur Erstattung eines Gutachtens über bestimmte vom Schiedsgericht festzulegende Fragen bestellen;

(2) die Parteien auffordern, dem Sachverständigen jede sachdienliche Auskunft zu erteilen oder alle für das Verfahren erheblichen Schriftstücke oder Sachen zur Aufnahme eines Befunds vorzulegen oder zugänglich zu machen.

2. Haben die Parteien nichts anderes vereinbart, so hat der Sachverständige, wenn eine Partei dies beantragt oder das Schiedsgericht es für erforderlich hält, nach Erstattung seines Gutachtens an einer mündlichen Verhandlung teilzunehmen. Bei der Verhandlung können die Parteien Fragen an den Sachverständigen stellen und eigene Sachverständige zu den streitigen Fragen aussagen lassen.

3. Auf den vom Schiedsgericht bestellten Sachverständigen sind §§ 588 und 589 Abs. 1 und 2 entsprechend anzuwenden.

4. Haben die Parteien nichts anderes vereinbart, so hat jede Partei das Recht, Gutachten eigener Sachverständiger vorzulegen. Abs. 2 gilt entsprechend.

GERICHTLICHE RECHTSHILFE

§ 602

Das Schiedsgericht, vom Schiedsgericht hiezu beauftrage Schiedsrichter oder eine der Parteien mit Zustimmung des Schiedsgerichts können bei Gericht die Vornahme richterlicher Handlungen beantragen, zu deren Vornahme das Schiedsgericht nicht befugt ist. Die Rechtshilfe kann auch darin bestehen, dass das Gericht ein ausländisches Gericht oder eine Behörde um die Vornahme solcher Handlungen ersucht. § 37 Abs. 2 bis 5 und §§ 38, 39 und 40 JN gelten entsprechend mit der Maßgabe, dass die Rechtsmittelbefugnis gemäß § 40 JN dem Schiedsgericht und den Parteien des Schiedsverfahrens zusteht. Das Schiedsgericht oder ein vom Schiedsgericht beauftragter Schiedsrichter und die Parteien sind berechtigt, an einer gerichtlichen Beweisaufnahme teilzunehmen und Fragen zu stellen. § 289 ist sinngemäß anzuwenden.

SECHSTER TITEL – SCHIEDSSPRUCH UND BEENDIGUNG DES VERFAHRENS

ANZUWENDENDES RECHT

§ 603

1. Das Schiedsgericht hat die Streitigkeit in Übereinstimmung mit den Rechtsvorschriften oder Rechtsregeln zu entscheiden, die von den Parteien

vereinbart worden sind. Die Vereinbarung des Rechts oder der Rechtsordnung eines bestimmten Staates ist, sofern die Parteien nicht ausdrücklich etwas anderes vereinbart haben, als unmittelbare Verweisung auf das materielle Recht dieses Staates und nicht auf sein Kollisionsrecht zu verstehen.

2. Haben die Parteien die anzuwendenden Rechtsvorschriften oder Rechtsregeln nicht bestimmt, so hat das Schiedsgericht jene Rechtsvorschriften anzuwenden, die es für angemessen erachtet.

3. Das Schiedsgericht hat nur dann nach Billigkeit zu entscheiden, wenn die Parteien es ausdrücklich dazu ermächtigt haben.

ENTSCHEIDUNG DURCH EIN SCHIEDSRICHTERKOLLEGIUM

§ 604

Haben die Parteien nichts anderes vereinbart, so gilt Folgendes:

1. In Schiedsverfahren mit mehr als einem Schiedsrichter ist jede Entscheidung des Schiedsgerichts mit Stimmenmehrheit aller Mitglieder zu treffen. In Verfahrensfragen kann der Vorsitzende allein entscheiden, wenn die Parteien oder alle Mitglieder des Schiedsgerichts ihn dazu ermächtigt haben.

2. Nehmen ein oder mehrere Schiedsrichter an einer Abstimmung ohne rechtfertigenden Grund nicht teil, so können die anderen Schiedsrichter ohne sie entscheiden. Auch in diesem Fall ist die erforderliche Stimmenmehrheit von der Gesamtzahl aller teilnehmenden und nicht teilnehmenden Schiedsrichter zu berechnen. Bei einer Abstimmung über einen Schiedsspruch ist die Absicht, so vorzugehen, den Parteien vorher mitzuteilen. Bei anderen Entscheidungen sind die Parteien von der Nichtteilnahme an der Abstimmung nachträglich in Kenntnis zu setzen.

VERGLEICH

§ 605

Vergleichen sich die Parteien während des Schiedsverfahrens über die Streitigkeit und sind die Parteien fähig, über den Gegenstand des Streits einen Vergleich abzuschließen, so können sie beantragen, dass

1. das Schiedsgericht den Vergleich protokolliert, sofern der Inhalt des Vergleichs nicht gegen Grundwertungen der österreichischen Rechtsordnung (ordre public) verstößt; es reicht aus, wenn das Protokoll von den Parteien und dem Vorsitzenden unterschrieben wird;

2. das Schiedsgericht den Vergleich in Form eines Schiedsspruchs mit vereinbartem Wortlaut festhält, sofern der Inhalt des Vergleichs nicht gegen Grundwertungen der österreichischen Rechtsordnung (ordre public) verstößt. Ein solcher Schiedsspruch ist gemäß § 606 zu erlassen. Er hat dieselbe Wirkung wie jeder Schiedsspruch in der Sache.

SCHIEDSSPRUCH

§ 606

1. Der Schiedsspruch ist schriftlich zu erlassen und durch den Schiedsrichter oder die Schiedsrichter zu unterschreiben. Haben die Parteien nichts anderes vereinbart, so genügen in Schiedsverfahren mit mehr als einem Schiedsrichter die Unterschriften der Mehrheit aller Mitglieder des Schiedsgerichts, sofern der Vorsitzende oder ein anderer Schiedsrichter am Schiedsspruch vermerkt, welches Hindernis fehlenden Unterschriften entgegensteht.

2. Haben die Parteien nichts anderes vereinbart, so ist der Schiedsspruch zu begründen.

3. Im Schiedsspruch sind der Tag, an dem er erlassen wurde, und der nach § 595 Abs. 1 bestimmte Sitz des Schiedsgerichts anzugeben. Der Schiedsspruch gilt als an diesem Tag und an diesem Ort erlassen.

4. Jeder Partei ist ein von den Schiedsrichtern nach Abs. 1 unterschriebenes Exemplar des Schiedsspruchs zu übersenden.

5. Der Schiedsspruch und die Urkunden über dessen Zustellung sind gemeinschaftliche Urkunden der Parteien und der Schiedsrichter. Das Schiedsgericht hat mit den Parteien eine allfällige Verwahrung des Schiedsspruchs sowie der Urkunden über dessen Zustellung zu erörtern.

6. Der Vorsitzende, im Falle seiner Verhinderung ein anderer Schiedsrichter, hat auf Verlangen einer Partei die Rechtskraft und Vollstreckbarkeit des Schiedsspruchs auf einem Exemplar des Schiedsspruchs zu bestätigen.

7. Durch Erlassung eines Schiedsspruchs tritt die zugrunde liegende Schiedsvereinbarung nicht außer Kraft.

WIRKUNG DES SCHIEDSSPRUCHS

§ 607

Der Schiedsspruch hat zwischen den Parteien die Wirkung eines rechtskräftigen gerichtlichen Urteils.

BEENDIGUNG DES SCHIEDSVERFAHRENS

§ 608

1. Das Schiedsverfahren wird mit dem Schiedsspruch in der Sache, einem Schiedsvergleich oder mit einem Beschluss des Schiedsgerichts nach Abs. 2 beendet.

2. Das Schiedsgericht hat das Schiedsverfahren zu beenden, wenn

(1) es der Kläger versäumt, die Klage nach § 597 Abs. l einzubringen;

(2) der Kläger seine Klage zurücknimmt, es sei denn, dass der Beklagte dem widerspricht und das Schiedsgericht ein berechtigtes Interesse des Beklagten an der endgültigen Beilegung der Streitigkeit anerkennt;

(3) die Parteien die Beendigung des Verfahrens vereinbaren und dies dem Schiedsgericht mitteilen;

(4) ihm die Fortsetzung des Verfahrens unmöglich geworden ist, insbesondere weil die bisher im Verfahren tätigen Parteien trotz schriftlicher Aufforderung des Schiedsgerichts, mit welcher dieses auf die Möglichkeit einer Beendigung des Schiedsverfahrens hinweist, das Schiedsverfahren nicht weiter betreiben.

3. Vorbehaltlich der §§ 606 Abs. 4 bis 6, 609 Abs. 5, und 610 sowie der Verpflichtung zur Aufhebung einer angeordneten vorläufigen oder sichernden Maßnahme endet das Amt des Schiedsgerichts mit der Beendigung des Schiedsverfahrens.

ENTSCHEIDUNG ÜBER DIE KOSTEN

§ 609

1. Wird das Schiedsverfahren beendet, so hat das Schiedsgericht über die Verpflichtung zum Kostenersatz zu entscheiden, sofern die Parteien nicht anderes vereinbart haben. Das Schiedsgericht hat dabei nach seinem Ermessen die Umstände des Einzelfalls, insbesondere den Ausgang des Verfahrens, zu berücksichtigen. Die Ersatzpflicht kann alle zur zweckentsprechenden Rechtsverfolgung oder Rechtsverteidigung angemessenen Kosten umfassen. Im Fall von § 608 Abs. 2 Z 3 hat eine solche Entscheidung nur zu ergehen, wenn eine Partei gleichzeitig mit der Mitteilung der Vereinbarung über die Beendigung des Verfahrens eine solche Entscheidung beantragt.

2. Das Schiedsgericht kann auf Antrag des Beklagten auch über eine Verpflichtung des Klägers zum Kostenersatz entscheiden, wenn es sich für unzuständig erklärt hat, weil keine Schiedsvereinbarung vorhanden ist.

3. Gleichzeitig mit der Entscheidung über die Verpflichtung zum Kostenersatz hat das Schiedsgericht, sofern dies bereits möglich ist und die Kosten nicht gegeneinander aufgehoben werden, den Betrag der zu ersetzenden Kosten festzusetzen.

4. In jedem Fall haben die Entscheidung über die Verpflichtung zum Kostenersatz und die Festsetzung des zu ersetzenden Betrags in Form eines Schiedsspruchs nach § 606 zu erfolgen.

5. Ist die Entscheidung über die Verpflichtung zum Kostenersatz oder die Festsetzung des zu ersetzenden Betrags unterblieben oder erst nach Beendigung des Schiedsverfahrens möglich, so wird darüber in einem gesonderten Schiedsspruch entschieden.

BERICHTIGUNG, ERLÄUTERUNG UND ERGÄNZUNG DES SCHIEDSSPRUCHS

§ 610

1. Sofern die Parteien keine andere Frist vereinbart haben, kann jede Partei innerhalb von vier Wochen nach Empfang des Schiedsspruchs beim Schiedsgericht beantragen,

    (1) Rechen-, Schreib- und Druckfehler oder Fehler ähnlicher Art im Schiedsspruch zu berichtigen;

    (2) bestimmte Teile des Schiedsspruchs zu erläutern, sofern die Parteien dies vereinbart haben;

    (3) einen ergänzenden Schiedsspruch über Ansprüche zu erlassen, die im Schiedsverfahren zwar geltend gemacht, im Schiedsspruch aber nicht erledigt worden sind.

2. Der Antrag nach Abs. 1 ist der anderen Partei zu übersenden. Vor der Entscheidung über einen solchen Antrag ist die andere Partei zu hören.

3. Das Schiedsgericht soll über die Berichtigung oder Erläuterung des Schiedsspruchs innerhalb von vier Wochen und über die Ergänzung des Schiedsspruchs innerhalb von acht Wochen entscheiden.

4. Eine Berichtigung des Schiedsspruchs nach Abs. 1 Z 1 kann das Schiedsgericht binnen vier Wochen ab dem Datum des Schiedsspruchs auch ohne Antrag vornehmen.

5. § 606 ist auf die Berichtigung, Erläuterung oder Ergänzung des Schiedsspruchs anzuwenden. Die Erläuterung oder Berichtigung ist Bestandteil des Schiedsspruchs.

SIEBENTER TITEL – RECHTSBEHELF GEGEN DEN SCHIEDSSPRUCH

ANTRAG AUF AUFHEBUNG EINES SCHIEDSSPRUCHS

§ 611

1. Gegen einen Schiedsspruch kann nur eine Klage auf gerichtliche Aufhebung gestellt werden. Dies gilt auch für Schiedssprüche, mit welchen das Schiedsgericht über seine Zuständigkeit abgesprochen hat.

2. Ein Schiedsspruch ist aufzuheben, wenn

(1) eine gültige Schiedsvereinbarung nicht vorhanden ist, oder wenn das Schiedsgericht seine Zuständigkeit verneint hat, eine gültige Schiedsvereinbarung aber doch vorhanden ist, oder wenn eine Partei nach dem Recht, das für sie persönlich maßgebend ist, zum Abschluss einer gültigen Schiedsvereinbarung nicht fähig war;

(2) eine Partei von der Bestellung eines Schiedsrichters oder vom Schiedsverfahren nicht gehörig in Kenntnis gesetzt wurde oder sie aus einem anderen Grund ihre Angriffs- oder Verteidigungsmittel nicht geltend machen konnte;

(3) der Schiedsspruch eine Streitigkeit betrifft, für welche die Schiedsvereinbarung nicht gilt, oder er Entscheidungen enthält, welche die Grenzen der Schiedsvereinbarung oder das Rechtsschutzbegehren der Parteien überschreiten; betrifft der Mangel nur einen trennbaren Teil des Schiedsspruchs, so ist dieser Teil aufzuheben;

(4) die Bildung oder Zusammensetzung des Schiedsgerichts einer Bestimmung dieses Abschnitts oder einer zulässigen Vereinbarung der Parteien widerspricht;

(5) das Schiedsverfahren in einer Weise durchgeführt wurde, die Grundwertungen der österreichischen Rechtsordnung (ordre public) widerspricht;

(6) die Voraussetzungen vorhanden sind, unter denen nach § 530 Abs. 1 Z 1 bis 5 ein gerichtliches Urteil mittels Wiederaufnahmsklage angefochten werden kann;

(7) der Gegenstand des Streits nach inländischem Recht nicht schiedsfähig ist;

(8) der Schiedsspruch Grundwertungen der österreichischen Rechtsordnung (ordre public) widerspricht.

3. Die Aufhebungsgründe des Abs. 2 Z 7 und 8 sind auch von Amts wegen wahrzunehmen.

4. Die Klage auf Aufhebung ist innerhalb von drei Monaten zu erheben. Die Frist beginnt mit dem Tag, an welchem der Kläger den Schiedsspruch oder den ergänzenden Schiedsspruch empfangen hat. Ein Antrag nach § 610 Abs. 1 Z 1 oder 2 verlängert diese Frist nicht. Im Fall des Abs. 2 Z 6 ist die Frist für die Aufhebungsklage nach den Bestimmungen über die Wiederaufnahmsklage zu beurteilen.

5. Die Aufhebung eines Schiedsspruchs berührt nicht die Wirksamkeit der zugrunde liegenden Schiedsvereinbarung. Wurde bereits zweimal ein Schiedsspruch über den selben Gegenstand rechtskräftig aufgehoben und ist ein weiterer hierüber ergehender Schiedsspruch aufzuheben, so hat das Gericht auf Antrag einer der Parteien gleichzeitig die Schiedsvereinbarung hinsichtlich dieses Gegenstandes für unwirksam zu erklären.

Feststellung des Bestehens oder Nichtbestehens eines Schiedsspruchs

§ 612

Die Feststellung des Bestehens oder Nichtbestehens eines Schiedsspruchs kann begehrt werden, wenn der Antragsteller ein rechtliches Interesse daran hat.

Wahrnehmung von Aufhebungsgründen in einem anderen Verfahren

§ 613

Stellt ein Gericht oder eine Behörde in einem anderen Verfahren, etwa in einem Exekutionsverfahren, fest, dass ein Aufhebungsgrund nach § 611 Abs. 2 Z 7 und 8 besteht, so ist der Schiedsspruch in diesem Verfahren nicht zu beachten.

ACHTER TITEL – ANERKENNUNG UND VOLLSTRECKBARERKLÄRUNG

Ausländischer Schiedssprüche

§ 614

1. Die Anerkennung und Vollstreckbarerklärung ausländischer Schiedssprüche richten sich nach den Bestimmungen der Exekutionsordnung, soweit nicht nach Völkerrecht oder in Rechtsakten der Europäischen Union anderes bestimmt ist. Das Formerfordernis für die Schiedsvereinbarung gilt auch dann als erfüllt, wenn die Schiedsvereinbarung sowohl den Formvorschriften des § 583 als auch den Formvorschriften des auf die Schiedsvereinbarung anwendbaren Rechts entspricht.

2. Die Vorlage der Urschrift oder einer beglaubigten Abschrift der Schiedsvereinbarung nach Art IV Abs. 1 lit b des New Yorker UN-Übereinkommens über die Anerkennung und Vollstreckung ausländischer Schiedssprüche ist nur nach Aufforderung durch das Gericht erforderlich.

NEUNTER TITEL – GERICHTLICHES VERFAHREN

Zuständigkeit

§ 615

1. Für die Klage auf Aufhebung des Schiedsspruchs und die Klage auf Feststellung des Bestehens oder Nichtbestehens eines Schiedsspruchs sowie für Verfahren in

Angelegenheiten nach dem dritten Titel ist in erster Instanz ohne Rücksicht auf den Wert des Streitgegenstandes das die Gerichtsbarkeit in bürgerlichen Rechtssachen ausübende Landesgericht zuständig, das in der Schiedsvereinbarung bezeichnet oder dessen Zuständigkeit nach § 104 JN vereinbart wurde oder, wenn eine solche Bezeichnung oder Vereinbarung fehlt, in dessen Sprengel der Sitz des Schiedsgerichts liegt. Ist auch der Sitz des Schiedsgerichts noch nicht bestimmt oder liegt dieser im Fall des § 612 nicht in Österreich, so ist das Handelsgericht Wien zuständig.

2. Ist die dem Schiedsspruch zugrundliegende Rechtsstreitigkeit eine Handelssache im Sinn des § 51 JN, so entscheidet das Landesgericht in Ausübung der Gerichtsbarkeit in Handelssachen, in Wien das Handelsgericht Wien; handelt es sich um eine Arbeitsrechtssachen im Sinne des § 50 Abs. 1 ASGG, so entscheiden die Landesgerichte als Arbeits- und Sozialgerichte, in Wien das Arbeits- und Sozialgericht Wien.

VERFAHREN

§ 616

1. Das Verfahren über die Klage auf Aufhebung des Schiedsspruchs und die Klage auf Feststellung des Bestehens oder Nichtbestehens eines Schiedsspruchs richtet sich nach den Bestimmungen dieses Gesetzes, das Verfahren in Angelegenheiten nach dem dritten Titel richtet sich nach den allgemeinen Bestimmungen des Außerstreitgesetzes.

2. Auf Antrag einer Partei kann die Öffentlichkeit auch ausgeschlossen werden, wenn ein berechtigtes Interesse daran dargetan wird.

ZEHNTER TITEL – SONDERBESTIMMUNGEN

KONSUMENTEN

§ 617

1. Schiedsvereinbarungen zwischen einem Unternehmer und einem Verbraucher können wirksam nur für bereits entstandene Streitigkeiten abgeschlossen werden.

2. Schiedsvereinbarungen, an denen ein Verbraucher beteiligt ist, müssen in einem von diesem eigenhändig unterzeichneten Dokument enthalten sein. Andere Vereinbarungen als solche, die sich auf das Schiedsverfahren beziehen, darf dieses nicht enthalten.

3. Bei Schiedsvereinbarungen zwischen einem Unternehmer und einem Verbraucher ist dem Verbraucher vor Abschluss der Schiedsvereinbarung eine

schriftliche Rechtsbelehrung über die wesentlichen Unterschiede zwischen einem Schiedsverfahren und einem Gerichtsverfahren zu erteilen.

4. In Schiedsvereinbarungen zwischen Unternehmern und Verbrauchern muss der Sitz des Schiedsgerichts festgelegt werden. Das Schiedsgericht darf zur mündlichen Verhandlung und zur Beweisaufnahme nur dann an einem anderen Ort zusammentreten, wenn der Verbraucher dem zugestimmt hat oder der Beweisaufnahme am Sitz des Schiedsgerichts erhebliche Schwierigkeiten entgegenstehen.

5. Wurde die Schiedsvereinbarung zwischen einem Unternehmer und einem Verbraucher geschlossen, und hat der Verbraucher weder bei Abschluss der Schiedsvereinbarung noch zu dem Zeitpunkt, zu dem eine Klage anhängig gemacht wird, seinen Wohnsitz, gewöhnlichen Aufenthalt oder Beschäftigungsort in dem Staat, in welchem das Schiedsgericht seinen Sitz hat, so ist die Schiedsvereinbarung nur zu beachten, wenn sich der Verbraucher darauf beruft.

6. Ein Schiedsspruch ist auch dann aufzuheben, wenn in einem Schiedsverfahren, an dem ein Verbraucher beteiligt ist,

(1) gegen zwingende Rechtsvorschriften verstoßen wurde, deren Anwendung auch bei einem Sachverhalt mit Auslandsberührung durch Rechtswahl der Parteien nicht, abbedungen werden könnte, oder

(2) die Voraussetzungen vorhanden sind, unter denen nach § 530 Abs. 1 Z 6 und 7 ein gerichtliches Urteil mittels Wiederaufnahmsklage angefochten werden kann; diesfalls ist die Frist für die Aufhebungsklage nach den Bestimmungen über die Wiederaufnahmsklage zu beurteilen.

7. Hat das Schiedsverfahren zwischen einem Unternehmer und einem Verbraucher stattgefunden, so ist der Schiedsspruch auch aufzuheben, wenn die schriftliche Rechtsbelehrung nach Abs. 3 nicht erteilt wurde.

ARBEITSRECHTSSACHEN

§ 618

Für Schiedsverfahren in Arbeitsrechtssachen nach § 50 Abs. 1 ASGG gilt § 617 Abs. 2 bis Abs. 7 sinngemäß.

Annex 9a

Former Code of Civil Procedure*

ARBITRATION PROCEDURE – ARBITRATION AGREEMENT

Section 577

1. An agreement that a legal dispute shall be settled by one or more arbitrators (an arbitration agreement) is valid insofar as the parties are entitled to conclude a settlement concerning the subject matter of the dispute.

2. An arbitration agreement submitting future disputes arising from a specified legal relationship to arbitration by one or more arbitrators is also valid.

3. The arbitration agreement must be in writing or be contained in telegrams, telexes or in electronic representations exchanged by the parties.

Section 578

Judicial officers may not accept appointment as arbitrators during their tenure of judicial office.

Section 579

No one is obliged to accept appointment as arbitrator. If he has reasonable cause an arbitrator may resign even after accepting appointment.

---

*   Translation from the German, which is the authentic text. Reprinted with kind permission of the Vienna International Arbitration Centre (VIAC).

Section 580

If the arbitration agreement contains neither the names of the arbitrators nor a provision concerning number and appointment of arbitrators, each party shall appoint an arbitrator, and they in turn shall appoint the chairman of the arbitral tribunal.

Section 581

1. A party which is obliged to make an appointment of an arbitrator pursuant to an arbitration agreement can be required by the opposing party to appoint an arbitrator within 14 days and to give notice to the party making the demand. The demand may also be made if the arbitrator who has already been appointed pursuant to the arbitration agreement refuses to accept office as arbitrator or refuses to fulfil his obligations or dies or is challenged successfully or ceases to act for any other reason.

2. If the party making the demand also has to appoint an arbitrator, the demand shall also give notice of the person appointed as arbitrator.

3. The exchange of demands and notices can be made by post or through a public notary.

4. A person who is called on to appoint an arbitrator is bound by an appointment made by him as soon as the opposing party or one of the parties has received notice of the appointment.

Section 582

1. If an appointment is not made within the proper time or if the arbitrators cannot agree upon a chairman, the Court shall upon application make the appointment. The application should be brought before the Court which would have been competent to hear the dispute in first instance in the absence of an arbitration agreement; however, if a Court has been indicated in the arbitration agreement as being competent for this purpose and if it would be possible for that Court to be given competence by agreement of the parties (Section 104(1) and (2) Judicature Act), or if the arbitration agreement indicates the venue of the arbitral procedure, then that Court is competent, or in the absence of such indication, the Court under whose jurisdiction this venue comes. If there is no Court with local jurisdiction, or if such Court cannot be ascertained, the application should be brought before the Court which has local jurisdiction for the 1st municipal district of Vienna, insofar as the arbitration agreement requires the arbitral tribunal to meet within Austria. The application may be made by the parties and under Section 580 by either of the arbitrators. The applicant does not need to be represented by an attorney, even before the Superior Court of First Instance.

2. The order on the application is not subject to appeal.

Section 583

1. If the parties cannot agree on the arbitrator to be appointed by them jointly, the Court mentioned in Section 582 shall pronounce the rescission of the arbitration agreement.

2. The same procedure shall be followed

   (1) if named persons are appointed as arbitrators in the arbitration agreement and one of these arbitrators dies, ceases to act consequent upon a challenge or for any other reason, refuses to accept office as arbitrator or withdraws from the contract concluded with him because of his appointment; or
   (2) if an arbitrator who is named in the arbitration agreement or appointed by a party pursuant to the arbitration agreement or by the Court pursuant to Section 582 refuses to fulfil the obligations assumed by his acceptance of office as arbitrator, or delays unreasonably in their fulfilment.

3. If the arbitration agreement is concluded with reference to all disputes arising out of a particular legal relationship and the circumstances in which the Court is to declare the arbitration agreement as rescinded are such that submission to arbitration of possible disputes arising in the future is not excluded, the Court shall only declare the arbitration agreement of no effect for the case in question.

Section 584

1. The decision on an application under Section 583 shall be made by order after an oral hearing. This decision and the decision on an application under Section 582 may be made in the Superior Court of First Instance by the President of the Court or by a judge authorized by him.

2. An arbitrator who does not fulfil in time or at all the obligations assumed by his acceptance of office is liable to the parties for all the loss caused by his wrongful refusal or delay, without prejudice to the parties' rights to claim rescission of the arbitration agreement.

Section 585

The provisions of Sections 582 and 583 are not applicable insofar as the parties have agreed otherwise in the arbitration agreement or in a written agreement made after the conclusion of the arbitration agreement.

Section 586

1. An arbitrator may be challenged for the same reasons that a judge may be challenged (Sections 19 and 20 Judicature Act).

2. A party which appoints an arbitrator alone or jointly with the opposing party is entitled to challenge him only if the reason for the challenge arose or became known to the party after the appointment.

PROCEDURE BEFORE THE ARBITRATORS

Section 587

1. The arbitrators shall hear the parties and investigate the facts of the case before making their award. The procedure shall be determined by the arbitrators in their discretion unless the parties have agreed otherwise in the arbitration agreement or in a subsequent written agreement.

2. If a party refuses to attend the hearing before the arbitrators, the hearing shall continue in the presence of the other party.

Section 588

The arbitrators are not entitled to administer the oath to the parties, witnesses and experts, who appear voluntarily before them. They may not apply coercive measures or award punishments against parties or other persons.

Section 589

1. Those judicial acts considered necessary by the arbitrators but which they have no jurisdiction to undertake will be carried out by the State Court which has jurisdiction on the application of the arbitrators. In case of doubt the application is to be made to the District Court in whose district the act is to be carried out or the evidence to be taken.

2. The Court to which the application is made shall accede to it insofar as it is not legally inadmissible. In particular the Court shall also take those decisions regarding taking of evidence which are reserved by the present statute in the case of taking of evidence on commission to the Court hearing the case.

Section 590

If more than two arbitrators are to decide, the award shall be made by an absolute majority unless the arbitration agreement contains anything to the contrary.

Section 591

1. If the necessary majority for taking a decision, or where there are only two arbitrators, unanimity cannot be reached the arbitrators must inform the parties.

2. If no other provision for this case is contained in the arbitration agreement or in a subsequent written agreement of the parties, any party may apply to the Court mentioned inn Section 582 for a declaration that the arbitration agreement is rescinded or of no effect in the particular case.

Section 592

1. Copies of the award shall be served on the parties either in person before the arbitral tribunal or by post or by a public notary.

2. These copies and the original of the award shall mention the date of the making of the award and shall be signed by the arbitrators. The signature of the majority of the arbitrators shall suffice if there is a statement in the award that the minority refuses to sign or if signature of the minority cannot be obtained because of an obstacle which cannot be overcome within a reasonable period of time.

Section 593

1. The original award and documents recording the service of copies on the parties shall be kept in safe custody by the person named in the arbitration agreement. If no such agreement has been made or the named custodian has died, the arbitrators shall determine the method of deposit. In case of doubt these documents shall be deposited with a public notary of the district where the arbitral tribunal has its seat.

2. The original of the award and the documents recording service are to be deemed documents common to the parties.

Section 594

1. The arbitral award has the effect between the parties of a final and binding Court judgment unless the parties have agreed in the arbitration agreement that there shall be the possibility of an appeal against the award to a second-tier arbitral body.

2. The chairman of the tribunal, or if he is unable to act, any other arbitrator, shall at the request of a party confirm in writing on a copy of the award the final and binding nature and the enforceability of the award.

CANCELLATION OF THE AWARD

Section 595

1. The award shall be set aside,

    (1) if an arbitration agreement according to Section 577 does not exist, if the arbitration agreement has become invalid before the making of the award

or ceased to have effect for the particular case or if a party was unable to conclude the arbitration agreement because of its status;

(2) if the party applying to have the award set aside was unable to present its case in the proceedings before the arbitrators or if required by statute to be represented by an agent or guardian was not so represented in those proceedings unless in the latter case the procedure has been subsequently properly ratified;

(3) if statutory or contractual provisions regarding the composition of the arbitral tribunal or the method of reaching a decision have been infringed or if the original of the award has not been signed in accordance with the provisions of Section 592 (2);

(4) if a challenge to an arbitrator has been rejected unjustifiably by the arbitral tribunal;

(5) if the arbitral tribunal dealt with matters beyond those referred to it;

(6) if the award is incompatible with the basic principles of the Austrian legal system or if it infringes mandatory provisions of the law, the application of which cannot be set aside by a choice of law of the parties even in a case where a foreign contact according to Section 35 of the International Private Law Act is involved;

(7) if the conditions are present in which a request can be made under Section 530 (1) figures 1 to 7 for a Court judgment to be set aside and the case re-opened.*

2. In the cases set out in section (1) above, figures 2 to 7, the arbitration agreement will become invalid in respect of the subject matter of the arbitration procedure if an arbitral award thereupon has been set aside twice by final and binding judgment.

Section 596

1. If an applicant is made to set aside an award, the application shall be made to the Court specified in Section 582.

2. If the application is based on one of the grounds set out in Section 595 (1) figures 1 to 6, it must be made within a time limit of three months failing which the application will be time barred. The time limit begins to run on the day of service of the award on the party concerned, or, if the ground for rescission only came to the party's notice later, from the day when the party became aware of the said ground.

3. The time limit for applications under Section 595 (1) figure 7 is governed by the provisions concerning the application to re-open the case.

Section 597

The procedure on an application to set aside the award shall be in accordance with the general provisions of the present statute.

Section 598

1. A party cannot waive the application of Sections 586, 592 and 595, either in the arbitration agreement or any other agreement.

2. If both parties have concluded the arbitration agreement as businessmen (Section 1 (1) figure 1 of the Consumer Protection Act), they may waive the application of Section 595 (1) figure 7.

Section 599

1. The provisions of this chapter are applicable *mutatis mutandis* to arbitral tribunals constituted in ways permitted by statute whether by will or other dispositions not being based on the agreement of the parties to the dispute or by Sections of association. The provisions of Sections 586, 592 and 595 may not be waived by unilateral dispositions or provisions of Sections of association.

2. Arbitral tribunals constituted in accordance with the Act for the Settlement of Differences in Associations 1951, Official Gazette No. 233/1951 (*Vereinsgesetz* 1951, BGBl. Nr. 233/1951), are not subject to the provisions of this chapter.

---

*   Section 530 Application to re-open a case:

1. A case concluded by a judgement can be re-opened on application of a party,
    1. if a document on which the judgement was based was completely or partially forged;
    2. if a witness or expert of the opposing party has given false testimony during his examination and the judgementis based on this testimony;
    3. if the judgement was given as a result of an act punishable at law, whether as willful misrepresentation (Section 108 StGB), embezzlement (Section 134 StGB), fraud (Section 146 StGB), forgery of documents (Section 223 StGB), forgery of documents especially protected by the law (as defined in Section 224 StGB), forgery of public seals (Section 225 StGB), indirect false recording or certification (Section 228 StGB), suppression of documents (Section 229 StGB), or of displacement of boundary marks (Section 230 StGB), on the part of the representative of the party, or of the opposing party or its representative;
    4. if the judge has been guilty of criminal negligence of his official duties to the prejudice of the applicant in giving judgement or in a previous decision relating to the case on which the judgement or in a previous decision relating to the case on which the judgement is based;
    5. if a decision by a criminal court on which the judgement is based has been set aside by a subsequent final judgement;
    6. if the applicant discovers the existence of, or is placed in a position to use previous judgement concerning the same claim or the same legal relationship which is already final and which determines the rights of and between the parties of the case to be re-opened;
    7. if the applicant has discovered or is placed in a position to use new facts or evidence which would have resulted in a more favourable decision for the applicant on the merits, if they had been presented in the previous hearing.
2. The re-opening of the case under figures 6 and 7 is only permissible if the applicant was unable without fault on his part to assert the finality of the judgement or the new facts or evidence before the end of the oral hearing after which the judgement of First Instance was given.

Annex 9b

Zivilprozessordnung (in der Fassung vor der Schiedsrechtsänderungsreform 2006 'Alte Fassung')*

SCHIEDSRICHTERLICHES VERFAHREN – SCHIEDSVERTRAG

§ 577

1. Die Vereinbarung, dass die Entscheidung einer Rechtsstreitigkeit durch einen oder mehrere Schiedsrichter erfolgen solle (Schiedsvertrag), hat insoweit rechtliche Wirkung, als die Parteien über den Gegenstand des Streites einen Vergleich abzuschließen fähig sind.

2. In einem Schiedsvertrag kann auch wirksam vereinbart werden, dass aus einem bestimmten Rechtsverhältnisse künftig entstehende Streitigkeiten durch einen oder mehrere Schiedsrichter entschieden werden sollen.

3. Der Schiedsvertrag muss schriftlich errichtet werden oder in Telegrammen, Fernschreiben oder elektronischen Erklärungen enthalten sein, die die Parteien gewechselt haben.

§ 578

Richterliche Beamte dürfen, solange sie im richterlichen Dienste stehen, die Bestellung als Schiedsrichter nicht annehmen.

---

* Gilt für Verfahren, die vor dem 1.7.2006 begonnen wurden.

§ 579

Niemand ist verpflichtet, die Bestellung als Schiedsrichter anzunehmen. Aus trif-
tigen Gründen kann der Schiedsrichter auch nach Annahme der Bestellung von der
übernommenen Verpflichtung zurücktreten.

§ 580

Wenn in dem Schiedsvertrage weder die Schiedsrichter benannt, noch eine
Bestimmung über die Zahl und Ernennung der Schiedsrichter enthalten ist, so wird
von jeder Partei ein Schiedsrichter bestellt. Diese haben einen Obmann zu wählen.

§ 581

1. Wer zufolge eines Schiedsvertrages die Bestellung eines Schiedsrichters vorzunehmen hat, kann von dem Gegner oder, wenn die Bestellung des Schiedsrichters
einem Dritten obliegt, von jeder der Parteien aufgefordert werden, binnen vierzehn
Tagen diesen Schiedsrichter zu bestellen und hievon der auffordernden Partei
Mittheilung zu machen. Eine gleiche Aufforderung ist dann zulässig, wenn der
auf Grund des Schiedsvertrages bereits bestellt Schiedsrichter die Annahme des
Schiedsrichteramtes oder die Erfüllung seiner Verpflichtungen verweigert, wenn
er stirbt, mit Erfolg abgelehnt wird, oder aus einem anderen Grunde wegfällt.

2. Hat auch die auffordernde Partei einen Schiedsrichter zu bestellen, so hat sie
mit ihrer Aufforderung die Anzeige zu verbinden, welche Person sie selbst zum
Schiedsrichter bestellt hat.

3. Diese gegenseitigen Aufforderungen und Anzeigen können durch die Post oder
einen Notar vorgenommen werden.

4. Die zur Bestellung eines Schiedsrichters berufene Person ist an die von ihr
vorgenommene Bestellung gebunden, sobald der Gegner oder eine der Parteien
die Anzeige dieser Bestellung erhalten hat.

§ 582

1. Wenn die Bestellung eines Schiedsrichters nicht rechtzeitig vorgenommen wird
oder wenn die beiden Schiedsrichter sich über die Person des Obmannes nicht einigen können, so erfolgt die Bestellung auf Antrag durch das Gericht. Der Antrag ist bei
dem Gericht zu stellen, welches mangels eines Schiedsvertrages für den Rechtsstreit
in erster Instanz zuständig wäre; ist jedoch im Schiedsvertrag das Gericht, das hiefür
zuständig sein soll, bezeichnet und könnte es durch Vereinbarung der Parteien
zuständig gemacht werden (§ 104 Abs. 1 und 2 JN) oder ist im Schiedsvertrag der
Ort bezeichnet, an dem das Schiedsgericht tagen soll, so ist jenes Gericht oder in
Ermangelung einer solchen Bezeichnung das für diesen Ort zuständige Gericht
zuständig. Fehlt ein örtlich zuständiges Gericht oder ist es nicht zu ermitteln, so

ist der Antrag, sofern das Schiedsgericht nach dem Schiedsvertrag im Inland tagen soll, bei dem örtlich für den ersten Wiener Gemeindebezirk zuständigen Gericht zu stellen. Zur Antragstellung sind die Parteien und im Fall des § 580 auch jeder der beiden Schiedsrichter berechtigt. Zur Antragstellung ist auch vor Gerichtshöfen die Vertretung durch einen Rechtsanwalt nicht notwendig.

2. Der über den Antrag ergehende Beschluss kann durch ein Rechtsmittel nicht angefochten werden.

§ 583

1. Können sich die Parteien über von ihnen gemeinschaftlich zu bestellende Schiedsrichter nicht einigen, so hat das im § 582 bezeichnete Gericht auf Antrag auszusprechen, dass der Schiedsvertrag außer Kraft trete.

2. Gleiches hat dann zu geschehen, wenn:

(1) bestimmte Personen in dem Schiedsvertrage zu Schiedsrichtern bestellt sind und einer dieser Schiedsrichter stirbt, infolge Ablehnung oder aus einem anderen Grunde wegfällt, die Übernahme des Schiedsrichteramtes verweigert oder von dem mit ihm deshalb geschlossenen Vertrage zurücktritt, oder wenn

(2) ein im Schiedsvertrage ernannter oder auf Grund des Schiedsvertrages von einer Partei oder gemäß § 582 vom Gericht bestellter Schiedsrichter die Erfüllung seiner durch die Annahme der Bestellung übernommenen Verpflichtung verweigert oder ungebührlich verzögert.

3. Wenn der Schiedsvertrag in Ansehung aller aus einem bestimmten Rechtsverhältnisse entstehenden Streitigkeiten geschlossen ist, und der Umstand, wegen dessen das Gericht den Schiedsvertrag für unwirksam erklären soll, so beschaffen ist, dass er die schiedsrichterliche Erledigung der sich in Zukunft aus diesem Rechtsverhältnisse etwa noch ergebenden Streitigkeiten nicht ausschließt, so hat das Gericht seinen Ausspruch dahin zu beschränken, dass der Schiedsvertrag nur für diesen bestimmten Fall unwirksam ist.

§ 584

1. Über einen im Sinne des § 583 gestellten Antrag ist nach vorgängiger mündlicher Verhandlung durch Beschluss zu entscheiden. Diese Entscheidung sowie die Entscheidung über einen gemäß § 582 gestellten Antrag kann bei Gerichtshöfen auch von dem Vorsteher des Gerichtshofes oder von einem seitens des Vorstehers beauftragten Richter gefällt werden.

2. Ein Schiedsrichter, welcher die durch Annahme der Bestellung übernommene Verpflichtung gar nicht oder nicht rechtzeitig erfüllt, haftet den Parteien, unbeschadet ihres Rechtes, die Außerkraftsetzung des Schiedsvertrages zu begehren, für allen durch seine schuldbare Weigerung oder Verzögerung verursachten Schaden.

§ 585

Die Bestimmungen der §§ 582 und 583 finden insoweit keine Anwendung, als im Schiedsvertrage oder in einer dem Abschluss des Schiedsvertrages nachgefolgten schriftlichen Vereinbarung von den Parteien für die bezeichneten Fälle etwas anderes festgesetzt ist.

§ 586

1. Ein Schiedsrichter kann aus denselben Gründen abgelehnt werden, welche zur Ablehnung eines Richters berechtigen (§§ 19 und 20 Jur.- Norm).

2. Eine Partei, welche einen Schiedsrichter allein oder in Gemeinschaft mit ihrem Gegner bestellt hat, ist zur Ablehnung desselben nur dann berechtigt, wenn der Ablehnungsgrund erst nach der Bestellung entstanden oder der Partei bekannt geworden ist.

VERFAHREN VOR DEN SCHIEDSRICHTERN

§ 587

1. Die Schiedsrichter haben vor Erlassung des Schiedsspruches die Parteien zu hören und den dem Streite zugrunde liegenden Sachverhalt zu ermitteln. Das Verfahren wird, sofern durch den Schiedsvertrag oder eine nachträgliche schriftliche Vereinbarung der Parteien nichts anderes festgesetzt ist, von den Schiedsrichtern nach freiem Ermessen bestimmt.

2. Wenn sich eine Partei in die Verhandlung vor den Schiedsrichtern nicht einlässt, ist mit der anderen Partei allein zu verhandeln.

§ 588

Die Schiedsrichter dürfen die Parteien, sowie die Zeugen und Sachverständigen, welche freiwillig vor ihnen erscheinen, nur unbeeidet vernehmen. Sie dürfen weder gegen Parteien noch gegen andere Personen Zwangsmittel anwenden oder Strafen verhängen.

§ 589

1. Von den Schiedsrichtern für erforderlich erachtete richterliche Handlungen, zu deren Vornahme dieselben nicht befugt sind, werden auf Ersuchen der Schiedsrichter von dem zuständigen staatlichen Gerichte vorgenommen. Im Zweifel ist das Ersuchen an das Bezirksgericht zu stellen, in dessen Sprengel die Handlung vorgenommen werden soll oder der Beweis aufzunehmen ist.

2. Das ersuchte Gericht hat dem Ersuchen zu entsprechen, sofern dasselbe nicht gesetzlich unzulässig ist. In Ansehung einer Beweisaufnahme stehen diesem

Gerichte insbesondere auch die Entscheidungen zu, welche für den Fall der Beweisaufnahme durch einen ersuchten Richter durch die Bestimmungen des gegenwärtigen Gesetzes dem erkennenden Gerichte oder dem Processgerichte vorbehalten sind.

§ 590

Wenn mehr als zwei Schiedsrichter zur Entscheidung berufen sind, ist der Schiedsspruch nach der absoluten Mehrheit der Stimmen zu fällen, sofern nicht in dem Schiedsvertrage etwas anderes bestimmt ist.

§ 591

1. Wenn bei einer Entscheidung die für die Beschlussfassung erforderliche Stimmenmehrheit oder, falls nur zwei Schiedsrichter bestellt sind, Stimmeneinhelligkeit nicht zu erreichen ist, so haben die Schiedsrichter dies den Parteien bekannt zu geben.

2. Wenn nicht im Schiedsvertrage oder in einer nachträglichen schriftlichen Vereinbarung der Parteien für einen solchen Fall eine andere Vorsorge getroffen ist, kann jede der Parteien bei dem im § 582 bezeichneten Gerichte den Antrag auf Erlassung eines Ausspruches stellen, dass der Schiedsvertrag außer Kraft trete oder für den einzelnen Fall unwirksam sei (§ 584).

§ 592

1. Den Parteien sind Ausfertigungen des Schiedsspruchs, und zwar, falls sie dieselben nicht vor dem Schiedsgericht persönlich in Empfang nehmen, durch die Post, einen Notar oder im Weg der elektronischen Post zuzustellen.

2. Diese Ausfertigungen und die Urschrift des Schiedsspruches sind mit der Angabe des Tages der Abfassung des Schiedsspruches zu versehen und von den Schiedsrichtern zu unterschreiben. Die Unterschrift der Mehrheit der Schiedsrichter genügt, wenn im Schiedsspruch vermerkt wird, daß die anderen die Unterschrift verweigern oder daß der Unterzeichnung durch sie ein Hindernis entgegensteht, das nicht in angemessener Frist überwunden werden kann.

§ 593

1. Die Urschrift des Schiedsspruches ist nebst den Beurkundungen über die an die Parteien erfolgte Zustellung der Ausfertigungen von der im Schiedsvertrage bezeichneten Person zu verwahren. Fehlt es an einer solchen Vereinbarung oder ist der benannte Verwahrer verstorben, so haben die Schiedsrichter die Art der Verwahrung zu bestimmen. Im Zweifel sind diese Schriftstücke bei einem Notar des Bezirkes zu hinterlegen, in welchem das Schiedsgericht seinen Sitz hatte.

2. Die Urschrift des Schiedsspruches, sowie die Zustellungsbeurkundungen haben als den Parteien gemeinschaftliche Urkunden zu gelten.

§ 594

1. Der Schiedsspruch hat unter den Parteien die Wirkung eines rechtskräftigen gerichtlichen Urtheiles, sofern die Parteien in dem Schiedsvertrage nicht die Zulässigkeit der Anfechtung des Urtheiles vor einer höheren schiedsrichterlichen Instanz vereinbart haben.

2. Der Obmann, im Fall seiner Verhinderung ein anderer Schiedsrichter, hat auf Verlangen einer Partei die Rechtskraft und die Vollstreckbarkeit des Schiedsspruches auf einer Ausfertigung zu bestätigen.

AUFHEBUNG DES SCHIEDSSPRUCHES

§ 595

1. Der Schiedsspruch ist aufzuheben,

   (1) wenn ein dem § 577 entsprechender Schiedsvertrag nicht vorhanden ist, der Schiedsvertrag vor der Fällung des Schiedsspruches außer Kraft getreten oder für den einzelnen Fall unwirksam geworden ist oder wenn eine Partei nach ihrem Personalstatut zur Eingehung des Schiedsvertrages nicht fähig war;

   (2) wenn der Partei, die die Aufhebung des Schiedsspruches begehrt, im Verfahren vor den Schiedsrichtern das rechtliche Gehör nicht gewährt wurde oder wenn sie, falls sie eines gesetzlichen Vertreters bedarf, in diesem Verfahren nicht durch einen solchen vertreten war, sofern nicht im letzten Fall die Prozeßführung nachträglich ordnungsgemäß genehmigt worden ist;

   (3) wenn gesetzliche oder vertragliche Bestimmungen über die Besetzung des Schiedsgerichtes oder die Beschlußfassung verletzt worden sind oder wenn die Urschrift des Schiedsspruches nicht entsprechend dem § 592 Abs. 2 unterschrieben worden ist;

   (4) wenn die Ablehnung eines Schiedsrichters vom Schiedsgericht ungerechtfertigt zurückgewiesen worden ist;

   (5) wenn das Schiedsgericht die Grenzen seiner Aufgabe überschritten hat;

   (6) wenn der Schiedsspruch mit den Grundwertungen der österreichischen Rechtsordnung unvereinbar ist oder gegen zwingende Rechtsvorschriften verstößt, deren Anwendung auch bei einem Sachverhalt mit Auslandsberührung nach § 35 IPR-Gesetz durch eine Rechtswahl der Parteien nicht abbedungen werden kann;

   (7) wenn die Voraussetzungen vorhanden sind, unter denen nach § 530 Abs. 1 Z 1 bis 7 ein gerichtliches Urteil mittels der Wiederaufnahmsklage angefochten werden kann.

2. In den Fällen des Abs. 1 Z 2 bis 7 wird der Schiedsvertrag für den Gegenstand des Schiedsverfahrens unwirksam, wenn bereits zweimal ein Schiedsspruch hierüber rechtskräftig aufgehoben worden ist.

§ 596

1. Wird auf Aufhebung eines Schiedsspruches geklagt, so ist die Klage bei dem im § 582 bezeichneten Gerichte anzubringen.

2. Sie ist, wenn sie auf einen der im § 595, Abs. 1 Z 1 bis 6 angegebenen Gründe gestützt wird, bei sonstigem Ausschlusse binnen der Frist von drei Monaten zu erheben. Diese Frist beginnt mit dem Tage, an welchem der Partei der Schiedsspruch zugestellt wurde, wenn aber der Anfechtungsgrund erst später bekannt wurde, mit dem Tage, an welchem die Partei vom Anfechtungsgrund Kenntnis erlangt hat.

3. Im Falle des § 595 Abs. 1 Z 7 ist die Frist für die Klage nach den Bestimmungen über die Wiederaufnahmsklage zu beurtheilen.

§ 597

Über die Klage auf Aufhebung eines Schiedsspruches ist nach den allgemeinen Vorschriften dieses Gesetzes zu verfahren.

§ 598

1. Auf die Anwendung der Bestimmungen der §§ 586, 592 und 595 kann von den Parteien weder im Schiedsvertrag, noch im Wege einer anderen Vereinbarung verzichtet werden.

2. Haben beide Parteien den Schiedsvertrag als Unternehmer (§ 1 Abs. 1 Z 1 KSchG) geschlossen, so können sie auf die Anwendung des § 595 Abs. 1 Z 7 verzichten.

§ 599

1. Die Vorschriften dieses Abschnittes finden auf Schiedsgerichte sinngemäße Anwendung, die in gesetzlich zulässiger Weise durch letztwillige oder andere nicht auf Vereinbarung der streitenden Theile beruhende Verfügungen oder durch Statuten angeordnet werden. Die Anwendung der §§ 586, 592 und 595 kann auch nicht durch einseitige Verfügungen oder durch Statutenbestimmungen wirksam ausgeschlossen werden.

2. Die in Gemäßheit des Gesetzes vom 15. November 1867, R. G. Bl. Nr. 134, zur Schlichtung von Streitigkeiten aus dem Vereinsverhältnisse errichteten Schiedsgerichte sind den Bestimmungen dieses Abschnittes nicht unterworfen.

Annex 10

European Convention on International Commercial Arbitration 1961 (European Convention)*

Preamble

The undersigned, duly authorized,

Convened under the auspices of the Economic Commission for Europe of the United Nations,

Having noted that on 10th June 1958 at the United Nations Conference on International Commercial Arbitration has been signed in New York a Convention on the Recognition and Enforcement of Foreign Arbitral Awards,

Desirous of promoting the development of European trade by, as far as possible, removing certain difficulties that may impede the organization and operation of international commercial arbitration in relations between physical or legal persons of different European countries,

Have agreed on the following provisions:

Article I – Scope of the Convention

1. This Convention shall apply:

    a. to arbitration agreements concluded for the purpose of settling disputes arising from international trade between physical or legal persons having,

---

*   Done at Geneva, 21 April 1961.

when concluding the agreement, their habitual place of residence or their seat in different Contracting States;

b. to arbitral procedures and awards based on agreements referred to in paragraph 1(a) above.

2. For the purpose of this Convention,

a. the term 'arbitration agreement' shall mean either an arbitral clause in a contract or an arbitration agreement being signed by the parties, or contained in an exchange of letters, telegrams, or in a communication by teleprinter and, in relations between States whose laws do not require that an arbitration agreement be made in writing, any arbitration agreement concluded in the form authorized by these laws;

b. the term 'arbitration' shall mean not only settlement by arbitrators appointed for each case (ad hoc arbitration) but also by permanent arbitral institutions;

c. the term 'seat' shall mean the place of the situation of the establishment that has made the arbitration agreement.

Article II – Right of legal persons of public law to resort to arbitration

1. In the cases referred to in Article I, paragraph 1, of this Convention, legal persons considered by the law which is applicable to them as 'legal persons of public law' have the right to conclude valid arbitration agreements.

2. On signing, ratifying or acceding to this Convention any State shall be entitled to declare that it limits the above faculty to such conditions as may be stated in its declaration.

Article III – Right of foreign nationals to be designated as arbitrators

In arbitration covered by this Convention, foreign nationals may be designated as arbitrators.

Article IV – Organization of the arbitration

1. The parties to an arbitration agreement shall be free to submit their disputes:

a. to a permanent arbitral institution; in this case, the arbitration proceedings shall be held in conformity with the rules of the said institution;

b. to an ad hoc arbitral procedure; in this case, they shall be free inter alia:

i. to appoint arbitrators or to establish means for their appointment in the event of an actual dispute;

ii. to determine the place of arbitration; and

iii. to lay down the procedure to be followed by the arbitrators.

2. Where the parties have agreed to submit any disputes to an ad hoc arbitration, and where within thirty days of the notification of the request for arbitration to the respondent one of the parties fails to appoint his arbitrator, the latter shall, unless otherwise provided, be appointed at the request of the other party by the President of the competent Chamber of Commerce of the country of the defaulting party's habitual place of residence or seat at the time of the introduction of the request for arbitration. This paragraph shall also apply to the replacement of the arbitrator(s) appointed by one of the parties or by the President of the Chamber of Commerce above referred to.

3. Where the parties have agreed to submit any disputes to an ad hoc arbitration by one or more arbitrators and the arbitration agreement contains no indication regarding the organization of the arbitration, as mentioned in paragraph 1 of this article, the necessary steps shall be taken by the arbitrator(s) already appointed, unless the parties are able to agree thereon and without prejudice to the case referred to in paragraph 2 above. Where the parties cannot agree on the appointment of the sole arbitrator or where the arbitrators appointed cannot agree on the measures to be taken, the claimant shall apply for the necessary action, where the place of arbitration has been agreed upon by the parties, at his option to the President of the Chamber of Commerce of the place of arbitration agreed upon or to the President of the competent Chamber of Commerce of the respondent's habitual place of residence or seat at the time of the introduction of the request for arbitration. Where such a place has not been agreed upon, the claimant shall be entitled at his option to apply for the necessary action either to the President of the competent Chamber of Commerce of the country of the respondent's habitual place of residence or seat at the time of the introduction of the request for arbitration, or to the Special Committee whose composition and procedure are specified in the Annex to this Convention. Where the claimant fails to exercise the rights given to him under this paragraph the respondent or the arbitrator(s) shall be entitled to do so.

4. When seized of a request the President or the Special Committee shall be entitled as need be:

    a. to appoint the sole arbitrator, presiding arbitrator, umpire, or referee;
    b. to replace the arbitrator(s) appointed under any procedure other than that referred to in paragraph 2 above;
    c. to determine the place of arbitration, provided that the arbitrator(s) may fix another place of arbitration;
    d. to establish directly or by reference to the rules and statutes of a permanent arbitral institution the rules of procedure to be followed by the arbitrator(s), provided that the arbitrators have not established these rules themselves in the absence of any agreement thereon between the parties.

5. Where the parties have agreed to submit their disputes to a permanent arbitral institution without determining the institution in question and cannot agree thereon, the claimant may request the determination of such institution in conformity with the procedure referred to in paragraph 3 above.

6. Where the arbitration agreement does not specify the mode of arbitration (arbitration by a permanent arbitral institution or an ad hoc arbitration) to which the parties have agreed to submit their dispute, and where the parties cannot agree thereon, the claimant shall be entitled to have recourse in this case to the procedure referred to in paragraph 3 above to determine the question. The President of the competent Chamber of Commerce or the Special Committee, shall be entitled either to refer the parties to a permanent arbitral institution or to request the parties to appoint their arbitrators within such time-limits as the President of the competent Chamber of Commerce or the Special Committee may have fixed and to agree within such time-limits on the necessary measures for the functioning of the arbitration. In the latter case, the provisions of paragraphs 2, 3 and 4 of this Article shall apply.

7. Where within a period of sixty days from the moment when he was requested to fulfil one of the functions set out in paragraphs 2, 3, 4, 5 and 6 of this Article, the President of the Chamber of Commerce designated by virtue of these paragraphs has not fulfilled one of these functions, the party requesting shall be entitled to ask the Special Committee to do so.

Article V – Plea as to arbitral jurisdiction

1. The party which intends to raise a plea as to the arbitrator's jurisdiction based on the fact that the arbitration agreement was either non-existent or null and void or had lapsed shall do so during the arbitration proceedings, not later than the delivery of its statement of claim or defence relating to the substance of the dispute; those based on the fact that an arbitrator has exceeded his terms of reference shall be raised during the arbitration proceedings as soon as the question on which the arbitrator is alleged to have no jurisdiction is raised during the arbitral procedure. Where the delay in raising the plea is due to a cause which the arbitrator deems justified, the arbitrator shall declare the plea admissible.

2. Pleas to the jurisdiction referred to in paragraph 1 above that have not been raised during the time-limits there referred to, may not be entered either during a subsequent stage of the arbitral proceedings where they are pleas left to the sole discretion of the parties under the law applicable by the arbitrator, or during subsequent court proceedings concerning the substance or the enforcement of the award where such pleas are left to the discretion of the parties under the rule of conflict of the court seized of the substance of the dispute or the enforcement of the award. The arbitrator's decision on the delay in raising the plea, will, however, be subject to judicial control.

3. Subject to any subsequent judicial control provided for under the lex fori, the arbitrator whose jurisdiction is called in question shall be entitled to proceed with the arbitration, to rule on his own jurisdiction and to decide upon the existence or the validity of the arbitration agreement or of the contract of which the agreement forms part.

Article VI – Jurisdiction of courts of law

1. A plea as to the jurisdiction of the court made before the court seized by either party to the arbitration agreement, on the basis of the fact that an arbitration agreement exists shall, under penalty of estoppel, be presented by the respondent before or at the same time as the presentation of his substantial defence, depending upon whether the law of the court seized regards this plea as one of procedure or of substance.

2. In taking a decision concerning the existence or the validity of an arbitration agreement, courts of Contracting States shall examine the validity of such agreement with reference to the capacity of the parties, under the law applicable to them, and with reference to other questions:

    a. under the law to which the parties have subjected their arbitration agreement;

    b. failing any indication thereon, under the law of the country in which the award is to be made;

    c. failing any indication as to the law to which the parties have subjected the agreement, and where at the time when the question is raised in court the country in which the award is to be made cannot be determined, under the competent law by virtue of the rules of conflict of the court seized of the dispute.

The courts may also refuse recognition of the arbitration agreement if under the law of their country the dispute is not capable of settlement by arbitration.

3. Where either party to an arbitration agreement has initiated arbitration proceedings before any resort is had to a court, courts of Contracting States subsequently asked to deal with the same subject-matter between the same parties or with the question whether the arbitration agreement was non-existent or null and void or had lapsed, shall stay their ruling on the arbitrator's jurisdiction until the arbitral award is made, unless they have good and substantial reasons to the contrary.

4. A request for interim measures or measures of conservation addressed to a judicial authority shall not be deemed incompatible with the arbitration agreement, or regarded as a submission of the substance of the case to the court.

Article VII – Applicable law

1. The parties shall be free to determine, by agreement, the law to be applied by the arbitrators to the substance of the dispute. Failing any indication by the parties as to the applicable law, the arbitrators shall apply the proper law under the rule of conflict that the arbitrators deem applicable. In both cases the arbitrators shall take account of the terms of the contract and trade usages.

2. The arbitrators shall act as amiables compositeurs if the parties so decide and if they may do so under the law applicable to the arbitration.

Article VIII – Reasons for the award

The parties shall be presumed to have agreed that reasons shall be given for the award unless they:

a. either expressly declare that reasons shall not be given; or
b. have assented to an arbitral procedure under which it is not customary to give reasons for awards, provided that in this case neither party requests before the end of the hearing, or if there has not been a hearing then before the making of the award, that reasons be given.

Article IX – Setting aside of the arbitral award

1. The setting aside in a Contracting State of an arbitral award covered by this Convention shall only constitute a ground for the refusal of recognition or enforcement in another Contracting State where such setting aside took place in a State in which, or under the law of which, the award has been made and for one of the following reasons:

a. the parties to the arbitration agreement were under the law applicable to them, under some incapacity or the said agreement is not valid under the law to which the parties have subjected it or, failing any indication thereon, under the law of the country where the award was made, or
b. the party requesting the setting aside of the award was not given proper notice of the appointment of the arbitrator or of the arbitration proceedings or was otherwise unable to present his case; or
c. the award deals with a difference not contemplated by or not falling within the terms of the submission to arbitration, or it contains decisions on matters beyond the scope of the submission to arbitration, provided that, if the decisions on matters submitted to arbitration can be separated from those not so submitted, that part of the award which contains decisions on matters submitted to arbitration need not be set aside;
d. the composition of the arbitral authority or the arbitral procedure was not in accordance with the agreement of the parties, or failing such agreement, with the provisions of Article IV of this Convention.

2. In relations between Contracting States that are also parties to the New York Convention on the Recognition and Enforcement of Foreign Arbitral Awards of 10th June 1958, paragraph 1 of this Article limits the application of Article V(1)(e) of the New York Convention solely to the cases of setting aside set out under paragraph 1 above.

Article X – Final clauses

1. This Convention is open for signature or accession by countries members of the Economic Commission for Europe and countries admitted to the Commission in a consultative capacity under paragraph 8 of the Commission's terms of reference.

2. Such countries as may participate in certain activities of the Economic Commission for Europe in accordance with paragraph 11 of the Commission's terms of reference may become Contracting Parties to this Convention by acceding thereto after its entry into force.

3. The Convention shall be open for signature until 31 December 1961 inclusive. Thereafter, it shall be open for accession.

4. This Convention shall be ratified.

5. Ratification or accession shall be effected by the deposit of an instrument with the Secretary-General of the United Nations.

6. When signing, ratifying or acceding to this Convention, the Contracting Parties shall communicate to the Secretary-General of the United Nations a list of the Chambers of Commerce or other institutions in their country who will exercise the functions conferred by virtue of Article IV of this Convention on Presidents of the competent Chambers of Commerce.

7. The provisions of the present Convention shall not affect the validity of multilateral or bilateral agreements concerning arbitration entered into by Contracting States.

8. This Convention shall come into force on the ninetieth day after five of the countries referred to in paragraph 1 above have deposited their instruments of ratification or accession. For any country ratifying or acceding to it later this Convention shall enter into force on the ninetieth day after the said country has deposited its instrument of ratification or accession.

9. Any Contracting Party may denounce this Convention by so notifying the Secretary-General of the United Nations. Denunciation shall take effect twelve months after the date of receipt by the Secretary-General of the notification of denunciation.

10. If, after the entry into force of this Convention, the number of Contracting Parties is reduced, as a result of denunciations, to less than five, the Convention shall cease to be in force from the date on which the last of such denunciations takes effect.

11. The Secretary-General of the United Nations shall notify the countries referred to in paragraph 1, and the countries which have become Contracting Parties under paragraph 2 above, of:

    a. declarations made under Article II, paragraph 2;
    b. ratifications and accessions under paragraphs 1 and 2 above;
    c. communications received in pursuance of paragraph 6 above;
    d. the dates of entry into force of this Convention in accordance with paragraph 8 above;
    e. denunciations under paragraph 9 above;
    f. the termination of this Convention in accordance with paragraph 10 above.

12. After 31 December 1961, the original of this Convention shall be deposited with the Secretary-General of the United Nations, who shall transmit certified true copies to each of the countries mentioned in paragraphs 1 and 2 above.

ANNEX: COMPOSITION AND PROCEDURE OF THE SPECIAL COMMITTEE REFERRED TO IN ARTICLE IV OF THE CONVENTION

1. The Special Committee referred to in Article IV of the Convention shall consist of two regular members and a Chairman. One of the regular members shall be elected by the Chambers of Commerce or other institutions designated, under Article X, paragraph 6, of the Convention, by States in which at the time when the Convention is open to signature National Committees of the International Chamber of Commerce exist, and which at the time of the election are parties to the Convention. The other member shall be elected by the Chambers of Commerce or other institutions designated, under Article X, paragraph 6, of the Convention, by States in which at the time when the Convention is open to signature no National Committees of the International Chamber of Commerce exist and which at the time of the election are parties to the Convention.

2. The persons who are to act as Chairman of the Special Committee pursuant to paragraph 7 of this Annex shall also be elected in like manner by the Chambers of Commerce or other institutions referred to in paragraph 1 of this Annex.

3. The Chambers of Commerce or other institutions referred to in paragraph 1 of this Annex shall elect alternates at the same time and in the same manner as they elect the Chairman and other regular members, in case of the temporary inability of the Chairman or regular members to act. In the event of the permanent inability to act or of the resignation of a Chairman or of a regular member, then the alternate elected to replace him shall become, as the case may be, the Chairman or regular member, and the group of Chambers of Commerce or other institutions which had elected the alternate who has become Chairman or regular member shall elect another alternate.

4. The first elections to the Committee shall be held within ninety days from the date of the deposit of the fifth instrument of ratification or accession. Chambers of Commerce and other institutions designated by Signatory States who are not yet parties to the Convention shall also be entitled to take part in these elections. If however it should not be possible to hold elections within the prescribed period, the entry into force of paragraphs 3 to 7 of Article IV of the Convention shall be postponed until elections are held as provided for above.

5. Subject to the provisions of paragraph 7 below, the members of the Special Committee shall be elected for a term of four years. New elections shall be held within the first six months of the fourth year following the previous elections. Nevertheless, if a new procedure for the election of the members of the Special Committee has not produced results, the members previously elected shall continue to exercise their functions until the election of new members.

6. The results of the elections of the members of the Special Committee shall be communicated to the Secretary-General of the United Nations who shall notify the States referred to in Article X, paragraph 1, of the Convention and the States which have become Contracting Parties under Article X, paragraph 2. The Secretary-General shall likewise notify the said States of any postponement and of the entry into force of paragraphs 3 to 7 of Article IV of the Convention in pursuance of paragraph 4 of this Annex.

7. The persons elected to the office of Chairman shall exercise their functions in rotation, each during a period of two years. The question which of these two persons shall act as Chairman during the first two-year period after the entry into force of the Convention shall be decided by the drawing of lots. The office of Chairman shall thereafter be vested, for each successive two-year period, in the person elected Chairman by the group of countries other than that by which the Chairman exercising his functions during the immediately preceding two-year period was elected.

8. The reference to the Special Committee of one of the requests referred to in paragraphs 3 to 7 of the aforesaid Article IV shall be addressed to the Executive Secretary of the Economic Commission for Europe. The Executive Secretary shall in the first instance lay the request before the member of the Special Committee elected by the group of countries other than that by which the Chairman holding office at the time of the introduction of the request was elected. The proposal of the member applied to in the first instance shall be communicated by the Executive Secretary to the other member of the Committee and, if that other member agrees to this proposal, it shall be deemed to be the Committee's ruling and shall be communicated as such by the Executive Secretary to the person who made the request.

9. If the two members of the Special Committee applied to by the Executive Secretary are unable to agree on a ruling by correspondence, the Executive Secretary of the Economic Commission for Europe shall convene a meeting of the said Committee at Geneva in an attempt to secure a unanimous decision on the request. In the absence of unanimity, the Committee's decision shall be given by a majority vote and shall be communicated by the Executive Secretary to the person who made the request.

10. The expenses connected with the Special Committee's action shall be advanced by the person requesting such action but shall be considered as costs in the cause.

Annex 11

Convention on the Recognition and Enforcement of Foreign Arbitral Awards 1958 (New York Convention)*

Article I

1. This Convention shall apply to the recognition and enforcement of arbitral awards made in the territory of a State other than the State where the recognition and enforcement of such awards are sought, and arising out of differences between persons, whether physical or legal. It shall also apply to arbitral awards not considered as domestic awards in the State where their recognition and enforcement are sought.

2. The term 'arbitral awards' shall include not only awards made by arbitrators appointed for each case but also those made by permanent arbitral bodies to which the parties have submitted.

3. When signing, ratifying or acceding to this Convention, or notifying extension under article X hereof, any State may on the basis of reciprocity declare that it will apply the Convention to the recognition and enforcement of awards made only in the territory of another Contracting State. It may also declare that it will apply the Convention only to differences arising out of legal relationships, whether contractual or not, which are considered as commercial under the national law of the State making such declaration.

Article II

1. Each Contracting State shall recognize an agreement in writing under which the parties undertake to submit to arbitration all or any differences which have arisen

---

* Done at New York, on 10 June 1958. Reprinted with kind permission of UNCITRAL.

or which may arise between them in respect of a defined legal relationship, whether contractual or not, concerning a subject matter capable of settlement by arbitration.

2. The term 'agreement in writing' shall include an arbitral clause in a contract or an arbitration agreement, signed by the parties or contained in an exchange of letters or telegrams.

3. The court of a Contracting State, when seized of an action in a matter in respect of which the parties have made an agreement within the meaning of this article, shall, at the request of one of the parties, refer the parties to arbitration, unless it finds that the said agreement is null and void, inoperative or incapable of being performed.

Article III

Each Contracting State shall recognize arbitral awards as binding and enforce them in accordance with the rules of procedure of the territory where the award is relied upon, under the conditions laid down in the following articles. There shall not be imposed substantially more onerous conditions or higher fees or charges on the recognition or enforcement of arbitral awards to which this Convention applies than are imposed on the recognition or enforcement of domestic arbitral awards.

Article IV

1. To obtain the recognition and enforcement mentioned in the preceding article, the party applying for recognition and enforcement shall, at the time of the application, supply:

    a. The duly authenticated original award or a duly certified copy thereof;
    b. The original agreement referred to in article II or a duly certified copy thereof.

2. If the said award or agreement is not made in an official language of the country in which the award is relied upon, the party applying for recognition and enforcement of the award shall produce a translation of these documents into such language. The translation shall be certified by an official or sworn translator or by a diplomatic or consular agent.

Article V

1. Recognition and enforcement of the award may be refused, at the request of the party against whom it is invoked, only if that party furnishes to the competent authority where the recognition and enforcement is sought, proof that:

    a. The parties to the agreement referred to in article II were, under the law applicable to them, under some incapacity, or the said agreement is not valid under the law to which the parties have subjected it or, failing any indication thereon, under the law of the country where the award was made; or

b. The party against whom the award is invoked was not given proper notice of the appointment of the arbitrator or of the arbitration proceedings or was otherwise unable to present his case; or

c. The award deals with a difference not contemplated by or not falling within the terms of the submission to arbitration, or it contains decisions on matters beyond the scope of the submission to arbitration, provided that, if the decisions on matters submitted to arbitration can be separated from those not so submitted, that part of the award which contains decisions on matters submitted to arbitration may be recognized and enforced; or

d. The composition of the arbitral authority or the arbitral procedure was not in accordance with the agreement of the parties, or, failing such agreement, was not in accordance with the law of the country where the arbitration took place; or

e. The award has not yet become binding on the parties, or has been set aside or suspended by a competent authority of the country in which, or under the law of which, that award was made.

2. Recognition and enforcement of an arbitral award may also be refused if the competent authority in the country where recognition and enforcement is sought finds that:

a. The subject matter of the difference is not capable of settlement by arbitration under the law of that country; or

b. The recognition or enforcement of the award would be contrary to the public policy of that country.

Article VI

If an application for the setting aside or suspension of the award has been made to a competent authority referred to in article V(1)(e), the authority before which the award is sought to be relied upon may, if it considers it proper, adjourn the decision on the enforcement of the award and may also, on the application of the party claiming enforcement of the award, order the other party to give suitable security.

Article VII

1. The provisions of the present Convention shall not affect the validity of multilateral or bilateral agreements concerning the recognition and enforcement of arbitral awards entered into by the Contracting States nor deprive any interested party of any right he may have to avail himself of an arbitral award in the manner and to the extent allowed by the law or the treaties of the country where such award is sought to be relied upon.

2. The Geneva Protocol on Arbitration Clauses of 1923 and the Geneva Convention on the Execution of Foreign Arbitral Awards of 1927 shall cease to have effect

between Contracting States on their becoming bound and to the extent that they become bound, by this Convention.

Article VIII

1. This Convention shall be open until 31 December 1958 for signature on behalf of any Member of the United Nations and also on behalf of any other State which is or hereafter becomes a member of any specialized agency of the United Nations, or which is or hereafter becomes a party to the Statute of the International Court of Justice, or any other State to which an invitation has been addressed by the General Assembly of the United Nations.

2. This Convention shall be ratified and the instrument of ratification shall be deposited with the Secretary-General of the United Nations.

Article IX

1. This Convention shall be open for accession to all States referred to in article VIII.

2. Accession shall be effected by the deposit of an instrument of accession with the Secretary-General of the United Nations.

Article X

1. Any State may, at the time of signature, ratification or accession, declare that this Convention shall extend to all or any of the territories for the international relations of which it is responsible. Such a declaration shall take effect when the Convention enters into force for the State concerned.

2. At any time thereafter any such extension shall be made by notification addressed to the Secretary-General of the United Nations and shall take effect as from the ninetieth day after the day of receipt by the Secretary-General of the United Nations of this notification, or as from the date of entry into force of the Convention for the State concerned, whichever is the later.

3. With respect to those territories to which this Convention is not extended at the time of signature, ratification or accession, each State concerned shall consider the possibility of taking the necessary steps in order to extend the application of this Convention to such territories, subject, where necessary for constitutional reasons, to the consent of the Governments of such territories.

Article XI

In the case of a federal or non-unitary State, the following provisions shall apply:

    a. With respect to those articles of this Convention that come within the legislative jurisdiction of the federal authority, the obligations of the federal

Government shall to this extent be the same as those of Contracting States which are not federal States;

b. With respect to those articles of this Convention that come within the legislative jurisdiction of constituent states or provinces which are not, under the constitutional system of the federation, bound to take legislative action, the federal Government shall bring such articles with a favourable recommendation to the notice of the appropriate authorities of constituent states or provinces at the earliest possible moment;

c. A federal State Party to this Convention shall, at the request of any other Contracting State transmitted through the Secretary-General of the United Nations, supply a statement of the law and practice of the federation and its constituent units in regard to any particular provision of this Convention, showing the extent to which effect has been given to that provision by legislative or other action.

Article XII

1. This Convention shall come into force on the ninetieth day following the date of deposit of the third instrument of ratification or accession.

2. For each State ratifying or acceding to this Convention after the deposit of the third instrument of ratification or accession, this Convention shall enter into force on the ninetieth day after deposit by such State of its instrument of ratification or accession.

Article XIII

1. Any Contracting State may denounce this Convention by a written notification to the Secretary-General of the United Nations. Denunciation shall take effect one year after the date of receipt of the notification by the Secretary-General.

2. Any State which has made a declaration or notification under article X may, at any time thereafter, by notification to the Secretary-General of the United Nations, declare that this Convention shall cease to extend to the territory concerned one year after the date of the receipt of the notification by the Secretary-General.

3. This Convention shall continue to be applicable to arbitral awards in respect of which recognition or enforcement proceedings have been instituted before the denunciation takes effect.

Article XIV

A Contracting State shall not be entitled to avail itself of the present Convention against other Contracting States except to the extent that it is itself bound to apply the Convention.

Article XV

The Secretary-General of the United Nations shall notify the States contemplated in article VIII of the following:

    a. Signatures and ratifications in accordance with article VIII;
    b. Accessions in accordance with article IX;
    c. Declarations and notifications under articles I, X and XI;
    d. The date upon which this Convention enters into force in accordance with article XII;
    e. Denunciations and notifications in accordance with article XIII.

Article XVI

1. This Convention, of which the Chinese, English, French, Russian and Spanish texts shall be equally authentic, shall be deposited in the archives of the United Nations.

2. The Secretary-General of the United Nations shall transmit a certified copy of this Convention to the States contemplated in article VIII.

Annex 12

List of Bilateral Agreements Concluded by Austria That Refer to Arbitration

Bilateral Agreement	Signed	BGBl. No.
Treaty between Austria and the USSR (now applicable in relation to the Russian Federation) on Commerce and Shipping	17 October 1955	193/1956
Treaty on German Foreign Debts	27 February 1959	203/1958
Treaty between Austria and the Federal Republic of Germany on the Mutual Recognition and Enforcement of Judgments, Settlements and Public Certificates in Civil and Commercial law	6 June 1959	105/1960
Convention between Austria and the Federal People's Republic of Yugoslavia on the Recognition and Enforcement of Arbitral Awards and Arbitral Settlements in Commercial Matters	18 March 1960	115/1961
Treaty between Austria and the Kingdom of Belgium on the Mutual Recognition and Enforcement of Judgments, Arbitral Awards and Public Certificates in Civil and Commercial Law	16 June 1959	287/1961
Treaty between Austria and Switzerland on the Recognition and Enforcements of Judgments	16 December 1960	125/1962

Bilateral Agreement	*Signed*	*BGBl. No.*
Agreement between the Austrian federal government and the Royal Hellenic government on commercial scheduled air transport	15 January 1962	224/1963
Agreement between the Austrian federal government and the government of the Republic of Finland for air services between and beyond their respective territories	4 June 1969	257/1969
Order of the Austrian Ministry of Justice in Relation to the Canadian Province of British Columbia on the Recognition and Enforcement of Judgments and Arbitral Awards in Civil Law and Judgments in Alimony matters	28 September 1970	314/1970
Treaty between Austria and Liechtenstein on the Recognition and Enforcements of Judgments, Arbitral Awards, Settlements and Public Certificates	5 July 1973	114/1975
Agreement between the Austrian federal government and the government of the Republic of Kenya for air services between and beyond their respective territories	15 May 1985	527/1985
Agreement between the Austrian federal government and the government of the Federal Republic of Brazil on air traffic	16 July 1993	630/1995
Announcement of the federal chancellor regarding bilateral agreements between the Republic of Austria and the Republic of Croatia	8 October 1991	474/1996
Announcement of the federal chancellor regarding bilateral agreements between the Republic of Austria and the Former Yugoslavian Republic of Macedonia	8 September 1991	III 92/ 1997

Annex 13

List of Multilateral Agreements Concluded by Austria That Refer to Arbitration

Multilateral Agreement	Signed	BGBl. No.
Protocol on Arbitration Clauses	Geneva, 24 September 1923	57/1928
Convention on the Execution of Foreign Arbitral Awards	Geneva, 26 September-1927	343/1930
European Convention on International Commercial Arbitration	21 April 1961	107/1964
Convention on the Application of the European Convention on International Commercial Arbitration	17 December 1962	19/1965
Convention on the Settlement of Investment Disputes between States and Nationals of other States	18 March 1965	357/1971
***	***	***
Convention on the contract for the international carriage of goods by road (CMR)	19 May 1956	138/1961
Convention for the unification of certain rules relating to international carriage by air (signed at Warsaw, October 12, 1929)	12 October 1929	286/1961
International convention concerning the carriage of goods by rail (CIM)	25 February 1961	266/1964

Multilateral Agreement	*Signed*	*BGBl. No.*
International convention concerning the carriage of passengers and luggage by rail (CIV)	25 February 1961	267/1964
Convention supplementary to the Warsaw Convention, for the unification of certain rules relating to international carriage by air performed by a person other than the contracting carrier	18 September 1961	46/1966
Convention establishing the European centre for medium-range weather forecasts	11 October 1973	29/1976
Convention on the conservation of European wildlife and natural habitats	19 September 1979	372/1983
United Nations convention on the law of the sea	10 December 1982	885/1995
International convention on the harmonization of frontier controls of goods	1 April 1983	467/1987
International agreement on the procedure for the establishment of tariffs for intra-European scheduled air services	16 June 1987	489/1988
Agreement establishing the common fund for commodities	27 June 1980	507/1989
European convention for the protection of animals during international transport	13 December 1968	BGBl No. 597/ 1973, amended by BGBl No. 591/ 1989
Basel Convention on the control of transboundary movements of hazardous wastes and their disposal	22 March 1989	229/1993
United Nations convention on the carriage of goods by sea, 1978	30 April 1979	836/1993
Convention on biological diversity	5 June 1992	213/1995
Convention on the protection and use of transboundary watercourses and international lakes	17 March 1992	578/1996
Convention on environmental impact assessment in a transboundary context	25 February 1991	201/1997

Multilateral Agreement	*Signed*	*BGBl. No.*
Convention for the establishment of the European Radiocommunications Office (ERO)	23 June 1993	III 73/1998
The energy charter treaty	17 December 1994	81/1998
Convention on cooperation for the protection and sustainable use of the Danube river (Danube river protection convention)	29 June 1994	III 139/1998
Convention on the transboundary effects of industrial accidents	17 March 1992	119/2000
Convention establishing the European Telecommunications Satellite organization 'EUTELSAT'	15 July 1982	BGBl No. 350/ 1985, amended by BGBl No. III 265/ 2001
Protocol on the privileges and immunities of the European Telecommunications Satellite organization (EUTELSAT)	13 February 1987	BGBl No. 176/ 1989, amended by BGBl No. III 46/ 2004
Agreement between the Republic of Austria, the Republic of Bulgaria, the Republic of Croatia, the Czech Republic, the Republic of Hungary, the Republic of Poland, Romania, the Slovak Republic and the Republic of Slovenia promoting cooperation in the field of higher education within the framework of the Central European Exchange Programme for University Studies ('CEEPUS II')	1 August 2004	III 2004/104
Convention on access to information, public participation in decision-making and access to justice in environmental matters	25 June 1998	88/2005
Agreement establishing an association between the European Community and its member states, of the one part, and the Republic of Chile, of the other part	18 November 2002	III 132/2005
International treaty on plant genetic resources for food and agriculture	3 November 2001	III 98/2006

List of Bilateral Investment Treaties Concluded Between Austria and Other Countries

Country	Signed	BGBl. No.	Enacted
Albania	18.03.1993	372/1995	01.08.1995
Algeria	17.06.2003	III/5/2006	01.01.2006
Argentina	07.08.1992	893/1994	01.01.1995
Armenia	17.10.2001	III/12/2003	12.11.2002
Azerbaijan	04.07.2000	III/85/2001	28.05.2001
Bangladesh	21.12.2000	III/256/2001	01.12.2001
Belarus	16.05.2001	III/74/2002	01.06.2002
Belize	17.07.2001	III/2/2002	01.02.2002
Bolivia	04.04.1997	III/148/2002	01.07.2002
Bosnia and Herzegovina	02.10.2000	III/229/2002	20.10.2002
Bulgaria	22.01.1997	III/162/1997	01.11.1997
Cambodia	17.12.2004	–	–
Cape Verde	03.09.1991	83/1993	01.04.1993
Chile	08.09.1997	III/161/2000	22.10.2000
China	12.09.1985	537/1986	11.10.1986
Croatia	19.02.1997	III/180/1999	01.11.1999
Cuba	19.05.2000	III/232/2001	01.12.2001
Czech Republic	15.10.1990	513/1991	01.10.1991
Egypt	12.04.2001	III/73/2002	29.04.2002
Estonia	16.05.1994	725/1995	01.10.1995
Ethiopia	12.11.2004	III/206/2005	01.11.2005
Georgia	01.10.2001	III/45/2004	01.03.2004
Guatemala	16.01.2006	–	–
Hong Kong, China	11.10.1996	III/198/1997	01.10.1997

Country	Signed	BGBl. No.	Enacted
Hungary	26.05.1988	339/1989	01.09.1989
India	08.11.1999	III/27/2001	01.03.2001
Iran, Islamic Republic of	15.02.2001	III/96/2004	11.07.2004
Jordan	23.01.2001	III/261/2001	25.11.2001
Korea, Republic of	14.03.1991	523/1991	01.11.1991
Kuwait	16.11.1996	III/154/1998	22.09.1998
Latvia	17.11.1994	137/1996	01.05.1996
Lebanon	26.05.2001	III/201/2002	30.09.2002
Libyan Arab Jamahiriya	18.06.2002	III/127/2003	01.01.2004
Lithuania	28.06.1996	III/74/1997	01.07.1997
Macedonia, TFYR	28.03.2001	III/65/2002	14.04.2002
Malaysia	12.04.1985	601/1986	01.01.1987
Malta	29.05.2002	III/38/2004	01.03.2004
Mexico	29.06.1998	III/41/2001	26.03.2001
Moldova, Republic of	05.06.2001	III/142/2002	01.08.2002
Mongolia	22.05.2001	III/66/2002	01.05.2002
Montenegro	12.10.2001	III/151/2002 III/124/2007	01.08.2002
Morocco	02.11.1992	295/1995	01.07.1995
Namibia	28.05.2003	III/108/2008	01.09.2008
Oman	01.04.2001	III/241/2001	01.12.2001
Paraguay	13.08.1993 –	III/226/1999 and III/227/ 1999	01.01.2000 –
Philippines	11.04.2002	III/128/2003	01.12.2003
Poland	24.11.1988	473/1989	01.11.1989
Romania	15.05.1996	III/73/1997	01.07.1997
Russian Federation	08.02.1990	387/1991	01.09.1991
Saudi-Arabia	30.06.2001	III/85/2003	25.07.2003
Serbia	12.10.2001	III/151/2002	01.08.2002
Slovakia	15.10.1990 –	513/91 and 1046/1994	01.10.1991 –
Slovenia	07.03.2001	III/1/2002	01.02.2002
South Africa	28.11.1996	III/193/1997	01.01.1998
Tajikistan	08.02.1990	387/1991 and III/4/1998	01.09.1991
Tunisia	01.06.1995	694/1996	01.01.1997
Turkey	16.09.1988	612/1991	01.01.1992
Ukraine	08.11.1996	III/170/1997	01.12.1997
United Arab Emirates	17.06.2001	III/129/2003	01.12.2003
Uzbekistan	02.06.2000	III/167/2001	18.08.2001
Vietnam	27.03.1995	571/1996	01.10.1996
Yemen	30.05.2003	III/44/2004	01.07.2004
Zimbabwe	10.11.2000	–	–

Annex 15

UNCITRAL Notes on Organizing Arbitral Proceedings 1996 (UNCITRAL Notes)*

PREFACE

The United Nations Commission on International Trade Law (UNCITRAL) finalized the Notes at its twenty-ninth session (New York, 28 May – 14 June 1996). In addition to the 36 member States of the Commission, representatives of many other States and of a number of international organizations had participated in the deliberations. In preparing the draft materials, the Secretariat consulted with experts from various legal systems, national arbitration bodies, as well as international professional associations.

The Commission, after an initial discussion on the project in 1993,[1] considered in 1994 a draft entitled 'Draft Guidelines for Preparatory Conferences in Arbitral Proceedings'.[2] That draft was also discussed at several meetings of arbitration practitioners, including the XIIth International Arbitration Congress, held by the International Council for Commercial Arbitration (ICCA) at Vienna from 3 to

---

*   Reprinted with kind permission of UNCITRAL.
1. Report of the United Nations Commission on International Trade Law on the work of its twenty-sixth session, Official Records of the General Assembly, Forty-eighth Session, Supplement No. 17 (A/48/17) (reproduced in UNCITRAL Yearbook, vol. XXIV: 1993, part one), paras. 291-296.
2. The draft Guidelines have been published as document A/CN. 9/396/Add. 1 (reproduced in UNCITRAL Yearbook, vol. XXV: 1994, part two, IV); the considerations of the Commission are reflected in the report of the United Nations Commission on International Trade Law on the work of its twenty-seventh session, Official Records of the General Assembly, Forty-ninth Session Supplement No. 17 (A/49/17) (reproduced in UNCITRAL Yearbook, Vol. XXV: 1994, part two, IV), paras. 111-195.

6 November 1994.[3] On the basis of those discussions in the Commission and elsewhere, the Secretariat prepared 'draft Notes on Organizing Arbitral Proceedings'.[4] The Commission considered the draft Notes in 1995,[5] and a revised draft in 1996,[6] when the Notes were finalized.[7]

INTRODUCTION

PURPOSE OF THE NOTES

1. The purpose of the Notes is to assist arbitration practitioners by listing and briefly describing questions on which appropriately timed decisions on organizing arbitral proceedings may be useful. The text, prepared with a particular view to international arbitrations, may be used whether or not the arbitration is administered by an arbitral institution.

NON-BINDING CHARACTER OF THE NOTES

2. No legal requirement binding on the arbitrators or the parties is imposed by the Notes. The arbitral tribunal remains free to use the Notes as it sees fit and is not required to give reasons for disregarding them.

3. The Notes are not suitable to be used as arbitration rules, since they do not establish any obligation of the arbitral tribunal or the parties to act in a particular way. Accordingly, the use of the Notes cannot imply any modification of the arbitration rules that the parties may have agreed upon.

---

3. The proceedings of the Congress are published in *Planning Efficient Arbitration Proceedings/ The Law Applicable in International Arbitration*, ICCA Congress Series No. 7, Kluwer Law International, The Hague, 1996.
4. The draft Notes have been published as document A/CN. 9/410 (and will be reproduced in UNCITRAL Yearbook, vol. XXVI: 1995, part two, III).
5. Report of the United Nations Commission on International Trade Law on the work of its twentyeighth session, Official Records of the General Assembly, Fiftieth Session, Supplement No. 17 (A/50/17) (and will be reproduced in UNCITRAL Yearbook, vol. XXVI: 1995, part one), paras. 314-373.
6. The revised draft Notes have been published as document A/CN. 9/423 (and will be reproduced in UNCITRAL Yearbook, vol. XXVII: 1996, part two).
7. Report of the United Nations Commission on International Trade Law on the work of its twentyninth session, Official Records of the General Assembly, Fifty-first Session, Supplement No. 17 (A/51/17) (and will be reproduced in UNCITRAL Yearbook, vol. XXVII: 1996, part one), paras. 11 to 54.

DISCRETION IN CONDUCT OF PROCEEDINGS AND USEFULNESS OF TIMELY DECISIONS ON ORGANIZING PROCEEDINGS

4. Laws governing the arbitral procedure and arbitration rules that parties may agree upon typically allow the arbitral tribunal broad discretion and flexibility in the conduct of arbitral proceedings.[8] This is useful in that it enables the arbitral tribunal to take decisions on the organization of proceedings that take into account the circumstances of the case, the expectations of the parties and of the members of the arbitral tribunal, and the need for a just and cost-efficient resolution of the dispute.

5. Such discretion may make it desirable for the arbitral tribunal to give the parties a timely indication as to the organization of the proceedings and the manner in which the tribunal intends to proceed. This is particularly desirable in international arbitrations, where the participants may be accustomed to differing styles of conducting arbitrations. Without such guidance, a party may find aspects of the proceedings unpredictable and difficult to prepare for. That may lead to misunderstandings, delays and increased costs.

MULTI-PARTY ARBITRATION

6. These Notes are intended for use not only in arbitrations with two parties but also in arbitrations with three or more parties. Use of the Notes in multi-party arbitration is referred to below in paragraphs 86-88 (item 18).

PROCESS OF MAKING DECISIONS ON ORGANIZING ARBITRAL PROCEEDINGS

7. Decisions by the arbitral tribunal on organizing arbitral proceedings may be taken with or without previous consultations with the parties. The method chosen depends on whether, in view of the type of the question to be decided, the arbitral tribunal considers that consultations are not necessary or that hearing the views of the parties would be beneficial for increasing the predictability of the proceedings or improving the procedural atmosphere.

8. The consultations, whether they involve only the arbitrators or also the parties, can be held in one or more meetings, or can be carried out by correspondence or telecommunications such as telefax or conference telephone calls or other

---

8.   A prominent example of such rules are the UNCITRAL Arbitration Rules, which provide in article 15(1): 'Subject to these Rules, the arbitral tribunal may conduct the arbitration in such manner as it considers appropriate, provided that the parties are treated with equality and that at any stage of the proceedings each party is given a full opportunity of presenting his case.'

electronic means. Meetings may be held at the venue of arbitration or at some other appropriate location.

9. In some arbitrations a special meeting may be devoted exclusively to such procedural consultations; alternatively, the consultations may be held in conjunction with a hearing on the substance of the dispute. Practices differ as to whether such special meetings should be held and how they should be organized. Special procedural meetings of the arbitrators and the parties separate from hearings are in practice referred to by expressions such as 'preliminary meeting', 'pre-hearing conference', 'preparatory conference', 'pre-hearing review', or terms of similar meaning. The terms used partly depend on the stage of the proceedings at which the meeting is taking place.

LIST OF MATTERS FOR POSSIBLE CONSIDERATION IN ORGANIZING ARBITRAL PROCEEDINGS

10. The Notes provide a list, followed by annotations, of matters on which the arbitral tribunal may wish to formulate decisions on organizing arbitral proceedings.

11. Given that procedural styles and practices in arbitration vary widely, that the purpose of the Notes is not to promote any practice as best practice, and that the Notes are designed for universal use, it is not attempted in the Notes to describe in detail different arbitral practices or express a preference for any of them.

12. The list, while not exhaustive, covers a broad range of situations that may arise in an arbitration. In many arbitrations, however, only a limited number of the matters mentioned in the list need to be considered. It also depends on the circumstances of the case at which stage or stages of the proceedings it would be useful to consider matters concerning the organization of the proceedings. Generally, in order not to create opportunities for unnecessary discussions and delay, it is advisable not to raise a matter prematurely, i. e. before it is clear that a decision is needed.

13. When the Notes are used, it should be borne in mind that the discretion of the arbitral tribunal in organizing the proceedings may be limited by arbitration rules, by other provisions agreed to by the parties and by the law applicable to the arbitral procedure. When an arbitration is administered by an arbitral institution, various matters discussed in the Notes may be covered by the rules and practices of that institution.

LIST OF MATTERS FOR POSSIBLE CONSIDERATION IN ORGANIZING ARBITRAL PROCEEDINGS

		Paragraphs
(1)	Set of arbitration rules	14-16
	If the parties have not agreed on a set of arbitration rules, would they wish to do so	14-16
(2)	Language of proceedings	17-20
	(a) Possible need for translation of documents, in full or in part	18
	(b) Possible need for interpretation of oral presentations	19
	(c) Cost of translation and interpretation	20
(3)	Place of arbitration	21-23
	(a) Determination of the place of arbitration, if not already agreed upon by the parties	21-22
	(b) Possibility of meetings outside the place of arbitration	23
(4)	Administrative services that may be needed for the arbitral tribunal to carry out its functions	24-27
(5)	Deposits in respect of costs	28-30
	(a) Amount to be deposited	28
	(b) Management of deposits	29
	(c) Supplementary deposits	30
(6)	Confidentiality of information relating to the arbitration; possible agreement thereon	31-32
(7)	Routing of written communications among the parties and the arbitrators	33-34
(8)	Telefax and other electronic means of sending documents	35-37
	(a) Telefax	35
	(b) Other electronic means (e. g. electronic mail and magnetic or optical disk)	36-37
(9)	Arrangements for the exchange of written submissions	38-41
	(a) Scheduling of written submissions	39-40
	(b) Consecutive or simultaneous submissions	41
(10)	Practical details concerning written submissions and evidence (e.g. method of submission, copies, numbering, references)	42
(11)	Defining points at issue; order of deciding issues; defining relief or remedy sought	43-46
	(a) Should a list of points at issue be prepared	43
	(b) In which order should the points at issue be decided	44-45
	(c) Is there a need to define more precisely the relief or remedy sought	46
(12)	Possible settlement negotiations and their effect on scheduling proceedings	47

(13) Documentary evidence   48-54
      (a)   Time-limits for submission of documentary
            evidence intended to be submitted by the parties;
            consequences of late submission   48-49
      (b)   Whether the arbitral tribunal intends to require a
            party to produce documentary evidence...................   50-51
      (c)   Should assertions about the origin and receipt of
            documents and about the correctness of photocopies
            be assumed as accurate   52
      (d)   Are the parties willing to submit jointly a single set
            of documentary evidence   53
      (e)   Should voluminous and complicated documentary
            evidence be presented through summaries,
            tabulations, charts, extracts or samples   54
(14) Physical evidence other than documents...........................   55-58
      (a)   What arrangements should be made if physical
            evidence will be submitted   56
      (b)   What arrangements should be made if an on-site
            inspection is necessary...   57-58
(15) Witnesses   59-68
      (a)   Advance notice about a witness whom a party
            intends to present; written witnesses' statements   60-62
      (b)   Manner of taking oral evidence of witnesses   63-65
            (i)   Order in which questions will be asked and
                   the manner in which the hearing of
                   witnesses will be conducted......................   63
            (ii)   Whether oral testimony will be given under
                   oath or affirmation and, if so, in what form
                   an oath or affirmation should be made   64
            (iii) May witnesses be in the hearing room when
                   they are not testifying   65
      (c)   The order in which the witnesses will be called   66
      (d)   Interviewing witnesses prior to their appearance at a
            hearing   67
      (e)   Hearing representatives of a party............................   68
(16) Experts and expert witnesses.......................................   69-73
      (a)   Expert appointed by the arbitral tribunal   70-72
            (i)   The expert's terms of reference.................   71
            (ii)   The opportunity of the parties to comment
                   on the expert's report, including by
                   presenting expert testimony   72
      (b)   Expert opinion presented by a party (expert witness)   73
(17) Hearings   74-85
      (a)   Decision whether to hold hearings   74-75
      (b)   Whether one period of hearings should be held or
            separate periods of hearings......................................   76
      (c)   Setting dates for hearings..   77

(d) Whether there should be a limit on the aggregate
amount of time each party will have for oral
arguments and questioning witnesses...................... 78-79
(e) The order in which the parties will present their
arguments and evidence.. 80
(f) Length of hearings... 81
(g) Arrangements for a record of the hearings 82-83
(h) Whether and when the parties are permitted to
submit notes summarizing their oral arguments 84-85
(18) Multi-party arbitration.. 86-88
(19) Possible requirements concerning filing or delivering the
award... 89-90
Who should take steps to fulfil any requirement............. 90

ANNOTATIONS

(1)   SET OF ARBITRATION RULES

If the parties have not agreed on a set of arbitration rules, would they wish to do so

14. Sometimes parties who have not included in their arbitration agreement a stipulation that a set of arbitration rules will govern their arbitral proceedings might wish to do so after the arbitration has begun. If that occurs, the UNCITRAL Arbitration Rules may be used either without modification or with such modifications as the parties might wish to agree upon. In the alternative, the parties might wish to adopt the rules of an arbitral institution; in that case, it may be necessary to secure the agreement of that institution and to stipulate the terms under which the arbitration could be carried out in accordance with the rules of that institution.

15. However, caution is advised as consideration of a set of arbitration rules might delay the proceedings or give rise to unnecessary controversy.

16. It should be noted that agreement on arbitration rules is not a necessity and that, if the parties do not agree on a set of arbitration rules, the arbitral tribunal has the power to continue the proceedings and determine how the case will be conducted.

(2)   LANGUAGE OF PROCEEDINGS

17. Many rules and laws on arbitral procedure empower the arbitral tribunal to determine the language or languages to be used in the proceedings, if the parties have not reached an agreement thereon.

(a)   **Possible Need for Translation of Documents,
                            in Full or in Part**

18. Some documents annexed to the statements of claim and defence or submitted later may not be in the language of the proceedings. Bearing in mind the needs of the proceedings and economy, it may be considered whether the arbitral tribunal should order that any of those documents or parts thereof should be accompanied by a translation into the language of the proceedings.

(b)   **Possible Need for Interpretation of Oral Presentations**

19. If interpretation will be necessary during oral hearings, it is advisable to consider whether the interpretation will be simultaneous or consecutive and whether the arrangements should be the responsibility of a party or the arbitral tribunal. In an arbitration administered by an institution, interpretation as well as translation services are often arranged by the arbitral institution.

(c)   **Cost of Translation and Interpretation**

20. In taking decisions about translation or interpretation, it is advisable to decide whether any or all of the costs are to be paid directly by a party or whether they will be paid out of the deposits and apportioned between the parties along with the other arbitration costs.

(3)   PLACE OF ARBITRATION

(a)   **Determination of the Place of Arbitration, if not Already
                            Agreed upon by the Parties**

21. Arbitration rules usually allow the parties to agree on the place of arbitration, subject to the requirement of some arbitral institutions that arbitrations under their rules be conducted at a particular place, usually the location of the institution. If the place has not been so agreed upon, the rules governing the arbitration typically provide that it is in the power of the arbitral tribunal or the institution administering the arbitration to determine the place. If the arbitral tribunal is to make that determination, it may wish to hear the views of the parties before doing so.

22. Various factual and legal factors influence the choice of the place of arbitration, and their relative importance varies from case to case. Among the more prominent factors are: (a) suitability of the law on arbitral procedure of the place of arbitration; (b) whether there is a multilateral or bilateral treaty on enforcement of arbitral awards between the State where the arbitration takes place and the State or States where the award may have to be enforced; (c) convenience of the parties and the arbitrators, including the travel distances; (d) availability and cost of support services needed; and (e) location of the subjectmatter in dispute and proximity of evidence.

(b)   Possibility of Meetings Outside the Place of Arbitration

23. Many sets of arbitration rules and laws on arbitral procedure expressly allow the arbitral tribunal to hold meetings elsewhere than at the place of arbitration. For example, under the UNCITRAL Model Law on International Commercial Arbitration 'the arbitral tribunal may, unless otherwise agreed by the parties, meet at any place it considers appropriate for consultation among its members, for hearing witnesses, experts or the parties, or for inspection of goods, other property or documents' (article 20(2)). The purpose of this discretion is to permit arbitral proceedings to be carried out in a manner that is most efficient and economical.

(4)   ADMINISTRATIVE SERVICES THAT MAY BE NEEDED FOR THE
               ARBITRAL TRIBUNAL TO CARRY OUT ITS FUNCTIONS

24. Various administrative services (e. g. hearing rooms or secretarial services) may need to be procured for the arbitral tribunal to be able to carry out its functions. When the arbitration is administered by an arbitral institution, the institution will usually provide all or a good part of the required administrative support to the arbitral tribunal. When an arbitration administered by an arbitral institution takes place away from the seat of the institution, the institution may be able to arrange for administrative services to be obtained from another source, often an arbitral institution; some arbitral institutions have entered into cooperation agreements with a view to providing mutual assistance in servicing arbitral proceedings.

25. When the case is not administered by an institution, or the involvement of the institution does not include providing administrative support, usually the administrative arrangements for the proceedings will be made by the arbitral tribunal or the presiding arbitrator; it may also be acceptable to leave some of the arrangements to the parties, or to one of the parties subject to agreement of the other party or parties. Even in such cases, a convenient source of administrative support might be found in arbitral institutions, which often offer their facilities to arbitrations not governed by the rules of the institution. Otherwise, some services could be procured from entities such as chambers of commerce, hotels or specialized firms providing secretarial or other support services.

26. Administrative services might be secured by engaging a secretary of the arbitral tribunal (also referred to as registrar, clerk, administrator or rapporteur), who carries out the tasks under the direction of the arbitral tribunal. Some arbitral institutions routinely assign such persons to the cases administered by them. In arbitrations not administered by an institution or where the arbitral institution does not appoint a secretary, some arbitrators frequently engage such persons, at least in certain types of cases, whereas many others normally conduct the proceedings without them.

27. To the extent the tasks of the secretary are purely organizational (e. g. obtaining meeting rooms and providing or coordinating secretarial services), this is usually not controversial. Differences in views, however, may arise if the tasks include legal research and other professional assistance to the arbitral tribunal (e. g. collecting case law or published commentaries on legal issues defined by the arbitral tribunal, preparing summaries from case law and publications, and sometimes also preparing drafts of procedural decisions or drafts of certain parts of the award, in particular those concerning the facts of the case). Views or expectations may differ especially where a task of the secretary is similar to professional functions of the arbitrators. Such a role of the secretary is in the view of some commentators inappropriate or is appropriate only under certain conditions, such as that the parties agree thereto. However, it is typically recognized that it is important to ensure that the secretary does not perform any decision-making function of the arbitral tribunal.

(5)   DEPOSITS IN RESPECT OF COSTS

(a)   Amount to be Deposited

28. In an arbitration administered by an institution, the institution often sets, on the basis of an estimate of the costs of the proceedings, the amount to be deposited as an advance for the costs of the arbitration. In other cases it is customary for the arbitral tribunal to make such an estimate and request a deposit. The estimate typically includes travel and other expenses by the arbitrators, expenditures for administrative assistance required by the arbitral tribunal, costs of any expert advice required by the arbitral tribunal, and the fees for the arbitrators. Many arbitration rules have provisions on this matter, including on whether the deposit should be made by the two parties (or all parties in a multi-party case) or only by the claimant.

(b)   Management of Deposits

29. When the arbitration is administered by an institution, the institution's services may include managing and accounting for the deposited money. Where that is not the case, it might be useful to clarify matters such as the type and location of the account in which the money will be kept and how the deposits will be managed.

(c)   Supplementary Deposits

30. If during the course of proceedings it emerges that the costs will be higher than anticipated, supplementary deposits may be required (e. g. because the arbitral tribunal decides pursuant to the arbitration rules to appoint an expert).

(6)   CONFIDENTIALITY OF INFORMATION RELATING TO THE ARBITRATION; POSSIBLE AGREEMENT THEREON

31. It is widely viewed that confidentiality is one of the advantageous and helpful features of arbitration. Nevertheless, there is no uniform answer in national laws as to the extent to which the participants in an arbitration are under the duty to observe the confidentiality of information relating to the case. Moreover, parties that have agreed on arbitration rules or other provisions that do not expressly address the issue of confidentiality cannot assume that all jurisdictions would recognize an implied commitment to confidentiality. Furthermore, the participants in an arbitration might not have the same understanding as regards the extent of confidentiality that is expected. Therefore, the arbitral tribunal might wish to discuss that with the parties and, if considered appropriate, record any agreed principles on the duty of confidentiality.

32. An agreement on confidentiality might cover, for example, one or more of the following matters: the material or information that is to be kept confidential (e. g. pieces of evidence, written and oral arguments, the fact that the arbitration is taking place, identity of the arbitrators, content of the award); measures for maintaining confidentiality of such information and hearings; whether any special procedures should be employed for maintaining the confidentiality of information transmitted by electronic means (e. g. because communication equipment is shared by several users, or because electronic mail over public networks is considered not sufficiently protected against unauthorized access); circumstances in which confidential information may be disclosed in part or in whole (e. g. in the context of disclosures of information in the public domain, or if required by law or a regulatory body).

(7)   ROUTING OF WRITTEN COMMUNICATIONS AMONG THE PARTIES AND THE ARBITRATORS

33. To the extent the question how documents and other written communications should be routed among the parties and the arbitrators is not settled by the agreed rules, or, if an institution administers the case, by the practices of the institution, it is useful for the arbitral tribunal to clarify the question suitably early so as to avoid misunderstandings and delays.

34. Among various possible patterns of routing, one example is that a party transmits the appropriate number of copies to the arbitral tribunal, or to the arbitral institution, if one is involved, which then forwards them as appropriate. Another example is that a party is to send copies simultaneously to the arbitrators and the other party or parties. Documents and other written communications directed by the arbitral tribunal or the presiding arbitrator to one or more parties may also follow a determined pattern, such as through the arbitral institution or by direct transmission. For some communications, in particular those on organizational matters (e. g. dates for hearings), more direct routes of communication may be agreed, even if, for example, the arbitral institution acts as an intermediary for documents such as the statements of claim and defence, evidence or written arguments.

(8)   TELEFAX AND OTHER ELECTRONIC MEANS OF SENDING DOCUMENTS

(a)   **Telefax**

35. Telefax, which offers many advantages over traditional means of communication, is widely used in arbitral proceedings. Nevertheless, should it be thought that, because of the characteristics of the equipment used, it would be preferable not to rely only on a telefacsimile of a document, special arrangements may be considered, such as that a particular piece of written evidence should be mailed or otherwise physically delivered, or that certain telefax messages should be confirmed by mailing or otherwise delivering documents whose facsimile were transmitted by electronic means. When a document should not be sent by telefax, it may, however, be appropriate, in order to avoid an unnecessarily rigid procedure, for the arbitral tribunal to retain discretion to accept an advance copy of a document by telefax for the purposes of meeting a deadline, provided that the document itself is received within a reasonable time thereafter.

(b)   **Other Electronic Means (e. g. Electronic Mail and Magnetic or Optical Disk)**

36. It might be agreed that documents, or some of them, will be exchanged not only in paper-based form, but in addition also in an electronic form other than telefax (e. g. as electronic mail, or on a magnetic or optical disk), or only in electronic form. Since the use of electronic means depends on the aptitude of the persons involved and the availability of equipment and computer programs, agreement is necessary for such means to be used. If both paper-based and electronic means are to be used, it is advisable to decide which one is controlling and, if there is a time-limit for submitting a document, which act constitutes submission.

37. When the exchange of documents in electronic form is planned, it is useful, in order to avoid technical difficulties, to agree on matters such as: data carriers (e. g. electronic mail or computer disks) and their technical characteristics; computer programs to be used in preparing the electronic records; instructions for transforming the electronic records into human-readable form; keeping of logs and backup records of communications sent and received; information in human-readable form that should accompany the disks (e. g. the names of the originator and recipient, computer program, titles of the electronic files and the back-up methods used); procedures when a message is lost or the communication system otherwise fails; and identification of persons who can be contacted if a problem occurs.

(9)   ARRANGEMENTS FOR THE EXCHANGE OF WRITTEN SUBMISSIONS

38. After the parties have initially stated their claims and defences, they may wish, or the arbitral tribunal might request them, to present further written submissions so as to prepare for the hearings or to provide the basis for a decision without hearings. In such submissions, the parties, for example, present or comment on allegations and evidence, cite or explain law, or make or react to proposals. In practice such submissions are referred to variously as, for example, statement, memorial, counter-memorial, brief, counter-brief, reply, réplique, duplique, rebuttal or rejoinder; the terminology is a matter of linguistic usage and the scope or sequence of the submission.

(a)   Scheduling of Written Submissions

39. It is advisable that the arbitral tribunal set time-limits for written submissions. In enforcing the timelimits, the arbitral tribunal may wish, on the one hand, to make sure that the case is not unduly protracted and, on the other hand, to reserve a degree of discretion and allow late submissions if appropriate under the circumstances. In some cases the arbitral tribunal might prefer not to plan the written submissions in advance, thus leaving such matters, including time-limits, to be decided in light of the developments in the proceedings. In other cases, the arbitral tribunal may wish to determine, when scheduling the first written submissions, the number of subsequent submissions.

40. Practices differ as to whether, after the hearings have been held, written submissions are still acceptable. While some arbitral tribunals consider post-hearing submissions unacceptable, others might request or allow them on a particular issue. Some arbitral tribunals follow the procedure according to which the parties are not requested to present written evidence and legal arguments to the arbitral tribunal before the hearings; in such a case, the arbitral tribunal may regard it as appropriate that written submissions be made after the hearings.

(b)   Consecutive or Simultaneous Submissions

41. Written submissions on an issue may be made consecutively, i. e. the party who receives a submission is given a period of time to react with its counter-submission. Another possibility is to request each party to make the submission within the same time period to the arbitral tribunal or the institution administering the case; the received submissions are then forwarded simultaneously to the respective other party or parties. The approach used may depend on the type of issues to be commented upon and the time in which the views should be clarified. With consecutive submissions, it may take longer than with simultaneous ones to obtain views of the parties on a given issue. Consecutive submissions, however, allow the reacting party to comment on all points raised by the other party or parties, which simultaneous submissions do not; thus, simultaneous submissions might possibly necessitate further submissions.

(10)   PRACTICAL DETAILS CONCERNING WRITTEN SUBMISSIONS AND EVIDENCE (E.G. METHOD OF SUBMISSION, COPIES, NUMBERING, REFERENCES)

42. Depending on the volume and kind of documents to be handled, it might be considered whether practical arrangements on details such as the following would be helpful:

- Whether the submissions will be made as paper documents or by electronic means, or both (see paragraphs 35-37);
- The number of copies in which each document is to be submitted;
- A system for numbering documents and items of evidence, and a method for marking them, including by tabs;
- The form of references to documents (e. g. by the heading and the number assigned to the document or its date);
- Paragraph numbering in written submissions, in order to facilitate precise references to parts of a text;
- When translations are to be submitted as paper documents, whether the translations are to be contained in the same volume as the original texts or included in separate volumes.

(11)   DEFINING POINTS AT ISSUE; ORDER OF DECIDING ISSUES; DEFINING RELIEF OR REMEDY SOUGHT

(a)   Should a List of Points at Issue be Prepared

43. In considering the parties' allegations and arguments, the arbitral tribunal may come to the conclusion that it would be useful for it or for the parties to prepare, for analytical purposes and for ease of discussion, a list of the points at issue, as opposed to those that are undisputed. If the arbitral tribunal determines that the advantages of working on the basis of such a list outweigh the disadvantages, it chooses the appropriate stage of the proceedings for preparing a list, bearing in mind also that subsequent developments in the proceedings may require a revision of the points at issue. Such an identification of points at issue might help to concentrate on the essential matters, to reduce the number of points at issue by agreement of the parties, and to select the best and most economical process for resolving the dispute. However, possible disadvantages of preparing such a list include delay, adverse effect on the flexibility of the proceedings, or unnecessary disagreements about whether the arbitral tribunal has decided all issues submitted to it or whether the award contains decisions on matters beyond the scope of the submission to arbitration. The terms of reference required under some arbitration rules, or in agreements of parties, may serve the same purpose as the above-described list of points at issue.

(b)   In which Order Should the Points at Issue be Decided

44. While it is often appropriate to deal with all the points at issue collectively, the arbitral tribunal might decide to take them up during the proceedings in a particular order. The order may be due to a point being preliminary relative to another (e. g. a decision on the jurisdiction of the arbitral tribunal is preliminary to consideration of substantive issues, or the issue of responsibility for a breach of contract is preliminary to the issue of the resulting damages). A particular order may be decided also when the breach of various contracts is in dispute or when damages arising from various events are claimed.

45. If the arbitral tribunal has adopted a particular order of deciding points at issue, it might consider it appropriate to issue a decision on one of the points earlier than on the other ones. This might be done, for example, when a discrete part of a claim is ready for decision while the other parts still require extensive consideration, or when it is expected that after deciding certain issues the parties might be more inclined to settle the remaining ones. Such earlier decisions are referred to by expressions such as 'partial', 'interlocutory' or 'interim' awards or decisions, depending on the type of issue dealt with and on whether the decision is final with respect to the issue it resolves. Questions that might be the subject of such decisions are, for example, jurisdiction of the arbitral tribunal, interim measures of protection, or the liability of a party.

(c)   Is there a Need to Define More Precisely the Relief or Remedy Sought

46. If the arbitral tribunal considers that the relief or remedy sought is insufficiently definite, it may wish to explain to the parties the degree of definiteness with which their claims should be formulated. Such an explanation may be useful since criteria are not uniform as to how specific the claimant must be in formulating a relief or remedy.

(12)   POSSIBLE SETTLEMENT NEGOTIATIONS AND THEIR EFFECT ON
            SCHEDULING PROCEEDINGS

47. Attitudes differ as to whether it is appropriate for the arbitral tribunal to bring up the possibility of settlement. Given the divergence of practices in this regard, the arbitral tribunal should only suggest settlement negotiations with caution. However, it may be opportune for the arbitral tribunal to schedule the proceedings in a way that might facilitate the continuation or initiation of settlement negotiations.

(13)   Documentary Evidence

(a)   **Time-Limits for Submission of Documentary Evidence Intended to be Submitted by the Parties; Consequences of Late Submission**

48. Often the written submissions of the parties contain sufficient information for the arbitral tribunal to fix the time-limit for submitting evidence. Otherwise, in order to set realistic time periods, the arbitral tribunal may wish to consult with the parties about the time that they would reasonably need.

49. The arbitral tribunal may wish to clarify that evidence submitted late will as a rule not be accepted. It may wish not to preclude itself from accepting a late submission of evidence if the party shows sufficient cause for the delay.

(b)   **Whether the Arbitral Tribunal Intends to Require a Party to Produce Documentary Evidence**

50. Procedures and practices differ widely as to the conditions under which the arbitral tribunal may require a party to produce documents. Therefore, the arbitral tribunal might consider it useful, when the agreed arbitration rules do not provide specific conditions, to clarify to the parties the manner in which it intends to proceed.

51. The arbitral tribunal may wish to establish time-limits for the production of documents. The parties might be reminded that, if the requested party duly invited to produce documentary evidence fails to do so within the established period of time, without showing sufficient cause for such failure, the arbitral tribunal is free to draw its conclusions from the failure and may make the award on the evidence before it.

(c)   **Should Assertions About the Origin and Receipt of Documents and About the Correctness of Photocopies be Assumed as Accurate**

52. It may be helpful for the arbitral tribunal to inform the parties that it intends to conduct the proceedings on the basis that, unless a party raises an objection to any of the following conclusions within a specified period of time: (a) a document is accepted as having originated from the source indicated in the document; (b) a copy of a dispatched communication (e. g. letter, telex, telefax or other electronic message) is accepted without further proof as having been received by the addressee; and (c) a copy is accepted as correct. A statement by the arbitral tribunal to that effect can simplify the introduction of documentary evidence and discourage unfounded and dilatory objections, at a late stage of the proceedings, to the probative value of documents. It is advisable to provide that the time-limit for objections will not be enforced if the arbitral tribunal considers the delay justified.

(d)   Are the Parties Willing to Submit Jointly a Single Set of Documentary Evidence

53. The parties may consider submitting jointly a single set of documentary evidence whose authenticity is not disputed. The purpose would be to avoid duplicate submissions and unnecessary discussions concerning the authenticity of documents, without prejudicing the position of the parties concerning the content of the documents. Additional documents may be inserted later if the parties agree. When a single set of documents would be too voluminous to be easily manageable, it might be practical to select a number of frequently used documents and establish a set of 'working' documents. A convenient arrangement of documents in the set may be according to chronological order or subject-matter. It is useful to keep a table of contents of the documents, for example, by their short headings and dates, and to provide that the parties will refer to documents by those headings and dates.

(e)   Should Voluminous and Complicated Documentary Evidence be Presented Through Summaries, Tabulations, Charts, Extracts or Samples

54. When documentary evidence is voluminous and complicated, it may save time and costs if such evidence is presented by a report of a person competent in the relevant field (e. g. public accountant or consulting engineer). The report may present the information in the form of summaries, tabulations, charts, extracts or samples. Such presentation of evidence should be combined with arrangements that give the interested party the opportunity to review the underlying data and the methodology of preparing the report.

(14)   PHYSICAL EVIDENCE OTHER THAN DOCUMENTS

55. In some arbitrations the arbitral tribunal is called upon to assess physical evidence other than documents, for example, by inspecting samples of goods, viewing a video recording or observing the functioning of a machine.

(a)   What Arrangements should be Made if Physical Evidence will be Submitted

56. If physical evidence will be submitted, the arbitral tribunal may wish to fix the time schedule for presenting the evidence, make arrangements for the other party or parties to have a suitable opportunity to prepare itself for the presentation of the evidence, and possibly take measures for safekeeping the items of evidence.

(b)   **What Arrangements should be Made if an On-Site**
                      Inspection is Necessary

57. If an on-site inspection of property or goods will take place, the arbitral tribunal may consider matters such as timing, meeting places, other arrangements to provide the opportunity for all parties to be present, and the need to avoid communications between arbitrators and a party about points at issue without the presence of the other party or parties.

58. The site to be inspected is often under the control of one of the parties, which typically means that employees or representatives of that party will be present to give guidance and explanations. It should be borne in mind that statements of those representatives or employees made during an on-site inspection, as contrasted with statements those persons might make as witnesses in a hearing, should not be treated as evidence in the proceedings.

(15)   WITNESSES

59. While laws and rules on arbitral procedure typically leave broad freedom concerning the manner of taking evidence of witnesses, practices on procedural points are varied. In order to facilitate the preparations of the parties for the hearings, the arbitral tribunal may consider it appropriate to clarify, in advance of the hearings, some or all of the following issues.

(a)   **Advance Notice about a Witness whom a Party Intends to**
                      Present; Written Witnesses' Statements

60. To the extent the applicable arbitration rules do not deal with the matter, the arbitral tribunal may wish to require that each party give advance notice to the arbitral tribunal and the other party or parties of any witness it intends to present. As to the content of the notice, the following is an example of what might be required, in addition to the names and addresses of the witnesses: (a) the subject upon which the witnesses will testify; (b) the language in which the witnesses will testify; and (c) the nature of the relationship with any of the parties, qualifications and experience of the witnesses if and to the extent these are relevant to the dispute or the testimony, and how the witnesses learned about the facts on which they will testify. However, it may not be necessary to require such a notice, in particular if the thrust of the testimony can be clearly ascertained from the party's allegations.

61. Some practitioners favour the procedure according to which the party presenting witness evidence submits a signed witness's statement containing testimony itself. It should be noted, however, that such practice, which implies interviewing the witness by the party presenting the testimony, is not known in all parts of the world and, moreover, that some practitioners disapprove of it on the ground that such contacts between the party and the witness may compromise the credibility of the testimony and are therefore improper (see paragraph 67). Notwithstanding these reservations, signed witness's testimony has advantages in that it may expedite the proceedings by making it easier for the other party or parties to prepare for the hearings or for the parties to identify uncontested matters. However, those advantages might be outweighed by the time and expense involved in obtaining the written testimony.

62. If a signed witness's statement should be made under oath or similar affirmation of truthfulness, it may be necessary to clarify by whom the oath or affirmation should be administered and whether any formal authentication will be required by the arbitral tribunal.

(b)   Manner of Taking Oral Evidence of Witnesses

(i)   Order in which Questions will be Asked and the Manner in which the Hearing of Witnesses will be Conducted

63. To the extent that the applicable rules do not provide an answer, it may be useful for the arbitral tribunal to clarify how witnesses will be heard. One of the various possibilities is that a witness is first questioned by the arbitral tribunal, whereupon questions are asked by the parties, first by the party who called the witness. Another possibility is for the witness to be questioned by the party presenting the witness and then by the other party or parties, while the arbitral tribunal might pose questions during the questioning or after the parties on points that in the tribunal's view have not been sufficiently clarified. Differences exist also as to the degree of control the arbitral tribunal exercises over the hearing of witnesses. For example, some arbitrators prefer to permit the parties to pose questions freely and directly to the witness, but may disallow a question if a party objects; other arbitrators tend to exercise more control and may disallow a question on their initiative or even require that questions from the parties be asked through the arbitral tribunal.

(ii)   Whether Oral Testimony will be Given Under Oath or Affirmation and, if so, in what Form an Oath or Affirmation should be Made

64. Practices and laws differ as to whether or not oral testimony is to be given under oath or affirmation. In some legal systems, the arbitrators are empowered to put witnesses on oath, but it is usually in their discretion whether they want to do so. In other systems, oral testimony under oath is either unknown or may even be considered improper as only an official such as a judge or notary may have the authority to administer oaths.

(iii)   *May Witnesses be in the Hearing Room when they are Not Testifying*

65. Some arbitrators favour the procedure that, except if the circumstances suggest otherwise, the presence of a witness in the hearing room is limited to the time the witness is testifying; the purpose is to prevent the witness from being influenced by what is said in the hearing room, or to prevent that the presence of the witness would influence another witness. Other arbitrators consider that the presence of a witness during the testimony of other witnesses may be beneficial in that possible contradictions may be readily clarified or that their presence may act as a deterrent against untrue statements. Other possible approaches may be that witnesses are not present in the hearing room before their testimony, but stay in the room after they have testified, or that the arbitral tribunal decides the question for each witness individually depending on what the arbitral tribunal considers most appropriate. The arbitral tribunal may leave the procedure to be decided during the hearings, or may give guidance on the question in advance of the hearings.

(c)   **The Order in which the Witnesses will be Called**

66. When several witnesses are to be heard and longer testimony is expected, it is likely to reduce costs if the order in which they will be called is known in advance and their presence can be scheduled accordingly. Each party might be invited to suggest the order in which it intends to present the witnesses, while it would be up to the arbitral tribunal to approve the scheduling and to make departures from it.

(d)   **Interviewing Witnesses Prior to their Appearance at a Hearing**

67. In some legal systems, parties or their representatives are permitted to interview witnesses, prior to their appearance at the hearing, as to such matters as their recollection of the relevant events, their experience, qualifications or relation with a participant in the proceedings. In those legal systems such contacts are usually not permitted once the witness's oral testimony has begun. In other systems such contacts with witnesses are considered improper. In order to avoid misunderstandings, the arbitral tribunal may consider it useful to clarify what kind of contacts a party is permitted to have with a witness in the preparations for the hearings.

(e)   **Hearing Representatives of a Party**

68. According to some legal systems, certain persons affiliated with a party may only be heard as representatives of the party but not as witnesses. In such a case, it may be necessary to consider ground rules for determining which persons may not testify as witnesses (e. g. certain executives, employees or agents) and for hearing statements of those persons and for questioning them.

(16)   EXPERTS AND EXPERT WITNESSES

69. Many arbitration rules and laws on arbitral procedure address the participation of experts in arbitral proceedings. A frequent solution is that the arbitral tribunal has the power to appoint an expert to report on issues determined by the tribunal; in addition, the parties may be permitted to present expert witnesses on points at issue. In other cases, it is for the parties to present expert testimony, and it is not expected that the arbitral tribunal will appoint an expert.

(a)   Expert Appointed by the Arbitral Tribunal

70. If the arbitral tribunal is empowered to appoint an expert, one possible approach is for the tribunal to proceed directly to selecting the expert. Another possibility is to consult the parties as to who should be the expert; this may be done, for example, without mentioning a candidate, by presenting to the parties a list of candidates, soliciting proposals from the parties, or by discussing with the parties the 'profile' of the expert the arbitral tribunal intends to appoint, i. e. the qualifications, experience and abilities of the expert.

(i)   The Expert's Terms of Reference

71. The purpose of the expert's terms of reference is to indicate the questions on which the expert is to provide clarification, to avoid opinions on points that are not for the expert to assess and to commit the expert to a time schedule. While the discretion to appoint an expert normally includes the determination of the expert's terms of reference, the arbitral tribunal may decide to consult the parties before finalizing the terms. It might also be useful to determine details about how the expert will receive from the parties any relevant information or have access to any relevant documents, goods or other property, so as to enable the expert to prepare the report. In order to facilitate the evaluation of the expert's report, it is advisable to require the expert to include in the report information on the method used in arriving at the conclusions and the evidence and information used in preparing the report.

(ii)   The Opportunity of the Parties to Comment on the Expert's Report, Including by Presenting Expert Testimony

72. Arbitration rules that contain provisions on experts usually also have provisions on the right of a party to comment on the report of the expert appointed by the arbitral tribunal. If no such provisions apply or more specific procedures than those prescribed are deemed necessary, the arbitral tribunal may, in light of those provisions, consider it opportune to determine, for example, the time period for presenting written comments of the parties, or, if hearings are to be held for the purpose of hearing the expert, the procedures for interrogating the expert by the parties or for the participation of any expert witnesses presented by the parties.

(b)   **Expert Opinion Presented by a Party (Expert Witness)**

73. If a party presents an expert opinion, the arbitral tribunal might consider requiring, for example, that the opinion be in writing, that the expert should be available to answer questions at hearings, and that, if a party will present an expert witness at a hearing, advance notice must be given or that the written opinion must be presented in advance, as in the case of other witnesses (see paragraphs 60-62).

(17)   Hearings

(a)   **Decision Whether to Hold Hearings**

74. Laws on arbitral procedure and arbitration rules often have provisions as to the cases in which oral hearings must be held and as to when the arbitral tribunal has discretion to decide whether to hold hearings.

75. If it is up to the arbitral tribunal to decide whether to hold hearings, the decision is likely to be influenced by factors such as, on the one hand, that it is usually quicker and easier to clarify points at issue pursuant to a direct confrontation of arguments than on the basis of correspondence and, on the other hand, the travel and other cost of holding hearings, and that the need of finding acceptable dates for the hearings might delay the proceedings. The arbitral tribunal may wish to consult the parties on this matter.

(b)   **Whether One Period of Hearings should be Held or
                       Separate Periods of Hearings**

76. Attitudes vary as to whether hearings should be held in a single period of hearings or in separate periods, especially when more than a few days are needed to complete the hearings. According to some arbitrators, the entire hearings should normally be held in a single period, even if the hearings are to last for more than a week. Other arbitrators in such cases tend to schedule separate periods of hearings. In some cases issues to be decided are separated, and separate hearings set for those issues, with the aim that oral presentation on those issues will be completed within the allotted time. Among the advantages of one period of hearings are that it involves less travel costs, memory will not fade, and it is unlikely that people representing a party will change. On the other hand, the longer the hearings, the more difficult it may be to find early dates acceptable to all participants. Furthermore, separate periods of hearings may be easier to schedule, the subsequent hearings may be tailored to the development of the case, and the period between the hearings leaves time for analysing the records and negotiations between the parties aimed at narrowing the points at issue by agreement.

(c)   **Setting Dates for Hearings**

77. Typically, firm dates will be fixed for hearings. Exceptionally, the arbitral tribunal may initially wish to set only 'target dates' as opposed to definitive dates. This may be done at a stage of the proceedings when not all information necessary to schedule hearings is yet available, with the understanding that the target dates will either be confirmed or rescheduled within a reasonably short period. Such provisional planning can be useful to participants who are generally not available on short notice.

(d)   **Whether there should be a Limit on the Aggregate Amount of Time Each Party will have for Oral Arguments and Questioning Witnesses**

78. Some arbitrators consider it useful to limit the aggregate amount of time each party has for any of the following: (a) making oral statements; (b) questioning its witnesses; and (c) questioning the witnesses of the other party or parties. In general, the same aggregate amount of time is considered appropriate for each party, unless the arbitral tribunal considers that a different allocation is justified. Before deciding, the arbitral tribunal may wish to consult the parties as to how much time they think they will need.

79. Such planning of time, provided it is realistic, fair and subject to judiciously firm control by the arbitral tribunal, will make it easier for the parties to plan the presentation of the various items of evidence and arguments, reduce the likelihood of running out of time towards the end of the hearings and avoid that one party would unfairly use up a disproportionate amount of time.

(e)   **The Order in Which the Parties will Present their Arguments and Evidence**

80. Arbitration rules typically give broad latitude to the arbitral tribunal to determine the order of presentations at the hearings. Within that latitude, practices differ, for example, as to whether opening or closing statements are heard and their level of detail; the sequence in which the claimant and the respondent present their opening statements, arguments, witnesses and other evidence; and whether the respondent or the claimant has the last word. In view of such differences, or when no arbitration rules apply, it may foster efficiency of the proceedings if the arbitral tribunal clarifies to the parties, in advance of the hearings, the manner in which it will conduct the hearings, at least in broad lines.

(f)   **Length of Hearings**

81. The length of a hearing primarily depends on the complexity of the issues to be argued and the amount of witness evidence to be presented. The length also depends on the procedural style used in the arbitration. Some practitioners prefer to have written evidence and written arguments presented before the hearings, which thus can focus on the issues that have not been sufficiently clarified. Those practitioners generally tend to plan shorter hearings than those practitioners who prefer that most if not all evidence and arguments are presented to the arbitral tribunal orally and in full detail. In order to facilitate the parties' preparations and avoid misunderstandings, the arbitral tribunal may wish to clarify to the parties, in advance of the hearings, the intended use of time and style of work at the hearings.

(g)   Arrangements for a Record of the Hearings

82. The arbitral tribunal should decide, possibly after consulting with the parties, on the method of preparing a record of oral statements and testimony during hearings. Among different possibilities, one method is that the members of the arbitral tribunal take personal notes. Another is that the presiding arbitrator during the hearing dictates to a typist a summary of oral statements and testimony. A further method, possible when a secretary of the arbitral tribunal has been appointed, may be to leave to that person the preparation of a summary record. A useful, though costly, method is for professional stenographers to prepare verbatim transcripts, often within the next day or a similarly short time period. A written record may be combined with tape-recording, so as to enable reference to the tape in case of a disagreement over the written record.

83. If transcripts are to be produced, it may be considered how the persons who made the statements will be given an opportunity to check the transcripts. For example, it may be determined that the changes to the record would be approved by the parties or, failing their agreement, would be referred for decision to the arbitral tribunal.

**(h)   Whether and when the Parties are Permitted to Submit
                Notes Summarizing their Oral Arguments**

84. Some legal counsel are accustomed to giving notes summarizing their oral arguments to the arbitral tribunal and to the other party or parties. If such notes are presented, this is usually done during the hearings or shortly thereafter; in some cases, the notes are sent before the hearing. In order to avoid surprise, foster equal treatment of the parties and facilitate preparations for the hearings, advance clarification is advisable as to whether submitting such notes is acceptable and the time for doing so.

85. In closing the hearings, the arbitral tribunal will normally assume that no further proof is to be offered or submission to be made. Therefore, if notes are to be presented to be read after the closure of the hearings, the arbitral tribunal may find it worthwhile to stress that the notes should be limited to summarizing what was said orally and in particular should not refer to new evidence or new argument.

(18)   MULTI-PARTY ARBITRATION

86. When a single arbitration involves more than two parties (multi-party arbitration), considerations regarding the need to organize arbitral proceedings, and matters that may be considered in that connection, are generally not different from two-party arbitrations. A possible difference may be that, because of the need to deal with more than two parties, multi-party proceedings can be more complicated to manage than bilateral proceedings. The Notes, notwithstanding a possible greater complexity of multi-party arbitration, can be used in multi-party as well as in two-party proceedings.

87. The areas of possibly increased complexity in multi-party arbitration are, for example, the flow of communications among the parties and the arbitral tribunal (see paragraphs 33, 34 and 38-41); if points at issue are to be decided at different points in time, the order of deciding them (paragraphs 44-45); the manner in which the parties will participate in hearing witnesses (paragraph 63); the appointment of experts and the participation of the parties in considering their reports (paragraphs 70-72); the scheduling of hearings (paragraph 76); the order in which the parties will present their arguments and evidence at hearings (paragraph 80).

88. The Notes, which are limited to pointing out matters that may be considered in organizing arbitral proceedings in general, do not cover the drafting of the arbitration agreement or the constitution of the arbitral tribunal, both issues that give rise to special questions in multi-party arbitration as compared to two-party arbitration.

(19)   POSSIBLE REQUIREMENTS CONCERNING FILING OR DELIVERING THE AWARD

89. Some national laws require that arbitral awards be filed or registered with a court or similar authority, or that they be delivered in a particular manner or through a particular authority. Those laws differ with respect to, for example, the type of award to which the requirement applies (e. g. to all awards or only to awards not rendered under the auspices of an arbitral institution); time periods for filing, registering or delivering the award (in some cases those time periods may be rather short); or consequences for failing to comply with the requirement (which might be, for example, invalidity of the award or inability to enforce it in a particular manner).

Who should take steps to fulfil any requirement

90. If such a requirement exists, it is useful, some time before the award is to be issued, to plan who should take the necessary steps to meet the requirement and how the costs are to be borne.

Annex 16

IBA Rules on the Taking of Evidence in International Commercial Arbitration (IBA Rules of Evidence)*

Preamble

1. These IBA Rules on the Taking of Evidence in International Commercial Arbitration (the 'IBA Rules of Evidence') are intended to govern in an efficient and economical manner the taking of evidence in international commercial arbitrations, particularly those between Parties from different legal traditions. They are designed to supplement the legal provisions and the institutional or *ad hoc* rules according to which the Parties are conducting their arbitration.

2. Parties and Arbitral Tribunals may adopt the IBA Rules of Evidence, in whole or in part, to govern arbitration proceedings, or they may vary them or use them as guidelines in developing their own procedures. The Rules are not intended to limit the flexibility that is inherent in, and an advantage of, international arbitration, and Parties and Arbitral Tribunals are free to adapt them to the particular circumstances of each arbitration.

3. Each Arbitral Tribunal is encouraged to identify to the Parties, as soon as it considers it to be appropriate, the issues that it may regard as relevant and material to the outcome of the case, including issues where a preliminary determination may be appropriate.

---

4. The taking of evidence shall be conducted on the principle that each Party shall be entitled to know, reasonably in advance of any Evidentiary Hearing, the evidence on which the other Parties rely.

Article 1 – Definitions

In the IBA Rules of Evidence:

- *'Arbitral Tribunal'* means a sole arbitrator or a panel of arbitrators validly deciding by majority or otherwise;
- *'Claimant'* means the Party or Parties who commenced the arbitration and any Party who, through joinder or otherwise, becomes aligned with such Party or Parties;
- *'Document'* means a writing of any kind, whether recorded on paper, electronic means, audio or visual recordings or any other mechanical or electronic means of storing or recording information;
- *'Evidentiary Hearing'* means any hearing, whether or not held on consecutive days, at which the Arbitral Tribunal receives oral evidence;
- *'Expert Report'* means a written statement by a Tribunal-Appointed Expert or a Party-Appointed Expert submitted pursuant to the IBA Rules of Evidence;
- *'General Rules'* mean the institutional or *ad hoc* rules according to which the Parties are conducting their arbitration;
- *'Party'* means a party to the arbitration;
- *'Party-Appointed Expert'* means an expert witness presented by a Party;
- *'Request to Produce'* means a request by a Party for a procedural order by which the Arbitral Tribunal would direct another Party to produce documents;
- *'Respondent'* means the Party or Parties against whom the Claimant made its claim, and any Party who, through joinder or otherwise, becomes aligned with such Party or Parties, and includes a Respondent making a counter-claim;
- *'Tribunal-Appointed Expert'* means a person or organization appointed by the Arbitral Tribunal in order to report to it on specific issues determined by the Arbitral Tribunal.

Article 2 – Scope of Application

1. Whenever the Parties have agreed or the Arbitral Tribunal has determined to apply the IBA Rules of Evidence, the Rules shall govern the taking of evidence, except to the extent that any specific provision of them may be found to be in conflict with any mandatory provision of law determined to be applicable to the case by the Parties or by the Arbitral Tribunal.

2. In case of conflict between any provisions of the IBA Rules of Evidence and the General Rules, the Arbitral Tribunal shall apply the IBA Rules of Evidence in the

manner that it determines best in order to accomplish the purposes of both the General Rules and the IBA Rules of Evidence, unless the Parties agree to the contrary.

3. In the event of any dispute regarding the meaning of the IBA Rules of Evidence, the Arbitral Tribunal shall interpret them according to their purpose and in the manner most appropriate for the particular arbitration.

4. Insofar as the IBA Rules of Evidence and the General Rules are silent on any matter concerning the taking of evidence and the Parties have not agreed otherwise, the Arbitral Tribunal may conduct the taking of evidence as it deems appropriate, in accordance with the general principles of the IBA Rules of Evidence.

Article 3 – Documents

1. Within the time ordered by the Arbitral Tribunal, each Party shall submit to the Arbitral Tribunal and to the other Parties all documents available to it on which it relies, including public documents and those in the public domain, except for any documents that have already been submitted by another Party.

2. Within the time ordered by the Arbitral Tribunal, any Party may submit to the Arbitral Tribunal a Request to Produce.

3. A Request to Produce shall contain:

   (a) *(i)* a description of a requested document sufficient to identify it, or *(ii)* a description in sufficient detail (including subject matter) of a narrow and specific requested category of documents that are reasonably believed to exist;
   (b) a description of how the documents requested are relevant and material to the outcome of the case; and
   (c) a statement that the documents requested are not in the possession, custody or control of the requesting Party, and of the reason why that Party assumes the documents requested to be in the possession, custody or control of the other Party.

4. Within the time ordered by the Arbitral Tribunal, the Party to whom the Request to Produce is addressed shall produce to the Arbitral Tribunal and to the other Parties all the documents requested in its possession, custody or control as to which no objection is made.

5. If the Party to whom the Request to Produce is addressed has objections to some or all of the documents requested, it shall state them in writing to the Arbitral Tribunal within the time ordered by the Arbitral Tribunal. The reasons for such objections shall be any of those set forth in Article 9.2.

6. The Arbitral Tribunal shall, in consultation with the Parties and in timely fashion, consider the Request to Produce and the objections. The Arbitral Tribunal may order the Party to whom such Request is addressed to produce to

the Arbitral Tribunal and to the other Parties those requested documents in its possession, custody or control as to which the Arbitral Tribunal determines that *(i)* the issues that the requesting Party wishes to prove are relevant and material to the outcome of the case, and *(ii)* none of the reasons for objection set forth in Article 9.2 apply.

7. In exceptional circumstances, if the propriety of an objection can only be determined by review of the document, the Arbitral Tribunal may determine that it should not review the document. In that event, the Arbitral Tribunal may, after consultation with the Parties, appoint an independent and impartial expert, bound to confidentiality, to review any such document and to report on the objection. To the extent that the objection is upheld by the Arbitral Tribunal, the expert shall not disclose to the Arbitral Tribunal and to the other Parties the contents of the document reviewed.

8. If a Party wishes to obtain the production of documents from a person or organization who is not a Party to the arbitration and from whom the Party cannot obtain the documents on its own, the Party may, within the time ordered by the Arbitral Tribunal, ask it to take whatever steps are legally available to obtain the requested documents. The Party shall identify the documents in sufficient detail and state why such documents are relevant and material to the outcome of the case. The Arbitral Tribunal shall decide on this request and shall take the necessary steps if in its discretion it determines that the documents would be relevant and material.

9. The Arbitral Tribunal, at any time before the arbitration is concluded, may request a Party to produce to the Arbitral Tribunal and to the other Parties any documents that it believes to be relevant and material to the outcome of the case. A Party may object to such a request based on any of the reasons set forth in Article 9.2. If a Party raises such an objection, the Arbitral Tribunal shall decide whether to order the production of such documents based upon the considerations set forth in Article 3.6 and, if the Arbitral Tribunal considers it appropriate, through the use of the procedures set forth in Article 3.7.

10. Within the time ordered by the Arbitral Tribunal, the Parties may submit to the Arbitral Tribunal and to the other Parties any additional documents which they believe have become relevant and material as a consequence of the issues raised in documents, Witness Statements or Expert Reports submitted or produced by another Party or in other submissions of the Parties.

11. If copies are submitted or produced, they must conform fully to the originals. At the request of the Arbitral Tribunal, any original must be presented for inspection.

12. All documents produced by a Party pursuant to the IBA Rules of Evidence (or by a non-Party pursuant to Article 3.8) shall be kept confidential by the Arbitral Tribunal and by the other Parties, and they shall be used only in connection with the arbitration. The Arbitral Tribunal may issue orders to set forth the terms of this confidentiality. This requirement is without prejudice to all other obligations of confidentiality in arbitration.

Article 4 – Witnesses of Fact

1. Within the time ordered by the Arbitral Tribunal, each Party shall identify the witnesses on whose testimony it relies and the subject matter of that testimony.

2. Any person may present evidence as a witness, including a Party or a Party's officer, employee or other representative.

3. It shall not be improper for a Party, its officers, employees, legal advisors or other representatives to interview its witnesses or potential witnesses.

4. The Arbitral Tribunal may order each Party to submit within a specified time to the Arbitral Tribunal and to the other Parties a written statement by each witness on whose testimony it relies, except for those witnesses whose testimony is sought pursuant to Article 4.10 (the 'Witness Statement'). If Evidentiary Hearings are organized on separate issues (such as liability and damages), the Arbitral Tribunal or the Parties by agreement may schedule the submission of Witness Statements separately for each Evidentiary Hearing.

5. Each Witness Statement shall contain:

    (a) the full name and address of the witness, his or her present and past relationship (if any) with any of the Parties, and a description of his or her background, qualifications, training and experience, if such a description may be relevant and material to the dispute or to the contents of the statement;

    (b) a full and detailed description of the facts, and the source of the witness's information as to those facts, sufficient to serve as that witness's evidence in the matter in dispute;

    (c) an affirmation of the truth of the statement; and

    (d) the signature of the witness and its date and place.

6. If Witness Statements are submitted, any Party may, within the time ordered by the Arbitral Tribunal, submit to the Arbitral Tribunal and to the other Parties revised or additional Witness Statements, including statements from persons not previously named as witnesses, so long as any such revisions or additions only respond to matters contained in another Party's Witness Statement or Expert Report and such matters have not been previously presented in the arbitration.

7. Each witness who has submitted a Witness Statement shall appear for testimony at an Evidentiary Hearing, unless the Parties agree otherwise.

8. If a witness who has submitted a Witness Statement does not appear without a valid reason for testimony at an Evidentiary Hearing, except by agreement of the Parties, the Arbitral Tribunal shall disregard that Witness Statement unless, in exceptional circumstances, the Arbitral Tribunal determines otherwise.

9. If the Parties agree that a witness who has submitted a Witness Statement does not need to appear for testimony at an Evidentiary Hearing, such an agreement

shall not be considered to reflect an agreement as to the correctness of the content of the Witness Statement.

10. If a Party wishes to present evidence from a person who will not appear voluntarily at its request, the Party may, within the time ordered by the Arbitral Tribunal, ask it to take whatever steps are legally available to obtain the testimony of that person. The Party shall identify the intended witness, shall describe the subjects on which the witness's testimony is sought and shall state why such subjects are relevant and material to the outcome of the case. The Arbitral Tribunal shall decide on this request and shall take the necessary steps if in its discretion it determines that the testimony of that witness would be relevant and material.

11. The Arbitral Tribunal may, at any time before the arbitration is concluded, order any Party to provide, or to use its best efforts to provide, the appearance for testimony at an Evidentiary Hearing of any person, including one whose testimony has not yet been offered.

Article 5 – Party-Appointed Experts

1. A Party may rely on a Party-Appointed Expert as a means of evidence on specific issues. Within the time ordered by the Arbitral Tribunal, a Party- Appointed Expert shall submit an Expert Report.

2. The Expert Report shall contain:

    (a) the full name and address of the Party- Appointed Expert, his or her present and past relationship (if any) with any of the Parties, and a description of his or her background, qualifications, training and experience;

    (b) a statement of the facts on which he or she is basing his or her expert opinions and conclusions;

    (c) his or her expert opinions and conclusions, including a description of the method, evidence and information used in arriving at the conclusions;

    (d) an affirmation of the truth of the Expert Report; and

    (e) the signature of the Party-Appointed Expert and its date and place.

3. The Arbitral Tribunal in its discretion may order that any Party-Appointed Experts who have submitted Expert Reports on the same or related issues meet and confer on such issues. At such meeting, the Party-Appointed Experts shall attempt to reach agreement on those issues as to which they had differences of opinion in their Expert Reports, and they shall record in writing any such issues on which they reach agreement.

4. Each Party-Appointed Expert shall appear for testimony at an Evidentiary Hearing, unless the Parties agree otherwise and the Arbitral Tribunal accepts this agreement.

5. If a Party-Appointed Expert does not appear without a valid reason for testimony at an Evidentiary Hearing, except by agreement of the Parties accepted by the

Arbitral Tribunal, the Arbitral Tribunal shall disregard his or her Expert Report unless, in exceptional circumstances, the Arbitral Tribunal determines otherwise.

6. If the Parties agree that a Party-Appointed Expert does not need to appear for testimony at an Evidentiary Hearing, such an agreement shall not be considered to reflect an agreement as to the correctness of the content of the Expert Report.

Article 6 – Tribunal-Appointed Experts

1. The Arbitral Tribunal, after having consulted with the Parties, may appoint one or more independent Tribunal-Appointed Experts to report to it on specific issues designated by the Arbitral Tribunal. The Arbitral Tribunal shall establish the terms of reference for any Tribunal-Appointed Expert report after having consulted with the Parties. A copy of the final terms of reference shall be sent by the Arbitral Tribunal to the Parties.

2. The Tribunal-Appointed Expert shall, before accepting appointment, submit to the Arbitral Tribunal and to the Parties a statement of his or her independence from the Parties and the Arbitral Tribunal. Within the time ordered by the Arbitral Tribunal, the Parties shall inform the Arbitral Tribunal whether they have any objections to the Tribunal-Appointed Expert's independence. The Arbitral Tribunal shall decide promptly whether to accept any such objection.

3. Subject to the provisions of Article 9.2, the Tribunal-Appointed Expert may request a Party to provide any relevant and material information or to provide access to any relevant documents, goods, samples, property or site for inspection. The authority of a Tribunal-Appointed Expert to request such information or access shall be the same as the authority of the Arbitral Tribunal. The Parties and their representatives shall have the right to receive any such information and to attend any such inspection. Any disagreement between a Tribunal-Appointed Expert and a Party as to the relevance, materiality or appropriateness of such a request shall be decided by the Arbitral Tribunal, in the manner provided in Articles 3.5 through 3.7. The Tribunal- Appointed Expert shall record in the report any non-compliance by a Party with an appropriate request or decision by the Arbitral Tribunal and shall describe its effects on the determination of the specific issue.

4. The Tribunal-Appointed Expert shall report in writing to the Arbitral Tribunal. The Tribunal- Appointed Expert shall describe in the report the method, evidence and information used in arriving at the conclusions.

5. The Arbitral Tribunal shall send a copy of such Expert Report to the Parties. The Parties may examine any document that the Tribunal- Appointed Expert has examined and any correspondence between the Arbitral Tribunal and the Tribunal, Appointed Expert. Within the time ordered by the Arbitral Tribunal, any Party shall have the opportunity to respond to the report in a submission by the Party or through an Expert Report by a Party-Appointed Expert. The Arbitral Tribunal shall

send the submission or Expert Report to the Tribunal-Appointed Expert and to the other Parties.

6. At the request of a Party or of the Arbitral Tribunal, the Tribunal-Appointed Expert shall be present at an Evidentiary Hearing. The Arbitral Tribunal may question the Tribunal-Appointed Expert, and he or she may be questioned by the Parties or by any Party- Appointed Expert on issues raised in the Parties' submissions or in the Expert Reports made by the Party-Appointed Experts pursuant to Article 6.5.

7. Any Expert Report made by a Tribunal-Appointed Expert and its conclusions shall be assessed by the Arbitral Tribunal with due regard to all circumstances of the case.

8. The fees and expenses of a Tribunal-Appointed Expert, to be funded in a manner determined by the Arbitral Tribunal, shall form part of the costs of the arbitration.

Article 7 – On Site Inspection

Subject to the provisions of Article 9.2, the Arbitral Tribunal may, at the request of a Party or on its own motion, inspect or require the inspection by a Tribunal-Appointed Expert of any site, property, machinery or any other goods or process, or documents, as it deems appropriate. The Arbitral Tribunal shall, in consultation with the Parties, determine the timing and arrangement for the inspection. The Parties and their representatives shall have the right to attend any such inspection.

Article 8 – Evidentiary Hearing

1. The Arbitral Tribunal shall at all times have complete control over the Evidentiary Hearing. The Arbitral Tribunal may limit or exclude any question to, answer by or appearance of a witness (which term includes, for the purposes of this Article, witnesses of fact and any Experts), if it considers such question, answer or appearance to be irrelevant, immaterial, burdensome, duplicative or covered by a reason for objection set forth in Article 9.2. Questions to a witness during direct and redirect testimony may not be unreasonably leading.

2. The Claimant shall ordinarily first present the testimony of its witnesses, followed by the Respondent presenting testimony of its witnesses, and then by the presentation by Claimant of rebuttal witnesses, if any. Following direct testimony, any other Party may question such witness, in an order to be determined by the Arbitral Tribunal. The Party who initially presented the witness shall subsequently have the opportunity to ask additional questions on the matters raised in the other Parties' questioning. The Arbitral Tribunal, upon request of a Party or on its own motion, may vary this order of proceeding, including the arrangement of testimony by particular issues or in such a manner that witnesses presented by different Parties be questioned at the same time and in confrontation with each other. The Arbitral Tribunal may ask questions to a witness at any time.

3. Any witness providing testimony shall first affirm, in a manner determined appropriate by the Arbitral Tribunal, that he or she is telling the truth. If the witness has submitted a Witness Statement or an Expert Report, the witness shall confirm it. The Parties may agree or the Arbitral Tribunal may order that the Witness Statement or Expert Report shall serve as that witness's direct testimony.

4. Subject to the provisions of Article 9.2, the Arbitral Tribunal may request any person to give oral or written evidence on any issue that the Arbitral Tribunal considers to be relevant and material. Any witness called and questioned by the Arbitral Tribunal may also be questioned by the Parties.

Article 9 – Admissibility and Assessment of Evidence

1. The Arbitral Tribunal shall determine the admissibility, relevance, materiality and weight of evidence.

2. The Arbitral Tribunal shall, at the request of a Party or on its own motion, exclude from evidence or production any document, statement, oral testimony or inspection for any of the following reasons: (a) lack of sufficient relevance or materiality; (b) legal impediment or privilege under the legal or ethical rules determined by the Arbitral Tribunal to be applicable; (c) unreasonable burden to produce the requested evidence; (d) loss or destruction of the document that has been reasonably shown to have occurred; (e) grounds of commercial or technical confidentiality that the Arbitral Tribunal determines to be compelling; (f) grounds of special political or institutional sensitivity (including evidence that has been classified as secret by a government or a public international institution) that the Arbitral Tribunal determines to be compelling; or (g) considerations of fairness or equality of the Parties that the Arbitral Tribunal determines to be compelling.

3. The Arbitral Tribunal may, where appropriate, make necessary arrangements to permit evidence to be considered subject to suitable confidentiality protection.

4. If a Party fails without satisfactory explanation to produce any document requested in a Request to Produce to which it has not objected in due time or fails to produce any document ordered to be produced by the Arbitral Tribunal, the Arbitral Tribunal may infer that such document would be adverse to the interests of that Party.

5. If a Party fails without satisfactory explanation to make available any other relevant evidence, including testimony, sought by one Party to which the Party to whom the request was addressed has not objected in due time or fails to make available any evidence, including testimony, ordered by the Arbitral Tribunal to be produced, the Arbitral Tribunal may infer that such evidence would be adverse to the interests of that Party.

Annex 17

IBA Guidelines on Conflicts of Interest in International Arbitration (IBA Conflict Guidelines)*

INTRODUCTION

Problems of conflicts of interest increasingly challenge international arbitration. Arbitrators are often unsure about what facts need to be disclosed, and they may make different choices about disclosures than other arbitrators in the same situation. The growth of international business and the manner in which it is conducted, including interlocking corporate relationships and larger international law firms, have caused more disclosures and have created more difficult conflict of interest issues to determine. Reluctant parties have more opportunities to use challenges of arbitrators to delay arbitrations or to deny the opposing party the arbitrator of its choice. Disclosure of any relationship, no matter how minor or serious, has too often led to objections, challenge and withdrawal or removal of the arbitrator.

Thus, parties, arbitrators, institutions and courts face complex decisions about what to disclose and what standards to apply. In addition, institutions and courts face difficult decisions if an objection or a challenge is made after a disclosure. There is a tension between, on the one hand, the parties' right to disclosure of situations that may reasonably call into question an arbitrator's impartiality or independence and their right to a fair hearing and, on the other hand, the parties' right to select arbitrators of their choosing. Even though laws and arbitration rules provide some standards, there is a lack of detail in their guidance and of uniformity in

* Approved on 22 May 2004 by the Council of the IBA. © 2004, International Bar Association. Reprinted with kind permission of the IBA. The text is available at the IBA website http://www.ibanet.org.

their application. As a result, quite often members of the international arbitration community apply different standards in making decisions concerning disclosure, objections and challenges.

It is in the interest of everyone in the international arbitration community that international arbitration proceedings not be hindered by these growing conflicts of interest issues. The Committee on Arbitration and ADR of the International Bar Association appointed a Working Group of 19 experts[1] in international arbitration from 14 countries to study, with the intent of helping this decision-making process, national laws, judicial decisions, arbitration rules and practical considerations and applications regarding impartiality and independence and disclosure in international arbitration. The Working Group has determined that existing standards lack sufficient clarity and uniformity in their application. It has therefore prepared these Guidelines, which set forth some General Standards and Explanatory Notes on the Standards. Moreover, the Working Group believes that greater consistency and fewer unnecessary challenges and arbitrator withdrawals and removals could be achieved by providing lists of specific situations that, in the view of the Working Group, do or do not warrant disclosure or disqualification of an arbitrator. Such lists – designated Red, Orange and Green (the 'Application Lists') – appear at the end of these Guidelines.[2]

The Guidelines reflect the Working Group's understanding of the best current international practice firmly rooted in the principles expressed in the General Standards. The Working Group has based the General Standards and the Application Lists upon statutes and case law in jurisdictions and upon the judgment and experience of members of the Working Group and others involved in international commercial arbitration. The Working Group has attempted to balance the various interests of parties, representatives, arbitrators and arbitration institutions, all of whom have a responsibility for ensuring the integrity, reputation and efficiency of international commercial arbitration. In particular, the Working Group has sought and considered the views of many leading arbitration institutions, as well as corporate counsel and other persons involved in international arbitration. The Working Group also published drafts of the Guidelines and sought comments at two annual meetings of the International Bar Association and other

---

1. The members of the Working Group are: (1) Henri Alvarez, Canada; (2) John Beechey, England; (3) Jim Carter, United States; (4) Emmanuel Gaillard, France, (5) Emilio Gonzales de Castilla, Mexico; (6) Bernard Hanotiau, Belgium; (7) Michael Hwang, Singapore; (8) Albert Jan van den Berg, Belgium; (9) Doug Jones, Australia; (10) Gabrielle Kaufmann-Kohler, Switzerland; (11) Arthur Marriott, England; (12) Tore Wiwen Nilsson, Sweden; (13) Hilmar Raeschke-Kessler, Germany; (14) David W. Rivkin, United States; (15) Klaus Sachs, Germany; (16) Nathalie Voser, Switzerland (Rapporteur); (17) David Williams, New Zealand; (18) Des Williams, South Africa; (19); Otto de Witt Wijnen, The Netherlands (Chair).

2. Detailed Background Information to the Guidelines has been published in *Business Law International* at BLI Vol 5, No 3, September 2004, pp 433-458 and is available at the IBA website http://www.ibanet.org.

meetings of arbitrators. While the comments received by the Working Group varied, and included some points of criticisms, the arbitration community generally supported and encouraged these efforts to help reduce the growing problems of conflicts of interests. The Working Group has studied all the comments received and has adopted many of the proposals that it has received. The Working Group is very grateful indeed for the serious considerations given to its proposals by so many institutions and individuals all over the globe and for the comments and proposals received.

Originally, the Working Group developed the Guidelines for international commercial arbitration. However, in the light of comments received, it realized that the Guidelines should equally apply to other types of arbitration, such as investment arbitrations (insofar as these may not be considered as commercial arbitrations).[3]

These Guidelines are not legal provisions and do not override any applicable national law or arbitral rules chosen by the parties. However, the Working Group hopes that these Guidelines will find general acceptance within the international arbitration community (as was the case with the IBA Rules on the Taking of Evidence in International Commercial Arbitration) and that they thus will help parties, practitioners, arbitrators, institutions and the courts in their decision-making process on these very important questions of impartiality, independence, disclosure, objections and challenges made in that connection. The Working Group trusts that the Guidelines will be applied with robust common sense and without pedantic and unduly formalistic interpretation. The Working Group is also publishing a Background and History, which describes the studies made by the Working Group and may be helpful in interpreting the Guidelines.

The IBA and the Working Group view these Guidelines as a beginning, rather than an end, of the process. The Application Lists cover many of the varied situations that commonly arise in practice, but they do not purport to be comprehensive, nor could they be. Nevertheless, the Working Group is confident that the Application Lists provide better concrete guidance than the General Standards (and certainly more than existing standards). The IBA and the Working Group seek comments on the actual use of the Guidelines, and they plan to supplement, revise and refine the Guidelines based on that practical experience.

In 1987, the IBA published Rules of Ethics for International Arbitrators. Those Rules cover more topics than these Guidelines, and they remain in effect as to subjects that are not discussed in the Guidelines. The Guidelines supersede the Rules of Ethics as to the matters treated here.

---

3. Similarly, the Working Group is of the opinion that these Guidelines should apply by analogy to civil servants and government officers who are appointed as arbitrators by States or State entities that are parties to arbitration proceedings.

PART I GENERAL STANDARDS REGARDING IMPARTIALITY,
INDEPENDENCE AND DISCLOSURE

(1) General Principle

*Every arbitrator shall be impartial and independent of the parties at the time of
accepting an appointment to serve and shall remain so during the entire arbitration proceeding until the final award has been rendered or the proceeding has
otherwise finally terminated.*

Explanation to General Standard 1:

The Working Group is guided by the fundamental principle in international
arbitration that each arbitrator must be impartial and independent of the parties
at the time he or she accepts an appointment to act as arbitrator and must remain
so during the entire course of the arbitration proceedings. The Working Group
considered whether this obligation should extend even during the period that the
award may be challenged but has decided against this. The Working Group
takes the view that the arbitrator's duty ends when the Arbitral Tribunal has
rendered the final award or the proceedings have otherwise been finally terminated (e.g., because of a settlement). If, after setting aside or other proceedings,
the dispute is referred back to the same arbitrator, a fresh round of disclosure
may be necessary.

(2) Conflicts of Interest

(a) *An arbitrator shall decline to accept an appointment or, if the arbitration has
already been commenced, refuse to continue to act as an arbitrator if he or she has
any doubts as to his or her ability to be impartial or independent.*

(b) *The same principle applies if facts or circumstances exist, or have arisen since
the appointment, that, from a reasonable third person's point of view having
knowledge of the relevant facts, give rise to justifiable doubts as to the arbitrator's
impartiality or independence, unless the parties have accepted the arbitrator in
accordance with the requirements set out in General Standard (4).*

(c) *Doubts are justifiable if a reasonable and informed third party would reach the
conclusion that there was a likelihood that the arbitrator may be influenced by
factors other than the merits of the case as presented by the parties in reaching his
or her decision.*

(d) *Justifiable doubts necessarily exist as to the arbitrator's impartiality or
independence if there is an identity between a party and the arbitrator, if the
arbitrator is a legal representative of a legal entity that is a party in the
arbitration, or if the arbitrator has a significant financial or personal interest
in the matter at stake.*

Explanation to General Standard 2:

(a) It is the main ethical guiding principle of every arbitrator that actual bias from the arbitrator's own point of view must lead to that arbitrator declining his or her appointment. This standard should apply regardless of the stage of the proceedings. This principle is so selfevident that many national laws do not explicitly say so. See e.g. Article 12, UNCITRAL Model Law. The Working Group, however, has included it in the General Standards because explicit expression in these Guidelines helps to avoid confusion and to create confidence in procedures before arbitral tribunals. In addition, the Working Group believes that the broad standard of 'any doubts as to an ability to be impartial and independent' should lead to the arbitrator declining the appointment.

(b) In order for standards to be applied as consistently as possible, the Working Group believes that the test for disqualification should be an objective one. The Working Group uses the wording 'impartiality or independence' derived from the broadly adopted Article 12 of the UNCITRAL Model Law, and the use of an appearance test, based on justifiable doubts as to the impartiality or independence of the arbitrator, as provided in Article 12(2) of the UNCITRAL Model Law, to be applied objectively (a 'reasonable third person test'). As described in the Explanation to General Standard 3(d), this standard should apply regardless of the stage of the proceedings.

(c) Most laws and rules that apply the standard of justifiable doubts do not further define that standard. The Working Group believes that this General Standard provides some context for making this determination.

(d) The Working Group supports the view that no one is allowed to be his or her own judge; i.e., there cannot be identity between an arbitrator and a party. The Working Group believes that this situation cannot be waived by the parties. The same principle should apply to persons who are legal representatives of a legal entity that is a party in the arbitration, like board members, or who have a significant economic interest in the matter at stake. Because of the importance of this principle, this non-waivable situation is made a General Standard, and examples are provided in the non-waivable Red List. The General Standard purposely uses the terms 'identity' and 'legal representatives.' In the light of comments received, the Working Group considered whether these terms should be extended or further defined, but decided against doing so. It realizes that there are situations in which an employee of a party or a civil servant can be in a position similar, if not identical, to the position of an official legal representative. The Working Group decided that it should suffice to state the principle.

(3) Disclosure by the Arbitrator

(a) *If facts or circumstances exist that may, in the eyes of the parties, give rise to doubts as to the arbitrator's impartiality or independence, the arbitrator shall disclose such facts or circumstances to the parties, the arbitration institution or other appointing authority (if any, and if so required by the applicable institutional rules) and to the co-arbitrators, if any, prior to accepting his or her appointment or, if thereafter, as soon as he or she learns about them.*

(b) *It follows from General Standards 1 and 2(a) that an arbitrator who has made a disclosure considers himself or herself to be impartial and independent of the parties despite the disclosed facts and therefore capable of performing his or her duties as arbitrator. Otherwise, he or she would have declined the nomination or appointment at the outset or resigned.*

(c) *Any doubt as to whether an arbitrator should disclose certain facts or circumstances should be resolved in favour of disclosure.*

(d) *When considering whether or not facts or circumstances exist that should be disclosed, the arbitrator shall not take into account whether the arbitration proceeding is at the beginning or at a later stage.*

Explanation to General Standard 3:

(a) General Standard 2(b) above sets out an objective test for disqualification of an arbitrator. However, because of varying considerations with respect to disclosure, the proper standard for disclosure may be different. A purely objective test for disclosure exists in the majority of the jurisdictions analyzed and in the UNCITRAL Model Law. Nevertheless, the Working Group recognizes that the parties have an interest in being fully informed about any circumstances that may be relevant in their view. Because of the strongly held views of many arbitration institutions (as reflected in their rules and as stated to the Working Group) that the disclosure test should reflect the perspectives of the parties, the Working Group in principle accepted, after much debate, a subjective approach for disclosure. The Working Group has adapted the language of Article 7(2) of the ICC Rules for this standard. However, the Working Group believes that this principle should not be applied without limitations. Because some situations should never lead to disqualification under the objective test, such situations need not be disclosed, regardless of the parties' perspective. These limitations to the subjective test are reflected in the Green List, which lists some situations in which disclosure is not required. Similarly, the Working Group emphasizes that the two tests (objective test for disqualification and subjective test for disclosure) are clearly distinct from each other, and that a disclosure shall not automatically lead to disqualification, as reflected in General Standard 3(b). In determining what facts should be disclosed, an arbitrator should take into account all circumstances known to him or her, including to the extent known the culture and the customs of the country of which the parties are domiciled or nationals.

(b) Disclosure is not an admission of a conflict of interest. An arbitrator who has made a disclosure to the parties considers himself or herself to be impartial and independent of the parties, despite the disclosed facts, or else he or she would have declined the nomination or resigned. An arbitrator making disclosure thus feels capable of performing his or her duties. It is the purpose of disclosure to allow the parties to judge whether or not they agree with the evaluation of the arbitrator and, if they so wish, to explore the situation further. The Working Group hopes that the promulgation of this General Standard will eliminate the misunderstanding that disclosure demonstrates doubts sufficient to disqualify the arbitrator. Instead, any challenge should be successful only if an objective test, as set forth above, is met.

(c) Unnecessary disclosure sometimes raises an incorrect implication in the minds of the parties that the disclosed circumstances would affect his or her impartiality or independence. Excessive disclosures thus unnecessarily undermine the parties' confidence in the process. Nevertheless, after some debate, the Working Group believes it important to provide expressly in the General Standards that in case of doubt the arbitrator should disclose. If the arbitrator feels that he or she should disclose but that professional secrecy rules or other rules of practice prevent such disclosure, he or she should not accept the appointment or should resign.

(d) The Working Group has concluded that disclosure or disqualification (as set out in General Standard 2) should not depend on the particular stage of the arbitration. In order to determine whether the arbitrator should disclose, decline the appointment or refuse to continue to act or whether a challenge by a party should be successful, the facts and circumstances alone are relevant and not the current stage of the procedure or the consequences of the withdrawal. As a practical matter, institutions make a distinction between the commencement of an arbitration proceeding and a later stage. Also, courts tend to apply different standards. Nevertheless, the Working Group believes it important to clarify that no distinction should be made regarding the stage of the arbitral procedure. While there are practical concerns if an arbitrator must withdraw after an arbitration has commenced, a distinction based on the stage of arbitration would be inconsistent with the General Standards.

(4) Waiver by the Parties

(a) *If, within 30 days after the receipt of any disclosure by the arbitrator or after a party learns of facts or circumstances that could constitute a potential conflict of interest for an arbitrator, a party does not raise an express objection with regard to that arbitrator, subject to paragraphs (b) and (c) of this General Standard, the party is deemed to have waived any potential conflict of interest by the arbitrator based on such facts or circumstances and may not raise any objection to such facts or circumstances at a later stage.*

(b) *However, if facts or circumstances exist as described in General Standard 2(d), any waiver by a party or any agreement by the parties to have such a person serve as arbitrator shall be regarded as invalid.*

(c) *A person should not serve as an arbitrator when a conflict of interest such as those exemplified in the waivable Red List, exists. Nevertheless, such a person may accept appointment as arbitrator or continue to act as an arbitrator, if the following conditions are met:*

    (i) *All parties, all arbitrators and the arbitration institution or other appointing authority (if any) must have full knowledge of the conflict of interest; and*

    (ii) *All parties must expressly agree that such person may serve as arbitrator despite the conflict of interest.*

(d) *An arbitrator may assist the parties in reaching a settlement of the dispute at any stage of the proceedings. However, before doing so, the arbitrator should receive an express agreement by the parties that acting in such a manner shall not disqualify the arbitrator from continuing to serve as arbitrator. Such express agreement shall be considered to be an effective waiver of any potential conflict of interest that may arise from the arbitrator's participation in such process or from information that the arbitrator may learn in the process. If the assistance by the arbitrator does not lead to final settlement of the case, the parties remain bound by their waiver. However, consistent with General Standard 2(a) and notwithstanding such agreement, the arbitrator shall resign if, as a consequence of his or her involvement in the settlement process, the arbitrator develops doubts as to his or her ability to remain impartial or independent in the future course of the arbitration proceedings.*

Explanation to General Standard 4:

(a) The Working Group suggests a requirement of an explicit objection by the parties within a certain time limit. In the view of the Working Group, this time limit should also apply to a party who refuses to be involved.

(b) This General Standard is included to make General Standard 4(a) consistent with the non-waivable provisions of General Standard 2(d). Examples of such circumstances are described in the non-waivable Red List.

(c) In a serious conflict of interest, such as those that are described by way of example in the waivable Red List, the parties may nevertheless wish to use such a person as an arbitrator. Here, party autonomy and the desire to have only impartial and independent arbitrators must be balanced. The Working Group believes persons with such a serious conflict of interests may serve as arbitrators only if the parties make fully informed, explicit waivers.

(d) The concept of the Arbitral Tribunal assisting the parties in reaching a settlement of their dispute in the course of the arbitration proceedings is well established in some jurisdictions but not in others. Informed consent by the parties to such a process prior to its beginning should be regarded as effective waiver of a potential conflict of interest. Express consent is generally sufficient, as opposed to a consent made in writing which in certain jurisdictions requires signature. In practice, the requirement of an express waiver allows such consent to be made in the minutes or transcript of a hearing. In addition, in order to avoid parties using an arbitrator as mediator as a means of disqualifying the arbitrator, the General Standard makes clear that the waiver should remain effective if the mediation is unsuccessful. Thus, parties assume the risk of what the arbitrator may learn in the settlement process. In giving their express consent, the parties should realize the consequences of the arbitrator assisting the parties in a settlement process and agree on regulating this special position further where appropriate.

(5) Scope

These Guidelines apply equally to tribunal chairs, sole arbitrators and party-appointed arbitrators. These Guidelines do not apply to nonneutral arbitrators, who do not have an obligation to be independent and impartial, as may be permitted by some arbitration rules or national laws.

Explanation to General Standard 5:

Because each member of an Arbitral Tribunal has an obligation to be impartial and independent, the General Standards should not distinguish among sole arbitrators, party-appointed arbitrators and tribunal chairs. With regard to secretaries of Arbitral Tribunals, the Working Group takes the view that it is the responsibility of the arbitrator to ensure that the secretary is and remains impartial and independent. Some arbitration rules and domestic laws permit partyappointed arbitrators to be non-neutral. When an arbitrator is serving in such a role, these Guidelines should not apply to him or her, since their purpose is to protect impartiality and independence.

(6) Relationships

(a) *When considering the relevance of facts or circumstances to determine whether a potential conflict of interest exists or whether disclosure should be made, the activities of an arbitrator's law firm, if any, should be reasonably considered in each individual case. Therefore, the fact that the activities of the arbitrator's firm involve one of the parties shall not automatically constitute a source of such conflict or a reason for disclosure.*

(b) *Similarly, if one of the parties is a legal entity which is a member of a group with which the arbitrator's firm has an involvement, such facts or circumstances should be reasonably considered in each individual case. Therefore, this fact alone shall not automatically constitute a source of a conflict of interest or a reason for disclosure.*

(c) *If one of the parties is a legal entity, the managers, directors and members of a supervisory board of such legal entity and any person having a similar controlling influence on the legal entity shall be considered to be the equivalent of the legal entity.*

Explanation to General Standard 6:

(a) The growing size of law firms should be taken into account as part of today's reality in international arbitration. There is a need to balance the interests of a party to use the arbitrator of its choice and the importance of maintaining confidence in the impartiality and independence of international arbitration. In the opinion of the Working Group, the arbitrator must in principle be considered as identical to his or her law firm, but nevertheless the activities of the arbitrator's firm should not automatically constitute a conflict of interest. The relevance of such activities, such as the nature, timing and scope of the work by the law firm, should be reasonably considered in each individual case. The Working Group uses the term 'involvement' rather than 'acting for' because a law firm's relevant connections with a party may include activities other than representation on a legal matter.

(b) When a party to an arbitration is a member of a group of companies, special questions regarding conflict of interest arise. As in the prior paragraph, the Working Group believes that because individual corporate structure arrangements vary so widely an automatic rule is not appropriate. Instead, the particular circumstances of an affiliation with another entity within the same group of companies should be reasonably considered in each individual case.

(c) The party in international arbitration is usually a legal entity. Therefore, this General Standard clarifies which individuals should be considered effectively to be that party.

(7) Duty of Arbitrator and Parties

(a) *A party shall inform an arbitrator, the Arbitral Tribunal, the other parties and the arbitration institution or other appointing authority (if any) about any direct or indirect relationship between it (or another company of the same group of companies) and the arbitrator. The party shall do so on its own initiative before the beginning of the proceeding or as soon as it becomes aware of such relationship.*

(b) *In order to comply with General Standard 7(a), a party shall provide any information already available to it and shall perform a reasonable search of publicly available information.*

(c) *An arbitrator is under a duty to make reasonable enquiries to investigate any potential conflict of interest, as well as any facts or circumstances that may cause his or her impartiality or independence to be questioned. Failure to disclose a potential conflict is not excused by lack of knowledge if the arbitrator makes no reasonable attempt to investigate.*

Explanation to General Standard 7:

To reduce the risk of abuse by unmeritorious challenge of an arbitrator's impartiality or independence, it is necessary that the parties disclose any relevant relationship with the arbitrator. In addition, any party or potential party to an arbitration is, at the outset, required to make a reasonable effort to ascertain and to disclose publicly available information that, applying the general standard, might affect the arbitrator's impartiality and independence. It is the arbitrator or putative arbitrator's obligation to make similar enquiries and to disclose any information that may cause his or her impartiality or independence to be called into question.

PART II PRACTICAL APPLICATION OF THE GENERAL STANDARDS

1. The Working Group believes that if the Guidelines are to have an important practical influence, they should reflect situations that are likely to occur in today's arbitration practice. The Guidelines should provide specific guidance to arbitrators, parties, institutions and courts as to what situations do or do not constitute conflicts of interest or should be disclosed. For this purpose, the members of the Working Group analyzed their respective case law and categorized situations that can occur in the following Application Lists. These lists obviously cannot contain every situation, but they provide guidance in many circumstances, and the Working Group has sought to make them as comprehensive as possible. In all cases, the General Standards should control.

2. The Red List consists of two parts: 'a non-waivable Red List' (see General Standards 2(c) and 4(b)) and 'a waivable Red List' (see General Standard 4(c)). These lists are a non-exhaustive enumeration of specific situations which, depending on the facts of a given case, give rise to justifiable doubts as to the arbitrator's impartiality and independence; ie, in these circumstances an objective conflict of interest exists from the point of view of a reasonable third person having knowledge of the relevant facts (*see* General Standard 2(b)). The non-waivable Red List includes situations deriving from the overriding principle that no person can be his or her own judge. Therefore, disclosure of such a situation cannot cure the conflict. The waivable Red List encompasses situations that are serious but not as severe. Because of their seriousness, unlike circumstances described in the Orange List, these situations should be considered waivable only if and when the parties, being aware of the conflict of interest situation, nevertheless expressly state their willingness to have such a person act as arbitrator, as set forth in General Standard 4(c).

3. The Orange List is a non-exhaustive enumeration of specific situations which (depending on the facts of a given case) in the eyes of the parties may give rise to justifiable doubts as to the arbitrator's impartiality or independence. The Orange List thus reflects situations that would fall under General Standard 3(a), so that the arbitrator has a duty to disclose such situations. In all these situations, the parties are deemed to have accepted the arbitrator if, after disclosure, no timely objection is made. (General Standard 4(a)).

4. It should be stressed that, as stated above, such disclosure should not automatically result in a disqualification of the arbitrator; no presumption regarding disqualification should arise from a disclosure. The purpose of the disclosure is to inform the parties of a situation that they may wish to explore further in order to determine whether objectively – i.e., from a reasonable third person's point of view having knowledge of the relevant facts – there is a justifiable doubt as to the arbitrator's impartiality or independence. If the conclusion is that there is no justifiable doubt, the arbitrator can act. He or she can also act if there is no timely objection by the parties or, in situations covered by the waivable Red List, a specific acceptance by the parties in accordance with General Standard 4(c). Of course, if a party challenges the appointment of the arbitrator, he or she can nevertheless act if the authority that has to rule on the challenge decides that the challenge does not meet the objective test for disqualification.

5. In addition, a later challenge based on the fact that an arbitrator did not disclose such facts or circumstances should not result automatically in either non-appointment, later disqualification or a successful challenge to any award. In the view of the Working Group, non-disclosure cannot make an arbitrator partial or lacking independence; only the facts or circumstances that he or she did not disclose can do so.

6. The Green List contains a non-exhaustive enumeration of specific situations where no appearance of, and no actual, conflict of interest exists from the relevant objective point of view. Thus, the arbitrator has no duty to disclose situations falling within the Green List. In the opinion of the Working Group, as already expressed in the Explanation to General Standard 3(a), there should be a limit to disclosure, based on reasonableness; in some situations, an objective test should prevail over the purely subjective test of 'the eyes of the parties.'

7. Situations falling outside the time limit used in some of the Orange List situations should generally be considered as falling in the Green List, even though they are not specifically stated. An arbitrator may nevertheless wish to make disclosure if, under the General Standards, he or she believes it to be appropriate. While there has been much debate with respect to the time limits used in the Lists, the Working Group has concluded that the limits indicated are appropriate and provide guidance where none exists now. For example, the three-year period in Orange List 3.1 may be too long in certain circumstances and too short in others, but the Working Group believes that the period is an appropriate general criterion, subject to the special circumstances of any case.

8. The borderline between the situations indicated is often thin. It can be debated whether a certain situation should be on one List of instead of another. Also, the Lists contain, for various situations, open norms like 'significant'. The Working Group has extensively and repeatedly discussed both of these issues, in the light of comments received. It believes that the decisions reflected in the Lists reflect international principles to the best extent possible and that further definition of the norms, which should be interpreted reasonably in light of the facts and circumstances in each case, would be counter-productive.

9. There has been much debate as to whether there should be a Green List at all and also, with respect to the Red List, whether the situations on the Non-Waivable Red List should be waivable in light of party autonomy. With respect to the first question, the Working Group has maintained its decision that the subjective test for disclosure should not be the absolute criterion but that some objective thresholds should be added. With respect to the second question, the conclusion of the Working Group was that party autonomy, in this respect, has its limits.

1. NON-WAIVABLE RED LIST

1.1 There is an identity between a party and the arbitrator, or the arbitrator is a legal representative of an entity that is a party in the arbitration.

1.2 The arbitrator is a manager, director or member of the supervisory board, or has a similar controlling influence in one of the parties.

1.3 The arbitrator has a significant financial interest in one of the parties or the outcome of the case.

1.4 The arbitrator regularly advises the appointing party or an affiliate of the appointing party, and the arbitrator or his or her firm derives a significant financial income therefrom.

2. WAIVABLE RED LIST

2.1 Relationship of the Arbitrator to the Dispute

2.1.1 The arbitrator has given legal advice or provided an expert opinion on the dispute to a party or an affiliate of one of the parties.

2.1.2 The arbitrator has previous involvement in the case.

2.2 Arbitrator's Direct or Indirect Interest in the Dispute

2.2.1 The arbitrator holds shares, either directly or indirectly, in one of the parties or an affiliate of one of the parties that is privately held.

2.2.2 A close family member[4] of the arbitrator has a significant financial interest in the outcome of the dispute.

2.2.3 The arbitrator or a close family member of the arbitrator has a close relationship with a third party who may be liable to recourse on the part of the unsuccessful party in the dispute.

---

4. Throughout the Application Lists, the term 'close family member' refers to a spouse, sibling, child, parent or life partner.

2.3 Arbitrator's Relationship with the Parties or Counsel

2.3.1 The arbitrator currently represents or advises one of the parties or an affiliate of one of the parties.

2.3.2 The arbitrator currently represents the lawyer or law firm acting as counsel for one of the parties.

2.3.3 The arbitrator is a lawyer in the same law firm as the counsel to one of the parties.

2.3.4 The arbitrator is a manager, director or member of the supervisory board, or has a similar controlling influence, in an affiliate[5] of one of the parties if the affiliate is directly involved in the matters in dispute in the arbitration.

2.3.5 The arbitrator's law firm had a previous but terminated involvement in the case without the arbitrator being involved himself or herself.

2.3.6 The arbitrator's law firm currently has a significant commercial relationship with one of the parties or an affiliate of one of the parties.

2.3.7 The arbitrator regularly advises the appointing party or an affiliate of the appointing party, but neither the arbitrator nor his or her firm derives a significant financial income therefrom.

2.3.8 The arbitrator has a close family relationship with one of the parties or with a manager, director or member of the supervisory board or any person having a similar controlling influence in one of the parties or an affiliate of one of the parties or with a counsel representing a party.

2.3.9 A close family member of the arbitrator has a significant financial interest in one of the parties or an affiliate of one of the parties.

3. ORANGE LIST

3.1 Previous Services for One of the Parties or Other Involvement in the Case

3.1.1 The arbitrator has within the past three years served as counsel for one of the parties or an affiliate of one of the parties or has previously advised or been consulted by the party or an affiliate of the party making the appointment in an unrelated matter, but the arbitrator and the party or the affiliate of the party have no ongoing relationship.

---

5. Throughout the Application Lists, the term 'affiliate' encompasses all companies in one group of companies including the parent company.

3.1.2 The arbitrator has within the past three years served as counsel against one of the parties or an affiliate of one of the parties in an unrelated matter.

3.1.3 The arbitrator has within the past three years been appointed as arbitrator on two or more occasions by one of the parties or an affiliate of one of the parties.[6]

3.1.4 The arbitrator's law firm has within the past three years acted for one of the parties or an affiliate of one of the parties in an unrelated matter without the involvement of the arbitrator.

3.1.5 The arbitrator currently serves, or has served within the past three years, as arbitrator in another arbitration on a related issue involving one of the parties or an affiliate of one of the parties.

3.2 Current Services for One of the Parties

3.2.1 The arbitrator's law firm is currently rendering services to one of the parties or to an affiliate of one of the parties without creating a significant commercial relationship and without the involvement of the arbitrator.

3.2.2 A law firm that shares revenues or fees with the arbitrator's law firm renders services to one of the parties or an affiliate of one of the parties before the arbitral tribunal.

3.2.3 The arbitrator or his or her firm represents a party or an affiliate to the arbitration on a regular basis but is not involved in the current dispute.

3.3 Relationship between an Arbitrator and another Arbitrator or Counsel.

3.3.1 The arbitrator and another arbitrator are lawyers in the same law firm.

3.3.2 The arbitrator and another arbitrator or the counsel for one of the parties are members of the same barristers' chambers.[7]

3.3.3 The arbitrator was within the past three years a partner of, or otherwise affiliated with, another arbitrator or any of the counsel in the same arbitration.

3.3.4 A lawyer in the arbitrator's law firm is an arbitrator in another dispute involving the same party or parties or an affiliate of one of the parties.

---

6. It may be the practice in certain specific kinds of arbitration, such as maritime or commodities arbitration, to draw arbitrators from a small, specialized pool. If in such fields it is the custom and practice for parties frequently to appoint the same arbitrator in different cases, no disclosure of this fact is required where all parties in the arbitration should be familiar with such custom and practice.
7. Issues concerning special considerations involving barristers in England are discussed in the Background Information issued by the Working Group.

3.3.5 A close family member of the arbitrator is a partner or employee of the law firm representing one of the parties, but is not assisting with the dispute.

3.3.6 A close personal friendship exists between an arbitrator and a counsel of one party, as demonstrated by the fact that the arbitrator and the counsel regularly spend considerable time together unrelated to professional work commitments or the activities of professional associations or social organizations.

3.3.7 The arbitrator has within the past three years received more than three appointments by the same counsel or the same law firm.

3.4 Relationship between Arbitrator and Party and Others Involved in the Arbitration

3.4.1 The arbitrator's law firm is currently acting adverse to one of the parties or an affiliate of one of the parties.

3.4.2 The arbitrator had been associated within the past three years with a party or an affiliate of one of the parties in a professional capacity, such as a former employee or partner.

3.4.3 A close personal friendship exists between an arbitrator and a manager or director or a member of the supervisory board or any person having a similar controlling influence in one of the parties or an affiliate of one of the parties or a witness or expert, as demonstrated by the fact that the arbitrator and such director, manager, other person, witness or expert regularly spend considerable time together unrelated to professional work commitments or the activities of professional associations or social organizations.

3.4.4 If the arbitrator is a former judge, he or she has within the past three years heard a significant case involving one of the parties.

3.5 Other Circumstances

3.5.1 The arbitrator holds shares, either directly or indirectly, which by reason of number or denomination constitute a material holding in one of the parties or an affiliate of one of the parties that is publicly listed.

3.5.2 The arbitrator has publicly advocated a specific position regarding the case that is being arbitrated, whether in a published paper or speech or otherwise.

3.5.3 The arbitrator holds one position in an arbitration institution with appointing authority over the dispute.

3.5.4 The arbitrator is a manager, director or member of the supervisory board, or has a similar controlling influence, in an affiliate of one of the parties, where the affiliate is not directly involved in the matters in dispute in the arbitration.

4. GREEN LIST

4.1 Previously Expressed Legal Opinions

4.1.1 The arbitrator has previously published a general opinion (such as in a law review article or public lecture) concerning an issue which also arises in the arbitration (but this opinion is not focused on the case that is being arbitrated).

4.2 Previous Services against One Party

4.2.1 The arbitrator's law firm has acted against one of the parties or an affiliate of one of the parties in an unrelated matter without the involvement of the arbitrator.

4.3 Current Services for One of the Parties

4.3.1 A firm in association or in alliance with the arbitrator's law firm, but which does not share fees or other revenues with the arbitrator's law firm, renders services to one of the parties or an affiliate of one of the parties in an unrelated matter.

4.4 Contacts with another Arbitrator or with Counsel for One of the Parties

4.4.1 The arbitrator has a relationship with another arbitrator or with the counsel for one of the parties through membership in the same professional association or social organization.

4.4.2 The arbitrator and counsel for one of the parties or another arbitrator have previously served together as arbitrators or as co-counsel.

4.5. Contacts between the Arbitrator and One of the Parties

4.5.1 The arbitrator has had an initial contact with the appointing party or an affiliate of the appointing party (or the respective counsels) prior to appointment, if this contact is limited to the arbitrator's availability and qualifications to serve or to the names of possible candidates for a chairperson and did not address the merits or procedural aspects of the dispute.

4.5.2 The arbitrator holds an insignificant amount of shares in one of the parties or an affiliate of one of the parties, which is publicly listed.

4.5.3 The arbitrator and a manager, director or member of the supervisory board, or any person having a similar controlling influence, in one of the parties or an affiliate of one of the parties, have worked together as joint experts or in another professional capacity, including as arbitrators in the same case.

A flow chart is attached to these Guidelines for easy reference to the application of the Lists. However, it should be stressed that this is only a schematic reflection of the very complex reality. Always, the specific circumstances of the case prevail.

Flow chart IBA Guidelines on Conflicts of Interest in International Arbitration

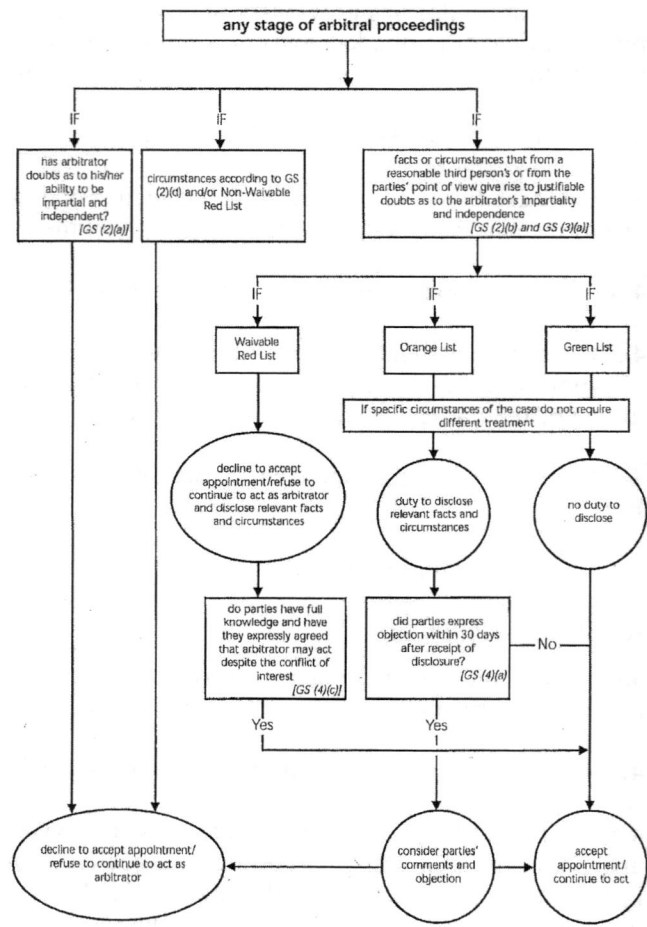

Annex 18

IBA Rules of Ethics for International Arbitrators (IBA Rules of Ethics)*

INTRODUCTORY NOTE

International arbitrators should be impartial, independent, competent, diligent and discreet. These rules seek to establish the manner in which these abstract qualities may be assessed in practice. Rather than rigid rules, they reflect internationally acceptable guidelines developed by practising lawyers from all continents. They will attain their objectives only if they are applied in good faith.

The rules cannot be directly binding either on arbitrators, or on the parties themselves, unless they are adopted by agreement. Whilst the International Bar Association hopes that they will be taken into account in the context of challenges to arbitrators, it is emphasised that these guidelines are not intended to create grounds for the setting aside of awards by national courts.

If parties wish to adopt the rules they may add the following to their arbitration clause or arbitration agreement:

> The parties agree that the Rules of Ethics for International Arbitrators established by the International Bar Association, in force at the date of the commencement of any arbitration under this clause, shall be applicable to the arbitrators appointed in respect of such arbitration.

The International Bar Association takes the position that (whatever may be the case in domestic arbitration) international arbitrators should in principle be granted immunity from suit under national laws, except in extreme cases of wilful or

---

reckless disregard of their legal obligations. Accordingly, the International Bar Association wishes to make it clear that it is not the intention of these rules to create opportunities for aggrieved parties to sue international arbitrators in national courts. The normal sanction for breach of an ethical duty is removal from office, with consequent loss of entitlement to remuneration. The International Bar Association also emphasises that these rules do not affect, and are intended to be consistent with, the International Code of Ethics for lawyers, adopted at Oslo on 25 July 1956, and amended by the General Meeting of the International Bar Association at Mexico City on 24 July 1964.

1. FUNDAMENTAL RULE

Arbitrators shall proceed diligently and efficiently to provide the parties with a just and effective resolution of their disputes, and shall be and shall remain free from bias.

2. ACCEPTANCE OF APPOINTMENT

2.1 A prospective arbitrator shall accept an appointment only if he is fully satisfied that he is able to discharge his duties without bias.

2.2 A prospective arbitrator shall accept an appointment only if he is fully satisfied that he is competent to determine the issues in dispute, and has an adequate knowledge of the language of the arbitration.

2.3 A prospective arbitrator should accept an appointment only if he is able to give to the arbitration the time and attention which the parties are reasonably entitled to expect.

2.4 It is inappropriate to contact parties in order to solicit appointment as arbitrator.

3. ELEMENTS OF BIAS

3.1 The criteria for assessing questions relating to bias are impartiality and independence. Partiality arises when an arbitrator favours one of the parties, or where he is prejudiced in relation to the subject-matter of the dispute. Dependence arises from relationships between an arbitrator and one of the parties, or with someone closely connected with one of the parties.

3.2 Facts which might lead a reasonable person, not knowing the arbitrator's true state of mind, to consider that he is dependent on a party create an appearance of bias. The same is true if an arbitrator has a material interest in the outcome of the dispute, or if he has already taken a position in relation to it. The appearance of bias is best overcome by full disclosure as described in Article 4 below.

3.3 Any current direct or indirect business relationship between an arbitrator and a party, or with a person who is known to be a potentially important witness, will normally give rise to justifiable doubts as to a prospective arbitrator's impartiality or independence. He should decline to accept an appointment in such circumstances unless the parties agree in writing that he may proceed. Examples of indirect relationships are where a member of the prospective arbitrator's family, his firm, or any business partner has a business relationship with one of the parties.

3.4 Past business relationships will not operate as an absolute bar to acceptance of appointment, unless they are of such magnitude or nature as to be likely to affect a prospective arbitrator's judgment.

3.5 Continuous and substantial social or professional relationships between a prospective arbitrator and a party, or with a person who is known to be a potentially important witness in the arbitration, will normally give rise to justifiable doubts as to the impartiality or independence of a prospective arbitrator.

4. DUTY OF DISCLOSURE

4.1 A prospective arbitrator should disclose all facts or circumstances that may give rise to justifiable doubts as to his impartiality or independence. Failure to make such disclosure creates an appearance of bias, and may of itself be a ground for disqualification even though he non-disclosed facts or circumstances would not of themselves justify disqualification.

4.2 A prospective arbitrator should disclose:

a. any past or present business relationship, whether direct or indirect as illustrated in Article 3.3, including prior appointment as arbitrator, with any party to the dispute, or any representative of a party, or any person known to be a potentially important witness in the arbitration. With regard to present relationships, the duty of disclosure applies irrespective of their magnitude, but with regard to past relationships only if they were of more than a trivial nature in relation to the arbitrator's professional or business affairs. Non-disclosure of an indirect relationship unknown to a prospective arbitrator will not be a ground for disqualification unless it could have been ascertained by making reasonable enquiries;
b. the nature and duration of any substantial social relationships with any party or any person known to be likely to be an important witness in the arbitration;
c. the nature of any previous relationship with any fellow arbitrator (including prior joint service as an arbitrator);
d. the extent of any prior knowledge he may have of the dispute;
e. the extent of any commitments which may affect his availability to perform his duties as arbitrator as may be reasonably anticipated.

4.3 The duty of disclosure continues throughout the arbitral proceedings as regards new facts or circumstances.

4.4 Disclosure should be made in writing and communicated to all parties and arbitrators. When an arbitrator has been appointed, any previous disclosure made to the parties should be communicated to the other arbitrators.

5. COMMUNICATIONS WITH PARTIES

5.1 When approached with a view to appointment, a prospective arbitrator should make sufficient enquiries in order to inform himself whether there may be any justifiable doubts regarding his impartiality or independence; whether he is competent to determine the issues in dispute; and whether he is able to give the arbitration the time and attention required. He may also respond to enquiries from those approaching him, provided that such enquiries are designed to determine his suitability and availability for the appointment and provided that the merits of the case are not discussed. In the event that a prospective sole arbitrator or presiding arbitrator is approached by one party alone, or by one arbitrator chosen unilaterally by a party (a 'party-nominated' arbitrator), he should ascertain that the other party or parties, or the other arbitrator, has consented to the manner in which he has been approached. In such circumstances he should, in writing or orally, inform the other party or parties, or the other arbitrator, of the substance of the initial conversation.

5.2 If a party-nominated arbitrator is required to participate in the selection of a third or presiding arbitrator, it is acceptable for him (although he is not so required) to obtain the views of the party who nominated him as to the acceptability of candidates being considered.

5.3 Throughout the arbitral proceedings, an arbitrator should avoid any unilateral communications regarding the case with any party, or its representatives. If such communication should occur, the arbitrator should inform the other party or parties and arbitrators of its substance.

5.4 If an arbitrator becomes aware that a fellow arbitrator has been in improper communication with a party, he may inform the remaining arbitrators and they should together determine what action should be taken. Normally, the appropriate initial course of action is for the offending arbitrator to be requested to refrain from making any further improper communications with the party. Where the offending arbitrator fails or refuses to refrain from improper communications, the remaining arbitrators may inform the innocent party in order that he may consider what action he should take. An arbitrator may act unilaterally to inform a party of the conduct of another arbitrator in order to allow the said party to consider a challenge of the offending arbitrator only in extreme circumstances, and after communicating his intention to his fellow arbitrators in writing.

5.5 No arbitrator should accept any gift or substantial, hospitality, directly or indirectly, from any party to the arbitration. Sole arbitrators and presiding arbitrators should be particularly meticulous in avoiding significant social or professional contacts with any party to the arbitration other than in the presence of the other parties.

6. FEES

Unless the parties agree otherwise or a party defaults, an arbitrator shall make no unilateral arrangements for fees or expenses.

7. DUTY OF DILIGENCE

All arbitrators should devote such time and attention as the parties may reasonably require having regard to all the circumstances of the case, and shall do their best to conduct the arbitration in such a manner that costs do not rise to an unreasonable proportion of the interests at stake.

8. INVOLVEMENT IN SETTLEMENT PROPOSALS

Where the parties have so requested, or consented to a suggestion to this effect by the arbitral tribunal, the tribunal as a whole (or the presiding arbitrator where appropriate), may make proposals for settlement to both parties simultaneously, and preferably in the presence of each other. Although any procedure is possible with the agreement of the parties, the arbitral tribunal should point out to the parties that it is undesirable that any arbitrator should discuss settlement terms with a party in the absence of the other parties since this will normally have the result that any arbitrator involved in such discussions will become disqualified from any future participation in the arbitration.

9. CONFIDENTIALITY OF THE DELIBERATIONS

The deliberations of the arbitral tribunal, and the contents of the award itself, remain confidential in perpetuity unless the parties release the arbitrators from this obligation. An arbitrator should not participate in, or give any information for the purpose of assistance in, any proceedings to consider the award unless, exceptionally, he considers it his duty to disclose any material misconduct or fraud on the part of his fellow arbitrators.

Index

The numbers here refer to paragraph numbers.

ABGB (Austrian Civil Code)   1-072,
    1-074–1-075, 1-093, 7-052, 8-011,
    8-013, 9-017, 11-044, 14-043, 15-046,
    15-085, 34-007
additional party   9-069, 15-063, 15-075,
    33-006, 34-020, 36-011
adjudicate   11-038, 11-044, 11-046, 22-138
administration   1-009, 1-017, 1-105–1-148,
    3-015, 3-034, 5-001, 5-006–5-007,
    5-010, 5-016, 5-018, 5-027, 5-029,
    8-032, 9-013–9-014, 9-060, 9-075,
    9-077, 9-089, 9-090–9-092, 9-098,
    9-102, 10-003, 12-025, 20-018,
    20-253, 33-001, 34-003–34-004
administrative costs   1-019, 11-041, 12-011,
    31-002, 31-004, 32-002, 33-001,
    33-003, 33-006, 34-003–34-006,
    34-019–34-020, 34-056,
    36-002–36-003, 36-010–36-011,
    36-027, 36-033–36-034
administrator   3-033, 7-154
admissibility of multi-party arbitration
    15-005, 15-006–15-025
admissibility of multi-party proceedings
    15-118–15-121
advisers   21-011, 21-019, 23-007–23-008
advisory board   4-001–4-004

AFCC (Austrian Federal Chamber of
    Commerce)   1-004, 1-016, 1-148,
    1-151, 3-003, 5-016
AFEC (Austrian Federal Economic
    Chamber)   1-004–1-008,
    1-016–1-017, 1-103, 3-003–3-004,
    3-008, 3-028, 5-002–5-003, 5-016,
    5-020, 5-022, 9-006, 9-054, 9-091,
    11-001, 11-015, 11-017, 27-017
affiliate   1-100, 15-083, 15-104, 15-107
affirmation   19-021, 20-024, 20-204
age   3-008–3-009
agency   1-021–1-022, 1-071–1-072,
    1-074–1-075, 2-055, 2-062, 7-009,
    7-052, 9-100, 15-107, 20-252, 20-254,
    24-015–24-016, 34-029
aggrieved party   7-103–7-104, 7-107, 8-005,
    16-019, 16-028, 16-035, 16-052,
    17-010, 20-052, 20-056, 20-067,
    20-069, 20-069, 20-126–20-127
agreement, express   7-127, 15-054,
    20-131–20-132, 20-168, 21-009,
    24-048, 24-050
AHG (Austrian Public Liability Act)   8-005,
    8-027
Allgemeines Bürgerliches Gesetzbuch, see
    ABGB

amendment, of claim 11-001–11-052
Amtshaftungsgesetz, see AHG
a-national arbitration 2-020
applicable law, arbitration agreement
    2-032–2-036
applicable law, procedural 2-041–2-044
applicable law, substantive 1-029, 1-069,
    2-072, 7-021, 11-044, 14-062,
    15-015–15-016, 15-018, 20-135,
    20-160, 24-001–24-003, 24-005,
    24-024, 24-047, 25-024, 26-035,
    28-008, 34-016, 35-015
applicant 15-078, 17-017, 22-063–22-064,
    22-066, 22-069, 22-074, 22-122,
    22-137, 22-144, 22-157, 27-064
appointing party 7-111–7-112, 7-114, 7-118,
    16-017, 16-042, 16-054
appointment, institutional 1-021, 6-004,
    7-045, 8-031, 14-060, 15-043, 15-045,
    15-053
appointment, joint 15-039, 15-043, 15-045,
    15-051
arbitrability, objective 1-109– 1-129,
    1-132–1-136, 1-138, 1-140–1-141,
    27-063, 31-052
appointment procedure 1-009, 1-016, 3-030,
    5-002, 5-004, 5-016, 9-063, 9-074,
    9-086, 10-025, 12-019, 14-008,
    14-014–14-015, 14-019, 14-043,
    14-045, 14-056, 15-047
arbitrability, subjective 1-32–1-33,
    1-35–1-36, 1-046–1-047
arbitral centre 1-001, 1-004, 1-006, 1-103,
    5-001, 9-070, 9-088, 9-091, 11-001,
    11-015, 11-017, 27-017
arbitral institutions 1-004, 1-011–1-013,
    1-149, 1-155, 2-063, 3-001–3-002,
    3-010, 3-014, 3-016, 5-016, 7-002,
    7-087, 7-154, 8-001–8-002, 8-029,
    8-030, 9-015, 9-040, 9-059, 9-071,
    9-076, 9-080, 9-085, 9-088, 14-020,
    14-023, 14-025, 20-165, 22-029,
    26-036, 31-036, 33-001, 33-008,
    36-041
arbitral seat 2-001–2-072, 15-113,
    27-010–27-013
arbitral tribunal, constitution 2-059, 11-021,
    15-036, 19-008, 19-024, 19-026

arbitration agreement, conferring
    jurisdiction 11-044, 15-008, 15-020,
    15-025
arbitration agreement, formal validity of
    1-080, 2-036, 13-032, 15-117
arbitration agreement, substantive
    validity of 2-035, 15-100, 19-039,
    19-045
arbitration clause 1-004, 1-016, 1-023,
    1-031, 1-050, 1-056–1-058, 1-062,
    1-068, 1-076–1-078, 1-102–1-104,
    1-129–1-130, 1-147, 2.042, 7-015,
    14-008, 14-013–14-014, 15-001,
    15-012, 15-022, 15-035, 15-058,
    15-064, 15-069, 15-072,
    15-083–15-084, 15-086,
    15-090–15-093, 15-095,
    15-100–15-102, 15-106,
    15-112–15-113, 19-035, 19-038,
    19-044–19-045, 19-048, 20-279,
    24-022, 27-044, 31-013, 37-009
arbitration clause, recommended
    1-102–1-104, 14-013–14-014
arbitration, costs of 1-009, 12-022, 22-085,
    31-003, 31-013, 31-059, 33-007,
    34-001, 34-015, 36-001–36-044
arbitration, institutional 1-004, 1-102,
    2-021, 7-090, 8-027, 9-096, 11-009,
    11-020, 12-021, 15-041, 16-013,
    20-001, 20-110, 20-164, 21-007,
    22-043, 24-004, 30-007, 31-013
arbitration institutions 1-004, 1-149,
    23-003, 23-006, 27-024, 27-030,
    37-008
arbitration, place of 1-070, 2-001–2-072,
    9-019, 9-022, 9-046, 22-111–22-116,
    24-033, 26-003, 27-010–27-013,
    27-065, 31-012–31-013, 31-048
arbitration, seat of 2-001–2-072, 20-110,
    22-094, 23-003
arbitrator immunity 8-010, 8-013
arbitrator liability 8-001–8-027, 8-034
arbitrator, challenge of 3-013, 7-114,
    14-068, 16-001–16-057, 17-022,
    20-287, 21-013, 36-032
arbitrator, defaulting 26-010–26-011,
    26-013
arbitrator, duties 7-046–7-132

arbitrator, fees   9-060, 12-023, 31-006,
    34-004–34-005, 34-007–34-014,
    34-020, 36-006, 36-010, 36-011,
    36-027, 36-032, 36-041,
    36-043–36-044
arbitrator, impartiality of   3-015, 3-017, 7-020,
    7-080, 7-082, 7-093, 7-099–7-100,
    7-113, 16-002–16-003, 16-027
arbitrator, procedural discretion of   20-268,
    20-281, 35-003, 35-012
arbitrators, guidelines for   1-029, 12-011
arbitrators, independence of   7-020, 7-082,
    7-099, 7-113
arbitrators, non-neutral   7-098, 7-118
arbitrators, replaced   1-009, 3-035, 7-056,
    16-017, 16-042, 17-009,
    18-002–18-006, 18-010–18-011
attorney, commercial power of   1-072, 1-074
attorney, oral power of   1-073–1-074, 23-009
Attorney Tariff Act, see RATG
attorneys' fees   31-013
Ausschließungsgründe   7-100–7-101, 7-104,
    7-108, 7-110
Austrian Civil Code, see ABGB
Austrian Enforcement Act, see EO
Austrian enforcement law   22-142–22-143
Austrian Federal Chamber of Commerce,
    see AFCC
Austrian Federal Economic Chamber, see AFEC
Austrian Public Liability Act, see AHG
Austrian Attorney Tariff Act, see RATG
authority, appointing   1-013, 1-016–1-017,
    5-016, 7-140, 7-149, 9-096
authority, evidentiary   20-180–20-181,
    20-186, 20-188, 21-014
authorization   1-161, 2-055, 14-035, 20-252,
    20-266, 22-007, 22-014, 22-022,
    22-026, 22-036, 23-009–23-010,
    24-017, 24-048–24-049, 25-025,
    26-036, 27-024, 27-050, 31-013,
    31-050
authorized agents   23-001–23-010
award, additional   25-026, 29-001, 29-009,
    29-012, 29-015, 29-018
award, annulment of   8-018, 9-037, 13-029,
    20-033
award, by consent   1-019, 7-075, 25-004,
    28-002, 28-005

award, default   20-257, 20-260, 20-261
award, interim   22-065, 22-115, 27-024,
    27-026, 27-028, 34-039, 34-042,
    34-045
award, partial   15-036, 19-026, 19-028,
    27-027, 27-037, 34-038, 34-042,
    34-046, 34-048, 36-032
awarding costs   31-013, 31-042

beneficiary, third-party   15-086–15-093
bias   7-024, 7-058, 7-080–7-082, 7-091,
    7-093, 7-095, 7-103, 7-110, 7-112,
    7-118–7-120, 7-123–7-124, 7-128,
    7-143, 7-148, 15-073, 16-001, 16-003,
    16-019, 16-021, 16-025–16-028,
    16-030, 16-032–16-033, 16-035,
    16-037, 16-039, 16-052, 17-006,
    17-010, 17-023, 17-026, 21-002,
    30-006
bills, hotel   30-036–30-067
board decision   3-012, 3-014–3-015,
    9-097–9-098, 14-032–14-034
board members   1-007, 3-003, 3-005–3-010,
    3-014, 3-017–3-018, 3-020, 3-023,
    3-025–3-028, 3-030–3-031,
    4-002–4-003, 5-003, 5-019–5-020,
    5-024, 7-044, 14-043
Böckstiegel Method   20-146
briefs   9-051, 20-137–20-139, 20-143, 31-054

calculation, of costs   12-001, 36-009
capacity, subjective   1-032–1-033, 1-045
cash outlays   5-009, 31-006, 34-012, 34-017,
    34-020–34-021, 34-059, 34-061,
    36-035–36-036, 36-039–36-040,
    36-043
causality   20-067–20-069, 20-126
Chamber of Commerce, see AFCC
chambers, regional economic   1-004, 1-161
Civil Code, see ABGB
civil law countries   8-006, 9-022–9-023,
    20-176, 20-207, 20-209
civil law jurisdictions   8-002, 8-004,
    9-025–9-026, 15-094, 20-043, 20-045,
    20-069, 20-119, 20-196, 20-199,
    20-205, 20-209, 20-223, 20-229,
    20-232, 20-235, 20-237,
    26-027–26-028

civil law practitioners   20-197, 20-212,
    20-220, 20-226
claimants, multiple   15-008–15-009,
    15-028–15-029, 15-042
co-arbitrators   7-009, 7-140, 10-030, 14-002,
    14-046, 14-054, 14-058–14-061,
    14-065, 15-073, 16-011, 16-044,
    18-004–18-005, 20-045, 26-004,
    26-015, 26-018, 26-022, 26-037,
    36-031
Code of Conduct   20-218–20-219, 20-221
commercial enterprise   1-044
companies doctrine, group of   15-109–15-110
competence-competence   19-015–19-018,
    19-022, 19-039, 31-051–31-052
conciliation proceedings   1-018–1-019
conciliator   1-018–1-019
confidentiality   3-031–3-032, 5-003, 5-005,
    5-024, 59-028, 7-063, 7-066–7-067,
    14-061, 20-109, 20-144, 20-152,
    20-156–20-167, 20-190,
    20-244–20-245, 30-002
confidentiality agreement   20-156–20-157,
    20-162–20-164
confidentiality of arbitration   20-152,
    20-156–20-167
confidentiality obligations   3-031–3-032,
    5-024, 20-161–20-162
conflict of laws rules   1-073, 2-014, 2-016,
    24-015, 24-039–24-043
conflicts of interest in international
    arbitration   7-048, 7-086, 7-140
conflicts, potential   12-015
consent award   25-006, 28-002,
    28-004–28-007, 28-009–28-010
conservatory measures   22-004, 22-006,
    22-049, 22-067, 22-083
consolidation   15-005, 15-010, 15-056, 15-058,
    15-060–15-062, 15-064–15-067,
    15-073, 15-077, 15-081
constitution   1-033, 1-041, 1-052, 1-059,
    1-068, 1-085–1-086, 1-097, 1-105,
    1-112, 7-015, 7-017, 7-041, 7-052,
    7-071, 7-099, 7-111, 7-113, 7-129,
    7-148, 7-155, 9-016, 9-032, 9-043,
    9-062, 7-071, 7-075, 7-078,
    15-033–15-040
consumers   1-037, 1-039–1-040, 1-042,
    1-044, 1-050, 1-125

content requirements   9-002, 9-046–9-047,
    9-064, 10-017–10-018, 11-013
contract, arbitrator's   1-021, 5-008, 7-041,
    7-052, 8-007, 8-013, 8-021,
    8-025–8-027, 9-074
contract, international   24-007, 24-038
contract law   1-059, 8-003, 8-021,
    15-098, 34-053–34-054
contract, procedural   1-034, 1-059,
    15-098–15-100
contracting states   9-028
contractual approach   8-003, 8-006–8-007,
contractual liability   8-006–8-008, 8-010,
    8-012–8-013
contractual nature   1-008, 1-140, 8-006,
    8-018, 8-026–8-027, 9-074, 9-079,
    20-154, 27-030, 34-035, 36-016
contractual obligations   1-046, 8-017,
    15-0107, 22-044, 22-095
contractual relationship   1-021, 1-023, 1-025,
    1-050, 1-155, 7-041, 7-047, 7-053,
    8-003, 8-031, 9-100, 9-102, 11-018,
    12-011, 15-055, 15-060, 19-036,
    19-042, 19-047, 20-153, 20-160,
    22-138
control over arbitration   2-018, 7-099,
    20-025, 20-082–20-084, 20-093,
    20-187, 20-256, 31-008, 34-034,
    36-011
correction of award   7-055, 7-119, 8-012, 29-
    007, 29-011, 29-015–29-017,
    34-013
correspondence   1-022, 1-084, 3-022, 3-024,
    5-011, 6-001–6-002, 6-004–6-005,
    7-029, 7-067, 9-066, 12-006, 12-020,
    13-018, 13-021, 13-022, 13-025,
    13-027–13-028, 14-007, 14-018,
    20-101, 20-124, 20-128, 20-142,
    20-232
cost allocation   13-013, 13-041,
    31-042–31-050
costs, deposit of   5-008, 9-056, 10-005,
    11-014, 12-023, 12-025, 33-007,
    34-001, 34-006, 34-022, 34-024,
    35-003, 36-011, 36-015, 36-031,
    36-043–36-044
costs, legal   31-004, 31-016, 31-040,
    31-043–31-044, 31-059
costs, security of   22-101–22-107

counter-claim   1-009, 9-014, 10-018, 10-021,
        11-001–11-002, 11-004–11-017,
        11-019–11-029, 11-039–11-040,
        11-043, 14-014, 22-097, 31-021,
        31-043, 33-008–33-009,
        34-029–34-030, 34-056,
        36-014–36-015, 36-018–36-019
counter-claimant   11-013, 11-016, 11-020,
        11-026, 33-005, 34-029
counter-respondent   11-019, 11-027–11-028,
        34-034
country of origin   7-054
court review   17-002, 17-021–17-027,
        19-003, 19-018, 19-021–19-029
cross-examination   20-009, 20-146,
        20-195, 20-197, 20-200, 20-202,
        20-208, 20-211–20-213, 21-011,
        21-016
custody   20-228, 20-243–20-244
cut-off date   20-031, 20-072–20-075,
        20-183, 20-186, 20-289

damages   3-033, 7-011, 7-046, 8-012, 8-017,
        8-021, 8-028, 9-022, 9-059, 19-043,
        20-045, 20-203, 21-001, 22-040,
        22-042, 22-044–22-045, 22-064,
        22-066, 22-070, 22-073, 22-138,
        22-157, 24-015–24-017, 25-003,
        27-027, 27-031, 29-002, 31-013,
        34-045
defaulting party   1-016, 10-034, 14-056,
        14-066, 19-011, 20-148, 20-259,
        20-260, 20-268, 20-270–20-271,
        25-016, 34-041–34-042,
        34-045–34-046, 34-050–34-052
defects, formal   1-59–1-60, 1-084, 15-097,
        15-102–15-103, 19-014
delay, unjustified   9-018, 11-026
deletion from list   9-084, 33-009, 34-029
deliberations, secrecy of   26-028,
        26-032–26-033
delivery   5-008, 9-055–9-056, 10-008,
        10-030, 13-005, 13-015, 13-029,
        13-032, 13-035–13-047, 13-050,
        19-004, 22-118, 25-019, 33-004,
        34-013
deposit, additional   11-041, 34-037,
        34-056–34-058, 34-060, 35-003,
        35-008–35-009, 35-013, 36-018

deposit, initial   34-057, 34-059, 35-003,
        35-005, 35-008
deposit of costs   5-008, 9-056, 10-005,
        11-013, 12-023, 12-025, 33-007,
        34-001, 34-006, 34-022, 34-024,
        35-003, 36-011, 36-015, 36-031,
        36-043–36-044
diem, per   36-037
discretion, equitable   24-050, 36-007,
        36-009,
discretion, evidentiary   20-178–20-179
disqualification   7-080, 7-084, 7-085, 7-102,
        7-107, 7-110, 7-116, 7-130,
        7-143–7-144, 7-146, 12-015, 16-003,
        16-022, 16-027, 16-038
disqualifying circumstances   7-148,
        16-016–16-017, 16-019, 16-024,
        16-026, 16-028, 16-030,
        16-041–16-042, 16-054, 17-008
dissenting opinions   26-024–26-033
doctrine of lis pendens   9-023,
        9-026–9-027
document disclosure   20-227–20-249
documentary evidence   20-224–20-241
documents, joint   20-170, 20-232, 20-234,
        22-118, 27-021
documents, request for   20-178, 20-189,
        20-191–20-192, 20-229,
        20-233–20-236, 20-238,
        20-241–20-244, 20-256, 20-276
disclosure of documents   20-231, 20-234
discretion, procedural   20-268, 20-281,
        35-003, 35-012
due process   2-015, 2-068, 7-054, 7-057,
        7-066, 7-080, 9-037, 11-042, 16-043,
        17-018, 18-009, 20-016–20-017,
        20-029, 20-031, 20-036, 20-073,
        20-075, 20-101, 20-147, 20-191,
        20-035, 20-059, 23-005
Dutco   15-034–15-036, 15-038–15-042,
        15-044–15-045,

ECHR (European Convention on Human
        Rights)   7-099, 9-031, 14-012,
        15-046, 16-027, 20-017–20-018,
        20-021, 20-023–20-027, 20-036,
        20-044, 20-052, 20-057–20-058,
        20-061, 20-064–20-065, 20-131,
        20-248, 22-107, 22-125, 27-008

employees   1-125, 3-004, 8-001, 8-035,
        13-032, 20-220
enclosures   9-021, 9-041–9-042, 9-080,
        10-026, 12-021
Enforcement Act, see EO
enforcement of award   2-015, 2-051,
        24-001
enforcement of interim measures   22-005,
        22-023, 22-037, 22-114, 22-131,
        22-134
enforcement powers   22-010, 22-012
entrepreneur   1-039, 1-041
EO (Austrian Enforcement Act)   1-116,
        2-070, 15-085, 22-010, 22-048,
        22-138, 22-140, 22-153, 22-156,
        27-066
equality   7-100, 14-001, 15-036,
        15-039–15-040, 15-044, 15-046,
        15-048, 20-015–20-017, 20-019,
        20-021–20-022, 20-028, 20-099,
        20-223, 20-227, 20-244, 24-019
equity   1-045, 15-095, 24-003, 24-010,
        24-017–24-019, 24-047–24-048,
        24-050–24-051
ex aequo et bono   7-055, 24-049, 27-050
amiable compositeur   24-049
European Convention on International
        Commercial Arbitration   1-016
evidence, documentary   7-029, 10-013,
        20-052, 20-071, 20-096, 20-114,
        20-124, 20-177, 20-193, 20-195,
        20-209, 20-224–20-24
evidence in international commercial
        arbitration   20-011, 20-174–20-175,
        21-005
evidence, witness testimony   6-003, 7-063,
        20-048, 20-096, 20-101, 20-109,
        20-110, 20-114, 20-131–20-132,
        20-143, 20-171, 20-193–20-215
evidentiary applications   8-017,
        20-051–20-052, 20-055–20-056
evidentiary hearing   11-023, 18-009, 20-001,
        20-054, 20-189, 20-203, 20-211,
        20-213
examination, direct   2-061, 20-208,
        20-211–20-212
examination, re-direct   20-208
examination-in-chief   20-208, 20-211

Exekutionsordnung, see EO
exequatur   1-136, 1-139, 2-069–2-071,
        27-023, 27-032, 27-065–27-066
expenses, appropriate   31-018–31-019,
        31-029–31-030, 32-003
experience   3-020, 7-003, 7-018, 7-026,
        7-029–7-030, 7-033, 7-036, 9-088,
        14-005, 14-038, 18-007, 20-096,
        20-107, 20-204–20-205, 20-213,
        20-223, 20-248, 21-017, 26-019,
        35-004, 36-031, 36-035
expert evidence   20-177, 21-002–21-003,
        21-006–21-007, 21-015, 21-018,
        21-020
expert report   20-071, 20-135, 21-011,
        21-016
expert witnesses   20-214, 21-001–21-020
expertise   1-005, 4-001, 7-023, 7-026, 7-033,
        14-005, 14-064, 23-008
experts, legal   21-019–21-020
extension   1-031, 9-081, 10-012–10-015,
        10-033, 13-009–13-012, 13-023,
        14-022, 14-037, 14-037, 14-052,
        15-005, 15-017, 15-053, 15-058,
        15-106, 20-113, 20-179–20-180,
        20-266, 31-055, 33-002, 33-010,
        34-030, 34-033, 34-057, 36-011

fact-finding   20-227
fair treatment   20-016–20-024, 20-029,
        20-064, 27-006
fairness, procedural   7-116, 20-009, 20-107,
        20-213, 20-238, 20-249
fees, additional   33-004, 36-014–36-015
fees, administrative   35-008
fees, total   34-011
file number   1-163, 9-014
final award   1-090, 1-116, 6-006, 7-046,
        7-054, 7-058, 7-121, 7-151, 9-053,
        15-078, 16-001, 16-057, 17-001,
        17-016, 19-003, 19-019, 19-021,
        19-028, 20-031, 20-054, 20-181,
        20-278, 20-286, 22-001–22-002,
        22-010, 22-016, 22-034, 22-045,
        22-054, 22-057–22-058, 22-061,
        22-063, 22-085, 22-097,
        22-099–22-100, 22-108–22-109,
        27-025–27-026, 27-043, 28-001,

28-005, 29-006, 31-058, 34-003,
34-017, 34-045, 34-046, 36-006
Final Report on Lis Pendens and
Arbitration 9-033
foreign arbitral awards 27-032
foreign counsel 23-001, 23-003,
formal (or form) requirements, of arbitration
agreement 1-031, 1-052–1-055,
1-059–1-061, 1-063–1-065,
1-067–1-068, 1-072–1-073, 1-075,
1-078, 1-080, 1-099, 1-125,
1-158, 2-032, 2-0597-017, 7-055,
9-050, 10-026–10-028, 15-091,
15-100, 15-102–15-103, 27-067,
37-005
formal (or form) requirements, of award
1-063, 2-046, 7-055, 22-108, 22-111,
27-066, 29-015
function of arbitral institutions 1-007, 1-009,
1-011–1-013, 1-016, 1-021–1-022,
1-028, 1-155, 2-063, 2-065,
3-001–3-002, 3-009, 3-033, 5-014,
7-133, 7-136, 8-029, 9-046, 9-080,
14-020, 22-029, 36-041

Green List 7-034, 7-088, 7-111
group of companies 1-009, 1-101, 15-083,
15-109–15-111, 15-113
group of companies doctrine
15-109–15-110

Handelsgericht Wien 2-060, 7-108–7-109,
7-113, 14-047, 27-033–27-034
harmonization, of international arbitration
rules 7-083–7-089

IBA (International Bar Association) 20-011,
20-174
ILA (International Law Association) 9-033,
9-036–9-037, 9-039
impartiality 2-063, 3-015–3-017, 7-009,
7-015, 7-020, 7-042–7-043, 7-058,
7-073, 7-080, 7-082–7-083,
7-085–7-086, 7-088–7-093,
7-095–7-097, 7-099–7-106,
7-108–7-111, 7-113–7-117, 7-119,
7-122, 7-128, 7-132–7-134, 7-136,
7-139–7-141, 7-147, 7-150–7-151,

12-012–12-103, 12-016, 14-029,
14-044, 14-060, 16-001–16-004,
16-013, 15-016, 16-019, 16-027,
16-041, 15-052, 17-010, 17-021,
18-006, 21-002, 21-013, 21-016,
26-026, 26-033, 27-052,
30-006–30-007
independence 2-063, 3-003, 3-008 3-015,
3-017, 3-028, 3-030, 5-001, 5-003,
5-012, 5-020–5-022, 7-009, 7-020,
7-042–7-043, 7-058, 7-082–7-083,
7-085–7-086, 7-089, 7-090–7-092,
7-094–7-096, 7-099–7-100, 7-105,
7-107–7-109, 7-113, 7-115, 7-117,
7-122, 7-134, 7-136–7-141, 7-144,
7-147, 7-150–7-151, 12-012–12-013,
12-015–12-016, 12-020, 14-042,
14-044, 14-060, 14-063–14-064,
15-111, 16-001–16-004, 16-013,
16-016, 16-019, 16-041, 17-010,
17-021, 18-006, 21-002, 21-013,
21-016, 2-026, 27-052, 30-006,
31-005, 34-027, 35-001
immunity of arbitrator 8-003, 8-023
independence, declaration of 5-001, 12-015,
12-020, 14-042, 14-044,
14-063–14-064, 31-006
injunctions 2-066–2-067, 9-029, 22-006,
22-010, 22-048
injunctive relief 20-120, 22-023,
22-133
institutional rules 1-022, 1-149, 2-020,
7-006, 7-019, 7-046–7-047 7-051,
7-070, 7-092, 7-098, 7-137, 7-140,
9-044, 9-050, 9-073, 9-089, 9-090,
10-016, 11-008, 14-001, 15-048,
15-072, 16-015, 16-030, 16-054,
19-046, 20-004, 20-074,
20-087–20-088, 20-094–20-095,
20-120, 20-156, 20-195, 20-248,
20-260 21-015, 22-002, 22-041,
22-050 22-125, 23-006, 23-008,
26-007, 27-005, 28-002, 32-003,
34-041, 34-043, 36-011, 37-009,
37-010
interim award 22-065, 22-115, 27-024,
27-026, 27-028, 34-039, 34-042,
34-045

interim measures   1-118, 2-064–2-067,
     22-001–22-012, 22-015–22-019,
     22-022–22-031, 22-035–22-042,
     22-046–22-055, 22-059–22-075,
     22-077, 22-079–22-083, 22-088,
     22-104, 22-108, 22-112–22-117,
     22-119–22-129, 22-131, 22-134,
     22-136, 22-138–22-140, 22-142,
     22-144–22-148, 22-151–22-157,
     25-026
interim measures, enforcement of   22-005,
     22-023, 22-037, 22-114, 22-131,
     22-134
interim relief   2-015, 2-030, 2-065–2-066,
     22-004–22-010, 22-012–22-014,
     22-016, 22-018–22-019, 22-021,
     22-023, 22-025–22-027,
     22-029–22-034, 22-036–22-038,
     22-041, 22-044, 22-050–22-051,
     22-053, 22-055–22-058,
     22-060–22-062, 22-067, 22-069,
     22-072, 22-074, 22-076, 22-079,
     22-083–22-085, 22-087, 22-089,
     22-101, 22-114, 22-119, 22-122,
     22-125, 22-128, 22-132, 22-134,
     22-138–22-139, 22-148, 26-035,
     27-026
interim relief, enforcement of   22-132
interim relief, ex parte   22-036
international advisory board   4-001–4-004
international arbitration community   3-009,
     24-014
international arbitration, context of   2-039,
     7-129, 15-116, 22-104
International Bar Association, see IBA
International Law Association, see ILA
interpretation of award   29-001–29-018
interruption   9-017–9-018, 9-087
intervener   15-076
intervention   1-128–1-129, 2-002, 2-015,
     2-030–2-031, 2-051–2-052, 2-068,
     15-005, 15-052, 15-076, 17-019,
     19-023, 20-250–20-256
interview of prospective arbitrators
     7-031–7-037
irreparable harm   22-001, 22-063–22-066,
     22-077, 22-079, 22-083,
     22-085–22-086

joinder   15-005, 15-014–15-015, 15-020,
     15-057–15-058, 15-061,
     15-074–15-117, 30-011
judicial acts   2-055, 20-252–20-253
judicial assistance   20-192,
     20-252–20-253
judicial immunity   8-002–8-005,
     8-007–8-008, 8-015, 8-020,
     8-022–8-023, 8-027
jurisdiction, subject-matter   7-017, 22-016,
     22-056, 22-058
justice, natural   20-016

late submissions   20-270–20-271
law, abuse of   15-094–15-103,
     15-105–15-107, 22-150
legal authorities   26-012
legal capacity   1-034–1-035, 1-047,
     7-005–7-009, 7-020, 7-023
legal entity   1-007, 1-034, 7-008, 7-129,
     15-020, 15-105
legal position   1-108, 7-119, 8-014, 15-084,
     15-087, 15-089–15-090, 15-101,
     24-033,
legal representation   27-046, 31-002, 31-016,
     31-018, 31-059, 32-003
legal successor   1-078, 15-084–15-087,
     15-100
lex arbitri   2-013, 2-024, 2-038–2-040,
     2-043, 7-049, 7-054, 20-087, 20-181,
     20-272, 20-286, 22-008, 22-123,
     24-001, 26-031, 31-012, 31-042,
     31-048–31-049
lex loci arbitri   1-140, 2-002, 2-014–2-015,
     2-021–2-024, 2-026, 2-037, 2-045,
     2-051, 2-072
lex mercatoria   24-009, 24-011–24-019,
     24-045
liability, arbitrator's   7-040, 8-007, 8-012,
     8-022, 8-025, 8-027
liability, exclusion of   8-021, 8-027
limitations   9-001–9-002, 9-015–9-018,
     9-020–9-021, 9-045, 9-087, 12-001,
     19-046, 20-070, 20-119, 25-024,
     33-012
limitations, statute of   9-001–9-002, 9-016,
     9-022, 9-087, 12-001, 20-119, 25-024,
     33-012

limited liability companies   1-125
lis pendens   1-090, 9-002, 9-023–9-040,
    12-001, 22-147, 37-002

materiality   20-079, 20-244, 20-247,
    20-249
material and relevant   20-079, 20-189,
    20-243–20-244, 20-247, 20-256,
    21-008,
memorandum in reply   1-009, 1-022, 1-082,
    5-001, 9-009, 10-010–10-014,
    10-016–10-017, 10-019,
    10-023–10-024, 10-026–10-035,
    11-027, 12-004–12-004, 12-009,
    13-020, 14-006, 14-016, 14-022,
    14-033, 14-039, 14-052, 15-008,
    15-024–15-025, 19007, 20-134,
    23-010
multi-contract arbitration   15-001
multi-party arbitration   1-101, 15-005,
    15-006–15-025, 15-032, 15-052,
    15-082, 15-120
multi-party proceedings   11-022, 14-032,
    15-007, 15-013, 15-019, 15-021,
    15-023–15-025, 15-118, 15-121,
    34-025, 36-011

nationality   1-033, 2-018–2-020, 2-027,
    6-007, 7-018–7-022, 7-097,
    14-033, 14-038, 14-060, 20-124,
    23-003
natural person   1-033–1-034, 1-044–1-045,
    9-053
New York Convention   1-033, 1-061–1-062,
    1-073, 2-002, 2-013, 2-019,
    2-022–2-023, 2-034, 2-036,
    2-041, 2-070, 7-054, 9-028,
    15-117, 20-029, 20-031,
    20-052–20-053, 20-069, 20-088,
    22-105, 22-115, 22-131,
    22-146, 27-026, 27-041, 27-066,
    28-005
nomination, joint   14-031–14-037,
    14-057, 14-060, 14-062–14-063,
    14-065, 15-010, 15-028–15-029,
    15-032, 15-039, 15-043–15-044,
    15-049, 15-053–15-054, 16-011,
    18-004

non-lawyers   23-001, 23-003, 23-006,
    23-008
non-signatories   1-100, 15-082–15-117
Norsolor SA   24-014, 24-019, 24-050

oath of witness   20-215, 20-224
objection(s) (or objecting)   1-055, 1-060,
    1-079–1-084, 1-087, 1-089, 1-100,
    1-148, 2-071, 7-148, 9-030–9-031,
    9-075, 9-096, 10-002, 10-025, 11-015,
    14-008–14-009, 15-008, 15-023,
    15-083, 15-120, 16-029, 16-049,
    19-002–19-004, 19-008–19-011,
    19-013–19-014, 19-017, 20-117,
    20-127, 20-244–20-245,
    20-272–20-287, 22-036, 22-077,
    22-140, 22-144, 24-022, 27-067,
    30-003, 31-043, 37-005, 37-009
objections, timely   1-083, 1-087, 1-089,
    15-023, 16-029, 19-009–19-010,
    20-278, 20-283
objective arbitrability   1-109–1-129,
    1-133–1-136, 1-138, 1-140–1-141,
    27-063, 31-052
objective test   7-107, 31-022
objectivity   12-004, 12-010, 12-012, 31-018
obligation, ethical   7-074–7-075, 23-001
office   1-033, 1-072, 1-123, 1-144,
    3-004–3-007, 3-028, 3-031, 3-034,
    4-003, 5-003–5-004, 5-020, 5-023,
    5-027, 7-013–7-015, 7-081, 8-011,
    8-036, 9-054, 13-005, 14-071, 16-001,
    16-014, 16-016–16-017, 16-042,
    17-002, 17-004, 17-007–17-010,
    17-012–17-013, 17-22–17-23,
    18-003, 20-220, 25-001, 25-021,
    36-041
officio authority, ex   17-019–17-020,
    22-030, 29-013
omission   8-021, 8-025, 9-059
Orange List   7-088, 7-111
oral hearing   1-042, 1-087, 2-010, 16-044,
    17-015, 20-020, 20-031, 20-034,
    20-043, 20-113, 20-116, 20-130–
    20-134, 20-138, 20-141, 20-148,
    20-151, 20-196, 20-200, 20-202,
    20-211, 21-010, 21-012, 21-015,
    28-010, 36-008

order, procedural 2-054, 10-033, 12-021,
    13-020, 13-022, 19-020, 20-036,
    20-092, 20-108, 20-111, 20-122,
    20-183, 20-190, 20-282, 22-113,
    25-002, 25-006, 25-012, 26-011,
    26-036–26-037, 27-028, 30-005,
    34-054, 34-054, 35-003, 36-008,
organizing arbitral proceedings 7-048,
    7-062

parallel proceedings 1-089, 9-031, 9-033,
    9-036–9-038
partial award 15-036, 19-026, 19-028,
    27-027, 27-037, 34-038, 34-042,
    34-046, 34-048, 36-032
parties, nominating 1-018, 1-021, 7-093,
    7-120, 14-031, 14-033–14-034,
    14-037, 14-051, 14-053, 14-055,
    14-056–14-057, 14-062,
    14-069–14-070, 15-004, 15-029,
    16-010, 18-004
parties, non-defaulting 20-268, 34-042,
    34-045, 34-050, 34-052
parties, winning 22-069, 31-013, 31-017
party-appointed arbitrators 7-093, 7-098,
    7-112, 7-116–7-120
party-appointed expert(s) 21-005,
    21-015–21-020
party autonomy 1-107, 1-141, 2-034, 2-045,
    7-001, 7-023, 7-104, 13-003, 14-006,
    14-010–14-012, 14-057, 14-070,
    16-007, 16-027–16-028, 16-035,
    20-006, 20-010, 20-095–20-096,
    22-037, 22-139, 24-004–24-005,
    24-010, 24-037–24-038, 26-007,
    27-007, 27-016
payment obligations 34-029, 34-034,
    34-037, 34-048, 34-050–34-051,
    34-053, 34-057
pendency 9-001, 9-006, 9-029, 9-047,
    9-049, 22-003, 22-095, 33-011
phases of arbitration 36-008, 36-021
physical evidence 22-092
piercing the corporate veil 1-100, 15-015,
    15-083, 15-105
place of business 1-004, 1-143–1-146,
    1-161, 36-042
place of incorporation 15-114–15-115

plea 9-073, 11-043, 19-004, 19-006, 19-008,
    19-012, 22-135, 31-052
pleadings 1-087, 7-007, 9-048,
    10-018–10-020, 11-004,
    11-029–11-030, 11-035–11-036,
    12-016, 19-006, 20-031, 20-043,
    20-047, 20-071, 20-116, 20-135,
    20-141, 20-146, 20-169, 20-191,
    20-206, 20-019, 21-020, 24-031,
    24-033
possession 7-002, 7-105, 16-003,
    20-227–20-228, 20-235,
    20-243–20-244, 22-003
power of attorney 1-072–1-075, 9-068,
    10-028, 15-102, 23-007,
    23-009–23-010
power, discretionary 1-128, 19-013, 20-118,
    20-130, 20-177, 20-179, 24-046
pre-judgment 22-067–22-068
preservation of evidence 22-019, 22-045,
    22-062, 22-092–22-094
presiding arbitrator 7-018–7-019, 7-030,
    7-097, 7-116–7-119, 7-131, 9-049,
    14-002, 14-054, 14-057–14-058,
    14-060, 14-063, 16-011,
    18-004–18-006, 20-145,
    22-108–22-110, 22-119–22-120,
    26-003, 26-007, 26-011, 26-015,
    26-018–22-020, 26-022, 26-029,
    27-010, 27-016, 27-022, 28-003,
    28-009, 34-011
privacy 20-026, 20-152–20-167,
    30-002
procedural actions 31-027, 31-040, 34-057,
    35-002–35-003, 35-006, 35-014,
    36-011
procedural irregularities 15-035, 20-016,
    20-052, 20-126, 20-272–20-287
procedural order 2-054, 10-033, 12-021,
    13-020, 13-022, 19-020, 20-036,
    20-092, 20-108, 20-111, 20-122,
    20-183, 20-190, 20-282, 22-113,
    25-002, 25-006, 25-012, 26-011,
    26-036–26-037, 27-028, 30-005,
    34-054, 35-003, 36-008
procedural public policy 20-016,
    20-024–20-025, 20-247, 20-286,
    27-006–27-007

procedural ordre public   7-110, 15-046,
    16-027, 16-031–16-039, 20-015,
    20-018, 20-068, 20-185–20-286,
    23-005, 24-050, 27-051,
    27-054–24-055
proceedings, non-contentious   1-117
proceedings, parallel   1-089, 9-031–9-033,
    9-036–9-038
prohibition   2-046, 2-060, 7-014, 7-016,
    7-033, 7-094, 7-101, 7-103, 7-110,
    9-047, 10-033, 15-101–15-102,
    16-027, 16-029, 19-006, 20-126,
    20-169, 20-183, 20-196, 20-210,
    20-221, 20-261–20-263, 20-281,
    22-012, 22-037, 22-047, 22-057,
    22-066, 22-095, 26-028, 27-048,
    36-011
Prokura   1-072, 1-074
prospective arbitrators   1-029, 7-002, 7-004,
    7-021, 7-027, 7-031–7-036, 7-068,
    7-094, 7-112, 7-131–7-132, 7-135,
    7-137, 7-144, 7-147, 7-151–7-152,
    12-014, 12-017–12-019
protective measures   22-002, 22-006,
    22-022–22-023, 22-043, 22-056,
    22-079, 22-082, 25-026
provisional measures   2-030,
    22-003–22-006, 22-029, 22-065,
    22-070, 22-098, 22-100, 22-115
provisional measures, enforcement of
    2-030
provisions, non-mandatory   2-048, 2-049,
    20-087, 20-284–20-285, 26-007
provisions, mandatory   1-043, 2-002,
    2-044–2-050, 5-021, 7-049, 7-054,
    7-100, 8-009, 14-011, 16-020,
    17-009, 20-003–20-004, 20-028,
    20-087–20-089, 20-127, 20-151,
    20-181, 20-185, 20-261, 20-268,
    20-271, 20-283, 20-284–20-286,
    21-011, 24-017, 24-029, 24-044,
    25-002, 25-008, 26-007, 27-061,
    31-027
provisions, transitional   1-053, 1-132,
    37-001–37-010
Public Liability Act, see AHG

quorum   3-010, 3-019, 26-001–26-017

RATG (Austrian Attorney Tariff
    Act)   31-027
reasonableness   31-013, 31-019,
    31-021–31-022, 31-025
Rechtsanwaltstarifgesetz, see RATG
recipient   3-023, 9-006–9-007, 13-005,
    13-035–13-047
recognition, of awards   2-022–2-023, 2-030,
    2-034, 2-070, 7-014, 9-037, 9-053,
    20-088, 22-145, 24-001, 27-017,
    27-066
recognition, of arbitration
    agreements   1-062, 2-022, 2-030,
    20-088, 24-001
Red List, waivable   7-088, 7-101, 7-110,
    16-027, 16-032
Red List, non-waivable   7-088, 7-101, 7-110,
    16-027
registration fee   1-009, 1-163, 5-001, 8-032,
    9-069, 9-080, 33-001–33-012, 34-004
relief   1-140, 2-015, 2-030, 2-042,
    2-065–2-066, 7-055, 9-025–9-026,
    9-035, 9-037, 9-048, 9-050, 9-057,
    9-061, 9-098, 11-032, 11-036,
    20-119–20-120, 20-191, 20-229,
    22-003–22-011, 22-012–22-014,
    22-016, 22-018–22-019,
    22-021–22-027, 22-029–22-038,
    22-041–22-042, 22-044,
    22-048–22-051, 22-053,
    22-055–22-058, 22-060–22-063,
    22-067–22-070, 22-072–22-074,
    22-076, 22-077, 22-079–22-080,
    22-083–22-085, 22-087, 22-089,
    22-095, 22-101, 22-114, 22-119,
    22-122–22-123, 22-125, 22-128,
    22-132–2-135, 22-138–22-148,
    25-005, 26-035, 27-026, 27-049,
    35-050, 36-026
replacement   1-009, 1-061, 3-035, 7-056,
    7-152, 11-006, 16-007, 16-017,
    16-042, 17-009, 18-002–18-011,
    19-013, 20-202, 20-211, 25-002
representation   1-061, 1-082, 7-008, 9-068,
    20-033, 20-041, 23-005–23-010,
    27-046, 31-002, 31-013, 31-016,
    31-018–31-019, 31-030–31-032,
    31-059, 32-001–32-003

representatives   1-021, 1-035, 1-117, 1-127,
      7-101, 7-112, 7-129, 9-011, 9-046,
      9-068, 10-027, 13-004, 13-035–13-036,
      13-048, 13-050, 16-029, 20-033,
      20-056, 20-096, 20-105, 20-208,
      20-210, 20-213, 20-220,
      23-001–23-002, 23-004–23-010
requirements, procedural   20-280, 20-282,
      20-285
requirements, elective   15-011–15-025
requirements, mandatory   7-057, 9-004,
      9-011–9-012, 9-047, 9-053, 9-062,
      9-066, 9-070, 10-003, 10-005, 10-027,
      14-051, 15-008–15-011, 20-039,
      33-002, 33-011
requirements, in writing   1-041, 1-052,
      1-055–1-057, 1-061–1-070, 1-075,
      1-078, 7-042, 7-128, 9-071, 15-098,
      16-044, 20-130, 27-040
res judicata   1-128–1-129, 9-032, 9-035,
      11-027, 15-017, 25-009, 27-007,
      27-020
residence, habitual place of   1-043, 22-135
residence, normal   1-143, 1-145
respondents, multiple   15-008–15-009,
      15-032, 15-042, 15-053, 15-121
right to be heard   1-128, 1-131, 2-015, 2-046,
      2-049, 7-059, 7-132, 7-156, 9-067,
      11-027–11-028, 11-042, 13-001,
      13-011, 13-037, 15-076,
      20-015–20-017, 20-019, 20-023,
      20-026, 20-029–20-081, 20-101,
      20-123, 20-126–20-127, 20-129,
      20-132, 20-141, 20-151, 20-169,
      20-181, 20-183, 20-185, 20-202,
      20-211, 20-270, 20-279, 20-288,
      21-011, 21-015, 22-033, 23-005,
      27-003, 27-046–27-047, 27-054,
      31-054–31-055, 32-002
Rome Convention   20-047, 24-004–24-005,
      24-007, 24-031, 24-039
rules, conflict   24-036, 24-040, 24-043
rules, first-in-time   9-026, 9-035, 9-037
rules, institution's   37-001
rules, mandatory   20-099, 24-016
rules of law   7-092, 20-006, 20-088, 24-005,
      24-009, 24-020, 24-044–24-045,
      30-005

seat, of the arbitration   1-042, 1-140,
      2-001–2-072, 5-016, 7-071,
      14-047, 15-117, 20-007, 20-066,
      20-099, 20-109, 20-172, 20-181,
      20-250, 20-252, 20-254, 22-145,
      24-037, 24-039, 26-023,
      27-010–27-012, 27-030,
      27-034, 27-064–27-065,
      36-029
secrecy   3-025, 5-018, 7-063–7-067,
      26-027–26-028, 26-032–26-033
secretariat   1-018, 5-001, 5-005–5-006,
      5-014–5-017, 5-027, 6-006, 7-137,
      9-003, 9-006, 9-015, 9-017,
      9-052, 9-063, 10-007–10-008,
      10-014, 10-026, 10-29, 11-013,
      11-015, 11-041, 12-001, 12-010,
      12-012, 12-021, 13-025,
      22-129–22-130, 22-148, 31-041,
      34-017–34-018
secretary, administrative   7-152–7-153,
      7-157–7-158, 36-038
secretary general   1-002, 1-007, 1-015,
      1-017, 1-019, 1-027, 1-029, 1-148,
      1-155, 1-163, 3-001, 3-009, 3-010,
      3-023, 3-029, 5-001–5-016,
      5-018–5-029, 6-001–6-002,
      6-004–6-005, 7-041, 7-072, 7-158,
      8-035, 9-002–9-010, 9-013, 9-043,
      9-052–9-054, 9-056–9-057, 9-059,
      9-061–9-062, 9-066, 9-068, 9-070,
      9-072, 9-080–9-087, 9-094,
      9-097–9-098, 10-003–10-04,
      10-008, 10-010–10-012, 10-014,
      10-020, 10-022, 10-029–10-033,
      11-013–11-014, 11-052,
      12-001–12-006, 12-008–12-025,
      13-002, 13-009–13-010,
      13-018–13-021, 13-025–13-028,
      14-006–14-007, 14-009,
      14-015–14-016, 14-022, 14-032,
      14-037, 14-042, 14-052–14-053,
      14-056, 14-063, 15-030, 16-021,
      17-017, 18-004, 20-167, 20-277,
      21-009, 22-117, 23-010, 27-017,
      31-001–31-006, 31-059, 32-002,
      33-002, 33-004, 33-006, 33-008,
      33-010–33-012, 34-001–34-003,

34-006, 34-009, 34-012,
34-014–34-022, 34-026–34-027,
34-030, 34-032–34-033, 34-050,
34-052, 34-056–34-061, 35-001,
35-003, 35-007, 36-001,
36-006–36-011, 36-014–36-015,
36-017, 36-019, 36-022,
36-024–36-027, 36-029–36-031,
36-034–36-035, 36-040–36-041,
36-043–36-044

security, for costs   2-040, 22-101–22-102
sender   13-032, 13-046–13-047
separability doctrine   19-034–19-035,
19-039, 19-042, 19-045–19-046
services   1-005, 1-008, 1-014–1-015, 1-017,
1-021–1-024, 3-004, 5-016, 7-005,
7-010–7-012, 7-052, 7-072, 7-136,
7-154–7-155, 8-004, 8-006–8-007,
8-029, 9-006, 9-010, 9-054, 9-074,
9-092, 9-100, 10-003–10-008,
10-026, 10-029, 12-007, 13-006,
13-015–13-032, 13-036–13-049,
15-026–15-027, 18-011, 20-110,
20-169, 22-117, 23-002, 25-024,
27-019, 27-021, 27-028, 31-022,
33-011, 34-029, 35-007, 35-015,
36-038, 36-042
services, administrative   7-154
services, voluntary   7-010–7-012
set-off   10-021, 11-043–11-052, 14-014,
31-040, 34-056, 36-012–36-015,
36-018–36-019
set-off claim   11-043, 11-046–11-049,
11-051–11-052
set-off declarations   36-013
set-off defence   10-021, 11-043–11-045,
11-049, 34-056, 36-013,
36-018–33-019
settlement agreement   28-005
settlement negotiations   7-123–7-124
sequencing   20-136, 20-138
shareholders   1-078, 1-127–1-129, 15-015,
15-022, 15-115
signature   1-061, 1-065, 9-011, 10-028,
13-033, 15-095, 15-100, 18-002,
20-204, 22-107, 22-109,
26-016–26-017, 26-029,
27-014–27-016, 27-019, 28-006

statement of claims   1-009, 1-022, 1-148,
1-155, 1-163, 5-002, 5-010, 6-004,
7-041, 9-001–9-004, 9-006–9-013,
9-015, 9-017–9-018, 9-021–9-022,
9-041, 9-047, 9-050, 9-052–9-053,
9-055, 9-057–9-059, 9-061–9-069,
9-072, 9-075, 9-080, 9-083–9-084,
9-086, 9-091, 9-096–9-097,
10-002–10-011, 10-016, 10-019,
10-022, 10-024, 10-026–10-027,
10-030–10-031, 11-013, 11-020,
12-001, 12-004, 12-006–12-009,
13-009, 13-020, 13-028,
14-006–14-007, 14-016, 14-022,
14-033, 14-039, 14-051–14-052,
14-069, 15-027–15-028, 20-134,
20-258, 20-265–20-266, 20-268,
25-016, 25-019, 25-022–25-023,
31-045, 33-001–33-002, 3-004,
33-008, 33-011, 34-019
statement of defense   15-025, 15-030,
15-053
status quo   22-014, 22-019, 22-024,
22-046, 22-048, 22-057, 22-061,
22-087–22-090, 22-095
statute of limitations   9-001–9-002,
9-016–9-022, 9-046, 9-087, 12-001,
12-119, 25-024, 33-012
submissions   1-022, 1-039, 1-048, 1-050,
1-082, 5-022, 6-003, 6-005, 7-063,
9-001, 9-003, 9-008, 9-010, 9-012,
9-014, 9-022, 9-048, 9-050–9-051,
9-055, 9-059, 9-069, 9-097, 10-006,
10-016–10-017, 10-026,
10-032–10-035, 11-007, 11-024,
12-011, 12-014, 12-021, 13-002,
13-015, 13-019–13-020,
13-031–13-032, 13-034–13-038,
13-045–13-050, 14-006,
14-016–14-017, 14-054, 15-008,
15-036, 15-072, 15-120, 16-021,
16-044, 18-009, 19-007–19-008,
19-014, 20-001, 20-031, 20-034,
20-043–20-044, 20-053–20-054,
20-056, 20-061, 20-070–20-071,
20-075, 20-109–20-110, 20-113,
20-116, 20-125, 20-133–20-142,
20-161, 20-169, 20-181–20-183,

20-186, 20-199, 20-202–20-203,
20-224, 20-230–20-231–20-232,
20-235, 20-238, 20-241, 20-261,
20-268, 20-270–20-271, 20-288,
21-015, 21-019, 22-028, 22-143,
23-010, 27-003, 29-009, 31-022,
31-027, 33-001–33-003, 33-011,
36-033
submissions, electronic   9-010, 13-047
submissions, initial   9-012, 14-006, 14-017,
14-054, 22-028
submissions, legal   20-031, 20-043, 20-053,
20-056
submissions, simultaneous   1-022, 3-004,
4-003, 12-015, 13-042, 20-137–
20-138, 20-142, 27-055, 36-005
subsidiary   1-144, 5-007, 15-104,
15-107, 15-111, 15-115, 22-127,
27-064

tariffs   31-027, 36-032, 36-041
termination, early   3-013, 17-001–17-003,
18-001, 30-006, 34-014, 34-016,
36-003, 36-006, 36-010
termination of arbitrator's mandate   2-063,
3-035, 17-001–17-002, 17-004–
17-006, 17-015, 17-021–17-022,
17-024–17-025, 18-003, 18-006,
18-011, 26-011, 26-013, 30-006
termination of arbitration   20-265,
25-007–25-008, 25-017, 25-025
territoriality   2-003, 2-013, 2-016–2-031
testimony   1-067, 6-003, 7-063, 7-067,
20-001, 20-009, 20-048, 20-079,
20-096, 20-101, 20-109–20-110,
20-114, 20-131–20-132, 20-143,
20-169, 20-171, 20-176, 20-189,
20-193–20-203, 20-208–20-209,
20-211, 20-214–20-215, 20-219,
20-223–20-224, 20-288, 22-004,
22-009
third party beneficiaries   1-101,
15-086–15-093, 15-101
trade usage   1-094, 24-009,
24-020–24-024
transmission   1-061, 9-010, 9-052, 9-060,
10-001, 10-006, 10-026, 10-033,
11-023, 11-040, 12-001–12-025,

13-006, 13-013, 13-015, 13-020,
13-024, 13-030, 13-032–13-034,
13-046, 13-048, 20-123, 20-028,
33-006, 34-004, 36-008,
36-010–36-011, 36-033
tribunal-appointed expert   21-006, 21-009,
21-011, 21-013–21-014,
21-018–21-019
tribunal, three-member   14-003–14-005,
14-007, 14-026–14-028, 14-052

United Nations Commission on International
Trade Law, see UNCITRAL
UNCITRAL (United Nations Commission on
International Trade Law)   1-013,
1-017, 1-064, 1-107, 1-144, 1-146,
2-007, 5-016, 7-019, 7-022, 7-048,
7-062, 7-090, 7-109, 7-154–7-155,
9-029, 9-045, 9-048, 11-031, 11-036,
19-005, 19-016, 19-023, 19-025,
19-027, 19-035, 19-040, 20-019,
20-021, 20-034–20-035,
20-108–20-109, 20-267,
20-274–24-279, 20-282–20-284,
22-019, 22-022, 22-031,
22-035–22-036
UNCITRAL Arbitration Rules   1-012, 1-017,
5-016, 7-090, 9-048, 9-094, 11-010,
20-016, 20-164, 27-002, 28-002,
34-041
UNCITRAL Model Law   1-064, 1-108,
1-144, 1-146, 7-019, 7-022, 7-109,
7-134, 7-144, 19-016, 19-023, 19-025,
19-027, 19-035, 19-040, 20-019,
20-021, 20-023, 20-034–20-035,
20-282–20-283, 22-019, 22-022,
22-031, 22-035, 24-006, 24-020,
24-036, 24-045

valid arbitration agreement   1-018–1-019,
1-030, 1-036, 1-047, 1-067, 1-073,
1-079, 1-089, 1-127, 1-0134, 1-160,
19-001, 19-009, 19-024, 19-027,
27-042–27-044
validity, substantive, of arbitration
agreement   2-035–2-036,
15-100–15-101, 15-117, 19-039,
37-004

validity, formal, of arbitration
agreement 1-053, 1-080, 2-014,
2-036, 13-032, 15-117
value added tax, see VAT
VAT (value added taxes) 7-072, 12-023,
34-014, 34-020, 35-015, 36-041–36-044
venire contra factum proprium 1-059, 1-084,
15-094, 15-099, 15-102, 24-051
VIAC (Vienna International Arbitration
Centre) 1-001, 1-004, 1-006, 1-029
VIAC Board 1-018, 3-001–3-004, 3-008,
3-010, 3-021, 4-002, 5-002–5-003,
5-010–5-013, 5-019, 5-021,
5-023–5-029, 7-021, 7-038,
7-043–7-045, 9-003, 9-043, 9-049,
9-063, 9-072, 9-094, 9-096
VIAC Board members 3-003, 3-008, 5-019,
5-024, 7-043

Vienna International Arbitration Centre,
see VIAC
vote, decisive 3-010, 26-004,
26-006–26-008, 26-011, 26-017,
26-019–26-020, 27-016

withdrawal, voluntary 3-005,
16-016–16-018, 16-041–16-042,
17-007–17-010, 17-013
witness statements 16-044, 20-071, 20-125,
20-135, 20-177, 20-197,
20-199–20-206, 20-211, 20-218,
21-011
witness testimony 6-003, 7-063,
20-048, 20-096, 20-101,
20-109–20-110, 20-114,
20-131–20-132, 20-143, 20-171,
20-193–20-223